LDS Preparedness Manual

Version 8.0

May 1st, 2012

"15th Aniversary Edition"

Book 1: Temporal Preparedness

Ward and Stake Leadership Edition

Restricted Version
For Ward or Stake Evaluation
Only.

Dear Brother / Sister:

Thank you for your interest in the Ward & Stake leadership edition of the LDS Preparedness Manual.

This handbook has been prepared solely for evaluation by general and local Church officers who administer the affairs of the Church. It should not be duplicated or given to any other person without explicit approval.

Members holding the following callings are authorized to request this leadership copy.

General Authorities, Area Seventies,
Members of General Auxiliary Presidencies,
Church department heads, directors of temporal affairs
Mission presidency
Stake or district presidency
Stake or district clerk
Stake or district executive secretary
Stake High council members
Stake Young Men, Relief Society, Young Women, Primary, and Sunday School presidencies
Bishopric or Branch presidency
Ward or Branch clerk
Ward or Branch executive secretary
High Priest Group leadership
Elders Quorum Presidency
Ward Young Men, Relief Society, Young Women, Primary, and Sunday School presidencies
Ward Mission Leader
Ward or Stake Emergency Preparedness, Communications or Cannery specialists.

All evaluation copies are presented as Printed-Bound editions ONLY. No Electronic versions of the evaluation copy are available for download, as this would allow for unauthorized mass distribution.

After your Ward / Stake has reviewed the content of this manual and approved it for use (Note: You are free to request any material in this manual that you find objectionable be removed from your customized version), your Ward / Stake name and or Unit designation will be placed on this page of the manual clearly showing that it is now approved and authorized for distribution within your specific Ward/Stake. I will then create a new PDF of the final manual and send it to you for local Printing/Binding/Distribution to your Ward / Stake members, this way your unit will not have to incur any additional costs in having me Print and Ship it in bulk. However, should you want me to print and ship, I would be happy to do so. **Please Note:** Wards and Stake are REQUIRED to use church authorized funds for the reproduction of this manual. Members are specificly forbiden from paying for or contributing to any costs associated with this!

If there is anything else I can do to assist you, please let me know.

Brother Christopher M. Parrett
Rigby East Stake, Idaho

"chris@ldsavow.com"

P. O. Box 100, Rigby Idaho, 83442 USA

Please Note:
This book is NOT an original work

Rather, it is a compilation of many different author's works that have been gathered from the public domain of the Internet over the course of many years. These articles have been bound together and are presented here to simplify your access to them.

A FREE generic version of this manual that does <u>NOT</u> contain any Church Copyrighted materials can be downloaded at my online LDS Preparedness forums

WWW.LDSAVOW.COM

Any and all questions or comments abut this manual should be directed to its compiler
Brother Christopher M. Parrett
Rigby East Stake, Idaho

"chris@ldsavow.com"
P. O. Box 100, Rigby Idaho, 83442 USA

If you would like further information about any topic covered in this manual, please visit my LDS Preparedness website.

Another Voice of Warning
WWW.LDSAVOW.COM

Note to my readers.

This book is <u>WORTHLESS</u> if you put it in your bookshelf with the intention of only reading it after an emergency strikes. It is <u>NOT</u> a Survival manual intended to be used after the fact.

This is a PREPAREDNESS manual that can only help you if you read it in advance and follow it's suggestions to prepare and get ready for the emergency BEFORE IT HAPPENS!

At some point while reading this manual you ARE going to have questions, and I am happy to offer my assistence to you, your family, your church or your preparedness group <u>REGARDLESS of your religious affiliation!</u> While I am LDS, preparedness doesn't care what your religious affiliation is! If I or any of the AVOW members can help, we all stand ready to do so!

Please come and take a look at LDSAVOW (*Another Voice of Warning*)
Members of ALL Judeo-Christian denominations are warmly welcomed!

As of the date of publication we currently have
200 Topic Specific Discussion Forums containing
103,000+ unique discussions with over
938,000+ member posts/comments from our
12,000+ preparedness members.

Suffice it to say, we have a staggering **WEALTH OF INFORMATION** ready to share with you on any topic related to preparedness!!

NOTE: If you are reading the Internet PDF version
we offer a **BOUND PRINTED** edition of this manual at <u>COST</u> of Printing.

ANOTHER VOICE OF WARNING
...if ye are prepared, ye shall not fear
www.ldsavow.com

Table of Contents

Section 3: Every Needful Thing

72 Hour Emergency Kit (Get Out Of Dodge / Bug Out Bag)

Evacuation

Communication

PANDEMICS

Terrorist Attack

Church Guidelines Pertaining to Disasters

Section 4: PREPAREDNESS OUTSIDE YOUR COMFORT ZONE

EPILOGUE

Preface

The Lord Warns and Forewarns

"In mercy the Lord warns and forewarns. He sees the coming storm, knows the forces operating to produce it, and calls aloud through His prophets, advises, counsels, exhorts, even commands—that we prepare for what is about to befall and take shelter while yet there is time. But we go our several ways, feasting and making merry, consoling conscience with the easy fancy of 'time enough' and in idle hope that the tempest will pass us by, or that, when it begins to gather thick and black about us we can turn back and find shelter."
- *James E Talmage, The Parables of James E. Talmage, p. 50*

The Lord Holds Us Accountable

"Then whosoever heareth the sound of the trumpet, and taketh not warning; if the sword come, and take him away, his blood shall be upon his own head. He heard the sound of the trumpet, and took not warning; his blood shall be upon him. But he that taketh warning shall deliver his soul. ***But if the watchman see the sword come, and blow not the trumpet, and the people be not warned; if the sword come, and take [any] person from among them, he is taken away in his iniquity; <u>but his blood will I require at the watchman's hand</u>.***" *Ezekiel 33:4*

It wasn't raining when Noah built the Ark

BOOK OF GOMER PARABLE

These are the generations of Gomer, son of Homer, son of Omer. And in the days of Gomer, Noah, the Prophet, went unto the people saying, "Prepare ye for the flood which is to come, yea, build yourselves a boat, that ye may not perish."

Now, Gomer was a member of the Church, and taught Sunday School and played, yea, even on the ward softball team. And Gomer's wife said unto him, "Come, let us build unto ourselves a boat as the Prophet commandeth, that we may not perish in the flood." But behold, Gomer saith unto his wife, "Worry not, dear wife, for if the flood comes the government will provide boats for us."

And Gomer did not build a boat. And Gomer's wife went unto Noah and she returned saying, "Behold, Honey, the Prophet saith unto us, "Build a boat, that we may preserve ourselves, for the government pays men not to grow trees, wherefore the government hath not the lumber to build for you a boat." And Gomer answered saying, "Fear not, oh wife, for am I not the star pitcher on the ward softball team? Wherefore, the Church will provide for us a boat, that we will perish not."

And Gomer's wife went again unto Noah, and she returned unto Gomer, saying, "Behold, mine husband, the Prophet saith that the Church hath not enough lumber to build a boat for everyone, wherefore, mine husband, build for us a boat that we might not perish in the flood." And Gomer answered her saying, "Behold, if we build a boat, when the flood cometh, will not our neighbors overpower us and take from us our boat; wherefore, what doth it profit a man to build a boat?"

And Gomer's wife went again unto Noah and she returned, saying, "Behold, the Prophet saith, build unto yourselves a boat, and have faith, for if ye do the Lord's bidding, He will preserve your boat for you." But Gomer answered his wife, saying, "Behold, with this inflation, the price of wood has gone sky high, and if we wait awhile, perhaps the price will go down again. And then I will build for us a boat."

And Gomer's wife went again unto Noah, and she returned saying, "Thus saith the Prophet, build for yourselves a boat RIGHT NOW, for the price of wood will not go down, but will continue to go up. Wherefore, oh husband, build for ourselves a boat, that we may perish not." But Gomer answered his wife, saying, "Behold, for 120 years Noah hath told us to build a boat, to preserve us from the flood, but hath the flood come? Yea, I say, nay. Wherefore, perhaps the flood will not come for another hundred and twenty years.

And Gomer's wife went again unto Noah and returned saying, "The Prophet saith, he knows it has been 120 years, but nevertheless, the flood will come, wherefore, build unto yourselves a boat."

And Gomer answered her saying, "Wherewith shall we get the money to build ourselves a boat, for are we not now making monthly payments on our snazzy new four horsepower chariot? Wherefore, when our payments end, perhaps we shall build ourselves a boat."

And Gomer's wife went again unto Noah and returned saying, "Behold, the Prophet saith that we should cut down on our recreation, and our vacations, and even give each other lumber for Christmas, that we might thereby get enough lumber to build a boat." But Gomer saith unto her, "What a drag! Are we to cease enjoying life, just because we must build a boat?"

Wherefore, Gomer built not a boat. But behold, one afternoon Gomer heard thunder in the sky, and he feared exceedingly and he ran, yea, even to the lumber yard to buy lumber. But behold, the lumber store was crowded with great multitudes, all seeking to buy lumber, and there was not enough lumber to be found for the multitudes.

And on the same day were all the fountains of the deep opened, and the windows of heaven were broken up, and the floods came -- and behold, Gomer had no boat. And as the water rose above Gomer's waist, his wife saith unto him, "Behold, Honey, I told thee so!"

A SENSE OF FEAR AND URGENCY ABOUT PREPARING.

It is my personal belief that this fear, or sense of sudden urgency, is a very natural outgrowth of the awakening to our awful situation. As members come to more fully understand the true nature of the world we live in, and how fragile it actually is, the urge to prepare grows strong and hot. As they first begin to see their nakedness, they are overcome with their vulnerability and may panic in their attempts to get ready as quickly as possible.

Consider one of LDS Author Roger K. Young's stories: **The Farm Hand Who Could Sleep Through Anything**
There once was a farmer looking for a young man to help out at the farm. There were several young men who interviewed for the job and as far as the farmer could tell, they were about equally well qualified. He then asked them each one final question, "Tell me," he would say, "why should I hire you above the others?"

Of all of the applicants and their replies, there was one that was really different. One young man said, "Because I can sleep through anything." At first the farmer thought it was just strange. The more he thought, the more he was intrigued and mystified by the response. So he figured, well I will give this young man a chance, and hired him.

Weeks went by and the farmer was pretty happy with the young man's work. He still wondered sometimes what the young man had meant by his strange reply, but he never got around to asking about it. Then one night the farmer was awakened in the middle of the night with a phone call from a neighbor. "There's a big storm coming in with lots of wind, maybe a tornado. Better get ready for it." was the quick message.

Indeed as the farmer went to the door and looked out, he found that the wind was strong and rising, and rain had started. He quickly ran and tried to awaken the young man to help him get everything ready for the blow. Try as he might, the young man couldn't be stirred. Muttering to himself about what a stupid thing he had done in hiring a lazy boy who wouldn't wake up when he really needed him, the farmer went out to the farm.

He went out to tie down the hay, but discovered that the hay was already tied down securely. Next he went to the barn and the corrals. Everywhere he looked, everything had already been prepared. After a time of just wandering around the farm, learning that there was nothing that needed to be done at the last minute, because it had all been done (prepared) before, the farmer returned to his house, but instead of muttering, he actually found himself singing the praises of this young man. He had realized, to his great joy, that the reason the young man could sleep through anything was because before he went to bed each and every night he had already prepared for the very worst. And so the farmer followed the example of the young man, since everything was already prepared, he undressed and was soon fast asleep, with a huge smile of peace on his face.

This young man had nothing to fear and was not stricken with panic at the onset of the storm because he was fully prepared. He had put forth the necessary time and effort to secure everything well in advance so he could rest the night through with little concern for the howling winds outside.

For those who are feeling overwhelmed with the task of becoming prepared, or for those who are concerned that they simply cannot accomplish the tasks laid out before them to become prepared for the events to come, please remember the words of the great prophet Nephi when he taught us that "the Lord giveth no commandments unto the children of men, save he shall prepare a way for them that they may accomplish the thing which he commandeth them." (1Ne 3:7). No matter what our level of preparedness, fear and panic are not necessary if we are striving to be obedient, for we have this promise from the Lord.

We are all familiar with that statement "If ye are prepared, ye shall not fear" (D&C 38:30). But we must also bear in mind that this most powerful statement in the preparedness community has an equally powerful but completely opposite meaning – "If ye are not prepared, ye shall fear."

To take this a step further, it saddens me that we have so many members who struggle to enjoy their lives after having "awakened" to our awful situation. When the events of the last days seem closer than we imagined, it's difficult not to become pre-occupied with the future. While it's easy to "not fear" for ourselves if we are prepared, we can still feel saddened for our loved ones who are not prepared. Such emotional preoccupation can quickly become overwhelming if we're not careful. I encourage each and every one of us to prepare like the world will end tomorrow, but plan and live our lives as though the time is yet far away. If we can successfully find balance between these two activities, it is my opinion that we will each find comfort and peace in the days to come, regardless of what happens around us.

President Woodruff was known for doing today what needed to be done, without undue concern for what might occur in the future. On one occasion he was asked when the world was coming to an end. He replied, "Well, I don't know, but I am still planting cherry trees."

Now, please consider the following parable about preparedness from LDS Author Roger K. Young.

Once there was a group of people traveling on a long and often difficult road in the wilderness, making their way towards a very special place. They had a map and some instructions on how to use the map to get to their destination, but now the road led upward into the mountains, becoming steeper, rockier and generally more difficult to travel. None of them had ever been on this road before, and there was some confusion about where they were according to the map. Some had even become discouraged because the storms were becoming stronger and more frequent. As they rounded a bend they came to a little spring where a family of fellow travelers were resting and preparing to travel on. Sitting on a nearby rock was one of the family members studying the map. Pausing to refresh themselves, they joined in conversation with the traveler and his family.

After finding out that the man had been sitting for several hours, map in hand, studying the surrounding wilderness, they asked him what his opinion was concerning their exact location according to the map. "Well," said he, "I've never been on this road before either, but I will share with you some of the things that I think I have figured out. I am by no means an expert or a guide, and so I would encourage you to take some time to ponder these things for yourselves." He then took the map and began indicating some of the landmarks on the map, pointing out various mountain peaks, passes, cliffs, rock slides, swamps, forests and other places, while at the same time gesturing at the surrounding countryside. "See this mountain peak on the map," he would say, "I believe that it refers to that very tall mountain over there."

After pointing out a dozen or so landmarks he went on to say, pointing to a spot on the map, "After looking at all of these landmarks, I believe that this spring where we are is right here. If that is correct, then actually we are pretty close to our destination. However, the road from now on becomes very steep, rocky, narrow, and treacherous, with almost no opportunity to obtain food or water until we finish the journey. As you know, the Master has sent some guides out, and for the last little while they have been indicating that we need to start packing some extra water and food in case we get caught in one of the storms. The legend on the map says that as we go on from here, the storms will increase and become very severe making this final part of the journey extremely difficult and dangerous. I would advise that if you haven't already picked up an extra supply of food and water, and made the final preparations for the last part of the journey, that you do so quickly."

"Oh, one last thing," said the traveler as his family began to load up and journey on, "the map says that there will probably be road washouts, bridges damaged or down, flash floods, unmarked quick sands, as well as other dangers up ahead. The Master's guides will be set along the way with directions and instructions on how to avoid or make it through these dangers, and so I would advise you to listen to them and follow their advice very carefully and quickly."

The travelers, weary from the steady climb over rocky ground made slippery from the now almost constant rain, came round a large rock outcropping and noticed a small shelter on the other side. As they headed towards it, they noticed a small group of people, among them the friend they had met earlier, further down the trail. As they drew closer, they realized that the group and their friend were just getting ready to leave, and were in the process of tying themselves together with rope.

Their friend saluted them with a warm greeting and expressed joy that they had arrived to join him and his family, if even for a brief moment. "Rest for a minute while you can, and get ready for what is ahead," he advised them. "The next part of the journey is extremely difficult and treacherous, and the Master has sent one of his Guides to come and show us the way. They alone know the way and are in constant contact with the Master, receiving the information needed to pass through the perils ahead. We have decided that the only way to make it the rest of the way is to rope ourselves to the Guide in order to not get lost in the darkness of the storms and chaos ahead."

"Take heart," their friend continued, "the guide has told us that though the path ahead, over the mountain, will be extremely dangerous and will test the endurance and faith of the best of us, in a relatively short time we will pass through the trials ahead and be in the very lush and beautiful Millennial valley on the other side."

"Unfortunately, the map of this part of the journey is not very clear, hence the need to stay extremely close to the guides. I'll share with you what I think I have learned about the trail ahead, for whatever benefit it might do you, but my understanding is very fragmented and unsure. Again, the only real safety is to follow the Master's Guides, obeying immediately every word of direction and counsel they give as if it were from the Master himself. To do anything less will surely invite disaster. I don't know if I will see you again along the trail ahead, but if not, hopefully we will have a great reunion in the valley on the other side." With that, their friend handed over to them a small packet of papers. Then he, his family, and the others all roped together in their group with one of the Guides, slowly trudged off into the rain and darkness...

"And so we now say to all men everywhere, to men of all sects, parties, and denominations, but more particularly to those who believe: Hear ye the words of the watchmen, and be ye ready for that which is soon to be. 'For there shall be a day'—and as the Lord lives, that day is now—'that the watchmen upon the mount Ephraim shall cry, Arise ye, and let us go up to Zion unto the Lord our God.' (Jer. 31:6.) Go ye, go ye up to Zion; find refuge in one of her stakes, and be ye one with those who are pure in heart." – Bruce R. McConkie (The Millenial Messiah).

My brothers and sisters, please remember that I am but a fellow traveler on this journey. I hope, quite simply, that this book can act as a tool and an aid in your preparations. I am not privy to information from the Lord that you do not have. I am not a prophet, a seer, or a revelator. I do not have any stewardship or authority over you. I simply interpret what I have been given for myself and occasionally, when prompted, share my conclusions and ideas. We have all been given the same map, the same directions, and the same destination.

As the brethren have taught us many times in the past, all the money and all the preparations in the world will not save you in the events to come unless you are spiritually prepared. Temporal preparedness should be your second priority after your spiritual preparations.

I humbly ask that you do not treat anything in this book, especially me, as bigger than life, nor should you regard anything I say or do with any special "weight." We are all equals before the Lord. I have no special calling or authority over you. The Lord is our Master. His prophets are our guides. The Holy Ghost is our watchman. We are in this together.

May God bless you all in your efforts!   Brother Christopher Michael Parrett

SECTION 1:
Emergency Preparedness
WHY?

THE CHURCH OF JESUS CHRIST OF LATTER DAY SAINTS
SALT LAKE CITY, UTAH 84150

June 24, 1988

To: General Authorities and the following Priesthood leaders in the United States and Canada: Area Authorities (formerly Regional Reps.); Stake, Mission, and District Presidents; Bishops and Branch Presidents.

Dear Brethren:

OFFICE OF THE FIRST PRESIDENCY

Preparing for Emergencies (To be read in Sacrament Meeting.)

Occasionally people speculate about possible disasters, which speculation engenders fear and can cause members to become caught up in emergency preparedness efforts that are not only costly but go beyond the basics consistently taught by the First Presidency. Leaders should refer to *Preparing for and Responding to Emergencies: Guidelines for Church Leaders*. Member preparations require wise planning, diligence, and provident living. If circumstances warrant, the First Presidency and Council of the Twelve will provide additional guidance on such matters through established Priesthood channels.

We continue to encourage members to store sufficient food, clothing, and, where possible, fuel for at least one year. We have not laid down an exact formula for what should be stored. However, we suggest that members concentrate on essential foods that sustain life, such as grains, legumes, cooking oil, powdered milk, salt, sugar or honey, and water. Most families can achieve and maintain this basic level of preparedness. The decision to do more than this rests with the individual.

We encourage you to follow this counsel with the assurance that a people prepared through obedience to the commandments of God need not fear.

Sincerely your Brethren,

Ezra Taft Benson
Gordon B. Hinckley
Thomas S. Monson
The First Presidency

THE CHURCH OF JESUS CHRIST OF LATTER DAY SAINTS
SALT LAKE CITY, UTAH 84150

January 20, 2002

To: General Authorities; Area Authority Seventies: Stake, Mission and District Presidents; Bishops and Branch presidents

Dear Brethren:

OFFICE OF THE FIRST PRESIDENCY

Home Storage and Financial Reserves.

Priesthood and Relief Society leaders should teach the importance of home storage and securing a financial reserve. These principles may be taught in ward councils or on a fifth Sunday in Priesthood and Relief Society meetings.

Church members can begin their home storage by storing the basic foods that would be required to keep them alive if they did not have anything else to eat. Depending on where members live, those basics might include water, wheat or other grains, legumes, salt, honey or sugar, powdered milk, and cooking oil. (See reverse for suggested amounts.) When members have stored enough of these essentials to meet the needs of their family for one year, they may decide to add other items that they are accustomed to using day to day.

Some members do not have the money or space for such storage, and some are prohibited by law from storing a year's supply of food. These members should store as much as their circumstances allow. Families who do not have the resources to acquire a year's supply can begin their storage by obtaining supplies to last for a few months. Members should be prudent and not panic or go to extremes in this effort. Through careful planning, most Church members can, over time, establish both a financial reserve and a year's supply of essentials.

Sincerely yours,
The First Presidency

THE CHURCH OF JESUS CHRIST OF LATTER DAY SAINTS
SALT LAKE CITY, UTAH 84150

February 1, 2007

To: General Authorities; Area Authority Seventies: Stake, Mission and District Presidents; Bishops and Branch presidents

Dear Brothers and Sisters:

OFFICE OF THE FIRST PRESIDENCY

Family Home Storage

Our Heavenly Father created this beautiful earth, with all its abundance, for our benefit and use. His purpose is to provide for our needs as we walk in faith and obedience. He has lovingly commanded us to "prepare every needful thing" (see D&C 109:8) so that, should adversity come, we may care for ourselves and our neighbors and support bishops as they care for others.

We encourage Church members worldwide to prepare for adversity in life by having a basic supply of food and water and some money in savings.

We ask that you be wise as you store food and water and build your savings. Do not go to extremes; it is not prudent, for example, to go into debt to establish your food storage all at once. With careful planning, you can, over time, establish a home storage supply and a financial reserve.

We realize that some of you may not have financial resources or space for such storage. Some of you may be prohibited by law from storing large amounts of food. We encourage you to store as much as circumstances allow.

May the Lord bless you in your home storage efforts.

The First Presidency

18

If Ye Are Prepared Ye Shall Not Fear

Selected Excerpts from President Gordon B. Hinckley,
Oct 2005 General Conference, Priesthood Session

I do not hesitate to say that this old world is no stranger to calamities and catastrophes. Those of us who read and believe the scriptures are aware of the warnings of prophets concerning catastrophes that have come to pass and are yet to come to pass... There was the great Flood, when waters covered the earth and when, as Peter says, only "eight souls were saved" (1 Peter 3:20).

If anyone has any doubt concerning the terrible things that can and will afflict mankind, let him read the 24th chapter of Matthew. Among other things the Lord says: *"Ye shall hear of wars and rumours of wars. . . .*

"For nation shall rise against nation, and kingdom against kingdom: and there shall be famines, and pestilences, and earthquakes, in divers places. All these are the beginning of sorrows. . . ."

"And woe unto them that are with child, and to them that give suck in those days! . . ."

"For then shall be great tribulation, such as was not since the beginning of the world to this time, no, nor ever shall be. And except those days should be shortened, there should no flesh be saved: but for the elect's sake those days shall be shortened" (Matthew 24:6–8, 19, 21–22).

In the Book of Mormon we read of unimaginable destruction in the Western Hemisphere at the time of the Savior's death in Jerusalem. Again I quote:

"And it came to pass in the thirty and fourth year, in the first month, on the fourth day of the month, there arose a great storm, such an one as never had been known in all the land. And there was also a great and terrible tempest; and there was terrible thunder, insomuch that it did shake the whole earth as if it was about to divide asunder. And there were exceedingly sharp lightnings, such as never had been known in all the land. And the city of Zarahemla did take fire. And the city of Moroni did sink into the depths of the sea, and the inhabitants thereof were drowned. And the earth was carried up upon the city of Moronihah, that in the place of the city there became a great mountain. . . . "

". . . The whole face of the land was changed, because of the tempest and the whirlwinds, and the thunderings and the lightnings, and the exceedingly great quaking of the whole earth; And the highways were broken up, and the level roads were spoiled, and many smooth places became rough. And many great and notable cities were sunk, and many were burned, and many were shaken till the buildings thereof had fallen to the earth, and the inhabitants thereof were slain, and the places were left desolate" (3 Nephi 8:5–10, 12–14).

What a terrible catastrophe that must have been.

How portentous are the words of revelation found in the 88th section of the Doctrine and Covenants concerning the calamities that should befall after the testimonies of the elders.

The Lord says:
"For after your testimony cometh the testimony of earthquakes, that shall cause groanings in the midst of her, and men shall fall upon the ground and shall not be able to stand. And also cometh the testimony of the voice of thunderings, and the voice of lightnings, and the voice of tempests, and the voice of the waves of the sea heaving themselves beyond their bounds. And all things shall be in commotion; and surely, men's hearts shall fail them; for fear shall come upon all people" (D&C 88:89–91).

How interesting are descriptions of the tsunami and the recent hurricanes in terms of the language of this revelation, which says, *"The voice of the waves of the sea heaving themselves beyond their bounds."*

Man's inhumanity to man expressed in past and present conflict has and continues to bring unspeakable suffering. In the Darfur region of Sudan, tens of thousands have been killed and well over a million have been left homeless.

What we have experienced in the past was all foretold, and the end is not yet. Just as there have been calamities in the past, we expect more in the future. What do we do?

Someone has said it was not raining when Noah built the ark. But he built it, and the rains came.

The Lord has said, *"If ye are prepared ye shall not fear"* (D&C 38:30).

The primary preparation is also set forth in the Doctrine and Covenants, wherein it says, "Wherefore, stand ye in holy places, and be not moved, until the day of the Lord come" (D&C 87:8).

We sing the song:

> When the earth begins to tremble, Bid our fearful thoughts be still;When thy judgments spread destruction, Keep us safe on Zion's hill.

("Guide Us, O Thou Great Jehovah," *Hymns,* no. 83)

We can so live that we can call upon the Lord for His protection and guidance. This is a first priority. **We cannot expect His help if we are unwilling to keep His commandments.** We in this Church have evidence enough of the penalties of disobedience in the examples of both the Jaredite and the Nephite nations. Each went from glory to utter destruction because of wickedness.

We can heed warnings. We have been told that many had been given concerning the vulnerability of New Orleans. We are told by seismologists that the Salt Lake Valley is a potential earthquake zone. This is the primary reason that we are extensively renovating the Tabernacle on Temple Square. **This historic and remarkable building must be made to withstand the shaking of the earth.**

We have built grain storage and storehouses and stocked them with the necessities of life in the event of a disaster. **But the best storehouse is the family storeroom.** In words of revelation the Lord has said, *"Organize yourselves; prepare every needful thing"* (D&C 109:8).

Our people for three-quarters of a century have been counseled and encouraged to make such preparation as will assure survival should a calamity come.

We can set aside some water, basic food, medicine, and clothing to keep us warm. We ought to have a little money laid aside in case of a rainy day...

I am saying nothing that has not been said for a very long time.

Let us never lose sight of the dream of Pharaoh concerning the fat cattle and the lean, the full ears of corn, and the blasted ears; the meaning of which was interpreted by Joseph to indicate years of plenty and years of scarcity (see Genesis 41:1–36).

I have faith, my dear brethren, that the Lord will bless us, and watch over us, and assist us if we walk in obedience to His light, His gospel, and His commandments. He is our Father and our God, and we are His children, and we must be in every way deserving of His love and concern. That we may do so is my humble prayer, in the name of Jesus Christ, amen.

President Gordon B. Hinckley, October Conference 2001.

"I am suggesting that the time has come to get our houses in order...**avoid debt** to the extent possible. **Pay off debt** as quickly as you can, and free yourselves from bondage... **There is a portent of stormy weather ahead to which we had better give heed**" (Gordon B. Hinckley, October Conference 1998.

"Peace is fragile, civilization itself is fragile. **The economy is particularly vulnerable...**
"I do not know what the future holds. I do not wish to sound negative, but I wish to remind you of the **warnings of scripture** and the **teachings of the prophets** which we have had constantly before us.

I cannot forget the great lesson of **Pharaoh's dream** of the fat and lean kine and of the full and withered stalks of corn.
I cannot dismiss from my mind the **grim warnings** of the Lord as set forth in the **24th chapter of Matthew.**

I am familiar, as are you, with the declarations of modem revelation that the time will come when the **earth will be cleansed** and there will be **indescribable distress**, with weeping and mourning and lamentation. . . . Now, I do not wish to be an alarmist. I do not wish to be a prophet of doom. I am optimistic. I do not believe the time is here when an all-consuming calamity will overtake us. I earnestly pray that it may not.

"As we have been continuously counseled for more than 60 years, let us have some **food set aside that would sustain us for a time in case of need.** But let us not panic nor go to extremes. Let us be prudent in every respect. And, above all, my brothers and sisters, let us move forward with faith in the Living God and His Beloved Son...

Prepare for the Days of Tribulation

Ensign Magazine, November 1980,
President Ezra Taft Benson, of the Quorum of the Twelve Apostles

For over forty years, in a spirit of love, members of the Church have been counseled to be thrifty and self-reliant; to avoid debt; pay tithes and a generous fast offering; be industrious; and have sufficient food, clothing, and fuel on hand to last at least one year.

Today there are compelling reasons to reemphasize this counsel. We heard it done effectively in that great welfare meeting this morning. May I add just a word.

Members of the Church are feeling the economic pinch of higher taxes and inflation coupled with conditions of continuing recession. Some have come to their bishops seeking assistance to pay for house payments, car loans, and utilities.

Unfortunately, there has been fostered in the minds of some an expectation that when we experience hard times, when we have been unwise and extravagant with our resources and have lived beyond our means, we should look to either the Church or government to bail us out. Forgotten by some of our members is an underlying principle of the Church welfare plan that *"no true Latter-day Saint will, while physically able, voluntarily shift from himself the burden of his own support"* (Marion G. Romney, in Conference Report, Oct. 1973, p. 106).

One of the first principles revealed to father Adam when he was driven out of the Garden of Eden was this: *"In the sweat of thy face shalt thou eat bread, till thou return unto the ground"* (Gen. 3:19). All we obtain in life of a material nature comes as a product of labor and the providence of God. Work alone produces life's necessities.

In saying this, I am aware of and sympathetic to the plight of many young families who are struggling to make ends meet. They are faced with the financial burden of providing for the three great necessities of life: food, clothing, and shelter. I am also sympathetic to the situation of widows and other sisters who rear families alone. By revelation, the

Lord made provision for their care and support. (See D&C 83:1–2, 4–6.)

More than ever before, we need to learn and apply the principles of economic self-reliance. We do not know when the crisis involving sickness or unemployment may affect our own circumstances. We do know that the Lord has decreed global calamities for the future and has warned and forewarned us to be prepared. For this reason the Brethren have repeatedly stressed a "back to basics" program for temporal and spiritual welfare.

Today, I emphasize a most basic principle: home production and storage. Have you ever paused to realize what would happen to your community or nation if transportation were paralyzed or if we had a war or depression? How would you and your neighbors obtain food? How long would the corner grocery store—or supermarket—sustain the needs of the community?

Shortly after World War II, I was called by the First Presidency to go to Europe to reestablish our missions and set up a program for the distribution of food and clothing to the Saints. Vivid in my memory are the people who got on trains each morning with all kinds of bric-a-brac in their arms to go out to the countryside to trade their possessions for food. At evening time, the train station was filled with people with arms full of vegetables and fruits, and a menagerie of squealing pigs and chickens. You never heard such a commotion. These people were, of course, willing to barter practically anything for that commodity which sustains life—food.

An almost forgotten means of economic self-reliance is the home production of food. We are too accustomed to going to stores and purchasing what we need. By producing some of our food we reduce, to a great extent, the impact of inflation on our money. More importantly, we learn how to produce our own food and involve all family members in a beneficial project. No more timely counsel, I feel, has been given by President Kimball than his repeated emphasis to grow our own gardens. Here is one sample of his emphasis over the past seven years:

"We encourage you to grow all the food that you feasibly can on your own property. Berry bushes, grapevines, fruit trees—plant them if your climate is right for their growth. Grow vegetables and eat them from your own yard." (Ensign, May 1976, p. 124).

Many of you have listened and done as President Kimball counseled, and you have been blessed for it. Others have rationalized that they had no time or space. May I suggest you do what others have done. Get together with others and seek permission to use a vacant lot for a garden, or rent a plot of ground and grow your gardens. Some elders quorums have done this as a quorum, and all who have participated have reaped the benefits of a vegetable and fruit harvest and the blessings of cooperation and family involvement. Many families have dug up lawn space for gardens.

We encourage you to be more self-reliant so that, as the Lord has declared, *"notwithstanding the tribulation which shall descend upon you, … the church may stand independent above all other creatures beneath the celestial world"* (D&C 78:14). The Lord wants us to be independent and self-reliant because these will be days of tribulation. He has warned and forewarned us of the eventuality.

President Brigham Young said, *"If you are without bread, how much wisdom can you boast, and of what real utility are your talents, if you cannot procure for yourselves and save against a day of scarcity those substances designed to sustain your natural lives?"* (In Journal of Discourses, 8:68.)

Food production is just one part of the repeated emphasis that you store a provision of food which will last for at least a year wherever it is legally permissible to do so. The Church has not told you what foods should be stored. This decision is left up to individual members. However, some excellent suggestions are available in the booklet produced by the Church entitled "Essentials of Home Production & Storage" (stock no. PGWE1125; 35¢ each). There are also booklets available on gardening from BYU.

From the standpoint of food production, storage, handling, and the Lord's counsel, wheat should have high priority. *"There is more salvation and security in wheat,"* said Orson Hyde years ago, *"than in all the political schemes of the world"* (in Journal of Discourses, 2:207). Water, of course, is essential. Other basics could include honey or sugar, legumes, milk products or substitutes, and salt or its equivalent. The revelation to produce and store food may be as essential to our temporal welfare today as boarding the ark was to the people in the days of Noah.

Elder Harold B. Lee counseled,

"Perhaps if we think not in terms of a year's supply of what we ordinarily would use, and think more in terms of what it would take to keep us alive in case we didn't have anything else to eat, that last would be very easy to put in storage for a year … just enough to keep us alive if we didn't have anything else to eat. We wouldn't get fat on it, but we would live; and if you think in terms of that kind of annual storage rather than a whole year's supply of everything that you are accustomed to eat which, in most cases, is utterly impossible for the average family, I think we will come nearer to what President J. Reuben Clark, Jr., advised us way back in 1937." (In Welfare Conference, 1 October 1966.)

There are blessings in being close to the soil, in raising your own food even if it is only a garden in your yard and a fruit tree or two. Those families will be fortunate who, in the last days, have an adequate supply of food because of their foresight and ability to produce their own.

The counsel from Church authorities has been consistent over the years and is well summarized in these words:

"First, and above and beyond everything else, let us live righteously. …

"Let us avoid debt as we would avoid a plague; where we are now in debt, let us get out of debt; if not today, then tomorrow.

"Let us straitly and strictly live within our incomes, and save a little.

"Let every head of every household see to it that he has on hand enough food and clothing, and, where possible, fuel also, for at least a year ahead. You of small means put your money in foodstuffs and wearing apparel, not in stocks and bonds; you of large means will think you know how to care for yourselves, but I may venture to suggest that you do not speculate. Let every head of every household aim to own his own home, free from mortgage. Let every man who has a garden spot, garden it; every man who owns a farm, farm it." (President J. Reuben Clark, Jr., in Conference Report, Apr. 1937, p. 26.)

You do not need to go into debt, may I add, to obtain a year's supply. Plan to build up your food supply just as you would a savings account. Save a little for storage each paycheck. Can or bottle fruit and vegetables from your gardens and orchards. Learn how to preserve food through drying and possibly freezing. Make your storage a part of your budget. Store seeds and have sufficient tools on hand to do the job. If you are saving and planning for a second car or a TV set or some item which merely adds to your comfort or pleasure, you may need to change your priorities. We urge you to do this prayerfully and do it now.

I speak with a feeling of great urgency. I have seen what the days of tribulation can do to people. I have seen hunger stalk the streets of Europe. I have witnessed the appalling, emaciated shadows of human figures. I have seen women and children scavenge army garbage dumps for scraps of food. Those scenes and nameless faces cannot be erased from my memory.

I shall never forget the Saints of Hamburg who appeared on the verge of collapse from starvation, or their small children whom I invited to come to the stand as we emptied our pockets of edibles. Most had never seen these items before because of the wartime conditions. Nor can I forget the expectant and nursing mothers whose eyes watered with tears when we gave them each an orange. We saw the terrible physical and social side effects of hunger and malnutrition. One sister walked over a thousand miles with four small children, leaving her home in Poland. She lost all four to starvation and the freezing conditions. Yet she stood before us in her emaciated condition, her clothing shredded, and her feet wrapped in burlap, and bore testimony of how blessed she was.

I cannot forget the French Saints who, unable to obtain bread, used potato peelings for the emblems of the sacrament. Nor will I ever forget the faith of the Dutch Saints who accepted our suggestion to grow potatoes to alleviate their own starving conditions, and then sent a portion of their first harvest to the German people who had been their bitter enemies. The following year they sent them the entire harvest. The annals of Church history have seldom recorded a more Christlike act of love and compassion.

Too often we bask in our comfortable complacency and rationalize that the ravages of war, economic disaster, famine, and earthquake cannot happen here. Those who believe this are either not acquainted with the revelations of the Lord, or they do not believe them. Those who smugly think these calamities will not happen, that they somehow will be set aside because of the righteousness of the Saints, are deceived and will rue the day they harbored such a delusion.

The Lord has warned and forewarned us against a day of great tribulation and given us counsel, through His servants, on how we can be prepared for these difficult times. Have we heeded His counsel?

I bear you my testimony that President Heber J. Grant was inspired of the Lord in establishing the Church Welfare program. The First Presidency was inspired when they made the first public announcement in 1936 and declared the prime purpose of Church welfare was "*to help the people help themselves*" (in Conference Report, Oct. 1936, p. 3). I bear witness to that inspired counsel from 1936 to the present day that the Saints lay up a year's supply of food. When President Spencer W. Kimball persistently admonishes the members to plant gardens and fruit trees and produce our own food, he is likewise inspired of the Lord.

Be faithful, my brothers and sisters, to this counsel and you will be blessed—yes, the most blessed people in all the earth. You are good people. I know that. But all of us need to be better than we are. Let us be in a position so we are able to not only feed ourselves through the home production and storage, but others as well.

May God bless us to be prepared for the days which lie ahead, which may be the most severe yet. In the name of Jesus Christ, amen.

> *"Today, I emphasize a most basic principle: home production and storage. Have you ever paused to realize what would happen to your community or nation if transportation were paralyzed or if we had a war or depression? How would you and your neighbors obtain food? How long would the corner grocery store—or supermarket—sustain the needs of the community?"*

GETTING SET FOR A MODERN DAY REPEAT OF HAUN'S MILL

We all know the tragic story of Haun's mill.

Joseph Smith had counseled all of the Church members living around Far West to drop everything and come into Far West for safety. It wasn't a commandment...it was simply a request and counsel. Almost all the members of the Church immediately followed the counsel of the prophet. However, brother Jacob Haun, upon hearing this counsel, came and argued with the Prophet about the counsel at least 3 times during one day. Brother Haun's point was that he did not see the reason for it and he felt that he and his people could defend themselves if necessary. According to John Lee who was present for the conversations, on 26 October 1838 The Prophet said,

> "Move in, by all means, if you wish to save your lives." Haun replied that if the settlers left their homes all of their property would be lost and the Gentiles would burn their houses and other buildings. Joseph replied, "You had better lose your property than your lives, but there is no danger of losing either if you will do as you are commanded."

Again, brother Haun thought he and his neighbors could protect and defend themselves, and Smith finally gave them permission to remain, and is recorded as saying;

> "they would consider him a tyrant if he <u>forced</u> them to leave and abandon their property and come to Far West."

Years later, on 8 June 1867 John Lee reaffirmed in his diary that;

> "Jos. permitted Haun to gather the Brethren and defend their Mill but stated at the same time that they would be massacred & sure enough it was done."[1]

Four years later after the incident Joseph himself recounted:

> "Up to this day God had given me wisdom to save the people who took Council. None had ever been killed who abode by my Council. At Haun's Mill the brethren went contrary to my Council; if they had not, their lives would have been spared." [2]

The lesson here for us to learn from is that brother Haun, the righteous local leader of a group of good saints...felt he knew better than to obey all of the counsel of the living prophet. After all, Joseph hadn't made it an enforced commandment... he phrased it as counsel and advice. In fact, it is important to note that Joseph **REFUSED** to make it a **COMMANDMENT** and force the people to gather, even though he knew it would save their lives. Many of the good and righteous people who trusted in their own wisdom and their local leader and refused to give full heed to the words of the prophet, sadly, paid the terrible price four days later. That they were good people who were righteous and had great faith is not disputed as some of them performed miracles later even in the very day of their distress. But it was to help alleviate some of the suffering their disobedient actions had brought down upon them. The problem was they thought it was a little more important to try and save their material positions in the world, than to obey the suggestions of a living prophet. This brings up another point of discussion.

LABORING UNDER A FALSE DOCTRINE
Does personal spiritual righteousness and gospel zeal guarantee the temporal protection of the Lord and excuse an individual from obeying counsel of the Prophets and Apostles?

On the face of it the answer would seem obvious...absolutely not. We must obey all of the counsel of the Lord's anointed...all of the time. We can't pick and choose without facing the resulting consequences. But throughout history and even today many of the saints and their local leaders believe, work under and teach this false doctrine in an important aspect of their lives.

Let me rephrase this question in another way. Can a member or a leader be trying so hard in so many areas and be doing a tremendous amount of good while yet at the same time ignore counsel given again and again by prophets...and then suffer terrible consequences because of his lack of obedience in something very small he personally did not see the benefit of?

The answer is of course...yes. Let me use one more famous historical example of this very issue. The Martin and Willey handcart experience is again, like Haun's mill, a story of a group of good, righteous individuals and their local leaders ignoring counsel from Prophets and Apostles and suffering the consequences. They specifically, and falsely, applied the idea that their personal righteousness would protect them in their disregard for following the counsel of the Apostles. In fact they actually used as an excuse their gospel enthusiasm, zeal, faith and obedience as some of the primary reasons in their arguments to disobey the advice of the brethren.[3] After all, it wasn't a commandment that was enforced...it was just counsel. Again, history proved them to be tragically wrong.

> "The decision to send out the Willie and Martin companies so late in the season was extremely reckless and based upon false doctrine. That decision cost the lives of nearly one-fourth of the entire group; about 220 people died before the rescue party sent by President Young could reach them." [4]

Of course we have the story of those who survived the Willie and Martin experience who drew closer to the Lord. But, according to Brigham Young, it wasn't what the Lord wanted:

> "In mid-November President Brigham Young angrily reproved those who had authorized the late start or who had not ordered the several parties back to Florence when they still had the opportunity, charging "ignorance," "mismanagement," and "misconduct." Though terrible, the suffering could have been far worse. Had the rescue effort not been launched immediately—well before the storm struck—the handcart companies would probably have been totally destroyed."[5]

SETTING UP A MODERN DAY REPEAT
Are too many of us as members and local leaders setting ourselves up for another Haun's Mill and Willie and Martin handcart disaster...only on a tremendously much larger scale?

I can't tell you how many times I have talked with people who are wonderful, faithful members of the Church, some even who are ward and stake leaders, who don't have enough food storage to last more than a week or so. Often this is because they have been well blessed in material possessions and income. In our discussions about how the counsel for food storage has been repeated by every prophet for over 60 years they commonly respond that with all of the other issues that they are dealing with, it just isn't very high on the priority list. Temple work, family history, missionary work are all much more important than food storage. However, some explain that if the Prophet made it a commandment, like they did with the Word of Wisdom by including it on the temple recommend interview, instead of just counsel, then they would move it up on the priority list.

These people, and I am convinced they represent a very large portion of the membership of the Church, believe the very same false doctrines as did the members of the two ill fated groups mentioned above. First, they falsely believe that their personal righteousness will save them. After all, they are busy going to the temple, fulfilling Church callings, sending missionaries out, etc. in other words...doing the works of the righteous. Surely, the Lord will be merciful to them and take care of them despite their lack of attention to this small item. They discount what president Benson taught on this point:

> "Should the Lord decide at this time to cleanse the Church—and the need for that cleansing seems to be increasing—a famine in this land of one year's duration could wipe out a large percentage of slothful members, including some ward

and stake officers. Yet we cannot say we have not been warned."[6]

Additionally, they commonly believe and have heard it actually taught over the pulpit by others that those terrible things that have been prophesied won't happen to the righteous and so they need not prepare for them. Many prophets, including President Lee and President Kimball addressed this terribly false notion, but President Benson said it best in his "Rue The Day" statement:

> "Too often we bask in our comfortable complacency and rationalize that the ravages of war, economic disaster, famine, and earthquake cannot happen here. Those who believe this are either not acquainted with the revelations of the Lord, or they do not believe them. *Those who smugly think these calamities will not happen, that they somehow will be set aside because of the righteousness of the Saints, are deceived and will rue the day they harbored such a delusion.* The Lord has warned and forewarned us against a day of great tribulation and given us counsel, through His servants, on how we can be prepared for these difficult times. Have we heeded His counsel?[7]

It is hard for me to understand why or how so many good and wonderful people can discount what the prophets have said, again, and again, and again, and again concerning what will suddenly happen to the world in the future. President Benson said:

> "The revelation to produce and store food may be as essential to our temporal welfare today as boarding the ark was to the people in the days of Noah."[8]

It is important to note that the people who didn't get on the ark, suffered and died by the very calamity that for 300 years had been prophesied would come upon them. People, including members of the Church, have always had a habit of believing that things won't change drastically, or that terrible things could happen to them. It is a part of human nature.

However, the scriptures are very clear that these terrible cataclysmic events, some perhaps 20-30 years prior to the actual return of the Savior in power and great glory, will come suddenly upon the heart of the Church, and then be poured out upon the rest of the world.

> *"Behold, vengeance cometh speedily upon the inhabitants of the earth, a day of wrath,*

> *a day of burning, a day of desolation, of weeping, of mourning, and of lamentation; and as a whirlwind it shall come upon all the face of the earth, saith the Lord.*
>
> *"And upon my house shall it begin, and from my house shall it go forth, saith the Lord;*
>
> *"First among those among you, saith the Lord, who have professed to know my name and have not known me, and have blasphemed against me in the midst of my house, saith the Lord."[9]*

It is noteworthy that President Hinckley quoted from this scripture in his famous Sunday morning talk given in General conference following the September 11, 2001 terrorist attack and subsequent beginning of the war in Iraq.

Additionally, this scripture was supposed to have been discussed in great detail recently throughout the Church as it was contained in the Priesthood/Relief Society manuals when we studied Joseph F. Smith. A few quotes from that lesson:

> **"The many eruptions, earthquakes and tidal waves which have occurred...are signs which the Savior declared would foreshadow his second coming, although he said his advent should be as thief in the night...The wise and prudent will heed the warning and prepare themselves that they be not taken unawares."**

> **"I...testify, that [the Latter-Day Saints]...will be the first to fall beneath the judgments of the Almighty, for his judgments will begin at his own house."[10]**

Wilford Woodruff commented that he believed that the dreadful calamities described in the second half of the third Chapter of Isaiah is a direct description of some of the aftermath of this and other unpleasant prophetic fulfillments specifically upon the Church members because of their participation in the fashions of Babylon which showed where their hearts really were:

> "There are some prophecies pertaining to these latter days that are unpleasant to contemplate. President Young has been calling upon the daughters of Zion day after day, now, for years, to lay aside these Babylonish fashions. I have been reading the third chapter of Isaiah, and I have been hoping, all the days of my ministry, that the

26

sayings contained in that chapter would never apply to the daughters of Zion in our day; but I believe they will, and inasmuch as they will not listen to President Young and to the prophets, apostles and elders of Israel with regard to throwing off these nonsensical things, I hope they will hasten the lengthening out of their skirts and drag them in the streets; that they will increase their round tires like the moon, increase their hoops, and their headbands, increase their Grecian bends at once and carry it out until they get through with it, so that we can turn to the Lord as a people. Some of the daughters of Zion do not seem willing to forsake the fashions of Babylon. I to such would say hasten it, and let the woe that is threatened on this account come, that we may get through with it, then we can go on and build up the Zion of God on the earth."[11]

Imagine what he would say if he saw the fashions of today that include the nose rings, the leg ornaments, the tinkling ornaments about the feet that were not present during his day, but are now very prevalent in ours, even among many of our members?

BUT WHAT ABOUT A YEARS SUPPLY OF BASIC FOOD STORAGE?

I believe that every prophet over the last 60 years has talked about having the Church members get a bare minimum of at least a one year's supply of basic food items. Though it is not addressed directly in every conference, it is published in a tremendous amount of Church literature, pamphlets, Church handbook of instructions, monthly messages for home teachers and visiting teachers, instruction manuals, etc.

Again, after 9/11, in the following October General Conference, President Hinckley talked about food storage.

"**We cannot provide against every contingency. But we can provide against many contingencies. Let the present situation remind us that this we should do. As we have been continuously counseled for more than 60 years, let us have some food set aside that would sustain us for a time in case of need. But let us not panic nor go to extremes. Let us be prudent in every respect.**"[12]

Three months later, the First Presidency then took the unprecedented step of issuing a special letter (January 20, 2002) clarifying his remarks so that there would be no misunderstanding, asking that food storage preparation, specifically concerning having minimally a one year supply for every member in the world where ever possible, be taught in every branch, ward, district and stake in the Church. In it, for the first time, it outlined the minimum of basic food items to be included in such storage. Unfortunately, it is estimated that 25% of the membership in North America, still have never even heard of the letter because it was not taught to them by their local leaders. Quoting from the letter (underlining is mine):

"Priesthood and Relief Society leaders should teach the importance of home storage and securing a financial reserve. These principles may be taught in ward councils or on a fifth Sunday in priesthood and Relief Society meetings.

"**Church members can begin their home storage by storing the basic foods that would be required to keep them alive if they did not have anything else to eat. Depending on where members live, those basics might include water, wheat or other grains, legumes, salt, honey or sugar, powdered milk, and cooking oil. ...** When members have stored enough of these essentials to meet the needs of their family for one year, they may decide to add other items that they are accustomed to using day to day.

"**Some members do not have the money or space for such storage, and some are prohibited by law from storing a year's supply of food. These members should store as much as their circumstances allow. Families who do not have the resources to acquire a year's supply can begin their storage by obtaining supplies to last for a few months. Members should be prudent and not panic or go to extremes in this effort.** Through careful planning, most Church members can, over time, establish both a financial reserve and a year's supply of essentials."[13]

Following this, the Church made a major change at the Bishops storehouses, creating monthly survival food storage boxes for one person at tremendously low prices. A person could purchase 12 of these boxes and have a years supply of food storage...allowing the step by step completion of President Hinckley's counsel by almost any member.

The preparedness message was also echoed by other Church leaders as well. In a Jan 31, 2002 letter by President Packer, acting President of the Quorum of the Twelve, to General Authorities, Area Authority Seventies, Stake, Mission and District Presidents part of the emphasis for 2002 stake conference training was "please instruct members of the importance of reducing debt, living within their means, and storing food and other essentials that enable them to remain self-reliant in times of need."

A year later to reemphasize the importance of obtaining a years supply of food storage, it was the main topic for the visiting teaching message for January 2003, "If ye are prepared ye shall not fear."

And so we get to the heart of the matter:

ARE TOO MANY MEMBERS, INCLUDING LOCAL AND STAKE LEADERS, IGNORING THE COUNSEL TO TEACH AND ENCOURAGE THAT <u>EVERY</u> **MEMBER SHOULD HAVE AT LEAST A 1 YEAR SUPPLY OF BASICS?**

Is there a chance that because of their lack of attention in this one small area...that they and their trusting members might one day in the future suffer terrible consequences such as watching their families and friends slowly starve to death? President Kimball said:

> **"How often do Church members arise early in the morning to do the will of the Lord?... How often do we say, "Yes, I will obey the commandment to store food and to help others, but just now I have neither the time nor the money to spare; I will obey later"? Oh, foolish people! While we procrastinate, the harvest will be over and we will not be saved. Now is the time to follow Abraham's example; now is the time to repent; now is the time for prompt obedience to God's will."[14]**

It is important to note that many of the prophets, including President Kimball in the preceding quote, call it <u>THE COMMANDMENT</u> to store food.

As one reads the scriptures, the talks, the manuals and all that has been said upon the subject, it isn't a matter of <u>IF</u> the famine comes, it is a matter of only <u>WHEN</u> the famine comes. President Benson stated:

> **"Not only should we have strong spiritual homes, but we should have strong temporal homes. We should avoid bondage by getting out of debt as soon as we can, pay as we go, and live within our incomes. There is wisdom in having on hand a year's supply of food, clothing, fuel (if possible), and in being prepared to defend our families and our possessions and to take care of ourselves. I believe a man should prepare for the worst while working for the best. Some people prepare and don't work, while others work but don't prepare. Both are needed if we would be of maximum service to our God, our family, and our country."**
>
> **"We must do more to get our people prepared for the difficult days we face in the future. Our major concern should be their spiritual preparation so they will respond with faith and not fear. "If ye are prepared, ye shall not fear" (D&C 38:21). Our next concern should be for their temporal preparation. When the economies of nations fail, when famine and other disasters prevent people from buying food in stores, the Saints must be prepared to handle these emergencies. This is a matter of concern for area, region, and stake councils."[15]**

What do we do after we have a basic year's supply of food for ourselves and our family? Simply, we have been counseled to think about going beyond just the basics of food and extend the principle to clothing, fuel, seeds, tools, shelters (tents) and other items necessary to sustain ourselves and our families for a year.

> **"A man should not only be prepared to protect himself physically, but he should also have on hand sufficient supplies to sustain himself and his family in an emergency. For many years the leaders of the Mormon Church have recommended, with instructions, that every family have on hand at least a year's supply of basic food, clothing, fuel (where possible), and provisions for shelter. This has been most helpful to families suffering temporary reverses. It can and will be useful in many circumstances in the days ahead. We also need to get out of financial bondage, to be debt-free."[16]**

Some believe falsely that when things get bad...the Church has stored enough for all of the members. The Church leadership has been very clear on this issue:

"Our bishop's storehouses are not intended to stock enough commodities to care for all the members of the Church. Storehouses are only established to care for the poor and the needy. For this reason, members of the Church have been instructed to personally store a year's supply of food, clothing, and, where possible, fuel. By following this counsel, most members will be prepared and able to care for themselves and their family members, and be able to share with others as may be needed." [17]

Finally, in summary:

"You do not need to go into debt to obtain a year's supply. Plan to build up your food supply just as you would a savings account. Save a little for storage each paycheck. Can or bottle fruit and vegetables from your gardens and orchards. Learn how to preserve food through drying and possibly freezing. Make your storage a part of your budget. Store seeds and have sufficient tools on hand to do the job. If you are saving and planning for a second car or a television set or some item which merely adds to your comfort or pleasure, you may need to change your priorities. We urge you to do this prayerfully and do it now. I speak with a feeling of great urgency." [18]

"When we really get into hard times," said President J. Reuben Clark, Jr., "where food is scarce or there is none at all, and so with clothing and shelter, money may be no good for there may be nothing to buy, and you cannot eat money, you cannot get enough of it together to burn to keep warm, and you cannot wear it." [19]

"For more than a hundred years, Church leaders have taught the members to store grain and other essentials that would sustain life in times of drought or famine. The current guidelines for home storage are intended to apply internationally. They include having a supply of food, clothing, and, where possible, the fuel necessary to sustain life for one year. Church guidance states, "We have never laid down an exact formula for what anybody should store. Perhaps if we think not in terms of a year's supply of what we ordinarily would use, and think more in terms of what it would take to keep us alive in case we didn't have anything else to eat, that last would be very easy to put in storage for a year"." [20]

President Joseph Fielding Smith said:
"The distress and perplexity, bloodshed and terror, selfish ambition of despotic rulers, such as the world has never before seen, all indicate that the great and dreadful day of the Lord is very near, even at our doors. We have been warned by the prophets from the beginning of time. They have declared, by revelation from the Lord, that in this present day, confusion, bloodshed, misery, plague, famine, earthquake, and other calamities, would cover the face of the earth. The Lord told his disciples of these dreadful scenes and said men's hearts would fail them because of these things coming upon the earth. . . ." [21]

"President Wilford Woodruff and the Prophet Joseph Smith declare that it was their duty and should be the duty of every righteous man to raise the warning voice and proclaim the fact that these calamities are at our doors, and I have been condemned because I have done that. I heard one good man say, "There are too many good things to think about without talking about these troubles, these plagues, or worrying about the coming of the Lord." Here is what the Lord says in Section 45 of the Doctrine and Covenants, verses 39 to 43.

"And it shall come to pass that he that feareth me shall be looking forth for the great day of the Lord to come, even for the signs of the coming of the Son of Man.
"And they shall see signs and wonders, for they shall be shown forth in the heavens above, and in the earth beneath.
"And they shall behold blood, and fire, and vapors of smoke."

"Now, when the Lord says that, don't you think I am justified in raising my voice and do you think I am doing wrong when I am... watching the signs of the times and these calamities and troubles that are coming? Am I doing wrong? And yet one good brother said that. Too many things to do.

We haven't time to worry about the coming of Christ. I hope he is here. Now, here is something from President Brigham Young.

"Do you think there is calamity abroad now among the people?...All we have yet heard and all we have experienced is scarcely a preface to the sermon that is going to be preached. When the testimony of the Elders ceases to be given, and the Lord says to them, 'come home; I will now preach My own sermons to the nations of the earth,' all you now know can scarcely be called a preface to the sermon that will be preached with fire and sword, tempests, earthquakes, hail, rain, thunders, and lightnings and fearful destruction. What matters the destruction of a few railway cars? You will hear of magnificent cities, now idolized by the people, sinking in the earth, entombing the inhabitants. The sea will heave itself beyond its bounds, engulfing mighty cities. Famine will spread over the nations, and nation will rise up against nation, kingdom against kingdom, and states against states, in our own country and in foreign lands; and they will destroy each other, caring not for the blood and lives of their neighbors, of their families, or for their own lives. They will be like the Jaredites who preceded the Nephites upon this continent, and will destroy each other to the last man, through the anger that the devil will place in their hearts, because they have rejected the words of life and are given over to Satan to do whatever he listeth to do with them. You may think that the little you hear of now is grievous; yet the faithful of God's people will see days that will cause them to close their eyes because of the sorrow that will come upon the wicked nations. The hearts of the faithful will be filled with pain and anguish for them."

"Why is the Lord angry? Why are all these things coming upon the world? President Young said in this article that I read and the Lord says in the revelations I have read to you, it is because they have turned away from the Gospel of Jesus Christ, because they have rebelled against God, and because they have refused to hear the testimony of those who have been sent to preach the Gospel to them. That is why. They have rejected the message. The nations are full of iniquity."

"Now, there is our danger. We must not forsake God. If we are not on His side, you may be sure He is not going to be on our side. He will leave us to ourselves. Now, these calamities are here. They are upon us. The whole world is in commotion. I have had to leave unsaid about two-thirds of what I have prepared to say, but next week, which will be the concluding talk, I am going to turn to these Scriptures and show you what the old prophets have said in regard to our day. I have told you now what the Lord said and what the prophets of our own day have said. I have shown you the fulfillment of the prediction by President Wilford Woodruff, that the angels are sent forth to reap the earth. They are on that mission. This I have presented to you tonight, and we will get the other things next time."[22]

"If ye are prepared ye shall not fear."[23]

Copyright, Roger K. Young

(Footnotes)

[1] Regional Studies, Missouri, Benson—Haun's Mill, p.107
[2] Ehat & Cook, Words, Manuscript History of the Church: 29 August 1842 (Monday Morning), p.127–129
[3] See B. H. Roberts, Comprehensive History of the Church, Vol.4, Ch.98, p.91
[4] Encyclopedia of Mormonism, Vol.2, HANDCART COMPANIES
[5] Ibid
[6] Teachings of Ezra Taft Benson, p.265
[7] Teachings of Ezra Taft Benson, p.706
[8] (CR October 1980, Ensign 10 [November 1980]: 33.) Teachings of Ezra Taft Benson, p.266
[9] D&C 112:24-26
[10] President Joseph F. Smith quotes from Lesson 44 Preparing For The Second Coming of Christ, page 393
[11] The Discourses of Wilford Woodruff, p.226 - p.227
[12] Oct 6, 2002 Sunday morning Session, President Hinckley
[13] Jan 20, 2002 First Presidency Letter
[14] The Teachings of Spencer W. Kimball, p.174
[15] Teachings of Ezra Taft Benson, p.264
[16] President Benson, God, Family, Country, p. 331.)
[17] Teachings of Ezra Taft Benson, p.263-264, 267
[18] President Benson, CR October 1980, Ensign 10 [November 1980]: 33.)
[19] Teachings of Ezra Taft Benson, p.268
[20] Encyclopedia of Mormonism, Vol.2, EMERGENCY PREPAREDNESS
[21] Joseph Fielding Smith Jr., Doctrines of Salvation, Vol.3, p.19
[22] Joseph Fielding Smith, The Signs of the Times, p.124-137
[23] D&C 38:30

Copyright 2005, Roger K. Young

Normalcy Bias – *It's All in Your Head*

Human bodies don't normally fly through the air, but last year that's exactly what I witnessed while waiting for a red light to turn green.

I was sitting in my Tahoe at an intersection not far from home when I heard the loud rumble of a truck engine. I couldn't quite believe my eyes when a green pick-up veered around me, raced into the intersection and plowed into a white sedan. While my mind was registering this violent accident, I saw a scarecrow fly through the air. I took a few deep breaths, tried to remember the details of how the accident happened and waited to give my eyewitness account to the police who appeared on the scene within minutes.

My mind re-played the scene, always with that scarecrow flying out of the truck and into the adjacent field. It wasn't until a half hour later, when I saw EMTs trying to revive a young man did I realize that what I had actually seen was his body at the moment it was ejected from the front seat. Even now, when I remember the accident, I don't see a human. Instead, the image of a scarecrow is imprinted in my brain because humans don't fly through the air!

Normalcy Bias defined

This is an example of Normalcy Bias, a survival mechanism our brains are equipped with that can place us in grave danger when we're faced with something traumatic. Simply put, it causes our brains to insist that all is okay. Everything will return to normal. For most of us who have never faced true peril, Normalcy Bias tells us that nothing bad will ever happen. "This is America!," some people insist when I tell them about the possibility of a deeper Depression or hyperinflation. Incredibly, the most obvious warning signs are ignored.

This explains why so many Jews continued living in Germany, even after they were forced to wear identifying yellow stars and discriminatory laws were passed against Jewish people. Life had been so good for so long that, surely, things would get better. Jews who could have easily afforded to move out of the country stayed, and perished.

Oncoming hurricanes and similar disasters elicit similar reactions. We simply expect life to go on as it always has, and our brains are wired to accept that and nothing else. A driver attempts to cross a flooded river. Thousands of New Orleans residents faced with Hurricane Katrina refuse to leave the city, and city officials don't even make an attempt to evacuate them. One survivor from 9/11 tells of going blind as she saw dozens of human bodies hitting the ground outside the Twin Towers. Our brains can accommodate billions of bits of information each day, but apparently, there are some things too terrible to comprehend.
image by richardmasoner

Those of us who believe in preparedness, whether beginners or veterans, know the frustration of trying to convince loved ones that the future is not at all secure, but the Normalcy Bias isn't something we can debate. It's not based on logic or rational thought. It's the brain, doing its best to help its human owner deal with terrifying events and possibilities, as well as with escalating situations whose logical, final outcomes can't be accepted.

Here's another example from just last month…

If you had told me two months ago that American citizens would meekly line up to walk through powerful x-ray machines that would strip them bare before low-level TSA employees, I would have said, "Never!" If you had told me that, as an option, they would stand with arms raised while their crotches were groped and would allow their pre-schoolers to be similarly molested, I would have laughed. Yet, that is exactly what is happening, and we hear of similar searches planned for train stations, hotels, and more.

The water is heating up and most of the frogs are oblivious.
"Life will get back to normal."
"There's nothing wrong with this!"

Each week brings another repressive ruling, and still, most American citizens insist there is no reason for concern. New legislators will make everything right again. This is just temporary.

Whatever comes next will, again, be excused and accepted. Darn that Normalcy Bias!

Eleven Tips for Banishing Normalcy Bias

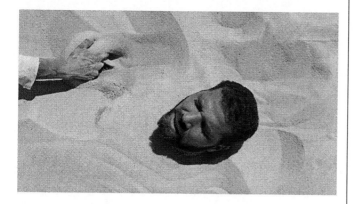

Here's the bottom line. As SurvivalMoms, we don't have the luxury of looking at a catastrophe before us and saying over and over again, "I can't believe this is happening. I can't believe this." If our kids can't rely on us when all hell is breaking loose, then who can they depend on? Law enforcement and first responders are quickly overwhelmed, and your family is hardly at the top of their list. Normalcy Bias can place those we love most in grave danger.

I think a conversation about overcoming Normalcy Bias will be important and valuable in the Comment section following this article, but here are eleven ways we can begin to condition our minds to accept the unacceptable.

1. Be willing to go through the painful process of acknowledging the uncertainty of our future. I compare it with the Kubler-Ross grief process: denial (Normalcy Bias rearing its ugly head!), anger (at politicians, circumstances, family members), bargaining ("If I can just buy enough precious metals, we'll be okay."), depression (our children aren't facing the same, sunny future that we did, America is changing before our eyes), and finally, acceptance (I can't do everything, but I can be proactive and do what I can.)

2. Face facts, don't hide from them. Confront financial difficulties, acknowledge your limits. Only when you face reality can you prepare for it.

3. Trust your instincts. Headlines change on a dime. Take in a much bigger picture than a single, optimistic headline or the words of a politician seeking re-election. Trust your own five senses and what your gut is telling you.

4. Start where you are with what you have.

5. Fight feeling overwhelmed with lists and organization. Focus on what you will do today, this week, this month. Little by little it will all come together.

6. Reach out to others. Start your own SurvivalMom meet-up group. Spend time on preparedness and survival forums, as long as they don't feed your fears. If there was ever a time for people to come together, this is it.

7. It's better to over-prepare than to be under-prepared. Normalcy Bias assures us that everything will be okay. A few extra bottles of water is all you really need. Those ten cans of tuna will be plenty! Go ahead and stock up more than you think you'll need to. Make plans for scenarios that may be a bit far out but still within the realm of possibility.

8. Make plans. Have an evacuation plan, and prepare for it. Have a hunker-down plan, and prepare for it. Decide ahead of time how you will face the most likely crises and communicate those plans with those who need-to-know. Write down your plans! Panic and stress have a way of erasing the logical parts of our brains!

9. Be ready to act quickly and decisively. It's better to take action too soon than too late.

10. Take time off. Forget you ever heard of the word, 'preparedness'. Go shopping and blow a few bucks on something completely unnecessary. Go out to lunch. Play with the kids. Spend an hour on the phone gossiping with your best friend. Give yourself a mental break! Your family needs you to be strong. You need to take care of yourself, body, soul, and spirit.

11. Get physically fit. There is a huge connection between physical and mental fitness. Start with some sort of exercise and start today.

Normalcy Bias, although deeply ingrained in the human brain, doesn't have to control our futures or place us in harm's way. The first step in being prepared is becoming educated. Knowing about this bias, what it can do, and how it can be controlled will help you become a SurvivalMom in every sense of the word!

Understanding the Normalcy Bias Could Save Your Life.

I am going to tell you a true story of personal tragedy. It was one of the most valuable learning experiences of my life. I have one regret…**I wish I would have understood a strange phenomenon called the normalcy bias.**

The formal definition is the phenomenon of disbelieving one's situation when faced with grave and imminent danger and/or catastrophe. One tends to over focus on the actual phenomenon instead of taking evasive action and enters a state of paralysis.

On October 27th, 1993, my home, along with 350 others in Laguna Beach, California burned to the ground. It was our first house. My husband and I hadn't even unpacked all our wedding gifts.

Early that afternoon, I went home to evacuate. My husband was out of town. As I made the long drive to the top of the hill where my house overlooked the ocean, the scene was surreal. Most of my neighbors were on their roof tops, watching the fire burn along the north side of the 133.

The fire was raging less than one thousand feet across the gorge, yet no one was packing their cars or preparing to evacuate. They were standing, like deer in the headlights, facing their inevitable doom. I hit the accelerator, pushing my old car to the limits of its capabilities, desperate to get to my home so I could get my important things. I promised myself to be out in 30 minutes or less.

But, something strange happened. I went from being focused on an efficient evacuation, to a complete state of disbelief. For the next three hours, I paced frantically back and forth, glued to the TV. I was biting my nails while wondering if it was really worth the trouble to pack up my car since the chances of something like this actually happening to me were so slim. Hello!

That, my friends, is the normalcy bias in action. I was paralyzed with indecision even though the facts of my situation were undisputable. I learned many life lessons with that experience. I no longer hesitate to evacuate immediately when we are threatened with a natural disaster, which is about once every other year in California.

In some ways, I feel like Americans are under the influence of the normalcy bias as it relates to the state of our economy, our currency and the security of our nation. Convincing facts are piling up like fire across the gorge. **All it will take is one little shift in the wind to send us into a tailspin** that is incomprehensible. Yet, most people I speak with don't seem the least bit concerned. **Could this be the normalcy bias at work?**

My story didn't end well. I was jolted back to reality when I literally felt the heat from the fire. During the last 10 minutes in our home, I was too flustered to function. In the end, I left with only the dogs and my life, trying to escape the 100 foot high wall of flame that was swallowing homes.

The Great Laguna Fire - 1993
seen from El Camino Street
Steve Turnout

I have always questioned my behavior that day. Why did I ignore my initial instinct to get out? Why did I go into such a powerful state of denial? Now, I know—it was a textbook case of the normalcy bias.

I could be completely wrong about the state of our nation. I am no expert. But I see signs everywhere and I can't shake the feeling that we are in for a big shakedown. I have vowed that 2011 is my year to get prepared for an emergency, whatever it may be. Maybe next time, I won't be caught with my proverbial pants down.

The normalcy bias is alive and well during every crisis and natural disaster. Just look at the events of hurricane Katrina and the recent BP oil crisis or any atrocity. Now, I realize that the normalcy bias played a huge role in individual behavior, corporate behavior and the behavior of our government.

Things would have been much different for me Oct. 27, 1993 if I had known about the normalcy bias. If you haven't been through a major disaster or crisis, it's difficult to comprehend. **Understanding this phenomenon could save your life.** Use it as a resource to get prepared and to overcome the denial that happens when faced with crisis, so you can act with a clear head and possibly save your life.

The Five Principles of Preparedness

by Phil Burns

americanpreppersnetwork.com

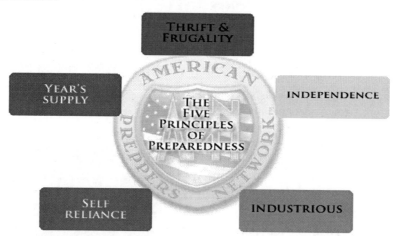

There are basic principles that keep us and our families grounded that are key to our happiness as a family unit while we Walk the Path of the Prepper. There is safety and peace that comes from having car insurance, home insurance, medical insurance,etc. What many families frequently ignore is "Standard of Living Insurance". At its heart, this is what Preparedness, Self-Reliance, Prepping – however you want to call it – is. By Getting Started in Prepping, or continuing in Prepping as the case may be, and following these five Principles of Preparedness we can provide our families with the assurance that we will be able to maintain a certain standard of living. This standard of living is dictated by the level of preparedness we are able to achieve and maintain.

For example, if a family falls into crisis and they have no preparations then once the average two weeks of supplies they have on hand has been used up, they will drop to a poverty standard of living. If that same family had a month's worth of supplies stored up, they would have a buffer of a little more than a month before they suffered consequences of their situation. Likewise, if they had a year's supply of essentials stored, they would effectively be giving themselves a year to be able to recover and plan in the event of a paradigm changing event.

Standard of Living Insurance, or Prepping, provides us with a hedge against calamity. There is much talk recently of "Doomsday" events – which are inappropriately and improperly titled. After all, Doomsday literally means the last day before the end of the earth. What point is there in preparing for that? Massive, widespread crisis, such as; an EMP, Nuclear War, Coronal Mass Ejection, Economic Collapse, and so on is a frequent topic as well. While these things are important to consider in preparing, it is a mistake to hyper-focus on them. There are many other immediate,

closer and more likely scenarios that make sense to focus on such as the loss or major injury of a breadwinner, loss of a primary job, extended sickness, accidents and other personal calamities. These happen every single day and each of us likely knows someone to whom this has happened. These are the things that are most essential to develop a "Standard of Living Insurance" against.

The most common effect of living an abundant life, as many of us do, is complacency. As we progress and develop disposable income the complacent tendency is to adjust our standard of living upwards by purchasing a bigger house, a new vehicle, a boat or other recreational toys instead of investing that money to insure the standard of living that we previously grew accustomed to. It is most prudent to instead, in times of largess, not expand your standard of living right away but to choose to ensure that if the current boon withdraws the family is not affected by it. Complacency however, leads us down the path of seeing increased income to the home as play, expendable, or rewarding money – all of which it can be with the proper perspective. That perspective is to view this blessing as an opportunity to 'play' at increasing our stores as much as possible, to purchase as many 'expendable' goods as possible – that can go into storage, or to 'reward' ourselves by adding a more expensive item to our storage that will significantly increase the amount of coverage our Standard of Living Insurance provides us. It also gives us the opportunity to scrutinize our funds and storage to determine if the family can splurge a little and enjoy some recreational time without it impacting the bottom line of our Standard of Living – but adamantly without changing our cost of living.

Following the Principles of Preparedness allows heads of households to reduce stress, find peace and be comfortable in an ever-changing and tumultuous world.

Principle 1
Practice thrift and frugality

The depression era saying of "Use it up, Wear it out, Make it do, or Do without" sums up the practice of Thrift. Living thriftily is not a popular concept in our "Staying up with the Jones's" mentality, but the folly of that mentality is that if one thing goes wrong and your family slips into crisis, you will have to learn all about "Staying above water". Living thriftily is a very simple, effective and immediate method to increase your spending power. Imagine being, instead of a consumer; a creator, a repairer, or simply abstaining. It is phenomenally financially wasteful to eat at restaurants on a regular basis, in addition to being typically un-healthy; it also takes away from time spent together as a family creating a personal dining experience at home, together. Thrift is a practice of not wasting anything including time and money.

Frugality dictates that we live within our means and "Waste not, want not". It requires us to be prudent with how we spend our money and to cautiously and guardedly decide how to distribute it. Why do Americans work themselves so hard and as soon as the paycheck comes in, they throw it to the wind as quickly as they can – leaving them with no reserves, no safety and no peace? It is because we have come to accept abundance as our standard. We foolishly assure ourselves that there will be a check next pay period – which there normally is, until there is not. It is the high possibility that at some point something critical will happen in our lives that brings us to the conclusion that it is very likely that at some point, that check will not be there.

One massive waste that Americans have become very comfortable with is living on credit. We have become extremely complacent with our finances in this regard. Instead of doing without for a short time while we save, we finance everything and as a consequence, pay financing fees and interest that we somehow justify as necessary. It is not necessary that we ever pay financing fees or interest for anything, even a house, if we are willing to be prudent. Instant gratification is the bane of thrift and frugality. We Americans have deceived ourselves into believing that we 'deserve' to live a better lifestyle than our parents (which took them a lifetime to achieve) – when in reality – we DESERVE to be secure and at peace in our lifestyle. It is ironic that as a society, we will dicker over $3,000 on a new vehicle and then finance it for 5 years – wherein we condemn ourselves to paying several times that in financing fees and interest.

What good have we done ourselves by shaving $3,000 of off $30,000 when we just finance it? If you're willing to pay astronomical fees for the pleasure of immediate gratification, amortizing $3,000 does NOTHING to our monthly bill. A frugal person would take 3 years and save monthly as much as they would have paid out on their car payment with a little bonus savings here and there over time. In that short period of time they would accumulate enough cash that they could go into the car dealership and lay down a pile of $23,000 in cash and say they want to walk out with either their money or that $30,000 car. They're going to walk out with the car because the dealer wants the instant gratification of the cash versus selling an amortized note at a discount.

Living a thrifty and frugal lifestyle is truly simple. Use it up. Wear it out. Make it do. Do without. Waste not. These things lead us to not being left wanting when a crisis strikes our family. These two highly empowering tools not only give us the ability to build up our Standard of Living Insurance, they also bring an assured peace and allow us to live a truly abundant lifestyle where we are in control of our money instead being a slave to lenders.

A Prepper who successfully follows this principle for a few years will find themselves in a position where they are able to spend time not working without it affecting the family in an adverse manner.

*"Not only should we have strong spiritual homes, but we should have strong temporal homes. We should avoid bondage by getting out of debt as soon as we can, pay as we go, and live within our incomes. There is wisdom in having on hand a year's supply of food, clothing, fuel (if possible), and in being preparing to defend our families and our possessions and to take care of ourselves. **I believe a man should prepare for the worst while working for the best**."*
Teachings of Ezra Taft Benson, p. 263-264.

Principle Two
Seek to be Independent

Debt can be crippling and crushing to a family, making them unable to move forward due to the demands of making payments on things they potentially don't even own anymore. Seek to become Independent from debt! Learn to abhor the idea of being forced to labor and earn money that is not yours as a consequence of choosing to "live a little better" by going into debt. Living independently means being free to choose what is pertinent for you and your family to do with your money.

As you avoid going into debt and gain greater control of your money, establish savings that will grow and serve you as you become the master of your money. Learn to budget and responsibly manage your money as it is a very powerful tool to either enslave or empower you. You can begin to build wealth while you're getting out of debt by putting together a wise plan like the ones Dave Ramsey teaches in his Financial Peace University.

Independence doesn't just mean money though. Seek to be Independent of the influences of the world such as; caffeine, alcohol, drugs, tobacco, un-healthy yet addictive food, medications (where possible) and so on. All of these things not only make you a personal slave to addictions, it also indentures your wallet to spending wasteful amounts of money to satiate your personal weaknesses. Strive to become Independent of all these things and you will not only find a healthier you, you will also increase your income as you free a daily outgo to servicing your demons.

Live Independent of the entrapping influences of society as much as possible. Free your mind of thinking you need a better looking car, a prettier house or better clothes. Do what works for YOU, not what you think others will think highly of. Live independent of the fear of judgment of others and become secure in your own person. There seems to be a farcical belief in our society that we should appear as wealthy as possible. The idiocy of this belief is that it fails to take into account just how damaging it is to our self-

esteem, our lives and our livelihood. Break free of these childish societal 'norms' and live a life independent of the influence of advertisers, marketers and peer pressure!

Prepper families who learn to live independently will find themselves prospering greatly – in ways that may not be apparent to the enslaved masses of society.

Principle Three
Become Industrious

Learn, Explore, Do. Manage your circumstance to your advantage, be enterprising and fully explore opportunities that come your way. Seek always to discover ways to create benefit to you and your family. When opportunity presents itself, work hard at redefining and reshaping yourself, your position and your knowledge to be worthy of the success that opportunity can provide. Be resourceful, always looking for a new way to create what you need in order to succeed.

Common ways to be industrious include furthering your education – your whole life – and constantly working to develop new skills. By exploring opportunities, we are able to assess their potential, weigh risk and make a decision as to whether our conclusions merit committing to an opportunity or walking away from it. By improving ourselves constantly, we open up even more opportunity that can potentially bring success.

Idly standing by and waiting for success to land in your lap is a poor strategy. Being industrious means getting up and attempting something – even if it has the potential to fail. The Farmer who fails to put in a crop because he doesn't think there was enough snowfall during the winter loses out when spring rains finally bring plenty of water. When you commit to something, work hard at it; throw in everything you've got. Getting up and going is truly the only way to end up somewhere else.

Preppers who industriously seek out opportunity will soon find the one that will create a change in the direction their lives have been heading.

Principle Four
Strive Towards Self-Reliance

The Principle of Self-Reliance is predicated by and builds upon the first three principles. They are unavoidably intertwined and interdependent. Self-Reliance is, in its simplest form, being able to create or provide all needed things as the result of labor using a developed skill or talent and being able to provide resources as a result of a judicious practice of storing needful things. Therefore, becoming Self-Reliant is the actual process of developing skills and talents while putting away resources.

When combined with Thrift and Frugality, Self-Reliance is providing needed things for yourself that you would otherwise have had to pay money for such as; growing a garden, sewing or repairing clothes, building furniture, building a home, fixing your vehicle and so on. It is being willing to enjoy the fruits of your labor versus the blandness of buying something commercially produced. It is accepting things for their functionality, not for the logo that was stamped on them in a plant somewhere. It is being willing to use something that may be less than perfect in its manufacture but is pure in intent and purpose, knowing that the next one you create you will be able to work out flaws and produce something better.

Self-Reliance, when combined with Independence, drives us to be truly reliant on ourselves in all areas. It teaches us to discover a vocation where we are able to create an expandable income using our talents and labor instead of falling into a career where our income is constricted by salaries and our progress in hindered by being boxed into a job description. A truly independent person creates income opportunities for themselves and others while staying free and clear of debt and interest. A Self-Reliant person builds their own storage and is not dependent on a grocery store to be stocked and operational for them to feed themselves and their family.

Your Industriousness should be more than simply financially motivated. Self-Reliance is the act of being free of needing others, including companies, the government, or your community to provide for or support you. It is learning how to; make soap, grow your own food, provide your own energy, defend yourself, create the things you need and so on. It requires research, learning, experimenting, failing, experimenting more and finally succeeding – in gaining a new skill, accomplishing something new or developing a new vocation. An industrious and Self-Reliant person is truly a creator and experiences the joy of creation on a daily basis.

A Prepper who begins to become Self-Reliant experiences a mental shift and begins to see things such as a grocery store as a warehouse that is utilized to stock up their own storage.

Principle Five
Aspire to have a year's supply of every needful thing

The natural outgrowth of becoming truly Self-Reliant is to feel compelled to store things up that are essential for our family's ensured safety, comfort and existence. Every needful thing teaches us to consider the possibility of storing up a supply of every item that we purchase which we truly need. What is a need? Simply put, it is something that it would be difficult or impacting to have to live without. This includes; food, clothing, water, heat, power, home medical supplies, fire starters, light and so on.

It is obviously not prudent to just purchase a year's supply of every needful thing. Instead, it is a goal that is pursued relentlessly by the Self Reliant Person and is adjusted for each item of consideration. For example, it is quite inexpensive and easy to acquire a year's supply of ketchup – at most a family will probably use 2 bottles a month. Therefore, purchasing 24 bottles would give you a year's supply. However, a year supply of something like water, which is consumed every day, requires a very different approach. It is not feasible to store a year supply of water unless you have your own water tower. There are other options available though which include such things as; drilling a well, installing a rain catchment system, being situated near a body of water. Several of these options would require filtering the water that you acquire. For the money spent on a filtering system, such as a Berkey filter, it becomes prudent to purchase filtering capability for the system that will last several years. Each item is adjusted in quantity and time by its own consideration.

One year is not a magic number. It is, however, a measure which provides us with a lengthy buffer to recover from whatever has happened. It also allows us to be charitable towards others who have fallen on hard times without it creating a severe impact on us. Imagine an unprepared neighbor or friend having their bread winner incapacitated for a period of time and not being able to provide for themselves. You are not impacted by their crisis and because you have a year's supply stored up, you have the opportunity to assist them by opening your storage to them and allowing them to take what they need without it causing you an economic impact and with very little added risk to yourself.

Begin by striving to build up a 3 month supply, then double it and double it again. Once you've accomplished the first three months, you will have an idea of the amount of time and money it will take to acquire a year's supply.

The Prepper who is striving to build a year's supply of every needful thing will experience a dramatic reduction in stress and inverse increase in peace as they begin meeting goals on the path to achieving this principle.

The impact of living The Principles of Preparedness

When teaching these Principles, the question is inevitably asked "What if nothing ever happens that I need my supplies for?" To which I respond, "That would be wonderful!" Most people don't get it right away, but let's consider it.

Consider if you adjusted your life and lived for years under these principles. What impact would there be if nothing happened that required you to survive off your stores? Might it be possible that in following these principles you will have created a new life for yourself that is infinitely better than it would be otherwise? Would you possibly have spent that time living in peace, without stress and with a much higher level of confidence, satisfaction and self -esteem? I can testify to you that this is indeed what will happen! In fact, the mere application of these principles in your life will allow you to weather small crises without them even registering a bump in the continuity of your life. When you are living a Self-Reliance lifestyle with a full year's supply, not having an income for a month is inconsequential. If you fully commit to living these principles, do you see how this would be the outcome? Would that serve you to be able to live that way?

Consider also that as you develop a year supply of every needful thing, you are to live off of that supply. You don't just package things up and leave them in a corner to gather dust. You consume your supply each month and at the end of four weeks, go to the "warehouse" (aka grocery store, etc.) and replenish your supply with six weeks worth of what was consumed. This allows you to continuously grow your storage with little to no visible impact to you. And, if times are tough financially, you can extend to 8 or 12 weeks without it stressing your family.

As you become these Principles, you will experience breaking free of the slavery of debt, a 'career', of "keeping up with the Jones's" and most importantly, the stress of trying to live month to month. What you will find instead is that you are able to fully experience life and truly enjoy the blessings of your family.

All the while knowing that the secret to a happy life is wrapped up in a little concept called being a "Prepper"!

- Inspired by a talk by James E. Faust

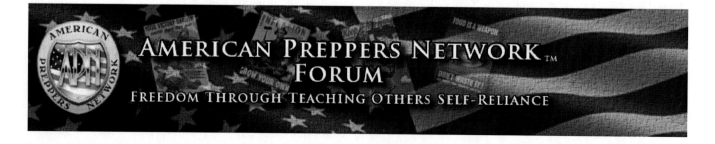

Mental & Spiritual Preparations for Survival

Originally posted at www.SurvivalBlog.com
Copyright 2012

For many people preparing to survive has become an obsession; a pursuit placed above all else in their lives. Others feel as if survival prep should be more of a priority if they could only afford to do more. Still others feel as if they may have already gone overboard in their preparations. Preparing for survival after TEOTWAWKI can make you feel overwhelmed, under-supplied, overspent, under-funded, over-your-head, or under-the-gun (no pun intended).

There are those who have the ability to purchase a retreat, stock it with supplies and equipment for a year or more, and have enough to share with those in need at will. They expect to support parents, siblings and spouses, nieces and nephews, grandkids, and several families of friends, and have already stocked their retreat with all the food, water, and supplies for all of them to start completely over. Most of us, however, fall far short of that ability, and hope that we can simply prepare for ourselves and our immediate family.

Please understand, I am not criticizing those who are able to prepare in this way. That's what this country is all about – the chance to make and keep your fortunes. As Christians we don't believe in luck, but we do believe in hard work and good fortune. We can only hope that most, many, or all of these fortunate people have the Christian outlook of sharing with those in need.

Whether you are a preparedness guru (PG) or a "newbie" (NP – for New Preparer), getting prepared to survive after any disaster, or even a total collapse, seems like a daunting task. PGs know just how expensive and time consuming preparing can be, and many NP's have become discouraged as they begin to realize what they are facing. It is for that reason that mental preparedness (MP) is so important.

Mental Preparedness involves many aspects and the first and foremost of these is an individual's Spiritual preparation. Are you a Christian? Have you accepted Jesus Christ as your Lord and Savior? Are you ready to die if that's what God's will for you is? Christianity – that is, evangelical Christianity (Christians who believe that Jesus died for their sins, was buried, and rose again as a living Savior sitting at the right hand of God) offers living hope for our future. We worship a living Savior, one Who has gone before us to prepare a place for us in heaven.

If you have not already done so, accept Jesus into your life as Lord and Savior. It's so easy to do. Any good Christian can help you or go to www.sbc.net and click on the small green

link at the top of the page "I want to know Jesus." Until you make Christ real in your life the rest of the preparations are just going through the motions.

Once you are Spiritually prepared, the next step is prayer. Ask God to guide you in your preparation, to give you insight into the survival mindset, to lead you to the resources you need to get your mind ready for the preparation task, and to guide and help you in the decisions that must be made to prepare yourself and your family for survival. Ask Him how you can become a better Christian and person through this process – He will show you if you are open to receiving the answers. Finally, ask the Lord help you communicate the urgency and necessity to others to prepare to survive.

Is there Biblical mandate for survival? For preparation? Yes, God has given us instructions in His Word for survival and preparation. Following is a list of Scriptures for you to look up for yourself rather than quoting them here for brevity, but please take the time to look up each one and understand what God is trying to tell us, tell you, about being prepared and surviving.

Proverbs 6:6–11 – tells us that we are responsible to do the work of preparation while we are able.

2 Thessalonians 3:10 – basically says that if you don't work, you don't eat. Of course that does not include the sick or the aged; those should be taken care of by family or Christian charity. It plainly teaches that indolence or laziness should not be rewarded. In other words, if we could have

prepared for the crisis but we didn't, we can't expect anyone else to take care of us. It is a principle that applies in every-day-life or in crisis situations.

1 John 3:17 – 18 – exhorts us to help others in need. Yet, you can not help someone who is in need if you haven't prepared for or can't help yourself. If we are to obey this verse then some sort of preparation is not only called for, but required.

Some great thoughts from another (unknown) Christian author:

" With regard to fleeing from life-threatening situations - what one brother sarcastically refers to as 'hidey hole' theology - Both Peter and Paul escaped from life-threatening situations. Peter fled from Jerusalem after his miraculous deliverance from prison by the angel. Paul was let down over the walls of Damascus when a plot against his life was uncovered. Both of these were escapes from the physical persecution that arose against them because of their testimony and preaching of the Gospel. Are we supposed to believe that God is only interested in preserving His people if they are in danger as a result of their following Jesus? That if the shortsightedness or greed of the world, places Christians in danger, that somehow that is not sufficient reason to escape in order to continue to serve, worship and love God and those around us? I can't speak for others, but I know my purpose in preparing for eventualities. It is not merely to save my hide; it's not worth that much anyway; but to do what Christians have done throughout the centuries, namely to maintain a living witness to the redemptive love of God in Christ, and to continue nurturing the Church which God has called me.

Some Christians believe that it is wrong to leave your urban or suburban home to find a rural setting where survival would be more likely. Again, this is called, 'hidey hole' theology. Yet, after the stoning of Stephen much of the Church in Jerusalem dispersed precisely to preserve their lives, to continue to care for each other and spread the Gospel in the new surroundings. God called Stephen to martyrdom, but not the whole Church. The Church in Rome met in the catacombs. Some lived in the catacombs. Was that 'hidey-hole' theology? When Jesus began his ministry He read from Isaiah in the synagogue, 'The Spirit of the Lord is upon me....This day the Scripture is fulfilled in your hearing.' They wanted to kill Him, but He 'passed through them.' He escaped. Was that 'hidey-hole' theology?

In 1 Kings 17:8 - 16, Elijah instructed the widow of Zarephath to give him her last cup of flour and last bit of oil. He told her don't be afraid, God will provide. God caused there to be a daily miracle provision of flour and oil for her

survival. But another widow and her son in *2 Kings 4: 1 - 7, were instructed by Elisha to gather many containers, for God was about to provide for her needs.* There was an immediate miracle of multiplication of the oil, part of which she was told to pay off her debts with, but the remainder she was to store. Thus, there was preparation, provision, and then storage in order for this woman and her son to survive. Sure, the provision was miraculous; but her use of God's provision was quite normal and mundane. Nor did Elisha criticize her for storing her oil for her family's future needs. [This author adds: it could be that your provisions may be provided in an equally miraculous fashion.]

Am I stupid, sinful and unbiblical because I want to see that my family survives? Am I supposed to believe that God doesn't want me to do anything about the survival of those whom I love, whom He has given to me? Have I no responsibility? Do I just stand with my eyes scrunched closed and say, 'OK God, you take care of me and mine?' Survival is not the ultimate value or goal for me or my family. It never was or will be. 'Glorifying God and enjoying Him forever' is. If God wants me and mine dead, so be it, and may He be praised forever. But I don't see that glorifying God and staying alive are mutually exclusive, especially when He seems to be graciously giving us advanced warning precisely so that we may continue to survive, so that we may serve Him and others.

And you, O mortal, do not be afraid of their words, though briers and thorns surround you and you live among scorpions; do not be afraid of their words, and do not be dismayed at their looks. Ezekiel 2:6

The clever see danger and hide; but the simple go on, and suffer for it. - Proverbs 22:3.

A closing thought (on Spiritual Preparedness): "When Noah built the ark, it wasn't raining."

Get your life right with God and prepare for tomorrow.

Many other aspects of survival require mental preparation as well. Too many people believe that because they witnessed some depravity that man had wrought on an individual, or on others, that they are now prepared to go through the hard times a severe crisis or even TEOTWAWKI can bring. Witnessing a tragic car accident, a shooting or murder, a knife fight in a bar, a shootout with the police, or even trying to help a rape victim can not begin to prepare you for the mental anguish of long-term crises. For the few who have had to kill in self-defense or seen the starvation and disease in some Third World country first hand as a missionary, these only begin to understand. If you served in combat – Iraq, Afghanistan, Korea, Vietnam, or WWII – and you had to kill or be killed, you had to care for a wounded and dying fellow soldier, or you had to survive as a prisoner of war, you understand some of what will be faced in an end of the world situation. Many of you may have loved ones or know someone who suffered with or still suffers from Post Traumatic Stress Disorder (PTSD) and can understand the mental stressors the individual endures. Unless you have been through it too you can't really comprehend all that this individual, these individuals, is/are going through.

So how do we prepare ourselves for what is to come? Everything starts with planning! And, it all hinges on organization. If you're a NP, start a list of preparations that need to be made. Do research on the Internet to find lists of the things you will need to do and what you will need to have on hand. Don't be overwhelmed by the lists of supplies — all of these things can be obtained one item at a time. Remember, if you start today you're still ahead of the majority of people. Continue to remind yourself that whatever you do today to prepare, won't be a need tomorrow.

Prepare your mind through the research you do. Read everything you can get your hands on about preparedness and survival, but read with a "grain of salt" so that you can discern good advice from bad. Read books and articles that are recommended by friends or reliable sources. Even other people who are preparedness minded can get and give bad advice — proceed with caution, but proceed.

One reliable and trusted Internet resource is www.SurvivalBlog.com, written and maintained by Jim Rawles. He is also the author of one of the best survival preparedness books on the market called Patriots – Surviving the Coming Collapse. While the book is a novel, there are many, many good references and teachings throughout. He has numerous other resources of his own and others on the web site.

To continue mental preparations for survival the NP must understand that they are basically on their own. Of course, they may have a supportive spouse, other family members, or a friend or two who understands survival prep, but beyond that you won't find individuals who are willing to open up their homes or retreats and say, "come see how I've done it." Because of the secretive nature of our preparations for ourselves and our families, and because we want to protect those preps from those that would steal them or want to show up at our front gate when TSHTF, we just don't let others know what we've got. Thus, we are on our own. It is a very difficult position to be in when a best friend refuses to recognize the importance and urgency or preparation. PGs understand this and have developed techniques and questions to discern how a person feels about preparedness and survival without really asking. Only time, practice, and mental preparedness can help in this area.

Preparing Standard Operating Procedures (SOPs) that outline what every family member will do in a crisis will ease your mental state as your preps continue. SOPs are nothing more than written directions to cover every contingency for every person. Make sure you have instructions written for all members who will be with you in a disaster situation. Different situations call for different SOPs – try to cover all the bases for at least 72 hours. This is not something you will accomplish overnight or even in the first few weeks. As you study and prepare you will continue to rewrite and edit your SOPs. Some may take years to finish while others may never be done.

Once your lists are in order you should begin putting together a BoB (Bug-out-Bag). This is a bag – a backpack, a duffel bag, a pillow case (although I think you will discover that a pillow case just isn't big enough) with everything in it you'll need to survive for three days to one week (or more). Every family member should have his/her own BoB, even children (as long as they are big enough to carry it). Weight for each BoB is obviously determined by each individual's size and ability. When you know everyone has the things they need to survive for several days, your mind is much more at ease.

The BoBs are like everything else involved with prep and survival – they will evolve through shrinking and growing for months before you are satisfied with all the preps for them. Only you can determine what is best for you to carry in the end, but there are literally 100's of list suggestions for BoBs on the Internet. Again, be prepared to sift through and decide what is best for you.

By prioritizing your purchases you can buy a little at a time – in fact, you can buy one item at a time if that is all your budget (or your wife [I'll address this issue further down] will allow). For instance, water must be a top priority for everyone in preparing for disaster. You can go for days without food but only hours (in comparison) without water. If you have a free-flowing spring in your yard then you are obviously covered, but for most of us water is something we must prepare for. Do we try to store enough bottled water for our family? Do we depend on our neighbors? (I think we know the answer to that one – remember, we depend on no one but ourselves) Storing bottled water is impractical for long-term preparedness. Water is needed at the rate of at least one gallon per person per day. In hot or humid conditions or if you are working outside strenuously, you will need more – maybe even twice that amount. So, a water filter, with extra filters, is an obvious priority. You may have to save for a couple of weeks or more to buy one, but since it is an important item it will clearly be worth it.

Food is a relatively easy category to begin to fill out your supply of. If you will make a list of items that you and your family regularly eat (in dry or canned items) and then begin to buy one or two extra items each time you go to the grocery store, you will find that your food supply will grow quickly. Don't forget things like toilet paper, tissues, baby items, feminine products, and the like; if you will buy these two at a time when you need them – one goes on the shelf to be used and the other goes in the prep closet or tub. These type products will also add to your stash quickly. P. S. You can never have enough toilet paper if TSHTF (no pun intended).

Continue to move down your Priority List is similar fashion and you will suddenly find yourself short of space to store things and your mental attitude eased by the fact that you are becoming prepared much quicker than you ever thought possible. Remember, organization is the key. Once you begin to buy items for prep or survival you must be organized. Lists are required, and keeping up with them is paramount for making sure you get what is necessary. It is very easy to buy things twice (or even more) if you are trying to keep up with your purchases by memory, or to think you bought something and miss the chance to buy it. Use lists!

Lists and organization are important to your MP in other ways as well. If you have your mind cluttered with mental lists, past or future purchases, and trying to keep up with all of your preps, family, work, etc., your going to be stressed beyond belief. Good MP calls for good organization.

I mentioned above that I would address the problem of a spouse who is a non-believer in preparedness or survival. When you want to talk about prep or survival all they do is change the subject or patronize you quickly and then dismiss it as unnecessary. They don't want to waste money on it.

Many spouses believe there's plenty of time to get what's needed if an emergency comes up later. Some will say that God will provide for us, so we don't have to do that. And, the excuses and objections goes on . . .
My own wife is one of those, or was one of those types. I went ahead with some small purchases a few years ago and

she would question them, but I never hid my purchases from her, lied to her about them, or dismissed her inquisitions. I simply explained that I had bought the item so we would be prepared in case of an emergency and what it was for. I would try to talk to her about it each time SHE brought something up, but she always changed the subject or said we'd talk about it another time. I never forced the issue.

Whenever she would hear a news story about some crisis situation (hurricane, tornado, lost hiker, violent robbery or home invasion) I would take the opportunity to point out the lack of preparation on the part of the individuals involved or what they needed instead of what they had, and I would say, "You know, I think I'll get one of those (whatever was mentioned that someone else needed) for us next time I get a chance so we won't be caught unprepared." She would usually agree we needed it, and the next day (or even that very day) I would buy whatever it was and add it to my supplies. She never questioned those purchases and eventually became (a little) more interested in our preps. I'm now trying to get her interested in a piece of retreat property by explaining the exact things I'm looking for (wooded acreage with room for house, barn & garden, a spring or free-flowing creek, isolated, defensible, etc.) and why. It has caused a few arguments (of course, the making up is fun), and she still won't read "Patriots" or any of the other books I've bought on the subject, but our (my) prep supplies are steadily growing and she's beginning to understand slowly. I'm still open to new suggestions in this area if anyone has any, but I know this has worked for me so far.

Mental preparedness for survival is very important if you are to ever feel like you're well on the way to being prepared. I'm one of those who believes that you can never be 100 percent prepared, but you can be well prepared. You can get to a point of calling yourself prepared and feeling good about your preps as long as you continue to monitor expiration dates, rotate fuel supplies, grow and can your own crops, and have all the things needed for starting over after TEOTWAWKI. A survival mindset is the first step. Making lists, prioritizing those lists for purchase or acquisition, and organizing the lists and acquisitions will help to keep you mentally prepared for survival.

Originally posted at
www.SurvivalBlog.com
Copyright 2012

How Long until You Starve?

by Mr. Yankee

*Originally posted at www.**SurvivalBlog**.com*
Copyright 2012

How long would you survive if you could never buy groceries again? Now consider how much worse that scenario would be if everyone you know was faced with the same question. It may have more relevance than you think. The food distribution system in industrialized nations has a complexity which baffles the mind. Thousands of suppliers coordinate with thousands of distributors to send food to millions of retailers for billions of consumers. But is there enough redundancy in the system to ensure the continued viability of commercially delivered food to your table? What if that incredibly complex system bottlenecked or crashed? Would you literally starve to death?

It has been estimated that the average grocery store has less than a one week supply of food. We have all seen shelves stripped bare following hurricanes or other natural disasters. There is rarely starvation in those settings because aide pours in from unaffected surrounding areas. But what if the shortages were on a regional or national level?

What could possibly cause such a disruption?

There are three steps involved in getting commercially produced food to your home. The food must be produced. It must be moved from the farm to the retailer (often involving several middlemen including turning raw wheat into boxed cereal etc.). And ownership must be transferred to you.

At the very source of food farmers could stop producing food if it becomes unsafe or unprofitable to do so. A pandemic might shut down the production of food on a regional scale. Any large natural disaster would have the same effect. A super volcano or large meteor strike would simply destroy every thing in the effected area including crops, farmers, and distributors or any food that might be produced or shipped through the effected area. Even a single nuclear detonation would effectively eliminate food production in the many miles polluted by windblown fallout. Nobody farms when they are putting their lives back together after disaster or fighting for survival against a pandemic.

More likely than those violent extremes are natural fluctuations of weather. Most of us agree that weather extremes seem more common today than in decades past. Climate change (from whatever source) is evident. Drought, too much rain, excessive heat, or unseasonably cold weather may all prevent crops from germinating, kill seeds in the ground, stunt growth, delay harvest, or out right kill plants and animals. Our very lives depend on predictably mild weather.

But dangers to food production exist in even more mundane forms. The lowly honey bee is the most prolific and productive pollinator of crops. It is actually threatened with extinction by a new wave of parasites and bee diseases. In the same way that "avian flu" endangers the global bird population (and to a lesser extent humans) bee diseases have the potential to destroy that essential link in the production of food for human consumption. Diseases in the crops and animals themselves could be just as devastating. The famous Irish potato famine of the 1840s was the result of a naturally occurring plant disease that destroyed the potato crops. It alone killed thousands of people even when no other crop was affected. A similar blight in rice or wheat could have a massive impact on the food supply globally.

All these factors apply not only to domestically produced food, but to imported food as well. In addition, the importation may be negatively influenced by war, economic, and other political factors. The effect of scarce resources and impaired distribution systems for food gave rise to the need for ration cards and "victory gardens" to combat hunger in the 1940s.

Modern commercial farming is dependent on commercially produced hybrid seeds (which are not capable of reproducing true to form), commercially produced fertilizers, and especially abundant supplies of fuel. If the supplies of gasoline and diesel fuels are interrupted, commercial farming will stop. Think about that for a moment. Even changes in the market price of fuel affect the profitability of farming. If a farmer earns $1,000 per ton of food produced, but it will cost $1,000 more in fuel costs next season, why would he plant the next crop? All factors affecting oil production and distribution (let alone the growing scarcity of cheaply refined oil) affect the viability of commercial farming. Any time a farmer chooses to not produce food, the supply available for market decreases.

What about distribution?

From Wikipedia: Food distribution, "a method of distributing (or transporting) food from one place to another, is a very important factor in public nutrition. Where it breaks down, famine, malnutrition or illness can occur. There are three main components of food distribution:

Transport infrastructure, such as roads, vehicles, rail transport, airports, and ports.

Food handling technology and regulation, such as refrigeration, and storage, warehousing.

Adequate source and supply logistics, based on demand and need."

All of the factors affecting food production may also adversely affect food distribution. Anything that interrupts the movement of food by road or rail or sea could stop food from reaching your market. A trucking strike, a port closure, a breakdown in communication technology would have impacts. A spike in fuel prices may slow distribution as well, but the major danger I see is a terrorists' electro magnetic pulse. There are theories which say that a single nuclear detonation at the correct altitude could blanket the continental United States with an electromagnetic pulse (EMP) sufficient to bring down the power grid and destroy the electronic ignitions in most automobiles, trucks, and other machinery. Stop the machines and you stop food distribution. Such an EMP would not only cripple hundred of thousands of machines, but would wipe out the communication networks. Framers, distributors, and retailers would not be able to communicate.

Business would literally stop when no telephones, faxes, or emails could take place. If the grid was down for two weeks, people would literally begin to starve and that doesn't even address the water shortage that would occur when the pumps stop, let alone sanitation and security issues.
The same is true of food processing and refining. Turning wheat into breakfast cereal and flour, pigs into bacon, chicken into nuggets etc all require machinery run on fuel and electricity. Each processor needs to coordinate an incoming supply of food from the farms and coordinate shipment to distribution centers and retailers.

Can you buy it?
Even if the food is on the grocery shelves, you need to be able to reach it before you can make use of it. Simple transportation from your home to the retailer and home again might be a challenge in a world where transportation has been disrupted by natural disaster, attack, or technological failure.

Some very intelligent people warn of an economic collapse on the scale of the Great Depression or worse. Hyper inflation is a reality in third world nations. It has happened in civilized and developed Europe several times in the last century as well. What if your paycheck loses 90% of its buying power in a month's time? What if the markets lose faith in the imaginary value of currency? Such things have happened repeatedly in the past. If the store shelves are full but a can of soup costs $100, how long can you eat? How long until rioting empties the stores and stops distribution?

Most of the scenarios described above are less than likely. In fact, most will never happen. But they are possible. When you consider the combined likelihood of each small possibility you may feel that it is prudent to prepare.

Why be concerned?

Early in the twentieth century the United States weathered the Great Depression and the effects of two World Wars. Why be concerned now? 50 years ago it was common for rural households to keep a garden and home can the produce to be used until the next harvest. Many rural families kept a cow for milk, raised poultry for meat and eggs, or at least raised feeder pigs to butcher each fall. My family did all those things through the 1980s but just try to find ten homes keeping a family milk cow today!

Even five years ago, I was not terribly concerned with the challenge of finding livestock to raise my own steak, eggs, milk, butter, pork, chicken, etc. But a US government program to microchip and register every single domestic animal (including poultry) has since been undertaken. The National Animal Identification System (NAIS) proposes to ID and track every single food animal in America. This program will make it illegal to keep unregistered livestock. This may not only prompt some people to avoid keeping stock (who needs more paperwork?) but also creates the real potential for government abuse. NAIS is already in the pilot test phase. It is currently being carried out "on a voluntary basis" in several states. I'm not surprised if you've never heard of it. It is amazing how little press it is getting. Libertarians should be screaming warnings from the roof tops, but the media is ignoring it. If you haven't heard about NAIS you can find info on in the Survivalblog archives and information on how to protest against it here: www.nonais.org

As late as the 1970s open pollinated (heirloom) seeds were common in backyard gardens. As you know, hybrid seeds are far more popular than open pollinated seeds today. Of the people you know who keep gardens, how many of them plant even half their crops from seeds they save themselves? The majority of the commercial seed stock worldwide is owned and distributed by just a handful of corporations? Those corporations are rapidly buying up the smaller seed companies on a global scale. A neighbor of mine owns a seed company that has bought twenty five competitors in the past decade! It would take very few corporate buyouts or mergers to put control of the majority of the world food supply under one board of directors. If the majority of seeds in circulation for producing grain crops are hybrids (and I think they are). We have no choice but to pay whatever they ask for next year's seeds. If you let that sink in for a moment and you will realize a terrifying potential for the abuse of power.

What can you do?

As in preparing for any danger, emergency or shortage, you should provide for your basic needs in advance.

#1 Store a food and water reserve to see you through the initial crisis. If you are reading Survivalblog, chances are good that you already consider storage food as a basic preparation. Consider storing as much as you can up to the limit of food that you will consume before proper rotation prevents spoilage. The easiest way to acquire a reserve is to buy more of what you normally use when it is on sale at discounted prices. Instead of buying pasta at 99 cents per pound each week, buy a case when it is on sale at 33 cents per pound. Do the same for soup, rice, canned fruit, etc. In a short time you will not only have a reserve of food ready for use, but your overall food bill will decrease because you are paying less for the same amount of goods over time.

You may choose to buy food prepackaged for long term storage. These dehydrated and freeze-dried products offer shelf lives of five years and longer. One source for long term storage foods is SurvivalBlog advertiser Ready Made Resources. I have done business in the past with Walton Feed. They offer a reasonably priced basic year's supply of food for under $1,000. A year's supply for your family is not an unreasonable amount. Five years of the shelf stable basics for your family would not be too much. But even this would be a short term solution. Should the tyranny we are discussing last longer than whatever food you have stored you must be prepared to feed yourself beyond then.

#2 Open pollinated "heirloom" seeds and the ability to raise your own crops (at least "gardening") are part of the answer. Buy your seeds now, practice planting, harvesting, storing the food, and saving your own seeds to plant for the next season. It is worth noting that some varieties thrive in one climate or soil type, but fail miserably in other locations. It would be prudent to test the crops you hope to survive on. Ideally you could establish a large number of perennial crops such as Jerusalem artichokes, asparagus, berry bushes, and fruit trees to harvest from in the future. Non-hybrid seeds are still available from many sources including The Ark Institute, Heirloomseeds.com, and The Seedsavers Exchange.

#3 Don't overlook unconventional sources of food. With a little research you should be able to recognize wild forage plants and prepare them for your table. Dandelions can be found almost anywhere including in urban areas from earliest spring through late fall. Their leaves can be eaten raw or boiled as vitamin laden greens. Even if you don't care for the taste of the greens, the nectar bearing yellow flower is a slightly sweet wild treat. Every part of the wild onion (a.k.a. "ramps" or "leeks") is edible (wild onions) but they may be hard to find in winter. One truly four season food is the cat-tail. It has edible shoots in spring, leaves and pollen in summer, and roots in autumn and winter (cat-tail). As an example of what a little knowledge can do to put food on your table, I recently saw "gobo" (a.k.a. burdock roots) for sale in large chain grocery store for $4 per pound.

#4 If keeping domestic livestock or poultry is an option that you would like to explore, I highly recommend Countryside and Small Stock Journal. My public library carries ten years of back issues and I read every one before I became one of the contributing authors. Even if you can't find it for free, check your newsstand or go to www.countrysidemag.com. But remember that the time to buy your flocks, herds, and the equipment to care for them, is long before you need to harvest.

#5 If keeping small stock isn't practical you may resort to foraging for wild game or fishing. Snares are silent and extremely effective, but they do not last forever. You will need to learn how to build and rebuild them and have the materials available to do so. Buckshot's Camp is a great source for snares and materials as well as instructional videos. Leg hold traps are less effective (at least for me) but they last much longer than wire or cable snares. Fish traps can be an extremely effective way to gather protein silently as well. Many can be camouflaged as stream littering debris (such as discarded PVC pipe) if necessary. If you are not blessed to live in an area of natural abundance, you may wish to install and stock your own "decorative" fish pond well in advance of any time of need.

Many grains store well for months if they are stored in pest proof containers. To rodent proof your stored grains store them within steel drums, or galvanized garbage cans with secure lids. Speaking of storing animal feed, I once read an article by someone who worked in the management of a major pet food company. That author stated that in a life or death situation they would not hesitate to feed themselves on the company product. Yep, lightweight, inexpensive dry kibble and water can sustain your life for weeks if you need it to. That's just something to keep in mind when you store those big bags of nuggets for Rover.

I hope that the above will provoke enough thought to generate a few comments including tips that I haven't thought of, because no matter how much we have stored against times of future need, it is primarily our knowledge and the ability to apply it that will help us to survive.

And what if nothing happens? What if none of the dangers described above materialize in the near future? Are your efforts wasted? They are not! Because even absent disaster, you will still need to eat! In a best case scenario you will use the tips above to save money, eat a healthier, and sleep with more peace of mind.God bless you and yours, - Mr. Yankee

Originally posted at
www.SurvivalBlog.com
Copyright 2012

THE CHURCH OF
JESUS CHRIST
OF LATTER-DAY SAINTS

Stake and Ward Emergency Planning Guide

Stake and ward councils can use this planning guide to create or update emergency response plans (see *Handbook 1: Stake Presidents and Bishops* [2010] 5.1.3 and 5.2.11). Stake and ward plans should be coordinated with plans in the community. Leaders may consider calling welfare specialists to assist with emergency response efforts. The most effective plans are brief and not overly complex. It is recommended that councils review and update plans regularly.

Step 1: Identify Likely Disasters

List the disasters (natural or man-made) that are most likely to occur in your area. For each type of disaster, identify specific response actions that would be needed. (*For example:* In a disaster that can damage homes—such as an earthquake, fire, flood, or hurricane—a key action would be to find temporary shelter for displaced families.)

Step 2: Gather Critical Information

Compile and maintain the following information:

- ☐ Contact data for all members and missionaries living within stake or ward boundaries.
- ☐ A map of the area, including the locations of member and missionary residences.
- ☐ A list of members with special needs, such as the disabled and the elderly.
- ☐ A list of members with equipment or skills (such as medical or emergency response training) that would be critical in a disaster.
- ☐ Contact information for public safety agencies (e.g., police, fire, medical).
- ☐ Contact information for community organizations (e.g., the Red Cross or Red Crescent) that provide emergency services, such as food, shelter, and medical care.
- ☐ Contact information for area welfare leaders and, where available, local Church welfare operations.

Step 3: Outline Assignments and Procedures

Plan how the council will organize and carry out each of the tasks listed below, identifying who will be responsible for each and what procedures they will follow. Designate a primary and an alternate central location where council members will gather after an emergency to direct relief efforts.

Prior to a disaster

- ☐ Develop working relationships with civil authorities and other community relief organizations.

Immediately after a disaster

- ☐ Determine and report the condition of members and missionaries.
  Reports on member needs generally come from home teachers to quorum leaders, who then report them to the bishop. Bishops, in turn, report them to the stake president.
- ☐ Help to locate and reunite family members who have become separated.
- ☐ Obtain medical care for those who have been injured or who have other health challenges.
- ☐ Coordinate response efforts with civil authorities and community relief organizations.
- ☐ Assess needs and arrange for the supply of basic provisions and services—such as food, temporary shelter, sanitation, and clothing—for members and others.
  Area welfare leaders and, where available, Church welfare operations can be called upon to assist with provisions and services.
- ☐ Determine and report the condition of Church buildings and property.

In the period following a disaster

- ☐ Provide assistance to members who have suffered damage to homes or belongings, emotional trauma, or loss of livelihood.
- ☐ Work with civil authorities and relief organizations to identify and respond to opportunities for the Church to assist with community needs.

47

Step 4: Identify Emergency Communication Methods

Identify and plan for alternative communication methods that can be used in case phone lines, cellular phone service, or vehicle transportation routes are disrupted during a disaster. Such methods may include:

- Internet communications (including e-mail, social media, and Internet telephony).
- Text messaging via cellular phone (which may be available even if voice service is not).
- Amateur radio.
- Personal contact via foot, bicycle, etc. (Full-time missionaries can also help.)

As needed, priesthood leaders may call members of their units to be communication specialists. Qualified specialists often own communications equipment and possess valuable experience.

Step 5: Encourage Member Preparation

Regularly encourage members to engage in preparedness efforts and to follow the counsel outlined in the pamphlets *All Is Safely Gathered In: Family Home Storage* (04008) and *All Is Safely Gathered In: Family Finances* (04007). Channels for doing this might include:

- Quorum and Relief Society meetings.
- Sacrament meeting or stake conference talks.
- Home and visiting teaching messages.

From President Thomas S. Monson.

"Many more people could ride out the storm-tossed waves in their economic lives if they had their year's supply of food ... and were debt-free. Today we find that many have followed this counsel in reverse: they have at least a year's supply of debt and are food-free."

"Noah heeded God's command to build an ark...that they might be saved from the floodwaters...Yet there was no evidence of rain and flood...His actions were considered irrational...The sun was shining and life moved forward as usual. But time ran out...The floods came, the disobedient were drowned... When God speaks and we obey, we will always be right" T.S.Monson Ensign 10-07

General Preparedness Survey

The intent of this survey is to give you a quick sence of where some of your preparedness shortcomings may be. No One is expected to score 100%!!

BOOKS
I have assembled a well rounded preparedness library covering all major topics: Yes, No
I have READ the books in my preparedness Library: Yes, No.
I read those books AND actually put their preparedness suggestions to use!! Yes, No.

CLOTHING

I have a Summer & a Winter sleeping bag for each member of my family: Yes, No.
Everyone in my family has a pair of readily available sturdy shoes/boots: Yes, No.
I have a pair of shoes at my bedside I could put on with no light at night: Yes, No.

COMMUNICATIONS
I have a AM/FM/Shortwave radio that is Battery or Solar Powered: Yes, No.
I have 2-Way radios (CB, FRS, GMRS) for my family members: Yes, No
I have spare batteries or Solar Chargers for my radios for: None, 3 days, 7 days, 15 Days, 30 Days +
Each member of my family has a Cell Phone: Yes, No
I have 2nd way to charge each phone without Utility Power: Yes, No.
I have my HAM License and a HAM Radio: Yes, No.

DEFENSE
I own a Dog: Yes, No
My Yard is fully fenced: yes, No.
I have Deadbolts on all my doors and locks on all windows: Yes, No
I have a burglar alarm and arm and use it daily/nightly: Yes, No
I have a Handgun for each member of my family (age appropriate): Yes, No
I have a Rifle for each member of my family (age appropriate): Yes, No.
I have at least 1,000 rounds of ammunition for each weapon: Yes, No.
I have a Safe Room in my home: Yes, No
My family has a Home Invasion Plan and we have drilled it: Yes, No.
I have a concealed Carry Permit and carry my weapon with me at all times: Yes, No.

DRILLS
I have staged a Fire Drill in my home for my family in the last 24 months: Yes, No
I have staged an Emergency Evacuation (Bugout) Drill for my family in the last 24 months: Yes, No
I have staged an Intruder/Robbery/Break in Drill for my family in the last 24 months: Yes, No
I have staged a 48 hour Power Outage Drill for my family in the last 24 months: Yes, No
I have staged a 48 hour Water Outage Drill for my family in the last 24 months: Yes, No

DOCUMENTS
I have paper copies of all important documents: Yes, No
I have a paper list of contacts, Phone, Names, Addresses, ect: Yes, No.
Each member of my family has a current valid Passport: Yes, No.

EVACUATION

I have a specific planned destination to go to for emergency relocation: Yes, No
I have an appropriatly packed 72hr Kit for each member of my family: Yes, No
I have a Bug Out Bag for my family: Yes, No.
I have paper maps for my City, County, State and route to planned destination: Yes, No

FINANCES

I keep the following "Cash On Hand" in my home: <$250, $500, $1000, $2,500, $5,000+
I have Silver or Gold coins for emergency use: Yes, No.
I have an Emergency Fund for all monthly expenses for: None, 1 Month, 3 Months, 6 Months, 1 Year+
I have paid off all of my credit card debt: Yes, No.
I have paid off ALL my debts: Yes, No

FOOD

For every member of my family, I have at least
Canned: None, <15 Days, 30 Days, 90 Days, 1 Year+
Dehydrated/Freeze Dried: None, <15 days, 30 Days, 90 Days, 1 Year+
MRE/Retort: None, 3 days, 7 days, 15 Days, 30 Days +
I regularly rotate my food and never allow any to expire: Yes, No.
I have a way to cook my food (camp stove/grill/ect) without any utility power or Natural Gas: Yes, No.

FUEL

I have stored stabilized gasoline: None, 5 gallons, 10 Gallons, 25 Gallons, 50 Gallons +
I have backup fuel, such as Butane, White Gas, wood, Propane or Charcoal for emergency cooking: Yes, No.
I have backup fuel, such as wood or propane for emergency home heating: Yes, No.

LIGHTING

I have a flashlight in every bedroom: Yes, No.
I have backup lighting (LED Lamps, Kerosene Lamps, Solar Lights, ect): Yes, No
I have Long Burning candles for: None, 3 days, 7 days, 15 Days, 30 Days +
I have spare batteries to power my flashlights for: None, 3 days, 7 days, 15 Days, 30 Days +

MEDICAL

I know and am trained in First Aid: Yes, No.
I have a well stocked first aid kit in my home: Yes, No.
I have my prescriptions on hand for: <2 weeks, 1 Month, 2 Months, 3 Months, 6 Months+
I have well rounded supply of Over The Counter Medications: Yes, No.
I regularly exercise and maintain my physical health: Yes, No.
My family has a Medical Emergency Response Plan and knows what to do: Yes, No.

NUCLEAR / BIOLOGIAL / CHEMICAL

I have a Geiger Counter or radiological survey meter: Yes, No.
I have assembled a decontamination kit for NBC exposure: Yes, No
I have an appropriate Gas Mask for each member of my family: Yes, No
I have an NBC Suit for each member of my family: Yes, No.

PANDEMIC

My family is ready to impose a "Self Issolation Reverse Quarentine" for: None, 15, 30, 60, 90 Days
I have a substancial supply of disspoable: Gloves, Masks, Booties, Suits, Goggles, ect: Yes, No
My family is fully prepared to create, supply and staff an issolation/sick room in our home: Yes, No.

POWER

I have a portable electric Generator: Yes, No.
I have started and run my generator in the last: Week, Month, Quarter, Year, Don't remember
I have a solar/Wind/Hydro electric system in my home: Yes, No.

SANITATION

I have a chemical or Organic toilet: Yes, No.
I have a "Lugable Loo" or other disposable emergency Toilet: Yes, No
I have an Outhouse on my property: Yes, No.
I have stored Lime to use with an emergency outdoor pit toilet: Yes, No
I have stored lots of extra toilet paper: Yes, No.

SHELTER

I have a fire extinguisher in my home and know how to use it: Yes, No
I have a Carbon Monoxide Detector for use in an emergency: Yes, No.
I know my neighbors and could count on them in an emergency: Yes, No.

SPIRITUAL

I have personal prayer every day: Yes, No.
I have personal scripture study every day: Yes, No.
I participate in Family prayer every day: Yes, No.
I participate in Family scripture study every day: Yes, No.
I participate in Family Home Evening every week: Yes, No.
I attend my church every week: Yes, No.
I donate generously in my Tithes and Offerings to my church: Yes, No.

TRAINING:

I am CERT (Community Emergency Responce Training) certified: Yes, No

TRANSPORTATION

My vehicle fuel tank is currently: Near Empty, 1/4, 1/2, 3/4, Full.
I have a 4 wheel drive vehicle: Yes, No.
I have a fire extinguisher in my car and know how to use it: Yes, No.
I keep a Bug Out Bag in my vehicle at all times: Yes, No.
I have a GPS unit in my vehicle or readily available: Yes, No.
I have a well stocked first aid kit in my vehicle: Yes, No.

WATER

I have enough stored water for each member of my family for: None, 3 days, 7 days, 15 Days, 30 Days +
I have water treatment chemicals (bleach, iodine, aerobic oxygen, etc.) stored: Yes, No.
I have a water purification system (filter): Yes, No.

I AM PREPARED WELL ENOUGH TO BE ABLE TO SHARE WITH OTHERS AROUND ME: Yes, No.

BECAUSE I AM WELL PREPARED, I WILL BE AN ASSET AND NOT A LIABILITY TO MY COMMUNITY: Yes, No.

BECAUSE I AM WELL PREPARED, I AM HELPING OTHERS BECOME PREPARED: Yes, No.

5 Levels of Preparation

There are five levels of preparedness.

Level 0: _Every emergency is a disaster_

Less than two weeks of food in the house
No water purification system
No bug-out bag
No defensive weapons
No way to produce their own food
No physical gold or silver
No tangible assets to barter

Level 1: _Can Survive Two Weeks of Minor Emergency_
(such as ice storm)

Have sufficient food and water for two weeks of
emergency
Able to heat their home for two weeks without relying
on the power grid by use of kerosene heater or
fireplace
Able to cook their meals for two weeks without relying
on the power grid
Has a first aid kit
Likely has no defensive weapons
Must leave their home after two weeks due to lack of
preparation

Level 2: _Can Survive One Month of an Emergency_
(such as major hurricane)

Likely has a portable power generator and sufficient fuel
for one month of operation
Has handguns or shotgun to defend their home
Has a month's work of canned goods to eat from
Has sufficient prescription medicines for 30 days
Has enough batteries for power a portable radio for 30
days

Level 3: _Can Survive Three Months of an Emergency_
(such as martial law or impacting earthquake)

Has a deep-short term pantry
Likely has a water purification system
Likely has defensive weapon for each family member
Likely has some type of neighborhood safety watch or
24 hour security watch rotation at the home
Has stocked wood to burn in fireplace and/or iron stove
Has communication gear to keep track of local and
world events
Has means to recharge batteries without relying on
power grid

Has three months of prescription medicines

Level 4: _Can Survive One Year of an Emergency_
(such as currency devaluation, economic depression)

Has a deep short- and long-term food pantry
Likely has their own garden to produce food
Likely has small-sized farm animals to produce protein
(chickens, goats, rabbits)
Has a deep supply of ammo (2000+ rounds per weapon)
Is a spare weapon in event of damage
Has mean to produce herbal medicines to replace
prescriptions
Has a long-term store of antibiotics
Likely has dog for security watch
Has full 24 hour rotation of security watch on the home
(requires 6 adults)
Show have secondary off-site storage of food, weapons,
and ammo
Is ready to bug-out with full hiking and camping gear, if
security situation degrades
Is able to educate their children at home

Level 5: _Can Survive Indefinitely from their Home_
during an multi-year SHTF or TEOTWAWKI situation

Has a fully functioning large garden or small farm for
food production
Is able to can and store the results of food harvest for
the coming year
Is able to harvest seeds for next year's planting
Is able to raise multiple generations of farm animals
(cattle, sheep, horses)
Has horses for local and distance travel
Has enough ammo to last a generation (10,000+ rounds
per weapon)
Has spares of each weapon and lots of extra magazines
Able to generate their own fuel (bio-diesel, alcohol)
Likely has fully functional solar power bank with deep
storage batteries
Has natural on-site water sources for farm and home
Has home-based business to generate income
Is able to build new building and make any necessary
repairs to existing buildings
Is able to provide excess food for charity
Has a secondary residency (such as mountain cabin) for
full bug-out
Is prepared for minor surgery and child birth at home
Has stores of gold and silver for barter
Is able to produce their own clothing (from raw wool or
raw cotton with spinning wheel and small loom)

http://survival5x5.com/?page_id=14

SECTION 2:
Getting Started

Don't have any food storage at all?? Start here with the new

LDS Church FAMILY HOME STORAGE KITS!
This is the most food you can buy for the lowest possible price to get your food storage started.

LDS Members: **store.lds.com**

Non LDS Members:
Visit one of our Home Storage Centers (open to the public)
www.providentliving.org/location/ map/0,12566,2026-1-4,00.html

EMERGENCY FOOD STORAGE

"...and he will have his eyes fixed on the signs of the times, and that day will not overtake him unawares." - JD 7:189.

We do seem to be undergoing a **quickening of the times** and that may be an important indication for each of us to evaluate our personal and family storage needs again.

As members of the Church we have been counseled for many many years to prepare and keep on hand at least a **one-year supply of food.** In the early days of our church the Saints were admonished to have a **7 year** food supply. Then, for many years there was a time when a two-year supply was recommended, (and it undoubtedly would be a good idea for each of us to still keep a two-year supply if at all possible as this will allow us to share with others). But in the meantime it is imperative that we heed the current counsel to **obtain and maintain at least a one-year minimum emergency food supply**.

According to figures gathered by one of the food storage manufacturing firms, less than 6% of the members of the Church have an adequate emergency program. *Where do you fit into this figure?*

Let's enjoy life as much as we can - but let's also **be prepared**. As we have recently seen, an unexpected disaster or loss of income can strike every *s-o-o* quickly.

"When the emergency is upon us, the time of preparation has passed."

<u>BARE-MINIMUM</u> LDS Food storage requirements
for

1 adult male for 1 year Appx. 2,300 calories per day. (only 695lbs total)
This will keep you fed, but leave you hungry. **TOTAL FOOD PER DAY = 24.65 Ounces**

Grains (400lbs)

Unless your family already eats 100% whole wheat homemade bread, white flour should be used in the transition process to whole wheat. Adding rye flour (10%) helps make wheat bread a more complete protein. Dent corn is used to make tortillas.

Beans & Legumes (90lbs) {Absolute Bare minimum reduced by LDS church to only 60lbs in 2002}

Black beans cook quickly, make a good salad complement with a vinaigrette dressing over them. Soybeans can be used to make soy milk and tofu, a protein food you should be prepared to make. Familiarize yourself with sprouting techniques. Learn how to make wheat grass juice - the best vitamin supplement you can use.

Milk-Dair products (75lbs) {Absolute Bare minimum reduced by LDS church to only 16lbs in 2002}

Milk powder can be used to make cottage cheese, cream cheese and hard cheeses. Ideally your milk should be fortified with Vitamins A & D. When reconstituting aerate to improve flavor (special mixing pitchers can accomplish this). Whole eggs are the best all-purpose egg product. Powdered sour cream has a limited shelf life unless frozen.

Meats / Meat substitute (20lbs) {Absolute Bare minimum reduced by LDS church to only ZERO in 2002}

Use meat in soups, stews and beans for flavor. Freeze dried is the best option for real meat. Textured Vegetable protein is the main alternative to freeze dried meats.

Fats / Oils (20lbs)

This group can boost the calories one is getting from food storage products, and supply essential fatty acids.

Sugars (60lbs)

Store your honey in 5 gallon pails. Candy and other sweets can help with appetite fatigue.

Fruits / Vegetables (90lbs) {Absolute Bare minimum reduced by LDS church to only ZERO in 2002}

Some fruits and vegetables are best dehydrated, others freeze dried (strawberries & blueberries). Fruits are a nice addition to hot cereal, muffins, pancakes and breads.

Auxiliary foods (weight varies)

Vanilla extract improves the flavor of powdered milk. The production of tofu requires a precipitator such as nigari, epsom salt, calcium chloride or calcium sulfide (good calcium source). Learn how to make and use wheat gluten (liquid smoke adds good flavor). Chocolate syrup and powdered drink mixes help with appetite fatigue. Vitamins and protein powders will boost the nutrition levels of foods that may have suffered losses during processing.

Note:

For an average adult Female - multiply the weight by 0.75
For children ages 1-3 multiply by 0.3, 4-6 multiply by 0.5, 7-9 multiply by 0.75
For adults engaged in manual labor multiply by 1.25-1.50

If you follow the "Bare Minimum" recomen-dations from the LDS church this is all the food that you will have to live on for a full year.

Ask yourself this simple question.

Are you ready to live on a loaf of bread and 1/3 cup of beans a day?

NOW is the time to stock up and fill out your food storage!!

For example, with a days rations you could make a loaf of bread and have a 1/3 cup of beans

This is the basic recommendation for a 1 year supply for 1 person

Salt
8 lbs

Cooking Oil
10 Quarts

Legumes
60 lbs

Storage Rack
Sam's Club
$70

Powdered Milk
16 lbs

Sugar or Honey
60 lbs

Grains
400 lbs

Our food supply is fragile

Grocery stores don't stock weeks of food anymore. Most keep only 72 hours of food on the shelves. They re-stock based on just-in-time delivery of food supplies. If the trucks stop rolling in your part of the country during a crisis, the store shelves will be emptied almost immediately. In fact, expect a shortage of mainstay items like milk and bread to occur similar to what happens before an approaching hurricane hits. Those who are aware of the problem but who haven't already made preparations will engage in a last-minute rush to buy a few extra supplies.

Transportation is the key to food

Without transportation, farmers can't get their crops to the wholesalers or food processing facilities. Food is heavy, generally speaking, and it requires trucks and trains to move it around — a literal ARMY of trucks and trains, weaving their way from city to city, optimized and prioritized by computers. If the computers freeze, the whole transportation infrastructure will shut down.

Transportation also depends heavily on fuel, which means the oil-producing countries in the Middle East have to be able to produce the oil that gets refined into diesel fuel here in America. So, in other words, **your food supply depends on Saudi Arabia being alive and well.** Do you trust the people in charge in Saudi Arabia, Iraq, Iran, and Kuwait with your life? If you don't **make preparations now**, you're trusting them by default.

Cities depend entirely on rural land

Did you know cities would be ghost towns without the supporting imports of food from the country? We should all thank the farmers a little more, because they literally keep us all alive. Cities are like concrete islands. You might think a city is self-sustaining until you really think about it, but underneath it all, that city is a ghost town without the people in the country supporting it.

You may already know that city people and country people have very different views on politics and life in general. Country people tend to be more religious and more conservative. City people tend to be more liberal. So there's more than a little animosity between country people and city people. When a crisis hits, and the country people find they are without electricity and fuel, they will still survive, for the most part, because they're used to surviving. But do you think they will really put "saving city people" high on their list of priorities? I don't think so. Any food that's harvested from the fields will be kept and stored by the farmers themselves. They will NOT be shipping this stuff to the cities unless they have excess goods and can find a transportation method that still works (and has fuel). Unfortunately, if some emergency powers acts are signed into place by the President, the Federal Emergency Management Association will have the legal power to actually confiscate and redistribute food. This makes it all the more likely that farmers will harvest it and HIDE IT in order to keep it. And that means even less food making it to the cities. Bottom line? Cities where food can't be delivered will eventually be gutted, looted, evacuated and likely burned to the ground.

You need to start stocking food

You can do a lot if you start early. Unfortunately, "early" might have been yesterday. Now we're way past early, and you need a reasonable plan to get food supplies that will store well and don't cost too much.

You've probably already realized that buying up extra cans of soup at the grocery store is a really stupid way to spend your preparedness money. You need a better plan. Every $10 you spend at the store might feed a person for a few days. You need more leverage, where you can spend $10 and feed a person for a few weeks.

Buy extra, use FIFO

Go ahead and buy more food than normal when you're out shopping, and set it aside. Use the "first in, first out" rule to eat your older supplies first. Keep rotating your supplies so you never abandon food "way in the back."

Buy ingredients, not prepared foods

Ingredients such as salt, honey, oatmeal and wheat will last a lot longer than prepared foods like TV dinners, cereals, and food mixes. Naturally, as you purchase food ingredients, you'll want to practice actually using them! And remember the basics. For example, if you purchase a bag of wheat, how exactly do you plan to make flour out of it? I've personally seen plans in a survival book that described throwing some wheat in a coffee can and pounding it into flour with a blunt stick. You can make a few cups of flour after ten of fifteen minutes of noisemaking.

Do you REALLY have a year's supply?

Just how big is a Year's Supply of food? As explained on the previous page, our Church is now suggesting the following <u>absolute bare minimums</u> for each adult:

400 lbs.	Grains	(17.5oz / day)
60 lbs.	Beans	(2.6oz / day)
10 quarts	Cooking oil	(0.87oz / day)
60 lbs.	Honey	(2.63oz / day)
8 lbs.	Salt	(0.35oz / day)
16 lbs	Powdered milk	(0.70oz / day)
14 gallons	of drinking water (for 2 weeks)	

So, just how much is this?
Two 5 gallon buckets will hold about 75lbs of wheat, rice or other grains.
This means you need *11 buckets of grain* for each person in your family.

If you store all your grains in #10 cans...

Wheat, Rice, Corn, etc..
You would need 64 cans or 10.5 cases per person.

Pasta
You would need 32 cans or 5.25 cases per person.

Rolled oats
These are lighter but bulkier, so they require more storage containers and space.
You would need 124 cans or 21 cases person.

Beans
A 25 lb bag of beans will about fit in a single 5 gallon bucket, with a little space over, so 2 buckets would hold a one person supply, or 12 -13 # 10 cans or about 2 cases.

Daily Food
Dividing 400lbs by 365days, equals out to 1.09589lbs, or just over 1 lb of grain, per person, per day. That is approximately 2 cups of unground grain to cover your breakfast lunch and dinner.

Dividing 60lbs by 365, this works out to 0.16 lbs of beans per day, or 2.6 oz—approximately 3/4 cup.

The other foods listed would also need to be used in limited amounts.

This is not much food, folks. Get the basics, then immediately begin to add more kinds of grain, soup mix, canned and/or dehydrated vegetables and fruit, etc to add variety and provide more than the minimal survival diet.

As an example, the minimum recommended amount of grain, when ground and prepared will yield about 6 small biscuits or a plateful of pancakes. Its enough to keep you alive, but a far cry from being satisfied and not hungry.

Basic Food Storage List

GRAINS = 400 lbs per adult

_____ Barley
_____ Cereal
_____ Corn (meal or Dent)
_____ Cous Cous
_____ *Flour* (4lb/can)
_____ Millet
_____ *Multi grain soup mix*(5lb/can)
_____ *Oats, rolled quick*(3lb/can)
_____ *Oats, rolled regular*(3lb/can)
_____ Popcorn
_____ Rye
_____ Sprouting Seeds
_____ *Wheat*(6lb/can)
_____ *White Rice*(6lb/can)

Pastas

_____ *Macaroni*(3lb/can)
_____ Noodles

_____ *Spaghetti*(4lb/can)

MILK / DAIRY = 75 lbs per adult

_____ Brick cheese
_____ Canned Milk
_____ Canned sour cream
_____ Cheese spreads
_____ Condensed milk
_____ Dried cheese
_____ Dried eggs
_____ Infant formula
_____ Non-dairy creamer
_____ *Non-fat dry milk*(4lb/can)
_____ Powdered cheese
_____ Powdered sour cream

JUICES/BEVERAGES = 25 lbs

_____ Apple juice
_____ Apricot nectar
_____ Baby strained juices
_____ *Cocoa drink mix*(4lb/can)
_____ Cranberry juice
_____ *Dried juice mix*(6lb/can)
_____ Grapefruit juice
_____ Grape juice
_____ Kool-aid
_____ Lemonaid

_____ Orange juice
_____ Pineapple juice
_____ Plum juice
_____ Prune juice
_____ Punch crystals
_____ Soft drink mixes
_____ Soft drinks
_____ Tomato juice
_____ V-8 juice

FATS / OILS = 20 lbs per adult

_____ Butter
_____ Cooking oil
_____ Lard
_____ Margarine
_____ Mayonnaise
_____ Olive Oil (extra virgin)
_____ Peanut butter
_____ Powdered butter
_____ Powdered margarine
_____ Powdered shortening
_____ Salad dressing
_____ Shortening

CANNED or DRIED MEATS

(20 lbs per adult)

_____ Bacon
_____ Beef
_____ Beef jerky
_____ Chicken
_____ Clams
_____ Corned beef
_____ Crabmeat
_____ Deviled meats
_____ Fish
_____ Ham
_____ Hamburger
_____ Lamb
_____ Lunch meats
_____ Mutton
_____ Pepperoni
_____ Pork
_____ Tuna
_____ Salmon
_____ Sandwich spreads
_____ Sardines

_____ Sausage
_____ Shrimp
_____ Spam
_____ Treet
_____ Turkey
_____ TVP- Textured vegi Protein
_____ Veal
_____ Venison jerky
_____ Vienna sausage

AUXILIARY FOODS

_____ Baking powder
_____ Baking soda
_____ Cake mixes
_____ Calcium supplement
_____ Casserole mixes
_____ Chow mein noodles
_____ Cookies
_____ Cookie mixes
_____ Cornstarch
_____ Crackers
_____ Cream of tartar
_____ Hot roll mixes
_____ Hydrated lime (for tortillas)
_____ Instant breakfast
_____ Instant yeast
_____ Iron supplement
_____ Marshmallows
_____ MREs
_____ Muffin mixes
_____ Non perishable pet foods
_____ Pancake mixes
_____ Pastry mixes
_____ Pectin
_____ Pie crust mixes
_____ Pie fillings
_____ Pizza mixes
_____ Plain gelatin
_____ Rennin tablets
_____ Salt
_____ Sourdough starter
_____ Survival bars
_____ Tofu Solidifier
_____ Vitamins and minerals
_____ Whipped topping mixes

FRUITS and VEGETABLES
90 lbs Dried, 370qts canned, 370Lbs fresh

Fruits
_____ ***Apples*** *(2lb/can)*
_____ Applesauce
_____ Apricots
_____ Peaches
_____ Berries
_____ Cherries
_____ Coconut
_____ Currants
_____ Figs
_____ Fruit cocktail
_____ Grapefruit
_____ Grapes
_____ Mandarin oranges
_____ Nectarines
_____ Olives
_____ Pears
_____ Peaches
_____ Pineapples
_____ Plums
_____ Prunes
_____ Raisins
_____ Tomatoes

BEANS & LEGUMES
(90 lbs per adult)
_____ ***Beans,*** *pink(5lb/can)*
_____ ***Beans,*** *pinto(5lb/can)*
_____ ***Beans,*** *white(5lb/can)*
_____ Lentils
_____ Nuts
_____ Peas
_____ Sprouting beans and seeds
_____ Soybeans

Vegetables
_____ Artichoke hearts
_____ Asparagus
_____ Beans
_____ Beets
_____ Broccoli
_____ Brussels sprouts
_____ ***Carrots*** *(3lb/can)*
_____ Cauliflower

_____ Celery
_____ Corn-sweet
_____ Green beans
_____ Hominy
_____ Mushrooms
_____ Okra
_____ ***Onions*** *(2lb/can)*
_____ Parsnips
_____ Peas
_____ Peppers
_____ Pickles
_____ ***Potatoes, flakes*** *(1.5lb/can)*
_____ ***Potatoes, pearls*** *(3lb/can)*
_____ Pumpkins
_____ Rhubarb
_____ Rutabagas
_____ Salsify
_____ Sauerkraut
_____ Soups
_____ Spinach
_____ Squash
_____ Sweet potatoes (yams)
_____ Tomatos
_____ Tomato powder
_____ Turnips
_____ Water chestnuts

SPICES / CONDIMENTS
_____ Almond extract
_____ Allspice
_____ Baking chocolate
_____ Basil
_____ BBQ sauce
_____ Bouillon cubes / granules
Beef, chicken, onion, vegetable flavors
_____ Cayenne pepper
_____ Celery salt
_____ Chili powder
_____ Chives
_____ Chocolate chips
_____ Chocolate syrup
_____ Cinnamon
_____ Cloves
_____ Cocoa
_____ Coriander
_____ Cumin
_____ Curry
_____ Dill weed
_____ Garlic salt

_____ Ginger
_____ Gravy mixes
_____ Herbs
_____ Ketchup
_____ Lemon extract
_____ Lemon / lime juice
_____ Liquid smoke
_____ Majoram
_____ Maple extract
_____ Nutmeg
_____ Onion flakes
_____ Onion salt
_____ Orange peel

_____ Oregano
_____ Paprika
_____ Pepper
_____ Poultry Seasoning
_____ protein supplement
_____ Sage
_____ Salad dressings
_____ Salt (**5 lbs per adult**)
_____ Sauce mixes
_____ Seasoned salt
_____ Spaghetti sauce
_____ Soy sauce
_____ Steak sauce
_____ Tarragon
_____ Thyme
_____ Turmeric
_____ Vanilla extract
_____ Vinegar

_____ Worcestershire sauce

SUGARS = 60 lbs per adult
_____ Corn syrup
_____ Hard candy
_____ Honey
_____ Jello
_____ Jelly or jam
_____ Maple syrup
_____ Molasses
_____ ***Pudding,*** *chocolate (5lb/can)*
_____ ***Pudding,*** *vanilla (5lb/can)*
_____ ***Sugar*** *(6lb/can)*

Long Term Storage - MASTER FOOD LIST

___6 GRAIN PANCAKE MIX
___6 WAY ROLLED GRAIN, 6 TYPES OF GRAIN
___9 GRAIN CRACKED CEREAL
___ALFALFA FOR SPROUTING
___ALFALFA, POWDER
___ALFALFA, CUT
___Almonds, Raw
___ALLSPICE (JAMAICAN) POWDER
___ALLSPICE (JAMAICAN) WHOLE
___Amaranth, Organic
___ANISE (STAR), WHOLE
___ANISE SEED, WHOLE
___APPLE FLAKES, PEACH FLAVOR, DEHYDRATED
___APPLE FLAKES, STRAWBERRY FLAVOR
___APPLE SLICES,
___APPLESAUCE, DEHYDRATED
___ARROWROOT POWDER
___BAKING POWDER,
___BAKING SODA,
___BANANA SLICES, DEHYDRATED,
___BARBECUE SPICE BLEND - GROUND
___BARLEY FLAKES
___BARLEY FOR SPROUTING
___BARLEY, HULLED,
___Barley, Hulless Waxy
___BARLEY, PEARL
___BASIL (EGYPTIAN) - CUT
___BASIL (SWEET CALIFORNIA), CUT
___BAY LEAVES, CUT
___BAY LEAVES, WHOLE
___BEANS, BLACK, BULK, FREEZE DRIED
___BEANS, 10-BEAN MIX,
___ Anasazi Beans
___BEANS, AUZZUKIE
___BEANS, BABY LIMAS,
___BEANS, BLACK EYED,
___BEANS, BLACK TURTLE,
___BEANS, GARBANZO,
___BEANS, GREAT NORTHERN WHITE,
___BEANS, GREEN, DEHYDRATED,
___BEANS, KIDNEY,
___BEANS, LARGE LIMA,
___BEANS, MUNG,
___BEANS, NAVY, BULK, DEHYDRATED,
___BEANS, PINK,
___BEANS, PINTO,
___ Refried Beans
___ Refried Beans w/corn oil
___BEANS, SMALL RED
___BEANS, SMALL WHITE, NAVY
___BEANS, SOY,
___BEANS, SPROUTING, AUZZUKIE,
___BEANS, SPROUTING, GARBANZO,
___BEANS, SPROUTING, MUNG,
___BEANS, SPROUTING, SOY,
___BEE POLLEN

___Bouillon, Beef
___Bouillon, Chicken
___BROCCOLI, DEHYDRATED
___BUCK WHEAT, HULLED,
___BURDOCK ROOT CUT
___BUTTER POWDER,
___BUTTERMILK POWDER
___CABBAGE
___CABBAGE SEED,
___CAJUN SPICE BLEND, GROUND
___CAKE MIX, GINGERBREAD (ADD WATER)
___CAKE MIX, BROWNIE (ADD WATER)
___CAKE MIX, CARROT (ADD WATER)
___CAKE MIX, DEVIL'S FOOD
___CAKE MIX, LEMON
___CAKE MIX, POUND CAKE (ADD WATER)
___CAKE MIX, SPICE
___CAKE MIX, SWISS CHOC (ADD WATER)
___CAKE MIX, WHITE
___CAKE MIX, YELLOW
___CAKE, FUNNEL (ADD WATER)
___CARAWAY SEED
___CARDAMOM (DECORTICATED) WHOLE
___CARDAMOM (WHOLE GREEN PODS)
___CARDAMOM (GROUND)
___CAROB (ROASTED), POWDERED
___CARROT DICES, DEHYDRATED,
___CAYENNE (40 HEAT UNIT) DOMESTIC
___CAYENNE (60 HEAT UNIT) IMPORTED
___CAYENNE (90 HEAT UNIT)
___CELERY
___CELERY SEED - GROUND
___CELERY SEED - WHOLE
___CHAMOMILE TEA BAGS
___CHEESE SAUCE, DEHYDRATED, BULK
___CHEESE, CHEDDAR, DEHYDRATED, BAG
___CHIA SEEDS (FOR SPROUTING)
___CHICKWEED
___CHILI BLEND, GROUND
___CHILI PEPPERS, GROUND
___CHILI, CRUSHED
___CHINESE FIVE SPICE,
___CHIVES, CUT
___CHOCOLATE CHIPS, MILK CHOCOLATE
___CHOCOLATE CHIPS, SEMI SWEET
___CILANTRO CUT
___CINNAMON CHIPS, SMALL CUT
___CINNAMON POWDER
___CINNAMON STICKS, 1 INCH,
___CLOVES (SMALL VERY FRAGRANT)
___CLOVES POWDER
___Cocoa Mix
___Cocoa Mix Chocolate Mint Truffle
___Cocoa Mix Mint
___Cocoa Mix, Orange Creme
___COCOA FOR COOKING,
___COCONUT (UNSWEETENED) - MEDIUM

___CORIANDER SEED, GROUND
___CORIANDER SEED, WHOLE
___CORN MEAL, BAG
___CORN, SWEET, DEHYDRATED
___CORN, WHOLE YELLOW, PAPER BAG
___ Corn, Yellow Grit-hominy polenta
___CORNSTARCH
___ Corn Syrup Solids
___CREAM OF TARTAR
___CUMIN SEED, GROUND
___CUMIN SEED, WHOLE
___CURRY POWDER, HOT BLEND
___CURRY POWDER, REGULAR BLEND
___DILL SEED, WHOLE
___DILL WEED, (DOMESTIC) CUT
___DOUGH ENHANCER, NATURAL
___DRESSING, 1000 ISLAND
___DRESSING, BLEU CHEESE,
___DRESSING, OUR HOUSE DRESSING
___DRINK BASE, APPLE CIDER, INSTANT,
___DRINK MIX, APPLE, DEHYDRATED,
___DRINK MIX, CHERRY,
___DRINK MIX, Fruit Punch
___DRINK MIX, GRAPE,
___DRINK MIX, HOT CIDER,
___DRINK MIX, LEMONADE,
___DRINK MIX, ORANGE,
___DRINK MIX, Peach
___DRINK MIX, PINK LEMONADE,
___DRINK MIX, STRAWBERRY,
___DRINK MIX. Tofu
___DRINK, APPLE, W/FRUIT JUICE
___DRINK, PEACH, DEHYDRATED, BG
___EGG MIX, DEHYDRATED,
___EGG WHITES, DEHYDRATED,
___EGGS, Whole
___FAJITA SEASONING,
___FENNEL SEED, POWDER
___FENNEL SEED, WHOLE
___FENUGREEK SEED, WHOLE
___ FLAVOR CRYSTALS, MAPLE, NATURAL & ART
___ FLAVOR CRYSTALS, VANILLA, NATURAL & AR
___ FLAVOR CRYSTALS, WALNUT, NATURAL & AR
___ FLAX SEED,
___ FLOUR, ALL PURPOSE,
___ FLOUR, BAKERS BLEND high protein
___ FLOUR, Whole Wheat
___ FLOUR, Whole Wheat Red
___ FLOUR, UNBLEACHED,
___ FLOUR, UNBLEACHED, Hard White
___ FLOUR, UNBLEACHED-Red
___ FLOUR, UNBLEACHED-White
___ FRANKINCENSE
___ FROSTING MIX, CHOCOLATE
___ FROSTING MIX, FUDGE
___ FRUCTOSE,
___ FRUIT BLEND (TASTY TEA) NO CAFFEINE
___ FRUIT BLEND TEA BAG
___ FRUIT GALAXY, DEHYDRATED BAG
___ FRUIT WHIRLS

___ GARLIC (DOMESTIC),
___ GARLIC GRANULES (CALIFORNIA)
___ GARLIC POWDER (DOMESTIC)
___ GARLIC MINCED
___ G EL CAPS -00-
___ GELATIN, CHERRY,
___ GELATIN, LEMON,
___ GELATIN, LIME,
___ GELATIN, ORANGE,
___ GELATIN, PEACH,
___ GELATIN, RASPBERRY,
___ GELATIN, STRAWBERRY,
___ GERMADE,
___ GINGER ROOT PIECES, 1/4 IN PIECES
___ GINGER ROOT POWDER
___ GINSENG POWDER
___ GOTU KOLA POWDER
___ GRANOLA, 25 LB BAG
___ GRAVY MIX, BROWN,
___ GRAVY MIX, CHICKEN,
___ GRAVY MIX, TURKEY,
___ GRAVY, COUNTRY STYLE,
___GREEK SEASONING, GROUND
___HERB MIX (SALT SUBSTITUTE)
___HONEY, Clover
___HONEY, Creamy Whipped
___HONEY, COX'S (CREAMED)
___ITALIAN SEASONING, CUT
___ITALIAN SEASONING, GROUND
___KELP POWDER
___Kamut
___LECITHIN GRANULES
___LEMON GRANULES
___LEMON JUICE POWDER (INSTANT)
___LEMON PEEL CUT
___LEMON PEPPER BLEND, GROUND
___LENTILS, 100 LB BAG
___LICORICE MINT BLEND (TEA) NO CAFFEINE
___LICORICE ROOT POWDER
___LICORICE SPICE BLEND (TEA) CAFFEINE FREE
___LICORICE STICKS
___MACE, GROUND
___Macaroni & Cheese
___MAPLE LEAF
___MARGARINE POWDER,
___MARJORAM, CUT
___MEAT TENDERIZER, SEASONED,
___MEAT TENDERIZER, UNSEASONED,
___MICROWAVE POPCORN CINCH BUTTER
___MILK, INSTANT, NON FAT DRY,
___MILK, REGULAR, NON FAT DRY,
___MILLET,
___MILLET, HULLED,
___MIX, BELGIAN WAFFLE
___MIX, BLUEBERRY MUFFIN
___MIX, BROWNIE
___MIX, BUTTERMILK BISCUIT
___MIX, Cheasecake
___MIX, CHOCOLATE CHIP COOKIE
___MIX, COOKIE, CHOCOLATE CHIP

___MIX, Fudge Brownie
___MIX, Honeywheat Bread & Roll
___MIX,Scones
___MIX, WHITE FROSTING,
___MOLASSES, HOME MADE,
___MRE, COMPLETE MEAL,
___MRE, Applesauce
___MRE, Beef Frankfurters
___MRE, Beef Ravioli
___MRE, Beef Steak (chunked & formed)
___MRE, Beef Teriyaki
___MRE, Cheese Spread
___MRE, Cheese Tortellini
___MRE, Cherry Beverage Powder
___MRE, Solid Chicken Breast Patties
___MRE, Chicken Noodle
___MRE, Chicken Salsa
___MRE, Chili Macaroni
___MRE, Chocolate covered cookies
___MRE, Cocoa
___MRE, Crackers
___MRE, Ham Slices
___MRE, Lemon Pound Cake
___MRE, Meat Loaf W/Brown Onion Gravy
___MRE, Mexican Rice
___MRE, Oatmeal Cookie Bar
___MRE, Pasta Vegetable
___MRE, Pasta & Vegetable Alfredo Sauce
___MRE, Peanut Butter
___MRE, Pork w/Rice
___MRE, Pork Chow Mein
___MRE, Escalloped Potato W/Ham
___MRE, Potato Sticks
___MRE, Spaghetti
___MRE, Grilled Turkey Breast & Potatoes
___MRE, Turkey Breast & Potatoes
___MRE, Western Beans
___MRE, White Rice
___MUFFIN, BLUEBERRY
___MUFFIN, CORN,
___MUNG BEANS (FOR SPROUTING)
___MUSHROOM SLICES, DEHYDRATED,
___MUSTARD SEED (BROWN) WHOLE
___MUSTARD SEED (YELLOW) POWDER
___MUSTARD SEED (YELLOW) WHOLE
___MYRRH GUM PCS
___Noodles, Egg
___NUTMEG, GROUND
___NUTMEG, WHOLE
___OAT BRAN,
___OAT GROATS,
___OATS
___OIL, 100% CANOLA FRYING OIL,
___ONION, CHOPPED
___ONION, GRANULES
___ONION, POWDER, DOMESTIC
___ORANGE PEEL GRANULES
___ORANGE SPICE
___OREGANO (GREEK), CUT
___OREGANO (MEXICAN), CUT

___OREGANO (MEXICAN), GROUND
___OREGANO (MEXICAN), WHOLE,
___PAN D'ARCO (CUT)
___PANCAKE MIX, 6 Grain
___PANCAKE MIX, Blueberry
___PANCAKE MIX, BUTTERMILK,
___PANCAKE OLD FASHIONED,
___PAPRIKA GROUND
___PARSLEY FLAKES (CALIFORNIA)
___PARSLEY HERB POWDER
___PASTA, EGG NOODLES,
___PASTA, LASAGNA, WIDE CUT,
___PASTA, MACARONI, JUMBO SHELL,
___PASTA, MACARONI, LARGE SHELL,
___PASTA, MACARONI, ELBOW,
___PASTA, MACARONI, SALAD,
___PASTA, MACARONI, SMALL ELBOW
___PASTA, MACARONI, SMALL SHELL,
___PASTA, MACARONI, Whole Wheat
___Pasta-Pizza Sauce Mix
___PASTA, SPAGHETTI,
___Peach Slices
___ peach Flavor Apple Slices
___PEANUT BUTTER POWDER, DEHYDRATED
___PEAS, Alaskan
___PEAS, BLACK EYED,
___PEAS, SPLIT GREEN,
___PEAS, SPLIT YELLOW,
___PEAS, SWEET GARDEN, DEHYDRATED
___PEAS, WHOLE GREEN,
___PEPPER (BLACK) 1/4 CRACKED
___PEPPER (BLACK) TABLE GRIND
___PEPPER (WHITE), FINE GROUND
___PEPPERCORNS (BLACK), WHOLE
___PEPPERMINT, DOMESTIC
___PEPPERMINT TEA BAGS
___PEPPERS (GREEN BELL)
___PICKLING SPICE BLEND, WHOLE
___POPCORN, RABBIT EARS,
___POPPY SEED
___POPPY SEED, (BLUE), WHOLE
___POTATO DICES, DEHYDRATED
___POTATO FLAKES, DEHYDRATED,
___POTATO GRANULES,
___POTATO SLICES, DEHYDRATED,
___POTATO, HASHBROWNS, DEHYDRATED,
___POULTRY SEASONING, GROUND
___PSYLLIUM HUSKS
___PUDDING, BANANA, ADD MILK/INST
___PUDDING, BUTTERSCOTCH, MILK/INS *
___PUDDING, Custard
___PUDDING, CHOCOLATE, MILK/COOK *
___PUDDING, CHOCOLATE, MILK/INST *
___PUDDING, COCONUT, MILK/INST *
___PUDDING, LEMON, MILK/INST *
___PUDDING, Tapioca
___PUDDING, VANILLA, ADD MILK/INST *
___PUDDING, VANILLA, MILK/COOK
___PUMPKIN PIE SPICE,
___PUMPKIN SEEDS, SHELLED

___Quinoa,
___RADISH SEED,
___RADISH SEED, (FOR SPROUTING)
___RAISINS, Select
___RAISINS, Golden
___RASPBERRY LEAF
___RED CLOVER SEEDS (FOR SPROUTING)
___ RICE, Basmati Brown-Organic
___RICE, BROWN, LONG GRAIN
___RICE, Par Boiled
___RICE, WHITE, LONG GRAIN
___ROSE HIP POWDER
___ROSEMARY, CUT
___ROSEMARY, GROUND
___ROSEMARY, WHOLE
___RYE FLAKES, PAPER BAG
___RYE, PAPER BAG
___SAGE, FINE POWDER
___SAGE, RUBBED
___SAGE, WHOLE
___SALAD SUPREME SEASONING
___SALT
___SAUCE, AU JUS INSTANT
___SAUSAGE SEASONING,
___SESAME SEED (NATURAL) WHOLE
___SHEPHERDS PURSE
___SHORTENING POWDER, DEHYDRATED
___SLIPPERY ELM POWDER
___SOUP BASE, BEEF FLAVOR
___SOUP BASE, CHICKEN FLAVOR,
___SOUP BASE, CREAM, NON DAIRY
___SOUP MIX, ABC,
___SOUP MIX, BEEF BARLEY
___SOUP MIX, OLD FASHIONED,
___SOUP, AU-JUS SAUCE
___SOUP, BEEF, BARLEY, VEGETABLE
___SOUP, BEEF Noodle
___SOUP, BEEF Flovored Stew
___SOUP, CHICKEN NOODLE, (GREAT FLAVOR)
___SOUP, CORN CHOWDER BASE, MAKES
___SOUP, CREAM OF CHICKEN, MAKES
___SOUP, CREAM OF MUSHROOM, MAKES
___SOUP, CREAM PEA CHOWDER, MAKES
___SOUP, CREAMY CHEDDAR CHWD,
___SOUP, Creamy Potato
___SOUP, FRENCH ONION SOUP,
___SOUP, ITALIAN TOMATO/VEG,
___SOUP, MINESTRONE,
___SOUP, Mountain Stew Blend
___SOUP, NE CHOWDER BASE,
___SOUP, OLD FASHIONED SOUP MIX
___SOUP, ORIGINAL CREAM SOUP BASE
___SOUP, VEGETABLE BEEF #
___Sour Cream Powder
___SOUTHERN BUTTERMILK BISCUIT MIX
___SOUTHERN CORNBREAD II (YELLOW)
___SOY SAUCE,
___SPEARMINT SPICE BLEND (TEA) NO CAFFEIN
___SPELT, (ORGANIC)
___SPINACH FLAKES

___SUGAR, BROWN,
___SUGAR, POWDERED,
___SUGAR, WHITE
___SUNFLOWER SEED, RAW,
___Sweet Potato
___SYRUP, APRICOT,
___SYRUP, BLUEBERRY,
___SYRUP, BOYSENBERRY,
___SYRUP, NATURAL BUTTER FLAVOR,
___SYRUP, STRAWBERRY,
___SYRUP, LIGHT CORN,
___T.V.P. BACON FLAVORED,
___T.V.P. BEEF FLAVORED, DEHYDRATED
___T.V.P. CHICKEN FLAVORED,
___T.V.P. IMAGIC BARBECUE MIX
___T.V.P. IMAGIC BBQ FLAVOR,
___T.V.P. IMAGIC SLOPPY JOE MIX
___T.V.P. IMITATION HAM FLAVOR CHIPLETS
___T.V.P. PEPPERONI, IMITATION FLAVOR
___T.V.P. SAUSAGE FLAVOR
___T.V.P. TACO BEEF FLAVOR
___T.V.P. ULTRA-SOY, MINCED, NATURAL *FLAVOR*
___TACO SEASONING, GROUND
___TAPIOCA PEARLS (MEDIUM) WHOLE
___TARRAGON (CALIFORNIA), CUT
___TEA STRAINER(S)
___THYME, GROUND
___THYME LEAVES
___TOMATO POWDER, DEHYDRATED,
___TUMERIC POWDER
___VALERIAN ROOT CUT
___VALERIAN ROOT POWDER
___VANILLA EXTRACT
___VEGETABLE FLAKES, MIXED
___VEGETABLE SOUP BLEND
___VEGETABLE STEW BLEND
___WHEAT BRAN, PAPER BAG
___WHEAT FLAKES, WHITE,
___WHEAT GERM
___WHEAT, CRACKED,
___WHEAT, GOLDEN 86,
___WHEAT, HARD RED STORAGE,
___WHEAT, HARD WHITE,
___WHEAT, SOFT WHEAT,
___WHEAT, VITAL GLUTEN,
___WHEAT, WHITE, GOLDEN 86,
___WHEY,
___WHITE CREAM SAUCE
___WHITE PEPPER, WHOLE
___YEAST, INSTANT

One Year Supply Guide

Suggested Amounts of Basic Foods for Home Storage-Per Adult for One Year

Basic Food Storage		Extras	
Grains	300 lbs.	Fruits	185 lbs. Family Totals
Legumes	60 lbs.	(Veg) Vegetables	185 lbs. Family Totals
Powdered Milk	16 lbs.	(CE) Cooking Essentials	8 lbs. Per Person
Cooking Oil	25 lbs.	Meats/Meat Substitutes	20 lbs. Per Person
Sugar or Honey	60 lbs.	(Aux.) Auxiliary Foods	-
Salt	8 lbs.	(Cond.) Spices/Condiments	-
Water (2 wks.)	14 gallons	*Quantities are _estimates_ and should be adjusted to individual needs & likes.	

Food Storage Item	Amount	Shelf Life	Storage
GRAINS:	**300 lbs.+**	*Keep all grains away from weevil & rodents!	
Cereal	5 lbs./5 boxes cereal	2-3 years	Dry & weevil proof
Cornmeal	10 lbs.	30 years+*	*See below
Flour	75 lbs./ 3 bags(25lb.)	8-10 years	Dry & weevil proof
Mixes (pancake, muffin, etc.)	10 lbs.	2 years	Dry & weevil proof
Oats	20 lbs./ 7 (48oz.)bag	30 years+*	*See below
Pasta	40 lbs./40 bags(1lb.)	30 years+*	*See below
Rice	40 lbs./ 2 bags(20lb.)	30 years+*	*See below
Wheat	100 lbs./4 bags(25lb)	30 years+*	*See below

*According to the LDS church website, www.providentliving.com it states:
"Properly packaged, low moisture foods stored at room temperature or cooler (75 F or lower) remain nutritious and edible MUCH longer than previously thought according to findings of recent scientific studies. Estimated shelf life for many products has increased to 30 years or more." See website for more detailed information.

Food Storage Item	Amount	Shelf Life	Storage
LEGUMES/BEANS:	**60 lbs.**	*If beans are **DRIED**, they will last over 30 years!	
Black Beans	10 lbs./10 cans	Canned/ 2 years	Cool, dry place
Chili	5 lbs./5 cans	Canned/ 2 years	Cool, dry place
Kidney Beans	10 lbs./10 cans	Canned/ 2 years	Cool, dry place
Lentils	5 lb. bag	30 years+	Cool, dry place
Pinto Beans	15 lb. bag/15 cans	Canned/ 2 years	Cool, dry place
Pork n' Beans	5 lbs./5 cans	Canned/ 2 years	Cool, dry place
Refried Beans	10 lbs./10 cans	Canned/ 2 years	Cool, dry place

Food Storage Item	Amount	Shelf Life	Storage
MILK/DAIRY:	**16 lbs.**		
Evaporated Milk	2 lbs./ 3 (12oz.) cans	2 years	Cool, dry place
Other	1 lb.	Expirations	Cool, dry place
Powdered Milk	12 lbs.	20 years+	*See Above Statement
Sweetened Condensed	1lb./2 cans	2 years	Cool, dry place

Food Storage Item	Amount	Shelf Life	Storage
SUGAR:	**60 lbs.**		
Brown Sugar	6 lbs./ 3 (32oz.)bags	2 years+	Tightly sealed & dry
Corn Syrup	1 lb.	2 years+	Sealed

Honey	3 lbs.	Indefinite	Cool, tightly sealed, dark
Jam/Jellies	3 lbs./3 jars	2 years	Cool, tightly sealed, dark
Jello	1 lb./6 (3oz.) boxes	18 months	Cool & very dry
Maple Syrup	3 lbs./2 bottles	2 years	Cool, dry place
Molasses	1 lb.	2 years	Cool, dry place
Powdered Sugar	6 lbs./ 3 (32oz.)bags	2 years+	Tightly sealed & dry
Pudding	1 lb./6 (3oz.) boxes	18 months	Cool, dry place
White Granulated Sugar	35 lbs.	Indefinite	Tightly sealed & dry

OILS/FATS: 25 lbs.

Butter	2 lbs./2 (1lb.) boxes	1 year in the freezer	Freezer
Cooking Oil (Veg., Canola, etc.)	5 lbs./1.5 (48oz.) oils	2-3 years	Cool, dry place
Margarine	2 lbs./2 (1lb.) boxes	1 year in the freezer	Freezer
Mayonaise	4 lbs./2 (32oz.) Jars	1-2 years/expiration date	Sealed, dark & cool
Olive Oil	3 lbs./ 1 (48oz.)	1-2 years	Sealed, dark & cool
Peanut Butter	4 lbs./4 (18oz.) jars	4 years	Sealed, dark & cool
Salad Dressing	2 lbs./ 2 (19oz.) jars	1 year	Sealed, dark & cool
Shortening	3 lbs./ 1 (48oz.) tub	2-3 years	Cool, dry place

SALT: 8 lbs.

Salt	8 lbs.	Indefinite	Sealed & BONE dry

WATER: 28 gallons (2 week supply)

Drinking	14 gallons +	1 year	No contact w/ cement.
Washing/Cleaning	14 gallons +	1 year	No contact w/ cement.

MEATS/SUBSTITUTES: 20 lbs.

Canned Chicken	2 lbs./5 cans (6oz.)	2 years	Cool, dry place
Canned Tuna	5 lbs./13 cans (6oz.)	2 years	Cool, dry place
Canned Turkey	1 lb./2 cans (6oz.)	2 years	Cool, dry place
Chicken Noodle Soup/Meat soups	2 lbs./2 cans (15oz.)	2 years	Cool, dry place
Clams	.5 lbs./2 cans (4oz.)	2 years	Cool, dry place
Spam	1 lb./2 cans (8oz.)	2 years	Cool, dry place
Stew	2 lbs./ 2 cans	2 years	Cool, dry place
Vienna Sausages	.5 lbs./2 cans (4oz.)	2 years	Cool, dry place
TVP	1 lb.	20 years	Cool, dry place
Fresh Meat/1 month supply/Freezer:			
Bacon	1 lb.+	1 year/freezer	Freezer bags/containers
Beef/Roast	1 lb.+	1 year/freezer	Freezer bags/containers
Chicken	1 lb.+	1 year/freezer	Freezer bags/containers
Pork	1 lb.+	1 year/freezer	Freezer bags/containers
Sausage	1 lb.+	1 year/freezer	Freezer bags/containers
Seafood	1 lb.+	1 year/freezer	Freezer bags/containers

FRUITS: 185 lbs. (Totals for the ENTIRE family)

Applesauce	36 lbs./ 36 cans	2 years	Cool, dry place
Dry Fruit (raisins, coconut, apples)	17 lbs./ 17 1lb. Bags	2 years	Cool, dry place

Fruit Cocktail	12 lbs./ 12 cans	2 years	Cool, dry place
Mandarin Oranges	36 lbs./52cans(11oz)	2 years	Cool, dry place
Peaches	24 lbs./ 24 cans	2 years	Cool, dry place
Pears	24 lbs./ 24 cans	2 years	Cool, dry place
Pineapple	36 lbs./45cans(20oz)	2 years	Cool, dry place

VEGETABLES: 185 lbs. (Totals for the ENTIRE family)

*If vegetables are dried and packaged properly they will last anywhere from 18-24 months, or longer.

Beets	1 lb./ 1 can	2 years	Cool, dry place
Carrots	5 lbs./ 5 cans/or dried	2 years	Cool, dry place
Corn	24 lbs./ 24 cans	2 years	Cool, dry place
Green Beans	24 lbs./ 24 cans	2 years	Cool, dry place
Green Chilies	3 lbs./ 12 cans(4oz)	2 years	Cool, dry place
Instant Potatoes	30 lbs.	30 years+*	*See Above Statement
Mixed Vegetables	5 lbs/5 cans (15oz.)	2 years	Cool, dry place
Mushrooms	1 lb./ 4 cans (8oz.)	2 years	Cool, dry place
Onions	5 lbs.	18-24 months	Cool, dry place
Peas	6 lbs./ 6 cans (15oz.)	2 years	Cool, dry place
Pickles	6 lbs. / 4 jars (24oz.)	2 years	Cool, dry place
Pumpkin	10 lbs./ 5 cans(29oz)	2 years	Cool, dry place
Salsa	6 lbs./ 6 jars (16oz.)	2 years	Cool, dry place
Spaghetti Sauce	30 lbs./19 jars(26oz.)	2-3 years if in glass jar	Cool, dry place
Tomato Paste	2.5 lbs./7 cans (6oz.)	2 years	Cool, dry place
Tomato Sauce	2.5 lbs./7 cans (6oz.)	2 years	Cool, dry place
Tomato Soup	6 lbs./ 6 cans (15oz.)	2 years	Cool, dry place
Tomatoes	27 lbs/27 cans(15oz)	2 years	Cool, dry place
Yams	1 lb./ 1 can (15oz)	2 years	Cool, dry place

COOKING ESSENTIALS: 6 lbs.

Baking Powder	2 lbs./ 3 cans(10oz.)	3 years	Sealed & BONE dry
Baking Soda	1 lb./ 1 box (16oz.)	3 years	Sealed & BONE dry
Cocoa	1 lb./ 2 cans (8oz.)	3 years	Sealed & cool
Vanilla	As desired	3 years	Cool, dry place
Vinegar	2 quarts/.5 gallon	2 years+	Sealed
Yeast	2 lbs./ 2 pkgs. (16oz)	1 year in the freezer	Freezer or cool place

AUXILIARY FOODS:

Brownie & Cookie Mixes	1 year	Dry & Weevil proofed
Cake Mixes	1 year	Dry & Weevil proofed
Casserole Mixes	1 year	Dry & Weevil proofed
Crackers	1 year	Dry & Weevil proofed
Marshmallows	1 year	Cool, dry place
Pie Fillings	2 years	Cool, dry place
Spices	3 years+	Dry & Weevil proofed
Vitamins & Minerals	1 year+	Cool, dark, dry place
Chocolate Chips	18 months	Cool, dry place

CONDIMENTS:

BBQ Sauce	2 years	Tightly sealed, Dry
Ketchup	2 years	Tightly sealed, Dry
Mustard	2 years	Tightly sealed, Dry
Specialty Mustards	2 years	Tightly sealed, Dry

http://www.dealstomeals.com/uploads/show/One_Year_Supply_Guide.pdf

Our Prophet Gordon B Hinckley, said, "In words of revelation the Lord has said, "Organize yourselves; prepare every needful thing" ([D&C 109:8](#)). Our people for three-quarters of a century have been counseled and encouraged to make such preparation as will assure survival should a calamity come. We can set aside some water, basic food, medicine, and clothing to keep us warm. We ought to have a little money laid aside in case of a rainy day."

"The best place to have some food set aside is within our homes, together with a little money in savings. The best welfare program is our own welfare program. Five or six cans of wheat in the home are better than a bushel in the welfare granary. ...

"We can begin with a one week's food supply and gradually build it to a month, and then to three months. I am speaking now of food to cover basic needs" ("To Men of the Priesthood," *Ensign,* Nov. 2002,

" 'And there shall arise after them seven years of famine...And God will shortly bring it to pass.' Now brethren, I want to make it very clear that I am not prophesying, that I am not predicting *years* of famine in the future. But, I am suggesting that the time has come to get our houses in order...**avoid debt** to the extent possible. **Pay off debt** as quickly as you can, and free yourselves from bondage... **There is a portent of stormy weather ahead to which we had better give heed.** We are carrying a message of self-reliance throughout the Church... I urge you brethren to look to the condition of your finances..." (Gordon B. Hinckley, **October Conference 1998**

ANOTHER VOICE OF WARNING

...if ye are prepared, ye shall not fear

www.ldsavow.com

Monthly Food Storage Purchasing Calendar

Compiled by Andrea Chapman

If you are just starting out, this calendar can be used any year.
Just start with the current month's items.

We have tried to keep the costs down to between $35 and $45 per week. This might seem rather costly, but if you want to build a good food storage in only one year, it will cost you more each week than if you spread out acquiring it over several years. Be certain to buy only items your family will use, and rotate and use the items in your storage throughout the year. Milk is an expensive item and prices keep soaring, so you might need to invest in a bit higher food storage bill to buy it right now.
* The items in the first few months are basic essentials and are the most important to purchase and store.

It is vital to get <u>WATER - STORAGE</u> . If you don't have water, you will not be able to use many of the foods you have that are dehydrated or require water to cook. Many times in natural disasters, the electricity goes down and you will not be able to access your water. Sometimes the water is contaminated from flooding and cross-contamination from sewage. You will need water, at very least, you will need 3 days worth.

January

Week #1
1 case canned fruit
2 #10 cans instant potatoes

Week #2
3 #10 cans dry milk

Week #3
3 #10 cans dry milk

Week #4
9 pounds yeast

Week #5
Anything you have missed from above

February

Week #1

Water Storage Containers-buy either 55 gallon drums, 5 gallon water containers (available at all emergency preparedness stores and some super markets) and spigot, or start to save water in pop bottles and plastic juice containers. Also purchase 100 lbs. hard white wheat and three plastic storage buckets with tight fitting lids.
Check out the local mills in your area for best prices.

Week #2
25 lbs of **sugar** or 20 lbs of **honey**
5 lbs **salt** per person
bucket opener

Week #3
4 #10 cans **shortening** or 4 - 48 oz bottles **oil**
2 #10 cans of **dry instant milk**

Week #4
2 case **canned beans** (like refried pinto, black, kidney, white, pink etc.) or
25 lbs **dry beans** (preferable) and bucket to store them in.
50 lbs dried **corn or popcorn**
(about $10.00 from a mill or food storage company) and a bucket to store it in.
(Can be ground into cornmeal as well as for popcorn.)

(*All grains and beans can be put into #10 cans at the LDS cannery.*)
(If not, the buckets work well.)

March

(please note that many of these items are repeats because we want to be SURE you have enough of the essentials!)

Week #1
Enough **water** containers for 14 gallons per person in the family.
(This was mentioned last month-but we want to be sure you have this)
(*Water is your most important item!*)
If you didn't get enough containers last month, you can get them this month.
White Rice, at least 15 pounds per person in the family and if possible buckets to store it.
(*Brown Rice goes rancid faster.*)

Week #2
2 jars **mayonnaise**
1 gallon **oil**
2 tubs **shortening**

Week #3
25 pounds **sugar**
1- 25 pound bag of **legumes** (pinto, lentils, white, pink etc.)

Week #4
Salt 5 more lbs
2 bottles of **bleach**
1 #10 can or 1 box of **dry milk.**

Week #5
Check your list for the last 8 weeks and purchase any items you fell short on.
These items are essential ones and you will need to be sure you have enough.

April

Week #1
100 pounds **wheat**
10 lbs. **brown sugar**

Week #2
2 #10 size cans **dried fruit** or 1 case **canned fruit**
1 pound **yeast**

Week #3
1 case **tuna or salmon**
2 #10 **cans milk**
3 lbs **sprouting seeds**
1 80 oz can Rumsford baking powder

Week #4
2 large jars **peanut butter** or
1 #10 can **peanut butter powder** (last longer)
2 cans **dried whole egg** (keep in a cool dry place)

May

Week #1
2 to 3 bottles of **multi-vitamins**
2 #10 cans of **rolled oats**
(if #10 cans are not available in your area, buy the largest packages available)
(in your local store, and also purchase a small bucket to store it in.)

Week #2
100 lbs. of **wheat**
3 buckets

Week #3
#10 can **margarine powder -** or shortening if marg. powder is unavailable
2 #10 cans **rolled oats**
(or equivalent, and a storage bucket)

Week #4
4 #10 cans **instant potatoes**
1 bottle **black pepper**

June

Week #1

2 cans **dry milk**, 2 boxes of **Rennet**
(used for making cottage cheese and other dairy products from dry milk.)
1 bottle **lemon juice**,
1 bottle **vinegar**. (also used in making dairy products from dry milk

Week #2

100 lbs **wheat**
25 lbs. **white flour**

Week #3

Baking **soda** (try to buy in bulk in places like Sam's Club or Cosco) Buy about 10 lbs.
25 lbs. or **legumes** (choose those you are willing to eat.
Remember you can sprout legumes and almost quadruple the nutritional value of them.
Buy one large box Knox or other gelatin to be used in place of eggs in baking.

Week #4

Tomato products (try to buy them by the case in normal size cans. Spaghetti sauce, tomato sauce, and whole and chopped tomatoes. Buy a combination of flavored and not flavored to matoes. Buy paste if you can get a good deal on it. It is less expensive to add water to paste to make sauce than it is just to buy sauce sometimes. *Buy three cases if possible.*)

Week #5

Be on the look out for **garden seeds** that are NON- Hybrid.
That way you can use the seeds from the plants you grow to grow a garden the next season.
A good price for them is about $18-20 per can with about 10 varieties per can.

July

Week #1

200# **wheat**
(buckets to store it in if needed)
[keep filling pop bottles, Gallon syrup containers, etc. with water - basically no cost to this)

Week #2

20 lbs. **Peanut butter**
[keep filling those water containers]

Week #3

4 #10 cans **shortening**
2 # 10 cans **dry milk**
[keep filling water containers - make this a habit - when you empty something worthy of water storage, wash it and fill it right away]

Week #4

6 #10 cans **dry milk**
[**more water!**]

August

Week #1

25# **rice**
25# **sugar**
1 # 10 can **instant potatoes**
5 lbs. **salt**

Week #2

1 case **tuna** or **salmon** or other **meat**
2 # 10 cans **dry milk**

Week #3

2 #10 cans **dry milk**
2 cans **shortening**
1 #10 can **instant potatoes**

Week #4

In late August and early September, many stores have sales on canned fruits and vegetables.
Ask your local store when these sales will be, and switch the weeks of this calendar as needed.
2 cases **fruit**
5 lbs. **salt**

Week #5	2 cases **canned fruit** 1 case misc. **vegetables** (green beans, peas, carrots, etc.)

September

Week # 1	2 cases canned **fruit** 1 case misc. **vegetables**
Week # 2	2 cases canned **fruit** 2 cans **shortening**
Week #3	2 cases **fruit** 1 case **vegetables**
Week #4	2 cans **shortening** 25# **rice** buckets to store rice if it did not come in #10 cans

October

Week #1	100 lbs. **wheat** and 3 buckets
Week #2	1 case **tuna** or other **meat**
Week #3	25 lbs. **Sugar** 2 large cans **fruit juice powder**
Week #4	3 #10 cans **dry milk**
Week #5	9 #10 cans **potato flakes**

November

Week #1	4 large jars **peanut butter**
Week #2	1 case canned **fruit** 15 pounds **rice**
Week #3	7 #10 cans **shortening**
Week #4	50 pounds **rice** and buckets to store

December

Week #1	100 lbs. **wheat** and 3 buckets
Week #2	1 large can **fruit juice powder** 3 large jars **peanut butter**
Week #3	3 #10 cans **dry milk**
Week #4	50 pounds of **rice**, **oats**, or **barley** buckets to store

A 30-Day Emergency Food Supply
(3,000 Calories per Day for one Adult)

Introduction

30 Day Emergency Food Supply It would be nice to have two different types of emergency food supplies as follows:

A 30-day or one-month emergency food supply.
A one-year emergency food supply.

Some emergencies are short-term and they do not last very long. A 30-day food supply would be very useful in this type of situation. In most short-term emergencies electrical power is not available, and water may or may not be available. Under these conditions cooking a meal from scratch would be extremely challenging. In this type of situation it would be nice if you had a decent variety of canned foods that you could simply heat and eat.

On the other hand, a long-term hard times event is different. Although eating from a can is a reasonable option for a short period of time, after awhile it becomes very boring. That is when your body will crave "real food" that you prepare from scratch. Therefore, a one-year emergency food supply will need to contain a broad variety of food items that include some canned foods and some foods that you can prepare from scratch, such as a loaf of fresh baked bread.

One reasonable option for storing your emergency food supplies would be as follows:

Store your 30-day food supply at your current residence. If something unexpected happens then you would have immediate access to your food and you could make the decision to either stay exactly where you are, or you could quickly load your 30-day food supply into your car and go somewhere safer.

Store your one-year food supply with your parents or children or close relatives who live in a country area. You could arrange this with them ahead of time and perhaps they could set aside a spare bedroom just for your family in the event of an emergency. Then you could stack your one-year emergency food supply in the closet of that bedroom, or put some of it under the bed or beds in that bedroom. This would provide you with food to eat when you arrived at your more desirable back-up location. (Or you could store some of your food at a temperature controlled warehouse in a distant small rural town.)

Important Criteria for Selecting Food Items for an Emergency 30-Day Food Supply

If an emergency were to occur unexpectedly and you had to provide for your family until the emergency was over, then you should have enough fresh drinking water and enough food stored ahead of time to get you through the emergency.

If the electrical power is off, then cooking a meal from scratch would be far more challenging than simply opening a can of food, heating it, and then serving it to your family.

In this type of situation your canned foods should meet all of the following criteria:

The food item should be one that your family members have enjoyed eating in the past. During a short-term emergency it would be really nice if your family knew that their daily meals would be something they have enjoyed eating in the past. It is okay if different members of your family have different taste preferences. You should consider purchasing and storing the food items that each person in your family really likes because in most situations one can of food is just barely enough for one person.

The food item should have a reasonably long shelf life, preferably at least five-years or more.

The food item should not require refrigeration or freezing. You should be able to safely store the food item at normal room temperatures.

The food item should be relatively affordable.

The food item should be ready to heat and eat.

The food item should be a complete meal in a can that includes meat, vegetables, and a few vitamins.

The food item should contain a lot of calories, fat, carbohydrates, and protein. Your body will need and crave all of these basic ingredients and therefore your food items should contain all of them. In other words, don't just look at the calorie content of the food item. Also consider the fat, carbohydrates, and protein of the food in order to provide a truly balanced meal that will satisfy your family's hunger. After you have eaten a meal you should not feel hungry again for several hours. This is extremely important because some foods only relieve your hunger for a very short period of time and you become extremely hungry again rather quickly. Therefore, the foods you select should be ones that can keep you from feeling hunger for at least 5 or 6 hours. If the food contains reasonable levels of calories, fat, carbohydrates, and protein then hunger should not be a problem for several hours.

For each food item read the nutritional data on the label. Multiply the number of servings in the container by the number of calories, fat, carbohydrates, and protein per serving. This will yield the total nutritional value of the entire food container. This is important because different canned foods show a different number of "servings per can" and therefore you must convert this into the total food value of the can instead of just comparing the food value per serving. For example, consider the following:

Food Item	Servings Per Can	Calories per Serving	Total Calories per Can
18.8 ounces Chunky Soup	2	170	340
12.5 ounces Canned Chicken	6	60	360
15 ounces Canned Pasta	2	250	500
16 ounces Canned Ham	8	80	640
15 ounces Chili with Beans	2	350	700
12 ounces Canned Spam	6	180	1,080

The last column in the above table is the important column because it shows the total number of Calories in the entire Can. You would need to do the same calculation for the total Fat per Can, the total Carbohydrates per Can, and the Total Protein per Can.

Your food supply should contain a wide assortment of foods. If possible, you should not have to eat the same exact food item until at least seven days have passed. This means you should have enough variety so you could serve different meals to your family every day for one week.

A Recommended 30-Day Emergency Food Supply for One Adult

In my opinion the following food items are ones you should consider for your 30-day emergency food supply. I strongly recommend that you purchase one can of each of the following foods and serve it to your family during normal times to determine if they enjoy it. If they like it then you could purchase additional cans of that food item for your 30-day emergency food supply.

The following suggestions would be a reasonable starting position for the average family. However, since each family has unique taste and dietary requirements, each family will probably need to remove some items from the following list and add other items that they enjoy more.

Note: All costs, package sizes, and nutritional data in the following table were obtained on September 1, 2010.

Quantity	Item	Size	Cost	Total	Total Nutrition/Container
3 Cans	Campbell's Chunky "Beef Base" Soup	18.8 ounces	$ 1.50	$ 4.50	280Cal, 9Ft, 38Crb, 14Pro
3 Cans	Campbell's Chunky "Chicken Base" Soup	18.8 ounces	$ 1.50	$ 4.50	360Cal, 16 Ft, 38 Crb, 16 Pro
2 Cans	Campbell's Chunky "Other Base" Soup	18.8 ounces	$ 1.50	$ 3.00	380Cal, 5 Ft, 60 Crb, 24 Pro
8 Cans	Chef Boyardee Pasta (Spaghetti/Ravioli/Lasagna)	15 ounces	$ 1.00	$ 8.00	500Cal, 24 Ft, 54 Crb, 18 Pro
4 Cans	LaChoy Asian "Meat and Vegetables"	42 ounces	$ 2.50	$ 10.00	360 Cal, 10 Ft, 54 Crb, 15 Pro
4 Cans	Armour Beef Stew	24 ounces	$ 2.40	$ 9.60	630 Cal, 33 Ft, 60 Crb, 24 Pro
4 Cans	Hormel Roast Beef Hash	15 ounces	$ 2.00	$ 8.00	780 Cal, 48 Ft, 44 Crb, 42 Pro
4 Cans	Van Camps Chili with Beans	15 ounces	$ 1.16	$ 4.64	700 Cal, 36 Ft, 62 Crb, 34 Pro
2 Cans	Ranch Style Black Beans (or Pinto or Kidney)	15 ounces	$ 0.68	$ 1.36	385 Cal, 2 Ft, 66 Crb, 21 Pro
2 Cans	Taco Bell Refried Beans	16 ounces	$ 0.98	$ 1.96	420 Cal, 3 Ft, 70 Crb, 24 Pro
4 Pcks	Taco Bell Taco Seasoning Mix	1.25 ounces	$ 0.50	$ 2.00	120 Cal, 0 Ft, 18 Crb, 0 Pro
4 Cans	Hereford Roast Beef	12 ounces	$ 2.98	$ 11.92	350 Cal, 7 Ft, 5 Crb, 65 Pro
2 Cans	Van Camps Pork and Beans	15 ounces	$ 0.50	$ 1.00	385 Cal, 3 Ft, 88 Crb, 21 Pro
4 Cans	Armour Vienna Sausage	5 ounces	$ 0.47	$ 1.88	330 Cal, 30 Ft, 3 Crb, 15 Pro
4 Cans	Veg-All Mixed Vegetables (Corn, Peas & Carrots)	15 ounces	$ 0.88	$ 3.52	140 Cal, 0 Ft, 28 Crb, 3 Pro
6 Pks	Idahoan Instant Potatoes (Add Water Only)	4 ounces	$ 0.92	$ 5.52	440 Cal, 12 Ft, 80 Crb, 8 Pro

Qty	Item	Size	Unit $	Total $	Nutrition
2 Bags	Enriched White Rice	16 ounces	$ 0.68	$ 1.36	1,600 Cal, 0 Ft, 350 Crb, 30 Pro
2 Boxes	Maggi Small Bouillon Cubes (beef and chicken)	2.82 ounces	$ 1.28	$ 2.56	100 Cal, 0 Ft, 0 Crb, 0 Pro
4 Pks	Country Gravy Dry Mix (or Brown Gravy)	2.64 ounces	$ 0.98	$ 3.92	320 Cal, 16 Ft, 40 Crb, 8 Pro
8 Cans	Chef Boyardee Mac & Cheese	15 ounces	$ 1.00	$ 8.00	480 Cal, 20 Ft, 56 Crb, 18 Pro
4 Cans	Double "Q" Pink Alaskan Salmon	14.75 ounces	$ 2.26	$ 9.04	630 Cal, 21 Ft, 0 Crb, 100 Pro
4 Cans	Bumble Bee Solid White Albacore (Tuna in Oil)	5 ounces	$ 1.34	$ 5.36	160 Cal, 6 Ft, 0 Crb, 28 Pro
4 Cans	Great Value Chunk Chicken Breast	12.5 ounces	$ 1.98	$ 7.92	360 Cal, 6 Ft, 6 Crb, 66 Pro
4 Cans	Spam Lunch Meat (or Dak Canned Ham)	12 ounces	$ 2.44	$ 9.76	1,080 Cal, 96 Ft, 6 Crb, 42 Pro
1 Cntr	Quaker Quick Oats (or Breakfast Bars)	42 ounces	$ 3.18	$ 3.18	4,500 Cal, 90 Ft, 810 Crb, 150 Pro
4 Cntr	Tang Orange Drink Mix	20 ounces	$ 2.66	$ 10.64	2,160 Cal, 0 Ft, 520 Crb, 0 Pro
15 Pcgs	Kool-Aid Drink Mix (Assorted Flavors)	0.13 ounces	$ 0.20	$ 3.00	0 Cal, 0 Ft, 0 Crb, 0 Pro
10 lbs	Granulated Sugar	5 pounds	$ 2.54	$ 5.08	8,500 Cal, 0 Ft, 2,270 Crb, 0 Pro
1 Box	Instant Powdered Milk	64 ounces	$ 15.63	$ 15.63	6,400 Cal, 0 Ft, 960 Carbs, 640 Pro
Crb1 Cntnr	Hershey's Cocoa Powder	8 ounces	$ 2.96	$ 2.96	900 Cal, 22 Ft, 135 Crb, 45 Pro
8 Cans	Del Monte Fruit Cocktail (or Peaches or Pears)	15.25 ounces	$ 1.46	$ 11.68	350 Cal, 0 Ft, 84 Carbs, 0 Pro
3.5lb	Child's Play Candy Assortment (150 Pieces)	3.5 pounds	$ 7.34	$ 7.34	6k Cal, 150 Ft, 1,350 Crb, 50 Pro
30 Each	Complete Multivitamin Tablets	30 Each	$ 1.40	$ 1.40	0 Calories, 0 Fat, 0 Crb, 0 Pro

Totals . . . $ 190.23

89,020 Calories, 2,023 Fat, 14,707 Carbs, 3,319 Protein.

If you do not want to cook then omit the rice and potatoes and buy more of the complete meals in a can (Chunky Soups, Pasta, Chili with Beans, Beef Stew, etc.). Usually one can of food is just enough for one good meal for one person. However, some of the above canned foods contain enough food for two meals (lunch and supper), or for two people at the same time.

Discussion of Some of the Recommended Food Items

The powdered milk and the cocoa powder may be used to make either chocolate milk or hot chocolate.
On the other hand, if your family doesn't like milk then don't buy it. If you prefer coffee or tea then buy it instead.
If you don't like Kool-Aid or Tang and you prefer soft drinks or beer or wine then buy them instead.

White rice can be enhanced with bouillon cubes (either beef or chicken) or with gravy (either white country gravy or brown gravy).

Instant potatoes can be enhanced with brown gravy or white country gravy.

Armour Roast Beef can be converted into a "Mexican" meal by combining it with approximately one-half package of Taco Mix and then serving it with either Refried Beans or Black Beans. If you have some flour then you could make a burrito or tortilla shell.

Chef Boyardee Macaroni and Cheese may be eaten as a side dish by itself, or it can be converted into a casserole by adding canned tuna, or canned chicken, or sliced Vienna Sausages, or diced Spam.

Pork and Beans can be made into "Beanie Wienies" by adding sliced pieces of Vienna Sausage.

The Vienna Sausages may be eaten as a simple meat item, or converted into "mini corn dogs" if you have some cornmeal, or into "pigs in a blanket" if you have some flour.

The Spam may be sliced and fried for breakfast, lunch, or supper.

The Salmon can be made into "Salmon Patties" if you add a little cornmeal.

Canned fruit may be eaten as a dessert item, or you could eat from the bag of candy.

The candy could be hard candies (peppermints, spearmints, butterscotch disks, or cinnamon disks), or caramels, or tootsie rolls or any combination your family prefers.

Note: If you use a standard Vacuum Food Sealer to vacuum seal some of the above items (candy, vitamins, white rice, instant milk, sugar, cocoa powder, and quick oats), then you could extend the normal shelf life of these items by a multiple of approximately five.

Suggestions for Preparing Meals During a Short-Term Hard Times Event

To prepare a meal from scratch normally takes more time, more fuel, and as the food slowly cooks it emits a stronger aroma than when you simply open a can of food, heat it, and then immediately eat it.

Therefore, having canned foods that you simply heat and eat means you will need less cooking fuel and you will be keeping your cooking aromas to the absolute minimum. The absence of strong cooking aromas may help you to avoid attracting unnecessary attention to your family during a difficult short-term hard times event.

As a practical example,

Breakfast could be oatmeal, or breakfast bars, or fried Spam or fried ham, or you could skip breakfast and eat lunch at 10:00 AM and supper at 5:00 PM.

Lunch could be a complete meal from a can.

Supper could be more like a normal meal such as boiled rice or instant potatoes or beans or vegetables, plus a meat item from a can, such as salmon patties.

Remember, canned foods have been fully cooked and they only need to be heated and served. However, whenever possible it is advisable to heat your food to at least 185 degrees Fahrenheit (85 degrees Celsius) to kill any potential harmful microorganisms that might be in the food.

It would also be a good idea to put a lid on the cook pot or skillet when you are heating the food. The lid will help to keep the heat and the aroma inside the cook pot. This means you will need less fuel to heat the food to an acceptable temperature, and it will prevent most of the delicious cooking aromas (odors) from escaping and attracting unnecessary attention to your location.

It should also be noted that some foods emit a powerful aroma while they are being prepared, such as coffee and bacon. Therefore, if you truly love coffee then during a short-term emergency it might be advisable to have a small supply of "instant coffee" instead of "regular coffee." I know there is a difference between the flavor of instant coffee and regular coffee but you need to consider your priorities during a short-term emergency. For example,

Would a cup of instant coffee be okay if it did not attract any attention to your location?

Or would you prefer for everyone within a half-block radius to be knocking on your door and asking you to please, please share some of your fresh brewed coffee?

Some Options for Heating Canned Foods

It is possible to heat some food items while they are still in the can. This would mean no dirty cook pots to wash. However, after heating the can of food you will still need to transfer the food to a bowl or plate so you can stir the food to more evenly blend its ingredients in order to make it a more enjoyable eating experience.

If you decide to heat your food while it is still inside the can then you should first remove the exterior paper label, if the can has a paper label. Then you should remove the top of the can to allow the pressure to escape. Some people recommend simply punching one or two holes in the top of the can with a can opener in order to prevent the ashes from a campfire from getting into the food. However, trying to remove the lid from a can that has been heated to 120 degrees or higher can be a very challenging task.

Microwave Oven Coleman Stove Charcoal Grill Fireplace Sterno Cooking Fuel Oil Lamp Candle in Glass Holder

Following are some options for heating canned foods:

Microwave Oven: If the power is still on a microwave oven will control the cooking aromas, and it uses very little power, and it is very fast. However, you must remove the food from the can and put it into a microwave safe container before heating the food inside the microwave oven.

Coleman Camp Stove: Another obvious option would be a Coleman Camp Stove. One model uses Coleman fuel and a different model uses the small propane tanks. The major shortcoming is the initial investment in the grill itself and in the fuel, and the fact that they are designed to be used outdoors because they release poisonous gas fumes while in operation. Another disadvantage is that when you run out of fuel the Coleman grill will cease to function. Finally, if you are forced to evacuate your home then which would you rather have in the trunk of your car: (1) a Coleman Grill and some spare fuel, or (2) an extra case or two of canned foods?

Charcoal Grill: A small portable charcoal grill can be used to heat food. You should consider lining the bottom of the grill with a thin layer of sand, or dirt, or small gravel before starting a fire in the charcoal grill. You could use ordinary charcoal briquettes, or you could collect some small sticks from a nearby wooded area and use them to start a very small fire inside your charcoal grill.

If you use sticks, then you should consider collecting sticks that have fallen off the trees and are caught in some bushes or are leaning against something else. These sticks will be extremely dry and they will burn well. If you collect sticks lying flat on the ground then you will probably discover that many of them are damp, or moldy, or rotten and they will not burn well.

The primary shortcoming of both charcoal and sticks is that they must be used outside, and as they burn they will release an odor, or smoke, that will attract a lot of attention to your cooking area.

Grill Surface: All you really need is the top metal grill cooking surface off a charcoal grill. You could support this metal grill piece in a variety of different ways and place a heat source below it to heat your food. For example, if you were indoors you could support the metal grill piece on top of four cans of food, and then put a can of "Sterno Cooking Fuel" below the metal grill piece, and you could then heat your food in a skillet on top of the metal grill piece. If you were outdoors you could use four rocks for support and start a fire using some wood sticks from a nearby wooded area.

Fireplace: If you have a wood burning fireplace then you could build a very small fire in your fireplace and heat your meals there. Remember that you only need to heat your food so it would be okay to heat the food over a small flame. In other words, you would not need to wait for the wood sticks to burn down into red hot coals to heat your food. This is one of the differences between simply heating a can of food and cooking from scratch. The major disadvantage of heating food in your fireplace will be the column of chimney smoke that everyone can see. During the cool or cold winter months this would not be an unusual sight. But during the warm summer months a column of chimney smoke will be a "very unusual sight" and almost everyone will notice it and immediately realize you are probably cooking something inside your fireplace.

Solar Oven: You could purchase a pre-made solar oven, or you could build your own "solar oven." Or you could simply line the inside of a small cardboard box with some aluminum foil and then put a piece of glass or a piece of clear plastic on top of the box. The box should be at least twice as big as your can of food. Place the small solar oven in front of a southern facing window to heat your canned foods. The major shortcoming of this method is that the sun must be shining which may not be the case during a short-term hard times event.

Window and a Dark Cloth: Do not remove the lid from the canned food, and do not punch any holes in the lid. Place the can of food under a dark cloth in front of a window in direct sunlight for several hours. You could also use this method by placing the wrapped can of food below the rear window of your car. The dark cloth will achieve two objectives: (1) It will collect and capture more of the sun's energy and do a better job of heating the food, and (2) It will prevent anyone who might pass by from seeing that you are heating a can of food underneath the dark cloth. The major shortcoming of this method is that the sun must be shining which may not be the case during a short-term hard times event.

Sterno Cooking Fuel: The twin packs of Sterno Cooking Fuel may be purchased in the camping section of most sporting goods stores, including most Walmarts. Remove the lid from the can, light the fuel, heat your food, put out the flame, put the top back on the can of fuel, and save the rest of the fuel for your next meal. Since you will only be heating your canned foods, a single can of Sterno Cooking Fuel will last a lot longer as compared to using it to cook a meal from scratch.

Oil Lamp: Remove the glass top from the oil lamp, light the wick, adjust the wick to achieve a very short flame, and then put the flame below a campfire grill and heat the food on top of the campfire grill.

Candle: Place a short round candle inside a candle holder and light it. The short round candles are better because they will last a lot longer inside a candle holder than a long thin candle that will burn down very quickly. You can heat your food above the flame of a candle similar to a "fondue" pot. The glass candle holder in the above picture has a long glass stem on its bottom. The long glass stem allows you to move the candle holder to a different location while the candle is still burning. Some candle holders have a flat bottom and the sides of the glass candle holder get extremely hot and it is very challenging to move the lit candle to a different location.

When you stop and think about the above options carefully, the ones that would be the most dependable in the widest variety of short-term hard times events and which would attract the least amount of attention would be the last four options above. On the other hand, if the power was still on, then the microwave oven would be my first choice.

Note: Several of the above options are only a reasonable choice for heating a can of precooked food. Cooking a food item from scratch will require significantly more heat for a much longer period of time.

Conclusion

There may not be very much to do during a short-term emergency and everyone in your family will be truly looking forward to each meal in order to relieve their boredom and to satisfy their hunger.

It is okay to talk about unpleasant topics at other times during the day but each member of your family should understand that all discussions at the dining table will be about pleasant topics. This will facilitate their enjoyment of their meal and it will aid in the digestive process.

Finally, please remember to thank God for every meal before your family starts eating.

Chef Boyardee Canned Pasta Note:

I have tried the Overstuffed Ravioli, and the Giant Meatballs, and the Regular Ravioli, and the Mini Ravioli and the Mini Spaghetti with Meatballs.

In my opinion the Mini Ravioli and the Mini Spaghetti with Meatballs are better than the regular pastas or the giant pastas. The "mini pastas" contain more sauce, and all the food heats more evenly in less time, and the overall taste is superior.

Therefore I strongly recommend the "mini pastas" instead of the regular pastas or the giant pastas. However, since taste is a very individual experience, your family may completely disagree with me and there is nothing wrong with that.

If you have young children then they will probably prefer the Chef Boyardee "ABC" and "Dinosaur" pastas because they are significantly more fun to eat. The nutritional value of these pastas is almost the same as the other pastas so there is nothing wrong will adding these special pastas to your emergency food supply for your young children.

Real-World One-Year Emergency Food Supply
(*3,000 Calories per Day for one Adult*)

The original retail price for each food item was established at the beginning of the year 2008 on January 9, 2008. The Total Retail Cost for the entire one-year emergency food supply on January 9, 2008 was $1,385 in the Southeastern United States.

Year 2008 Inflation: The total cost of the one-year emergency food supply increased in price by 15.3% or $212 in twelve-months from January 9, 2008 ($1,385) to January 3, 2009 ($1,597).

Year 2009 Inflation: The total cost of the one-year emergency food supply increased in price by 6.1% or $97 in twelve-months from January 3, 2009 ($1,597) to January 4, 2010 ($1,694).

Year 2010 Deflation: The total cost of the one-year emergency food supply decreased in price by -1.4% or $-23 in twelve-months from January 4, 2010 ($1,694) to January 3, 2011 ($1,671).

Year 2011 Inflation: The total cost of the one-year emergency food supply increased in price by 9.3% or $165 in twelve-months from January 3, 2011 ($1,768) to January 2, 2012 ($1,933).

Combined Four Year Inflation: Over the entire four year period beginning on January 9, 2008 and ending on January 2, 2012 the total combined impact of inflation on the One-Year Emergency Food Supply has been 32.6%. In other words, in the United States of America we are paying approximately **33% more for our food every week** than we were four years ago. This is significant because most of us in the United States, myself included, have not received any type of pay increase over that same four year period. Although my pay has not changed for four years I still consider myself extremely fortunate because I still have a job and I know that an overwhelming number of people cannot find work of any kind.

The One-Year Emergency Food Supply List
The retail Cost of the following "One-Year Emergency Food Supply" is based on prices as of **March 1, 2012.**

Quantity	Calories	Cost	Item (Number In Parenthesis = Total Calories per One Bag, Jar, or Can)
70 Pounds	105,000	$ 40	Long Grain White Rice in 10 or 20 pound Bags (very long shelf life)
70 Pounds	105,000	$ 28	Whole Wheat Berries or Flour (not self-rising) (7,500 Calories per 5 lbs.)
30 Pounds	48,240	$ 16	5 lb. Bag Corn Meal (8,040 Calories per 5 lb. Bag)
4 Boxes	12,800	$ 10	32 oz. Box Aunt Jemima Buttermilk Complete Pancake/Waffle Mix (3,200)
4 Boxes	18,000	$ 15	42 oz. Box Quaker Quick 1 Minute Oats (4,500)
4 Boxes 3	1,720	$ 8	5 lb. Box Quaker Quick Grits (7,930)
36 Boxes	60,480	$ 39	16 oz. Box Spaghetti Noodles (Angel hair or thin cooks faster) (1,680 Calories)
24 Cans	11,520	$ 24	15 oz. Can Chef Boyardee Brand Macaroni and Cheese (480)
24 Cans	12,000	$ 24	15 oz. Can Chef Boyardee Brand Pasta (lasagna, ravioli, spaghetti wi etc.) (500)
24 Cans	8,640	$ 36	18.8 oz. Can Campbell's Chunky Soup (buy the soups with chicken) (360)
48 Cans	9,000	$ 66	5 oz. Can Bumble Bee Brand Tuna in Oil (water pack has fewer calories) (187)
12 Cans	9,600	$ 46	16 oz. Can Dak Brand Canned Ham (no refrigeration required) (800)
24 Cans	24,480	$ 60	12 oz. Can Spam (1,020)
24 Cans	9,000	$ 12	5 oz. Can Vienna Sausage (375)
24 Cans	9,000	$ 96	12 oz. Can Roast Beef (375)
24 Cans	18,720	$ 50	15 oz. Can Hormel Roast Beef Hash (Corned Beef Hash) (beef & potatoes) (780)
48 Cans	30,240	$ 119	24 oz. Can Armour Brand Beef Stew (with potatoes & carrots) (630)
48 Cans	33,600	$ 56	15 oz. Can Chili with Beans (700)
96 Cans	35,520	$ 65	15 oz. Can Beans (assorted different varieties) (370)
180 Cans	25,200	$ 122	15 oz. Can Mixed Vegetables (note: green beans have very few calories) (140)
12 Boxes	41,280	$ 33	32 oz. Box Instant Potatoes (add water only preferred) (3,440)
48 Cans	15,120	$ 47	15 oz. Can Fruit Cocktail (or peaches, pears, pineapple, etc.) (315)

24 Cans	3,000	$ 11	6 oz. Can Tomato Paste (125)
36 Cans	15,120	$ 42	26.5 oz. Can Del Monte Spaghetti Sauce (Do not buy the Hunt's Brand) (420)
12 Cans	480	$ 12	4 oz. Can Sliced Mushrooms (not pieces) (40)
12 Cans	3,600	$ 12	10.75 oz. Can Cream of Chicken Soup (Chicken Noodle) (eat if you get sick) (300)
12 Boxes	76,800	$ 219	64 oz. Box Powdered Instant Non-fat Dry Milk (long shelf life) (6,400)
24 Cans	11,520	$ 21	12 oz. Can Evaporated Milk (480)
3 Boxes	7,680	$ 14	32 oz. Box Velvetta Brand Cheese (short shelf life) (2,560)
12 Boxes	38,400	$ 36	1 lb. Box Butter (short shelf life unless frozen) (no margarine) (3,200)
5 Jars	60,000	$ 57	50.7 oz. Jar Extra-Virgin Olive Oil (indefinite shelf life) (12,000)
2 Cans	24,860	$ 10	3 lb. Can Crisco Shortening (very short shelf life) (12,430)
12 Cans	10,800	$ 33	8 oz. Container Hershey's Cocoa Powder (900)
8 Cans	9,600	$ 15	16 oz. Can Hershey's Cocoa Syrup (1,200)
25 Pounds	42,500	$ 15	5 lb. Bag White Granulated Sugar (indefinite shelf life) (8,500)
12 Pounds	10,200	$ 15	1 lb. Box Light Brown or Dark Brown Sugar (indefinite shelf life) (1,700)
12 Pounds	10,800	$ 15	1 lb. Box Confectioners Sugar (indefinite shelf life) (1,800)
12 Boxes	26,400	$ 18	20 oz. Box Brownie Mix (or Cake Mix) (2,200)
6 Jars	11,520	$ 10	16 oz. Jar Light Corn Syrup (indefinite shelf life) (1,920)
6 Jars	7,200	$ 39	12.5 oz. Jar 100% Pure Maple Syrup (indefinite shelf life) (1,200)
9 Jars	10,240	$ 57	16 oz. Jar "Sue Bee Brand" Clover Honey (indefinite shelf life) (1,280)
12 Jars	36,480	$ 31	18 oz. Jar Peanut Butter (3,040)
12 Jars	15,600	$ 19	16 oz. Jar Jelly or Preserves (very long shelf life) (1,300)
48 Each	960	$ 11	Beef Bouillon Large Cubes (20 per large cube) (1 large cube = 4 small cubes)
48 Each	960	$ 11	Chicken Bouillon Large Cubes (20 per large cube) (1 large cube = 4 small cubes)
12 Boxes	20,160	$ 12	16 oz. Box Corn Starch (indefinite shelf life) (1,680)
24 Boxes	0	$ 17	16 oz. Box Baking Soda (indefinite shelf life)
12 Jars	0	$ 72	2.62 oz. Cream of Tartar (indefinite shelf life)
24 Pkgs.	0	$ 12	5/16 oz. Package Hodgson Mill Brand Yeast (store in Ziploc bag in the freezer)
6 Bottles	0	$ 22	2 oz. Bottle Vanilla Extract (indefinite shelf life)
24 Pounds	0	$ 8	4 lb. Box Pure Salt (Morton Brand Canning and Pickling Salt) (indefinite shelf life)
12 Jars	0	$ 12	2.6 oz. Ground Black Pepper (or Whole Peppercorns have an indefinite shelf life)
12 Jars	0	$ 6	5.5 oz. Seasoned Meat Tenderizer (Walmart)
12 Jars	0	$ 6	3.12 oz. Onion Powder (Walmart)
2 Jars	0	$ 1	0.9 oz. Oregano (Walmart)
2 Jars	0	$ 2	2.5 oz. Garlic Powder (or Garlic Salt) (Walmart)
2 Jars	0	$ 1	2.37 oz. Cinnamon (Walmart)
1 Jar	0	$ 5	1.75 oz. Cayenne Red Pepper
2 Bottles	0	$ 4	15 oz. Bottle Lemon Juice (short shelf life)
1 Jug	0	$ 4	1 Gallon Apple Cider Vinegar (indefinite life if stored in glass at 40°F-70°F in dark)

------ ------ ------ ------

Totals = 1,129,040   **$1,931** One-Year Emergency Food Supply for One Adult

Explanation of the Foods Included in the One-Year Emergency Food Supply

Special Note: On January 3, 2011 a few minor changes were made to the above list. During the year 2010 some package sizes were discontinued by the manufacturer and replaced by other package sizes. Therefore the above data was revised to match the package sizes that are currently available for sale. A list of the changes appears at the very end of this article in the "Revision History." This changed the total price from $1,671 to $1,768.

Frozen Foods: Do not invest in frozen foods for a long-term hard times event. Do not invest in a big freezer for a long-term hard times event. During a long-term hard times event you may not have any electricity. If you produce your own electricity using solar panels or a generator then you will need to use that electricity in the most efficient manner possible. A food freezer is not a good way to use that electricity. The reason is because you can currently purchase a huge variety of delicious foods that do not require refrigeration or freezing. The money you would have invested in a food freezer would be much better invested in a larger inventory of foods that do not need to be refrigerated or frozen.

Comfort Foods: The above list contains 60 different food items. However, you should also purchase some Kool-Aid, Tang, Coffee, Tea, Soft Drinks, Beer, Wine, Miniature Tootsie Rolls, Caramels, Assorted Hard Candies, or whatever else appeals to you. These are referred to as "comfort foods" and they can definitely help make the hard times more bearable.

Can Opener: Every family should invest in an old-fashioned manually operated can opener. This type of can opener is placed on the top of the can, then the handles are squeezed together to puncture a hole in the top of the can, and then the crank is rotated to open the can. If the electricity is off then you will be very glad you have one of these manually operated can openers. It is okay to have a "Dollar Store" quality manual can opener as a backup but each family should also own a high quality stainless steel can opener. Being able to open your canned foods safely and quickly will help to prevent a wide variety of accidents during hard times. (Note: Rinse the piercing/cutting edge in clean water after each use to keep the can opener clean and sanitary and to significantly extend its useful life.)

Canned Spaghetti Sauce: Although the Del Monte Brand and the Hunt's Brand both contain 26.5 ounces of spaghetti sauce, and they sell for the same price per can, the Del Monte Brand has 420 calories per can whereas the Hunt's Brand only has 300 calories per can. The Del Monte Brand is thick spaghetti sauce. The Hunt's Brand is watery spaghetti sauce. I do not know when Hunt's decided to change the consistency of their spaghetti sauce but it now contains a lot more water than the Del Monte Brand. When I recently opened a can of the Hunt's spaghetti sauce I was shocked that the sauce poured out of the can almost like water. I was expecting it to flow out slowly like thick spaghetti sauce should. It didn't. That was when I checked the number of total calories per can for both the Del Monte and the Hunt's Brands. The Hunt's Brand now has 120 fewer calories per can than the Del Monte Brand because the Hunt's Brand now contains more water. Adding more water is one method a company may use to keep the can size the same, and the number of total ounces the same, and keep the selling price the same, but actually deliver a cheaper product to its customers. I mention this because with the economy being depressed, then more companies may decide to use a similar strategy. Therefore if you are buying a lot of food for future consumption then you would be well advised to check the total calories inside the can and compare it to the number in parentheses in the above list before you invest a lot of your money.

Quantities: You should have enough food for each member of your family for at least six-months. If you are an experienced farmer or rancher living on your own land, then you should also have enough seeds to replenish your food supplies on an annual basis. You will also need your own canning jars and lids or you will need to know how your ancestors preserved food without electricity or canning jars. If you have no previous experience with farming then you would probably be better off with a two or three-years supply of food for each family member.

Appetite Fatigue: Your emergency food supply must have a reasonable variety of different food items. If you only have a limited number of different food items to eat then appetite fatigue will result in your starvation even though you have food. Your mind and your body will simply reject the thought of eating the same food again and again and again. If you doubt the truth of this statement then conduct a simple test. Pick your favorite four food items that you enjoy eating more than anything else and then only eat those four food items for one-month. Before one-week has passed you will be repulsed at the thought of eating those foods again. Try it and see if you can force yourself to only eat those four foods for an entire month.

Appetite fatigue does not occur when there is no food available. For example, long-term war prisoners in a P.O.W. camp will generally eat almost anything. Each day they do not have the option to eat or not eat. On many days they get nothing to eat. When they do get fed there is never enough food to satisfy their hunger and therefore they will eat almost anything at any time and be grateful for whatever it happens to be.

Appetite fatigue occurs when you have food to eat and you have the choice to eat or not eat. This is one of the reasons old people in a retirement home usually lose weight and their health. The cafeteria serves the same basic bland food over and over again.

Therefore you should have some reasonable variety in your emergency food supplies.

Substitutions: If you are allergic to a food then do not buy it. If you do not enjoy the taste of one of the above recommended foods then do not buy it. Feel free to substitute any food item and name brands you prefer. However, you should try to keep a reasonable balance of meat, carbohydrates, vegetables, fruits, grains, and dairy products.

For example, instead of buying 48 cans of Fruit Cocktail you may wish to buy a few cans of apples, peaches, pears, cherries, and pineapple based on your own individual taste preferences. The important issue is to have some canned fruits in your food storage plan.

The same concept applies to vegetables. The above list recommends 180 cans of mixed vegetables, 96 cans of beans, 12 boxes of instant potatoes, 48 cans of beef stew (meat, potatoes, and carrots), 24 cans of roast beef hash (meat and potatoes), and 48 cans of chili with beans. If you like the canned "Mixed Vegetables" then purchase them. But you could purchase cans of corn, peas, spinach, or any other vegetable you wish. However, you should consider the nutritional value of each vegetable by reading the nutrition label. For example, green beans cost almost the same as all the other vegetables but they have very few calories. Therefore, green beans would be a poor choice from a nutritional value standpoint. There would be nothing wrong with having a few cans of green beans in your pantry for variety but the number of those cans should be very small compared to the other vegetables. However, most other canned beans have relatively high levels of protein and calories.

You should also adjust the recommended quantities based on your family's actual needs. If you have several family members who drink a lot of milk, then you should purchase more dry powdered milk than suggested.

Calories: An active adult engaged in normal physical labor can burn 3,000 calories per day without gaining weight. However, an adult who has a desk job would gain weight. Therefore the concept of a "One-Year Food Supply" is based on the average physically active adult. If you were not very active during a disaster event then you could easily reduce your calorie intake to 2,000 calories per day and still maintain your weight. Therefore, the above food reserves would last a non-active adult for 18 months with no weight loss. If you wanted to lose a little weight, then the above food could last for 24 to 30 months. (Note: For an investment of approximately $1,931 one adult could stay alive and in good health for two and one-half years. Or the above food could feed two adults for 15 months.)

Brand Names: All the above foods are generic brand or store brand except where brand names are specifically indicated. For example, in my opinion Armour Brand Beef Stew is pleasant to eat but the cheaper brands are disgusting. Therefore, purchase and eat one can of each of the above food items to see if the flavor of that brand is agreeable to you before you purchase a year's supply of that item and then discover it tastes horrible.

Taste is a very personal experience. Two people in the same exact family can have entirely different opinions about the same exact food. The limited number of brand name foods I recommend are based on my individual taste preferences and I do not have any financial interest in any of those food companies. You will need to make your own decision about which brands of food you prefer.

If you are already happy with a specific name brand then it would probably be a better investment than a generic brand you are not familiar with. However, if there is a big price difference between the brands, such as 52 cents for the generic and 94 cents for your brand, then it would be a good idea to buy one can of the generic brand and take it home and eat it to see how it compares to your preferred name brand food item.

Prices: All the above prices are the average retail price in United States Dollars in the southeast United States. None of the prices are special temporary sale prices. If you can find any of the above items offered at a really good discount, then you should stock up on that item during the week it is on sale.

Package Sizes: Larger packages are usually a little cheaper per ounce, but if half the package spoils after you open it and before it can all be used, then you lose. Therefore resist the temptation to buy the large one-gallon size cans of food. If you need more food per meal than one regular size can then you can always open two cans. However, instead of opening two cans of the same thing you might consider opening one can of two different food items to provide more variety during the meal.

Storage Area: You should carefully consider where you will keep your emergency food stored for the following reasons:

It takes a lot of space to store a one-year supply of food.

It will take a significant amount of time and effort to move all the food between locations.

The food should not be located where it may be accidentally discovered by anyone.

Absolutely no one, except your spouse, should know about your emergency food reserves.

The above recommended foods need to be stored in a temperature controlled environment for a variety of reasons.

If a disaster unfolds rapidly and unexpectedly, you will need to be able to get to your food without drawing attention to your family.

If possible, always purchase your food on cardboard flats for easy convenient stacking when you put it into a storage area. In other words, purchase canned goods in multiples of 6, 12, or 24 depending on the number that fit onto a standard cardboard flat. Take the cardboard flat with you through the check-out line when you pay for the food. If your store cuts one side off the front of the cardboard flats then take two cardboard flats and turn them end-to-end one inside the other to make one new cardboard flat that will hold your canned goods without collapsing.

When items are on sale at your local grocery store they sometimes leave them on cardboard flats at the end of an aisle. Just pick up an entire cardboard flat of food and put it into your shopping cart. If appropriate, put two, three, or more flats of food into your shopping cart and then pay for them at the cashier station. It would not hurt to have a little more food than you think you might need.

Usually it is much easier to buy large quantities of food at a place like Sam's Club or Costco. You can pick up entire cases of food already enclosed in plastic wrap and put them on your flatbed cart and take them to the checkout area. However, food items are very, very heavy so resist the temptation to purchase an entire year's food supply in one trip. Your vehicle may not be able to move 2,000 pounds of food in one trip. The only disadvantage of purchasing at a "Membership Warehouse" is that the store keeps a permanent record of all your purchases in its computer, even if you pay with cash. On the other hand, if you pay with cash at a grocery store and do not use a "Store Shopping Card" then there will be no permanent record of your food purchases. The lack of an electronic trail to your emergency food supplies may allow you to keep your food if the government decides to collect all the food purchased by "unethical hoarders" who made their food purchases just prior to a worldwide food shortage. If you need to use a credit card to finance your food purchases, then you should consider going to your local bank and asking your bank teller to give you a "cash advance" against your credit card. Most banks will do this regardless of which bank issued the credit card.

Each time you go to the store it is usually better to purchase food in more than one food category instead of investing all your money in only one food item. This way you could gradually build your emergency food reserves. If a disaster were to occur before you finished, you would still have some food in each major food group, instead of having lots of rice and no vegetables, as an example.

Either write or tape a simple label onto each cardboard flat of food indicating the date you purchased it.

It is very easy to forget what you have already purchased so you should keep a written list of all the food items you have added to your reserves. This list will help you to strategi-cally build your food stores without overlooking something or buying too much of something else.

The shelf life of most of the above items is five years or more, regardless of the expiration date printed on the package.

Store food at temperatures between 40ºF to 70°F if possible. Higher storage temperatures shortens the shelf life, reduces the vitamins and calories, and changes the taste.

Mix It Up: If most of your cans are approximately the same size such as 15 ounces, then you should consider mixing your canned foods together on a single cardboard flat. For example, some people have canned corn, pinto beans, mixed vegetables, fruit cocktail, spaghetti with meatballs, and chili with beans, and these cans are stored 24 cans per cardboard flat. However, instead of having 24 cans of exactly the same thing on a single cardboard flat it would be smarter to mix the canned foods together and put some of each type of canned food on each cardboard flat. For example, a cardboard flat that contains 24 cans could hold:

4 cans of corn,
4 cans of pinto beans,
4 cans of mixed vegetables,
4 cans of fruit cocktail,
4 cans of spaghetti with meatballs, and
4 cans of chili with beans.

This would be advantageous for all the following reasons:

Plan A (Staying Home): If a hard times tragedy event were to occur and you were forced to start consuming your emergency food, then some of each type of food would be in the cardboard flat on top of a stack. You would not have to move everything to get to a food item that was on the bottom of the stack. This would also help you to use your emergency food in a more balanced nutritional manner because you would know you should consume all the food on one cardboard flat before eating food items off the next cardboard flat.

Plan B (Living with a Relative): If you were going to transfer some of your canned food to the home of a close relative, or into a storage area at a distant small rural town, then you could move a few cardboard flats of food to that location and you would know you had a reasonable assortment of foods on each cardboard flat.

Plan C (Disappearing into the Wilderness): If you were forced to quickly evacuate your current home and you only had a few minutes to load your vehicle, then you could add as many cardboard flats of food as you could and you would know each cardboard flat contained a reasonable variety of canned foods.

Rotation: Long-term food storage advice usually includes the recommendation that you use your emergency food on a regular basis and replace it as you use it by employing a first-in first-out inventory strategy. This is good advice but it is very difficult for most families to execute. The sheer volume of any reasonable emergency food supply makes it very difficult to rotate your food without a tremendous investment in time and energy. Therefore most families simply buy their emergency food, put it into a suitable storage area, and then forget about it. May I suggest a compromise between these two extremes. Most of the recommended long-term storage food items have a shelf life of five-years or longer. The major exceptions are yeast, spices, lemon juice, fresh butter, Velvetta Brand cheese, flour, and corn meal. If you will store these items where you can easily get to them then you could gradually use these items and replace them as they are consumed. If you discover that two or three years have passed and some of these items have not been used then you should consider replacing them with fresh food. However the balance of your emergency storage food should still be safe and enjoyable to eat, even though you did not rotate it the same way you did your short shelf life foods.

Consumption: Carefully ration your food at the beginning of hard times. Don't wait until half your food is gone before you consider rationing.

Chef Boyardee Macaroni and Cheese: The Chef Boyardee Brand Macaroni and Cheese is recommended instead of the boxed macaroni and cheese because it contains almost twice the calories and it is already cooked so it only needs to be heated before you eat it (you don't have to add both milk and butter to cook it). In addition, the powdered cheese packages in the boxes of macaroni and cheese have a relatively short shelf life and they will go bad long before the dry macaroni noodles. Therefore, the canned macaroni and cheese is a better value from a nutritional perspective and an ease of preparation perspective and a shelf life perspective.

Campbell's Chunky Brand Soup: Canned chicken was removed from the list because many families, including my own, do not find the taste of canned chicken to be very enjoyable. However, the Campbell's Chunky Brand Soups that contain chicken also contain a lot of other tasty foods, and they have more volume, and they have more nutrients, and they cost less than a can of chicken. Therefore, in order to add chicken to the menu in addition to beef, tuna, and ham, the Campbell's Chunky Brand Chicken Based Soups are perfect. Some examples would be: Chicken Broccoli

Cheese with Potato, Chicken Corn Chowder, Chicken and Dumplings, Grilled Chicken and Sausage Gumbo, and Fajita Chicken with Rice and Beans.

Cooking From Scratch: At the current time you may not use some of the food items in the recommended food list. However, in the event of an emergency you will probably discover you will need all the foods in the list, including the spices. I recommend you access the recipes on my web site and print a hard copy of all my recipes. Then store those recipes in a three-ring binder with your emergency food supplies. During an actual emergency those recipes will help you to prepare an interesting and pleasant variety of meals using the basic staple foods and spices in the above recommended list of foods.

Additional Food Items: If you have the money and the space, then purchase extra white rice, beans, and wheat.

White Rice: Ordinary white rice should be one of the primary emergency foods every family has stored in their home. White rice goes well as a side dish with almost any meal (including wild game and fresh fish). White rice is normally enriched with several vitamins and it is a complex carbohydrate which is something the human body needs.

White rice is extremely cheap when compared to other foods. A ten-pound bag of white rice can be purchased at many grocery stores for about six-dollars (or a twenty-pound bag for about twelve-dollars). At approximately 60-cents per pound you are buying 1,500 calories per pound or 15,000 calories per ten-pound bag. That is a true bargain. And white rice has a shelf life between twenty to thirty-years if stored in a cool, dry area that is kept between 40 to 70 degrees year round. (Note: Brown rice has a shelf life of six-months or less.)

In a hard times survival situation a ten-pound bag of white rice would feed one person for about 52 days if the person ate 1.5-cup of cooked rice per day (equal to 1/2 cup uncooked rice). This would be approximately 300 calories per day from rice. A recommended one-year food supply of white rice for one person would be approximately 70 pounds of white rice. Obviously other foods would also need to be eaten but the white rice could serve as an inexpensive part of the daily menu.

However it should be noted that white rice has two disadvantages in a hard times survival situation:

White rice needs to be prepared with fresh clean water. Therefore each family must determine how they are going to address the water issue. Additional information about water is on this web site at: How to Find Water and How to

Make Water Safe to Drink.
White rice has a tendency to become very unexciting after it has been eaten on a regular basis for an extended period of time.

There are a vast multitude of recipes that use white rice as a primary ingredient. Unfortunately most of those recipes require an assortment of herbs, spices, and many other ingredients that most of us don't have in our kitchen pantries. The recipes listed on this web site are unique in that respect. Most of the white rice recipes on this web site only require a few ingredients, and many of those ingredients are ones that most of us already have in our kitchen pantries. Therefore the white rice recipes on this web site will help to relieve the problem of dietary boredom or appetite fatigue.

Beans: A small quantity of dry beans may be substituted for some of the canned beans. Dry beans can be planted as seed in a garden and they will produce a new crop of beans at the end of the summer growing season. Dry beans are sold at most grocery stores inside 1, 2, and 4 pound plastic bags. However, it should be noted that dry beans will continue to get drier and drier with the passage of time and they will gradually become too hard to cook and eat after about 3 or 4 years in storage. Therefore, if you anticipate storing your beans for an extended period of time then the canned beans are a better option. Canned beans are already fully cooked inside the can and they will be edible many, many years after the printed expiration date on the can. (Note: I have personally eaten canned beans that were ten years old and they tasted just like they had been recently canned.)

Salt: The above food list recommends the purchase of more salt than you would need in one-year because almost all the canned and processed foods already contain adequate salt. The reason salt is on the list is to provide the option to cook, season, and/or preserve any fresh vegetables or meat you may be able to obtain during a long-term disaster event. Salt is one of the basic ingredients the human body requires to maintain good long-term health. At the present time salt is very cheap but during a disaster event it may become very difficult to acquire.

Pure Salt may be used to help preserve food. Iodized salt should not be used as a food preservative. However, iodized salt is the best salt to use when adding salt to your food just before you eat it. Your body needs a little iodine on a regular basis and a good way to get iodine is by adding a little iodized salt onto your food at the table. I recommend the Morton Lite Iodized Salt because it can also be used to create an "electrolyte beverage." Therefore, in addition to Pure Salt, it would probably also be a good idea to purchase one or two 11-ounce Morton Lite Salt containers and add them to your one-year emergency food supply.

Pepper: If your family enjoys the taste of pepper then you will need to store some pepper as part of your emergency food supplies. You have two options: ground black pepper or whole peppercorns. Whole peppercorns have an indefinite shelf life if stored in their original packaging in the dark in a temperature controlled environment. Or you can vacuum seal the peppercorns to completely eliminate any aroma or taste loss as a result of exposure to the air or humidity. If you invest in peppercorns then you will also need to invest in a pepper grinder. I suggest you purchase a refillable normal pepper grinder and not one of those little pepper grinders in the spice rack of your grocery store that contains a small amount of peppercorns. The majority of those little pepper grinders cannot be opened and refilled.

Yeast: Freeze store bought yeast until it is needed. Stir a little crumbled yeast into some warm water (105ºF to 115ºF or 40ºC to 46ºC). Test the water on your wrist. It should feel warm but not hot. If the water is too hot it will kill the yeast. If the water is too cold it will slow down the process. Adding a little sugar to the water will speed up the process. Adding salt or fat will slow it down. Good yeast will become foamy and creamy after about 10 to 12 minutes.

Don't waste your package yeast. After you have added yeast to some bread dough, pinch off one handful of the bread dough after the first rise and save it in an airtight container in a cool dark place. The next day thoroughly mix (knead) the old dough into a new batch of dough. The yeast will multiply and spread throughout the new batch. After the first rise, pinch off a handful of dough and save it. Continue this process each time you make yeast bread and you will be able to make bread for a very long time from that one original package of yeast.

Baking Powder: Both yeast and baking powder will cause your bread dough to rise. But both yeast and baking powder have relatively short shelf lives. The good news is that you can make your own baking powder as follows:

    1 part baking soda.
    1 part corn starch.
    2 parts cream of tartar.
    Mix together to make fresh baking powder.

Baking soda, corn starch, and cream of tartar have an indefinite shelf life if properly stored.

However, after you mix them together a slow chemical reaction begins and the shelf life of the resulting baking powder is much less.

Therefore make your baking powder as you need it and do not make more than you will need in a specific recipe.

Coleman Camp Oven Baking Options: During a serious hard times event you may need to cook and bake using a wood burning fire.
For baking you have two options as follows:

Cast Iron Dutch Oven: Instructions for using a Dutch oven for baking are at the following link on my web site: Cast Iron Cookware.

Folding Camp Oven: You could purchase a folding metal camp oven and bake over a propane stove or a campfire. These folding ovens come in a variety of different sizes and they may be purchased at some Army/Navy stores, some hardware stores, and some Walmarts.

Seasoned Meat Tenderizer: The reason the seasoned meat tenderizer is on the list is because it is really cheap at the current time and it will make it a lot easier for your entire family to gradually adjust to the flavor of any "wild game meat" you may be able to acquire during a long-term hard times event.

Bouillon Cubes: Bouillon cubes are also a seasoning. A large cube should be cut into quarter sections so each piece is the same size as a regular small cube. These cubes may be used to enhance or improve the flavor of a variety of different foods. For example, a cube may be used to enhance the flavor of white rice by adding it to some boiling water before you add the white rice, or it may be used to enhance the flavor of a casserole. A large cube only contains twenty calories and a small cube only contains five calories. Some of the different brands of cubes do not contain any calories. Bouillon cubes do not contain any carbohydrates, or protein, or vitamins. Therefore their food value is negligible, the same as any other seasoning or flavoring. If you simply add a bouillon cube to some water then you will change the taste of that water but you will not be creating a full-bodied soup that will sustain you and restore your energy. You will only be creating some flavored water.

Long-Term Storage Foods: Freeze-dried and dehydrated foods are also an outstanding choice for long-term food storage and you should include them in your food storage plan if you can find them available at a price you can afford. Occasionally these items are on backorder and it may take weeks or months before the food is delivered to you. That is one of the advantages of buying food at your local grocery store. You take possession of your food immediately and you don't have to worry about receiving a very polite notice at some future date that your order has been can

celed and it will not be shipped to you for reasons beyond the control of the seller.

Vitamins

The following is not medical advice nor is it a medical recommendation. If you have a medical question then please consult a licensed medical professional.

During a long-term hard times event the nutritional value of your daily meals will probably not be as high as during normal times. To help maintain your health and to help prevent a number of vitamin deficiency health problems, your family should have a reasonable supply of complete multivitamins. The health benefits of vitamins is usually not fully appreciated by people in the United States until they have a vitamin deficiency and a health problem develops as a result of that deficiency, such as bleeding gums and loose teeth. Therefore each member of your family should take a complete multivitamin on a regular basis, unless they have been advised not to by a medical professional.

During a hard times event if you are not sure how long it will be before you can replenish your supply of vitamins then you may need to ration your vitamins and only take one vitamin every two or three days. This is a decision you will need to make yourself.

Vacuum Food Sealer

Many foods can be protected from insects, oxygen, and humidity by sealing them inside a vacuum seal bag. Some examples would be salt, peppercorns, baking soda, corn starch, corn meal, sugar, dry noodles, grits, instant potatoes, instant milk, oatmeal flakes, white rice, tootsie rolls, and hard candies.

Vacuum sealing will preserve the freshness and the original flavor of the sealed food approximately three to five times longer than if the food is not sealed.

Vacuum sealing will also significantly extend the shelf life of some foods because you eliminate the oxygen and the humidity that can gradually destroy the food.

If you use vacuum sealed storage bags you will not need to purchase any of the "oxygen absorber packets" because the vacuum sealing process will remove all the oxygen from inside the specially designed bags.

A cheap good quality food vacuum sealer will cost about $40 and a two-roll box of vacuum seal bags will cost about $22.

If you buy the 11-inch wide rolls that are 16-feet long then you can cut individuals bags from the roll to the exact length you need. Therefore there will be very little waste because:

You won't need to seal a small item inside a large bag, and You can seal the foods in the quantities you think you will need so you can open one bag at a time and the rest of your food will remain fresh inside its own vacuum sealed bag.

Immediately after you vacuum seal an item inside a vacuum storage bag use a medium tip permanent black magic marker to write a brief description of the contents on the top of the bag and the date you sealed the bag, such as: 16 ounces Pure Salt, Sealed Feb. 2010.

Note: Vacuum sealing is not a substitute for refrigeration or freezing. Any food item than needs to be refrigerated or frozen will still need to be kept in the refrigerator or freezer after you vacuum seal it. However, vacuum sealing will help that food item to remain edible about 3 to 5 times longer than if it wasn't sealed. It will eliminate the problem with freezer burn because you will have isolated the food from the cold dry air inside the freezer.

Instant Non-Fat Dry Powdered Milk
Instant Nonfat Powdered Milk will last at least 20 years if properly stored.

The easiest way to store and preserve instant milk for future consumption is to use a vacuum food sealer. However, if you simply pour some instant milk powder into a vacuum seal bag and then you attempt to draw a vacuum on the bag you will discover that some of the milk powder will be sucked into the seam area. This will result in the bag not being properly sealed and air will gradually enter the bag and your instant milk will deteriorate more rapidly.

The simple solution to this problem is to purchase instant powdered milk in the one-quart paper packs. There are usually several of these one-quart packs in a box of instant milk. Open the box and remove the one-quart packs of instant milk. Select a vacuum bag of a matching size or cut a bag that will work from a long roll of vacuum seal material. Either two or four of the one-quart instant milk packs will usually fit nicely in one vacuum bag, depending on the size of the bag. Use some scissors to snip a very short cut (about 1/4 inch long) into the edge of each paper milk pack to break the seal of the pack. Then place the milk packs inside the vacuum bag and draw a vacuum on the bag. The air inside the paper milk packs will be withdrawn but almost none of the dry milk powder will escape. This means you will have succeeded in vacuum sealing your instant milk.

Then store your sealed instant milk inside a suitable container with a lid in a dark cool dry place.

Wheat Berries
I recommend the Golden 86 or White Wheat in a six-gallon pail. This type of wheat is closer in flavor to the average bread that most people in the United States now eat.

A six-gallon pail of wheat berries will cost about $72 (which includes the shipping fee) and a six-gallon pail contains about 72,000 calories.

One internet store that sells wheat berries is:
http://www.pleasanthillgrain.com/buy_wheat_whole_grain_red_white_wheat_berries_making_bread_flour.aspx

The wheat is vacuum sealed inside a mylar bag and then sealed inside the six-gallon pail.

Therefore the shelf life of the wheat inside one of these pails will be more than 30 years.

You will also need a hand-operated wheat grinder.

If you can afford it then you should consider buying an equal amount of red wheat berries and white wheat berries. One type of wheat is better for loaves of bread and one type of wheat is better for cakes, cookies, and donuts. The above web site has some good information on the different types of wheat berries.

Unlike some of the other food items, if a hard times event does not force you to eat your wheat berries, then your wheat pails can be an investment that you can pass on to your children and grandchildren.

The Seven Major Mistakes in Food Storage

By Vickie Tate

A month or two ago I met a cute little gal who was talking to me about her newly begun food storage. "You know," she began, "I've dreaded doing my food storage for years, its seems so blah, but the way national events are going my husband and I decided we couldn't put it off anymore. And, do you know, it really hasn't been hard. We just bought 20 bags of wheat, my husband found a place to get 60 pound cans of honey, and now all we have to do is get a couple of cases of powdered milk. Could you tell me where to get the milk?" After I suggested several distributors, I asked, "Do you know how to cook with your wheat?" "Oh," she laughed, "if we ever need it I'll learn how. My kids only like white bread and I don't have a wheat grinder." She had just made every major mistake in storing food (other than not storing anything at all.) But she's not alone. Through 14 years of helping people prepare, I found most people's storage starts out looking just like hers. So what's wrong with this storage plan? **There are seven serious problems that may occur trying to live on these basics:**

1.) VARIETY -

Most people don't have enough variety in their storage. 95% of the people I've worked with only stored the 4 basic items we mentioned earlier: *wheat, milk, honey, and salt.* Statistics show most of us won't survive on such a diet for several reasons. a.) **Many people are allergic to wheat** and may not be aware of it until they are eating it meal after meal. b.) **Wheat is too harsh for young children.** They can tolerate it in small amounts but not as their main staple. c.) **We get tired of eating the same foods** over and over and many times prefer not to eat than to sample that particular food again. This is called *appetite fatigue.* Young children and older people are particularly susceptible to it. Store *less* wheat than is generally suggest and put the difference into a variety of other grains, particularly ones your family likes to eat. Also store a variety of beans. This will add variety of color, texture and flavor. **Variety is the key to a successful storage program.** It is essential that you *store flavorings* such as tomato, bouilion, cheese, and onion.

Also, *include a good supply of the spices* you like to cook with. These flavorings and spices allow you to do many creative things with your grains and beans. Without them you are severely limited. One of the best suggestions I can give you is **buy a good food storage cookbook.** Go through it and see what your family would really eat. Notice the ingredients as you do it. This will help you more than anything else to know what items to store.

2.) EXTENDED STAPLES -

Few people get beyond storing the four basic items, but it is extremely important that you do so. *Never put all your eggs in one basket.* Store **dehydrated and/or freeze-dried foods** as well as home canned and store bought canned goods. Make sure you add cooking oil, shortening, baking powder, soda, yeast and powdered eggs. You can't cook even the most basic recipes without these items. Because of limited space I won't list all the items that should be included in a well-balanced storage program. They are all included in the *The New Cookin With Home Storage* cookbook, as well as information on how much to store, and where to purchase it.

3.) VITAMINS -

Vitamins are important, especially if you have children, since children do not store body reserves of nutrients as adults do. *A good quality multi-vitamin and vitamin C are the most vital.* Others may be added as your budget permits.

4.) QUICK, EASY AND PSYCHOLOGICAL FOODS

Quick and easy foods help you through times when you are psychologically or physically unable to prepare your basic storage items. **No cook foods such as freeze-dried** are wonderful since they require little preparation. **MRE's** (Meals Ready to Eat), such as many preparedness outlets carry, canned goods, etc. are also very good. Psychological Foods are the goodies - Jello, pudding, candy, etc. - you should add to your storage.

These may sound frivolous, but through the years I've talked with many people who have lived entirely on their storage for extended periods of time. Nearly all of them say these were the most helpful items in their storage to normalize their situations and make it more bearable. These are especially important if you have children.

5.) BALANCE -

Time and time again I've seen families buy all of their wheat, then buy all of another item, and so on. Don't do that. It's important to **keep well-balanced as you build your storage.** Buy several items, rather than a large quantity of one item. If something happens and you have to live on your present storage, you''ll fare much better having a one-month supply of a variety of items than a year's supply of two to three items.

6.) CONTAINERS -

Always store your bulk foods in food storage containers. I have seen literally tons and tons of food thrown away because they were left in sacks, where they became highly susceptible to moisture, insects and rodents. If you are using plastic buckets make sure they are lined with a food grade plastic liner available from companies that carry packaging supplies. **Never use trash can liners** as these are treated with pesticides. Don't stack them too high. In an earthquake they may topple, the lids pop open, or they may crack. A better container is the #10 tin can which most preparedness companies use when they package their foods. Note: Mice and Rats can know their way through plastic buckest if given the opportunity. If this is a concern, go with the #10 Tin Cans for added security.

7.) USE YOUR STORAGE -

In all the years I've worked with preparedness one of the biggest problems I've seen is people storing food and not knowing what to do with it. It's vital that you and your family become familiar with the things you are storing. You need to know how to prepare these foods. This is not something you want to learn under stress. Your family needs to be used to eating these foods. A stressful period is not a good time to totally change your diet. Get a food storage cookbook and learn to use these foods!

It's easy to solve these food storage problems once you know what they are. The lady I talked about at the first of the article left realizing what she had stored was a good beginning, but not enough. As she said, "It's better to find out the mistakes I've made now while there's still time to make corrections." This makes a lot more sense.

If you're one who needs to make some adjustments, that's okay. Look at these suggestions and add the things you're missing. It's easy to take a basic storage and add the essentials to make it liveable, but it needs to be done. As I did the research for my cookbook I wanted to include recipes that gave help to families no matter what they had stored. As I put the material together it was fascinating to discover what the pioneers ate is the type of things we store. But if you have stored only the 4 basics, there's very, very little you can do with it. By adding even just a few things it greatly increases your options, and the prospect of your family surviving on it. As I studied how the pioneers lived and ate, my whole feeling for food changed. I realized our storage is what most of the world has always lived on. If it's put together the right way we'll be returning to good basic living with a few goodies thrown in.

Bishop Keith B. McMullin, 2nd Counselor Presiding Bishopric

"A cardinal principle of the gospel is to prepare for the day of scarcity… And, brethren, we *lay up in store!* Then, "through [the Lord's] providence, notwithstanding the tribulation … the church [and its people will] stand independent.".and …

we *lay up in store!* By doing these things, "the Lord shall have power over his saints, and shall reign in [our] midst."
(Lay Up in Store, May 2007, Ensign)

Elder L. Tom Perry of the Quorum of the Twelve Apostles taught:

"Acquire and store a reserve of food and supplies that will sustain life. . . . As long as I can remember, we have been taught to prepare for the future and to obtain a year's supply of necessities. I would guess that the years of plenty have almost universally caused us to set aside this counsel. I believe the time to disregard this counsel is over. With events in the world today, it must be considered with all seriousness" ("If Ye Are Prepared Ye Shall Not Fear," *Ensign,* Nov. 1995)

COMMON STORAGE FOODS

Herein is covered a range of foods suited for incorporation into home storage programs.

As you review them there are several considerations you should keep in mind when deciding on what foods you want to include.

The first is *variety in the diet*. This is of great importance but many do not give it adequate thought. Some simply buy however much wheat, corn, rice, or beans they think is necessary to meet their needs and leave it at that. Others rely on prepackaged decisions made for them by their storage food retailer who put together a "year's supply of food" to buy all at once. Either decision could possibly be a mistake.

There are many food storage plans one may use as a guide. Some are based on the so-called "Mormon Four" of wheat, milk, honey and salt, with as many additional foods as the planner found desirable. This plan was developed in the 1930's and we've learned a great deal about workable food storage in the decades hence. Among which are the food allergies that an unfortunate number of people in our society develop.

One of the more common food allergens is wheat. Even more unfortunate is the fact that many who have such an allergy are unaware of it. They won't become aware until they try to live with whole grain wheat as a large part of their diet and their latent allergy reveals itself. Another thing we have learned is that many adults suffer from an intolerance to the milk sugar lactose, especially those of certain ethnic backgrounds. For these reasons and more you should always make it a practice to **store what you eat** AND TO **eat what you store**, so that ugly surprises such as these do not arise after it's too late to easily avoid them.

A second reason to think about storing a wide variety of foods is *appetite fatigue*. There are those who think providing variety in the diet is relatively unimportant and that if and when the time comes they'll eat what they've got and that will be that. For healthy, well adjusted adults under ordinary circumstances or for those who have the vital *survival mindset* this might be possible without too much difficulty. However, the reason for having a home food storage program in the first place is for when circumstances aren't ordinary.

Times of crisis produce stress - possibly physical, but always mental. If you are suddenly forced to eat a diet both alien and monotonous, it is going to add that much more stress on top of what you are already dealing with. If your planning includes the elderly, young children, and/or infants there is a significant risk they will quit eating or refuse to eat sufficient amounts of the right foods leaving them unable to survive. *This is not a trivial problem and should be given serious consideration*. When it's wheat, day in and day out, wheat's going to start becoming unpopular fast. Far better to have a variety of foods on hand to forestall appetite fatigue and, more importantly, *to use those storable foods in your everyday diet so that you'll be accustomed to eating them*. In his book, ***Making the Best of Basics***, James Stevens mentions a post-WWII study by Dr. Norman Wright, of the British Food Ministry, which found the people of England and Europe were more likely to reject unfamiliar or distasteful foods during times of stress than under normal conditions. *Consider the positive aspects of adding variety and comfort foods to your storage program.*

A last thought that I want to give for ALL foods you might put into your program. Unless you are already familiar with **and** eating a particular type and brand of food do not put large quantities of it into your pantry until you – preferably everyone who will be depending on that food – have eaten some of it first. It's not always as easy to pick up a new food as it may first appear. Differences between brands of foods alone can sometimes be enough to disappoint you when consumed. You'd hate to discover that you cannot abide a particular food item after you've brought home a case of Brand X. Seriously relying on any food that you are not already familiar with is making a fools bet.

GRAINS AND FLOURS

ABOUT GLUTEN:

As you read through the grain descriptions below you will come across frequent mention of "gluten". Gluten is a combination of proteins found in some grains which enables the dough made from them to rise by trapping the gases produced by yeast fermentation or chemical reaction of baking powder or soda. The amount of these proteins varies depending on the species of grain and varieties within a species. Some grains such as rice have virtually no gluten at all and will not produce a raised loaf by itself while others like hard winter wheat have a great deal and make excellent raised bread. As a general rule yeast raised breads need a fair amount of gluten to attain good dough volumes while non-yeast raised breads may need little or none at all. Whether gluten content is of importance to you will depend upon the end uses you intend for your grain.

Some of the common and relatively uncommon types of grains are listed below.

AMARANTH:

Amaranth is not a true cereal grain at all, but is a relative of the pigweeds and the ornamental flowers we call "cockscomb". It's grown not only for its seed, but for its leaves that can be cooked and eaten as greens. The seed is high in protein, particularly the amino acid lysine which is limited in the true cereal grains. It can be milled as-is, or toasted to provide more flavor. The flour lacks gluten, so is not suited for raised breads by itself, but can be made into any of a number of flat breads. Some varieties can be popped like popcorn, boiled and eaten as a cereal, used in soups, granolas, and the like. Toasted or untoasted, it blends well with other grain flours.

NOTE: Like some other edible seeds, raw amaranth contains biological factors that can inhibit proper absorption of some nutrients. For this reason amaranth seeds or flour should always be cooked before consumption, whether for human food or animal feed.

BARLEY:

Barley is thought by some to be the first grain intentionally cultivated by man. It has short, stubby kernels with a hull that is difficult to remove. Excluding barley intended for malting or animal feed, this grain is generally consumed directly by humans in two forms. Most common is the white, highly processed pearl barley with much of its bran and germ milled off along with its hull. It is the least nutritious form of barley. The second offering is called pot or hulled barley and it has been subjected to the same milling process as pearled, but with fewer trips through the polisher. Because of this, it

retains more of the nutritious germ and bran, but does not keep as well as the more refined product without special packaging. Unless you are prepared to try to get the hulls off I don't recommend buying unhulled barley. Although it can be milled into flour, barley's low gluten content will not make a good loaf of raised bread. It can be combined with other flours that do have sufficient gluten to make leavened bread or used in flat breads. Barley flour and flakes have a light nutty flavor that is enhanced by toasting. Whole barley is commonly used to add thickness to soups and stews.

Recently, a hull-less form has become available on the market through a few suppliers. This is whole grain barley with all of its bran and germ intact and should have the most nutrients of any form of this grain available. I don't know yet how suitable it is for long term storage.

BUCKWHEAT:

Buckwheat is another of those seeds commonly considered to be a grain, but which is not a true cereal. It is, in fact, a close relative to the docks and sorrels. The "grain" itself is a dark, three cornered seed resembling a tiny beechnut. It has a hard, fibrous hull requiring a special buckwheat huller to remove. Here in the U.S., buckwheat is most often used in pancakes, biscuits and muffins. In Eastern Europe and Russia it is known in its toasted form as kasha. In the Far East, it's often made into soba or noodles. It's also a good bee plant, producing a dark, strongly flavored honey. The flour is light or dark depending on how much of the hull has been removed before grinding. Dark flour is much more strongly flavored than lighter flour, but because of the high fiber and tannin content of its hull, which can interfere with nutrient absorption, it is not necessarily more nutritious. Buckwheat is one of those foods with no middle ground in peoples opinions — they either love it or they hate it. Like amaranth, it's high in lysine, an amino acid commonly lacking in the true cereal grains.

CORN (maize):

Corn is the largest grain crop in the U.S., but is mostly consumed indirectly as animal feed or even industrial feedstock rather than directly as food. As one of the Three Sisters (maize, squash and beans) corn was the staple grain of nearly all of the indigenous peoples of the American continents before the advent of European colonization. This American grain has an amazing variety of forms. Major classes are the flint, dent, flour, and popcorns. To a certain extent, they're all interchangeable for milling into meal (sometimes known as polenta meal) or flour (very finely ground corn, not cornstarch). The varieties intended to be eaten as sweet corn (fresh green corn) are high in sugar content so do not dry or store well relative to the other corns but instead are usually preserved as a vegetable. There are a number of lesser corn varieties with specialized uses that do not lend themselves to direct food use, but these are seldom found in the open market.

As a general rule of thumb, the flint varieties make better meal as they have a grittier texture than most other corns. If meal, hominy and hominy grits (commonly called just "grits") are what you are interested in then use the flint type if you can find a source. If you intend to make corn masa for tortillas and tamales, then the flour corns are what you want, but these are fairly uncommon on the commercial market so the dent corns are next best. Yellow dent seems to be the most commonly available and will work for almost any purpose except popping.

Popcorn is for snacks or used as a cold cereal after popping or can be ground into quite acceptable meal. In my experience I have found it difficult to hull popcorn with alkali treatment for making hominy (posolé, nixtamal) though your mileage may vary. Popcorn is one form of a whole grain available to nearly everyone in the U.S. It is so common a snack food, particularly at movie theaters, fairs, and ball games, that the smallest of towns will often have at least one business selling it cleaned, dried, and ready to pop in twenty-five or fifty pound bags. Popcorn is harder than other varieties of corn so if your mill is not of the heavy duty sort you may want to consider cracking the kernels into coarse pieces first then grinding into finer textured meal. The Family Grain Mill states that it should not be used to mill popcorn at all and the Back To Basics mill should not be used for any great quantity. All other manual and electric mills that I am aware of will mill popcorn without problem.

Once you've decided on your preferred corn type you may also be able to choose your preferred color. There are yellow, white, blue, red, and multicolored varieties. The yellow and whites are the most common by far with the blues, reds, and parti-colored varieties mostly being relegated to curiosities, though the blue and red corns have been gaining in popularity these last few years. These would be worth investigating if you can find a good source. It should be kept in mind that white corn does not have the carotene content (converts into vitamin A) of yellow corn. As vitamin A is one of the major limiting nutrients in long term food storage, any possible source of it should be utilized. For this reason I suggest storing yellow rather than white corn. Additionally, much of the niacin content of corn is chemically bound up in a form not available for human nutrition unless it has been treated with an alkali. This is really of importance only if most of your sustained daily calorie intake will come from corn, but grits, hominy (posolé) or corn masa (for tortillas and tamales) are traditional uses of this grain and can go

a long way toward increasing the number of recipes you can make with corn. Give them a try, they're quite good.

Any grain as widely grown as corn is naturally going to be processed into many products. Here are a few suited for use in home storage programs.

Corn Meal (polenta meal):

This is simply dry corn ground into a meal. Corn meal intended for polenta may be found in either a coarse or a fine grind. In the U.S. corn meal for making corn bread and most other uses is typically ground to a fairly fine meal. Very finely milled corn is often used for breading foods to be fried and is known as corn flour to distinguish it from coarser meals. This sometimes causes confusion because corn starch (see below)is also known as corn flour in Great Britain - a very different product and not really interchangeable.

The germ of the corn kernel contains about twice the oil content of wheat and is highly susceptible to rancidity once the kernel is broken in the milling process. Because of this most commercially available corn meal will have had the germ and hull removed to extend shelf-life then nutritionally enriched to make up for some of the vitamins and minerals lost with the grain germ. This is desirable for the miller and the grocer, but for the diner it comes at a cost of flavor and some of the nutrition of the whole grain. Some grocers may offer a whole grain corn meal that keeps the grain germ and bran which gives a superior flavored product and retains the full nutrition of the grain but makes for a more perishable commodity. If you go this route be sure of your product's freshness then store it in your refrigerator or freezer.

The grocer's corn meal is mostly milled from yellow or white corn, but some suppliers are now offering blue or even red corn meals. The flavor of the degerminated yellow and white meals are largely indistinguishable from each other, but blue and red corns are interestingly different. Might be worth investigating if you can find them.

Storage life of degerminated corn meal is about one year in average conditions in store packaging and a good deal longer if you repackage it for long term storage. Whole grain meal is good for about four weeks on the shelf, months in the refrigerator, and several years in the freezer or if carefully put up in oxygen free packaging. If you have a grain mill I recommend storing your corn meal in the form of whole corn and milling it as needed. This is what we do, milling a few weeks worth of meal at a time then keeping it in the freezer until needed. The fresh whole grain meal has a much fuller corn flavor than the degerminated meal from the grocery store.

Hominy (posolé'):

This is corn with the hull, and possibly the germ, removed. Hominy cooks faster than unhulled whole corn, is easier to digest, and in some circumstances the alkali peeled varieties can present a superior nutritional profile to whole corn. There are two methods of producing hominy: Mechanical dehulling in a wet milling process or by treating with one of a number of various alkalis such as industrial lye (sodium hydroxide), wood ash lye (mostly potassium hydroxides) or by using some form of lime (calcium hydroxide).

Dry lye peeled hominy is now seldom found for sale, but canned white or yellow hominy is still common across the Southern U.S. and many other areas as well as in Latin American groceries. Generally speaking hominy produced using lime is known by its Spanish name – posole' – but this will not always be clear on labels. I have seen can labels of lime peeled hominy simply called hominy. Whether this is important to you depends on the particular flavor you are trying to achieve in the dish you are preparing. Freshly hulled corn using the lime process that is to be ground to make masa (dough) for corn tortillas is called nixtamal. Dry posole' can be found in Latin American groceries or ordered from the Internet in nearly any color that corn offers. There's a world of things that can be done with hominy other than simply heating it up and serving with butter and salt. A few minutes spent searching the Internet will produce dozens of recipes using hominy as a major ingredient. It's an excellent ingredient in hearty soups and stews.

Hominy Grits:

Usually just called "grits" this coarsely ground meal can be either simple whole corn ground coarse or corn that has been hulled in a process using a form of lye to make hominy then dried and coarsely ground. Grits produced from lye peeled corn typically cook faster, have a longer shelf life, and presents a different, possibly superior, nutritional profile than the whole grain product. Grits produced from whole corn take much longer to cook, have a short shelf life if not refrigerated or put up in special packaging, a superior flavor to the lye peeled product, and retains the nutrition of the whole grain. Very coarsely ground grits is also known as samp.

Hominy grits in the U.S. must be enriched like many other refined grain products and are now typically industrially produced. They are usually what you will find at your local grocers. Whole grain grits are primarily the product of grist mills making stone ground products and are often found in living history demonstrations, heritage fairs, pioneer day celebrations, and so on. Both yellow and white corns are commonly milled for grits and which one you should buy probably depends on what you ate growing up. If you're indifferent as to the color of your grits then I suggest buy-ing yellow corn grits as the beta carotene content of yellow corn can be converted by our bodies into Vitamin A whereas white corn has none.

Masa Harina:

In Spanish "masa" means "dough" and "harina" means "flour" which is a straight forward description of what masa harina is: A lime peeled corn that has been dried and milled into meal to be made into tortilla dough. It's flavor is distinctively different from either corn meal or hominy grits and is used in making tortillas, tamales, and many other Southwestern, Mexican, Central and South American dishes. Can often be found in mainstream grocery stores and grocers catering to a Latin American trade. Will store on the shelf for about a year and even longer if refrigerated or put up in good storage packaging. If you have a mind to try making your own tortillas you will save yourself much time and effort by using a tortilla press. These can be found in some groceries catering to a Latin American clientèle or ordered over the Internet.

Corn Starch:

A common starch used as a thickener. Made by a roller milling process removing the hull and germ leaving behind a nearly pure starch. Storage life is indefinite if kept dry. In the United Kingdom and some other areas it is known as corn flour which occasionally causes confusion with very finely milled corn also known as corn flour here in the States. The two products are largely not interchangeable.

MILLET:

Millet is an important staple grain in North China and India, but is little known in the U.S, where we mostly use it as bird feed. The grain kernels are very small, round, and usually ivory colored or yellow, though some varieties are darker. A lack of gluten and a rather bland flavor may account for the anonymity of this cereal. Millet has a more alkaline pH (and a higher iron content) than other grains which makes it very easy to digest. A major advantage of millet is that it swells a great deal when cooked and supplies more servings per pound than any other grain. When cooked like rice millet makes an excellent breakfast cereal. It has little gluten of its own, but mixes well with other flours. Adding whole millet kernels to the dough can add a pleasant crunch to your home made breads.

OATS:

Though the Scots and the Irish have made a cuisine of oats, it is mostly thought of in the U.S. as a bland breakfast food. Seldom found as a whole grain, it's usually sold processed in one form or another. Much like barley, the oat is a difficult grain to separate from its hull. Besides its longtime role as a breakfast food, oats make an excellent thickener of soups and stews and a filler in meat loafs and casseroles. Probably the second most common use for oats in America is in cookies and granolas. A little creative thought can really increase their culinary range. Listed below are the forms of oats found in the U.S. Rolled and cut oats retain both their bran and their germ.

Oat groats:

These are whole oats with the hulls removed. They are not often found in this form, but can sometimes be had from natural food stores and some storage food dealers. Oats are not the easiest thing to obtain a consistent grind from so producing your own oat flour takes a bit of experience. If you have a roller mill or attachment you can produce your own oatmeal using whole oat groats.

Steel cut oats:

Also known as Irish, pinhead or porridge oats. They are oat groats cut into chunks with steel blades. They're not rolled and look like coarse bits of grain. Steel cut oats can be found in many supermarkets and natural food stores. They take longer to cook than rolled oats, but retain more texture. They need oxygen free packaging to be kept at their best for long term storage.

Rolled oats:

These are also commonly called old fashioned, thick cut or porridge oats. To produce them, oat groats are steamed and then rolled to flatten. They can generally be found wherever oats are sold. They take slightly longer to cook than do the quick cooking oats, but they retain more flavor, texture and nutrition. This is what most people will call to mind when they think of oatmeal.

Quick cooking rolled oats:

These are just steamed oat groats rolled thinner than the old fashioned kind above so that they will cook faster. They can usually be found right next to the thicker rolled oats.

Instant rolled oats:

These are the "just add hot water" or microwave type of oat cereals and are not particularly suited for a storage program. They do, however, have uses in "bug out" and 72 hour food kits for short term crises.

Whole oats:

This is with the hulls still on. They are sold in feed & seed stores and sometimes straight from the farmer who grew them. Unless you have some means of getting the hulls off, I don't recommend buying oats in this form. If you do buy from a seed supplier, make certain that they have not been treated with any chemicals that are toxic to humans.

QUINOA:

Quinoa is yet another of the grains that is not a true cereal. It's botanical name is Chenopodium quinoa (pronounced "keen-wah"), and is a relative of the common weed Lambs-quarter. The individual kernels are about 1.5-2 mm in size and are shaped rather like small flattened spheres. When quinoa is cooked, the germ of the grain coils into a small "tail" that lends a pleasant crunch when eaten. Some forms of this grain have a bitter tasting water soluble component that should be removed by a thorough washing unless this was already done by the processor as most of the quinoa sold in the U.S. apparently has. There are several varieties of quinoa that have color ranging from near white to a dark brown. The larger white varieties are considered superior and are the most common.

RICE:

Rice is the most widely consumed food grain in the world with the U.S. being the leading exporter of this important staple, though we actually only produce about 1% of the global supply. The majority of the world's rice is eaten within five miles of where it was grown.

Much like wheat and corn, rice comes in a number of varieties, each with different characteristics. They are typically divided into classes by the length of their kernel grains; short, medium and long.

Short grain rice:

The short grain variety is a little softer and bit moister when it cooks and tends to stick together more than the longer rices. It has a sweeter, somewhat stronger flavor than long grain rice.

Medium grain rice: The medium grain variety is not very common in the States. It has flavor like the short variety, but with a texture more like long.

Long grain rice:

The long grain variety cooks up into a drier, flakier dish than the shorter types and the flavor tends to be blander. It is the most commonly found size of rice on American grocery shelves.

Each of the above may be processed into brown, white, parboiled or converted, and instant rice. Below is a short discussion of the differences between the various types.

Brown rice:

This is whole grain rice with only the hull removed. It retains all of the nutrition and has a pleasant nutty flavor. From a nutritional standpoint it is by far the best, but it has one flaw: The essential oil in the germ is very susceptible to oxidation and soon goes rancid. As a result, brown rice has a shelf life of only about six months unless given special packaging or storage. Freezing or refrigeration will greatly extend this. It's possible to purchase brown rice from long term food suppliers already specially packaged in air tight containers with an inert nitrogen atmosphere or you can do it yourself. In this kind of packaging, (if properly done), the storage life can be extended for several years.

Converted rice:

Converted rice starts as whole rice still in the hull which undergoes a process of soaking and steaming until it is partially cooked. It is then dried, hulled and polished to remove the bran and germ. The steaming process drives some of the vitamins and minerals from the outer layers into the white inner layers. This makes it more nutritious than polished white rice, but also makes it more expensive. Its storage life is the same as regular white rice.

White rice:

This is raw rice that has had its outer layers milled off, taking with it about 10% of its protein, 85% of its fat and 70% of its mineral content. Because so much of the nutrition is lost, white rice sold in the U.S. has to be "enriched" with vitamins to partially replace what was removed. It stores very well and is generally the cheapest form of rice to be found in the market place making it a very common storage food.

Instant rice:

The type of rice is fully cooked and then dehydrated needing nothing more than the addition of water to reconstitute it. In a pinch, it's not even necessary to use hot water. It's not particularly suitable for inclusion in storage programs, but may have a place in "seventy-two hour" and other short-term emergency kits. The white variety is by far the most common, but in the last few years instant brown rice has made an appearance on the market.

RYE:

Rye is well known as a bread grain in the U.S. It has dark brown kernels longer and thinner than wheat, but less gluten. Rye flours can be found in varying stages of refinement from dark whole grain flour to semi-refined medium to pale fully refined offerings. Bread made from this grain tends to be dense unless gluten is added (often in the form of a lot of wheat flour). German pumpernickels and Russian black breads, made with unrefined rye flour and molasses, are two of the darkest, densest forms of rye bread. Many sourdoughs are built upon a rye base with a resulting interesting, intense flavor.

SORGHUM:

Sorghum is probably more widely known here in the States for the syrup made from the sweet juice squeezed from the stalks of some varieties of this grain. Also known as "milo", it is one of the principle cereal grains of Africa. Its seeds are somewhat round, a little smaller than peppercorns, of an overall brown color with a bit of red and yellow mixed in. The varieties called "yellow endosperm sorghum" are considered to have a better taste. It is a major feed grain in the Southwestern U.S. and is where the vast majority of the national production goes. Like most of the other grains, sorghum is low in gluten, but the seeds can be milled into flour and mixed with higher gluten flours or made into flat breads, pancakes or cookies. In the Far East, it is cooked and eaten like rice, while in Africa it is ground into meal for porridge. It's also fermented for alcoholic beverages.

TEFF:

Easily the smallest of the grains, teff kernels are only about 1/32nd inch in diameter. The name itself means "lost" because if dropped on the ground, it's too small to recover. It's been very little known until recently, but has been a staple grain in Ethiopia for nearly five millennia. Small amounts are now being grown in South Africa and the United States. This grain ranges in color from reddish brown to near white. It has a protein content in the 10-12% range, good calcium and a useful source of iron. It is traditionally used in making the Ethiopian flat bread "injera", but has no gluten content of its own. It'll combine well with wheat flour though and has something of a sweetish flavor.

TRITICALE:

Triticale is not a creation sprung from the smooth brows of Star Trek script writers. It is, in fact, a cross between durum wheat and rye. This youngest of grains combines the productivity of wheat with the ruggedness of rye and has a high nutrition value. The kernels are gray-brown, oval shaped larger-than-wheat and plumper than rye. It can be used in much the same way as either of its two parents. It will make a raised bread like wheat does, but its gluten is a bit weak so wheat flour is frequently added to strengthen it. Because of the delicate nature of its gluten, excessive kneading must be avoided.

WHEAT:

The most widely consumed grain in the United States and along with rice and corn one of the three most widely grown in the world. Wheat is also one of the most intensively processed to turn into food of all the grains. It comes in a number of different varieties each more suitable for some purposes than others based on its particular characteristics. The most common classifications of these varieties are based on their respective growing season, hardness of kernel, and color of their bran layers - spring or winter, hard or soft, red or white.

The hard wheats have kernels that tend to be small, hard in texture, and with high protein (primarily gluten) contents. As a general rule, hard varieties have more protein than soft varieties. Yeast raised breads that need a lot of gluten are where it's at for the hard wheats.

The soft wheats have kernels tending to be larger, plumper and softer in texture than hard wheats. As their gluten content is lower they are primarily used in biscuits, pastries, quick breads, some pastas, and breakfast cereals where a higher gluten content would contribute an undesirable tougher texture. Soft wheats do not produce as fine a loaf

Ezra Taft Benson (1899–1994) Thirteenth President of the Church

"The revelation to store food may be as essential to our temporal salvation today as boarding the ark was to the people in the days of Noah" ("Prepare Ye," *Ensign,* Jan. 1974, 69).

The Lord has warned and forewarned us against a day of great tribulation and given us counsel, through His Servants, on how we can be prepared for these difficult times. Have we heeded His counsel?" (Ezra Taft Benson, Ensign, November 1980)

"When the economies of nations fail, when famine and other disasters prevent people from buying food in stores, the Saints must be prepared to handle these emergencies." (*The Teachings of Ezra Taft Benson*, p. 264.)

of yeast raised bread as high gluten hard wheat, though it can still be used for yeast breads by combining with higher gluten flours or using methods suitable for its protein level. Many traditional European yeast raised breads are made with lower protein flours.

Durum wheat also has a very hard kernel and a high protein content, but of a somewhat different nature than the other hard wheats. Durum is not primarily used for breads but is instead consumed mostly in the manufacture of pasta where it lends its characteristic yellowish color to the finished product. There are some specialty breads that call for durum/semolina flour so it can be used for bread making even if it's not best suited to the task.

Winter wheats are planted in the Fall, over winter in the field, grow through the Spring and are harvested early the next Summer. Spring wheats are planted in the early Spring and are harvested the following Fall. Red wheats comprise most of the hard varieties while white wheats comprise most of the soft. Recently, hard white wheats have been developed that are very suitable for yeast raised bread making. Some feel the hard white varieties make a better tasting whole wheat bread than the hard reds and I am inclined to agree. When milled, whole grain hard white wheat flour looks somewhat like unbleached refined white flour in appearance.

The hard red varieties, either spring or winter, are commonly chosen for storage programs because of their high protein content which should be no less than 12% with 14% or more being excellent. The hard white spring wheats are still relatively new and not yet as widespread but are steadily growing in popularity. They have the same excellent storage characteristics as the hard red wheats and should be selected with the same protein contents as well.

With so many different varieties of wheat it should come as no surprise that there are a number of different types of wheat flour offered to the home baker. Distinguishing between the array of products available through both retail grocery stores and commercial supply houses catering to bakers nearly requires the knowledge of a professional baker or a cereal chemist and would take up page after page to explain it all. Instead I will briefly cover only those flours or flour products that one can usually find in supermarkets in the U.S. and elsewhere. If you need more advanced knowledge in order to purchase through commercial or institutional food channels I recommend taking your questions to the Usenet newsgroups rec.food.baking, sci.bio.food-science, or alt.bread.recipes where you may be able to get answers from professionals in the field.

All Purpose Flour:

Of all the flours in the retail market all-purpose flour is the one most subject to major differences between brands, regions of the U.S., and/or other nations. This refined flour is typically made from a blend of hard and soft wheats with a protein content that can range from as low as 8% to as high as 12%. The regional brands of the Southern U.S. have traditionally been on the lower end of the protein scale. This is due to the fact that historically only soft wheats were grown in the South and the resulting flour was best used is in making biscuits and other types of non-yeast raised breads that did not require high gluten levels. The regional brands of the Northern U.S., and Canada are typically at the high end of the protein scale at or approaching 12%. This is because hard wheats are primarily northern grown and are well suited to making yeast raised breads which need higher gluten levels as were customarily made there. The national brands either differ by region or are in the 10-11% range in an effort to try to satisfy all markets.

In the U.S. all-purpose flour is enriched and can be had either bleached or unbleached and may possibly have small quantities of malt added as well (see below about enrichment, bleaching and malting).

As the name implies all-purpose is meant to serve as a general all-around flour from which you can make anything from cakes and pie crusts to sandwich bread. So far as it goes you can, but it's a lot like one-size-fits-all clothing in that chances are it won't work as well for a given project as a flour milled with that particular use in mind. The lower protein all-purpose flours sold in the Southern U.S. will produce a more tender biscuit, cake, or pie crust than the higher protein all-purpose flours of the Northern U.S. and Canada, but unless you use some special techniques (like how true French bread is made) it won't produce a very satisfying loaf of yeast bread. The flours in 10-11% range try to strike a happy medium between the two, but still won't serve as well as flour produced specifically with a given end use in mind. If you want to limit the number of types of flour you put into your storage program I'd recommend going with the 10-11% flours and either plan on adding gluten as needed to make the best yeast raised breads or cornstarch to produce more tender cakes and pie crusts.

In the United Kingdom and Canada all-purpose flour is oft times labeled as "plain flour", "top patent", "general purpose", or "family flour."

Bread Flour:

A refined white flour with a higher protein (gluten) content than most all-purpose flours to achieve better performance in making yeast raised breads. Protein levels should be at least 12% with 13-14% better still.

As this is a refined flour in the U.S. it will be enriched with added vitamins and iron, and can be found either bleached or unbleached. Because it is intended primarily for use in yeast raised breads this flour will usually have other additives such as small amounts of malt to improve yeast performance and vitamin C (ascorbic acid) to improve dough volume and texture. Some bread flours may also be treated with potassium bromate to improve gluten qualities, but concerns over possible toxicity of this additive is leading to its diminished use.

A high gluten refined bread flour is commonly added to whole wheat doughs to strengthen them which can improve loaf rises and volume. Bread flour is most commonly used in the production of yeast raised breads, pizza crusts, and some specialty baked goods. In Great Britain bread flour is often labeled as "Strong Flour" meaning it has a high protein content.

Whole Wheat Flour:

Real whole wheat flour should include 100% of the bran and germ so read your ingredient labels carefully to be sure this is so. This flour is mostly milled from hard red wheats, but whole grain hard white flour is available from some mills and will produce a bread that looks closer to refined white bread if that is what you are accustomed to eating. Protein contents can vary, but as most whole wheat flour is used in yeast bread making it should be at least 12% with 13-14% being better still. This is good because the bran and the germ can interfere with good gluten development as the dough is mixed and kneaded. Some do not mind this while others strengthen their flour by adding vital wheat gluten or high protein refined bread flours to achieve the rise and volume they are accustomed to in yeast breads. Approximately 90% of the total protein of a kernel of wheat is gluten with the remaining 10% other proteins being mostly found in the grain germ. Refined flours have had the germ removed so a statement of protein content can be taken as an indication of that flour's suitability for making raised yeast breads. With whole wheat flours one must remember that ten percent of non-gluten germ proteins and judge that flour's protein content accordingly. Whole wheat flour milled from lower protein soft wheats may be offered as "whole wheat pastry flour" so be sure of what you are buying. Some whole-wheat flours are also enriched.

Whole wheat flour may also be called "Graham Flour", sometimes simply "Stone Ground Wheat Flour" and in Great Britain, Canada, and Australia may be known as "Whole Meal Flour." In Britain there is also a "Brown Flour" which is midway between whole meal and white flour in that it retains about 85% of the wheat kernel rather than only the 72-75% that is typical of refined white flours.

The real disadvantage to storing whole wheat flour is that like other processed grain products that includes the oil rich germ it wants to go rancid. How fast this can happen depends upon temperature, moisture, etc, but four to six weeks is generally enough time for rancidity to become noticeable. One can, of course, package the flour in good containers with oxygen absorbers and the like, but better still would be to buy the flour in the form of whole wheat berries and mill them yourself. This is exactly what I and many other folks with food storage programs do. Baking with fresh, whole wheat flour is something of an art so the time to get good with it is right NOW while you can toss your failures to the chickens rather than having to eat them regardless because you can't afford to waste the food.

Vital Wheat Gluten:

Sometimes labeled as simply "wheat gluten." This is the purified gluten of hard wheat extracted from flour. It is generally 75-80% protein and is used to strengthen weak or whole grain flours for making yeast raised breads or made into "seitan" a wheat protein meat substitute. Somewhat confusing the issue is "High Gluten Flour" which is available in some markets. Careful investigation is needed here because this flour can range from a mere high gluten bread flour (approx 14%) to a gluten enriched flour typically 40%+) all the way up to purified wheat gluten (75%+). Be clear as to what it is you're buying and if you're not certain contact the manufacturer. If your whole wheat bread is not rising for you as much as you'd like then an addition of a few spoonfuls of gluten or some high gluten flour may perk it up a bit.

Cake Flour:

Typically the lowest protein content (6-8%) flour available to the home baker. This highly processed flour will make the tenderest cakes, cookies, and biscuits but performs poorly for yeasted breads. The flour is nearly always bleached (chlorinated) both to give it a bright whiteness and to improve its moisture holding capacity for cakes calling for a high ratio of sugars or fats. Unless you make a lot of cakes this is a rather specialized item to store.

Pastry Flour:

Similar to cake flour, but generally slightly higher in protein, not chlorinated, and may be found bleached or unbleached. Used to produce tender pie crusts, biscuits, etc. Very similar to the regional all-purpose flours of the Southern U.S. Can also sometimes be found in a whole-wheat version as well. In Great Britain, Canada, and Australia may be known as "soft flour."

Semolina/Durum:

Produced from durum wheat this flour is typically high in protein, 12% or more, enriched, unbleached with a distinctive pale yellow color. Texture depends largely on brand and can range from fairly coarse to bread flour fine. Most commonly used in the production of pastas, noodles, and couscous, but some specialty bread types call for semolina flour. May also be known as "alimentary flour", "macaroni flour", or "pasta flour." Farina, a coarse meal used as a breakfast cereal, is made from durum wheat.

Self-Rising Flour:

This is ordinary refined and enriched all-purpose flour to which approximately 1.5 teaspoons of baking powder and 0.5 teaspoons of salt have been added to each cup of flour. This flour has its fans, but it's not well suited to long storage as the baking powder wants to go flat over time even with special packaging. Nor is it suited to making yeast raised breads. Most self-rising flours are in the mid to low end of the protein scale (8-10%) because this is where chemically leavened quick breads perform best to achieve good rises and textures. You can make your own self-rising flour by adding in the requisite amount of double acting baking powder and salt mentioned above which is what I recommend doing rather than trying to store the ready-made product. Self-rising flour is sometimes known as phosphated flour (for the baking powder used in it) and in Great Britain, Canada, and Australia may be known as "self-raising flour" or "raising flour."

Instant Flour:

This specialized flour product is also sometimes known as "shaker flour" for the shaker can in which it's usually found This is a low-protein flour in a granular form processed for easy and rapid dissolution into hot or cold liquids for making sauces, gravies, and batters. A fairly specialized item which any worthy cook can use ordinary flour to replace.

FLOUR TREATMENTS AND ADDITIVES

Flour milling companies (and home bakers) use a variety of additives and treatments in their flours to improve or suppress a particular quality in their product. If you read the package labels carefully you can discern quite a lot about what has and has not been done. Here are a few of the more common:

Enrichment:

U.S. law (and some other nations) requires that refined flours which have had their bran and germ portions removed to be "enriched" by adding back a portion of the niacin, thiamin, riboflavin, folic acid, and iron that were lost in the refining process. Some milling companies go even further by adding vitamins A & D as well. There are various opinions about the value of this enrichment, but it's there. It has no affect on the taste, color, texture, caloric value, or baking qualities of the flour. Outside of the U.S. refined white flours may or may not be enriched so study your package labels carefully if this concerns you.

Bleaching:

White bread and white cakes come by their snowy beauty thanks to bleaching. This is a process by which the yellowish carotenoid pigments that naturally occur in wheat are bleached white in order to improve the appearance of the flour and perhaps to change some of its physical characteristics as well. This would occur naturally by itself were the refined flour allowed to sit around for several months, but it's an uneven process and time is money to the milling companies who cannot afford to have large stocks of product sitting around in their warehouses for long periods of time.

Beyond making naturally off-white flour snowy in appearance bleaching can perform several other functions which the individual baker must decide if they are important to his needs. Until fairly recently much refined flour was also "bromated" using potassium bromate both to lighten the color, and to improve the qualities of the gluten. Concerns over the toxicity of this chemical has led to its gradual decline or outright ban on its use. Other bleaching agents are now used such as chlorine gas, chlorine dioxide, benzoyl peroxide and possibly others as well. Flours treated in this fashion will often exhibit improved loaf volume, finer grain, and look better in the finished product.

Cake flour is generally chlorinated not only whiten but also to improve its moisture holding ability when used in cakes with a high ratio of sugar and fat to flour. This bleaching also further tempers the already low gluten of the flour to produce the tenderest possible texture.

For the folks who do not care to buy bleached flours, small amounts of ascorbic acid (vitamin C) are often added as a dough conditioner and yeast nutrient. Home bakers often add their own vitamin C to their breads when they make them for the same reasons. A mere 1/8 tsp of ascorbic acid per cup of flour is all that is necessary.

All bleached flours must be so labeled in the U.S.

Malting:

Many bread flours and some all-purpose flours will have small amounts of malt, malted barley flour, malt flour, or diastatic malt added to them. This additive improves the performance of the yeast by providing enzymes which speed the conversion of some of the flour starches into the digestible sugars the yeast use as fuel which can improve both the rise of the dough and the flavor of the finished product. The malt can also serve to improve the appearance of the bread when baked and lengthen its shelf life. You can add your own diastatic malt in the ratio of about 0.5-1.0 teaspoons for every three cups of flour.

Organic:

This is flour produced and processed under the guidelines of the U.S. Department of Agriculture's Organic foods program. Most of the basic flour types (all-purpose, bread, pastry, etc.) can be found in organic forms though you may have to search a bit to find them.

Pre-Sifted:

This is flour sifted at the mill before it was packaged. Supposedly this means you do not need to sift it again at home, but many feel that due to settling during transport and storage if the recipe calls for sifted flour it should be done again.

Other Additives: There are many other potential additives that you may potentially come across in flour which would require more space than is possible here to cover them. Most are for use within the commercial/industrial baking fields and you would need to contact the supplier to determine precisely what it is they can do for you.

STORING FLOUR PRODUCTS

As already mentioned above whole wheat flour wants to go rancid rather quickly after it has been milled. Once ground it will stay fresh for about four to six weeks sitting on your room temperature kitchen shelf. In a sealed container in the refrigerator the flour will stay good for a year or so. In the freezer it will keep for years. Personally, I think it best to store your whole wheat flour in the form of wheat berries and only mill as much flour as you will use in a week or two and keep that in the refrigerator or freezer until you do. If for some reason you cannot do this then buy the freshest product you can and package it well in Mylar bags, glass jars, or metal cans with oxygen absorbers. Due to the fine texture of flour it will not gas flush very well at all.

Even the refined white flours have limited shelf-lives. In spite of what some would have you believe they are not "dead foods." The bran and germ may have been removed, but a minute portion of the germ oils will remain as well as the naturally occurring enzymes found in the grain. Refined white flour won't noticeably go off on you the way whole wheat flour will, but given sufficient time and exposure to heat and atmospheric humidity the protein content of the flour will slowly breakdown. Your first indications of trouble may be a slowly developing musty smell or degraded dough performance – poor rises and bad loaf volumes. In a sealed, air tight container you should easily achieve six months to a year at room temperatures. Sealed containers in the refrigerator or freezer will last for at least several years. If you want your white flour to stay at its best for the longest possible time then package it in Mylar bags, glass jars, or metal cans air tight with oxygen absorbers. At a decent storage temperature sealed in a low oxygen environment you should easily achieve five years of shelf life or more.

LEGUME VARIETIES

If you're willing to spend what it takes on preserved meats and dairy products it's not necessary to store legumes at all. But most people do choose to keep a selection of beans, peas, and lentils in their larders either for reasons of economy, because they like them, or both. There are few non-animal foods that contain the amount of protein to be found in legumes with the varieties commonly available in the U.S. ranging from 20%-35%. As with most non-animal proteins, they are not complete in themselves for purposes of human nutrition, but become so when they are combined with the incomplete proteins found in grains. This is why grains and legumes are so often served together the world around.

The legume family, of which all beans, peas, lentils, and peanuts are a part, is one of the largest in the plant kingdom. Because of this and the many thousands of years of cultivation and development that man has given them on several continents the variety of edible legumes available to us is huge. Both their appearance and their names are colorful and varied. They range from "adzuki beans", a type of soybean from the Orient, to "zipper peas", a common field-pea here in the Southern U.S. Their color can range from a clean white, to deep red, dull green to flat black with thousands of mixtures and patterns in between.

In spite of this incredible variety, many legumes are largely interchangeable in cooking, although some dishes just wouldn't be the same if a different type were used. Below is a partial list of common legumes.

ADZUKI BEANS:

These small, deep red beans are very popular in Japan, China and other Asian nations, but are not as well known in the U.S. They are actually a cousin of the soybean and are commonly used in producing sweet bean paste for Chinese buns and other dishes. Pressure cooking will sometimes impart a bitter flavor so they are best presoaked then boiled in the conventional fashion. Their flavor is somewhat milder than kidney or small red beans, but they can serve as an adequate substitute for either in chili and other dishes in which those beans are commonly used.

BLACK BEANS:

Also known as "turtle beans", they are small, dark brownish-black and oval-shaped. Well known in Cuban black bean soup and commonly used in Central and South America and in China. They tend to bleed darkly when cooked so they are not well suited to being combined with other beans, lest they give the entire pot a muddy appearance. The skins of black beans also slip off easily so for this reason they are generally not recommended for pressure cooking for fear of clogging the vent. This can be lessened by not presoaking before cooking.

BLACK-EYED PEAS:

Also known as "cowpeas" or "field peas" there are many varieties these peas eaten across the Southern United States, Mexico, and Africa with black-eyed peas being the most commonly known in the U.S. The coloring of field-peas is as varied as the rest of the legume family, with black-eyed peas being small, oval shaped with an overall creamy color and, of course, their distinctive black-eye. Dried field-peas cook very quickly and combine very tastily with either rice or cornbread and are often eaten as Hoppin' John every New Years for luck. They're also reputed to produce less flatulence than many other beans.

CHICKPEAS:

Also known as the "garbanzo bean" or "cecci pea" (or bean), they tend to be a creamy or tan color, rather lumpily roundish and larger than dried garden peas. Many have eaten the nutty flavored chick-pea, even if they've never seen a whole one. They are the prime ingredient in hummus and falafel and are one of the oldest cultivated legume species known, going back as far as 5400 B.C. in the Near East. Chickpeas tend to remain firmer when cooked than other legumes and can add a pleasant texture to many foods. I like them in red spaghetti sauces in particular and they are often used in Spanish cuisine in a tomato based sauce. Roasted brown then ground they have also served as a coffee substitute.

FAVA BEANS:

Not as well known in the U.S. as in Europe and the Mediterranean favas are also known as "broad beans" or "horse beans" being broad in shape, flat and reddish brown in color. This is one of the oldest legume species in European cultivation, but it does require more effort to consume. The hull of the bean is tough and not conducive to being tenderized by cooking so is often peeled away. The skinless bean falls apart so is made into a puree. A small number of people with Mediterranean ancestry have a genetic sensitivity to the blossom pollens and undercooked beans, a condition known as "favism" so should avoid consuming them.

GREAT NORTHERN BEANS:

A large white bean about twice the size of navy beans they are typically bean flavored and are frequently favored for soups, salads, casseroles, and baked beans. One of the more commonly eaten in the U.S. Milled into meal these mild flavored beans can be included in many baked goods as a protein booster or used to thicken soups and stews.

KIDNEY BEANS:

Like the rest of the family, kidney beans can be found in wide variety. They may be white, mottled or a light or dark red color with their distinctive kidney shape. Probably best known here in the U.S. for their use in chili and bean salads, they figure prominently in Mexican, Brazilian and Chinese cuisine.

LENTILS:

Lentils are an odd lot. They don't fit in with either the beans or the peas and occupy a place by themselves. Their shape is different from other legumes being roundish little discs with colors ranging from muddy brown, to green to a rather bright orangish-red. They cook very quickly and have a distinctive mildly peppery flavor. They are much used in Far Eastern cuisine from India to China. Next to mung beans they make excellent sprouts though their peppery flavor tends to strengthen somewhat so are best mixed with milder sprouts.

LIMA BEANS:

In the Southern U.S., they are also commonly called "butter beans". Limas are one of the most common legumes, found in this country in all manner of preservation from the young small beans to the large fully mature type. Their flavor is pleasant, but a little bland. Their shape is rather flat and broad with colors ranging from pale green to speckled cream and purple. They combine very well with rice.

MUNG BEANS:

Best known here in the States in their sprouted form, they are quite common in Indian and other Asian cuisines and are a close relative of the field peas (cowpeas). Their shape is generally round, fairly small with color ranging from a medium green to so dark as to be nearly black. They cook quickly and presoaking is not generally needed.

NAVY BEANS:

Smaller than Great Northerns these petite sized beans are also sometimes knows as pea beans. They are the stars of Navy and Senate Bean Soups, favored for many baked bean dishes, and are most often chosen for use in commercial pork and beans. They retain their shape well when cooked. Ground into meal they can be added to many soups and stews without overpowering them.

PEANUTS (Groundnuts):

The peanut is not actually a nut at all, but a legume. They are another odd species not much like the more familiar beans and peas. Peanuts have a high protein percentage and even more fat. Whatever their classification peanuts are certainly not unfamiliar to U.S. eaters. They are one of the two legume species commonly grown for oilseed in this country, and are also used for peanut butter, and boiled or roasted peanuts. Peanut butter (without excessive added sweeteners) can add body and flavor to sauces, gravies, soups, and stews. Many Central and South American, African, Chinese, and Thai dishes incorporate peanuts so they are useful for much more than just a snack food or cooking oil.

PEAS, GREEN OR YELLOW:

More often found as split peas though whole peas can sometimes be had. The yellow variety has become some-what uncommon but has a milder flavor than the green types which well lends them to blending inconspicuously into other foods. Probably best known in split pea soup, particularly with a smoky chunk of ham added. They are also used in Indian cuisine, especially dals. Whole peas need soaking, but split peas can be cooked as is. Split peas and pea meal makes an excellent thickener for soups and stews. Because splitting damages the pea, this more processed form does not keep for as long as whole peas unless given special packaging.

PINK AND RED BEANS:

Related to the kidney bean these are smaller in size but similar in flavor. The pink bean has a more delicate flavor than the red. The are both often favored for use in chili and widely used across the American Southwest, Mexico, and Latin America. They can add nicely to the color variety in multi-bean soups.

PINTO BEANS:

Anyone who has eaten Tex-Mex food has likely had the pinto bean. It is probably the most widely consumed legume in the U.S., particularly in the Southwestern portion of the country. Stereotypically bean shaped, it has a dappled pattern of tans and browns on its shell. Pintos have a flavor that blends well with many foods. When ground together with great northern or navy beans they make my favorite homemade version of falafel. When milled into a meal pintos will cook in mere minutes, making a near instant form of refried beans.

SOYBEANS:

The soybean is by far the legume with the highest protein content in large scale commercial production and it's amino acid profile is the most nearly complete for human nutrition. Alongside the peanut it is the other common legume oilseed. The beans themselves are small, round, and with a multitude of different shades though tan seems to be the most common that I've seen. Because of their high oil content, they are more sensitive to oxygen exposure than other legumes and precautions should be taken accordingly if they are to be kept for more than a year in storage, especially if they are to be processed for soymilk or tofu. Although the U.S. grows a large percentage of the global supply, we consume virtually none of them directly. Most go into cattle feed, are used by industry, or exported. What does get eaten directly has usually been intensively processed. Soybean products range from soymilk to tofu, to tempeh, to textured vegetable protein (TVP) and hundreds of other forms. They don't lend themselves well to merely being boiled until done then eaten the way other beans and peas do. For this reason, if you plan on keeping some as a part of your storage program you would be well served to begin to learn how to process and prepare them now while you're not under pressure to produce. This way you can throw out your failures and order pizza, rather than having to choke them down, regardless.

AVAILABILITY OF GRAINS AND LEGUMES

Grains and legumes of all types may be purchased in a number of different ways depending largely on where you live and the time of year. The following will cover the various steps of the processing chain starting with the forms most immediately suitable for storage and progressing all the way back to the farmer.

Each type of availability has its good and bad points. As you might expect, the more processing a product receives, the higher its price is likely to be. The further back along the processing chain you go the cheaper a product should become in terms of purchase price. It will, however, cost you more in time and effort to get it ready for storage.

The easiest and simplest way to incorporate grains and legumes into your storage program is to purchase your items pre-cleaned and prepackaged. These are products that have been harvested, passed through fans and screens to remove chaff, smut balls, insect parts, mouse droppings and other debris, then put up in retail sized bags or other containers - possibly even going so far as to already be packaged for long-term storage. This would be either from your local grocer or a storage food dealer. If you don't live in the area where what you want is grown it may be your only option. If you want to purchase in bulk then you may be able to find pre-cleaned but not yet packaged products. These sources would be commercial or institutional food suppliers, food co-ops, warehouse grocers like Sam's Club or Costco, local food companies that package their own product lines, and the like. If what you want is not already in 50-100 lb bags you may have to provide your own container and there may be minimum purchase amounts as well. If the moisture content is in the right range then nothing will need to be done other than to put it up in your own storage packaging. If you don't buy it from some sort of foods dealer then be certain read the cautionary text below.

Should you happen to live in the area where the type of grain or legume that you are interested in purchasing is grown you may be able to purchase direct from the producer or distributor.

If you are interested in doing this, it may be possible to find your product field-run which simply means that it's been harvested and sold shortly thereafter. It will not have been given any cleaning or processing and is likely to be rather dirty depending upon the conditions under which it was grown and harvested.

A second form called field-run from storage is product that has been harvested then put into storage for a time. It will have the dirt and debris of field run grain and whatever it may have picked up from the grain elevator as well.

IMPORTANT NOTE: If you have purchased your grains and legumes from a foods dealer then you needn't worry about hidden mold infections, fungicides or insecticides that are unsafe for human consumption. In the U.S., the products will have been checked several times by Federal and State agriculture departments and probably by the major foods dealers as well, to ensure its quality.

This is not necessarily the case when you purchase your grains or legumes directly from the farmer or elevator operator as field-run or field-run from storage grain. Nor is it necessarily the case if you've made the decision to utilize grains marketed as animal feed. Inspection procedures vary from nation to nation, so if you buy outside of the U.S. inquire of your supplier.

If you are buying your grains and legumes from some place other than a foods dealer, you need to know the history of what you are buying. There is the remote possibility that field-run from storage or any grade of grain not specifically sold for human consumption may have had fumigants, fungicides or insecticides not certified as safe for human foods added while it was in the bin. It is important to know what it has been treated with before you buy it.

Straight field-run grain, other than being dirty, is not likely to have had anything added that would make it undesirable for human consumption. There is, however, the also remote possibility it may have been infected with fungi that would make it unsafe for eating.

One of these fungal infections of grain is called "ergot". This fungal disease affects the flowering parts of some members of the grass family, mostly confined to rye. Consuming the fungus causes a nervous disorder known as St. Anthony's Fire. When eaten in large quantities the ergot alkaloids may cause constriction of the blood vessels, particularly in the extremities. The effects of ergot poisoning are cumulative and lead to numbness of the limbs and other, frequently serious, symptoms.

The fungus bodies are hard, spur like, purple-black structures that replace the kernel in the grain head. The ergot bodies can vary in size from the length of the kernel to as much as several times as long. They don't crush as easily as smut bodies of other funguses. When they are cracked open, the inner broken faces can be off-white, yellow, or tan. The infected grain looks very different from ordinary, healthy rye grains and can be spotted easily. Ergot only rarely affects other grains and will generally afflict rye only when the growing conditions were damp. If you purchase field run rye, you should closely examine it first for the presence of ergot bodies. If you find more than a very, very few pass up that grain and look elsewhere.

Ergot is typically not a problem in the U.S and is easily spotted when it does occur. Other grain fungi, however, are much harder to spot and also have serious consequences should they be consumed. The various species of Aspergillus and Fusarium molds can be a problem almost anywhere.

Animal feed grains or seed grain/legumes are widely available and there are those who want to consider using these sources. Keep in mind that animal feeds are typically dirtier than food grains and may have a higher contaminant level than what is permissible for human consumption. The USDA allows the sale of grain or legumes for animal feed that could not be sold for direct human food use. It may even be mixed varieties of one grain and not all one type. In the case of feed wheat it may have an acceptable protein content but still make miserable raised bread so try milling and baking with a small amount before you put a lot of it away. Seed grains, in particular, must be investigated carefully to find out what they may have been treated with. It is quite common for seed to be coated with fungicides, and possibly other chemicals as well. Once treated, they are no longer safe for human or animal consumption. Be sure to inquire of your supplier.

If you do purchase field-run grain of any sort, examine it closely for contamination and moldy grain. Ask the farmer or distributor whether it has been tested for mold or myco-toxin (fungal toxin) content. This is especially the case if you are buying field-run CORN, RYE, SOYBEANS or RICE. When you purchase direct from the field, you may be getting it before it has been checked. Be certain of what it is that you are buying and ask questions if you choose to go this route. Know who you are dealing with. Unless you just can't find any other source, I don't recommend using animal feed or seed grains for human food use.

MOISTURE CONTENT

The moisture content of the grain or legume you want to put by has a major impact on how long you will be able to profitably keep it in storage. Some of the available literature states that grain with a moisture content as high as 13% can be safely put up, but there is a risk to keeping it at that level that should be understood.

The outside of every kernel of grain and bean you buy or grow hosts thousands of fungi spores and bacteria. This is all perfectly natural and is not a cause for alarm. The problem is that at moisture levels between 13.5% to 15% some fungal species are able to grow and reproduce. Aerobic bacteria (needing free oxygen to survive) require moisture in the 20% range. If you have grain with a moisture content as high as 13% you are perilously close to having enough moisture to enable mold growth which could lead to the spoilage and loss of your product. For this reason, I suggest you keep all grains and legumes to a moisture content of no more than 10%. An exception to this is raw peanuts which are particularly susceptible to an Aspergillus mold growth that produces aflatoxin (a type of mycotoxin) so should be stored with an 8% moisture content or less.

If you do not have a clue as to what the moisture level of your grain is here are several methods to determine it. The first method is quick, simple and will usually give you a close enough idea to work with of how much moisture there is in your grain or legume. The last two require a great deal more time and effort, but give more precise results.

METHOD ONE

This is the method I use myself. It's quick and dirty requiring nothing more than crushing a kernel of grain or a bean between two solid objects like a hammer and a brick. You don't have to hit it like you're driving spikes, just give it a sharp rap. If the grain shatters nicely into powdery debris or many small bits then the moisture level ought to be in the right range and you can package as-is. If the kernel just mashes flat or only reluctantly breaks into pieces it probably has too much moisture. If you're not sure of what you're seeing try drying a small amount overnight at only a warm temperature (100º Fahrenheit) such as you'd get from the pilot light in a gas oven. The next day take another sample from the same container and rinse in warm water for a few seconds, rub dry on a towel and let sit for about ten minutes. Now try the crush test on both samples. One should give you a good result and the other should be much different. Any seed with a high fat content such as soybeans and peanuts will not work well with this method.

COMMON TO METHODS TWO AND THREE
The more precise moisture content measurements require more time and effort. Nevertheless, you can make useful determinations with home equipment and I include them here for those who find Method One to be unsatisfactory.

You'll need some way to measure weight with a fair degree of accuracy. The better the scale you use, the more reliability you'll have in your determinations. Provided that it will weigh accurately to the half-ounce or less, any scale that can be calibrated with a known check weight will do. Postal scales can be made to serve if they are carefully calibrated against a known weight. Many individuals interested in starting storage programs may have grain weight scales used in ammunition reloading that might serve well.

Also necessary is a thermometer capable of withstanding and accurately measuring oven temperatures. As many bakers can tell you, home oven thermostats are often notoriously inaccurate so it is better to rely on a decent thermometer. Most kitchen supply stores can supply one that is oven safe and will accurately measure to the degree Fahrenheit or Celsius.

Proper technique calls for preheating the oven for a half-hour or more before starting the dehydrating process so that it will be of a uniform heat throughout. The sample pan should be placed on the middle rack as close to the vertical and horizontal center of the oven as possible. The bulb or dial of the thermometer should be placed next to the pan.

METHOD TWO

This method is for measuring moisture content in whole grains and legumes. Grain flours or meals, milk powders and any other finely textured foods should use Method Three detailed below.

To be done prior to measuring — choose a shallow heat resistant container that has a close fitting lid. Clean it thoroughly and dry completely in your oven for 10-15 minutes. Allow it to cool and then weigh it carefully. This will give you the tare weight or what your container weighs empty.

Depending on how your scale is calibrated you can use a smaller sample size than what is indicated below. Using the twenty-ounce sample mentioned in the following text will allow for fairly accurate readings with the average postal scale. A scale that will measure to the gram could use as small a sample as 20 grams. A powder scale could use even less, but the smaller your sample size becomes the more finicky care you must exercise not to allow error to creep in. Keep your sample size large enough to easily work with.

Allowing for the weight of the sample pan, measure out a weighed twenty-ounce representative sample of the grain or legumes in question. Ideally, you should thoroughly mix the entire lot immediately before removing the sample, but if this is not possible then take it from the middle center of the container. It is important that you use care in this measurement since it will affect all following determinations.

Put the sample in the container making sure it is not more than an inch deep. Place it in the oven with the lid off and allow to heat. Below is a table giving the oven temperatures and times per grain or legume type:

Time and Temperature Settings for Determining Moisture Contents of Whole Seeds

Seed	Oven Temperature F*	Oven Temp C*	Time
Barley	266	130	20
Beans	217	103	72
Corn	217	103	72
Oats	266	130	22
Rye	266	130	16
Sorghum, millet	266	130	18
Soybeans, peanuts	217	103	72
Wheat, rice	266	130	19

*No home oven that I am aware of will allow for such precise temperature control. Try to keep the temperature within ten degrees either way of what is listed and you will still achieve useful results. When the dehydration period is over place the close fitting lid on the sample pan and allow to cool in the oven with the door closed. Remove and carefully weigh the pan.

A one ounce loss in weight indicates your grain has a roughly five percent moisture content, 2 ounces indicates that it has a 10% moisture content, etc., etc. You might even be able to cut it as fine as a half-ounce loss, but I wouldn't try to take it further than that. Obviously, this is only a rough measure, but it works and can be done with postal or dietetic scales that are available virtually everywhere. As I mentioned above, if you have a scale with a finer calibration it is possible to use a smaller sample size and achieve the same result.

METHOD THREE

This method is much faster to use than the first, but greater care must be taken to prevent error. It can be used to determine moisture contents of whole grains and legumes, flours, meals and various food powders.

The same equipment as was used in Method Two will be required here as well as a low-RPM grain mill or some other device that can reduce a quantity of the grain to a meal consistency with only minimal heating of the sample. If the food to be tested is already at a meal consistency or finer then it can be used as-is.

Grind a quantity of product from which you want to measure the moisture content. Take care to grind the sample slowly enough to keep friction heat build up to a minimum (should not be more than mildly warm) or else moisture will be lost due to heat evaporation before it can be weighed. Immediately upon finishing the grinding, weigh out your sample so as to minimize unmeasured moisture loss.

Place the sample in the oven and dehydrate in the manner used in Method Two for a period of two hours at a temperature setting of 275º F (135º C). When the heating period is finished cover with the tight-fitting lid and allow to cool in the oven. Remove and weigh carefully. Moisture determination is the same as above. If anyone has a better way of measuring moisture levels which can be done without a lab or special equipment I'd surely like to hear from you.

CLEANING IT YOURSELF

If you've chosen to purchase field-run grain or if the pre-cleaned product you've bought isn't clean enough to suit you it can be given further cleaning.

The fastest and easiest method is "fanning", a form of winnowing. This is done by pouring the grain slowly through the air stream of a fan or blower into a clean, deep container such as a cardboard box or trash can. The wind blowing through the falling grain will blow out most of the broken kernels, chaff, smut balls, mouse droppings, etc. If you're losing too much good grain, try turning the fan down or moving it further back from the container. The deep container will cut down on the amount of kernels that bounce out. Repeat fanning as necessary until the grain is clean enough to suit or you've blown all of the lighter contaminants out.

If the fanning didn't get the grain clean enough it can be further cleaned by running it through a screen or sieve. This should be made with holes just big enough to pass an average sized grain of what it is you're cleaning. Obviously, the size of the holes will necessarily vary depending upon the kernel size of the grain.

Should the kernels still not be clean enough to suit then you'll just have to resort to hand picking out the offending particles. I'd strongly suggest doing this just prior to grinding where it can be done in small batches rather than trying to do your entire storage all at once. It's much easier to do a few pounds at a time than fifty or a hundred.

If you have it in mind to wash the grain, this should not be done prior to storage, but rather just before use. After rinsing, dry the grain immediately in an oven heated to 150º F (117 º C) for an hour in a layer no deeper than 1/2 inch deep stirring often.

George Albert Smith (1870–1951) Eighth President of the Church

"How on the face of the earth could a man enjoy his religion when he had been told by the Lord how to prepare for a day of famine, when instead of doing so he had fooled away that which would have sustained him and his family" (*Deseret News,* Mar. 4, 1868, 26).

GRAINS COOKING CHART

GRAIN (1 cup dry)	CUPS WATER	COOK TIME	CUPS YIELD
Amaranth	2 1/2	20 - 25 min.	2 1/2
Barley, pearled	3	50 - 60 min.	3 1/2
Barley, hulled	3	1 hr. 15 min.	3 1/2
Barley, flakes	2	30 - 40 min.	2 1/2
Buckwheat groats *	2	15 min..	2 1/2
Cornmeal (fine grind)	4 - 4 1/2	8 - 10 min.	2 1/2
Cornmeal (polenta, coarse)	4 - 4 1/2	20 - 25 min.	2 1/2
Millet, hulled	3 - 4	20 - 25 min.	3 1/2
Oat Groats	3	30 - 40 min.	3 1/2
Oat, bran	2 1/2	5 min.	2
Quinoa *	2	15 - 20 min.	2 3/4
Rice, brown basmati	2 1/2	35 - 40 min.	3
Rice, brown, long grain	2 1/2	45 - 55 min.	3
Rice, brown, short grain*	2 - 2 1/2	45 - 55 min.	3
Rice, brown, quick	1 1/4	10 min.	2
Rice, wild	3	50 - 60 min.	4
Rye, berries	3 - 4	1 hr.	3
Rye, flakes	2	10 - 15 min.	3
Spelt	3 - 4	40 - 50 min.	2 1/2
Teff *	3	5 - 20 min.	3 1/2
Triticale	3	1 hr. 45 min.	2 1/2
Wheat, whole berries	3	2 hrs.	2 1/2
Wheat, couscous	1	5 min.	2
Wheat, cracked	2	20 - 25 min.	2 1/4
Wheat, bulgur *	2	15 min.	2 1/2

BASIC COOKING INSTRUCTIONS FOR GRAINS & LEGUMES.

A basic cooking direction for all grains begins with measuring the grains and water into a saucepan. If you are cooking 1 cup (240 ml) of grains, use a 2-quart (2 liter) saucepan.
Add 1/2 to 1 teaspoon salt if desired.

Cover the saucepan and bring to a boil over high heat. Turn the heat down to low, and steam for the recommended cooking time. Lift the lid and test the grains for tenderness. If the grains need more time, cover the saucepan and steam 5 to 10 minutes longer. If the grains need more cooking time and all the water has been absorbed, add up to 1/4 cup (60 ml) of water, cover, and continue steaming.

If tender, turn off the heat and allow the grains to rest 5 to 10 minutes before serving to fluff.

Buckwheat is the exception to the basic directions. Because the grain is so porous and absorbs water quickly, it's best to bring the water to a boil first. Then, add the buckwheat.
When the water returns to a boil, cover the saucepan, turn the heat down to low, and time the steaming process.

*Buckwheat groats are available toasted and untoasted. Cooking times are the same.

* Quinoa should be well rinsed in a fine strainer for 1 to 2 minutes to remove the saponens, a natural, protective coating which will give a bitter flavor if not rinsed off.

* Short grain brown rice is sometimes labeled sweet, glutinous, or sticky brown rice.

*Teff can be enjoyed raw as well as cooked. Sprinkle it on salads or over cooked cereals to increase fiber and nutrition.

*Bulgur wheat can be covered with 1-inch of warm water and soaked for 1 hour to soften. It is then ready to use in raw salads such as tabbouli.

PREPARING BEANS & LEGUMES

Begin by washing beans and discarding any which are discolored or badly formed. Check for debris in the package such as small rocks or twigs and discard them. Beans cook more quickly and their digestibility benefits with soaking in water to cover by about 3 inches (7.5 cm) for 8 hours or overnight. Discard the soak water and cook the beans in fresh water.

Some bean cookery aficionados feel that salt and seasonings added during the cooking tends to make beans cook more slowly. Since beans require lengthy cooking, we recommend adding salt and seasonings during the last few minutes and find they absorb flavor quite readily.

There are other factors which contribute to the length of cooking, such as, hard water and beans that have been dried for a long period of time. For some of the longer cooking beans we have found that soaking 24 hours and changing the soak water 2 or 3 times hastens the cooking time.

Many people are concerned with the reputation that beans have for causing flatulence.

Starting your bean ventures with small amounts helps to increase your body's enzyme production gradually. Soaking and cooking the beans thoroughly helps to break down the complex sugars (oligosaccharides) which challenge our digestive systems.

Some herbs that help the digestion of beans can be added during the cooking process.

These include bay leaf, cumin, and winter or summer savory, fresh epazote (available in Hispanic markets). Many people from India maintain the tradition of chewing on dried fennel seeds or drinking a cup of fennel tea at the end of a legume meal to aid the digestion.

QUICK-SOAK METHOD:

When time is limited, you can wash and pick over beans and put them into a stock pot with water to cover by 3 inches (7.5 cm). Bring to a boil and boil for 10 minutes to remove toxins. Then cover and allow to

BEANS AND LEGUMES COOKING CHART

BEAN (1 cup dry)	CUPS WATER	COOK TIME	CUPS YIELD
Adzuki (Aduki)	4	45 - 55 min.	3
Anasazi	2 1/2 - 3	45 - 55 min.	2 1/4
Black Beans	4	1 hr. - 1 1/2 hrs.	2 1/4
Black-eyed Peas	3	1 hr.	2
Cannellini (White Kidney Beans)	3	45 min.	2 1/2
Cranberry Bean	3	40 - 45 min.	3
Fava Beans, skins removed	3	40 - 50 min.	1 2/3
Garbanzos (Chick Peas)	4	1 - 3 hrs.	2
Great Northern Beans	3 1/2	1 1/2 hrs.	2 2/3
Green Split Peas	4	45 min.	2
Yellow Split Peas	4	1 - 1 1/2 hrs.	2
Green Peas, whole	6	1 - 2 hrs.	2
Kidney Beans	3	1 hr.	2 1/4
Lentils, brown	2 1/4	45 min. - 1 hr.	2 1/4
Lentils, green	2	30-45 min.	2
Lentils, red	3	20 - 30 min.	2-2 1/2
Lima Beans, large	4	45 - 1 hr.	2
Lima Beans, small	4	50 - 60 min.	3
Lima Beans, Christmas	4	1 hr.	2
Mung Beans	2 1/2	1 hr.	2
Navy Beans	3	45-60 min.	2 2/3
Pink Beans	3	50 - 60 min.	2 3/4
Pinto Beans	3	1 - 1/2 hrs.	2 2/3
Soybeans	4	3 - 4 hrs	3

soak for 1 hour. Discard soak water, add fresh water, and cook until tender.

As a general rule of thumb, 1 cup of dried beans will yield about 2 1/2 - 3 cups (.5 to .75 liters) of cooked beans.

PRESSURE COOKING

For pressure-cooking beans you can choose to soak the beans overnight, use the quicksoak method, or forego soaking altogether. There are well-known chefs, like Emeril Lagasse, who do not soak beans before pressure-cooking.

Whether you choose to soak or eliminate that step, put the beans in the pressure cooker with 3 times as much water as beans. Cook at 15 pounds of pressure for 30 minutes for small beans. For large beans, such as limas or fava beans, pressure cook for about 40 minutes.

COOKING FRESH BEANS

Because few people actually grow beans and go through the time-consuming process of shelling and cooking them, most of the information about preparing beans refers to dried beans. However, fresh beans are delicious and easy to prepare and can often be found at farmers' markets. Fresh black-eyed peas, garbanzos, cannellini, limas, and others offer excellent flavor and nutrition.

There are two methods of cooking fresh beans: boiling or steaming. To boil, drop the shelled beans into boiling water to cover, and boil gently for 5 to 10 minutes. You may want to add some onions, garlic, herbs of your choice, and a dash of salt to the water to flavor the beans.

To steam, put about an inch of water into the bottom of a saucepan, and place the beans into a steamer basket that fits into the saucepan. Cover the pan, and steam over boiling water for 5 to 10 minutes.

After fresh fava beans are cooked, their tough skins are usually peeled and discarded.

When left on, they give the beans a bitter flavor. To peel the skins, use a small paring knife and peel away one end. Then squeeze the opposite end and the bean will slip out easily.

SUGAR, HONEY AND OTHER SWEETENERS

There are a wide number of sugars to be found for purposes of sweetening foods. Fructose is the primary sugar in fruit and honey; maltose is one of the sugars in malted grains; pimentose is found in olives, and sucrose is what we know as granulated or table sugar. Sucrose is a highly refined product made primarily from sugar cane though sugar beets still contribute a fair amount of the world supply. Modern table sugar is now so highly refined as to be virtually 100% pure and nearly indestructible if protected from moisture. Powdered sugar and brown sugar are simple variations on granulated sugar and share its long life.

Liquid sweeteners do not have quite the longevity of dry sugars. Honey, cane syrup, molasses, corn syrup and maple syrup may crystallize or mold during long storage. These syrups are chemically not as simple as table sugar and therefore lose flavor and otherwise break down over time.

GRANULATED SUGARS:

Buying refined sugar is a simple matter. Select a brand you know you can trust, be certain the package is clean, dry and has no insect infestation. There's little that can go wrong with it.

GRANULATED:

Granulated sugar does not spoil, but if it gets damp it will grow lumpy or turn into a sugar rock. If it does, it can be pulverized into smaller pieces and used. Granulated sugar can be found in varying textures, coarser or finer. "Castor/caster sugar" is a finer granulation than what is commonly sold as table sugar in the U.S. and is more closely equivalent to our super fine or berry sugar.

POWDERED, CONFECTIONERS, ICING:

All names refer to the same kind of sugar, that is white granulated sugar very finely ground. For commercial use there is a range of textures from coarse to ultra-fine. For home consumption, what is generally found is either Very Fine (6X) or Ultra-Fine (10X), but this can vary from nation to nation. Not all manufacturers will indicate the grind on the package. Sugar refiners usually add a small amount of cornstarch to prevent caking which will make it undesirable for use in sugar syrups or solutions where clarity is needed.

Powdered sugar is as inert as granulated sugar, but it is even more hygroscopic and will adsorb any moisture present. If it soaks up more than a little it will cake and become hard. It's difficult to reclaim hardened powdered sugar, but it can still be used like granulated sugar where clarity in solution (syrups) is not important.

BROWN, LIGHT & DARK:

In the United States brown sugar is generally refined white sugar that has had a bit of molasses or sugar syrup and caramel coloring added to it. Dark brown sugar has more molasses which gives it a stronger flavor, a darker color and makes it damp. Light brown sugar has less molasses which gives it a milder flavor, a blonder color and is slightly dryer than the dark variety. Light brown sugar can be made by combining one fourth to one third white sugar to the remainder dark brown sugar and blend thoroughly.

Both varieties need to be protected from drying out, or they will become hard and difficult to deal with. Nor do you want to allow them to become damper than what they already are.

There are dry granulated and liquid brown sugars available, but they don't have the same cooking qualities as ordinary brown sugars. They also don't dry out and harden quite so readily either.

RAW, NATURAL, TURBINADO & OTHERS:

In recent years, refiners have realized there is a market for less processed forms of cane sugar in the U.S. so have begun to sell these under various names and packaging. None of them are actually raw sugar as it is illegal to sell in the States due to the high impurities level in the truly raw product. All will have been processed to some degree, perhaps to remove the sticky surface molasses or to lighten the color, but will not have been subjected to the full refining and whitening processes of ordinary white table sugar. This leaves some of the natural hue and a strength of flavor that deepens with the color. All of these less refined sugars may be stored and handled like brown sugar.

Outside of the United States it is possible to buy cane sugars from the truly raw product with all of the detritus remaining from the cane juice extraction process up through various stages of refinement much like we have here in the United States. Many can be found with names such as "muscavado", "jaggery" (usually a raw palm or date sugar), "demerara", "succanat," and others. Colors will range from quite dark to blonde and may or may not be sticky with molasses. Generally the darker the color the stronger the flavor will be. In spite of any impurities they can be stored like brown sugar since their sugar content is high enough to inhibit most microbial growth. Recently I have found demerara sugar for sale here in the U.S.

STORING GRANULATED SUGARS

All granulated sugars have basically the same storage requirements. They need to be kept in air tight, insect and moisture proof containers. For powdered, and granulated sugar you might want to consider using some desiccant in the storage container if your local climate is damp. Since brown sugars and raw sugars are supposed to be moist, they do not need desiccants. Shelf life is indefinite if kept dry, but anything you intend to eat really should be rotated occasionally. Time has a way of affecting even the most durable of foods.

I've used brown sugar that was six years old at the time it was removed from storage and, other than the molasses settling somewhat toward the bottom, it was fine. A friend to whom I gave a bucket of the brown sugar finished it off three years later which was nine years after it was packaged and it, too, was fine.

HONEY

Honey may be the oldest sweetener known to man - its use predates recorded history. Remains of honey have been found in the Egyptian pyramids. This product of honeybees is typically sweeter than granulated sugar by a factor of 25%-40% depending upon the specific flowers from which the bees gathered their nectar. This means a smaller amount of honey can give the same amount of sweetening as sugar. The source flowers also dictate the flavor and the color as well. Honey color can range from very dark (nearly black) to almost colorless. As a general rule, the lighter the color and the more delicate the flavor, the greater the price the honey will bring. As you might expect, since honey is sweeter than table sugar, it also has more calories as well — an average of twenty two per teaspoon compared to granulated sugar's sixteen. There are also trivial amounts of minerals and vitamins in the bee product while white sugar has none. Honey is not a direct substitute for table sugar however, its use in recipes may call for a bit of alteration to make them to turn out right.

Although the chance is remote, raw honey may also contain minute quantities of *Clostridium botulinum* spores so should not be fed to children under one year of age. PLEASE READ THE POST FROM GERI GUIDETTI CONCERNING THIS BELOW. Raw honey is OK for older children and adults.

Honey comes in a number of forms in the retail market and all with somewhat different storage characteristics:

WHOLE-COMB:

This is the bee product straight from the hive. It is the most unprocessed form of honey, being large pieces of waxy comb floating in raw honey. The comb itself will contain many unopened honey cells.

RAW:

This is unheated honey that has been removed from the comb. It may contain bits of wax and other small particles.

FILTERED:

This is raw honey that has been warmed slightly to make it easier to filter out small particles and impurities. Other than being somewhat cleaner than raw honey it is essentially the same. Most of the trace amounts of nutrients remain intact.

LIQUID/PURE:

This is honey that has been heated to higher temperatures to allow for easier filtering and to kill any microorganisms. Usually lighter in color, this form is milder in flavor, resists crystallization and generally clearer. It stores the best of the various forms of honey. Much of the trace amounts of vitamins, however, are lost.

SPUN, CRYSTALLIZED or CREAMED:

This honey has had some of its moisture content removed to make a creamy spread. It is the most processed form of honey. It keeps quite well. Also available in various flavors.

BUYING HONEY

Much of the honey sold in supermarkets has been blended from a variety of different honeys and some may have even had other sweeteners added as well. Like anything involving humans, buying honey can be a tricky business. It pays to deal with individuals and brands you know you can trust. In the United States you should buy products labeled U.S. GRADE A or U.S. FANCY if buying in retail outlets. However, be aware there are no federal labeling laws governing the sale of honey, so only honey labeled pure is entirely honey and not blended with other sweeteners. Honey grading is a matter of voluntary compliance which means some producers may be lax in their practices. Some may also use words like "organic", "raw", "uncooked" and "unfiltered" on their labels, possibly to mislead. Fortunately, most honey producers are quite honest in their product labeling so if you're not certain of who to deal with, it is worthwhile to ask around to find out who produces a good product.

Honey may also contain trace amounts of drugs used in treating various bee ailments, including antibiotics. If this is a concern to you, then it would be wise to investigate with your local honey producer what they may have used.

STORING HONEY

Honey is much easier to store than to select and buy. Pure honey won't mold, but may crystallize over time. Exposure to air and moisture may cause color to darken, flavor to intensify and may speed crystallization as well. Comb honey doesn't store as well liquid honey so you should not expect it to last as long.

Storage temperature is not as important for honey, but it should not be allowed to freeze or exposed to high temperatures if possible. Either can cause crystallization and heat may cause flavor to strengthen undesirably.

Filtered liquid honey will last the longest in storage. Storage containers should be opaque, airtight, moisture and odor-proof. Like any other stored food, honey should be rotated through the storage cycle and replaced with fresh product.

If crystallization does occur, honey can be reliquified by placing the container in a larger container of hot water until it has melted. Avoid adding water to honey you intend to keep in storage or it may ferment.

Avoid storing honey near heat sources or petroleum products (including gasoline/diesel engines), chemicals or any other odor-producing products which may infuse through plastic packaging.

RAW HONEY AND BOTULISM
From: Geri Guidetti arkinst@concentric.net

Duane Miles wrote:

If I recall correctly, honey contains very, very small amounts of the bacteria that cause botulism. For adults, this seldom causes problems. Our immune system is capable of dealing with small numbers of even nasty bacteria, they do it all the time. The problem is when we get large numbers of bacteria, or when our immune system is damaged or not yet developed.

That is where the problem with honey comes in. Some people used to use honey to sweeten milk or other foods for infants. Infants immune systems sometimes cannot handle the bacteria that cause botulism, and, of course, those infants became seriously ill. So pediatricians now advise strongly against using honey for children under a certain age.

Yes, raw honey can contain the temperature resistant spores of *Clostridium botulinum*, the bacterium that causes botulism. The organism is a strict anaerobe, meaning that it only grows in the absence of molecular oxygen. The problem with infants and honey is that the small, intestinal tract of an infant apparently is sufficiently anaerobic to allow the spores to germinate into actively growing *C. botulinum* organisms. Essentially, the infant serves the same role as a sealed, airtight, contaminated can of beans as far as the organisms are concerned. There in the infant's body the bacteria secrete the dangerous toxin that causes the symptoms of botulism. There have been quite a few documented infant deaths due to honey. As I recall, the studies identifying honey as the source were done in the '80s. Most pediatricians recommend no honey for the first year. It is probably best to check with your own for even later updates...Geri Guidetti, The Ark Institute

EDITOR'S NOTE: The advice not to give raw honey or foods containing raw honey to infants under one year of age still stands. Do please understand, though, that honey is not the only means by which infants can suffer from botulism, in many of which cases no certain source of contagion could ever be determined. The actual chances of any infant being stricken is very, very small and keeping the child's colon open, active and healthy can reduce it still more. Breast-fed children seem to be more resistant as well.

HONEY OUTGASSING

Q: My can of honey is bulging. Is it safe to use?

A: Honey can react with the can lining to release a gas especially when stored over a long period of time. Honey's high sugar content prevents bacteria growth. If there is no sign of mold growth, it is safe to eat. FREQUENTLY ASKED FOOD QUESTIONS, FN250

CANE SYRUPS

CANE SYRUP:

Seldom found in supermarkets pure cane syrup is a sweet symbol of the U.S. Deep South. Produced by boiling down the extracted juice of the sugarcane in much the same fashion as sorghum and maple syrups are produced. The best syrup is clear with a dark amber color and a smooth intense flavor. Cane syrup usually has to be purchased from roadside stands, living history recreations, farm festivals, or state and county fairs. Some syrup makers will add small quantities of lemon juice or corn syrup to deter crystallization. Flavored cane syrups can sometimes be found, but are usually a sign of inferior syrup.

MOLASSES:

A by-product of sugar refining, molasses is generally composed of sugars such as glucose that are resistant to crystallization, browning reaction products resulting from the syrup reduction process, and small amounts of minerals. Flavor can vary between brands, but is usually strong and the color dark and opaque. Sulfured molasses can sometimes be found but its intense flavor is unappealing to most. Brands labeled as 'blackstrap molasses' are intensely flavored.

SORGHUM SYRUP:

This is produced in the same manner as cane syrup, but sweet sorghum cane, rather than sugar cane, is used. Sorghum tends to have a thinner, slightly sourer taste than cane syrup. Good syrup should be a clear dark amber with a smooth flavor. It can sometimes be found in the supermarket, but more often is found in the same types of places as genuine sugar cane syrup.

TREACLE:

This sweetener comes in varying colors from a rather dark version, similar to, but not quite the same as blackstrap molasses, to paler versions more similar to golden syrup. If you cannot find it in your store's syrup area check in their imported foods section.

All of the above syrups are generally dark with a rich, heavy flavor.

GOLDEN SYRUP:

This syrup is both lighter and paler in color than any of the above four, more similar to what we would call a table syrup here in the U.S. Can usually be found in the same areas as treacle above.

TABLE SYRUP:

There are many table syrups sold in supermarkets, some with flavorings of one sort or another such as maple, various fruits, butter, etc. A close examination of the ingredients list will reveal mixtures usually of cane syrup, cane sugar syrup or corn syrup along with preservatives, colorings and other additives. Table syrup usually has a much less pronounced flavor than molasses, cane or sorghum syrup or the darker treacles. Any syrup containing corn syrup should be stored as corn syrup.

STORING CANE SYRUPS

All of the above syrups, except for those having corn syrup in their makeup, have the same storage characteristics. They can be stored on the shelf for about two years and up to a year after opening. Once they are opened, they are best kept in the refrigerator to retard mold growth. If mold growth does occur, the syrup should be discarded. The outside of the bottle should be cleaned of drips after each use. Some pure cane and sorghum syrups may crystallize in storage, but this causes no harm and they can be reliquified using the same method as for honey. Molasses or other sugar refining by-products won't usually crystallize, but will dry into an unmanageable tar unless kept sealed.

CORN SYRUP

Corn syrup is a liquid sweetener made by breaking down cornstarch into its constituent sugars through an enzyme reaction. Available in both a light and a dark form, the darker variety has a flavor similar to molasses and contains refiners syrup (a by-product of sugar refining). Both types often contain flavorings and preservatives. It is commonly used in baking and candy making because it does not crystallize when heated. Corn syrup is common in the U.S., but less so elsewhere.

Corn syrup stores poorly compared to other sweeteners and because of this it often has a best if used by date on the bottle. It should be stored in its original bottle, tightly capped, in a cool, dry place. New unopened bottles can be expected to keep about six months past the date on the label and sometimes longer.

After opening, keep the corn syrup four to six months. These syrups are prone to mold and to fermentation so be on the lookout for bubbling or a mold haze. If these present themselves, throw the syrup out. You should wipe off any drips from the bottle after every use.

MAPLE SYRUP

Maple syrup is produced by boiling down the sap of the maple tree (and a lot of it too) collected at certain times in the early Spring until it reaches a syrup consistency. This native American sweetener is slightly sweeter than table sugar and is judged by much the same criteria as honey: Lightness of color, clarity and taste. Making the syrup is energy and labor intensive so pure maple is generally expensive. Maple flavored pancake syrups are usually mixtures of corn and cane sugar syrups with either natural or artificial flavorings and should be kept and stored as corn syrups.

New unopened bottles of maple syrup may be kept on a cool, dark, shelf for up to two years. The sweetener may darken and the flavor get stronger, but it is still usable.

After the bottle has been opened, it should be refrigerated. It will last about a year. Be careful to look out for mold growth. If mold occurs, discard the syrup.

DAIRY PRODUCTS

Got milk? Butter? Cheese? In the refrigerator, right? Dairy products are a great source of essential amino acids, vitamin D, and calcium, but in their usual forms found in the refrigerator case of your local supermarkets are perishable commodities. Fortunately, there are a number of dairy products that lend themselves to food storage.

DRY MILKS

Dry, powdered milk is available in nearly as many varieties as the fresh fluid product. Most can be found on the shelves of your local supermarket while a few may have to come from rather more specialized suppliers. Skillfully and knowledgeably used they can vastly improve the quality of your food storage program.

NONFAT (skim):

This is pasteurized skim milk reduced to a powdered concentrate and is found in two forms - regular and instant. They are both made from the same type of milk, but the instant variety has been given further processing to make it more easily soluble in water than regular dry milk. Both types have essentially the same nutrient composition. The regular variety is more compact, requires less storage space than the instantized variety, usually costs somewhat less, but is a little more difficult to reconstitute. Instant dry milk is commonly available in nearly any grocery store. The regular type generally has to be sought out from baking and restaurant suppliers or storage food dealers. There is a retail brand by the name of "Milkman" that has a bit of fat content that makes it similar to 1% milk. The fat content means it should be stored like whole milk, described below.

It takes 3.2 oz or about 3 tablespoons of instant nonfat dry milk added to 32 oz of water to make 1 quart of milk you can drink or cook with like fresh milk. Combining the dry milk with water at least several hours before you plan to use it gives it time to dissolve fully and to develop a fresher flavor. Shaking the fluid milk vigorously will incorporate air and will also help to improve flavor. Add the powder to baked goods, gravies, smoothies, hot cereals, casseroles and meat loaf as a nutrition booster. It can also be used to make yogurt, cheese and most any cultured dairy product that does not require a high fat content. Several of the ways that we use dry milk powder is in making grits, oatmeal, and our favorite whole wheat bread. A few tablespoons of dry milk greatly improves the amino acid composition of any grain product.

FLAVORED NONFAT:

This may be found packaged in a variety of forms from a low calorie diet drink (artificially sweetened) to the other end of the scale, as cocoa mix or malted milk. The key ingredient is the dry milk so buy and store these products accordingly.

WHOLE MILK:

This is whole dry milk with all of its fat content (roughly 28% milkfat) and therefore has a shorter shelf life than nonfat. Other than that, it may be reconstituted and used in exactly the same way as nonfat dry milk. Dry whole milk can sometimes be found in the Hispanic foods area of grocery stores (Nido and Klim by Nestlé are the two brands I know), natural or health food stores, and some storage food suppliers carry it as well as institutional and restaurant foods businesses. It can also sometimes be found where camping and outback supplies are sold. Because of the high fat content this form of dry milk really needs to be either vacuum sealed or packaged with oxygen absorbers in gas impermeable containers such as canning jars, Mylar bags, etc. Rotate and use dry whole milk within two years, less if not packaged for long-term storage.

BUTTERMILK:

Dry buttermilk is for use in recipes calling for buttermilk. It can be reconstituted into liquid buttermilk, but it's not much like the fresh liquid product and is best used in baked goods. Since it has a slightly higher fat content than nonfat dry milk, it generally does not keep as long. If properly packaged it should keep for several years.

SOUR CREAM:

Made from cultured sweet cream like the fresh product then dried and processed into a powder. Like the real thing it has a high milkfat content (25-28%) and should be stored like whole milk using vacuum sealing and/or oxygen absorbers and kept in a cool place. Mixed with the proper amount of cold water it can be reconstituted into a rich, thick product much like fresh sour cream and can be used in a similar manner or just used as a powder to add a tangy richness to many foods. Properly stored in oxygen free packaging and kept in a cool environment it is possible to achieve about a three year shelf life.

MILK SUBSTITUTES:

There are a number of products on the market that purport to take the place of cow or goats milk. They range from soy "milk", rice or other grain "milks", and beverages based on milk components such as whey. If there is not a substantial fat content they may all be stored as you would nonfat dry milk. Those products with a significant fat content (above 1% by weight) should be stored as you would whole dry milk. Do keep in mind that nearly all of these products DO NOT have the same nutritional composition as either nonfat or whole milk. In storage food programs dairy products serve as important sources of high quality complete proteins, calcium, vitamin D and possibly vitamin A. If the milk substitute you're considering does not you'll need to find another adequate source of these important nutrients.

BUYING DRY MILK PRODUCTS

(a) - Be sure the dry milk you are buying has been fortified with vitamins A and D. All of the whole and nonfat dry milks I've seen come fortified with these two vitamins. The dry buttermilk does not come this way, at least the SACO brand does not. The flavored dry milks vary by manufacturer.

(b) - There should be no artificial colors or flavors. I believe it is illegal to add preservatives to any dry milk sold in the U.S. so a claim of "no preservatives" on the label is of no consequence. Other nations may be different, however.

(c) - "Extra Grade" on the label indicates the manufacturer has held to higher processing and quality standards and the milk is somewhat lower in fat, moisture and bacterial content, is more soluble, and has fewer scorched particles.

There are still some manufacturers of dry milk that sell ordinary Grade A product, but they are becoming fewer. Every brand of instant powdered milk in my local grocery store is the Extra Grade, even the generic store brand. This, too, may vary outside of the States.

(d) - If you'll be buying your milk in bulk from businesses such as restaurant and institutional foods suppliers be sure to specify "low-temperature spray process" dry milk. The high-temperature process dry milks will not give you a very desirable product unless you intend to use it solely for baking.

(e) - Try to buy your dried milk in containers of a size that makes sense for the level of consumption in the household. Once it is opened, powdered milk has a short shelf life before undesirable changes in flavor and nutrient content occurs. If you buy large packages and do not use much at one time, consider breaking it down and repackaging into smaller containers at the time of purchase. I vacuum seal mine in glass canning jars.

(f) - As with any storage food you buy, try to deal only with reputable dealers. It is particularly important to do this with dry milk because of its short shelf life and sensitivity to storage conditions. Check expiration dates, then date and rotate packages.

STORING DRY MILKS

Dry milk products are highly sensitive to environmental conditions, particularly temperature and moisture. Their vitamins A and D are also photosensitive and break down rapidly if exposed to light.

The area where your dry milk is stored should be kept as cool as possible. Air-conditioning or even refrigeration can greatly extend the nutrient shelf life.

If the storage container is transparent or translucent then it should be put into a second container opaque to light or stored in a dark room.

Dry milk will absorb moisture and odors from the air so storage containers should be impervious to both air and moisture. The drier it can be kept, the better it will keep which makes the use of desiccants is an excellent idea. Oxygen also speeds decomposition so vacuum sealing or oxygen absorbers will decrease the available oxygen. Because of its fine powdery texture gas flushing with nitrogen or carbon dioxide generally yields poor results.

If the dry milk you purchased was not packaged for long term storage then it should be repackaged right away.

I purchase the instant variety of dry skim, whole milk, and sometimes buttermilk powder at my local grocery and repack it at home. The method I now use is to pour the powder into clean, dry canning jars then vacuum seal them with my Tilia Foodsaver using the jar adapter then storing in the ubiquitous cool, dark place. They must be guarded against breakage, but they offer the advantage of not holding odors, thus allowing for reuse after cleaning. Since the glass is transparent they must be protected against light.

Clean, sound plastic one and two liter soda bottles can also be used, but probably should be used just once since the plastic is somewhat permeable and will hold odors.

If you have access to a can sealer, #10 cans make wonderful storage containers for dry milk, particularly if used in conjunction with O2 absorbers.

SHELF LIFE OF DRY MILKS

Dear Mr. Hagan:

Thank you for your e-mail today and for your interest in SACO Mix'nDrink Pure Skim Milk.

Our Mix'n Drink will keep its nutrition value for up to about two years if kept cool and dry, and the only vitamins that actually decrease over time are the vitamins A and D. These are not shelf-stable vitamins and are sensitive to heat and light. A good rule of thumb to follow is that the vitamins A and D will dissipate at a rate of about 20% every year if stored properly. The less heat and moisture the milk is exposed to, the better the vitamins will keep. A freezer could extend the shelf life, as long as the powder does not get moisture in it. If you had to put a time limit on the Mix'nDrink, for rotation purposes, I would date it at two years after the date of purchase.

After opening a package of dry milk, transfer the powder to a tightly covered glass or metal container (dry milk can pick up odors from plastic containers) and keep it in the refrigerator. Unsealed nonfat dry milk keeps for a few months; dry whole milk for a few weeks.

CANNED FLUID MILKS AND CREAMS

Preserved liquid milk comes in a number of forms, none of which are very similar to each other. The most common are as follows:

CANNED MILKS: These are commonly called UHT milks (Ultra High Temperature) for the packaging technique used to preserve them. They come in the same varieties as fresh liquid milks: Whole, 2%, 1% and skim. I've even found whipping cream in UHT packaging (Grand Chef - Parmalat), though this may be offered only in the commercial and restaurant trade. In the U.S. they all have vitamin D added. The lesser fat content milks do not keep as long as whole milk and their use by dates are correspondingly shorter term. This milk is packaged in aseptic laminated paper cartons. It has the same composition as fresh milk of the same type, and can be stored at room temperature because of the special pasteurizing process used. The milk has a boiled flavor, but less so than evaporated milk. The dates are usually for approximately six months. The milk is still usable past its date, but the flavor soon begins to go stale and the cream separates.

With a six-month shelf life this type of canned milk naturally requires a much faster rotation cycle than other types. Several companies sell flavored milks (chocolate, etc.) in this packaging, usually in the smaller single-serving sizes. UHT milk makes excellent yogurt, losing the boiled flavor.

EVAPORATED MILK: Made from fresh, unpasteurized milk using a vacuum-heating process that removes 60% of the water, the concentrate is heated, homogenized, and in the States, vitamin D is added. It is then sealed in cans and heated again to sterilize the contents. Some brands may have other nutrients and/or chemical stabilizers added so read can labels closely. A mixture of one part water and one part evaporated milk will have about the same nutritional value as an equal amount of fresh milk. It does not taste like fresh milk but many do not find the flavor to be disagreeable. Both whole and skim milk varieties are available with the higher fat content type having the best storage life. The typical recommended storage time is six months. There is generally no date or use by code on evaporated milk.

Some grocers along with health food stores carry canned, evaporated goat's milk, in a similar concentration.

SWEETENED CONDENSED MILK: A less processed product than evaporated milk. It starts with pasteurized milk combined with a sugar solution. The water is then extracted until the mixture is less than half its original weight. It is not heated because the high sugar content prevents spoilage. It's very rich as well: 8 oz contains 980 calories. Obviously with a greatly reduced water content and a high sugar level it won't taste like fresh milk but it does have many uses in cooking. Some use condensed milk to cream their coffee. This type too is available in whole and skim varieties.

A fairly new entry into the sweetened condensed milk field is Dulce de Leche a popular dessert item in Latin America. It's basically sweetened condensed milk that has been heated to the point that the sugar begins to brown which produces a rich tasting caramel dessert. In the past you had to make it yourself, but now it can be purchased ready made in the can. I have seen it in the canned/dry milk areas or the Hispanic/ethnic foods areas of many grocery stores here in Florida.

Although it is often hard to find, the condensed milk can label should have a stamped date code which indicates the date by which it should be consumed. Condensed milk may thicken and darken as it ages, but it is still edible.

CANNED CREAM: So far as I have found here in the U.S. only the Nestlé company produces canned creams, both being imports. One is "Media Crema" produced in Mexico with a pull-top can and the other is "Table Cream" produced in Australia in a standard (as in use an opener) can. There is a slight difference in preservatives and thickeners, but basically both are a shelf stable light cream which can be used in any way that you would use fresh light cream. I haven't yet determined a shelf-life for these products, but it seems to be in excess of two years in any decent storage environment. Like the Dulce de Leche above I found them either in the dry/canned milk areas or the Hispanic/ethnic areas of my local grocery stores. Would be worth looking or asking for in your local markets.

BUTTER

Butter can be found in several forms each with their particular strengths and weaknesses.

BUTTER POWDER: Probably the easiest to find of the shelf-stable butters the powder is a moisture free product consisting of butter fat condensed on milk solids generally with added antioxidants. It can be reconstituted by mixing with water to make a spread similar to whipped butter, but it cannot be used for frying or other applications requiring high heat that would burn the milk solids. Most butter powders have something of a milky taste due to the additional milk solids necessary to create the powder, but many do not find this objectionable. Because it is a powder (lots of surface area) with a high fat content it needs good packaging to keep it at its best. Vacuum sealing and/or oxygen absorbers will work well if you are doing your own packaging.

CLARIFIED BUTTER (GHEE): Another form of butter suitable for storage programs is clarified butter or ghee as it is known in India. This is fresh, unsalted butter gently heated to drive off the moisture with the remaining fat poured off of the butter solids. It can be purchased commercially but most choose to make it themselves. As it's essentially pure butterfat with no water there is little to spoil so will keep for years in a glass jar protected from oxygen, heat, and light. A good source of fat calories and useful in cooking, but maybe not something you'd want to spread on a biscuit.

CANNED BUTTER: For those whom only the real thing will do it's now possible to find shelf stable real butter. It seems mostly to be sold in those nations where home refrigeration is not as common as it is here in the U.S. As a rule I do not single out suppliers for any given product but at the time of this writing (11/2003) the only U.S. importer of shelf stable canned butter I've been able to find is Bruce Hopkin's Internet Grocer (http://www.internet-grocer.com). His product is Red Feather brand canned butter from New Zealand. It is salted though not as heavily as most salted butter in the U.S. The manufacturer claims an eighteen month shelf-stable storage life though they do advise keeping it in a cool, dry place. Like all butter it will liquefy it allowed to warm too much. Each can contains twelve ounces (equivalent to about three sticks of butter) and once opened should be handled like any other butter.

CHEESE

There are a number of shelf-stable cheese products that are suited for storage programs. Each of them have particular strengths or weaknesses for given uses. The basic forms storage cheeses can take are:

CANNED CHEESE: Actually, it's "Pasteurized Processed Cheddar Cheese Product" but it's the closest thing to a shelf-stable real cheese that I've yet found. It's another one of those products produced for use in countries where home refrigeration is scarcer than it is here in the U.S. The only brand available in the States that I know of at this time is made by Kraft's Australian division whose product most resembles a mild white cheddar or perhaps an American cheese. The only U.S. source for this cheese that I have found thus far is again Bruce Hopkin's Internet Grocer (http://www.internet-grocer.com). It comes in an eight ounce can and the manufacturer claims it will keep "indefinitely" at any reasonable storage temperature.

DRIED GRATED CHEESES: These are the familiar grated dry Parmesan and Romano cheeses, possibly others as well. They're generally a coarse dry powder, low or nonfat, and often with a fair amount of salt. Kept dry, cool, and dark they'll keep as they come from the store for several years though to get the maximum possible shelf life you should vacuum seal them in glass. Usually fairly expensive for the amount you get but as they're also strongly flavored a little will go a long way.

CHEESE SAUCES AND SOUPS: These are products such as Cheez Whiz, Campbell's Cheddar Cheese Soup, chip dips and related. They're not really cheese, but a mixture of cheese, milk, flour, and other ingredients. Depending on what your end uses may be they can provide a cheese flavor, calories, and a degree of protein, fat, and calcium. In any decent storage conditions they'll keep for several years at least. Aerosol cheese is an abomination that will not be discussed here.

POWDERED CHEESE: Used in products such as boxed macaroni and cheese, au gratin potatoes, snacks, and the like, this is basically cheese that has had its moisture removed leaving behind mostly protein, fat, a fair amount of calcium and various flavoring and coloring compounds (naturally occurring or added) along with a fair amount of salt. It can't really be melted, but it can add a nice cheese flavor where a real cheese texture is not needed.

There are also cheese powder blends, typically a mixture of cheese powder, food starch, whey, milk solids and other non-cheese ingredients. It has less fat than true cheese powder, about the same protein, but less calcium. You can make it yourself with dry milk and cornstarch so there's little point in not getting real cheese powder.

Cheese powder will keep for many years in sealed metal cans kept at cool temperatures. You'll probably have to get it from restaurant foods suppliers or order it from storage foods dealers. It's high fat content means that it needs low-oxygen packaging.

EGGS

The noble fruit of the hen, eggs play an important role in the kitchen arts. Unfortunately, outside of regular runs to the store to buy fresh eggs or keeping your own hens (which is what I do) they're problematical to store. There are two basic ways to keep eggs for those times when fresh eggs may be hard to come by. One is to preserve them in the shell, a process which must be done at home as there are no commercial sources of preserved shell eggs that I know of. The second is to buy dry, or powdered, eggs. I may address home shell egg preservation in a future FAQ update but for now I will concentrate on dry eggs which anyone can buy.

DRY EGGS
Dry eggs are generally available in four different forms – whole eggs, egg whites, egg yolks, and as a mix for making scrambled eggs and omelets. Which you should buy depends on how you expect to use them. As a general rule I find dry eggs reconstitute more easily when mixed with warm (not hot) water. Mixing the dry powder with other dry ingredients before adding liquids also increases the ease by which they can be reconstituted. Allowing the eggs to sit a few minutes before using improves water adsorption.

WHOLE EGGS: This is everything but the shell and the water. Usually found in the form of a somewhat clumpy, eggy smelling yellow powder. Typically one tablespoon of whole egg powder mixed with two tablespoons of water will equal one large fresh egg. Can be used to make most anything you'd make with fresh eggs though personally I prefer to use them in baking rather than as scrambled eggs or omelets. Whole egg powder is commonly used in baking mixes of all kinds, but I've never seen plain powdered eggs for sale in any grocery. Fortunately, they're easy to come by from mail order suppliers. A #10 can of powdered eggs is quite a lot so give some thought as to how fast you might use them and either order smaller cans, repackage an opened can into smaller containers, or plan on eating eggs often.

EGG WHITES: Nearly pure protein, egg white powder can add a high-protein boost to anything you put it in. The powder itself is whitish in color and not as clumpy as whole egg powder. When properly reconstituted it will whip into meringue like fresh egg whites and can be used in producing angel food and sponge cakes. Dry egg whites are often found in the baking section of many supermarkets. The brand name I have seen is "Just Whites" by Deb El. Powdered egg whites are also available from many mail order suppliers.

EGG YOLKS: High protein, high fat, and a source of lecithin (a natural emulsifier). Egg yolk powder can add richness and flavor to any number of foods, used to make custards, sauces, noodles, even mayonnaise. Not generally as easy to find as whole eggs and whites, but can be mail ordered. Being pure yolks this powder has a high fat content and most be appropriately packaged to achieve a good shelf life.

EGG MIX OR SCRAMBLING MIX: Typically a mix of whole egg powder, nonfat milk powder, oil, and salt. Used for making scrambled eggs, omelets, or general egg cookery. This mix does offer a degree of convenience but you can easily make it yourself and save the trouble of having to store it as a separate product.

STORING DRY EGGS

All dry egg products are exceedingly sensitive to moisture and will go off quickly if allowed to become the least bit damp. Whole eggs, egg yolks, and egg mix have high fat contents which make them very sensitive to oxygen. I highly recommend vacuum sealing in glass jars or using oxygen absorbers in conjunction with some other form of high barrier property packaging to keep these products at their best. If you bought quality products, packaged them well in oxygen free packaging, and put them away in a good storage environment then whole eggs, egg yolks, and egg mix should be able to achieve at least a three year shelf life, possibly more. Egg whites will easily achieve five years. Naturally, if you're packaging your eggs in any sort of transparent or translucent packaging then they should be stored in a dark place.

INFANT FORMULA

While not universal, it's safe to say that most folks interested in food storage are planning for families, real or as yet hypothetical. Many of these families include children (or hope to) under the age of two. Very young children such as this have nutritional requirements that are different from adults and require somewhat different preparations than adults or even older children.

If at all possible, it's best for children up to the age of six months to be breast fed by their mothers and up to the age of one year breast milk should contribute a significant portion of the child's nutritional intake. Indeed, breast feeding can supplement a child's diet in an important way until age two. Even the American Academy of Pediatrics now recognizes and recommends this. There are those who nurse even longer, but I mention this only as an observation, not necessarily as a recommendation. For the preparedness-minded breast feeding makes particularly good sense as mama can consume a far wider range of storable foods than a baby can, and she can produce from those foods a nutrition source perfectly suited to her child.

To promote this end here is the contact information for the largest and best known breast feeding support group.

La Leche League International 1400 N. Meacham Road Schaumburg, IL (USA) 60173-4808 Web: http://www.lalecheleague.org

They can help you to find local chapters of the League in your area and point out useful books and sources of information. When our daughter was born my wife has attended a number of our local chapter's meetings and borrowed books with which to educate ourselves.

Also in this same line, there is a useful document put out by the World Health Organization titled How to Breastfeed During an Emergency. It apparently is no longer hosted on any WHO sites so I have taken the liberty of hosting it myself at:

http://athagan.members.atlantic.net/PFSFAQ/Breastfeeding_in_an_emergency.html

It would be an excellent idea to print out a few copies and put them away. You never know who you might come across who'll desperately such information should there come a Fall.

ALTERNATIVES TO BREASTFEEDING

If breastfeeding should not be a viable option you'll need to find another source of infant nutrition. I STRONGLY RECOMMEND AGAINST USING HOME-MADE INFANT FORMULAS AS A SOLE SOURCE OF NUTRITION FOR A BABY. If you know you're going to have a nursing infant on your hands, if and when the balloon should go up, you should take steps in advance of the crisis to put away a suitable food supply for the child. Young children have nutritional needs that are different from those of adults or even older children. Lacking human breast milk, you should put by a store of commercially made infant formula. Evaporated milk, dry milk, sweetened condensed milk, goat's milk and all the rest can be an important *supplement* for children over the age of six months, particularly over one year of age. For children under six months of age these products simply do not contain sufficient amounts of the appropriate nutrients to provide adequate nutrition when used as the sole source of sustenance.

As for soy milk, there are considerable important differences in soy nutritional content compared to cow's milk which is to say nothing of human milk. Soy milk alone is simply not nutritious enough to serve as a sole source of nutrition for children under the age of six months and should not be used as more than a *supplement* for children over six months of age. This does not apply to commercially made *soy protein infant formula* which is a very different product than soy milk.

SELECTING AND FEEDING AN INFANT FORMULA

If the child you're concerned with is already on the scene then you probably already know which formula you need to put away. Unless instructed against doing so by your doctor, my only suggestion here is to make sure the formula has iron in it. The problems of iron in formulas from the nineteen fifties and sixties have long ago been solved and young children very much need this nutrient.

If you feel the need to store formula in advance for a child not yet on the scene (or who is only a contingency to plan against) I suggest storing one of the *cow's milk based lactose-free formulas*. Two brand names that will work well are "Lactofree" from Mead Johnson and "Similac Lactose Free" from Ross Laboratories. Lactose is the sugar found in milk and an inability to properly digest lactose is the most common source of infant formula feeding problems. Of course, there is the remote chance the child could have a true allergy to cow's milk protein, but the child could be allergic to soy protein too. It's been known to happen for a child to be allergic to both at the same time. There is no absolute certainty in preparedness, but you can plan for the most likely problems which is why I suggest storing lactose free cow's milk formula.

Unless you store only disposable bottles and "ready to feed" formula, don't forget that both reconstituting formula from dry powder or liquid concentrates and washing feeding equipment requires the use of clean, safe drinking water. You'll need to carefully examine your water storage in this regard.

STORING INFANT FORMULAS AND BABY FOODS

Storing infant formula and baby food is easy. Infant foods are one of the few areas in which the (US) Federal government regulates shelf life labeling. All containers of infant formula and baby food should have a clear "best used by" or similar date somewhere on the container which is generally longer than a child will require such food. Unopened containers of formula should be stored the same way you would keep dry milk, in a dark, cool, dry place and used before the date on the container is reached. Opened containers of dry formula powder should be used within one month of opening and the contents should be kept bone dry, cool and in the dark.

If it hasn't been needed by the time the expiration date begins to near it's an excellent idea to donate the infant formula to a nursing infant or organization like a food bank that can put it to use before it expires. There's too much valuable high quality nutrition in infant formula to allow it to go to waste.

Spencer W. Kimball (1895–1985) Twelfth President of the Church

"We encourage you to grow all the food that you feasibly can on your own property. Berry bushes, grapevines, fruit trees—plant them if your climate is right for their growth. Grow vegetables and eat them from your own yard. Even those residing in apartments or condominiums can generally grow a little food in pots and planters. … Make your garden as neat and attractive as well as productive. If there are children in your home, involve them in the process with assigned responsibilities" ("Family Preparedness," *Ensign,* May 1976, 124).

"We want you to be ready with your personal storehouse filled with at least a year's supply. You don't argue why it cannot be done, you just plan to organize and get it done" Spencer W. Kimball, Aug 1976

FATS AND OILS

All oils are fats, but not all fats are oils. They are similar to each other in their chemical makeup, but what makes one an oil and another a fat is the percentage of hydrogen saturation in the fatty acids of which they are composed. The fats which are available to us for culinary purposes are actually mixtures of differing fatty acids so for practical purposes we'll say saturated fats are solid at room temperature (70ºF, 21º C) and the unsaturated fats we call oils are liquid at room temperature. For dietary and nutrition purposes fats are generally classified as saturated, monounsaturated and polyunsaturated, which is a further refinement of the amount of saturation of the particular compositions of fatty acids in the fats.

BUYING AND STORING OILS AND FATS

There is a problem with storing oils and fats for the long term and that is they want to go rancid. Rancid fats have been implicated in increased rates of heart disease, arteriosclerosis and are carcinogenic (cancer causing) so are best avoided whenever possible.

Oxygen is eight times more soluble in fat than in water and it is the oxidation resulting from this exposure that is the primary cause of rancidity. The less saturated a fat is, the faster it will go off. This may not, at first, be readily apparent because vegetable oils have to become several times more rancid than animal fats before our noses can easily detect it. An extreme example of rancidity is the linseed oil (flaxseed) that we use as a wood finish and a base for oil paints. In a matter of hours the oil oxidizes into a solid polymer. This is very desirable for wood and paint, very undesirable for food.

Because of this difficulty in storing fats and oils for any long period of time many books and articles on the subject of food storage make only passing mention of them, if they say anything at all. This is unfortunate because fat contains *nine* calories to the gram compared to the *four* calories contained by either carbohydrates or protein. This makes fat a valuable source of concentrated calories that could be of real importance if faced with a diet consisting largely of unrefined grains and legumes. For small children, infants, nursing mothers, and the elderly, they may not be able to consume the volume of food that would be necessary in the course of a day to get all of the calories they would need to avoid weight loss and possible malnutrition. Additionally, fats play an important role in our perception of taste and texture and their absence would make many foods more difficult to prepare and consume. Furthermore, a small amount of dietary fat is necessary for our bodies to properly absorb fat soluble vitamins like A,D,E and K.

Long term storage of fats may be problematical, but it is not impossible. There are some general rules you can follow to get the most life out of your stored cooking oils and fats.

#1 - Exposure to oxygen, light and heat are the greatest factors to rancidity. If you can, refrigerate your stored oil, particularly after it's been opened. If possible, buy your oils in opaque, airtight containers. If you purchase it in plastic, particularly clear plastic, then transfer it to a gas impermeable glass or metal container that can be sealed airtight. If you have a means of doing so, vacuum sealing the storage container is an excellent idea as it removes most of the air remaining inside, taking much of the oxygen with it. Transparent glass and plastic containers should be stored in the dark, such as in a box or cabinet. Regardless of the storage container, it should be stored at as cool a temperature as possible and rotated as fast as is practical. All other considerations being equal, oils and fats with preservatives will have a greater shelf life than those without, provided they are fresh when purchased.

#2 - Unless they have been specially treated, most unopened cooking oils have a shelf life of about a year to a year and a half, depending upon the above conditions. Some specialty oils such as sesame and flax seed have shorter usable lives. If you don't use a lot, try to not buy your fats in big containers. This way you won't be exposing a large quantity to the air after opening, to grow old and possibly rancid, before you can use it all up. Once opened, it is an excellent idea to refrigerate cooking fats. If it turns cloudy or solid, the fat is still perfectly usable and will return to its normal liquid, clear state after it has warmed to room temperature. Left at room temperatures, opened bottles of cooking oils can begin to rancid in anywhere from a week to a couple of months, though it may take several more months to reach such a point of rancidity that it can be noticeably smelled.

#3 - Although darker colored oils have more flavor than paler colored, the agents that contribute to that flavor and color also contribute to faster rancidity. For maximum shelf life buy paler colored oils.

EXTENDING SHELF LIFE BY ADDING

ANTI-OXIDANTS

I take no position on doing this, but if obtaining the maximum possible shelf life in your cooking fats is important to you, it is possible to add antioxidant preservatives to the fat you have purchased. Used in conjunction with a gas impermeable container, either opaque in color or stored in a dark place, and cool storage temperatures (70º F 21ºC or less) then shelf life can be extended to about five years, possibly longer.

The antioxidant in question is Butylated HydroxyToluene (BHT). It is often used in the food industry to slow the development of off-flavors, odors and color changes caused by oxidation, mostly in foods with significant fat contents. BHT is on the U.S. Food and Drug Administration's Generally Recognized As Safe (GRAS) list as a common preservative. The FDA limits the use of BHT to 0.02% or 200 parts per million (ppm) of the oil or fat content of a food product. The directions that I give below will be for the FDA limit. BHT is available over the counter in the retail trade, typically found in health or natural foods stores or vitamin and nutritional supplement suppliers. It may also be found from various suppliers on the Internet.

To get the best results you will need the freshest oil you can find. Purchasing from a large, busy supermarket will usually suffice. You'll also need containers that are gas impermeable such as glass jars, or metal cans. There may be plastic containers with high gas barrier properties that will also serve, but I cannot knowledgeably say about this. It is important that your containers be food grade, clean, dry and dust-free. In keeping with the FDA's GRAS guidelines you want to add 5.3mg of BHT crystals per fluid ounce of oil or fat. If you're using a scale calibrated in grains, such as a reloading powder scale, you may use the following table.

HT in grains	OIL	BHT in milligrams
0.1 grain	1 fl oz	5.3 mg
0.7 grain	8 fl oz (1 cup)	42.4 mg
1.3 grain	16 fl oz (1 pint)	84.8 mg
2.6 grain	32 fl oz (1 quart)	169.6 mg
5.2 grain	64 fl oz (1/2 gal)	339.2 mg
10.3 grain	128 fl oz (1 gallon)	678.4 mg

*NOTE: The grain weight measurements have been rounded up to the nearest tenth grain since most powder scales will not accurately measure less than one-tenth of a grain. **IMPORTANT NOTE:** If you are using a reloading powder scale, be sure the balance pan is clean and the balance has been calibrated recently with a reliable set of check weights.*

Remove the BHT crystals from their gelatin capsules and weigh them, if you're going to. Once you have the appropriate amount, add the crystals to a pint or so of the oil, shaking vigorously. It may take several hours for the preservative to dissolve completely. Bringing the oil up to a warm, NOT HOT, temperature will speed the process. Once completely dissolved, pour the antioxidant laden oil into the rest of the oil and mix thoroughly. Once mixed, the oil can then be poured into its storage containers leaving approximately 1/2 inch of headspace. If you have a vacuum sealer the jars or cans may be vacuum sealed to remove most of the oxygen laden air from the container, otherwise just seal the lid. Store in a cool place and if using transparent jars, be certain to put them in a larger container such as a box to keep the contents in the dark. Don't forget to label and date the jars.

Before I close out this section on fats and oils, please allow me to reemphasize that no amount of preservatives that can be added to your stored fats will substitute for proper storage and rotation. *Don't sit on your oil supply for years without rotating it.* **A little bit rancid is a little bit poisonous.** *'Nuff said.*

COOKING ADJUNCTS

BAKING POWDER
Baking powder is a combination of an acid and an alkali with starch added to keep the other two ingredients stable and dry. The powder reacts with liquid by foaming and the resulting bubbles of carbon dioxide can aerate and raise dough. Almost all baking powder now on the market is double acting, meaning it has one acid that bubbles at room temperature and another acid which only reacts at oven temperatures. Unless a recipe specifies otherwise, this is the type to use.

Don't expose baking powder to steam, humid air, wet spoons, or other moisture. Store in a tightly lidded container for no more than a year. Even when kept bone dry it will eventually loses its potency. To test its strength, measure 1 tsp powder into 1/3 cup hot water. The mixture should fizz and bubble furiously. If it doesn't, throw it out.

For those folks concerned with aluminum in the diet, the Rumford brand has none and there may be others.

BAKING SODA
This gritty powder is sodium bicarbonate also known as sodium acid bicarbonate ($NaHCO3$), a mild alkali. When combined with an acid ingredient such as buttermilk it is used in baking to leaven quick breads and other baked foods working in the same manner as baking powder. It can also be used to make hominy. When combined with an acid ingredient, the bicarbonate reacts to give off carbon dioxide bubbles which causes the baked good to rise. If kept well sealed in an air- and moisture-proof container its storage life is indefinite. If kept in the cardboard box it usually comes in, it will keep for about eighteen months. Do keep in mind that baking soda is a wonderful odor absorber. If you don't want your baked goods tasting of whatever smells it absorbed then keeping it in an airtight container is a good idea.

HERBS AND SPICES
It is difficult to give exact instructions on how best to store culinary herbs and spices because there are dozens of different seeds, leaves, roots, barks, etc., we call an herb or

L Tom Perry Nov. 1995

Quote: *"Now you ask where do I get the money for these things. I agree I need them, but I'm having a hard time making ends meet. Here is how you do it: Use one or more of the following suggestions: <u>Food Storage Christmas</u>: Use 25-50% of money for food storage, <u>New Clothes</u>: Don't buy instead make it last a few more months, use that money for FS, <u>Vacation/Holiday</u>: no vacation or holiday until FS complete, <u>Recreation</u>: Cut by 50%, use money for FS, find fun, free things to make lasting memories, <u>Snowmobiles/campers/boats</u>: sell or trade to get year supply, <u>Change Diet</u>: Eat cheaper foods and use extra money for food storage....*

"The Lord will make it possible, if we make a firm commitment, for every LDS family to have a year's supply of food reserves...

"I believe it is time, and perhaps with some *urgency*, to review the counsel we have received in dealing with our personal and family preparedness. ...With events in the world today, *it must be considered with all seriousness*. We are not in a situation that requires panic buying but the instability in the world today makes it imperative that we take heed this counsel and prepare for the future."

a spice. There are, however, some general rules that may be followed to best preserve their flavors. All spices, particularly dried, are especially sensitive to heat, air, moisture, and light. Room temperature is satisfactory for storage but refrigeration or freezing is even better. What ever you do they should be kept away from heat sources. It is common for the household spice cabinet or shelf to be located over the stove, but this is really about the worst possible place to keep herbs and spices even if it is convenient. Dark opaque glass is best for storage, but failing that, keeping a tightly sealed glass container in a dark place is next best. The cellophane packets some products come in won't do. Tightly sealed metal containers will work as well. Even dense plastic will do, but glass is best.

Where possible, buy spices whole. Whole nutmegs will keep their flavor far longer than ground nutmeg, the same for other seeds and roots. You'll have to use a grater, grinder or whatever, but the difference in flavor is worth it.

If you buy spices in bulk containers (which is certainly cheaper) consider transferring some into smaller containers and keeping the larger one tightly sealed in a cool, dark place. This will prevent unwanted light and air from continually getting in and playing havoc. My large jars of reserve spices are kept in vacuum sealed jars with smaller jars of ready spices kept in the kitchen.

There are many mail order or online suppliers of bulk herbs and spices. My personal favorite is Penzey's (http://www.penzeys.com). Their products have been consistently excellent with good prices. It's worth investigating some of these companies as they can really take the sting out of purchasing large quantities.

SALT

Storage life for salt is indefinite. So long as you do not let it become contaminated with dirt or whatever, it will never go bad. Over time, iodized salt may turn yellow, but this is harmless and can still be used. Salt is rather hygroscopic and will adsorb moisture from the air if not sealed in an airtight container. If it does cake up, it can be dried in the oven and then pulverized again with no harm done.

All salt, however, is not the same. Salt comes in a number of different varieties, and very little of what is produced in the U.S. is intended for use in food. The rest of it, about 98%, has other uses. Therefore, it is important to be certain the salt you have is intended for human consumption. Once you are satisfied it is, you should then determine its appropriateness for the tasks to which you might want to set it to. Below is a list of some of the available salts

TABLE SALT: This is by far the most widely known type of salt. It comes in two varieties; iodized and non-iodized. There is an ingredient added to adsorb moisture so the salt will stay free flowing in damp weather. This non-caking agent does not dissolve in water and can cause cloudiness in solutions if sufficiently large quantities are used. In canning this won't cause a problem since little per jar is used. For pickling, though, it would be noticeable. If you are storing salt for this purpose, you should be sure to choose plain pickling salt, or other food grade pure salt such as kosher salt. In the iodized varieties, the iodine can cause discoloration or darkening of pickled foods. For folks in areas that are historically iodine deficient a store of iodized salt for table consumption should be kept.

CANNING SALT: This is pure salt and nothing but salt. It can usually be found in the canning supplies section of most grocery stores. This is the preferred salt for most food preservation or storage uses. It is generally about the same grain size as table salt.

KOSHER SALT: This salt is not really, in itself, kosher, but is used in "kashering" meat to make the flesh kosher for eating. This involves first soaking the meat then rubbing it with the salt to draw out the blood which is not-kosher and is subsequently washed off along with the salt. The cleansed meat is then kosher. What makes it of interest for food storage and preservation is that it is generally pure salt suitable for canning, pickling and meat curing. It is of a larger grain size than table or canning salt, and usually rolled to flake the grains for easier dissolving. Frequently it is slightly cheaper than canning salt and usually easier to find in urban/suburban areas.

NOTE: Not all brands of kosher salt are exactly alike. Diamond Crystal Kosher Salt is the only brand that I'm aware of that is not flaked, but still in its unaltered crystal form. The Morton brand of Coarse Kosher Salt has "yellow prussiate of soda" added as an anti-caking agent but unlike other anti-caking agents it does not cause cloudiness in solution. Morton even gives a kosher dill pickle recipe on the box.

Whether flaked or in its unaltered crystal form, kosher salt takes up more volume for an equivalent amount of mass than does canning salt. If it is important to get a precise amount of salt in your pickling or curing recipe you may want to weigh the salt to get the correct amount.

SEA SALT: This type of salt comes in about as many different varieties as coffee and from many different places around the world. The "gourmet" versions can be rather expensive. In general, the types sold in grocery stores, natural food markets and gourmet shops have been purified enough to use in food. It's not suitable for food preservation, though, because the mineral content it contains (other than the sodium chloride) may cause discoloration of the food.

ROCK or ICE CREAM SALT: This salt comes in large chunky crystals and is intended primarily for use in home ice cream churns to lower the temperature of the ice filled water in which the churn sits. It's also sometimes used in icing down beer kegs or watermelons. It is used in food preservation by some, but none of the brands I have been able to find label it as food grade nor do they specifically mention its use in foods so I would not use it for this purpose.

SOLAR SALT: This is also sometimes confusingly called "sea salt". It is not, however, the same thing as the sea salt found in food stores. Most importantly, it is not food grade. It's main purpose is for use in water softeners. The reason it is called "solar" and sometimes "sea salt" is that it is produced by evaporation of sea water in large ponds in various arid areas of the world. This salt type is not purified and still contains the desiccated remains of whatever aquatic life might have been trapped in it. Those organic remains might react with the proteins in the foods you are attempting to preserve and cause it to spoil.

HALITE: For those of us fortunate enough to live where it is warm, halite is the salt that is used on roads to melt snow and ice. It, too, is not food grade and should not be used in food preservation. This form of salt is also frequently called rock salt, like the rock salt above, but neither are suitable for food use.

SALT SUBSTITUTES: These are other kinds of metal salts such as potassium chloride used to substitute for the ordinary sodium chloride (NaCl) salt we are familiar with. They have their uses, but should not be used in foods undergoing a heated preservation processing, as they can cause the product to taste bad. Even the heat from normal cooking is sometimes sufficient to cause this.

VINEGAR

There is vinegar and then there is vinegar and it is not all alike. The active ingredient in all vinegars is *acetic acid*, but how the sour stuff was made can vary widely. The most common vinegar is *white distilled* which is actually diluted distilled acetic acid and not true vinegar at all. It keeps pretty much indefinitely if tightly sealed in a plastic or glass bottle with a plastic cap. The enamel coated metal caps always seem to get eaten by the acid over time. It is usually about 5-6% acetic acid and for pickling it is the type most often called for.

The next most common is *apple cider vinegar* which is available in two varieties. A cider *flavored* distilled acetic acid type and a *true cider vinegar* fermented from hard cider. Either will store indefinitely at room temperature until a sediment begins to appear on the bottom. Non-distilled vinegar will sometimes develop a cloudy substance. This is called a *mother of vinegar* and it is harmless. As long as the liquid does not begin to smell foul it can be filtered out through cheesecloth or a coffee filter and rebottled in a clean container. The mother can even be used to make more vinegar. If it begins to smell bad, however, it's gone over and should be tossed out.

The more exotic *wine, balsalmic, malt, rice* and other vinegars can be stored like cider vinegar. Age and exposure to light and air, however, eventually begin to take their toll on their delicate flavors. Tightly capped in a cool, dark cabinet or refrigerator is best for their storage.

YEAST

Yeast is just not a product you can stow away and forget about until you need it in a few years. After all, this single celled microscopic fungus is a living organism so if it's not alive at the time you need it, you'll get no action. When we incorporate yeast into our bread dough, beer wort or fruit juice it begins to ferment madly (we hope) and produce several by-products. If you're baking, the by-product you want is carbon dioxide which is trapped by the dough and subsequently causes it to rise. In brewing or vintning what is wanted is the ethyl alcohol and, if the drink is to be carbonated, the carbon dioxide as well.

Almost all yeasts used for these purposes are in the same genus (*Saccharomyces* or sugar fungi), but several different species or strains within species have evolved and some are more suitable for a particular task than others. It's entirely possible to use grocery store bread yeast to brew beer or ferment wine, but the flavor may leave a great deal to be desired. It's also possible to use yeast from ale brewing to make bread. From my limited experience with trying it myself the results were pretty much indistinguishable from bread yeast.

Types of Baking Yeasts

Leaving aside the brewing and vintning yeasts that are outside the scope of this FAQ I am going to concentrate on bread yeast. It comes in two generally available forms; *compressed* or *fresh yeast* and *dried yeast* which is further broken down into *active dry yeast* and *rapid acting* also known as *rapid rise* or *bread machine yeasts*. Although both of the dry yeasts are in the same species they come from different genetic strains with different performance characteristics and are processed somewhat differently from each other.

COMPRESSED (FRESH) YEAST: Compressed yeast is only partly dried (about 70% moisture), requires refrigeration and keeps even better in a deep freezer. If kept in an air- and moisture-tight container to prevent desiccation this type of yeast will keep for a year in the freezer (0ºF, −17ºC or less), but only about two weeks in the refrigerator. Unless your kitchen is quite chilly it will not keep on the shelf. It should

not have a mottled color or a sour odor. Compressed Yeast is generally available in 0.6-ounce and 2-ounce foil-wrapped cakes. For traditional baking, dissolve compressed yeast in warm (90°-95°F, 32º-35ºC) liquids. A 0.6-ounce cake will leaven up to 4 cups of flour (about a pound). A 2-ounce cake will leaven about 12 cups or roughly three pounds of flour.

ACTIVE DRY YEAST: A granular powder with about an 8% moisture content, active dry yeast can be found in either single use foil packets or vacuum packed foil covered one pound 'bricks'. In general bread making active dry yeast is typically dissolved in water (105º-115ºF, 40º-46ºC) along with an equal amount of sugar to give it time to resuscitate and actively begin growing before being mixed into the dry ingredients. Bread machines, however, are often different in this regard and you should follow the directions your particular machine's manufacturer gives. Mine calls for putting the dry yeast atop the other dry ingredients completely out of contact with the liquid ingredients until the machine mixes them together. One envelope (roughly 2 ¼ teaspoons) is sufficient to leaven about four cups or roughly one pound of flour.

RAPID ACTING & BREAD MACHINE YEAST: A more finely granulated powder with a lower moisture content than standard active dry yeast the rapid acting version is designed to raise bread as much as fifty percent faster. This lends it to the 'quick' or 'rapid' cycles of many bread machines that eliminate one rise cycle of the bread dough to facilitate faster production. This form of yeast is also generally mixed with a small amount of ascorbic acid which acts as a dough conditioner to give improved rise performance. Rapid Acting yeasts often perform poorly in recipes calling for long fermentation periods. Because of its finer granulation it does not need to be dissolved in liquid first and should be added to the dry ingredients instead. In the case of bread machines follow the manufacturer's directions. One envelope (roughly 2 ¼ teaspoons) is sufficient to leaven about four cups or roughly one pound of flour.

Interchanging Yeast Types

Can fresh, active dry, and rapid acting yeasts be used interchangeably?

Yes, to a certain extent. To substitute Rapid Acting yeasts for Active Dry yeasts reduce the amount of Rapid Acting used by 25% from the amount of Active Dry the recipe calls for then add the dry yeast to the dry ingredients before mixing.

To substitute Active Dry for Rapid Acting increase the amount of Active Dry by 25% over what the recipe calls for of Rapid Acting yeast and dissolve in warm water (105º-115ºF, 40º-46ºC) with an equal amount of sugar before mixing in with the dry ingredients.

Once 0.6 ounce cake of fresh, compressed yeast is roughly equivalent to one pack of active dry yeast (2 1/4 teaspoons) or to about 1 3/4 teaspoons of Rapid Acting yeast.

NOTE: Substituting one yeast type for another can be done, but will oft times require a bit of tweaking. If at all possible use the yeast type specified in the recipe. If you can't be prepared to make adjustments where necessary.

PROOFING YEAST: Although it's generally not necessary anymore if you are concerned that your yeast may be dead due to age or poor storage conditions any type of yeast can be tested for viability by *proofing*. This is nothing more than mixing a small amount of the yeast with an equal amount of sugar in warm water 105º-115ºF, 40º-46ºC for dried; 90°-95°F, 32º-35ºC for fresh. Within about five to ten minutes active yeast will become bubbly and begin to expand (at normal room temperature). Yeast which only slowly becomes active can still be used, but you will have to use more. If there is no activity at all, the yeast is dead and should be tossed. If you've stored your yeast in half-way decent conditions, or better yet in the freezer, proofing will usually not be necessary.

NOTE: Rapid Acting yeast loses its fast rising capabilities if dissolved in liquid for proofing, and will require two complete rises like standard active dry yeast.

STORING YEAST: All of the dry yeasts will last for months on the shelf, until the expiration date which should be clearly stamped on the package. If packaged in an air/moisture tight container and kept in the freezer it may last for several years though one year is the general recommendation most often found among various authorities. I'm presently (12/2003) using yeast stored in my refrigerator freezer in a tightly sealed canning jar with a "Best Used By" date of June, 1998 that is still going strong. The larger packs of yeast should be transferred to an air and moisture tight container after opening. A canning jar with a decent lid will suffice.

There is another means of providing leavening for breads besides buying yeast from a grocery store and that is by using a sourdough starter. I'm not going to address it here, but I will point out that it has a Usenet newsgroup all its own (*rec. food.sourdough*) which has several FAQ's devoted to it. You can find addresses for these FAQs in the Resources section. Drop in and read for awhile and you'll learn more than you thought you could ever want to know.

Ezra Taft Benson (1899–1994) Thirteenth President of the Church

"Too often we bask in the comfortable complacency and rationalize that the ravages of war, economic disaster, famine and earthquake cannot happen here. Those who believe this are either not acquainted with the revelations of the Lord or they do not believe them. Those who smugly think these calamities will not happen, that they will somehow be set aside because of the righteousness of the Saints, are deceived and will rue the day they harbored such a delusion. The Lord has warned and forewarned us against a day of great tribulation and given us counsel, through His Servants, on how we can be prepared for these difficult times. Have you(we) heeded His counsel? (Ezra Taft Benson, Jun '80)

Storage Life of Dehydrated Foods

Determining the storage life of foods is at best an inexact science **as there are so many variables. These range from the condition your food was in when you first purchased it and includes many other factors. This page was written with input by Mr. Stephen Portela who has over 30 years of professional food storage experience. This information should be used as a general guide only, and should not be followed "as the gospel truth" because your results may be different.**

Four Factors that effect food storage:

Factor #1: The Temperature:

Temperature has more to do with how long well dried foods store than anything else. The USDA states, *"Each 5.6 C. (10.08F) drop in temperature doubles the storage life of the seeds."* Obviously, there is a limit as to how far this statement can be taken. However I expect it basically holds true from room temperature down to freezing. No doubt, the inverse could also be considered true. *"Each 5.6C. (10.08F) rise in temperature halves the storage life of seeds."* This theory holds true for non-garden seeds as well.

Storage Life Differences Depending on Temperature

Constant Storage Temp in degrees F	Storage life In Years
39.76	40
49.84	30
59.92	20
70.00	10
80.08	5
90.16	2.5
100.24	1.25

Note: the above chart is not for a specific food but shows the relationship between temperature and storage life.

Lets look at a couple of real life examples of good and poor food storage practices:

About a year ago we got an unopened paper bag of white flour which had been stored at 70 degrees F, in a dry climate. It had been sitting for 3 years in a closet. It made fine looking bread but had such an 'old' and bad flavor that it was difficult to eat. For another example, a couple of years ago in the Puget Sound area we were given a 4 gallon can of wheat that had been stored up high in a garage for about 30 years. This part of the country is not as hot as some places, yet in the summers the average garage still gets up into the 90's. Even

though wheat will store for 30+ years under good conditions, the bread from this particular wheat was very bad tasting and after a few batches we ended up throwing the wheat away (something I always dislike doing).

Counter these stories with several examples told by Mr. Stephen Portela, Walton Feed's manager: He stores his long term food storage in his basement where the temperature hovers around 60 degrees F. The experts give brown rice a 6 month storage life because of all the oils in it that go rancid. Yet, Mr. Portela has been eating from a supply of brown rice that has been in his basement over 10 years. It is still wholesome! In another example, there is a family living near him who purchased a supply of food in #10 cans 30 years ago. Their basement hovers around 58 degrees F. After 28 years, Mr. Portela took a sample of many of these items to the Benson Institute at BYU to have it tested. The results can be seen at the bottom of Mr. Portela's welcome page. You will see everything tested had a 'good' to 'satisfactory' rating except for the eggs which had a 'minimum passing' rating. After 28 years I think it is most interesting that it passed at all. Mr. Portela tells me as 30 years have now passed, their storage is still in very good condition.

The bottom line is even with the very best packaging methods, if you are planning on storing your food in a warm environment, it will only last a fraction of the time it would last if stored in a cool, dry place. You can expect good storage life if your storage temperature is at 60 degrees F or below. Optimum storage temperature is at 40 degrees F or less. It is important you also find a place where the temperature remains constant. Frequent temperature changes shorten storage life. If you don't have a cool place for your food storage, plan on rotating your storage quickly enough to prevent food loss.

Factor #2: Product moisture content:

By looking at the USDA nutritional tables, dry beans, grains, and flours contain an average of 10% moisture. Although it is very difficult and unnecessary to remove all moisture from dry foods, it is imperative that any food be stored as dry as possible. Foods with excess moisture can spoil right in their containers. This is an important consideration when packing food with dry ice as moisture condenses and freezes on the outer surface of the dry ice. For long term storage, grains should have a moisture content of 10% or less. It is difficult to accurately measure this without special equipment. See the misc.survivalism faqs for a quick and easy way of getting a rough estimate of the water content in your foods. It is also important to know that you can not dehydrate foods at home that reach these levels. Food that is dried to a moisture level of 10% moisture crisply snap when bent. Those of you who dehydrate foods at home know dehydrated foods from your dehydrator are quite pliable when bent, especially fruits. These will not store well long term.

Factor #3: Atmosphere the product is stored in:

Foods packed in air don't store as well as in oxygen free gasses. This is because air contains oxygen which oxidizes many of the compounds in food. Bacteria, one of several agents which make food go rancid also needs oxygen to grow. Food storage companies have a couple of different processes for removing the oxygen:

·**Displacing the oxygen:** This is done by purging out all the air in the product with an inert gas. Nitrogen is almost always used because it is the most inert gas known. People doing their own packing occasionally use dry ice which gives off carbon dioxide gas, and probably works just about as well.

·**Absorb the oxygen:** Oxygen absorber packets do just that. Air contains about 78% nitrogen and 21% oxygen, leaving about 1% for the other gasses. If the oxygen is absorbed, what remains is 99% pure nitrogen in a partial vacuum.

If oxygen absorber packets are used, care must be taken to use a storage container that can stand some vacuum. If it's not air tight, air will be sucked into your container as the oxygen is absorbed, reintroducing more oxygen that must be absorbed. Before long, the oxygen absorbers will have absorbed all the oxygen they can. Obviously, your product won't be oxygen free under these circumstances.

Seeds store better in nitrogen. On the other hand, seeds you plan on sprouting, such as garden seed, or seeds set aside for growing your own sprouts store better in air. For this reason Walton cans their garden seed packs in air. Oxygen absorbers also contain a minute amount of moisture to activate the absorber. Sometimes, with the heat generated by the absorber, they can cause sweating if you use glass bottles or tupperware type containers.

Factor #4: The container the product is stored in:

To get the best storage life out of your product it must have a hermetic (air tight) seal. Containers that do this well are:
·#10 Cans (Use only cans that are enamel lined, otherwise your food flavor will be tainted by the steel it comes in contact with. An enamel lined can also prevents the inside of the can from rusting.)
·Sealable food storage buckets
·Sealable food quality metal (lined) or plastic drums.
Whatever container you use, be sure it is food grade as your product can be tainted with whatever the container is made

from. Plastic sacks are not good air tight containers, for even if they are sealed, the relatively thin plastic 'breathes,' allowing air to pass through. Paper sacks are of course even worse.

There is some concern as to how good a seal is made by the lids on plastic buckets used by food storage companies. Manufacturer studies show an extremely small amount of air transfer. This amount is so small, however, that it can be considered a hermetic seal. It has also been found that the lids can be re-used several times without dramatically degrading the performance of the seal.

People who purchase products from food storage providers are often concerned about receiving their buckets bulging or with one side collapsed in. Collapsed buckets occasionally occur when ordering from Walton's as the elevation of their packing facility is above 6,000 feet. As the buckets are shipped to a lower elevation, the increased ambient air pressure can sometimes push in one side. If a side is popped in, it is a great indication that the bucket is indeed sealed. And this also holds true for buckets that might be under a slight amount of pressure. If either condition concerns you, crack the lid to equalize the air pressure. You can do this without seriously degrading the storageability of the product within the bucket. Remember to re-seal the lid after doing this.

Bulging cans:

Some bulging cans have been returned to Waltons. In almost every case, these cans held mixes that contained baking powder or soda. It is believed that occasionally the extremely small amount of moisture found in the product interacts over time with the baking powder or soda and creates a small amount of carbon dioxide gas. Oxyten absorbers can also react with the baking powder causing the cans to buldge. These cans have been sent off for bacteria analysis and and in each case came back negative.

Storage Life Notes About Specific Foods:

The Soft Grains
Barley Hulled or Pearled, Oat Groats, Rolled Oats, Quinoa Rye.

Soft Grains have softer outer shells which don't protect the seed interior as well as hard shelled seeds and therefore won't store as long. Hermetically sealed in the absence of oxygen, plan on a storage life of 8 years at a stable temperature of 70 degrees F. They should keep proportionally longer if stored at cooler temperatures.

The Hard Grains

Buckwheat, Corn, Dry Flax, Kamut, Millet, Durum wheat, Hard red wheat, Hard white wheat, Soft wheat, Special bake wheat, Spelt, Triticale.

The Hard Grains all store well because of their hard outer shell which is nature's near perfect container. Remove that container and the contents rapidly deteriorate. Wheat, probably nature's longest storing seed, has been known to be edible after scores of years when stored in a cool dry place. As a general rule for hard grains, hermetically sealed in the absence of oxygen, plan on a storage life of 15-20 years at a stable temperature of 70 degrees F. They should keep proportionately longer if stored at cooler temperatures.

Beans

Adzuki Beans, Blackeye Beans, Black Turtle Beans, Garbanzo Beans, Great Northern, Kidney Beans, Lentils, Lima Beans, Mung Beans, Pink Beans, Pinto Beans, Small Red Beans, Soy Beans. As beans age they lose their oils, resist water absorbtion and won't swell. Worst case, they must be ground to be used. Storing beans in nitrogenhelps prolong the loss of these oils as does cool temperatures. Hermetically sealed in the absence of oxygen, plan on a storage life of 8-10 years ata stable temperature of 70 degrees F. They should keep proportionately longer if stored 10-20 degree F cooler temperatures.

Dehydrated Vegitables

Broccoli, Cabbage, Carrots, Celery, Onions, Peppers, Potatoes.

Dehydrated vegetables store well if hermetically sealed in the absence of oxygen. Plan on a storage life of 8-10 years at a stable temperature of 70 degrees F. They should keep proportionately longer if stored at cooler temperatures.

Dehydrated Dairy Products

Cheese Powder, Cocoa Powder, Powdered Eggs, Butter/ margarine Powder, Powdered Milk, Morning Moo, Whey Powder.

Dehydrated Dairy Products generally store very well if stored dry in hermetically sealed containers with the oxygen removed. Plan on a storage life of 5 to 10 years if stored at a stable temperature of 70 degrees F. They should keep, probably 5 years longer, if stored at cooler temperatures. One exception is Morning Moo. As a new whey based product, it hasn't been tested for long term storage. Plan on rotating this product after 5 years. Our dairy powders (excluding our sour cream powder) contain no fat, an agent that markedly decreases the storage life of dairy products.

Flours and Other Products made from Cracked / Ground Seed.

All Purpose Flour, Bakers Flour, Unbleached Flour, White Flour, Whole Wheat Flour, Cornmeal, Mixes, Refried Beans, Cracked wheat, Germade, Gluten, Wheat flakes.

After seeds are broken open their outer shells can no longer protect the seed contents and seed nutrients start to degrade. Don't try to store unprotected flours longer than a year. Hermetically sealed in the absence of oxygen, plan on a storage life of 5 years at a stable temperature of 70 degrees F. They should keep proportionately longer if stored at cooler temperatures.Note: Granola is not a long storing food because of the nuts. They contain high concentrations of oil which go rancid over the short term. Expect granola to last about 6-9 months.

Pasta

Macaroni, Noodles, Ribbons, Spaghetti.

Pasta will store longer than flour if kept dry. Hermetically sealed in the absence of oxygen, plan on a storage life of 10 - 15 years at a stable temperature of 70 degrees F. Pasta should keep proportionately longer if stored at cooler temperatures.

Dehydrated Fruit

Fruit doesn't keep as well as many dehydrated items. Hermetically sealed in the absence of oxygen, plan on a storage life of 10-15 years at a stable temperature of 70 degrees F. They should keep proportionately longer if stored at cooler temperatures.

Honey, Salt and Sugar

Honey, Salt and Sugar should keep indefinitely if stored free of moisture. Watch out for additives in the honey. It is possible to buy honey with water and sugar added. This honey generally doesn't crystallize like pure 100% honey does when stored for a long time. If there are additives, there is no saying how long it will last.

Peanut Butter Powder

Peanut Butter Powder will not store as long as wheat flour. Hermetically sealed in the absence of oxygen, plan on a storage life of 4-5 years at a stable temperature of 70 degrees F. It should keep proportionately longer if stored at cooler temperatures.

Brown and White Rices

Brown and white rices store very differently. Brown rice is only expected to store for 6 months under average conditions. This is because of the essential fatty acids in brown rice. These oils quickly go rancid as they oxidize. It will store much longer if refrigerated. White rice has the outer shell removed along with those fats. Because of this, white rice isn't nearly as good for you, but will store longer. Hermetically sealed in the absence of oxygen, plan on a storage life for white rice of 8-10 years at a stable temperature of 70 degrees F. It should keep proportionately longer if stored at cooler temperatures. Stored in the absence of oxygen, brown rice will last longer than if it was stored in air. Plan on 1 to 2 years. It is very important to store brown rice as cool as possible, for if you can get the temperature down another ten degrees, it will double the storage life again.

Garden Seedor Sprouting Seed

All viable seeds are hibernating tiny living plants that only need moisture and warmth to sprout. And much like a chick in an egg, all the nutrients this little life needs to spring into existence is contained within it's shell. Like boiling an egg, heating a seed will kill that little life within it. However, unlike an egg, a seed can withstand cold temperatures. As seeds usually remain edible after the life within it dies, we must use different criteria when determining sproutable seed storage life. And again the big deciding factor is temperature. Plan on a storage life of 2 to 3 years at a stable temperature of 70 degrees F. They should keep proportionately longer if stored at cooler temperatures. And remember, you want to store all of these seeds in air. Packed in nitrogen, the viability of some seeds will last longer than others. This is still to a large degree an unexplored science, and therefore we recommend you store all the seeds you plan on sprouting in air. Alfalfa is a unique seed as it actually germinates better if the seed is 2 or 3 years old. Most any sample of alfalfa contains 'hard' seed and 'soft' seed. Soft seed germinates within two days while hard seed germinates in about a week. The problem is, by the time the soft seed sprouts are ready to harvest, the hard seed may not have germinated yet. As storage time draws on, the hard seed turns into soft seed. Older seed germinates closer together. Stored in cool conditions, alfalfa seed should have a good percentage of germination up until it is 8 years old.

Total Vegetable Protein

Total Vegetable Protein, made from soy beans, has an unusually long storage life. Hermetically sealed in the absence of oxygen, plan on a storage life of 15-20 years at a stable temperature of 70 degrees F. meat substitute should keep proportionately longer if stored at cooler temperatures.

Yeast

Yeast, a living organism, has a relatively short storage life. Keep yeast in the original metal foil storage containers. If the seal remains intact, yeast should last 2 years at 70 degrees F. However it is strongly recommended that you refrigerate it, which should give you a storage life of 5 years. Frozen yeast should store for a long time.

Wilford Woodruff (1807–1898) Fourth President of the Church

"We feel led to caution the Latter-day Saints against forming the bad habit of incurring debt and taking upon themselves obligations which frequently burden them heavier than they can bear, and lead to the loss of their homes and other possessions. … Our business should be done, as much as possible, on the principle of paying for that which we purchase, and our needs should be brought within the limit of our resources" (*Teachings of Presidents of the Church: Wilford Woodruff* [2004], 232–33).

"The Lord is not going to disappoint either Babylon or Zion, with regard to famine, pestilence, earthquake or storms. . . . Lay up your wheat and other provisions against a day of need, for the day will come when they will be wanted, and no mistake about it. We shall want bread, and the Gentiles will want bread, and if we are wise we shall have something to feed them and ourselves when famine comes." (*Journal of Discourses*, 18:121.)

Shelf Life Studies:

Canned Food Study One

A Food and Drug Administration Article about a shelf life test that was conducted on **100-year old canned foods** that were retrieved from the Steamboat Bertrand can be read at the following link:

http://web.archive.org/web/20070509153848/http://www.fda.gov/bbs/topics/CONSUMER/CON00043.html

Following is a brief summary of a very small portion of the above article:

"Among the canned food items retrieved from the Bertrand in 1968 were brandied peaches, oysters, plum tomatoes, honey, and mixed vegetables. In 1974, chemists at the National Food Processors Association (NFPA) analyzed the products for bacterial contamination and nutrient value. Although the food had lost its fresh smell and appearance, the NFPA chemists detected no microbial growth and determined that **the foods were as safe to eat as they had been when canned more than 100 years earlier.** The nutrient values varied depending upon the product and nutrient. NFPA chemists Janet Dudek and Edgar Elkins report that significant amounts of vitamins C and A were lost. But protein levels remained high, and all calcium values 'were comparable to today's products.'"

"NFPA chemists also analyzed a 40-year-old can of corn found in the basement of a home in California. Again, **the canning process had kept the corn safe from contaminants and from much nutrient loss.** In addition, Dudek says, the kernels looked and smelled like recently canned corn."

"According to a recent study cosponsored by the U.S. Department of Agriculture and NFPA, canned foods provide the same nutritional value as fresh grocery produce and their frozen counterparts when prepared for the table. NFPA researchers compared six vegetables in three forms: home-cooked fresh, warmed canned, and prepared frozen. 'Levels of 13 minerals, eight vitamins, and fiber in the foods were similar,' says Dudek. In fact, in some cases the canned product contained high levels of some vitamins that in fresh produce are destroyed by light or exposure to air."

Canned Food Study Two

A canned food shelf life study conducted by the U.S. Army revealed that **canned meats, vegetables, and jam were in an excellent state of preservation after 46 years.**
The Washington State University summary article can be read at:
http://www.whatcom.wsu.edu/family/facts/shelflif.htm

Dry Food Study One

A scientific study conducted at Brigham Young University on the shelf life of a variety of different dry foods can be read at both of the following links:

http://ce.byu.edu/cw/womensconference/archive/2005/sharing_stations/pdf/52a.pdf

http://www.providentliving.org/content/display/0,11666,7797-1-4222-1,00.html

A brief summary of the above web site information shows the following estimated shelf life per dry food item:

Over 30 years for wheat and white rice. 30 years for pinto beans, macaroni, rolled oats, and potato flakes. 20 years for powdered milk.

All dry food items should be stored in airtight moisture proof containers at a temperature between 40ºF to 70ºF. Salt, baking soda, and granulated sugar still in their original containers have no known shelf life limit if properly stored.

Dry Food Study Two

http://www.sciencedaily.com/videos/2007/0208-keeping_food_for_years.htm

Food scientists now know that, when properly sealed, some dried food that's been sitting on shelves for years, could still be OK to eat.

"It lasts a lot longer than we thought," Oscar Pike a food scientist at Brigham Young University in Provo, Utah, tells DBIS.

Scientists have known certain foods like sugar and salt can be stored indefinitely, but wanted to learn the shelf life of other food like dried apples -- stored since 1973 -- tried by taste testers.

"I like to call it the emergency shelf life of the food, food that you'd still be willing to eat in an emergency," Pike says. "It's not as though it were freshly canned, but it's certainly edible."

Pros and Cons of Freeze-Dried, Dehydrated, MRE, Food Bars, & Basic Commodities.

Pros   **_Cons_**

Freeze-Dried / Instant

Very low moisture   Most expensive food storage option
Very lightweight   Most items require water to prepare
Long shelf life   Items are bulkier than if dehydrated
Reconstitutes quickly
Retains original shape, texture, color after resonstitution
Best way to dry meat items

Dehydrated (most items)

Low moisture   Requires water to prepare
Lightweight   Some items take a long time to reconstitute
Long shelf life   Some items loose taste after recontitution
No waste   Dehydration process can affect nutritional value
Not easily spoiled   Some items have poor visual appeal

MRE (Meal Ready to Eat)

Can be eaten right from pouch without preparation   Taste of MREs considered poor by some
Requires no water to prepare   Artificial additives added in many recipes
Can be heated for hot meal by many methods   Expensive considering actual food received
Convenient to use   Many entrees more like sauces & require additional
Familiar foods available   quality carbohydrates for a filling meal
No mixing or blending required   Entrees alone will not supply adequate nutritional value
                                                                     Because of foil pouch, they are susceptable to puncture
                                                                     Can be heavy if larger quantities need to be
                                                                     transportated

Emergency food bars

Compact - convenient   Limited nutritional value
Low cost   Not a satisfying substitute for a hot meal
5 year shelf life   Not adequate for prolonged use
Can take exposure to high heat

Grains, Beans, Basic Commodities

Very familiar   Not generally appropriate for shorter term emergencies
Low cost   Very heavy weight
Long storage life   Requires large quantities of water and fuel to prepare
Traditional basic foods   More time consuming to prepare
Good nutritional value   Time is required to adapt to basic comodity oriented
                                                                     diet
Many sproutable seeds, grains, and beans increase   For higher calorie requirements a fairly large quantity of
nutritional value   grains/beans must be consumed when eaten
                                                                     exclusively.

MREs: MEALS, READY TO EAT

This category includes more than the modern day military rations known by the above acronym, but also their civilian equivalents which are marketed by two of the major U.S. military MRE contractors, and a number of other products on the civilian market that fit better into this category than any other. Over the last several years the number of self-contained meals available in either the new style flexible pouches or old fashioned metal cans has greatly increased. I can't cover them all in detail so for this section I will cover only those meals that also include some form of self-contained heating device to warm the food to serving temperature. This allows one to have a hot meal yet needing no equipment other than a spoon to eat with. Whether you buy self-heating meals or supply the heat yourself to non-self heating meals you should investigate the offerings your local grocer may now be carrying. They have great potential for those situations where cooking food would be difficult or impossible.

U.S. MILITARY MREs

The Meal, Ready to Eat (MRE) is the current U.S. military field ration for those times when troops are out of contact with their regular mess facilities. In the early 1980's they replaced the older C & K-rations that had honorably served since the Second World War. These new rations represented a major leap forward in food preservation technology by disposing of the heavy, unwieldy metal can and replacing it with the much lighter, flexible "retort pouch." These pouches are the beefier cousins of the aluminized Mylar bag much used in long-term food storage and are basically constructed the same way. A thick outer layer of tough polyester film, a thin middle layer of aluminum foil for its excellent gas barrier properties, and an inner layer of food safe polypropylene film to allow heat sealing. Food is placed in the pouch then specially heat processed for preservation which renders it microbiologically shelf-stable, fully cooked, and ready to eat.

What's in an MRE?

From the Defense Logistics Agency Subsistence web site (http://www.dscp.dla.mil/subs/rations/meals/mres.htm) we find this:

The twenty-four different varieties of meals can be seen in the menu table. Components are selected to complement each entrée as well as provide necessary nutrition. The components vary among menus and include both Mexican and white rice, fruits, bakery items, crackers, spreads, beverages, snacks, candy, hot sauce, and chow mein noodles for the pork chow mein entrée. The fruits may be applesauce, pears, peaches, pineapple, or strawberry. The bakery items include a fudge brownie, cookies, fruit bars, a

toaster pastry, and pound cake in flavors of lemon, vanilla, orange, pineapple, and chocolate mint. Each meal also contains an accessory packet. The contents of one MRE meal bag provides an average of 1250 kilocalories (13 % protein, 36 % fat, and 51 % carbohydrates). It also provides 1/3 of the Military Recommended Daily Allowance of vitamins and minerals determined essential by the Surgeon General of the United States.

All of which is then placed inside of a heavy plastic pouch and sealed. Being field rations they had to be designed to take considerable punishment in packs, air drops, and other forms of abuse remaining safely intact until consumed. By and large they do just that.

All of this sounds rather attractive to the person interested in emergency preparedness and they are. So much so, in fact, that several years ago the U.S. military finally said "enough!" to the continuing losses of their rations to the civilian market and banned any further civilian sale. All new MRE complete ration packs now bear the words "U.S. Government Property. Commercial Resale Is Unlawful."

This did slow the loss rate somewhat, but anyone that wants the real thing can still get them from military personnel they may know, at gun shows, some military surplus shops, or via E-Bay. Whether you should do this is up to you, but I will give a couple of cautions here:

#1 – Being a back channel acquisition chances are you have no way of knowing the storage history of what you're buying. Maybe it's been sitting in some nice cool warehouse since it was produced or maybe it bounced around in the back of a deuce-and-a-half in the Nevada desert for a month last summer. If you don't know where it's been how can you estimate how much useful shelf-life it may have left?

#2 – Make sure what you're buying really is a military MRE or MRE component. Some of the civilian commercial products can look remarkably similar, but are not quite the same. Know what you're looking at and make it clear with the person you're buying from that you want genuine military issue (if that's what you want).

MRE Heaters: These devices will either come with your MRE at the time of purchase or they can be bought separately. They contain a small amount of salt, magnesium, and iron and when you add a small amount of water they undergo a flameless chemical reaction that will heat an 8 oz MRE entrée by roughly 100° Fahrenheit (37°C) in about ten minutes. As water is what starts the reaction it is imperative the heaters be kept dry until used. If stored in an area of high humidity the heaters can undergo a slow reaction leading to degraded performance later or even complete failure over time. As a part of the chemical reaction the heaters release small amounts of hydrogen gas which is generally harmless but large numbers of heaters in a damp, sealed storage area could conceivably present a danger. This is unlikely unless you're storing many cases of heaters. In such an event keep them in an air tight storage container with some desiccant.

While any MRE can be eaten cold these heaters can certainly improve the palatability of the food. Lacking a heater you can simply boil the individual retort pouches in water for a few minutes, lay them in the sun to warm, or tuck them in your shirt. The one thing you should not do is expose them to direct flame.

For more detailed information on U.S. military, civilian, some foreign military MREs, and other rations please see the excellent MRE Info website at   http://www.mreinfo. com/index.html

U.S. MILITARY MRE SHELF LIFE

Much discussion has gone into how long one should keep MREs on hand before rotating them out of stock. In this regard they're no different than any other type of preserved food. The longer you keep them on hand the more unpalatable and non-nutritious they will become with heat playing a large role in shortening their useful lifespan.

The short answer to the shelf-life question (from http://www.dscp.dla.mil/subs/rations/meals/mres.htm) is simply "The shelf life of the MRE is three (3) years at 80 degrees F. However, the shelf life can be extended through the use of cold storage facilities prior to distribution." Of course, that's at 80° Fahrenheit (27°C). What if your storage temperature is different? Then you need the storage life chart that was developed by the U.S. Army's NATIC Research Laboratories which basically says that at a given storage temperature an MRE will remain palatable for so many months as illustrated below:

Storage Temperature	Shelf Life
120° F (49°C)	1 month
110° F (43°C)	2 months
100° F (37°C)	6 months
90° F (32°C)	18 motnhs
80° F (27°C)	36 months
70° F (21°C)	40 months
60° F (15°C)	48 months
50° F	60 months

Note: As with any other stored food, time and temperature have a cumulative effect. *A complete shelf-life chart for all U.S. military rations may be found here:*

U.S. CIVILIAN MREs (WORNICK, SOPAKCO, OTHERS?)

Except for contract overruns on individual components actual military MREs, especially complete MRE ration packs, are not legal for sale on the civilian market. Recognizing there was a civilian market for such rations both Wornick and Sopakco through its Crown Point, limited, subsidiary brought out similar products for commercial sale. Their complete civilian ration packs are not precisely the same as their military cousins, but the individual components are usually produced on the same production lines.

Because there are no legal restrictions on their sale these civilian MREs are easier to find and are generally available in three basic forms —individual components, complete ration packs, and multi-serving tray packs meant for group feeding. Exact menus vary over time, usually being a subset of whatever the companies are producing for the military at the time of their production so I'm not going to try to address specific menus.

Some of the typical differences between military and civilian MREs are:

Menu choice. Military MREs presently have twenty four different menu choices. Their civilian equivalents are currently limited to twelve.

Ration heaters. These are standard with military MREs, but you may have to pay extra to get them with the civilian equivalents.

Total amount of food. Many of the civilian offerings contain less total food than military MREs, typically in the form of fewer side items. One notable difference is that fewer of the civilian rations contain the little Tabasco packets than their military counterparts.

The spoon. The spoons in the civilian packets are not the same as in the military rations. The civilian spoon is white plastic while the military spoon is brown and of a longer length which makes it easier to get to the bottom of the pouches without getting food on your fingers. This strikes me as particularly chintzy on the manufacturer's part.

For more detailed information on U.S. military, civilian, and some foreign military MREs, and other rations please see the excellent MRE Info website at http://www.mreinfo.com/index.html

U.S. CIVILIAN MRE SHELF LIVES

One would think that the shelf lives of U.S. military and civilian MREs would be the same, but are they? If you look at the manufacturer's websites for what they say about their civilian equivalent rations we find:

Crown Point, Ltd (SOPAKCO)
From http://www.crownpt.com/Q&As.htm
How long will these products last? < /p>

SOPAKCO Packaging uses an estimated shelf life figure of "3-5 years, plus or minus" for its MRE-type pouched food products. Actual shelf life may vary from this estimate. A key factor effecting actual shelf life is the temperature of the storage environment. Storage at temperatures higher than 85F (85 degrees Fahrenheit) may shorten the shelf life of MRE-type food products. On the other hand, lowering the storage temperature will help extend the products' shelf life. This effect is common to most processed food products.

The shelf life figures given below for MRE's are based on studies conducted by the U.S. Army's NATIC Research Laboratories. This study was conducted by NATIC without participation of the MRE manufacturers. As such, SOPAKCO Packaging cannot verify the test procedures used by the NATIC labs, nor do we adopt these shelf life figures as a guarantee of any sort. The data is useful, though, as a general indication of the effects of storage temperatures on the shelf life of MRE-type food products.

The above storage data and time periods were based on "acceptable taste" measures, which is a subjective standard that may vary among each individual. Test participants were asked to indicate which products they were presented would be rated to still be of "acceptable taste". Responses were noted, and average values were calculated to yield the data above.

The above data does not indicate the maximum useful life of MRE food products. The NATIC study noted that nutritional value and product safety value of the products often extended far beyond these time points.

Again, SOPAKCO Packaging in no way adopts the NATIC shelf life figures as any form of express or implied guarantee of the actual shelf life of its MRE food products. This information is provided as a general indication of the effects of storage temperature on MRE-type packaged foods.

Long Life Food Depot (The Wornick Company's civilian sales agent)

How long do MRE products last - what is their Shelf Life

We guarantee our MRE products to last 5 years from the date of sale, in a room temperature environment (70 deg. F), no matter what the production date.

Of course, the production date is visible on all our entrees and on most side dishes, desserts, and other components.

The production date is a four digit number (date code) on each item, example "2156." In this example the 2 represents the year 2002 (a "3" would represent 2003, etc.), the 156 represents the 156th day of the year. See the top of the individual box or look on pouch for the Date Code.

At this time nearly all of our MRE products were manufactured between 2002 and 2003 and have always been kept in a climate-controlled warehouse to ensure freshness.

The official MRE Shelf Life Chart, created by the Army's Natick Research Lab, gives the whole picture and explains why we are prepared to guarantee our products for 5 years from date of sale. It is clear that the wholesomeness of the products extends well beyond 5 years. To see this chart and a more complete discussion of MRE Shelf LIfe, click here.

MRE Shelf Life:

A main concern in the development and testing of rations for our armed forces has always been SHELF LIFE. An amazing amount of research has been done in the development of the retort pouch and the MRE to determine the exact length of time and the exact conditions under which it is safe to store the entrees and the side dishes.

The main thing we have to work with is the shelf life chart (shown below) compiled by the Army's Natick Research labs. This gives a very good overview and summary of all the findings gathered from all the testing of MRE products. However, it leaves many questions unanswered. Here are additional facts and observations we have gathered about MRE shelf life:

1) The shelf life ratings shown in the chart below were determined by taste panels, panels of "average" people, mostly office personnel at the Natick labs. Their opinions were combined to determine when a particular component or, in this case, the entire MRE ration, was no longer acceptable.

2) The shelf life determinations were made solely on the basis of taste, as it was discovered that acceptable nutritional content and basic product safety would extend way beyond the point where taste degradation would occur. This means that MREs would be safe and give a high degree of food value long after the official expiration of the products as determined by taste.

3) MRE pouches have been tested and redesigned where necessary according to standards much more strict than for commercial food. They must be able to stand up to abuse tests such as obstacle course traversals in field clothing pockets, storage outdoors anywhere in the world, shipping under extremely rough circumstances, 100% survival of parachute drops, 75% survival of free-fall air drops, severe repetitive vibration (1 hour at 1 G vibration), 7,920 individual pouch drops from 20 inches, and individual pouches being subjected to a static load of 200 lbs for 3 minutes.

4) Freezing an MRE retort pouch does not destroy the food inside, but repeated freezing increases the chances that the stretching and stressing of the pouch will cause a break in a layer of the laminated pouch. These pouches are made to withstand 1,000 flexes, but repetitive freezing does increase the failure rate by a small fraction of a percent.

MRE Storage Life Chart A graphic of the chart I have reproduced above.

As we can see both company's refer to the NATIC shelf-life chart then give qualifiers *"The NATIC study noted that nutritional value and product safety value of the products often extended far beyond these time points."* and *"This means that MREs would be safe and give a high degree of food value long after the official expiration of the products as determined by taste."* Neither state how much or what kinds of nutrition would remain once the food goes beyond it's recommended shelf life, but it can be safely assumed the most sensitive nutrients (notably vitamins A and C among others) will have significantly declined. Old food is not likely to be attractive food, nor will it give long term nutrition, but if it's all you've got it'll still be safe to eat it.

BRITISH/CANADIAN MREs

These are basically MREs little different in form than the American made product but made by companies in these respective nations. Shelf-life is the same. Menu choices reflect British/Canadian tastes, of course. Company contact information can be found in the Suppliers Section.

One minor difference seems to be with the Hot Pack company of U.K./Canada in that they claim their ration heaters are somewhat larger than the ones packaged with U.S. MREs

From the company's web site:

Will defrost ice or snow for drinking water.
Will heat 300 g (10.6 oz.) of food or water from room temperature to 80°C (178°F) in 12 minutes.
Will provide a source of heat for up to forty five minutes after activation.

Is sometimes reusable for a limited heat cycle (dependent on how much of the heating element was exhausted in the first cycle).

The chemical reaction is totally safe. When water is added to the heater, the mixture bubbling away inside the sleeve (magnesium hydroxide) is a pharmaceutical chemical used by doctors to treat stomach acidity.

Food grade ingredients are used in the manufacturing of the heater.

Once activated, the heater will keep hot for approximately 45 minutes.
It can be used as a body warmer or to heat a drink after heating the meal.

OTHER SELF-HEATING READY TO EAT TYPE PRODUCTS

As one might expect once the bugs were worked out of retort pouch and flameless ration heater technologies the manufacturing companies that produce them would try them on the civilian market. This has been a little slow in coming, mostly because in the modern day 'fresh is best and refrigeration is cheap' world their market segment is somewhat small, but they are arriving. At the time of this writing there are several products now available, some of them quite new.

HEATERMEALS

HeaterMeals are a type of MRE in casual clothing. Like the rations above they are a retort pouch preserved meal with its own built in heater. The heater itself is the same technology as the MRE heaters (the company makes them for the military), but a little different in form, to include having its own self-contained water to start the heating reaction. The meals themselves aren't packaged with the idea of rough handling in mind, but they'll keep well on the shelf.

The meals themselves come in two basic forms:

An entrée pack with the heater, seasoning packet and cutlery

A complete meal pack with the heater, entrée, seasoning packet, cutlery, side items like fruit, snack, and dessert, and a bottle of water to drink.

If you're not having to use them under rough field conditions they represent a self-heating, completely self contained meal.

These meals can be ordered from the manufacturer, a number of dealers which are listed on the company website, or you can often find them at truck stops, some supermarkets, sporting goods stores, and other such businesses.

Shelf life info for HeaterMeals was found at: http://www.heatermeals.com/faq.html#shelflife

What is the shelf-life of HeaterMeals and HeaterMeals Plus Meals?

HeaterMeals are a high quality canned food, so storage is easy.

HeaterMeals Dinner entrees do not require refrigeration, and are shelf-stable for approximately 2 years. HeaterMeals entrees come with a "Please use by" date stamped on each box. This date is two years after we package the meals, as this is the optimum time to eat your HeaterMeals.

The HeaterMeals Breakfast "Pancakes, Syrup & Sausage Links" and all HeaterMeals Plus meals have a one year shelf-life.

HeaterMeals dinner entrees are designed to safely store (at 80 degrees Fahrenheit) for at least two years; three years or more, if stored at a temperature of 60ºF or cooler. The shelf-life of HeaterMeals can be even longer; and the unique packaging of the entree and water pouch permits freezing for unlimited storage.

HOT CANS – UNITED KINGDOM

In the United Kingdom there is another entry in the self-heating meal field. This is the Hot Can from Hot Can UK, Limited. It's an interesting blend of old and different new tech in that the food itself is contained in a run-of-the-mill pop-top metal can, but the food can is contained in a sealed larger can filled with calcium oxide (quicklime) and a separate water capsule. When needed the self-contained water capsule is pierced with the provided tool allowing moisture to seep into the dry quicklime below and the food can pop-top is removed. In twelve to fifteen minutes the can will have heated to 65°-70° Celsius and remains at that temperature for roughly forty five minutes which means once you've finished the food inside you can quickly rinse the can and heat something else, perhaps a beverage.

There are a variety of meals available from the company, each weighing about 400 grams (roughly 14 ozs). Shelf life is *"Three years from manufacturing date, or as indicated on printed bottom end of can."* The heater itself releases no harmful or dangerous gasses and if for some reason you should break one open and spill some of the quicklime on yourself it can simply be washed off again with water.

Company contact information can be found in the Suppliers Section. Hot Cans are probably also available through retail dealers in the U.K. and elsewhere.

ALPINEAIRE INSTANT – SELF HEATING MEALS

New on the market from AlpineAire is their entry into the self-heating meal arena. Uses the same retort and flameless heater technology as MREs but in different packaging. Snap the bottom of the package and in eight minutes your entrée is hot and ready to go. As I write this there are only two entrees with more coming in the near future. They're rather pricey at a suggested retail of $8.95 for a mere 240 calories worth of vegetarian food. Still, it's a start and with time they may both lower the price and increase the menu choices.

Alpineaire advises an eighteen month shelf life for this particular product line. They may be ordered directly from AlpineAire or through their many stocking dealers.

MOUNTAIN HOUSE MOUNTAIN OVEN

Mountain House isn't really offering a true Meal, Ready to Eat since you still have to add water to their freeze dried/dehydrated food, but I'm including it here since it's close. Basically, what they're offering is their own version of a flameless ration heater and some new packaging of a few of their entrees that allows the pouches to be put into their heaters to be warmed. They call their heater a "Mountain Oven" though they really don't bake anything, just warms things up.

To use their heater you dissolve one of the furnished salt tablets in a plastic bottle that comes in the kit. Place a "heat activation pad" in the bottom of the insulated over pouch then pour the salt water on it. Open up the food pouch, pour in the required amount of water then put the pouch inside the insulated bag and zip it closed (the outer bag is vented). Twenty minutes later the food should be about 100° F. (38°C) hotter than when you started.

Each Mountain Oven kit is good for five uses. At a suggested retail of $11.99 per kit that's about $2.40 per use which makes it rather pricey compared to the ordinary MRE heaters already on the market which can usually be purchased for about a buck apiece or less. Still, like the AlpineAire entry it's a start and with time they may come down in price and perhaps be easier to use as well.

The Mountain Oven kits can be ordered from Mountain House directly or purchased from one of their many dealers as they are distributed.

RATION BARS

U.S. Coast Guard approved lifeboat ration bars are not common storage foods. Nevertheless they have a specific use important enough to warrant inclusion in personal preparedness programs.

As many involved with emergency preparedness discover, finding foods capable of being stored for long periods of time under harsh conditions that will remain both palatable and nutritious is a real undertaking. This is especially a problem with vehicle emergency kits where interior temperatures in the Spring, Summer, or Fall may exceed 120°F (50°C) for hours at a time each day. Very little in the way of anything usefully edible will survive such sustained temperatures for long before it breaks down, becomes unpalatable, with most or all of its nutrients damaged or destroyed.

This is a problem not only for those of us trying to build vehicle emergency kits but also for mariners needing to provision life boats that might be exposed to anything from desert temperatures to artic climates. In reaction to this and a number of other marine emergency preparedness needs most of the world's maritime nations met to develop the Safety Of Life At Sea (SOLAS) conventions, one of which concerns itself with emergency provisions for lifeboats. In the United States responsibility for implementing the SOLAS regulations falls to the U.S. Coast Guard and they have developed guidelines by which manufacturers must abide in order to become Coast Guard approved suppliers of life boat rations.

Among the guideline requirements are:

- Lifeboat rations must be capable of withstanding long periods of high temperatures or sub freezing weather without significant deterioration;

- must not increase bodily water needs with high protein or salt levels yet provide sufficient calories to keep the body from burning its fat reserves which also increases bodily water needs;

- be compact in size and lightweight;

- be sufficiently palatable that injured or ill passengers would be able to eat them;

- not constipate nor cause diarrhea;

- use packaging that is sufficiently durable to withstand rough conditions.

Those manufacturers that meet these guidelines can submit their products for approval to be placed on the *U.S. Coast Guard Equipment List 160.046 - Emergency Provisions for Merchant Vessels* which may be found here: http://www.uscg.mil/hq/g-m/mse/equiplists/160046.pdf

Each of these companies produces lifeboat rations. In the U.S. the two most commonly available product lines are the Mainstay Emergency Food Ration and the Datrex Red (or White) or Blue ration.

The Mainstay rations are lemon flavored and available in 1200, 2400, and 3600 calorie packages. The Datrex rations are coconut flavored and available in 2400 (red or white ration) or 3600 (blue ration) calorie packages. As per regulations both have a five year shelf life. Each package from either company has been tabletized and subpackaged to make it easier to serve them out in controlled portions.

Both are primarily composed of complex carbohydrates, fairly low protein, enriched with extra vitamins and minerals then vacuum sealed in heavy aluminized plastic pouches similar to military MREs. Flavors are noted above, textures are similar to a fairly dense pound cake. I've sampled both and while I wouldn't care to eat them for a week straight for the relative few days a vehicle or similar emergency kit is intended to get you through they'll get the job done and not turn into something nasty after a few months of hot weather. In the cool times of the year when vehicle interiors do not climb into oven temperature ranges food options increase considerably with some form of military or civilian-equivalent MRE being well suited to the task.

Something to consider if you're building emergency kits or bug-out bags.

Growing and Using Sprouts

Sprouts are great to eat for everyday living and especially so in an emergency situation. Typical foods set aside for storage are traditionally low or nonexistent in vitamin C and many of the B vitamins. Yet it is exciting to know the seeds from those same storage foods can be sprouted to give a rich source of these important nutrients. Sprouts are an excellent source of vitamin C and also contain many good B vitamins. And you probably won't find a less expensive way to get these vitamins than from low calorie sprouts. Green leafy sprouts are also a good source of vitamin A. Sprouts are a good source of fiber, protein, and contain enzymes that aid digestion. In addition, sprouting destroys the seed's natural preservative enzymes that inhibit digestion.

Different kinds of seeds you can sprout: (This list gives the popularly sprouted seeds and is not all enclusive as you can sprout almost any kind of seed.)

Generally eaten raw: Alfalfa, radish, mung bean, sunflower, clover, cabbage.

Generally cooked: Kidney, Pinto and other miscellaneous beans.

Eaten raw or cooked: Lentils, Soy beans, green peas and wheat. (In addition, all the sprouts that are generally eaten raw can be easily cooked.)

Alfalfa: Alfalfa, one of the most popular sprouts, is a good source of vitamins A, B, C, D, E, F, and K and is rich in many minerals, as well as many enzymes needed for digestion.

Radish sprouts are high in vitamin C and potassium and have a rich flavor.

Wheat is high in Vitamins B, C, and E and has three times the vitamin E of dry wheat. Wheat also has many minerals.

Mung Beans: These sprouts should be sprouted under pressure to produce long and juicy sprouts. Mung bean sprouts are an excellent source of protein, vitamin C, A and E, along with many minerals.

Green Pea sprouts are rich in many of the B vitamins and vitamin C. Green pea sprouts make a rich addition to any green salad.

Soybeans: An extremely rich source of protein and vitamins A, B, C and E. Soybeans are rich in minerals and lecithin. They can be sprouted under pressure like mung beans.

Kidney beans, pinto beans and miscellaneous beans: They are a good source of vitamin C, many of the B vitamins and many minerals. Sprouting these beans also changes their indigestible carbohydrates to digestible carbohydrates thereby greatly reducing the intestinal gas they otherwise cause.

Lentils: Rich in protein, vitamin C and the B vitamins. They have a mild ground pepper flavor.

Buckwheat: Makes a great salad green. High in vitamins A, B, C and D.

Sunflower: Rich in vitamins B, D, and E, many minerals, and Linoleic Acid, the W6 EFA.

Do Not eat tomato, peppers or potato sprouts as they are poisonous.

Growing Sprouts:

Sprouts are easy to produce and require no special equipment or knowledge. All that is required to produce sprouts is seeds, moisture, warmth, darkness and maybe 10 minutes of your time every day. Methods vary from high tech production to something as simple as quart jar or a cloth covered pan. Perhaps the simplest method is to take your seeds, place them in a quart jar, and cover them with water to start the process.

Seed amounts to use per quart jar:
1/2 Cup Seeds: Wheat, All Beans, Rye, Oats, Rice, Sunflower, Lentil, Hulled Buckwheat, and Garbanzo Beans.
2 Tablespoons: Alfalfa, radish, clover, cabbage.

Be aware that seeds soak up 2 or 3 times their dry volume in water. After they have absorbed all the water they are going to absorb (2-12 hours depending on the size of the seed), drain the water off, rinse them, and put them in a dark, warm place, with the bottle upside down and tipped up against a corner so water can drip out. Of course you need to put something under the bottle to catch the dripping water. Use a lid that permits air to move in and out of the jar. You can use a thin cloth, a nylon stocking, or anything you have that's handy. Fasten it down around the opening of the jar using an elastic or bottle ring. After the seeds have stopped draining, if you are sprouting very small seeds like alfalfa, cabbage or radish seeds, roll the bottle, coating the outer wall of the bottle with seeds. Leave the bottle on it's side in the dark. Room temperature is best for growing sprouts, around 70 degrees F. Rinse the seeds twice a day, being sure to drain them well.

(Do not neglect to rinse them. They will sour and be useless.) Within two days your seeds should begin sprouting.

For sprouts you are going to cook, let the sprout grow only as long as the seed. For sprouts you will eat raw (except wheat) let them grow up to 2-3 inches. Expose mature alfalfa, wheatgrass, buckwheat or sunflower sprouts to indirect sunlight for 4-5 hours. As they turn dark green their vitamin A content dramatically increases. (This is an important step, for if you don't, your sprouts will have only about 1 percent of this vitamin's RDA. Don't expose bean sprouts to sunlight as this will give them an unpleasant bitter taste.) When your sprouts have grown to the desired length, rinse them again, then put them in a sealed container with something to absorb the water on the bottom and store them in the refrigerator.

Sprouting mung beans under pressure

Place soaked beans in a small colander inside another container. Place several layers of burlap over the top of the seeds, then place a 3-5 pound bag of marbles or small stones on top of this. Water every two or three hours to ensure adequate moisture (this prevents the root systems from over developing in their search for water). Keep them in the dark at all times or they will turn bitter as they begin to green. When they are 2 to 3 inches long, remove them from the colander and refrigerate.

Using your sprouts

After sprouts reach their peak, they immediately begin to loose their vitamin C. Because of this, don't attempt to store sprouts longer than a week. Only grow small quantities of sprouts that can be used in a short period of time. If you plan on getting many of your vitamins from sprouts, it would be a good idea to have one or two small batches of sprouts growing all the time.

Cook sprouted beans using the same recipes you normally use. Sprouted beans cook in 2/3rds the time of unsprouted beans. Heat kills a percentage of the vitamins and enzymes gained by sprouting, so simmer or steam slowly depending on your recipe, and don't cook longer than necessary.

You can sprout a mixture of seeds to make great green salads all by themselves. You can also use raw sprouts in just about anything:

> Blended in drinks.
> Added to bean or lettuce salads.
> Mixed with already cooked breakfast cereals.
> Wrapped in tortilla or taco shells and smothered in your favorite sauce.
> Added to soups and stews just before eating.
> Sprout filled Won Tons.
> Put into sandwiches.

Raw sprouts are so versatile that they can also be thrown into just about anything then cooked, such as:

> Breads and biscuits.
> Soups.
> Pancakes.
> Eggs and omelets.
> Oatmeal or cracked wheat.
> Sauces.
> Mexican or Chinese foods.
> Potato Patties.
> Casseroles.
> Dips.
> Meatloaf.
> Any vegetable.
> Stir fried all by themselves.
> Even desserts. Really, the sky's the limit.

When cooking sprouts, it is better to steam or stir fry them than to boil them and discard the water. You only lose 20-30 percent of the vitamin C compared to 60 percent.

How much sprouting seed you should store and tips on purchasing.

It is suggested that if you plan to get all your vitamins from sprouts alone, that you store up to 125 lbs of a variety of seeds per year per person. If you have other sources for your vitamins, it is suggested you have 30 lbs of seeds set aside for sprouts to be eaten raw, and 30 lbs of sprouts intended to be cooked per year per person.

Many specialty companies exist that deal exclusively in sprout seed. Usually these seeds cost several times more than other seeds of the same type. One study shows that mung beans sold exclusively for sprouting cost 4.5 times more than regular mung beans. Yet 99 percent of the time the cheaper seed will sprout and grow as quickly as the more expensive seed. It is the web page author's opinion that it is a waste of money to buy 'sprouting seed' over regular seed. Before purchasing a large amount of storage seed intended for sprouting, purchase a small amount and test it to see if it sprouts well.

Do not attempt to store your sprouting seed for more than 5 years unless it is stored in a cool (at least 60-65 degrees F) dry place. If you are storing large seed, it may be packed in the absence of oxygen. Seed may last up to 15 years stored in this way. As your seeds get old they will take longer to sprout, and you will progressively get more seeds that won't sprout. The key again is rotate, rotate, rotate.

Use several different kinds of sprouts to find what you like before purchasing a large quantity of seed. Do not purchase seeds intended for anything except human consumption. Many seeds processed by farmers and gardeners for planting have been **treated with fungicide and or insecticide** agents and are very **poisonous**. These seeds are usually, but not always dyed red. If in doubt, ask.

All contents copyright © Al Durtschi.

Ark Institute Seed List

Eventually you will need to start raising your own food. To do this, you will need seeds, but <u>not</u> the kind of seeds you buy at the store. Why? Because those are hybrid seeds, and most hybrid seeds have no capacity to reproduce.

Hybrid seeds are a cruel trick played out on humanity. Seeds are God's gift to mankind, and for corporations and marketing people to purposely create seeds that can't produce offspring seems criminal. Yet this is exactly what goes on every day, all over the world. It's all about protecting patents and "profits." Well, those profits might get you killed if you're dumb enough to go along with the mainstream and buy hybrid seeds.

You need <u>non-hybrid seeds</u>. These are genetically-pure seeds, grown for hundreds or thousands of years, that consistently produce viable offspring. There's only one place I know of to get a complete garden-package of non-hybrid seeds at an affordable price: the **Ark Institute**. Buy their non-hybrid seed package and store it away as if it were gold. If civilization breaks down, these seeds may be the key to your survival and prosperity. While everyone else is scratching their heads wondering why their green beans won't sprout, you'll be reaping a huge harvest of self-proliferating, non-hybrid fruits and vegetables.

When you buy the non-hybrid seed package from the **Ark Institute**, you'll receive these seeds:

- Asparagus
- Green Bush Beans
- Yellow Bush Beans
- Red Kidney Beans
- White Navy Beans
- Pinto Beans
- Sweet Green Peas
- Snow Peas
- Red Beets
- White Sweet Corn
- Yellow Sweet Corn
- Spring Broccoli
- Fall Broccoli
- Red Cabbage for Salads
- Cabbage for coleslaw/kraut
- Early Carrots
- Mid-Season/Late Carrots
- Salad Cucumbers
- Pickling Cucumbers
- Eggplants
- Butterhead Lettuce
- Red Lettuce
- Mildew-resistant Cantaloupe
- Summer Oak Leaf Lettuce
- Basil

- Spanish Onions
- Red Onions
- Yellow Onions
- Scallions
- Green/Red Sweet Pepper
- Long Yellow Sweet Peppers
- Cayenne Hot Pepper
- Pie Pumpkins
- Giant Radish
- Spinach
- Canning/Catsup Tomato
- Yellow Summer Squash
- Zucchini Summer Squash
- Butternut Squash
- Acorn Winter Squash
- Solid Salad/Canning Tomato
- Italian Plum Tomato
- Large Salad Tomato
- Heirloom Slicing Tomato
- Flour/Meal Corn
- Wheat
- Drought-resistant Cantaloupe
- Romaine Lettuce
- Parsley

Survival Seeds — *Every family should have a robust store of garden seeds*

by suburbanprep   http://survival5x5.com/?p=239

I love tomatoes. Love fresh tomatoes in salads, tomato sauce over pasta, pizza with tomato sauce and topping's — all wonderful. Tomato with fresh mozzarella, basil, and aged balsamic vinegar is truly a gift from god and nature.

For those who are over age 30, as I well am, you might remember the taste of tomatoes from your childhood. I remember the robust sweetness and rich flavor of vine ripen local tomatoes.

How does your store bought tomatoes taste today?? In my opinion, store tomatoes are utterly tasteless. Store tomatoes have been breed and modified to survive transportation from far distances to your store. Today's typical store tomato is produced form genetically modified seeds. (Reference to GMO tomatoes from wikipedia: "Variety in which the production of the enzyme polygalacturonase (PG) is suppressed, retarding fruit softening after harvesting")

Tomatoes can be raised in nearly any climate, including hot houses and greenhouses in the very Northern cold climates. So it does not make sense to buy tomatoes, which were grown 1000 miles away.

Genetically modified organism (GMO) is found throughout our food chain. There is good and bad in the GMO concept. I believe technology is needed to increase the amount of food needed to feed 7 billion people on this planet. Without GMO grains (rice, wheat, corn), the world would be starving. India and China have become self-sufficient in their food production in large part to GMO technology. The bad aspects of GMO is the loss of flavor, micronuturients, and natural reproduction. The major problem with many GMO seeds is their lack of ability to create new productive seeds for the next year's planting.

When you harvest seeds from your own garden, and those seeds originated from a GMO plant, there is a high likelihood that the seed will not be productive. GMO seeds are often not open pollinating.

For the home gardener and survival prepper, GMO garden seeds are a bad thing. The reason for having a garden is provide fresh, natural, nutritious, and flavorful food to your family. Home gardening is a way to provide food for your family in a cost effective manner. During World War I, the Great Depression of 1930's, and World War II, many family had their own gardens, also known as Victory Gardens.

With the economy degrading, unemployment high, and the potential of various SHTF/TEOTWAWKI events, it is time for all of us to establish our own Victory Gardens. As a suburban prepper, I am very land constrained. No doubt, many of you also have limited space. But there are various solutions to lack of land for a garden. Flower boxes and window boxes allow many of us to raise small vegetables, such as tomatoes, green beans, herbs, and peppers. I highly recommend that you acquire the book: The Backyard Homestead: Produce all the food you need on just a quarter acre! by Carleen Madigan, (Editor).

Every survival prepper needs a large reserve of non-GMO garden seeds. This is an absolute must requirement for long-term survival plans. After a SHTF or TEOTWAWKI event, you must be able to produce your own food. You cannot count on government or the global food supply-chain to feed you. As I see a TEOTWAWKI world unfolding, you will need about 3 years of long-term food storage. This is a lot, but you can build up to it slowly over time. Here is the rational for needing 3 years of food storage:

During the first year of TEOTWAWKI or SHTF, you need to hunker down and maintain a low profile. Security and defending your family will be the focus of your days and nights. Spending your days gardening will be a high risk endeavor, as you are an easy target. You need enough food not be become a refugee. The first year will have you primarily eating from your food storage.

During the second year after TEOTWAWKI or SHTF event, you will need to start your own food production and be able to survive until through a full planting and harvesting cycle. You need enough food to survival through a full harvest.

A third year of long-term food storage will give you the capacity to survive a bad harvest or to provide charity to your local community.

A must for this long-term survival scenario is a rich and deep reserve of non-GMO seeds. You should store and rotate on an annual basis enough seeds to feed your family for years.

There are many source for non-GMO seeds. Many survival food providers sell packaged non-GMO seeds in #10 metal cans. This is a quick and easy solution. Buy a couple cans and then you have a modest supply. One of my favorite places to obtain non-GMO seeds is on eBay. Search for "survival seeds" on ebay to find numerous providers. Nearly all retail seed companies now offer non-GMO seeds. A couple providers include:

http://www.arkinstitute.com/seed.html
http://rareseeds.com/
http://www.victoryseeds.com/
http://www.heirloomseeds.com/
http://www.seedsnow.com/
Many many more – do a web search for "non-GMO seeds"

Personally, I have no problem with seed companies that provide both GMO and non-GMO seeds. GMO seeds have their place. GMO plants grow quickly and uniformly. But you cannot harvest the seeds from GMO plants for the next year's planting.

So how much seeds to store? In my opinion, a lot. Garden seeds, even non-GMO seeds, are cheap, cheap, cheap. For $50, you can obtain thousands of seeds for a wide variety of different grains, fruits, and vegetables. Of the grains, I recommend rye, because rye is very tolerant of climate extremes. If properly stored in a cool, dry place away from any sunlight, garden seeds should last for 5 years. I recommend that you buy a new package of non-GMO seeds every year, and rotate. Seeds older that 5 years are to be discarded or given to charity. After 5 years of rotation, you will have a rich and deep reserve of seeds.

Another important aspect of storing seeds is sprouting. Sprouting is a hugely valuable way to provide your family with vitamins and nutrients. During the winter, when perhaps there is little other ways to produce fresh food, anyone can do sprouting. It is very easy!!! You should definitely include sprouting seeds in your long-term food storage plans. Even folks in small apartments can do sprouting. Recommend that you store many, many months worth of sprouting seeds and have a sprouting kit.

Another reason stock up on garden seeds is for charity and barter. After a TEOTWAWKI or SHTF event, the most important barter items will be ammunition, food, garden seeds, medicines, gold and silver. If these, garden seeds will be the most important, since everyone will revert to having their own victory garden. My plan for after a TEOTWAWKI or SHTF event is to provide all my neighbors with non-GMO seeds, so that we may all grow robust gardens. In the future, I'll provide a blog posting on the concept of stealth or "guerrilla" gardening, which will be important if there ever becomes a break-down in civil society or a long-termWROL situation.

Wish you all a thriving garden and thriving family...

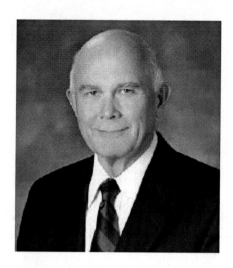

Elder Dallin H. Oaks

"Signs of the Second Coming are all around us and seem to be increasing in frequency and intensity. . . . While we are powerless to alter the fact of the Second Coming and unable to know its exact time, we can accelerate our own preparation and try to influence the preparation of those around us. We need to make both temporal and spiritual preparationfor the events prophesied at the time of the Second Coming." "Preparation for the Second Coming" Elder Dallin H. Oaks (2004)

Elder Dallin H. Oaks "We are living in the prophesied time "when peace shall be taken from the earth," (D&C 1:35) when "all things shall be in commotion," and "men's hearts shall fail them." (D&C 88:91) These signs of the Second coming are all around us and seem to be increasing in frequency and intensity." Conference, *April, 2004,*

STORAGE CONTAINERS

WHAT IS FOOD GRADE PACKAGING?

Q: *OK, I'm ready to start my storage program. What should I put the food in?*

A: You should use food grade packaging for storing anything you intend to eat. A food grade container is one that will not transfer noxious or toxic substances into the food it is holding. If you are uncertain whether a package type is food grade you can contact the manufacturer. Ask if that particular container is (US) FDA approved meaning that it is safe for food use. When inquiring be sure to specify the characteristics of the food you are storing; wet, dry, strongly acidic or alkaline, alcoholic or a high fat content. A container that is approved for one of the above types of food may not be approved for another.

The major functions of a food storage container are to:

#1. Protect its contents from outside environmental influences such as moisture, and oxygen, but possibly also heat or cold, light, insects and/or rodents as well.

#2. Prevent damage during handling and shipping.

#3. Establish and/or maintain microbiological stability. The container should not allow microorganisms such as fungi and bacteria from outside the container to come into contact with its contents. This is of critical importance to wet-pack foods such as canned vegetables, fruits and meats.

#4. Withstand the temperatures and pressures it will be exposed to. This is necessary if the contents are to be pasteurized or sterilized, either immediately before or after filling. It must not have any structural failures nor release any noxious or toxic breakdown chemicals into the food it contains. This is the reason why purpose built canning jars are recommended for home canning and mayonnaise jars aren't. The former are made heavier to withstand high temperatures and handling whereas the latter are not and have an increased risk of breakage if used for that purpose.

Virtually all containers used in home food preservation involving exposure to high temperatures are made of glass or metal, with the exception of some specialized "heat & seal" type of plastic bags. Glass can be used with any food type providing it is clean and in sound condition but the lids, particularly the liner inside the lid, may not be so you'll need to investigate suitability.

Metal cans are more specialized. They must be intended for food use and must also have a lining or coating of the inside that is suitable for the pH level of the food it will be in contact with.

If the foods are not subjected to some form of heat processing before or after packaging your selection of container types for home use is a great deal larger. Virtually any kind of clean, sound glass jar can be used and many types of new metal containers. Several sorts of plastics have become popular. These various kinds of plastics are each suited for different purposes, making selection a more complex task.

WHERE DO I FIND FOOD GRADE CONTAINERS?

Food grade packaging is everywhere. Every time you go into the grocery store you are surrounded by it. Many well known companies such as Tupperware and Rubbermaid manufacture and sell empty packaging for the express purpose of containing repackaged foods. The kinds of containers you are interested in and the types of foods you want to put in those containers will dictate where you need to look for a particular packaging system.

For food storage purposes most folks are usually interested in five and six gallon plastic pails, certain recycled plastic containers such as soda or juice bottles, glass jars from half pint to gallon sizes, metal containers such as the institutional sized #10 cans, and Mylar or other high barrier property plastic bags. Those are the containers most often used, but virtually anything that can protect foods from outside environmental influences, safely contain something you're going to later eat and have a volume capacity large enough to be worthwhile may be used.

A number of food storage retailers such as those listed in the Resources section sell plastic buckets, Mylar bags and a few even sell new #10 cans with lids. It may also be possible to purchase #10 cans through the LDS Family Canneries and dealers such as *Lehman's Hardware, Cumberland General Store* or *Home Canning Specialty and Supply*. On the local scene, plastic five gallon buckets are widely available, but only if you purchase them through a company catering to a food related trade will you likely be able to tell if they're safe to keep food in. If you can locate a customer service number for the manufacturer of a container that interests you call them and ask. Many times manufacturers will make products that are FDA approved and sell them as general purpose containers, but you need to ask to be sure.

Packaging supply houses have large FDA approved packaging lines. Several such companies are listed in the Resources section and a bit of detective work will certainly turn up more. Some require minimum orders and others don't. The cost of shipping the containers will probably play a major role in your decision making. If you are going to package a great deal of food all at once, perhaps for a group, some of the companies that require minimum purchases may save you a fair amount of money and supply packaging you might otherwise have a difficult time finding. Some time spent searching the *Thomas Register*, available both online (http://www.thomasregister.com) and in library reference sections, might turn up some valuable leads.

For glass jars, don't overlook flea markets, yard sales, thrift shops and similar places. Canning jars can sometimes be had for very little. Delicatessens, sub shops and restaurants of all sorts can be a source of one gallon glass jars formerly containing pickles, peppers, etc. If the lids are still in good condition, they are well suited to bulk storage and can be reused over and over. When I need new buckets I go to a neighboring town to buy them from a beekeeping supply house which sells them for bulk honey storage. A bit of looking will turn up other potential sources as well.

Metal cans, by and large, are not reusable for food storage, but some companies might be able to sell you new cans. The traditional single use #10 can is only the beginning of what might be available with a little looking. Gallon sized or larger cans with double friction lids (like paint comes in) make excellent storage containers and some companies make them food safe. One gallon and larger cans with wide diameter screw caps are available from some companies as well. You might have seen some of these holding edible oils, soy sauce, honey and other liquid food. If they come with a cap that will seal air tight they would be well suited for bulk storage of grains and legumes, particularly if they come in a four to six gallon size.

Pick up your local phone book, log on to your favorite search engine or head to your local public library and explore the possibilities. Make it clear that what you want must be FDA approved and be up front about how many you need or can deal with. If one company won't deal with you, try another. You'll eventually get what you want.

PLASTIC PACKAGING

Before we can discuss plastic packaging it is necessary to understand what is the substance we call "plastic." Plastics are produced from basic polymers called "resins", each of which have differing physical properties. Additives may be blended in for color or to modify particular properties such as moldability, structural rigidity, resistance to light or heat or oxidation. Additionally, it is common for several different kinds of plastic to be laminated together each performing a particular desired task. One might offer structural rigidity and the other might be more impermeable to the transfer of gasses and odors. When bonded together a rigid, gas impermeable package can be made.

Whether that package is safe for food use will depend on the exact nature of the additives blended into the plastic. Some of them, notably *plasticizers* and *dyes*, can migrate from the packaging material into the food it's containing. This may be exacerbated by the food it's in contact with especially if it is high in fat, strongly acidic, or alcoholic in nature. Time and temperature may also play a prominent role in the migration of plastic additives into food. For this reason, the (US) FDA assesses the safety of packaging materials for food contact and conducts toxicological studies to establish safety standards. Only plastics that are FDA approved for a particular food type should be used for direct contact with that food.

Being FDA approved, however, may not be all of the story. It must still be determined whether the particular plastic in question has the physical properties that would make it desirable for your purpose.

As mentioned above each base resin has somewhat differing physical properties that may be modified with additives or combined by laminating with another plastic or even completely unrelated materials such as metal foils. An example of this is "Mylar", a type of polyester film. By itself, it has moderate barrier resistance to moisture and oxygen. When laminated together with aluminum foil it has very high resistance and makes an excellent material for creating long term food storage packaging. One or more other kinds of plastic with low melting points and good flow characteristics are typically bonded on the opposite side of the foil to act as a sealant ply so that the aluminized Mylar can be fashioned into bags or sealed across container openings. The combined materials have properties that make them useful for long term storage that each separately do not have.

The most common plastic that raises suitability questions is *High Density PolyEthylene* (HDPE). It's used in a wide array of packaging and is the material from which most plastic five and six gallon buckets are made. It has a moderate rigidity, a good resistance to fats, oils, moisture and impacts, a fair resistance to acids, but is a relatively poor barrier to oxygen.

Whether it is suitable for your purpose depends on how sensitive to oxygen your product is and how long you need it to stay in optimal condition. Foods such as whole grains are not particularly delicate in nature and will easily keep for years in nothing more than a tightly sealed HDPE bucket. Most legumes are the same way, but those that have high fat contents such as peanuts and soybeans are more sensitive to O_2. Other foods such as dry milk powder might only go a year before deleterious changes are noticed. If that milk were sealed in an air-tight aluminized Mylar bag with the oxygen inside removed, the milk would keep for much longer. Better still would be to seal the milk in a metal can or glass jar. HDPE alone can be used for long term storage with one or more of the following precautions to keep a high food quality: The food should either be put on a shorter rotation cycle than packaging also using a second gas barrier such as Mylar; be periodically opened and re-purged or fresh absorbers should be inserted.

Another common plastic used in food storage is *polyethylene terephthalate* commonly known as PETE or PET plastic. Used to make soda, juice, and some water bottles among other products it is available for recycling into food storage containers in nearly every home. Properly cleaned and with intact screw-on lids PETE plastic containers will serve for keeping nearly any kind of food providing the containers are stored in a dark location. PETE has good barrier properties against oxygen and moisture and when used in combination with oxygen absorbers presents a complete dry-pack canning system in itself. About the only drawbacks to PETE plastics are that they are nearly always transparent to light, container volumes typically are limited to a gallon or less, and when used in conjunction with oxygen absorbers the sides will flex sufficiently to make stacking difficult though you could simply lay them on their sides.

There are other plastics and plastic laminates with good oxygen and moisture barrier properties that are suited for long term food storage, but they are not as easy to find, though some used containers might be available for reuse.

HOW DO I GET THE ODOR OUT OF PICKLE BUCKETS?

I've had fairly good luck doing it in the following way. As vinegar is the primary smell in pickles and it's acidic in nature, we use a base to counteract it. First we scrubbed the bucket well, inside and out, with dish detergent, most any sort will do. Then we filled the buckets with hot water and dissolved a cup of baking soda in each. Stir well, get the bucket as full as you can and put the top on. Put the bucket in the sun to keep it warm so the plastic pores stay open as much as possible. In a couple of days come back and empty the buckets. Rinse them out, fill with warm water again and add about a cup of bleach and reseal. Put back in the sun for another couple of days. Empty out and let dry with the tops off. We completely eliminated the vinegar smell this way. It might be possible to cut the time down a lot, but we haven't experimented that much.

METAL CANS

Metal cans and glass jars being heat resistant, can both be used for heat processed, wet-pack foods and for non-heat treated dry pack canning. Relative to glass jars though, metal cans have several disadvantages for the do-it-yourselfer. They are hard to come by, and they need specialized equipment to seal them that can be difficult to locate. The greatest flaw which makes them unpopular for home canning is they can only be used once. As the commercial canning industry is not interested in reusing the containers, metal cans make great sense for their purposes. The cans are both cheaper (for them) and lighter than glass jars. This adds to the economy of scale that makes canned foods as cheap as they are in the grocery store.

For home canning, glass jars are better because even the smallest of towns will usually have at least one business that carries pressure and boiling water canners along with jars, rings and lids. With metal cans a sealer is also necessary which usually has to be ordered from the manufacturer or a mail-order distributor. A few of which are listed in the Resources section.

Tin cans are not really made of tin. They're actually steel cans with a tin coating on the inside and outside. Some kinds of strongly colored acidic foods will fade from long exposure to tin so an enamel liner called "R-enamel" is used to forestall this. Certain other kinds of food that are high in sulfur or that are close to neutral in pH will also discolor from prolonged contact with tin. For those foods, cans with "C-enamel" are used.

The excellent food preservation book, *Putting Food By* Chapter 6 (see reference list) has a section on the use of metal cans for wet packed foods as does the *Ball Blue Book*.

Probably the most common use of metal containers is the #10 cans such as are used by the LDS Family Canneries discussed below. This is not the only way metal containers may be used though. It will probably take a bit of searching, but there are various food grade metal containers available of sufficient volume to make them useful for food storage. They usually have double friction lids similar to paint cans or screw caps like jars that can achieve an air-tight seal. If you can find them with a sufficient volume capacity they can be of real use for storing bulky foods such as grains, legumes and sugar. Smaller cans of a gallon or less would be useful for storing items like dry milks. If properly sealed, metal cans have a far higher barrier resistance to gasses such as oxygen, CO_2, and nitrogen than any plastic.

Although they can hardly be considered portable the use of clean metal drums (not garbage or trash cans), either themselves food grade or used with food grade liners, is also a possibility. A fifty five gallon drum of grain will weigh several hundred pounds, but may make for a much easier storage solution than multiple buckets. The advantage of using such a large container is that a great amount of a single product can be kept in a smaller amount of space and fumigating or purging the storage atmosphere would be simpler. The disadvantages are the difficulties of moving it and rotating the stock in the drum. If using oxygen absorbers make sure the drum you want to use is capable of making an air-tight seal, otherwise you should stick with carbon dioxide fumigation.

POOLING RESOURCES:
THE CHURCH OF JESUS CHRIST OF LATTER DAY SAINTS — THE MORMONS

Although the purchase of a can sealer and metal cans for home use is not generally economically feasible for most people there is one method by which it can be made practical. This is by pooling community resources to purchase the equipment and supplies. It may even not be necessary to form your own community to do this. If you live in the right area your local Latter Day Saints church may have facilities they will allow you to use. They may even have suitable food products to sell you. This is an offshoot of the church's welfare programs and is done in their Family Canneries also known as Home Storage Centers. Rather than using plastic buckets they have gone over to using metal cans and aluminized Mylar bags church-wide for dry-pack canning. By sharing the cost of the equipment and purchasing the cans in bulk quantities, they are able to enjoy the advantages of metal cans and professional equipment over plastic containers while minimizing the disadvantages of cost.

Any food products you want to have sealed in cans or pouches will need to fall within the LDS cannery guidelines of suitability for that type of packaging. This is for reasons of spoilage control as many types of foods aren't suitable for simply being sealed into a container without further processing. If you purchase food products from them, they will already be within those guidelines.

Once you have your foodstuffs on hand, either supplying your own or by purchasing them from the cannery you're ready to package them. It is here that using some forethought concerning your packaging system can save you much time and aggravation.

IMPORTANT NOTE: Please keep in mind that the individuals responsible for the family canneries are all volunteers with demands on their time from many areas. Be courteous when speaking with them and, if there are facilities for use, flexible in making arrangements to use them. You will, of course, have to pay for the supplies that you use, cans and lids at the least, and any food products you get from them. As a general rule they cannot put your food in storage for you. Be ready to pay for your purchases in advance. They do not take credit cards and probably cannot make change so take a check with you.

The following is a list of suggestions to make the most efficient use of your access time:

#1 - Make your appointment well in advance. Possibly you may be able to go with another church member if you cannot go for yourself alone. Many people may be trying to make use of the canneries so making advanced reservations is a must.

#2 - Have enough people to set up an assembly line type operation. Make sure each of your people knows what they need to do and how to do it. At least four people for any serious amount of food is a good number. Ask the cannery volunteer to go over the process with you and your crew.

#3 - Make sure you have enough muscular helpers to do the heavy lifting so you don't wear yourself out or hurt your back. Some of the supplies you will be working with, such as wheat, come in fifty pound bags and a box of #10 cans or pouches full of sugar or other weighty food is heavy.

#4 - Make labels in advance for any foods you bring with you to pack that the cannery does not carry. This will save time and possibly much confusion after the cans or pouches are filled. Once sealed one anonymous looking can or pouch looks like another.

#5 - Take out only as many as oxygen absorbers as you will use in fifteen minutes. They use most of their adsorptive capacity within two to three hours depending on temperature and humidity so you don't want to waste any by soaking up the oxygen in the room. The ones you don't use right away should be tightly sealed in a gas proof container.

#6 - Save powdery food items such as dry milk powder, pudding mixes, grain flours and meals till last. They can be messy to can and this will keep them out of your other foods. Dust masks may not be a bad idea.

#7 - Leave time to clean up after yourself. The cannery is doing you the courtesy of allowing you to use their equipment and selling you the supplies at cost. You should return the favor by leaving the place *at least* as clean as you found it. If they give you a set amount of time to work in then *finished or not* honor that time slot. Others may be waiting to use the equipment too.

#8 - Always keep in the back of your mind how much volume and weight your vehicle can haul. You'd hate to find you had canned more than you could carry home.

PREVENTING EXTERIOR CORROSION OF CANNED GOODS

Some areas have difficulty storing metal canned goods for long periods of time. This is usually caused by high humidity or exposure to salt in a marine environment. If this is a problem, it is possible to extend the life of metal cans by coating their outsides. I've seen this used on boats here in Florida, especially when loading for a long trip. There are at least five methods that can be used to do this, but for cans that require a can opener only the paraffin or mineral oil methods should be used.

PARAFFIN METHOD: Using a double boiler, paraffin is melted and brushed on the clean, unrusted cans. Be certain to get a good coat on all seams, particularly the joints. If the can is small enough, it can be dipped directly into the wax. Care must be taken to not cause the labels to separate from the cans. Do not leave in long enough for the can contents to warm.

MINERAL OIL METHOD: Use only food grade or drug store (medicinal) mineral oil. Wipe down the outside of each can with only enough oil to leave a barely visible sheen. Paper labels will have to be removed to wipe underneath with the contents written on the outside beforehand with a marker or leave the under label areas uncoated. Even with a barely visible sheen of oil the cans will tend to attract dust so you will need to wipe off the can tops before opening.

PASTE WAX METHOD: Combine 2-3 oz. of paste or jelly wax with a quart of mineral spirits. Warm the mixture CAREFULLY in its container by immersing it in a larger container of hot water. DO NOT HEAT OVER AN OPEN FLAME! Stir the wax/spirits thoroughly until it is well mixed and dissolved. Paint the cans with a brush in the same manner as above. Place the cans on a wire rack until dry.

B: A light coating of ordinary spray silicone may be used to deter rust. Spray lightly, allow to dry, wipe gently with a clean cloth to remove excess silicone.

CLEAR COATING: A clear type of spray or brush on coating such as Rustoleum may be applied. This is best suited for larger resealable cans, but will keep them protected from corrosion for years.

GLASS JARS

Compared to metal cans, glass jars are very stable, although they obviously don't take being banged around well. Fortunately the cardboard boxes most jars come in are well designed to cushion them from shocks. The box also has the added bonus of keeping damaging light away from food.

The major advantage of glass jars is they are reusable. For wet-pack canning the lids should be replaced, but the rings can be reused until they finally rust away or become too dented to use. For dry pack canning even the lids may be reused nearly indefinitely if you're careful in removing them. In my personal experience I've grown to prefer Ball lids rather than Kerr, especially for vacuum sealed dry pack canning. The red sealing compound Ball uses seems to more reliably achieve a seal than the gray compound Kerr uses.

When you get right down to the bottom line, it is seldom practical strictly in terms of dollars and cents to wet-pack your own food in jars. When you count the cost of your equipment, including the jars, rings, lids and all the rest, along with a not inconsiderable amount of your personal time, the cost of purchasing or growing your produce, you'll almost always come out ahead to buy food canned for you by the commercial canning industry. That said, forget about the strict bottom line and examine more closely why you want to put up your own food. For many, gardening is a pleasure and they have to have something to do with the food they've grown! There's also the fact that for many, you simply cannot buy the quality of the food you can put up for yourself. The canning industry tries to appeal to a broad spectrum of the general public while you can put up food to your own family's specific tastes. Home canning is not so much about saving money as it is about satisfaction. You get what you pay for.

If home canning appeals to you, please allow me to point you toward the rec.food.preserving FAQ where much good information about methods and techniques may be found.

Dry-pack canning using glass jars, on the other hand, may well make a great deal of economic sense. It is usually far cheaper per pound to purchase dry foods in bulk quantities, but often unsuitable to store it that way. Breaking the food down into smaller units allows for easier handling and exposes a smaller quantity to oxygen and moisture before it can be eaten. Of course, packaging used for doing this can be made of many different materials, but glass is often the easiest and most convenient to acquire and use. Used containers are often free or of little cost. One source of gallon sized glass jars are sandwich shops and restaurants that use pickles, peppers and other sandwich condiments. There are also half-gallon canning jars, though they are sometimes difficult to find. Both Ball and Kerr make these jars and I have a local Ace hardware order mine.

MYLAR BAGS

The word "Mylar" is a trademark of the DuPont corporation for a special type of polyester film. Typically made in thin sheets, it has a high tensile strength and is used in a wide variety of industrial settings.

In food storage, particularly for the long term, it is commonly found as a laminate with Mylar as the top layer, a very thin aluminum foil in the middle and one or more other types of plastic films on the bottom acting as sealant plies. This laminate combination possesses a high resistance to the passage of oxygen, carbon dioxide, nitrogen, other gasses, water vapor, and light which is what makes it valuable for our purposes. Unfortunately, it has a poor puncture resistance so must be used as an interior liner for more puncture resistant containers rather than as a stand-alone package.

Food grade aluminized Mylar complies with US FDA requirements and is safe to be in contact with all food types except alcoholic.

For food use, Mylar is most commonly available as pre-made bags of various sizes. Flat sheets or rolls of the material might also be found from which bags could be fashioned as well.

When Mylar bags are used by the storage food industry they are generally for products sealed in plastic buckets. The reason for doing this is the High Density PolyEthylene (HDPE) from which the pails are made is somewhat porous to gasses. This means that small molecules, such as oxygen (O_2), can slowly pass through the plastic and come into contact with the food inside. The problem is further compounded if oxygen absorbers are used, as the result of their absorbing action is to lower the air pressure inside the container unless it has first been carefully flushed with an inert gas such as nitrogen. How fast this migration activity will occur is a function of the specific plastic formulation, its wall thickness and the air pressure inside the container. In order to gain the maximum possible shelf life a second gas barrier, the Mylar bag, is used inside the pail.

Whether the use of these bags is necessary for your home packaged storage foods depends on how oxygen sensitive the food item is and how long you want it to stay at its best. If the container is made of a gas impervious material such as metal or glass then a second gas barrier inside is not needed. If it is HDPE or a plastic with similar properties and you want to get the longest possible storage life (say 10+ yrs for grain) then Mylar is a good idea. If you're going to use the grain in four to five years or less then it is not needed. Provided the oxygen has been purged from the container in the first place, either with a proper flushing technique, or by absorption, there will not have been sufficient O_2 infiltration to seriously impact the food. Particularly oxygen sensitive foods such as dry milk powders that are to be kept in plastic containers for more than two years would benefit from the use of Mylar. Naturally, storage temperature and moisture content is going to play a major role as well.

There is also the question of the seal integrity of the outer container. If you are using thin walled plastic buckets in conjunction with oxygen absorbers the resulting drop in air pressure inside the pail may cause the walls to buckle. If this should occur, there would be a risk of losing seal integrity, particularly if the buckets are stacked two or more deep. If the food was packed in Mylar bags with the absorbers inside this would keep the vacuum from seriously stressing the container walls. Better still would be not to have the problem at all by either using containers of sufficient wall thickness or flushing with inert gas before sealing. Heavy wall thickness is one reason why the six gallon Super Pails have become so widespread. It should be noted that Mylar is not strongly resistant to insect penetration and not resistant at all to rodents. If mice chew through your buckets, they'll go right through the bags.

HOW DO I USE MYLAR BAGS?

Sealing food in Mylar bags is a straight-forward affair, but it may take a bit of practice to get it right, so purchase one or two more bags than you think you'll need in case you don't immediately get the hang of it.

#1 - The bags typically sold by storage food dealers look rather large when you compare them to the five or six gallons buckets they are commonly used in. That extra material is necessary though if you are to have enough bag material left over after filling to be able to work with. Unless you are sure of what you are doing, don't trim off any material until after the sealing operation is completed.

#2 - Place the bag inside the outer container and fill with the food product. Resist filling it all the way to the top. You need at least an inch or so below the bucket rim left open to get the lid to seat completely. If you'll be using desiccants and oxygen absorbers together place the desiccant on the bottom of the bag before filling.

#3 - When the pail seems to be full, gently thump it on the floor a few times to pack the product and reduce air pockets. Add any makeup food necessary to bring level back to where it should be.

#4 - Take the bag by the corners and pull out any slack in the material so that all sides can be pulled together evenly. Place your oxygen absorbers inside if you are going to use them. Now place a board over the top of the bucket and fold the bag end down over it keeping it straight and even. Place a piece of thin cotton fabric such as sheet or t-shirt material over the edge of the bag mouth. Using a clothes iron set on the cotton, wool or high setting run it over the cloth-covered Mylar about a half-inch from the edge for about twenty seconds or so until it seals. You'll probably have to do the bag in sections. Temperature settings on irons vary so experimenting on a left-over strip to find the right setting is a good idea.

#5 - When you've done the entire bag allow it to cool then try to pull the mouth of the bag open. If moderate pressure doesn't open it, fold the bag down into the pail until you feel the trapped air pillowing up against the material and wait to see if it deflates. If it stays buoyant, your seal is good. You can seal on the bucket lid at this point or take the further step to vacuum or gas flush the bag.

Once a seal has been obtained the bags can be left as-is, vacuum sealed or gas flushed. To obtain the most efficient oxygen removal the bags can be first drawn down with a vacuum pump and then purged using an inert gas.

Vacuum Sealing Mylar Bags

Once you have obtained a good seal on the bag, pulling a vacuum on the contents is straight forward.

First you'll need something to make a vacuum with. This can be either a regular vacuum pump, a vacuum sealer such as the Tilia Food Saver or even the suction end of your household vacuum cleaner. The end to be inserted into the bag will need to be of fairly small diameter in order to keep the hole in the Mylar from being any larger than necessary. This means that if you use a vacuum cleaner you'll need to fashion some form of reduction fitting. One such that I've seen is a plastic film canister with a hole drilled in the bottom and a piece of plastic tubing epoxied in place.

Cut a hole into the Mylar bag on a corner, making the opening only just large enough to admit the vacuum probe. Insert the nozzle and using a sponge, or something similar, push down on the material over the probe to make a seal. Now draw down a vacuum on the bag. When it's drawn down as much as possible, run a hot iron diagonally across the cut corner resealing the bag.

Gas Flushing Mylar Bags

Flushing with inert gas works essentially like vacuum sealing except that you're putting more gas into the bag rather than taking it out. You'll want to keep the entry hole small, but don't make a seal around it as above. Beyond that, follow the directions as given in *Section III.B.2 - CO₂ and Nitrogen*. When you feel that the bag has been sufficiently flushed, run the iron across the corner as above to seal.

Flushing with dry ice can also be done, but it is important to wait until the frozen carbon dioxide has completely sublimated into gas before making the final seal otherwise the bag will burst like an overfilled balloon.

REUSING OR RECYCLING PACKAGING

In an effort to save money or because new packaging may be hard to come by, it is common for many people to want to re-use previously used containers. There is nothing wrong with this, but it is sometimes more complicated than using new containers would be. Here are some general rules if you have an interest in doing this.

#1. Do not use containers that have previously contained products other than food. There are two risks this can expose you to. The first is that the particular package type may not have been tested for food use and may allow the transfer of chemicals from the packaging into your food. The second is

that all plastics are porous to some degree. Small amounts of the previous contents may have been absorbed by the packaging material only to be released into your food, particularly if it is wet, oily or alcoholic.

#2. Previously used containers should only be used with foods of a similar nature and exposed to similar processes. This means that if a container previously held a material high in fat, such as cooking oil, then it should not be used to store a strong acid such as vinegar. Nor should a container be exposed to extreme conditions, such as heat, if the original use of the package did not subject it to that treatment. An exception to this is glass which is covered below. Generally speaking, dry, non-oily, non-acidic or alkaline, non-alcoholic foods may be safely contained in any food safe container. An example of this is keeping grains and legumes in HDPE buckets formerly containing pickles.

#3. Glass may be used to store any food provided it is in sound condition and has only been used to store food previously. The lid or cap, however, that seals the jar is subject to the cautions given above. Glass jars not specifically made for home canning, either boiling water bath or pressure canning, have a significant risk of breakage if used for that purpose.

#4. Porous packaging materials such as paper, cardboard and Styrofoam should not be reused. Their open texture can trap food particles and are difficult to adequately clean. Packaging formerly holding raw meats, seafoods, or egg products are particularly at risk.

#5. Containers previously holding odorous foods may trap those odors and transfer them to foods later stored. Pickle flavored milk leaves a lot to be desired. Foods such as dry milk powders, fats and oils, flours and meals will absorb any odors seeping from your container material. Be sure to get the smell out before you fill them.

CARBON DIOXIDE AND NITROGEN

Carbon dioxide (CO_2) and nitrogen (N_2) are commonly used in packaging both fresh and shelf-stable foods, in order to extend their shelf lives. Fresh foods are outside the scope of this work so attention shall be focused on those foods suitable for use in storage programs.

The most common use of these gasses is for excluding oxygen (O_2) from the atmosphere contained inside of a storage container (called head gas). When head gas oxygen levels can be dropped below 2% the amount of undesirable oxidation reactions in stored foods can be greatly decreased resulting in longer shelf lives. Actually achieving this is not a simple matter when limited to the equipment and facilities typically available in the home. Still, with careful technique and proper packaging materials it is possible to achieve useful results.

In order for either gas to be used most effectively it is should be contained inside of packaging with high barrier properties to prevent outward diffusion over time or allowing oxygen to infuse in. Examples of this kind of packaging are aluminized Mylar or other high barrier property plastics, metal cans or glass jars. Buckets made of HDPE plastic are relatively poor gas barriers and will, over time, allow oxygen to infuse into the container. In order for foods to be kept for their maximum shelf lives the containers would need to be re-purged every three to four years. Foods that are particularly oxygen sensitive, such as dry milk powders, should not be stored in HDPE without a secondary gas barrier. It is possible to use HDPE buckets alone when gas purging if a shorter rotation period is used. An example would be using wheat in four to five years instead of the eight to ten that would be achievable if a high barrier container were used.

Purging efficiency can be greatly improved when used with a vacuum device. By first drawing down the head gas of the container and then flooding with the purging gas much more oxygen can be removed. Repeating the process once more will improve removal efficiency even more. If a true vacuum pump is not available, the suction end of a home vacuum-cleaner can be made to serve and still achieve useful results. With careful technique, oxygen levels can be dropped to between 0.5-2%. Finely textured materials such as grain flours and meals, dry milk powders, dry eggs, and similar textured foods will purge poorly and are better packaged with oxygen absorbers. Instructions for vacuum usage are given in *A.5.1 Using Mylar Bags*. Instructions for gas purging are given below in *B.1 Dry Ice* and *B.2 Compressed Nitrogen*.

A less common, but important use for carbon dioxide is fumigation. This is killing or retarding insect life contained in a product. Many chemical fumigants are available to do this but are not thought desirable by many who have foodstuffs they want to put into storage. CO_2 is not as certain as the more toxic fumigants, but it can be made to work and will not leave potentially harmful residues behind. It is possible for nitrogen to work in a similar manner, but it must be in a head gas concentration of 99%+ whereas carbon dioxide can be effective over time at levels as low as 3%. The precise amount of time necessary for the gas to do its work will vary according to the specific insect species and its growth stage along with the temperature and humidity level of the product being fumigated. In general, the more active the growth stage and the warmer the temperature the more effective CO_2 is in killing weevil infestations. The gas also exhibits bacterial and fungal inhibiting properties, but for our purposes this will be of little moment since all foods should be too dry to support such growth in the first place.

The procedure for fumigating foodstuffs with carbon dioxide is precisely the same as the one used in purging oxygen from storage containers mentioned below. The only change is that for the fastest effectiveness the sealed container should be left in a warm place for a week or so before moving it into its final storage location. The gas is still effective at cooler temperatures, but because insect life is slowed by lower temperatures the carbon dioxide takes longer to complete its mission.

NOTE: Both Mitsubishi Gas-Chemical, maker of the Ageless line of oxygen absorbers, and Multisorb, manufacturer of the FreshPax D 750 absorbers, state the their products should not be used in a high carbon dioxide environment. There are absorbers that will work well in high carbon dioxide atmospheres but they require an external moisture source which would make them difficult to use for our purposes.

DRY ICE
Using dry ice to displace oxygen from food storage containers is straightforward. To get the best results it is recommended that all foodstuffs and packaging materials be put in a warm location for a few hours before beginning the purging process. The reason for this is that the cold CO_2 sublimating from the dry ice will be denser than the warmer, lighter oxygen containing air. The cold gas will tend to stay on the bottom, gradually filling the container and pushing the warm air out the top.

When you first pick up your dry ice from the supplier, put it in a moisture proof container so that air humidity will be less able to condense and freeze on it. The sublimating gas will prevent you from achieving a tight seal, but you can slow down the water ice accumulation.

Gather your containers and any interior packaging materials. Break off a piece of dry ice of sufficient size for the volume to be purged. One pound of dry ice will produce about 8.3 cubic feet of carbon dioxide gas so approximately two ounces per five gallon bucket will do. Wipe off any accumulated water frost which should look whiter than the somewhat bluish frozen gas. Wrap in a paper towel to keep foodstuffs out of direct contact. Place in the bottom of the container that will actually contain the food, i.e. the bag. Fill the package with the food product, shaking and vibrating while doing so to achieve the maximum packing density.

If a vacuum process is not to be used then place the lid on the container, but do not fully seal. If a liner bag is being used then gather the top together or heat seal and cut off a small corner. This is to allow the air being purged to escape as it is pushed upward by the expanding gas from the dry ice. Do not move or shake the container while the ice is sublimating so as to minimize turbulence and mixing. After about two hours feel the bottom of the container immediately below where you put the ice. If it's not still icy cold complete the seal. Check the container every fifteen minutes or so to be sure that a pressure build up is not occurring. A small amount of positive pressure is OK, but do not allow the container to bulge.

If a vacuum process is used then cut off a corner of the bag and insert the probe or place the container in the vacuum chamber. Draw a vacuum and when it has reached the desired point shut it off, but do not allow air back inside. When the dry ice has finished sublimating seal the container. If a slightly larger piece of dry ice is used this process may be repeated once more to improve oxygen removal. Watch for pressure signs as above.

NOTE: It is natural for some grains and legumes to adsorb carbon dioxide when stored in an atmosphere with high levels of the gas. This will result in a drop in head space air pressure much like using oxygen absorbers will cause as they absorb oxygen. Precautions should be taken in thin walled containers against buckling and possible loss of seal integrity. When the food products are removed from the container they will release the adsorbed CO_2 and suffer no harm.

WARNING: Dry ice is extremely cold (about −110° degrees F.) and can cause burns to the skin with prolonged contact.

Because of this you should wear gloves whenever handling it. Also, dry ice evaporates into carbon dioxide gas, which is why we want it. CO_2 is not inherently dangerous, we breath it out with every breath we exhale, but you should make sure the area where you are packing your storage containers is adequately ventilated so the escaping gas will not build to a level dangerous enough to asphyxiate you. If you must pack your containers in a coat closet, leave the door open <grin>.

IMPORTANT NOTE: *Because dry ice is very cold, if there is much moisture (humidity) in the air trapped in the container with your food, it will condense. Try to pack your containers on a day when the relative humidity is low or in an area with low humidity, such as in an air-conditioned house. Use of a desiccant package when using dry ice to purge storage containers may be a good idea.*

DRY ICE SUPPLIERS

Dry ice may be found at ice houses, welding supply shops, some ice cream stores, meat packers or you could look in your local phone book under the headings "ice", "dry ice" or "gasses". If you are still unable to locate a source, contact your local hospital and ask to speak to the laboratory manager. Ask where the hospital gets the dry ice they use to ship biological specimens. You may be able to use the same source.

153

Plastic Buckets for Longer-Term Food Storage

Plastic buckets may be used to store food commodities that are dry (about 10 percent moisture or less) and low in oil content. Only buckets made of food-grade plastic with gaskets in the lid seals should be used. Buckets that have held nonfood items should not be used.

To prevent insect infestation, dry ice (frozen carbon dioxide) should be used to treat grains and dry beans stored in plastic buckets. Treatment methods that depend on the absence of oxygen to kill insects, such as oxygen absorbers or nitrogen gas flushing, are not effective in plastic buckets. Avoid exposing food to humid, damp conditions when packaging them.

Dry Ice Treatment Instructions

1. Use approximately one ounce of dry ice per gallon (7 grams per liter) capacity of the container. Do not use dry ice in metal containers of any kind or size because of the potential for inadequate seals or excessive buildup of pressure.
2. Wear gloves when handling dry ice.
3. Wipe frost crystals from the dry ice, using a clean dry towel.
4. Place the dry ice in the center of the container bottom.
5. Pour the grain or dry beans on top of the dry ice. Fill the bucket to within one inch (25 mm) of the top.
6. Place the lid on top of the container and snap it down only about halfway around the container. The partially sealed lid will allow the carbon dioxide gas to escape from the bucket as the dry ice sublimates (changes from a solid to a gas).
7. Allow the dry ice to sublimate completely before sealing the bucket. Feel the bottom of the container to see if the dry ice is all gone. If the bottom of the container is very cold, dry ice is still present.
8. Monitor the bucket for a few minutes after sealing the lid. If the bucket or lid bulges, slightly lift the edge of the lid to relieve pressure.
9. It is normal for the lid of the bucket to pull down slightly as a result of the partial vacuum caused when carbon dioxide is absorbed into the product.

Storage of Plastic Buckets

- Store plastic buckets off the floor by at least ½ inch (1.3 cm) to allow air to circulate under the bucket.
- Do not stack plastic buckets over three high. If buckets are stacked, check them periodically to ensure that the lids have not broken from the weight.

Visit providentliving.org for additional information.

Pouch Sealer Instructions

For Portable Operation of AIE (and ME) 305 A1 Sealers

Please read the entire sheet before starting.

Setting up

1. Place the sealer on a sturdy surface about 5 inches (13 cm) above the table top. This will place the sealer jaw opening about 8½ inches (22 cm) above the table for the correct sealing position. Connect the foot switch to the back of the sealer, and place the foot switch on the floor. Plug in the power cord. *Caution: Do not allow children in the area when the sealer is plugged in.*

2. Set **Recycle** dial to 2, **Congealing** dial to 6, **Sealing** dial to 4, and **Action Selector** switch to Manual.

3. Open the bag containing oxygen absorbers. Remove the number of packets that you will use in the next 20–30 minutes. Reseal the bag with the impulse sealer. Open and reseal the bag as you need additional groups of absorbers.

Filling pouches

1. Fill a pouch with one gallon (4 liters) of product. (Overfilling will result in a poor seal.) A two-quart (2-liter) pitcher, cut off at the two-quart (2-liter) line, is a good measure to use in when you are filling pouches. Fill with two level measures, tapped down.

2. Place an oxygen absorber packet on top of the product in each pouch.

3. For powdered products, wipe product dust from inside the seal area using a dry towel.

Sealing pouches

1. Turn the **Power** switch on. (Do not allow small children in the area when the sealer is on.)

2. Place the pouch in an upright position in front of the sealer. Rest its weight on the table or shelf; do not let it hang.

3. Close the pouch by grasping the side seams and firmly pulling them outward. Fold the top 1½ inches of the pouch (30–40 mm) over at a right angle, and push down on the pouch to expel extra air from the package. Settle the product, and flatten the pouch opening. If the top will not flatten and fold over easily, check if the pouch is too full.

4. Hold the pouch by the side seams, and insert the top edge of the pouch into the jaw opening. Keep fingers clear of the jaw.

5. Position the pouch to seal it near the top. Stretch outward on the side seams to remove wrinkles. Press the foot switch to activate the sealer. Release hold on the pouch after the jaw closes. Remove the pouch when the cycle is finished.

6. Label the pouch with contents and packaging date.

Testing seals

1. Inspect the seams to ensure that they are adequate and without burned spots. The seam should resemble factory seams.

2. Check to see if the seam can be pulled apart.

3. Push on the pouch to see if air or product can be forced out.

4. If seams pull apart, check for inadequate cleaning of seam area or for overfill. If necessary, increase sealing setting by ¼ step (for example, from 4 to 4.25). Verify that the congealing setting is at 6.

5. If seams are burned, decrease the sealing setting by ¼ step.

Notes

1. The sealer comes from the factory with two bolts protruding from the front of the machine. These bolts are for holding the shelf provided in the box. Remove the bolts, and do not use the shelf unless it is used as part of a separate stand.

2. If the Teflon cover on the lower jaw is burned, unplug the sealer, loosen and lift up the cover, and carefully clean off any burrs that may be on the heat strip. Advance the cover approximately ½ inch (12 mm), trim excess, and retighten.

3. If the sealer fails to operate, check the two fuses mounted in the lower back of the case. If necessary, replace them with fuses of the correct size.

4. Dry foods that are packaged for long-term storage should be limited to those that best retain flavor and nutritional value. These foods should be low in moisture (approximately 10 percent or less), of good quality, and insect free. Avoid exposing dry foods to humid, damp conditions when packaging them. *Warning: Products that are too high in moisture should not be stored in reduced oxygen packaging because botulism poisoning may result.* Visit providentliving.org for specific product guidelines.

For Portable Operation of AIE (and ME) 305 A1 Sealers

Please read the entire sheet before starting.

Setting up

1. Place the sealer on a sturdy surface about 5 inches (13 cm) above the table top. This will place the sealer jaw opening about 8½ inches (22 cm) above the table for the correct sealing position. Connect the foot switch to the back of the sealer, and place the foot switch on the floor. Plug in the power cord. *Caution: Do not allow children in the area when the sealer is plugged in.*
2. Set **Recycle** dial to 2, **Congealing** dial to 6, **Sealing** dial to 4, and **Action Selector** switch to Manual.
3. Open the bag containing oxygen absorbers. Remove the number of packets that you will use in the next 20–30 minutes. Reseal the bag with the impulse sealer. Open and reseal the bag as you need additional groups of absorbers.

Filling pouches

1. Fill a pouch with one gallon (4 liters) of product. (Overfilling will result in a poor seal.) A two-quart (2-liter) pitcher, cut off at the two-quart (2-liter) line, is a good measure to use in when you are filling pouches. Fill with two level measures, tapped down.
2. Place an oxygen absorber packet on top of the product in each pouch.
3. For powdered products, wipe product dust from inside the seal area using a dry towel.

Sealing pouches

1. Turn the **Power** switch on. (Do not allow small children in the area when the sealer is on.)
2. Place the pouch in an upright position in front of the sealer. Rest its weight on the table or shelf; do not let it hang.
3. Close the pouch by grasping the side seams and firmly pulling them outward. Fold the top 1½ inches of the pouch (30–40 mm) over at a right angle, and push down on the pouch to expel extra air from the package. Settle the product, and flatten the pouch opening. If the top will not flatten and fold over easily, check if the pouch is too full.
4. Hold the pouch by the side seams, and insert the top edge of the pouch into the jaw opening. Keep fingers clear of the jaw.
5. Position the pouch to seal it near the top. Stretch outward on the side seams to remove wrinkles. Press the foot switch to activate the sealer. Release hold on the pouch after the jaw closes. Remove the pouch when the cycle is finished.
6. Label the pouch with contents and packaging date.

Testing seals

1. Inspect the seams to ensure that they are adequate and without burned spots. The seam should resemble factory seams.
2. Check to see if the seam can be pulled apart.
3. Push on the pouch to see if air or product can be forced out.
4. If seams pull apart, check for inadequate cleaning of seam area or for overfill. If necessary, increase sealing setting by ¼ step (for example, from 4 to 4.25). Verify that the congealing setting is at 6.
5. If seams are burned, decrease the sealing setting by ¼ step.

Notes

1. The sealer comes from the factory with two bolts protruding from the front of the machine. These bolts are for holding the shelf provided in the box. Remove the bolts, and do not use the shelf unless it is used as part of a separate stand.
2. If the Teflon cover on the lower jaw is burned, unplug the sealer, loosen and lift up the cover, and carefully clean off any burrs that may be on the heat strip. Advance the cover approximately ½ inch (12 mm), trim excess, and retighten.
3. If the sealer fails to operate, check the two fuses mounted in the lower back of the case. If necessary, replace them with fuses of the correct size.
4. Dry foods that are packaged for long-term storage should be limited to those that best retain flavor and nutritional value. These foods should be low in moisture (approximately 10 percent or less), of good quality, and insect free. Avoid exposing dry foods to humid, damp conditions when packaging them. *Warning: Products that are too high in moisture should not be stored in reduced oxygen packaging because botulism poisoning may result.* Visit providentliving.org for specific product guidelines.

Pouch Sealer Instructions

1

Elevate the sealer five inches (130 mm).

Sealer Settings
- Set **Selector** to Manual.
- Set **Recycle** dial to 2.
- Set **Congealing** dial to 6.
- Set **Sealing** dial to 4.
- Turn the power on.

Caution: Do not allow children in area when the sealer is plugged in.

2

Use a measuring pitcher to fill pouch.

3

Fill pouch with only one gallon (4 liters) of product.

4

Place the oxygen packet in the filled pouch.

5

Wipe off top inside edge of the pouch (for powdered products).

6

Grasp side seams of pouch.

Pull outward on sides to close pouch opening.

Fold the top of the pouch over.

7

Insert top edge of pouch into jaw opening.

Position pouch to seal it near the top.

Stretch outward on side seams to remove wrinkles.

Make certain that fingers are not in jaw opening.

8

Activate the foot switch.

Release hold on pouch after jaw closes.

Remove pouch when cycle is finished.

Inspect pouch to verify that it has sealed properly.

9

Label pouch with contents and packaging date.

PERIODIC SEAL EVALUATION

A

Proper seal. The seal should be similar to the factory seams.

B

If the sealing time is too long, the seal will degloss and may melt.

Decrease **Sealing** dial setting slightly and reseal pouch.

C

DO NOT overfill pouches. A poor seal will result.

D

Seam should not pull apart. Increase **Sealing** dial setting slightly and reseal pouch.

E

Pressing on bag should not cause leaks.

OXYGEN ABSORBERS

WHAT IS AN OXYGEN ABSORBER?

Oxygen absorbers are a relatively recent food storage tool whose arrival has been a real boon to the person wanting to put up oxygen sensitive dry foods at home. The packets absorb free oxygen from the air around them and chemically bind it by oxidizing finely divided iron into iron oxide. This removes oxygen from being available for other purposes such as oxidative rancidity and respiration by insects, fungi or aerobic bacteria. The practical upshot of all this is that by removing the free oxygen from your storage containers, you can extend the storage life of the foods inside. Not all foods are particularly oxygen sensitive but for those that are the absorbers truly simplify getting the job done.

The absorbers themselves have only a relatively short life span, roughly about six months from the time they were manufactured for the types that do not need an external moisture source. They don't suddenly become ineffective all at once, it's just at that point you will begin to notice (if you can measure it) that the absorbers no longer soak up as much as they would when they were new. Better to use them while they're fresh.

HOW ARE OXYGEN ABSORBERS USED?

In order to make the best use of your absorbers you need to know three things:

#1 – *Is the food I want to put by particularly oxygen sensitive for the time I want to keep it in storage?* Whole grains that have not been polished or hulled such as wheat, corn, and rye are not especially oxygen sensitive. If you intend to use them up in five years or so, there's no great advantage to using oxygen absorbers, unless used to deter weevil infestations. The same for most beans and peas. Processed or high fat grains and legumes such as oats, barley, brown rice, soybeans, peanuts and split peas would benefit from their use if they are to be kept for more than a year. Whole grain products such as whole wheat flour and rolled oats would as well. Refined grain products such as white rice, white flour, degerminated cornmeal will keep fine for a year or so, possibly longer, without oxygen absorbers if kept dry and protected from weevils. Dry milk, dry eggs, dry meats, and many kinds of dehydrated foods and any kind of freeze dried foods would benefit from oxygen absorbers. Foods with an easily transferable fat content should not be used with oxygen absorbers, nor should they be used with foods that are high in moisture or with free liquids in the storage container. These should be preserved using pressure or boiling water bath canning as appropriate.

#2 – *Will the packaging I want to use seal air-tight and is the packaging material itself a good gas barrier?* Obviously if the container won't seal air tight you're wasting your time trying to use oxygen absorbers but the barrier properties of a container stump many folks. Canning jars with good lids, properly sealed #10 (or other size) cans, properly sealed Mylar bags, PETE plastics with appropriate lids or caps, military surplus ammo cans with good gaskets, and many other types of packaging will seal air-tight and provide good barrier properties against oxygen infusing through the packaging material. Non-laminated flexible plastic packaging (bags, sheets, etc.), HDPE plastic buckets and any kind of non-laminated paper or cardboard container have poor gas barrier properties. "Poor" is a relative term, though, and if you're going to use the food up in two or three years, even oxygen sensitive foods can be kept in unlined HDPE buckets if you use an appropriately sized absorber and make sure the bucket is well sealed. You'll be using the food before sufficient oxygen has been able to infuse through the walls of the container to make a significant impact.

#3 – *What is the volume of the container and how much air volume remains after I've filled it with food?* This is important to know if you want to make the most efficient use of your absorbers and be certain your food is adequately protected. Taking the question in two parts, here is how to determine the answer:

A. Absorber capacity is rated by the amount of oxygen in milliliters that each will absorb so you'll need to know what the volume of your container is in milliliters. The table below gives conversions between common U.S. container sizes and their milliliter equivalents.

Pint jar (16 fl oz)	475 milliliters
Quart jar (32 fl oz)	950 milliliters
Half-gallon jar (64 fl oz)	1,900 milliliters
#10 can (112 fl oz)	3,300 milliliters
One gallon jar (128 fl oz)	3,800 milliliters
Five gallon pail (640 fl oz)	19,000 milliliters
Six gallon pail (768 fl oz)	22,800 milliliters
Fifty-five gallon drum (7,040 fl oz)	208,175 milliliters

Fluid ounces x 29.57 = milliliters = cubic centimeters

Now multiply the volume of your container times the 21% (0.21) of the atmosphere that oxygen constitutes and you'll come up with the volume of oxygen, in milliliters, that your container holds when it's empty.

An example: A quart jar (32 ozs) is approximately 950 milliliters in volume. Multiply 950 x 0.21 (21%) and you get 199.5 milliliters of oxygen in an empty quart jar. This leads to the second half of the above question.

B. Determining remaining air volume in a container that has been filled can be difficult. Foods vary widely in their density and porosity from flour, which will pack tightly to elbow macaroni which is mostly air even if you pack it to just short of crushing. The following are three rough and ready rules that can be used and will work.

i> Foods that have a lot of open space between the food particles (called *intersitial space*) such as macaroni, pasta, instant dry milk, instant potato flakes, many coarsely chunky dehydrated foods, cold cereals, etc. should use *one half* the container volume as the remaining air space. Using the example above with the quart jar, there would be approximately 100 milliliters of oxygen remaining.

ii> Foods that pack more densely such as non-instant milk, dry eggs, flours and meals, grains with small kernels, dehydrated foods with fine particles and the like should use *one-third* the container volume as the remaining air space. Using the

example above, there would be 66 milliliters of oxygen remaining.

iii> Alternatively, you could do what many of the commercial storage food packagers do and use the *entire container volume.* This is not as efficient as more closely determining remaining air volume but it does add certainty that your absorbers will soak up all available free oxygen and still leave some capacity to deal with any microscopic leaks or infusion through the packaging material.

NOTES: #1 — Both Multisorb and Mitsubishi corporations advise that their oxygen absorbers should not be used in a high carbon dioxide environment. This is apparently for reasons that the absorbers will also absorb carbon dioxide as well as oxygen and may run out of capacity before all of the oxygen in the container has been absorbed.

#2 — If you do choose to use oxygen absorbers in packing your food give some consideration to the sturdiness of your containers. In doing its job the absorber is going be removing the 21% of the atmosphere that oxygen constitutes. Since nothing is replacing the absorbed gas this will leave the storage container with a lower atmospheric pressure inside than outside. If the container is sufficiently sturdy this pressure differential will be of little consequence. For containers with thinner walls the pressure drop could cause them partially collapse or buckle, particularly if other containers are stacked upon them. Should this occur the entire stack could fall causing one or more to burst. Metal cans and glass jars should have no problems, but some plastic buckets made of HDPE have relatively thin walls which can buckle when the internal air pressure drops. To deter this, a liner bag of Mylar or other high gas barrier plastic should used. Heavier walled buckets won't need a liner unless you're trying to achieve the maximum possible shelf life. Seal the absorbers inside of the liner bag so that the pressure drop with not stress the walls of the container. Other containers should probably be tested or first flushed with an inert gas (N2) before the absorber is sealed in.

#3 — If the pack of absorbers you need to open contains more than you are going to use in fifteen minutes or so, you should minimize exposure of the remaining packets. This can be done by heat sealing the bag they came in with an iron after expelling as much air as possible or better yet by vacuum sealing the bag. You can also put the remaining absorbers in as small a jar or metal can as they will fit in and closing with an air tight lid.

#4 — The chemical reaction that absorbs the oxygen releases minor amounts of heat. This heat release is trivial in an individual packet but if they are piled one atop another as you're using them they can warm each other and speed the absorptive reaction. This costs you capacity lost to open room air so it's best to spread the packets in immediate use out on a tray so they lay atop each other.

#5 — If absorbers are sealed in a package with desiccants some thought should be given to how low the relative humidity will become. Silica gel will reduce humidity to approximately 40% which should not interfere with the absorbers oxidation reaction. Other desiccants, however, are capable of reducing relative humidity to very low levels. This might adversely affect your absorber's ability to carry out its mission by removing moisture from the absorber package that is necessary to sustain the oxidation reaction. If you do use desiccants and oxygen absorbers in the same package, place the desiccant on the bottom, fill the package and then place the oxygen absorber on top of the food before sealing.

MOISTURE IN PACKAGING AND FOOD STORAGE

WHY MOISTURE IS IMPORTANT
Moisture in inappropriate amounts and places is damaging to food. Because of this, much effort is put into reducing the water content of dry foods in order to prolong their shelf lives. Once it is reduced to the desired level the product can then be packaged for storage. Unfortunately, merely reducing moisture content is not always sufficient. Environmental conditions can play a role as well.

There are four mechanisms by which environmental conditions may cause a moisture problem in your food storage:

1. - The air trapped in the container with the food may have held sufficient humidity to raise the moisture content of the food to undesirable levels.

2. - Even if the water vapor content wasn't too high, a falling temperature level may cause the trapped humidity to reach its dew point causing water to be squeezed out of the air to condense on your food much the same way as dew forms on your lawn on cool mornings after a warm, humid night. This can be a particular problem if the condensation is localized – say, only the portion of the food next to the walls of the container – resulting in excessive moisture in that local area even though the contents as a whole would be at a satisfactorily low moisture level.

3. - The seal of the container may not be sufficiently tight enough to prevent moisture laden air from leaking in.

4. - The packaging material itself may be porous to water vapor to one degree or another. All paper, wood and cardboard has this fault. Depending upon their particular physical properties some plastics do as well. Metal and glass containers have excellent barrier properties though their seals may not.

The solution for moisture problems is multi-faceted.

1 - Make sure the product to be stored is at an appropriate water content for that particular foodstuff. Beans and grains store well at a 10% moisture level, but milk powders, dried eggs and dehydrated or freeze dried foods should be lower for best results. As a general rule, nearly any dry food will store well at moisture contents between 3%-10% with the lower the better. Don't get carried away with this though. Extreme low moisture levels (below 3%) can make some foods difficult or impossible to reconstitute and damage the viability of seeds.

Ideally, the dry foodstuffs you have on hand will have no more than a 10% moisture content. If they do not then you will need to reduce moisture to a level appropriate for the kind of food you are storing.

One of the following methods might be of use in lowering moisture content.

A - The least involved is to wait until the driest time of year for your location making sure there is plenty of free air circulation around the food product. If this doesn't suit, then turn your air conditioning on a little high. Bring in your buckets, lids, and the storage food. Let everything sit in a well-ventilated place where it's going to get plenty of cool, dry air from the A/C (avoid anywhere near the kitchen or bathroom areas, as they put out a lot of moisture). Stir the food frequently to maximize moisture loss. A few days of cool, constant air flow and low humidity ought to dry things out. Due to its odor absorptive nature, I would not do this with any dried milk products or other powdered foods, flours or meals . This method works best with coarse particles such as grain, legumes and dried foods.

B - Warm, dry air can also be used to lower moisture content and works well if you have large quantities of grains and legumes. This is similar to what is used on farms for drying harvested grain. You'll need a source of forced, warm, *not hot*, air. Place the grain in a drum or barrel and blow the heat from the bottom so that the warm and the moisture it will carry can exit from the top. It's important to not let the bottom product get too hot. You should also monitor the top, center of the drum to be certain the product there is not getting damp from the moisture escaping other areas. Stirring occasionally may be necessary. I've seen this done with an old, drum style vacuum cleaner that put off fairly warm exhaust air and it worked pretty well. Do be sure to clean the vacuum thoroughly so you don't blow the grain full of dust.

C - If the above methods won't do or you have powdery foods to dry, you can put the food and a large quantity of desiccant (see below) in a storage container. The desiccant should be in its own container placed on top of the food and the container lid sealed on. After about a week, unseal and check the desiccant. If it's saturated, change it out with dry desiccant and reseal. Continue to do this until the contents are sufficiently dry. If it doesn't become saturated the first time, change it anyway before sealing the bucket permanently to deter saturation in storage.

If your food products are sufficiently dry you can pack them in storage containers using the packaging method of your choice and have a reasonable expectation of your food staying in good condition. Whether you will need to use a desiccant will be dependent upon the conditions discussed below.

2 - Try to package your goods in a dry atmosphere and do not allow extreme temperature swings in storage areas. Warm temperatures and a high relative humidity when a container is sealed means the air trapped inside the container will have a high dew point. This will lead to condensation should storage temperatures fall below that dew point. An example of this would be a container sealed on a day that was 70º F and 40% relative humidity. At that temperature the relative humidity would be quite reasonable for all but the most moisture sensitive food. However, should the temperature fall to 44º F the capacity of the air to hold water vapor would

have dropped to the point that it could not contain what was sealed in at 77º F and the excess would be squeezed out to condense on the food, i.e. - it will grow moister. Possibly the food will be able to adsorb this moisture without harm and then again, it may not.

3 - Use appropriate packaging materials and make certain it is sealed correctly. If you are going to consume them in four to five years, storing grains, beans and peas in unlined HDPE buckets at normal humidities is fine. If you want to keep them at their best for many years beyond that, the plastic the pail is made of is too porous to water vapor for best results and should have an interior liner of a material with better barrier properties. Dry milk powders should not be kept for more than a year in unlined HDPE, but can be kept for much longer in #10 metal cans, glass jars or Mylar bags. Naturally, even the most highly resistant packaging material is useless if its seal isn't good so be sure you use good technique when making closures.

Lastly, you may wish to consider using a desiccant if good humidity control at the time of packing is difficult or if the storage area is in a high humidity environment or if the packaging material does not have sufficiently high barrier properties.

NOTE: There has been some confusion in the past over the appropriate use of desiccants in food storage which I would like to address here. Any desiccants you may seal in your storage containers (if you use them) are not for lowering the moisture content of the foods therein, but for moderating any shifts in moisture levels caused by those factors I mention above. If the food you want to put up is too high in moisture for good storage this needs to be dealt with BEFORE you seal the packaging. An example of what I'm trying to communicate here would be 10lbs of wheat with a 15% moisture content. That's too high for safe storage and needs to be lowered, preferably to 10% or less. To lower the moisture content of that grain to 10% you need to remove the 5% excess. 5% of 10lbs is eight ounces of water. Good dry silica gel (one of the most common desiccants) will hold 40% of its mass in moisture so to soak up that extra water you would need 20 ounces of silica gel – quite a large amount – all to remove that 5% excess moisture in ten pounds of grain. Fifty pounds of grain at that same moisture level would require 100 ounces or *six and a quarter pounds of silica gel*. Clearly no practical amount of desiccant you can put inside your storage packaging will do for you what should have been done before the food was put by. Desiccants can be used for lowering food moisture content, but this will involve rotating packages of desiccant in and out of the foodstuff until the desired moisture content has been reached. Once the package is sealed any desiccant you leave inside should be there to control moisture fluctuations or to guard against moisture infiltration from the outside.

WHAT IS A DESICCANT?

A desiccant is a substance with strong *hygroscopic* properties, meaning it will soak up water vapor from the surrounding air. A number of different substances are capable of doing this, but only a relative few of them are of practical use and fewer still are going to be readily available to the average person. Before elaborating on the different types that might be useful for our purposes it's necessary to explain how to choose a desiccant.

The U.S. military has done much of the best research on the use of desiccants in packaging and have largely set the standards by which they are judged. Each type of desiccant has temperature and humidity ranges where it performs best and particular physical and chemical characteristics that may need to be considered in relation to what you propose to do with them.

The most applicable standard for home food storage defines a unit of desiccant as *the amount of desiccant that will adsorb at least 6 grams of water vapor at 40% relative humidity at 77º F (25º C).*

Desiccant Needed to Adsorb 6 Grams of Water Vapor

Desiccant Type Needed	Mass (weight) of Desiccant
Silica Gel	15 grams
Indicating Silica Gel	75 grams [1]
Montmorillonite Clay	24 grams
Calcium Oxide (quicklime)	21.5 grams
Calcium Sulfate (gypsum, Drierite)	60 grams
Wood	43 grams [1]

[1] See desiccant descriptions for clarification.

In order to maximize surface area to obtain optimal adsorption, desiccants are manufactured in granular or powder forms. This presents a problem of keeping the desiccant, which may not be safe for direct contact with food, out of the product while still allowing sufficient air flow for it to carry out its task. Manufacturers call this "dusting" and deal with it by packaging the adsorbent in materials such as uncoated Tyvek, a spunbonded high-density polyethylene material produced by the Dupont corporation. Unfortunately, I have not yet been able to locate a retail source of uncoated Tyvek, just the coated variety such as is used in postal envelopes. Second best, and what I use, is two or more layers of coffee filter paper securely sealed over the mouth of the container holding the desiccant. I've also made "cartridges" of filter paper for use in narrow necked containers such as two-liter bottles. For this I used ordinary white glue. Getting a good seal all the way around requires some care in execution. Brown Kraft (butcher paper) may be used as well.

For coarse granular materials tightly woven fabrics might serve the purpose providing the seams are tightly stitched.

TYPES OF DESICCANTS

SILICA GEL

The most commonly known and used desiccant is silica gel which is a form of silica dioxide (SiO_2), a naturally occurring mineral. It will work from below freezing to past the boiling point of water, but performs best at room temperatures (70-90º F) and high humidity (60-90%). Its performance begins to drop off over 100º F, but will continue to work until approximately 220º F. It will lower the relative humidity in a container to around 40% at any temperature in its range until it is saturated. Silica gel will absorb up to 40% of its weight in moisture. Some forms are approved by the FDA for direct food use (check with your supplier to be sure). It recharges easily (see below in the indicating silica gel text) and does not swell in size as it adsorbs moisture.

INDICATING SILICA GEL

In the retail trade, the most common form of silica gel is indicating silica gel composed of small white crystals looking much like granulated sugar with pink or blue colored crystals scattered throughout. This is ordinary silica gel with the colored specks being coated with cobalt chloride, a heavy metal salt. When the gel has absorbed approximately eight percent of its weight in water the colored crystals will turn from blue to pink making an easy visual indicator of whether the gel has become saturated with moisture. *Because cobalt is a heavy metal,* **indicating silica gel** *is not food safe and should be kept from spilling into anything edible.*

The indicating silica gel will still adsorb up to 40% of its weight in water vapor like the non-indicating type will but once it has gone past the 8% level and the crystals have turned pink there is no way to tell how close it is to saturation. This isn't necessarily a problem, you'll just have to treat like the other non-indicating desiccants and either weigh it to determine adsorption or use a *humidity indicator card*. These cards are made to show various humidity ranges and can be had from many desiccant and packaging suppliers.

When saturated, both varieties of silica gel can be dried out and used again. This is done by heating the crystals in an oven at a temperature of no more than 300° F (149° C) for approximately three hours or until the crystals turn blue. Dehydrating the desiccant may also be accomplished by heating in a microwave oven. Using a 900 watt oven heat the crystals for three minute intervals until the color change occurs. The exact amount of time necessary will depend upon the oven wattage. Spreading the desiccant in a broad pan in a shallow layer will speed the process. Heating to 325° F (149° C) or more, or using a microwave oven over 900 watts can damage the gel and render it unable to adsorb moisture.

If your desiccant is packaged in Tyvek, do not heat above 250° F (121° C) or you could damage the material. This leaves a fairly narrow temperature window since silica gel will not begin to desorb moisture below 220° F (104° C). It's a good idea to use a reliable oven thermometer to check your oven temperature as the thermostats in home ovens are often off by more than twenty five degrees. Start with the packets in a cold oven and raise the temperature to 245° F (118° C), keeping it there for twenty four hours. Spread the packets so they are not touching and keep them at least 16 inches from any heating elements or flames so that radiant heat does not damage the packaging. Tyvek should not be microwaved.

HOW DO I USE DESICCANTS?

Before you get to this point you should have already used the charts above and determined how much of the particular desiccant you're interested in you need for the size of the storage containers you'll be using. Once you know that you're ready to put them it into use.

Although they perform different functions, desiccants and oxygen absorbers are used in a similar fashion. They both begin to adsorb their respective targets as soon as they are exposed to them so you want to only keep out in the open air as much desiccant as you are going to use up in fifteen minutes or so. If you'll be using oxygen absorbers in the same package, place the desiccant on the bottom of the package and the oxygen absorber on the top. This is to keep the desiccants from robbing needed moisture from your oxygen absorbers which will hinder their operation.

If your desiccant is pre-packaged, that's all there is to it, put it in the package and seal it up. If you have purchased bulk desiccant you'll first need to make your own containers.

I use indicating silica gel for practically everything. My usual procedure is to save or scrounge clear plastic pill bottles, such as aspirin bottles or small plastic jars. Fill the bottle with the desiccant (remember to dry the gel first) and then use a double thickness of coffee filter paper carefully and securely tied around the neck of the bottle to keep any from leaking out (remember the indicating type of silica gel is not food safe). The paper is permeable to moisture, but it's tight enough not to let the crystals out. I use several winds of plain cotton string for this as both adhesive tapes and rubber bands have a way of going bad over time which might allow the cap to come off spilling the desiccant into the food.

For containers that have openings too narrow to use a desiccant container such as described above you can make desiccant packets with the same filter paper. The easiest way I've found is to wrap at least a double layer of paper around the barrel of a marker pen and use a thin bead of white glue to seal. Slide the packet off the pen and allow to dry. When ready, fill with the necessary amount of desiccant. You can then fold the top over twice and tie with string or staple closed. Take care that the top is closed securely enough not to allow any desiccant to leak out. Virgin (not recycled) brown Kraft paper can be used to make the packets with as well.

The above method will also work other desiccants, subject to whatever precautions the individual type may have.

IMPORTANT NOTE: *The indicating form of silica gel (has small blue or pink specks in it) is not edible so you want to use care when putting together your desiccant package to insure that is does not spill into your food.*

WHERE DO I FIND DESICCANTS?
I buy indicating silica gel at Wal-Mart in their dry flower section where it is sold in one and five pound cans for flower drying. I've seen it sold the same way in crafts stores and other department type stores that carry flower-arranging supplies. You can also buy it from many other businesses already prepackaged in one form or another to be used as an adsorbent. All of the desiccant that I've found packaged this way has been rather expensive (to me) so shop carefully. There are a number of Internet sources available which will probably provide your best route for finding what you want.

Businesses carrying packaging supplies sometimes also sell desiccants. Some businesses commonly receive packets or bags of desiccants packaged along with the products they receive. I've seen montmorillonite clay in bags as large as a pound shipped with pianos coming in from Japan. Small packets of silica gel seem to be packed in nearly everything. Naturally, any salvaged or recycled desiccant should be of a type appropriate for use with the product you want to package.

It is possible to make your own desiccants using gypsum from drywall and maybe Plaster of Paris. Calcium oxide can also be produced from limestone (calcium carbonate) or slaked or pickling lime (calcium hydroxide) by roasting to drive off the adsorbed water and carbon dioxide. I don't have any clear instructions, as of yet, on how to go about this. Please do keep in mind that calcium oxide (quicklime) is caustic in nature and is hazardous if handled incorrectly.

DIATOMACEOUS EARTH

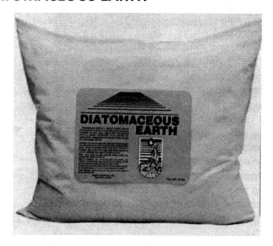

WHAT IS DIATOMACEOUS EARTH?

Diatomaceous earth is a naturally occurring substance partially comprised of the fossilized remains of diatoms. Diatoms are microscopic sized hard shelled creatures found in both marine and fresh waters. The diatom shells are covered in sharp spines that make them dangerous to exoskeletal insects, but not to animals with internal skeletons. The spines of the diatom skeletons pierce the soft body tissues of insects between their hard exoskeletal plates and it is through these numerous microscopic wounds that the insect loses bodily moisture to the point of desiccating and dying. Creatures with internal skeletons such as humans, cattle and pets have means of resisting such damage and are not harmed. Thus, it is possible to mix a small amount of DE into your stored grains and beans to deter insect infestations without having to remove the dust again before you consume them. *Diatomaceous earth works in a purely physical, not chemical, manner thus has no chemical toxicity.*

As neat as this sounds, in the limited number of controlled studies that I have been able to find it seems that DE is not as effective in controlling food storage insects as properly used freezing techniques, fumigation with carbon dioxide (dry ice) or sealing in air-tight containers with oxygen absorbers. This is primarily for reasons that most of the insects that cause a problem in grain storage are hard-shelled weevils which have only a limited amount of soft tissue exposure. I now mostly use DE for controlling ants and roaches in areas where I feed my animals and bedding areas. Still, some folks want to use DE in their food storage so the following information is provided.

WHERE DO I FIND D.E. AND WHAT TYPE SHOULD I BUY?

IMPORTANT NOTE: There are two kinds of diatomaceous earth to be found on the market and only one of them is suitable for use as an insecticide in your stored grains. *The type you DO NOT WANT FOR FOOD USE is sold by swimming pool suppliers as a filtering agent. DE to be used for filtering* has been subjected to a heat treatment that dramatically increases it's crystalline silicate content which makes it unsuitable for use with your foodstuffs. *The diatomaceous earth that is needed for use in food storage has not been heat treated and has a crystalline silica content of no more than 1-1.5%.* It is commonly sold in hardware and garden stores as an "organic pesticide" and is available from a number of storage food dealers. A few of these suppliers are listed in the *Resources* section.

I have always purchased my DE from my local hardware store and have had no concerns about its safety. However, a number of correspondents have reported to me that their local suppliers keep their DE in the same area as their chemical pesticides. This causes some concern about possible contamination and I no longer recommend using DE from these sources. Since the actual amount of DE (by weight) that is necessary to protect grains is fairly small I recommend ordering yours from suppliers who will guarantee their product is *food grade* as stipulated by the US FDA. This will insure you receive a product that has no deleterious contaminants and is safe to use.

HOW DO I USE D.E. IN FOOD STORAGE?

To use, you should mix thoroughly one cup (8 fl ozs) of DE to every forty pounds of grain, grain products or legumes. This works out to approximately one cup of DE to every five gallon bucket of food you want to treat. You need to make certain that every kernel is coated so it is better to do the mixing in small batches where you can insure more even coating. Both the grain and the DE should be quite dry when doing the mixing otherwise you'll get an uneven distribution.

WARNING: DE is a powdery dust which you need to take steps to keep out of your lungs and eyes. A paint or hardware store filter mask and a pair of goggles will do the job. It's a good idea to do the actual mixing outside in a slight breeze otherwise you'll get DE all over everything. Even whole wheat flour dust can cause lung irritation if you breathe in a sufficient amount.

Being inactive and usually covered in a hard shell, DE works poorly on insect eggs or pupae. It has more effectiveness on larvae and adult insects with a fair amount of soft tissue exposure.

SPOILAGE

INSECT INFESTATIONS

PESTS OF STORED GRAINS, LEGUMES AND DRY FOODSTUFFS

Insect infestations can occur in a wide variety of foodstuffs such as flours, meals, pastas, dried fruits or vegetables, nuts, sweets, whole grains, beans, sugars, TVP, jerky, bird seed and pet foods.

Naturally, the best way to deal with an insect infestation is not to have one in the first place. Try to purchase your goods from suppliers who are clean and who turn over their inventory quickly so the products you purchase will be less likely to have bugs.

When you buy foodstuffs examine them closely to be sure they are insect free. Check for any packaging or use by dates to insure their freshness. Don't shake the package, most adult insects will be found in the top couple of inches of the product and shaking the package will mix them into the contents disguising their appearance. If the package does turn out to be infested, return it for replacement.

If not already packaged for storage when you buy them transfer your foods into air- and moisture-tight containers so they cannot be invaded after you have brought them home. With sufficient time, some adult and larval insect forms can penetrate paper, cardboard and thin plastic packaging. Storage containers should be glass, metal, or heavy plastic with tight fitting lids. As with everything in food storage, you should use older packages before newer ones and opened packages before unopened ones.

Storage areas should be kept clean. Don't allow grain, flour, beans, bits of pasta or other food particles to accumulate on shelves or floors. Cracks and crevices should be sealed or otherwise blocked. Except for sticky spills, vacuuming is the best method of cleaning as soap and water can wash food particles into cracks.

Insects may also get their start in chairs, sofas and carpets where food is dropped and not cleaned up. Don't forget to replace the filter bag on the vacuum as some insects can survive and reproduce in the bag.

Bags of dry pet food and bird seed can harbor insect infestation. Decorative foodstuffs such as ears of colorful Indian corn, colored beans and hard squashes can carry insects that may infest your edible food. Even poison baits can harbor flour beetles.

CONTROL OF INSECT INFESTATIONS

Should you find that in spite of buying fresh products and using careful packaging techniques you have an insect infestation, you can try some of the following steps:

1. If the food is too heavily infested to try to save it should be disposed of as soon as possible. Remove from the kitchen or food storage area immediately so as to not infest other foods.

2. Large bugs can be sifted or winnowed out if the food's not too heavily infested and you want to try to save it. Then treat by placing into a deep freezer at 0º F (-18º C) for three to seven days depending upon the size of the package. Refrigerator freezers usually do not freeze low enough to effectively kill all of the life stages of insects, but if left there, will slow their development. If freezing is not workable then the product could be spread on baking sheets and heated to 150º F for fifteen to twenty minutes, cooled and repackaged. This will shorten shelf life so heat treated foods should be consumed shortly thereafter.

3. The surface areas where the food containers are stored can be treated with an insecticide. This is not a replacement for clean storage habits and good containers, but is rather a supplement. This will not control insect infestations already in your stored foods.

Spray the shelf surface with 0.5% chlorpyrifos (Dursban), 1% propoxur (Baygon), 0.5 percent diazinon, or 0.25 percent resmethrin. You can find any of these in the hardware store in ready to apply packages. If a sprayer isn't feasible then they can be applied with a paint brush. Allow the solution to dry thoroughly. Cover the shelves with clean, untreated shelf paper then put properly packaged foods back on shelves. READ THE PRODUCT LABEL FOR SAFETY INFORMATION CONCERNING CHILDREN AND PETS.

Household bleach, Lysol and other sterilizers will not control insect infestation, though they can be used for mold, mildew and algae.

You may continue to find some insects after the cleanup is finished. This could be for several reasons. It may be they escaped from the packages they were infesting and did not get cleaned up. There may be more packages infested than were originally found or, there may be hiding places in the storage area that need attention. Once you have carefully eliminated all food sources, the bugs should disappear in a few weeks.

MOLDS IN FOOD

Molds are fungi like mushrooms and yeast. Also like mushrooms, they reproduce by releasing spores into the air that land on everything, including your food and food storage containers. If those spores begin to grow, they create thin threads that spread through their growing medium. These threads are the roots of the mold fungus, called *mycelium*. The stalk of a mold fungus is the portion above or on the surface of the food. It produces the spores and gives the mold its color. We've all seen examples of this when we discover a dish of something or other left too long in the refrigerator only to become covered in a mold fuzz.

Molds can grow anywhere they have a growing medium (their food), sufficient moisture and warmth. Some can even grow at refrigerator temperatures, albeit more slowly than they would if it were warmer. These fungi can also withstand more salt and sugar than bacteria, which is why you sometimes find mold in jellies and jams with their high sugar content and on dry cured products like ham or bacon with their high salt content.

In the past, a slight amount of mold was commonly felt to be harmless and the food consumed anyway. For molds that were intentionally introduced, such as the mold in bleu cheese, this is fine. For the unintentional molds, it could possibly be a serious error in judgment. These unwanted molds could be producing toxic substances called *mycotoxins* which can be very bad indeed. Mycotoxins are produced around the root or mycelium of molds and these mold roots can penetrate deeply into the food. Mycotoxins can survive for a long time and most are not destroyed by cooking. The molds probably best known for this dangerous spoilage are the various *Aspergillus* species which produces a mycotoxin known as *aflatoxin*, but there are other dangerous fungi as well, such as the *Fusarium* molds. Both of the above affect grains and some legumes. See *B.3 Molds In Grains and Legumes.*

IMPORTANT NOTE: In wet pack foods such as your home canned goodies, molds can do something else as well, possibly with lethal consequences. If they find their way into wet pack acid foods canned by the boiling water bath method, whether by reasons of improper procedure or contamination after the fact, they can consume the natural acids present in the food. The effect of this is to raise the pH of the food in the container, perhaps to the point that it becomes possible for spores of *Clostridium botulinum*, better known as *botulism*, to become active and reproduce. For this reason, moldy wet pack foods should be *safely* discarded. This most deadly kind of food poisoning has an entry of its own in the bacterial spoilage section.

Molds in low acid foods canned by the pressure canning method are equally dangerous and should also be discarded in a safe manner.

MINIMIZING MOLDS

You can do a number of things to minimize unwanted mold growth in your kitchen, food storage areas and refrigerators. If your kitchen is at all like mine, it is the refrigerator that is going to collect the most fungal growth. This can be dealt with by washing the inside every couple of months with a tablespoon of baking soda dissolved in a quart of warm water. Rinse clean and allow to dry. The black mildew that grows on the rubber door gaskets and other places can be dealt with by wiping down with a solution of three tablespoons of household bleach in a quart of water. I generally use a soft bristle brush for this. A really bad case will not bleach back to a white color, at least it won't for me, but will instead turn pink or red after the bleach has carried out its disinfection mission.

The rest of the kitchen can be kept mold free by keeping the area clean, dry, and spraying occasionally with a product such as Lysol. Patches of mold can be eliminated with the bleach solution used on the refrigerator doors.

Try not to purchase more fresh food than you'll be able to eat in a short period of time. This will keep you from having to deal with the moldy remains that didn't get eaten. If food does go moldy, don't sniff it. This is a good way to give yourself respiratory difficulties if you are at all susceptible to mold allergies. Moldy food should be disposed in such a manner that your animals and children won't be able to get into it. Mycotoxins are every bit as bad for your animals as they are for you.

Obviously, you don't have to throw out everything that shows a spot of mold on it. Some foods can be safely dealt with and still partially saved if they show signs of fungal growth. Below is a set of guideline from M. Susan Brewer, Ph.D., R.D., a specialist in food safety. Her articles and works are found in many state university extension services publications lists.

If the food shows even a tiny mold spot, follow these guidelines:

1. Hard or firm foods with tiny mold spots can be trimmed; cut away the area around the mold (at least an inch) and rewrap in clean wrap. Make sure that knife does not touch the mold.

TRIM:
Hard Cheese (Cheddar, Swiss, etc.)
Bell Peppers, Carrots, Cabbage
Broccoli, Cauliflower,
Brussels Sprouts
Garlic,   Onions
Potatoes, Turnips
Zucchini
Apples, Pears

2. Soft foods such as cheese slices, cream cheese, sour cream and yogurt should be thrown away.

TOSS:
Soft Cheeses, (Mozzarella, Brie, etc.)
Sour Cream, Yogurt, Cottage cheese
Bacon, Hot d   ogs, Sliced lunch meats
Meat pies
Opened canned ham
Most left-over food
Bread, Cakes, rolls, flour, pastry
Peanut butter
Juices, berries
Jam, Jellies, Syrups
Cucumbers, Tomatoes
Spinach, Lettuce, other leafy vegetables
Bananas, Peaches, Melons
Corn-on-the-cob
Stored nuts, whole grains, rice

MOLDS IN CANNED GOODS

If good equipment and proper technique are used, it is unlikely you will ever have mold growth in your unopened canned goods. If you do have such, there was either a flaw in the procedure used, or something affected the jar or can after the fact to break its seal. In any event, once the food has molded, it is past saving and should be discarded in such a way that children and animals will not be able to get into it. The most likely home canned products to show mold growth are jams and jellies sealed with paraffin wax.

There are a number of points in the canning process where this can occur:

(1) In the time after the jar is taken out of its boiling water bath, but before it is filled.
(2) In the time between when the jar is filled and covered with the melted wax.
(3) When the wax cools, if it pulls away from the side of the jar, leaving an opening for the mold to get in.
(4) If bubbles form in the paraffin, which break and leave holes.

For these reasons most canning authorities no longer recommend using this technique. If you must do so, the jars should be boiled for at least 10 minutes before the jelly is poured. The filled and wax capped jars should then be covered with some sort of protective lid. The book, *Putting Food By* has excellent instructions on this or see the applicable section of the *rec. food.preserving FAQ*.

MOLDS IN GRAINS AND LEGUMES

It has long been known that eating moldy grain is bad for your health with the ugly consequences of eating ergot-infected rye being a well known example. It has only been about thirty years, though, that intensive study has been carried out on other species of grain fungi and their respective mycotoxins. Fortunately, for those of us in the U.S., the USDA and the various state departments of agriculture go to a great deal of trouble to detect grain and legumes infected with these toxic fungi. In some of the less developed countries, the citizenry are not so lucky. It is good to have something of an understanding of what one should do to prevent mold growth in ones stored grains and to have an idea of what to look for and ask about when purchasing grains and legumes.

The one fungal group that has caused the most commotion in recent history are the various *Aspergillus* species of molds. Under certain conditions with certain grains, legumes, and to a lesser extent, nuts, they can produce a mycotoxin called *aflatoxin*. This is a serious problem in some parts of the world, most especially in peanuts, occasionally in corn. I am not aware of any documented deaths in the United States from aflatoxicity, but other nations have not been so fortunate. What makes aflatoxin worrisome in this country is that it is also a potent carcinogen (cancer causing agent).

In addition to the Aspergillus molds, there is also a large family of molds known as *Fusarium* which can produce mycotoxins of their own, none of which do you want to be eating directly or feeding to your food animals where you will get the toxins back indirectly when the animal is slaughtered and eaten.

The Federal and state governments continuously monitor food and forage crops entering the marketplace. Those products found to be contaminated with mold or mycotoxins are not allowed to be sold for food. Once purchased however, the responsibility is yours to keep your food safe from mold growth. If you have already found mold growth in your whole grains, meals, flours or other grain products, they should be discarded. Most mycotoxins are not broken down or destroyed by cooking temperatures and there is no safe way to salvage grain that has molded.

PREVENTING MOLD GROWTH IN STORED GRAINS AND LEGUMES

The easiest method to prevent mold growth in your stored grains and legumes is to keep them too dry for mold to grow. The *Aspergillus* and *Fusarium* molds require moisture contents of 18% and above to reproduce. This is subject to some variability, but in all grains and soybeans, they must have a moisture content of that level. If you are storing raw (not roasted) peanuts, in the shell or shelled, you want to get the moisture content to less than 8% as peanuts are particularly susceptible to mold growth. The recommended moisture content for all other grain and legume storage is no more than 10%. Please see part *Grains and Legumes* for a method to determine moisture content. At 10% moisture, there is simply too little water for fungi to grow.

BACTERIAL SPOILAGE

Like the fungi, bacteria are everywhere, in the water, soil, air, on you, your food and your food storage containers. Fortunately, the vast majority of the bacteria we encounter are relatively harmless or even benign and only a few represent a danger to us and our stored foods.

Bacteria can be much more difficult to kill than molds and insects. Some are capable of continued growth at temperatures that would kill other spoilage organisms. When conditions are such that they are unable to grow, some bacteria can go dormant and form spores. These spores can be quite hardy, even to the point of surviving boiling water temperatures.

In order to grow, bacteria must have water, some species needing as little as a 20% moisture. For properly packaged dry grains, legumes, powdered milk and other low moisture foodstuffs bacterial spoilage will never be a problem as their moisture levels should be too scant to support growth.

WARNING: It is in wet pack canned goods (where the container has free liquid in it) and fresh foods we must be the most concerned about spoilage bacteria. It is here that a little bad luck and a moment's inattention to what you are doing could kill or seriously injure you or some other person who eats the foods you've put by. In both home-canned and commercially-canned goods, **IF THE CAN IS BULGING, LEAKING, SMELLS BAD, OR SPEWS LIQUID WHEN YOU OPEN IT THEN THROW IT OUT!** But, throw it out safely so that children and animals cannot get into it.

BOTULISM

Clostridium botulinum is one of the oldest life forms on this planet dating from a time before the Earth had an abundant oxygen atmosphere. Like the gangrene bacteria, it is an anaerobic organism meaning it lives and grows only in the absence of free oxygen. When conditions are not suitable for growth the bacteria can form durable seed like spores which are commonly found in the soil. This means that *C. botulinum* can be brought into your life on raw produce, tools, hands or anything else that came into contact with dirt. To further complicate matters, botulinum spores are extremely heat-hardy. The bacteria itself can be killed by a short exposure to boiling water (212º F AT SEA LEVEL PRESSURE), but its spores can not. To kill them, the food product and container must be exposed to temperatures of 240º F (AGAIN AT SEA LEVEL PRESSURE) for a long enough period of time to allow all of the food in each container to come completely up to the proper temperature. Only a pressure-canner can reach the necessary temperature.

It's not the bacteria or its spores which are directly deadly, but the toxin the bacteria creates when it grows and reproduces. In its pure form, botulism toxin is so potent that a mere teaspoon would be enough to provide a fatal dose to hundreds of thousands of people. It is this lethality that is why every responsible book on home canning, food preservation, and food storage hammers constantly on the need for care in technique and method and why spoilage must be taken seriously.

Like any other life form *Clostridium botulinum* must have suitable conditions for its growth to become a danger. One of the most important of these is water - the botulism bacterium needs moisture in the 35% range to grow making it a danger only in improperly processed high moisture foods. Another requirement is suitable pH, which is the measure of acidity or alkalinity in a substance and is measured on a scale of 1-14. Anything above 7 is considered alkaline and everything below 7 is considered acid. If the acidity of your wet pack food is BELOW pH4.6 then *C. botulinum* is unable to grow. Keep in mind that in foods pH is not necessarily stable and could possibly change if other spoilers like mold are able to grow. If the product should change to a lesser acidity than pH4.6 your previously botulinum proof food may start allowing the lethal spoiler to grow (see *molds in canned goods*). This is why it is vital to use proper technique, even for acid foods like tomatoes. It has been found that when this pH shift occurs allowing *C. botulinum* to become active producing its lethal toxin the bacterium also produces minute amounts of acid which can lower the pH of the poisoned food back into what should have been the safe zone had the pH not jumped up and allowed the bacteria to grow. Again and again — use good technique and pay attention to what you are doing.

Unlike fungal mycotoxins Botulinum toxin can be destroyed by boiling food briskly in an open vessel for fifteen minutes. Because of this, if your canned food shows any safety problems you should follow this procedure. If the food shows even the slightest mold growth, keep in mind that mycotoxins are not for the most part broken down by heat and dispose of the food safely.

I won't go into the hows of home canning here. For that I strongly recommend that you read the *rec.food.preserving FAQ*, the *Ball Blue Book* or most especially the book *Putting Food By* for in depth information on this subject.

ENZYMATIC ACTION IN FOOD SPOILAGE

Every living organism uses enzymes of many sorts in its bodily functions as part of its normal life cycle. Enzymes are used in creating life. After death, enzymes play a role in the decomposition of once living tissue. The enzymes in a tomato help it to ripen and enzymes produced by the tomato and whatever fungal and bacterial spoilers are on it cause it to decay.

Fortunately, slowing down or stopping the action of a food's enzymes is much easier than slowing or stopping some of the bacterial spoilers mentioned above. Enzymes are most active in a temperature range between 85-120º F and begin to be destroyed when the temperature goes above 140º F. Cold also slows down the action of enzymes, which is why fresh tomatoes last longer in the refrigerator than they do on the kitchen table. Most enzymatic action also requires moisture to occur. In foods stored at 10% moisture or less, there is not enough moisture for most enzymes to be active.

RECOMMENDED FOOD STORAGE TIMES

Food		Keep	Comments
Baking powder		Till can date	Sealed & bone dry
Baking soda		2 years	Sealed & dry
Biscuit, brownie, muffin mix		9 months	Sealed, cool, dry, weevil proofed
Bouillon, cubes or granules		2 years	Sealed, cool and dry
Cake mixes,	regular	9 months	Sealed, cool, dry, weevil proofed
	angel food	1 year	Sealed, cool, dry, weevil proofed
Canned food:	metal can, Non-Acidic	2 years	Cool & Dry
	Metal Can, Acidic	12-18months	Cool & Dry
	Glass jars	2-3 years	Dark, Cool & Dry
Chocolate, semi-sweet or unsweetened, bars or chips		18 months	Cool and dark
Chocolate syrup		2 years	Cool & tightly sealed
Cocoa,	powder or mixes	8 months	Sealed and cool
Coffee creamers, powdered		9 months	Sealed and cool
Cornmeal		1 year	Keep dry & weevil proofed
Cornstarch		18 months	Keep dry
Crackers		3 months	Keep dry & weevil proofed
Flour,	refined white	8-12 months	Dry & weevil proofed,
	whole wheat	4-6 weeks	refrigerate/freeze for longer shelf life
Frostings,	canned	3 months	Cool
	Mix	8 months	Dry and cool
Fruits, dried		6-12 months	Cool, sealed, weevil proofed
Gelatin, all types		18 months	Protect from moisture
Grains, whole		2 years	Dry and weevil proofed
Hominy, hominy grits, masa harina		1 year	Dry and weevil proofed
Honey		2 years	Cool, tightly sealed, dark
Jellies, jams, preserves		2 years	Dark, cool, tightly sealed.
Molasses & syrups		2 years	Tightly sealed
Mayonnaise		6 months	Cool & dark
Milk,	condensed or evaporated	1 year	Turn over every 2 months
	non-fat dry	6 months	Bone dry and cool
Nuts,	vacuum canned	1 year	Cool and Dark
	other packaging	3 months	Cool and dark – better Refrigerated in shell
		4 months	Cool, dry & dark, better refrigerated or frozen
Pancake mix		6-9 months	Dry and weevil proofed
Pastas (macaroni, noodles, etc)		2 years	Dry and weevil proofed
Peanut butter		6-9 months	Sealed, cool, dark
Peas and beans, dry (not soybeans)		2 years	Dry and weevil proofed
Potatoes, instant		6-12 months	Dry and weevil proofed
Pudding mixes		1 year	Cool and very dry
Rice,	white	2+ years	Dry and weevil proofed
	brown	3-6 months	Dry & weevil proofed, better refrigerated or frozen
	flavored or herb	6 months	Sealed, dry and weevil proofed
Salad dressings		10-12 months	Sealed, dark, cool. Better refrigerated
Salad oils		6 months	Sealed, dark, cool. Better refrigerated
Sauce and gravy mixes		6-12 months	Cool and dry
Shortening, solid		1 year	Cool, dark, tightly sealed.
Soup mixes		1 year	Cool, dry, and weevil proofed
Sugar,	brown	2 years	Tightly sealed, Dry.
	confectioners	18 months	Tightly sealed, Dry.
	granulated	2+years	Dry
Syrups (corn syrup based)		8-12 months	Sealed and cool
Vegetables, dried		1 year	Cool, dark, dry, weevil proofed
Vinegar		2+ years	Sealed

Space Cramp???

(er.. cramped space...
where to hide all that Food Storage!)
by Kim Hicken

Storage space got you down? Do you feel as though you are tripping over your food storage? Never fear - there is a light at the end of the storage tunnel! Storage space seems to be a never ending problem these days. Many new homes are built with terrific vaulted ceilings, great views, and NO storage space!!! Older homes can also have a shortage of space. With a little creative thinking, and some planning, Saints can have space to store the important things in your life.

The first thing that must be done, (and this is the very hardest part) is that you must de-junk your home. Saints are all pack-rats to a certain extent. At a speech regarding the de-junking of our homes, the presenter asked how many people present had a watch at home that did not work. Every single person in the room held up his hand. Do YOU have one of these treasures in your home? (Be honest, now!) We all have things in our homes that were once priceless treasures, but have now become a nuisance. Get rid of them! There are probably a million suggestions of ways to de-junk. Choose one that fits with your life style. A book that can help you with this is **Clutter's Last Stand: It's time to de-Junk Your Life by Don Aslett.** Check your local library for this, and other books on this subject.

Once you have gotten rid of some of the non-essentials, you must become creative.

Stand in each room of your home and take a good look around.

- Is there storage space that is currently not being utilized?
- Is there space that is being used ineffieciently?
- Are there shelves that could be built taller?
- Are there shelves that are deep that are only filled partially?
- Making efficient use of the storage space you already have may net you enough new space to store quite a bit.
- There are a lot of nice, new plastic storage containers on the market that may help you store things more easily, and stack them a bit deeper. Sturdy carboard boxes can also help. Grocery stores will generally give you fruit boxes if you ask.

One Saint who is raising four children in a very small turn-of-the-century stone house has come up with some very creative storage space. She built her own couches using a basic toy-box type design. She purchased thick foam rubber, and made cushions to go on top of the boxes. Then she made coordinating pillows to add more comfort to the couch. The hollow bottoms have given her lots of extra space.

When she moved into the home, the cupboards had space above them. She modified them so that now her kitchen cupboards go all the way to the ceiling. No space has been wasted. She completely utilizes the space under her stairs. An upstairs bedroom built into the attic space still has some space (under the eves) that she utilizes for additional storage.

Since she does not care for crawling around in dark places, she built small doors into the wall approximately every four feet. When she needs to put something in the space or take something out, she simply reaches in the closest door.

She does not like to move things to vaccuum, so she puts many shelves on the walls, and up off the floor. By building shelves in this manner, she has moved miscellaneous family items out of prime food-storage space, allowing her to store more food. In many cases, our best food-storage space is full of things that could be stored elsewhere.

Another Saint who has six children in a modular home has learned to be creative with her space as well. She stood in her rooms and looked around, and before long, she discovered that there was a hollow space between two walls. This was not a huge space, but it was enough to provide her some more storage space. She took the paneling off that portion of the wall, and put a cupboard door on. Cupboard doors are not expensive, nor are they difficult to install. Now she has a storage closet where non existed originally.

The floor in a small bedroom has a trap door in it that allows her to actually go under her home. There she has found a lot of great space to store things that need to be kept cool. Even in the heat of summer, this space is cool. She uses it to store potatoes, and foods that are in air-tight containers. She has buckets of honey, buckets of wheat, and buckets of beans under this room.

One good trick is to use garbage cans as bedside tables. This is done by purchasing regular garbage cans at a discount store. New ones are recommended because they have no odd smells or dirt attached! One sheet of plywood is then used to cut two circles four to five inches bigger in diameter than the top of the can. The lids to the garbage cans are not used. Let the kids use them as shields when they play. Place the plywood circles over the top of the garbage cans, and then cover your new bedside tables with nice round covers (called "table rounds") that coordinate with your bedspread. Nobody will know that your lovely bedside tables are actually garbage cans! This provides wonderful food storage space for some of the items that need to be stored in bulk, such as beans or wheat.

Don't forget the space under your beds! There are lots of food items that can be stored in the small spaces under your beds. Salt, peanut butter, cans of potato flakes, canned vegetables, and cans of shortening can all be stored easily under the beds. They are also easily accessible.

Take a look at your closets. Is there room on the floor of the closet? There are many commercial closet storage systems on the market that can help you more efficiently use your space. But you can also build your own for less expense. Five gallon buckets can be stored on the floor of the closet, and a board put across the top of them to make a handy shelf for shoes and boots. Does the space in the top of the closet go all the way to the ceiling? Five gallon buckets could be stored up there as well, but it is not recommended to store heavy things in them. This may be a good place to store tissue, paper towels, or toilet paper. If you buy your laundry detergent in big buckets, these make terrific storage containers for such items.

One Saint who struggled with a tiny dining area solved two problems with one solution. She built her own benches with hollow bottoms (the toy box design again).

She put colorful cushions on top, and then used her own dining room table. Benches generally seat more people than traditional chairs. Now her entire family can fit in her small dining area, and she has extra storage space as well. Don't let storage problems scare you! You are smarter than the things you own! A little creativity and elbow grease can go a long way toward providing more storage space in your home. Now roll up those sleeves and take a good look at YOUR home!

Here are a few more ideas sent by Food Storage Editor, Andrea Chapman:
"I have some ideas for storing in small places. One idea is a little radical, but my husband and I did it and it worked well. We **took apart our bed frame** and used buckets, about 12-16 to hold up our bed. It was a little higher than before, but it looked fine. I have a friend who used the **#10 cans in boxes** that the fit in 6 at a time. She stacked those and used that under the bed. Also, you can stack those three high and put a table cloth over it for a nice little table in the Living Room or Family room. I have also put food storage in the boys room, in their closet on the floor. Not many little kids use all their closet space."

SECTION 3:
Every Needful Thing

Preparedness Is Peace

You can't control world events, but you can control your families preparedness.

Ready Level

No Fear

Complete Self Reliant Lifestyle
2+ Year Supply of Long Term Food Storage with the knowledge and resources to produce more food
Knowledge of livestock, farming, bees, medicinal herbs, soap making, candle making, fabric weaving, sewing, survival, building and other esential skills, etc, etc
and a continued desire to learn more
Emergency Shelter(like a 4 season canvas tent and tent stove) and Fuel for Heat.

Resource

1 Year+ Supply of Long Term Food Storage of Grains, Legumes, and basic survival foods
Seed Storage, Gardening Tools, Canning supplies
YOU have been doing this long enough to TEACH others how to do it
Ability to purify water for up to a year
Emergency Toilet, Lighting, Cooking Fuel(indoor and outdoor)
All IMPORTANT information has been printed off in Hard Paper Copies in case of loss of internet
Cash on hand, Longer term Medicine and CERT Training

Progress

90 Day Supply of Foods you Already Eat that you can rotate through
90 days of DRINKING water stored
Spouting Seeds stored to use for Fresh Vegitables if you can't get any
Savings in the Bank, Debt Free from Consumer Debt
Sleeping Bags, Basic Camping Gear, Fire Starters,
Warm Clothing, including coats and boots for your whole family
Special supplies like feminine products, infant products, and medical supplies
Ability to use alternative cooking methods, like solar or thermal or dutch oven

Started

Two Weeks of Food in Pantry (fat pantry), Two Weeks of income in the Bank
Two weeks of drinking water, Two Weeks of Fuel
Paying off debts, Over coming addictions
72 hour kits for fleeing & car kits in the car for incidents on the road
First Aid Supplies and Training
A Family Emergency Plan, written down and discussed with the family
Know your Neighbors, Know your Community Resources
Have all contact numbers available on hand, easy to find place
Home prepared for earthquakes

Not Ready

I am COMPLETELY at the mercy of others if an event happens today
I have no current resources to care for myself or others
POSSIBLE REASONS:
I have done nothing to prepare
I live pay check to pay check
I am in debt
I struggle with an addiction
I am a little child, elderly, disabled, ill, out of work
or have lost everything in fire, death, divorce, personal emergency

Event Level

SEVERE
Fatalities
Major Structural Damage
No Travel
Stores Empty, Looting
Long Term Recovery

HIGH
Major Injuries
Loss of Services
No Water, Sewer, Gas, Electric
Medical, Banks, Fuel
Limited Travel

ELEVATED
Minor Injuries
Minor Structural Damage
Possible Prolonged Shelter/Isolation
Possible Outbreak- or Inclement Weather
Conservation of Resources

GUARDED
Threat of Reduced Resources or Economic Instability
Local City Wide Event (like fire, or gas leak)
Travel Still Available (Peope may evacuate until safe to return)
Scare of an Event or Threat of Event

LOW
Relative Safety and Peace
Private Family Emergencies are occurring
like sickness, job losses, on a case by case
Best Time to Prepare your family

In emergency preparedness, a "72 hour kit" is widely considered the

first step in becoming prepared. Sitting in a closet or some other area close to the front door, it can be grabbed in a moment's notice, should you have to depart your home with little or no warning. Two days ago, only a block from my house, a neighbor's home caught fire at 3 AM. After getting everyone out, the fire hastily spread and quickly destroyed this family's home. Everything inside it was totally destroyed. What did they have left? Only the pajamas on their backs. They lost literally everything. They didn't even have shoes on their feet. They wish they'd had a good 72 hour kit. Fortunately, the whole community is pulling together for them. But not everyone is this lucky. Sometimes, whole communities are affected at the same time. This same tiny farming village back in 1978 had to be immediately evacuated for several days because of derailed and leaking butane cars. Before that, everyone here thought this was a place where disasters 'never happened.' Seventy-two hour kits would have been really handy then as well. It's not necessary that you live in a tornado or hurricane alley to need a 72 hour kit. Every family needs one for the unexpected.

A deluxe "72" hour kit should contain all the essential things your family would need to take you through 3-4 days of being on your own. There's a reason behind the length of time the kit's contents should last. It generally takes the disaster relief agencies at least 3-4 days to move in and set up before offering assistance. Generally speaking, you're on your own during this time. Depending on how bad the situation is, it could even be longer. Whether you start with our kit or put one together yourself from scratch, it's important for your family's welfare to have one. In any type of disaster things will be bad. Not having the necessities to sustain your life and the lives of your family members could turn an otherwise manageable problem into a personal cataclysm you could never recover from. **Prepare now for life's surprises.**

PLAN FIRST!

Building The Right Bug Out Bag for You

Factors When Building a Bug Out Bag

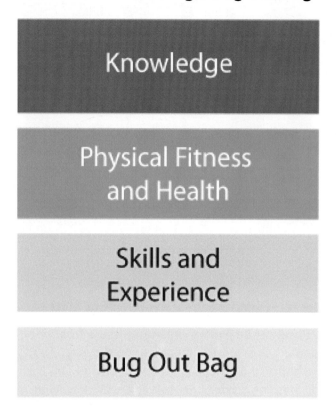

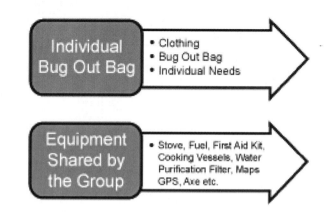

Factor 1: You

As I see it the most important aspect of making it through a Survival Situation is You. It's your effort, your Skills, your Knowledge, your Experience and your Will to Survive that will ultimately make biggest difference if you make it or not. The Bug Out Bag is important, but this is only a tool that will help you get the job done. It's still you that will have to get the job done. It's easy to discuss equipment, what items to store and other physical aspect of crisis preparedness and survivalism. But it's important to not lose track of your prioritize and to continue to work on yourself as much as you work on your gear. Your Physical Fitness and Health are also crucial factors that will determine how much you can carry and how long distances you can carry it.

Factor 2: Going At It Alone Or As A Group?

The next important factor is if you are creating a kit just for you or for a group or family. This will affect your setup in many ways. I suggest that you build your setup so that you can cover your own basic needs if you would be unable to meet up with your group or get separated from them. For more advice on this subject check out the article Bugging Out As a Group.

Factor 3: Climate and Terrain

Your climate and terrain will affect the choice for Shelter, Clothing, how much water you have to carry, what food that is most appropriate and what type of source for light you should bring. Some people may have to travel through different types of terrains so solution for clothing and shelter must work for all this types of terrains.

Factor 4: Season

In many parts of the world the temperature, rain and wind vary over the seasons and the setup must be adjusted depending if it's spring, summer, autumn or winter. This can affect factors like:
• Clothing and Footwear
• Shelter
• What type of Stove and Food you should bring
• The Access to Water

Factor 5: Your Every Day Carry and Pocket Survival Kit

Most Survivalists will most likely have some form of Every Day Carry or even a Pocket Survival Kit that they carry on an Every Day Basis. You should build your Bug Out Bag so that it complements your EDC and Pocket Survival Kit. Examples can be:
• Trying to find products that use the same type of batteries for Flashlight, Headlamps, Radios, GPS units and other electronics.
• Use different types of Equipment to Build a Fire in your Bug Out Bag, Pocket Survival Kit and in your Every Day Carry.

Factor 6: Do You Use Your Bug Out Bag For Other Activities?

Building a fully equipped Bug Out Bag can be a very costly process especially if high quality equipment is preferred. The equipment in your Bug Out Bag can also be used for a number of other activities like hiking, camping, hunting, fishing and other outdoor activities. If you engage in this type of activities I suggest that you try to find solutions and equipment that will the same functions both during this type of activities and during an evacuation. Using the same gear for different activities also give you the chance to get familiar with your equipment, learn how to use properly and see what works well and not. But most importantly it gives you the opportunity to enjoy the investment that you have made.

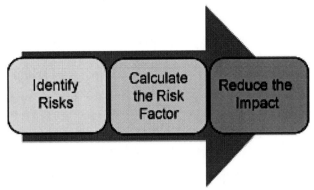

Factor 7: What Kind Of Scenarios Do You Prepare For?

What types of situations that you are trying to prepare for is also a critical aspect for what type of Bug Out Bag that you should put together. There is big difference if you are putting together a kit to assist for hurricane evacuation or to function as tool during a total breakdown of modern society. I suggest that you make a comprehensive Risk Assessment before you make up your mind about what type of situations that you base your BOB upon.

Factor 8: Budget

For most people the economical aspect will also limit what kind of setup that they can build. If one has an almost unlimited budget this is of little concern but for most people this will be a factor when deciding what setup they will build. I recommend that you try to prioritize the items that you will use often and try to build a basic well functioning setup that you can upgrade as you go. For the budget it can also be important that you get the right equipment the first time, it's even more expensive to have to buy a completely new solution if you get a cheap piece of equipment that does not work.

177

The Process of Building a Bug Out Bag

Step1: Decide what you want the Bug Out Bag to Perform for You

After you have taken these factors into consideration you will face the process of putting the Bug Out Bag together. Taking a look at the different factors presented above can give you a basic idea of what you want the bag to do for you and what functions you want it to have.

Step 2: Research

From this perspective you will first have to make some research in order to find items that can allow you to perform these tasks. Picking the tools that can provide you with shelter, water and water purification, help you to build a fire, light, food and ability to prepare food, hygiene, first aid, navigation, a survival knife and other tools can be quite a long process. Here you also have to take factors like price, weight, quality and function into consideration. You should also consider how the different items that you have complement the other items that you choose and how they can help to reinforce your skills. I suggest that you try to check out equipment like clothing, tents, knives and other gear in a physical store before you purchase them, or check out what equipment, friends, family or professionals that work in your area use.

Step 3: Acquire the Equipment

After you decided what items you want to get you still have process of finding the items and buying them. You might already have some of the equipment needed in your possession or you might have to buy the equipment. Make sure that you check with your family, friends, at E-Bay and the second hand market and multiple sources before you buy a piece of equipment, you can often save allot of money by doing some research.

Step 4: Test the Bug Out Bag

After you have put the kit together you still have to test the kit so that you actually know if it performs as intended. Taking the Bag for a longer hike in your local terrain can give you the chance to practice skills but also to see what items that you really need and what items that you don't need.

Step 5: Adjust the Setup

After you have tested the Bug Out Bag you normally make adjustments to the setup and question comes back again: What do you want your Bag to perform?

One Size Does Not Fit All

This article is written to give you some ideas of what factors that you have to take into consideration when building a Bug Out Bag. There can of course be more factors that have to be taken into consideration than the ones that have been mentioned above, every person has specific consideration that must govern what a specific setup should contain. The important aspect is that your BOB will reflect what you need and be designed for your particular situation. One Size does not fit all; this is something that applies to all kinds of crisis preparedness and survival situations. Others can often provide good suggestions and feedback but in the end you have to make the decisions for yourself. http://sibitotique.blogspot.com/2011/04/building-right-bug-out-bag-for-you.html

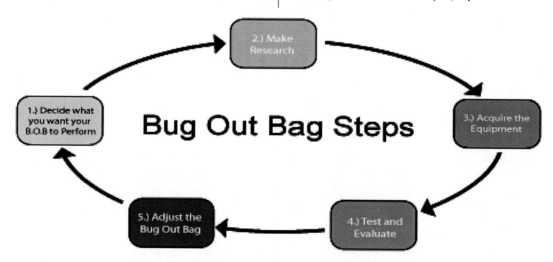

OK, But What Do I Prepare For?

Before you can prepare, you must determine what you are preparing to survive and how each disaster threatens you, your safety and survival. That will give you the parameters necessary for the following steps.

This initial exercise isn't tough, it only takes a few minutes of thought. We suggest you jot notes or switch into your word processor while you work.

But first, it's important to realize that you cannot prepare for everything — only the army tries to do that, and we've yet to meet anyone with their resources. Captain Dave suggests you prepare only for those potential disasters that are likely to occur within the next five years. Sure, you may wait seven years for the next earthquake, but remember the survivalists creed: *better safe than sorry*.

What's going to happen in the next five years? If we knew, our web page would look different. You'll have to extrapolate, evaluate trends, read the newspaper, conduct your own research. At the very least, take a few minutes and consider your location. Pull out a map and look what's within a two-mile, five-mile 10-mile and 25-mile radius of your home and place of work. Put on your pessimist hat and consider what might go wrong that could directly impact you. Decide if that's something you want to prepare for (see questions one and two, below).

For example, if you live a "safe" distance outside of a flood plain, your house might still gets flooded in the 100-year flood, should you prepare for it? We would, but it's your call. It's your ass on the line, so you have to decide.

That nuclear plant 20 miles away has an excellent safety record. Should a nuclear disaster be on your list? Again, you make the call.

Are you worried about a meteorite crashing into your house? Well, it has happened, but it's probably not worth preparing for.

Finally, if you've been afraid of something since you were a child — whether it's a raging fire or nuclear war — prepare for it. At the very least, you'll sleep better at nights knowing you have done all you can.

Here are some questions to ask yourself:

What natural disasters or extreme conditions am I (we) I likely to face in the next five years?

Make a list and rank them in order of most to least likely to impact you. Your list might look like this:

Natural Disasters

Weather-related

Hurricanes	Tornadoes
Heavy thunder storms	
Flash flooding	Flooding
Mud/rock slides	
High winds	Hail
Severe winter weather	
Avalanche	Extreme high heat
Drought	
Wildfire	

Non Weather-related

Earthquake	Volcano eruption
Tidal wave/Tsunami	

Man-made Disasters

War (*conventional, biological, chemical or nuclear*)
Toxic material emission or spill (*from a train, semi-truck or nearby plant*)
Riot or other civil disorder
Nuclear plant melt down or other nuclear disaster
Terrorism   Fire
Government action against you
Stock market crash
Sever depression

Other

Plague or disease outbreak
Comet strike or giant meteor

Personal Emergencies

Kidnapping	Mugging,
robbery or other criminal attack	
Unemployment	
financial disaster	
Death in family	
Home destroyed by fire	
Random acts of violence	

What are the ramifications of each item on my list.??

Now, take your list and create a second column. Put the ramifications of each disaster in the second column. What do we mean by ramification? How the disaster or emergency situation could affect you. Think this one through very carefully, as everyone's situation is different. For example, families with children have different concerns than those without or singles.

Potential Disaster Ramifications
Thunder storm with electrical outage for 2 (average)
to 48 hours (severe)
Food spoilage possible
Lack of air conditioning/furnace
Damage to house or car from nearby trees
Possible local flooding (see below)
Local transportation impaired by fallen trees, wires
Lightning damage/fire potential

Severe winter weather, Electrical power outage
for 4hrs (average) to 72 hours (severe)
Would affect furnace operation
Exposure problems
Frozen pipes
Disruption of travel, transportation
Self or family members possibly stranded away from home
Possible food shortages and empty shelves at local markets

Nearby flash flooding
Local transportation disrupted
Danger while traveling in car or by foot
Possible loss of some utilities

Nearby train derailment
Possible leak or spill of chemicals
Short-term exposure problem
Long-term cancer concerns
Evacuation may be necessary

Riot or other civil disorder Disruption of commute
(ala Los Angeles)
Stranded in car or office while family is at home and/or school
Danger of riot spreading to my neighborhood
Danger of local kids/low lives taking advantage of situation
Attack or threat to personal safety
Looting and rampaging by otherwise lawful citizens

Fire with potentially no response by authorities
Police are overwhelmed, cannot protect law-abiding citizens

Nuclear plant problems
Reactor vessel damage could result in release of radioactive chemicals to atmosphere
Evacuation necessary

Terrorism Threat to safety at work and during business travel
Disruption of commerce, travel
Less personal freedom, privacy as a result of government reaction to terrorism

Once you've created a chart like the one above, you know what situations you are most likely to face and can prepare your survival plan

Survival Priorities:
The Rule of Three

While I took issue with the conclusions drawn from the facts employed in a recent article titled _The Coming Food Armageddon', the truth is you could find yourself and your loved ones in a struggle for survival at any time. For what it's worth, not only am I a big booster of _prepping', I have a realistic strategy if the SHTF and my outdoor skills are better than most, although that's not really saying much given our predominantly urban population. But prepping is not what I want to talk to you about. I want to talk to you about Survival. And I'm not going to offer you any strategies, tactics or supply sources. Rather, I just want you to get your head into a slightly different place than it probably is right now. For some of you, this might be a remedial review. You may be military, firefighter, law enforcement, rescue worker or just plain folk with an inordinate amount of common sense. Regardless, it never hurts to revisit the basics.

And all of the basics can be summed-up in —The Rule of Three which says, absent sudden death (such as an accident) or terminal illness, your survival is generally contingent upon you not exceeding:
3 minutes without breathing (drowning, asphyxiation)
3 hours without shelter in an extreme environment (exposure)
3 days without water (dehydration)
3 weeks without food (starvation)

We'll leave accident avoidance and healthy lifestyle choices for another discussion and just focus on the ramifications of the Rule of Three. However, this essay is offered merely to encourage you in proactively conducting your own ongoing risk assessment.

Nothing in this essay is intended nor is to be construed as advice, professional or otherwise. Any information contained in this essay is not to be relied upon. You're going to have to go find it out for yourself!

Starvation

Most _preppers' are stocking food. You will note that starvation is the slowest form of death among the Rule of Three. You would likely have three weeks before you starve. Your level of physical exertion has an impact on the body's caloric requirements. Personally, I might survive starvation for five or six weeks if I stay in repose as I'm carrying a lot of extra weight (just in case!). Don't call me obese. Call me prepped! Keep in mind, too, that your survival strategy must consider the likelihood of you being separated from your food supply in an emergency. When that happens, stay calm, focus on any immediate threats or hazards and remember that you have three weeks to implement Food Plan B or Plan C. You do have a Food Plan B and Plan C, don't you?

Dehydration

Dehydration occurs much more quickly than starvation. As such, water supply is much more critical to address in an emergency. Consider that in a temperate climate and without exertion, the human body requires approximately 2.5 liters of fluids per day. In extreme heat this requirement goes up significantly. Diarrhea can lead to rapid, catastrophic dehydration as well. Given that water is far bulkier to store and/or transport than food, and that dehydration is potentially a far more pressing concern than starvation, your ability to procure water in an emergency should supplant food in your ranking of Survival priorities. Stated simply, water is far more important than food. What is your base plan for water? What is your mobile plan for water?

Exposure

Exposure occurs far more rapidly than dehydration. Hot or cold, you could find yourself unable to function in less than three hours. Immersion in cold water, such as breaking through ice, could reduce your time to act down to mere minutes. So what's your shelter strategy when you're away from base? Here in TheNorth, we've already had temps below minus 40 this winter. February is typically our coldest month where I've personally experienced minus 52 F actual. If you have an accident on a slick road late at night in such conditions, you will likely not be waking up ever again unless you have prepared for such an eventuality. Exposure kills in hours, or less. Countering exposure is your number two priority for survival in any emergency situation. Yet most preppers are not thinking about exposure while stocking their pantries. Prepare for exposure.

Asphyxiation

Asphyxiation kills in three minutes. This is the emergency situation that gives you the least amount of time to react for your survival. This is your Priority One Survival issue. An interior fire is the most common cause of asphyxiation. How many of you have a home escape plan in the event of a fire? I thought so. Make one. It's free. It takes minutes.

And it might save your life. Unless you've been in a burning building, I guarantee that you cannot imagine how blinding the smoke is nor how quickly a structure can become fully engulfed. If you have children, periodic rehearsal of the escape plan is mandatory. In the unthinkable event of a fire, panic is inevitable. Rehearsal helps to moderate the flight reaction, which might otherwise lead to death. Also, test your smoke detectors. Notwithstanding my disclaimer above, check them regularly. I mean it! Our friends out West can attest to the power, speed and terror of a large scale wildfire.

Most of us assume such an occurrence will provide adequate forewarning, thereby allowing avoidance. While normally that's true, you wouldn't be prepping if you only planned for _typical' events. The Peshtigo, WS Fire of 1871 is an example of a wildfire that _upgraded' to firestorm. While obviously a confluence of enabling conditions is required in order for a firestorm to occur, be assured that this could occur in most parts of the country. While the development of those enabling conditions will be obvious (i.e. extreme drought) to anyone on the lookout, once commenced, the firestorm expands far too quickly to allow for evacuation. 1.5 million acres burned that day.

While fire is a common cause, there are other causes of asphyxiation worth your consideration:

Carbon monoxide poisoning – usually from a combustion source in the home. This has also occurred in vehicles stranded in snowstorms. Vehicles were run for heat. Accumulating snow shrouded the tailpipe resulting in vehicle exhaust entering the passenger compartment.

Other poisonous fumes – tanker trucks, rail cars and chemical & other industrial plants often have hazardous materials that, in an emergency situation, could cause you grave bodily harm if exposed.

Smothering- confined space entrapment, such as a building collapse (snow or volcanic ash loads on roofs, earthquakes, etc). Consider also avalanches, landslides and mudslides.

Drowning – while common sense on and around bodies of water is presumed, consider also flash floods, tsunami, the aforementioned breaking ice, catastrophic dam failure, bridge failure while crossing. Flash floods are relatively common and often deadly. While a tsunami is much less common, consider the scale of the 2004 Indian Ocean tsunami before you dismiss its' likelihood. If you live in a coastal region, it would only take one to bring all of your pantry efforts to naught.

All of these events are sudden, unexpected and leave you minutes or less to choose a course of action. Taking the proper action may save your life.

Perils, Perils Everywhere

As you continually assess and prioritize your survival risks, take into account those risks specific to the area where you happen to be. Weather patterns for example. Hurricanes in coastal regions, tornados on the plains and thunderstorms or blizzards in the mountains are all hazards to be anticipated and prepped for. Also, consider geologic perils. Earthquakes, volcanoes and rapidly moving lahars are hazards to be aware of and plan for, even if you are merely passing through.

Therefore, if you are inclined to take a proactive approach in preparing for what economists might refer to as _outlier occurrences', then it behooves you to prioritize your risks and review appropriate responses to them in a rational fashion. The scenarios resulting in your death most quickly should command your immediate attention. When you have sufficiently addressed those, by all means move down your list. We all believe in the Boy Scout motto of —Be Prepared . However oftentimes it's the obvious peril that gets overlooked.

Author TomOfTheNorth is a Volunteer Firefighter with a small rural FD in northeastern MN, where he is also Vice President of the Department and President of the Department's meager pension association.

A High-Mobility 72 Hour Kit

By Ward Dorrity

"You can ignore reality, but you cannot ignore the consequences of ignoring reality." – Ayn Rand

The history of much of the last century was written in the blood of the victims of war, genocide, political upheaval and social unrest. One of the lessons of modern history – lost on most Americans, unfortunately – is that our circumstances can change literally overnight. Consider Beirut, Sarajevo, the Islamic mass murders at the Twin Towers and the Pentagon, and lately - the riots in Greece, Spain, Italy and London. These events were all harbingers of an abrupt, irrevocable and often brutal change in peoples' lives.

It Can't Happen Here? Think again. More unarmed citizens guilty of nothing more than being who they were have been killed by their own governments in modern times than all of the casualties of all of the wars ever fought throughout recorded history. If you regard this as hyperbole or exaggeration, then please visit Professor R. J. Rummel's Wikipedia entry at http://en.wikipedia.org/wiki/R._J._Rummel , the contents of which are correct, and as the evidence emerges, are understated. His website at http://www.hawaii.edu/powerkills/welcome.html delivers these horrendous statistics in irrefutable detail. Rummel coined the term democide for murder by government. Loosely rendered, Prof. Rummel's research shows that six times as many people died of democide during the 20th century than in all that century's wars combined.

Mass murder, atrocity and cruelty against civilian populations and on a scale that beggars the imagination was the one of the main recurrent themes of the last century; it has continued virtually unabated in the 21st century, largely unreported and, one might suspect, deliberately covered up. Daniel Jonah Goldhagen, in his landmark Worse Than War: Genocide, Eliminationism, and the Ongoing Assault on Humanity, delivers a grisly panorama of recent history that should put to rest any illusions that you may have concerning the madness that haunts our modern world. We are all at risk, no matter how sunny or benign your day to day world might seem.

Consider a Jewish tailor living in Prague in the late 1930's. He could scarcely have understood what was happening to him when he and his family were rounded up by the National Socialists and packed into a cattle car – they were told that they were being 'relocated for their own safety'. "But, that was World War 2," you say. So let's move forward: in the early 1970s, and in the span of 72 hours, the Khmer Rouge emptied every major city in Cambodia and before they were done, they had slaughtered over a third of the country – more than a million people - over the next few years. "But, that was during the Vietnam War years and in Asia," you say. "Surely," you say, "that's over". But nothing could be further from the truth – as Goldhagen points out, the slaughter, the 're-education' camps, the slave labor prisons never stopped; it only diminished in intensity. Most of us have forgotten Sarajevo, host of the 1984 Winter Olympics and formerly known as "the jewel of the Adriatic." Sarajevo fell into a flame-shot hell of barbarism with a rapidity that stunned its inhabitants. The so-called 'siege of Sarajevo' earned the dubious distinction of being the longest such siege in modern times – it lasted almost 4 years. Modern high-rise buildings became death traps as services failed and snipers picked off anyone who tried to leave in search of food, water or something to burn for warmth. World War 2, again? No – the siege of Sarajevo took place from 1992 through 1996. "But, but - those were Serbs and Croats – we're not like that," you say. But if you thought that we here in America have some special immunity to circumstances like those, you would be wrong.

Here in America, the Watts and Rodney King riots, and hurricane Katrina serve as examples of just how quickly our own civil order can vanish. The recent ' flash mob' robbery/ assault phenomenon - where groups of blacks make use of cell phone texting and social networks such as Twitter to organize and to swarm retail establishments in order to overwhelm them and to loot them - are becoming increasingly bolder and more violent here in the good old USA. Lately, and in a more ominous turn of events, those same flash mobs have begun to target individual people for racially motivated robbery and assault. You can even see this on YouTube, where many of these incidents are published for 'bragging rights'! Even though the flash rob-mob phenomenon has largely fallen off the media radar (and some might say that it is being deliberately suppressed), it hasn't stopped. It just hasn't been reported by a compliant media with an agenda. And with few exceptions, nobody's going to jail for it.

The recent 'Occupy' movement with its shadowy organizational origins and even more ambiguous sources of funding are another harbinger of social unrest to come. Merely another situation under-reported and misrepresented by a media strangely uninterested in the whole story, but the sentiment of those participating is easy enough to discern: "Capitalism has taught us that no one is ever going to give us anything," said OSC spokesperson Mark Paschal. "You have to take it." His comments and many, many others like it have an old familiar ring:

"We are socialists, we are enemies of today's capitalistic economic system for the exploitation of the economically weak, with its unfair salaries, with its unseemly evaluation of a human being according to wealth and property instead of responsibility and performance, and we are all determined to destroy this system under all conditions."

This is almost word-for-word what is coming from the mouths of the OWS crowd, and you would find few among them who would disagree with it. In fact, you would find few among our intelligentsia, our artists, our journalists, even our preachers and pastors who would find fault with it. But it's old news, as the quote comes from a speech made in May 1, 1927 by one of the true nemeses and monsters of the last century, one Adolf Hitler. "It can't happen here," you say? Don't bet on it. It already has. The "low level ethnic conflict," of the flash mobs, the increasingly violent theater of the Occupy movement, and the systematic abrogation of the rule of law and the disregard for the Constitution and the Bill of Rights by the Obama regime are merely sign posts along the way to something far, far worse.

Who am I to say these things? Well, I'm just the guy on the block who sees his neighbor's house on fire and tries to do something about it, rather than wait for the fire department to show up.

But in this case, what's burning is our own civilization. Those who want to "burn the old world to reveal the new," will get nothing but ashes and their own extinction. That's the lesson of history that so many of us have failed to learn. As Will Durant put it in The Story of Civilization, "...civilization is a precious good, whose delicate complex order and freedom can at any moment be overthrown by barbarians invading from without and multiplying from within."

It's become increasingly obvious that those barbarians of which Durant spoke are already well inside our gates. They occupy offices in the House and Senate, they enjoy positions of power and influence in the arts, media and our educational institutions. They preach from our pulpits. Their goal? Power. Power over thee and me. Their outlook? That human beings are nothing more than things, animals or machines to be ruled, managed and yes, slaughtered.

"We are fast approaching the stage of the ultimate inversion: the stage where the government is free to do anything it pleases, while the citizens may act only by permission; which is the stage of the darkest periods of human history, the stage of rule by brute force."
— Ayn Rand

Erosion of Trust and Social Cohesion and the One Hour Meltdown.

We like to think of ourselves as fairly civilized. But the bonds that have held us together as a society, as a people, and as Americans have been systematically – and again, some might say deliberately - eroded over the past few generations. If you consider social capital as composed of mutual trust and respect for the rule of law, then our account is seriously overdrawn. The Obama regime is already operating well outside the constraints of the Constitution and the rule of law and continues to do so with impunity. When such behavior becomes the norm for a state, bad things – very bad things – usually happen.

The "Bank Holiday" Scenario.

Consider the following scenario: abruptly, and in the middle of a workday, a "bank holiday" is declared by the current regime. In today's context, a bank holiday declaration will most likely be the leading edge of a far broader and deep economic collapse - things are not likely to improve any time soon from that point on. For those who consider this unlikely or impossible, think again: it's been done. Here, during the beginning of the Great Depression. Also understand that at the beginning of the Great Depression of 1929, Americans had a great deal more social cohesion and were possessed of substantially more self-restraint back then. Read Amity Shlaes' The Forgotten Man: A New History of the Great Depression for an accurate account of those times. For all the hard times, the Great Depression era was relatively orderly. Now – not so much. And that has consequences.

You will do well to pay close attention to news feeds from now on – because, when you hear a declaration of a 'bank holiday' (or martial law, for that matter), you'll have about an hour, perhaps less. An hour for what, you might ask. The answer is: you'll have about an hour – perhaps less - before ordinary, everyday people around you flip right out and go crazy, some of them homicidally so. Here's one way that it might go down, and it will all happen in parallel. I've borrowed and expanded upon some of these concepts that another writer/blogger outlined in his essay, The One Hour Meltdown. The following 'bank holiday' scenario will have a grave and immediate impact on you and everyone else that you know.

1. Retail Businesses:

This is the area that will likely have the most immediate effect on you. A declaration of a 'bank holiday' will effectively halt all electronic transfers of money. Since businesses will be unable to process even simple debit card- or check-based transactions, many retail establishments will have no choice but to shut down. They will attempt to lock their doors to prevent anyone else from entering. If possible, they will complete any transactions for customers already inside the building, but on a cash-only basis. Any customers wishing to pay by check or with a credit/debit card will be told that the system is down and that, sorry, their transaction can't be honored. Now – picture this happening in an establishment like Target, Wal-Mart or your local grocery store. Imagine the scene at the checkout lines: people with shopping carts full of stuff they want are suddenly told that, no - they can't have their stuff. To put it mildly, this will not be taken well. Let's face it – some of the frustrated clientele will NOT leave empty-handed and in an orderly fashion. Thus, the establishment can and will move from order to disorder in a matter of minutes. Once the first item is simply taken without paying for it, once the first window is broken, once the first punch is thrown, all hell will break loose. The looting and the violence will start and spread like wildfire.

Even if the retail establishment has prepared for this eventuality – and rest assured that most of them have not – they will have little or no control over the ensuing chaos. For chaos there will be. It will take 5 or 10 minutes - perhaps even less - for the implications of the retail shutdown to sink into the consciousness of everyone in the store. Again, cases where the frustrated clientele will leave in an orderly fashion will be few and far between. Your best option, if you are paying attention to what's happening around you, is to vacate the premises as quickly as you possibly can. Leave your shopping cart behind – it doesn't matter now, as it's far less important than your life. Speed, mobility and decisive action will be your only friends. Take your purse or wallet and immediately slip out of the checkout line and head for the exits. If you're in the middle of the store, then hit the nearest exit, alarms be damned. Should those doors already be locked, head out through the back and exit through the loading dock area. You'll have a small window of time in which to act. Trust me - this is the last place you'll want to be. Don't count on store employees, store security or local law enforcement to maintain order. The first two aren't paid enough to risk their lives, nor are they well-trained enough to deal with what's coming at them. Local law enforcement are going to have their hands full elsewhere and everywhere. Because whatever's happening in your location will be happening all over the place. In spades.

It won't take long for the mob mentality to take over. And some of these mobs will begin seeking vengeance on anyone or any establishment they feel has wronged them. Banks, and government buildings, courthouses or any perceived seat of authority will be the most obvious targets of opportunity. Anyone still inside those buildings will be in serious danger. Consider the recent events in Greece, where four Athens bank employees – one of them a pregnant woman – were beaten and then burned alive in their bank building. Why? Because there were riots in all major Greek cities over a proposed 'austerity program.' Imagine that. But you don't have to imagine it, because it's true. So what about banks? If you think that they've got lots of cash, and that you can get some or all of yours, you would be wrong. And here's why:

2. Banks:
Banks today don't have anywhere nearly enough currency on hand to sustain a bank run, much less the outcomes of a declaration of a 'bank holiday'. Unlike retail stores, most major financial institutions have contingency plans to shut down the instant they are told to do so – and yes, they will be told to do so in no uncertain terms by the Obama regime. Within minutes, and all across America, ATM machines will be offline, credit card and debit card terminals will become unresponsive. Banks and credit unions will close their vaults, lock their doors, and their personnel will be hastily dismissed from the premises, except perhaps for some special security guards. Telephone inquiries to any of the financial institutions will be automatically answered by a computer with a pre-recorded message similar to the following: "Our system is currently experiencing an extremely high call volume and therefore we are unable to answer your call at this time. Please try again later when our call volume returns to normal." Bank web sites will become unresponsive and otherwise unavailable. Bottom line: you will NOT have access to your money or to the contents of your safety deposit boxes. Period. Neither will anyone else. Now is the time to ponder the implications of that last statement and to prepare accordingly. To put it bluntly, if you're one of those people who live off their credit/debit cards, you are screwed. Again, if you happen to be on bank premises when the deal goes down, leave immediately and head

home or to your pre-arranged rendezvous point. Because it'll get ugly even more quickly inside the bank. It'll take only 15-30 minutes before an angry mob begins to gather outside the bank. And that's no place for you.

3. Gas stations:
Most people today don't remember the Mid-East oil crisis of the 1970s (thanks for the memories, Jimmy Carter), or the long lines that developed when gasoline and other fuels ran short. For the most part, though, we behaved ourselves. That will not be the case today. Most gas stations will close in fairly short order, and there will be a run on fuel. The stations that remain open will immediately shift to a cash-only, high-dollar basis, and you can just imagine how that'll affect those who live on their plastic cards. Thus, the scenes in the lines waiting to get to the now-closed pumps will quickly devolve into something… unpleasant. This why you must never, never let your gas tank go below half-full, and why you must always carry at least $100 in cash. That $100 may only buy you five gallons or perhaps even just one in those circumstances, but that's more than you'd have otherwise. It's best not to be in that position in the first place. You need to be able to pass those gas stations by if you can.

4. Government offices:
The vast majority of our government leaders all over the world are relatively intelligent individuals – despite all evidence to the contrary. Perhaps it's more accurate to say that they are cunning individuals, which is not the same thing as intelligence. If nothing else, they are possessed of a keen sense of self-interest and self-preservation. In any case, they completely understand the ramifications of a "bank holiday" in our electronically-based financial economy and what it might mean for their continued safety. They also hold ordinary people like you and me in complete and total contempt. Therefore, government offices will also be immediately shut down, and those in charge will empty their buildings and lock their doors. Any transaction in progress, including any trials or other legal proceedings, will halt and will be 'postponed until some future date'. High-level government officials, including judges and especially tax officials, will immediately begin to make their way to imagined places of safety. In any case, government offices will go into a 'lockdown' mode. If you happen to be in or near one of these places, get out as quickly as you can. They will soon become targets for retribution and retaliation along with anyone unfortunate enough to be there.

5. Criminals:
Anyone and everyone who has criminal tendencies will see civil disorder as a golden opportunity to improve their situation. More than likely, some of these criminals have al-

ready made detailed plans that include exactly which businesses they are going to hit first, second, third, and so on. We don't think that way – but they do. Any business with a reasonable level of cash-on-hand will be very high on every criminal's list. Every jewelry store and pawn shop that has any type of silver or gold coins or jewelry, or precious stones (diamonds, rubies, emeralds, etc.) will be very high on everyone's list, along with stores that sell firearms and ammunition. The warfare that breaks out at these establishments between competing criminals and/or gangs will be vicious and brutal beyond belief. You don't want to be anywhere near these places.

6. Normal People:

The ethical and moral constraints binding regular folks will fall away fairly quickly – desperation and lack of understanding does odd things to people. Especially the unprepared ones who suddenly realize that they are well and truly screwed. It won't take long before some average people panic and begin to loot and to engage in the most desperate sort of mayhem. Grocery stores will be completely emptied from wall-to-wall, including the rear storage area within a few hours or less. Stores that sell firearms, ammunition, appliances, clothing, shoes, or anything else the average citizen thinks they need will be stripped in less than an hour. As targets of looting opportunity diminish, it won't take long for fighting to begin over the few remaining resources. Many who have lost their jobs, their vehicles, their homes, and their life savings will now have nothing more to lose by seeking some form of retribution against the society that they believe has taken everything away from them. Everyone who felt they got a raw deal from a traffic cop will be in a very unpleasant mood. Everyone who has had their property taxes increased at the same time their income AND the value of their home decreased will not be in a good mood. Everyone who has had their credit card interest rate increased at the same time their employer was reducing the number of hours they worked each week will not be in a good mood. Everyone who has been reduced from a two-family income down to a one-family income or less will not be in a good mood. Everyone who lost their job because their employer went bankrupt will not be in a good mood. This will not be a good time to engage any of these folks in a conversation.

7. The Entitled Classes:

There is no lack of people who have been just barely surviving in a situation where they were living hand-to-mouth on government welfare or the charity of the local community (unemployment checks, welfare checks, food stamps, food banks, etc.). You probably know some of these folks yourself. Most of them have made absolutely NO preparation for a calamity of the type that we have been discussing. They will not have any extended stores of provisions,

fuel, water, etc. The instant it dawns on them that there will be no more government welfare or charity, then these individuals will have no hope for survival unless they are able to immediately acquire the food and other resources they need before it is all gone. This will be particularly true for what we have come to know as the inner-city 'entitled classes.' Anyone who tries to stand in their way, or who tries to reason with them will find that their own life will become nasty, brutish and short. And once they've reduced their cities into wastelands and slaughterhouses, they'll come boiling out of those urban areas and into the countryside looking for fresh 'opportunities' - that being you and yours and your carefully managed preparations. There will be only one way to deal with them. Best to have your neighborhood 'un-welcoming committee' on 24/7 watch. But that's an entirely different subject.

8. Revolutionary Wanna-bes:

This lot can be dangerous. Most of them are ignorant sheep, but there's an edgy, violent side to some of them. The events that follow the One Hour Meltdown will present an opportunity for the more megalomaniac and messianic of the bunch to act out their savage revolutionary fantasies. Think Occupy [where-ever] on meth. Come to think of it, many of them will be. Who will be among their targets of choice? You will. Because you drive a decent car. Or wear decent clothes. Or have nice shoes. Or have an iPod or an iPad. Or are seen coming out of a building housing one of their hated businesses. Or just because it's Tuesday. After a while, the excuses and the justifications fall by the wayside and savagery rules the day. Very, very bad for you unless you're either already gone or are prepared to deal with them in the only way they can - and should - be dealt with.

The upshot is: The only resources that you'll be able to count on when things become… unpleasant are the ones you'll have with you. It's your choice to be prepared and to have a chance to live through this – or not, and have no chance at all.

Now what?

Time to think the unthinkable.

If you have not previously thought about the above scenarios, or if you are not intellectually and emotionally prepared to deal with it, then the chances are not very good for your long-term survival. Let me say that again: *If you have not previously thought about the above scenario, or if you are not intellectually and emotionally prepared to deal with it, then the chances are not very good for your long-term survival.* In other words, you and anyone depending on you are going to wind up <u>dead</u> - or worse (yes, there's worse than dead) - and in fairly short order unless you are phenomenally lucky. Many of the above events will happen simultaneously during the first hour of the crisis. After that first hour has passed, then things will begin to get really nasty. It will begin to dawn on folks that there are not enough law enforcement personnel to protect everyone and everything. In fact, a sizeable percentage of law enforcement personnel will think of family first and the rest of us as a very distant second priority – if they even bother to think of us at all. Remember – most police hold us 'civilians' in contempt. Although the military will probably be ordered to protect specific high priority/high value establishments and resources, there will simply not be enough military personnel to protect individual civilians, neighborhoods or businesses. In any case, you simply don't want to be anywhere near these places and situations. You'll have to be <u>mentally</u>, <u>emotionally</u> and <u>physically</u> prepared to get away from them and fast. *Plan in advance* to have a safe place to go (preferably more than one) or a rendezvous with others for mutual support. And have more than one plan.

The Best Defense. Your best defense against catastrophe is to PAY ATTENTION! Take those iPod plugs out of your ears, you fool! Self-absorption in trivialities *will get you killed* at a time when immediate and decisive action is called for. No one has a crystal ball, but keeping a "weather eye" out for trouble is just pure common sense. Now, if all of this seems like too much trouble, then ask yourself a simple question: what's your life worth? Or the lives of your loved ones? If you choose not to consider this question and its implications out of fear, or out of scorn for what you believe is unthinkable, or if it all seems like too much work, or if you're simply in denial about the events happening around you, then you've sold your life and theirs cheap. And believe me, there will be many, many who will do just that. If you're reading this, then you've taken the first step towards not being 'that guy'. Don't be 'that guy'. Do you want to live? Decide now.

Get Out of Dodge!

So here's your picture: Everyone – and I mean <u>everyone</u> should have within reach a kit that will help them to leave wherever they are and proceed to a place of relative safety. DO NOT stick around to see what happens once things start to get dodgy. There will be no neutral spectators in this game. In fact, if you're watchful and prudent, you won't even show them your taillights before the party gets started. If you have planned well (and you do have a plan, don't you?), then you will have a fighting chance to make your way home or to your rally point. To accomplish that in relative comfort and safety, you'll need something more than a bag of Doritos and your car keys. You'll need a Get

Out Of Dodge kit. This is at its most fundamental, a bag of food, water and gear that'll sustain you for three days 'in the field.' Most of the gear used to build these kits is off-the-shelf and relatively cheap. You'll be out about $300 - $600 for a complete kit, minus weapons and ammunition. Cheap insurance, any way you look at it. Check out *Cabela's, CheaperThanDirt.com* and *SportsMansGuide.com* for the best deals.

So ask yourself: what are you going to do when and if

Civil unrest / breakdown occurs.

Communications go down. The recent flash mob phenomenon just about guarantees that cell phone services will be shut down by the authorities.

Law and order becomes sporadic or non-existent. Remember: even in the best of times, when seconds count, the police are only minutes away.

You have to fight to preserve your own life or protect others' lives in order to get where you're going.

You have to abandon your vehicle in the face of mobs or roadblocks.

You have to walk to a prearranged safe place or rendezvous/rally point.

You need to move quickly and not 'camp out'. Rest, yes. Camp, no.

The weather may not be your friend – hot, cold, wet, snowy. Prepare accordingly.

What's your plan?

As I've said, you're going to have to get the hell out of Dodge, and quickly, too. That's what you're going to have to do. And to do that, you're going to have to be prepared with the means to sustain yourself for at least three days 'in the field'. Now, if you're lucky, AND you've been paying attention, then you'll be able to quietly get up from your workplace, excuse yourself and drive home without incident. But don't plan on it.

187

Why Do it <u>This</u> Way?

This is a layered approach, with duplication of key items at every layer where practical. Strategy for this assumes that you may lose your backpack and/or your sling bag. Or that you may not have time to suit up, and that you can only grab your sling bag and/or backpack and weapons. Yes, I said *weapons*. How do you plan to deter thugs or other riff-raff who are intent on robbing and killing you? Or worse (yes, there's worse). Harsh language? The voice of sweet reason? Get real. Don't kid yourself.

Some key points follow:

Be Good to Your Feet

When it comes to your feet, you must treat them as royalty. So think: *can I run, climb, fight and walk long distances with what I have on my feet right <u>now</u>*? If the answer is **no** to *any* of these questions, you may be – no, you WILL BE in for a world of hurt. In fact, under the scenario outlined above, you will probably be *dead* sooner rather than later. You've got to be able to move away from trouble as quickly as you can. Your every-day footwear should be a pair of decent hiking shoes or durable shoes in case you can't put your boots on in time. Boots with puncture-proof soles could save your life. You <u>do</u> have good, broken-in boots or durable footwear for the current season, don't you? If not, get some NOW and break 'em in.

Figure 1 - Men's Bates infantry boots - about $80

A Word for Womenfolk

Yeah, I know – the shoe thing. But here's the cold, hard, immutable truth: in a bad situation, *those flip flops, Jimmy Choos or Manolo Blahniks will get you <u>killed</u>*. Why? Because you will not be able to do the things that you absolutely must be able to do when things get ugly: specifically, run, climb, fight and walk long distances in those cute, but now worse-than-useless shoes. Without question, <u>you will be a liability to yourself and to anyone you're with</u> if you don't have <u>sturdy, well broken-in footwear</u>. The term 'fashion victim' takes on a whole new meaning here, doesn't it? Don't be one.

Figure 2 - Women's Bates side-zip duty boots - about $80

Protect Your Eyes.

If you're near an outbreak of civil disorder, the air will soon become filled with debris and other unpleasant things. As I mentioned earlier, gunfire will shatter glass and send it flying, and impact with masonry will spall shards and splinters of material everywhere. Get hit in your eyes with anything like that, and you'll be blind, perhaps permanently. If you can't see, you can't fight, flee or do much of anything that you'll need to do in order to stay alive. Ordinary glasses, if you wear them, offer better-than-nothing protection for your eyes, but not much else. So don't rely on them. It will be worth your while and your eyes – and perhaps your life – to acquire an inexpensive set of eye protection. It's a common industrial item, readily available. Better still, get a set of protective goggles like the ones used by our troops in Iraq - they are also less than $20, and will accommodate most eyeglass wearers. See to live – and live to see.

Figure 3 - GI Issue Sun, Wind and Dust Goggles – about $20

Be Good to Your Hands

Most people don't think of this. You need good gloves in order to protect your hands. Here's why:

One of the by-products of civil unrest is rubble, broken glass and large quantities of other debris. All of which can turn your hands into hamburger in fairly short order when you come into contact with it. And you WILL come into contact with it. Why? Think about it – you're almost certainly to have to make your way through areas that have taken the brunt of destruction from a variety of sources. This means that you're going to have to climb, crawl, and go prone or otherwise come into contact with your environment. If you're in an urban area experiencing civil unrest, storefronts, office buildings and vehicle windshields will generate an astonishing amount of broken glass, jagged metal shards and other debris in fairly short order. Gunfire will spall sharp hand-shredding, foot-puncturing, eye-blinding shards of concrete, masonry and other debris everywhere. If heavy weapons come into play, this destruction and its accompanying rubble will be even greater, deadlier and even more widespread.

The point of this is that good, durable gloves that allow you both dexterity and protection are absolutely essential, no matter what the season. Cost – about $30-$40 for a good set of Kevlar-constructed gloves. The ones shown in figure 4 are a bit more, as they also incorporate hardened knuckle protection.

Cold weather calls for a warmer glove, but leaves you with the problem of weapons handling. Experiment until you find a glove that keeps your fingers warm but allows you enough freedom of movement and sensitivity to hand le tools and weapons.

Knees and elbows next.

Figure 4 - BlackHawk Fury Comando HD Gloves – about $60

These are warm weather gloves. Use a variant with Thinsulate Insulation for colder weather. Make sure that you can handle all of your gear, especially weapons, with gloves on.

Figure 5 - Frabill® Performance Task Gloves about $36

A less expensive, but still highly functional pair of gloves. Don't compromise by going cheaper.

Be Good to Your Knees and Elbows.

Most of us never think of having to protect these indispensable parts of our anatomy. If you ever have to kneel, crawl or go prone in gravel, broken glass or riot debris, you'll be very sorry indeed if you don't have some sort of protection for your knees and elbows. The first time you spend some time firing a rifle in the prone position out in the field, you'll immediately understand the issue. Knee and elbow protectors are pretty inexpensive, and you should find those that will match the clothing you're wearing. And get them on immediately as part of your dress-out/load-out routine. You may not get a chance later. You'll have a huge edge where others won't. And in some circumstances, you could even make broken glass and other debris work in your favor to discourage unwanted company from following you. Be creative.

Figure 6 - Tru-Spec Tactical Elbow Pads Nylon Polymer – about $15

First layer – Combat Uniform or Inconspicuous Durable Clothing

You may or may not wish to put on BDUs (Battle Dress Uniform) depending upon the circumstances. If you're going to remain in an urban area (very *bad* idea, BTW), or wish to escape from one (a very *good* idea), dark or gray inconspicuous clothing may be best. Even the latest digital Army camo can stand out <u>if no one else is wearing it</u>.

You want to be as inconspicuous as you can be in whatever environment you find yourself. *The important thing is to have comfortable, durable clothing that can take some abuse and that you can wear for days.*

For example, Carhartt makes very sturdy double-fronted work jeans that wear very, very well, and come in colors that will blend a variety of environments. Usually about $40. Irregulars can be had on sale for about $10-$15 less.

Filson makes expensive but incredibly tough outdoor clothing. Filson's what you buy if you only want to buy it once. "Might as well have the best," is their motto and it also should be yours.

Figure 7- Carhartt double front loggers jeans

For another example, the **Outback Trading Company Long Unlined Drover** (or duster) is tough and durable with an oilskin shell. Wearable in all but the hottest weather and with a wool liner for colder weather, this will keep you dry, cut the wind and offer concealment for short rifles, shotguns and other weapons. The length will tend to keep your legs from getting soaked in windy, rainy weather. Available from Cabela's, it's gotten great reviews. Check it out. About $130. Not cheap, but it is definitely worth the money.

Filson offers first-rate outdoor clothing. As I mentioned before, their motto is, "Might as well have the best." And they're not kidding. Not cheap, either

Their **Shelter Cloth Duster** shown below can be configured with a hood and various weights of zip-in liners. It's the last outdoor coat you'll ever buy. www.filson.com

In general, dark(er) clothing will serve you well in an urban environment. But don't go for dead black. Black stands out more than you might believe, ninja stories notwithstanding. Flat grays, olive drabs and tan/khaki work pretty well. In fact, grayish clothing may be one of the best choices for an urban environment. Bright colors or otherwise shiny fabrics are right out – unless you want to look like a target.

Some tactical clothing manufacturers make inconspicuous pants with inserts for kneepads – well worth checking out. If you ever have to kneel or crawl on gravel, debris or broken glass – and you almost certainly will at some point in a civil unrest scenario - you'll be very glad you had this particular fashion accessory. Same goes for your elbows. Get protection for these important parts of your body.

Figure 8 - Outback Unlined drover coat. About $130.

Filson Tin Cloth Packer coat – extra-long - about $320

I own this one - tough as nails and supremely comfortable.

Filson Shelter Cloth Duster coat – about $350

For full-up combat dress, I prefer 80's era Swiss Alpenflage. This is what works for my area. Cheap and readily available (or used to be), works great for the inland Pacific NW environment. The important thing is to rig for your area and circumstances.

Again, I strongly recommend good, *well broken-in* boots with puncture-proof steel shank soles (for reasons we've already discussed) and a PASGT helmet with appropriate cover. A good helmet will save your life – without one you stand an excellent chance of becoming another piece of bio-degradable scenery. You can somewhat conceal the fact that you're wearing one by flipping the hood of your coat or poncho over it. There's plenty of PASGT gear on eBay if you don't have a local source. Avoid the stuff with bullet holes in it, though. Probably bad luck. So think it through and wear what will work for your environment and will help to reduce your profile.

Figure 9 - Alpenflage combat blouse

Figure 12 - PASGT helmet without cover - around $70-$90 on eBay

Figure 10 - Alpenflage combat pants

Figure 11 - Swiss Alpenflage. 80s era camo gear.

First Layer - combat uniform pocket contents

Assume that you may not be able to reach your bug-out bags. Assume that you may lose one or both of them for one reason or another. Then, whatever you have in your pockets is what you'll have.

1. **Strike-anywhere matches.** Best to put them in a waterproof case. UCO Stormproof Matches are the best matches available for harsh conditions. Each match burns for about 15 seconds even if it is windy, rainy, or cold. The matches even burn underwater. Extra strikers are included.

Figure 13 – Strike anywhere matches

2. **Fire Starter.** BlastMatch with tinder of some sort. Yes, it's redundant, but you can't have too many ways to make a fire. WetFire Tinder is one of the best fire-starting materials available to help you get a blaze going even in a downpour! They extinguish instantly leaving no residue, odor, or smoke. 8 Cubes burn for 12 minutes each.

Figure 14 - Blastmatch fire starter

Figure 15 - WetFire tinder

3. **Maps.** Topo maps or even Jeppesen charts (standard aviation charts) are very useful. Create a custom Google or Bing map of your E&E routes. If you do, then laminate them for durability and to make them waterproof. You DO have more than one escape route worked out, don't you?

4. **Compass.** In a worst case scenario, you may not be able to rely upon a GPS device. Learn how to follow a compass bearing. With this knowledge, you can guide yourself through thickly forested areas, featureless winter landscapes, foggy and/or overgrown areas, etc. An orienteering class or two will put this knowledge in practical focus.

Figure 16 - Standard military compass

5. **LED Flashlight and extra batteries.** Use what works best for you. Carry at least two. Most run on 3 AAA batteries. You should also consider the use of a headlamp. There are times when having both hands free AND having a light source directed at your work can literally be a life-saver.

Figure 17 – Life Gear LED flashlights – 80 lumens – about $25 for 2 from Costco. Sold in 2, 3, and 4 pack units. Good quality.

I like the Streamlight Trident® Headlamp. It has 3 different beam options including a powerful 300 mA Xenon bi-pin bulb for 18 lumens, 2 standard white LEDs and 1 safety green LED for low light work. This is the gold standard of headlamps and it's a lifesaver. About $25 at 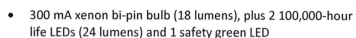 www.sportsmansguide.com

- 300 mA xenon bi-pin bulb (18 lumens), plus 2 100,000-hour life LEDs (24 lumens) and 1 safety green LED
- 3-position lighting: xenon bulb, 1 safety green LED, 2 white LEDs
- Spot to flood focus
- Adjustable elastic head strap and rubber hard hat strap
- 90 degrees tilting head
- Durable compact ABS body
- Powered by 3 AAA alkaline batteries run up to 150 hrs (single LED)

Figure 18 – Streamlight Trident® Headlamp

6. **Energy bars.** Easy to consume on the go. Always have something like this in your pockets. Forget the low-fat stuff. You're going to need the calories, and this is no time to diet. Stuff 2-4 of these in your pockets. Wrap them in a zip-lock or two to protect them. The zip-locks themselves are useful items.

Figure 19 - Millennium Energy Bars - 400 calories each

A reviewer at Amazon.com had the following to say about the Pemmican bar shown here in Figure 19a:

"This product will keep you alive. Significant calorie count. Fairly high carb/protein ratio for energy. Oddly nice, mild taste; reminiscent of fruit cake. 10g (40% daily) of fiber! It will power through your digestive system with the inexorable force of a fruit-n'-nut-flavored glacier. You know that saying about the bear doing something in the woods? That'll be you. Not a bad thing, just keep it in mind."

I happen to like these, and I can tell you from direct and personal experience that they'll keep for a very long time.

Figure 19a - Pemmican energy bars - 12 pack about $21.00/12 at Amazon.com

7. **Extra Clothing Layer.** Refer to the Outback duster mentioned previously. Failing that, or if local weather conditions make such gear impractical, consider a poncho and/or a parka. You could even use a Mylar emergency blanket or even a 3 mil contractor's bag in a pinch. Naturally, this is all area / climate / season specific. A light poncho will fold up into one of your pockets. So will an extra pair of socks in a waterproof bag, and those could be a lifesaver because they may save your feet at some point. Remember – even at the height of summer, it can still get coolish-cold at night, even in the desert and especially in the northern tier of states and/or latitudes. If you stop to rest, you've got to keep warm, even if it's not wise to make a fire at the time.

195

8. **Gloves.** Save your hands. You need to be able to use your hands. This means protecting them from the elements and from hard use. Make sure your winter gloves will do what they are supposed to do AND allow you enough dexterity to use your weapons effectively. Lightweight gloves for summer, warm ones for winter.

Give serious thought to investing a bit extra to get gloves with plastic knuckle protectors. .

Figure 20 – Frabill® Performance Task Gloves – warm weather only.

9. **Knee and elbow pads.** Save your knees and elbows. Cuts, abrasions and other light injuries can quickly become infected. You don't want that.

Figure 22 - Elbow pads

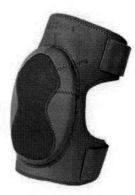

Figure 21 - Knee pads

10. **Sunglasses / goggles.** Save your eyes. Look for shatter-proof lenses. Prescription if you need them. Some combat style goggles allow for glasses or other eyewear, but I assure you that it is not comfortable.

Figure 24 - US military issue combat eye protection

Figure 23 - Wiley sunglasses

11. **Individual First Aid Kit (IFAK).** Carry basic first aid supplies such as sterile gauze and pads, Band-Aids, moleskin (always, always protect your feet), quickclot bandage, etc. Be sure to include some sort of eyewash like Visine. A small kit of the basics will fit in one of your pockets. You get the picture. **Be smart and take a first aid course** or two at your local community college – the knowledge you gain can literally be a life saver for you and others. The one shown here will fit in a cargo pants pocket. A typical IFAK might contain:

- EMT shears (*very* important – should be in the top of the kit, as you'll need them to cut away clothing to get to a wound)
- Tweezers (again, top of the kit)
- Eye Patch Dressing
- 4" Israeli Battle Dressing – HIGHLY recommended
- Quickclot powder
- Water Purification Tablets
- SuperGlue (refresh often – great for closing cuts)
- Disinfectant – betadyne or hydrogen peroxide
- Lip Balm
- Muslin for bandage, wrap or sling (2)
- Tampons – great for gunshot wounds
- Moleskin – lots of moleskin
- Assorted Adhesive Bandages (10)

Figure 25 - Individual First Aid Kit (IFAK)

12. **Knife / multi-tool.** Preferably one of each. An extra knife on a lanyard around your neck or clipped to an inner pocket is good insurance. You can't have too many knives. Carry at least one knife heavy enough for fighting and light shelter construction.

Figure 27 - Remington 1911 Multi Tool Black

Figure 26 - CRKT folder with clip

13. **A pair of heavy lineman's pliers/wire-cutters.** This tool will handle situations that are beyond the capabilities of your multi-tool. Very useful for getting through obstacles like small chain link or wire fence. Can also be used to make obstacles and traps out of heavy gauge wire. Be creative and think out of the box.

Figure 28 - Irwin 7" lineman's pliers/wire cutters

14. **Water. Do not allow yourself to get dehydrated!** Adopt/adapt your water carrier for your circumstances. You should have a pouch or space for a Camelback-style water bladder. Best thing to do is to keep a gallon jug of fresh water in your kit so that you can fill your water bladder(s) or bottle(s) on the spot before you depart. You don't want to keep water in your canteen / water bladder for an extended length of time. So you can keep your main water supply fresh by dumping the jug once a week and refilling it with fresh.

Figure 29 -100 oz water bladder

- **Water purification.** Clean water is a must! But you won't always be able to count on having it handy and clean. One of the best products I've encountered is the Polar Pure water disinfectant system. Compact, effective and inexpensive. One unit will treat 2000 quarts of water. Available on Amazon.com. Get several. You won't be good for much if you're blowing your guts out of both ends. Caveat: the Polar Pure iodine-based system and others like it are of limited value against protozoa cysts. Cryptosporidium in particular is resistant to halogen treatments. You may need to pre-filter your water before you treat it – depends on your operating area.

15. **Ammunition.** At least one full rifle mag and one pistol mag. Dedicate a secure pocket for one of each of these. One is better than none. Most pistol rigs will have places for an extra magazine or two.

NOTE: There's a small emergency kit that works very well and can be modified for your own use. About $60, it is waterproof and fits nicely in cargo pants or BDU pockets. This kit measures 6-1/2" x 3-7/8" x 1-5/8" and comes with the following items:

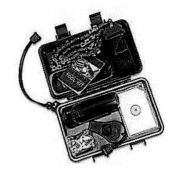

BlastMatch fire starter
WetFire tinder
StarFlash signal mirror
JetScream whistle
SaberCut saw
HardCache carrying case

Figure 30 - Compact emergency survival kit

I would be inclined to lose the mirror and the whistle, as you're not going to be interested in advertising your whereabouts in the sort of situations we're contemplating here. Substitute water purification tablets and/or more tinder or small first aid items for the mirror and the whistle. Add a Smith's PP1 pocket sharpener for less than $10.

My version of this kit has the following items packed in the HardCache carrying case:

- BlastMatch fire starter
- WetFire tinder
- Trioxane bar (burns nicely with little or no smoke)
- Small Gerber clip knife
- Small LED flashlight (single AA battery)
- SaberCut saw
- Mylar emergency blanket
- 20 lb fishing line – good for repairs or traps

Figure 31 – Smiths PP1 pocket sharpener

A word about the SabreCut saw: It sells for about $25 and is essentially a chain saw in your pocket. Check out Amazon.com for user reviews. It's truly amazing how well this works.

Nice package for a single cargo pocket. If you can afford it, add one to your sling bag, too.

You can get it here:
http://www.cheaperthandirt.com/CAMP224-1.html

Extras if you've got the pockets or the inclination:

1. **Small radio w/extra batteries.** Why carry a radio? Because your cell phone may become unusable in fairly short order. Or worse, your cell phone may serve as a means for people who are not your friends to locate you. Look for a 22+ mile range GMRS/NOAA weather combo. If you've made arrangements with others to meet up, that type of radio can be invaluable. Be secure about using one, though. Learn its use and its useable range in advance. Practice.

2. **25-50 ft of parachute cord.** Whatever and wherever it fits. Very, very useful. That cord, some branches and your poncho or a couple of 3 mil contractors' bags can construct a decent impromptu shelter. Which could be a life-saver for you or someone else.

Figure 31 - Midland GMRS radio set - about $60

I've left off fishing kit - but not fishing line - and items like that because you're probably not going to have the time for fishing and in any case, you have room for that sort of thing in either your sling bag or your small backpack if you really must have it.

Practice and test. Finally, when you've got that all together, field test it. See how fast you can get it all on, boots and helmet included. Speed counts, and in a tense situation, your training here will definitely pay off. Do it again and again. Then do it at least once a week. Walk, trot, run and see what rattles. Quiet the rattles. Then roll down an embankment, throw yourself down flat, tumble if you're capable and see what you've got left. Fix what you have to. Walk, trot, run. Still quiet? Still have everything? Good.

Break in Your Boots! I'll say this again - you've got to be kind to your feet. The time you are obliged to take a 40 mile trek home is NOT the time to break in your boots, or to find out where the problem areas are. Break them in *with all the gear you're going to carry*. And carry moleskin for blisters. Lots of moleskin.

Second Layer – Sling Bag

The sling bags / messenger bags offered by places like *Cheaper Than Dirt* and *Sportsman's Guide* are great. They're light, easily snatched up, relatively inconspicuous and the contents will afford you an extra day or two of operation in the field. Plenty of MOLLE webbing attachments for your customization pleasure, but *don't* overload it or bulk it out.

The premise is that even if you don't have time to suit up, you can still grab your weapons and sling bag and make a decent go of it. Yet you want stuff handy if you must fight. I wear mine on the left, since I'm a right- hander. The one I use also has a waist strap to keep it from flapping in the breeze – I consider that essential.

Figure 32 - Messenger bag with MOLLE attachment base

To a certain extent, I replicate the items listed for in the bag and the list below reflects that. But it differs in some details and sports a few additions. Ammo, for instance. I hang a 3 mag pouch hanging on the exterior front strap for my AR carbine, and there's more ammo and an extra full rifle and pistol magazine in the bag. Again, you're not looking to camp out – you want to keep moving towards your destination. Rest, but don't set up housekeeping. Even if this is all you can grab, then you have <u>greatly</u> improved your odds.

Some survival advocates are big on chest rigs. And for good reason. Once you've 'gone to ground,' then a full-on combat rig is a very good idea, for all the reasons that the military like them. I have one myself. But not for a bug-out situation where you'd like to be as unremarkable as is practical. A loaded chest rig says that you're ready for a fight. An individual with a full load-out chest rig is going to attract unwanted attention, and our goal here is to remain as inconspicuous as possible. A guy in a long coat with a sling bag and a small backpack won't look as immediately threatening as a guy in full-up combat gear. If you're smart, you'll keep your carbine or shotgun slung under your coat, but in such a manner that you can be 'at the ready' when circumstances call for it. Looking like just another scared refugee can work to your advantage. No point in giving the game away if you don't have to.

Second Layer - Sling Bag Contents

Try your best to leave with at least the contents of your pockets as discussed above and your sling bag. If you've gotten your co-workers used to seeing you with it, then you're far more likely to have it at your side when it comes time to beat feet.

1. **Strike-anywhere matches** in a waterproof case.

2. **Fire Starter. BlastMatch** with tinder of some sort.

3. **Maps.** Same as above

4. **Compass.** Yep, another one.

5. **LED Flashlight and extra batteries.** Where practical, your radio, flashlight and any other electronic device you might carry *will all use the same batteries*. Still, you're probably going to wind up with a combination of AAA and AA batteries.

6. **MRE** of your choice. A good *hot* meal (some familiar with MREs may dispute even the possibility) can make a big difference to your outlook. Even the (ugh) omelet ones. Make sure that your MRE comes with a heater. Not all of them do.

7. **Energy bar(s).** Something to eat on the go. Forget diet stuff – you're eating to live, and you're going to be burning a lot of calories while on the move.

8. **Extra Clothing Layer.** Same as above. Don't forget those socks!

9. **Extra pair of season-appropriate, durable gloves**. If you need them, you'll be *very* sorry if you don't have them.

10. **Contractor's bag(s).** Throw in a couple of these 3 mil bags if you have room and they don't take much. Makes a great emergency shelter and/or an impromptu poncho. Use one to catch rainwater. Lots of other uses.

11. **Sunglasses AND regular glasses.** For those of us who need glasses, the investment in an extra pair of each could be a life-saver. The messenger bag version of the sling bag accommodates glasses in hard cases nicely. In any case, make sure that you have some sort of eye protection.

12. **Binoculars.** No need to explain why you might want this. Compact, decent quality and easy to get to. Hang 'em in their case on your sling bag strap.

13. **First Aid Kit.** Carry additional first aid items as mentioned above. Another compact IFAK will do nicely.

14. **Knife / multi-tool.** Preferably one of each. Again. You can't have too many knives.

15. **Fishing line.** Small spool of 20 # test line. Useful for making alerts or making repairs.

16. **Empty Water container.** You can fill it later. It'll add to the one on/in your backpack or on your belt.

17. **Water purification system**. Now, you're up to two of them. Lose one, you've still got one.

18. **Rifle / pistol mag.** Full, and one of each. They'll be inside the pack along with as much extra ammo on strippers as you deem fit or have room. Don't overload it, though.

19. **Rifle ammo on strippers.** .223 / 5.56 mm doesn't take up that much room and you can probably carry an extra 2 or 3 magazines worth. Remember to include a couple of extra stripper guides. Wear one around your neck; keep the other in a zipper compartment in the bag.

20. **Rifle mag pouch.** Hang this in an easy-to-get-to place on the outside of the bag. Most will hold three AR-style mags. The fundamental thought here is that you should carry as much ammo as you comfortably can. You'll burn through it quickly in a firefight.

   Again, practice and test. Same as above. Still have everything? Still quiet? Good.

Third Layer – Small Backpack

Cheaper Than Dirt and *Sportsman's Guide* offer some nice compact backpacks. I like the Level III assault pack. It's big enough to hold more of what you need for an extra two or three days in the field, expands your available food and ammo, provides for a change of socks, underwear and t-shirt, insect repellent, a small folding shovel, a mess kit and a hydration pack. I include a small camping stove like the foldable pocket cooker shown here - $13 from http://www.sportsmansguide.com/:

Figure 33 - Level III Assault Pack

Figure 34 - folding pocket cooker

Very compact, burns any fuel, although trioxane bars or military fuel tabs don't give off smoke. Combined with a small mess kit and a tin

204

cup, you can produce hot food and drink very quickly. Well worth the carry weight.

Personal hygiene stuff. Depending upon what you feel like stuffing in there, you can add a waterproof bag with a small towel and some baby wipes. Yes, baby wipes. Ask any of our troops who have been in the field overseas and they'll tell you that they're indispensable for staying clean in tough environments. Getting clean is a real morale booster – don't overlook it. A small traveler's toothbrush with a small tube of toothpaste and a disposable razor and a small bar of soap are all items that can do wonders for your outlook. But don't go for a big fat backpack that'll hold everything including the kitchen sink. You want to stay light on your feet and to be able to move fast. Can't do that with a big monkey on your back.

Again, practice and test. Same as above. Still have everything? Still quiet?

Weaponry

When things get dicey, don't assume that you're going to just drive off or stroll home without incident. The longer you remain in troubled areas, the harder it's going to be to avoid a fight. A rifle, a pistol and a good fighting knife (that is, a knife that you actually know how to fight with) are essentials. The sane among us know that the last thing you want to do is to get into a firefight – or any kind of fight for that matter. But if you do, you want to have a chance to prevail. Again, *carry* ONLY *what you know how to use*. Otherwise it's likely to be taken away and used against you. You don't want that.

This will be no time for on-the-job training. If you don't have the skills AND the mind set to *kill* your opponents without hesitation, take a <u>practical</u> martial arts class of some sort (NOT tai chi, dammit – try Krav Maga or Kung Fu San Soo) and get thee to an Appleseed event taco pronto to learn how to shoot like a rifleman. <u>www.appleseedinfo.org</u>. Follow that with a <u>practical</u> self-defense pistol course.

Here's the thing: none of this is worth a <u>damn</u> *if you aren't prepared to use it*. And it's not just a matter of skill. <u>It's your willingness to incapacitate and kill your opponent as quickly as you can</u>. Short, brutal and nasty. Do you want to live? Decide now. If the answer is 'yes,' then you've got a chance. If the answer is 'no,' then you won't be going home.

As for weapons, everyone's got an opinion – so I'll just tell you what I pack and why.

1. **Rifle.** M4 carbine or equivalent. Decent ones are round $750 in 'plain Jane' configurations. Light, compact, accurate within reason and you can carry *lots* of 5.56mm ammo. I carry many loaded magazines – one in the rifle with another taped to it, three in a quick-access pouch on the sling bag, one inside it and two more in the backpack. Plus more ammo on strippers for a total load-out of 420 rounds. My rifle's in a soft padded case with a sling, so I can carry it in a slightly more inconspicuous fashion during the initial part of my journey out of my semi-industrial work area. You can customize this kind of rifle to your heart's content. My recommendation: keep it simple. It's more important to learn to shoot like a rifleman over iron sights and to maintain the skills than to play with accessories or to drop big bucks on fancy optics that will either approximate or exceed the value of the rifle.

   The Appleseed program (www.appleseedinfo.org) will be the best weekend you and your rifle will ever spend. And it can - no, it *will* - save your life.

Figure 35- my AR15 carbine with sling

2. **Pistol.** Glock mod 20 (10mm) with one 15 round mag in the pistol, two in the carry rig, one in the sling bag and two more in the backpack. This is a full-sized hard-hitting pistol, a real fight-stopper. I won't debate my choice of caliber here - it's been done to death in too many other places. What you should do is to carry the biggest, hardest-hitting caliber you can handle with skill. Here's a hint: any caliber starting with at least '4' is usually a good bet. Here's the deal: you're not going to be firing warning shots; you are going to your absolute very best to KILL the son of a bitch who's trying to harm you and yours. Anyway, if you're down to your pistol, then you've got other things to worry about besides calibers. But don't discount the value of a good pistol in a fight. Lots of good pistols out there. Find one. Learn it. Love it. Master it.

Figure 36 - 1911 45 auto and Glock model 20 10mm

3. **Tomahawk OR Stanley FUBAR forcible entry tool.** One 'hawk MOLLE'd to my backpack. Personally, I <u>like</u> tomahawks. Very nasty weapon for a close-quarters fight. If you're facing more than one opponent, the sudden and terrible damage you can visit on the first opponent is instantly instructional to the others and may end the fight right there. Learn it, love it, and kill with it if you have to. Or use it to make a nice temporary shelter. Works either way.

The tomahawk shown here has the advantage of being very light and fast, qualities that go a long way towards making it a superior fighting tool. Just as with a knife, you will seldom achieve an instant kill with one of these, especially in a straight-up fight, but you can deliver sufficiently painful and serious wounds to your opponent that will buy you valuable time to finish the job.

Figure 38 – SOG Fusion Tomahawk – about $35

If you're not skilled with the tomahawk, there are very useful alternatives. We're talking here about the **Stanley FUBAR forcible entry tool.** The Stanley FUBAR Forcible Entry tool is, like the tomahawk, a dual-purpose tool. They're about $70-$80 bucks and are extremely versatile – and *very* nasty as a weapon in practiced hands. Look it up and get one if you're not a 'hawk aficionado. It's not too hard to think of situations where a good demo tool could be a life-saver. For example, if you're strong and determined, you can in short order use the 18" the Stanley FUBAR to smash through sheetrock, wrench 2x4 studs apart and out of the way – and presto – you've just made yourself an impromptu exit or entrance. A wall is only a wall until it has a hole in it.

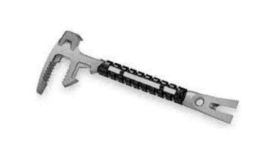

Figure 39 - Stanley FUBAR Forcible Entry Tool – about $80

4. **Fighting knife.** A Cold Steel Tanto Recon MOLLE'd to my sling bag. I've had mine for over 35 years, and it is well-used and well loved. When it comes to fighting knives, I favor single-edged designs like the Cold Steel Tanto or the Becker TAC Tool. This allows you to hold the knife edge-out against your forearm for a very nasty blocking move, from which you can transition to close-quarters smash and slash. Sounds ugly, doesn't it? It is.

Here's the thing about knife fighting – knife wounds are seldom *instantly* fatal. That's a key qualification. And *you* are likely to take damage. If you're close enough to stab or cut your opponent, then they're close enough to do the same thing to you. I've been taught to use a knife to deliver a quick and surprise strike that inflicts great pain or otherwise interferes with my opponent's vision. This distraction simply buys time for me to either get away or arrange something rather more permanent for my enemy. Don't like to think that way? Better start now and get used to it. If you want to live,

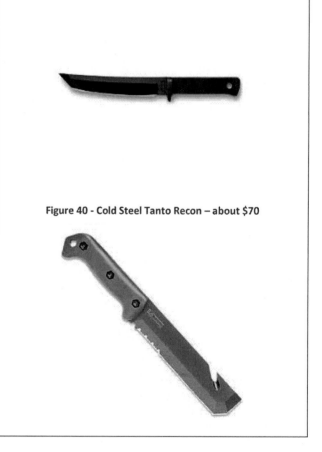

Figure 40 - Cold Steel Tanto Recon – about $70

Tools For Your Vehicle

If you're lucky enough to be able to drive away in advance of whatever unpleasantness begins to develop, there are some items that you might want to keep in your vehicle. Just in case. What we're talking about here are basic pioneering tools – pick, shovel, 6' pry bar – and a few other things that will smooth your path and get you past most common barricades. Be creative in the use of your tools, but also be sensible. Always use the right tool for the job at hand.

Here's the deal – ordinarily, you wouldn't carry <u>all</u> of this around in your vehicle. Although, if you live in a rural area and/or snow country, none of this will come as a surprise. You'll already have most, if not all of it aboard as a matter of course. But if you've got your nose to the wind, you'll get the sense that trouble's on the horizon – and that calls for a higher level of preparedness and anticipation of trouble. Trust your gut on this. You may already have snow chains, a basic mechanic's tool set and a highway safety kit in your car, but we're talking about going well beyond that for special circumstances. Make use of wooden boxes or heavy-duty plastic cases to contain and organize your tools, chains and spare batteries. Cover items with heavy contractor's bags to keep them dry. Lightly oil exposed metal shovel blades, etc. Inspect everything regularly. Take care of your tools and they'll take care of you. More importantly, it's a good habit of mind that generalizes to other areas. An old saying goes something like this: "90% of life is maintenance."

Note that a lot of what's in the following list can be had for pennies on the dollar at garage sales or swap meets

1. Pick.
Nothing fancy here. Just a good old-fashioned digging instrument. Gets through stuff shovels won't.

2. Shovel.
Again, nothing fancy. Also carry an aluminum grain scoop in the winter time if you're in a snowy area. Makes a great snow shovel.

3. 5' pry bar / breaker bar, 17 - 18 lbs.
Tamp on one end, wedge on the other. Great for prying things open or other sundry demolition tasks. One good whack with the wedge end will blast open most small locks. Also a nasty weapon if you're strong enough to wield it. When it comes to locks securing gates or fences, think ahead – if you come to a chained gate and you must remove the lock, carry a spare lock or two to re-secure the gate after you're through. Hang the re-secured lock

and chain just the way you found it. Be sure to remove the opened lock from the scene. This may buy you some additional time and discourage pursuit.

4. Sledge hammer.
Too many uses to detail here. Be creative. Even a small three pound short sledge can be a very useful companion tool.

5. Chisel.
Throw in one of these while you're at it. Put that three pound short sledge behind a good chisel and very little will stand in your way.

6. Sawzall.
The king of demolition tools. This should be an 18v-24v battery-powered Sawzall reciprocating saw with at least one spare battery pack. Make sure that you have an assortment of spare blades suitable for differing materials in the case that it comes in. If you have to pick one blade, go for the metal cutter. It'll work on wood, too, just not as well as once designed for wood. Practice with it on different materials to get a feel for how it works. There are very few problems that can't be solved with a Sawzall and the right blade.

7. Medium drill / rotohammer.
More powerful than a regular drill. Obvious uses. Indispensible if and when you need one. Battery powered - should also be an 18v-24v unit, preferably with an extra battery of the same type used by your Sawzall.

8. Chainsaw.
If you've got room for one and/or if you live in a rural area. Make sure you have at least a chain guard for it, if not a complete case. Carry a small container with bar oil, preferably one with a nozzle or spout. Same for fuel for the saw. Got a tree across the road? Here's your answer. Make sure that you've dealt with whoever might be waiting behind it first if there aren't too many of them. Always size up an obstacle like that first before you tackle it.

9. Chains.
One pair each of a 6' set and a 12' set with heavy duty hooks on each end. Learn how to quickly 'set a chain' in a choker loop if you don't know how. Allows you to use your vehicle as a force-multiplier for all sorts of interesting and useful things.

10. Pins and shackles.
A few of these can be a real problem solver when used with your chains.

11. Come along.

Have at least one. Use this with your chains to secure an item or to apply pressure. If you've used one, you know what I'm talking about. If you haven't then a new world will open up to you.

12. 2' x 4' roll of chain link fence.

A couple of these can be lifesavers. If you get stuck in sand, snow or mud, one or two of these can give your wheels enough purchase to get out. I know, because I've used them for just that purpose.

Your Vehicle

As a final thought, consider what you're driving. Can it take a beating? Are you willing to let it take a beating if it means your life or your loved ones' lives? You people who drive these little eco-fart mobiles will live – if only for a few minutes - to regret it. A sturdy, *well-maintained* 4WD vehicle is far more likely to get you out of trouble than one of those underpowered Smart Car cheese boxes. Fuel economy and eco-consciousness should always take a back seat to survivability – and that's what we're talking about there. Don't hesitate to think of your vehicle as a tool – a tool for removing obstacles. Or as a tool for dealing with people with bad intent. Some considerations:

1. High ground clearance – for obvious reasons.

2. Sturdy mud and snow-rated tires in good condition – forget the fancy wheels.

3. Cargo capacity – for the kit we just outlined above. Preferably covered and lockable.

4. 4 wheel drive with a really deep 4-low. Pay the extra for one with a limited-slip differential.

5. Sizeable gas tank.

6. Cattle guard bumper extensions

Also: you're a fool if you think your vehicle can provide protection from gunfire. Everyday vehicles offer you none. Let me repeat that: NONE! Hand gun projectiles and especially rifle projectiles will basically zip right through a car door or body – and you, too if you're unfortunate enough to be inside at the time. Worse still, projectiles that strike any part of your vehicle before they strike you will almost certainly begin to tumble, turning them into nasty little buzz saws of death. Your engine block will afford you some protection, but your opponents won't be aiming for the engine – they'll be aiming at whoever's behind that windshield and that'll be you and/or anyone with you. Vehicle ambushes are bad news for those reasons and others. Be vigilant. A barricade is almost always a set-up for just that sort of thing. Watch for them and turn the hell around as soon you or your passenger/lookout spots one. Remember – aside from getting to your home or rally point, avoidance of conflict is your primary goal. Only fight if you absolutely must. There's no glory in it – only survival.

What's a good bug-out vehicle? A lot of this is personal taste. Jeep, Subaru, most pickups, Hummers, etc. What do I drive? A well-maintained Chevy Avalanche 1500 with a Z71 off-road package. A lot of folks love these vehicles for a variety of good reasons.

Final Thoughts

None of this gear, no amount of preparedness is a guarantee. Fate can be a fickle mistress indeed. If your number is up, then I hope that you can meet your Creator with a good conscience. But there can be an awful lot of time and opportunity between now and then. Within the time your Creator has granted you, there is a lot that you can do to affect your destiny. Why not do as much as you can? You'll be saving your own life, and by extension, you'll be able to use that life to save others like your family and friends.

As to the cost? The money you'll spend on the items I've outlined here is money better spent by far than on trivialities and junk.

"Get Out Of Dodge / Bug Out Bag", Checklist.

The following list is intended to assist you in building up your specific "GOOD-BOB". It is not suggested that everyone have everything on this list, but rather that you pick and choose from it "Ala-Cart" as dictated by your personal family needs and requirements.

Check	Item	Quantity	Comment
	G.O.O.D Bag Paperwork		
	Cash, Dollars	$250-$500	ATMs will not be working. Include a roll of Quarters for vending machines.
	Cash, Gold Coins	As affordable	The highest store of wealth the average person can carry and use.
	Cash, Silver Coins	1 roll of 20	If the USA dollar collapses, Silver will always be accepted
	Contact List (printed on paper)		List of all your contacts: friends, family, banks, brokerage, employers, utilities, insurance, etc.
	Notepad and 2 Pens		A small "Water Proof" spiral bound notepad
	Recent Photo of each person		In case you need to provide to emergency authorizes
	Secure USB Flash Drive	Every Person	With a digital copy of EVERYTHING on this list in case you get seperated.
	Water Proof Document Bag		To carry and protect your documents
	Government identification (photo copies) including:		
	Birth Certificate		***Store ALL Document copies in water proof sealable bag or Mapcase***
	CCW License or Gun Permits		***If in doubt, LAMINATE the documents.***
	Change of Name		**SCAN/DIGITIZE all document copies and store on a secure Flash Drive.**
	Court Orders		
	Drivers License		
	Medicare / Medicaid Cards		
	Military ID		Could be highly usefull in an evacuation situation
	Passport	Every Person	Get the new "wallet" passport card so you always have Federal ID with you.
	Social Security Card		
	Photo copies of Important Documents		
	A recent Bank statement		***Store ALL Document copies in water proof sealable bag or Mapcase***
	Adoption Certificate		***SCAN/DIGITIZE all document copies and store on a secure Flash Drive.***
	Any important court orders		
	Business Licenses		
	Divorce Decree		
	Eye Glass Prescriptions		
	Genealogy Records		
	Insurance Policies		
	Land Deeds		
	Legal Custody of Minors		
	List of Credit Card Accounts		
	Living Will		
	Marriage License		
	Medical Insurance Cards		
	Medicine Prescriptions		
	Mortgage Agreement		
	Patriarchal Blessing		
	Power of Attorney Documents		
	Proof of employment		such as a Paystub
	Property / Real Estate Deeds		
	Rental Agreements		
	Stocks & Bonds		
	Vacination Report		
	Wills		
	Copy of the following		
	Concealed Carry Laws		Get one of the books that covers every state in the nation.
	Local and state maps (on paper)		Ideally a "Gazetter" of your state, Sealed in Zip Lock bag or "Mapcase"
	Pocket Constitution		References for debates and legal situations. Stored in zip lock bag to protect against moisture.
	Set of Scriptures		Small "military" style that will fit in a breast pocket (w/waterproof case)
	Survival Instruction Book		Recommend the SAS survival hand book

Done	Item	Quantity	Comment
		G.O.O.D. Bag - Essential Equipment	
	Aluminum Foil, Heavy Duty	One roll	100's of uses
	Batteries	Many	Sizes for ALL of your power needs, perfer Pure Lithium over Alkaline for long term storability and Cold Weather use.
	Binoculars	one	Small Lightweight waterproof "Mini" (lets you see trouble in advance)
	Camp Ax or Hatchet	One	For collecting fire wood or constructing temporary shelter
	Camp Saw	One	Small Folding style
	Can Opener	One for each	Small military knife edge style
	Carabiners	a few	Come in very handy to attaching things and rope use.
	Cell Phone	One for each	
	Collapsible Shovel	One	Need to bury the food and human wastes.
	Compass	One	Lensatic, Tritium-illuminated w/ pouch
	Deck of Playing Cards	one per family	Something to help pass the down time.
	Digital Camera	At least one per family	Take pictures of important events
	Duct Tape	One for each	All purpose fix-it and sealer. Also quick temporary seal for wounds.
	Extra batteries	As needed	Double the count of all batteries used in your electronic equipment
	Extra House Keys		
	Extra Vehicle Keys		
	Filled metal fuel cans	At least 10 gallons	spare fuel for your vehicle
	Firestarter	One Pack	See "Wetfire"
	Fishing kit		(if appropriate in your area)
	Flare, Road	Couple	Worst Case Scenario, this will light ANYTHING on fire even if wet.
	GPS Unit	One	With rechargeable batteries
	Knife	One for each	Sturdy fixed blade
	LED Flashlight	One for each	With Pure Lithium Batteries for Max Shelf Life and Duration
	LED Headlamp	One for each	With Pure Lithium Batteries (very nice to have hands free directed light)
	Lighter, Butane	One for each	See "Storm Lighter"
	Machete	One	Clearing brush and self defense
	Magic Marker	one	To clearly mark items if needed
	Magnifying Glass	one per family	Small plastic style.
	Matches	50+	Water Proof/Storm Proof in sealed Match container
	Matches, Magnesium	One	see "Blastmatch" (magnesium striking block w/flint)
	Mosquito net	One for each	
	Multi-tool, such as Leatherman	One for each	100's of uses
	Nylon rope or "550" parachute cord	100+ feet	100's of uses
	Pedometer	one	For estimating distance traveled on foot.
	Pen and Pencil	two	For taking notes on your waterproof notepad
	Pre-Paid Phone Card	One	
	Radio (Hand Crank / Solar)	At least one	AM, FM, Shortwave and NOAA bands
	Rain Poncho	One for each	
	Rubber Bands	One pack	
	Satellite Phone	One for family	Very good way of staying in touch in a local Grid-Down scenario
	Saw	one per family	Small Folding or Wire Style
	Signal Mirror	one per family	can be used for personal hygeine as well.
	Snare Thin Metal Wire	10+ feet	100's of uses, including vehicle repairs
	Solar battery recharger	One	See "Goal Zero Guide"
	Spare external battery for cell phone	one for each	See "iGo PowerExtender"
	Spare eye glasses	As needed	Keep your old eye glasses as a backup or obtain a cheap spare. Avoid contact lens, if possible, in emergency situation.
	Sunglasses	One for each	
	Trash Bags	3 for each	Large Heavy Duty "Yard" bags
	Trash Bags, Large Heavy Duty	One dozen	100's of uses
	Walkie-talkies	One for each	With rechargeable batteries
	Water Filter	one per family	see "Katadyn Pocket, Vario or Hiker"
	Water Filter, "Coffee Filter"	Several	Coffee Filters to remove sediment before mechanical filter
	Whistle	One for each	Get a "Storm Safety Whistle" it's the loudest there is.
	Wrist Watch	One for each	Illuminated for night time viewing
	Zip-Lock Bags, Quart and Gallon size	One dozen	100's of uses
	Zip Ties	A Dozen	Get the strong ones that will hold anything together.

Check	Item	Quantity	Comment
		CLOTHING, BEDDING, CAMPING GEAR	
	Backpack	one for each	Size and Fit accordingly to each person
	Bandanna	1 for each	
	Belt	1 for each	Strong Sturdy Belt
	Fanny Pack	One for each	Carry small items at your waist
	Fun games		Something to help fight boredom and pass down time.
	Gloves	one for each	Sturdy comfortable leather work gloves
	Groud Pad	one for each	Foam Pad or Self Inflating Air Matress. See "ThermaRest"
	Hiking / Walking shoes	one pair for each	
	Long Pants	1 set for each	
	Mosquetto Netting	1 for each	At least a head cover for sleeping at night
	Outdoor Sleeping Bag	One for each	Rated for the lowest winter temperatures in your area
	Pillow	one for each	TINY camping pillow, *some people can't sleep without one.*
	Plastic Tarp		Ground cover for tent or sleeping bags
	Portable Tent		Preferable a 4 season tent with enough capacity for your family or Bivowac Bags for each sleeping bag. See "Bivy Bag"
	Rain Gear, Pants & Jacket	one for each	Upgraded Better Alternative to poncho, Gortex if possible
	Rain Gear, Ponch	one for each	Large full coverage Poncho for hiking in the rain
	Repair Kit: Awl	One	For sewing any heavy materials
	Repair Kit: Buttons	One Pack	Assorted Buttons for sewing repairs
	Repair Kit: Goop	One Tube	For shoe soul repair
	Repair Kit: Mink Oil / SnoSeal	One bottle	For waterproofing leather boots
	Repair Kit: Needles	One Pack	Assorted Needles for sewing repairs
	Repair Kit: Nylon Thread	One Roll	
	Repair Kit: Patch Material		Some material to repair major tears in clothing or gear
	Repair Kit: Waxed Cotton Thread	One Roll	
	Short axe		Clear brush and chop good
	Shorts	1 set for each	(in warmer climates)
	Socks	3 pairs for each	wool/sythetic, NOT cotton, Tall will offer more support & protection
	Socks, Liner	2 pairs for each	Comes in very handy if your feet are prone to blisters from hiking
	Space Blanket	one for each	Emergency Mylar Blanket, see "*SOL Sport Utility Blanket*"
	Space Blanket, "Bivvy Bag"	one for each	Space Blanket sleeping bag, see "*SOL Thermal Bivvy*"
	Spare Shoe Laces	one pair for each	
	Tee-shirts	2 for each	Long Sleave
	Tent pegs and Tent Hammer		To secure the tent
	Underwear	2 spare sets for each	
	Wide-brimmed hat	one for each	
	Winter: Balaclava	1 each	
	Winter: Boots	1 pair each	Suitable for the lowest winter temperatures you might encounter
	Winter: Cap	1 each	Classic wool/synthetic watchman cap
	Winter: Fleece (for severe cold)	1 each	Fleece Jacket and Pants to be worn under outerwear/rainwear
	Winter: Gloves	1 pair each	Waterproof & Insulated
	Winter: Jacket	1 each	Sturdy all weather "outdoors" winter jacket
	Winter: Long Underwear	one for each	Polypropylene Top and Bottom, NOT Cotton
	Winter: Scarf	1 each	Polypropylene scarf to seal your neck.
	Winter: Socks	3 pairs for each	Heavy Duty, Tall and Warm, Wool/Synthetic, NOT Cotton
	Winter: Sweater	1 each	Wool or Synthetic, NOT Cotton
	Wool Blankets	1 for each	

Check	Item	Quantity	Comment
			G.O.O.D Bag Paperwork
	Cash, Dollars	$250-$500	ATMs will not be working. Include a roll of Quarters for vending machines.
	Cash, Gold Coins	As affordable	The highest store of wealth the average person can carry and use.
	Cash, Silver Coins	1 roll of 20	If the USA dollar collapses, Silver will always be accepted
	Contact List (printed on paper)		List of all your contacts: friends, family, banks, brokerage, employers, utilities, insurance, etc.
	Notepad and 2 Pens		A small "Water Proof" spiral bound notepad
	Recent Photo of each person		In case you need to provide to emergency authorizes
	Secure USB Flash Drive	Every Person	With a digital copy of EVERYTHING on this list in case you get seperated.
	Water Proof Document Bag		To carry and protect your documents
			Government identification (photo copies) including:
	Birth Certificate		***Store ALL Document copies in water proof sealable bag or Mapcase***
	CCW License or Gun Permits		***If in doubt, LAMINATE the documents.***
	Change of Name		***SCAN/DIGITIZE all document copies and store on a secure Flash Drive.***
	Court Orders		
	Drivers License		
	Medicare / Medicaid Cards		
	Military ID		Could be highly usefull in an evacuation situation
	Passport	Every Person	Get the new "wallet" passport card so you always have Federal ID with you.
	Social Security Card		
			Photo copies of Important Documents
	A recent Bank statement		***Store ALL Document copies in water proof sealable bag or Mapcase***
	Adoption Certificate		***SCAN/DIGITIZE all document copies and store on a secure Flash Drive.***
	Any important court orders		
	Business Licenses		
	Divorce Decree		
	Eye Glass Prescriptions		
	Genealogy Records		
	Insurance Policies		
	Land Deeds		
	Legal Custody of Minors		
	List of Credit Card Accounts		
	Living Will		
	Marriage License		
	Medical Insurance Cards		
	Medicine Prescriptions		
	Mortgage Agreement		
	Patriarchal Blessing		
	Power of Attorney Documents		
	Proof of employment		such as a Paystub
	Property / Real Estate Deeds		
	Rental Agreements		
	Stocks & Bonds		
	Vacination Report		
	Wills		
			Copy of the following
	Concealed Carry Laws		Get one of the books that covers every state in the nation.
	Local and state maps (on paper)		Ideally a "Gazetter" of your state, Sealed in Zip Lock bag or "Mapcase"
	Pocket Constitution		References for debates and legal situations. Stored in zip lock bag to protect against moisture.
	Set of Scriptures		Small "military" style that will fit in a breast pocket (w/waterproof case)
	Survival Instruction Book		Recommend the SAS survival hand book

Check	Things to do before you leave Home	
	Item	**Comment**
	Call ahead for motel or hotel room reservations	Expect hotels to be filled quickly
	Call your alarm system monitoring company	Let them know that you are away and that any entries into your home should be reported to police, prior to your return home
	Call your extended family	Only if you have time
	Call your insurance agents	Only if you have time
	Close all interior doors	Lessen smoke damage in event of fire
	Close all window blinds and curtains	Do not let outsider see into your home
	Fill your water carriers and canteens	
	Fill vehicle fuel tank and spare fuel cans	
	Gather prescription medicines	
	Gather spare eyeglasses	
	Grab favorite doll or toy for each child	For comforting the little ones
	Have your mail forwarded or placed on hold.	Do not let mail stack up at your home. Can do this once you arrive at your destination, if you are in a hurry.
	Leave one light on in home	Gives the appearance that the home is lived in
	Load bicycles onto vehicle, if possible	
	Load camping equipment into vehicle	
	Load extra food into vehicle	
	Load family picture library into vehicle	
	Load GOOD Bag into vehicle	
	Load spare fuel cans into vehicle	
	Lock all Windows	Secure your home
	Lock the Doors!!!	Secure your home
	Lock up any weapons that you are not taking with you	
	Pre-Pay any coming due bills	Can do this once you arrive at your destination, if you are in a hurry.
	Monitor the news for traffic congestion	Have three alternative routes out of your neighborhood. Sometime side streets and back roads are less congested. Test your bug out routes during rush hour
	Move valuables to the second floor	Move any art, collectibles, rugs and furniture to the 2nd floor, if there is a possibility of flooding.
	Notify local police, if possible	Local police will often patrol unattended homes
	Notify your trusted neighbors of your plans	Give them forwarding addresses and cell phone numbers
	Pack your check book and all credit cards	
	Pack extra batteries	
	Pack & Load your money, gold and silver for transport	The amount you pack will be determined by your personal situation. Don't pack more than you will likely need. Leave the rest secured.
	Post "No Trespassing" signs in your yard	Let it be known that no one is legally permitted to entry your home.
	Stop delivery of fuel oil or propane for home heating,	if applicable
	Stop newspaper delivery	Do not let newspapers stack up at your home.
	Turn down furnace to 62 degree F	Lower home heating expenses, but do not let pipes freeze
	Turn off automated water sprinkler	
	Turn off home connect to public sewer	To prevent backup of sewer into home
	Turn off main electrical circuit breaker	if applicable
	Turn off main water valve	
	Turn off natural gas valve to house	if applicable
	Turn off power strips throughout your home	In case of power surges
	Unload refrigerator and freezer, if not returning for a long time	Food will spoil and reek when you return
	Unload trash from kitchen	Will stink upon return
	Unplug all electronic equipment	Avoid damage from power spikes if circuit breaker left ON
	Say a prayer	

Check	Item	Quantity	Comment
	G.O.O.D. Bag -WEAPONS		
	22LR Rifle	At least one per family	allow for sharing and redundancy. (preferably a break down model for compact transportation)
	Ammunition	200 rounds for each gun	Carry more if possible
	Body Armor	Level III Vest for each	"High-Dollar" bug-out option, but highly encouraged if you think you might get shot at!!
	Cleaning Kit	One per Family	One for Pistol, One for Rifle, See "Otis Cleaning"
	Fixed Blade Knife	One for each adult	Previous mentioned in gear above
	Holsters	One for each pistol	
	Pepper Spray	One for each	For when you need "less than leathal" deterence
	Pistol or Revolver	One for each legal adult	Get your Concealed Carry License now!!! Best to standardize your family on the same pistol and caliber of ammunition to
	Semi-automatic rifle	One for each adult	Recommend .223 NATO for each legal adult. Experienced larger shooters may prefer .308 NATO. Again, attempt to standardize your group with identical rifle and caliber if at all possible.
	Shotgun	One per Family	12 gauge
	Sling	One for each rifle	
	Spare magazines for guns	Three extra for each weapon	4 magazines total per weapon, always loaded.

Check	Item	Quantity	Comment
	G.O.O.D. Bag -FOOD, BEVERAGES & Cookware		
	Bouillon and/or tea bags		
	Breakfast, Instant Oatmeal	Box	Hot Water and you have a hot breakfast to start your day with.
	Camping tea pot or coffee pot	One	To heat/Boil water at camp or melt snow
	Can Opener		
	Canned Meats		Example: Spam, Tuna Fish, Vienna Sausages
	Canteen, water bottles, camel back	Two for each adult, one for each child	Camel back is ideal if integrated into your backpack.
	Cooking utensils	One Set	Spatula, Ladle, ect..
	Dehydrated/Freeze Dried Food		Backpacking / Camping meals
	Dried Soup Mixes		
	Energy Food Bars	Many	
	Food	As Desired	storable foods that your family prefers & will eat in an emergency. All should be as Heat & Cold impervious as possible for storability.
	Funnel	one per family	
	Hard Candies	MANY	
	Hot Chocolate Drink Mixes	As Desired	It gets cold at night.
	Meals Ready-to-eat (MRE)	**MANY**	The amount you carry depends on the space you have available.
	Metal Camping cup	One for each	See "Sierra Cup"
	Metal Camping fork and spoon	One for each	
	Metal Camping Plate	One for each	
	Metal Pot & Skillet, Nesting	one per family	To cook one-pot meal (soups, stews) for the group or melt snow.
	MRE Components	As Desired	Side Dishes, Spreads, Crackers, Desserts, Candies, Beverages
	MRE Heaters	As Desired	Its nice to have a quick Hot Meal. (Flameless Ration Heaters)
	Portable Water Filter	At least one per family	You can only carry so much water. (with filter replacement)
	Powdered Drink Mixes	Many	Gatoraid style powders that add flavor, electrolytes and Calories.
	Seasoning Kit	one per family	One of the small round multi-seasoning dispensers
	Stove	one per family	Small backpacking style stove with spare fuel canisters
	Top Ramen Noodles	Several Packs	
	Water Purification Tablets	One Bottle	
	Water: Bagged or Bottled	Min 1 Gallon each	As much as you can fit into your vehicle. For easy Long Term Storage, consider the metalized foil pouches of survival water.
	Windscreen	one per family	For stove

Check	Item	Quantity	Comment
		G.O.O.D. Bag -PERSONAL HYGIENE & SANITATION	
	Baby Wipes	1 Box	More if you have small children
	Brush & Comb	One	
	Camp Toilet, Honey Bucket, Lugable Loo	One	Choose the most appropriate style for your family situation
	Chemical Toilet Disinfectant	One Pack	See "Reliance Bio-Blue"
	Chewable multi-vitamin	One bttle	
	Collapsible Basin		Small cloth/plastic foldable "bowl" for personal cleaning
	Dental Floss	One	Oral hygiene and 100's of other uses
	Denture Supplies	as needed	
	Deodarant	One for each	
	Diapers (or pull-ups)		Two week's supply for each infant
	Dish Soap	One small Bottle	To keep your cookware clean
	Elastic Hair Bands		To help the ladies keep their hair up and clean
	Eye Drops	One	
	Eye Glasses	as needed	Spare pair of Eye Glasses, especially if you wear contact lens
	Female Urination Device	One for each Female	See "Gogirl or P-Mate"
	Feminine Sanitary Supplies	Two week's supply for each	(Tampons, sanitary napkins, Ect)
	Foot Powder		See "Army Foot Powder" you may be doing A LOT of walking.
	Hand Lotion	One Bottle	
	Hand sanitizer	A couple small bottles	Do NOT underestimate the importance of HYGENE in an emergency.
	Kleenex	one pack each	Small pack that fits in your shirt pocket
	Laytex Gloves	One Pair each	For when you have to touch things you really don't want to
	Lip Balm	One for each	See "Chapstick"
	Mosquito & Chigger repellant	Full bottle	Adjust quantity as needed for your location.
	Mouthwash or Breath Strips	One small Bottle or pack	Your family will appreciate it!
	Nail Clipper & File	One	
	Perri Bottle	One for each Female	For when the toilet paper runs out.
	Q-Tips	Small Pack	
	Razor	One for each Adult	One pack of spare blades
	Saline Solution / Spare Contact Lenses	as needed	Make up a small case with everything in it.
	Scissors	One	One small pair
	Scouring Pad	One	To keep your cookware clean
	Shampoo		
	Shaving Cream	one	
	Soap	One	1 bar of "Anti-Bacterial" soap
	Solar Shower	One per Family	A nice luxury if water is plentiful
	Sunscreen Lotion (SPF 30+)	One for each	Prepare to be outdoors a lot!
	Toilet Paper	2 rolls each	Some camping toilet paper is vacuum packed to reduce size
	Toilet Waste Bags	One Pack	See "Reliance Double Doodie"
	Toothbrush and tooth paste	1 for each	
	Towel (Military Field Towel)	2 each	Sealed, pre soaped/pre-wetted, See "Hoo-Aahs"
	Towel, Microfiber	1 each	Ultra-Compact, see "Outgo"
	Towels, Paper	1 Roll	
	Washcloth	One	

THE SUPPLY TABLE (*The Master Preparedness List*)

This list is based on a **family** of *two/three adults and two/three childrent* that want to take their preparedness beyond the simple 96 hour kits and become more fully prepared for whatever may come. The items within each category are listed by "Purchase Priority". The quantities listed are for a 30 day to one-year crisis. Because some items are impossible to store indefinitely or it would not be cost-effective to store the quantities necessary to maintain our current lifestyle, it is assumed that alternate sources or substitutes will be found or changes in lifestyle will occur if the crisis lasts over one year. Quantities could be adjusted for other estimated lengths of crisis.

There are 3 major groupings that are based on the duration of the "Crisis", 30 Days, 90 Days and 1 Year. (*I know the list looks daunting at first glance, but just focus in on one group at a time*). Within each of these three durations, items are prioritized. It should be your goal to Obtain all of the "30 Day" items in sequence from Priority 1 to 3, by April 1st. Then move onto your "90 Day" items in the same manner obtaining them by July 1st, and finally onto your "1 Year" items by October 1st. This will allow you to build up your preparedness in stages, 30 Days first (as these items would be needed in EVERY scenario) 90 Days second (as they build on the 30 day list), and finally your 1 Year equipment that rounds out your preperations.

The purchase priority is **not** how important the item is. I believe everything on this list is important. The purchase priority is how soon the item should be purchased *to avoid shortages should other people decide to start "stocking up" on the same items*. I firmly believe that there will be a wake up call for a lot of people. A priority "1" item should be purchased ASAP. A priority "2" item should be purchased before most people figure out what is going on. Priority "3" items should be available until later. These are common household items which should be manufactured and shipped right up until the last minute. The purchase date is my guideline of when to make purchases. Items with a "Last minute" listing are perishable and you want as long a shelf life as possible. Signs of shortages or panic should be watched closely to avoid missing out on these items. The final three columns indicate whether I think the item would be necessary for a 1 month, three month, one year to indefinite crisis.

Clothing
Keep in mind that a crises will likely be during the winter and adjust this list for your climate. Warm, Waterproof, Windproof clothing. Think *Wool, Gore-Tex, Polarfleece, Polypro, Thinsulate. Avoid Cotton!*

Item	Quantity Required	Purchase Priority	Purchase by Date	Planned Duration		
Bandanas	24 each	3				
(*inexpensive shield face, head cover, wash cloth, bandage, sanitary pad*)						
Blaclava	1/person	3	4-1-12	30 Day		
Boots	2/person	2	4-1-12	30 Day		
Boots, (insulated)	1/person	2	4-1-12	30 Day		
Bra athletic	2/female	3	4-1-12	30 Day		
Clothes line	100 ft	3	4-1-12	30 Day		
Clothes pins	250	3	4-1-12	30 Day		
Clothes Wringer (hand crank)	1	2	7-1-12		90 Day	
Coats	1/person	2	4-1-12	30 Day		
Hats	1/person	3	7-1-12		90 Day	
Iron-on patches.	2 packages	3	4-1-12	30 Day		
Laundry detergent	5 (5gal)	3	4-1-12	30 Day		
Long sleeve shirt/high collar	5/person	3	4-1-12	30 Day		
Long underwear	3/person	2	4-1-12	30 Day		
Needles	Assortment	3	7-1-12		90 Day	
Non-electric washing machine	1	1	4-1-12	30 Day		
Jean Pants	6/person	3	4-1-12	30 Day		
Rain Parka/Rain Pants	2/person	2	4-1-12	30 Day		
Safety pins	Assortment	3	7-1-12		90 Day	
Sewing patterns	Assortment	3	10-1-12			1 Year

Item	Quantity Required	Purchase Priority	Purchase by Date	Planned Duration
Sewing supplies	Assortment	2	4-1-12	30 Day
Shirts	6/person	3	4-1-12	30 Day
Shoelaces	20	3	7-1-12	90 Day
Snow Jacket	1/person	3	4-1-12	30 Day
Socks heavy	12/person	3	4-1-12	30 Day
Stove iron	1	1	7-1-12	90 Day
Sweats/nightclothes	2/person	3	4-1-12	30 Day
Tennis Shoes	2pair/person	3	4-1-12	30 Day
Thread	Assortment	3	7-1-12	90 Day
Underwear	12/person	3	4-1-12	30 Day
Wash board	2	1	7-1-12	90 Day
Wash tub	2	1	7-1-12	90 Day
Winter gloves	1/person	2	4-1-12	30 Day
Work Gloves	3	2	7-1-12	90 Day
Zippers and buttons	Assortment	3	4-1-12	30 Day

Communications

The phone/address books are of friends and family so that you can look them up after the worst has passed. If phones are not working you may have to travel to their home to check on them.

*Keep these items in waterproof containers. Many survival and camping stores sell flat, water tight pouches. If you have a food vacuum sealer, this is another great use for it!

Item	Quantity Required	Purchase Priority	Purchase by Date	Planned Duration
Addresses of friends/family	1 set			
CB Radio	1	2	4-1-12	30 Day
Cell phone				
Frequency lists/books	1	2	7-1-12	90 Day
Map of your local area	2	2	4-1-12	30 Day
Phone numbersof friends/family	1 set			
Pre-addressed, stamped postcards	1 set			
Radio (hand cranked)	1	1	4-1-12	30 Day
Road Flares	8	3	7-1-12	90 Day
Short-wave Radio	1	1	7-1-12	90 Day
Signal Flares	12	2	7-1-12	90 Day
Signal Mirror	1/person	3	7-1-12	90 Day
Signal Whistle	2/person	3	7-1-12	90 Day

Documents

Item	Quantity Required	Purchase Priority	Purchase by Date	Planned Duration
bank account numbers,			Now	30 & 90 & Year
birth, death, marriage certificates and divorce decrees,			Now	30 & 90 & Year
charge card account numbers, "lost or stolen" notification numbers			Now	30 & 90 & Year
deeds and contracts,			Now	30 & 90 & Year
house and life insurance policies,			Now	30 & 90 & Year
inventory of valuable household items,		Now	30 & 90 & Year	
medical records including immunizations		Now	30 & 90 & Year	
passports, where pertinent for each family member			Now	30 & 90 & Year
social security numbers			Now	30 & 90 & Year
stocks and bonds			Now	30 & 90 & Year
Vaccination records			Now	30 & 90 & Year
wills			Now	30 & 90 & Year

Entertainment & Education

Disasters may provide excellent opportunities to share Christ with others so extra scriptures would be a good thing to have.

Item	Quantity Required	Purchase Priority	Purchase by Date	Planned Duration	
Bible & scriptures	1/person	3	4-1-12	30 Day	
Bibles & BOM	6	1	4-1-12	30 Day	
Board Games	1 set	3	4-1-12	30 Day	
Books for pleasure reading	Many	3	4-1-12	30 Day	
Book on Edible plants	1	3	10-1-12		1 Year
Card game book	1	3	4-1-12	30 Day	
Cards	4 sets	3	4-1-12	30 Day	
Crayons	2	3	4-1-12	30 Day	
Domino game book	1	3	4-1-12	30 Day	
Dominoes	1	3	4-1-12	30 Day	
Erasers	10	3	4-1-12	30 Day	
Home School Curriculum	1/child	2	10-1-12		1 Year
How to books	Many	1	7-1-12	90 Day	
Hoyle game rule book	1	3	4-1-12	30 Day	
Magnifying Glass	1 each	3	4-1-12	30 Day	
Non-electric pencil sharpener	2	3	4-1-12	30 Day	
Paper	100 pads	3	4-1-12	30 Day	
Paper Clips, assorted sizes	1 box	3	4-1-12	30 Day	
Pencils	100	3	4-1-12	30 Day	
Pencil Sharpner	2	3	7-1-12	90 Day	
Pens	50	3	4-1-12	30 Day	
Reference books		1	7-1-12	90 Day	
Rubber Bands, assorted sizes	1 box	3	4-1-12	30 Day	
Safety Pins, assorted sizes	1 box	3	4-1-12	30 Day	
Toys		3	4-1-12	30 Day	

First Aid Supplies

Item	Quantity Required	Purchase Priority	Purchase by Date	Planned Duration	
Ace bandage	5	3	4-1-12	30 Day	
Band aids	6 large assort	3	4-1-12	30 Day	
Band aids Finger tip	1 large box	3	4-1-12	30 Day	
Band aids Knuckle	1 large box	3	4-1-12	30 Day	
Bandages (Ace) elastic, 4"	2	3	4-1-12	30 Day	
Bandages, gauze, 2", 3", 4"	4 boxes	3	4-1-12	30 Day	
Bandages, gauze, 18" x 36"	1	3	4-1-12	30 Day	
Bandages, burns (Second Skin)	1 box	2	4-1-12	30 Day	
Bandages Triangular	3	3	4-1-12	30 Day	
Birth supply kit	1	3	7-1-12	90 Day	
Burn Dressings (Burn Free)	Assorted	2	4-1-12	30 Day	
Butterfly closures/Leukostrips	1 large box	3	4-1-12	30 Day	
Cold/heat Pack, instant	5 each	3	4-1-12	30 Day	
Cold/heat Pack, reusable	1	3	4-1-12	30 Day	
Cotton Balls	1 box	3	4-1-12	30 Day	
Cotton Swabs	1 large box	3	4-1-12	30 Day	
Eyedropper	1	3	4-1-12	30 Day	
Eye pads	1 large box	3	4-1-12	30 Day	

Item	Quantity Required	Purchase Priority	Purchase by Date	Planned Duration	
First aid manual	1	3	10-1-12		1 Year
Gauze 2"	5 rolls	3	4-1-12	30 Day	
Gauze 3"	5 rolls	3	4-1-12	30 Day	
Latex gloves	1 box	3	4-1-12	30 Day	
SAM splint	1	3	10-1-12		1 Year
Scalpel	1 box	3	4-1-12	30 Day	
Scissors, Surgical pointed	1	3	10-1-12		1 Year
Shears	2	3	10-1-12		1 Year
Snake bite kit	1	3	7-1-12		90 Day
Space Blankets	4	3	4-1-12	30 Day	
Sterile pads 4" x 4"	1 large box	3	4-1-12	30 Day	
Sterile pads 5" x 9"	1 large box	3	4-1-12	30 Day	
Surgical tape	10 rolls	3	4-1-12	30 Day	
Thermometer	4	3	4-1-12	30 Day	
Tongue Depressors	6	3	4-1-12	30 Day	
Tweezers	4	3	4-1-12	30 Day	

First Aid, Perishables

Item	Quantity Required	Purchase Priority	Purchase by Date	Planned Duration	
Alcohol	6	3	7-1-12		90 Day
Alcohol Moist Towelettes	100	3	Last minute	30 Day	
Analgesic Cream (*Camphophenique*)	1 tube	2	Last minute	30 Day	
Antacid (*Mylanta, Tums, Pepto-Bismal*)	1 box	2	Last minute	30 Day	
Antibiotic (*Amoxicillin /Erythromycin/Tetracycline for general infections*)	1 set	2	Last minute	30 Day	
Anti-Diarrheal (*Imodium, Diasorb, Lomotil*)	1 box	2	Last minute	30 Day	
Anti-fungal (*Desenex, Micatin, Tinactin, Lotrimin*)	1 box	2	Last minute	30 Day	
Antihistamine (*Benadryl, Claratyne*)	1 box	2	Last minute	30 Day	
Antiseptic Ointment (*Neosporin*)	3 tube	2	Last minute	30 Day	
Aspirin	6 (100)	3	Last minute		90 Day
Bee sting ointment	6 tubes	3	Last minute	30 Day	
Bicarbonate of Soda	1 box	2	7-1-12		90 Day
Bronco Dialator (*Primatine Mist*)	1	2	Last Minute	30 Day	
Burn Ointment (*Hydrocortisone, Derm-Aid*)	1 tube	2	Last minute	30 Day	
Cold/Flu Tablets (*Nyquil*)	1 box	2	Last minute	30 Day	
Constipation (*Ex-Lax, Dulcolax, Durolax*)	1 box	2	Last minute	30 Day	
Cough Syrup (*Robitussen, Dimetap*)	1 bottle	2	Last minute	30 Day	
Epsom Salts	1 box	2	7-1-12		90 Day
Eye Drops (*Visine*)	1 bottle	2	Last minute	30 Day	
Eye Wash	1 bottle	2	Last minute	30 Day	
Hemorrhoid Relief (*Preparation H, Anusol*)	1 tube	2	Last minute	30 Day	
Hydrogen peroxide	6 bottles	3	7-1-12		90 Day

Item	Quantity Required	Purchase Priority	Purchase by Date	Planned Duration	
Ibuprofen (*Advil, Motrin*)	1 box	2	Last minute	30 Day	
Itching, Insect/Rash (*Caladril, Calamine*)	1 bottle	2	Last minute	30 Day	
Itching (*Dibucaine, Lanacane*)	1 tube	2	Last minute	30 Day	
Lice (*Nix or RID Lice Shampoo*)	1 tube	2	Last minute	30 Day	
Lip Balm (*ChapStick, Blistex*)	1 tube	2	Last minute	30 Day	
Lubricant, Water Soluble (*K-Y Jelly*)	1 tube	2	Last minute		90 Day
Meat Tenderizer bites & stings	1 bottle	2	7-1-12		90 Day
Nasal Decongestant (*Actifed, Sudafed Sinex*)	1 bottle	2	Last minute	30 Day	
Nausea, Motion Sickness (*Kwells, Dramamine, Meclizine*)	1 box	2	Last minute	30 Day	
Non-Aspirin Pain Reliever (*Tylenol*)	1 box	2	Last minute	30 Day	
Pain, Fever Reducer (*Panadeine, Mobigesic*)	1 box	2	Last minute	30 Day	
Pain Reliever with Codeine (*Tylenol 3*)	1 box	2	Last minute	30 Day	
Prescriptions	(as needed)	1	Last minute	30 Day	
Petroleum Jelly (*Vaseline*)	1 jar	2	Last minute	30 Day	
Poison Ivy/Oak (*Neoxyn*)	6 bottle	2	Last minute	30 Day	
Poison Absorber (*Activated Charcoal*)	1 bottle	2	Last minute		90 Day
Soap, liquid, antibacterial	1 bottle	3	Last minute	30 Day	
Sunburn Relief (*Solarcaine*)	1 can	2	Last minute	30 Day	
Sunscreen (SPF 15 at least)	1 bottle	2	Last minute	30 Day	
Vomit Inducer (*Ipecac*)	1 bottle	2	Last minute	30 Day	
Yeast Infection Treatment (Gyne-Lotrimin, Monistat)	1 tube	2	Last minute	30 Day	

Food Preparation

The fire place insert would ideally be designed to cook on. The fire grate is for cooking outside over an open fire. Crisco shortening is listed because it can be stored for a long time.

Item	Quantity Required	Purchase Priority	Purchase by Date	Planned Duration	
1 roll Plastic Wrap					
Aluminum foil, Heavy	6 large rolls	3	4-1-12	30 Day	
BBQ grill (charcoal/propane)	1	3	7-1-12		90 Day
Boning Knife	2	3	4-1-12	30 Day	
Bread Loaf Pan	4	3	4-1-12	30 Day	
Butcher Knife	1	3	4-1-12	30 Day	
Butter churn	1	2	10-1-12		1 year
Camp Stove	1	2	4-1-12	30 Day	
Can opener (hand cranked)	2	3	4-1-12	30 Day	
Can Opener, heavy duty	1	3	4-1-12	30 Day	
Canning books	1 set	2	7-1-12		90 Day
Cast iron cook set - (*Complete!*)	1 set	2	4-1-12	30 Day	
Cheesecloth	1 roll	3	4-1-12	30 Day	
Cheese press	1	2	10-1-12		1 Year
Coffee filters	100	3	4-1-12	30 Day	
Coffe maker, metal	1	3	4-1-12	30 Day	
Coleman metal dinner plates	1 set	2	4-1-12	30 Day	

Item	Quantity Required	Purchase Priority	Purchase by Date	Planned Duration	
Coleman Cooler	2	3	4-1-12	30 Day	
Corkscrew	1	3	4-1-12	30 Day	
Crock pot, Large	1	1	10-1-12		1 Year
Cultures	1 set	3	Last Minute	90 Day	
Dish Cloths	6	3	4-1-12	30 Day	
Dishwashing liquid	5 gal	3	4-1-12	30 Day	
Dutch Oven, small with lid	1	2	4-1-12	30 Day	
Dutch Oven, large with lid,	1	2	7-1-12	90 Day	
Fire grate	1	1	7-1-12	90 Day	
Fireplace insert	1	1	4-1-12	30 Day	
Grain mill (hand cranked)	1	1	4-1-12	30 Day	
Grater	1	3	4-1-12	30 Day	
Hot Pad	1 set	3	4-1-12	30 Day	
Kettle, huge, for boiling water	1	2	7-1-12	90 Day	
Latex disposable gloves	1 box	2	7-1-12	90 Day	
Mixing Bowl, Large	1 each	3	4-1-12	30 Day	
Mixing Bowl, Small	1 each	3	4-1-12	30 Day	
Molds	1 set	3	4-1-12	30 Day	
Napkins	10	3	4-1-12	30 Day	
Pancake Turners, metal	2	3	4-1-12	30 Day	
Paper cups	100	3	4-1-12	30 Day	
Paring Knife	1	3	4-1-12	30 Day	
Plastic knives, forks, spoons	200	3	4-1-12	30 Day	
Pressure cooker	1	2	7-1-12	90 Day	
Rennet	1	3	10-1-12		1 Year
Rubber dish gloves	4 Sets	3	4-1-12	30 Day	
Sauce Pan, large with lid,	1	3	4-1-12	30 Day	
Sauce Pan, small with lid,	1	3	4-1-12	30 Day	
Scrub pads	50	3	4-1-12	30 Day	
Skillet, large with lid,	1	3	4-1-12	30 Day	
Spoons, large metal	2	3	4-1-12	30 Day	
Spoons, Wooden	2	3	4-1-12	30 Day	
Strainer	1	3	4-1-12	30 Day	
Thermos	1/person	2	4-1-12	30 Day	
Yeast	1 box	3	Last minute	30 Day	
Yogurt culture,	1 box	3	Last Minute	90 Day	
Ziploc Bags - Sandwich	100	3	4-1-12	30 Day	
Ziploc Bags - Storage	50	3	7-1-12	90 Day	
Ziploc Freezer Bags, gallon	2 boxes	3	7-1-12	90 Day	
Ziploc Freezer Bags, quart	2 boxes	3	4-1-12	30 Day	

Food Storage

Item	Quantity Required	Purchase Priority	Purchase by Date	Planned Duration	
1 gal. plastic bags	300	3	7-1-12	90 Day	
Baskets/crates	24	1	10-1-12		1 year
Boiling canner	1	1	10-1-12		1 year
Bucket opener	2	1	10-1-12		1 year
Canning book	1	1	10-1-12		1 year
Canning jars	100	1	10-1-12		1 year
Canning lids	500	1	10-1-12		1 year
Canning salt	20lb	1	10-1-12		1 year
Canning supplies (Misc)	Assortment	1	10-1-12		1 year
Canning Utensils	Assortment	1	10-1-12		1 year

Item	Quantity Required	Purchase Priority	Purchase by Date	Planned Duration	
Colander	1	1	10-1-12		1 year
Desiccants	60 (66gm)	1	4-1-12	30 Day	
Food storage buckets	30 (5 gal)	1	7-1-12		90 Day
Jar lifter	1	1	10-1-12		1 year
Jars	Assortment	1	10-1-12		1 year
Lids	Assortment	1	10-1-12		1 year
Mesh bags	24	1	10-1-12		1 year
Oxygen absorbers	50 (500ml)	1	7-1-12		90 Day
Parafin Wax	5lb	1	10-1-12		1 Year
Pressure canner	1	1	10-1-12		1 year
Saucepan	2	1	10-1-12		1 year
Saucepot	3	1	10-1-12		1 year
Scale	1	1	10-1-12		1 year
Storage/garden books	Assortment	2	10-1-12		1 year
Timer	1	1	10-1-12		1 year
Tongs to remove jars	2	2	4-1-12	30 Day	
Water storage	10 (5 gal)	1	4-1-12	30 Day	
Water storage	2 (55 gal)	1	4-1-12	30 Day	
Wax for canning					

Fuel & Power

The amount of firewood will depend on your climate and the efficiency of your stove or fireplace. The kerosene is for the lamps under "General Household". Sta-bil is an additive which allows gasoline to be stored longer than normal. The barrel is to transport gasoline in if it can be purchased.

Item	Quantity Required	Purchase Priority	Purchase by Date	Planned Duration	
Barrel (55 gal)	1	1	7-1-12		90 Day
Charcoal	500 lb.	1	4-1-12	30 Day	
Fire starters	2	1	7-1-12		90 Day
(jelly, ribbon, tablets, impregnated peat bricks, wax-coated pine cones, magnesium block, flint)					
Fire wood	10 cords	2	4-1-12		90 Day
Fuel filter for generator	1	2	4-1-12	30 Day	
Fuel pump	1	1	4-1-12	30 Day	
Gasoline	500 gal	2	10-1-12		1 Year
Gas cans (5 gal)	6	2	4-1-12	30 Day	
Kerosene	50 gal	2	7-1-12		90 Day
Kerosene storage barrel	1 (55gal)	2	7-1-12		90 Day
Lighter Fluid	5 cans	2	4-1-12	30 Day	
Matches	20 (250)	1	4-1-12	30 Day	
Propane	500 gal	2	7-1-12		90 Day
Spark plug for generator	1	2	4-1-12	30 Day	
Sta-bil	8 qt	1	4-1-12	30 Day	
Starter fluid	5 gal	1	4-1-12	30 Day	
White Gas Coleman (for campstove)	10 (1 gal)	2	4-1-12	30 Day	

Gardening

Non-hybrid seeds will reproduce true to the parent plant. Hybrid seeds may reproduce with a recessive gene. The polyethylene is for covering young plants to maintain warmth and moisture. The styrofoam cups are for coverings seedlings during late winter frosts.

Item	Quantity Required	Purchase Priority	Purchase by Date	Planned Duration	
Black polyethylene	1	2	10-1-12		1 year
Bleach	5 gal	2	10-1-12		1 year
Clear polyethylene	1	2	10-1-12		1 year

Item	Quantity Required	Purchase Priority	Purchase by Date	Planned Duration
Garden hoses	2	3	4-1-12	30 Day
Herb Seeds	Assortment	2	10-1-12	1 year
Hoe	2	3	7-1-12	90 Day
Misters for seedlings	2	2	10-1-12	1 year
Miracle Gro		2	10-1-12	1 year
Non-hybrid seeds	Assortment	1	10-1-12	1 year
Organic fertilizers	Assortment	2	10-1-12	1 year
Perennial flowerseeds	Assortment	3	10-1-12	1 year
Pull wagon	1	3	7-1-12	90 Day
Rototiller	1	2	10-1-12	1 year
Seed starting containers	Assortment	2	10-1-12	1 year
Seed starting medium	Assortment	2	10-1-12	1 year
Thermometers	2	2	10-1-12	1 year
Soil testing equipment.	1	1	10-1-12	1 year
Sprayer/Pumper - 2 gallon size	1	3	7-1-12	90 Day
Styrofoam cups	1000	2	10-1-12	1 year
Watering can	1	2	10-1-12	1 year
Wheel barrel	2	2	10-1-12	1 year

Bug spray. Malathion, Sevin, Dursban and Diazanon. Dursban and Diazanon can have severe side effects in humans, for use outside of house, not necessarily on the garden. Fine for flower gardens. Sevin is safer to use on the vegetables.

Hardware & Building supplies

Item	Quantity Required	Purchase Priority	Purchase by Date	Planned Duration
A few cases of silicone caulk. (If you are like me and your carpentry isn't perfect.)				
Bolts	Assortment	3	7-1-12	90 Day
Bricks, rocks	Assortment	3	10-1-12	1 Year
Cable	100 ft	3	7-1-12	90 Day
Cable clamps	8	3	7-1-12	90 Day
Cement	10 bags	3	10-1-12	1 year
Chains and padlocks.	several	3	7-1-12	90 Day
Chicken wire, barbed wire, etc.	2 rolls	3	10-1-12	1 Year
Duct tape	10 rolls	3	4-1-12	30 Day
Extra axe handles	2	3	10-1-12	1 year
Long polls	10	3	10-1-12	1 Year
Fencing material.	Assortment	3	10-1-12	1 year
Lumber	Assorted	3	10-1-12	1 Year
Mouse traps	5	3	4-1-12	30 Day
Nails	100 lbs.	3	7-1-12	90 Day
Nuts and bolts	Assorted	3	4-1-12	30 Day
Pipe	Assorted	3	4-1-12	30 Day
Plumbing repair supplies	Assorted	3	4-1-12	30 Day
Polyethylene Black	2	3	7-1-12	90 Day
Polyethylene Clear	2	3	7-1-12	90 Day
Pulleys	4	3	7-1-12	90 Day
Rigging book	1	3	7-1-12	90 Day
Rope	Assorted	3	4-1-12	30 Day
Screws	Assorted	3	7-1-12	90 Day
Spare keys to all of your locks.	1 set	2	4-1-12	30 Day
(*Better yet, have them all set up to take the same key*).				
Spare parts for your wheelbarrow	1 set	3	7-1-12	90 Day
Spare toilet parts	1 set	3	7-1-12	90 Day

Tarps	4	3	4-1-12	30 Day
WD-40	1 gal	3	7-1-12	90 Day
Wire	Assorted	3	4-1-12	30 Day

Household Items

The water filter is assuming you have a stream or other reliable source of water. The ni-cad batteries are rechargeable for the radio. Other batteries should be sized according to your needs.

Item	Quantity Required	Purchase Priority	Purchase by Date	Planned Duration
Backpack with Frame (for Hauling)	1/person	2	4-1-12	30 Day
Batteries AA	100	1	Last minute	30 Day
Batteries AA, Ni-Cad	8	1	4-1-12	30 Day
Batteries C	20	1	Last minute	30 Day
Batteries C, Ni-Cad	8	1	4-1-12	30 Day
Batteries D	100	1	Last minute	30 Day
Batteries D, Ni-Cad	8	1	4-1-12	30 Day
Battery Charger, SOLAR	2	1	4-1-12	30 Day
Blankets	10	1	4-1-12	30 Day
Camera	1	3	7-1-12	90 Day
Camera batteries	1 set	3	Last minute	90 Day
Candles 10 hour	50	1	4-1-12	30 Day
Candles 36 hour	25	1	4-1-12	30 Day
Candles 100 hour (liquid parafin)	25	1	4-1-12	30 Day
Candle holders	1 set	2	4-1-12	30 Day
Candle wax/wick	10lbs	2	7-1-12	90 Day
carpet sweeper hand operated	1	3	4-1-12	30 Day
Clocks wind up	3	3	4-1-12	30 Day
Fanny pack for short excursions	1/person	2	4-1-12	30 Day
Fire extinguishers	4	3	4-1-12	30 Day
Flashlights	5	2	4-1-12	30 Day
Flashlight bulbs	2/light	3	4-1-12	30 Day
Handwarmer, lighter fuled	1	3	4-1-12	30 Day
Kerosene Heater	2	1	4-1-12	30 Day
Kerosene lamps	4	1	4-1-12	30 Day
Kerosene lamp wicks	10	1	4-1-12	30 Day
Lighters (disposable)	50	2	4-1-12	30 Day
Light sticks (12 hour)	18	3	4-1-12	30 Day
Matches stick	20 boxes of 250	2	4-1-12	30 Day
Matches, water/windproof	5 boxes of 20	2	7-1-12	90 Day
Mosquito Netting	1 roll	3	7-1-12	90 Day
Paper towels	100	3	4-1-12	30 Day
Pet Food	as needed	3	4-1-12	30 Day
Permanent Ink Makrer	2	3	4-1-12	30 Day
Propane Heater	2	2	4-1-12	30 Day
Sleeping bags	1/person	1	4-1-12	30 Day
Sleeping Bag Mattress Pads	1/person	1	4-1-12	30 Day
Tents (2 person)	2	2	4-1-12	30 Day
Trash bags	10 boxes	3	4-1-12	30 Day
Treadle Sowing Machine	1	2	7-1-12	90 Day
Walkie talkies	1 pair	1	4-1-12	30 Day
Watches	5	3	4-1-12	30 Day
Wool Blankets, heavy	2/person	2	4-1-12	30 Day

Infant Supplies

Item	Quantity Required	Purchase Priority	Purchase by Date	Planned Duration
Baby Food	????	2	Last Minute	30 Day
Baby Clothes	3 sets	1	4-1-12	30 Day
Baby Powder	2 bottles	1	4-1-12	30 Day
Baby Wash	2 bottles	1	4-1-12	30 Day
Blankets	2 each	1	4-1-12	30 Day
Bottles	3 each	1	4-1-12	30 Day
Diaper Cover		1	4-1-12	30 Day
Diapers, disposable (24 count)	26 boxes	1	4-1-12	30 Day
Diaper Rash Ointment	1 bottle	1	4-1-12	30 Day
Formula	? cans	1	Last Minute	30 Day
Lotion	2 bottles	1	4-1-12	30 Day
nursing bras	1 each	1	4-1-12	30 Day
Nursing pads	4 each	1	4-1-12	30 Day
Teething Ring	1 each	1	4-1-12	30 Day
Towelettes, Pre-moistened	2 boxes	1	4-1-12	30 Day
Toys	As needed	1	4-1-12	30 Day

Miscellaneous

The maps should be very detailing showing back roads in case major highways are closed or clogged. I always wanted a night vision scope, so I threw it in for good measure. A burn barrel is for disposing of household garbage and a spark arrestor is a grated top to prevent accidental fires.

Item	Quantity Required	Purchase Priority	Purchase by Date	Planned Duration
5 gallon emergency toilet	1	2	4-1-12	30 Day
Ant spray concentrate	1	3	4-1-12	30 Day
Binoculars	2	3	4-1-12	30 Day
Book on using compass	1	1	4-1-12	30 Day
Burn barrel	2	3	7-1-12	90 Day
Compass	2	1	4-1-12	30 Day
Fishing tackle	Assortment	3	10-1-12	1 year
Knives	Assortment	1	4-1-12	30 Day
Metal bucket - for charcoals/ashes	1	3	4-1-12	30 Day
Night vision scope	1	1	4-1-12	30 Day
O.D. parachute cord	200ft	3	7-1-12	90 Day
Safe	1	1	4-1-12	30 Day
Spark arrestor	2	3	4-1-12	30 Day
Sponges	10	3	4-1-12	30 Day
Toilet seat	1	3	7-1-12	90 Day
Trash bags - 13 gallon size	1 box	3	4-1-12	30 Day
Trash bags - 33 gallon size	1 box	3	4-1-12	30 Day
Water buckets 5 gal	2	3	4-1-12	30 Day
Glue of various types	several	3	7-1-12	90 Day
(wood glue, super glue, weather stripping adhesive, etc.)				
Paint	10 gal	3	10-1-12	1 year
Rolls of 10 mil "Visqueen"	3	3	4-1-12	30 Day
Tape	assortment	3	4-1-12	30 Day
(especially duct tape, masking tape, packing tape, etc.)				
Window screen.	2 Rolls	3	10-1-12	90 Day

Money

$1000. in cash and change (during times of disaster charge cards and checks will not be honored*

*Money is always hard to tuck away and pretend it isn't there, but in this instance, it is a necessity. One can't assume to put expenditures on credit cards during a crisis. Think about it. Whenever you make a purchase, it is always verified by a telephoned authorization number. If phone lines are down and these numbers are not obtainable, chances are your purchase won't be allowed.

Item	Quantity Required	Purchase Priority	Purchase by Date	Planned Duration	
Cash	$1000/person	1	4-1-12	30 Day	
Gold	10oz/person	1	10-1-12		1 Year
Silver	100oz/person	1	7-1-12		90 Day

Personal Toiletries

Solar showers use the sun to heat water for bathing. Lime is used to keep down odors from human waste. Quantities are not given for feminine or baby needs because I am not familiar with them.

Item	Quantity Required	Purchase Priority	Purchase by Date	Planned Duration	
Baby wipes	1 box	3	4-1-12	30 Day	
Bar soap	100	3	4-1-12	30 Day	
Barber scissors	2 pair	3	4-1-12	30 Day	
Birth Control	3 boxes	3	7-1-12		90 Day
Brushes	3/person	3	4-1-12	30 Day	
Camping Potty	1	2	4-1-12	30 Day	
Chapstick	24	3	4-1-12	30 Day	
Combs	3/person	3	4-1-12	30 Day	
Contact cleaning supplies	1 set	3	last minute	30 Day	
Cotton swabs	4 (500)	3	4-1-12	30 Day	
Dental floss	12	3	4-1-12	30 Day	
Deodorant (men's)	12	3	4-1-12	30 Day	
Deodorant (women's)	12	3	4-1-12	30 Day	
Fingernail clippers	1/person	3	4-1-12	30 Day	
Fingernail file metal	1/person	3	4-1-12	30 Day	
Fluoride Rinse	2 bottles	3	7-1-12		90 Day
Glasses	2 pair	2	7-1-12		90 Day
Insect Repellent	4 cans	3	7-1-12		90 Day
Kleenex	50 boxes	3	4-1-12	30 Day	
Lime	100 lbs.	3	7-1-12		90 Day
Liquid Hair Shampoo (Adult)	2 bottles	3	4-1-12	30 Day	
Liquid Hair Shampoo (Child)	2 bottles	3	4-1-12	30 Day	
Liquid Hand Soap (antibacterial)	5 bottles	3	4-1-12	30 Day	
Lotion	12	3	4-1-12	30 Day	
Mouthwash	2 bottles	3	7-1-12		90 Day
Panty Liners	1 box	3	4-1-12	30 Day	
Razor blades (men's)	30	3	4-1-12	30 Day	
Razor blades (women's)	30	3	4-1-12	30 Day	
Sanitary Pads	1 box	3	4-1-12	30 Day	
Shampoo	24	3	4-1-12	30 Day	
Shaving Cream	2 cans	3	4-1-12	30 Day	
Solar Shower	2	1	7-1-12		90 Day
Sunglasses	2/person	3	4-1-12	30 Day	
Tampons	1 box	3	4-1-12	30 Day	
Toenail clippers	3	3	4-1-12	30 Day	
Toilet paper	100 rolls	3	4-1-12	30 Day	
Toothbrushes	2	3	4-1-12	30 Day	

Item	Quantity	Priority	Date	Duration
Toothpaste	5 tubes	3	4-1-12	30 Day
Towelettes, Pre-moistened	2 boxes	3	4-1-12	30 Day
Towels	15	3	4-1-12	30 Day
Tweezers, pointed	2	3	4-1-12	30 Day
Wash Cloths & Towel	4/person	3	4-1-12	30 Day

Security Supplies

Guns are like tools, it's difficult to have to many. The quanity and types of guns required will vary tremendously from one person to another. No amount of supplies will do you any good if someone else takes them from you by force. Self defense is an important consideration and, if wild game is in the area, hunting can provide fresh meat. The safe is for storing records, documents, cash, and gold or silver. *Common Caliber Ammunition. I've always felt that common caliber ammunition is the best all-around barter item. Top choices are: .22 long rifle, .223 Remington (5.56 mm NATO), .308 Winchester (7.62 mm NATO), .30-06, 12 gauge (#00 Buckshot), .45 ACP, and 9mm Parabellum*

Item	Quantity Required	Purchase Priority	Purchase by Date	Planned Duration
.22 shells	1000	2	7-1-12	90 Day
Gun safe	1	1	4-1-12	30 Day
Guns/Ammo	Assortment	1	4-1-12	30 Day
military rifle bore cleaner	10 1 oz. bottles	2	7-1-12	90 Day
Ammo reloader	1	2	10-1-12	1 Year
Ammo Cans	5	2	4-1-12	30 Day
Gun accessories	1 set/weapon	2	4-1-12	30 Day
Gun cleaning equipment	1 set/weapon	2	4-1-12	30 day
Military web gear	2/person	2	4-1-12	30 Day
(lots of folks may *suddenly* need pistol belts, magazine pouches, et cetera.)				
Perimeter alarm of some sort	1 set	2	4-1-12	30 Day
Solar powered perimieter Lights	5	3	4-1-12	30 day
Waterproof dufflebags ("dry bags")	1/person	2	4-1-12	30 Day

Tools

The generator is for emergencies and occasional use like pumping water from a well. I do not think it is feasible to store enough fuel to run a generator full time to maintain our current lifestyle. A cant hook is a tool for rolling logs so that you can move them in to position to cut them for firewood. This assumes a source of timber to be cut for firewood. A list of hand tools could be as long as the rest of the list. At a minimum it should include pliers, wrenches, screwdrivers, and a hammer. The funnels are for transferring fuel and other liquids from bulk storage containers to daily use containers. A come-a-long is a portable cable winch. It could be used for moving heavy objects like dead cars or fallen trees.

Item	Quantity Required	Purchase Priority	Purchase by Date	Planned Duration
1 gallon gas can for mixed gas	1	3	4-1-12	30 Day
10" Wire Cutters	1	3	4-1-12	30 Day
2 cycle oil	6	3	7-1-12	90 Day
24" or 30" Bolt Cutters	1	2	7-1-12	90 Day
Axe	1	3	4-1-12	30 Day
Bar oil	1	3	7-1-12	90 Day
Blades	Assortment	3	4-1-12	30 Day
Bow saw	2	3	4-1-12	30 Day
Bow saw blades	2	3	4-1-12	30 Day
Bungee Straps (variety of lengths)	6	3	4-1-12	30 Day
Bush or Tree Saw	1	3	7-1-12	90 Day
Caulking gun	1	3	4-1-12	30 Day
Chain	1	3	4-1-12	30 Day
Chainsaw	1	3	7-1-12	90 Day
Chainsaw extra chain	2	3	7-1-12	90 Day
Chimney cleaning brush	1	3	10-1-12	1 year

Chisel/Wedge	1	3	4-1-12	30 Day	
CO Detector, battery powered	2	3	4-1-12	30 Day	
Come-a-long	1	3	4-1-12	30 Day	
Crowbar	1	3	4-1-12	30 day	
Drill, Hand-operated	1	3	4-1-12	30 day	
Dust Mask	1box	3	4-1-12	30 day	
Duct/100 MPH Tape	1 box	3	7-1-12		90 Day
Extra air filter	2	3	7-1-12		90 Day
Extra spark plug	2	3	7-1-12		90 Day
Funnels	Assortment	3	4-1-12	30 Day	
Garden fork	2	3	7-1-12		90 Day
Generator	1	1	4-1-12	30 Day	
Hacksaw	1	3	4-1-12	30 day	
Hammer	1	3	4-1-12	30 day	
Hand tools	Assortment	3	4-1-12	30 Day	
Hatchet	1	3	4-1-12	30 Day	
Ladder	1	3	4-1-12	30 Day	
Maul	1	3	4-1-12	30 Day	
Oil for generator	12 qt	3	4-1-12	30 Day	
Paint brushes	2	3	10-1-12		1 year
Pick	1	3	4-1-12	30 Day	
Pins	1 box	3	4-1-12	30 day	
Pliers, needle nose	1	3	4-1-12	30 day	
Pliers, regular	1	3	4-1-12	30 day	
Post Hole Digger, auger type	1	3	4-1-12	30 day	
Rope, Nylon	100 feet	3	4-1-12	30 day	
Saw horses	2	3	4-1-12	30 day	
Scissors	2	3	4-1-12	30 day	
Screwdriver, Flat Head	2	3	4-1-12	30 day	
Screwdriver, Phillips	2	3	4-1-12	30 day	
Sharpening files	1	3	4-1-12	30 Day	
Sharpening instruments	1 set	3	7-1-12		90 day
Sharpening stone	Assortment	3	4-1-12	30 Day	
Shovel, round	2	3	4-1-12	30 Day	
Shovel, sharpshooter	2	3	4-1-12	30 Day	
Shovel, Snow	1	3	4-1-12	30 Day	
Shovel, square	2	3	4-1-12	30 Day	
Sledgehammer	1	3	4-1-12	30 Day	
Smoke Detector, bettery powered	2	3	4-1-12	30 day	
Staple Gun and Staples	1	3	4-1-12	30 day	
Swiss Army Knife	1/person	3	4-1-12	30 day	
Tin snips	1	3	4-1-12	30 day	
Tow Chain/Straps	1	3	4-1-12	30 day	
Twine or Heavy String	100feet	3	4-1-12	30 day	
Two man tree saw	1	3	10-1-12		1 year
Vice Grips	1	3	4-1-12	30 day	
Wedge	1	3	4-1-12	30 Day	
welding outfit	1	3	7-1-12		90 Day
Wench and Cable (come along)	1	3	7-1-12		90 day
Wire Cutters	1	3	4-1-12	30 day	
Wood Saw	2	3	7-1-12		90 day
Wood Screws	Assorted	3	4-1-12	30 day	
Wrenches	Assorted	3	4-1-12	30 day	

Transportation

Vehicle maintenance shouldn't be a problem in the short run or the long run if fuel supplies dry up. A "mid-length" crisis could call for some basic maintenance though. Bicycles should come in hand for short trips and to avoid drawing attention to yourself when most people are walking. An old rebuilt car. No electronic ignition. .

Item	Quantity Required	Purchase Priority	Purchase by Date	Planned Duration	
12 volt air compressor	1	3	4-1-12	30 Day	
Antifreeze	2 gals	3	4-1-12	30 Day	
Bicycle	1/person	3	4-1-12	30 Day	
Bicyle chain repair kit	1/bike	3	4-1-12	30 Day	
bicycle tire repair kit	1/bike	3	4-1-12	30 Day	
Bicycle tube hand air pump	1/bike	3	4-1-12	30 day	
Fan belts	1set/auto	3	7-1-12		90 Day
Fuses	1 set	3	4-1-12	30 Day	
Handlebar Basket	1/bike	3	4-1-12	30 Day	
Hi-Lift Jack	1	3	4-1-12	30 Day	
Hoses	1set/auto	3	7-1-12		90 Day
Jacks and stands	1 set	3	4-1-12	30 day	
Jumper Cables	1	3	4-1-12	30 Day	
Manuals	1 set/auto	3	7-1-12		90 day
Oil filter	4	3	7-1-12		90 Day
Oil	24 quarts	3	7-1-12		90 Day
Ramps	1 set	3	7-1-12		90 day
Snow Chains	1set/auto	3	4-1-12	30 day	
Spare bicycle tires	2/bike	3	4-1-12	30 Day	
Spare bicycle tubes	2/bike	3	4-1-12	30 Day	
Spare replacement parts for the car	1 set	3	4-1-12	30 day	
Tire pressure gauge	1	3	4-1-12	30 day	
Tires and blocks	1/auto	3	4-1-12	30 day	
Tire sealer/inflator (can)	2/auto	3	4-1-12	30 Day	
Tire wrench	1/auto	3	4-1-12	30 Day	
Tools that your particular car needs	1 set	2	4-1-12	30 day	
Torx screwdrivers	1 set	3	4-1-12	30 Day	
Tow chain	1	3	4-1-12	30 Day	
Tow strap	1	3	4-1-12	30 Day	
Tube repair kits	1/bike	3	4-1-12	30 Day	

Water

Item	Quantity Required	Purchase Priority	Purchase by Date	Planned Duration	
55 gallon water drums	2/person	2	4-1-12	30 day	
Bleach - 1 gallon (5.25%)	1	3	4-1-12	30 day	
Bung Wrench					
Hand pumps for drum	2	2	4-1-12	30 day	
Pool tarp - 12 x 16 ft.	1	3	4-1-12	30 day	
Pool water testing kit	1	3	4-1-12	30 day	
Water bag (collapsible) - 5 gallon	1	3	4-1-12	30 day	
Water can - 5 gallon	2	3	4-1-12	30 day	
Water chlorinating granules (pool)	1 box	3	7-1-12		90 day
Water Distiller	1	3	10-1-12		1 Year
Water filter	1	1	4-1-12	30 Day	
Water filter, replacement cartridge	1	1	4-1-12	30 Day	
Water funnels	2	3	4-1-12	30 day	
Water jug bottles, 2qt	2/person	2	4-1-12	30 Day	
Water pump	1	1	7-1-12		90 Day

The 3rd Wave, Evacuation From A Disaster Location

The subject of evacuation from a disaster location, or evacuation in advance of a potential disaster (such as a storm), has been written about here and on other sites ad nauseum. But the timing of an evacuation isn't usually discussed in detail. That is the topic of this article.

In general, during an SHTF event there is likely going to be 3 waves of evacuations.

1st Wave

These are mostly going to be the people who already live their lives on a hair-pin trigger just waiting for any small sign that a disaster is brewing. "Neurotic" is certainly an accurate if not flattering description. It also includes a small number of people, either by gifted insight or blind luck, connect the dots early and come to the conclusion that a major SHTF event is approaching.

The number of people evacuating probably will be very low. Most people will either refuse to believe anything bad is going to happen ("normalcy bias") or fail to see the early warning signs and connect the dots.

Supplies like food, water, fuel etc will be at normal levels of availability and you should make every effort to top-off with fresh supplies before leaving. Similarly, currency will still be readily available and accepted. Retailers should have little problem resupplying at normal schedules (if you choose to risk waiting a bit longer for additional supplies).

Traffic will be light to normal with little or no additional law enforcement/government control issues. People in surrounding communities will likely not even notice you as you pass through, perhaps pausing for more supplies, refueling etc.

2nd Wave

By this stage the danger (or at least the signs of the danger) is becoming far more apparent and harder to ignore, though many more will still refuse to accept what events seem to be leading up to (footnote: Some argue we are already in this stage). This wave will be characterized by a much wider swath of people taking their leave of the affected area(s). Not just preppers but "average" (non-preppers) too will be getting nervous and start leaving. Early signs of panic may be setting in too.

Supplies, especially of food, water, and fuel will start becoming noticeably harder to find (and likely more expensive) with less products on the shelves, even some empty shelves, and longer lines. Resupply to retailers will be slower. ATMs will start running out of cash. Bank branches themselves will run low or out of cash as branches only keep a small amount of actual currency on hand every day (for security and liquidity reasons).

Services too may become harder to obtain as "the [pick a color] flu" mysteriously falls upon employees in all manner of government and private business (i.e. people choose not to come into work to either stay home with their families or evacuate – a topic for another article soon).

A much larger number of people will be on the roads and other transportation methods. Traffic will be much greater and nerves tenser (more road rage). Also, the availability of other means of transport (train tickets, bus tickets etc) will be in greater demand and less available. There may be an increased law enforcement presence on the roads especially at bridges and tunnels, probably more for traffic control.

Surrounding communities and even further out from the affected area will see a rapidly growing influx of out of area people. Initially there may be some welcome as they bring a fast economic boost to the community, buying supplies etc. But that will likely switch over to resentment and possibly forceful rejection as smaller community supplies dwindle and people just keep coming and demanding more.

3rd Wave

In this wave all your neighbors, preppers or not, have reached the same conclusion: **Time to get out of Dodge!**

At this point the danger is upon you. The SHTF event has happened or is on the cusp of happening. It is acknowledged (perhaps begrudgingly but still acknowledged) by all but the most intransigent people who still refuse to accept the reality of the situation and cling to hopeless ideas everything will be fine and/or someone (i.e. government) will do something to make it all better. At this point these people are likely never going to be convinced and, cruel as it may sound, don't waste any more time trying to. They may already be beyond helping.

Supplies will be very hard if not impossible to get. Store shelves will be wiped clean. Fuel may be unavailable as retailers have drained their tanks and resupply unlikely. There may even be fuel rationing as whatever local supplies are ordered saved for "official use only". Bank branches will likely be closed and ATMs long since emptied of cash.

The roads will likely be packed and tempers will be high. Fear and panic will set otherwise calm people off at any little provocation. Some level of civil unrest may ensue especially if it is perceived there is an official policy to slow or prevent people from leaving (such as some kind of check point or vehicle searches).

The masses of evacuees will spread throughout the surrounding geography and likely overrun smaller surrounding communities thereby overwhelming their own stocks of retail supplies and services. Tempers will be high, violence likely. Don't be surprised if small communities even try to block the main roads into their areas.

By the time the 3rd wave of evacuees comes if you still haven't left most likely it's too late to even try. For all the reasons above and more it will be impossible, or at the very least highly risky, to even attempt to leave. You are probably better off digging in and trying to wait out the event (depending what the event is).

I believe the key to success in this is to determine your "trigger event". Determine clearly and precisely what actions or events prior to an SHTF event will prompt you to implement your evacuation plan. You have to be reasonable and specific. Life is full of daily unexpected events and you can't be "bugging out" every time there's a news flash.

Above all, I believe it comes down to trusting your gut instincts. Don't be ruled by what others are doing, or more likely not doing. Don't be afraid to make the decision to leave. You may get ribbed for it later if nothing bad happens. But I assure you deep down a lot of those people jabbing you wish they had thought to leave too and had the strength of character to actually do it themselves.

Copyright 2012 by ST
http://suburbansurvivalblog.com/

Bug Out Trigger Criteria

This is a guest post by a new contributing Author Mr-Jones. Mr-Jones and I know each other primarily from Facebook, and some of the same forums, and have become fast friends, online. I have asked him to contribute when he can, and I greatly appreciate it. Please welcome him...

What exactly would it take to trigger a bug out?
Just like you have, I have read a ton on bug out bags, bug out routes, and bug out destinations, but I seldom receive a satisfactory answer to the question: If it came down to it, what exactly would trigger you to pack up and leave your primary residence? I ask this for a reason. In my mind, any exit strategy has to have a trigger. In a business, it's usually a monetary trigger. But it could be an milestone event in the cycle of decline, such as, when your distributors freeze your credit lines. What would have to happen to trigger your bug out contingency plan? If you plan to leave before the hordes of sheeple exit your city then you have you to beat them to it, right? If you plan to bug out before the roadblocks go up, you need to leave before that ... or do you have a contingency plan for that? What if, in this age of information, you don't beat them? This could happen because of geography or it could happen because some of the sheeple are not packing anything or it could happen because you were either too lazy or too uninformed to identify possible triggers and waited too long. I want to focus on that last bit.

I had some events that caused me to rethink my positioning. At the time, I owned a business located in a couple suites of a strip mall in the Phoenix-Metro area. One of the events was a power outage ... the power turned off, (this is not an abnormal occurrence, all of us have probably been through power outages) but the power usually turned back on in a few seconds or a few minutes. Seconds turned into minutes and minutes turned into hours. And I realized ... "Hey, dummy, the backup batteries for my business alarm systems should be running out about now." So I found myself in a prison of my own making. I had envisioned myself bugging in at home, or bugging out to one of a few destinations. Instead, I went down and guarded my livelyhood until the power came on ... not unlike the Korean shop owners in the LA riots. Since then, I eventually repositioned, accepting lower pay, but bettering my footing in an emergency. Now I live in a rural community that, in all likelyhood, (and unlike Phoenix) won't have riots, and will have water post-SHTF event. I'm not saying that no one will be able to survive in Phoenix. I'm just saying I traded something good for something better. I've already "bugged in" outside of major metro areas, and severed my ties to my business, so that frees me up and decreases the chance I will have to bug out in the first place. But it's always a possibility.

Do you do drills?

If so, do you time yourself? Have you triggered a bug out before? I have done some "surprise" drills. I say that tongue-in-cheek because, how can you surprise yourself? One Friday, I just say, OK, "Go!" I look at the clock and see how it turns out. How fast can you even go on a camping trip? Can you do it without stopping at the store or stop for gas? If not, that gives you a pretty good idea of where you need to focus your preparations. Stop for gas will surely turn into wait in line for gas, and then you're too late. What is a reasonable goal for you to shoot for? It's probably going to be slightly diferent for a single fellow than for a couple, and different still for a family. Do you know where you're headed? I think it's healthy to focus on the basics and to have repetition in skill training. Some numbers on that … the first time you train or are trained on a given topic, retention is something like 13% on average … second time, it goes up to say 21% … but the third time, it goes up into the high 60's percentile-wise. Just a tidbit on skill training to help you train smart. Another thing that might help is to have a followup mechanism. For me, it's a small Rite-In-The-Rain journal. I volunteer with my Community Emergency Response Team and the Amateur Radio Emergency Service. Every time I practice bugging out, go on an outing, do a major training excercise with CERT or ARES, or I'm deployed, I sit down afterward and make a journal entry. I include the date, how long it was, what the weather was like, a short review of my performance, how my gear performed, and anything I could subtract from my gear or that I need for my gear. Eventually, making your gear lightweight will be as important as buying new gear … age will eventually catch up to you. Or, if you're a new prepper, you'll very quickly find that you can't carry all your gear with you. That very quickly turns into "you can't carry everything you'd like" with you. By now you have probably noticed that I'm a gear junky and I need to improve on that.

What goes into identifying my triggers?

My background is in business, so how I do it, its how I would develop a trigger for an exit strategy. I Identify qualitative and quantitative triggers … or triggers that are both. For qualatative triggers, think about the "qualities" or conditions such as "mobs in the street." For quantitative triggers, think: "a mob is 5 or more people." For both, think: mobs (5 or more people) within 10 blocks of my apartment. Then, I make my trigger a conditional (If/Then) action statement: If I have reliable reports of mobs (of 5 or more) within 10 blocks of my apartment, then I will implement bug out strategy Alpha. That's just how I do it. I'd love to hear ideas

to improve my method. I will steal them and never give you any credit for them. That's what I learned in self-defense classes … when lives are on the line, it's OK to lie, steal, and cheat to win.

I think the actual triggers vary greatly based on your geographical location and the threats you face.

Do you live in a seizmically active area? I do. My house could be rendered unsafe by an earthquake and I could have to bug out. In this case, it might not even be that far. Often one house is destroyed and the one next to it is fine. It could be a fire … that could affect most of us. It could be an NBC event. I'm not really in a fallout zone (given normal wind patterns) for any high value targets, but my little city does have a meat packing plant that stores ammonia. Do you know where you live in relation to targets and wind-patterns? How much radiation would cause you to bug out? Can you measure it? That reminds me that it's time to have my instruments re-calibrated. Could it be drought? Famine? If so, what would the trigger be? How long would the power have to be off? Would you EVER have to bug out because of a power outage? Perhaps a localized EMP from a solar flare for you people with your own micro-hydro plant, solar panels and wind generators. How about an influx of refugees? How soon would you leave, or would you, in a government ordered evacuation? How about a pandemic? Could your home be rendered unsafe by a tornado or a micro-burst? How about a weather event with a warning like a hurricane? How big would it have to be or is that a consideration? Could it be flooded? Could your water supply become contaminated? Yes, the list is endless, but what is in the top 10 for your local?

In summary …

what if the unthinkable does happen? What are those triggers we talked about? Is there just one? Is it different for different contigencies? I'm going to leave you with these questions, because I haven't been able to come up with any one answer that is right for everyone in every situation. But I hopefully have given you some ideas of how to identify some triggers and I challenge you to think about your top 10, write some trigger statements and respond. If you do it in the form of a qualitative and quantitative action statement, browine points for you. If you do it in your own way, good for you, you're still better off than before you identified your bug out triggers.

Understanding Everyone In the City Will Be a Refugee Post SHTF

Not often spoken of, I think in the survivalist or prepper circle, is how to avoid becoming a refugee post SHTF. We talk a lot about prepping, we talk a lot about bugging out or bugging in, but we never really talk about the situation where we do find ourselves shut off from our gear and are in a situation where our preps don't help us much. For instance, what if you are in NYC or on Long Island and there is some emergency and the tunnels and bridges are shut down for an undetermined amount of time. You're stuck on one of the islands maybe without anywhere to go. Almost immediately you are a trapped refugee.

I should also preface this with some of your decisions as a refugee may or may not be the most ethical decisions based on you need to survive.

I should probably also define SHTF. SHTF does not have to be an invasion by a foreign power, earthquake, hurricane, etc. It could be something as simple as losing your job and being forced out of your home. For the purposes of this post, however, feel free to apply whatever situation you might think you would most likely put you in a situation where you might actually be a refugee. Let's also assume you are in a highly populated area like the suburbs of a major city or the major city itself.

Apply your situation, and you find yourself homeless with little cash. Communications systems are up and down, and there is still law enforcement and security of some sort. Assume you have your EDC on you, and a backpack with minimal supplies. Where would you go? What would you do? Would you live on the street? Enter a shelter? Find an abandon building?

First, let me tell you what will happen if you enter a shelter. Chances are you will be searched upon entering, no weapons, knives, food, multi-tools, etc. Nada. How do I know this? Remember my friend who was in the shelter, and that kit I made him? Well, they confiscated half the stuff out of the kit. Including the multi-tool and the ER Bar that I had in the kit. You will have to cache many of your supplies and hope they are there the next day when you return for them. Try doing that in the city, and feel good about it. Second, should you choose to live on the street during a SHTF in the city, you better be good at urban evasion tactics, and I am not just talking about from authorities. I am talking other refugees, existing homeless, gangs, etc.

To that end, if the bridges and tunnels to NYC are shut down, chances are it is going to be a while before any fresh medical supplies, bottled water (because no one from the city drinks from the tap), food (as the public knows it), etc. makes its way into the city and properly distributed. And properly distributed during a SHTF is clearly government distribution and rationed supplies. Now, if food and supplies can come in, then they will clearly be evacuating those out of the city to wherever they set up camp. That's a lot additional refugees and locusts that will be filling in the suburbs. I hope some or many are prepared for that. What to do when the locusts evacuate the city into the suburbs will be another post altogether.

Not to mention there will be a mass exodus to try to get out of the city. Everyone with a country home in NY State, PA, or elsewhere will be trying to get out of the city. Those that have family outside the city will be trying to get outside the city. There will be refugees floating around everywhere. And when they find out they cannot get off the island of Manhattan, they are going to get angry. Those that have completely adapted to the urban lifestyle will have very few resources in their apartment. They will run out of food and water quickly. Then comes desperate measure.

If they keep the bridges and tunnels open, good luck getting over or through them at any speed. People will be walking, biking, running, in their car, etc. Think of the stories about how hard it was to evacuate before Hurricane Katrina. The roads were packed going about two MPH for miles and miles. By the time anyone gets from one side of the tunnel or bridge walking or going so slowly it takes hours, there are going to be a lot of angry people. If you are going into NJ and you are walking, to get as far as the Meadowlands you have to go over at least one more bridge over a river. Assuming the NJ State police do not have these roads blocked off, you may be able to make it to your destination. If it six hours to go six miles it might take a lot longer than that if you try to get to your destination.

If you get stuck in the city (any city) it is likely you will also be deprived of the basic necessity of sleep, since you will be on a heightened state of alert most of the time. Some of the things you might encounter would be yelling, screaming, sirens, megaphones talking as they are driving down the road, people crying, localized riots and civil unrest. Along with your sleep deprivation will be your diminished decision making capacity that follows it.

99% of the people in a city or the suburbs are not going to be prepared for any emergency. Most people aren't going to get 10 miles. They are going to get hungry, tired, angry, or worse hostile towards other refugees around them.

The truth is, I am not even sure I would make it. There are a lot of variables, and I am constantly trying to prep and prepare for the uncertain.
So, with all those thoughts, (because that is what they really were, a collection of what if thoughts) if any SHTF occurs, what will you do about it? How will you handle it? What will your level of preparation be?

Is there a need for emergency communication in my ward or stake?

When an emergency occurs, leaders need the ability to immediately communicate with members, missionaries, and civil and Church authorities to provide status reports or to request assistance. A reliable emergency communication system should be in place if regular telephone or cell phone service fails.

If we typically do not have natural disasters in our area, why should we include emergency communication in our ward and stake emergency plans?

In addition to a natural disaster, an emergency may occur anywhere and without warning. Examples include hazardous material spills, fires, power failure, and terrorist attacks. Consider which emergencies are possible in your location and identify specific ways to communicate in these types of emergencies.

What is the job description of a ward or stake emergency communication specialist?

Leaders may choose to call a ward or stake emergency communication specialist from their community to assist with planning and implementing communication plans. Emergency communication specialists provide training and ensure the readiness of communication equipment. Emergency communication specialists may be invited to participate in ward and stake communication discussions as directed by leaders.

Will my mobile telephone work in an emergency?

The mobile telephone is an effective tool for communication under normal circumstances. However, in a disaster, mobile telephone systems often fail due to overload, damage, and loss of power. Mobile telephone providers will restore service following a disaster, but it may take several hours, days, or weeks.

Should wards and stakes purchase or accept a donated satellite telephone or amateur radio equipment for use in an emergency?

No. The ward and stake budget allowance does not include expenses for the purchase of equipment, repair, maintenance fees, or service contracts associated with satellite telephones and radio equipment. Leaders are encouraged to identify individuals who may already have their own equipment to assist with specific ward and stake communication needs.

What information should be reported to leaders following an emergency?

Leaders should be prepared to report the nature of the disaster, the welfare of members and missionaries, the condition of meetinghouses, and any requests for assistance.

A member of the Mercury Amateur Radio Association (MARA) approached me with an offer to provide communication services and an emergency communications plan template for my stake. What relationship does the Church have with MARA, and is it appropriate to utilize MARA or other similar organizations in my emergency planning?

Priesthood leaders may utilize resources outside of the Church organization to assist in emergency communication planning as appropriate. A leader may also choose to call a member of MARA or another amateur radio organization to serve as a ward or stake communication specialist under priesthood direction. The Church of Jesus Christ of Latter-day Saints has no formal relationship with any amateur radio organizations or clubs, but may find the training and experience of Church members who belong to these organizations useful during an actual emergency. As a reminder, amateur radio clubs or associations, including MARA, may not use church meetinghouses to hold association meetings or other club events as this could be interpreted as a form of remuneration, and could possibly be a violation of Federal Communications Commission (FCC) regulations.

During an emergency, normal means of communication may become inoperable. Priesthood leaders should consider:

- How to contact missionaries and members following a disaster.
- How to communicate the status of missionaries, members, buildings, and other necessary information to area leaders.
- Available communication personnel and equipment.

Communication Specialists

Priesthood leaders may call communication specialists as needed. Individuals interested in communications often own radio equipment and possess valuable experience.

Additional Resources

Satellite Telephones - Storehouses in the United States and Canada have satellite telephones. In other Church areas, satellite telephones are available in administration offices for emergency use.

Amateur Radio – Some storehouses in the United States and Canada have amateur radio equipment and conduct regular network exercises. For information, contact your priesthood leader or regional welfare specialist.

Organize Yourself, Prepare Every Needful Thing...

DID YOU THINK TO PRAY?

Communications
FAMILY READY

PEACE

Long Range Ham Radio & Satalite Systems are not cheap, and you have to be willing to get licensed. It is a disiplined form of communicatin where chatter isn't tolerated. But they work over hundreds of miles through repeaters, and can bring the news of safety of loved ones, or can be used to reach out when you are in distress and need help. There is a Ham Operators system in place worldwide to communicate post disaster. Your family can also invest time, resources, & energy into learning how to do this too. For More Info: go to aarl.org

Amateur Radio License

RESOURCE

Establish Block Captains. Use runners in a neighborhood, to send messages. Cheaper Shorter Two Way Radios work great In a neighborhood communication system. Family members locally, can use them like walkie talkies. Get ones with enough sub-frequency channels to avoid stepping on others (too many talking at one time) who will be using them locally too. These work by line of site and most likely only cover a few miles at best. Plan also for a way to Recharge Radios. Solar? Extra Batteries? etc?

Two Way Radios Block Captains Runners

PROGRESS

Old Land Line Phones are Great in an emergency because they are low frequency fiber optics, OFTEN they do not loose power when everthing else does. If you have an older push button phone that doesn't require recharging or batteries (not a cordless phone) often these land lines will work for at least out of state calls. Local lines get bogged down during a disaster, but out of state family members can often get through or vise versa, when nothing else is working.

Land Lines

STARTED

Establish a Family Contengency Communicatin Plan Now, while you can communicate. Where would you meet if you were seperated in a large scale disaster. Kids at school? Dad traveling or at work? Mom? Have an Out of State Contact Family member, that can relay info to you and other family members as a go between, if local lines are down. (See Land Lines above) Write out your plan. Make sure everyone has this info. Also get a wind up or other rechargable AM/FM Radio so you can recieve news. (Great gift.)

Family Plan EP Contact AM/FM Radio

NOT READY

Conviently Use Email Systems & Facebook Group Pages, Internet Blogs, & cell phones, including texting, for pre disaster communication. Use to teach preparedness, keep people in the loop, and to communicate in minor emergencies. After a Major Disaster, if there is long term loss of power most of these will become useless. Texting May Continue... texting works sometimes, even when you can't get a dialtone.

Cell Phone Email Internet

Radio Spectrum

	Medium Frequency (MF) 0.3 to 3mhz	High Frequency (HF) 3 to 30mhz	Very High Frequency (VHF) 30 to 300mhz	Ultra High Frequency (UHF) 300 to 3,000mhz
Range	Signals travel with ease over hundreds or thousands of miles with even small amounts of power. Band is highly reliable and works well regardless of solar activity.	Depends on solar activity (needed to charge the ionosphere, which these signals bounce), time of day, and season. No solar activity makes this band nearly useless, but with solar activity, signals can travel world-wide.	High-power signal can travel a few hundred miles. More typical range is 1 to 20 miles, depending on the amount of transmitter power. (1-watt usually translates to about a half-mile, line of site, depending on antenna efficiency).	Line-of-site only. Signals are blocked by buildings, trees, people, mountains, and other structures. If you can't see it with a pair of binoculars, you probably won't be able to get a signal to it.
Antenna	A minimal efficiency antenna will be 82 to 820 feet – and could be twice or 4x that size for a highly efficient antenna.	Antennas can be very long (300+ feet) towards the 3mhz range, and 30+ feet towards the 30mhz range.	High-efficiency antennas might be 6 to 20 feet. Low-efficiency antennas could be as short as a few inches.	A few feet to a few inches.
Typical Use	AM Broadcast, coast guard distress, maritime ship-to-shore, Ham Radio (160-meter band)	Shortwave radio, CB, military, trans-oceanic aviation, Ham Radio (10-meter through 80-meter bands). ** CB range limited to around 5 miles due to power restrictions and mode.	Police, fire, aviation, military, CAP, MURS, FM broadcast radio, marine, television, Ham Radio (6-meter, 2-meter, 1.25-meter).	Police, fire, cell phones, broadcast television, WiFi, FRS, GMRS, cordless phones, digital television, military, pagers, Ham Radio (70-cm, 23cm, 13cm).

LDS Emergency Communications

by
Dennis Bartholomew

The Church of Jesus Christ of Latter Day Saints has long encouraged its members to assemble and maintain a 72 hour kit that can be utilized in an emergency. In addition, members have been encouraged to acquire a long-term supply of food, water and other necessities for emergencies. In any emergency, communications are also essential. This paper will address alternate forms of communication that can be used if such an event warrants it.

In most emergencies, normal forms of communication are still available, namely telephone, cell service and the internet. However, there may be limited service. For example, voice cell service may be spotty, but texting is more reliable. On land lines, incoming calls may be possible, but outgoing calls will be limited or impossible.

In the case of a widespread emergency or disaster, all forms of regular communication are simply nonexistent. Katrina is one such example. Communication is essential in everyday life, and especially so in any type of disaster. The question is raised, "What type of communication will work all the time and can be independent of the power grid and other conventional infrastructure, and still operate efficiently?"

The answer to this question is ham radio, also called amateur radio. Ham radio has been in existence since the 1920's. It is extremely reliable. All ham radios operate on 12 volts DC, and therefore, can operate for days, weeks or longer on battery power from automobiles. It is relatively inexpensive to get started in ham radio. For many, ham radio is a hobby. But it is already recognized by the ham radio community as an emergency mode of communication.

Since the 1970's, the Church has had an informal group of member ham radio operators organized throughout the United States and some parts of Canada. This organization is known as ERC, or Emergency Response Communica-

tions. They routinely conduct meetings on the air (called nets), which have allowed them to practice their craft on a weekly basis in being prepared to communicate in any situation. This is the 'big picture' view of the program. Let's talk about the local concept of this form of communication.

When disaster strikes, the bishop will want to obtain information about his ward members. He will want to know who, and how many were affected, what the status of Church owned buildings are, and he will also want to know the status of the full-time missionaries. If this information cannot be provided through normal means of communications, members of the ward who are ham radio operators, would collect this information and pass it to the bishop via ham radio. (This process would be outlined in advance in the Ward Emergency Plan.) This information would then need to be forwarded to the stake president. The information may need to be passed further up the Priesthood chain – possibly to Headquarters in Salt Lake City – depending on the severity of the disaster and the needs of the members.

When organized well, this form of communication can function quite efficiently and satisfy the needs that Church leaders have to obtain this vital information in such an event.

What is the process of being a ham radio operator?

There are some simple, but needed requirements to operate a ham radio. First, in the United States, the Federal Communications Commission (FCC) governs the use of ham radio frequencies. Similar agencies direct communications in most countries in the world. The FCC requires that a ham radio operator possess a ham radio license. This license is acquired by successfully passing a 35 question multiple choice test. Books are available to study for this test, which teach the essentials of ham radio and are good reference books for after-the-test use. After the test has been passed, the individual will be issued a ham radio license by the FCC. The license will show the call sign that was issued, which is used in all transmissions on a ham radio.

For study books, locations of testing sites and other resources, see 'Resources' at the end of this article.

After obtaining the license, you will want to invest in a ham radio. There is a large variety of ham radios that are available from many sources. The key in owning your first ham radio is to find equipment that is reliable, but isn't extremely expensive. The author recommends a handheld-type of radio as your first investment. Also called an HT, or handheld transceiver, HT's are very portable and easy to use. They will provide you with years of service – even after you purchase additional, more expensive equipment, if you so desire. An HT typically costs about $130. An HT may be the only radio you will ever require to provide the needed communication for your situation.

As mentioned, additional equipment may be desired, depending on your need to communicate in a wider area. Typically, a person can invest in additional equipment that enhances the use of the HT. For example, adding a discrete antenna to the roof of your house can greatly extend the range of the HT. An HT usually transmits between 1 and 5 watts of power. Other radios are available that transmit between 50 and 75 watts. These radios are called mobile radios. As the name implies, they are often permanently mounted in a vehicle. They are also used as a 'base station' in homes or other stationary locations. A mobile radio will need a 12 volt power supply if used as a base station. This can be accomplished by using a sealed 12 volt battery that is being charged by a trickle charger or battery maintainer. This method allows the use of the base station without the need for power from the grid. A mobile radio is a good investment, because it can easily be moved into any vehicle and used as a mobile, in the literal sense. As in all cases, an antenna is required. When using a mobile radio in a temporary vehicle installation, the use of a magnetic mounted antenna would work quite well.

As you can see, the list of equipment can grow quickly. As a review, the above mentioned items include a handheld radio, a mobile radio, a house mounted antenna and a magnetic mounted antenna. Do not let this list overwhelm you. As mentioned, an HT may be all that is necessary for your needs. If you wish to increase your capabilities with additional equipment, you can do so incrementally and over a period of time.

During the process of learning about ham radio, you will want to locate ham radio operators in your community. They are a valuable source of information to you, and most are quite willing to help you. You can locate clubs that are established in your area, through the ARRL. (See 'Resources' below)

Let's talk about the range of ham radios. The range will vary tremendously, depending on terrain, how much power you are transmitting and how high your antenna is. Typically, a handheld's range will be 1 to 2 miles. With a roof mounted antenna, the range will increase approximately ten-fold, in most cases. The transmit range of a mobile radio is more than that of an HT, because it is capable of transmitting

more power. Range can be increased even further, through the use of what is called a repeater.

A repeater is a ham radio with some unique properties. It is typically installed at a high location – usually a mountain or high building. As an operator, you transmit to the repeater. The repeater, then, receives your signal and re-transmits it in all directions and with a much greater range than what is typical for your own radio. This allows other operators to hear your signal and for you to hear theirs, over a much larger area than is possible with a base radio by itself. Repeaters are usually owned by a person or ham radio club. If you wish to transmit using a repeater, it is recommended that you ask the repeater owner or trustee for permission to do so. This can be done simply by finding out the name of the repeater owner and making a verbal request via the repeater. After that, you are most likely going to be welcome to transmit on the repeater.

When using a ham radio, bear in mind that whenever you transmit, anyone can hear what you are saying if they are on the same frequency as you are. It is a 'party line' and should be treated as such.

Let's talk now about bands. The definition of a band is a group of consecutive frequencies that are grouped for a specific purpose. For example, your car radio has two bands – the FM band and the AM band. The range of frequencies of the FM band is from 87.5 to 107.9. These numbers are expressed in megahertz, or MHz. Interestingly, immediately following the FM band is the aviation band, which starts at 108.0 and ends at 135.0 MHz. All aircraft communications take place within that range of frequencies. There are hundreds of bands that are used for dozens of purposes like commercial radio and television, ham radio, government, cell phone, garage door openers, model airplanes, and many other purposes.

One of the more popular ham radio bands is called the '2 meter' band. Its frequency range is from 144.0 to 148.0 MHz. You will notice that it is not far from the FM band in your vehicle. It is called the 2 meter band because the antenna has a theoretical length of 2 meters, or just over 6 feet. This is not the actual length of the antennas used. There are many ways to make an antenna a convenient length, but is electrically compatible with the band.

Many other bands are available for ham radio – about 15 in all. Each band has its own advantages, which allow communications of various types. Some bands offer high quality sound, but with a short range. Other bands allow a lower quality sound, but with extreme distance capabilities – 12,000 miles or more.

There are many 'modes' – or forms of communication via ham radio. The most common is voice. When you transmit, someone hears you. Examples of other forms are data, ATV and IRLP. The mode called data, allows a ham to transmit and receive information. Instead of transmitting or receiving a voice, you transmit or receive computer files – a spreadsheet or a Word® document, for example. ATV, or Amateur Television is also possible. This allows hams to transmit and receive video signals using ham frequencies. IRLP, or Internet Radio Linking Project, is part of the voice mode, except it joins ham radio with the internet, allowing a ham to transmit to distant locations through the use of the internet. You will notice that Morse Code is not mentioned as a mode. That is because, although it is still used in ham radio, it is no longer required, and consequently, it is not necessary for new hams to learn Morse Code.

As you can see, ham radio is many things. But, one thing that it is for us – that is, a very capable form of communication in an emergency situation when no other method is available. It is the desire of this author that you consider ham radio as a serious step in being better prepared for what may come our way.

Resources

The American Radio Relay League (ARRL) is the largest ham radio 'club' in the United States. This organization represents approximately one-third of all ham radio operators in the U.S. The ARRL produces an excellent manual for preparing for the FCC license test. They have testing dates and locations listed. They also have a list of clubs that meet in your area. Their site is http://www.arrl.org

Another source of study materials is at http://www.w5yi.org

Radio supply houses are numerous. Some of the more popular ones follow:
Ham Radio Outlet - http://hamradio.com
Amateur Electronic Supply - http://aesham.com
Texas Towers - http://texastowers.com/index.htm
Ham City - https://www.hamcity.com/store/pc/home.asp
Gigaparts - http://www.gigaparts.com/radioindex.php

This article was written by Dennis Bartholomew, AF6TR. He has been involved with ham radio for over 15 years. His Church assignment involves the organization of emergency communications, using ham radio, in 60 stakes in the northern California and western Nevada areas. The content and opinions expressed in this article are the sole responsibility of Dennis Bartholomew.

You may view his web site at http://ercinfo.webs.com or email him at dennis7400@sbcglobal.net

General Radio Primer

There are a lot of options when it comes to communications. Some require licenses, and some do not. I will riefly describe some of the aspects here, but if you want more information, then I suggest that you get one of the beginning radio books on the subject. These can be found anywhere from your local library to websites (www.aesham.com, www.hamradio.com, www.arrl.org) just to name a few.

Things to consider:
budget
distance
portable or base station
power supply
weight
usability

Options that do not require a license

CB

Inexpensive and easy to obtain, but also crowded, and in the high HF frequencies (27 MHz). There are portable handhelds (rather large), mobile, and desktop models. CB's have a decent range, around 25 to 30 miles for a 4 watt model with a good antenna. Handheld units will be less. With CB you also can get "skip", which is a bounce of the signal off of the ionosphere. That means that you can talk, or hear, stations many hundreds to thousands of miles away. The amount of skip is cyclical, by about 11 years. It also varies by time of day, usually starting around midday, and lasting into the evening.

FRS

Inexpensive and easy to obtain. Low power, handheld with some base style units. Due to the frequency range (UHF 460 MHz) they do not have a lot of range. Depending on the terrian, up to 2 miles. In hilly areas, expect a mile or less. What makes a big difference in these radios (or any radio for that matter) is a good receiver. My pair of Motorola can get more "range" than my bargain town radios. The fact that they are of limited range can also be put to good use. That means that the signals that you do transmit won't make it far, and you have far less problems with "skip" from a long distance interfereing with your local communications.

Options that require a license

GMRS (business band)
GMRS is very similar to FRS as they are easy to obtain. They operate on a different band, and most commonly employed by businesses. They are usually handheld in nature, but you can also get base stations. They use more power,have a 5 mile range, and may employ repeaters if you are subscribed to one of the commercial ones. You are required to have a license, but there are many operators that do not get the license ($70 fee), and operate anyway. According to reports you are not bothered unless you interfere with a business user who will report the problem to the FCC.

Ham Radio (HF VHF UHF)
Operation in this range requires an FCC license, which is easy to obtain, and basically costs nothing beyond the testing. They are monitored by the FCC, but mostly by the ham radio operators themselves.

HF
This is long what has been thought of as where ham radio operator reside, and to an extent that is true. The areas where you can operate start just above the AM radio (160 meters or 1.8MHz) section and continue to just above the CB band in what is known as 10 meters (28 to 30MHz). Each part of this section has it's own abilities and detractions. The higher you go in frequency, the more it tends to be only available during the day, and the lower in frequency the more available during the night (for long range communications). Of course you can reverse that for short comms and security. The best all around, and most used segment, is that of 20 meters or 14MHz. You will notice that it falls in the middle of this section. These bands, given that you use the correct band, mode of communication, antennas and such, will give you comms around the world, somtimes with very little power. I have a small home built radio, that uses morse code, operates on a small battery pack, and is able to communicate over a very long distance (thousands of miles). It's power output is less than what would be used to power a maglight. Most units here are of the base station type, although mobiles are common. Most units manufactured in the last 20 years or so operate on 12v which makes our job much easier. My current radio, at full power of 100 watts, needs 20 amps at 12 volts to function, so you must plan accordingly. You can also build very simple, portable radios such as those described above that can do a very good job.

VHF and UHF
These bands are very popular, and is the easiest to get licensed for. All that is required is some basic electronic theory and regulations. Average study time is about 8 hours, so can easily be done in a week. There is no code requirement.

VHF
This band goes from 50MHz to approximately 220MHz. The relevant parts for us is the 6M (50MHz), 2M (144MHZ), and 220MHz portions. There are a lot of government use of this band, especially around the 50MHz portion. For years the darling of this has been 2 meters for mobile and handheld use. That has begun to change in recent years with the addition of good cheap radios for the 6 meter portion of the band.

50MHz or 6 meters
Long considered the best of the VHF bands, there are a lot of government use of the surrounding frequencies, including the military. This band has good range, even for a handheld radio, and due to increasing popularity, an increase in the types of radios that you can get for a very resonable price. Since this band is very close to the HF range, it does experience some 'skip' due to atmospheric and sunspot conditions, so range will vary accordingly. Handheld units are typically 5 watts, and range out to 30 or more miles. A mobile unit at 25 watts and a good antenna can range out to the hundreds of miles. This is currently seeing lots of activity within the patriot community due to this fact, and the fact that it is widely used by the military. Hence it is becoming a standard capability to posess. Base station and mobile radios can be bought that will operate using all the available modes (AM, FM, CW, SSB, DATA).

144MHz or 2 meters
Base station and mobile radios can be bought that will operate using all the available modes (AM, FM, CW, SSB, DATA). Range for handhelds is around 15 miles, less depending on terrain, mobiles have about 25 to 60 miles depending on the power of the unit. A good antenna, as elsewhere, really helps your range. Most radiowaves here are vertical, but a handheld beam can be used both ways. Since this is a popular ham radio band, and has been for quite some time, there are lots of repeaters to extend your range, and most have

some backup capability (at least for a while anyway). Equipment is common on the used market as well.

220MHz
Not a lot of use on this band, and hence not a lot of equipment to choose from. Range falls between 2 meters and 440MHz.

UHF
This band is primarily in use by amateurs in the 440MHz portion. This is also where the FRS and GMRS users reside (just above). Less users, and less crowded, this is a good band for limited range commnuications, and mobile, base station, and handheld units can be bought, some at a very resonable price. The primary users are handheld or mobiles to repeaters, although this is where sattelite use really comes into play. Handheld radios typically can output 5 watts, and depending on terrain have a range to about 10 miles. Base station and mobile radios can be bought that will operate using all the available modes (AM, FM, CW, SSB, DATA).

Beyond
There are frequencies beyond the UHF spectrum that go will into the microwave region (above 1GHz). They are very useful for point to point communications, but usually it is line of sight. This range is affected by such things as rain. It is not uncommon to use transverters to gain access to this band, which will allow the use of your better equipped VHF or UHF station (the signal is converted up and down). You can get handhelds and mobiles for this band, but you are limited.

Equipment Options

There are several different types of radio selections, and the line is blurred with the newer electronics. Some of the mobile radios will boast features that were not long ago only available to base station type radios.

Base Stations
These usually have more features, better filtering (audio and signal), but are large and require a substantial amount of power to run. Older, but very good radio's can be had on the used market for a resonable price. Normally found for the HF spectrum, they can also be found for VHF and UHF.

Handhelds
These are just what you think. Generally low power, and lacking base station features. But, they are readily portable, which is nice when you want to pack it around all day.

Portable (mobiles)
These have less power than base stations (usually), but more than handhelds. They are larger than what a handheld would be, but can get you a host of features above a handheld. Depending on the frequency, this option can cost you some in weight and space, but give you a lot more operational range. Of course you will have to lug around bigger batteries.

Antennas
Antennas come in three basic configurations: vertical, dipole, and beam. There are literally many variations of these antennas, but that is beyond what is required knowledge at this time. There are some very good books written on the subject, including design theory, or just how to build them with dimensions and such.

Vertical
These antennas are what people are most familiar with. Car radio antennas, CB antennas, your handheld radio, cellular phones. They can be very tall, or short, depending on the frequency range. Easy to deploy, but cumbersome due to materials. Generally good antennas for use in the VHF and UHF bands, but quite large for HF work. There are ones on the market for HF that will work quite well. Usually will provide some signal gain.

Dipole
These are usually made of wire, and strung between to vertical points (trees, houses, etc...). Easy to make, can be concealed, lightweight if needed, and normally used on HF, but could be used on VHF and above. Most will provide no signal gain, and in fact a dipole is used as a zero refernce. For portability these are an excellent choice on HF and 6 meters. There are some models of wire antennas that can provide gain, but they add weight, are not easy to make, and are easier to see. This is the type of antenna that I primarily use for HF.

Beam

These are usually made out of tubing, and put on top of a tower (like a TV antenna). They provide gain, and can be used on all bands, but the lower HF portion can be quite large and use tricks to electrically make them larger. For VHF use, they can be quite small and portable. For this band they are also a very good choice since you can get a good boost by using them.

Modes of Communication

AM

This is the mode that standard CB uses, and some ham activity. This mode uses more energy for a given amount of output power. AM uses a continuous carrier that is modulated by voice. If you want to conserve power, and get distance, this is not the mode to use.

SSB

Single Sideband is the stepchild of AM. What SSB does is eliminate the continuous carrier, and then output one of the modulated sidebands (hence the term Lower Sideband (LSB) and Upper Sideband (USB)). What that means is that it uses less power, and gives you a greater range. This is what most form of HF communications utilizes for voice, as well as some CB's that have the capability.

CW

Continuous Wave is best known as Morse Code. This is sending a carrier wave in bursts, long and short. The familiar dit dah's that you hear. It is fairly easy to learn, uses very little power, easy to build transmitters and receivers, and can go for a very long distance. It is also easier to understand if there is a lot of atmosphereic noise, far greater than that of SSB.

FM

Frequency Modulation is similar to AM, but uses a different method of sending and interpreting the signal. This mode is most common on the FRS, GMRS, handheld and mobile radios for ham use. Again it uses more power, and will not get a signal as far, but when you do get a signal, it will tend to be very clear.

DATA

Sending data via a radio is very similar to using your modem to connect to the internet. The method of communication may use SSB or FM, but then delves very deep from there as to how the communication is sent and received. Depending on the mode used, this can go quite a distance, but is generally about the same as voice.

Satellite

Similar to using a repeater situated on a mountain or building, you are using a sattelite to repeat your signal within the path that it can 'see'. So, you have to be able to get into it, and also the person that you are trying to contact. There are also store and forward types, that would be similar to a bulletin board, or email. This can use some sophisticated equipment depending on which one you are trying to use, but can be done with a dual band handheld unit. Generally the use of FM (which handhelds use) is discouraged due to the bandwidth of the signal, and how much power is used by the sattelite to bring the signal back to earth.

Powering your Radio Setup

Oh, the choices that you can have. Depending on how much power is required by your setup, and whether you want it to be portable, luggable, or need a forklift and commercial power is up to you. For portability the gel cell reigns king. They are usually inexpensive, and provide a good power to weight ratio. Most of the batteries that you would need can be found on the used market. Such places as phone switching equipment swap out there batteries long before they are worn out. Don't overlook a good marine battery either. You can use regular automotive batteries but they will not last nearly as long since they are not designed for deep discharge cycles. I also prefer batteries that are sealed, but that does not limit what I could use. To charge, you can make your own chargers, buy commercail ones, or setup some solar panels and control unit. While solar panels are not quite there in portability, they have come a long way in the last decade.

-bidah
http://www.survivalfiles.info

Basics of 2-Way RadioCommunications

Why?

2-way radios provide the opportunity to relay information about a tactical situation, maintain contact with others in your group, and to whatever extent might be possible, maintain contact with the outside world. They are the life-blood of every major operational vocation in the world. Construction workers, taxi drivers, police, firefighters, aviation, hospitals, and, of course, our military would be nearly useless without the constant use of 2-way radios.

Most preparedness experts will tell you to focus on things that don't require long-term power to sustain. Any power you can find (batteries) or produce (via generators / fuel) will be extraordinarily valuable, thus anything that requires electricity should rank towards the top of your essentials list. With this in mind, it's no surprise that communications equipment (2-way radios) remain among the few items most are willing to consider "essential enough" to justify storing or creating electricity.

What are my options?

Similar to firearms, there's no such thing as a single solution to every problem. Issues to consider when selecting a framework for your communications:

1) **Cost:** You'll find the price of each solution varies widely, and, in general, you get what you pay for when it comes to communications equipment. You can spend as little as a few dollars (FRS / GMRS radios) to tens of thousands of dollars (high-end ham equipment), and everything in between.

2) **Ease of Use:** How much training and experience do you need to successfully operate the equipment? Most people equate 2-way radios with "turn it on and press the talk button", which is definitely true in the case of simpler, shorter-range systems (such as FRS). However, as you expand into more complex radio systems, you may find that simply "having the radio" isn't enough. Sometimes years of training and experience are required to really operate high-end gear.

3) **Quiet and Privacy:** When you turn on your radio, what is the likelihood that you will be sharing your frequencies with others? What is the likeliehood that someone else can eavesdrop? Without spending hundreds of thousands in communications infrastructure, assume there's no such thing as a private conversation and decide how important it is to you that you be able to find a clear frequency at ANY time.

4) **Range:** As you're likely already well aware, the "range" printed on the brochure for most radios is not only inaccurate, it's often comical. Know that with distance comes trade-offs. The less distance you need, the less you'll have ti spend, and the smaller the equipment, antennas, and power requirements.

5) **Legality:** While certainly in a grue apocalyptic scenario, we all assume the laws will be open to a little more interpretation than they are right now, many like to take into account the legal use of their equipment when considering where to invest. The reality is that very few methods of communications are legally open to the public for general use. Most are either strictly forbidden for non-official use (such as aviation), and others require some sort of license (ham radio and GMRS). Note that just because something requires a license doesn't mean you shouldn't use it – just that you should take this into account when making your decisions.

	Cost	Ease of Use	Quiet / Private	Range (Normal Conditions / Equipment)	Legal to Use
CB	$	★★★★★	★	★★	Yes
Ham	$$$$	★	★★★	★★★★★	Licensed
FRS	$	★★★★	★★	★	Yes
GMRS	$	★★★★	★★	★★	Licensed
MARS	$$$	★★	★★★	★★★	No
Marine	$$	★★★★	★★★★	★★★	No
Aviation	$$$	★★★	★★★	★★★	No
Commercial	$$	★★★★	★★★	★★	No

Other Features You Should Consider

1) Is it water-proof? (Many high-end radios are – and most marine radios definitely are).
2) Is it dust and mud proof?
3) Can I attach a hands-free headset to the radio so that it can be used in tactical situations?
4) How long will the batteries last?
5) Can I set the radio to vibrate, instead of make noise, if someone is trying to call me?
6) Can I use it with the power sources I'm already investing in? (e.g. AA batteries, 12V DC Solar Panels, etc.)
7) Do I need a fixed-station setup for longer range? If so, do I have room for the antenna it's going to require?
8) Is my radio gear going to be compatible with others in my group? (e.g. can you talk to each other?)
9) Is the radio easy to use / program? Can I teach everyone in my group how to program their radios?
10) Can the keypad be "locked" to prevent it from being bumped off channel?

You may want to consider creating a reference card for your various radios. Each reference card should detail exactly how to program the radio, what each button and menu-item is for, and any specific communications procedures for your group.

Reference Cards

With the exception of FRS, every type of 2-way radio discussed in this list comes in two different varieties (Mobile, and Hand-Held). I mention that FRS is an exception only because under current FCC regulations, FRS radios are required to be hand-held. (Walkie-talkie style).

In each scenario, keep in mind that the handheld radios can talk to the mobile radios, and vice versa. Also keep in mind that the mobile radios don't necessarily need to be installed in a vehicle. As long as you've got a power source and a properly installed antenna, they can be used anywhere. Many use them as fixed "base station" radios. You'll see from the chart below that if you want any amount of range, you'll need a real mobile radio. However, you can't beat the flexibility of a hand-held.

If you purchase hand-held (walkie-talkie) style radios, it's best to find radios that allow you to operate off standard AA batteries if needed. Many radios will do this out of the box, or allow you to purchase a separate "tray adapter" that lets you remove a pre-installed NiMH pack, and use straight AA batteries instead. This is ESSENTIAL to making sure you can continue to power your radios, even in unforeseen circumstances. (NiMH packs have a limited life, whereas AA batteries are easily replaced and easily found). Also note that NiMH packs will slowly discharge over time. So if you rely solely on the NiMH packs to power your gear, you may find that all of your batteries are dead when you need them. If you go with AA batteries, DO NOT store them inside the radio. They will also be dead when you need them, and they may even corrode over time, damaging the radio itself.

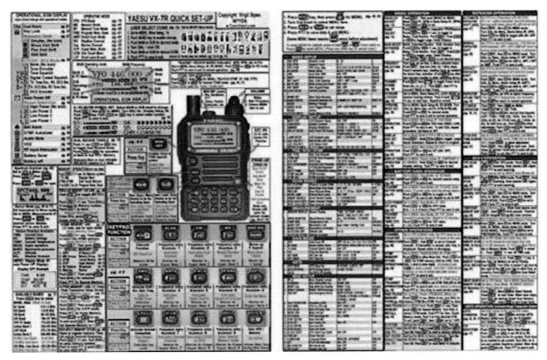

Sample Reference Card for a Yaesu VX-7R Ham Radio
Mobile vs. Fixed vs. Hand-Held

Ham Radio: Is it worth it?

If you're serious about high-end communications, the answer is "probably". Getting involved in ham radio will teach you how to build highly-efficient antennas, basic electronics and troubleshooting, RF safety, good operating techniques, and even give you a chance to experiment with other potentially useful communications methods, such as morse code, computer/digital, satellite communications, shortwave, and more.

The down-side to ham radio is that the equipment is extremely complex. You will not (and let me make this absolutely, 100% clear), you will NOT simply pull a ham radio out of the box, turn it on, and start using it. It takes a few weeks to master the basics, and years to become truly proficient. These radios often have thousands of features, require detailed programming, and complex antenna configurations. The likelihood of damaging your equipment (or hurting someone) is also relatively high if you don't understand the science behind it. Too many people get their ham license, buy a radio, and tuck it in their go-bag, never to think about it again. I can safely say they're in for a nasty awakening if it ever comes time to use that radio.

If you have the time and the desire to really invest into ham radio (e.g. you have an interest in electronics, radios, engineering, etc.) then you'll find great return on your investment in terms of being prepared to communicate in a difficult situation. However, if you lack the desire to really get started in "another hobby", I would strongly recommend that you pick an alternative form of communications. (Seriously consider Marine and/or GMRS).

Stake Emergency Communications QuickTalk Kit

This plan provides "continuity of communications" during a time of disaster in the Stake. The plan provides for a stake-wide communications network wherein bishops can communicate with each other, and directly with the Stake President. This plan will be implemented when normal communications are down, and is designed to allow Bishop's to communicate the needs of their wards to the Stake, and allows the Stake President to communicate instructions to bishops and coordinate response efforts.

The plan will be activated during and following: any major disaster which results in the loss of normal communications (cell phones, telephones, etc.) and the welfare of stake and ward members is threatened. Examples of such a scenario include earthquakes, tornados, floods, fires, and other such scenarios. If you are unable to communicate using normal methods, and you believe members of your ward may have special needs that threaten life or property, or you believe members of your ward may be able to lend assistance to others, please consider the plan "activated".

Getting Started

1. Open your QuickTalk kit,
2. Install the 4 Lithium AA batteries
3. Turn your radio to channel 18, privacy code 18.
4. Check in with the Stake President.

Your radio should be pre-programmed to 18 / 18 when you turn it on. If not, see reverse side for instructions.

All Bishops, the Stake President, and the Stake Emergency Communications Specialist will be communicating on the Stake Channel

We use Channel 18, Privacy Code 18
This is 462.6250 MHz PL 123.0

Do not share channel / contact information with ward members. It's very important that only one representative that only one representative from each ward (the bishop) be communicating on this channel.

Communication Tips

1. All transmissions should be as short as necessary to communicate the information. "Chatter" makes things difficult for everyone.

2. Do not use ten-codes (10-4, 10-20, etc.). Speak in plain English so that everyone listening clearly understands you.

3. End each transmission with the word "Over". It seems silly, but this really helps to eliminate double-up (when two stations attempt to talk at the same time).

4. When calling another person, state your name, and then state the name of the person you are calling. (Example: "This is Bishop Jones calling President Smith").

5. When replying to a call, state your name, and the person who called you. (Example: "This is President Smith. Go ahead Bishop Jones.").

6. Your radio should be carried with you and turned on at all times during an emergency.

Roles and Responsibilities

Bishops: Your job is to establish and maintain communications with the Stake Emergency Communications Specialist and/or the Stake President to communicate the emergency welfare needs of your ward and report on available resources (both people and items). You should implement and manage your intra-ward emergency communications plan to help accomplish this goal.

Stake Emergency Communications Specialist:
You will work under the direction of the Stake President to act as the hub of stake-wide communications, providing a station capable of operating over a long period of time and over long distances without the need for grid power. You will manage the intra-stake communications as well as communications to the Bishops Storehouse or directly to church headquarters as required.

Stake President and Stake Leaders: Your immediate priority is to establish the emergency welfare requirements of the individual wards and determine what requests need to be escalated to the Bishop's Storehouse, versus what needs can be fulfilled locally. In addition, you will also work to understand what resources (people and items) are available in each ward in order to quickly respond to situations as they are made known.

Additional Tips

1. Keep in mind that your Lithium AA batteries will not last forever. As quickly as prudent, locate spare batteries.

2. Your radio will work better outside and away from large buildings or structures. If you are having trouble communicating, find an open area and try again.

3. Avoid changing any settings on your radio. You risk changing something that will cause the radio to stop working properly.

4. Use your existing priesthood hierarchy to determine welfare needs and resource availability. Use the Aaronic priesthood to deliver and collect information.

5. If you have problems with your radio, contact the Stake President immediately (using a runner, if necessary). Spare radios might be available.

Please store this kit in a cool, dry area that will be accessible in the event of a disaster.
Do not install or open the batteries until needed

Additional Help and Instructions (Side 2)

- Battery Level
- High Power (H = 5 watts)
- Headphone Connector
- Privacy Code
- Channel
- On/Off/Volume
- Push to Talk
- Lock Button (Hold for 4 seconds to lock keypad / prevent accidentally changing settings)

Setting the Channel

Your radio should be pre-programmed for channel 18, privacy code 18. If not, follow these instructions to set the channel.

1. Turn the radio off and back on. This will reset the radio back to the main screen.
2. Unlock the radio (if locked) by holding down the "Call/Lock" button for 4 seconds (until the "lock" icon disappears from the screen). Repeat to lock / unlock the radio.
3. Once unlocked, press the "MENU" button ONE time. The large number will begin flashing (this is the channel).
4. Set the channel to "18" by pressing the up or down arrow keys.
5. Press the menu button TWO MORE TIMES until "18" is on the screen and the word "oF" is flashing.
6. Press the UP arrow until the screen reads "ctcss / ct", then press MENU again.
7. Push the up/down arrows until the small number reads "18". This is the privacy code.
8. Press MENU 9 more times until you reach the home screen again.
9. Lock the radio to prevent bumping it off channel (See Step 2).

Please store this kit in a cool, dry area that will be accessible in the event of a disaster.
Do not install or open the batteries until needed

Survival Communications Primer

By Vector_Joe

Ver. 3.0

22-June 2007

This FAQ, wiki or primer is a compilation of information gathered on various internet websites as well as FCC and ARRL sources. Subjective opinions are included in this document. Inspirations or ideas have also been taken from **AR-Jedi**, **Scoutmaster**, and **GySgtD** and others without their permission (screen names from various forums are used to protect privacy). While a lot of information here is ham related, almost all of it can be applied or applies to non-ham radio systems.

One thing I have to mention here. We are not trying to be or sound like ham radio snobs. We highly suggest a diversity in communications systems. I personally have computers, internet, landlines, cell phones, frs/gmrs radios as well as amateur radio equipment. The key is to understand how each works and the limitations of the equipment.

Why do I need comms?

Well, unless you want to be a hermit during an emergency situation, you need at least some sort of rudimentary communication system. At the very least some sort of receiver system is necessary. Depending on the situation, you may need information on how to take shelter (inclement weather), how to leave an area (terrorist, chemical spill, etc.) or many other considerations.

Your options are basically one way or two way comms. One way consists of am/fm radio, television, shortwave radio, internet websites and other radio services, etc. Two way comms consists of am/fm/ssb/cw/digital radio on ham bands and other radio services, cell phones, satellite phones, internet email and instant messaging, etc.

If you follow the rule of 3's, then you should have at least 3 methods of distance communications (not including yelling across the road or 2 cans on a string).

Do I need 2 way comms?

That is a bit subjective depending on your situation. However, it is highly recommended. Needed for communication with friends and family in a disaster situation where you are not together. Needed to call for help. Needed to ask for specific information from others who may have information.

Considerations when using the transmit (tx) part of 2 way comms.

There are a couple of considerations one should consider when transmitting. In general, all things being equal, more power equals more range. But there are many reasons why one should limit the power of transmissions. The general rule is to use the MINIMUM power required to communicate. For one, this reduces airwave pollution. If you are talking on your radio, you don't want some other radio operator talking over your conversation booming out 1000's of watts of power for no reason. Second, especially in emergency situations, minimum power means longer battery life. Another consideration is that when communicating, you may not want 'everyone' to hear what you are saying, particularly in an emergency situation. By using the minimum power, you will limit the number of 'ears' that can hear your comms.

A second consideration when transmitting is the *reason* and *to whom* you are transmitting. This generally falls into 2 categories in emergency/survival situations.
1) Calling for help. In this situation, you need to transmit with enough power so that 'aid' can year your call but low enough that you can conserve your battery for extended use. Perhaps you will need to guide any aid to your location, that would require using the radio for enough time for help to arrive. In this situation, where lives are on the line, using any method of wireless communication with any equipment is allowed.
2) Calling within your group. You may need to communicate with your group after some sort of disaster or emergency situation where the communications are not dealing with life and death. In this case, in general, you want to keep your power low. Also, as long as there is some sort of governmental entity, you will probably want to stay within the legal limits of your radio equipment. The FCC uses a system of 'Type Acceptance' where specific equipment is authorized for use with specific bands of air spectrum. This basically means that for most bands, you need a radio that is qualified for use on those frequencies. In general, amateur radio equipment is not type accepted for any of the services. You also, for example, would not be able to use a radio that is type accepted for the AIR band on the Marine band frequencies (unless the radio happens to be type accepted for both- I don't know if they exist) NOTE: For use on amateur radio bands, there is no type accepted equipment. You can build or modify any equipment and use it on the ham bands as long as you follow the other ham regulations in terms of operation.

Background on wireless communications and the FCC (thanks Jim –ARJedi)

This part is excerpted from a thread by AR-Jedi.
Also, most of the text can be downloaded from http://cynthion.com/tacoma.txt

The usable-for-communications electromagnetic spectrum spans a frequency range from about 100 KHz to 100GHz. (aside, only a portion of that is usable by inexpensive equipment). In the USA, the federal communications commission (FCC) is responsible for administering the spectrum for US users; however, the FCC works closely on this with international bodies, for reasons which will soon become clear. The "administering" that the FCC performs includes dictating what frequency bands are to be used for what purposes, and also specifying operational requirements for those bands (e.g. TX power output, ERP, modulation type, etc).

Since examples are worth thousands of words, I'll provide a few. 1) The FCC has decided that broadcast FM stations are to exist in the 88MHz to 108MHz range. There are certainly power limits however I've no idea at hand what they are. 2) The FCC has decided that CB exists at around 27MHz, and that the maximum TX power output is 4W. 3) The FCC has decided that FRS exists around 462/467MHz, with a maximum ERP specified. And for the last example, 4) ham (amateur radio) has a number of bands allocated, each with associated limitations on power/modulation etc. I could go on and on with cell phones, marine radios, garage door openers, key fobs, microwave towers, etc etc etc. basically, if the device is what is referred to by the FCC as an "intentional radiator", they have an assigned slot (band) for it and constraints on it's operation.

Why the constraints? Well, one reason is for your physiological protection. High RF power can cause burns, blindness, and other problems. (The "invention" of the microwave oven was an accident -- technicians working on early radar antennas were developing burns when the units were powered). Another reason for the constraints is public safety. The last thing a 747 pilot on emergency approach into Kennedy airport needs is crosstalk with taxi dispatchers in NYC. Hence the wide berth the FCC gives around police, fire, and EMS frequencies.

Now then, we see that the FCC regulates intentional radiator use by dividing the frequency spectrum into bands, and then sets characteristics for each of those bands that users must obey by.

A common question is, "is one frequency band 'better' than another"? The answer is "sometimes". For certain applications (more on this in a moment), a given frequency band may provide better range, fidelity, immunity to interference, and so forth. These factors, and others, that make a frequency usable for a given application were taken into consideration when the spectrum was allocated.

It is important to note here that transmitter power output is one of many, many factors that influence the range at which you can communicate over a given transmission path. While important, transmitter power output plays only one role in a multi-faceted problem. Antenna gain, antenna polarization, modulation type, receiver sensitivity, background noise level, path loss, and a dozen other issues factor into the equation. Show me a well designed 2W transmitter and I will show you a way to communicate ~6.5 billion miles. NASA does this every day with their Voyager 1 & 2 probes -- they are now twice as far away as Pluto. ......Much more in the links above.

Should I get my ham (amateur radio operator) license?

I think this is sort of a no brainer and there is a general consensus that everyone who is serious about being prepared for emergencies should get their ham license. I can see maybe 2 'legitimate' reasons why not to get licensed, but I would discount them both.

One is that no one else you know is licensed. I discount this 'reason' because once you get on the air you will meet many other people and many will have the same attitude about being prepared as you and I. Also, once you get into communications, you *may* be able to get other friends or family interested.

The other 'reason' that I can image that may hold some water is that you don't want to get on another government list. Well, you are probably on so many government lists, one more isn't going to make a difference. I think (IMO) that this is a bit on the too paranoid side, but I don't like to judge people.

Even if you decided that ham radio is not for you, I suggest you read over the next few sections to get a better understanding of frequencies/bands/modes and equipment. Starting with about page 8, we start discussing other non-ham specifics.

How do I get a license?

Go to http://www.ARRL.org to get much more general information about getting licensed to operate as a ham. On that site is listed the local radio clubs in your area. It also lists the times and locations for taking the FCC exams http://www.arrl.org/arrlvec/examsearch.phtml . The exams are given by other hams that have been certified to give the exams. There are four (4) testing elements.

Element 1 is a 5 word per minute Morse code exam. As far as I know, this is no longer adminstered and is no longer a requirement for any of the license classifications.

Element 2 is the technician level exam. It is 35 questions with some basic electronics theory, radio safety and some FCC operator's rules.

Element 3 is the general class exam. It is also 35 questions. The content is similar to the technician exam except that it requires a bit more in depth knowledge. The question pools are different.

Element 4 is the final exam and is used to get your extra class license. It is 50 questions long with very in depth knowledge required about different operating modes, techniques, theory, safety and rules.

<u>To be licensed as an amateur radio operator, you must take and pass a minimum of element 2.</u>

When you go into a testing session, you can take as many of the four tests as you want for the single session fee of $14.00. However, if you want to retake any tests that you fail, you need to pay the $14.00 again.

As for studying, the technician license is fairly simple. This site has several free resources to study elements 1, 2 and 3: http://www.frrl.org/education/ . Here is a link to the July 1, 2006 element 2 test question pool: http://www.ncvec.org/downloads/2006tech.pdf.

As for the General and Extra exams, I personally suggest the ARRL 'License Manuals'. See here: http://www.arrl.org/catalog/lm/ . There are also Q&A books available, however, they seem to be just covering the question pools (which are available for free on the internet) rather than actually covering the complete theory behind the operating modes and rules.

Also, go here http://www.qrz.com/p/testing.pl to take practice tests (elements 2, 3 and/or 4).

If you want to learn Morse code, *and I suggest you do*, you can download one of the many freeware programs that generate random letters at specified speeds. They also generate regular words and full conversations (QSOs). Here is the one I like:
http://www.g4fon.net/CW%20Trainer.htm
Note: I personally am still working on learning it because it is a great thing to know...

What is with the different license classes and bands?

For hams, there are basically 4 bands, HF (high frequency), VHF (very hf), UHF (ultra hf), and microwave. At this point microwave is mainly for experimental communications, so you will not see a lot of emergency communications on these frequencies.

Jim- what does 2M mean? Why is it seemingly used interchangeably with 146MHz?

Hams simultaneously use one of two terms to describe the band they are discussing: frequency or wavelength. The two are related by a constant known as C, the speed of light. It turns out that after you crunch the numbers, you can easily convert between the two terms using the following rule of thumb...

300/freq in MHz = wavelength in meters
Or the same rule but turned around,
300/wavelength in meters = freq in MHz

Hence:
300/146MHz ~= 2 meters

And now you see why 146MHz and 2M are used interchangeably.

Similarly, some wavelength to frequency conversions for other popular HF and
VHF/UHF ham bands...

40M	--> 300/40	~=	7.5MHz
20M	--> 300/20	~=	15MHz
10M	--> 300/10	~=	30MHz
6M	--> 300/6	~=	50MHz
1.25M	--> 300/1.25	~=	220MHz
70cm	--> 300/0.70	~=	440MHz

HF is the region of the electromagnetic spectrum that goes from about 30MHz and lower frequencies. VHF goes from 30 to 300 MHz and UHF goes from 300 MHz up to the bottom of the microwave range.

VHF and UHF are basically line of sight methods of communications (not counting sporadic-e, grey line, aurora, meteor scatter, eme and other less than common propagation methods). So if your antenna can 'see' the antenna you want to talk to then you should be good to go. UHF and VHF make extensive use of repeaters which are radios which are usually connected to antennas in highly elevated positions. These repeater radios receive on one frequency and transmit simultaneously on another frequency. This allows a user to transmit and his antenna can see the repeater antenna because of its elevated position. Also the retransmitted signal is sent from an elevated position so that it has a much broader range. A repeaters range can be up in the 10's of miles (30, 40, 50 or more). Typical handheld transmitters (HT), which usually max at about 5-6 watts of power, can maybe get 5 miles depending on the terrain without using a repeater.

HF on the other hand is suited for medium to long range communications. HF frequencies (depending on the season, time of day, and solar activity) will bounce off the upper atmosphere. So a signal from your location may go up, bounce off the ionosphere and come back down several hundred or thousand miles away. Communications between the North America and Europe, Asia, Antarctica, pretty much anywhere, is possible and happens all the time. You can set up your antenna system to send your main signal toward the horizon to try and get the furthest contacts, or you can point your signal mostly straight up (NVIS-Near Vertical Incident Skywave) and get the signal to bounce back down relatively near your location to get communications within 40-600 miles.

During emergencies such as tornados, earthquakes, flooding,etc. 80-95% of emergency communications will take place at the local level with VHF/UHF frequencies. There will probably be less use by volume of HF because of the nature of the operations. This will vary of course depending on the situation. In a more regional disaster such as a hurricane or the SE Asian tsunami, the use of HF may be a greater percentage as communication over greater distances and into and out of the affected area will be needed.

More from Jim- first, I hate to break this to you, but THE EARTH IS ROUND. No, I'm not kidding -- it really is spherical despite what they told you in school or at church. Ok, now that you are past that, you should visualize in your head that radio waves travel in a straight line. Since the earth curves, it is not possible to talk over distances of over about 20 miles without "help". this "help" can come in a multitude of ways, and is somewhat dependent on the height of the transmitter and receiver, the gain of their respective antennae, the frequency of transmission, the weather and other atmospheric conditions, the sun cycle, hams around you erecting things called repeaters, and a few dozen other things. Nevertheless, the key point here is that the further you are away from each other, the more likely it is that the curvature of the earth is going to be the limiting factor. Always remember that without "help", radio communications are "line of sight".

HF, or high frequency (roughly defined as everything below about 30MHz [10 meters wavelength]) signals can bounce off of a charged belt (called the ionosphere) which completely envelopes the earth. HF thus can communicate over long distances by using one or more "bounces" -- you may have heard the CB term "skip". With just a few dozen watts, and a proper antenna, it's possible for you to talk (or more likely communicate using mores) with a station 2000 miles away. Interestingly, it is sometimes difficult to talk to nearby stations that are "under the skip", that is they are too close to you to hear the reflected wave. One primary disadvantage of HF communications is that the antenna has to be physically long. Nevertheless, HF can be a valuable asset in emergency communications -- like it was during hurricane Katrina when everything else was tits up. In general, when you think of HF you should think of long distance comms. With some exceptions, most HF rigs are designed for desktop use and the supporting equipment (power supplies, antenna tuner, etc) is heavy and not so portable. But there is a class of mobile and low power HF rigs which allow you to talk over great distances with just a few pounds of equipment. ...

... the primary limitation of VHF/UHF is the short range imposed by the curvature of the earth combined with the fact that VHF/UHF signals do not bounce off of the ionosphere (in case you were wondering, they pass right through it). Of course it helps greatly with VHF/UHF to be up as high as possible, as this gives more "line of sight" distance -- the same way you can see much farther when atop a tall building. But that's not always practical. e.g., I live right at sea level -- no kidding. How can I, the low lying ham, communicate with any distance using VHF or UHF? Am I stuck trying to use HF for comms more than a few miles?

Enter the "repeater". Simply put, a repeater is an unattended radio advantageously located on a hill or with the antenna high up on a tower. The purpose of the repeater is to retransmit your signal in real time. It does this by listening on one frequency, called the input, and simultaneously transmitting the input audio on a second frequency, called the output. Accordingly, my radio would be set to transmit on the repeater's input frequency, and listen on the repeater's output frequency. (The difference is known as the "offset".) All that is required from a radio implementation standpoint is a little bit of frequency agility -- when you press the transmit button, your radio tunes it's transmitter to the required new frequency. When you unkey, it changes back. All this happens in milliseconds and without your involvement save for some initial settings. The beauty of this set up is that with a low power HT (typ, 0.5W to 5W) you can talk for perhaps hundreds of miles! The repeater provides the "help" for VHF and UHF, just like the ionosphere provided the "help" for HF.

There are 3 basic ham licenses and one sort of sub group (at this time). There is Technician, General and Extra. The sub group is this: if you have passed the 5 word per minute Morse code test, then as a Technician, you have some limited access to the HF bands.

A technician license allows the operator to use any UHF or VHF frequency with any mode.

A general licensee is allowed to use almost all of the HF bands (all modes) as well as all of the UHF and VHF. Some small sections of each HF band are reserved for extra and advanced licensees.

An extra class license allows the full use of all amateur bands with all modes.

For the actual US code regulations that govern amateur radio, see http://www.access.gpo.gov/nara/cfr/waisidx_05/47cfr97_05.html which lists 'PART 97-- AMATEUR RADIO SERVICE'.

What are these modes?

Modes are basically the way we modify a signal to carry information. The most common modes that everyone knows about are AM (amplitude modulation) and FM (frequency modulation). Others common modes include SSB, CW, and digital.

SSB is a method of amplitude modulation (AM) where the carrier wave and one of the side bands (there are 2 – upper and lower) is suppressed. This means that the signal you are sending out takes up smaller bandwidth and has higher power (relatively) than a traditional AM signal.

CW is short for continuous wave or the method for sending Morse code. This is the traditional method of communication with a very small bandwidth and is useful when communications conditions are poor.

Digital modes are various and include RTTY (radio teletype), PSK31, PSK63, Hellschreiber, packet modes, sstv, fstv and many others. There are new digital modes being invented everyday. In general these are text based modes that use some sort of computer interface to a radio. This is **not** at all internet based. It is simply a computer interfacing with a radio to send a signal. SSTV and FSTV are video modes with allow the transmission of pictures. There is also D-STAR which is a new digital mode based on the Japanese protocal. It is designed for simplex and repeater use on 2m, 70cm, 1.2 GHz.

There is also a hybrid mode of communication which does interface with the internet. The main types are IRLP, echolink and Wires. These are simply interfaces that allow radio users to send their signals to other users, radios or repeaters in other parts of the world. However, this relies on an internet connection and should not be relied on in emergency situations.

What sort of equipment is available? (just a small sampling)

HT (handi-talkies/handheld transceivers) – available for VHF/UHF, single band/dual band/triband/quad band. Transmit powers range from 300milliwatts (.3 watts) to 6 watts in general. Pros - Extremely portable, light weight, low power consumption, available with extremely wide receive frequencies (to pick up broadcast, shortwave, public service, aircraft and other services). Cons – relatively low transmit power with respect to other types of equipment. Stock rubber duck antennas are generally very poor radiators.

Mobile/Portable rigs – These can be used in an automobile, out in the field or in a backpack or on a bench as a base station. They are smaller an lighter than dedicated base stations, but are usually more suited for emergency communications because they may be more robust and easier to transport in different disaster situations. They may be low power (QRP) with only 5, 10 or 20 watts or up to about 100 watts full power. These are mainly available for HF, HF+ VHF/UHF, VHF only, UHF only or VHF/UHF.

Base stations – These typically have the most features of all radios including digital processing, filters to improve signals as well as other enhancements. Power on these rigs may go up to about 250 watts without the use of an external amplifier. These are mainly available for HF, or HF+ VHF/UHF.

Antenna – Basically the most important part of the radio system is the antenna. Without a good antenna system, your transmitter is just going to heat up the 'antenna' like a resistor.

Antenna length, is inversely proportional to the frequency being transmitted:
CB=	27 MHz
MURS=	151 MHz
GMRS=	462 MHz

So the CB antenna will be longest and the GMRS will be the shortest.

Antennas can come in almost any form and with a good antenna tuner, almost anything can be made to radiate (including a barbed wire fence or your aluminum house gutters). Some of the basic forms are wire dipoles,verticals and beams. Antennas are usually defined by the wavelength at which the antenna is designed to operate. The most basic is a ½ wavelength dipole fed with ladderline or coax at the center. If it is mounted low to the ground it is good for NVIS. Up higher at ¼ wavelength up, then better for DX (distance comms). Another basic form is a ¼ wavelength vertical. This is basically ½ of a ½ wave dipole. It is fed at the end and relies on a reflection from a ground plane or grounding radials. An ht antenna is sometimes a ¼ wave vertical without a good ground plane. Beams are directional antennas which allow the main power from the antenna to be directed in one directions. This lowers the amount of noise coming from other directions and increases the power toward your intended target. Beams can be in the form of a Yagi or a quad or several other types. A promising option (that I haven't tried) for emergency comms is a 'hamstick dipole'. See:
http://www.varaces.org/techrefs/HamstickDipoleFactSheet.pdf

Antenna tuners – these are devices that allow antennas that are not designed for a specified frequency to operate on that frequency. There are automatic and manual and they work by matching the impedance (by altering the capacitance and inductance) of the antenna and feedline to the transceiver.

Repeaters – not something that most hams will 'buy' or build, but may help pay for the upkeep and use of the repeaters. Most are open to use by any licensed ham with priority given to any emergency traffic. Most repeaters are owned and maintained by local ham clubs.

Jim- the disadvantage of repeaters is simple: in order for the repeater to work, you need power and the antenna has to be upright. These are not likely conditions in areas overcome by, for example, a category 4 or 5 hurricane. while tons of lead acid batteries may delay the inevitable, there is a finite amount of no-AC-power operation time for any repeater unless expensive measures have been taken (e.g. a diesel genset and good sized fuel tank, as you would find mounted behind a police station). Nevertheless, hams are resourceful people and generally fixing the repeaters is an immediate priority in disaster areas. Moreover, all the equipment necessary for a repeater can be carried in the back of a Tacoma, with room to spare. So if a makeshift antenna can be erected on the mountainside, a substitute repeater can be up and running in a few hours to replace the one crushed by the flying oak tree.

One way to look at a ham repeater is as an analog of a cell site. Having many cell sites make it possible for your low power cell phone to communicate anywhere the global phone network reaches. Similarly, hams link repeaters using point-to-point RF, the phone network, or these days using the internet. all of these methods allow greater "reach" from your low power HT. with the exception of point-to-point RF, the other methods require public infrastructure that may or may not be available when the SHTF.

Where do I get specific information about equipment?

Go to http://www.eham.net/reviews/ (ham as well as some commercial) and look there for reviews.
For details on the specifications of each rig, you can go to the manufacturers' websites. The 4 main UHF/VHF ham equipment manufacturers are Alinco, Icom, Kenwood and Yaesu. For HF, there are also many other manufacturers including Tentec, Elecraft, Hallicrafters, Heath, Drake, SGC and others. For commercial, some of the above as well as Motorola and Uniden.

For pictures and other information, you can try: http://www.rigpix.com/

What about power off the grid?

Most modern rigs run off of 12v dc power (13.8v really). So these can be run off of car batteries, gel cells, or ac-dc power supplies. The bigger rigs (mobile or base stations) should have a power supply that gives 20-25 amps continuous current. You could also run off of a generator, but this would also generally require an ac-dc power supply as well. You should have a way to recharge these batteries, so in a real outage situation, you need to be able to get access to 1) a generator, 2) a larger battery or 3) a solar or other charging supply. If you anticipate running off of batteries for an extended amount of time, you should consider using an ht to do most of your monitoring since they consume the least amount of power. See here for more:
http://losdos.dyndns.org:8080/public/ham/RACES-box.html

5, 7, 12 amp-hour sealed lead acid batteries are available at many sources, through the internet or computer electronics stores. At one time radio shack carried them, but I am not sure about their current stocking situation.

Whether I decide to get or not get my license what are my other options?

GMRS, MURS, FRS, Marine band, cell phones, internet, satellite phones.

GMRS requires a $80 license that covers you and all your extended family. It is a set of channelized frequencies in the UHF band utilizing FM, a few hertz above the UHF 440 band. There are GMRS repeater systems, but these are usually private and do no allow public access. They are allowed up to 50 watts and detachable antennae; however these are not common in consumer products. The type of radios you can get at a department or electronics store is typically in the 1-4 watt range with fixed antennas in the form of HT's. Commercial mobile and base stations are available at greater cost.

One issue to consider with GMRS is that it *will* be heavily congested during emergency situations since they are cheap and easy to get and licensing is some/many people don't even bother with. (I advocate getting your gmrs license if you have the radios as it covers the whole family and there is no testing involved.)

Name	Lower Frequency (MHz)	Upper Frequency	Motorola convention
"550"	462.550	467.550	ch 15
"575"	462.575	467.575	ch 16
"600"	462.600	467.600	ch 17
"625"	462.625	467.625	ch 18
"650"	462.650	467.650	ch 19
"675"	462.675	467.675	ch 20
"700"	462.700	467.700	ch 21
"725"	462.725	467.725	ch 22

This second set of frequencies shows the interstitial ranges shared with the FRS. These frequencies can only be used for simplex operations.

Name	Frequency (MHz)	Motorola convention
"5625" or "FRS 1"	462.5625	ch 1
"5875" or "FRS 2"	462.5875	ch 2
"6125" or "FRS 3"	462.6125	ch 3
"6375" or "FRS 4"	462.6375	ch 4
"6625" or "FRS 5"	462.6625	ch 5
"6875" or "FRS 6"	462.6875	ch 6
"7125" or "FRS 7"	462.7125	ch 7

FRS is a UHF citizens band (CB). No license is required. It is in the same range as the GMRS frequencies. FRS radios are limited to 500mW (.5 watts) and cannot have detachable antennae. Repeaters are not available.

```
Channel No.              (MHz)

1.................... 462.5625
2.................... 462.5875
3.................... 462.6125
4.................... 462.6375
5.................... 462.6625
6.................... 462.6875
7.................... 462.7125
8.................... 467.5625
9.................... 467.5875
10................. 467.6125
11................. 467.6375
12................. 467.6625
13................. 467.6875
14................. 467.7125
```

Multi Use Radio Service (MURS) is VHF CB. No license required. There are 5 MURS channels a few hertz above the 144 ham band. Power is limited to 2 watts, but types or gain on antennas are not restricted. Repeater systems are prohibited, and antennas are restricted to 20 feet above the structure or 60 above ground (whichever is greater).

One note to consider is that at the moment, MURS is not a heavily used band. So if you are looking to be able to use the radios with minimal interference, that is a benefit. It also means that if you are trying to reach out to someone for help, there will be less of a chance of anyone being able to respond to you. The frequencies are listed:

151.820 MHz
151.880 MHz
151.940 MHz
154.570 MHz
154.600 MHz

Marine band radios are similar to ham vhf radios. However, (from the FCC) *to operate on land, you must have a special license, called a marine utility station license, to operate a hand-held marine radio from land -- a ship station license IS NOT sufficient. You may apply for this license by filing FCC Form 601 with the FCC. To be eligible for a marine utility station license, you must generally provide some sort of service to ships or have control over a bridge or waterway. Additionally, you must show a need to communicate using hand-held portable equipment from both a ship and from coast locations. Each unit must be capable of operation while being hand-carried by an individual. The station operates under the rules applicable to ship stations when the unit is aboard a ship, and under the rules applicable to private coast stations when the unit is on land.*

Citizens Band (CB) old standby. Popularity and use seems to have fallen to a degree, however there are probably plenty of people still using this band. Power limit is 4w (12w SSB), but you can use external antennae. 27MHz band or 11meter.

Channel	Frequency		Channel	Frequency
Channel 01	26.965 MHz		Channel 21	27.215 MHz
Channel 02	26.975 MHz		Channel 22	27.225 MHz
Channel 03	26.985 MHz		Channel 23	27.255 MHz
Channel 04	27.005 MHz		Channel 24	27.235 MHz
Channel 05	27.015 MHz		Channel 25	27.245 MHz
Channel 06	27.025 MHz		Channel 26	27.265 MHz
Channel 07	27.035 MHz		Channel 27	27.275 MHz
Channel 08	27.055 MHz		Channel 28	27.285 MHz
Channel 09	27.065 MHz *(emergency channel)*		Channel 29	27.295 MHz
Channel 10	27.075 MHz		Channel 30	27.305 MHz
Channel 11	27.085 MHz		Channel 31	27.315 MHz
Channel 12	27.105 MHz		Channel 32	27.325 MHz
Channel 13	27.115 MHz		Channel 33	27.335 MHz
Channel 14	27.125 MHz		Channel 34	27.345 MHz
Channel 15	27.135 MHz		Channel 35	27.355 MHz
Channel 16	27.155 MHz		Channel 36	27.365 MHz
Channel 17	27.165 MHz		Channel 37	27.375 MHz
Channel 18	27.175 MHz		Channel 38	27.385 MHz *(lsb, national calling frequency)*
Channel 19	27.185 MHz *(unofficial trucker's channel)*		Channel 39	27.395 MHz
Channel 20	27.205 MHz		Channel 40	27.405 MHz

Cell phones and Internet. We all know about those. Good during normal times. Possibly unreliable during emergencies.

Cell and Landlines (AR-Jedi): (why is ham better than cell phones?) for two reasons:

1) the POTS (plain old telephone service) phone network is designed around a premise of about 0.16 erlangs, or 6 century call seconds (CCS). this is equivalent to about a 16% "occupancy rate" of the network. not all interLATA nor CO-to-CO trunks can accept this high of a rate however. once these occupancy rates are exceeded, you will just get a "fast busy" tone or a "your call can not be completed" message. in telecommunications circles, this is known as "oversubscription" -- that is, you have more customers than capacity. it is perfectly ok, as not everyone is on the phone at the same time. and if you build your network for 100% of your subscribers, you will be out of money. but when there is huge calling demand, there will be some problems.

2) the various cellular systems are even more oversubscribed; they are designed around a peak occupancy rate of about 5% (2 CCS). note that there is no "standard" number for this; in downtown NYC, a cell network may be engineered for a much higher occupancy; whereas in a farmland area, it will be engineered for a lower occupancy. this is simple economics for the service provider -- more subscriber capacity means more equipment (towers, sector antennas, base station switches, call handoff computers, etc) and more backhaul bandwidth. this translates to increased initial capital and also higher recurring costs (electricity, land/tower leases, etc). from an economic standpoint, the service provider puts "just enough" equipment in place for normal everyday traffic. but when the SHTF, the cell networks are quickly overburdened.

as alluded to in the post above, this is why the cell (and POTS) networks sag during "events". and indeed, here in northern NJ, the phone networks were all but useless for about 24 hours post 9/11. between the massive calling volume and the loss of a major NYC central office, the networks were simply overwhelmed. it was a peak traffic profile that was never engineered for; sort of like putting double the weight onto a container ship and then wondering why it sank.

Satellite phones. High initial cost and high monthly service cost. But can be a good alternative if you have the resources.

TV audio receive:

Channel	MHz	Channel	MHz
2	59.75	36	607.75
3	65.75	37	613.75
4	71.75	38	619.75
5	81.75	39	625.75
6	87.75	40	631.75
7	179.75	41	637.75
8	185.75	42	643.75
9	191.75	43	649.75
10	197.75	44	655.75
11	203.75	45	661.75
12	209.75	46	667.75
13	215.75	47	673.75
14	475.75	48	679.75
15	481.75	49	685.75
16	487.75	50	691.75
17	493.75	51	697.75
18	499.75	52	703.75

19	505.75	53	709.75
20	511.75	54	715.75
21	517.75	55	721.75
22	523.75	56	727.75
23	529.75	57	733.75
24	535.75	58	739.75
25	541.75	59	745.75
26	547.75	60	751.75
27	553.75	61	757.75
28	559.75	62	763.75
29	565.75	63	769.75
30	571.75	64	775.75
31	577.75	65	781.75
32	583.75	66	787.75
33	589.75	67	793.75
34	595.75	68	799.75
35	601.75	69	805.75

Other:

What frequencies should I be listening to?

If you have a scanner or other wideband receive radio, you can program frequencies to be saved. You can certainly program the frs, gmrs, murs and cb frequencies in to monitor them if the radio is capable. However, there are other channels/sources to listen to.

First off, go here or someplace similar:
http://www.radioreference.com/modules.php?name=RR

This is a user maintained database with as many public frequencies as commonly known. It gives the frequencies for police, fire, municipal, county and state agencies. It also lists the type of radio system they use. Program in any that you think might be useful now or for the future. Many modern radios now have several hundred memory slots, so you should be able to get plenty in.

Note: many municipalities, especially the larger ones have or are going to 'trunked' or digital radio systems. This means that the frequency or channel that a specific group is using may jump to another frequency or channel. This is done to make the use of frequencies by a city or agency more efficient. However listening on a simple ham radio is a bit difficult to monitor this. If the system is trunked, and you can find out the list of frequencies that an agency uses, you can still monitor their transmissions, however in some cases, the conversation will switch to another channel. Usually as a listener, you can get the gist of the conversation just by the few seconds that are available. This is not ideal, but it can work. Another option is to listen to the neighboring safety frequencies such as smaller municipalities or county sheriff's. Also, you may be able to find out the interdepartmental 'aid' frequency that allows different departments/cities to talk to each other and call for assistance.

Second, go here or someplace similar:
http://www.artscipub.com/repeaters/

This is a relatively good list of ham repeaters across the US. Even if you are only listening or not even a ham, listening to ham operators will probably keep you well informed during times of emergency. Pay particular attention to any repeaters that are listed as OEM (office of emergency management), EMA (emergency management agency), ARES (amateur radio emergency service), or RACES (radio amateur civil emergency service) affiliated.

Below are some somewhat standardized alphabets in use by emergency services.

	Law Enforcement				NATO/Military/International		
A	Adam	N	Nora	A	Alpha	N	November
B	Boy	O	Ocean	B	Bravo	O	Oscar
C	Charles	P	Paul	C	Charlie	P	Papa
D	David	Q	Queen	D	Delta	Q	Quebec
E	Edward	R	Robert	E	Echo	R	Romeo
F	Frank	S	Sam	F	Foxtrot	S	Sierra
G	George	T	Tom	G	Golf	T	Tango
H	Henry	U	Union	H	Hotel	U	Uniform
I	Ida	V	Victor	I	India	V	Victor
J	John	W	William	J	Juliet	W	Whiskey
K	King	X	X-ray	K	Kilo	X	X-ray
L	Lincoln	Y	Young	L	Lima	Y	Yankee
M	Mary	Z	Zebra	M	Mike	Z	Zulu

Applications and Case Studies:

CASE 1 - bluduk15 -Okay, I've read through most of this thread and still have a few newbie questions. I have two Icom F-21GM radios that are FRS/GRMS. I actually even paid the fee and got the requisite FCC GMRS license (probably the only one in the country to do so).

Anyway, these radios are great with an upgraded whip and other features, but they just don't have the range I need. I have some property in W. Texas that is mainly canyonland and need at least 5-10 mile range capability. The terrain has low foliage, but does have some canyon lands.

Can I use a mobile as a repeater on GMRS or do I need to get a ticket and upgrade to 2m? Would a Yaesu FX 170 give me the range I need, even in canyons from HT to HT? What setup would you suggest?

Thanks in advance.

GlockTiger-Jedi was right when he said lots of options with ham. A very easy route -- don't fear the licensing. As you can see arfcommers are popping up with new ham licenses every day!

He's right about a crossband repeater. All you need is one radio in about the $400 range and the ability to read an owners manual to program it. You can slap a commercial dual band antenna on your windmill and leave her there with coax already run, so when you get to the location you just set up your radio and power source and you have an instant repeater for your HT's.

Here are some example figures (all new gear):
Yaesu FT-8800 dual band mobile w/ cross band repeat $370
Power Supply $100 or 12v deep cycle/agm/gel cell battery $50-100
Dual band base antenna -- $80-200
Feed line (coax) -- $.50/ft
Yaesu FT-60R dual band HT's $189 ea.

That said, I'd recommend you use mobiles in lieu of handhelds. You can always get HT's later, but might as well start with the extra power of mobile-mobile. Then as long as the terrain between you isn't hellacious, 8-10 miles will work just fine without a repeater.

You could buy an x-band capable mobile for each vehicle if you want, then you get HT's down the road and let the vehicle radio x-band repeat for you while you're away from the vehicle. Then you don't have to ever set up a base station repeater.

Application 1: Cross band repeating

In many circumstances, using an HT is the handiest way to go, but also has the least amount of power to get your signal out. One option is to use cross band repeating. Cross band repeating is in essence a way to amplify your signal using a more powerful transciever. Typically it is done to reach a repeater that cannot be accessed by your radio from your current position.

The typical way this is setup is to use an HT in conjuction with a dual band Mobile (which may be in an automobile). The user communicates from the HT to the Mobile (cross band repeater) to a distant main repeater. The HT transmits on channel uhf-a, the Mobile unit receives on uhf-a and retransmits simultaneously on vhf-a. The base repeater then recieves on vhf-a and simultaneously retransmits on vhf-b. Finally, for the user with the HT to receive, there are 2 options. 1)HT receives the signal directly from the base repeater on vhf-b or 2) the mobile receives vhf-b and retransmits simultaneously on uhf-b and the ht receives on on uhf-b. This second option is much harder on the mobile and will increase the 'wear and tear' on the equipment. There is also some debate as to whether 2) is entirely legal.

In this way, if you are inside a building or blocked by topography, you may be able to communicate with the main 'base' repeater.

Application 2: Encryption

Encryption on the amateur bands is strictly prohibited. There are some radio services that do allow encryption, but not on the ham bands. However, there are legal ways to limit the amount of people that will understand your transmissions when using ham frequencies. These all require that there be an openly published protcol for the mode you are using.

For example text messaging, you can send a text message over the ham bands. If you interface a computer to your radio, you can send text messages either live or with packets and someone listening in would not understand the message unless they were running the same type of software to translate the data. (see digital modes on page 6)

There is also morse code. While there are still many people who use it and many others learning, it does exclude those who do not know the code.

Sample
Family Emergency Communications Plan

This sample plan is designed to be used by families with reasonable distance between them, who have ham radio licenses and training, and have ham radio gear.

Participants and Callsigns:

Gary: N1NNN (General)

Brian: W2WWW (Extra)

Jennie: A3AAA (Technician)

Kari: K4KKK (Technician)

Beverly: N4BBB (Technician)

Where to Listen

1) If it is believed that the other party is within simplex range, that channel should be used first. Both parties should know whether this is a possibility and, if it is believed to be possible, always attempt a contact on 2m simplex first.

    2-Meter Simplex: **145.790 (FM)**

    If it is not believed the other party is in simplex range, it is not necessary to monitor this channel.

2) A 2-meter repeater is the second option, and should only be used if 1) the repeater is operational and 2) it is believed the other party is possibly within range of the repeater. If both of these are believed to be true, attempt to contact on the following repeaters:

    a) **Big Mountain Repeater**   **146.660 (FM / 88.5 PL / -)**
    b) **Docs Flat Repeater**   **147.040 (FM / 123.0 PL / +)**

    If both repeaters are up, contact should only be attempted on the FIRST repeater. If only one of the two repeaters is up, contact should only be attempted on the available repeater. ***If none of the repeaters are up, it is assumed that neither party will be attempting repeater contact and it is not necessary to monitor these channels.***

3) 40 meters is the chosen band for all other fall-back communications. 40-meters is ideal because a) it can be used over both short and long distances b) it does not require a massive antenna to operate, and c) it is usually open during all times of the day.

    a) **40-meter "voice" channel**   **7.2260.00 MHz (LSB)   (If the band is open)**
    b) **40-meter PSK31 channel**   **7.065.00 MHz (USB) (If the band is NOT open)**

When to Listen

Contact should always be attempted as soon as possible following a major incident that impacts one or more parties.

If initial contact following an emergency is not possible, contact should be attempted during dawn or dusk in Colorado. Remember that dawn and dusk happen during different times depending on the season. Also remember that if you happen to be in another part of the country, you'll need to do the math to figure out what time sunrise and sunset takes places according to Colorado time. Contacts should be attempted 30 minutes prior to, up to 30 minutes after, the time of the sunrise and sunset. This leaves a full 1-hour window twice a day when contact is likely to occur based on the above schedule.

Once contact has been established, a more convenient schedule can be established verbally.

If the communicated / new schedule is missed 3 or more times in a row, both parties should resume the emergency / first-contact schedule outlined here!!!

Communicating Locations

Never communicate your exact location over the air during distressed times. Doing so may put you or the party you're speaking to at risk. The risk is that someone listening may discover that you have resources of value (if you're operating a radio, they will likely assume you have other resources as well).

With this understood, it may be necessary to let the other person know your exact location. In this case, **it should be done prefaced with the phrase "trying to get to" and then all numbers should be multipled by 9.** The phrase "trying to get to" will let the other party know that you have multiplied your location numbers by 9.

In other words, if you were going to tell someone that you were currently at 1421 South 5210 West, you would say "I am trying to get to 12789 South 46890 West". This will allow you to safely communicate your location in an "encrypted" fashion without anyone knowing it's encrypted, and without risk of your location being known to others. While it is technically illegal for HAMs to obscure the meaning of their message, I don't think we really care. ☺

Examples:

"I am on 6th street and Vine" becomes "I am approximately on 54th street and Vine"

"My GPS coordinates are 41.10.26 North 112.06.28 West" becomes "My GPS coordinates are approximately 1008.90.234 North 1008.54.252 West".

Out of Range / No RF Capabilities

If you are out of range of local repeaters, simplex is not possible, and you do not have access to 40-meters, attempts should be made to contact someone who has access to 40-meters, and the above schedule should be communicated to that person, along with whatever message should be relayed. If possible, give that person instructions on how to contact you again so they can relay any messages back to you if needed. Make sure if they communicate your location, they do so using the "code" mentioned above (you don't need to mention it's in code unless necessary – in which case you can explain why. Be sure they use the phrase "trying to get to" to designate it's been encoded).

REMEMBER: In a true emergency where life or property are at stake, the FCC grants you permission to transmit on any frequency with any amount of power at our disposal, regardless of your license status!!

Money

The first thing to understand is that nearly all of the current money supply is in the form of electronic data entries on computers rather than in cash. Most of the wealth of the world is in promises to pay (credit) rather than in cash. Of the approximately $460 billion U.S. money supply, only about 4%, $17.9 billion, in cash is currently circulating in the U.S. (according to the St. Louis Fed figures for June, 1998). The rest is held by individuals, companies, banks and governments in foreign countries. When a disaster hits and the computers in the banks or ATMs go down, or if there are bank runs, all that electronic wealth could evaporate overnight. In the event of a national disaster, the total money supply could shrink by 96%.

Most people (Saints and non-members alike) currently thought of as wealthy have their wealth tied up in credit-related investments of one kind or another—the stock market, bonds, CD's, real estate, etc. Almost nobody keeps a big stash of cash around because there's been no need for large amounts of cash for a long, long time. All these currently wealthy people could suddenly become poor if a financial crash were to hit us. I don't mean metaphorically poor, I mean really freezing, starving poor, broke, destitute. All their resources will be in the wrong form for the new conditions. Only those who have cash will be wealthy after a national disaster; survival requires cash.

Can't the government simply print enough paper money to replace all the electronic money ? The answer is no, it's impossible. The presses at the Bureau of Engraving and Printing are already running at capacity 24 hours a day just to replace the paper money that wears out each year. To replace just the $17.9 billion of paper currency currently circulating would take 2 years at the current BEP printing capacity. It would take several decades to replace the entire $460 billion.

Joseph Fielding Smith (1876–1972) Tenth President of the Church

"[The pioneers] were taught by their leaders to produce, as far as possible, all that they consumed, and to be frugal and not wasteful of their substance. This is still excellent counsel" ("The Pioneer Spirit," *Improvement Era,* July 1970, 3).

It has been reported that the Fed has been printing and stockpiling cash in case of a bank run, and they will have an extra $50 billion on hand along with $150 billion they have apparently been secretly stockpiling for years. This makes a possible total of $218 billion just in case. Even if this is true, $218 billion is a long, long way from $460 billion and light years away from $7 trillion, which is the total value of the entire U.S. economy. Note that if the total U.S. economy is worth $7 trillion but that only $460 billion of that total exists as physical cash (and only $17.9 billion is circulating within our borders), then the vast majority of the wealth of America is obviously only electronic, credit money. After a major disaster or financial crash, no banks or no electricity or no oil or coal or no trains means no electronic wealth. We're back to an all-cash economy.

Cash For Survival

The answer to the money question is a simple one: *Have Cash*—coins and green pieces of paper with pictures of dead presidents on them. Start converting some of your credit investments and electronic forms of money into cash. If you have cash after the disaster, you will be one of the few wealthy people in the world. Not only will you be able to survive the disastrous times, you will be able to use your cash to build a prosperous future for you and your family.

A word of warning: you must be very careful to keep a low profile both now and in the future. You want to attract as little attention as possible now while you convert to cash and later when you use your cash , for two different but equally vital reasons.

First, although you have every right to convert all your investments and savings into cash, doing so may invite the attention of the government DEA agents who may think you're some kind of drug dealer. The drug laws are so powerful regarding the confiscation of suspected drug dealers' wealth that you could find yourself in a protracted legal battle to get back the money that belongs to you. You want to avoid attracting the attention of bank tellers or branch managers who might report to the DEA that you are withdrawing large sums of cash.

Secondly, when everyone around you is impoverished and hungry, it's very prudent to keep your own wealth out of sight. A desperate man will go to extremes to feed his family and keep them sheltered and warm; a hungry man will do what is necessary to procure food. Someone who flashes a lot of cash is courting danger.

Get your cash in tens and twenties and a few fifties. If you receive any crisp new bills, stop off at a convenience store and buy a candy bar or something, hand the clerk a new bill and you will receive older, worn bills in change. Afterwards, anyone with brand new money may invite envy as a hoarder or may become a target for robbers. You want to avoid attracting attention to yourself both now and then.

You will need ones and fives after a disaster, but it's too noticeable to cash a large check and ask for a lot of very small bills.

Coins

You will also need coins. Gold and silver might be useful during the rebuilding stage several years after the crisis, but for the first couple of years, ordinary dimes and quarters, nickels and pennies will be the most easily traded form of money. In a massive deflation, which is what a financial crash would create, real hard money becomes far more valuable. A loaf of bread that costs $1.25 today may cost 5 cents afterwards

assuming there's any bread to be had. People are completely used to ordinary pocket change coins, so that's what they will most readily accept for local transactions—and I believe nearly all transactions will be local after a major national disaster.

You need to start saving up a coin stash. Once a month or so, take a few $20 bills to a bank in which you do not have an account and trade them for rolls of quarters or dollar coins. Any bank will exchange paper for coins without question.

Gold And Silver

Gold and silver coins are real money, based on their standard precious metal content; they have always been a historical refuge in times of crisis and because of increased public awareness about a possible disasters, gold and silver coins are becoming more desireable to have. You are not interested in nusmismatic collectible coins; you're only interested in gold and silver coins for their precious metal content.

The cheapest way to hold silver coins is to buy pre-1965 junk silver dimes and quarters. No one knows the future value ratio of silver coins to copper-clad coins (our currently circulating ones) after a disaster, but there's no doubt that silver coins will be worth considerably more than clads once people get used to having them.

You pay a higher premium for silver dollars than you do for silver dimes and quarters but it would be wise to have some silver dollars on hand as part of your survival plan. They are bigger and more impressive looking than dimes and quarters; even though a silver dollar may have the same metal content as ten silver dimes or four silver quarters, it justs looks more valuable. The alternative is to buy brand new American Silver Eagles. These are current manufacture pure Silver coins from the US Mint. Though not commonly seen in circulation, they are legal tender and worth far more than their face value. US Silver Eagles and pure Bullion Coins are an excellent way to build up an inventory of silver.

Gold

Gold coins are the most desirable, most valuable, form of real, hard money. Gold is scarce, it does not rust or corrode, it's very beautiful to look at, it's highly desirable as jewelry, it has industrial uses, and a long, long monetary history in many cultures worldwide. It's the real deal.

Right now the price of gold is higher than it's been for 25 years, which should warn us that inflation is on the way (Inflation or the threat of inflation causes an immediate rise in the price of gold).

The best gold coins are American coins in one oz., 1/2 oz., 1/4 oz. and 1/10 oz. denominations. People have no experience with real gold money and they will probably more readily accept U.S. gold coins than foreign coins. Although the U.S. 1 oz. Liberty coin is slightly more expensive to buy than the South African Kruger Rand, for example, when you go to spend gold, you'll find it easier to move the American coins.

Get more smaller denomination gold coins than larger ones. In other words, buy more 1/10 oz. coins than 1/4 oz. coins, and more 1/4 oz. coins than 1/2 oz. coins, etc. The reason for this is that gold is an immense store of value for its size and weight. You will not be able to go into a local flea market or general store with a one oz. gold coin and be able to buy a few loaves of bread and some local cheese. How will the store owner make change for such a high value coin? You will use the fraying paper money, followed by clad coins and then silver coins before you'll place any gold on the counter. Gold is for large purchases so a small gold coin will be of far greater use on most occasions than a larger one. Save your 1 oz. gold coins to purchase major items.

Storing Cash

Now you need to find a safe place to hide your cash. First, tell no one that you have a load of cash, except possibly your spouse, and don't tell your spouse unless you're absolutely certain of the strength of your marriage. I'm not kidding. Hard times drive people to do things they would not do ordinarily, and if the hammer hits hard as it may well do, these will be the hardest times in our country's history. If your spouse is a full and completely trustworthy celestial partner in your life, consider yourself fortunate and keep no secrets; otherwise, be careful.

If you plan to hide your cash somewhere in your house, you want to make sure to protect it from fire, so go to a Walmart or a similar discount store and buy a fireproof storage box. You should be able to get one for under $40. It will protect your cash from burning for a half hour of direct flame. Put your paper money and your gold and silver in the box. If you fill it up, buy another one and fill that one up too. As you begin changing some of your electronic credit wealth into cash, gold and silver, your money is fully under your control. As long as you keep it safe, it will always be there for you.

Captain Moroni 1oz Silver Bullion Preparedness Coin

SETTING UP AN EMERGENCY CASH STASH

By "RusherJim"

Worried about world financial markets?
Do your banking online?
Got a dozen credit/debit cards?
Rarely carry cash?

You need an "emergency cash stash" in your home to guard against emergency situations when traditional methods of commerce have failed. Such situations are rare, but do occur regularly as regional and temporary events (think: Hurricane Katrina or one of the famous New York city/northeastern U.S. blackouts, or even the occasional glitch in a communications satellite).

Even ignoring the turbulent financial markets, just imagine if the electricity shut down in your region due to acts of terrorism, a natural disaster--or even a widespread and lingering system malfunction or virus.

• You won't be getting online to do your banking, and no one will accept credit cards or personal checks because they won't be able to verify the transaction.

• Hackers mess with financial networks for fun...and even if the entire financial network in your region doesn't go down, YOUR bank's online/electronic capabilities may go down for a few, or even several, days.

• These modern commerce methods will almost surely fail you during at least the early phases of any disaster or emergency—there will simply be too many users!

• If you haven't stored enough food/water or they were damaged in the disaster, you may need that money to buy food for your family, or medicines for your kids.

You should have an "emergency cash stash."
In your home or yard, protected, out-of-sight and well-secured, you should cache a reasonable amount of paper currency and coins.

• Some folks buy a home safe and place it in the basement or garage, anchoring it to the concrete with appropriate bolts, or install a wall safe.

• Others buy a small water-tight container, which they nest within larger-size waterproof containers, and bury in the yard or sink within a pond.

o If you do this, make sure you can retrieve your stash quickly if you must evacuate. You may not have time to dig three feet or move a huge rock.

• Some do the "half-empty cocoa can" in the back of the pantry, with the money tucked inside layers of Ziploc bags and buried beneath the remaining hot cocoa mix.

• Others buy fake books with hidden storage space, or similar containers, and try the "hiding in plain sight" approach.

• Some folks bury/cache their cash stash in nearby parkland, national forests or wilderness areas (that one's a little extreme for most of us).

• There are thousands of ways & places to store your cash stash...and obviously, we wouldn't reveal all of them here.

o Use your imagination...be creative...be proactive in protecting your cash stash's existence and location..

• Make do with a coffee can and duct tape if you must--just get it done. You'll sleep better.

Your "Cash Stash" container (or multiple containers, if needed) should be kept confidential.

• Children & teens generally shouldn't be aware of its location; such funds occasionally have become ice cream money or date funds.

• And definitely, don't brag to your neighbors about the money you've hidden.

Whichever approach you choose for your Cash Stash, make it something you can "grab and go" during an evacuation or emergency.

• Make sure it is on your list of "emergency to-go items" (AKA: "bug-out kit) coded so you don't give it away to burglars. Call it something like: "Derricks' Special Medication," or "Suzie's Scrapbook."

How much money should you keep in your cash stash?

An amount consistent with your economic circumstances, the most likely hazards/risks in your region and your perceived needs.

• Budget limitations are important; if you can only stash $50, then stash $50.

• We've read about folks that keep $10,000 or more in their cash stash, including some in silver and/or gold, because during emergencies they plan to travel to another region and might need the cash while on the road.

• **$300 to $500 is a good number for many families in most situations,** broken into various denominations (including lots of dollar bills, but certainly nothing higher than a $50). At least $40 should be in coins; probably quarters, but some folks like $1 or $2 coins. Again, you can, and probably should, accumulate these sums gradually and **_NEVER go into debt to do so._**

• Coins are a great idea for several reasons:

o Using them in vending machines in a temporary shelter, or to use a pay phone once your cell phone battery runs down.

o Avoiding pulling out a wad of cash in front of folks during emergencies.

o Some folks will trust "hard" assets like coins more than paper currency.

In closing: ABSOLUTELY and without exception, every family should have a modest CASH STASH in their home for use during emergencies.

• It should be VERY well-hidden but readily accessible, for temporary use in extreme emergencies, when banks might be closed temporarily.

• You might consider $300 to $500 kept in a home safe or a hidden storage location.

o If you can only stash $50, that may be the money that gets you the taxi ride to the emergency room when your husband or wife has a heart attack during a major, lengthy regional electrical blackout.

o Keep it in small bills and/or coins.

\• And, you should NOT advertise the location (or even the existence!) of your cash stash to friends or neighbors...this is one of those good family secrets.
Good luck, and may you never need to use your emergency cash stash.

Debt and Preparedness

With such uncertain times around us, I've noticed a trend of desperation as families work towards getting prepared. That desperation sometimes results in incurring debt to purchase preparedness items.

Over and over, we have been told by living prophets not to go into debt in order to get prepared. Instead we should be working towards getting debt-free as part of our preparedness efforts. Here are just a few sources:

We urge all Latter-day Saints to be prudent in their planning, to be conservative in their living, and to avoid excessive or unnecessary debt. (President Thomas S. Monson, October 2008 general conference)

"We ask that you be wise as you store food and water and build your savings. Do not go to extremes; it is not prudent, for example, to go into debt to establish your food storage all at once. With careful planning, you can, over time, establish a home storage supply and a financial reserve." (All

Is Safely Gathered In: Family Home Storage (2007), First Presidency, President Gordon B. Hinckley, President Thomas S. Monson, President James E. Faust)

"I am suggesting that the time has come to get our houses in order … Self-reliance cannot obtain when there is serious debt hanging over a household." (President Gordon B. Hinckley, General Conference, October, 199

Wisely we have been counseled to avoid debt as we would avoid the plague. (Elder L. Tom Perry referencing President J. Reuben Clark, October 1995 general conference)

You do not need to go into debt, may I add, to obtain a year's supply. Plan to build up your food supply just as you would a savings account. (President Ezra Taft Benson, October 1980 general conference)

A huge chunk of being prepared is also having your financial houses in order. You might reason that in an economic downturn, or the end-of-the-world, that money might be meaningless. But it's much more likely, that whatever the emergency circumstances, your house payment will still be due.

And it's not enough to be debt free. Make plans to ensure that you have a financial reserve to get you through potentially tough times:

"We encourage you wherever you may live in the world to prepare for adversity by looking to the condition of your finances. We urge you to be modest in your expenditures. . . Pay off debt as quickly as you can, and free yourselves from this bondage. Save a little money regularly to gradually build a financial reserve. If you have paid your debts and have a financial reserve, even though it be small, you and your family will feel more secure and enjoy greater peace in your hearts.(All Is Safely Gathered In: Family Finances (2007), First Presidency, President Gordon B. Hinckley, President Thomas S. Monson, President James E. Faust)

"Set your houses in order. If you have paid your debts, if you have a reserve, even though it be small, then should storms howl about your head, you will have shelter for your wives and children and peace in your hearts" (President Gordon B. Hinckley, October 1998 general conference).

So, before you go and purchase that new generator, farm land, long-term food storage, or gun, make sure that you can afford it without using credit, that you have a financial reserve and that you are working towards being debt-free.

http://iprepared.blogspot.com/2011/12/debt-and-getting-prepared.html

Get Out Of Debt While You Can

Debt, even under the best of circumstances, can be stifling and worrisome. It can lead to many sleepless nights fretting over how to make the next month's payments. Problems with debt are even more profound when the end of the world as we know it (TEOTWAWKI) happens.

Our current way of life depends on a widely-accepted set of principles that are deeply woven into the fabric of our modern society. The standards for acceptable behavior are but a thread in that thin fabric. If those principles change, the threads begins to unravel and our way of life is forever altered.

Money After TEOTWAWKI

TEOTWAWKI changes everything. The rules that currently govern our financial, legal, and other systems will no longer apply post-TEOTWAWKI. Cash on hand will be very valuable at first since ATMs and other forms of electronic money will be limited or unavailable.

As time passes, the value of the paper-based currency will diminish. It's the physical assets that will matter most. Bartering will become the norm.

Creditors will quickly become aware of this new reality and take action to protect their investments. Unscrupulous institutions may send "agents" to collect the balance due on a loan or repossess the item used as collateral.

That EMP-proof 1970's model Jeep that you financed may not be there for you when you need it most. The Credit Union that holds the note may come calling, taking it by force if you can't pay off the loan. "But that's not fair!", you say. In the new post-TEOTWAWKI world, there's a new definition of "fair".

Preparing For The New World

As a prepper, there are things that we can do to protect ourselves from the coming collapse.

Make a budget. Fiscal responsibility before the collapse is one of the best ways to prepare for the life after the collapse. Get your financial house in order by creating a monthly budget. Be intentional about your spending. Know where your money is going. Track your expenditures for a couple of months. Then change your buying habits to match your priorities.

Identify the what you need to buy. Regardless of how long you've been preparing, it's doubtful that you have everything that you'd like to have for the coming collapse. There's alway more ammunition, more food, more hand tools, and more training that you'd like to have. Inventory what you have; identify what you lack. Prioritize the items that are missing so that you know what to work toward first.

Prioritize your expenses. Once you recognize that your own preparedness is not where you would like to be, it's tempting to immediately rush in to fill the gap using money that you don't have. That's foolish, short-sighted, and could be costly in the long run. Make it a priority to pay off debt as you collect the items you'll need post-TEOTWAWKI. As with most things, balance is key.

Keep paper copies. Going paperless for the environment is a worthy goal. But what happens if the electronic devices that store all of your financial documents fail? Can you prove that you've paid off your auto loan? Can you prove that you own your house? Keep paper copies of key financial documents. They may not carry a lot of way in the new, post-collapse economy. But then again, they may mean the difference in keeping your Jeep and having the guys from the Credit Union driving off in it.

If a lot of us are wrong and TEOTWAWKI is not just around the corner, reducing your debt is still a good thing. But if we are right and TEOTWAWKI is looming just over the horizon, reducing your debt now could be the difference between having the supplies you need and being out of the street.

http://preppingtosurvive.com/2011/03...while-you-can/

Medical kits for self-reliant families

By Jackie Clay

There may be a time, as close as tomorrow, when your loved ones need medication or medical treatment and there is no drug store open or doctor available. This may be as simple a situation as a head cold coming on during a weekend night, or more drastic, such as nothing available after a civil or natural disaster.

Family medical kits

Here at home, we've always had a medical kit. Several, in fact. One is quite large, made up of a poly box, originally designed as a field box for trap and skeet shooters. This "drug store on wheels" is a well-packed medical utility box that will handle nearly everything from a cold to severe lacerations. This one we carry when traveling in remote locations.

But while it is loaded with most medical needs, far surpassing a first-aid "kit," it is heavy, weighing over 30 pounds, and it is not something we carry for short trips, pack in our canoe, or carry on horseback. Our medical kit.

An intermediate kit is lighter and fits into a flat, moderate-sized fishing tackle box. While this does not contain such a wide variety of medical supplies and medications, it is a very well thought out first-aid-and then some-medical kit. This is light enough to pack in the canoe (if we don't foresee many lengthy portages, when every ounce counts), with camp supplies on a horse packing trip, or small enough to take up little room in the truck.

Besides this kit, we also carry a small first aid kit under the seat of the truck and Suburban, containing bandages, antibiotic ointment, burn medication, sterile gauze, tweezers,

aspirin, sterile eye wash, and cold tablets for ourselves and our eight- year-old son, David. In the glove box is a smaller snap-open plastic box with Bob's oral diabetes medication, my blood pressure pills, and a few aspirin. This has come in handy many times when someone forgot to take prescribed daily medication or a headache suddenly popped up. As the glove box does get hot during the summer, this small stash of meds is rotated routinely to make sure the strength does not fade.

Learning to use your kit.

No matter how comprehensive your medical kit is it can be useless or even harmful if you do not know how to use it safely. You don't have to have extensive medical treatment to handle most emergencies that occur in real life. Most of ours consist of splinters, minor cuts and scrapes, sprains, and an occasional head cold or the flu. While these are scarcely life-threatening, they are uncomfortable and the afflicted party sure appreciates quick, competent aid.

Our family is lucky; I have spent a lifetime as a veterinary field technician riding on calls and acting as an assistant on everything from broken legs to pneumonia. Bob is a Certified Nurses Assistant (CNA) with additional military medical training in Vietnam. But you'd be surprised at how much free medical training is out there for you to pick up. Many communities provide first-aid classes, including invaluable cardiopulmonary resuscitation (CPR) training.

During these classes, ask questions to boot up the amount of knowledge you receive. Attend volunteer firemen's training sessions, as available (again, ask around). Ask your veterinarian if you could accompany him/her on calls one or more days a week free in exchange for the knowledge you gain. Yep, I know, they're animals, not people, but basically, a mammal is a mammal, especially when it comes to shock, wounds, and common illnesses such as pneumonia.

Pick up a good first-aid manual (which should be in your large medical kit at all times) and a book or two from a preparedness company which details medical treatment when no doctor or dentist is available. Then read these manuals carefully. I know they're not great reading, but they can save someone's life. Share the reading with your spouse or older children, and even practice at home. It can be interesting, learning to suture gaping wounds on a piece of that chicken you're having for dinner. After it's butchered and ready to cook, of course. I'm not that morbid.

Real life medical treatment basics.

While some survival first aid manuals assume your family's injuries will need treatment for nuclear blast and gaping wounds, in reality most will be of a much more mundane level no matter where you are, from arctic tundra to urban sprawl. They will consist of minor cuts, scrapes, slivers, blisters, the flu, colds, a fish hook in the skin, etc. We have lived for years in very remote locations and, although the worst injury any of us sustained was Bob's green stick fracture of his leg in a snowmobile accident, the most painful was my severely sprained ankle, suffered when I missed a step going downstairs in our farmhouse in "civilization."

Let's look at some real-life possibilities and what to do about them, assuming that there is no doctor or hospital available. Remember that if trained medical help is available, one should always consider this course first as many conditions can be made worse by incorrect diagnosis and treatment.

Hypothermia

Believe it or not, hypothermia (the condition where the body temperature is lowered below normal) kills more people in survival/stress situations than does gunfire, wild animal attacks, poisonous reptiles and spiders, wounds, or drowning.

The large medical kit is portable. We carry it on all remote trips

Hypothermia has many causes, from shock following an accident to remaining outside in cold weather without adequate clothing or shelter to getting dunked in icy water- even for short periods of time. It is definitely something to watch for in any survival situation.

Identifying hypothermia can be a problem with the uninitiated, as it comes on slowly and the person still can walk and talk. But by paying careful attention, one can usually notice body shaking, paleness, and a tendency toward poor judgement and/or speech that doesn't make sense.

Taking the victim's temperature, you will quickly see that it is subnormal.

Hypothermia must be treated vigorously and immediately. Warmth is the key. As the body has lost it's ability to warm itself, simply putting a blanket around the person is not enough. Build a warm fire. If the victim is wet, get them into warm dry clothes quickly. Warm a blanket or sleeping bag, then wrap it around them while they sit or lie in front of the fire. If they are not too bad, a drink of warm coffee or tea often helps. But do not give anything to eat or drink to a victim that is dazed or unconscious.

If nothing else is available, have one or more persons crawl into a sleeping bag or blankets to provide bodily warmth to the victim. Then keep the person warm and dry until they are fully recovered. You don't have to be a mountaineer to suffer hypothermia. I have had several encounters: falling through thin ice while crossing a beaver dam, getting stuck out in an unexpected blizzard in June, and getting drenched in the rain while making a mile and a half canoe portage in Minnesota's Boundary Waters. Hypothermia can be just plain uncomfortably miserable, but it can also kill.

Wounds

Most wounds that folks suffer in a survival situation are relatively minor, and though they may be uncomfortable and even bleeding, they are not usually life-threatening. The thing is not to panic. A little blood looks like a lot, especially when it is on yourself or a loved one.

If the wound is combined with possible other injuries, such as following a tumble down a rocky slope, you have to first assess the possible damage.

Could there be a broken bone? A concussion? Internal injuries?

Don't panic. However, if you suspect such complications, do not move the injured party unless absolutely necessary, and then do it with great care.

Talk to the victim. He can usually tell you a lot about where he hurts and how much pain he is in. If the only injury seems to be the wound, reassure the victim and begin treatment.

Check the wound. Is it visibly dirty? Is the blood simply flowing from the wound or is it spurting? In survival situations, more people die from infected wounds than bleeding to death.

If the wound is relatively minor and the bleeding is minimal, you'll want to gently clean it before any attempt is made to bandage it. Nothing causes infection more than bandaging an unclean wound, even if it contains no visible dirt. Remember that deadly staph organisms are commonly found on human skin.

A good way to clean most wounds is to gently bathe the area with mild soap and water. Mop away from the wound, as one would sweep a floor, instead of scrubbing back and forth. The latter only moves bacteria around rather than removing it from the area. Rinse or soak the area well, removing any debris carefully with sterile tweezers.

When the area is clean, pat it dry with sterile gauze or air-dry it, then apply Betadine or antibiotic salve. We use Betadine for deeper wounds, and antibiotic salve for lesser injuries. Minor wounds seldom require bandaging, healing quicker by air exposure. Deeper wounds and ones in areas where they will be constantly irritated by clothing or work should be bandaged. A simple adhesive strip usually does the trick.

If the wound is bleeding quite a bit, simply applying pressure to the area with a sterile gauze pad will usually stop it within a few minutes. Where tourniquets were once advised, it has been found that more damage was done by the tourniquet than the bleeding would have caused in most instances. The application of firm pressure directly to the wound is very effective. After the severe bleeding has been stopped, gently clean the wound, but do not destroy the clot that has formed or bleeding will probably resume.

Should you be dealing with a more severe wound, covering it with a Betadine soaked (but not wet) sterile gauze, then a plain sterile gauze square, then adhesive tape is usually sufficient. If the edges of the wound gape or there is a flap of skin hanging down, either gently match the edges with butterfly adhesive strips or suture them, if you have the experience. Remember that most wounds will heal fine without suturing, especially with a little help from gentle butterfly adhesive strips. Sutures that are too tightly drawn will cause pain and scarring.

Never bandage a wound tightly with gauze bandage or anything else. This will restrict circulation and can cause pain and severe problems and even gangrene.

In the following days, keep the wound clean and dry. Change the dressing as needed, usually twice a day, leaving the dressing off and the area open to fresh air and sunlight as much as possible. This will greatly reduce the healing time and reduce chances of infection. Bacteria love damp, dark, warm areas, including a wound which is bandaged.

Our medical kit comes in handy in daily life, from cuts to colds.

Watch for ugly redness or a fever in the patient, which would indicate infection in the wound. In this case, keep the area soaked in Betadine and give the patient antibiotics for 10 days, even if they seem better within a day or two. Immersing the infected wound in a hot Epsom salts solution also helps reduce pain and swelling along with cleansing the area.

Simple pain and swelling from the injury can be alleviated by plain aspirin, taken orally. Do not give aspirin immedi-ately following an injury if there is a possibility of internal injuries, as aspirin may enhance hemorrhage. Do not give aspirin to young children. Use Ibuprofen instead.

Colds and flu

These common conditions are bad enough when things are fine, but are downright miserable in a survival situation. And remember that stress helps these overcome your body.

At the first sign of a cold or the flu, do those things your grandmother told you: keep warm and dry, rest, and drink plenty of fluids. Then add vitamin C and zinc lozenges, and most folks can overcome that mean cold or flu in a few days. If you need to alleviate symptoms, such as fever, runny nose, or coughing, take a cold/flu medication that covers your symptoms. By now, you probably know what works best for you and your children. The key is to have the medication on hand.

If the cold or flu lasts for longer than 10 days or seems to get worse, it may have turned into bronchitis or pneumonia, and antibiotics are necessary. Remember that home treatment is only for when no doctor or hospital is available.

Sprains

Believe it or not, sprains are one of the most common injuries in a survival situation. And often one of the most painful. The sprain can arise from walking over debris, logs, rocks, and even urban curbs. It can come from a fall or even an ankle turning over. (Your family will experience less sprains if they wear good, sturdy footwear, not flats or sandals. Ankle support is very important.)

When a sprain is new, immerse the affected part in cold water or apply ice packs to reduce pain and inflammation. I've found that when I take two plain aspirin immediately following such an injury that it greatly reduces both pain and inflammation later on.

If possible, rest the sprain, keeping it immobile and elevated for as long as reasonably possible. I continue taking the aspirin to keep down the inflammation. If you must move about, gently wrap the area with an elastic bandage to support it. Do not wrap area tightly or you will restrict circulation and make the pain much worse. Use a cane or crutches if the sprain is in a foot, ankle, or knee to reduce the amount of weight put on the injury. If the sprain is in the hand, wrist, elbow, or shoulder, keeping the arm in a sling will greatly reduce the pain and help it heal.

After a day, begin using hot Epsom salts soaks or packs to reduce the swelling and pain. And remember, the more you use a sprained joint, the longer it will take to heal and it may not ever heal completely if you persist using it before it heals. Rest is the key.

Slivers and spines

Getting a sliver or sticker of some kind is awfully common, especially in a survival situation, when one may be building a wood fire or foraging for food. Most of the time you can simply get hold of it and pull it out and be no worse for wear. But sometimes it is in too deep and painful and seemingly impossible to remove.

For relatively minor, but painful slivers, I use a sterile hypodermic needle, choosing the gauge (diameter/size) to fit the sliver size. Most smaller slivers are removed very easily with a 20-gauge needle. Now I use a hypodermic needle for several reasons, as opposed to using a sewing needle.

First, and most important, they are hollow. This allows one to slip them into the sliver track with little pain, as less bulk is pressing on that tender skin. They are also sharp, which lets me carefully pick away the skin layer above the sliver which has no feeling because there are no nerves, until the sliver is exposed and can be either snagged with the needle and drawn out or picked up with a pair of sterile tweezers and removed.

With larger slivers, I use an 18-gauge needle, which does the same thing but is a bit stronger. When the sliver is very painful, using a local anesthetic, such as oral medication or antibiotic ointment containing an anesthetic on the area about 10 minutes before the procedure, helps a lot.

The main thing is to keep the sliver aligned with its track, and not to pry it upright in removal, which is extremely painful.

Once the sliver is out, a little alcohol or Betadine will disinfect the area and let it heal quickly.

I've discovered a great treatment for small stickers and cactus thorns which break off when you try to remove them from tender skin. Should you or a family member fall into a cactus or other plant with fine stickers, simply coat the area with Shoe-Goo or Sportsman's-Goo, which is a clear silicone-type produce. Just a thin coat is fine. In about fifteen minutes it will be dry, and you can just peel it off, complete with all of the painful stickers.

Of course, there are many other possible injuries and illnesses. With a little advance preparation and study, you'll be surprised at what you can glide smoothly through. There is seldom any benefit to panic; a positive mental outlook can save lives.

TEOTWAWKI Medical Kits

What you stock up on should be related to what you know how to use and what you can obtain. There are potentially thousands of drugs, and different pieces of medical equipment, and you can't stock everything. Fortunately it is possible to manage 90% of medical problems with only a moderate amount of basic equipment and drugs. Obviously the treatment may not be as high quality as that provided by a proper hospital but it may be life saving and reduce long term problems. For example; a general anaesthetic, an operation for an internal tibial nail, followed by pain management, and physiotherapy usually manages a broken tibia in a hospital setting. In a remote austere situation it can be managed by manipulation with analgesia, and immobilization with an external splint for 6-8 weeks, and as a result the patient may be in pain for a few weeks, and have a limp for life but still have a functioning leg. Also appendicitis has been treated with high-dose antibiotics when surgery has been unavailable such as on a submarine or in the Antarctic. Removal of an appendix has been done successfully many times under local anaesthesia. Although in each case management maybe sub-optimal and may have some risk in a survival situation it can be done and may be successful with limited medication and equipment.

Obtaining medical supplies:

Medications:

Obtaining medications can be difficult. The problem is two-fold. First is access and second is cost. Below are some suggestions for legally obtaining medicines for use in a survival medicine situation.

i. Talk to your doctor. Be honest explain exactly why and what you want, that you want to be prepared for any disaster and have some important basic meds available, for if medical care isn't freely available. Demonstrate an understanding of what each drug is for and that you know how to safely use it. This approach depends on your relationship with your doctor, and how comfortably you are discussing these issues. Although, I would suggest that you don't request narcotics the first time. Then return the meds when they have expired, this will confirm that you are not using them inappropriately.

ii. Discuss with your MD your plans for a trekking holiday. Most MDs recognise the importance of an adequate medical kit if you are travelling in the 3rd world or doing isolated backpacking. Most would prescribe antibiotics, rehydration fluid, simple pain killers, anti-diarrhoea meds, antibiotic and fungal creams, and if climbing steroids, acetazolamide and furosemide for AMS (although these last 2 have limited roles in a survival situation). It is also worth requesting

Malaria prophylaxis – the CDC recommends doxycycline for most regions.

Buy a boat. Australia, New Zealand, and the UK, require all boats sailing beyond coastal limits to carry a comprehensive medical kit. This includes antibiotics, strong narcotic analgesias, and a variety of other meds. Although not a legal requirement in the US, I imagine most MD's would happily equip an ocean going yacht with a comprehensive medical kit, especially if you can demonstrate a basic medical knowledge. The US Public Health service offers suggested medications and equipment, depending on numbers and expected isolation.

iv. Prescription medicines are available over the counter in many third world countries. While purchasing them certainly isn't illegal, importation into your own country may well be. While it is unlikely that a single course of antibiotics would be a problem, extreme care should be exercised with more uncommon drugs or large amounts. Narcotics shouldn't be imported under any circumstances. Should you purchase drugs in the third (or second) world you need to be absolutely sure you are getting what you believe you are, the best way is to ensure that the medications are still sealed in the original manufactures packaging.

v. "Not for human consumption": Veterinary meds are widely available and are relatively cheap – you can by human grade antibiotics from many fish supply stores. Several books discuss obtaining them (Survivalist Medicine Chest. Ragnar Benson. Paladin Press is one), so I won't cover it in detail here. We cannot recommend this method, but obviously for some it is the only viable option. Generally speaking most veterinary drugs come from the same batches and factories as the human version, the only difference being in the labelling. This is the case for most common single-component drugs such as antibiotics. If you are going to purchase veterinary medications I strongly suggest only purchasing antibiotics or topical preparations and with the following cautions: (1) Make sure you know exactly what drug you are buying, (2) avoid preparations which contain combinations of drugs and also obscure drugs for which you can find no identical human preparation and (3) avoid drug preparations for specific animal conditions for which there is no human equivalent. Buy drugs which are generically identical to their human counterparts, e.g. Amoxicillin 500mg (Vet) = Amoxicillin 500mg (Human), etc. You use these at your own risk.

A recent discussion with a number of doctors suggests that options ii and iii would be acceptable to the majority of those spoken too. In fact many were surprisingly broad in what they would be prepared to supply in those situations. However, be warned the majority of the same *group considered the preparedness/survivalism philosophy to be unhealthy!*

Other medical supplies:
Obtaining general medical supplies is often easier. Basic bandages, and stethoscopes, etc. can be bought from any medical supply house. In the USA there is no federal law prohibiting the purchase of things like sutures, syringes, needles, IVs, etc. but some states can make it difficult. In most other countries they are freely available. Try looking in the yellow pages for medical, or emergency medical supply houses, or veterinary supplies. A number of commercial survival outfitters offer first aid and medical supplies, however, I would shop around before purchasing from these companies as their prices, in my experience, are higher than standard medical suppliers. The above approaches for obtaining medicines can also be used for obtaining medical equipment if you do have problems. The most important point is to be able to demonstrate an understanding of how to use what you are requesting.

Pre-packaged Kits: Generally speaking it is considerably cheaper to purchase your own supplies and put together your own kit. The commercial kits cost 2-3 times more than the same kit would cost to put together yourself and frequently contain items which are of limited value. The more you buy the cheaper things become – consider buying in bulk.

Storage and Rotation of Medications
Medications can be one of the more expensive items in your storage inventory, and there can be a reluctance to rotate them due to this cost issue, and also due to difficulties in obtaining new stock.

Unfortunately drugs do have limited shelf life. It is a requirement for medications sold in the US (and most other first world countries) to display an expiration date. It is our experience that these are usually very easy to follow, without the confusing codes sometimes found on food products, e.g. -- Exp. 12/00=Expires December 2000.

We cannot endorse using medications which have expired, but having said that, the majority of medications are safe for at least 12 months following their expiration date. As with food the main problem with expired medicines is not that they become dangerous but that they lose potency over time and the manufacturer will no longer guarantee the dose/response effects of the drug. We discuss using expired medications in more detail in Chapter 11.

The important exception to this rule was always said to be the tetracycline group of antibiotics which could become toxic with time. However, it is thought that the toxicity with degrading tetracycline was due to citric acid which was part of the tablet composition. Citric acid is no longer used in the production of tetracycline, therefore, the dangers of toxicity with degradation of tetracycline is no longer a problem. Aspirin and Epinephrine do break down over time to toxic metabolites and extreme care should be taken using these medications beyond their expiry dates.

Despite the above comments "Let the buyer beware." The expiry dates ARE there for a reason, and there are almost certainly other medications which do break down, and become toxic after their expiry date.

In addition, we recommend that if you are acquiring medications on a doctor's prescription that when you have the prescription filled you explain the medications are for storage (you don't need to say exactly what for), and request recently manufactured stock with distant expiration dates.

The ideal storage conditions for most medications are in a cool, dark, dry environment. These conditions will optimise the shelf life of the drugs. A small number of drugs require refrigeration to avoid loss of potency.These include insulin, ergometrine, oxytocin, and some muscle relaxants. Others such as diazepam rapidly lose potency if exposed to the light.

How much?
This is a very individual question. It depends upon what you are preparing for and the number of people you will be looking after. It is impossible to say how much is enough. In order get a rough idea of what you should stock – think of your worse case scenario and at least double or triple the amounts you calculate. Items which never go as far as you think they will include – gauze, tape, antibiotics, and sutures. If you have ever been hospitalised or had a close relative in hospital for even a relatively minor problem take a look at the billing account for medical supplies and drugs to get an idea how much can be consumed with even a relatively small problem. It is simple mathematics; drugs which you need to take more than once or twice a day disappear extremely fast – penicillin 4 times a day for 10 days on a couple of occasions quickly erodes your "large stock" of 100 tablets! The same number of ciprofloxacin required only twice a day last longer. Dosing frequency is worth considering when deciding amounts.

Specific Medical Kits
Everyone has an idea of what his or her perfect kit is and what he or she thinks is vital - so there is no perfect kit-packing list. What is perfect for one person's situation and knowledge may not be perfect for yours. You need to build a kit that you are able to understand and use.

In this section we have looked at a basic first aid kit, a more broad-spectrum basic medical kit, and an advanced medical kit able to cope with most medical problems. These are not the perfect kits or the ideal packing list – but they give you some idea of what we consider are needed to provide varying levels of care.

There is also frequent confusion over which surgical instruments to buy, how many of each, and what some actually do so we have gone into more detail looking at some possible surgical and dental kits, and what level of care can be delivered with each.

Note:
1) We've tried to use the international generic names for drugs. However, there are some differences between the British and the US pharmacopoeias and where possible we have tried to include both e.g. Lignocaine (UK & Oz/NZ) = Lidocaine (US)

2) We have not included any quantities. This is dependent on what you are planning for and what you can afford. Unfortunately most medications require rotation with 1- 5 year shelf lives, making this a costly exercise, as they are not like food you can rotate into the kitchen

3) Always store a supply of any medicines you take regularly. These do not feature on the packing-lists. However, it is vital to remember the blood pressure pills, thyroid hormones, allergy pills, contraceptive pills, asthma inhalers, or what ever you take regularly. Most doctors will issue additional prescriptions for regular medication to allow an extra supply at a holiday home or to leave a supply at work. The main problem likely to arise is covering the cost of the extra medication which may be expensive and not covered by insurance. If you have previously had severe allergic reactions consider having a supply of Epi-pens

Medical Bags:
Before addressing what you need, it's worth looking at what you're going to put it in. There is large selection of medical bags on the market – military and civilian styles, rigid and soft construction. They vary in size from bum bags to large multi compartment backpacks and vary in price from less than $100 to more than $500 USD. We have selected 3-4 bags in each size range – personal use, first responder, and large multi-compartment bags. They cover a range of prices. What is right for you will depend on your individual requirements. If in a fixed location consider buying a rolling mechanics tool chest and using it as a "crash cart".

Personal size:
• Battle pack (Chinook Medical gear)
• Modular Medical Pouch (Tactical Tailor)
• Compact individual medical pouch (S.O Tech)

First responder size
• First response bag (Tactical Tailor)
• Modular bag system (Galls)
• Plano 747M Hard Case (Plano)
• NSW Medical Patrol bag (London Bridge Trading Company)
• Responder II (Conterra)
• Pelican waterproof case

Large kit bag:
• M5 style bag (Tactical tailor)
• MIII Medical pack (Eagle)
• NSW Training/Coverage Medical Backpack (London Bridge Trading Company) - one of the best large bags on the market. The STOMP II Medical Backpack from Blackhawk industries is very similar to the NSW training/coverage pack from LBTC – but significantly cheaper.
• ALS pack (Conterra)
• Kifaru back-packs (Kifaru) – not specifically medical, but can be customised inside and out. When you have selected the bags that suit you, one approach to organising your medical supplies is:

Personal bag: Carry this with you at all time. It contains basic first aid gear or in a tactical situation the equipment to deal with injuries from a gunshot wound or explosion.

First response bag: Carry this in your car; take it with you when you go camping etc. It contains more advanced first aid gear and some medical items.

Large kit bag: This is your home/retreat/bugging out medical kit. It contains your medical equipment as opposed to simple first aid supplies.

Storage area: In your home/retreat. It contains duplicate and bulk supplies. Large plastic storage bins are ideal for this.

Pack/organise/store items that are fragile, easily damaged by water, or can become messy (most liquids and ointments, ESPECIALLY tincture of benzoin in any form) in individual zip-lock plastic bags. For high-value water sensitive items (pulse oximeters, blood glucose meters, etc.) consider packing in water proof hard cases – such as the Pelican or Otter boxes.

Consider packing items that are used together into "battle-packs", ready to use packages – for example, pack an IV giving set with an IV start set with an Angio-Cath in zip-lock bag – so you can grab one thing and be ready to go.

Appendix 1 lists some medical suppliers.

EBay is a good source of medical supplies and surgical instruments but be careful to know what you are buying: Make certain you know what you want and what it would have cost from a supplier.

A brief note about airway management equipment

Before describing in detail packing lists for several possible kits we should discuss briefly airway management and the equipment associated with it. The details of this are best learnt in a First Aid /EMT class. The management of an airway has a number
of steps:

• Basic airway manoeuvres – head tilt, chin lift, jaw thrust.
• Simple airway adjuvants – oral airways, nasal airways.
• Advanced airway adjuvants – laryngeal masks, Combi-tubes.
• Endotracheal intubation – this is the gold standard of airway management. A plastic tube from the mouth into the trachea through which a patient can be
ventilated.

In addition once you have managed the airway you need to ventilate the patient either with mouth-to-mouth/mask or using a mask - self inflating bag combination (e.g. Ambubag).

The reason for discussing this is that you need to decide how much airway equipment to stock. Our view is that there is relatively little need to stock anything more than simple airway devices such as oral or nasal airways unless you are planning (and have the skills) to give an anaesthetic for the simple reason that anyone one who requires advanced airway management is likely to be unsalvageable in an austere situation. If
simple devices are not sufficient then they are likely to die regardless and introducing relatively complicated airway devices will not help. This, however, is an individual decision.

First Aid Kit

A comprehensive basic first aid kit is the building block of any medical preparations. With relatively simple equipment and supplies you can stop bleeding, splint a fracture, and provide basic patient assessment. Table 4.1 lists the suggested contents for a basic first air kit. The following are the key components of any kit albeit for a work, sport, or survival orientated first aid kit:

Dressings – Small gauze squares/large squares/Combined dressings/battle dressings/ non-adhesive dressings. There is a vast range. They serve two functions: - to cover and stop bleeding and to protect a wound. Exactly what you need is to a large degree personal preference – but whatever you buy you need small and large sizes, and they need to be absorbent.

Roller/Crepe Bandages – These go by various names (Crepe, Kerlix) – but we are talking about is some form of elasticised roller bandage. These are required to hold dressings in place, apply pressure to bleeding wounds, to help splint fractures, and to strap and support joint sprains. They come in a variety of sizes from 3 cm to 15 cm (1- 4") and you should stock a variety of sizes

Triangular bandages – These are triangular shapes of material which can be used for making slings, and splinting fractures, and sprains.

Band-Aids – Lots of them and in multiple sizes. They are useful for protecting minor wounds and skin damage.

Oral or nasal airways and a CPR face shield – We have already discussed supplies for airway management. Oral or nasal airways are the basics for assisting with airway management. Often when combined with basic airway opening manoeuvres these are sufficient to maintain the airway of an unconscious person. The face shield is if you need to perform mouth-to-mouth on someone. This only really an issue with strangers not close friends or family members.

Sterile normal saline (salt water) or water – You don't need expensive antiseptic solutions for cleaning wounds. Sterile saline or water (and to be honest – even tap water is fine for most wound cleaning) is all that's required to irrigate or clean contaminated wounds. There is no clear evidence that using antiseptics over sterile water in traumatic (as opposed to surgical) cuts or abrasions reduces the incidence of infection. The best way to clean a wound is with copious amounts of water or saline. It is also useful for irrigating eyes which have been exposed to chemical, dust, or other foreign bodies.

Tape – You can never have too much tape. It has 100s of uses. We recommend a strong sticky tape like Sleek™ or Elastoplast™. There are many other paper or plastic based tapes around – the main criterion is that it always sticks when required.

Gloves – Needed for two reasons. Firstly you have to assume that everyone you deal with has a blood borne disease. When you are dealing with family members in an austere situation this isn't so important. The second reason is to try and reduce infection when dealing with wounds. In the same way that using antiseptics over sterile water for irrigation of wounds has minimal impact on the incidence of infection – the same is true for sterile vs. non-sterile gloves. When managing traumatic wounds (again this isn't true for surgical incisions and operations) there appears to be minimal

difference in infection rates between wound management with sterile or non-sterile gloves. Exam gloves are not sterile, can be used on either hand, and are just casually sized (small, medium, large, etc.). They come in boxes of 50 or 100. Nitrile gloves are more than latex. Sterile gloves are packed individually and have specific sizes – 7.0, 7.5, 8.0, etc. Size is important – know your size.

That's it really, a very basic and limited range of supplies. As you can see this is considerably less than what is sold in many commercial first air kits but this is all that is required in a basic first aid kit. These supplies cover most first aid situations. They give you the ability to provide basic airway management, clean a wound, control bleeding, and splint, and immobilise fractures and sprains. It will also protect yourself from contamination with the gloves and face shield.

Basic Medical Kit

The basic medical kit is the next step you take from a basic first aid kit. The example here is designed for someone with a basic medical knowledge and a couple of good books. A lot of common problems can be managed with it; minor trauma (cuts and minor fractures), simple infections, and medical problems. Between this and the larger more comprehensive advanced kit wide spectrum dependent on knowledge or experience. Most begin with a first aid kit and expand as knowledge and finances allow.

A smaller medical kit for your bug-out bag could be made up from the above by adding some medications (such as acetaminophen, Benadryl, and some loperimide) and some instruments to a small first aid kit.

Advanced Medical kit

This is designed for someone with extensive medical training and would allow one to cope with 90% of common medical problems including some surgery, spinal and regional anaesthesia, and general anaesthesia with ketamine, treating most common infections and medical problems, and moderate trauma. This list may seem extreme, but is designed for a well-trained person in a worst-case scenario. Even though it is a long list, it all packs down. This sort of amount of equipment packs into two medium size nylon multi-compartment bags and a Plano rigid 747 box

Table 4.1 Basic First Aid Kit
Bandages and Dressings:
[__] Antiseptic Wipes
[__] Bandage (Crepe) – 50 mm (2")
[__] Bandage (Crepe) – 75 mm (2.5")
[__] Bandage (Crepe) – 100 mm (4")
[__] Bandage (Gauze) – 75 mm (2.5")
[__] Bandage (Gauze) – 100 mm (4")
[__] Bandage Triangular
[__] Dressing (Combine) 90 mm x 100 m m
[__] Dressing (Combine) 200 mm x 200 mm
[__] Dressing (Non Adhesive) 75 mm x 50 mm
[__] Dressing (Non Adhesive) 75 mm x 100 mm
[__] Dressing Strip - Elastoplast 75 mm x 1 m
[__] Eye Pads
[__] Gauze Swabs (Pkt 2) – 100 mm x 100 mm
[__] Sticking plasters

Personal protection
[__] Disposable Gloves
[__] CPR Face Shield

Instruments
[__] Clothing Shears
[__] Tweezers - Fine Point
[__] Splinter Probes

Other
[__] Saline Solution 30 mL Tubes
[__] Steri-Strips – 3 mm
[__] Survival Sheet
[__] Tape – 25 mm

Table 4.2. Basic medical kit
Bandages and Dressings
[__] Combat Dressings
[__] Large gauze dressings
[__] Small gauze squares
[__] Roller Bandages elastic + cotton (2in/4in/6in)
[__] Triangular Bandages

[__] Bandaids -assorted sizes and shapes (i.e. fin gertips)
[__] Sleek Tape 1 in.
(waterproof, plastic/elasticised tape)
[__] Cotton buds (Q-tips, cotton tips)

Personal protection / Antisepsis:
[__] Chlorhexidine (Hibiclens) or
[__] Povidone-iodine (Disinfectant)
[__] Antibacterial Soap
[__] Gloves
[__] Saline solution – for irrigation

Medication:
[__] Lignocaine 1% (Lidocaine) (local anaesthetic)
[__] Augmentin (broad spectrum antibiotic)
[__] Acetaminophen (Tylenol) (mild analgesic)
[__] Diclophenac (Voltaren)
(mod analgesic/antiinflammatory)
[__] Oral Rehydration powder
[__] Loperamide (Imodium) (antidiarrhoeal)
[__] Benadryl &/or Claritin
(antihistamines, short + long acting)
[__] Adrenaline auto injector (Epicene)
(USA = epinephrine)
[__] Morphine Sulphate
(strong pain killer) if available
[__] Gamma Benzene Hexachloride
(lice/scabies treatment)
[__] Co-timoxazole (antifungal)
[__] Contraceptive pills/Condoms

Instruments:
[__] Clothing shears
[__] Surgical scissors
[__] Needle holder) Enough to do basic minor
[__] Sm curved clamps) surgery - suturing, draining
[__] Tissue forceps) abscesses, cleaning a wound,
[__] Scalpel blades) etc.

Other:
[__] Thermometer (rectal or pacifier for children)
[__] Emergency Obstetric Kit
(includes bulb suction)
[__] Vicryl 2-0 suture material
(*Your choice of suture material is up to you – and is covered in detail elsewhere in this book. Vicryl is a synthetic dissolvable one, but takes up to 4-6 weeks to dissolve, so I think it is the ideal survival thread*)
[__] 5 mL syringes
[__] 20 gauge needles

Dental:

[__]   Oil of cloves (tooth ache)
[__]   Emergency dental kit
          (commercial preparation)

Table 4.3. The Deluxe Medical Kit

Bandages and dressings

[__]   Large gauze dressings
[__]   Small gauze squares
[__]   Combat dressings
[__]   Petroleum gauze squares
[__]   Plastic bags
[__]   Bandaids - assorted sizes and shapes
[__]   Elastoplast dressing
[__]   Steri-Strips - assorted sizes
[__]   Tincture of Benzoin
[__]   Roller (elasticised + cotton)
          bandages (2in/4in/6in)
[__]   Triangular bandages
[__]   Safety pins
[__]   Cotton buds
[__]   Paper tape (1/2 in/1in)
[__]   Sleek tape (1/2in/1in)
[__]   Plaster of Paris (or fibreglass)
          roller bandages (4in/6in)
[__]   Eye patches

Airway

[__]   Oropharyngeal airways
[__]   Nasal airways (nasal trumpet)
[__]   Resuscitation facemask with one-way valve
[__]   Self-inflating resuscitation bag
[__]   Endotracheal tube/ Laryngoscope

Assessment

[__]   BP cuff
[__]   Stethoscope
[__]   Otoscope
[__]   Small Torch (flash light)
[__]   Thermometer (rectal for children)
[__]   Multi-dip. urine test strips
[__]   Pregnancy test kits
[__]   Fluorescein eye strips
          (+ some liquid tears to wet the strips)

Other

[__]   Small eye magnet (for FB's)
[__]   Space blanket
[__]   Air splints (arm/long-leg/short-leg)
[__]   SAM splints
[__]   Sterile and un-sterile latex gloves
[__]   Scrub Suits

IV Kit

[__]   Normal Saline or Hartmans
[__]   Haemaccel or Pentaspan
          (a colloid resuscitation fluid)
[__]   IV giving sets - maxi-sets + standard sets
[__]   Blood collection bags + filter giving sets
[__]   Syringes 2/5/10/20 mL
[__]   Needles 20/22/24 gauge
[__]   IV cannulas 16/20/24 gauge
[__]   Spinal needles 22 gauge
[__]   Leur locks/Heparin locks
[__]   Saline for flushes
[__]   Tourniquet
[__]   Alcohol Wipes

Dental Kit

[__]   Oil of cloves
[__]   Zinc Oxide paste
[__]   Dental mirror
[__]   Sharp probe
[__]   Compactor
[__]   Extraction forceps
[__]   Elevators

Surgical Kit

[__]   Mayo scissors
[__]   Dissecting forceps
[__]   Small + medium needle holders
[__]   Small curved clamps
[__]   Small straight clamps
[__]   Large curved clamps
[__]   Scalpel Handle + Blades (size 11, 12, 15)
          or disposable scalpels
[__]   Small Bone Saw
[__]   Lift- Out obstetric forceps
[__]   Emergency Obstetric Kit
          (includes cord clamps, bulb suction etc)
[__]   Suture Material Vicryl; 0, 2-0
[__]   Chromic 0, 2-0
[__]   Dermalon 0, 2-0
[__]   Surgical stapler and remover
[__]   Heimlich flutter valve
[__]   Chest drains – various sizes
[__]   Drainage bottles or Flutter valves
[__]   Penrose drains
[__]   Foley Urethral Catheters –
          16 French (most useful size)
[__]   Urine Bags
[__]   Nasogastric (NG) tubes + spigots
[__]   Heavy duty scissors

Medications

[__] Povidone - iodine Prep antiseptic skin prep and/or Alcohol prep antiseptic skin prep Chlorhexidine and cetrimide anti

[__] septic hand wash

[__] Benalkium Chloride Antirabies skin wash

[__] Antibacterial Soap

[__] Paracetamol (Tylenol) oral mild analgesic

[__] Aspirin oral   wonder drug

[__] Diclophenac oral mod analgesic (NASID)

[__] Morphine IV/IMSC   strong analgesic

[__] Naroxone IV   antagonist to morphine

[__] Ketamine IV/IM IV   anaesthetic

[__] Diazepam IV   hypnotic/sedative

[__] Atropine IV   pre-med/poison anti

[__] Lignocaine (Lidocaine) IV local anaesthetic

[__] Metoclopramide (Reglan) anti-emetic

[__] Augmentin oral/IV   penicillin antibiotic

[__] Metronidazole oral   anaerobic antibiotic

[__] Cefaclor oral   cephalosporin antibiotic

[__] Ceftriaxone IV   cephalosporin antibiotic

[__] Ciprofloxacin oral   quinolone antibiotic

[__] Mebendazole oral   antiparasitic

[__] Co-trimoxazole top   antifungal

[__] Adrenaline IV/IM (USA = Epinephrine)

[__] Salbutamol inhaler   asthma/anaphylaxis

[__] Rehydration formula   dehydration

[__] Benadryl &/or Claritin oral antihistamine

[__] OTC Cough suppressant

[__] Betnesol oral   steroid

[__] Hydrocortisone IV/cream steroid

[__] Loperamide oral   antidiarrheal

[__] Ergometrine &/or Oxytocin IV/IM ecbolic for PPH

[__] Neomycin eye drops

[__] Prilocaine eye drops local anaesthetic

[__] Starr Otic Drops antibiotic ear drops

[__] Mupirocin (Bactroban) top topical antibacterial cream

[__] Gamma Benzene Hexachloride topical for scabies and lice

[__] Water for injection/normal saline for injection

[__] Oral Contraceptive Pills

[__] Condoms/Cervical Caps/Diaphragms

Surgical Instruments

The above kits are general medical kits – covering the multitude of medical problems and contain surgical instruments. However commonly asked questions relate specifically to surgical instruments – what and how many of them are required for various levels of surgical procedures. Below is a detailed list of surgical instruments with 4 levels of increasing complexity. Note that each level builds on the one before it. This instrument list reflects our own preferences and experience under austere conditions. There are many other instruments that would be helpful (for example ring forceps to hold sponges, larger retractors, etc.), but they are not considered vital. This is the bare minimum.

What is it?

Needle holders – shaped like scissors but instead of having a cutting surface they have two opposed plates with groves cut into them, and are designed to hold the needle, and stop it rolling or slipping as you sew. Once you have gripped the needle a ratchet holds the tips locked so the needle does not move

Haemostat/Clips/Clamps – Similar in shape to needle holders but the tips are designed to clamp onto tissue and to hold it. They have the same ratchet mechanism to keep them locked and attached once they are attached. They are used to clip bleeding blood vessels or hold onto tissues you are working with. There is a massive range of sizes and shapes depending on what they are designed to clip or clamp.

Forceps/Dissectors – are shaped like traditional tweezers and come in various sizes. They either have small teeth on their tips or are smooth tipped. They are designed to handle tissues and to help you move tissues round such as when suturing

Scissors – these are self-explanatory

Retractors – these are designed to hold tissues out of the way so that you can see what you are doing. They come in a huge range of sizes and shapes depending on what part of the body you are working with. Skin hooks or small right-angle retractors are most suitable for most minor wound repairs

Level 1: Field Wound Repair Kit

This is a minimal cost unit intended to be carried in a kit or pack, and be used for minor wound debridement, and closure of the types of injuries most commonly occurring. Although it is a pre-packaged "disposable" kit the instruments may be reused many times with appropriate sterilization and care. This easily goes in a ziplock bag, and can be widely distributed, and available among your group.

Level 2: Basic Suture Tray

This is composed of good quality instruments intended for long term use and resterilization. It is suitable for repair and debridement of minor wounds and injuries including simple two-layer closure. This is typical of the majority of wound care done in a hospital ER.

Level 3: Procedure kit

This kit is capable of complicated multilayer wound repair, OB repairs, plastic surgery closures, tendon repair, chest tube insertion. This is suitable for laymen with some training and experience, and is probably the recommended level for most as it has the greatest capability vs. expense. Those with adequate medical training could press this into service for more advanced problems with some improvisation. Note: if you anticipate a lot of OB or foreign body removal a Weitlaner retractor, 5-6" would be very helpful. A rongeur and rasp are very helpful for bone clean up, traumatic finger amputations, etc.

Level 4: Major procedures kit

This kit is capable of complicated multilayer wound repair, OB repairs, plastic surgery closures, tendon repair, chest tube insertion, emergency abdominal surgery, Caesarean sections, straightforward amputations, etc. With this kit a competent practitioner should be able to perform all the procedures that are likely to be possible in an austere environment.

Table 4.4 Field Wound repair kit

[__] 1 Tube Super-glue Gel
[__] 1 Steri-Strips, and Benzoin adhesive, or duct tape
[__] 1 Betadine swab packet, or skin cleaner of choice
[__] 1 Irrigation syringe and ability to purify at least 2 quarts water; tablets, etc.
[__] 1 Dressings of choice

Optional items to consider include:
[__] 1 Disposable laceration tray with needle driver, pickups, scissors, 4x4s, drape
[__] 1 Disposable scalpel, #10
[__] 1 Ethilon, or Prolene, or Silk 4-0 & 6-0
[__] 1 Vicryl or Chromic 4-0
[__] 1 skin stapler, 15 shot
[__] 1 staple remover
[__] 1 Sterile gloves your size
[__] 1 Lidocaine 1% or 2% WITHOUT epinephrine

Table 4.5 Basic suture tray

[__] 1 Needle driver, 5"
[__] 1 Adson forceps ,1x2 teeth
[__] 1 Sharp/blunt scissors, 5" straight
[__] 1 Iris tissue scissors, curved
[__] 1 Mosquito hemostat, curved
[__] 1 #3 Scalpel handle & #10, #11, #15 blades

[__] Ethilon, or Prolene, or Silk suture;
        2-0, 4-0, 6-0, cuticular needles
[__] Vicryl or Chromic suture 2-0, 4-0, 6-0 cuticular needles

[__] Skin staplers & remover
[__] Steri-Strips and Benzoin
[__] Several tubes Super-glue Gel
[__] Skin cleaner of choice
[__] Irrigation syringes & ability to purify water
[__] Sterile gloves appropriate sizes
[__] Sterile drapes, disposable or reusable
[__] Appropriate anaesthesia and dressing of choice

Table 4.6 Procedure set

[__] 1 Needle driver, 4-5"
[__] 1 Needle driver, 6-7"
[__] 1 Sharp/blunt scissors, 5" straight
[__] 1 Baby Metzenbaum or Mayo scissors ,5" curved
[__] 1 Iris tissue scissors, curved
[__] 1 Mosquito haemostat, straight
[__] 1 Mosquito haemostat, curved
[__] 1 Kelly haemostat, straight
[__] 1 Kelly haemostat, curved
[__] 1 Peon or Oschner haemostat; 7-8", curved
[__] 1 Adson, 1x2 teeth
[__] 1 Adson, no teeth
[__] 1 Splinter forceps
[__] 1 Senn 3 prong/blunt + right-angle double end retractor
[__] 1 Allis 4x5 clamp
[__] 2 #3 Scalpel handle and #10, #11, #15 blades
[__] 1 #4 Scalpel handle and #20 or #22 blades
[__] 1 Thin probe

[__] Ethilon, or Prolene, or Silk suture;
        0, 2-0, 4-0, 5-0, 6-0, 7-0 cuticular & plastic needles
[__] Vicryl or Chromic suture;
        0, 2-0, 4-0, 6-0 cuticular needles
[__] Skin staplers & remover
[__] Steri-Strips and Benzoin
[__] Several tubes Super-glue Gel
[__] Skin cleaner of choice
[__] Irrigation syringes & ability to purify water
[__] Sterile gloves appropriate sizes
[__] Sterile drapes, disposable or reusable
[__] Appropriate anaesthesia and dressing of choice

Table 4.7 Major Procedure kit

[__] 1 Needle driver, 4-5"
[__] 1 Needle driver, 6-7"
[__] 1 Sharp/blunt scissors, 5" straight
[__] 2 Baby Metzenbaum or Mayo scissors, 5" curved
[__] 1 Metzenbaum, 6-7" Curved
[__] 1 Mayo, 6-7" Curved
[__] 1 Iris tissue scissors, curved
[__] 1 Mosquito haemostat, straight
[__] 1 Mosquito haemostat, curved

[__] 2 Kelly haemostat, straight
[__] 2 Kelly haemostat, curved
[__] 2 Peon or Oschner haemostat, 7-8" curved
[__] 1 Adson, 1x2 teeth
[__] 1 Adson ,no teeth
[__] 1 Splinter forceps
[__] 1 Russian forceps, 6-7"
[__] 2 Senn 3 prong/blunt
        + right-angle double end retractor
[__] 2 Allis 4x5 clamp
[__] 1 Army-Navy retractor
[__] 1 Ribbon retractor
[__] 1 Weitlaner retractor
[__] 2 #3 Scalpel handle and #10, #11, #15 blades
[__] 1 #4 Scalpel handle and #20 or #22 blades
[__] 1 Thin probe
[__] 1 Wire (Gigli) amputation saw or Satterlee amputation saw
[__] 1 Adson type bone rongeur
[__] 1 Bone rasp

[__] Ethilon, or Prolene, or Silk suture;
        0, 2-0, 4-0, 5-0, 6-0, 7-0 cuticular, taper, & plastic needles
[__] Vicryl or Chromic suture;
        0, 2-0, 4-0, 6-0 cuticular & taper needles
[__] Skin staplers & remover
[__] Steri-Strips and Benzoin
[__] Several tubes Super-glue Gel
[__] Skin cleaner of choice
[__] Irrigation syringes & ability to purify water
[__] Sterile gloves appropriate sizes
[__] Sterile drapes, disposable or reusable
[__] Appropriate anaesthesia and dressings of choice
Copyright 2005
Survival and Austere Medicine: An Introduction
http://medtech.syrene.net/forum/

Seven Antibiotics to Stockpile and Why,

by Cynthia J. Koelker, MD

Assuming your personal physician will help you stockpile antibiotics for TEOTWAWKI, which should you request? Is there a logical reason to have amoxicillin on hand rather than doxycycline?

Here's what I would suggest and why.
No antibiotic is effective against every type of microbe. Certain ones will kill aerobic bacteria, others are used for anaerobic bacteria, still others are effective against resistant strains, and certain people are allergic to or intolerant of various antibiotics. The following are all generics, running about $10 for about a month's treatment.

Amoxicillin is the old standby for most respiratory infections (probably most of which are viral and don't even require antibiotics). It is excellent for strep throat and some strains of pneumococcal bacteria. It is also safe for children and pregnant women. It is well-tolerated, causing little stomach distress or diarrhea. The drawbacks are that some people are truly allergic, and many bacteria have developed resistance to amoxicillin (especially staph) through overuse among both humans and animals. Anyone truly allergic to amoxicillin should substitute erythromycin or another antibiotic.

Cephalexin works on most of the same bacteria as amoxicillin, plus is stronger against Staph aureus, which mostly causes skin infections. It rarely works against MRSA (resistant staph), however. It is also well-tolerated in children and is safe in pregnant women, causing few side-effects. Like any antibiotic, it carries the risk of allergy. People who develop anaphylaxis (a life-threatening allergy) with amoxicillin probably should not take cephalexin, as there is a good 10% cross-reactivity between the two. If I had to choose between stockpiling amoxicillin or cephalexin, I would choose cephalexin. The combination drug, amoxicillin-clavulanate (Augmentin), is as strong against staph, but more expensive and harder on the stomach.

Ciprofloxacin is useful for anthrax (which I've never seen), urinary tract and prostate infections (which are very common), and many forms of pneumonia and bronchitis. One of the more important and selective uses of ciprofloxacin is in combination with metronidazole for diverticulitis. This potentially life-threatening infection usually (or at least often) requires two antibiotics to resolve. (Levaquin and Avelox are a bit stronger than ciprofloxacin and could be substituted for this, but are much more expensive.) Ciprofloxacin is not used in women or children unless the benefit clearly outweighs the risk, although the risk of joint damage (seen in animals) appears minimal. Taking ciprofloxacin by mouth is nearly as effective as taking by IV.

Doxycycline is useful in penicillin/amoxicillin-allergic adults for respiratory infections and some urinary/prostate infections. It is avoided in children and pregnant women unless the benefit clearly outweighs the risk (of permanent tooth discoloration in children under the age of 8). Doxycycline is sometimes effective against penicillin-resistant bacteria. If I were limited to either doxycycline or erythromycin, I would choose erythromycin for stockpile.

Erythromycin is useful for most of the same infections amoxicillin is used for, and thus can be substituted in penicillin-allergic patients. However, erythromycin tends to cause the intestine to contract, often causing cramps or diarrhea. (This property is sometimes used to help patients with conditions that impair intestinal motility.) It can be safely used in children and pregnant women.

Metronidazole is an unusual antibiotic used for very specific infections. It is aimed primarily at anaerobic bacteria, primarily those found in the intestine. It is also used for certain STDs, including trichomonas. As mentioned above, it is very useful in combination with ciprofloxacin (or SMZ-TMP, below) for diverticulitis. It is the only inexpensive antibiotic effective for Clostridium difficile (c. diff, or antibiotic-related) colitis. It is also effective against certain amoeba. This drug is not used in children unless the benefit clearly outweighs the risk.

SMZ-TMP is a combination drug of sulfamethoxazole and trimethoprim. The latter antibiotic is used mainly for urinary infections. The sulfa component is effective against many respiratory bacteria and most urinary pathogens, although ciprofloxacin is somewhat stronger. The main reason to stockpile SMZ-TMP is due to its effectiveness against resistant staph (MRSA).

Of course, only the most understanding fellow-prepper physician is likely to prescribe all these in quantity. The list can be narrowed a bit, by dropping doxycycline (since erythromycin covers most microbes that doxycycline would kill, and can be used in young children) and amoxicillin (because cephalexin covers most amoxicillin-sensitive bacteria and has the benefit of effectiveness against staph aureus).

My top five antibiotics would therefore be:

Cephalexin
Ciprofloxacin
Erythromycin
Metronidazole
SMZ-TMP

Of these, SMZ-TMP and ciprofloxacin have the most duplicate coverage, as do cephalexin and erythromycin. Since the intolerance of erythromycin is much higher than is allergy to cephalexin, I would favor cephalexin. Ciprofloxacin is stronger for intra-abdominal infections than SMZ-TMP, and is less likely to develop resistance. Although its use in children is a bit of a concern due to the question of joint pain (although this is rare), I would favor ciprofloxacin over than SMZ-TMP, even though SMZ-TMP is effective against MRSA. However, when the use of antibiotics is severely curtailed, antibiotic resistance will also decrease, and therefore MRSA will become less of a concern.

Therefore, my top three antibiotics to stockpile would be:

Cephalexin
Ciprofloxacin
Metronidazole

Using these three alone or in combination would cover around 90% of the infections physicians commonly encounter, as well as several less-likely threats (including anthrax and C. diff).

Using Expired Medications – Antibiotics and Antiviral Medications

My first guest post on SurvivalBlog.com generated an abundance of questions and concerns. Among the most popular was that of using medications beyond their expiration date. Are they safe? Are they effective?

It's easy enough for me to say I think it's safe, but is there any science to support my opinion? I spent the week looking into the facts, and found some fascinating information.

To start with, just what is a drug expiration date? In short, the date (required since 1979) does not indicate when a drug goes bad, but rather a date through which the drug is guaranteed to be good. Compare this to what you might find on a can of beans: the "best if used by" date.

How are these dates determined? In two ways.

The first is by real-time testing. Medications are stored under manufacturer-recommended conditions (which does not mean in your hot, humid bathroom over the toilet). At given intervals the medications are tested for appearance, drug content, and stability. Nowhere could I find that they are tested for safety specifically, but if the drug itself is present in acceptable amounts, it seems reasonable to conclude it is still safe.

Secondly, drugs are tested under high-temperature stress conditions to simulate longer time periods. Logically, if a drug is only two years old, five years of stability testing is unlikely to have been performed. However, if a medication remains stable for a specified time period under adverse conditions, one may presume it likely stable and therefore safe for much longer periods.

Expiration dates are only found on the original packaging and apply to unopened meds that have been stored as directed. This is in contrast to the date on your actual prescription bottle, a "do not use beyond" date. Pharmacists commonly purchase pills in bottles of 1,000 then dispense them into smaller containers, generally with a shorter expiration date. The latest this will be is a year beyond the original prescription date. Although the original bottle may have a date 2-3 years in the future, your own bottle will be dated for 1 year or less from purchase, due to uncertainty about actual storage conditions and patient use.

One tip on stocking up, then, is to request your prescriptions in the original packaging, typically bottles of 100 (usually not 90, as insurance often prefers, though there are exceptions). Your doctor will not necessarily know this information, but you can look it up in a PDR to save time. A used Physicians Desk Reference (PDR) can be purchased on Amazon for under $5. Generic drugs are not in the PDR. You will have to ask the pharmacist for information regarding your own prescription.

The primary source of information regarding the prolonged stability of medications comes from the Shelf Life Extension Program (SLEP) database. Rather than discard millions of dollars worth of expired drugs stockpiled for emergency use, the government tested representative lots for extended stability. These stockpiled drugs are aimed at emergency use for injuries and infections rather than chronic diseases such as diabetes, heart disease, and asthma. The most useful data for the layman is related to drugs to combat bacterial and viral infections.

In 2009 as a result of the H1N1 scare, two anti-viral (anti-influenza) drugs were granted an Emergency Use Authorization (which has since expired). Relenza was granted approval for up to one year after the original expiration date, whereas Tamiflu products were approved for up to an additional 5 years. Tamiflu is easier to use, has fewer side-effects, and comes in blister-packs of 10. A full dose is one 75-mg tablet twice daily for 5 days, to be started within the first day or two of true influenza infection (which is not always known, a discussion for another day).

The following is excerpted from my upcoming book, Armageddon Medicine.

Does a can of tuna go bad overnight? What about a bottle of medicine? Common sense suggests the answer is no, but is there any evidence?

The primary source of information regarding the prolonged stability of medications comes from the Shelf Life Extension Program database. Rather than discard millions of dollars worth of expired drugs stockpiled for emergency use, the U.S. federal government tested representative lots of selected medications for extended stability. These stockpiled drugs are aimed at emergency use for injuries and infections rather than chronic diseases such as diabetes, heart disease, and asthma. The most useful data for the layman is related to drugs to combat bacterial and viral infections.

Of the antibiotics tested, all passed assays for stability, potency, and appearance for at least a year beyond the original expiration date.

Of the lots tested, the following had their expiration date extended by the number of months indicated.

Medication Name	Dosage Form	Average extension in months (range)
Amoxicillin sodium	Tablets	23 (22-23)
Ampicillin	Capsules	49 (22-64)
Cephalexin	Capsules	57 (28-135)
Ciprofloxacin	Tablets	55 (12-142)
Doxycycline Hyclate	Capsules	50 (37-66)
Erythromycin lactobionate	Powder	60 (38-83)
Sulfisoxasole	Tablets	56 (45-68)
Tetracycline HCl	Capsules	50 (17-133)
Silver sulfadiazine	Cream	57 (28-104)

A summary of the Shelf Life Extension Prorgarm (SLEP) data is available in The Journal of Pharmaceutical Sciences, Vol. 95, No. 7, July 2006.

The Medical Letter, a respected professional newsletter, addressed the topic of expired medications in both 1996 and 2002. Regarding safety, they say: "The only report of human toxicity that may have been caused by chemical or physical degradation of a pharmaceutical product is renal tubular damage that was associated with use of degraded tetracycline... Current tetracycline preparations have been reformulated with different fillers to minimize degradation and are unlikely to have this effect." (The Medical Letter, Vol. 44, Issue 1142, October 28, 2002.)

Liquid preparations may be much less stable, and degrade more quickly if frozen or heated. The Medical Letter advises that "Drugs in solution, particularly injectables, that have become cloudy or discolored or show signs of precipitation should not be used." For oral medications, color changes may also be related to the dyes rather than the drugs. The

primary concern pertaining to eye drops is microbial contamination once the preservative becomes ineffective.

Overall then, the concern is not regarding safety, but rather effectiveness. "Many drugs stored under reasonable conditions retain 90% of their potency for at least 5 years after the expiration date on the label, and sometimes much longer," per The Medical Letter.

The SLEP data does not describe testing for any controlled-release antibiotics, such as Biaxin XL and Augmentin XR. Controlled-release delivery systems vary from drug to drug and would require testing not only of the medication itself, but the delivery system as well, to assure adequate drug delivery. Therefore, the regular versions of both Biaxin and Augmentin may be preferable for stockpiling. Essentially the only advantage of controlled-release antibiotics is less frequent dosing.

In the case of antibiotics, a 10-25% loss of potency over time may make little difference in treatment, and could be made up for by higher dosing in serious infections. Even now, generic medications are only required to be within 20% of the stated amount, and so the dose administered may already vary as much as 50% from one generic to another, or from pill to pill. For example, a 100 mg brand-name tablet must contain 95-105 mg of the active drug, whereas a generic of the same is permitted to have 80-125% active compound. Also, generics may not be equivalent in terms of integrity, dissolution properties, or coatings. In the case of generics, "Made in the USA" is probably preferable to those manufactured elsewhere.

To sum it all up, the good news is that most tablets and capsules are very likely safe and quite likely effective for several years beyond the printed expiration date. Using expired medications may suffice for a decade beyond the end of the world as we know it. (But what then?)

Although antimicrobial medications are important, what about other common drugs used on a daily basis? If you or someone you know suffers from diabetes, chronic pain, arthritis, asthma, hypertension, heart disease, or other serious condition, will medications be safe and effective beyond their expiration dates?

The following is excerpted from my upcoming book, Armageddon Medicine:

Published data has documented the safety of many medications beyond their expirations dates. The Medical Letter (Vol. 44, Issue 1142, October 28, 2002) states: "84% of 1,122 lots of 96 different drug products stored in military facilities in their unopened original containers would be expected to remain stable for an average of 57 months after their original expiration date." However, the products tested were primarily antibiotics and other drugs used for emergency purposes.

What information is available regarding common medications for other acute conditions, or chronic conditions? Only scattered reports are available. Per the same issue of The Medical Letter, captopril and TheoDur tablets remained chemically and physically stable for 1.5-to-9 years beyond their expiration dates; amantadine and rimantidine remained stable after storage for 25 years; another theophylline preparation retained 90% potency for about 30 years. The Medical Letter concludes, "Many drugs stored under reasonable conditions retain 90% of their potency for at least 5 years after the expiration date on the label, and sometimes much longer." They also mention that there has only been one reported case of dangerous degradation of expired medication, and that was of a type of tetracycline product that is no longer in human use. [JWR Adds: As previously mentioned in SurvivalBlog, the issue with tetracycline tablets of that vintage was a degradation of the tablet binder, and that binder is no longer in use.] (I do not know if veterinary antibiotics might use the old preparation, however.) Overall then, the concern is not regarding safety, but rather effectiveness.

Additional concerns exist regarding liquid preparations, which may be much less stable, and degrade more quickly if frozen or heated. The Medical Letter advises that "Drugs in solution, particularly injectables, that have become cloudy or discolored or show signs of precipitation should not be used." For oral liquid medications, color changes may be related to the dyes rather than the active drugs, however. Epinephrine in EpiPens was noted to contain less than 90% potency at 10 months after the expiration date. A significant problem with eye drops is microbial contamination once the preservative becomes ineffective. In short, medications for chronic illnesses have not been tested.

Nevertheless, it seems reasonable to extrapolate from the known data on drugs that were included in the Shelf Life Extension Program, and conclude that most tablets and capsules would be both safe and effective for several years past their expiration date, when stored in the original packaging at the recommended temperatures.

However, there are a few additional questions that deserve attention: extended-release medications, generics, and drugs which require blood testing. Of the medications tested in the SLEP program, few if any were of the extended-release variety. Because Americans like the convenience of once-daily dosing, many drugs have been developed with delayed-release technology. This includes any medicine with the following in the name: XR or XL (extend-

ed release), SR (sustained or slow release), CR (controlled release), "slo," "dur," or "contin". The methods by which the medications are slowly released in the stomach or intestine may not be as stable as the active drug itself, and have the potential to be effected by extremes of temperature or humidity. The release may be via a semi-permeable membrane of the entire tablet, or on each individual granule within a capsule, or by a layered tablet designed to dissolve at different pH (acidity) levels. Under adverse conditions, the active drug may be released more quickly or more slowly than intended, yielding unpredictable clinical results. For example, an extended-release blood pressure medication that enters the blood stream too quickly may lower your blood pressure too much or too rapidly. If released too slowly, it may not reduce your blood pressure adequately or at all. The dose of medication in a delayed release narcotic may be lethal if absorbed all at once.

Although I could find no specific data regarding stability of delayed-release or extended-release medications, I question whether they would be as stable or reliably absorbed as the regular versions of the drugs. Having your doctor change your medication now to a non-delayed-release preparation is a consideration. Of course, these rapid-release medications often must be taken more than once a day. Examples include Toprol XL, Wellbutrin SR and XL, Biaxin XL, Diltiazem SR and XL, Xanax XR, Effexor XR, and many others. Fortunately, the older, immediate-release versions are usually less expensive.

Another question is the stability of generic versus name brand drugs. Although I expect brand-name drugs would exhibit greater stability, cost is significantly more for most (but not all) preparations. Also, brand-name drugs are allowed a 5% leeway in bioavailability, whereas generic drugs are permitted 20%. That said, according to the FDA's web site, recent studies showed "The average difference in absorption into the body between the generic and the brand name was only 3.5 percent [Davit et al. Comparing generic and innovator drugs: a review of 12 years of bioequivalence data from the United States Food and Drug Administration. Ann Pharmacother. 2009;43(10):1583-97]."

Whereas I believe the quality of most generic medications is excellent, I have, however, encountered some generic drugs that are difficult to swallow, or crumble easily, or stick together, or become discolored. Some of my patients swear by one generic and claim another is ineffective. If possible, investigate the country of origin of your generic prescriptions. In this case, "Made in the USA" is a good sign.

Yet another concern lies with medications where blood levels are usually monitored. Of course, at TEOTWAWKI it's unlikely that blood testing will be performed. Drugs with "narrow therapeutic windows" pose a special concern. These drugs are ineffective at low dose but toxic at higher doses, with a small window between where the drug is therapeutic. Such drugs include digoxin, lithium, and theophylline. When serum drug levels or other biologic indices cannot be measured, dosing must be determined by clinical result and side-effects. Anti-seizure medications, thyroid preparations, and even insulin may fall in this category.

To sum it all up, the good news is that most tablets and capsules are very likely safe and quite likely effective for several years beyond the printed expiration date. Using expired medications may do for a decade beyond the end of the world as we know it.

About the Author: Cynthia J. Koelker, MD is the author of the book 101 Ways to Save Money on Health Care. The book explains how to treat over 30 common medical conditions economically, and includes dozens of sections on treating yourself. Available for under $10 online, the book offers practical advice on treating: respiratory infections, pink eye, sore throats, nausea, diarrhea, heartburn, urinary infections, allergies, arthritis, acne, hemorrhoids, dermatitis, skin infection, lacerations, lice, carpal tunnel syndrome, warts, mental illness, asthma, COPD, depression, diabetes, enlarged prostate, high blood pressure, high cholesterol, and much more.

For more articles by Dr. Koelker visit
ArmageddonMedicine.net.

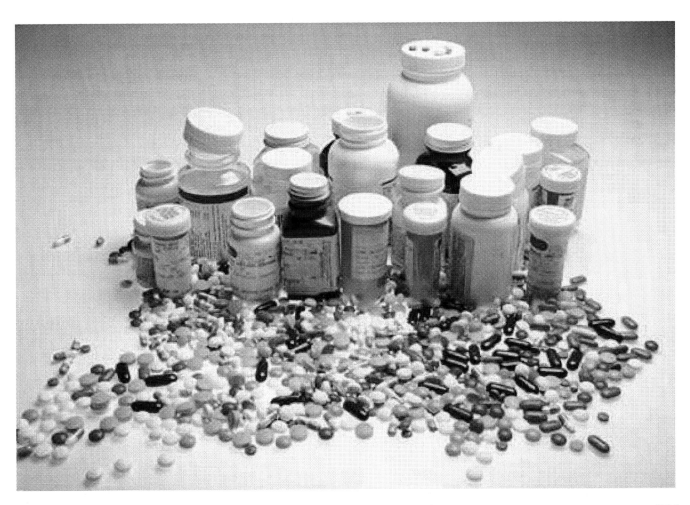

Prophetic Utterances on Defense

*"There is one principle which is eternal; **it is the duty of all men to protect their lives and the lives of the household**, whenever necessity requires, and no power has the right to forbid it, should the last extreme arrive, but I anticipate no such extreme, but caution is the parent of safety."*
Teachings of the Prophet Joseph Smith, Section Six, 1843-44, p. 391.

*"Not only should we have strong spiritual homes, but we should have strong temporal homes. We should avoid bondage by getting out of debt as soon as we can, pay as we go, and live within our incomes. There is wisdom in having on hand a year's supply of food, clothing, fuel (if possible), and **in being preparing to defend our families and our possessions** and to take care of ourselves. **I believe a man should prepare for the worst while working for the best**."* **Teachings of Ezra Taft Benson, p. 263-264.**

"As for this people fostering to themselves that the day has come for them to sell their guns and ammunition to their enemies, and sit down to sleep in peace, they will find themselves deceived and before they know, they will sleep until they are slain. They have got to carry weapons with them, to be ready to send their enemy to hell cross lots, whether they be Lamanites or mobs who may come to take their lives, or destroy their property. We must be prepared that they dare not come to us in a hostile manner without being assured they will meet a vigorous resistance and ten to one they will meet their grave." **Brigham Young, JD Vol 1, P . 171 - 172, July 31, 1853**

*"We all believe that the Lord will fight our battles; but how? Will He do it while we are unconcerned and make no effort whatever for our own safety when an enemy is upon us? If we make no effort to guard our towns, our houses, our cities, our wives and children, will the Lord guard them for us? He will not; but if we pursue the opposite course and strive to help Him to accomplish His designs, then will He fight our battles. We are baptized for the remission of sins; but it would be quite as unreasonable to expect a remission of sins without baptism, as to expect the Lord to fight our battles without our taking every precaution to be prepared to defend ourselves. The Lord requires us to be quite as willing to fight our own battles as to have Him fight them for us. **If we are not ready for an enemy when he comes upon us, we have not lived up to the requirements of Him who guides the ship of Zion, or who dictates the affairs of his kingdom**."* **Brigham Young, JD, Vol. 11, p. 131, August 1-10, 1865.**

*"And again, the Lord has said that: **Ye shall defend your families even unto bloodshed.** Therefore for this cause were the Nephites contending with the Lamanites, to defend themselves, and their families, and their lands, their country, and their rights, and their religion."*
Alma 43:47

*"We believe that men should appeal to the civil law for redress of all wrongs and grievances, where personal abuse is inflicted or the right of property or character infringed, where such laws exist as will protect the same; but **we believe that all men are justified in defending themselves, their friends, and property, and the government, from the unlawful assaults and encroachments of all persons in times of exigency, where immediate appeal cannot be made to the laws, and relief afforded**."* **Doctrine and Covenants 134:11**

Defense

"People who live in delightful, well-mannered suburbs, who never have to contest for their lives and property, often fail to grasp the subtle logic of violence. It is a mistake seldom made by hardened criminals." James Dale Davidson and Lord William Rees-Mogg in THE GREAT RECKONING

In a massive social collapse, most people will be able to keep only that which they can defend. This includes their lives, their homes, their food, their money, and if they're male, even their wives and perhaps their children. This is a thought that may disturb many people who are doing serious emergency planning; many members of our church do not have a "survivalist" background or mindset and they've never had any reason to think about physically defending that which is precious to them. A major disaster may change all that, just as it may change nearly everything else in the world for those living through it.

In an orderly, productive society with a stable division of labor, the harsh realities of life are not so obvious. You have laws that most people obey and you have professional police who enforce those laws. It's their job to defend the lives and property of the average citizen; if there's any violence to be done in that defense, the police handle that. The average person never has to consider defending what is his unless he is personally threatened by a criminal. The threat of force by the police keeps order in the society and tends to discourage aggressive criminal behavior (not always very well in today's world I'll admit). It also tends to hide a basic truth about the nature of human relations.

In a massive social collapse, law and public order break down and the truth about human rights is revealed: An individual has rights only as long as he can defend them. This is the subtle logic of violence. It has always been true but it's something to which most of us have never given a moment's thought. It's also a concept that makes some Saints uncomfortable because it contradicts much of the illusions by which we have lived all of our lives. However, unless you understand and accept this basic fact of life, you may not survive the coming challenges.

If a disaster crashes down hard upon us, it will destroy all the illusions and most of the rules we have lived by for the past hundred years or more. It will create harsh new rules. When the fundamental order of a society changes and new rules arise, those who fail to understand the new rules suffer the most.

There's a reason for the information in the above paragraphs: It may save your life. Why? Because it's not just having a weapon that's important, or even knowing how to use one; it's knowing full well why you need to use it

and therefore not hesitating to use it when needed. *A gun in your hand is totally worthless against an assailant unless you're fully willing to use it to defend yourself.* **You must understand that the new rules brought on by a major disaster may require you to defend your life personally.**

The information here meant for the average Saint; it's essentially one average Saint speaking to another. Most of us are not survivalists and we have not had much experience with guns. We have no particular interest in, and precious little time to learn about, exotic weapons with foreign sounding names. We need basic information about basic weapons that work dependably and don't cost a fortune.

In a bad scenario, it is not likely that things will deteriorate into some kind of violent chaos. The more likely worst case scenario is one in which there may be unrest and martial law in the urban areas and far less order than we're accustomed to everywhere (more akin to New Orleans) but nothing that resembles the Future War in *The Terminator*. Desperate people take desperate chances, the more base emotions become prominent in many people's behavior, and hunger, cold, lust, greed and fear take charge of people's actions. You probably won't have to worry about roving gangs; but your concern will be with one or two people breaking into your house for food or whatever may be available, stealing vegetables from your garden or firewood from your woodpile, etc. This is what you'll need to defend against and this is something you can handle.

The best weapon for home defense is a shotgun with a short barrel. There are three reasons why this is true. First, there is nothing scarier than looking at that big black hole at the end of the barrel of a shotgun when it's pointed at you. Second, when you fire a shotgun at close range it's impossible to miss; you're going to hit what you're aiming at. Third, when you hit someone with a shotgun, he doesn't get up and come at you. A short barrel gun is easier to handle than one with a long barrel.

There are several good basic shotguns on the market. One of the best is a 12 gauge Remington pump 870 Express Magnum with an 18" barrel. It's not fancy and it's not pretty but it will do the job. As someone told me not long ago, just hearing the unmistakable click of a pump shotgun being cocked will scare off most intruders. The Remington costs about $250 new. Mossberg also makes a good pump 12 gauge, along with several other manufacturers. If there is a good gun shop in your area, stop by and look at what's available. Ask questions; most gun shop employees are very knowledgable and willing to share that knowledge with you.

The other useful weapon for home or personal defense is a handgun. Although an automatic shoots faster and loads quicker than a revolver, it is a more complex mechanism and may jam occasionally, whereas a revolver almost never jams. Also for a novice, a revolver is less intimidating to hold and shoot. Maybe it's all those Roy Rogers and Gene Autry movies, but somehow a revolver just seems more familiar to someone who is not used to guns.

The best revolver to have is a .357 magnum with a 4 inch barrel. It can fire both .38 and .357 shells (use the .38 ammo for practice because it's cheaper than the .357). A .357 is powerful enough to kill or seriously injure an assailant and it's common enough to be affordable. I'd stick to a well-known brand such as a Smith & Wesson. Taurus makes a good handgun that is less expensive than the very top names. Again, ask at the gun shop.

If the gun is for a small female, the .357 may be too heavy and awkward to use effectively. In that case a .38 or even a .32 may be a better choice. Remember that a smaller caliber weapon does not have the stopping power of a larger one, so if you have to shoot someone to defend yourself, keep shooting until you empty the gun. Once you've wounded someone, he's going to try to kill you if he possibly can, so you don't want to inflict a minor wound; you must stop him!

No matter which guns you get, be sure to get lots of ammunition. Any ammo you don't use or need could be a great trade item after a disaster. Walmart generally has good prices on ammunition. Gun shows are always a good place to shop for ammo deals.

If you know someone who has a good bit of knowledge and experience with guns, get him to teach you how to shoot safely. It is a terrible mistake to have a gun and not know anything about proper shooting and gun safety. If there is a gun course offered in your area, take it; ask about this at your local gun shop.

Be sure to keep your guns away from your children! Put them where you can get to them quickly if needed but in a place to which they don't have access. There are lockable gun boxes on the market that are quick to get into if you know how, but impossible for a child to open; again, ask at the gun shop.

Finally, there is a cardinal rule about guns that should always be kept in mind: ***Never point a gun at someone unless you are completely willing to shoot.***

If your assailant senses hesitancy, he'll move quickly and take the gun away from you. Your life may depend upon this so it's essential to accept it completely. Go back and read the opening paragraphs above.

In a disaster the rules have changed; understand that and you will survive; fail to understand that and you will perish.

PREPAREDNESS
Has finally been achieved.

Selecting Preparedness Firearms

Sergeant
http://www.alpharubicon.com/leo/battofweps.htm

Raise your hand if you would try to adjust your carburetor with a crowbar. How many of you would try to build a cabin with only a saw, or treat a broken arm with epinephrine? These are similar tasks to trying to survive without a proper selection of firearms, and histrionics aside, are a proper analogy - for a firearm is a tool.

Given the societal changes that have occurred in this century, especially since the end of WW2, it is not especially surprising that a vast majority of folks are not well versed in firearms lore and the selection and use of weaponry. Having grown up on a farm in very rural country, I am more the exception than the rule, but a rural background by itself does not instill the knowledge to select a proper variety of firearms any more than living in Detroit makes you a car manufacturer. You have to apply yourself to the study of weapon usage and capability, and to their use in the field to gain insight that keeps you from wasting your money on things that don't appreciably help your chances of surviving.

Before you can make an intelligent choice, it would help if you knew what was out there, don't you think? While there are many hundreds of different firearms offered for sale today, and thousands of variations of barrel length, caliber, finish, sights, and other options, hopefully I can condense that down into a more digestible group that are most pertinent to survivalists today.

While every person has to decide just what role firearms will play in their own plans, I feel that automatically disqualifying any type from your battery for semantic reasons (i.e., "handguns are evil", or "assault rifles kill babies" or some such drivel) is both silly and dangerous. Without going into Second Amendment rights or discussion, I'd just like to say that if I need a pistol (for example), then I need it badly, and probably right now. Not having one because someone arbitrarily said I couldn't is just plain wrong. I can hear you now - "Will you quit BS-ing and get on with it?" Okay, okay!

Here's my version of the nitty-gritty: I think every would-be survivalist should have the ability to protect themselves in a variety of situations, and have the ability to hunt small game and whatever else is in their area, or the area where they will be (expect to be) in case of emergency. Redundancy is recommended, great variety is not, unless you can afford to do it right. My base line requirements are these:

Rifle for defense/offense
Rifle for hunting if fighting rifle is not suitable
Shotgun for defense/hunting
.22 Rifle for small game & plinking
        (informal target practice)
Handgun for defense
Handgun for field work
Handgun for concealment/defense

A couple of these, most notably the fieldwork handgun and the hunting rifle are of lower priority than the others, and if pressed, I could work with less. Obviously you can't carry all of these at the same time, so you may wonder why you need them. The answer is, you won't be fighting all the time, you won't be hunting all the time, you won't be carrying a rifle all the time and you won't need to conceal a handgun all the time. You get the picture. Also there are many other tasks that may need doing which I'll touch on later, but they are more specialized and not, to my mind, as likely to be important.

When considering what type of weapons to purchase, you also have to think about how many to get. While it seems prudent to get the defensive weapons first, at some point, if you accept the basic premise, you'll end up with the entire spectrum. At that point you should probably plan your

back-up package. Consider the current Special Forces logistical doctrine, which holds with the PACE concept - Primary, Alternate, Contingency, Extra. While we as individuals do not have the budget of the Federal Government, we should keep this in mind as an excellent method of planning, and build redundancy into our plans. If you've read the late Mel Tappan's definitive (though now somewhat dated) work Survival Guns, you are familiar with several precepts that should be nearly gospel. Some of these being have the right firearm (tool) for the job, have enough firearms, and have spare parts and plenty of ammunition. It is not necessary to get carried away with any thoughts of romanticism about weaponry, nor is it necessary to get one of everything, but do consider these thoughts from that signature volume: For every adult, contributing member he recommends you have (as a minimum):

one fighting rifle, plus a spare for every two (people)
a shotgun for every two
a fighting handgun each, plus a spare for every two
everyone should have one .22 and a working
        handgun
a concealment handgun for every two

If you think this looks a lot like what I wrote above, you're right on the money. While a lot of new and significantly improved firearms have been introduced since it was written, his words still carry a lot of wisdom.

Personally, I don't think that's enough, at least from a long-term perspective and neither did he. His "ideal" inventory of weapons for two people includes something on the order of 40 weapons, including a deluxe over/under hunting shotgun, and more calibers to stockpile than you're likely to find in your local gun shop!

I prefer a spare fighting rifle and handgun for each person and a shotgun and concealment handgun for each, plus more working weapons - albeit in calibers that, for the most part, are already in your inventory. I like the idea of having a complete battery both at home and at the retreat, and having at least one weapon available in many of the different locations that I may find myself temporarily stranded. If this sounds rather dramatic I apologize, but if I had the bucks, I could plan a pretty intensive war room! (Hello, Walter Mitty) Enough fluff, let's get on to the subject at hand.

The fighting rifle is where most controversy comes in. The entire family of semi-automatic, magazine fed rifles of suitable caliber (meaning 7.62 NATO, 7.62 x 39, or 5.56 NATO) is overpriced and over-restricted. In truth, however, pretty much all of the available choices are well constructed and serviceable, which makes selection mostly a matter of personal preference. The most commonly available weapons in this category are the AR-15, AK-47, SKS, M1A, FN-FAL, HK's 91 & 93, and Ruger's Mini-14. The M1 Garand is part of this group, but you'll not find a great selection of the more esoteric rifles (such as the Galil, Valmet, Beretta, Sig, etc.) in this country, and spare parts & magazines could prove difficult to find if you didn't stock enough for a protracted emergency.

There are those who hold the view that a magazine-fed semi-auto is not needed...that we are not likely to have to fight an infantry engagement. Regardless of who is right, they have some valuable insights in weaponry choices, and encourage the lever-action .30-30, .44 or .357 Magnum as a worthy alternative. After your initial reaction, listen to some of their arguments: Rapid fire repeater. Greater magazine capacity than most sporters. Much better trigger actions than most any battle rifle you'd care to name. Light weight. Cost is less than 20% of an assault rifle. These are, you have to admit, some pretty significant considerations. Think about it - you can buy two lever guns (at @ $200 each) and a thousand rounds of ammo (@ $500, if you shop around) for enough less than a state of the art auto ($1200 & up) to either get ANOTHER thousand rounds, or a handgun, shotgun, or a couple of .22's. Pretty convincing, especially when you consider it's increased versatility over a .223, better shooting rifles than the .30 Russian Short (7.62x39), and much lighter weight than any .308 battle rifle available.

The hunting rifle is, for most of us, a fairly easy choice - if you live in the lower 48 and don't plan to hunt elk, moose, or grizzly, then anything from the .243 to the .300 Winchester Magnum is suitable, with something in the middle probably most appropriate. I like the .308, mainly for it's universal availability and the wide choice of bullets available, both loaded and separately as components. And of course, for it's ammo interchangeability with a battle rifle.

The hunting rifle is probably a scope-sighted bolt-action job, with limited magazine capacity. It may be able to stand in for a "sniper" rifle, if it is accurate, your ammo and shooting skill are up to the task, and you don't have to drag it around on the ground, beat it against building walls, jump out of airplanes with it, or any of the myriad other tasks that military and law-enforcement professionals routinely encounter.

Some of the most common & popular rifles today are the Remington 700 (choice of the U.S. Army & Marine Corps as the M24 & M40A1), Winchester's M70, and Ruger's M77. Savage sells their M110 & 112, which are super deals, both in price and accuracy, and recently introduced a short action which should be even stiffer & thus more accurate,

while ending up lighter and shorter as well. There are lots of surplus Mausers on the market, of various model, manufacturer, and condition, as well as new production ones. As with all the other weapon types we'll discuss, there are many more types for sale than I could ever talk about in one article, so I'm only listing some of the most popular - don't think that your weapon, if it works for you, is somehow unsatisfactory. Just think about spare parts and ammo availability.

If you want to do some varmint hunting (coyote, groundhog, prairie dog, etc.) then you'll want a heavy-barreled .223 or .22-250, or something similar. If you think you can accurately shoot a deer or other large animal at long range, something more potent is called for. Starting at 7 millimeter (.28 caliber) magnums and working up through the .33 calibers, there are quite a few new cartridges that are very capable of taking out whatever you hit at ranges approaching 1000 meters. These cartridges send 160 to 250 grain bullets through the barrel at speeds up to 3600 FPS! Of course, to be able to hit anything at great distance requires immense amounts of practice and skill, but there you are.

If you feel that life doesn't begin until 600 meters, there are several .50 caliber rifles on the market that have been proven in battle in the last dozen years or so. There are several accounts of 2 MILE shots by Marine Corps snipers in Iraq during Desert Storm, and I personally laid behind a .50 on the Kuwaiti border in November of '90, looking at an Iraqi who, had we been shooting, would have been toast - at about 1200 meters. I was a guest of a Navy SEAL team, charged (later) with imitating a Marine battalion - just the dozen or so SEALs at that one Saudi Customs site. During those pre-shooting days, they were engaged with underwater reconnaissance - what they were originally developed to do.

The point I want to make about working rifles is that, given some realistic evaluations of what you will expect them to do, there are countless rifles out there that will work, and most of them will do everything you want. That is why I recommend sticking with one of the most popular calibers (.270, .30-06, .308, etc.), and spending the money saved for more ammo to practice with and stockpile. There's nothing wrong with having a spare working rifle, along with your spare "fighting" pieces, but have a real good reason if it's not the same model and caliber.

The shotgun, often called the "front door gun" where I come from, is the very picture of versatility. With slugs and a sighted, rifled barrel (is it still a shotgun if you put a rifled barrel on it?) it is deadly out to 125 yards or so. Everyone is familiar with its traditional bird-hunting role. With heavy loads of buckshot it is big medicine during building-clearing ops. With the near-universal availability of replacement barrels, chokes, stocks, and other options, they can be customized to suit your requirements, and rapidly and easily changed to do something else. Remington's 870 is the popular choice in this category, but hard on it's heels are Mossbergs 500 & 590 (choice of the Marine Corps in recent competition), and Winchester's 1200. These are all pump guns, but some autoloaders that make the cut are the HK/Benelli M1 Super 90, Beretta's 1201, and Remington's 11-87.

Probably the top shotgun accessories today are white light systems, the best of which is Laser Products Sure-Fire line. Available for most of the guns listed above, these units replace the factory forend with a completely self-contained flashlight/switch/forend combo that is extremely bright. It also allows single-hand control, something not possible before its introduction without dangling wires and taped-on switches. Additionally, the Side-Saddle spare ammo carrier that attaches to the side of the receiver and holds six extra rounds right at the balance point - accessible to either hand for tactical reloads while keeping the weapon on target - is virtually a standard addition to the tactical shotgun, and is well worth considering.

If you have ever lived or worked in the country, you'll immediately recognize the need for a .22 rifle. Whether you have rabbits in the garden, gophers in the yard, or starlings in the chicken feed, or simply want a way to spend an enjoyable afternoon, there is no other firearm that you will use as much or enjoy as much as a .22. Scopes are optional - I have several .22 rifles, about half of which are scoped. Marlin's line of bolt and semi-auto rifles have dominated the price wars for years, and are excellent buys, as is the Ruger 10/22 & bolt action 77/22, which is also available in .22 magnum, .22 Hornet, and now, .44 Magnum so strong is it's receiver. Ruger recently introduced its 96/22 lever-action rifle, and Winchester and Marlin also sell lever actions. Remington has a fine line (no surprises there) of bolt and semi-auto rifles as well. Don't overlook the variety of rifles that take-down for easier carry. These include Marlin's Papoose, the old Charter Arms AR-7 (now produced by Henry Arms), and Springfield Armoury's M6 combination .22/.410 shotgun. These are all lightweight rifles that are easily carried and offer a great improvement in accuracy for most shooters over trail handguns, while retaining the light weight that encourages their inclusion on your packing list for survival excursions or bug-out bags.

If you have the money, a top-drawer .22 rifle can be an immense joy to own and shoot. These rifles, by such makers as Kimber, Anshutz, and Walther can shoot rings around most anything going. With match ammo, these things go into groups that must be measured with a micrometer. The

downfall? The same one I keep bringing up. Call me a miser, but if I can accomplish the mission with a $200 rifle I don't see why I should pay $1000 for only marginally improved ability. Unless you are a serious competitor, you probably don't need the difference between a 50 yard, one-inch group, and one that goes into an eighth-inch. Assuming a squirrels-head target, if you can hold on it, you can hit it with either, and I'd rather spend the additional $800 on ammo and other things.

Nothing spells relief when things go bump in the night like a heavy handgun. The primary requirements are absolute reliability, adequate power and the accuracy to hit your target. The details are as numerous as the choices. The long-time favorite is the M1911A1-style .45. A large, heavy, and powerful handgun, its exploits are legendary. There are vastly more modern pistols, but very few approach the success of it's long heritage, and none has the wide base of knowledge, spare parts, or accessories. The Glock line is one that has been fantastically popular. There are those whom the lack of an external locking safety bothers, but the plastic Austrian gun's record doesn't reflect a problem. It's extreme reliability, light weight and accuracy have made converts of countless thousands of happy souls. Available in all the modern, effective calibers, in magazine capacities from 9 to 33 rounds, there is probably a Glock that is right for you. The U.S. Military has purchased the Beretta M92 and the Sig/Sauer P228 for our standard military pistols as the M9 and M11, respectively, and many Federal and State agencies have followed their lead. Smith & Wesson, Heckler & Koch (HK), Walther, Browning, Ruger and Taurus round out the most popular autos with a variety of models to fill any need.

All this talk about semi-auto's should not lead you to believe that revolvers somehow became ineffective the day everyone started switching to autos - far from it. A properly loaded revolver of quality design and manufacture is still potent medicine, and in the hands of a trained person can stand and deliver the goods. While autos will always have improved reload times and higher capacity, speedloaders and situational awareness, proper use of cover & concealment, and carrying the fastest reload of all - a spare weapon - will negate most of the arguments against them. No other handgun can compare with the .357's stopping record when using 125 grain hollow-points at a nominal 1400 FPS. And no other weapon is as versatile in as many conditions as a good four or six-inch barreled revolver.

The field handgun can double as the defense handgun, if you select carefully, and actually there is a lot to recommend such a course of action. This generally will be a revolver of suitable caliber, meaning either .357 Magnum, .44 Special or Magnum, .45 ACP or .45 Colt. The .38 Special is marginally acceptable, but since you can fire this cartridge in the .357, I see no need to limit yourself by choosing a .38 as your only chambering, at least in this larger revolver. In any case, if the field revolver is going to be your self-defense piece as well, it really must be a double action number with a swing-out cylinder for rapid reloading.

Some of the advantages of having a single weapon perform both missions are: You only have to store one caliber of ammo, You only need to practice with a single weapon to remain proficient, and initial procurement costs are cut in half or so - you'll still need a backup (ideally an identical duplicate), but generally a good revolver costs noticeably less than an equally good semi-auto, and it's ancillary items cost a lot less (speedloaders vs. magazines, anyway). If you opt for this course, I strongly urge you to stick with the .357, although you can get .44 Special (NOT magnum) guns built on medium frames these days, if you prefer big-bore bullet weights. You'll probably get tired of carrying the 50 oz. of a large frame .44 or .45 a lot quicker than a 32 oz. medium frame .357 or .44 Special.

If you do not require it to do double duty - and I recommend against it, if you can afford it - you can get away with a Single-Action revolver, preferably in a heavy caliber. I have a stainless steel Ruger Super Blackhawk in .44 Magnum, with a 5-1/2 inch barrel that I carry in a Bianchi Ranger convertible nylon holster. This holster allows you to carry it crossdraw, allowing easier carry of a slung rifle or backpack, while still permitting conventional carry when it is your only partner.

And finally, the hideout piece. A smaller, lighter, and usually less-powerful firearm than your primary handgun, it is often the one you have with you when the excrement impacts with the rotary oscillator. That being the case, don't neglect your training regimen with this weapon. It is probably more difficult to shoot well than your larger one, and, while marksmanship basics remain the same, they ARE more difficult to apply with grips and sights that are too small for most folks. Especially in dim or no light conditions, when your heart is racing, your hands are slippery and sweating, and you only went out for some milk for tomorrow's breakfast. This is a very important decision, but one that today is easier than ever before.

For most folks this will be a small frame .38 Special, but with the proliferation of sub-compact autos in serious calibers, more people are choosing autos than ever before. Kahr Arms' 9mm, and their new MK-9, are both smaller than just about anything out there, Kel-Tec's P-11, S&W's Sigma 9 & .380, Colt's Pony & Mustang - the list just goes on and on. Also there are scads of .32, .25, and .22 miniature autos, and Freedom Arms' incredibly small .22 single-ac-

tion revolver 5-shooters are wonders of micro-machining. For the traditionalist, or one who would rather depend on the proven .38, the S&W Centennial line are the ones to beat - concealed hammer, round grip frame, 2 inch barrel; at their best with an aluminum frame - they are also available in stainless and in .22, 9mm and .357 (stainless only) and with 3-inch barrels and adjustable sights. Colt has it's new DS-II .38 6-shot revolver (the Smiths are 5-shooters) and lots of it's old line such as the Agent and Detective Special are available used. Ruger's SP-101 is extremely robust for it's size and is available in the same calibers as the Smith & Wesson offerings, and also in .32 H&R Magnum. Taurus's M85 revolvers are very popular in this role, as well.

Having gone over the basics, let me touch on what I referred to as "Special" weapons in the table at the beginning of this article. There are a lot of firearms available that have a pretty narrow niche to fill. Some of them however - such as T/C's Contender, which, if you're not familiar with it, is a single shot pistol that breaks open like a shotgun, and allows you to change it's barrel with one of a wide-variety of other calibers & lengths - are very versatile. Consider that you can have scoped .223, .30-30 and .22 barrels, and a .45 Colt/.410 shotgun barrel, along with the frame, ammo for each, and cleaning & survival equipment, in a case 16 inches by 8 inches and weighing less than 10 pounds. This is an extremely versatile piece, and one that doesn't fit neatly into a pre-planned category, but rather may be at it's best in a Bug-Out Bag or kept in a vehicle. While there are other single-shots and break-open pistols available, none have the variety of calibers or widespread availability of the Contender. Additionally, if you purchase the optional 16 1/4 barrels, you can install the available buttstock to make a very lightweight, compact carbine that is even easier to shoot accurately.

There are those who live in states which allow civilian ownership of fully-automatic weapons who have or would like to have one. Personally I think this is a mistake - at least, if you are including it in your defense planning. Owning one as a part of your shooting hobby is something else entirely. But, for those who can afford their prodigious ammunition appetite and don't mind the Federal paperwork and giving up their privacy rights (legally possessing - and don't think about having one illegally - an automatic weapon gives the BATF the right to unannounced inspections of your storage of it, and brings in an entire new spectrum of Big Brother). Anyway, if you feel you really need it for your defense planning a sub-machine gun (a compact, fully automatic weapon which shoots a pistol cartridge) is most effective up close (up to 75 meters or so), and a .30 caliber medium machinegun on a tripod is pretty good out to a thousand meters or so - if you can afford to practice enough to get good enough to hit at that distance. Trust me - you can't just yank the trigger and "mow 'em down" - you still have to practice.

A silencer, or more properly a sound suppressor, is a horse of an entirely different color. Being restricted by the same laws as full-automatics, a suppressor is something that is much more user-friendly. It allows the shooter to hunt without giving away his position and to practice without earplugs. They ease the training of new shooters and help them avoid flinching, and in a more sinister context, allow such tasks as "sentry takedown" without alerting other guards. The military recognizes this and has a suppressor kit for the M9 Beretta, and the recent SOCOM (Special Operations COMmand) pistol contract specifies a sound suppressor as part of the package. EGW and Jonathan Arthur Ciener are two of the more widely known companies which sell suppressors in the States.

Along with decisions about what firearms to own, come more choices concerning ammunition. The caliber of weapon you have obviously narrows down the choices considerably, but they can still be nearly overwhelming. If you have made the wise choice of purchasing military caliber weapons, then by all means take advantage of the availability of surplus ammo. Round for round you won't find a better deal, and you can't even reload .308 or .223 ammo as cheaply as you can pick up surplus stuff - but. There's always a but in there somewhere, isn't there? In this case it is the sometimes questionable quality or reliability of ammo that may have been (and probably was) stored in very questionable conditions - widely varying temperature and humidity, perhaps contaminated with petroleum products - who knows? It may also be un-reloadable with Berdan primers, and could have corrosive primers as well. None of these are disqualifiers, but you need to know in advance and be prepared to compensate for these factors. In any case, it pays to check out a good sample of whatever lot you may purchase for reliability and accuracy, and make sure it's pressures don't exceed the strength of your rifle.

There is an old axiom that will hold true as long as we have firearms - you can never have too much ammunition. In any case, keep at least 500 rounds per weapon, and if you have battle rifles, I would rather have ten times that much. Or more. And 5,000 rounds would just be a starting point for a machinegun. Be sure, however, that your ammunition is stored properly and safely - you don't want to have all you've worked for destroyed because of carelessness.

Don't ignore cleaning supplies or spare parts. Keep large quantities of cleaning solvent, patches, bore brushes, Q-tips, pipe cleaners, and lubricating oil & gun grease on hand so you can keep those valuable investments doing their job. At the same time, wouldn't you hate to have that rifle inoperative because your firing pin broke, or mainspring went soft, and you couldn't replace it? We're talking $5 or $10 parts, which could cost you a lot if neglected. In general, purchase firing pins, extractors, ejectors, and all internal and magazine springs, and any other parts with a history of breakage or early replacement. Manufacturer's manuals, disassembly and repair books, and any other reference on your specific type should be gathered as well, for the inevitable necessary repairs down the line.

Please don't take the lack of mention of all the countless other manufacturers or models to mean they are somehow unsuited for use - the best gun in the world is the one you have when you need it. Take heart in the fact that, despite the best efforts of the anti-gunners we still have some of the most liberal gun laws of anyone anywhere in the world. Whatever your feelings are toward the NRA, if you own any firearms at all you should be a member - they are THE voice of law-abiding citizens in Congress's ear, and despite the negativity spread by it's detractors, it has been very effective in keeping our cause foremost in the American legislators mind. Join them and help support the right of all American citizens to keep and bear arms!

Survival Fire Safety

By Mr. F

In our preparations, we've all made an in depth survival plan. We have stocks of food items and a means to hunt or grow more. We know where we'll get water and how to treat it and have solutions for cooking, heating and lighting. Perhaps some will operate gasoline or propane-run electric generators and some may distill alcohol or use wood gasification for fuel. We also have adequate supplies of medications, vitamins and first-aid items. We've thought of everything, planned for any contingency. Right? What about Fire Safety? Our plans mostly or entirely rely on fire for cooking, heating and lighting. Do you have working fire extinguishers or another plan to deal with a fire if one erupts? If you are planning to use a generator it needs to be properly wired to prevent fire. And what about your fuel storage? Is it a hazard? After all, if services have deteriorated to this point, the local fire department isn't coming either.

Of all aspects of our daily life, Fire Safety is most commonly overlooked. The second step to mitigating any safety hazard, after removing the process entirely if possible, is to engineer out the hazard. Today, this is done for us in the form of model building codes, UL listings and other industry standards. Not surprisingly, it isn't forefront in our minds. But when SHTF, we'll be trading our electric lights for kerosene lamps and candles, electric ranges for camp stoves and wood fires. Many things will be home-built or improvised from available resources. Have we already, or will we, engineer in those safeguards? The Science of Fire To understand fire potential, and extinguishment, it is important to understand the dynamics of a fire. Some of you may recall learning about the —Fire Triangle in school. The theory being that combustion occurs when all three components (oxygen, fuel and heat) are present, and removing one or more will extinguish the fire. While this is a simplistic approach, it makes an appropriate foundation to start with. First off, this means that the fuel and oxygen components must attain proper geometric distribution or fuel to oxygen mixing. This usually requires that the fuel, though it may be in a liquid or solid form, must be heated until it vaporizes. This is where heat comes into play. —Flammable means that it will vaporize at temperatures below 105 degrees F and generally includes liquids such as gasoline, alcohol, propane, etc. —Combustible refers to fuels which vaporize at temperatures greater than 105 degrees F, thus requiring more heat input for the combustion process to occur. This is also why it is harder to start a campfire in the dead of a Canadian winter than summer in west Texas. As a fire burns, the combustion reaction produces large amounts of energy in the form of heat. This in turn becomes the heat necessary to sustain and/or grow the fire. The hotter the fire, the more fuel that becomes available and the more rapid the fire's growth. The only limitation now is the available air. It is important to note, however, that not all fuels need to be in vapor form. Fine dust particles, when airborne in high enough quantity, can attain the proper mixing with oxygen to burn quite rapidly. This is important for anyone with bulk storage of grains, coal, sawdust and even dusty hay.

The oxygen, or oxidizing agent, in the context to which we are concerned with comes from —standard atmospheric air – roughly 20% oxygen, 79% nitrogen, etc. As the fire burns, hot combustion gases expand and rise in a superheated plume. As these gases rise, fresh air is drawn into the fire at the base, heated, consumed in the fire and again released upward. This is what is referred to as convection currents and one reason why you aim a fire extinguisher at the base of the fire. Also note, however, that in some instances such as with gunpowder, no outside oxygen is required for combustion. Some chemicals, such as nitrates, contain sufficient quantities of oxygen within the molecules, and are easily released during the combustion process. These burn rapidly and are difficult to control. Okay, a fire just broke out! Now what do we do? First, we need to know what classification of fire it is (that is to say what materials are involved). This is important so we can determine the proper method of extinguishment.

Class A Fires involve —ordinary combustibles such as wood, paper, cloth, etc. This is the most common fire you can expect and will most likely occur from a campfire that got out of control, a lantern getting knocked over, a lit candle or some other similar incident. A little care can go a long way here.

Water is going to be the best means to put out a Class A fire but it's likely to be a precious commodity. Snow is another excellent media since it is also very effective at blanketing the fire. If it is small, you can also try smothering it with a blanket or jacket but make sure there is no flammable liquid involved (guarantee you'll set the blanket or jacket on fire if there is). In the case of a small to medium fire outdoors, sand or soil shoveled onto the fire is also effective. However, sometimes it may be best to simply let the fire burn itself out while you prevent it from spreading. Chimney Fires can creep up unwittingly. Unburned volatiles called creosote are given off primarily due to green/wet wood, low temperature fires and insufficient airflow. This creosote builds up until it either blocks the flue or is ignited by a hot fire. If a fire occurs, immediately close all inlet vents on the stove to smother the fire. If it is an open fireplace, extinguish the fire below then carefully try to close the damper if you can. Do not attempt to cover the chimney but do try to water down the roof if possible. There is otherwise very little that can be done for a chimney fire. Water sprayed into the flue will likely crack the flue liner. Even the extreme temperature generated is likely to cause damage to the chimney. Damaged flues and chimneys drastically increase the likelihood of a structure fire. It is best to take every precaution to avoid a chimney fire. [JWR Adds: Chimneys should be cleaned at least once per year!] Class B Fires involve generally flammable liquids such as gasoline, kerosene, paraffin, alcohol, etc. These pose a great risk because they ignite easily and spread quickly. Accumulated vapors can ignited with the smallest spark, even static electricity. If you encounter a flammable liquid pool fire, do not use water. Remember, most of the flammable liquids we will be using are hydrocarbon based and float on water.

Application of the water will cause ripples in the fuel, causing a flare up as well as spreading the fire. Flammable liquid fire must be extinguished by smothering. This is best accomplished by dry chemical of foam fire extinguishers though small fires in containers may be carefully covered. Now let's say you are refueling a hot generator and it flashes over. You now have flames coming out of the fuel tank as well as the gas can. Get away! It is important to keep your distance as explosion or eruption is possible. This is a bad situation and there is little you're going to be able to do. A pressurized hose could be used to cool surfaces but at the risk of overflowing the tank or can, thus spreading the fire. In the event of a leaking propane line that catches fire, shut off the gas at the source if it can be done safely. It is unlikely that anything else you try will be successful and even if it is, you'll be releasing raw fuel that is likely to re-ignite. Probably one of the most common and dangerous fires in this class is the grease fire. This generally occurs from superheating animal fats or vegetable oil and also applies to paraffin. Again, do not use water. Find something to cover it with, such as the lid to a pot if you are cooking. The next step is to do nothing. That's right, don't touch it. Let me repeat that. Do not touch it. Don't even think about. You see,

as oil, grease or paraffin burns, its' auto-ignition temperature decreases. That means that if any air is introduced, it will flash over again unless it has cooled sufficiently. Class C Fires involve energized electrical components such as wiring, motors, generators, etc.

In this case, the ignition source is the electricity and the fuel is usually the wiring. The first step in this situation is to kill the electricity – trip the disconnect, turn off the ignition, shut down the generator, what have you. Now it is simply a Class A or Class B fire. DO NOT use water around live electricity. Class D Fires involve metals, such as sodium, magnesium, aluminum, etc. These may be found in some fire starters and flares as well as around metal grinding and cutting. It is possible for two metals, along with a catalyst, to ignite. Such fires burn rapidly and extremely hot. However unlikely it is that you will encounter such a fire in a survival situation, this is one you can't affect without specialized firefighting equipment.

Fire Extinguishers are an indispensable safety item for every household. Each extinguisher will be labeled for the class of fire and fire size it is capable of being used on. There are several styles available so familiarize yourself with how yours operates before it is needed. There are also a number of different extinguishing agents so choose wisely. Water and water based foams will freeze and the powders used in dry chemical types wreak havoc with electronics. Do you homework. They also require some regular maintenance. For instance, dry chemical powders need to be —fluffed every so often to keep them from caking. This can be accomplished by turning it upside down and hitting the bottom with a rubber mallet. And also check to make sure the bottle is free of rust or other mechanical damage. I recall one incident in which a woman intended to operate a fire extinguisher on a small fire. However, the bottle was severely rusted and when she —charged it by firing off the supplied air cartridge, the top blew off and killed her. Also, with the exception of the old —Indian fire pumps , it's unlikely you'll be able to refill them. Doubtless, the most fearful fire of all is one that upon your person. In the event that your clothes become involved, don't run. STOP, DROP and ROLL to smother the fire. If you see someone else on fire, this is where your time on the high school football team comes in handy. Grab a blanket, preferably wool, and tackle them (albeit gently). The goal is to get them on the ground and covered with the blanket, smothering the fire. Depending on the circumstances and clothing involved, there will likely be some first aid required. Up in Smoke Aside from the inherent dangers of fire itself, combustion by-products may pose an even greater hazard. In complete combustion of organic materials, where adequate free air exists for the fire, carbon dioxide and water are produced. Carbon Dioxide (CO_2) is a colorless, odorless gas which, being heavier than air, collects in low areas. An increase of only 2-3% CO_2 in the air we breathe can result in impaired memory, loss of fine motor skills and weakness. Higher concentrations can cause unconsciousness and death. If you find someone a victim of CO_2 exposure, ventilate the area. Do not go rushing in and become a victim too (you won't do them or yourself any good like that). Remove the victim to an area with fresh clean air. In some cases, the victim may require further medical treatment my trained personnel.

If the fire is starved for oxygen, then carbon monoxide (CO) is produced. Again, CO is a colorless, odorless gas, but it is even more dangerous. Generally, CO exposure causes a feeling of sleepiness in the victim, but also nausea, headaches and vertigo. Once the victim becomes unconscious, death soon follows. The complicating factor here is that CO molecules bond to hemoglobin, the oxygen carriers in the bloodstream, preventing oxygen from getting to the cells. Simply getting the victim to fresh air will not adequately purge CO from the system. Treatment for CO exposure usually requires 100% oxygen or hyperbaric treatment. When inorganic materials such as plastic, paint, glue, particle board, wire insulation and other man-made materials burn, there is virtually no limit to the volatile and toxic chemicals that are released. These can result in serious illness and death very quickly and will almost certainly require medical treatment you cannot provide at your survival retreat. An Ounce of Prevention While we want to be prepared to deal with a fire if one starts, our best bet is to —engineer out the hazard and prevent a fire altogether. Make sure that lanterns, lamps and candles are placed on a flat, stable surface. Candles should be in a proper holder or on a porcelain or tin plate with sides to catch melted wax. An empty tuna can works well for this. Ensure that all combustibles are kept away and be mindful of shirt sleeves and loose clothing when working with or around such items. Also, be careful around children and animals (remember Mrs. O'Leary's cow). As I said before, chimney fires are best avoided and regular maintenance is the key to preventing them. This starts with regular cleanings. If you are burn strictly for heat in cold months, this means at least one cleaning before the burn season and possible more during the season. If you will be burning regularly for cooking, you'll probably be using a smaller fire, thus creating more creosote. Burning hot and staying away from — green wood or wood heavy with resins such as pines will drastically help reduce buildup. There are various products on the market which claim to help with creosote buildup. These products are simply burned periodically in the fire. However, while these would likely help, they are certainly no replacement for proper cleaning. Make sure you have a brush or two of the proper shape and size for each flue. In a pinch, a bundle of chain on a rope will work for small flues. Even as I write this, I received a call from a woman who just had a chimney fire last night. Today she is trying to make repairs so that it is again safe to burn. Metal chimneys are expensive but easily replaced if you have spare parts.

However, damage to masonry chimneys is much more difficult to repair. Take extra care with flammable liquids. When stored, ensure that they are in approved containers with good seals. On his 1911-12 journey to the South Pole, Robert Scott left caches of food and fuel. On the return trip, he found that many of the fuel cans were empty, having leaked at the seals. The lack of fuel eventually led to their deaths. Flammable liquids should be stored out of sunlight and in a well ventilated area. And for God's sake don't use anything with a flame around flammable liquids. Even a flashlight is a potential ignition source. If you need to have something for light, get a small flashlight with a Class 1, Div.1 rating. I use ones from Pelican and UA. Also avoid using gasoline and the like for starting fires. The accumulation of fumes can have deadly results. A good alternative is to use gel starting fluid for pellet stoves. The gel is less volatile and won't flash or explode like gasoline will.

Also be very mindful of the clothing you wear around or when starting a fire. Nylon, rayon and the multitudes of synthetic fibers used in clothing today are extremely dangerous. They ignite easily and melt even easier thus increasing the need for medical attention. Natural fibers such as cotton and wool are best. When possible, buy instead of building anything that uses a flame. This includes lanterns, stoves, burners, incubators, brooders and heaters. There are also several manufacturers of fire resistance coatings that can be applied to almost anything. Be careful with outdoor fires, especially when windy. The last thing you want to do is start a fire that burns your house or shelter down with your supplies in it. Remember the rule of 3's? You can survive 3 hours without shelter, 3 days without food. Don't use stoves or flames inside of tents unless both the tent and the stove are intended for such a purpose. If you are planning to use a wood framed structure for your survival shelter, you may want to think about fire resistance. A number of manufacturers offer concrete fiberboard siding that is fire proof as well as water, weather and insect proof. There are also a number of options for roof coverings such as metal, clay and cement fiberboard. Unless you are competent in electrical wiring, make sure to have everything checked out by a licensed electrician. If you plan to use an electric generator, use the proper connections and transfer switches. Don't try to jury rig this - the shock and fire potentials here are extremely high. Smokey Bear always said —Only you can prevent forest fires . This is essentially true in a survival situation too. Many of us will be living in somewhat primitive conditions compared to what we are used to. We need to be vigilant at every moment. Think Safe, Be Safe.

Emergency Heating & Cooking

HEATING

Coal stores well if kept in a dark place and away from moving air. Air speeds deterioration and breakdown, causing it to burn more rapidly. Coal may be stored in a plastic-lined pit or in sheds, bags, boxes, or barrels and should be kept away from circulating air, light, and moisture. Cover it to lend protection from weather and sun.

Wood. Hardwoods such as apple, cherry, and other fruit woods are slow burning and sustain coals. Hardwoods are more difficult to burn than softer woods, thus requiring a supply of kindling. Soft woods such as pine and cedar are light in weight and burn very rapidly, leaving ash and few coals for cooking. If you have a fireplace or a wood/coal burning stove, you will want to store several cords of firewood. Firewood is usually sold by the cord which is a neat pile that totals 128 cubic feet. This pile is four feet wide, four feet high, and eight feet long. Some dealers sell wood by the ton. As a general rule of thumb, a standard cord of air dried dense hardwood weighs about two tons and provides as much heat as one ton of coal. Be suspicious of any alleged cord delivered in a 1/2 or 3/4 ton pickup truck.

For best results, wood should be seasoned (dried) properly, usually at east a year. A plastic tarp, wood planks, or other plastic or metal sheeting over the woodpile is useful in keeping the wood dry. Other types of fuels are more practical to store and use than wood or coal.

Newspaper logs make a good and inexpensive source of fuel. You may prepare the logs in the following manner:

Use about eight pages of newspaper and open flat. Spread the stack, alternating the cut sides and folded sides. Place a 1" wood dowel or metal rod across one end and roll the paper around the rod very tightly. Roll it until there are 6-8 inches left to roll, then slip another 8 pages underneath the roll. Continue this procedure until you have a roll 4-6 inches in diameter. With a fine wire, tie the roll on both ends. Withdraw the rod. Your newspaper log is ready to use. Four of these logs will burn about 1 hour.

Propane is another excellent fuel for indoor use. Like kerosene, it produces carbon dioxide as it burns and is therefore not poisonous. It does consume oxygen so be sure to crack a window when burning propane.

Propane stores indefinitely, having no known shelf life. Propane stoves and small portable heaters are very economical, simple to use, and come the closest to approximating the type of convenience most of us are accustomed to using on a daily basis.

The storage of propane is governed by strict local laws. In this area you may store up to 1 gallon inside a building and up to 60 gallons stored outside. If you store more than these amounts, you will need a special permit from the fire marshal.

The primary hazard in using propane is that it is heavier than air and if a leak occurs it may "pool" which can create an explosive atmosphere. Furthermore, basement natural gas heating units CANNOT be legally converted for propane use. Again, the vapors are heavier than air and form "pockets." Ignition sources such as water heaters and electrical sources can cause an explosion.

White gas (Coleman fuel). Many families have camp stoves which burn Coleman Fuel or white gasoline. These stoves are fairly easy to use and produce a great amount of heat. However, they, like charcoal, produce vast amounts of carbon monoxide. **NEVER** use a Coleman Fuel stove indoors. It could be a fatal mistake to your entire family.

Never store fuels in the house or near a heater. Use a metal store cabinet which is vented on top and bottom and can be locked.

Kerosene (also known as Range Oil No. 1) is the cheapest of all the storage fuels and is also very forgiving if you make a mistake. Kerosene is not as explosive as gasoline and Coleman fuel. Kerosene stores well for long periods of time and by introducing some fuel additives it can be made to store even longer. However, do not store it in metal containers for extended time periods unless they are porcelain lined because the moisture in the kerosene will rust through the container causing the kerosene to leak out.

Most hardware stores and home improvement centers sell kerosene in five gallon plastic containers which store for many years. A 55 gallon drum stores in the back yard, or ten 5 gallon plastic containers will provide fuel enough to last an entire winter if used sparingly.

Caution: To burn kerosene you will need a kerosene heater. There are many models and sizes to choose from but remember that you are not trying to heat your entire home. The larger the heater the more fuel you will have to store. Most families should be able to get by on a heater that produces about 9,600 BTUs of heat, though kerosene heaters are made that will produce up to 25,000 to 30,000 BTUs. If you have the storage space to store the fuel required by these larger heaters they are excellent investments, but for most families the smaller heaters are more than adequate. When selecting a kerosene heater be sure to get one that can double as a cooking surface and source of light. Then when you are forced to use it be sure to plan your meals so that they can be cooked when you are using the heater for heat rather than wasting fuel used for cooking only.

When kerosene burns it requires very little oxygen, compared to charcoal. You must crack a window about 1/4 inch to allow enough oxygen to enter the room to prevent asphyxiation. During combustion, kerosene is not poisonous and is safe to use indoors. To prevent possible fires you should always fill it outside. The momentary incomplete combustion during lighting and extinguishing of kerosene heaters can cause some unpleasant odors. To prevent these odors from lingering in your home always light and extinguish the heater out of doors. During normal operation a kerosene heater is practically odorless.

Charcoal. *Never* use a charcoal burning device indoors. When charcoal burns it is a voracious consumer of oxygen and will quickly deplete the oxygen supply in your little "home within a home." Furthermore, as it burns it produces vast amounts of carbon monoxide which is a deadly poison. If you make the mistake of trying to heat your home by burning charcoal it could prove fatal to your entire family. Never burn charcoal indoors.

Cooking

To conserve your cooking fuel storage needs always do your emergency cooking in the most efficient manner possible. Don't boil more water than you need, extinguish the fire as soon as you finished, plan your meals ahead of time to consolidate as much cooking as possible, during the winter cook on top of your heating unit while heating your home, and cook in a pressure cooker or other fuel efficient container as much as possible. Keep enough fuel to provide outdoor cooking for at least 7-10 days.

It is even possible to cook without using fuel at all. For example, to cook dry beans you can place them inside a pressure cooker with the proper amount of water and other ingredients needed and place it on your heat source until it comes up to pressure. Then turn off the heat, remove the pressure cooker and place inside a large box filled with newspapers, blankets, or other insulating materials. Leave it for two and a half hours and then open it, your meal will be done, having cooked for two and a half hours with no heat. If you don't have a large box in which to place the pressure cooker, simply wrap it in several blankets and place it in the corner.

Store matches in waterproof airtight tin with each piece of equipment that must be lit with a flame.

Sterno fuel, a jellied petroleum product, is an excellent source of fuel for inclusion in your back pack as part of your 72 hour kit. Sterno is very light weight and easily ignited with a match or a spark from flint and steel but is not explosive. It is also safe for use indoors. A Sterno stove can be purchased at any sporting goods store and will retail between $3 and $8, depending upon the model you choose. They fold up into a very small, compact unit ideal for carrying in a pack. The fuel is readily available at all sporting goods stores and many drug stores. One can of Sterno fuel, about the diameter of a can of tuna fish and twice as high, will allow you to cook six meals if used frugally. Chafing dishes and fondue pots can also be used with Sterno.

Sterno is not without some problems. It will evaporate very easily, even when the lid is securely fastened. If you use Sterno in your 72 hour kit you should check it every six to eight months to insure that it has not evaporated beyond the point of usage. Because of this problem it is not a good fuel for long-term storage. It is a very expensive fuel to use compared to others fuel available, but is extremely convenient and portable.

Coleman fuel (white gas), when used with a Coleman stove is another excellent and convenient fuel for cooking. It is not as portable nor as lightweight as Sterno, but produces a much greater BTU value. Like Sterno, Coleman fuel has a tendency to evaporate even when the container is tightly sealed so it is not a good fuel for long-term storage. Unlike Sterno, however, it is highly volatile; it will explode under the right conditions and should therefore never be stored in the home. Because of its highly flammable nature great care should always be exercised when lighting stoves and lanterns that use Coleman fuel. Many serious burns have been caused by carelessness with this product. Always store Coleman fuel in the garage or shed, out of doors.

Charcoal is the least expensive fuel per BTU that the average family can store. Remember that it must always be used out of doors because of the vast amounts of poisonous carbon monoxide it produces. Charcoal will store for extended period of time if it is stored in air tight containers. It readily absorbs moisture from the surrounding air so do not store it in the paper bags it comes in for more than a few months or it may be difficult to light. Transfer it to airtight metal or plastic containers and it will keep almost forever.

Fifty or sixty dollars worth of charcoal will provide all the cooking fuel a family will need for an entire year if used sparingly. The best time to buy briquettes inexpensively is at the end of the summer. Broken or torn bags of briquettes are usually sold at a big discount. You will also want to store a small amount of charcoal lighter fluid (or kerosene). Newspapers will also provide an excellent ignition source for charcoal when used in a funnel type of lighting device.

To light charcoal using newspapers use two or three sheets, crumpled up, and a #10 tin can. Cut both ends out of the can. Punch holes every two inches around the lower edge of the can with a punch-type can opener (for opening juice cans). Set the can down so the punches holes are on the bottom. Place the crumpled newspaper in the bottom of the can and place the charcoal briquettes on top of the newspaper.

Lift the can slightly and light the newspaper. Prop a small rock under the bottom edge of the can to create a a good draft. The briquettes will be ready to use in about 20-30 minutes. When the coals are ready remove the chimney and place them in your cooker. Never place burning charcoal directly on concrete or cement because the heat will crack it. A wheelbarrow or old metal garbage can lid makes an excellent container for this type of fire.

One of the nice things about charcoal is that you can regulate the heat you will receive from them. Each briquette will produce about 40 degrees of heat. If you are baking bread, for example, and need 400 degrees of heat for your oven, simply use ten briquettes.

To conserve heat and thereby get the maximum heat value from your charcoal you must learn to funnel the heat where you want it rather than letting it dissipate into the air around you. One excellent way to do this is to cook inside a cardboard oven. Take a cardboard box, about the size of an orange crate, and cover it with aluminum foil inside and out. Be sure that the shiny side is visible so that maximum reflectivity is achieved. Turn the box on its side so that the opening is no longer on the top but is on the side. Place some small bricks or other noncombustible material inside upon which you can rest a cookie sheet about two or three inches above the bottom of the box. Place ten burning charcoal briquettes between the bricks (if you need 400 degrees), place the support for your cooking vessels, and then place your bread pans or whatever else you are using on top of the cookie sheet. Prop a foil-covered cardboard lid over the open side, leaving a large crack for air to get in (charcoal needs a lot of air to burn) and bake your bread, cake, cookies, etc. just like you would in your regular oven. Your results will amaze you.

To make your own charcoal, select twigs, limbs, and branches of fruit, nut and other hardwood trees; black walnuts and peach or apricot pits may also be used. Cut wood into desired size, place in a large can which has a few holes punched in it, put a lid on the can and place the can in a hot fire. When the flames from the holes in the can turn yellow-red, remove the can from the fire and allow it to cool. Store the briquettes in a moisture-proof container. Burn charcoal only in a well-ventilated area.

Wood and Coal. Many wood and coal burning stoves are made with cooking surface. These are excellent to use indoors during the winter because you may already be using it to heat the home. In the summer, however, they are unbearably hot and are simply not practical cooking appliances for indoor use. If you choose to build a campfire on the ground outside be sure to use caution and follow all the rules for safety. Little children, and even many adults, are not aware of the tremendous dangers that open fires may pose.

Kerosene. Many kerosene heaters will also double as a cooking unit. In fact, it is probably a good idea to not purchase a kerosene heater that cannot be used to cook on as well. Follow the same precautions for cooking over kerosene as was discussed under the section on heating your home with kerosene.

Propane. Many families have propane camp stoves. These are the most convenient and easy to use of all emergency cooking appliances available. They may be used indoors or out. As with other emergency fuel sources, cook with a pressure cooker whenever possible to conserve fuel.

By Greg Pope.

EMERGENCY LIGHTING

Should there be a temporary lapse in electrical power, alternative sources of lighting must be stored in advance. Before the event, this is relatively inexpensive and easy. After the event, it becomes very difficult, perhaps impossible. _____

In most emergencies with a several day time span (hurricanes, ice storms, etc.) battery operated lighting will often see us through. However, with a major emergency the duration can be much greater. There are many products on the market that will serve well for these longer emergencies.

There are now several solar products that can provide lighting, even after cloudy days. There are solar lanterns, solar flashlights, even solar battery chargers. The solar walkway lamps that line outdoor paths are available in home centers. These can be brought in at night to provide ambient lighting. Solar photovoltaic panels or wind generators, hooked to batteries, can provide lighting and cost as little as $100 per light. With solar or wind, once the power is restored, you still have free, non-polluting lighting.

Kerosene lanterns and gas lanterns are common choices. With these be sure you have enough fuel stored safely away from the house. Gas lantern are very noisy but give off lots of heat. Kerosene lanterns can smell but scented fuel is available.

Candles should not be ruled out. However, common decorative candles have a short life. Emergency candles can have up to 100 hours of burn time and an indefinite shelf life. Be sure to have a good quality fire extinguisher in each room where candles, kerosene and gas are being used. Most of the alternatives require a fire or flame, so use caution. More

home fires are caused by improper usage of fires used for light than for any other purpose. Especially use extra caution with children and flame. Teach them the proper safety procedures to follow under emergency conditions. Allow them to practice these skills under proper adult supervision now, rather than waiting until an emergency strikes.

Cyalume sticks are the safest form of indoor lighting available but very few people even know what they are. Cyalume sticks can be purchased at most sporting goods stores for about $2 per stick. They are a plastic stick about four inches in length and a half inch in diameter. To activate them, simply bend them until the glass tube inside them breaks, then shake to mix the chemicals inside and it will glow a bright green light for up to eight hours. Cyalume is the only form of light that is safe to turn on inside a home after an earthquake. One of the great dangers after a serious earthquake is caused by ruptured natural gas lines. If you flip on a light switch or even turn on a flashlight you run the risk of causing an explosion. Cyalume will not ignite natural gas. Cyalume sticks are so safe that a baby can even use them for a teether.

Two-Mantle Gas Lantern
A gallon of Coleman-type fuel utilized with a two-mantle gas lantern has a burning time of approximately 40 hours. Light output is approximately the same as a 200W light bulb. Assuming an operating or burning time of 5 hours per day, the following approximate amounts of fuel would be consumed: White gas may be substituted in some camping equipment, but read and follow the specific instructions of the equipment manufacturer. A gas lantern gives a high intensity light and lots of heat, too—though the pressurized gas delivery system is quite noisy when operating. Two-Mantle Gas Lantern Fuel Consumption

Period use.	Fuel Consumed per 5 Hours of
Day,	1 pint.
Week,	1 gallon.
Month,	4 gallons.
Year,	50 gallons.

Kerosene Lanterns
Given today's technology, a kerosene lantern seems a bit old-fashioned and out of place! However, a kerosene lantern with a 1" wick will burn approximately 45 hours per quart of kerosene, saving lots of natural resources and utilizing approximately one-fourth as much fuel as a gas lantern. Kerosene lanterns are an effective and fairly safe lighting source. There are now scented lamp oils which replace kerosene. This lamp oil is generally available in retail stores. Make sure

the oil is approved for use in your lamp.

There is a difference in lighting quantity and quality, as the kerosene lantern is quite dim when compared to the two-mantle gas lantern. The light output of a kerosene lantern is comparable to a 40W-60W light bulb. As a rule of thumb, the typical kerosene lantern burns approximately 1 ounce of fuel per hour. Burning at the rate of 5 hours each day, the following approximate amounts of kerosene would be used:

Kerosene Lantern Fuel Consumption

Period	Fuel Consumed per 5 Hr.
Day,	$1/4$ pint.
Week,	1 quart.
Month,	1 gallon.
Year,	12 gallons.

Kerosene lamps are excellent sources of light and will burn for approximately 45 hours on a quart of fuel. They burn bright and are inexpensive to operate. The main problem with using them is failure to properly trim the wicks and using the wrong size chimney. Wicks should be trimmed in an arch, a "V," an "A" or straight across the top. Failure to properly trim and maintain wicks will result in smoke and poor light.

Aladdin type lamps that use a circular wick and mantle do not need trimming and produce much more light (and heat) than conventional kerosene lamps. These lamps, however, produce a great amount of heat, getting up to 750 degrees F. If placed within 36 inches of any combustible object such as wooden cabinets, walls, etc. charring can occur. Great caution should therefore be exercised to prevent accidental fires.

The higher the elevation the taller the chimney should be. Most chimneys that come with kerosene lamps are made for use at sea level. At about 4500 feet above sea level the chimney should be about 18-20 inches high. If your chimney is not as tall as it should be you can improvise by wrapping aluminum foil around the top of it and extending it above the top. This will enable the light to still come out of the bottom portion and yet provide proper drawing of air for complete combustion. If the chimney is too short it will result in smoke and poor light. Be sure to store extra wicks, chimneys and mantles.

Tallow Candles

Tallow candles burn brighter, longer, and are fairly smoke-free when compared to wax candles. Tallow candles are generally available in specialty stores only, unless you make your own. Wax candles are available almost anywhere housewares are sold. Store tallow candles in a cool, dry location. Candles stored in the freezer will burn slower and without dripping.

Emergency Candles

There are two types of emergency candles available for camping, storage, and emergency purposes.

Candles. Every family should have a large supply of candles. Three hundred sixty-five candles, or one per day is not too many. The larger the better. Fifty-hour candles are available in both solid and liquid form. White or light colored candles burn brighter than dark candles. Tallow candles burn brighter, longer, and are fairly smoke free when compared to wax candles. Their lighting ability can be increased by placing an aluminum foil reflector behind them or by placing them in front of a mirror. However, candles are extremely dangerous indoors because of the high fire danger—especially around children. For this reason be sure to store several candle lanterns or broad-based candle holders. Be sure to store a goodly supply of wooden matches

Save your candle ends for emergency use. Votive candles set in empty jars will burn for up to 15 hours. Non-candles (plastic dish and paper wicks) and a bottle of salad oil will provide hundreds of hours of candle light.
The type made of hardened wax in a can has the capability of utilizing several wicks simultaneously. The other type is a liquid paraffin-filled bottle with a wick for easy lighting. The liquid paraffin burns without odor or smoke. This candle has a minimum 100-hour burning time and indefinite shelf life.

Tallow Candle Burning Rate

Height	Diameter	Approximate Burning Time in Hours
6"	$1/2$"	3
6"	1"	8
9"	2"	48

Trench candles can be used as fireplace fuel or as a candle for light. To make trench candles:
1. Place a narrow strip of cloth or twisted string (for a wick) on the edge of a stack of 6-10 newspapers.
2. Roll the papers very tightly, leaving about 3/4" of wick extending at each end.
3. Tie the roll firmly with string or wire at 2-4" intervals.
4. With a small saw, cut about 1" above each tie and pull the cut sections into cone shapes. Pull the center string in each piece toward the top of the cone to serve as a wick.
5. Melt paraffin in a large saucepan set inside a larger pan of hot water. Soak the pieces of candle in the paraffin for about 2 minutes.
6. Remove the candles and place on a newspaper to dry.

Emergency Electric Lighting

Electric lighting has several advantages over other types, and some drawbacks. It's more portable and safer than fire based light. It can be extremely light weight and reliable. It's major drawback is the requirement of a power source. The most portable and available power source we currently have on the market is the traditional battery.

Emergency Lights

Light role	Minimum Recommended	Recommended
EDC	1 per kit	1 per person and kit with spares
Low Level	2 per family	2 per family with spares
Thrower	1 per family	1 per adult
Headlamps	1 per family	1 per adult
Small Lantern	1 per family	2-3 per family
Large Lantern	1 per family	2-3 per family

Note, some lights can serve in more than one role. Especially multi level adjustable lights.

E.D.C

Short for Every Day Carry. These lights should be small enough that you won't mind carrying it around everywhere with you. You never know when you might need a light in an emergency. There will likely be no power and having a flashlight on you will give you additional flexibility in where you can go and when. You don't need to always always have it with you, but it's nice to have that option. Ideally it will run off a single cell, or two small cells. Having a bright mode is nice, but not essential, it can be just a low mode light, or just a high mode light. This light can also be multi role, act as a low level light and a thrower, maybe even a lantern when standing on it's tail indoors. There are some nice lights out there but they can get expensive quick. If you use flashlights be sure to use krypton or halogen light bulbs in them because they last much longer and give off several times more light than regular flashlight bulbs on the same energy consumption. Store at least two or three extra bulbs in a place where they will not be crushed or broken.

Low Level

This light is what you can get away with when traveling through known territory, around camp, through your house, a night trip to the out house/latrine, reading at home base. Conserves batteries, last a long time. Size is probably not important. This is probably the role that will see the most use, this is the easiest to find and is also the most important.

Thrower

This is your big light. You may need it for search and rescue, a security patrol around a camp site, illuminating an area a long distance away (hence the name, it "throws" light far). It probably won't be in use every day, and it will eat batteries fast so you wouldn't want to run it all the time anyway. It's likely to be a larger light and only carried when a need is anticipated. Probably the least important, but when you need it you need it.

Headlamp

This light will be used for night work or work in the dark where you need both hands free. If you've ever tried to do the dishes by hand, without power, or any other such similar task you will quickly appreciate what a headlamp can do for you. You may not have the ability to ask someone to hold a flashlight for you as you accomplish a task. It should be reasonably small and use small batteries. It is possible to rig up a flashlight to perform this role, for example, an EDC and a holder for it in a hat. A lantern can also perform this role to a degree, however, an actual headlamp still is a good idea.

Small Lantern

Sometimes you need to light up a room to socialize or you need a small light to read by. It mostly gives light to a small group of people. Other possibilities are using a flashlight in "candle mode", which is either with the bezel off the light exposing the lamp or just standing the flashlight on it's tail and letting the light reflect off the ceiling.

Large Lantern

When more light is required than a small lantern provides, allows a group of people to have light in a small, usually stationary, place. Eating a meal at night, or socializing would be good examples.

Types of lamps for lights

Incandescent/Halogen/Krypton

These are not recommended for general flashlight use. They are not very durable, prone to break easily – especially when dropped. They are inefficient, consume batteries rapidly and generally get dim quite quickly with use. Really they are only suitable for use in a thrower type of light, and even then should probably be avoided due to their fragility.

LED

These are excellent for most all uses, more efficient than incandescent/halogen bulbs. Highly durable and only get more efficient as batteries deplete. You get what you pay for with these lights, really nice flashlights can be had. Do some research and get what fits inside your budget and meets your needs. They are getting better every year. Regulated lights are more efficient than the cheaper lights with resisters. As of July 2006, I have in my hands high power production LEDs that are just as efficient as Fluorescents (finally!). So in 4 to 6 months I expect them to be on the shelves. Unfortunately they are expensive currently, this will change with time.

Fluorescent

Probably the best choice for large lanterns on a budget. Last a reasonably long time, they are not very expensive so you should own a few. The major drawback is they cannot be dimmed to save power, and don't work so well in cold weather.

Self Powered Lights

These are generally not recommended for several reasons. They are usually bulky and prone to mechanical failure. This is especially true since they are very cheaply made, making them more of a novelty item than actually useful. If you're really interested in these, I would recommend a shake light. They appear quite durable, the mechanical part is only a lose magnet that goes back and forth inside a sealed container. Not prone to breakage, though the light level is low. Be aware that there have been reports of shake lights on the market that have coin cell batteries in them, they look nice and bright when you pick them up. Once the batteries dies (a few hours) they run on shake power which is no where near as bright as the batteries were.

Solar lights are nice, but I would first buy a solar battery charger and not have to carry the bulk of a solar cell around with me when using the light. Internally a solar light is going to have a battery anyway.

Self powered lights can probably only fill the role of a low level light.

A short course in Battery Chemistries

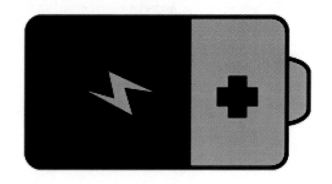

Primary Cells (single use, disposable cell)
The most common primary cells are Heavy-Duty and Alkaline, Lithium primary cells are also available but they can't always be used in devices that normally take Alkaline and Heavy-Duty batteries. Pure Lithium battery cells put out 3.0 volts rather than the normal 1.5. This requires either a different bulb or a "dummy" empty cell to be used to keep the overall voltage correct. But there are also new low voltage1.5v Lithium batteries as well.

Rechargeable Cells (multi use cells)
The most common today are probably NiMH cells. NiCd is an older technology. Lithium-ion is a newer technology, though it differs significantly from the more common cells.

Cell Type	Shelf Life	Capacity	Sizes Available	Cycles	Cold Weather
Heavy-Duty	8+ Years	Low	AAA, AA, C, D, 9V	1	Poor
Alkaline	8+ Years	Medium	AAA, AA, C, D, 9V	1	Poor
Lithium (Primary)	**15+ Years**	**High**	AAA, **AA**, C, **D**	1	***Excellant***
NiCd	3 Months	Med-Low	AAA, AA, C, D, 9V	1-2K	Good
NiMH	2 Months	Medium	AAA, AA, C, D, 9V	500-800	Poor
Lithium-ion	6 Months	High	R123A, other related sizes	300-500	Excellant

This table is a quick reference to some general comparisons of various cell types.

Other general notes on various cell types. Shelf Life improves if you store the batteries in a cooler environment. After a rechargeable battery loses it's charge due to shelf life, a simple recharge will put you back in business. Cold weather is defined as sub-freezing temperatures, and all cell types that got a "poor" rating can be warmed up in a pocket, put in an appliance and be expected to work again until they get too cold.

Battery cells should be treated like fuel. Take care of them, do not get them wet, do not throw them in fires, try not to drop them or get them banged up and they should be quite safe. Get water proof carry cases for your kits for them. You probably shouldn't store cells in devices if they are going to be packed away. If you store quantities of Lithium batteries in a house they should be stored in a fire proof box with vent holes drilled into a side of the box as a safety precaution (do not place vent holes near flammable objects). Do not store them in a tent. Don't get paranoid about Lithiums, you probably use them every day in devices like a cell phone, but you've probably hear a story or two of "exploding" batteries. What they really do is "vent rapidly with flame" (quite rare), use caution and don't buy knock offs.

Primary cells should be in your emergency kits as well as a small reserve for extended on the go emergencies, rechargeable cells will be more useful in a longer term emergency when you can settle down a bit but power still doesn't exist. AA cells are the most available with the best prices, adapters can also be found to make them fit into devices that use C and D batteries. AA rechargeable also don't require nearly as long as D cells to recharge.

Heavy Duty (Single use, Disposable)
Poor, not recommended. Cheap lights come with these batteries, it should also be taken as a sign that the light manufacture has cut every conceivable cost in the production and shipping of his light. Avoid them.

Alkaline (Single use, Disposable)
Good value. Costs are very reasonable, just stay away from poor brands as they are likely to leak and damage your devices and the residue is usually toxic. Duracell, Energizer, Rayovac, and most store-brand names are fine (Costco, Rite-aid). Stay away from Western Family and unknown brands.

Lithium (Single use, Disposable)

Expensive, but great cold weather performance for a primary cell, highest energy density. It would be good to have a few of these around for AA devices. Also in cases where weight, size, and capacity is more of an issue than cost.

NiCd (Recharagable)

Most durable type of rechargeable cell. There is a reason that in an era of NiMH and Li-ion batteries power tools and other such items that see regular hard use still use NiCDs. You can expect these cells to give you 5 years of use from the date of manufacture, if you care for them. And they do require care, suck them dry once every month or two and they'll hold out the longest. For longer term storage, put them in a cool place at about half charge. Not a bad value, good cold weather performance without a high cost. I would have some of these if you plan on using a standard rechargeable. Toxic, please use care when disposing of these cells.

NiMH (Recharagable)

Best value and convenience, an excellent value for what you receive with these batteries. They don't hold a charge long on the shelf but for regular battery use, they can't be beat. Some newer cells are available with a low self-discharge property at slightly reduced capacity (see Sanyo Eneloop or Titanium Enduro cells). They don't like the cold very much, so if it's cold outside you can put a flashlight in your pocket where it'll be warmer. Expect up to 3 years effective use from the date of manufacture, longer is possible but probably at reduced performance as the cell deteriorates.

Lithium-Ion (Recharagable)

Rather exotic and requires special care and attention. Special chargers are required, only really an option when you have a larger power source available to charge off of, like a car or off grid electrical system, or if you know how to build your own solar system to run the charger. Good cold weather performance, good power density (superior to even NiMH). However they deteriorate rapidly with time. Even 1 year will see reduced performance. You've probably noticed this with your cell phone and laptop computer batteries. Not the best long term option.

Lead Acid

Lowest self discharge of the rechargeable cells. Also the cheapest per unit of power. However they are also the least portable being the bulkiest. They can work well for area lighting and lanterns. Also for recharging smaller cells.

Once you have a good idea what you want and have acquired a few items. Run a family home evening off your battery devices only. Spend 1, 2, or even 3 days without the grid electric lights, learn what your needs are and use this information to fill them.

Copyright 2005
Brandon Mansfield

Off-Grid Power: What do I need?

Questions? Comments? brian@zyx.net

Energy Source

Why do I need it?

In order to live "off-grid" you need a source of electricity that is self-renewing (e.g. comes from the sun, wind, or water).

Solar panels, wind-mills, hydro-electric dams, and bicycle-generators are all examples of a renewable energy source you can use to create electricity.

The problem is that the electricity is created and disappears if it's not used immediately. The amount of power generated by these units is also constantly changing (on sunny days, for example, they generate more power). Wind mills change the amount of power they generate constantly. In other words, the power generated directly off these devices is not yet "useful", so we need some method of storing the electricity created by these units so that it can be delivered to our appliances with consistency.

How much will I pay?

Price depends 100% on how much power you want to generate. A very small set of solar panels will cost around $200.

Charge Controller

Why do I need it?

Charge controllers regulate (control) the amount of power coming from your energy source going into your batteries. Their job is to make sure you never have too much power being fed into your battery (on an especially windy day, you don't want your batteries charging too quickly). They also shut off the flow of electricity to the batteries when the batteries are full (over-charging will damage your batteries).

How much will I pay?

Charge controllers are the cheapest part of the system. You can buy a good charge controller for a low-end solar setup for as little as $20. High-end controllers used in homes cost a few hundred.

Power Storage

Why do I need it?

One of the challenges with renewable energy source is that most of them don't generate power 24x7, and when they do, the amount of power is inconsistent.

Using batteries to store the power allows you to have access to electricity when your energy-sources aren't working (example: when it's not windy, or at night when your solar panels aren't working).

How much will I pay?

Batteries also provide a clean, steady stream of power.

A typical "car battery" will run around $50. The more you spend, the more power you'll be able to store. The trick is balancing the amount of power your energy sources can produce with the amount of storage-capacity you have on-hand. Too much of one or the other and you're throwing money away.

Inverter

Why do I need it?

Most electrical devices run off AC voltage. (The stuff you have in your home). The problem is that batteries (and energy sources) produce DC voltage, so we need some way of converting (inverting) the DC from the battery into AC.

If you have items that run off DC (example: it uses a cigarette lighter adapter in your car) then you don't need an inverter to operate those items. They can be plugged directly into the battery (you can buy adapters at Radio Shack to do this).

How much will I pay?

The cost of the inverter, once again, depends 100% on how much power you need to run through it. A small inverter that can operate a laptop computer will cost around $20. A high-end inverter that can run a wheat grinder will cost around $200.

Appliances

Why do I need it?

These are your "things" that you are trying to power. Your wheat grinder, your ham radio, your iPod, your satellite TV, and your snow-cone machine.

How much will I pay?

The appliances are the final determining item in how big each of the other items in your power setup need to be.

If you have appliances that consume a lot of electricity, you'll need bigger inverters, bigger batteries, bigger charge controllers, and bigger energy sources. All of these translate into bigger cost.

A few Examples of Turn-Key Systems

Xantrex Xpower

Description

This is a TRUE all-in-one unit that includes your solar panel, charge controller, batteries and your inverter.

The battery is a 10amp/hour battery
The inverter is 400 watts

Note: It takes approximately 30 hours of sunlight to charge the battery off the included solar panel.

THIS UNIT WILL NOT RUN HEAVY APPLIANCES, SUCH AS A WHEAT GRINDER

Runtimes:

Laptop Computer: 2.5 hours
Fluorescent Light: 6 hours
3/8" Drill: 16 minutes

Cost

Amazon sells this unit for $126.25 with free shipping.

Xantrex 600

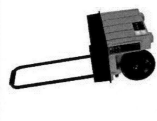

Description

This is unit that includes your charge controller, batteries and your inverter. The only thing missing is the actual energy source (e.g. solar panel)

The battery is a 28amp/hour battery
The inverter is 600 watts

Note: A 60-watt solar panel can charge this battery in about 8 hours. (This unit does not come with a solar panel)

THIS UNIT WILL NOT RUN HEAVY APPLIANCES, SUCH AS A WHEAT GRINDER

Runtimes:

Laptop Computer: 7 hours
Fluorescent Light: 20 hours
3/8" Drill: 50 minutes

Cost

Amazon sells this unit for $129.99 with free shipping.

Xantrex 1500

Description

This is unit that includes your charge controller, batteries and your inverter. The only thing missing is the actual energy source (e.g. solar panel)

The battery is a 60amp/hour battery
The inverter is 1,500 watts

Note: A 100-watt solar panel can charge this battery in about 10 hours. (This unit does not come with a solar panel)

Runtimes:

Laptop Computer: 17 hours
Fluorescent Light: 50 hours
3/8" Drill: 2 hours

Cost

Amazon sells this unit for $344.95 with free shipping.

Electric Generators

Generator Basics

Generators are shaft-driven machines that produce electric power. Broadly speaking, they range in size and capacity from the tiny devices used as sensors to the extremely large machines used at commercial power plants. The term "alternator" is also used and means essentially the same thing. The term "generator set" or "genset" is sometimes used to describe a generator along with a gasoline or diesel engine or other power source.

This article covers the use of generators to provide standby power in an emergency for a single family or small group.

Generators are rated in terms of the amount of power they can produce. This is measured in Watts (W) or Kilowatts (kW). A Kilowatt is equal to 1,000 Watts. Some household items list their power requirement in Watts, such as light bulbs and small appliances. Others only list Amperes (abbreviated A or Amps). Most household electrical loads (including all cord-connected appliances that plug into a standard outlet) run on 120 Volts, and since Watts = Amps X Volts, you can determine Watts by multiplying the amp requirement by 120. Large heating and cooling appliances, and well pumps, sometimes use 240 Volts. This can be determined from the nameplate. For these loads, wattage is determined by multiplying amps by 240.

Generator Types

Commercially available generators useful for small-scale standby power fall into these categories:

Type	Wattage	Price Range
Small portable units marketed primarily for camping	Generally less than 2 kW	$400-$600
Midsize portable units	3-5 kW.	$400-$2,000
Large trailer-mount units without engines, driven by a tractor PTO	15-60 kW	$2,000-$5,000
Large trailer-mount units designed for construction or industrial use	10 kW or more..	
Large standby units designed for permanent installation.	5-40 kW or more	$4,000-$12,000

Costs vary depending on ruggedness, reliability, and features.

The more expensive units typically include features like:

a. Better quality engines, with pressure lubrication, cast iron cylinder blocks (or cast iron sleeves), oil filters, and electronic ignition. The primary benefit of these is longevity, although the better engines may be somewhat more reliable.
b. Larger fuel tank for long, unattended runs.
c. Low oil shutdown to prevent engine damage
d. Electric start
e. Built in battery charger for 12V car batteries
f. Quieter design, achieved through better mufflers, soundproofing, and lower operating RPM
g. Ground fault circuit interrupters (GFCI) for safety
h. Wheels. Even the smaller generators are heavy.

There are a wide variety of brands available. All of them work, and most are adequate for occasional standby use.

The generators that are driven by a farm tractor are a good buy if you already own one or more farm tractors. Unlike car and truck mount generators, tractor-driven ones produce ample power. Tractors are better suited to continuous, stationary operation than cars and trucks.

Generator Uses

Generators can be useful in a long-duration power outage by providing power to run essential equipment, such as refrigerators, freezers, lighting, water pumps, sump pumps, and furnaces. They are also useful for providing power w here it is inconvenient, costly, or impossible to bring commercially produced power.

Sizing

Determining the exact size generator required for a household involves adding up the wattage required by each load, including the starting power required by the largest motor and any others that will be started at the same time. It is difficult to get accurate results since starting current requirements often vary and because nameplate ratings sometimes overstate the power required.

If a generator is too small for its load, the voltage will drop. This can cause damage to the generator, the load, or both. Circuit breakers and thermal protectors may trip and prevent damage, but cannot be relied upon. Do not connect loads to the generator that are too large for its capacity.

If you only want to run a few critical items, you can use this chart as a guide:

Generator size	Loads typically supported
1,000W or less	Lights, radio, battery chargers, clocks, fax, or computer
1,500W	Above items, also small manual defrost freezer or refrigerator
3,500W 240V	Same as 1500W, plus ½ H.P. well pump (if 240V)
3,500W 120V	Most refrigerators and freezers, clothes washer, gas clothes dryer, sump pump, ½ H.P. furnace blower, ½ H.P. well pump (if 120V), nearly any plug-connected appliance with a standard 120V plug
5,000W 240V	Same as 3500W, plus most well pumps up to 2 H.P.
15,000W 240V	Will run all the loads in most households including electric water heaters, dryers, well pumps, and ranges; will run many central air conditioning units. Electric heat systems need to be considered case by case as many larger systems use more power than even a big generator like this produces.

Measuring the Load

Sometimes it helps to measure the amount of power a particular piece of equipment (or an entire household) uses. This may be the only way to determine power requirements accurately if there is no nameplate listing the power required. Clamp-on ammeters are available at most building supply stores for about $50-$100 that will measure the number of amps flowing through a wire. They usually include an attachment that you can use for cord-and-plug connected devices. More sophisticated ammeters that measure starting current are available but are costly ($400) and require some expertise to use.

Electrical Hookup

There are three ways to hook up generators:

n   Plug in loads directly, using extension cords if necessary.
n   Transfer switch
n   Suicide wiring

Plugging in loads to the generator's outlets directly is the simplest and works OK when only a few small loads are used. This method is used in remote areas and for construction, where no electric wiring is present. It also works in standby situations for running a handful of things, say, a freezer, refrigerator, sump pump, and a couple lights. Generators must be operated outdoors unless specifically designed for indoor operation. Those designed for indoor use have an exhaust system that vents outside. Since the generator is usually outside and the load is inside, extension cords are needed. Be sure they're big enough. Most of the orange extension cords sold use 16 gauge wire and are rated for 13 amps. These are fine for a couple of small appliances but create a fire hazard when used for heavier loads.

Transfer switches

Transfer switches allow you to connect a load to either the generator or the commercial power source simply by flipping a switch. They are the only reasonable and safe alternative for running an entire house from a generator . They are also the only way to run equipment that can't be unplugged, such as furnace blowers, well pumps, and the like. Different configurations are available that allow switching of all or part of a household's electrical circuits. They are expensive a nd must be installed by an electrician or other qualified person. Some examples:

Transfer switches that have 4-6 different handles, each of which switches a single circuit, are available for around $200 from many retailers that sell generators. They wire into the house's breaker or fuse panel. You only hook up the circuits that you will need in an emergency, which reduces the cost, and you can switch them one at a time so all the motors don't start at once. Some designs include an ammeter so you can see how much power you're using.

Some designs, including one from Square D that I have seen, use circuit breakers to perform the switching and have an interlock so you can only turn on one circuit breaker – either the generator breaker or the commercial power breaker. I have seen the se for as little as $60 plus the cost of the circuit breakers. Again you only hook up the circuits that you think you will need in an emergency. These panels hook up to your main breaker panel as a sub-panel.

Large transfer switches switch the power to a house or group of buildings and are wired between the meter socket and breaker (or fuse) panel. These cost $300-$600 depending on capacity. They are costly to install as well.

Automatic transfer switches will start the generator and switch the load to it without intervention. Some standby systems have these built in. One catalog I have lists a 200A model as costing almost $2,000. Telephone companies, hospitals, radio and TV stations, and the like use larger versions of these.

Transfer switches are wired with a large, flexible cord and plug for use with portable generators. The cord and plug are not normally included with the transfer switch and must be purchased separately. Welding supply companies are a good, inexpensive source for the heavy gauge wire required. If you plan to connect the generator to building wiring, consider the transfer switch part of the cost of the generator.

Suicide wiring

Any method of connecting a generator to a building's electrical system, other than by using a transfer switch, falls under the category of suicide wiring.

You can be killed. And you can kill an electric lineman if you fail to isolate your generator from the power company's lines, by causing electricity to back-feed into the commercial power system. You can also burn up your generator or your house. It is also against the law in many jurisdictions.

Plan ahead. Buy a transfer switch. Get it installed. Don't use suicide wiring.

Safety

Here's some basic advice on generator safety. Read the instructions for your generator or check with a dealer or licensed electrician for authoritative safety rules.
1. Follow the safety instructions that come with the generator.
2. Keep the generator outside so you don't breathe carbon monoxide and die. Protected locations, such as a garage with the garage door open, are helpful if the weather is bad.
3. Follow whatever grounding instructions come with the generator. Generators should be grounded but the recommendations for how this is done vary depending on manufacturer.
4. You can get a bad shock by touching a wet power cord or plug while the generator is running. Shut off the engine before fiddling with the power connections if it is wet out.
5. Don't refuel a hot engine. If you refuel at night, use a source of light that won't ignite the gas. The cyalume sticks work well for this.
6. Don't overload extension cords.
7. Use a transfer switch.
8. Store gasoline outside, in a safe container.

More accidents happen during power outages than occur when power is available, particularly fires. Here are some general tips for safety during power outages:
1. Don't leave candles or oil or gasoline lanterns burning unattended.
2. Realize that smoke and carbon monoxide detectors will not work without power.
3. Have fire extinguishers at hand.
4. Have some water drawn up in buckets or pans to use in case the water supply fails.

Fuels and Fuel Storage

Most portable generators run on gasoline. But gasoline is a poor choice for standby use, because it is unsafe to store in residential areas and is prone to deterioration when stored for any length of time.

Gasoline is extremely flammable and should not be stored in any quantity in a house or garage. There is no safe way to store gasoline in a building. Building and zoning codes, and insurance requirements, vary; some municipalities prohibit permanently installed gasoline tanks and limit the size of portable ones.. In the author's area gasoline suppliers recommend that bulk storage tanks be at least 10' away from garages and other buildings. Some of the author's acquaintances store gasoline in 5 gallon ca ns in a little building not much larger than a doghouse, that is used for nothing else and is a long way from all the other buildings. Gasoline can be stored in full, sealed containers for 1-2 years or more without deterioration, provided that high temperatures are avoided. Air, water, and heat all contribute to deterioration.

The author uses a commercial fuel preserving additive in the gas tank for his generator, but there is no consensus on misc.survivalism that such additives materially improve the storage life of gasoline.

Some, mostly larger, generators are available with diesel engines. These engines are, as a rule, noisier than gasoline engines and are more difficult to start in cold weather. For standby use, they may be worth having because of fuel storage considerations.

Diesel fuel and kerosene are much safer to store than gasoline. It is still common to store fuel oil, which has similar properties, indoors in houses in quantities up to 250 gallons. Again, building and zoning codes and insurance rules may limit the amount or method of storage. These products should not be stored in red cans because of the potential for confusion with gasoline. These fuels can be stored 2-3 years before they deteriorate.

Midsize and larger generators designed for permanent installation and standby use are available for use with LP gas or natural gas. The engines are like gasoline engines in most respects but replace the carburetor with a mixing system designed for LP o r natural gas. LP gas standby generators are widely used in industrial/commercial settings. The chief benefit is that LP gas can be stored indefinitely without deterioration.

LP gas conversion kits are available for many small generators.

Readiness

There are no statistics available, but anecdotal evidence suggests that generators frequently fail to start when they are needed, even in industrial settings where regular maintenance and testing is performed. Electric start generators sometimes fail to start because the battery is dead. Batteries that are continuously trickle-charged may start the engine while being charged but fail when the charger is turned off, as in an actual emergency. Battery terminal s also have a way of getting corroded. Stale gasoline can contribute to starting problems, especially in cold weather. Using starting fluid will sometimes make up for this.

Spare parts and supplies should be kept on hand. At a minimum, some extra motor oil, suitable starting aids, air and oil filters (if used), and a spark plug should be available. You should periodically operate your generator, and hook up whatever loads you plan to use, to make sure that everything is ready if needed. Once a month is probably often enough to catch most problems.

How Practical Is a Generator?

The author has had to resort to using the generator during a couple of long-duration power outages. Severe weather can be extremely disruptive to power systems and the unlucky individuals whose own lines are knocked down in a storm end up at the end of the power company's list for repairs. Power losses can be costly if you stand to loose the contents of your freezer, or if cold weather and no heat threatens to freeze pipes.

On the other hand, unless you can afford a fully automatic, permanently installed system, you had better be able-bodied. It's work to pull out the generator and start it and hook it up even if you have a good setup.

Big generators are noisy. Everyone in the neighborhood will know that you're running one.

You may wish to consider running the generator during only part of a 24-hour period. Most refrigerators and freezers will maintain temperature if operated 50% of the time, depending on ambient temperature, condition of the door seal, and how often the door is opened.

Fuel availability is a thorny issue. Gas stations require electricity to be able to pump gas. The author is fortunate enough to live in a setting where it is possible to store ample quantities of fuel to run the generator for a week or more. Even the worst power outages are ordinarily corrected after a week, two at the most. Those of you concerned about other TEOTWAWKI scenarios should consider other alternatives that do not rely on fuel availability.

Other Ways to Produce Electricity

Several companies sell inverters that produce 120V electricity using the power from a car or truck's battery and alternator. These are not suitable for most standby uses because the output power is too low. The largest car and truck alternators produce no more than 2000 watts, and this only at high engine speeds. The really big inverters – 2000W and over, capable of running a refrigerator – are expensive, big, heavy, and require heavy cabling to the battery. The logistics of ope rating a vehicle while stationary must also be considered: how do you secure the vehicle, potential for damage due to low oil or high temperature while unattended, potential for transmission bearing damage due to extended idling, poor fuel economy.

There are some belt-driven and PTO-driven generators for cars and trucks that have similar problems. In addition, most of these units must be operated at a specific speed. Unless the vehicle is equipped with an engine governor, this is difficult.

Uninterruptable power supplies (UPS) are designed primarily for use with computers and communications equipment. They generally are designed for short-duration outages, 15 minutes or less.

Solar, hydroelectric, and wind generators are a topic in their own right and are beyond the scope of this FAQ. Many products marketed for use with alternative power systems are also useful for standby use. It might make sense in some cases to have low- voltage DC wiring for lights that can be operated from batteries in an emergency.

Non-electric Alternatives

There are a number of low-tech techniques that can reduce your dependence on electricity. Some are effective by themselves, and others will reduce the size generator you need or the hours you need to run it.

Use something besides electricity for the primary source of heat. Although any modern central heating system requires some electricity to operate, you can run a natural gas, LP gas, or oil-fired furnace from a generator of modest size. Electric heat systems can't be operated except by very large generators.

Replace electric appliances with gas. Houses that are served by a natural gas supplier rarely have gas outages and electric outages at the same time (except possibly in earthquake-prone areas). LP gas is stored in tanks and is independent of electrical and other utilities. A gas stove can be used without electricity if the burners are lit with a match. Most gas water heaters don't require electricity at all (except for horizontal exhaust and other power-vented units).

Have a wood stove or fireplace insert that is capable of heating your house. Have enough wood on hand to be able to use it in a power outage.

A wide variety of non-electric lighting is available. Aladdin lamps, which burn kerosene and produce a bright light, are practical and safer to use inside than gasoline lanterns. Lamps that operate on LP gas supplied through pipes are available. They mount permanently to a wall or ceiling, and are bright, safe, and cheap to operate. Inexpensive kerosene wick lamps are widely available and produce more light than candles. LP gas and kerosene operated refrigerators and freezers are available. Some will also operate on electricity. Full-size units are expensive but no more so than a good generator installation. Smaller refrigerators, such as those used in RVs, are available too – though some require a 12V DC power source to operate the controls and ignition system even when running on LP gas.
By Steve Dunlop.

HONDA EU200 portable 2,000 Watt Generator

Honda UE6500 Portable 6,500 Watt Generator

320

Clothing

Clothing is something that is not considered often enough by Latter Day Saints in planning for a disaster. You'll find many chat room and discussion board references to food, water, housing, etc., but very few references to clothes. Yet finding suitable clothing will be a very real concern in a long term disaster..

Clothes wear out or your kids grow out of them. In these normal times, you just drive to the mall or Walmart or wherever and buy what you need. There's always plenty available. This might not be true after a major disaster. It takes factories to make clothes; it takes international trade, a reliable banking system, dependable distribution systems, accurate billing systems, sophisticated telecommunications, the power grid, computers, computers, computers! Even in a less than worst case scenario, there will definitely be problems in some or all of these areas. If you want to have clothes for your family in 2006 or later, you will need to get them now.

If you have children, this will take some thought. Will the clothes your oldest child wears become too small before they can be worn out, which means they can be handed down to younger siblings, or has your oldest essentially finished growing? Do you have boys or girls or both? Boys tend to wear out their clothes sooner than girls. Do you live in a cool northern area or a warmer southern one? The best way to figure out your family's clothing needs is to pretend they have nothing whatsoever to wear and you have been given the job of outfitting the entire family from underwear to topcoat. Actually you have been given this job, just not all at once. A disaster changes all that as it changes so many things. The bright side is that you can forget about getting them what's fashionable this year. No one will have the slightest interest in fashion after a disaster ; we'll all be too concerned with getting enough food and keeping warm.

We don't know how long the really nasty times will be. I'm planning on at least 1 year of chaos followed by a couple years of rebuilding. This seems reasonable to me based on what I've learned about a large scale disaster. If you agree with this estimate, you'll need to have *at least* two full years of clothes for your family. I'm thinking in terms of three years of clothes just to be sure. Since you already have clothes for everyone, you have part of this job done. You may have three years worth of clothes for your family in your house right now. The only really tricky part is allowing for growth if you have children.

Make a list with each family member on it and write down what each one needs, beginning with the oldest child. If the oldest still has some growing to do, figure that there will be hand-me-downs available to younger siblings. Allow at least

five long sleeve and five short sleeve shirts per child and five pairs of pants also. The oldest male can always hand down his outgrown shirts and pants to both younger brothers and sisters. Five pairs of underpants and undershirts, five pairs of socks, two sweaters, a jacket and a heavy coat per child should be the minimum. A few dresses and skirts for the girls would be nice. As I said, you already have most of this. The only difference from your normal clothing concerns is the fact that you will need to buy clothes for growing children now instead of next year and the year after.

There may not be much joy in your children's lives for a few years—things will be so terribly different from what they're used to—so have a few nice things tucked away for them, particularly for daughters. Kids are still kids and they love an attractive surprise. There may be some local social events in your area they'd like to look nice for so plan ahead for this, which means don't take them clothes shopping with you.

Shoes may be the worst clothing problem we have. Unless there is a cobbler in your area, which is very rare these days, there will be no way to repair shoes or resole them when they're worn out. The shoe purchase procedure is the same as with your other clothing concerns: figure out what each child will need for two or three years, allowing for growth, buy it now and put it away. Each child will need several pairs of everyday shoes to play in (or work in if things get really bad), plus a pair of nicer shoes for church or whatever social occasions may occur and some sturdy boots for winter snows.

Buy in a similar manner for you and your spouse or any other adults in the family. You don't have to buy everything new for adults or children; go to thrift shops or yard sales and stock up. If you find a good source of inexpensive clothes, buy lots of things in all the average sizes. Remember that most people will not be at all prepared for a crash so any clothes you don't need will be excellent barter items.

Warm, Protected and Modest: What to Wear in Difficult Times

Copyright 2012 Survivalblog by Marilyn E.

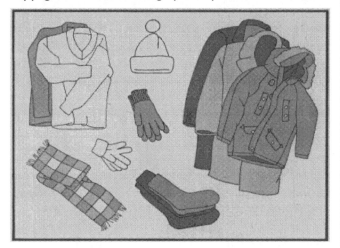

My father, a World War II veteran, suffered from trench foot, still suffers from its after effects. He contracted the condition in Europe by having cold, wet feet for days on end. A similar condition called immersion foot may be familiar to veterans who served in Vietnam where the water was warmer, but still caused loss of circulation. Dry socks are not a luxury. Warm, dry clothing is not only a joy and a comfort, it can save your body parts and your life. Protection from sun and wind, thorns and brush, cold and damp can be essential to your survival. But no matter how well prepared you are, sooner or later everything you own will wear out. When there is no thrift store, mall or internet with overnight delivery, you'll still need to protect yourself. In this article I will lay out some strategies for keeping you covered and comfortable. I will not address specialized clothing such as rain gear, armor and personal protective equipment. I will discuss what you wear every day: how to choose clothing and preserve. In future articles I hope to describe how to reuse and recycle clothing and, if necessary, create it from scratch.

The first question is what do you need to wear? What clothing is essential to your everyday tasks? I sit in an office most of the day. What I wear in that setting is not appropriate for mucking out stalls, tramping through heavy brush or digging in the garden, so I have two kinds of "working" wardrobes. The first step is deciding what activities you'll be performing in what kind of weather and determine if the clothing you have is going to keep you comfortable during those tasks. Will you be hunting, hunkering down, chopping wood, following a plow? Have you tried out your clothing in these situations and how is it working for you? Will you be outside in heat and cold, wet and dry? What do you currently own and what do you need to buy? What can be repurposed for the coming tasks? How much clothing do you need for how long? Can you make what you have

last until it can be replaced? What if it can't be replaced except by your own efforts? Inventory what you have and see where you are falling short. Decide if you need more of anything and make a plan to add, repair, replace or pare down if your closets are full of things that will do you no good.

What should your clothes be made of? There are basically three types of fabric: plant derived, animal derived and synthetic. Each has different characteristics. Natural fibers like cotton, hemp, bamboo, and linen, and some cellulose-based synthetics like rayon and its kin (modal and viscose) absorb moisture, breathe and allow you to stay cool. Wicking away moisture is important both in summer, when it helps keep your skin cool by allowing evaporation, and in the winter, when sweating under clothes can leave you clammy and chilled. Silk has properties similar to plant-derived materials with the added advantage that it can keep you cool in warm weather and warm in cool weather with very little added weight. My silk long underwear is dear to me. Historically silk has been used under armor to prevent chafing, aid in cooling and, so the story goes, to add an extra layer of protection, as well as making arrows easier to remove should they penetrate your armor.

Animal fibers like wool and hair can keep you warm even when they are wet. But a wool shirt, once soaked with your sweat, can also serve as a good evaporative cooling system. A closely woven or felted wool coat will keep you warmer than anything but heavy fur, with the added benefit that it can turn water for a considerable time. Fur, leather and hide, if treated correctly, can repel water and can be made soft enough to go next to the skin, although wet leather on skin, in my experience, is not a joy.

While synthetics, especially polyester, nylon and acrylic, have their place and are available in an amazing array of textures and weights, they may be less desirable than more natural fabrics. They often do not breathe and can leave you feeling clammy and damp, especially if worn close to the skin. Synthetics are often blended with natural fabrics to improve their handling, wrinkle resistance and cost. The more of the natural fiber blended into the fabric, the better it will likely feel next to your skin. If you ignite a tiny bit of fabric you can estimate the content of natural fibers: if it melts it is mostly petrochemical-derived synthetics, if it burns it has mostly natural fibers. You can imagine that fabric that melts into your skin during a fire is less than ideal. On the other hand, cotton gauze can burn furiously and be equally dangerous.

My vote is always for as much natural fiber as I can manage. Sometimes it's hard to find clothing made of natural fibers because synthetics have become ubiquitous and tend to be inexpensive. Cheap clothing cheaply constructed is not a bargain. Buy the best clothing you can afford, made of good fabrics and well constructed. It will last longer. Consignment shops often have excellent quality designer clothing made of high quality natural fabrics. Don't let the fashion fool you. These clothes are made of the best materials and built to last though they are usually worn for one season and tossed aside. That just means more for you and me at prices we can afford.

Accessorizing is not just for fashion mavens. You'll need gloves, hats, scarves and shoes or boots appropriate to whatever tasks you're performing. In the summer my husband and I use what we fondly call Amish sunscreen: long-sleeved shirts and hats with brims. Sunburn is painful; skin cancer is lethal. Grown-ups put on gloves before their hands start to blister, not after. Shoes that fit and are appropriate to the task should not need to be explained. And don't forget the dry socks.

A Side Note: In some unusual circumstances, the best clothes are no clothes at all. Two cases in point: 1) the five women who rowed across the Atlantic recently found that their seawater damp clothing caused sores where it rubbed. By rowing without clothes, they literally saved their skin; 2) while serving on a Pacific island, my father found that by placing his clothing under palm fronds during the brief daily monsoon, he had dry clothes for the rest of the day.

You've selected your clothing and tried it out in the sorts of situations where it will be expected to serve. Now how do you make it last? First, your clothes may need clothes. An apron, whether you're a cook or a blacksmith, will preserve your clothing. Protective sleeves, butchers' coats, and smocks can be washed repeatedly sparing your everyday clothing and making it last longer.

Clean clothes survive longer than dirty ones, but clothing doesn't need to be washed every time you wear it. Washing clothing too often wears it out. Clothing that is to be stored for any period of time must be clean because insects and mildew are attracted to body oil, deodorant, food stains, and other soil. Clothing should be completely dry before storing. To wash, sort fabrics by weight (towels should not be washed with sheets, for example) and by color, light colors separate from dark colors. Keep the red socks out of the whites to avoid having pink undies.

Soap or detergent? Detergent, made from petrochemicals, does a fairly good job of cleaning clothes, but you will find some types of grease stains will not be removed. Soap, made from natural fats or oils, will remove stains better, but soap forms a precipitate with hard water that can cause fabrics to become gray and dull. Vinegar or citrus juice added to the wash water will prevent this, as will washing in soft water (such as rain water). Baking soda also changes the pH of the water in the other direction (making it alkaline rather than acidic) and will make the detergent foam better in hard water making it clean more effectively. Dulling of dark colors is not caused by washing in hot water but by lint and residue clinging to the fabric. Vinegar in the final rinse will reduce this. Salt added to wash water can prevent yellowing of whites and combined with vinegar will remove mildew from fabric. If you are washing in a tub rather than in a machine, my friend tells me you are better off using a bathroom plunger than the metal one she bought for the job. It rusted and left stains on her clothes.

Never wash clothing in cold water. Cold water does not destroy bacteria or prevent mildew. Use the warmest water safe for the clothing, but not so hot it will degrade the fabric. However, you should use water hot enough to purify fabric that needs it, for example, clothing that has been in flood water or has been exposed to disease or infection.

I have often heard it said that line drying is better for clothing than using a drier. However, a woman of my acquaintance found the opposite to be true. This will depend somewhat on how you are drying your clothes and whether or not they are subject to wind and sun. Sunlight can degrade fabrics (especially silk) and cause colors to fade, but it can also destroy mildew. How you dry your clothes will depend on what is available to you. Clothing can be line dried in the winter as well as in the summer, but it may take longer. If drying takes so long the fabric mildews as during prolonged damp weather, find an alternative, such as drying indoors on lines or even furniture. A drying rack in or a retractable line over the bathtub works well.

Before washing clothes make any repairs that are required. Tears become worse while laundering. Also, close zippers, turn sweaters and trousers inside out, and empty pockets – pens and chap sticks in a washer or drier will do your clothing no good. Tie drawstrings loosely to prevent them from pulling out, hook bras or other items with hooks to keep them from snagging other garments (or wash them in a net bag or a pillow case).

Storing wool, other animal fibers and fur present a special problem because of clothing moths. The tiny larvae eat the protein in the hair or fiber and leave holes. Wool blended with synthetics is less attractive to them. They can be thwarted by several means. Freezing infested clothing for about two weeks or heating fabric to 120 degrees Fahrenheit for thirty minutes will kill the larvae. They do not like sun and movement so hanging clothes on a sunny, breezy clothes line will cause them to drop off. Also, soaking in soapy water for twelve hours will drown the little nibblers. Once you're sure the larvae are dead, store animal fiber clothing to prevent it from becoming reinfested. First, the clothing should be absolutely clean and dry. Avoid moth balls – they are toxic to more than moths, and the really awful smell is very difficult to banish. Old houses often have closets with windows in them specifically for storing woolens, but to be safe, add other precautions. Moths are deterred by the smell of cedar (the classic cedar trunk was designed to store woolens), eucalyptus, pennyroyal, lavender, rosemary, mint, cloves or lemon. Any non-edible barrier will stop the moths from getting to your clothes. This can be a paper bag tightly sealed or a well sealed cotton pillow case. Both of these allow air to circulate. I do not recommend plastic for storage as any trapped moisture can cause problems like mildew.

To repair and maintain your clothing you will need certain tools. Not enough can be said about the value of good needles. You should have them in several sizes, appropriate to whatever you're repairing, whether stockings or leather. Here is my basic tool kit. You'll obviously change it to suit your needs.

Needles in various weights and sizes: sharps sizes 3 through 9; yarn needles; others as needed such as darning, embroidery, sail maker's (also used for heavy leather), and upholstery

Thread in regular sewing weight and coat weight in an assortment of colors but at least white, black, and whatever most of your clothes are

A needle threader if you have poor eyesight

Safety pins in assorted sizes. Large ones can be used to thread elastic or draw strings through waistbands

Buttons of various sizes; snaps; hooks and eyes; grommets and a grommet setter. I have zippers, but I don't recommend them. More on this later.

Scissors, large for cutting fabric and small for snipping threads; scissors sharpener

Loop and hook tape; elastic in assorted widths; cording for draw strings and macramé buttons and frogs

Tape measure

Seam ripper – not essential but handy

Pins and pin cushion with an emery bag (the little metal-filing filled bag for sharpening pins)

Thimble – I rarely use mine, but they're nice to have

Patching material

Also handy but not essential are **seam tape, fusible bonding web** (Stitch Witchery), **liquid seam sealant** (Fray Check), **tailor's chalk**

A really good book on basic clothing repair and construction is worth the investment. Always make repairs as soon as possible. When adding a patch, make sure the edges are finished to prevent raveling and the patch is sufficiently large to be stitched to areas of strong fabric. A patch that is stronger than the material it is stitched to can tear out leaving a bigger hole. Creative patching can improve the appearance of worn garments, clever patching can be nearly invisible. Preemptive patches placed in areas of hard wear (leather patches on knees or elbows) can add years of life to garments.

Learn how to darn, practice doing it and wear the repaired clothing to see if the repair causes rubbing, blistering or discomfort. If so, toss or recycle the repaired item and try it again. Practice makes perfect and if you wait until you have nothing but holey socks to learn to repair them, you've waited too long. In most garments zippers are much harder to replace than you might think. Often to remove the old zipper and put in a new one requires nearly complete deconstruction of the item. Replacing the broken zipper with loop and hook (like Velcro) or with buttons is easier. For a coat, toggles with looped fasteners work well.

Choose your clothing wisely and take good care of it. Still, however careful you are, sooner or later everything you own will wear out. Reusing, repurposing, salvage and creation from scratch are the next steps. These require much more time and effort, so saving your clothes saves you both.

Copyright 2012 by Survivalblog.
http://survivalblog.com/2012/03/warm-protected-and-modest-what-to-wear-in-difficult-times-by-marilyn-e.html

Winter Clothes For Preparedness Survival

Winter clothes could be considered very important for survival preparedness to have in hard times if living in seasonal areas that cold weather is a normal thing. It should be classified up there with food and water storage. You can freeze to death faster than you can starve to death. It is a normal to have Arctic conditions exist when the wind is blowing and the temperature drops below 20 degrees F. There are only seven states in the US that do not experience Arctic weather. If there is no gas or propane to use that we are so accustom in using because of leaks or broken lines, we need to be prepared for these times. Having wood and wood stoves is also is something to consider.

So what preparation for winter clothes do you need for you and your family in those cold survival times? For winter clothes there are winter gloves, winter hats, winter coats, winter jackets, winter boots, long johns, and winter pants. Many of these winter clothes you might already have so you will be one step ahead here. Your clothing must allow your body moisture to escape from your body otherwise your own moister could cause you to freeze to death. So water proofing your winter clothes isn't a good idea being that it will cause the moister to stay in. What is better to do is to layer your winter clothes with the proper clothing materials which will allow your perspiration to escape or if you know anything about foam clothing you could consider having some made or make it yourself. It is very breathable and works great in those sub zero temperatures. If more sources on this are found it will be posted here. To keep warm you should consider having different layers of winter clothing on.

Long Johns

The layer closes to your body should be able to wick moisture away form your skin and trap a layer of warm air next to your skin during activities. Long johns or long underwear works well for this made of polyester, silk or polypropylene. Modern synthetics are nonabsorbent and will do the job Avoid cotton being that it will absorb your moister and trap it.

Winter Jackets

The middle layer of winter clothes provides insulation and affords you the most versatility as your activity intensifies or temps fluctuate. These winter jackets can be make of microfleece, wool, or "Polartec". Acrylic sweater, heavy wool jackets or button up shirts also work well for this. Keeping wind protection and capturing heated air space for warmth is what you want to consider.

Winter Coats

The outer layer is focused less on warmth and more on staying dry. It is the outer layer that protects insulating layers from wind & water - the 2 prime culprits in convective and conductive heat loss. Gore-Tex is something to consider that works well in allowing for venting of internal heat and and is still water and windproof. Nylon and Teflon coats offer good protection but have slightly less venting ability. PVC or plastic coated rain jacket will not breathe, nor will a nylon jacket repel rain for long periods of time if having to be out in wet and cold weather. Leather coats can keep you warm and breath well for a outer layer winter coat.

Winter Pants

Being dressed for warmth at our chest area will all know is important and do it but if you are only wearing cotton jeans, you will be very cold still. Cotton is just a bad insulator and doesn't hardly block the wind at all. Amazingly you have more surface area on your lower body than you do your upper body. So your upper body has to do more work in trying to keep your legs warm, but if your body can't maintain it, it will constrict your blood vessels to your legs trying to keep you core warm, so ultimately you get cold. Gore-Tex, Teflon, or nylon shell pants are great bottom layers for winter pants. With the lower body though, venting isn't as much of a priority as it is around the core of the body.

Winter Hats

Having a good winter hat on we all know is crucial in not losing a lot of our heat through our heads. Wool caps, fleece hats or a balaclava work great for this. Baseball caps do not provide adequate insulation and shouldn't be considered. Keeping your neck warm is also crucial and is usually neglected. You will find keeping your neck warm with a fleece scarf, neck gaiter or balaclava, which looks somewhat like a ski mask, will make a big difference in keeping the heat in.

Winter Gloves

Its been said that if you have your general body core warm that your hands and feet will easily stay warm being that your blood circulation will flow through out your body. Sometime mittens can be more effective than gloves being that you need airspace around your fingers to keep them warm. Gloves can be layered also to help this. Start with a lightweight poly or silk glove liner, then an intermediate glove (wool, windstopper) if you need it and finally an outer glove. If having to do detail work as with working with gun paraphernalia than mittens and the advise above should be considered.

Winter Boots

Having winter boots to fit you properly is important in keeping your feet warm or shoes if you have no winter boots. You need to be able have them large enough room inside to let you wiggle your toes and trap heat. If your shoes or winter boots are too small for these layers, you'll compress the insulation making it less effective and your toes will be jammed together, so they'll get cold. High insulated boots work well because they cover your ankles and calves. Keeping your feet warm also comes in layers like the rest of your body. First, put on a very light long sock made of either polyester or silk. Second, goes on a heavier sock that will cover your calves for the middle layer. Avoid cotton socks as they will trap the moister in which will cause your feet to get cold. Wool or wool blends for the middle layer will keep your feet warm and dry. Then of course the winter boots is next. Avoid the snug fit of most leather hiking boots which can limit the circulation of blood in the foot. The cloth stitching in leather boots can also wick moisture into the shoe. Nothing is worse than wet feet in the cold winter.

Clothing Checklist

- Bandanas 24 Each
- Blaclava 1 Each
- Boots 2 Each
- Boots – Insulated 1 Each
- Bra Athletic 2 Each Woman
- Clothes Line 100 ft
- Clothes Pins 250
- Clothes Wringer Hand Crank Version
- Coats 1 Each
- Hats 1 Each
- Iron-On Patches 2 Packages
- Jacket 2 Each
- Laundry Detergent 5 Gallons
- Long Sleeve/High Collar Shirt 5 Each
- Long Underwear 3 Each
- Needles Assortment
- Non-Electric Washing Machine
- Jean Pants 6 Each
- Rain Poncho/Parka/Pants 2 Each
- Safety Pins Assortment 3 Packages
- Sewing Supplies Assortment
- Shirts 6 Each
- Shoelaces 20 Each
- Socks Wool/Heavy 12 Each
- Stove Iron
- Sweats/Nightclothes 2 Each
- Tennis/Athletic Shoes 2 Each
- Underwear 12 Each
- Washboard
- Wash Tub 2
- Winter Gloves 1 Each
- Work Gloves 3 Pair
- Zippers and Buttons Assorted

Washing clothing after TEOTWAWKI

Good health is derived from good shelter, good nutrition, and good sanitation.

This topic is about good sanitation, specifically, clean clothing. After a SHTF or TEOTWAWKI event, expect to be dirtier. You are likely to be spending a lot of time in the outdoors for gardening, attending to your homestead, foraging and hunting for food, and conducting safety watches and patrols. You will be working harder than ever before. You will be wearing more clothing to keep warm, since the power grid is likely to be down. Feminine hygiene during monthly cycle and baby dirty diapers will add to the laundry. All this adds up to lots and lots of dirty clothes.

Washing clothes is one of the chores we all take for granted. Even if you must go to a laundromat, as I did during periods of my life, the process is very simple. Put clothing in the washing machine, add detergent, and start the machine. After washing, throw the clean, wet clothing into a drier. Remove dried clothing, fold, and store for future use. During my pre-married days, laundry took me a total of 3 hours once every other week. (I'll not discuss issues regarding dry cleaning, since wearing business suits after TEOTWAWKI is not likely.)

After a SHTF or TEOTWAWKI event, hand washing of clothing will become a necessary and time consuming endeavour. Dirty clothing will track waste and disease into your home. So now is the time to prepare for hand washing of your clothing. The effort is easily learned and conducted.

The first and most important issue is access to clean water. Clothes washing uses a lot of water. Need water for a pre-rinse of very dirty clothes, then water for the wash cycle, and then water for final rise. If your homestead is now using public water, be prepared to hand care water. If you homestead is utilizing a well, be prepared for grid-down and no electricity to supply an automated water pump. As a back-up, your well should have a hand pump for back up. Or obtain solar electrical panels and storage batteries for your well pump. Then you will need to purify your water. You can either: (1) boil the water, or (2) filter the water. Recommend the Big Berkey water filters for purify water. And have lots of clean buckets to store potable water. During TEOTWAWKI period, you will find that you are constantly filtering and sanitizing water for many uses – drinking, food preparation, laundry, toilets, cleaning home, …

Using hot water is a good method of sanitizing dirty clothing. In a grid-down situation, you are likely heating water over a fire or on a cast-iron stove.

After taking care of the issue of sourcing water, the next concern is vessels to conduct the washing. If you home has a bathtub, that is a great place to conduct the hand washing. Our you might want to obtain a galvanized steel tub and old fashion washboard. Ideally you should have one tub for washing and another tub for rising. Having a hand plunger for the manual washing efforts will save time.

Since many of us do not have the space wash tubs or the means to heat large amounts of water, I would highly recommend hand spun portable washing machine and an old fashion mop bucket with wringer to conduct small loads of clothing washing. The hand spun washing machine is great for small loads. Uses little water and little detergent. The wringer on the mop bucket is great for rising then squeezing the water out of the clean wet clothing.

The next matter to discuss in this topic is laundry detergent. Here I recommend the following:

Fels-Naptha Laundry Bar Soap - make your own laundry detergent (buy lots of it for long-term storage and barter)

Washing Soda - softens hard water and laundry booster

Borax - deodorizing and laundry booster

Pure Bleach – for purifying water or for sanitizating and brightening whites

Next concern is drying clothes. Here you will want clothespins, drying rack, and clothes line. To maintain a low profile during the first year of TEOTWAWKI, recommend that you conduct the washing and drying indoors. Also during the cold winter months, you must do the washing indoors. After when safety and security are established in your community, then you may do the washing and drying outdoors. Also, do not track dirty clothes into the house. When very dirty, remove boots and clothing immediately upon entering your home. Older farm houses had a mud room for a reason. Keep your outdoors clothing separate from your indoors clothing. Try to bath immediately after finishing your work day, so as to not track dirt through the home and into bed.

Prep Items:

Secure a good source of water, such as local stream or well.

Obtain washable feminine pads for the ladies monthly cycle

Obtain washable diapers for the babies

Obtain a wash tub (or two)

Have a Berkey water filter to purify water

Stock pure beach (liquid or solid) to sanitize water

Have a device to aggitated and mix dirty clothes, water and detergent

Stock dry laundry detergent or laundry bars to make your own detergent

Stock borax and baking soda to deodorize and boost the detergent

Have drying racks, clothes lines, and clothespins for drying

Have overalls (such as denim or duck bill overalls) to wear over your clothing while working outdoors. Let the overalls catch most of the dirt.

Hope all your days are safe and clean.

EMERGENCY SHELTER

In survival as in all aspects of life, it is easier to be organized if we prioritize. The priorities, in order, are shelter, water, heat, food, signal, and utility. You can live 4-6 weeks without food; 3-5 days without water; but hypothermia will kill you in 30 minutes. Therefore shelter is the first priority! Shelter may be defined as anything that protects the human element from nature's elements. I will not discuss clothing here, other than to say that a good coat can't be beat, and it is easier to survive in the summer with winter clothes than in the winter with summer clothes.

What You Need

A free-standing dome or A-frame tent is the only realistic option for a mobile shelter in a short-term emergency preparedness kit. There are several things to be aware of in selecting a tent. Construction should be of good quality, breathable materials. The rain fly should extend from the apex of the tent almost to the ground. A small rain fly like those found on many discount shelf specials is unsuitable, because it means the tent walls are made mostly of waterproof material. The human body passes 1-2 quarts of water vapor daily and if you are in a waterproof tent for an extended period of time that water vapor will condense on the walls. It is for this very reason that tube tents should be avoided like the plague.

A heavy-duty space blanket is recommended to put under the tent in order to protect the tent floor. It is much easier and cheaper to replace a $12 space blanket than a $100 tent. Avoid the pocket space blanket—another plague! Their usefulness is limited and they breed a false sense of security. **A sleeping bag** is the most critical piece of survival equipment you can possess, especially in winter. Fires are only 50% effective. You cook your front side while your buns freeze, or your toast your buns and your nose freezes—you just can't win! In a sleeping bag, however, you can efficiently maintain body heat.

A good sleeping bag will have the capability to form a hood. It will have a sizable draft tube along the length of the zipper to prevent snags. Another important feature is the ability to zip two bags together to share body heat or to put a child between parents. Select a synthetic insulation rather than down. Qualofill, Polarguard and some of the new materials recently released are excellent. The advantage of synthetic insulation is that when the bag gets wet, it can be wrung out and will still keep you warm. When down gets wet, the insulation value drops to nearly nothing. Emergency survival situations rarely occur on warm sunny days, and you can just about bet it will be on a dark, rainy or snowy night when the world comes apart.

A sleeping bag is the most critical piece of survival equipment you can possess, especially in winter. Fires are only 50% effective. You cook your front side while your buns freeze, or your toast your buns and your nose freezes—you just can't win! In a sleeping bag, however, you can efficiently maintain body heat.

A good sleeping bag will have the capability to form a hood. It will have a sizable draft tube along the length of the zipper to prevent snags. Another important feature is the ability to zip two bags together to share body heat or to put a child between parents. Select a synthetic insulation rather than down. Qualofill, Polarguard and some of the new materials recently released are excellent. The advantage of synthetic insulation is that when the bag gets wet, it can be wrung out and will still keep you warm. When down gets wet, the insulation value drops to nearly nothing. Emergency survival situations rarely occur on warm sunny days, and you can just about bet it will be on a dark, rainy or snowy night when the world comes apart.

An absolute must in a temperate climate is **a sleeping pad**. Ground cold can suck the heat right out of your body, through your sleeping bag. A closed-cell foam pad will provide the insulation required, but will give little if any comfort. An air mattress of the type you take to the beach or swimming pool will freeze your whole persona during the winter. For true comfort an air mattress such as Thermarest is expensive but worth every cent. For economy, a simple 3/4-length closed cell foam pad is all that you need. Avoid open-cell pads because they soak up water just like a sponge.

In putting together a good short-term preparedness kit, you may think it necessary to initially purchase items that are of inferior quality. Perhaps so, but at the first opportunity the higher quality equipment should be purchased. There is no economy in going second class. Tents and sleeping bags are expensive and should be considered a serious investment. After all, your life and the lives of your family are in the balance!
By Larry Bethers,

Elder Bruce R. McConkie, Quorum of the 12 Appostles.

"I stand before the Church this day and raise the warning voice. . . . It is a voice calling upon the Lord's people to prepare for the troubles and desolations which are about to be poured out upon the world without measure. For the moment we live in a day of peace and prosperity but it shall not ever be thus. Great trials lie ahead. All of the sorrows and perils of the past are but a foretaste of what is yet to be. And we must prepare ourselves temporally and spiritually." (*Ensign,* May 1979, pp. 92-93.)

"We do not know when the calamities and troubles of the last days will fall upon any of us as individuals or upon bodies of the Saints. . . . We can rest assured that if we have done all in our power to prepare for whatever lies ahead, He will then help us with whatever else we need. . . . We do not say that all of the Saints will be spared and saved from the coming day of desolation. But we do say there is no promise of safety and no promise of security except for those who love the Lord and who are seeking to do all that he commands." (*Ensign*, May 1979, p. 93.)

Emergency Sanitation

Care and Use of Water Supplies

If you are asked to shut off the service valve that controls the water supply to your home, or if the taps do not flow following a disaster, turn off all the water outlets. These include taps or faucets, valves on pipes supplying float-controlled equipment such as flush toilets, air cooling equipment, and heating equipment. Then when the water comes on again your home will not be flooded as these flotation devices sometimes stick after they have been allowed to dry out.

Turn off the gas or electricity that supplies your hot-water heater after closing your home water service valve, or when your water supply is interrupted for any other reason. Otherwise, if the limited supply of water remaining in your hot-water storage tank continues to be heated, an explosion may occur. Also, if no more water can reach the tank, continued heat will soon muddy its contents through oxidation and make the water useless for washing or drinking purposes.

If your water service is cut off following enemy attack or other natural disaster, do not try to telephone or otherwise communicate with your local water department or water company. Once service is restored, the water from your faucets may have a strong chlorine taste. Do not worry about this. It is a sign that extra precautions are being taken for your safety.

It is especially important to be sanitary in the storing, handling, and eating of food to avoid digestive upsets or other more serious illnesses.

Be sure to:
· Keep all food in covered containers.
· Keep cooking and eating utensils clean. Diarrhea may result from dish soap that is not thoroughly rinsed from dishes.
· Keep all garbage in a closed container or dispose of it outside the home when it is safe to go out. If possible, bury it. Avoid letting garbage or trash accumulate inside the shelter, both for fire and sanitation reasons.
· Wash hands and utensils frequently.
· Prepare only as much food as will be eaten at each meal.
· Paper cups and plates, paper towels and napkins are helpful if the water supply is cut off.
· Refrigerators and home freezer units should be kept closed as much as possible once the services they depend on are cut off. The food they contain will keep loner if you plan your meals well in advance so that you won't have to open the doors any more than necessary. If the gas or electric service is not restored within 12 hours, eat or cook the most perishable items in your refrigerator before they spoil. If foods show signs of decomposition, discard them before they contaminate other foods that keep better.

· Food will keep in home freezer units after they are shut off for varying periods depending on the amount and kind of food, the temperature at which it was kept, and the construction of the freezer. Frozen meats and other frozen foods can be preserved for later use by cooking them soon after they have thawed or by quick refreezing before they have completely thawed.

Official instructions regarding food will be issued locally in the event of an emergency. These instructions will tell you the type of disaster and its effect upon milk and other foods. Follow official instructions closely. Don't listen to rumors, and don't pass them on to others.

Laundry and Cleaning Supplies

During times of emergency it is critical that sanitation be strictly observed in the cleaning of clothing, bedding materials, and all kitchen and food preparation utensils. A book entitled *Housecleaning on a Shoestring* is available by writing to the Cooperative Extension Service, Utah State University, Logan, UT 84321. It contains useful recipes to make housecleaning products out of basic ingredients found in the home.

EMERGENCY TOILETS & GARBAGE DISPOSAL

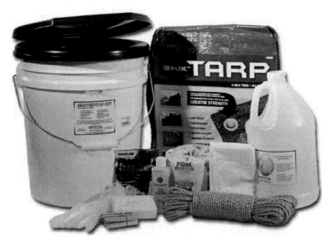

What will you do if your toilet stops flushing and you can't get anyone to take your garbage away? If an emergency causes your toilets or garbage service to stop working you MUST find a way to safely dispose of the human waste (sewage) and garbage yourself. **If you don't, you will soon be spending most of your time and energy treating sick people, including *yourself*.**

The three most important things to do are:
1. Bury or store all garbage and human waste at least 100 feet away from water wells or open water.
2. Keep flies, roaches and animals out of the sewage and garbage;
3. Wash or clean your hands whenever you handle something dirty and BEFORE you handle anything that you will be putting into your mouth or someone else's mouth.

TOILETS #1 - If the toilet bowl and seat in your home are still usable (not wrecked) scrub the bowl clean using one part of laundry bleach to ten parts of water (10:1). When clean, drain the bowl and dry it. Line the bowl with a plastic or paper bag. Line the inside of the first bag with a sturdy plastic bag and lay the toilet seat on it to keep it open. Use the toilet as you normally do. After every use, sprinkle the waste with the bleach/water solution mentioned above or cover it with a layer of sawdust, wood shavings, lime, dry dirt, grass clippings, etc. Limiting the liquids that go into the bowl will make it easier to change the bags. When the bag is full or you can't stand the smell anymore, carefully tie the top of the bag tightly closed, remove it and replace with another bag. Dispose of the waste using the instructions below. Other chemicals that can be used in place of liquid chlorine bleach are: HTH (calcium hypochlorite), which is available at swimming pool supply stores and is intended to be used in solution. Following the directions on the package it can be mixed and stored.

Caution: *Do not use calcium hypochlorite to disinfect drinking water as it kills all the beneficial bacteria in the intestinal tract and thus causes mild diarrhea. Portable toilet chemicals, both liquid and dry, are available at recreational vehicle (RV) supply stores. These chemicals are designed especially for toilets which are not connected to sewer lines. Use according to package directions. Powdered, chlorinated lime is available at building supply stores. It can be used dry. Be sure to get chlorinated lime, not quick lime which is highly alkaline and corrosive.* **Caution:** *Chlorinated products which are intended to be mixed with water for use can be dangerous if used dry. You may also use powdered laundry detergent, Lysol, Pinesol, ammonia, or other household cleaning and disinfecting products*

#2 - If your toilet bowl is not usable, use a five gallon bucket, wooden box or some other container sturdy enough to sit on. Sit the seat from your toilet on the bucket or make one from layers of heavy cardboard glued together, two boards laid across the top with a gap between them or cut a seat from plywood. Line with bags as outlined in #1 above. Dispose of the full bags using the instructions below.

#3 - If the emergency will only last for a day or two, you can use "cat holes" outside. These are small, onetime personal use holes you dig in the ground and squat over. The hole should be deep enough to cover your waste **at least six inches deep** when filled. Do not do this any closer than **100 feet** from open water or water wells or the germs in the sewage will get into the water.

#4 – If the emergency will last more than a week and your toilet or bucket commode no longer will do the job you need to make a latrine. Use a shovel or post-hole diggers to dig a pit four to six feet deep and about one foot wide. Place a bucket, box, barrel or anything with a hole in it that you can sit on over the pit. Whatever you use **must** cover the pit tightly so that flies cannot get in while no one is using it. The seat and box must be cleaned regularly with the bleach water solution mentioned above and kept tightly covered when not in use. When the pit fills to within eighteen inches of the top, fill the hole in with clean dirt and mound it over. Cover the mound to keep animals from digging it up.

DISPOSING OF WASTES: All wastes must be buried **no closer than 100 feet** from the nearest open water or water well or the germs will get into the water. Buried wastes must be covered with at least eighteen inches of dirt and protected from animals digging it up.

GARBAGE is trash that has food or anything else in it that would make attract insects, rats and other animals. It should not be allowed to accumulate where these pests can get into it. If garbage service is expected to resume in a few days then dry garbage should be tightly sealed in bags or kept in tightly covered garbage cans. Liquid wastes that don't have a lot of fat in them can be poured out outside if kept **more than 100 feet** away from open bodies of water and water wells. Liquids that do have a lot of fat should be buried to prevent attracting flies and roaches.

If garbage service is out for more several weeks and you are unable to store it, then it should be buried. Garbage should be buried **no closer than 100 feet** from open water or water wells. Crush containers to make them smaller. Garbage must be covered by at least eighteen inches of dirt. If burial is not possible then it will have to be burned. To burn garbage you must use a metal barrel with holes in the bottom and a grate or screen over the top to act as a spark arrester to prevent wildfires. Only dry garbage should be burned. Wet garbage should be buried.

If you have a baby in your home, it is best to keep an ample supply of disposable diapers on hand for emergency use. If these are not available, emergency diaper needs can be met by lining rubber pants with cleansing tissue, toilet paper, scraps of cloth, or other absorbent materials. To help insure proper sanitation it is imperative that you store a sufficient supply of disposable diapers, disposable wipes, and plastic garbage can liners. Change infants and toddlers regularly and keep them clean. Dispose of the soiled diapers in the plastic garbage can liners and keep them tightly sealed when not in use to help prevent the spread of disease. Be sure to wash your own hands regularly when working with infants (especially after each diaper change). Typhoid fever, amoebic dysentery, diarrhea, infectious hepatitis, salmonella and giardiasis are diseases that spread rapidly in times of emergency and threaten all, yet are all diseases that can easily be controlled by simply following the rules of good sanitation.

Disposal of Garbage and Rubbish

Garbage may sour or decompose, rubbish (trash) will not, but offers disposal problems in an emergency. The following suggestions will make it easier for you to take care of the refuse problem.

Garbage should be drained before being placed in storage containers. If liquids are strained away, garbage may be stored for a longer period of time without developing an unpleasant odor. After straining, wrap the garbage in several thicknesses of old newspapers before putting it into your container. This will absorb any remaining moisture. A tight-fitting lid is important to keep out flies and other insects. Final disposal of all stored garbage and refuse can be accomplished in the following manner, provided there is no danger from radioactive fallout:

1. All stored garbage should be buried if collection service is not restored and if unpaved yard areas are available—keep a shovel handy for this purpose. Dig a hole deep enough to cover it with at least 18-24 inches of dirt, which will prevent insect breeding and discourage animals from digging it up.

2. Other rubbish may be burned in open yard areas (if permission is granted by authorities under existing conditions) or left at dumps established by local authorities. Can should be flattened to reduce their bulk. Do not deposit ashes or rubbish in streets or alley ways without permission. Such material may interfere with the movement and operation of fire-fighting and other emergency equipment.

Harold B. Lee (1899–1973) Eleventh President of the Church

"We expect the individual to do all he can to help himself, whether it be an emergency for a single family or for a whole community, that the relatives will do all they can to help, then the Church steps in with commodities from the storehouse, with fast offerings to meet their needs that commodities from the storehouse will not supply, and finally, the Relief Society and the priesthood quorums will assist with rehabilitation" (*Teachings of Presidents of the Church: Harold B. Lee* [2000], 171).

Emergency Sanitation – The Scoop on Poop

A magnitude 7.5 earthquake has struck your area. All utilities have been interrupted and it may take months to restore them. An Electromagnetic Pulse (EMP) has crippled our country leaving most without basic utilities. A pandemic has incapacitated a significant portion of the population, crippling the infrastructure due to lack of manpower and leaving you without utilities for the duration. Pick a scenario or create your own. The result is the same. What are you going to do without water, sanitation, and garbage pick-up? The leading cause of illness and death in both natural and man-made disasters is inadequate sanitation, poor hygiene practice, and contaminated and insufficient water supplies.

In this post, we will focus on critically important sanitation practices. Due to the nature of this subject, or perhaps because we have become spoiled, we often neglect thinking and planning for sanitation needs in our preparedness efforts. Yet, it just might make the difference between life and death. Consider the following information as you plan for the sanitation needs of your family:

Personal Sanitation – It is vitally important to maintain good hygiene in an emergency situation. Use good standards of cleanliness including; brushing your teeth, washing your face, combing your hair, showering/bathing or washing your body with a clean wet cloth (or baby wipes) if water is scarce. Remember to wash your hands! Good personal hygiene will help prevent the spread of disease and help maintain personal health and comfort.

Basic Sanitation Kits- will vary from person to person depending on individual needs. Here are a few ideas: lots of toilet paper, feminine products, sanitizing chemicals, plastic buckets (with tight-fitting lids), a variety of garbage bags, disposable gloves, duct tape, disinfecting wipes, hand sanitizer, baby wipes, spray deodorizer, toothbrush and toothpaste, and soap. There are many other helpful products you can add to this list. This list is only a place to begin. Personalize your sanitation kits to the members of your family. Remember to include items for special needs such as diapers.

Low-Water Shower Options:

Solar Showers– are inexpensive and can provide a much needed warm shower by simply exposing the black shower bag to the sun for a few hours. While not a necessity, a warm shower can make life worth living.

Shower in a Box – is a good option when water is scarce. Baby wipes are a great way to take a sponge bath. Wipes are relatively inexpensive and have a long shelf life. They have many uses and can be discarded after use, preventing additional laundry. Regular bathing, even with baby wipes, can prevent the spread of germs, make others comfortable around you, and prevent sores from developing.

Tank Sprayer Shower- get a good pressure tank sprayer from the hardware store and fill it with clean water (NEVER use chemicals in this sprayer). If you leave it in the sun, you may get the added benefit of a nice sun warmed shower or fill it with warm water. Use the wand to shower with. It is a great way to conserve water and still enjoy the comforts of a warm shower.

Waste Disposal– We only need to look at the garbage cans of our neighbors (or perhaps ourselves), to realize most of us generate a significant amount of waste. What would you do if your faithful garbage man didn't come for weeks or possibly even months? Any type of disaster could easily disrupt that service. Garbage is a prime breeding ground for bacteria, insects, and rodents. It also attracts other unwanted pests. Develop a backup plan in the event you have to hold on to your garbage for awhile. Your plan may include some or all of the following strategies:

Waste Separation– Separate cans, glass, and plastic from burnable items and wet garbage. Wet garbage breeds bacteria and draws insects and animals. Mixing garbage contaminates all of it. Reduce bulk by smashing cans, flattening boxes, and compacting whenever possible. Store lots of quality garbage bags. Trash cans or barrels with tight-fitting lids have many uses and might come in handy for storing garbage.

Composting– Establish a composting area away from your home as it will attract insects and flies. You can compost yard waste, kitchen scraps, shredded paper products, and cardboard. Do not compost: human waste, dog or cat waste, meat or grease, and poisons or other chemicals. Compost any manure from animals that do not eat meat. Turn your compost pile to facilitate decomposition. This will create a rich, dark soil loaded with nutrients for gardening.

Trash Burning– Burning is not preferable due to safety and environmental concerns, but may become necessary. Cereal boxes, paper plates, cardboard, etc. may be used to fuel small fires for cooking. Cooled ashes may be added to a compost pit or used to control odors in an outhouse. Use great caution when burning anything to ensure safety of people and property. Burn trash in appropriate conditions and locations. Do not burn plastic, Styrofoam or other items that release toxins when burned. Consider storing real paper plates instead of Styrofoam because they can be burned.

Burying Trash– A prolonged crisis may require some garbage to be buried. If this becomes necessary, bury garbage as far away from your home as possible. Dig a hole at least four feet deep. Cover with at least 18 inches of soil to prevent insect and animal infestation. Consider digging the hole and covering with a large piece of plywood to allow additional garbage to be added as needed. You may need to secure it with large rocks or heavy objects to prevent animals from accessing it. Layering with soil, ashes, lime, or borax may help in controlling odors.

Human Waste Disposal– Mother Nature's call can not be put off for long regardless of the nature of the emergency or crisis. In fact, these circumstances may actually make the call more frequent and intense! Take time to carefully consider these basic toilet options or explore more of your own. Purchase an inexpensive option immediately and work toward a nicer option as funds permit.

Each person generates approximately five gallons of human waste each week. This waste, if not managed properly, becomes a source of odor, illness, and other problems. Never throw human waste on the open ground. If no other alternative is available, bury it in deep trenches and cover with at least 2-3 feet of soil. Make sure to avoid burying in high water tables as it may contaminate the water supply. Consider the toilet options listed below, make a plan, and get the supplies needed to ensure you can safely manage the waste your family creates.

Emergency Toilet Options:

Luggable Lou or bucket toilet– may be a good option for a lightweight portable toilet that you can grab along with your 72 hour kit. It may be difficult for the elderly, obese or very tall people to use this toilet safely. It is a good idea to practice to ensure this is a safe option for you.

Keep basic supplies inside so that it is ready to go - toilet paper, baby wipes, garbage bags, disinfecting wipes, feminine products, spray deodorizer, and chlorine bleach or sanitizing chemical. Line the bucket with a plastic garbage bag. Mix one cup liquid bleach (or sanitizing chemical) with two quarts of water and pour into the lined bucket. Add a little more disinfectant after each use. Change the bag when it is 1/3 - 1/2 full. Carefully tie the top and place in a larger lined can. Close the lid after each use to control odors. This will definitely work for an emergency, however, the smell is offensive and it is not our favorite option.

Possible disinfectants (sanitizing chemicals) include: Enzyme 300 (made for use with Luggable Lou), Luggable Lou liner with bio-gel, sodium hydroxide (blue liquid in chemical toilets), liquid chlorine bleach, Pine Sol, ammonia (never mix ammonia with bleach!!), baking soda, alcohol, laundry detergent, or other disinfectant. Poo Powder or WAG bags are nice, but pricey solutions. The Poo Powder instantly solidifies to prevent messy spills and controls germs and odors. A WAG bag contains Poo Powder and may be used multiple times. The bag is engineered to break down in 6-8 months to make disposal environmentally friendly. Some of these sanitizing chemicals work much better than others - the goal is to minimize odors and germs.

Permanent Port-a-Potty - your household toilet can be easily converted to a port-a-potty in an emergency and provide a familiar, inexpensive toilet option. This option assumes that you have been able to stay in your home and do not have sewage backing up through your toilet.

Turn off the water supply to the toilet tank. Then empty the toilet bowl. Lift the lid and seat. Place a garbage bag in the bowl and duct tape the edges around the back and sides of the bowl. Use the toilet as usual. Pour a small amount of disinfectant into the bag after each use to help prevent the spread of germs and disease. You may want to add sawdust or Poo Powder to solidify liquids. The bag may be used several times before changing.

Change the bag by lifting the lid and seat. Carefully remove the bag by loosening the taped edges, twisting the edges of the bag together and seal the bag. Place an empty plastic bucket right next to the toilet and lift the bag into the bucket. Use this bucket for transport to avoid accidental spills. Place bag in a large bucket with a tight-fitting lid. Store outside if possible. Cover entire toilet with a 30 gallon trash bag to control odor. Air fresheners or room deodorizers may also be helpful.

Chemical Toilets - These toilets are a great option and are regularly used by boaters and campers. They use very little water and the chemicals help to keep the smell and spread of disease to a minimum. Be sure to store plastic buckets with tight-fitting lids to store waste until you can safely dispose of it. . Be sure to store the appropriate chemicals for the toilet. The chemicals do have a limited shelf life. Check with the manufacturer.

Trench Latrine - If an outdoor toilet becomes necessary, a trench latrine can be constructed in a short amount of time. Be sure to locate it away from the home and all water sources. Create some type of shelter to provide protection from the weather and for privacy. Dig a trench 1 foot wide x 4 feet long and 2 1/2 feet deep. Add a little bit of soil or lime after each use to help control odor and flies. When the trench is filled within one foot of the surface, sprinkle with lime, fill with soil, and mound with an additional foot of soil. This toilet is used by squatting or straddling the trench.

Deep Pit Latrine- An extended crisis may require a more long term solution. A single-seat latrine may be built over a trench that is 2 feet wide x 2-6 feet long x 6 feet deep pit using available materials to create a shelter and seating area. Make sure the seating area is large enough to prevent it from collapsing into the pit. It is important to consider potential ground water contamination when locating a site or the depth of the latrine. Be sure to sprinkle with soil or lime after each use and before closing the pit.

Composting Toilet (sometimes called biological toilet, dry toilet, or waterless toilet) - is frequently used in remote locations such as cabins. A composting toilet system converts human waste into a fertilizer or useable soil through the natural breakdown of organic matter back into its essential minerals. This compost is not safe for use on vegetable gardens. Composting toilets are very expensive, but use little or no water and are nearly odorless.

Septic System– If you are fortunate enough to be on a septic system you may avoid the necessity for backup toilets if your system remains intact. Be sure to perform regular routine maintenance on your system. We recommend you still have a contingency plan in the event your system fails or you are required to evacuate.

Storage– In the event you are confined to a shelter, make sure you have buckets with tight-fitting lids for short-term storage of human waste. Remember to plan for 5 gallons of waste from each person. That can add up to a lot of buckets!

Sewage Backflow– There may be a potential for sewage to backflow into your home in some emergency situations. If this occurs, you have most likely lost your home due to the potential of disease and the stench associated with raw sewage. Evaluate your risk and, if necessary, consider installing some type of back-flow prevention valve.

Unwanted Critter Control:

Pest Control – Sharing our space and provisions with disease-spreading pests can make any situation worse. Our precious supplies can be quickly contaminated if pests are not controlled. Pest control must be an important consideration in your sanitation planning.

Insect control- Prevent breeding grounds by keeping the area clean. Standing water is a breeding ground for mosquitoes, which are known vectors for the spread of diseases. Carefully package all food storage to prevent infestation. Use care to prevent bedding from being contaminated through poor personal sanitation. Don't stop doing laundry! The old saying, "Good night, sleep tight, don't let the bed bugs bite" was adopted for a reason. Store insect repellent and insecticides safely and away from foods.

Fly control- Keep area free from garbage and waste products. Cover food and clean dishes to prevent contamination by flies. Store fly swatters, fly strips, fly traps, etc. for use as needed. Actively strive to keep living area free from flies as they are prone to spread disease.

Rodent control - Keep storage areas clean and organized. Store traps and poisons to use if necessary. Take time to package food storage to prevent infestation. Rodents can quickly access foods stored in Mylar bags. Consider putting the Mylar bags in plastic buckets for extra protection. Food stored in boxes, bags, and Mylar bags are at risk of infestation. Storing food in #10 cans is a great way to protect the contents.

The Challenge: Good sanitation practices always make sense. However, in an emergency situation, it is especially important to implement good sanitation techniques. It can make the difference between sickness and health, and possibly even life and death. Our challenge to you is to carefully think through the sanitation needs of your family. Educate family members as to the importance of good sanitation practice and how it applies to your family plan. Create a workable plan, set realistic goals, and get to work to accomplish those goals. We challenge you to do something TODAY!!

Controlling Odors

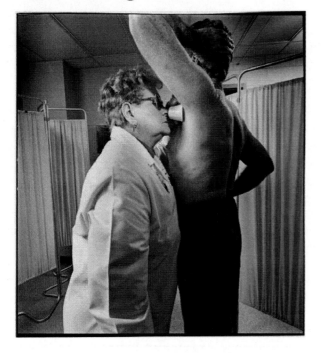

Our family loves to go camping. I don't mind the dirt, cold, lack of hot water, or even the bugs. However, I absolutely hate the outhouse! The concept is okay, but the smell is nauseating. The campground uses chemicals and empties it periodically. It still stinks! We have to pack out all of our garbage and by the end of the trip it is pretty nasty too. Camping with no electricity, no running water, no sewer, and limited resources is a great way to understand how to prepare for emergency situations.

In the event of an emergency situation, you may have to create and manage primitive facilities similar to our annual camping tip. Plan ahead to be able to control insects, animals, germs, and odors.

Let's explore some ways to control odors and make it a more tolerable experience for everyone:

Do not allow family members to defecate in the open, otherwise known as "free-ranging". Make sure that appropriate facilities are provided and used.

Plan for storage and disposal of human waste in healthy ways. Keep all waste away from water supplies and living areas.

Dispose of gray water (dirty dish water, washing water) away from the home as it will attract flies and smell.

Encourage family members to bath regularly, even if bathing consists only of wiping down with a damp cloth or baby wipes. Use deodorant.

Plan for a way to clean laundry using minimal water. "Airing out" clothing and bedding by hanging on a clothesline is helpful.

Separate trash and rubbish from wet garbage. Save space by crushing cans and plastic containers. If permissible, burn all burnable trash. Put all kitchen scraps in compost pile away from the home. Carefully store wet garbage in tightly-covered cans safe from animals and insects. Wet garbage is a breeding ground for germs and odors.

Store products that help reduce germs and odors. Practice using them. Discover what really works for you and your family.

Consider adding the following items to your storage:

Lime - is inexpensive, safe, and good for odor control. Available in 50 lb bags at hardware stores.

ZIX Zeolite Ion-Exchanger - reduces ammonia emissions. Removes offensive and harmful odors from air, soil, and liquids. A 100% all-natural product with no chemicals added. We use this in our dog kennel and chicken coop. It works great. May work well to control odors in a latrine.

OdoBan, Odor Eliminator (or similar product) - an industrial liquid that cleans, disinfects, sanitizes, and deodorizes all precleaned hard, nonporous household surfaces. OdoBan eliminates unpleasant odors on washable surfaces such as upholstery, carpets, bedding, showers, bathrooms, garbage areas, walls and floors while leaving a fresh scent. May be used in a bucket toilet in place of bleach (do not mix with bleach or any other chemical!). Dilute according to package directions. Do not allow to come in contact with skin. It has an indefinite shelf life.

Gloves - store gloves for personal protection while working with any chemicals.

TEOTWAWKI smells bad, get used to it !!
(...and get ready for it)

Before TEOTWAWKI, did you work in a nice clean office? After TEOTWAWKI, you will have your hands in the dirt to plant your garden, rooting through trash for recycle-ables, and cleaning the droppings from the chicken coup...where the smells are pronounced! The smells of the farm are the smells of abundance, which you will learn to love. (Prep item: Start immediately to plan your garden and acquire food long-term pantry to avoid eating from other's trash.)

Did you work now from 8:00 AM to 5:00 PM at a leisurely pace? After TEOTWAWKI, you will be working from sun up to sun down, then taking guard duty shifts at night. Hard work creates body odor. (Prep Item: Get ready for hard physical labor now with an exercise program. Acquire a set of outdoors work clothes, such as overalls or coveralls, so that you can keep your regular clothing free of dirt.)

Did you have a bath or shower everyday? After TEOT-WAWKI, you will be fortunate to have a weekly Saturday night bath. Hot water will be an absolute luxury. (Prep Item: Acquire a large metal wash basin from which you will take your baths. You will want to place the large metal wash basin next to your fireplace or cast iron stove to allow heated water to be poured directly for your weekly bath. Acquire old fashion water pitcher and wash basin to conduct daily personal cleaning. Stock up on pure Ivory soap, which will last a long time. Stock up on baby wipes for quick personal cleaning.)

Death and disease will be common place after TEOT-WAWKI. (Reference the Haitian earthquake as a small scale sample of what is likely after a full economic or societal collapse.) It will be important to quickly bury the dead to prevent disease. You will need to quickly secure clean water for drinking and bathing. (Prep item: Buy Berkey Water filter with extra filters. I recommend: http://www.direc-tive21.com. Prepare to lose indoor plumbing, so acquire

chamber pots to replace toilets. Have two good stovels for all the digging you will do. Acquire latex gloves and surgical masks for handling and aiding sick people. Also stock up on antibiotics and anti-diarrhea medication http://www.imodium.com. Quarantine any late arrivers of your family or survival group for two weeks to prevent the spread of infection. Bury the dead and human wastes at least 300 feet away from any water source and deep.)

Hungry, starving people will be searching for food. Desperate people will kill for a mouthful of food. It will be important for you to keep a low profile, hunker down, and yet be ready to defend your family. A good prepper is prepared to offer charity, but must stop at the point of taking food out of the mouths of their own children. You will need to defend your home and family from dirty, diseased, and desperate people. (Prep item: Acquire your defense weapons immediately. Get professional training. Stock lots of ammunition. Form a neighborhood watch or survival group of at least three full families now, in order to start a full-time security watch after TEOTWAWKI.)

You will be burning a lot of wood after TEOTWAWKI. Cooking your food and heating your water will primarily come from wood burning. I love the smell of a wood burning fireplace. But the smell of your home burned to the foundation is ghastly. Equally, the frost at the end of your nose is unpleasant, when you have no means to heat your home. You cannot expect the power grid and natural gas to be delivered after TEOTWAWKI. (Prep item: Replace the fancy natural gas fireplace with wood burning fireplace to provide sustainable heat for your home. Install a wood burning cook stove or pot belly Franklin stove for cooking and heating. Have your chimney cleaned and inspected on an annual basis before the start of the winter heating season. Always have a year's work of cured wood stocked and ready, prior to TEOTWAWKI. Chopping wood in the first year after TEOTWAWKI makes you an easy target.)

The requirements of Feminine sanitary needs are especially important to prepare for now. (Prep items: Acquire Menstrual cup and old fashion syringe douche to replace disposable productions. Acquire washable menstruation pad. Learn how to naturally care for yeast infections.)

Just as your body will be dirtier after TEOTWAWKI, your clothing will be even more filthy. Expect lots of outdoor work and manual labor after TEOTWAWKI. A day of gardening, hunting or foraging results in a day's worth of dirty clothes. It is impossible to rely on your automated washer and drier after TEOTWAWKI. You will be washing clothes by hand. That will be tedious work, but necessary to maintain good sanitation. (Prep items: Need a couple of galvanized metal wash tubs, such as Wash Tub 1 and Wash Tub 2. Learn how the washing method of boiling and rinsing. You will need to line dry the cleaned wet clothes, so acquire clothes pins, drying rack and laundry clothesline. Stock up on Fels-Naptha Laundry or other bar laundry soap, and borax to pretreat and deodorized.)

Before TEOTWAWKI, your home is fresh and clean. You have lovely sented candles and air freshening sprays to keep your home smelling like flowers all year round. Cleaning your home is not always the favorite chore, but easily done before TEOTWAWKI. After TEOTWAWKI, cleaning your home will be greatly challenged. Your home will be dirtier after TEOTWAWKI, as your family will track more dirt into your home. You can be expecting to butcher your own meat in your home, which can be a smelly endeavour in the best of times. Your electric vaccum will be a worthless piece of junk when the power grid is a memory. Obtaining enough fresh water to mop the floors will be a challenge. You expect to run out of cleaning supplies within the first year after TEOTWAWKI. (Prep items: Stock up on old fashion brooms, buckets and mops with replacement mop heads. Stock up on ammonia cleaner, pure bleach, vinegar, and baking soda. Vinegar is a very good cleaning agent in the kitchen and bathroom. Pure bleach is an excellent sanitizer. Ammonia cleaner stores for a long time and is good for floors and windows. These items are cheap now and worth their weight in gold after TEOTWAWKI.)

Hopefully TEOTWAWKI will never come and the bad smells will be avoided. For the preppers, preparing and becoming accustomed to bad smells is a way of life.

May all your smells be fresh, clean, and pleasant.

Copyright 2011, by suburbanprep
http://survival5x5.com/?author=1

3 Minutes Without Breathing

And the Lord God formed a man from the dust of the ground, and breathed into his nostrils the breath of life, and the man became a living soul.
Genesis 2:7

Install and test smoke alarms in your home. Most victims of fire succumb to the smoke and toxic gases and not to burns. Fire produces poisonous gases that can spread rapidly and far from the fire itself to claim victims who are asleep and not even aware of the fire. Even if residents awaken, the effects of exposure to these gases can cloud their thinking and slow their reactions so that they cannot make their escape. This is why it is so crucial for you and your family to have sufficient warning so that you can all escape before your ability to think and move is impaired. In addition, more than half of fatal fires in homes occur when people are asleep ' this represents only a third of a 24-hour day. Therefore, any fire protection system must be able to protect people who are asleep in their bedrooms when fire starts. If you have battery powered dectors make sure you replace batteries yearly as recommended by the U.S. Fire Administration.

Carbon monoxide (CO) is a deadly, colorless, odorless, poisonous gas. It is produced by the incomplete burning of various fuels, including coal, wood, charcoal, oil, kerosene, propane, and natural gas. Products and equipment powered by internal combustion engine-powered equipment such as portable generators, cars, lawn mowers, and power washers also produce CO. You will often read of people being sicken or dieing of carbon monoxide poisoning during times of emergecies. Often these accidents are the results of use of portable fuel-burning camping equipment inside a home, garage, vehicle or tent that is not specifically designed for use in an enclosed space or failure to follow manufacters instructions for safe use in an enclosed area. The burning of charcoal inside a home, garage, vehicle, or tent can also led to CO poisoning. Another common cause of carbon monoxide asphyxiation is from prolonged confinement in a running motor vehicle.

It is important to remember that you can be overcome by carbon monoxide poisoning if you do not have enough ventilation in your vehicle. Whether you are running your vehicle at intermittent times or burning one of the coffee can heaters, you still need to crack at least one of your windows for fresh air. You should only run your vehicle for no more than ten minutes every hour. You also need to make sure the exhaust pipe of your vehicle is free of snow or mud.

Moving water is very dangerous. Just 6 of fast moving water can knock you off your feet. Cars, including heavy trucks, can get swept away in less than 2-feet of swift water. Never drive through moving water. Nationwide, 70% of all flood-related fatalities are in vehicles. With so many of today's vehicles coming with electrical controlled power windows and doors you should consider keeping an emergency auto-glass breaking tool in your vehicle. A vehicle's submergence in water will quickly short out the electric controls which unlock doors and power open windows, leaving you trapped inside. These tools are especially designed to quickly and easily break auto glass allowing you to escape.

There are any number of other emergencies which can occur which pose the threat of asphyxiation and/or drowning including flash floods, mud slides, tsunamis, gas leaks (residential, commercial), inclosed use of chemical slovents, missues of common clean agents (the mixing of common chlorine bleach and household ammonia will cause a reaction that creates chlorine gas, chloramine and other noxious fumes. Accidental or deliberate mixing of bleach with fluids containing ammonia causes severe damage to the lungs.). Always consider those which seem the most likely to occur in your area and try to create a plan accordingly.
Cardiopulmonary resuscitation (CPR): First aid
Being trained in CPR and Rescue Breathing can in many of these instances literarily be the difference in life or death.

Cardiopulmonary resuscitation (CPR) is a lifesaving technique useful in many emergencies, including heart attack or near drowning, in which someone's breathing or heartbeat has stopped. Ideally, CPR involves two elements: chest compressions combined with mouth-to-mouth rescue breathing.

However, what you as a bystander should do in an emergency situation really depends on your knowledge and comfort level.

The bottom line is that it's far better to do something than to do nothing at all if you're fearful that your knowledge or abilities aren't 100 percent complete. Remember, the difference between your doing something and doing nothing could be someone's life.

Here's advice from the American Heart Association:

●**Untrained**. If you're not trained in CPR, then provide hands-only CPR. That means uninterrupted chest compressions of about 100 a minute until paramedics arrive (described in more detail below). You don't need to try rescue breathing.

●**Trained, and ready to go.** If you're well trained, and confident in your ability, then you can opt for one of two approaches: 1. Alternate between 30 chest compressions and two rescue breaths. 2. Just do chest compressions. (Details described below.)

●**Trained, but rusty.** If you've previously received CPR training, but you're not confident in your abilities, then just do chest compressions at a rate of about
100 a minute. (Details described below.)

The above advice applies only to adults needing CPR, not to children.

CPR can keep oxygenated blood flowing to the brain and other vital organs until more definitive medical treatment can restore a normal heart rhythm. When the heart stops, the absence of oxygenated blood can cause irreparable brain damage in only a few minutes. A person may die within eight to 10 minutes. To learn CPR properly, take an accredited first-aid training course, including CPR and how to use an automatic external defibrillator (AED).

Before you begin Before starting CPR, check:
●Is the person conscious or unconscious?
●If the person appears unconscious, tap or shake his or her shoulder and ask loudly, "Are you OK?"
●If the person doesn't respond and two people are available, one should call 911 or the local emergency number and one should begin CPR. If you are alone and have immediate access to a telephone, call 911 before beginning CPR — unless you think the person has become unresponsive because of suffocation (such as from drowning). In this special case, begin CPR for one minute and then call 911.

●If an AED is immediately available, deliver one shock if instructed by the device, then begin CPR.
Remember the ABCs

Think ABC — **airway**, **breathing** and **circulation** — to remember the steps explained below. Move quickly through airway and breathing to begin chest compressions.

Airway: Clear the airway
Put the person on his or her back on a firm surface.
Kneel next to the person's neck and shoulders.
Open the person's airway using the head-tilt, chin-lift maneuver. Put your palm on the person's forehead and gently tilt the head back. Then with the other hand, gently lift the chin forward to open the airway.

Check for normal breathing, taking no more than five or 10 seconds. Look for chest motion, listen for normal breath sounds, and feel for the person's breath on your cheek and ear. Gasping is not considered to be normal breathing. If the person isn't breathing normally and you are trained in

CPR, begin mouth-to-mouth breathing. If you believe the person is unconscious from a heart attack and you haven't been trained in emergency procedures, skip mouth-to-mouth rescue breathing and proceed directly to chest compressions.

Breathing: Breathe for the person Rescue breathing can be mouth-to-mouth breathing or mouth-to-nose breathing if the mouth is seriously injured or can't be opened.

With the airway open (using the head-tilt, chin-lift maneuver), pinch the nostrils shut for mouth-to-mouth breathing and cover the person's mouth with yours, making a seal.

Prepare to give two rescue breaths. Give the first rescue breath — lasting one second — and watch to see if the chest rises. If it does rise, give the second breath. If the chest doesn't rise, repeat the head-tilt, chin-lift maneuver and then give the second breath.

Begin chest compressions to restore circulation.

Circulation: Restore blood circulation with chest compressions

Place the heel of one hand over the center of the person's chest, between the nipples. Place your other hand on top of the first hand. Keep your elbows straight and position your shoulders directly above your hands.

Use your upper body weight (not just your arms) as you push straight down on (compress) the chest 2 inches (approximately 5 centimeters). Push hard at a rate of 100 compressions a minute. After 30 compressions, tilt the head back and lift the chin up to open the airway. Prepare to give two rescue breaths. Pinch the nose shut and breathe into the mouth for one second. If the chest rises, give a second rescue breath. If the chest doesn't rise, repeat the head-tilt, chin-lift maneuver and then give the second rescue breath. That's one cycle. If someone else is available, ask that person to give two breaths after you do 30 compressions. If you're not trained in CPR and feel comfortable performing only chest compressions, skip rescue breathing and continue chest compressions at a rate of 100 compressions a minute until medical personnel arrive.

If the person has not begun moving after five cycles (about two minutes) and an automatic external defibrillator (AED) is available, apply it and follow the prompts. Administer one shock, then resume CPR — starting with chest compressions — for two more minutes before administering a second shock. If you're not trained to use an AED, a 911 operator may be able to guide you in its use. Use pediatric pads, if available, for children ages 1 to 8. Do not use an

AED for babies younger than age 1. If an AED isn't available, go to step 5 below. Continue CPR until there are signs of movement or until emergency medical personnel take over.

To perform CPR on a child
The procedure for giving CPR to a child age 1 through 8 is essentially the same as that for an adult. The differences are as follows:

● If you're alone, perform five cycles of compressions and breaths on the child — this should take about two minutes — before calling 911 or your local emergency number or using an AED.

● Breathe more gently.

● After five cycles (about two minutes) of CPR, if there is no response and an AED is available, apply it and follow the prompts. Use pediatric pads if available. If pediatric pads aren't available, use adult pads.
Continue until the child moves or help arrives.

To perform CPR on a baby
Most cardiac arrests in babies occur from lack of oxygen, such as from drowning or choking. If you know the baby has an airway obstruction, perform first aid for choking. If you don't know why the baby isn't breathing, perform CPR.

To begin, examine the situation. Stroke the baby and watch for a response, such as movement, but don't shake the baby.

If there's no response, follow the ABC procedures below and time the call for help as follows:

● If you're the only rescuer and CPR is needed, do CPR for two minutes — about five cycles — before calling 911 or your local emergency number.

● If another person is available, have that person call for help immediately while you attend to the baby.

Airway: Clear the airway

Place the baby on his or her back on a firm, flat surface, such as a table. The floor or ground also will do. Gently tip the head back by lifting the chin with one hand and pushing down on the forehead with the other hand. In no more than 10 seconds, put your ear near the baby's mouth and check for breathing: Look for chest motion, listen for breath sounds, and feel for breath on your cheek and ear.

If the infant isn't breathing, begin mouth-to-mouth rescue breathing immediately.
Compressions-only CPR doesn't work for infants.

Breathing: Breathe for the infant
Cover the baby's mouth and nose with your mouth.
Prepare to give two rescue breaths. Use the strength of your cheeks to deliver gentle puffs of air (instead of deep breaths from your lungs) to slowly breathe into the baby's mouth one time, taking one second for the breath. Watch to see if the baby's chest rises. If it does, give a second rescue breath. If the chest does not rise, repeat the head-tilt, chin-lift maneuver and then give the second breath.

If the baby's chest still doesn't rise, examine the mouth to make sure no foreign material is inside. If the object is seen, sweep it out with your finger. If the airway seems blocked, perform first aid for a choking baby.

Begin chest compressions to restore blood circulation.
Circulation: Restore blood circulation

Imagine a horizontal line drawn between the baby's nipples. Place two fingers of one hand just below this line, in the center of the chest.

Gently compress the chest to about one-third to one-half the depth of the chest.

Count aloud as you pump in a fairly rapid rhythm. You should pump at a rate of 100 compressions a minute.
Give two breaths after every 30 chest compressions.
Perform CPR for about two minutes before calling for help unless someone else can make the call while you attend to the baby.

Continue CPR until you see signs of life or until medical personnel arrive.

Compiler"s Note:The American heart Association now recomends that you start with chest compression first and then do breaths as it is the chest compression which are the most important part of and lead to the best chances of recovery.

3 Hours without Shelter
Lack of Shelter
The major concern caused by the lack of shelter is that of hypothermia. There are any number of natural and man made disasters that can render your home unlivable. Without a back-up heat source loosing power/heat to your home in a snow storm can lead to temperatures quikly falling into the range where hypothermia can be a concern, every year a number of elderly die in their homes of hypothermia due to utility shutoffs and broken heating systems. In some cases your home could be flooded or so severely damaged to make it unsafe, especially in the case of a major earthquake (i.e.Haiti 2010) they may not be enough or even any safe and suitable buildings left in your area to even act as temporary shelters. This could quickly leave you and you family out to the mercy of the elements. You need to plan accordingly.

Hypothermia And You...
"Come, on finish that pasty or we'll all end up with hypothermia..." Yep, it's that time of year again, the nights are closing in, temperatures are dropping etc, ad nauseum. But what exactly is hypothermia, how do you spot it, what should you do if you get it and how should you avoid it in the first place?

What is hypothermia?
Pay attention now, hypopthermia, also known as 'exposure' is technically when your core body temperature drops below the normal 35 degrees centigrade, your normal body temperature is 37C. It happens when the amount of heat you're losing can't be replaced by your body, so your body temperature falls. The results are serious and can be fatal, one text book lists a drop of 4C as causing disorientation, 7C leaves you in a coma and a drop of 10C can be fatal.

So in very simple terms, it's a fall in body temperature cause because you're losing more heat than you can produce. It's not just feeling 'a bit cold', though that can be the start of it.

Spotting the symptons
Assuming you're not walking around with a thermometer permanently up your butt, you need to be aware of possible signs that you, or your mates are going hypothermic. Bear in mind that it's not always easy to spot, particularly early on, but watch out for: clumsiness - might look like drunkeness disorientation sudden bursts of energy exhaustion

Classically a quick test is to ask the suspected victim to do some quick mental arithmatic as a check on their mental function. Exhaustion and hypothermia go hand in hand by the way, if you're very tired, your metabolism slows, you don't kick out enough body heat and you become hypothermic...

Treating Hypothermia
Stop and take stock. It's essential that you don't push on regardless unless safety is very, very near. If the symptoms are mild, putting the casualty in some sort of shelter, adding dry, warm clothes and, in particular, a hat, and feeding them warm hot drinks and food may be enough.

● If things don't improve, put the casualty in a sleeping bag and insulate them from the cold ground with a sleeping mat.

● Recent research suggests that body to body warming can actually be counter-productive since pooled acidic blood in the muscles is warmed too quickly, reaches the heart and can cause cardiac arrest.

● Heat packs placed at the victim's armpits and groin are a better way of raising the core body temperature without risking shock as are a warm drink or soup if the victim is conscious.

● Do not give the victim alcohol or coffee since both can cause heat loss.

● Do not allow the victim to fall asleep.

● Treat the victim gently, in severe cases of hypothermia, rough handling can cause a chilled heart muscle to arrest.

● Even when the victim has apparently recovered, they mustn't be allowed to continue the hike. Instead, call or fetch help and, if possible, get them evacuated from the hill so they can receive professional treatment.

Avoiding Hypothermia
The best solution to hypothermia is to avoid it in the first place, which is doubly important when youre on your own, since disorientation makes the condition hard to spot.

Where correct and sufficient clothing. Wind chill and damp are both your enemy since both accelerate heat loss from the body, so wind and water-proof clothing and insulation layers are crucial.

● Cover your head - you lose a lot of heat through your noggin, while the body will restrict blood flow to, say, your feet, your brain needs a blood supply to function, so the stuff is always flowing up there. A warm, windproof hat will make a big difference. Carry a spare too, it's stupid dying because you dropped your hat...

● Eat high energy foods regularly as you go - your body is like an engine and if you don't fuel it, it'll stop running and stop producing heat.

● Don't be over ambitious - tired walklers and climbers are far more likely to get hypothermia, so be realistic about your day - if it's cold and wet or very windy, consider shortening your route or maybe cancelling altogether. If you're a little unfit, don't push yourself too hard.

Kit To Carry
Particularly if you're part of a group, carrying the right kit can make the difference between life and death. If you're backpacking, then you'll have most of what you need to survive already so...

● Your brain - no joke, pressing on regardless is what kills many hypothermia victims. Having the presence of mind to realise that you have a problem and need to deal with it is crucial, but difficult.

● Spare warm clothing and a sleeping bag / down jacket can be crucial in minimising heat loss in the victim. Bear in mind that other members of the group will also need warm clothing once you stop. Hats are crucial.

● An emergency shelter or bivvy bag - crucial to getting the victim out of the wind. Group survival shelters are excellent and can also be used for sheltered lunch stops and allow you to pool body heat.

● A sleeping or bivvy mat - ideally you want to insulate the casualty from cold ground, if you don't have these, improvise using a pack and / or spare clothing.

● Stove, drinks and food. A lightweight stove and some soup or hot drinks are a good move and you should always carry emergency, high energy food as a back-up measure.

● Heat pads - exothermic warming pads are a better way of warming a casualty than body contact. Well worth adding to a group kit list.

● We're not saying that you have to carry all of these in winter, but they could make the difference between a minor scare and a fatality, so, particularly if you're part of a group, think about sharing the above out between you.

And Finally...
Hypothermia's not just for winter, it's perfectly possible to cop it in spring or autumn, or even in summer, so let's be careful out there.

By Jon Doran outdoorsmagic.com

3 Days without Water

All the congregation of the people of Israel moved on from the wilderness of Sin by stages, according to the commandment of the LORD, and camped at Rephidim, but there was no water for the people to drink. Therefore the people quarreled with Moses and said, —Give us water to drink.|| And Moses said to them, —Why do you quarrel with me? Why do you test the LORD?|| But the people thirsted there for water, and the people grumbled against Moses and said, —Why did you bring us up out of Egypt, to kill us and our children and our livestock with thirst?|| So Moses cried to the LORD, —What shall I do with this people? They are almost ready to stone me.|| And the LORD said to Moses, —Pass on before the people, taking with you some of the elders of Israel, and take in your hand the staff with which you struck the Nile, and go. Behold, I will stand before you there on the rock at Horeb, and you shall strike the rock, and water shall come out of it, and the people will drink.|| And Moses did so, in the sight of the elders of Israel. And he called the name of the place Massah and Meribah, because of the quarreling of the people of Israel, and because they tested the LORD by saying, —Is the LORD among us or not?||
Exodus 17:1-7

Backcountry Water Treatment
Part 1: Proper Hydration

Prevent Dehydration with Proper Hydration

Dehydration is a serious concern during outdoor activities. It can happen in summer or winter, on a day hike or several days into a 50-miler, even on a canoe or kayak trip. Vigorous activity, excessive sun exposure, forgotten water breaks, higher altitudes (where humidity levels are lower), and medical conditions are a few factors that can affect your hydration level.

Some of the consequences of dehydration are loss of energy and motivation, irritability, headaches, difficulty sleeping, fainting, and, at high altitude, an increased likelihood of altitude sickness, hypothermia, and frostbite. In extreme cases, dehydration can lead to delirium and even death.

Essentially, if you're losing more fluids than you're taking in, dehydration is the result. So it's important to stay sufficiently hydrated while hiking, backpacking, or climbing.

However, water sources in the backcountry, or even at the trailhead, are not normally assured of being safe for consumption. So learning how to treat backcountry water is essential to ensure safe safe water supplies and proper hydration.

Dehydration Signs and Symptoms

The rule for judging whether someone is becoming dehydrated is the phrase —**Clear and Copious**. This means that one's urine should not have a strong color and that urination should be fairly frequent. If your urine is not clear like gin to pale yellow, you are dehydrated. Dark yellow indicates serious dehydration.

It takes time for the body to absorb fluids, so you must **drink early and often**. Make sure everyone, youths and adults, is drinking plenty of water. —Saving your water for later can result in dehydration instead. Trip leaders and other adults should make sure to not neglect their own hydration needs.

Thirst is not necessarily an indicator of dehydration. The body's thirst signal starts when you are 2 to 5 percent dehydrated, according to Dr. Eric Weiss. That person who is acting crankier than usual may be dehydrated, so take frequent water breaks (every 20 to 30 minutes). Consider using a hydration reservoir; its easy access means you never need to stop for a drink.

Rate of Moisture Loss

Some of us, especially those brought up in desert regions, were taught to —conserve our water, saving the small amounts available as long as possible; we were told we could quell the thirsty feeling by holding a small round pebble in our mouths and sucking on it. The problem with these misconceptions, is that we lose moisture in our breath and by sweating. For example, during eight hours of sleep about one liter of moisture is lost through breathing and another liter is lost through perspiration. The rate is even faster when exercising vigorously.

A good way to find your personal rate of moisture loss during exercise is the same as that used in professional and international competitions—weigh yourself before, during, and after an exercise session. It is, of course, impractical to weigh yourself during a hike, but you can weigh yourself before and after a training hike. Each pound you lose during exercise is a pint (half liter) of water lost. Be sure to account for any water and fluids you take in during the hike. In ultra-marathons and other endurance competitions, competitors are usually pulled from the event if they lose more than 5 percent of their body weight.

How Much Water?

The basic rule for avoiding dehydration is to drink plenty of fluids, but this doesn't means just any fluid. Diuretics (such as caffeine, alcohol, and a number of medicines, including Diamox commonly taken for altitude sickness) promote dehydration. The body does not absorb highly sugared or carbonated beverages as rapidly, which means that soft drinks are less efficient at quenching thirst than plain water. And some adults down a few malt beverages at the end of a hot day believing that they are rehydrating, but research shows quite the opposite.

The best way to keep hydrated or to rehydrate is with plain water or water with one of the specially developed rehydration mixes added.

Someone exercising hard may lose more than a liter (quart) of water an hour. So a good guideline for vigorous activities at altitude is a **minimum of 4 liters a day, up to as much as 8 liters**. For example, this might mean consuming a liter at breakfast (including hot drinks and fluids in cereal and fruit), one liter between breakfast and lunch (take frequent water breaks), a half-liter with lunch, a liter between lunch and supper (more water breaks), and a final liter at supper (including in the form of soups, hot drinks, and the main course). Many people find that staying well-hydrated is key to a good night's sleep. Remember that caffeine is a diuretic, so coffee, tea, and chocolate are not as effective as non-caffeinated drinks. -by Bill Straka

Part 2: Keeping Your Water Supply Safe In Camp

Whenever and wherever you camp, you must make sure your water supply is not contaminated, as well as take great care not to contaminate the water supply. To prevent contamination, separate your water source from the areas for bodily relief and washing dishes or yourself by at least 100 feet (or as specified by the land manager).

Designate a clean water source area and a separate latrine area when you set up camp. If there is a latrine or outhouse available, make this the designated latrine area. Emphasize to everyone in your party (adults and youth) that they must use the designated latrine area, and must not just step outside the tent during the night or first thing in the morning. When designating the latrine area, keep in mind that other people may be using the area in the future. In winter, consider the impact when the snow melts.

In Winter

It is tempting to think that snow, especially in winter, is uncontaminated, but this is not necessarily true. Avoid yellow or brown snow, but also keep in mind that animals roam the snowfields and can contaminate the snow, just as humans do. Purify the water, just as in summer. If you are melting snow, continue heating it up to the boiling point. While it's obvious when thinking about it, the shovel or scoop used for gathering snow to melt into water should be different from the shovel used for the latrine or other purposes.

In Wilderness Areas

In an increasing number of wilderness areas, camping and backpacking groups are required to carry out all human waste. This can be accomplished by using one of the commercial waste bags (RestStop or WAG Bags, for example) or by using doubled plastic garbage bags.

In the latter example, one garbage bag is used as a liner, either for a bucket carried in for that purpose (some groups carry a toilet seat for the can) or for a hole dug for that purpose. The person changing the liner bag should wear disposable gloves (the same type of surgical gloves everyone should have in their first aid kits), tightly close and tie-wrap the liner bag, and place it inside a second bag, which is also tightly closed and tie-wrapped. The now-contaminated gloves are disposed of in the new liner bag. A handful of cat litter can help reduce odor and will make the operation less unpleasant for the designee.

In winter, waste matter usually freezes quickly. To reduce volume, reserve the bags for fecal matter and have people urinate a short distance away. The bags can be emptied into a latrine or a dumpster at the trailhead (check with the local land managers for their standardized practices).

During a Natural Disaster

It is also important to be aware of the potential contamination of water supplies during natural disasters, such as earthquakes in California, floods in the Midwest, and hurricanes in the Gulf States. While this does not relate directly to camping, knowledge and practice in dealing with water supplies in the backcountry can help with preparedness for natural disasters or other interruptions of normal water supplies.

Clean Hands

Cleanliness is more difficult in the backcountry. It is important that the cook always has clean hands, as should everyone when eating (especially finger foods like sandwiches). Certainly, the person on latrine duty should not also be the cook. And when rotating duties, do not have the latrine person's next task involve food preparation. If possible, the latrine person should thoroughly wash his or her hands with soap and water.

Do not wash your hands in any stream, lake, or spring. That is your water supply and that of other parties and the local wildlife. You can carry a folding basin for this purpose; do the washing at least 100 feet from water sources. Alternatively, use the sterilizing solutions or gels, such as Pure Touch and Purell, found in many drug, grocery, and camping stores.

Clean Dishes

Rinsing soap off dishes, especially aluminum pots, requires enough hot water that the extra fuel to be carried becomes a significant factor. Part of the solution to having clean dishes is to prepare foods that produce minimal mess. Much of the mess can be cleaned off dishes and cooking utensils by scrubbing with snow and following with a hot water rinse (remember to pack out all food waste!). Also, remember to dispose of any soapy wash or rinse water in an ecologically sound manner, at least 100 feet from water sources.

You can also clean dishes as much as possible at the end of each meal, then sterilize dishes, cups, spoons, etc. in boiling water just before use in the water to be used for cooking.

Part 3: What is in Backcountry Water?

There are two major groups of contaminants found in water that can cause serious illness (potentially ruining a trip), and one aesthetic ingredient that makes water unattractive (and affects methods for removing the other two groups of contaminants).

The first two groups are biological contaminants and chemical contaminants. The aesthetic group is material suspended in the water that may not cause illness itself, but looks unattractive and can interfere with removal of the first two.

First, it should be noted that extensive testing of water in U.S. and Canadian areas popular for backpacking and canoeing, in all seasons, indicates that whether there is contamination and how dangerous it is varies widely from place to place, even within a given area. For example, studies in the Sierra have found front-country streams (at the trailhead) that have virtually no contamination, while some streams far from the trailhead and not frequented by humans or pack animals have a high concentration of biological contaminants. Some backcountry users take no precautions and do not get sick, while others diligently use filters and chemical purifiers and get extremely sick.

The most common thread for those who come down with digestive problems appears to be, not contaminated water, but carelessness in basic sanitation, particularly diligent washing and sterilizing of hands when handling food.

The situation is different in Third World countries. In tropical climates, especially, the abundance of wildlife living in potential water sources and the poor sanitation practices of local populations mean that there are many varieties of bacteria, viruses, and parasites that are unknown in colder climes, and against which those of us who live in North America have developed no resistance.

Biological Contaminants: Parasites, Bacteria, Viruses

The biological contaminants are generally grouped into parasites (or protozoa), bacteria, and viruses. Protozoa are the largest at about 1 micron, bacteria measure approximately 0.5 to 2 microns, and viruses measure around 0.02 - 0.3 microns.

The most infamous villain of backcountry water is the dreaded giardiasis, caused by the parasite giardia lamblia. Giardiasis was known among the pioneers and trappers as —beaver fever, since it was often associated with beaver ponds. This emphasizes the fact that biological contaminants in water come not only from human activity, but also from animals that live in the wilderness, as well as pack animals and domesticated animals that graze in such areas (sheep, goats, and cattle, among others). Some plant materials (certain algae in particular) can produce physical symptoms.

In areas where sanitation practices are poor, sewage seepage and runoff often include the organisms that cause cholera, hepatitis, and other diseases, along with a large variety of viruses.

Illness from biota can appear quickly, though most frequently; it takes several days for bacteria, viruses, and parasites to reproduce sufficiently to produce nausea, headaches, vomiting, and diarrhea. This delay in the appearance of symptoms often leads people to believe that they got away with drinking untreated water, and that the symptoms are due to something else not associated with their weekend trip.

Chemical Contaminants

Chemical contaminants can come from man-made or natural sources. Most common are man-made sources such as industrial and agricultural runoff. There are many —backcountry areas that are affected by such runoff into water sources. For example, mining operations took place throughout much of the Sierra Nevada and Rocky Mountains, resulting in seepage of heavy metal compounds and chemicals used in leeching operations. There was extensive mercury mining in the Santa Cruz Mountains until the 1960s. In the Almaden Valley, many streams are posted to warn fishermen not to eat any fish, because of the high concentrations of mercury in the fish in those streams. You should be aware of your water sources before going into any area, so you can prepare accordingly. Illness due to chemical contamination may be rapid, but more often is a very long-term problem. Heavy metals, such as mercury or selenium (found in areas of agricultural runoff), sometimes take several years of continual use of the contaminated water to show up. In some cases the available water may be highly saline. This includes ocean sailing trips or trips to offshore islands where your party is dropped off and later picked up. This article does not cover desalination. Critters do not pay attention to where they relieve themselves).

Basic sanitation—diligent washing and sterilizing hands when handling food—is as important as treating water.

Part 4: Methods for Making Water Safe

Short of transporting all your water from civilization and municipal water supplies, there are three general methods for treating your water for drinking and cooking, and two more recent additions:
Boiling
Filtering
Chemical Treatment
Ultraviolet Radiation
PUR Clean Drinking Water Kit

Chart: Which Treatment Methods Remove What

Boiling

Although sterilization by heating is referred to as —boiling, it is not necessary to actually bring water to a full rolling boil or to boil for 5 to 10 minutes, as is often stated. Raising the temperature of water to 155°F (70°C) is sufficient to kill most biota encountered by backpackers. This is also the temperature required for pasteurizing milk.

The temperature at which water boils decreases with altitude. However, the boiling temperature is higher than 155°F (70°C) at all altitudes that you would camp at (even on Mt. Everest with a boiling point of approximately 167°F / 75°C). Since few people carry a thermometer capable of measuring water temperature on a backpack, the most practical approach is to heat water until it starts bubbling.

Note: *the Environmental Protection Agency (EPA) and the Centers for Disease Control and Prevention (CDC) both recommend boiling water for one minute. If you are above 6,562 feet (2,000 meters), the recommended boiling time increases to three minutes.*

Advantages of Boiling:
Boiling kills most microorganisms.
Boiling is the most practical and simplest approach to sterilizing water for meals, since you have to raise the water to boiling for most backpacking foods anyway.
In winter, when you often must melt snow or ice, you usually will raise the water to boiling, as well.

Disadvantages of Boiling:
Boiling does not remove silt, glacial flour, or volcanic ash, though it will sometimes reduce turbidity from plant material in the water.

Boiling does not remove chemical contamination, though it can drive off some of the sulfur compounds.
Boiling requires burning fuel. Since you generally will be carrying your stove fuel with you , this means carrying extra weight.

Filtering

Filters depend primarily on forcing water through a medium with tiny holes to physically remove microbes and matter. Anything larger than the hole size is blocked, so a filter's effectiveness depends on its —pore size. Most filters available for backpackers remove all parasites and bacteria, plus some viruses. They remove most of the particles that cause turbidity. However, few filters for backpackers remove the smallest viruses.

Filters sold as —purifiers (First Need, for example) use a chemical purifier to kill viruses, usually an iodine resin. Purifiers must prove inactivation of all three biological contaminants (protozoa, bacteria, and viruses) to meet the EPA Guide Standard for Testing Microbiological Purifiers.

There are filters, known as —reverse-osmosis filters, available for desalination. However, their size makes them impractical for backpacking, though usable for ocean-going sailboats and other larger vessels.

Backpacking filters may work via a pump (a manual pump forces the water through the filter element), —straw (your suction pulls the water through the filter), or gravity. Ease of use and the speed of filtering are considerations when selecting a filter.

Advantages of Filtering:
Most filters are effective against bacteria and parasites.
Some filters remove larger viruses.
Filters remove some turbidity.
Filters are usually convenient and fast.

Disadvantages of Filtering:
In areas where viral contamination is present (Third World countries, for example), additional purification by boiling or chemical treatment is still required.

Few filters remove chemical contamination; those that do remove only a limited range of chemical contaminants (usually with an activated carbon element).
Fine particles like silt, glacial flour, and volcanic ash will clog any filter, requiring field maintenance (backflushing, cleaning with a brush made for the purpose, or replacement of the filter element). Many filters have pre-filters available to reduce the amount of material that will cause clogging — use them. Settling can also help.

If the filter freezes with even a tiny amount of water in the element, the element can crack, rendering the filter useless.

The moving parts of pump filters can break, rendering the pump useless.
Pumping can be tiring.

Proper Use of Filters:

Always store the intake hose separately from the rest of the pump.

Use the covers for the inlet and outlet to prevent contaminating the filter element on the outlet side.
Protect the filter from freezing.

Clean the filter regularly according to the manufacturer's specifications.

Use a bucket, pan, fold-up basin, or other container as the source of the water for the pump, rather than pumping directly out of the stream or lake (at least 100 feet from the water source). This is both for avoiding the watering area for local animals and to reduce the amount of suspended material entering the screen on the pickup and into the pre-filter.

If possible, let water stand overnight to allow suspended material to settle out.

Chemical Treatment: Iodine and Chlorine

The chemical treatment approach uses one of two halogens (chlorine or iodine) to kill biota. This is the method most used by municipal water supplies around the world. The backpacker's approach is to use a small amount of the halogen, rather than the massive treatment plant used by your local water company. The halogen may be applied in one of two forms – a tablet that is dissolved in the water to be treated or in a solution of the halogen in water. Both iodine and chlorine are very effective against the most common pathogens, but they require sufficient time to act. Like all chemical reactions, the time required increases as the temperature decreases.

Iodine

Iodine is most commonly used in the form of tablets, such as Potable Aqua water purification tablets. One or two tablets are added to each liter of water, with the time required being about 30 minutes for —room temperature water (always follow the manufacturer's instructions).

Alternatively, a small amount of a saturated solution made from iodine crystals is added to the water to be treated. The most common form of this treatment is Polar Pure.

With Polar Pure, the crystals are in a bottle that has a — trap in the mouth of the bottle to ensure that only the saturated solution of iodine in water and no crystals gets into your drinking water. One capful of the solution is measured out and poured into your one-liter water bottle. Then the Polar Pure bottle is refilled to allow a saturated solution to be formed for the next treatment.

Advantages of Iodine
Chemical treatments, like iodine, are very effective against most common pathogens.
Iodine is faster than chlorine, approximately 30 minutes versus up to 4 hours.

Disadvantages of Iodine
Does not kill the parasite cryptosporidium.
Chemical treatments do not remove chemical contaminants or turbidity.

Requires time to work (approximately 30 minutes); Temperatures below 70°F (20°C) and turbid water require increasingly longer times.

Some people react badly to iodine, particularly people with thyroid problems.

The medical community recommends that continuous usage of iodine-treated water last no more than 3 to 4 weeks.

Many people find the iodine taste objectionable (mixing in some citric acid in the form of lemon juice or tablets will kill the taste, but be sure to wait until sterilization has had plenty of time to take place).

Chlorine

Aquamira water treatment drops use chlorine. Chlorine is most commonly used in the form of chlorine dioxide tablets or drops, such as in Aquamira, Katadyn Micropur, and Potable Aqua Chlorine Dioxide. It can also be used in the form of laundry bleach (be sure it is pure hypochlorous acid and not mixed with perfumes or other chemicals) or a solution generated from rock salt, such as done by MSR's MIOX purifier.

While chlorine will kill most bacteria and parasites in a few minutes, a much longer time is required to kill the cysts of giardia and cryptosporidium, as well as many viruses. Typically 4 hours or more is the recommended time for room temperature water (70°F/20°C), with an increase for colder water, such as from mountain streams (always follow the manufacturer's instructions).

Chlorine can be used indefinitely, unlike iodine. It's what you drink in most city water systems. On the other hand, one of the joys of fresh stream water is its clean taste with no chemical smell or taste. The much longer time required for chlorine treatment is also a problem. The solution is to carry two water bottles, which are alternately refilled and the chlorine added at each water source. That way, you have a full bottle available when you empty the other.

Chemical treatments do not remove chemical contamination, and in fact can react with certain agricultural runoff. This is unlikely to be a significant problem for the backcountry traveler, however. Chemical treatment also does not remove turbidity. Turbid water requires longer treatment times or an increased amount of the halogen.

Advantages of Chlorine:
Chemical treatments are very effective against most common pathogens, and chlorine kills most bacteria and parasites in minutes.
Chlorine can be used indefinitely.

Disadvantages of Chlorine:
Chemical treatments do not remove chemical contaminants or turbidity.

Requires time to work, up to 4 hours, for full treatment; Temperatures below 70°F (20°C) and turbid water require increasingly longer times.

Ultraviolet Radiation

A recent addition to the quiver of techniques for purifying water in the field is ultraviolet (UV) radiation. The most widely available device for doing this is the SteriPen. This is a battery-operated device that is stirred in the water (preferably a one-liter water bottle with a wide mouth) for a short period of time (couple of minutes).

To prepare for purification, fill a bottle with water, press a button on the SteriPen according to the directions (single push for one liter), then insert the pen into the water. When the contacts on the side of the pen are immersed, the light will light up. Stir the water until the light extinguishes, and the water is sterilized. The UV radiation is extremely effective against biological contaminants.

However, like the other treatments mentioned above, UV radiation does not remove chemical contaminants or turbidity. The water should be fairly clear (it need not be crystal clear), so the water should be allowed to settle or a filter used to remove most of the sediment (a coffee filter is sufficient, according to the last word I had from the SteriPen people). If the water appears slightly milky from glacial flour or volcanic ash, you may want to run a second treatment. We used this approach on Kilimanjaro with the water taken from streams on the mountain.

A disadvantage of the SteriPen is that it requires batteries. However, one of the optional packages includes a carrying case with a solar charger in the lid. This requires 8 to 10 hours to recharge a pair of batteries. Since a charge will suffice for 10 liters or so of water (a couple day's worth), this is adequate. You can carry two or three sets of the batteries as backups, although the batteries (both primary and rechargeable) are lithium-based, hence subject to the TSA restrictions on carrying no more than two spare batteries in your carry-on baggage and none in your checked baggage.

Advantages of UV Radiation:
Effective against biological contaminants—parasites, bacteria, and viruses.
Fast and convenient.

Disadvantages of UV Radiation: Does not remove chemical contamination nor reduce turbidity.

Water should be fairly clear, though it does not have to be perfectly clear.

Requires batteries, but a solar charger is available.

PUR Water Treatment Kit

PUR, a Swiss division of Proctor and Gamble, developed a water treatment kit for use in Third World countries a couple of years ago. They have now made the PUR Clean Drinking Water Kit available in North America. This kit will purify water, removing biological and many chemical contaminants, along with suspended particulates.

The complete kit includes two 10-liter containers (one for the untreated water to be treated, the other for the treated water to be decanted into), a stirring tool, a cotton cloth filter to remove the flocculus with the trapped contaminants, packets of the treatment chemical, and a packet opening tool. The first container is filled with the water to be treated. The premeasured chemical packet, containing iron sulphate and calcium hypochlorite, is poured into the water and the stirring tool is used to stir the water to mix the chemical thoroughly. The container is then closed and let stand for 10 minutes.

The iron sulphate forms a flocculus (similar in appearance to fluffy cotton), which settles to the bottom, carrying most of the biological contaminants, silt and other suspended particulates, and most chemical contaminants (including heavy metal compounds) to the bottom. After 10 minutes, the water is carefully decanted through the cloth filter into the second container, which is allowed to sit for an additional 10 minutes, during which the remaining pathogens (viruses) are killed by the calcium hypochlorite acting as the purifying agent. At this point the water is pure enough to pass international standards for drinking water.

The two major problems with the PUR kit are that it is currently somewhat difficult to obtain, and that the packets are pre-measured for 10 liters. You cannot use a partial packet for a smaller amount of water (the powder does not necessarily have the components uniformly mixed throughout the packet, so you must empty the complete packet into the water). While this is ok for a group (or, in Third World communities, for a family group), this is inconvenient for the individual backpacker or a small group of backpackers. However, the cost is very small, less than the cost per liter of most of the other methods described.

The big advantage is that this is the only method available for water contaminated heavily with suspended particulates, many chemical contaminants, and virtually all biological contaminants. It would work well for larger backcountry groups, as well as in case of a natural or man-made disaster that interrupts municipal water supplies. It will not desalinate water.

Advantages of PUR Clean Drinking Water Kit:
Removes biological, particulate, and some chemical contamination.

Particularly good for Third World and highly contaminated water sources, and during natural or man-made disasters.

Inexpensive.
Simple procedure.

Treats 10 liters at a time, so is best for large groups.

Disadvantages of PUR Clean Drinking Water Kit:
Treats 10 liters at a time—no smaller, no larger—so inconvenient for most backpackers.
Takes 20 minutes total time for treatment.
Chart: Which Treatment Methods Remove What

The Bottom Line
As noted previously in —Part 3: What is in Backcountry Water, the strong evidence is that for backcountry travelers in the United States and Canada, the major source of digestive tract illness is not waterborne pathogens or other contamination, but poor sanitation. The best prevention is paying diligent attention to simple sanitation measures:

Wash your hands frequently, particularly after relieving yourself. Use soap and water and/or Purell or another alcohol-based purifier.

Wash and sterilize your hands before eating, particularly finger foods (sandwiches, bars, trail mix, etc.)
All individuals preparing or serving food for the group must wash and sterilize their hands, and should consider using gloves of the type now mandated for restaurant workers.

All dishes and utensils should be washed before meal preparation and serving. Sterilizing by dunking in boiling water is one of the easiest and quickest ways to assure sterile utensils.

It is all too easy to be careless and neglect simple sanitation while hiking, backpacking, and climbing. But, by treating your backcountry water, staying hydrated, and practicing proper hygiene, you'll help ensure that you, and everyone in your group, has a great trip and will be back on the trail again soon.

	Protozoa/Parasites	Bacteria	Viruses	Chemical Contaminants	Aesthetic Contaminants
Boiling	Yes	Yes	Yes	No	No
Filters	Yes	Yes	Remove some larger viruses, not smallest	A few remove a limited range of chemical contaminants	Removes some turbidity
Purifiers	Yes	Yes	Yes	No	No
Chemical: Iodine	Not cryptosporidium	Yes	Yes	No	No
Chemical: Chlorine	Yes	Yes	Yes	No	No
UV Radiation (SteriPen)	Yes	Yes	Yes	No	No
PUR Water Treatment Kit	Yes	Yes	Yes	Some	Yes

The information above is for general interest only. Always consult each manufacturer's specific product information for effectiveness of your treatment method against specific pathogens and contaminants.

Water

Water Storage
Quantity

A water ration of as little as a pint per day has allowed life raft survivors to live for weeks, but a more realistic figure is 1 gallon per person per day for survival. 4 gallons per person/day will allow personal hygiene, washing of dishes, counter tops, etc. 5 to 12 gallons per day would be needed for a conventional toilet, or 1/2 to two gallons for a pour flush latrine. For short-term emergencies, it will probably be more practical to store paper plates and utensils, and minimize food preparation, than to attempt to store more water.

In addition to stored water, there is quite a bit of water trapped in the piping of the average home. If the municipal water system was not contaminated before you shut the water off to your house, this water is still fit for consumption without treatment. To collect this water, open the lowest faucet in the system, and allow air into the system from a second faucet. Depending on the diameter of the piping, you may want to open every other faucet, to make sure all of the water is drained. This procedure will usually only drain the cold water side, the hot-water side will have to be drained from the water heater. Again, open all of the faucets to let air into the system, and be prepared to collect any water that comes out when the first faucet is opened. Toilet tanks (not the bowls) represent another source of water if a toilet bowl cleaner is not used in the tank.

Some people have plumbed old water heaters or other tanks in line with their cold water supply to add an always rotated source of water. *Two cautions are in order: 1) make sure the tanks can handle the pressure (50 psi min.), and 2) if the tanks are in series with the house plumbing, this method is susceptible to contamination of the municipal water system.* The system can be fed off the water lines with a shutoff valve (and a second drain line), preventing the water from being contaminated as long as the valve was closed at the time of contamination.

Water can only be realistically stored for short-term emergencies, after that some emergency supply of water needs to be developed

Water Collection

Wells

Water can only be moved by suction for an equivalent head of about 20′. After this cavitation occurs, that is the water boils off in tiny bubbles in the vacuum created by the pump rather than being lifted by the pump. At best no water is pumped, at worst the pump is destroyed. Well pumps in wells deeper than this work on one of the following principles:

1) The pump can be submerged in the well, this is usually the case for deep well pumps. Submersible pumps are available for depths up 1000 feet.

2) The pump can be located at the surface of the well, and two pipes go down the well: one carrying water down, and one returning it. A jet fixture called an ejector on the bottom of the two hoses causes well water to be lifted up the well with the returning pumped water. These pumps must have an efficient foot valve as there is no way for them to self-prime. These are commonly used in shallow wells, but can go as deep as 350 feet. Some pumps use the annular space between one pipe and the well casing as the second pipe this requires a packer (seal) at the ejector and at the top of the casing.

3) The pump cylinder can be located in the well, and the power source located above the well. This is the method used by windmills and most hand pumps. A few hand pumps pump the water from very shallow wells using an aboveground pump and suction line. A variety of primitive, but ingenious, pump designs also exist. One uses a chain with buckets to lift the water up. Another design uses a continuous loop rope dropping in the well and returning up a small diameter pipe. Sealing washers are located along the rope, such that water is pulled up the pipe with the rope. An ancient Chinese design used knots, but modern designs designed for village level maintenance in Africa use rubber washers made from tires, and will work to a much greater depth.

Obviously a bucket can be lowered down the well if the well is big enough, but this won't work with a modern drilled well. A better idea for a drilled well is to use a 2' length or so of galvanized pipe with end caps of a diameter that will fit in the well casing. The upper cap is drilled for a screw eye, and a small hole for ventilation. The lower end is drilled with a hole about half the diameter of the pipe, and on the inside a piece of rigid plastic or rubber is used as a flapper valve. This will allow water to enter the pipe, but not exit it. The whole assembly is lowered in the well casing, the weight of the pipe will cause it to fill with water, and it can then be lifted to the surface. The top pipe cap is there mostly to prevent the pipe from catching as it is lifted.

Springs

Springs or artesian wells are ideal sources of water. *Like a conventional well, the water should be tested for pathogens, VOCs (Volatile Organic Compounds such as fuel oil or benzene), pesticides and any other contaminants found in your area.* If the source is a spring it is very important to seal it in a spring box to prevent the water from becoming contaminated as it reaches the surface. It is also important to divert surface runoff around the spring box. As with a well, you will want to periodically treat the spring box with chlorine, particularly if the spring is slow moving. The spring may also be used for keeping food cool if a spring-house is built. If this is the case, it is still recommended to build a spring box inside the house to obtain potable water.

Surface water

Most US residents served by municipal water systems supplied with surface water, and many residents of underdeveloped countries rely on surface water. *While surface water will almost always need to be treated, a lot of the risk can be reduced by properly collecting the water.* Ideal sources of water are fast flowing creeks and rivers which don't have large sources of pollution in their watershed. With the small amounts of water needed by a family or small group, the most practical way to collect the water is though an infiltration gallery or well. Either method reduces the turbidity of the collected water making it easy for later treatment.

Water Purification

Heavy Metals

Heavy metals are only a problem is certain areas of the country. The best way to identify their presence is by a lab test of the water or by speaking with your county health department. Unless you are down stream of mining trailings or a factory, the problem will probably affect the whole county or region. Heavy metals are unlikely to be present in sufficient levels to cause problems with short-term use.

Turbidity

Turbidity refers to suspended solids, i.e. muddy water, is very turbid. Turbidity is undesirable for 3 reasons:

1) aesthetic considerations

2) solids may contain heavy metals, pathogens or other contaminants,

3) turbidity decreases the effectiveness of water treatment techniques by shielding pathogens from chemical or thermal damage, or in the case of UV treatment, absorbing the UV light itself.

Organic compounds

Water can be contaminated by a number of organic compound such as chloroform, gasoline, pesticides, and herbicides. These contaminants must be identified in a lab test. It is unlikely ground water will suddenly become contaminated unless a quantity of chemicals is allowed to enter a well or penetrating the aquifer. *One exception is when the aquifer is located in limestone.* Not only will water flow faster through limestone, but the rock is prone to forming vertical channels or sinkholes that will rapidly allow contamination from surface water. Surface water may show great swings in chemical levels due to differences in rainfall, seasonal crop cultivation, and industrial effluent levels

Pathogens

Protozoa

Protozoa cysts are the largest pathogens in drinking water, and are responsible for many of the waterborne disease cases in the US. Protozoa cysts range is size from 2 to 15 μm (**a micron is one millionth of a meter**), but can squeeze through smaller openings. In order to insure cyst filtration, filters with a absolute pore size of 1μm or less should be used. The two most common protozoa pathogens are *Giardia lamblia* (Giardia) and *Cryptosporidium* (Crypto). Both organisms have caused numerous deaths in recent years in the US, the deaths occurring in the young and elderly, and the sick and immune compromised. Many deaths were a result of more than one of these conditions. Neither disease is likely to be fatal to a healthy adult, even if untreated. For example in Milwaukee in April of 1993, of 400,000 who were diagnosed with Crypto, only 54 deaths were linked to the outbreak, 84% of whom were AIDS patients. Outside of the US and other developed countries, protozoa are responsible for many cases of amoebic dysentery, but so far this has not been a problem in the US, due to better wastewater treatment. This could change during a survival situation. Tests have found Giardia and/ or Crypto in up to 5% of vertical wells and 26% of springs in the US.

Bacteria

Bacteria are smaller than protozoa and are responsible for many diseases such as typhoid fever, cholera, diarrhea, and dysentery. Pathogenic bacteria range in size from 0.2 to 0.6 μm, and a 0.2 μm filter is necessary to prevent transmission. Contamination of water supplies by bacteria is blamed for the cholera epidemics which devastate undeveloped countries from time to time. Even in the US, *E. coli* is frequently found to contaminate water supplies. Fortunately E. coli is relatively harmless as pathogens go, and the problem isn't so much with E. coli found, but the fear that other bacteria may have contaminated the water as well. Never the less, dehydration from diarrhea caused by E. coli has resulted in fatalities.

Viruses

Viruses are the 2nd most problematic pathogen, behind protozoa. As with protozoa, most waterborne viral diseases don't present a lethal hazard to a healthy adult. Waterborne pathogenic viruses range in size from 0.020-0.030 μm, and are too small to be filtered out by a mechanical filter. All waterborne enteric viruses affecting humans occur solely in humans, thus animal waste doesn't present much of a viral threat. At the present viruses don't present a major hazard to people drinking surface water in the US, but this could change in a survival situation as the level of human sanitation is reduced. Viruses do tend to show up even in remote areas, so case can be made for eliminating them now.

Physical Treatment

Heat Treatment

Boiling is one guaranteed way to purify water of all pathogens. Most experts feel that if the water reaches a rolling boil it is safe. A few still hold out for maintaining the boiling for some length of time, commonly 5 or 10 minutes, plus an extra minute for every 1000 feet of elevation. If one wishes to do this, a pressure cooker would allow the water to be kept at boiling with out loosing the heat to evaporation. One reason for the long period of boiling may be to inactivate bacterial spores (which can survive boiling), but these spore are unlikely to be waterborne pathogens.

African aid agencies figure *it takes 1 kg of wood to boil 1 liter of water.* Hardwoods and efficient stoves would improve on this.

Water can also be treated at below boiling temperatures, if contact time is increased. A commercial unit has been developed that treats 500 gals of water per day at an estimated cost of $1/1000 gallons for the energy. The process is similar to milk pasteurization, and holds the water at 161° F for 15 seconds. Heat exchangers recover most of the energy used to warm the water. Solar pasteurizers have also been built that would heat three gallons of water to 65° C and hold the temperature for an hour. A higher temperature could be reached if the device was rotated east to west during the day to follow the sunlight.

Regardless of the method, heat treatment does not leave any form of residual to keep the water free of pathogens in storage.

Reverse Osmosis

Reverse osmosis forces water, under pressure, through a membrane that is impermeable to most contaminants. The most common use is aboard boats to produce fresh water from salt water. *The membrane is somewhat better at rejecting salts than it is at rejecting non-ionized weak acids and bases and smaller organic molecules (molecular weight below 200).* In the latter category are undissociated weak organic acids, amines, phenols, chlorinated hydrocarbons, some pesticides and low molecular weight alcohols. *Larger organic molecules, and all pathogens are rejected.* Of course it is possible to have a imperfection in the membrane that could allow molecules or whole pathogens to pass through.

Using reverse osmosis to desalinate seawater requires considerable pressure (1000 psi) to operate, and for a long time only electric models were available. Competing for a contract to build a hand powered model for the Navy, Recovery Engineering designed a model that could operate by hand, using the waste water (90 percent of the water is waste water, only 10% passes through the filter) to pressurize the back side of the piston. The design was later acquired by PUR. While there is little question that the devices work well, the considerable effort required to operate one has been questioned by some survival experts such as Michael Greenwald, himself a survivor of a shipwreck. On the other hand the people who have actually used them on a life raft credit the availability of water from their PUR watermaker for their survival.

PUR manual watermakers are available in two models: The Survivor 06 ($500) produces 2 pints per hour, and the Survivor 35 ($1350) produces 1.4 gal/hr. The latter model is also available as the Power Survivor 35 ($1700), which produces the same water volume from 4 Amps of 12 VDC, and can be disconnected and used as a hand held unit. A number of manufactures, including PUR, make DC powered models for shipboard use. PUR recommends replacing the O rings every 600 hours on its handheld units, and a kit is available to do this. Estimates for membrane life vary, but units designed for production use may last a year or more. *Every precaution should be taken to prevent petroleum products from contacting the membrane as they will damage or destroy the membrane.* The prefilter must also be regularly changed, and the membrane may need to be treated with a biocide occasionally

Reverse osmosis filter are also available that will use normal municipal or private water pressure to remove contaminates from water, as long as they aren't present in the levels found in sea water.

The water produced by reverse osmosis, like distilled water, will be close to pure H_2O. Therefore mineral intake may need to be increased to compensate for the normal mineral content of water in much of the world.

Distillation

Distillation is the evaporation and condensation of water to purify water. *Distillation has two disadvantages: 1) A large energy input is required and 2) If simple distillation is used, chemical contaminants with boiling points below water will be condensed along with the water.* Distillation is most commonly used to remove dissolved minerals and salts from water.

The simplest form of a distillation is a solar still. A solar still uses solar radiation to evaporate water below the boiling point, and the cooler ambient air to condense the vapor. The water can be extracted from the soil, vegetation piled in the still, or contaminated water (such as radiator fluid or salt water) can be added to the still. While per still output is low, they are an important technique if water is in short supply

Other forms of distillation require a concentrated heat source to boil water which is then condensed. Simple stills use a coiling coil to return this heat to the environment. These can be improvised with a boiler and tight fitting lid and some copper tubing (Avoid using lead soldered tubing if possible). FEMA suggests that, in an emergency, a hand towel can be used to collect steam above a container of boiling water. More efficient distillations plants use a vapor compression cycle where the water is boiled off at atmospheric pressure, the steam is compressed, and the condenser condenses the steam above the boiling point of the water in the boiler, returning the heat of fusion to the boiling water. The hot condensed water is run through a second heat exchanger which heats up the water feeding into the boiler. These plants normally use an internal combustion engine to run the compressor. Waste heat from the engine, including the exhaust, is used to start the process and make up any heat loss. This is the method used in most commercial and military desalinization plants

Inflatable solar stills are available from marine supply stores, but avoid the WW2 surplus models, as those who have used them have had a extremely high failure rate. Even new inflatable solar stills may only produce from 30-16 oz under actual conditions, compared to a rating of 48 oz/day under optimum conditions.

Jade Mountain also offers the following portable models in travel cases:

Traveler (WC106) 1 gpd, 23 lb., 24x26x10 folded $ 695

Base Camp (WC107) 2 gpd, 51 lb., 48x48x4 folded $ 895

Safari (WC108) 48x48x5 $1095 A ruggedized version of the Base Camp above.

Microfilters

Microfilters are small-scale filters designed to remove cysts, suspended solids, protozoa, and in some cases bacteria from water. Most filters use a ceramic or fiber element that can be cleaned to restore performance as the units are used. Most units and almost all made for camping use a hand pump to force the water through the filter. Others use gravity, either by placing the water to be filtered above the filter (e.g. the Katadyn drip filter), or by placing the filter in the water, and running a siphon hose to a collection vessel located below the filter (e.g. Katadyn siphon filter). Microfilters are the only method, other than boiling, to remove Cryptosporidia. Microfilters do not remove viruses, which many experts do not consider to be a problem in North America. Despite this the Katadyn microfilter has seen considerable use around the world by NATO-member militaries, WHO, UNHCR, and other aid organizations. Microfilters share a problem with charcoal filter in having bacteria grow on the filter medium. Some handle this by impregnating the filter element with silver such as the Katadyn, others advise against storage of a filter element after it has been used. The Sweetwater Guardian suggests using a freezer for short-term storage

Many microfilters may include silt prefilters, activated charcoal stages, or an iodine resin. Most filters come with a stainless steel prefilter, but other purchased or improvised filters can be added to reduce the loading on the main filter element. *Allowing time for solids to settle, and/or prefiltering with a coffee filter will also extend filter life.* Iodine matrix filters will kill viruses that will pass through the filter, and if a charcoal stage is used it will remove much of the iodine from the water. Charcoal filters will also remove other dissolved natural or manmade contaminates. Both the iodine and the charcoal stages do not indicate when they reach their useful life, which is much shorter than the filter element. If you are depending on the stage for filtering the water you will have to keep up with how much water passes through it.

New designs seem to be coming out every month. The best selling brands seem to be the PUR, and Sweetwater Guardian. The Katadyn doesn't sell as well to outdoor enthusiasts due to its high cost, but for years it was state of the art for water purification and still has a loyal following, especially among professionals in relief work. Below is the data on a few of the more common units, for a excellent field test of some common units, see the December 96 issue of Backpacker magazine.

Note that the first price is for the filter, the second for the replacement filter. The weight is from manufacturer's literature if it was not listed in the Backpacker article. Filter life is from manufacturer's literature and should be taken with a grain of salt.

[Alan's note: These prices are now several years out of date. You'll need to investigate current pricing]

Basic Designs Ceramic Filter Pump Cheap flimsy filter, claimed to filter up to 500 gallons with a 0.9 µm ceramic filter. Not EPA rated, may not have passed independent lab tests, prone to damage, filter element must be submerged in water.

General Ecology- First Need Deluxe This filter uses a structured matrix micro strainer, though General Ecology won't reveal what the structure is. It has survived independent lab tests, and filters particles to 4 µm, while actually removing viruses (the only filter capable of doing this) through electrostatic attraction. The filter cartridges can't be cleaned (other than by back flushing), but are good for 100 gallons. Pump design isn't the best. Other models are available from the manufacturer.

Katadyn PF. The original microfilter using a 0.2 µm silver impregnated ceramic candle. An extremely thick filter allows it to be cleaned many times for up to 14,000 gallons capacity. While the Katadyn seems well made, one reader of this list reported breaking the candle, and Backpacker Magazine broke the case during a field test. The pump, while probably indestructible, is somewhat slow and hard to use, requiring 20 lbs. of force on a small handle. The PF also lacks a output hose as the Katadyn engineers felt if would be a source of contamination.

Katadyn Combi, A cheaper version of the PF incorporating both ceramic and carbon stages. Much faster filter than the PF.

Katadyn Minifilter A smaller and cheaper version of the PF, easier to pump, but generally not well received. Good for 200 gallons.

Katadyn Expedition Similar filter to the PF (exact same cartridge as the Drip Filter Below), but designed for much higher production, stainless steel case with spade type D handle, produces 0.75 gpm. Filter good for 26,000 gallons.

Katadyn Drip Style Filter Filter elements similar to those in the PF are mounted vertically in top 3 gallon plastic bucket, water drips through filters into second 3 gallon bucket with faucet. 1 qt, per hour with the 2 filters included, a third filter can be added to increase rate 50%. Each filter good for 13,000 gallons. The mounting hardware for the filters is available for $10 to allow you to make your own filter of what ever size is needed. Each mounting kit requires a ½" hole in the bottom of the raw water container.

Katadyn Siphon Filter Similar design to PF filter element, but a siphon hose replaces the pump, filters 1-2 quarts per hour (allow 1 hour for the filter to "prime" itself via capillary action), but multiple filters can be used in the same container. Collection vessel must be lower than raw water container. Good for13,000 gallons.

MSR Miniworks MSR's smaller filter, using a 0.3 µm ceramic element. Pump is well designed, and easy to use. Main drawback is that the clean water discharge is from the bottom of the filter, and no hose is provided. While the bottom is threaded for a Nalgene bottle, it is a pain in the butt to fill a canteen or 2 liter bottle. Claimed to filter 100 gallons, Backpacker Magazine feels this may be one of the few filters without a grossly inflated rating.

MSR Waterworks MSR's first filter with a 0.2 µ ceramic and membrane stage and a carbon stage. Other wise similar to the Miniworks.

PUR Pioneer, newly introduced low-end microfilter. 0.5 µm, 1 lpm filter rate, 12 gallon capacity

PUR Hiker PUR's microfilter only design, filters to .5 µm. Well liked, as are the other PUR filters. Very compact. 200 gallon capacity

PUR Scout Combines a iodine resin stage, a 1.0 µm filter, and a activated charcoal filter. 200 gallon capacity

PUR Explorer PUR's top of the line model. Bulky, but well made, with a high output (1.4 lpm, faster than any of the hand held models listed and one of the easiest to pump) Has a 1.0 µm filter plus a iodine resin stage, 300 gallon capacity

Sweetwater Walkabout Sweetwater's low end filter, 0.2 µm, .7 lpm, 100 gal capacity

Sweetwater Guardian (Uses a glass fiber and carbon filter, filters to .2 µm, claimed to last for 200 gallons. An iodine resin stage can be added that will kill viruses, and will last for 90 gallons. Pump is well designed, but it takes a few seconds to pull a captive pin to fold for storage. Available in white or OD.

Timberline Eagle At 1 µm, this filter only does protozoa, but is much easier to pump, lighter, and cheaper. Filter is attached to pump, and must rest (but doesn't have to be submerged) in water to be purified. Looks flimsy, but seems to hold up. Claimed to last for 100 gallons.

It is also possible to build your own microfilter using *diatomaceous earth*, sold for swimming pool filters (DE). Usually pressure is required to achieve a reasonable flow rate. A DE filter will remove turbidity as well as pathogens larger than 1 um.

[Alan's note: This type of diatomaceous earth is **NOT** the type you want for food storage. Don't get them confused.

Slow Sand Filter

Slow sand filters pass water slowly through a bed of sand. Pathogens and turbidity are removed by natural die-off, biological action, and filtering. Typically the filter will consist of 24 inches of sand, then a gravel layer in which the drain pipe is embedded. The gravel doesn't touch the walls of the filter so that water can't run quickly down the wall of the filter and into the gravel. Building the walls with a rough surface also helps. A typical loading rate for the filter is 0.2 meters/hour day (the same as .2 m^3/m^2 of surface area). The filter can be cleaned several times before the sand has to be replaced.

Slow sand filter construction information:
Slow sand filters should only be used for continuous water treatment. If a continuous supply of raw water can't be insured (say using a holding tank), then another method should be chosen. It is also important for the water to have as low turbidity (suspended solids) as possible. Turbidity can be reduced by changing the method of collection (for example, building an infiltration gallery, rather than taking water directly from a creek), allowing time for the material to settle out (using a raw water tank), prefiltering or flocculation (adding a chemical such as alum to cause the suspended material to floc together.)

The SSF filter itself is a large box, at least 1.5 meters high. The walls should be as rough as possible to reduce the tendency for water to run down the walls of the filter, bypassing the sand. The bottom layer of the filter is a gravel bed in which a slotted pipe is placed to drain off the filtered water. The slots or the gravel should be no closer than 20 cm to the walls. again to prevent the water from bypassing the sand.

The sand for a SSF needs to be clean and uniform, and of the correct size. The sand can be cleaned in clean running water, even if it is in a creek. The ideal specs on sand are effective size (sieve size through which 10% of the sand passes) between 0.15 and 0.35 mm, uniformity coefficient (ratio of sieve sizes through which 60% pass and through which 10% pass) of less than 3, Maximum size of 3 mm, and minimum size of 0.1 mm.

The sand is added to a SSF to a minimum depth of 0.6 meters. Additional thickness will allow more cleanings before the sand must be replaced. 0.3 to 0.5 meters of extra sand will allow the filter to work for 3-4 years. An improved design uses a *geotextile* layer on top of the sand to reduce the frequency of cleaning. The outlet of a SSF must be above the sand level, and below the water level. The water must be maintained at a constant level to insure an even flow rate throughout the filter. The flow rate can be increased by lowering the outlet pipe, or increasing the water level. One common idea for maintaining the water level is to use a elevated raw water tank or pump, and a ball valve from a toilet.

While the SSF will begin to work at once, optimum treatment for pathogens will take a week or more. During this time the water should be chlorinated if at all possible (iodine can be substituted). After the filter has stabilized, the water should be safe to drink, but chlorinating of the output is still a good idea, particularly to prevent recontamination.

As the flow rate slows down the filter will have to be cleaned by draining and removing the top few inches of sand. If a geotextile filter is used, only the top ½" may have to be removed. As the filter is refilled, it will take a few days for the biological processes to reestablish themselves.

Activated Charcoal Filter

Activated charcoal filters water through adsorption, chemicals and some heavy metals are attracted to the surface of the charcoal, and are attached to it. Charcoal filters will filter some pathogens though they will quickly use up the filter adsorptive ability, and can even contribute to contamination as the charcoal provides an excellent breeding ground for bacteria and algae. Some charcoal filters are available impregnated with silver to prevent this, though current research concludes that the bacteria growing on the filter are harmless, even if the water wasn't disinfected before contacting the filter. The only filter I know of that uses only activated charcoal, and doesn't required pressurized water is the Water Washer ($59). Available from the Survival Center.

Activated charcoal can be used in conjunction with chemical treatment. The chemical (iodine or chlorine) will kill the pathogens, while the carbon filter will remove the treatment chemicals. In this case, as the filter reaches its capacity, a distinctive chlorine or iodine taste will be noted.

Activated charcoal can be made at home, though the product will be of varying quality compared to commercial products. Either purchased or homemade charcoal can be recycled by burning off the molecules adsorbed by the carbon (This won't work with heavy metals of course.)

The more activated charcoal in a filter, the longer it will last. The bed of carbon must be deep enough for adequate contact with the water. Production designs use granulated activated charcoal (effective size or 0.6 to 0.9 mm for maximum flow rate. Home or field models can also use a compressed carbon block or powered activated charcoal (effective size 0.01) to increase contact area. Powered charcoal can also be mixed with water and filtered out later. As far as life of the filter is concerned, carbon block filters will last the longest for a given size, simply due to their greater mass of carbon. A source of pressure is usually needed with carbon block filters to achieve a reasonable flow rate.

Sol-Air Water Treatment

If sufficient dissolved oxygen is available, sunlight will cause the temporary formation of reactive forms of oxygen such as hydrogen peroxide and oxygen free radicals. This form of water treatment is called *solar photooxidative disinfection* or sol-air water treatment. Sol-Air water treatment has been shown to dramatically reduce the level of fecal coliform bacteria. There is some evidence that other bacteria and viruses may be affected also. While not as reliable as other methods, it does offer a low-tech solution in emergencies. Sol-Air treatment requires bright sunlight, and has been shown to be effective when ever the sun causes a distinct shadow to be cast. Exposure to 4.5 hours of bright sunlight has been shown to cause a thousand fold reduction in fecal coliforms in lab tests.

In order for Sol-Air to be effective, oxygen must be present. Experiments have shown that shaking a bottle filled 3/4 with air will restore oxygen levels to near saturation. As the treatment continues, some of the oxygen will come out of solution, while other oxygen will be consumed by the killed pathogens, so the shaking should be repeated every few hours. Data shows that maximum activity occurs when the water temperature is above 50° C (122° F), so this method may be unsuitable in colder climates unless special solar collectors are used.

Either glass or plastic bottles may be used. Plastic bottles will allow short wave ultraviolet radiation to pass, increasing the rate of microbial inactivation, but may yellow with age, reducing light transmission, and may leach plasticizers into the water at the elevated temperatures that will occur. The leaching of plasticizers can be reduced by using bottles of PET (polyethlyene terephtalate) rather than PVC. Glass bottles on the other hand are more durable. Research has used bottles with 2 liters of capacity, but if the water is free of turbidity, larger containers can be used. Plastic bags, or some sort of flat glass container represent the ideal container as this maximizes the solar energy received per ounce of water.

Bottles should be filed 3/4 full in the early morning with water as free of turbidity as possible. After capping the bottles should be shaken vigorously for a few minutes then placed upright in the sun, where they will be not be shaded later in the day. The shaking should be repeated at least three times during the day. At the end of the day the water should be reasonably freed of bacteria, though it is most practical to let the water cool for consumption the following day. Each day a new batch should be treated due to the lack of a residual disinfected.

After consumption of the water the bottle should be air dried to prevent algae growth with continual use.

Improvised Mechanical Filter

If the materials aren't available to build a slow sand filter, or some other means of water treatment is preferred, it may still be advantageous to mechanically filter the water before treating it with chemicals or passing through a microfilter. Generally the idea is to allow the water to flow as slowly as possible through a bed of sand. In a municipal water treatment plant this is called a rapid sand filter. The particular design below is included, because the designer, a research engineer at Oak Ridge National Laboratories, found it particularly effective at removing fallout from water. The filter will do little or nothing to remove pathogens, though removing suspended solids allow others water treatment methods to work more effectively.

Expedient water filter, from *Nuclear War Survival Skills*, Cresson Kearny, ORNL

1) Perforate the bottom of a 5 gallon bucket, or similar container with a dozen nail holes even spread over a 4" diameter circle in the center of the container.

2) Place a 1.5" layer of small stones or pebbles in the bottom of the can. If pebbles aren't available, marbles, clean bottle caps, twisted coat hangers or clean twigs can be used.

3) Cover the pebbles with one thickness of terrycloth towel, burlap sackcloth, or other porous cloth. Curl the cloth in a roughly circular shape about three inches larger then the diameter of the can.

4) Take soil containing some clay (pure clay isn't porous enough, pure sand is too porous) from at least 4" below the surface of the ground (nearly all fallout particles remain near the surface except after disposition on sand or gravel.)

5) Pulverize the soil, then gently press it in layers over the cloth that covers the pebbles, so that the cloth is held snugly against the walls of the can. The soil should be 6-7" thick.

6) Completely cover the surface of the soil layer with one thickness of fabric as porous as a bath towel. This is to keep the soil from being eroded as water is being poured into the filter. A dozen small stones placed on the cloth near it's edges will secure it adequately.

7) Support the filter on rocks or sticks placed across the top of a container that is larger then the filter can (such as a dishpan)

The contaminated water should be poured into the filter can, preferably after allowing it to settle as described below. The filtered water should be disinfected by some method.

If the 6 or 7 inches of filtering soil is a sandy clay loam, the filter will initially deliver about 6 quarts/hour. If the filter is any faster than this then the fabric layer needs to be removed and the soil compressed more. The filtering rate will drop over time as the filter begins to clog up. When this happens the top 1/2" of soil can be removed to increase the filtering rate. After 50 or so quarts, the filter will need to be rebuilt with fresh soil.

As with any filter, optimum performance will be achieved if sediment in the water will be allowed to settle out before passing the water through the filter

If the water is contaminated with fallout, clay can be added to help the fallout particles to settle out. The procedure is as follows:

Fill a bucket or other deep container 3/4 full with contaminated water.

Dig pulverized clay or clayey soil from a depth of four or more inches below ground surface and stir it into the water.

Use about 1 inch of dry clay or clayey soil for every 4" depth of water. Stir until practically all of the clay particles are suspended in the water.

Let the clay settle for at least 6 hours. This will carry the fallout particles to the bottom and cover them. Carefully dip out or siphon the clear water and disinfect it.

Chemical Treatment

Chlorine: Chlorine is familiar to most Americans as it is used to treat virtually all municipal water systems in the United States. For a long time chlorine, in the form of Halazone tablets, was used to purify small batches of water for campers and military troops. Later questions emerged about the effectiveness of Halazone, and in 1989, Abbot labs pulled it off the market. If Halazone tablets are encountered outside the US, the nominal shelf life is 6 months, and the dosage is 2 tabs per liter. Until recently, there was no chlorine product designed for wilderness/survival use available in the US.

Chlorine has a number of problems when used for field treatment of water. When chlorine reacts with organic material, it attaches itself to nitrogen containing compounds (ammonium ions and amino acids), leaving less free chlorine to continue disinfection. Carcinogenic trihalomethanes are also produced, though this is only a problem with long-term exposure. Trihalomethanes can also be filtered out with a charcoal filter, though it is more efficient to use the same filter to remove organics before the water is chlorinated. ***Unless free chlorine is measured, disinfection can not be guaranteed with moderate doses of chlorine.*** One solution is superchlorination, the addition of far more chlorine than is needed. This must again be filtered through activated charcoal to remove the large amounts of chlorine, or hydrogen peroxide can be added to drive the chlorine off. Either way there is no residual chlorine left to prevent recontamination. This isn't a problem if the water is to be used at once.

Chlorine is sensitive to both the pH and temperature of the treated water. Temperature slows the reaction for any chemical treatment, but chlorine treatment is particularly susceptible to variations in the pH as at lower pHs, hypochlorous acid is formed, while at higher pHs, it will tend to dissociate into hydrogen and chlorite ions, which are less effective as a disinfectant. As a result, chlorine effectiveness drops off when the pH is greater than 8.

Chlorine, like iodine, will not kill Cryptosporidia.

Methods of chlorine treatment:

<u>Bleach</u>: Ordinary household bleach (such as Clorox) in the US contains 5.25% sodium hypochlorite ($NaOCL$) and can be used to purify water if it contains no other active ingredients, scents, or colorings. Bleach is far from an ideal source due to its bulkiness (only 5% active ingredient), and the instability over time of the chlorine content in bleach. Chlorine loss is farther increased by agitation or exposure to air. One source claims chlorine loss from a 5% solution at 10% over 6 months if stored at 70° F. Nevertheless, this may be the only chemical means available to purify water, and it is far better than nothing. Normal dosage is 8 drops (0.4 ml) per gallon. Allow the treated water to sit for 30 min., and if there isn't a slight chlorine smell, retreat. ***Note:*** USP standard medicine droppers are designed to dispense 0.045-0.055 ml per drop. Use of other solvents or some chemicals can change this. The dropper can be calibrated against a graduated cylinder for greater accuracy.

Some small treatment plants in Africa produce their own sodium hypochlorite on site from the electrolysis of brine. Power demands range from 1.7 to 4 kWh per lb. of NaOCL. 2 to 3.5 lbs. of salt are needed for each pound of NaOCL. These units are fairly simple and are made in both the US and the UK. Another system, designed for China, where the suitable raw materials were mined or manufactured locally, used a reaction between salt, manganese dioxide, and sulfuric acid to produce chlorine gas. The gas was then allowed to react with slaked lime to produce a bleaching powder that could then be used to treat water. A heat source is required to speed the reaction up.

AquaCure

AquaCure: Designed for the South African military, these tablets contain chlorine and alum. The alum causes the suspended solids to flocculate and the chlorine adds 8 PPM chlorine. This is a great way to treat turbid water, though it will leave a lot of chlorine in clear water (The one tablet/liter could be halved for clear water.)

The US distributor for Aqua Cure is:

Safesport Manufacturing, Box 11811, Denver, CO 80211 1 800 433 6506

Bleaching Powder

Bleaching Powder (Chlorinated Lime): Can also be purchased and used as a purification means if nothing else is available. Bleaching powder is 33-37% chlorine when produced, but losses its chlorine rapidly, particularly when exposed to air, light or moisture.

Calcium Hypochlorite:

Calcium Hypochlorite: Also known as High Test Hypochlorite (HTH). Supplied in crystal form, it is nearly 70% available chlorine. One product, the Sanitizer (formally the Sierra Water Purifier) uses these crystals to superchlorinate the water to insure pathogens were killed off, then hydrogen peroxide is added to drive off the residual chlorine. This is the most effective method of field chlorine treatment. The US military and most aid agencies also use HTH to treat their water, though a test kit, rather than superchlorination, is used to insure enough chlorine is added. This is preferable for large-scale systems as the residual chlorine will prevent recontamination.

Usually bulk water treatment plants first dilute to HTH to make a 1% working solution at the rate of 14g HTH per liter of water. *While testing to determine exact chlorine needs are preferable, the solution can be used at the dose rate of 8 drops/gallon, or for larger quantities, 1 part of 1% solution to 10,000 parts clear water.* Either of these doses will result in 1 PPM chlorine and may need to be increased if the water wasn't already filtered by other means.

When test kits are available, the WHO standard is a residual chlorine level of 0.2 to 0.5 mg/l after a 30 min. contact time.

The may require as much as 5 mg/l of chlorine to be added to the raw water.

Iodine:

Iodine: Iodine's use as a water purification method emerged after WW2, when the US military was looking for a replacement for Halazone tablets. *Iodine was found to be in many ways superior to chlorine for use in treating small batches of water.* Iodine is less sensitive to the pH and organic content of water, and is effective in lower doses. Some individuals are allergic to iodine, and there is some question about long term use of iodine. The safety of long-term exposure to low levels of iodine was proven when inmates of three Florida prisons were given water disinfected with 0.5 to 1.0 PPM iodine for 15 years. No effects on the health or thyroid function of previously healthy inmates was observed. Of 101 infants born to prisoners drinking the water for 122- 270 days, none showed detectable thyroid enlargement. However 4 individuals with preexisting cases of hyperthyroidism became more symptomatic while consuming the water.

Nevertheless experts are reluctant to recommend iodine for long term use. Average American iodine intake is estimated at 0.24 to 0.74 mg/day, higher than the RDA of 0.4 mg/day. Due to a recent National Academy of Science recommendation that iodine consumption be reduced to the RDA, the EPA discourages the use of iodized salt in areas where iodine is used to treat drinking water.

Iodine is normally used in doses of 8 PPM to treat clear water for a 10 minute contact time. The effectiveness of this dose has been shown in numerous studies. *Cloudy water needs twice as much iodine or twice as much contact time.* In cold water (Below 41° F or 5° C) the dose or time must also be doubled. In any case doubling the treatment time will allow the use of half as much iodine

These doses are calculated to remove all pathogens (other than cryptosporida) from the water. Of these, giardia cysts are the hardest to kill, and are what requires the high level of iodine. If the cysts are filtered out with a microfilter (any model will do since the cysts are 6 μm), only 0.5 PPM is needed to treat the resulting water.

Water treated with iodine can have any objectionable taste removed by treating the water with vitamin C (ascorbic acid), *but it must be added after the water has stood for the correct treatment time.* Flavored beverages containing vitamin C will accomplish the same thing. Sodium thiosulfate can also be used to combine with free iodine, and either of these chemicals will also help remove the taste of chlorine as well. Usually elemental iodine can't be tasted below 1 PPM, and below 2 PPM the taste isn't objectionable. Iodine ions have an even higher taste threshold of 5 PPM. Note that removing the iodine taste does not reduce the dose of iodine ingested by the body.

Sources of Iodine:

Tincture of Iodine: USP tincture of iodine contains 2% iodine and 2.4% sodium iodide dissolved in 50% ethyl alcohol. For water purification use, the sodium iodide has no purification effect, but contributes to the total iodine dose. Thus it is not a preferred source of iodine, but can be used if other sources are not available. 0.4 cc's (or 8 drops) of USP tincture (2% iodine) added to a liter of water will give the 8 mg/l (same as 8 PPM). If the iodine tincture isn't compounded to USP specs, then you will have to calculate an equal dose based on the iodine concentration.

Lugol's solution: Contains 5% iodine and 10% potassium iodide. 0.15 cc (3 drops) can be added per liter of water, but 3 times more iodine is consumed compared to sources without iodide.

Betadyne (povidone iodine): Some have recommended 8 drops of 10% povidone iodine per liter of water as a water treatment method, claiming that at low concentrations povidone iodine can be regarded as a solution of iodine. One study indicated that at 1:10,000 dilution (2 drops/liter), there was 2 PPM iodine, while another study resulted in conflicting results. However, at 8 drops/liter, there is little doubt that there is an antimicrobial effect. The manufacturer hasn't spent the money on testing this product against EPA standard tests, but in other countries it has been sold for use in field water treatment.

Kahn-Vassher solution: By adding a sufficient amount of iodine crystals to a small bottle, an almost unlimited supply of saturated iodine solution can be produced. As long as crystals remain in the bottle, the solution is saturated. Concentration of the iodine is dependent of temperature, either condition at ambient temperature can be assumed, or commercial models such as Polar Pure incorporate a liquid crystal thermometer to determine dose.

One criticism of this method is the chance of decanting iodine crystals into the water being treated. This isn't that much of a problem as iodine is very weakly toxic, but the Polar Pure incorporates a collar into the neck of the bottle to help prevent this. Another disadvantage to this method is that the saturated iodine solution must be kept in glass bottles, and is subject to freezing, but this is hardly an insurmountable problem. Freezing, of course, doesn't affect the crystals.

This is the method I use, but I do use the commercial Polar Pure bottle, and refill it as necessary with USP crystals. During a crisis, or extended camping trips I would microfilter the water first, so a much lower dose of iodine is needed.

With the Polar Pure bottle, dosage information is provided. Otherwise a 1 oz bottle can be used to carry the solution. The bottle is filled with water after use. At the next use, 1/2 of the supernate (15 cc) is poured off into a liter of water. At 68° F, this will yield a dose of 9 mg/l. To use this method with a microfilter to get a 0.5 PPM concentration, either large batches of water need to be treated (1/2 oz to 4.5 gallons would be 0.5 PPM), or a TB syringe or medicine dropper can be used to measure doses. A USP medicine dropper should give 20 drops per ml.

Iodine can also be dissolved in alcohol to make a solution of known concentration. I am not aware of any commercial products, but a pharmacy could compound one for you, or you could do it your self. One suggested formula is 8g iodine/100 cc ethyl alcohol which yields enough solution to disinfect 250 gallons of water. At the rate of 0.1 cc (2 drops)/liter to give a concentration of 8 mg/l.

Tetraglycine hydroperiodide (e.g. Potable Aqua): This is the form of iodine used by the US military for field treatment of water in canteen sized batches. Usual dose in one tablet per quart of water to give a concentration of 8 mg/l. Two tablets are used in cloudy or cold water or contact time is doubled. *The major downside of this product is that the product will loose its iodine rapidly when exposed to the air.* According to the manufacturer, they have a near indefinite life when sealed in the original bottle, but probably should be discarded within a few months of opening. The tablets will change color from gun metal gray to brown as they lose the iodine, and you should see a brown tint to the water after treating.

Iodine Resin Filter: Some commercial microfilters incorporate an iodine resin stage to kill viruses and bacteria, with out putting as much iodine in the water as if it had been added to the raw water. A few products rely exclusively on an iodine resin stage. Downside of these filters are their fragile nature, dependency of effectiveness on flow rate and the inability to identify when they need to be discarded. If you are going to use one where the water is known to be contaminated with viruses, then one of the better known brands such as the PUR or Sweetwater Viraguard is recommended. More than one pass through the filter may be necessary in cold weather.

Resins do have the advantage of producing less iodine in the water for the same antimicrobial effect as for the most part, they only release iodine when contacted by a microbe. The downside is that physical contact between the microbe and the resin is needed.

Silver: Silver has been suggested by some for water treatment and may still be available outside the US. Its use is currently out of favor due to the EPA's establishment of a 50 ppb MCL (Maximum Contaminate Level) limit on silver in drinking water. This limit is set to avoid *argyrosis*, a cosmetic blue/gray staining of the skin, eyes, and mucous membranes. As the disease requires a net accumulation of 1 g of silver in the body, one expert calculated that you could drink water treated at 50 ppb for 27 years before accumulating 1 g. Silver has only be proven to be effective against bacteria and protozoan cysts, though it is quite likely also effective against viruses.

Silver can be used in the form of a silver salt, commonly silver nitrate, a colloidal suspension, or a bed of metallic silver. Electrolysis can also be used to add metallic silver to a solution.

Some evidence has suggested that silver deposited on carbon block filters can kill pathogens without adding as much silver to the water.

Katadyn markets a silver based water treatment product called Micropur. The manufacturer recommends a 2 hr contact time at a dose of 1 tab per liter and states the product is "For the disinfection and storage of clear water. Reliably kills bacterial agents of enteric diseases, but not worm eggs, ameba, or viruses. Neutral to taste... insure protection against reinfection for 1-6 months."; The following forms are available:

Micropur Tablets

MT1 1 tablets/qt 25 gal MT2 1 tablet/5qts 62.5 gal

Micropur Fluid

MF 75 10 drops/gal 75 gals MF250 10 drops/gal 250 gals

Micropur Crystal

MC250 1 packet/gal 250 gal MC 2500 1 spoon/25 gal 2500 gal MC12500 1 spoon/250 gal 12500 gal

Potassium Permanganate: Potassium Permanganate is no longer commonly used in the developed world to kill pathogens. It is much weaker than the alternatives, more expensive, and leaves a objectionable pink or brown color. If it must be used, 1 gram per liter would probably be

sufficient against bacteria and viruses (no data is available on it effectiveness against protozoan cysts.

Hydrogen Peroxide: Hydrogen Peroxide can be used to purify water if nothing else is available. Studies have shown of 99 percent inactivation of poliovirus in 6 hr with 0.3 percent hydrogen peroxide and a 99% inactivation of rhinovirus with a 1.5% solution in 24 minutes. Hydrogen Peroxide is more effective against bacteria, though Fe^{+2} or Cu^{+2} needs to be present as a catalyst to get a reasonable concentration-time product.

Coagulation/Flocculation agents: While flocculation doesn't kill pathogens, it will reduce their levels along with removing particles that could shield the pathogens from chemical or thermal destruction, and organic matter that could tie up chlorine added for purification. 60-98% of coliform bacteria, 65-99% of viruses, and 60-90% of giardia will be removed from the water, along with organic matter and heavy metals.

Some of the advantages of coagulation/flocculation can be obtained by allowing the particles to settle out of the water with time (sedimentation), but it will take a while for them to do so. Adding coagulation chemicals such as alum will increase the rate at which the suspended particles settle out by combining many smaller particles into larger floc which will settle out faster. The usual dose for alum is 10-30 mg/liter of water. This dose must be rapidly mixed with the water, then the water must be agitated for 5 minutes to encourage the particles to form flocs. After this at least 30 minutes of settling time is need for the flocs to fall to the bottom, and them the clear water above the flocs may be poured off. Most of the flocculation agent is removed with the floc, nevertheless some question the safety of using alum due to the toxicity of the aluminum in it. There is little to no scientific evidence to back this up. Virtually all municipal plants in the US dose the water with alum.

In bulk water treatment, the alum dose can be varied until the idea dose is found. The needed dose varies with the pH of the water and the size of the particles. Increase turbidity makes the flocs easier to produce not harder, due to the increased number of collisions between particles.

Treatments requiring electricity:

Ozone: Ozone is used extensively in Europe to purify water. Ozone, a molecule composed of 3 atoms of oxygen rather than two, is formed by exposing air or oxygen to a high voltage electric arc. Ozone is much more effective as a disinfectant than chlorine, but no residual levels of disinfectant exist after ozone turns back into O2. (one source quotes a half life of only 120 minutes in distilled water at 20° C). Ozone is expected to see increased use in the US as a way to avoid the production of trihalomethanes. While ozone does break down organic molecules, sometimes this can be a disadvantage as ozone treatment can produce higher levels of smaller molecules that provide an energy source for microorganisms. If no residual disinfectant is present (as would happen if ozone were used as the only treatment method), these microorganisms will cause the water quality to deteriorate in storage.

Ozone also changes the surface charges of dissolved organics and colloidially suspended particles. This causes microflocculation of the dissolved organics and coagulation of the colloidal particles.

<u>UV light:</u> Ultraviolet light has been known to kill pathogens for a long time. A low pressure mercury bulb emits between 30 to 90 % of its energy at a wave length of 253.7 nm, right in the middle of the UV band. If water is exposed to enough light, pathogens will be killed. The problem is that some pathogens are hundreds of times less sensitive to UV light than others. The least sensitive pathogens to UV are protozoan cysts. Several studies show that Giardia will not be destroyed by many commercial UV treatment units. Fortunately these are the easiest pathogens to filter out with a mechanical filter.

The efficacy of UV treatment is very dependent on the turbidity of the water. The more opaque the water is, the less light that will be transmitted through it. The treatment units must be run at the designed flow rate to insure sufficient exposure, as well as insure turbulent flow rather than plug flow.

Another problem with UV treatment is that the damage done to the pathogens with UV light can be reversed if the water is exposed to visible light (specifically 330-500 nm) through a process known as photoreactivation.

UV treatment, like ozone or mechanical filtering leaves no residual component in the water to insure its continued disinfection. Any purchased UV filter should be checked to insure it at least complies with the 1966 HEW standard of 16 mW.s/cm^2 with a maximum water depth of 7.5 cm. ANSI/NSF require 38 mWs/cm^2 for primary water treatment systems. This level was chosen to give better than 3 log (99.9%) inactivation of Bacillus subtillis. This level is of little use against Giardia, and of no use against Crypto.

The US EPA explored UV light for small scale water treatment plants and found it compared unfavorably with chlorine due to 1) higher costs, 2) lower reliability, and 3) lack of a residual disinfectant.

Brigham Young (1801–77) Second President of the Church

"If you are without bread, how much wisdom can you boast and of what real utility are your talents, if you cannot procure for yourselves and save against a day of scarcity those substances designed to sustain your natural lives?" (*Deseret News,* July 18, 1860, 153).

"If we could only learn to be self-preserving and self-sustaining, we should then have learned what the Gods have learned before ue, and what we must eventually learn before we can be exalted." JD 9:169

"The time will come that **gold will hold no comparison in value to a bushel of wheat.**" (President Brigham Young, Discourses of Brigham Young, p.298.)

". . .save the wheat until we have one, two, five, or seven years provisions on hand, until there is enough of the staff of life saved by the people to bread themselves and those who will come here seeking for safety." (Discourses of Brigham Young, pp.291-293)

Three Weeks without Food

During the seven plentiful years the earth produced abundantly, and he gathered up all the food of these seven years, which occurred in the land of Egypt, and put the food in the cities. He put in every city the food from the fields around it. And Joseph stored up grain in great abundance, like the sand of the sea, until he ceased to measure it, for it could not be measured.
Genesis 41:47-49

In the house of the wise are stores of choice food and oil, but a foolish man devours all he has.
Proverbs 21:20

Store or Starve
A beginner's guide to food storage

Go to the ant, thou sluggard; consider her ways, and be wise.
~ Proverbs 6:6

I want people to store food not only for their sake, but for mine as well. I don't want to decide which of my kids have to go hungry when you and your unprepared kin come knocking on my door. Contrary to progressive-collectivist thinking, every individual who takes care of themselves and their families benefits society by not becoming a burden. So take responsibility now and start today. Don't expect the Feds to come by to hand you your ration of government-issued cheese. You could be in for a long wait. Wait too long, and you may end up with a green-stained mouth from eating grass, like the poor Irish during the potato famine in the mid 1800's. Or seriously reevaluate your aversion to cannibalism. Compared to those desperate methods, dumpster diving comes off as luxury cuisine.

An adult needs a minimum 2500 calories a day. More if you are physically active. This translates to about two pounds of food, plus a gallon of potable ("drinkable") water. To get started, follow this cardinal rule; Store what you eat, and eat what you store. Do not expect to suddenly acquire a taste for powered eggs or a jalapeno-spiced chili MRE in a long-term disaster. If you have children, they will be even more reluctant to eat such stuff. The next rule is not go into debt by spending thousands of dollars for pre-packaged foodstuffs. It kinda defeats the purpose if you have to eat your food supply because you have no money left after buying it.

Begin building your food storage by buying 2–3 extra items every time you shop at the grocery store. A few cans here, some bags and boxes there, and it will begin to add up. Look for sales, two-for-one specials, and coupon items. Set aside some space, and put the oldest stuff in front, and the newest in back. Rotate from back to front as you use it. If you have food items that are going to expire soon that you don't have time to eat, donate them to a local food pantry for Karma points. There. You now have established a simple but effective short term food storage system. Everything from here on will expand upon it.

The next step is to create a larger, stable environment to preserve your food supply over the long haul. Regardless if you live in a country mansion or a studio apartment, you need the following conditions to preserve food:

Keep it airtight
Keep it cool
Keep it dark
Keep it dry
Keep it protected

Now back to the oxygen problem. As long as the can does not have a tell-tale bulge, signaling spoiled contents, canned goods are viable for many years past their expiration dates, notwithstanding a loss in nutritional value. Dry food packed in paper, cardboard boxes, or plastic are subject to oxygen spoilage over time. One solution is to repackage dry food items using food grade Mylar bags. These bags are an inexpensive method for those on a budget to customize their food storage to their personal needs and taste. Mylar is an excellent air and moisture barrier. It is said one can jump on a filled sealed bag and it won't pop. But they need protection against punctures and gnawing vermin—hence they need to be stored in a protective container, like those mentioned above. The recommended base foods for long-term storage are wheat, oats, legumes, pasta, honey/sugar, and salt. These will easily last 20-30 years if packed and stored properly. Flour and dry milk are more finicky, and have a shelf life of only 5–10 years. If you or members of your family suffer from Celiac disease, and cannot consume gluten type foods such as wheat, substitute white rice instead. I do not recommend brown rice for long-term storage, as it contains oils that break down over time that causes it to spoil. Supplement your long term food with canned goods, MRE's and others sundries. The eventual goal is to build a diverse storage of food for health, variety, and if necessary, portability.

Items needed for packaging food:

Food grade Mylar bags. I recommend minimum 4.5mil thick bags in one-gallon size. These will hold about 4–6 lbs, depending on the bulk of the food products. Besides commercial vendors, the Church of Jesus Christ of Latter Day Saints also sells them online, along with other preparedness supplies. Their bags are 7mil thick. However, they only sell them in bulk, so 250 bags for $94 is probably more bags than you need. The church also has food canneries throughout the US that sells these in smaller quality. One can purchase pre-packaged food or bring their own food to seal at cost at these centers.

500cc Oxygen absorber packets. It takes two of these for each one gallon, 11" x 13" or similar sized Mylar bags full of food. These packets come in a sealed bag with all the oxygen sucked out. If the bag is not flat, but puffy with air, the oxygen packets have been compromised. You will need a glass jar with a metal (not plastic) lid to store them after you open the bag. Or you can seal them in a Mylar bag. Ordinary plastic bags are no good for storing oxygen packets – they provide a poor air barrier. Oxygen packets will start to feel warm when activated by exposure to air. Take them out only when you have everything else all set to bag and seal. Make sure to close the lid to preserve the others.

5-gram silica gel desiccant. These absorb any residue moisture that may reside in your food, to prevent mold. I've talked to the people at our local LDS cannery, and they and others who have stored food for years have experienced no problems not using desiccant packets. Everything I've read online suggest you should put them in. Your call. I purchase mine on eBay for around 25 cents each.

Sealer. This is a very expensive piece of equipment. I like to use the one at our local church. Contact the local Bishop or a Mormon friend to arrange a time to use one. It comes with a foot pedal, making it easier to seal bags. An alternative is using a hot iron set on wool or cotton (Not the wife's!) with a 2 x 4 piece of wood. Some find they can use conventional food sealers. But do your homework well, as it is for good reason that Mylar bags require industrial strength sealers compared to off-the-shelf food sealers.

Directions for sealing bags:

1. If using the LDS Church sealer, check that the settings are at Sealing: 3, Congealing: 6, Recycle: 2. Turn on the sealer and let it warm up for two minutes.

2. (Optional) Place two 5-gram silica gel packets at the bottom of the Mylar bag.

3. Pour flour, rice, grain, etc. in bag. This can be done single-handedly, but from experience, it is so much easier to have someone help holding the Mylar bag, as it is very slick and does not have a flat bottom to keep it upright. Flour and dry milk can be a pain because it "poufs" everywhere when pored in the bag. When it does, use a damp paper towel to clean up the inside of the top of the bags where it will be sealed together. Then apply a dry towel to remove any moisture. At this point, firmly bang the bag several times against the table to help settle the contents and reduce airspace between the food elements.

4. Place two 500cc oxygen packets on top of food. Be sure to keep the unused oxy packets sealed in an airtight container, so they will stay fresh.

5. Hold and pull tight both ends of the open bag, place in the sealer. Let the filled part of the bag drop down, to prevent food from coming up to opening and preventing a perfect seal. Hit the foot pedal. The seal bar will come down for 2–3 seconds to set the seal. I like to add a second seal to each bag for good measure. Check the seal by attempting to peel the opening apart. If the seal is secure, you won't be able too. Also push on the bag and watch if any air leaks out. None should. For using an iron, place the Mylar bag opening
on the 2 x 4, and press down. Some prefer to put a towel between the iron and the Mylar, but I've never scorched a bag yet.

6. Use a permanent marker to write the on bag the date, the weight, and the description on the bagged food. I like to include the brand name of the food, in case I have any problems with it, or is recalled by the FDA. For some things like powdered milk, I tape the mixing instructions on the bag.

Mylar bags may be cut in half or smaller to store smaller portions. Filled Mylar bags are very stiff and rigid. The bagged food will be a bit awkward to store in round containers like buckets and trashcans. Stack fragile food like pasta on top of the heavier, bulkier bagged foods. Large Mylar bags from vendors are available to store quantities up to 30 lbs in 5-gallon plastic buckets. Put one in, and fill up with the dry food product of your choice. Some recommend using dry ice on top of the food before sealing to displace oxygen in the bucket. I could not find any dry ice in my area, so put ten oxygen packets on top instead. Seal with a hot iron by pressing the Mylar against a 2 x 4 piece. Trim any excess from the sealed top edge of the bag with scissors to secure the Mylar bag into the bucket.

This YouTube video: http://www.youtube.com/watch?v=fk9b0dAtJ80

gives excellent demonstration. Cover with a lid. I prefer Gamma screw-top lids on my buckets. They cost from $7–10 each, but are so much easier than popping and hammering lids off and on every time.

Other food storage methods include canning, both traditional glass jars and #10 metal cans. The latter can be done at a local LDS cannery center. Dehydrating food is another valuable storage method.

A few more suggestions with building your food storage. Include fun foods to help break the monotony and uplift morale, such as hard candy, chocolate, powdered drinks, and dried fruit.

Pick up some recipes on cooking the food you store, to add variety to your diet. When possible, supplement your food storage meals with garden vegetables, home grown sprouts, or ordinary dandelion leaves. Be careful of depending on a diet of MRE's. While they are portable and convenient for traveling, they are short on fiber, and can be hard on the digestive system, especially with children and the elderly. They also negatively affect those who are gluten intolerant. On storing water, bottled water is okay if you are going to bug out, but for hunkering down, you need to think much bigger. For the cost of two cartons of bottled water, you can purchase a five-gallon water container. These are more practical if you need to go out and get your water replenished. Add half teaspoon of bleach per five gallons to keep it safe. Be sure to use only regular bleach, and not those with special or extra additives. If in doubt, boil it.

Whether a global disaster strikes or one becomes unemployed, food storage is the best insurance one can have in uncertain times. You will garner a better dividend on your food storage than any other investment. There's more to improve upon than mentioned here, such as progressing to the next level from food storage to food production. But you have enough info to get started. So no more excuses. Get working on your food storage today. And don't forget THE CAN OPENER.

By Ron Shirtz

Surviving in the City

Introduction
While we all want to do our best to prepare for a coming crisis, and many Saints realize the city is perhaps the worst place to live, very few of us are really prepared to pack up the old Winnebago and head for the hills. Most American Saints, whether they're aware or not, are going to stay in the cities.

This is not a hasty decision for most Saints. Most of us depend on the city for our livelihood, and we can be better prepared by continuing to live in the city, earn a good income, and make preparations for exiting the city at the appropriate time – or by staying in the city and living off existing supplies.

This special report explains some of the most critical dangers of living in a city and presents some solutions to surviving them. If you are one of the Saints who has decided to stay in the city, you'll benefit greatly from this information.

Cities are artificial
Every city is an artificial construct. Cities formed as people came together to conduct business, participate in social interaction, and benefit from efficiencies in public services (such as schools, sewers, water, etc.) and a common defense. Yet cities cannot survive alone. They need resources from the country; most notably, food, water and electricity. While electricity and water can sometimes be created or found within city limits, the acreage requirements of food dictate that no city could possibly feed its own people.

Read that last phrase carefully: "No city can feed its own people." Not one. Cities are, by their very nature, dependent on the importation of food. The advent of just-in-time delivery systems to our grocery stores means that most cities would run out of food within a week if supplies were for some reason disrupted.

Remember, cities are not self-sufficient. Although they may seem to be in 2005, they have for a long time been entirely dependent on the American farmer for their support – something almost all Americans take for granted (except the farmer, of course…)

Risks in the City
The city presents some serious risks during a crisis. The four most serious ones are 1. the collapse of social order (riots), 2. the failure of the water treatment and delivery systems, 3. the depletion of food supplies 4. the failure of the power grid and 5. you may be quarantined. While not every situation will appear in every city, every situation will most certainly appear in some cities. Will that include yours?
We'll tackle these one at a time:

1. The Collapse of Social Order

"Social order" is a delicate thing, and it exists as a psychological barrier that could easily collapse under the right conditions. We all saw this during the L.A. Riots following the Rodney King trial verdict as citizens of L.A. set fire to their own town, yanked people from vehicles and beat them literally to death, and even fired guns at firemen attempting to save their buildings! More recently we were all witness to the looting, violence and total breakdown of society following Hurricane Katrina in New Orleans.

What allowed this to happen? Simple: the simultaneous melting away of the psychological barrier of "order." Once people realized 911 couldn't handle the load, or was offline, that the local police were helpless or had simply abondoned their posts, "Law and Order" ceased to exist in their minds. They then conducted their lives in the way they always <u>wanted</u> to, but couldn't because of the police. That is, they ran out to the local stores and just took whatever they wanted (looting). They took our their racial frustration on innocent victims who happened to be driving through the area, and they let loose on a path of destruction that only stopped when men with rifles (the National Guard) were called in to settle things down. In other words, *only the threat of immediate death stopped the looting and violence.* Rifles work wonders.

Imagine store owners lying prone on the roofs of their stores with AK-47's, firing at anyone who approached. This is exactly what happened in Los Angeles. But worse, imagine the lawless horde firing at the rescue copters trying to bring in supplies to the desperate masses in New Orleans.

The National Guard eventually got things under control. This event was isolated, however, to one city. Imagine a hundred cities experiencing the same thing. Will the National Guard be able to handle the load? Not likely. What about local police? They aren't fools; if things look bad enough, they'll grab their families and head for the hills, just like they did in New Orleans. *No pension is worth getting killed for.* A few U.S. cities could be transformed into literal warzones overnight. It would require all-out martial law and military force to have any chance whatsoever of bringing order to these streets. And the reality is that there are not enough military in the USA to secure all of the cities if this happens.

This collapse of social order is perhaps the greatest risk of staying in the city during a crisis. What, exactly, would cause this collapse of social order? *Lack of three things: food, water, and money.* When people run out of food, some will begin ransacking their neighborhood, searching for something to eat. (Remember that in a city, a "neighbor" does not mean the same thing as a "neighbor" in the country. They are not necessarily your friends.) It won't take long, then, for vio-

lence to take over in some cities. While certain regions will certainly manage to keep things under control and people will form lines at the local (depleted) Red Cross shelter, other cities will see an explosion of violence. Imagine the gang-infested regions of L.A., Chicago, New York, St. Louis & New Orleans. Do you think those people are going to stand in line and wait? They already have guns; now they finally get to use them. Pent-up racial tensions & hostilities will simply serve as justification for shooting people of the same or other color in order to get their food.

Even if the food somehow gets into the cities, lack of money (due to the government not sending out checks) could cause the same thing. Eventually, lack of money results in looting and mass theft. As the stealing balloons, it also results in a collapse of social order. Water; the same thing (but faster). The collapse of social order is also very dangerous because it doesn't require any "actual" collapse of the power grid, telecommunications, transportation or banking. Social order is a psychological artifact. It is a frame of mind, and any global panic can quickly remove the mental barrier that right now keeps people basically "lawful."

2. The Failure of Water Treatment and Delivery Systems

Will the water treatment facilities fail during a crisis? Many will. Some won't. The problem lies in figuring out whether <u>yours</u> will. Certainly, they depend on electricity, and if the power goes down, so will the water.

The most important question here, though, is about what will happen when the water stops flowing (or if it is flowing, but it's not drinkable). As you are probably aware, while people can live without food for long periods of time (2-3 weeks), water is needed on a daily basis. You can go 2-3 days without it, at most, but beyond that, you'll quickly turn to dust.

That means people will do <u>anything</u> to get water, because to not have it means death. And guess where it's going to be the most difficult to actually get water? You guessed it: in the cities. During the first day of the water crisis, many people still won't figure out what's going on. They'll figure it's a temporary breakage of a water main and the government will get it fixed within hours. As those hours stretch into the next day, these people will get very worried.

By the second day, more and more people will realize the water isn't coming. At that point, you could easily see a breakdown of social order, as described in the previous section (as you can see, these things all tend to cause each other...). People will begin their "search for water," and the first place they're likely to go is where they always go for liquids: the grocery store, the local Walmart, the 7-11. The shelves will be cleaned out rather quickly.

Beyond that (because those liquids aren't going to last long), you're going to see people engaged in a mass-exodus from the cities. They'll take the gas they have left in their tanks and they'll leave the city in search of water. Some will go to "Grandma's house" out in the country where they might at least find a pond or stream to drink from. Others will simply go on an expanded looting mission, stopping at any house they see and asking the residents (with a gun in their face, likely) if they have any water to "donate."

As a result of all this, if water stops flowing, here are the events you can expect to see in some of the worse-off cities:

- Looting of all the grocery stores by the second or third day (remember New Orleans?)
- Minor outbreaks of violence during the looting. Shop owners, for example, may attempt to defend their shops with firearms (ala L.A. Riots)
- Mass exodus of residents from the city in search of water
- Ransacking of any houses or farms within a gas-tank radius of the city, presumably by desperate people with guns
- Mass traffic jams on the outbound highways as people run out of gas and abandon their vehicles (if bad enough, this could actually block the high-ways and trap people in the cities) (Remember Huricane Rita?)
- Mass outbreak of water-borne diseases as people use streams and rivers as both a water fountain and a bathroom. People crapping upstream are going to infect the people drinking downstream. Very few have any kind of water filtration device
-

That last point is really critical. Once the water flow stops, disease is going to strike.

3. The Depletion of Food Supplies
The food supplies will likely dwindle quickly as we approach a possible crisis due to people stocking up just in case. Once the crisis actually hits, expect to see breakdowns in the transportation sector that will result in major delays in food delivery. This means food may arrive in sporadic fashion in some cities (if at all).

Once this happens, food suddenly becomes really valuable to people (even though they take it for granted today). And that means any small shipment of food that arrives will be quickly grabbed and eaten or stored. It only takes one week without food to remind people how much they actually need it, so expect the atmosphere to be that of a "near panic" if food is delayed by as little as three days. The level of panic will vary from city to city. Some cities or towns may experi-ence very little difficulty receiving food. Others may face near-starvation circumstances.

Remember, the cities depend entirely on food shipped in from the farms and food processing companies. Also, note that if there's a water problem as mentioned in the previous section, and the mass exodus begins, the highways may be jammed up at critical locations, causing gridlock for the trucking industry. If we're lucky, some trucks will continue to roll. If we're not, assume that nothing gets through.

A shortage of food ultimately results in the same behavior as a shortage of water. First, people eat what's in the pantry, then they loot the grocery stores. After that, with all local supplies depleted and no hope on the horizon, they leave the city and start ransacking nearby homes. Some will hunt in nearby forests, but most city-dwellers don't know how to hunt. In any case, anyone with the means to leave the city will likely do so soon after their food shortage begins.

4. The Failure of the Power Grid
Nothing is as suddenly obvious – nor has such a gigantic psychological impact – as the failure of the power grid. When the electricity stops, almost everybody knows it at the same instant (unless it happens at night).

Naturally, during the first few hours of the power failure, if it occurs, people will assume it's a temporary situation. Maybe a tree fell on some power lines, or perhaps a transformer blew up somewhere nearby. They'll sit tight and wait for the power to come back on.

What if it doesn't? Then the city faces a severe problem. Without power, obviously, everything shuts down. Within hours, the looting begins in the more crime-ridden cities (we saw this in New York a few decades ago...). The longer the power stays off, the worse the social disorder.

The loss of power will bring the entire city to a halt. While vehicles may get around for a few more days (using whatever fuel they have left), businesses obviously won't be operating. Houses that depend on electricity for heat will quickly reach winter temperatures, freezing many occupants to death. While those that depend on electricity for Air Conditioning will just as quickly reach Summer temperatures, resulting in death from heat stroke. Hospitals and police stations may have generators on hand, with a few days' worth of fuel, but in short order, that will be depleted, too.

But the water treatment plant will almost certainly be off-line without power, causing all the events mentioned in the water section, above. *Let's face it, the power is the worst thing to be without in the city.* If you have power, you can survive a food shortage, perhaps even a short water shortage. But without power, all bets are off. If you have a "bug-out" vehicle stocked and ready to go (see below), this might be the time to bail.

5. Quarantine, Marshal Law or city has been sealed off.

A new threat that manifest itself in the aftermath of Hurican Katrina is the possibility that the government will Quarantine or Seal off the exits of a city to keep all of the residents contained within its boundaries so as not to allow them to flee or leave. This could be done for purely noble reasons like controlling an outbreak of disease/plague from spreading to nearby communities or for more diabolical reasons like exerting control over population centers by stopping the free movement of people. If you lived in New Orleans, the only time you could leave was before and during the Huricane. Afterwards you were trapped and could only leave when and where you were permitted. Countless people tried to walk out of the city and were turned back at gunpoint by the National Guard only to be sent back into the hell hole until they could be "outprocessed" and evacuated. Regardless of why, the issue is that should you choose to remain in the city, *you may not have the option of leaving once the disaster responce begins..*

Solutions in the City

Okay, so you're stuck in the city. You've made the decision to stay. You've read the problems above, you believe they make sense, and you're intelligently frightened. What now? You really have two strategies. You can:
· Stay and defend your house
· Bug out (leave the city and head for the hills)

Important! This is not an either/or situation. You can begin by staying in your house and assessing the situation. You'll want to have a "bug-out" vehicle stocked and ready, just in case, if you can afford one, but you may never actually choose to bug out. You'll have to be the ultimate judge of this. Just remember that when you bug out, you face major risks and disadvantages. Among these:
· 1. You're severely limited in how much you can carry
· 2. You have limited range due to fuel
· 3. You expose yourself to social chaos, roadblocks, random violence, etc.
· 4. Your house will certainly be looted while you're gone
· 5. You run the risk of mechanical breakdowns of your vehicle
· 6. You must have a place to go that you know is in better shape than where you currently are.

In general, unless you have a <u>specific, known safe place</u> as your final destination, I don't advise people to bug out. Just "heading for the hills" is a very poor plan. You might not make it. But heading for Grandma's house or some known, safe place could be a very good plan indeed, depending on whether Grandma is ready, willing and able to accept you!

For these reasons (and more), staying and defending your house is sometimes the only reasonable course of action, even if it <u>seems</u> dangerous. For the most part, looters and people looking for food are going to have plenty of easy victims, so if you show a little willingness to use force to defend your property, you'll likely send people on to the next house.

That is, until the next house is already empty and you appear to be the last house on the block with any food and water left. If you're in a bad enough area, your neighbors may "gang up" on you and demand your supplies or your life. This is truly a worst-case scenario, and unless you literally have a house full of battle rifles and people trained to use them (and the willingness to shoot your neighbors), you're sunk. *This is why the best situation by far is to keep your neighbors informed and help them get prepared.* Then you (both your member and non-member neighbors) can act as a group, defending your neighborhood and sharing the supplies you have with anyone willing to help defend you. (And don't think for a second that your non-member neighbors won't remember all that food storage in your garage!)

When you have this kind of situation going, your neighbors realize you are their lifeline. You supply them with food and water, and they will help support you because they are, in effect, supporting their own lives. The best situation is when your neighbors and other ward members have their own food and water supplies. That way, they aren't depleting yours, and they have a strong motivation for getting together with you defend your neighborhood. (More on this below...)

Storing (and Hiding) Your Food

Storing food is just as important in the city as in the country, but <u>hiding it</u> is far more important. That's because in the worst areas, marauders will be going from house to house, demanding your food or your life. If you're dumb enough to put everything you own in the obvious places, you might as well not buy it in the first place. They will find it. To count on having any amount of food left over after the marauders break in, you'll need to hide your food.

One alternative is to plan on defending your home with force. If you have enough gun-wise people in the house, and enough firearms and ammo, you can probably pull this off. But most Saints aren't nearly as experienced with firearms as the gang members. A better alternative might be to plan on bringing your supplies to your ward/stake building where all of the Saints can both pool and defend their resources. This of course will depend greatly on your local Bishop and Stake President.

Back to hiding: the best way to hide your food is to bury it. You'll need airtight containers, long-term food that won't rot and you'll need to plan ahead. Bury your food at night so nobody will notice, and make sure you don't leave the map on the refrigerator door! (Better to memorize it!) Try to get the ground to look normal after you're all finished. You'll want to bury your food as early as possible because it gives the grass time to regrow over the spot. If you're in an area that snows, you'll have a great concealment blanket! Most food marauders won't go to the trouble to dig up food, especially if you insist you don't have any.

Best plan: Have some smaller amount of food stashed around the house, letting them find something. Better to give them something and send them on their way. The art of hiding your food is an ancient one. You've got to get creative. Use the walls, the floors, and the structure of the house.

If hiding your food is simply not an available alternative, then try not to advertise it. Keep it put away in your house or garage in as descreet a manner as possible. Don't make a point of telling people that you have a years supply (or more). Word gets around fast that Bro. Jones has a ton of food in his garage. Boxes of food fit nicely under beds, behind furniture, in the attic, etc.. Be Creative!!

To sum up the food storage, you really have three strategies here:

· Store it all in your house and plan on defending it by force.
· Bury it in your yard in case you get overrun by looters.
· Store part of it in your house, and hide the bulk of it.
· Relocate all of it as soon as you recognize a major disaster is in progress

An alternative to burying that would be faster and easier-would be to simply build a false wall in your garage and seal up your food behind the false wall. Sure, you might loose 2-3 feet of useable space in your garage, but the tradeoff is knowing everything is safe and sound.

Storing Extra Water

Water can be stored in exactly the same way, although you might want to bury the barrel before you actually fill it with water. Make sure you treat your storage water, rotate it or have filters on hand when you get ready to use it.

If you don't have a yard, or it's not practical to bury your water, you'll have to store water inside your house. This can get very tricky because water takes up a lot of space and it's very difficult to conceal. It's best to get containers made for long-term storage, but in a pinch, use what you can find, just make sure its clean and food grade material. But a lot of these containers will deteriorate quickly, and they may break easily. Also, consider what happens if your water may be subjected to freezing. Will your containers survive? Be sure to leave enough air space to handle the expansion.

In order to prepare yourself for the water shortage, assuming you're going to stay in the city, stock at least six months of water at a minimum two gallons a day per person. That's nearly 400 gallons of water if you have two people.

Of course, even with the best in-house preparations, you may find yourself depleted of water supplies. In this situation, one of your best defenses is to have a really good water filter (like the Katadyn filter) that can remove parasites and bacteria from the water. You can also treat your water in other ways (iodine, distillation, silver solution, bleach, etc.). Armed with these items, you can safely use stream or river water (or even pond water) for drinking.

WATER WELLS

By far, the best solution for obtaining long-term water supplies is to drill a well. Buy the best-quality hand-pump available (cast-iron pumps available from Lehman's) and a good cylinder. They will last a lifetime if installed properly. With this setup, you'll have a near-unlimited supply of water.

The total cost of doing this, depending on where you live, ranges from about $4000 - $6000. Is it worth it? If you've got the money, I think so. However, many cities simply don't allow the drilling of wells, so you may not be able to get one drilled even if you want to.

The deeper your well, the more expensive it gets. Most well drilling companies charge by the foot. When water is deeper, you also need a bigger pump and a more powerful cylinder, so the costs tend to really grow the deeper you go. If you can find water at 20', you're very lucky and it might not cost you even $2000. If you have to go down to 200', it might cost you $7500, and you're at the depth limit of hand-powered pumps anyway.

Defending Your Life and Property

Let's talk about force. No doubt, there are plenty of nice people in this country, and I think that in small towns and rural areas, people are going to find ways to cooperate and get along. I also think, however, that some cities will suffer complete social breakdown and violence will rule. If you happen to be stuck in one of these cities, you're going to need to use force to defend your house. The section that follows discusses what I consider to be extreme responses to violence in the most dire situations. Hopefully, you won't find yourself in these circumstances, but if you do, the information below may be valuable.

Important: Do not use your lights at night. If you are stocking propane-powered lanterns, solar-powered flashlights, or other unusual supplies, using them at night will announce to everyone within line of sight that you have more than the "usual" supplies. Expect them to come knocking in your door. At most, let a fire burn in the fireplace, but in general, avoid drawing attention to your house.

Defending your house is a crucial element on your stay-in-the-city plan. Make your house your fortress, and hold drills to help other family members practice some of the more common activities such as hiding, defending, evacuating, etc. Some useful items for home defense include:

- A guard dog
- Pepper spray
- Firearms
- Smoke bombs (military-grade)
- Trip wires

Let's go over these:
The guard dog is certainly a welcome addition to any family trying to defend their house. Although he probably eats a lot of food, the investment is worth if. Dogs also tend to sleep light, so let them sleep right next to the food storage areas, and make sure you sleep within earshot. If the dog barks, don't consider it an annoyance, consider it an INTRUSION.

Pepper spray is a great alternative to the firearm. It will incapacitate people and certainly give them a painful experience to remember. On the downside (potentially), it might just remind them that next time they come back for food, they better kill you first. So understand the limitations of pepper spray.

Firearms are useful for obvious reasons. In the worst-case scenario, when looting is rampant, you may have to actually shoot someone to protect yourself or your family. If you're squeamish about pulling the trigger under these circumstances, don't plan to stay in the city. Use the "bug out" plan instead.

Smoke bombs can be useful for covering a planned escape from your house. You can purchase high-volume smoke bombs that will quickly fill up any house with an unbreathable cloud of military-grade white smoke.

Trip wires are great perimeter defenses. You can buy them from Cheaper Than Dirt (they run a few hundred dollars).

They will give you early warning if someone is approaching. You can connect the tripwires to flares, shotgun shells, lightsticks or other warning devices. This way, you can have an audible or visible alert, your choice.

In addition to these devices, you can make significant fortification-style improvements to your home. While none of these are very affordable, they certainly help defend your home:

- Replace glass windows with non-breakable plexiglass
- Add steel bars to the windows
- Replace all outside door locks with heavy-duty deadbolts
- Replace all outside doors with steel doors, preferably without windows
- Remove bushes and other shrubs where people might hide
- Black out the windows entirely to avoid light escaping at night (similar to what residents of London did during the WWII bombing raids)
- Build secret hiding places for food, coins, or even people
- Create escape hatches or passageways
- Rig pepper-spray booby traps

These aren't as absurd as they might at first sound. Many Saints living in rough cities already have steel bars covering their windows, and removing extra bushes and shrubs is a well-known tactic for making your home a safer place.

LIGHT
To light your home when there's no electricity, try the following:

- Use LED flashlights and rechargeable solar-charged batteries. You can buy all these items from the Real Goods catalog.
- Use propane-powered lanterns. You can find these in the camping section of your local Walmart. Be sure to purchase extra mantles and store lots of propane.
- Purchase quality oil lamps from Lehman's and stock up on oil. You can also purchase cheap kerosene lamps from the Sportman's Guide or Walmart, then simply purchase and store extra kerosene.
- Buy extra candles.
- Purchase lots of olive oil. Not only can you cook with it (and besides, it's a lot healthier than corn or vegetable oil), olive oil also burns as a clean candle fuel. You can float a wick in a jar half-full of olive oil and light the wick. Viola, a home-made candle. Olive oil is a fantastic item for your storage anyway because even if you purchase all the

grains in the world, you'll still need cooking oil, and you obviously can't buy powdered cooking oil. Well-stored olive oil can last for thousands of years.

STAYING WARM

Did you know that people won't steal giant logs? Although they may easily steal wood you've already chopped, most people won't have any way of stealing logs. They're too heavy, and the vehicles won't have any gas left. For this reason, your best bet in regards to stocking fuel for your house is to stock up on UNCUT wood logs.

It takes a lot of extra research to find out how to get them (took me a few weeks of asking around), but you can find a source if you look hard enough. Or you can usually get a permit to go out and cut your own. The effort is worth it, because this will give you a ready-to-go source of heat and fuel that cannot be easily stolen.

The catch, of course, is that you'll need equipment to cut and chop the wood. A chainsaw is REALLY nice in this way, but it requires fuel. Fortunately, chain saws don't use much fuel, so if you have a way to store as little as 50 gallons or so, you've got enough to power your chainsaw for a few years (at least!). You'll need fuel stabilizers, too, which you can buy at your local Walmart. (Be sure to buy extra chains for your chainsaw, too.)

You'll also need splitting hardware. You can buy log splitters or just buy an axe, a wedge, and a sledgehammer. Better yet, buy all four so you have a choice of what to use. And remember, wood splits much better when it's frozen, too, so you might just wait until the cold hits in Winter to start splitting your wood. Only split a little at a time, because you don't want to end up with a big pile of nicely-split wood sitting out in your yard. It will invite theft from people who don't have any. If you already have trees on your property, you're all set. Cut down about 4-5 cords right now, so they can start drying out, then chop them as you need 'em.

A "cord" of wood, by the way, is a volume measurement. It's 8' x 4' x 4', or 128 cubic feet of wood (stacked). Some people that sell wood will try to rip you off, so make sure you know what you're buying. If you purchase logs, it's better to get a price per linear foot, based on the diameter of the log. For example, you might ask for logs that are an average of 10" in diameter, and you'll ask how much the charge per linear foot would be. Something in the range of $1 - $2 would be great.

Relations With Neighbors

I've already mentioned the importance of getting along with your neighbors. It really is crucial to your city-based survival plan. The best situation to be in, as mentioned before, is to have neighbors & other church members who are aware of the issue and who are getting ready for it by stocking their own food, water, and other supplies. Every neighbor & member that becomes self-reliant is one less neighbor or member you'll have to support.

The range of neighbor situations, from best to worst, is as follows:

· Best case: your neighbor is current Recomend holder, is aware of and both temporaly & Spiritualy prepared for an emergency with their own supplies and training.
· Good case: your neighbor is aware of a potential crisis, and even though they don't have their own supplies, they're willing to help defend yours as long as you share
· Bad case: your neighbor is a non-member that didn't prepare for it, figuring they would just steal from you if things got bad. They are aware of YOUR supplies but don't have their own.
· Worst case: your neighbor isn't aware of anything, he is anti-mormon and he's a violent, angry neighbor just released from prison. He is going to be caught off guard by the ensuing events and will likely attempt to use violence to get what he needs or wants.

Your decision on whether to stay in the city may depend greatly on the quality and quantity of your neighbors. If you do live in a bad neighborhood, do what you can to relocate. If you live in a good neighborhood, do the best you can to educate and inform your neighbors. *This might well be the most important missionary work you ever do for your own temporal salvation!*

Gun Control in the Cities

No matter how you felt or thought about gun control in the past, it's time to face disaster-induced reality. The gun-control politicians (and the people who supported them) have placed Americans in a situation where not only can the police not protect us in a timely manner, but we cannot lawfully defend ourselves. Criminals unlawfully have firearms; citizens lawfully don't. Intentionally or otherwise, gun-control supporters have created a situation where an unfortunate number of innocent men, women and children are going to be in danger during a crisis simply because they could not obtain the tools of self-defense.

It also happens that the cities where the rioting will likely be the worst are precisely the cities where firearms are most likely to be banned from lawful ownership (and where criminals may wield near-absolute power for a while...). Perhaps when society recovers from it, we can review the fallacy in the cause / effect logic that keeps people voting for gun-control laws, but in the mean time, millions of people are going to have to resort to breaking the law in order to protect their families. And yes, you too will have to resort to breaking the law if you are to acquire a firearm in an area where guns are entirely banned from private citizens (like New York, Los Angeles, etc.).

After the disaster hits, if the rioting gets really bad, we're going to see local police begging law-abiding citizens for help. Your firearm will be a welcome addition to the force of law and order, believe me. No local cop is going to mind you having a handgun if you're manning a roadblock protecting a neighborhood of families with children. Act responsibly, tell them what you're doing, and they'll probably give you a big thanks. But if you're carrying a gun while you smash a window of the Walmart and walk off with a stereo; well that's a different story. Be prepare to get shot.

See, cops don't mind private ownership nearly as much as we've all been led to believe. I know, I work with law enforcement officers in a small town, and I ask them about topics like this. When the crisis hits, they'll be more than happy to have your cooperation. We're all going to need as many law-abiding gun-toting citizens as possible in order to fend off the criminals and establish some degree of order.

One More Reason To Move Out

If you really feel you need a firearm to protect yourself and your family, your best bet may be to move to a city or state where people are a lot more accepting of firearms. You'd be surprised what a difference the locale makes. Check the gun laws in any state you're considering moving to. Obviously, "cowboy" states like Arizona, Texas and Wyoming will have fewer restrictions on firearms (and, interestingly, they have less of a problem with gun violence). States where the population is more dense (like Florida, California, New York) tend to have much greater restrictions on private ownership of firearms.

Bugging Out

Suppose it's July 14, 2006, and you've changed your mind about this city thing. You happened to be right smack in the middle of one of the worst-hit cities in the country. The looting is getting worse, the power has been out for two weeks, and your water supplies are running low. You still have enough gas in your truck to make it out of town... if you can get past the gangs, that is. You've decided to BUG OUT!

Some basic pointers:
- Don't try to bug out in a Chevy Geo. You will likely need a big heavy 4x4 truck in order to go off-road and around stalled vehicles
- Get something that can carry at least 1000 pounds

of supplies. A big 4x4 pickup will do nicely! Yes, it requires more fuel, but you can carry the fuel as cargo.
- Don't bug out unless you can have someone ride shotgun, literally. You will need an armed passenger in case you run into not-so-nice people

WHAT TO TAKE

Ahh, the bug-out supply list. All this will fit in your truck. Here's what you should take if you're preparing to bug out with two people:
- Your 96 hour kits for each person in the vehicle
- 20 gallons of water
- 40 gallons of extra fuel or more (and a full gas tank)

WHERE TO GO

As mentioned earlier, if you have a designated place of refuge (Grandma's house, a cabin in the woods, etc.), head straight for it. If not, you're basically driving anywhere you can go, so try to head for an area that forested and near a creek or river where you can get some water.

Conclusion

Choosing to remain in the city is a rational choice for many Saints in many situations. However, as you have seen from the dangers described here, the further away you can get from the population centers in general, the better your chances of surviving.

Most Saints, perhaps yourself included, have a difficult time actually accepting that a major disaster is going to be as bad as described in this report. And after all, if you leave the city, sell out, quit your job, and move to the country – and then nothing bad happens – you will have disrupted your life, and you may find yourself broke, jobless, and homeless. You COULD assume it will be a mild event, which I suppose is also a credible possibility. In that case, surviving in the city will be quite feasible, especially if you have neighbors that can support your efforts and you don't live in a dangerous city with high racial tensions. However, the very nature of a major disaster means that if only one or two major infrastructure components goes down, the ripple effect will quickly create a much worse scenario. It seems there is very little room for "mild" effects unless they are miniscule. The most likely scenario at this point clearly points to massive disruptions, severe shortages in food and water, loss of power in some areas, and a breakdown of social order in certain areas where the population density is high.

But you can survive anything with good planning, an open mind, and plenty of practice. Why not start now?

Baby Gear for TEOTWAWKI

Food and Feeding

If you've had a baby join your family in the past few years, you are probably aware that there is A LOT of gear out there, and it's all supposed to be essential. A good parent puts their baby wipes into an electric warmer and buys a big "floor gym" for their immobile progeny, right?

baby supplies for teotwawki

It is wise to plan for the possible infant addition (since babies seem to show up unless concrete steps are taken to prevent their conception, and sometimes even then!). You may not be of an age or stage of life for that to be an issue, but someone close to you will be. (At the very least, these items would be great for bartering).

You probably have a long list of things you anticipate needing in the uncertain future, and baby items may not even be high on your list. Joe and I have been around the block a few times with regards to babies and the accompanying gear. I want to help steer you towards what is worthy of your money and storage space.

So, what is really essential?

It is easy to accumulate a lot of baby stuff and even easier to spend money unnecessarily on things that will be used for very short periods of time or not at all. Be aware of this when considering what to store.

Think about what you remember from your own childhood and the basics all humans need- food, clothing, shelter, and love- and go from there. In this installment, I am going to focus on the first one.

Food and Feeding Babies
Breast is Best
Hopefully, the new mother will be willing and able to nurse her newborn. She should be offered lots of encouragement and support because this is not always as easy as it looks on TV. I have heard and read that "if it hurts, you are doing it wrong." I'm hear to tell you that I know what I'm doing at this point and it still hurts for the first few weeks.

Don't let mom get discouraged. She has a lot going on in her body during this time and post-partum depression is common. She may need lots of extra TLC, especially because nursing may trigger painful contractions/cramps in mom in the days after giving birth.

It may take a number of tries before baby gets "latch-on" down, especially if he arrives early. Just keep trying. The more attempts the baby makes at suckling, the more milk is produced. If it's not offered often (or not at all) milk production will fall off or cease.

Be sure to stock lanolin. It is good for soothing sore nipples and it is the best diaper rash ointment I've found.

Back-up Plan: Formula
In case nursing doesn't work for whatever reason, powdered formula would be a good thing to have on hand until another lactating mother or different solution can be found (check online for recipes to make your own formula from food storage in a pinch).

The back of the formula can should give you an idea of how many feedings it contains. Keep in mind that newborns' appetites are small (maybe 2 oz. or less), but they feed frequently. Don't mix up more than can be used and risk it going to waste, especially if there is no refrigeration.

Formula comes in many different forms (powdered, liquid concentrate, ready-to-feed, etc) and made by a variety of companies. Some are cow's milk based, others are soy or other protein base. They are all required to have a minimum amount of nutrition however, no matter what company makes it. All but the "ready-to-feed" require clean safe water to mix with them.

To feed formula, you will need bottles. Glass ones are your best bet (I would probably stock at least 6). They can be sterilized by boiling and will not leach any harmful chemicals into the formula. There have been recent findings that even BPA-free plastics are not safe. Glass bottles have made a come-back. I have seen them in big box stores even. Be sure to stock bottle nipples and a bottle brush, too.

Is milk all they need?
Breastmilk is a very nourishing and complete meal for the developing baby for many months. The volume and ratios of nutrients in breastmilk change to meet the baby's needs as he grows. The most important thing is to be sure that mom is getting a good balance of healthy foods and lots of clean water. Her body will sacrifice itself in both pregnancy and lactation for the baby's sake, but it cannot give what it does not have. Try to make sure mom gets vitamin supplements too.

Though it is not required, a non-electric breastpump can be very useful. Sometimes mother makes more milk than baby can eat or she can get blocked ducts/mastitis. Using warm compresses and pumping surplus milk can help alleviate this. Offering surplus milk to another baby may literally save his life also.

Being able to pump and leave milk (refrigerated) for baby later can allow mom to do some things without carrying him along if someone else is caring for him. Again, bottles would be needed.

What about Solid Food?
In our culture, we push solid foods on babies at early ages and then we create endless varieties and consistencies at premium prices. It's not necessary.

Breastmilk contains all the nutrition a baby will need for months on end. Offering rice cereal may help a baby sleep longer at a stretch, but there is no magic age when babies must begin solid foods.

Common sense tells you that when a baby begins to reach for table food, he is probably ready to begin experimenting with it- in well-mashed, small amounts.

You should be able to find a non-electric food chopper. Steaming foods can add useful amounts of water to them, ensure they are safe from germs, and also make them easier to mash. For that reason, a steamer basket could be useful.

From there, you move to small pieces of finger foods. I have found a rotary pizza cutter to be very handy and a quick way to cut it all up at once.

"Sippy cups" are not absolutely necessary. Most of us are probably old enough that we predate them and we some-

how made it. Those spill-proof cups are extremely handy though in preventing a lot of wasted (precious) milk, etc. You can make your own decisions about those cups. As far as I know, they are all one kind of plastic or another and I have found that many of the valve systems on them are breeding grounds for icky things since they are very hard to clean well.

A few chunky handled spoons and forks would be helpful as toddlers begin to feed themselves, but you may have some silverware already that would be easy to grip (large handled things are easier for those with arthritis, tendinitis, and carpal tunnel syndrome to manage also).

By this point, baby is probably a year or more old. From this point on, it is mostly a matter of making sure that the food offered to baby is not a choking hazard. Beware of round things like grapes. When in doubt, cut it smaller.

Not Feeding Exactly...
I'm not sure exactly where the topic of pacifiers should fall in this series, but they seem to fit best here.

Some people have really strong feelings about this topic. We've only had one child that wanted a pacifier, but boy did she want it! And for about 2 years, she cried constantly if she didn't have it. A person can only take so much of that in the best of times. If everyone is under stress, everyone will need baby to have it!

I say stock a few varieties since they come in all kinds of shapes. Believe me, they will be very valuable barter items some day!

Be careful to monitor the condition of the pacifier because they can deteriorate and become choking hazards, especially once teeth come in.

This first part wasn't so hard and didn't break the bank. Gives you hope for the rest, right?

CLOTHING
The most basic item that most people think of is the diaper. That topic is at least one post of its own. I'll hold off on the discussion of disposable vs cloth and the types of cloth diapers and all the varieties of those.
What does an infant really need to wear?

With a little variation due to the seasons, infants need lots of pajama-type clothing. Most will go through quite a few of these in a day between spitting up and diapering accidents. Baby boys in particular are well known to sprinkle their own clothes (and probably yours) at every diaper change for a while.

Many people feel like babies should have pajamas and "day-time" clothes from the get-go. After a few times around, I'm not one of those. They sleep so much of the day at the beginning anyway and certainly don't choose their activities based on whether the sun is up or not. Save yourself some money. The babies don't care and they probably don't have any pressing social engagements early on anyway.

If anything, get different weights of pajamas so that, summer or winter, they are comfortable. If you buy all white , yellow, or green, any parent can be grateful for your forethought.

Babies are unpredictable size-wise. At the beginning, it may seem like forever before they even fill up their 0 – 3 month outfits. Then suddenly, you can hardly shoehorn them into 6 – 9 month sizes. Keep that in mind. It seems that all our 3 – 6 month clothes are pristine because the children only fit in them for two weeks. Growth spurts can be sudden and huge.

Beyond the Jammies
So, you have the PJs covered. Isn't there more to it? Well yes, especially given temperature fluctuations.

One of the best things to come along for babies was the Onesie. If you aren't familiar with them, they are essentially T-shirts that cover the entire diaper and snap at the crotch. They give an extra bit of warmth and also help keep diapers in place. They contain mess when diapers fail too. I stock these in every size up to at least 18 months. Expect to go through several of these in a day in the beginning also.

Layering
I'm not talking about high fashion- layering textures and colors on runway models. I mean the scientific principle of insulation. Warm air trapped next to the skin keeps the baby warmer. The more of this you can trap, the warmer he stays.

Babies have a lot to adjust to outside of the womb. There's all that breathing, eating, the bright lights, and then there is the temperature. They've been accustomed to a steady 98.6 generously provided for them by dear old mom. Now they are subjected to much cooler temperatures and drafts. In the early days especially, you want to keep baby warm enough.

Each layer you add will help him hold his own body heat in. Hands and feet in particular will turn a purplish color as they chill because the body instinctively decreases blood flow to the extremities to protect the core. It is fine (and

often quite helpful) to "swaddle" a newborn.

How to Wrap a Baby in a Blanket
Bear with me if this is a "Duh!" subject for you. I have found a lot of men in particular don't think it to be one. If you've never had your own baby, you may never have thought about it, either.

To swaddle a baby, get a receiving blanket (these are the lightweight ones hospitals use but they are available in any big box store). There are probably differing techniques for this, but this is what I do.

   Place it on a diagonal.
   Fold the top point down.
   Place baby in the center.
   Take one side and cross it over baby, tucking it underneath him.
   Fold up the bottom corner to cover him, tucking any long tail inside. It's fine (and usually better) if baby has his legs scrunched up inside.
   Cross the last corner over him and place it beneath him.

Babies are supposed to be laid down on their backs to prevent SIDS, so if the end of the blanket is beneath him, it should stay put since they can't move much yet.

You want the blanket to be pretty snug, but certainly not over the face or otherwise constricting breathing. This simulates the comforting close quarters of the womb while keeping him warm. It often calms a crying baby.

Other Layers
I have never found those stocking caps to be very helpful. It seems like they come off and end up over baby's face instead, so I just try to be very careful not to put baby down in a drafty place. A lot of heat can be lost through the scalp.

If your baby has purple hands and feet even when bundled, you may want to put baby socks over them also. This insulates them, but also keeps them from scratching their faces with their sharp fingernails. It seems impossible to trim them close enough that they can't scratch themselves while not injuring their tiny fingers.

By the time the sweet baby has need of more variety in this clothing, you will probably have found someone who will give you their hand-me-downs or be willing to barter. It's hard to try and outfit a child (of an unknown gender, that you don't even know yet) for years into his future when you have no idea what size he will be during the different seasons. I say don't sweat that yet.

SHELTER

You are probably wondering what I am planning to discuss under this category. "Shelter" is pretty obvious- keep the baby in a safe, climate-controlled place. But I want to expand a little bit to include the items you may need inside that shelter.

Where will baby sleep?

This may not be as obvious as it first seems. There are lots of possible answers to this actually.

Unless you intended to have a baby, you will likely not have a crib. They take up a noticeable amount of floor space and have no other real function. You need to consider where an unplanned baby will sleep.

Possibilities:

with mom and dad (sometimes called "co-sleeping)- this is popular with some people. It allows mom to nurse around the clock, losing the least amount of sleep. It can be very dangerou,s though. Many people have accidentally smothered the baby while sleeping.

in a cradle or bassinette – these are smaller and easier to store. In a pinch, you may be able to find a doll cradle that will work for a while. Our daughters were given a very nice handmade one.

the old fashioned "bureau drawer" – many a baby of poor parents have spent their early days in a dresser.

Another thing to keep in mind- anything you put baby in must have rails or sides with no spaces large enough for baby to get stuck in. Most old cribs (and even more recent drop-rail cribs) have been recalled or prohibited for sale due to the danger of strangulation.

How will you carry baby?

If it's by car, you know you will need some kind of carseat. I'll let you determine the likelihood of needing that and what kind you would want.

Beyond that, to get from place to place on foot or even around the house with hands full, how will you transport baby? I'd suggest looking into the various kinds of slings and wraps. Essentially, they allow you to carry baby in a snuggly way, hands-free. Some are more versatile than others, so look around and read reviews.

MobiwrapI have a Moby wrap, but I will confess to never fully mastering it. It seemed if I wrapped it so that baby and I were comfortable, within 30 minutes, it had stretched down to my knees and he risked tumbling out with my every movement. If I swaddled him any tighter, I worried he couldn't breathe well and I felt like I was cutting off my di-

gestive capabilities. I'm also an extremely active person- I ran the risk of whacking his head on things while I worked.

There are lots of choices out there, including some really great backpacks that will allow you to carry baby comfortably on foot without back strain, but some have steep price tags. One of the benefits of these snuggly forms of travel is that baby feels swaddled and close to Mom, so he often sleeps a lot and cries less.

The other thing to consider is a stroller of some kind. They are all over the board in price too. I would not recommend the cheap Chinese fold-up ones sold at StuffMart- they will fail when you need them most. But the boutique European ones are probably a big waste of money too. The "jogging" style with bicycle type tires roll quite easily over all terrain.

Consider how and where you may need to use one. Remember that if you have a backpack or wrap you could carry baby in, you may be able to bring along a lot more gear pushing the stuff in a stroller than you could otherwise.

Where will baby eat?

Most of us were fed our table food in a high chair. They are very handy, but again, space hogs. How about one of the collapsible types? We had one that attached to the table itself (needed a sturdy table without much lip on it), but it was great and portable.

Where will you set baby?

Here is where you can get into bunches of options and gobs of money. Obviously, you can't hold the baby constantly and it probably wouldn't be a good idea if you did. But where will you set him down?

In the beginning, it will probably just be in whatever he uses as a crib. Newborns sleep a lot.

bouncy seatBefore long, he will want to be propped up and watch what is going on. Swings are nice (expensive and big usually), but they often soothe colicky babies. Personally, I'd say borrow one when the time comes if you can. Otherwise, you'll get along without one.

If I could have only 1 piece of baby "seating", it would be the "bouncy seat." These are fabric chairs on metal frames that will bob up and down with baby's movements (or weary parents' foot-jiggling). The motion often lulls babies into naps everyone desperately needs them to take.

They come with all kinds of features like vibrations, ocean sounds, toy bars with flashing lights, etc. so you can spend as much or as little as you want. They typically store flat when disassembled.

376

Beyond the Bouncy Seat

johnny jumperBaby is trying out those legs and wants to entertain himself. There are all kinds of "gyms" and "exersaucers" and so on. They are nice for short periods of time, but I find they are not worth the expense of storage space. I'd opt for a "johnny jumper."

Essentially it is a bungee cord seat for babies that is suspended from a doorway. All but one of our children have thought this was the best thing ever. We hung it in a central doorway of the house (usually going into the kitchen) and the children could play moonwalking astronaut and watch everything else that went on in the family.

These jumpers don't take much space to store either. Our babies have enjoyed them from about 5 – 18 months, so we have gotten a lot of use out of them. Beyond that point, it's more of an issue of keeping baby out of places he shouldn't go than something to put them in. Baby gates would be helpful to keep baby back from the fireplace, etc. We have improvised with chairs across doorways when necessary, though we have semi-permanent gates at the top and bottom of stairways.

Conclusion

Don't let all this overwhelm you if you are new to baby gear. Parents did get along without most of this for ages, but if I had the option, a lot of it makes babyhood easier.

It doesn't have to require a loan to stock. You can pick up many of these items for just a few dollars at yard sales or keep an eye out for children's consignment sales. I hardly ever buy anything new, but "gently used" and hand-me-down has been a great help.

Getting Children Involved in Preparing

You've become convinced that it is wise to prepare for uncertainties in the future as best you can. You've been picking up extra canned goods each month and you are reducing debt wherever you can. You've started having some family discussions around the dinner table.

Last night, there was an interesting debated about how the tensions in Iran could affect the price of oil or what the reduced crop of peanuts will mean for lunch boxes in schools across the country. These are really good ways to get your children thinking about the bigger picture and the inter-related nature of things in the world around them. The next step is to actually enlist their help.

What are some appropriate ways to get children involved in preparing?

As I mentioned in a previous piece about what to tell your children about preparedness, it would be good if they saw benefits to the changes you intend to make. That full pantry may provide them the opportunity to decide what to have for dinner and even make it themselves on the spur of the moment. Enjoy that brownie mix you got for next to nothing with a coupon and make a dessert for supper. The next time someone comes down with a chest cold during the night, they will be glad they didn't have to wait until morning for relief because you already have some Mucinex on-hand.

Growing plants and raising animals are fun for children too. Even the smallest ones like to poke bean seeds into the ground and watch green shoots pop up a few days later. Our older ones love to enter their produce in the county fair in the fall. They've collected some ribbons, checks, and a year's worth of bragging rights for purple tomatoes and pie pumpkins among other things.

Developing Responsibilities and Problem-Solving Skills

We have been prepping for long enough now that even our oldest children don't really remember "before." For seven years now, we have been actively pursuing a lifestyle of increasing self-sufficiency. Once we moved to our farm, we began adding projects to meet our goals. The farm came with a small flock of chickens that the previous owners left behind. That spring we allowed our hens to set eggs and raise chicks. The following year, we began raising day-old chicks for meat and so on.

Many of these projects are perfect for children to get them introduced to the idea of planning ahead and anticipating needs. Experiences like these are really good for other reasons too. The children have to become more responsible. As we have reminded our children at times, those animals are completely dependent on you for their survival- if you don't give them food and water, they won't have any. If a predator gets one of your animals, you have to figure out how to keep it from happening again. Caring for farm animals also allows them to truly understand the life cycle that some movie-makers would rather obscure.

There are lots of smaller things they can do also. One of the most popular jobs in our house is writing the dates in permanent marker prominently on everything we purchase so that we can easily rotate it at a glance without squinting at tiny "sell by" dates in the semi-dark of a cabinet. Children can also be in charge of moving older items forward to load new items on the backs of the shelves. You can give them the occasional task of inventorying what you have, too. Some things, like wild rice or polenta, may get used infrequently enough that no one thinks to put it on the list when it gets low.

Encourage Hobbies with Prepping Potential

Cultivate their interests, especially if they have a preparedness link. One daughter has expressed an interest in knitting. This would be a great skill to have, so we want to encourage it. One son has really wanted to tan a deerskin to use for making belts or chaps or whatever. We still haven't followed through, but we have taken the step to find out how to do it by internet research and purchasing books. Leatherworking would be a fantastic profession in a post-collapse world. Personally, I think a set of fur-lined mittens sounds wonderful. We've got the rabbits- that's the first step.

Fishing, archery, marksmanship, baking, sewing, and so on would be great talents to encourage. One of the older children and I are registered to take a cheese-making class at a local dairy farm this spring. I am very excited about that. Once you start finding out what avenues are available through 4-H or the parks or the county ag office, you may be surprised what they take an interest in.

What Do You Tell the Children?

What to tell the kids about the prepping supplies

For most of us who are "prepping" for an uncertain future, our families are our primary motivation. I have often heard people say that they love their spouse/children/siblings/ etc., and so they prepare. Sometimes that is because those loved ones refuse to see the wisdom or are incapable of acquiring needed supplies for financial or other reasons. In the case of children, it is because they are dependent on us to provide for all their needs.

As you begin to take those steps to stock food and other needed items, you may have to get creative with where you will store it. There is a good possibility that they will notice if you begin storing bins of first aid supplies and rice under their beds. Then what do you do?

How much do you tell the children?

There is not one easy answer to that question. It will depend in part on your reasons for preparing. Your main motivation for preparing may be just to tide you over through an ice storm until power is restored. On the other end of the spectrum, you may be expecting the entire economy to come to an abrupt end any time now. Given those differences, how you present your reasons for preparedness could be pretty different.

Some things you may want to consider when deciding what to share with them and how to say it could be the following:

the age of the child(ren)

the temperament of the child(ren)

how much your plans will impact their everyday lives

1. Age

The age of your children will certainly factor into what you tell them. If you and your spouse are concerned that a spike in oil prices may set off a chain reaction of soaring food prices, riots, lay-offs, and so on, that will likely impact how you choose to spend available cash. You may think you should fill the pantry as soon as possible. Your 4 year old probably doesn't need to know all the reasons behind that. She will grow up soon enough. Besides, at that age, they are very adaptable and she'll adjust to the changes easily.

On the other hand, if your 16 year old is after you to buy the latest cool basketball shoes, it may be reasonable to just tell your teenager he could mow grass to buy them himself, but you may want to explain what he is probably hearing in the news anyhow. It's likely he is mature enough to appreciate the explanation.

2. Temperament
In the above example, you may have a happy-go-lucky teenager who always sees the glass half-full. You can tell him your observations about some unstable regions of the world and how events there could impact the U.S. It will give him some things to think about, but he won't lose any sleep. Even if you tell him that money may get a little tight, he will probably take it in stride.

On the other hand, if your child is more the pessimist or worrywart, you may choose your words differently. Your wording with this child may be more along the lines of how you've noticed that food prices seem to be slowly but steadily increasing and so you think it would be wise to go ahead and buy extra groceries now so you can save money in the long run. You'll have more opportunities to expand on this in future conversations once he has absorbed that.

3. The impact of your plans
If the changes you plan to implement will be subtle (like going "meatless" for dinner a few nights a week, trying new recipes using beans, and making a point to store water each month), these won't overly impact or concern the kids. When the topics come up, you can simply state that you are trying out some new things to trim the budget or become healthier and you think it's a good idea to have extra water on hand. Again, you can flesh out these reasons more as they come up again.

In a subsequent conversation, you may mention that you have been considering buying a pressure canner. If they say they'd rather go to the amusement park, you can point out that they are welcome to work towards a theme park trip, but that being able to preserve your own garden produce is important for reasons X and Y.

If your plans will have a larger impact like moving to a farm, miles away from all their friends, you will need to prepare for some opposition. The older the children are, the more resistance you will probably get. Bringing them around will probably go better if you can outline all the benefits to them.

What We Did
telling kids about preppingWhen we made the move our oldest ones were still pretty young, but we kept mentioning how nice it was going to be to have wide open spaces around- no more worrying about breaking the neighbors' windows just by tossing the ball around in your own back yard. And we can get more animals. And we can join 4-H. And there are big trees to climb. And ponds to fish in. And so on.

If we were moving at their present ages, I think we would tell them a lot of what they have come to know over the years we've been here, but in small chunks. We can grow our own food and know what goes in it. We can preserve it and largely insulate ourselves from wild food price fluctuations or shortages. We can save our seeds and not be dependent on GMO agribusiness. Being in a lower population density, we can be safer from violent crime and infectious diseases. You get the idea.

If they are very "wired in" and used to the instant conveniences of the present day big cities, they probably won't care much about any of those things initially. It may take pointing out how fragile and time-sensitive these conveniences are to get them to start thinking about "what if." A refresher on the Great Depression and some other pertinent history may help them understand a little better.

But don't be too shocked if your adolescents don't embrace your plan with open arms. That is the nature of being a teenager. Just do what you believe to be right as their parent- at worst, they tease you years from now because life as we presently know it continued to hum along without a hiccup. You can just smile and tell them how happy you are to have been wrong. At best, years from now they will be telling their own children how wise you are for your forethought.

Common Sense
A lot of this may seem like "Duh" kind of stuff, but I have been asked what people should tell their children quite a few times. It seems that many parents feel they should just do all their prepping on the sly and hope their children don't notice. I am definitely not advocating a "zombie apocalypse" type of approach with kids, but in reality, you want to introduce some changes to their thinking. They will be better mentally prepared if you explain your rationale for your physical preps.

Avoiding Fear

Teaching children without scaring them

Last week, I wrote a post about what you may want to tell your children about the reasons you have decided to prepare. I only touched briefly on the topic of fear, so I wanted to give that some more attention here.

There are a lot of unsettling things in the news these days. Some rate more as bothersome invasions of privacy (like TSA patdowns and strip-searches) and some could make a person lose sleep (like how far Iran may be from deploying nuclear missiles against the US). How we handle this information and how we relay it to our children is worth examining.

No "One Size Fits All" Approach

Depending on our personality types and our levels of awareness, we may have tendencies to react in certain ways. For example, when some people are told they "can't" do something, it will spur them to prove the speaker wrong. Others may be more prone to giving up and accepting another's judgment without trying. Considering the personality types of those around you may help you to know how to approach them about certain topics.

Avoiding Fear

Fear is not a nice place to live. It can be a useful survival instinct, but it is not an emotion we want to live with constantly. For some people, it is almost mentally paralyzing rather than motivating. So rather than having your loved ones (especially children) constantly watching for the sky to fall, you'd probably rather they think in healthier, problem-solving kinds of ways.

When we have talked to our children, we have tried to be careful to present what we do as a way of avoiding fear and panic in any circumstance. For example- the power may go out because of ice on the power lines? No problem- we have a wood-burning stove and propane heat back-up. A virulent strain of flu is making rounds quickly through the community? It's okay, we don't have to leave home and expose ourselves because we have food, water, medicine, etc. for months if need be.

How are you handling your concerns?

This doesn't apply only to children. Adults can really struggle with worry too. It's not healthy for us to live under self-imposed stress either.

I remember times when I became aware of an area we had not yet prepared for and how I would have brief periods of anxiety about getting that area addressed. Since they were things that were very concerning to me, I had to be careful to only discuss them with Joe in private. Children absorb a lot more than we think and will become worried and scared if they perceive their providers/protectors are worried and scared.

A fellow prepping friend of mine told me about something that had happened in her family that I think illustrates this well. She said she went into a grocery store once with her younger son. As they approached the back of the store, he noticed the refrigerated cases were dark and empty. The cases were just broken and the food had been removed, but he drew a very different conclusion.

His eyes got wide and immediately, in a terrified voice, he asked her if "it" had happened. She didn't understand his question or why he looked so alarmed. He pointed to the cases and asked if the grocery store was running out of food- should they get as many things as they can and hurry home?

Until that point, my friend did not realize how worried she had been and how the kids had obviously picked up on every concern she and her husband had discussed.

Easier Said Than Done

Sure, it's easy to tell someone else not to worry or be fearful. And you can know in that rational part of your head that it is not a healthy or happy way to live. It's so much harder in practice though. Adults have adult concerns. If the office grapevine says lay-offs are imminent, it sure is hard not to feel some anxiety about whether our names are on the chopping block. The mortgage has to be paid. The kids have gotten really used to eating 3 meals a day.

I don't have a panacea for this since I struggle with my own concerns. The ones that plague me the most are the things I have absolutely no power over, yet it's hard to just write them off and let them go.

The best advice I can give in this area is just to be aware of your thinking and how it's impacting you and others. Try to find balance. When I've struggled, sometimes it has helped to look at the list of things we have accomplished and focus on those. We don't have a greenhouse- well, we do have plenty of open-pollinated seeds. We haven't found a like-minded physician to help us stockpile medicines- well, we have been to the Medical Corps training class and gotten some more knowledge and practice.

Facts about Avian Influenza

Key Facts About Avian Influenza (Bird Flu) and Avian Influenza A (H5N1) Virus

This fact sheet provides general information about bird flu and information about one type of bird flu, called avian influenza A (H5N1) that is infecting birds in Asia and has infected some humans. Also see the Frequently Asked Questions (FAQs) on the World Health Organization (WHO) website.

What is avian influenza (bird flu)?

Bird flu is an infection caused by avian (bird) influenza (flu) viruses. These flu viruses occur naturally among birds. Wild birds worldwide carry the viruses in their intestines, but usually do not get sick from them. However, bird flu is very contagious among birds and can make some domesticated birds, including chickens, ducks, and turkeys, very sick and kill them.

Do bird flu viruses infect humans?

Bird flu viruses do not usually infect humans, but several cases of human infection with bird flu viruses have occurred since 1997.

How are bird flu viruses different from human flu viruses?

There are many different subtypes of type A influenza viruses. These subtypes differ because of certain proteins on the surface of the influenza A virus (hemagglutinin [HA] and neuraminidase [NA] proteins). There are 16 different HA subtypes and 9 different NA subtypes of flu A viruses. Many different combinations of HA and NA proteins are possible. Each combination is a different subtype. All known subtypes of flu A viruses can be found in birds. However, when we talk about "bird flu" viruses, we are referring to influenza A subtypes chiefly found in birds. They do not usually infect humans, even though we know they can. When we talk about "human flu viruses" we are referring to those subtypes that occur widely in humans. There are only three known A subtypes of human flu viruses (H1N1, H1N2, and H3N2); it is likely that some genetic parts of current human influenza A viruses came from birds originally. Influenza A viruses are constantly changing, and they might adapt over time to infect and spread among humans.

What are the symptoms of bird flu in humans?

Symptoms of bird flu in humans have ranged from typical flu-like symptoms (fever, cough, sore throat and muscle aches) to eye infections, pneumonia, severe respiratory diseases (such as acute respiratory distress), and other severe and life-threatening complications. The symptoms of bird flu may depend on which virus caused the infection.

How does bird flu spread?

Infected birds shed flu virus in their saliva, nasal secretions, and feces. Susceptible birds become infected when they have contact with contaminated excretions or surfaces that are contaminated with excretions. It is believed that most cases of bird flu infection in humans have resulted from contact with infected poultry or contaminated surfaces. The spread of avian influenza viruses from one ill person to another has been reported very rarely, and transmission has not been observed to continue beyond one person.

How is bird flu in humans treated?

Studies done in laboratories suggest that the prescription medicines approved for human flu viruses should work in preventing bird flu infection in humans. However, flu viruses can become resistant to these drugs, so these medications may not always work. Additional studies are needed to prove the effectiveness of these medicines.

What is the risk to humans from bird flu?

The risk from bird flu is generally low to most people because the viruses occur mainly among birds and do not usually infect humans. However, during an outbreak of bird flu among poultry (domesticated chicken, ducks, turkeys), there is a possible risk to people who have contact with infected birds or surfaces that have been contaminated with excretions from infected birds. The current outbreak of avian influenza A (H5N1) among poultry in Asia and Europe (see below) is an example of a bird flu outbreak that has caused human infections and deaths. In such situations, people should avoid contact with infected birds or contaminated surfaces, and should be careful when handling and cooking poultry. For more information about avian influenza and food safety issues, visit the World Health Organization website. In rare instances, limited human-to-human spread of H5N1 virus has occurred, and transmission has not been observed to continue beyond one person.

What is an avian influenza A (H5N1) virus?

Influenza A (H5N1) virus – also called "H5N1 virus" – is an influenza A virus subtype that occurs mainly in birds. Like all bird flu viruses, H5N1 virus circulates among birds worldwide, is very contagious among birds, and can be deadly.

What is the H5N1 bird flu that has been reported in Asia and Europe?

Outbreaks of influenza H5N1 occurred among poultry in eight countries in Asia (Cambodia, China, Indonesia, Japan, Laos , South Korea , Thailand , and Vietnam) during late 2003 and early 2004. At that time, more than 100 million birds in the affected countries either died from the disease or were killed in order to try to control the outbreak. By March 2004, the outbreak was reported to be under control. Beginning in late June 2004, however, new outbreaks of influenza H5N1 among poultry were reported by several countries in Asia (Cambodia, China [Tibet], Indonesia, Kazakhastan, Malaysia, Mongolia, Russia [Siberia], Thailand, and Vietnam). It is believed that these outbreaks are ongoing. Most recently, influenza H5N1 has been reported among poultry in Turkey and Romania. Human infections of influenza A (H5N1) have been reported in Cambodia, Indonesia, Thailand, and Vietnam.

What is the risk to humans from the H5N1 virus in Asia and Europe?

The H5N1 virus does not usually infect humans. In 1997. However, the first case of spread from a bird to a human was seen during an outbreak of bird flu in poultry in Hong Kong, Special Administrative Region. The virus caused severe respiratory illness in 18 people, 6 of whom died. Since that time, there have been other cases of H5N1 infection among humans. Recent human cases of H5N1 infection that have occurred in Cambodia, Thailand, and Vietnam have coincided with large H5N1 outbreaks in poultry. The World Health Organization (WHO) also has reported human cases in Indonesia. Most of these cases have occurred from contact with infected poultry or contaminated surfaces; however, it is thought that a few cases of human-to-human spread of H5N1 have occurred. So far, spread of H5N1 virus from person to person has been rare and has not continued beyond one person. However, because all influenza viruses have the ability to change, scientists are concerned that the H5N1 virus one day could be able to infect humans and spread easily from one person to another. Because these viruses do not commonly infect humans, there is little or no immune protection against them in the human population. If the H5N1 virus were able to infect people and spread easily from person to person, an influenza pandemic (worldwide outbreak of disease) could begin. No one can predict when a pandemic might occur. However, experts from around the world are watching the H5N1 situation in Asia very closely and are preparing for the possibility that the virus may begin to spread more easily and widely from person to person.

How is infection with H5N1 virus in humans treated?

The H5N1 virus currently infecting birds in Asia that has caused human illness and death is resistant to amantadine and rimantadine, two antiviral medications commonly used for influenza. Two other antiviral medications, oseltamavir and zanamavir, would probably work to treat flu caused by the H5N1 virus, but additional studies still need to be done to prove their effectiveness.

Is there a vaccine to protect humans from H5N1 virus?

There currently is no commercially available vaccine to protect humans against the H5N1 virus that is being seen in Asia and Europe . However, vaccine development efforts are taking place. Research studies to test a vaccine to protect humans against H5N1 virus began in April 2005, and a series of clinical trials is underway. For more information about the H5N1 vaccine development process, visit the National Institutes of Health website.

What is the risk to people in the United States from the H5N1 bird flu outbreak in Asia and Europe ?

The current risk to Americans from the H5N1 bird flu outbreak in Asia is low. The strain of H5N1 virus found in Asia and Europe has not been found in the United States . There have been no human cases of H5N1 flu in the United States . It is possible that travelers returning from affected countries in Asia could be infected if they were exposed to the virus. Since February 2004, medical and public health personnel have been watching closely to find any such cases.

What does CDC recommend regarding the H5N1 bird flu outbreak?

In February 2004, CDC provided U.S. health departments with recommendations for enhanced surveillance ("detection") in the U.S. of avian influenza A (H5N1). Follow-up messages, distributed via the Health Alert Network, were sent to the health departments on August 12, 2004 , and February 4, 2005 ; both alerts reminded health departments about how to detect (domestic surveillance), diagnose, and prevent the spread of avian influenza A (H5N1). The alerts also recommended measures for laboratory testing for H5N1 virus. CDC currently advises that travelers to countries with known outbreaks of influenza A (H5N1) avoid poultry farms, contact with animals in live food markets, and any surfaces that appear to be contaminated with feces from poultry or other animals. CDC does not recommend any travel restrictions to affected countries at this time. For more information, visit Travelers' Health.

What is CDC doing to prepare for a possible H5N1 flu pandemic?

CDC is taking part in a number of pandemic prevention and preparedness activities, including:

Providing leadership to the National Pandemic Influenza Preparedness and Response Task Force, created in May 2005 by the Secretary of the U.S. Department of Health and Human Services.

Working with the Association of Public Health Laboratories on training workshops for state laboratories on the use of special laboratory (molecular) techniques to identify H5 viruses.

Working with the Council of State and Territorial Epidemiologists and others to help states with their pandemic planning efforts.

Working with other agencies such as the Department of Defense and the Veterans Administration on antiviral stockpile issues.

Working with the World Health Organization (WHO) and Vietnamese Ministry of Health to investigate influenza H5N1 in Vietnam and to provide help in laboratory diagnostics and training to local authorities.

Performing laboratory testing of H5N1 viruses.

Starting a $5.5 million initiative to improve influenza surveillance in Asia .

Holding or taking part in training sessions to improve local capacities to conduct surveillance for possible human cases of H5N1 and to detect influenza A H5 viruses by using laboratory techniques.

Developing and distributing reagents kits to detect the currently circulating influenza A H5N1 viruses.

Working together with WHO and the National Institutes of Health (NIH) on safety testing of vaccine seed candidates and to develop additional vaccine virus seed candidates for influenza A (H5N1) and other subtypes of influenza A virus.

Recommendations for Avian Influenza

All patients who present to a health-care setting with fever and respiratory symptoms should be managed according to recommendations for Respiratory Hygiene and Cough Etiquette and questioned regarding their recent travel history.

Patients with a history of travel within 10 days to a country with avian influenza activity and are hospitalized with a severe febrile respiratory illness, or are otherwise under evaluation for avian influenza, should be managed using isolation precautions identical to those recommended for patients with known Severe Acute Respiratory Syndrome (SARS). These include:

Standard Precautions
Pay careful attention to hand hygiene before and after all patient contact or contact with items potentially contaminated with respiratory secretions.

Contact Precautions
Use gloves and gown for all patient contact.
Use dedicated equipment such as stethoscopes, disposable blood pressure cuffs, disposable thermometers, etc.

Eye protection *(i.e., goggles or face shields)*
Wear when within 3 feet of the patient.

Airborne Precautions
Place the patient in an airborne isolation room (AIR). Such rooms should have monitored negative air pressure in relation to corridor, with 6 to 12 air changes per hour (ACH), and exhaust air directly outside or have recirculated air filtered by a high efficiency particulate air (HEPA) filter. If an AIR is unavailable, contact the health-care facility engineer to assist or use portable HEPA filters.
Use a fit-tested respirator, at least as protective as a National Institute of Occupational Safety and Health (NIOSH)-approved N-95 filtering facepiece (i.e., disposable) respirator, when entering the room.

These precautions should be continued for 14 days after onset of symptoms or until either an alternative diagnosis is established or diagnostic test results indicate that the patient is not infected with influenza A virus. Patients managed as outpatients or hospitalized patients discharged before 14 days with suspected avian influenza should be isolated in the home setting.

Is the world adequately prepared for this pandemic ?
No.

Preparing for a Pandemic Influenza Outbreak
The Self Imposed Reverse Isolation (SIRQ) Plan

1) **Protecting the Family – Building a Safe Haven**
   a. Protecting the family from the influenza virus is central to the plan.
   b. This requires that families sequester themselves from the outside world in order to avoid infection.
      i. Children should not go to school or play with friends.
      i. Parents should work from home as much as possible.
      iii. The family should not attend public events (sporting events, cultural events, religious services, etc.).
      iv. If family members do have to leave sequestration, they must be educated and committed to maintaining protection.
   c. Parents
      i. Must establish their home as a protected cell.
      ii. Must understand that as long as their family is sequestered they are safe, but safety is only good AS LONG AS EVERY FAMILY MEMBER REMAINS SAFE AND DOES NOT BRING THE INFECTION HOME.
      iii. Must understand the importance of not allowing children to interact with others outside the family during the time the plan is in place.
      iv. Must know how to remain safe when they leave the home:
         1. Protective equipment,
         2. Protective methods of interacting in an infectious environment.
      v. Must have their homes prepared for a disruption in services.

   d. Children
      v. Are at high risk for transmission of disease because of less than ideal hygiene, close contact with others in closed environments, inadequate hand washing, etc.
      vi. Need to be sequestered in family groups.
      vii. Need to be isolated from others who are potentially infected.
      viii. Need to be trained in methods of protecting themselves from infection at their level.

2) **Protecting the Individual**
   a. During an influenza pandemic, any individual that has to interact with the outside world must consider all they come in contact with as being infected.
   b. Individuals must know how to interact in such an environment:
      i. Need education and training about how to protect themselves.
      ii. Need protective equipment to allow them to interact.

3) **Protecting the Community**
   a. Community leadership must support the SIRQ plan and strongly encourage its implementation:
      i. Educating leaders, families and individuals about the plan.
      i. Implementation of reverse quarantine protection early (BEFORE THE INFECTION HITS THE COMMUNITY).
      ii. Cancellation of schools, meetings, public venues, etc. (BEFORE THE INFECTION STARTS)
      iii. Identify key services and individuals essential to these services:
      1. Provide or strongly encourage personal protection use in all essential sectors early.
         1. Plan on contingencies
      b. Must provide venues for education of individuals and families.
         a. Should facilitate obtaining protective equipment for individuals or groups.
         b. Must lead by example.

This plan can be implemented without government or community support. A family or individual could use this plan and protect themselves as long as they are willing to keep themselves separate.

Quarantine, Quarantine, Quarantine

I have been ask repeatedly on how to quarantine properly and so this is being written to take care of that question.

I guess the first thing we need to consider is why we are quarantining. Remember quarantine is due to a biological event and not a chemical or nuclear. For these last two you should be sheltering in place.

A proper quarantine will protect you from what ever it is you are trying to protect against henceforth there will be different stages of quarantine.

1.   The first and most basic stage is to go home lock the doors and stay there. DO NOT try to seal up your home with duct tape and plastic as you will not have enough oxygen to breath within a very short time. This method is used for chemical events where you need to be indoors for a very short period of time. Most quarantines will last days if not weeks and months. At this stage you can actually go out in to your front yard or back yard and breathe the air just fine just as long as you do not breathe someone else's air that might be infected with an airborne communicable disease or virus. This could include certain animals and insects all depending on what the biological is. All infected people should remain a good distance (minimum 20 feet) away from you and anyone else sheltering with you. Anyone (again including certain animals) that has been in a possibly infected area should be kept separate (quarantined separate) from you until they have sough proper medical attention (if it is available) and been cleared or they have run the course of waiting the required length of time to be sure that symptoms will or will not show up. Remember in most biologicals symptoms do not show up for several days. For mothers and other care givers wishing to attend infected persons, especially children, during this time a full biological protection mask, gown, and gloves should be used and then disposed of properly. This really should be avoided at all costs but trying to tell a mother she cannot care for her children is sometimes near to impossible. Exposure time should be set at a bare minimum.

The proper shielding garments to be worn would be a disposable non-breathable (Tyvek) suit (available at most paints stores), a tight fitting (with two straps) N-95 or N-100 dust mask, and latex or rubber gloves. All of this needs to be disposable. A better face mask with biological filters is suggested.

It is important to remain quarantined for the suggest length of time that the certain biological requires. This will vary from biological to biological. This means no going to the store or to work or church or school or . . . STAY HOME.

2.   The second stage is for more serious conditions where being around certain biologicals, even on the oher side of a locked door, posses a more serious problem. Usually at this stage a gas mask with a biological filter is needed instead of a simple N-95 dust mask. Be wary of official warnings as when to move to this level.

3.   The third stage is the most serious and nothing other than a level one suit is required. Again be wary of official warning as when to move to this level although the common citizen should never be involved with such procedures that would require this level.

What more can I say about this other than . . . STAY HOME.
If you prepare now you can do this. It really is not that hard.

Medical Quarantine --
Protecting Your Family from Infection

Plague. Yellow fever. Cholera. Diphtheria. _Diseases which evoke images of death and despair._

Though less likely to transmit a fatal illness, would you open your door to someone with hepatitis, strep throat, or methacillin-resistant staph? What about a person suffering from vomiting, diarrhea, a cough, or lice, or a fever? Are you immune to measles, polio, and whooping cough – and would you even recognize these conditions? How will you know if someone is going to come down with influenza in the next day or two?

Before antibiotics, before anti-virals, before immune globulin, societies used quarantines to protect their populations. As early as the Middle Ages quarantines were imposed on potentially infected ships to reduce the risk of plague spreading to port cities.

What will you do if someone shows up, seeking shelter? Can you trust a child who appears healthy to be free of disease? Does loving your neighbor as yourself require you to put your entire family at risk?

In times of scarcity, when the marvels of modern medicine are unavailable, medical quarantine offers a possible solution. The term quarantine applies specifically to apparently well people who may have been exposed to a contagious disease, and therefore may (or may not) become ill. (For an obviously ill person, isolation procedures should be enacted, a topic for a future article.)

Almost every transmissible disease has an incubation period during which the person is infected but not yet showing signs of disease. Quite often, a person can be contagious for one to several days before exhibiting symptoms. Blood borne infections in asymptomatic individuals can sometimes be transmitted months or years before the infected person becomes symptomatic (as in HIV), hence the need for universal precautions.

In recent years the Haitian orphans provide an example of how the U.S. treats potentially contagious immigrants. Though not quarantined in the usual sense, per the CDC even the apparently healthy children were all examined for: bacterial and protozoal diarrhea, hepatitis A and E, typhoid fever, dengue fever, malaria, leptospirosis, tuberculosis, syphilis, intestinal parasites, Giardia spp., and Cryptosporidium. They also had their immunization status checked and updated for diphtheria, pertussis, tetanus, measles, rubella, polio, hepatitis A and B, Haemophilus influenzae type b, meningocococcus, pneumococcus, and varicella (chicken pox).

Lacking the means to do any of this, what constitutes a reasonable approach to strangers seeking help?

For the purposes of this article, I'll assume those seeking to join your group are not suffering from any apparent signs of infection including fever, chills, vomiting, diarrhea, cough, runny nose, peculiar behavior, or visible rash. Again, lack of apparent infection does not guarantee health. Certain illnesses such as chicken pox and influenza are often highly contagious even before symptoms have developed. With other microbes, such as strep and typhoid, occasionally a person will develop a carrier state where they are able to transmit an infection but are not themselves infected. In other cases an infection may be subclinical, that is, too mild to detect, as in the case of a toddler with infectious mononucleosis.

The above reasons are the basis for quarantining apparently healthy individuals, isolating them from your established, (hopefully) healthy group, until sufficient time has passed to convince you that the well-appearing newcomers are, indeed, most likely healthy. Even then, this cannot assure that an asymptomatic carrier is not in your presence, but the risk decreases as evidence of prolonged wellness accumulates.

Quarantine measures depend on potential routes of transmission: airborne, droplet-borne, direct contact, vector-borne (mosquitoes, fleas), fomite-borne (doorknobs, clothing, equipment, toys, or other inanimate object), food-borne, and feces-borne. Blood-borne infections should not be an issue without exposure to blood or other body fluids. (Warning: don't have sex with strangers.)

Ideally the quarantine area will be a separate building from your own living quarters, such as an outbuilding, garage, empty house, or barn. If you choose to offer a room within your home, choose one vented to the outside, without ductwork connecting to the rest of the house. Make sure the room has a negative pressure by leaving a window cracked, so the air flows into the room from the remainder of the house rather than vice versa. If you allow newcomers within your home, have them fold their arms across their chests as you lead them to the quarantine room, to prevent potential contamination of walls, doorknobs, and other surfaces.

Food utensils must be kept entirely separate. Do not offer to wash dishes nor remove waste. When offering food, do not touch a potentially contaminated dish with your own utensils. If this occurs, either leave them with the quarantined population, or sterilize them (by boiling or with a 10% bleach solution.)

A 5-gallon bucket with attached toilet seat and sturdy disposable bags is adequate for waste disposal, preferably with an adequate supply of sturdy disposable plastic bags until the quarantine is lifted.

Who should be quarantined? The answer could be anyone outside your group who wishes to join you. Of course, this will depend on several factors, including known epidemics, length of time since societal breakdown, potential resources of newcomers, etc. Even a few days of separation are better than none at all. People from unvaccinated populations may pose a greater threat than those likely to have had standard immunizations. No matter how long you wait, you may not know if an asymptomatic carrier is in your midst.

How long to impose a quarantine? Many latent viral infections will manifest themselves within a period of 3-5 days, and most within 10-14. A three-week period of wellness assures against most transmissible infections, though such a prolonged period may impose hardship on both host and guest. Certain viruses such as infectious mononucleosis and hepatitis A sometimes have an incubation period of 6 weeks before symptoms occur. Anyone over the age of 30, however, is presumed to have had mono whether they've

ever exhibited symptoms or not. A table at Wikipedia, culled from other sources, lists incubation periods of common illnesses.

Most illnesses are not truly airborne, but rather spread via droplet contamination of surfaces including hands, doorknobs, utensils, and tools (TB, anthrax, and influenza may be either airborne or droplet-borne.) It is not likely you will become infected by standing across the room from a person as long as you keep your hands to yourself. If you do touch something, do not, repeat, do not touch your face until you have washed your hands adequately. The mucus membranes of the eyes, nose, and mouth are the primary entry points for most contagious diseases.

If your newcomers still appear well at the end of whatever quarantine period you've chosen, don't neglect to do a rudimentary physical exam. Check their hair for nits (lice eggs) and their skin for rashes. Ask about known infections, including sexually transmitted diseases. Keep your ears open for a cough, or wheezing, or abnormal behavior.

This brings us, perhaps, to the point of turning someone away. Before you even start down the road of quarantine, you should have a plan in place. Will you turn away a child? A slow-moving grandmother? A hard-working adult? Will your decision be influenced by the potential contribution of the newcomer? Would you welcome a carpenter with lice? What about a gourmet cook with herpes? Or a doctor with shingles?

If I were a layman considering a post-Armageddon scenario, I would update my immunizations now, beginning with those protective against diphtheria, hepatitis A and B, tetanus, pertussis (whooping cough), polio, measles, mumps, rubella, meningitis, chicken pox, pneumonia, and influenza. Although other illness such as yellow fever, typhoid, and Japanese encephalitis are rare in the United States, immunizations are available. See the American Academy of Family Physicians recommendations for a list of vaccines and associated costs.

Dr. Cynthia Koelker
http://armageddonmedicine.net/

Basic Pandemic Supply List

- **5 gallons of liquid bleach** per person of the household to sanitize everything

- **4 boxes of latex gloves**
(different sizes for every member of the household)

- **2 boxes of 20 of N95 masks**
for every member of the household

- **antibacterial soap**
for meticulous hand washing

- **styrofoam "Take Out" containers**
to give to people that come to your door looking for food

- **100' roll of clear 4 mil plastic -**
for setting up an isolation room

- **duct tape -**
for setting up an isolation room

- **more HEPA filters -**
for my whole house air filtration system

- **several boxes of Borax -**
for provisional toilets

- **25 lbs. of lime per person -**
for provisional toilets

- **50 "yard waste" black garbage bags per person -**
for provisional toilets and garbage

- **100 "kitchen" bags per person -**
for provisional toilets and garbage

- **25 lbs. of kitty litter per person -**
for sick people's body fluids clean up

- **100 rolls of toilet paper per person -**
for personal sanitation

- **20 rolls of paper towels per person**

- **clothesline -**
for washing clothes by hand

- **laundry soap -**
for washing clothes by hand

- **good dish soap**
like "Dawn" or other aggressive anti-grease formula

- **water filtration and purification devices**

- **water collection, storage and carrying containers**

- **water, water, and more water**

I am sure there are more items but this is a good list to start with

Pandemic Planning - Home & Family Preparedness

For more information about this topic, call the Risk Management Division:
- 1-801-240-4049
- 1-800-453-3860, ext. 2-4049 (toll free in the United States and Canada)

This fact sheet provides information on how families can prepare themselves for a possible flu pandemic.

Background

A severe pandemic (defined as a world-wide epidemic) in a vulnerable population, such as the 1918 flu pandemic, represents a worst-case scenario for pandemic planning and preparedness. Communities, individuals, employers, schools, and other organizations are being asked to plan for the use of interventions that will help limit the spread of disease. At this time, there is concern because of continued spread of a highly pathogenic avian influenza (H5N1) virus among animals in Asia, Africa, the Middle East, and Europe which has the potential to significantly threaten human health. If a virus such as H5N1 mutates and spreads easily from one person to another, avian influenza may break out globally. While there are no reports of *sustained* human-to-human transmission of avian influenza, governments and international health agencies are preparing for a possible pandemic. A pandemic can originate from any "unknown" source, such as the H5N1 virus.

General Precautions

Observe general precautions including hand washing, avoiding contact with possibly infected poultry, or consuming undercooked poultry or poultry products.

If one of your family or household members becomes ill, they should be isolated in a separate room. If several members are sick, they can be isolated in the same room. When caring for those who are ill, you will need some appropriate personal protective equipment (PPE) including the following:

- Disposable vinyl, nitrile, or latex gloves or other reusable gloves that can be disinfected
- Protective clothing (long sleeved coveralls with a waterproof apron) or a disposable surgical gown
- Disposable shoe covers or those that can be disinfected
- Safety goggles or face shield
- Wear at least the minimum level of respiratory protection which is a surgical mask or preferably an N95 respirator
- These items must be removed in the proper sequence to avoid contaminating yourself (see *Pandemic Planning - Health Care Worker Preparedness* fact sheet for more details).

Disinfection

Cups, glasses, dishes, all eating utensils, thermometers, etc., must be disinfected after use by the ill person. The eating utensils can be disinfected either by use of a dishwasher or dishwater with 1.5 tsp. of household bleach to one gallon (3.8 liters) of water. Remember that handling these items while they are still contaminated will lead to possible infection. Therefore, wear gloves while handling potentially contaminated items.

Surfaces in the room of the infected persons should be cleaned with a solution of bleach water as noted above or with Lysol® or Clorox® spray, wipes or liquid. Pay particular attention to faucets, doorknobs, telephones, refrigerator, oven, and toilet flush handles. This should be done whenever there is contact by an infected person or otherwise 2-3 times a day. Linens and clothing need to be washed in warm water with detergent and preferably dried in a dryer. Remember if you are not careful in your personal protective wear and hygiene measures, you may carry infected material on your skin or clothing which may contaminate others or yourself. Designate a specific garbage bag for infected, disposable materials.

Isolation

If you develop flu-like symptoms, *stay home and isolated* from your household except to seek medical care. Remain at home for 7-10 days or until you are well and can no longer spread the infection. Seek medical care if you have signs of pneumonia or severe lung infection (difficulty breathing, wheezing, or a persistent fever over 102° F or 38.9° C)

If there are other cases of avian flu in your neighborhood, it would be safest to keep your children in your yard or home away from others who may be infected. Plan in advance what will need to be done or who you can call upon if you are either alone, ill and incapacitated, or if the adults in the household become ill and incapacitated. Talk with family members and loved ones about how they would be cared for if they got sick, or what will be needed to care for them in your home.

Schools and day care facilities will likely close. Plan your child care in advance and how you might function by working at home for example, or how college-age family members can assist in younger child care during the time their colleges and universities are closed. Having multiple younger children from several households in one home for day care is less than optimal due to the high risk of spreading the disease.

Limit your exposure to public places which may include a grocery trip only once a week rather than every few days. In addition to the recommended food and water storage items, keep a supply of your prescription medications, nonprescription drugs, and other health supplies on hand, including pain relievers, stomach remedies, cough and cold medicines, fluids with electrolytes, vitamins, rubbing alcohol, thermometers, garbage bags and cleaning supplies. Keep your car filled with gas and have cash on hand in case banks are closed or services limited. Use the over-the-counter medications as directed on the container.

Maintain social distancing (see *Pandemic Planning - Social Distancing* fact sheet for more details) and stay at least 6 feet away from others at all times particularly in public. Avoid handshaking and other forms of contact. Use proper cough and sneeze etiquette even if you are not ill (see *Pandemic Planning – Personal Hygiene* fact sheet for more details). Be sure to teach your children the proper hand washing and cough/sneeze behaviors as well. If you are ill, you need to be isolated from those who are healthy even in your own household.

References:

www.cdc.gov: Interim Pre-pandemic planning guidance: including individual planning, workplace planning, community planning, school planning, healthcare planning, community strategy for pandemic influenza mitigation
www.osha.gov: Guidance on Preparing Workplaces for an Influenza Pandemic
www.who.org: Avian Flu: Fact Sheet, pandemic preparedness plan, guidelines, WHO pandemic influenza draft protocol for rapid response and containment
www.epa.gov: Ground water and drinking water: emergency disinfection of drinking water

LDS Church, *Basic Self Reliance*, p.76, 1989

Pandemic Planning—Personal Hygiene

For more information about this topic, call the Risk Management Division:
- 1-801-240-4049
- 1-800-453-3860, ext. 2-4049 (toll free in the United States and Canada)

This fact sheet provides information on how to use good personal hygiene practices as a means to help control or minimize the spread of a possible pandemic virus among individuals and in the community.

Background

A severe pandemic (defined as a worldwide epidemic) in a vulnerable population, such as the 1918 flu pandemic, represents a worst-case scenario for pandemic planning and preparedness. Communities, individuals, employers, schools, and other organizations are being asked to plan for the use of interventions that will help limit the spread of disease. At this time, there is concern because of continued spread of a highly pathogenic avian influenza (H5N1) virus among animals in Asia, Africa, the Middle East and Europe that has the potential to significantly threaten human health. If a virus such as H5N1 mutates and spreads easily from one person to another, avian influenza may break out globally. While there are no reports of *sustained* human-to-human transmission of avian influenza, governments and international health agencies are preparing for a possible pandemic. A pandemic can originate from any unknown source, such as the H5N1 virus.

Personal Hygiene Basics

The best way to stop the spread of germs that cause the flu or other illnesses that can be spread from one person to another is to wash hands often and control the discharges associated with coughing and sneezing. According to the U.S. Centers for Disease Control Prevention, *"Hand washing is the single most important means of preventing the spread of infection."*

Hands should be washed with clean water and soap:
- When they are dirty
- After using the restroom
- Before and after preparing meals
- After cutting and handling uncooked meat
- Before eating
- After cleaning the house
- After caring for someone who is ill
- After changing an infant's diaper
- After cleaning up blood or body fluids
- After handling soiled bed linens and clothes
- Before and after flossing teeth
- After you cough or sneeze in them

How to Wash Hands

1. Adjust water to a comfortable level and wet hands. Dispense a small amount of soap into the palms of the hands creating lather.

2. Using as much friction as needed, thoroughly clean all surfaces of hands including between the fingers.

3. Pay attention to the nails and nail beds by rubbing the nails of one hand across the palm of the other, creating enough friction to clean underneath the nails. Hands should be washed for at least 20 seconds. Use of a memory aid, such as singing a song or reciting a familiar poem, may assist individuals in washing for an adequate period of time.

4. Rinse the hands under running water, being sure to hold the hands in a downward position.

5. Use paper towels to thoroughly dry the hands.

6. Using the same paper towel, turn off the water supply and open the door.

Other Hand Cleaning Options

Alcohol-based hand cleaners can also be used to clean hands. Put a small amount on the hands and rub all hand surfaces until the hands are dry.

If commercially prepared alcohol-based hand cleaners are not available or are too costly, an alcohol-based hand cleaner can be made by mixing 70% alcohol and glycerin (about 2% by volume of glycerin). The glycerin keeps the hands soft because the alcohol can dry them out. Hands will periodically need to be washed with soap and water because the hands will have a glycerin buildup with time.

Cough and Sneeze Etiquette

The following measures to contain respiratory secretions are recommended for all individuals with signs and symptoms of a respiratory infection.

- Cover the nose and mouth when coughing or sneezing.
- Provide and encourage use of tissues to contain respiratory secretions. If possible, dispose of tissues immediately in the nearest no-touch waste receptacle after use.
- If tissues are unavailable, cough or sneeze into a handkerchief or your arm or shoulder, not your hands.
- If you cough or sneeze in your hands, be sure to wash or clean them with an alcohol-based hand cleaner as soon as possible to stop the spread of germs.

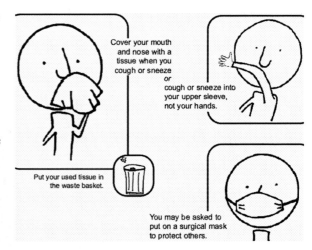

Pandemic Planning—Personal Protective Equipment

For more information about this topic, call the Risk Management Division:
- 1-801-240-4049
- 1-800-453-3860, ext. 2-4049 (toll free in the United States and Canada)

This fact sheet provides information on how individuals, such as employees and missionaries, can protect themselves from an infectious disease during a pandemic through the use of personal protective equipment (PPE).

Background

A severe pandemic (defined as a world-wide epidemic) in a vulnerable population, such as the 1918 flu pandemic, represents a worst-case scenario for pandemic planning and preparedness. Communities, individuals, employers, schools, and other organizations are being asked to plan for the use of interventions that will help limit the spread of disease. At this time, there is concern because of continued spread of a highly pathogenic avian influenza (H5N1) virus among animals in Asia, Africa, the Middle East, and Europe which has the potential to significantly threaten human health. If a virus such as H5N1 mutates and spreads easily from one person to another, avian influenza may break out globally. While there are no reports of *sustained* human-to-human transmission of avian influenza, governments and international health agencies are preparing for a possible pandemic. A pandemic can originate from any "unknown" source, such as the H5N1 virus.

General

Where contact with infected persons is not expected, individuals interacting with the general population should use basic PPE during a pandemic to prevent sprays of potentially infected liquid droplets (from talking, coughing, or sneezing) from contacting their nose or mouth. For caretakers in contact with possible avian influenza patients, refer to the *Pandemic Planning—Health Care Worker Preparedness* fact sheet or the *Pandemic Planning – Home and Family Preparedness* fact sheet.

Surgical Masks and Respirators

Surgical masks provide protection from liquid droplets and are generally recommended. Respirators, such as N95 respirators, may be considered if there is an expectation of close contact with persons who have symptomatic influenza infection. Follow the surgical mask or respirator manufacturer's fitting instructions to ensure proper fit and usage.

Eye Protection

Eye protection generally is not required to prevent influenza infection.

Hand Washing

Individuals should wash hands frequently with soap and water or a hand sanitizer to prevent hands from transferring potentially infectious material from surfaces to their mouths or noses.

Gloves

While individuals may choose to wear gloves, the exposure of concern is touching the mouth and nose with a contaminated hand and not exposure to the virus through broken skin (for example, cuts or scrapes). While the use of gloves may make individuals more aware of potential hand contamination, there is no difference between intentional or unintentional touching of the mouth, nose, or eyes with either a contaminated glove or a contaminated hand.

Proper Removal of PPE
Remove PPE in the proper sequence to avoid contamination.
1. Because gloves are considered the most contaminated piece of PPE, remove them first. Do not touch the outside of gloves with your bare hands during removal. If you contaminate your hands during the removal process, wash them before continuing.
2. Surgical masks or N95 respirators may be contaminated because droplets may have landed on them or you may have touched your face by mistake while wearing your PPE. Touch only the ties or straps at the back of your head. Slowly remove the straps, taking care that the respirator does not contaminate your bare skin or clothing.
3. Dispose of used PPE in a plastic lined trash can or a plastic bag. Seal the plastic bag for later disposal. Hold the bag by the outside and avoid any rush of air as you seal it.
4. Always wash your hands thoroughly with soap and water or a hand sanitizer immediately after PPE removal.

Summary
When selecting PPE, consider factors such as function, fit, long-term comfort, ability to be decontaminated, disposal, and cost. Sometimes, when a piece of PPE will have to be used repeatedly for a long period of time, a more expensive and durable piece of PPE may be less expensive in the long run than a disposable piece of PPE. During a pandemic, recommendations for PPE use may change, depending on information on PPE effectiveness in preventing the spread of influenza.

Reference
www.osha.gov/Publications/OSHA3327pandemic.pdf Guidance on Preparing Workplaces for an Influenza Pandemic. OSHA 3327-02N 2007.

Pandemic Planning—Social Distancing

For more information about this topic, call the Risk Management Division:
- 1-801-240-4049
- 1-800-453-3860, ext. 2-4049 (toll free in the United States and Canada)

This fact sheet provides information on how to utilize social distancing as a means to help control or minimize the spread of a possible pandemic virus among individuals and in the community.

Background

A severe pandemic (defined as a worldwide epidemic) in a vulnerable population, such as the 1918 flu pandemic, represents a worst-case scenario for pandemic planning and preparedness. Communities, individuals, employers, schools, and other organizations are being asked to plan for the use of interventions that will help limit the spread of disease. At this time, there is concern because of continued spread of a highly pathogenic avian influenza (H5N1) virus among animals in Asia, Africa, the Middle East, and Europe that has the potential to significantly threaten human health. If a virus such as H5N1 mutates and spreads easily from one person to another, an avian influenza may break out globally. While there are no reports of *sustained* human-to-human transmission of avian influenza, governments and international health agencies are preparing for a possible pandemic. A pandemic can originate from any unknown source, such as the H5N1 virus.

What Is Social Distancing?

Social distancing (SD), self-shielding, voluntary isolation, and reverse quarantine are all methods that attempt to limit close physical proximity between infected and healthy individuals. They provide individuals with some measure of personal control over their own exposure to a potential pandemic. SD can be instituted voluntarily by individuals or through actions taken by local, state, or government officials such as closure of schools, discontinuance of public transportation, and restrictions on large gatherings or public venues. During the 1918 pandemic, leaders of the Church were supportive of SD efforts to curtail public meetings and other social functions sponsored by the Church. Some examples of their efforts included the following:

- Postponing the April 1919 sessions of general conference until June
- Holding a nonpublic funeral for President Joseph F. Smith
- Suspending local Church meetings in areas affected by the pandemic
- Holding special fasts to help ease the pandemic
- Publishing articles in Saturday's edition of the *Deseret Evening News* to help fill the spiritual void left when Church meetings were suspended

Why Social Distancing?

Influenza is thought to be primarily spread through large respiratory droplets (droplet transmission) that directly contact the nose, mouth, or eyes. These droplets are produced when infected people cough, sneeze, or talk, sending the infectious droplets and very small sprays (aerosols) into the air and into contact with other people. Large droplets can only travel a limited distance; therefore, people should limit close contact (within 6 feet) with others when possible. To a lesser degree, human influenza is spread by touching objects contaminated with influenza viruses and then transferring the infected material from the hands to the nose, mouth, or eyes.

What Are the Benefits of Social Distancing?

Adults may decrease their risk of infection by practicing SD and minimizing their nonessential social contacts and exposure to highly populated environments. Low-cost and sustainable SD practices can be adopted by individuals within their community (for example, going to the grocery store once a week rather than every other day, avoiding large public gatherings) and at their workplace (for example, spacing people farther apart in the workplace, telecommuting when feasible, substituting teleconferences for meetings) for the duration of a community outbreak.

Children are a significant factor in the transmission of influenza for many reasons. Compared with adults, children usually shed more influenza virus and for a longer period. They also are less skilled in handling their secretions and are in close proximity with many other children for most of the day at school. Schools, in particular, clearly serve as a means to transmit seasonal community influenza epidemics. Infected children and parents are also thought to play a major role in introducing and transmitting influenza virus within their households.

Therefore, given the disproportionate contribution of children in spreading disease and viruses, targeting their social networks both within and outside of schools would be expected to help disrupt influenza spread. Given that children and teens are together at school for a significant portion of the day, dismissal of students from school could effectively disrupt a significant portion of influenza transmission within these age groups.

Mathematical modeling also suggests a reduction of overall disease especially when schools are closed early in the outbreak. Parents may determine to keep their children at home, therefore providing a form of voluntary SD. During this period, parents would be encouraged to consider child care arrangements that do not result in large gatherings of children outside the school setting.

What Are the Basics of Social Distancing

Social distancing may be a viable alternative for the general public to avoid the pandemic influenza infection until a vaccine becomes available. Below, in order of potential effectiveness, are various aspects of SD suggestions:

1. Limit exposure to other people within 6 feet.
2. Minimize exposure to enclosed spaces containing crowds, such as movie theatres, grocery stores, gas stations, schools, malls, and so forth.
3. Use personal protective equipment, such as N95 masks (see Pandemic Planning—Personal Protective Equipment fact sheet), if you must get within 6 feet of anyone outside your immediate family (or other individuals where you have intimate knowledge of their health conditions) or if you must go into an enclosed space containing crowds. It should be noted that there is limited information on the use of surgical masks for the control of a pandemic in settings where there is no identified source of infection.
4. Wash hands after touching any item that may have been touched by others or use disposable gloves (see Pandemic Planning—Personal Hygiene fact sheet for more details). Contaminated surfaces can transmit influenza for 24 hours.

Potential Impacts of Social Distancing

Closure of office buildings, stores, schools, and public transportation systems may be feasible community containment measures during a pandemic and are considered forms of forced SD. All of these have significant impact on the community and workforce. Careful consideration should be focused on their potential effectiveness and how to maintain critical supplies and infrastructure while limiting community interaction. For example, when public transportation is cancelled, other modes of transportation must be provided for emergency medical services and medical evaluation. The mandatory closure of public venues will have a direct and significant effect on worship services, as well as proselytizing efforts by missionaries.

Pandemic Planning—Sheltering in place

For more information about this fact sheet, contact Risk Management at
Salt Lake area: 240-4049
All other areas: 1-800-453-3860, ext. 2-4049

This fact sheet provides information on how to prepare for Sheltering in place in the event of a possible flu pandemic.

Background

A severe pandemic (defined as a worldwide epidemic) in a vulnerable population, such as the 1918 flu pandemic, represents a worst-case scenario for pandemic planning and preparedness. Communities, individuals, employers, schools, and other organizations are being asked to plan for the use of interventions that will help limit the spread of disease. At this time, there is concern because of continued spread of a highly pathogenic avian influenza (H5N1) virus among animals in Asia, Africa, the Middle East, and Europe that has the potential to significantly threaten human health. If a virus such as H5N1 mutates and spreads easily from one person to another, avian influenza may break out globally. While there are no reports of *sustained* human-to-human transmission of avian influenza, governments and international health agencies are preparing for a possible pandemic. A pandemic can originate from any unknown source, such as the H5N1 virus.

Depending on the severity of a pandemic, commercial airlines might drastically curtail or even cease operations. Travel restrictions could also impede people from returning to their home country or fleeing to other countries. For these reasons, it may make more sense to shelter in place (stay home and practice social distancing to avoid infection) for an appropriate period of time.

Preparation

Families should prepare at least two weeks of emergency supplies (food, water, medicines, and so forth) in order to shelter in place during an influenza pandemic. Consult "Preparation for Home Emergencies and Natural Disasters" under Provident Living at www.lds.org.

Living Internationally

Those living in areas with undependable infrastructure for water, electricity, and food availability should evaluate their situation and prepare emergency supplies accordingly (nonperishable food, potable water, medicines, and so forth.) for the possibility of sheltering in place for at least 2 and up to 12 weeks. Water purification techniques for drinking water such as boiling, filtering, and adding chlorine to locally available rainwater, lakes, rivers, and wells may replace the need to store large quantities of water.

Boiling water will kill most types of disease-causing organisms and is the most reliable method of purifying water easily. Bring the water to a rolling boil for two minutes. Add one minute for each 5,000 feet of elevation.

The addition of chlorine bleach to water is also a viable alternative. For clear water, add 8 drops per gallon (3.8 liters) and let stand for at least 15 minutes. If the water is cloudy, add twice as much bleach. Bleach used for water purification should be unscented and have a concentration of sodium hypochlorite of at least 4%.

What Can You Do on a Daily Basis?

Cover your cough. Wash your hands regularly with soap and water for at least 20 seconds to kill viruses and bacteria or apply a hand sanitizer with a minimum of 60% alcohol content when soap and water are not available (see Pandemic Planning—Personal Hygiene fact sheet for more details). Stay home if you are sick. Get a vaccination against seasonal flu.

Travel

Those living in or traveling to countries with human or animal cases of H5N1 virus should consider the potential risks. Keep informed of the latest medical guidance and practical information and plan accordingly. Consult www.travel.state.gov for the latest tips on international travel.

Sheltering of Missionaries

Missionaries serving in the local areas may require assistance if required to shelter in place for more than several days. Please contact the local mission president for instructions and assistance if requested to provide these services.

References

Information for this fact sheet was taken from the following the U.S. Department of State web site, www.travel.state.gov/travel/tips/health/health_3096.html.

Detailed information about suggested preparations, as well as planning checklists is available from:

- www.pandemicflu.gov.
- www.who.int/en/.
- www.cdc.gov.

Pandemic Planning—Infectious Disease Cleanup

For more information about this topic, call the Risk Management Division:
- 1-801-240-4049
- 1-800-453-3860, ext. 2-4049 (toll free in the United States and Canada)

This fact sheet provides information on how to perform clean-up measures in areas that may be contaminated by an infectious disease, such as avian influenza or severe acute respiratory syndrome (SARS). The procedures outlined will help control or minimize the spread of possible infectious diseases among individuals and in the community.

Background

A severe pandemic (defined as a worldwide epidemic) in a vulnerable population, such as the 1918 flu pandemic, represents a worst-case scenario for pandemic planning and preparedness. Communities, individuals, employers, schools, and other organizations are being asked to plan for the use of interventions that will help limit the spread of disease. At this time, there is concern because of continued spread of a highly pathogenic avian influenza (H5N1) virus among animals in Asia, Africa, the Middle East, and Europe that has the potential to significantly threaten human health. If a virus such as H5N1 mutates and spreads easily from one person to another, avian influenza may break out globally. While there are no reports of *sustained* human-to-human transmission of avian influenza, governments and international health agencies are preparing for a possible pandemic. A pandemic can originate from any unknown source, such as the H5N1 virus.

Personal Protective Equipment

Employees cleaning buildings in areas where contamination from an infectious disease is a concern should take the following precautions:

- Personnel doing general cleaning where infectious disease is a concern should wear disposable vinyl gloves and safety glasses but need not use protective clothing, masks, or respirators.

- Personnel who clean where a person suspected of having an infectious disease has been should wear disposable vinyl gloves; eye protection (goggles or face shield); and a NIOSH-certified, disposable N95 respirator (mask).

Hygiene and Housekeeping Practices

Supervisors of cleaning personnel should be aware of the symptoms of the suspected infectious disease that they are cleaning for. Any employee who cleans a building that has been occupied by a person suspected of having an infectious disease should notify their supervisor if he or she develops similar symptoms within 10 days of cleaning the building. The main source of airborne infectious particles will have been removed once a person suspected of having an infectious disease, such as SARS or avian influenza, leaves the building. It is unknown to what extent an infectious disease can be transmitted through contact with residual infectious materials on surfaces.

Personnel cleaning potentially contaminated facilities should frequently wash their hands with soap and water (see Pandemic Planning—Personal Personal Hygiene fact sheet). Cleaning personnel should also follow these additional recommendations:

- Remove and discard gloves if they become soiled or damaged while cleaning.
- Discard gloves after you have finished cleaning (do not wash or reuse gloves worn during cleaning).
- If soap and water are not available, use an alcohol-based hand wash to clean hands.
- Frequently touched surfaces in the building (such as armrests, doorknobs, and latches) and bathroom surfaces should be wiped down with an EPA-registered low- or intermediate-level chemical household germicide and allowed to air dry in accordance with the manufacturer's instructions.

The CDC advises that there are no disinfectant products currently registered by the EPA for SARS or avian influenza. The CDC recommends the use of EPA-registered chemical germicides that provide low- or intermediate-level disinfection during general use against infectious agents because these products are known to inactivate viruses with physical and biochemical properties similar to other viral agents. Disposable N95 respirators should be used in the context of a complete respiratory protection program. Refer to the Respiratory Protection Program in the *Church Safety, Health, and Environmental Manual*, U.S. or international version. A respiratory protection program includes medical determinations; fit-testing; training; and properly maintaining, cleaning, inspecting, and storing respirators. Order respirators through local safety suppliers. If respirators are not available locally, submit a purchase requisition to the area purchasing manager.

References
"Information Regarding Severe Acute Respiratory Syndrome (SARS)." Occupational Safety and Health Administration (OSHA). www.osha-slc.gov/dep/sars/index.html.
"Interim Recommendations for Cleaning and Disinfection of the SARS Patient Environment." CDC. www.cdc.gov/ncidod/sars/cleaningpatientenviro.htm.
"Interim Domestic Guidance on the Use of Respirators to Prevent Transmission of SARS." CDC. www.cdc.gov/ncidod/sars/respirators.htm.
"Interim Guidelines about Severe Acute Respiratory Syndrome (SARS) for Persons in the General Workplace Environment." CDC. www.cdc.gov/ncidod/sars/workplaceguidelines.htm.
"Guidance on Preparing Workplaces for an Influenza Pandemic," OSHA 3327-02N 2007 www.osha.gov/Publications/influenza pandemic.html.

Pandemic Planning—Workplace Preparedness

For more information about this topic, call the Risk Management Division:
- 1-801-240-4049
- 1-800-453-3860, ext. 2-4049 (toll free in the United States and Canada)

This fact sheet provides information on how employers can prepare for a possible flu pandemic.

Background

A severe pandemic (defined as a worldwide epidemic) in a vulnerable population, such as the 1918 flu pandemic, represents a worst-case scenario for pandemic planning and preparedness. Communities, individuals, employers, schools, and other organizations are being asked to plan for the use of interventions that will help limit the spread of disease. At this time, there is concern because of continued spread of a highly pathogenic avian influenza (H5N1) virus among animals in Asia, Africa, the Middle East, and Europe that has the potential to significantly threaten human health. If a virus such as H5N1 mutates and spreads easily from one person to another, avian influenza may break out globally. While there are no reports of *sustained* human-to-human transmission of avian influenza, governments and international health agencies are preparing for a possible pandemic. A pandemic can originate from any unknown source, such as the H5N1 virus.

Employers face several challenges in preparing their businesses for a possible pandemic:

- Section 5(a)(1) of the U.S. Occupational Safety and Health Act of 1970 requires that every working man and woman must be provided with a safe and healthful workplace.
- Absenteeism will increase due to illness of employees or their families.
- Changes in patterns of commerce may affect income and costs.
- Normal supply and delivery schedules will likely be interrupted.

Employers and employees should use this planning guidance to help identify levels of risk levels in workplace settings and apply appropriate control measures that include good hygiene, cough etiquette, social distancing, use of personal protective equipment (PPE), and staying home from work when ill. Other documents on these subjects are available through Risk Management. Employee risks may range from very high to lower risk depending on the nature of the business enterprise and the employee responsibilities. The OSHA document referenced at the end of this fact sheet can provide additional information.

Overview

The best way to reduce the risk of becoming infected with influenza during a pandemic is to avoid crowded settings and other situations that increase the risk of exposure to someone who may be infected. If it is necessary to be in a crowded setting, the time spent in a crowd should be as short as possible. It is the employer's obligation to consider and possibly provide additional methods of protection if employees and customers are required to be in close proximity to one another.

Incorporate Pandemic Planning into the Organization's Business Continuity Plan

- Develop a disaster plan that includes pandemic preparedness (see www.pandemicflu.gov/plan/businesschecklist.html.

- Make sure that your business continuity plan protects and supports your employees, customers, and the general public. Informed employees who feel safe at work are less likely to be absent.

- Prepare and plan for operations with a reduced workforce.

- Identify business-essential positions and the skills required to sustain essential business functions and operations. Be sure to cross-train three or more employees so they can function appropriately in these positions.

- Plan for downsizing services but also anticipate any scenario, that may require a surge in your services if they are critical in a pandemic situation.

- Organize and identify a central team of people or focal point to serve as a communication source so that your employees and customers can have accurate information during the crisis.

- Work with your suppliers to ensure that you can continue to operate and provide services.

Evaluate Personnel Risks and Concerns

- Identify possible exposure and health risks to employees. Will employees potentially be in contact with people with influenza? Are employees expected to have much contact with the general public or each other?

- Minimize exposure to fellow employees or the public. For example, can more employees work from home? This may require enhancement of technology and communications equipment.

- Develop a sick leave policy that does not penalize sick employees, thereby encouraging employees who have influenza-related symptoms (such as, fever, headache, cough, sore throat, runny or stuffy nose, muscle aches, or upset stomach) to stay home so that they do not infect other employees. Recognize that employees with ill family members may need to stay home to care for them.

- Recognize that, in the course of normal daily life, all employees will have nonoccupational risk factors at home and in community settings that should be reduced to the extent possible. Some employees will also have individual risk factors that should be considered by employers as they plan how the organization will respond to a potential pandemic (for example, immuno-compromised individuals and pregnant women).

- Assist employees in managing additional stressors related to the pandemic. These are likely to include distress related to personal or family illness; life disruption; grief related to loss of family, friends, or coworkers; loss of routine support systems; and other similar challenges. Assuring timely and accurate communication will also be important throughout the duration of the pandemic in decreasing fear or worry. Employers should provide opportunities for support, counseling, and mental health assessment and referral should these be necessary. If present, Employee Assistance Programs can offer training and provide resources and other guidance on mental health and resiliency before and during a pandemic.

- Work with DMBA and Risk Management as well as state and local health agencies to provide information to employees and customers about medical care in the event of a pandemic.

Employee Hygiene

- Develop policies and practices that distance employees from each other, customers, and the public (see the Pandemic Planning—Social Distancing fact sheet for more information). Consider practices to minimize face-to-face contact between employees such as e-mail, Web sites, and teleconferences. Policies and practices that allow employees to work from home or to stagger their work shifts may be important as absenteeism rises.

- Consider stockpiling items such as soap, tissue, hand sanitizer, cleaning supplies, and recommended PPE. When stockpiling items, be aware of each product's shelf life and storage conditions (avoid areas that are damp or have temperature extremes) and incorporate product rotation (consume oldest supplies first) into your stockpile management program.

- Encourage employees to wash their hands frequently with soap and water or with hand sanitizer if there is no soap or water available. Also, encourage your employees to avoid touching their noses, mouths, and eyes. Encourage employees to cover their coughs and sneezes with a tissue or to cough and sneeze into their upper sleeves if tissues are not available. All employees should wash their hands or use a hand sanitizer after they cough, sneeze, or blow their noses. See the Pandemic Planning—Personal Hygiene fact sheet for more information.

- Provide employees and customers in the workplace with easy access to infection control supplies, such as soap, hand sanitizers, PPE (such as gloves or surgical masks), tissues, and office cleaning supplies.

- Provide training, education and informational material about business-essential job functions and employee health and safety, including proper hygiene practices and the use of any PPE to be used in the workplace. Be sure that informational material is available in a usable format for individuals with sensory disabilities or limited English proficiency. Refer to fact sheets on hygiene, home preparedness, social distancing, and PPE for more information.

- Periodically disinfect work surfaces, telephones, computer equipment, and other frequently touched surfaces and office equipment.

- Discourage employees from using other employees' phones, desks, offices, or other work tools and equipment.

- Encourage employees to obtain a seasonal influenza vaccine (this helps to prevent illness from seasonal influenza strains that may continue to circulate).

Protecting Employees and Customers

- Educate and train employees in proper hand hygiene, cough etiquette, and social distancing techniques. Resource documents are available through Risk Management. Understand and develop work practice and engineering controls that can provide additional protection to employees and customers, such as drive-through service windows; clear plastic sneeze barriers; ventilation; and the proper selection, use, and disposal of PPE.

- Evaluate the types of measures that may be used to protect employees and customers (listed from most effective to least effective): engineering controls, administrative controls, work practices, and PPE.

- Employees should avoid close contact with their coworkers and customers (maintain a separation of at least 6 feet). They should avoid shaking hands and always wash their hands after contact with others. Even when employees wear gloves, they should wash their hands upon removal of the gloves in case their hands become contaminated during the removal process.

- Minimize situations where groups of people are crowded together, such as in a meeting. Use e-mail, phones, and text messages to communicate with each other. When meetings are necessary, avoid close contact by keeping a separation of at least 6 feet, where possible, and assure that there is proper ventilation in the meeting room.

- Reduce or eliminate unnecessary social interactions. This can be very effective in controlling the spread of infectious diseases. Reconsider all situations that permit or require employees, customers, and visitors (including family members) to enter the workplace.

- Promote healthy lifestyles, including good nutrition and exercise. A person's overall health impacts their body's immune system and can affect their ability to fight off or recover from an infectious disease.

Concerns When Living, Working, or Traveling Internationally
Employees living abroad and international business travelers should note that other geographic areas have different influenza seasons and will likely be affected by a pandemic at different times. The U.S. Department of State emphasizes that, in the event of a pandemic, its ability to assist Americans traveling and residing abroad may be severely limited by restrictions on local and international movement imposed for public health reasons, either by foreign governments and/or the United States. Furthermore, American citizens should take note that the Department of State cannot provide Americans traveling or living abroad with medications or supplies even in the event of a pandemic. These conditions will be similar to those found in most other countries. Each individual should contact their own country's Department of State for information specific to their country's policies and regulations.

The U.S. Department of State has asked its embassies and consulates to consider preparedness measures that take into consideration that travel into or out of a country may not be possible, safe, or medically advisable during a pandemic. Guidance on how private citizens can prepare is available in the Church's Pandemic Planning—Sheltering in Place fact sheet. Embassy stocks will typically not be made available to private citizens abroad. It is also likely that governments will respond to a pandemic by imposing public health measures that restrict domestic and international movement, further limiting the U.S. government's ability to assist Americans in these countries. As it is possible that these measures may be implemented very quickly, it is important that employers and employees plan appropriately.

Before any international travel:

- Consult the U.S. Government pandemic website at www.pandemicflu.gov or www.travel.state.gov/travel/travel or the World Health Organization's (WHO) Web site at www.who.int/csr/don/en/index.html to review countries with significant outbreaks of infectious disease.
- Find out how and where to get medical care in the country where you are traveling.
- Check your health insurance plan or get additional insurance that covers medical evacuation in case you become ill.
- Be sure your vaccinations are up-to-date at least 6 weeks before you travel.
- Assemble or purchase a travel health kit containing first aid and medical supplies. Be sure to include a thermometer and alcohol-based hand rub.

During travel:

- Avoid all direct contact with poultry or places where live poultry is raised or kept.
- Avoid handling surfaces contaminated with poultry feces or respiratory secretions.
- One of the most important preventive measures is careful and frequent hand washing. Please refer to the Pandemic Planning—Personal Hygiene fact sheet.
- It is important to understand that you might become infected in a country where the health care systems may be inadequate to cope with a serious infectious process.
- If you have an illness that requires prompt medical attention, a consular officer can assist you in locating medical services and communicating with your family and friends.

After your return:

- Monitor your health for 10 days.
- If you become ill with fever and develop a cough, difficulty breathing, or any illnesses during this period of time, consult a health care provider. Advise them of your symptoms, where you have traveled, and if you have had any contact with poultry or with a known case of any infectious disease.

References
www.osha.gov/Publications/influenza_pandemic.html
www.pandemicflu.gov
www.cdc.gov/niosh
www.cdc.gov
www.fda.gov/cdrh/ppe/fluoutbreaks.html

THE CHURCH OF
JESUS CHRIST
OF LATTER-DAY SAINTS

Pandemic Planning—Health Care Worker Preparedness

For more information about this topic, call the Risk Management Division:
- 1-801-240-4049
- 1-800-453-3860, ext. 2-4049 (toll free in the United States and Canada)

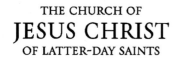

This fact sheet provides information on how health-care workers, such as missionary area medical advisors, physicians, nurses, respiratory therapists, etc. who may staff clinics and hospitals can prepare themselves for a possible flu pandemic.

Background

A severe pandemic (defined as a world-wide epidemic) in a vulnerable population, such as the 1918 flu pandemic, represents a worst-case scenario for pandemic planning and preparedness. Communities, individuals, employers, schools, and other organizations are being asked to plan for the use of interventions that will help limit the spread of disease. At this time, there is concern because of continued spread of a highly pathogenic avian influenza (H5N1) virus among animals in Asia, Africa, the Middle East, and Europe which has the potential to significantly threaten human health. If a virus such as H5N1 mutates and spreads easily from one person to another, avian influenza may break out globally. While there are no reports of *sustained* human-to-human transmission of avian influenza, governments and international health agencies are preparing for a possible pandemic. A pandemic can originate from any "unknown" source, such as the H5N1 virus.

When in contact with possible avian influenza patients, health-care providers should follow standard respiratory droplet precautions. At present, the transmission of flu virus is considered to be via droplet. If avian flu becomes easily transmissible via human-to-human contact, it will likely be via droplet or possible aerosol transmission.

General precautions

Wash hands carefully for 20 seconds before and after all patient contact, or contact with surfaces potentially contaminated with respiratory secretions.

Droplet Precautions:
- Use personal protective equipment (PPE) such as a surgical mask or preferably an N95 respirator, gloves and gown for all patient contact. Following established guidelines for the proper use of and the removal sequence for PPE is very important.
- Use disposable equipment if available, or other equipment such as blood pressure cuffs, thermometers, etc. that can be disinfected before use on another patient.
- Wear safety goggles or a face shield within 3 feet of the patient.

If there is concern of aerosol transmission, the patient should be placed in a negative-pressure, airborne infection isolation room. If such a room is unavailable, portable HEPA filters should be used if available. Workers should use at least a disposable N95 respirator when in the isolation room or other room containing the patient.

To help prevent transmission between patients:
- Group infected patients in the same room if private rooms are not available.
- Minimize transportation of patients outside the room.

- Limit the number of people caring for patients.
- Limit the numbers of visitors to the patient.

Proper Use and Removal of PPE

Proper surgical mask or respirator use and removal include the following:

- Prior to putting on PPE, wash hands thoroughly with soap and water or use a hand sanitizer to reduce the possibility of inadvertent contact between contaminated hands and mucous membranes.
- Follow the surgical mask or respirator manufacturer's fitting instructions to ensure proper fit and usage.
- If worn in the presence of infectious persons, a surgical mask or respirator may become contaminated with infectious material; therefore, avoid touching the outside of the device to help prevent contamination of hands.
- Once worn in the presence of a patient with an infectious disease, the surgical mask or disposable N95 respirator should be removed and appropriately discarded.

Remove PPE in the proper sequence to avoid contamination.

1. Because the gloves are considered the most contaminated piece of PPE, remove them first. Do not touch the outside of gloves with your bare hands during removal. If you contaminate your hands during the removal process, wash them before continuing.
2. The eye protection should be removed next because it is more cumbersome and might interfere with removal of the mask. Remember that it may be contaminated because droplets may have landed on it or you may have touched it by mistake while wearing your PPE. Remove eye protection by touching only the ear pieces or head band at the side of your head to lift away from your face. Discard it or deposit it into the soap and water container for washing later.
3. The gown is next; remember that the front is contaminated. Untie the back, then slip your hands under the gown at the neck and shoulders and peel it away from your body. Grasp cuffs one at a time by slipping your fingers underneath and then pull each arm out of the gown. Holding the gown at the shoulders, fold the outside contaminated part so that it is inside and then discard the gown. Then wash your hands or use hand sanitizer.
4. Surgical masks or N95 respirators may be contaminated because droplets may have landed on them or you may have touched your face by mistake while wearing your PPE. Touch only the ties or straps at the back of your head. Slowly remove the straps, taking care that the respirator does not contaminate your bare skin or clothing.
5. Dispose of used PPE in a plastic lined trash can or a plastic bag. Seal the plastic bag for later disposal. Hold the bag by the outside and avoid any rush of air as you seal it.
6. Always wash your hands thoroughly with soap and water or a hand sanitizer immediately after PPE removal.

References

www.cdc.gov: Interim pre-pandemic planning guidance, including individual planning, workplace planning, community planning, school planning, health-care planning, and community strategy for pandemic influenza mitigation
www.osha.gov: Guidance on Preparing Workplaces for an Influenza Pandemic
www.who.org: Avian Flu fact sheet, pandemic preparedness plan, guidelines, WHO pandemic influenza draft protocol for rapid response and containment

Isolation Room Setup
Preparation of the isolation room

- Ensure additional precautions by indicating with appropriate signage on the door (for example, bio-hazard logo).

- Place a log book at the entrance of the isolation room. All health care workers or visitors entering the isolation area must sign the log book.

- Remove all non-essential furniture. The remaining furniture should be easy to clean and should not conceal or retain dirt or moisture, either within or around it.

- Collect linen as needed.

- Stock the hand basin with suitable supplies for hand washing.

- Place appropriate waste bags in the room on a foot-operated bin.

- Place a puncture-proof container for sharps in the room.

- Keep the patient's personal belongings to a minimum. Keep water pitcher and cup, tissue wipes, and all items necessary for attending to personal hygiene within the patient's reach.

- The patient should be allocated his/her own non-critical items of patient care equipment, e.g. stethoscope, thermometer and sphygmomanometers. Any item of patient care equipment that is required for other patients should be thoroughly cleaned and disinfected prior to use.

- Set up a cart outside the door to hold personal protective equipment. A checklist may be useful to ensure all equipment is available.

- Place appropriate container with a lid outside the door for equipment that requires disinfection and sterilization. Once equipment has been appropriately cleaned it can be sent to the sterilizing service department.

- Keep adequate equipment required for cleaning and disinfection inside the patients' room.

Isolation Room Setup

Preparation of the isolation room in a residential home:

- Start by picking a room that preferably has an outside entrance and an interior bathroom. If this cannot be accomplished try an interior room with an interior bathroom and at least one outside operable window. Again these are ideals and we will work with what we have.
- Next clear out all furniture except the bare essential. Try to only leave furniture that can be sanitized. This means no unsealed or unpainted wood or cloth. Metal is preferable. The remaining furniture should be easy to clean and should not conceal or retain dirt or moisture, either within or around it.
- Remove all clothing from closets and anything else remaining that is not essential to the victims recovery. Also take down all drapes and curtains. Blinds are okay if they are plastic, metal or sealed wood.
- If the room is carpeted - remove carpet. If you cannot remove the carpet covering the floor with several layers of 4 or 6 mil plastic will do. If using this method make sure that you cut your plastic long enough to go at least 2 feet up the wall. Duct tape the plastic to the wall all the way around. Your are basically creating a plastic tub.
- BEFORE you lay plastic - seal up each floor or wall vent that will be below the plastic. this can be done be stuffing a towel down the uncovered vent and then with duct tape and plastic covering the vent so no air get blow out. This also includes any intake vents. If there are vents anywhere else in the room seal them as well. Do this even if you are not putting plastic on the floor.
- Seal all other entrances or holes or possible venting from the isolation room into the rest of the home. Do not forget attic accesses if they exit.
- Seal all exterior windows except two. One will be used as an air intake and the other as an exhaust. On the exhaust window place a fan (a box fan works good) in front of that window to blow out. If you have access to HEPA filters it would be a good idea to place one over the or in front of the fan to minimize problems with the exhaust to your neighbors and/or possible wind blowing contaminated air back into your other open window and doors to your house. All windows and doors with in 20' downwind of this exhaust window should be sealed with plastic. If your intake window is within 20' of your exhaust window it would be good to stretch a HEPA filter over that windows opening as well. Only open the exhaust window large enough for the fan. Open the intake window the same amount. If you only have one window use it for exhaust and use the intake from the home through the door.
- If you do not have an exterior entrance and are using the homes interior entrance to the room for entering and exiting the room your will need to create a clean room. This is a small chamber where you can change your clothes after exiting and before entering the room and decontaminate yourself before going into the rest of your home. This is done by removing the door first the draping plastic as a curtain in it's place. Cut the plastic down the middle to allow passage through the plastic. Try to overlap the two piece of the curtain. Duct taping the curtain to the header above the door will help ensure containment. Then into the hall about 4 or 5 feet hang another plastic curtain or curtains to create a small room. Cut and entrance/exit slit in that curtain as well. Duct taping this to the ceiling and wall will also help with containment.
- Place a chair and table in that room to aid with dressing and undressing and decontamination procedures. The table and chair should be cleanable as well. On the table should be a large water basin a bottle of spray water/bleach mixture (1 tablespoon of bleach to 1 quart of water solution) for decontamination several large plastic bags for placing contaminated discarded clothing. A foot operated hamper would be a good idea for convenience. Stock the basin with suitable supplies for hand washing. On the table leave room for personal protective equipment. A checklist may be useful to ensure all equipment is available.
- Ensure additional precautions by indicating with appropriate signage on the entrance (for example, bio-hazard logo). This is important so that if you have guests they can see clearly that the isolation room is not a normal room.
- Place a log book at the entrance of the isolation room. All health care workers or visitors entering the isolation area must sign the log book.
- Place appropriate waste bags in the room on a foot-operated bin.
- Place a puncture-proof container for sharps in the room.
- Keep the patient's personal belongings to a minimum. Keep water pitcher and cup, tissue wipes, and all items necessary for attending to personal hygiene within the patient's reach.
- Collect linen as needed.
- The patient should be allocated his/her own non-critical items of patient care equipment, e.g. stethoscope, thermometer and sphygmomanometers. Any item of patient care equipment that is required for other patients should be thoroughly cleaned and disinfected prior to use.
- Place appropriate container with a lid outside the door for equipment that requires disinfection and sterilization. Once equipment has been appropriately cleaned it will need to be sterilized.
- Keep adequate equipment required for cleaning and disinfection inside the patients' room.

National Security Emergencies

In addition to the natural and technological hazards described in this publication, Americans face threats posed by hostile governments or extremist groups. These threats to national security include acts of terrorism and acts of war. The following is general information about national security emergencies.

Terrorism

Terrorism is the use of force or violence against persons or property in violation of the criminal laws of the United States for purposes of intimidation, coercion or ransom. Terrorists often use threats to create fear among the public, to try to convince citizens that their government is powerless to prevent terrorism, and to get immediate publicity for their causes.

Acts of terrorism range from threats of terrorism, assassinations, kidnappings, hijackings, bomb scares and bombings, cyber attacks (computer-based), to the use of chemical, biological and nuclear weapons. High-risk targets include military and civilian government facilities, international airports, large cities and high-profile landmarks. Terrorists might also target large public gatherings, water and food supplies, utilities, and corporate centers. Further, they are capable of spreading fear by sending explosives or chemical and biological agents through the mail. In the immediate area of a terrorist event, you would need to rely on police, fire and other officials for instructions. However, you can prepare in much the same way you would prepare for other crisis events.

Preparing for terrorism

1. Wherever you are, be aware of your surroundings. The very nature of terrorism suggests there may be little or no warning.
2. Take precautions when traveling. Be aware of conspicuous or unusual behavior. Do not accept packages from strangers. Do not leave luggage unattended. Unusual behavior, suspicious packages and strange devices should be promptly reported to the police or security personnel.
3. Do not be afraid to move or leave if you feel uncomfortable or if something does not seem right.
4. Learn where emergency exits are located in buildings you frequent. Notice where exits are when you enter unfamiliar buildings. Plan how to get out of a building, subway or congested public area or traffic. Note where staircases are located. Notice heavy or breakable objects that could move, fall or break in an explosion.
5. Assemble a disaster supply kit at home and learn first aid. Separate the supplies you would take if you had to evacuate quickly, and put them in a backpac or container, ready to go.
6. Be familiar with different types of fire extinguishers and how to locate them. Know the location and availability of hard hats in buildings in which you spend a lot of time.

Protection against cyber attacks

Cyber attacks target computer or telecommunication networks of critical infrastructures such as power systems, traffic control systems, or financial systems. Cyber attacks target information technologies (IT) in three different ways. First, is a direct attack against an information system "through the wires alone (hacking). Second, the attack can be a physical assault against a critical IT element. Third, the attack can be from the inside as a result of compromising a trusted party with access to the system.

Be prepared to do without services you normally depend on that could be disrupted electricity, telephone, natural gas, gasoline pumps, cash registers, ATM machines, and internet transactions.

Be prepared to respond to official instructions if a cyber attack triggers other hazards, for example, general evacuation, evacuation to shelter, or shelter-in-place, because of hazardous materials releases, nuclear power plant incident, dam or flood control system failures.

Preparing for a building explosion

Explosions can collapse buildings and cause fires. People who live or work in a multi-level building can do the following:

1. Review emergency evacuation procedures. Know where emergency exits are located.

2. Keep fire extinguishers in working order. Know where they are located, and learn how to use them.

3. Learn first aid. Contact the local chapter of the American Red Cross for information and training.

4. Building owners should keep the following items in a designated place on each floor of the building.

* Portable, battery-operated radio and extra batteries
* Several flashlights and extra batteries
* First aid kit and manual
* Several hard hats
* Fluorescent tape to rope off dangerous areas

Bomb Threats

If you receive a bomb threat, get as much information from the caller as possible. Keep the caller on the line and record everything that is said. Then notify the police and the building management.

If you are notified of a bomb threat, do not touch any suspicious packages. Clear the area around suspicious packages and notify the police immediately. In evacuating a building, don't stand in front of windows, glass doors or other potentially hazardous areas. Do not block sidewalk or streets to be used by emergency officials or others still exiting the building.

Suspicious parcels and letters

Be wary of suspicious packages and letters. They can contain explosives, chemical or biological agents. Be particularly cautious at your place of employment.

Some typical characteristics postal inspectors have detected over the years, which ought to trigger suspicion, include parcels that

- *Are unexpected or from someone unfamiliar to you.*
- *Have no return address, or have one that can't be verified as legitimate.*
- *Are marked with restrictive endorsements, such as Personal, Confidential orDo not x-ray.*

- *Have protruding wires or aluminum foil, strange odors or stains.*
- *Show a city or state in the postmark that doesn't match the return address.*
- *Are of unusual weight, given their size, or are lopsided or oddly shaped.*
- *Are marked with any threatening language.*
- *Have inappropriate or unusual labeling.*
- *Have excessive postage or excessive packaging material such as masking tape and string.*
- *Have misspellings of common words.*
- *Are addressed to someone no longer with your organization or are otherwise outdated.*
- *Have incorrect titles or title without a name.*
- *Are not addressed to a specific person.*
- *Have handwritten or poorly typed addresses.*

With suspicious envelopes and packages other than those that might contain explosives, take these additional steps against possible biological and chemical agents.

- *Refrain from eating or drinking in a designated mail handling area.*
- *Place suspicious envelopes or packages in a plastic bag or some other type of container to prevent leakage of contents. Never sniff or smell suspect mail.*
- *If you do not have a container, then cover the envelope or package with anything available (e.g., clothing, paper, trash can, etc.) and do not remove the cover.*
- *Leave the room and close the door, or section off the area to prevent other from entering.*
- *Wash your hands with soap and water to prevent spreading any powder to your face.*
- *If you are at work, report the incident to your building security official or an available supervisor, who should notify police and other authorities without delay.*
- *List all people who were in the room or area when this suspicious letter or package was recognized. Give a copy of this list to both the local public health authorities and law enforcement officials for follow-up investigations and advice.*
- *If you are at home, report the incident to local police.*

What to do if there is an explosion

Leave the building as quickly as possible. Do not stop to retrieve personal possessions or make phone calls. If things are falling around you, get under a sturdy table or desk until they stop falling. Then leave quickly, watching for weakened floors and stairs and falling debris as you exit.

If there is a fire:
1. Stay low to the floor and exit the building as quickly as possible.

413

2. Cover your nose and mouth with a wet cloth.
3. When approaching a closed door, use the back of your hand to feel the lower, middle and upper parts of the door. Never use the palm of your hand or fingers to test for heat: burning those areas could impair your ability to escape a fire (i.e., ladders and crawling).
4. If the door is NOT hot, open slowly and ensure fire and/or smoke is not blocking your escape route. If your escape route is blocked, shut the door immediately and use an alternate escape route, such as a window. If clear, leave immediately through the door. Be prepared to crawl. Smoke and heat rise. The air is clearer and cooler near the floor.
5. If the door is hot, do not open it. Escape through a window. If you cannot escape, hang a white or light-colored sheet outside the window, alerting fire fighters to your presence.
6. Heavy smoke and poisonous gases collect first along the ceiling. Stay below the smoke at all times.

If you are trapped in debris:
1. Do not light a match.
2. Do not move about or kick up dust. Cover your mouth with a handkerchiefor clothing.
3. Rhythmically tap on a pipe or wall so that rescuers can hear where you are. Usea whistle if one is available. Shout only as a last resort when you hear sounds and think someone will hear you—shouting can causea person to inhale dangerous amounts of dust.

Chemical and Biological Weapons

In case of a chemical or biological weapon attack near you, authorities will instruct you on the best course of action. This may be to evacuate the area immediately,
to seek shelter at a designated location, or to take immediate shelter where you are and seal the premises. The best way to protect yourself is to take emergency preparedness measures ahead of time and to get medical attention as soon as possible, if needed.

Chemical

Chemical warfare agents are poisonous vapors, aerosols, liquids or solids that have toxic effects on people, animals or plants. They can be released by bombs, sprayed from aircraft, boats, or vehicles, or used as a liquid to create a hazard to people and the environment. Some chemical agents may be odorless and tasteless. They can have an immediate effect (a few seconds to a few minutes) or a delayed effect (several hours to several days). While potentially lethal, chemical agents are difficult to deliver in lethal concentrations. Outdoors, the agents often dissipate rapidly.

Chemical agents are also difficult to produce.

There are six types of agents:

1. Lung-damaging (pulmonary) agents such as phosgene,
2. Cyanide,
3. Vesicants or blister agents such as mustard,
4. Nerve agents such as GA (tabun), GB (sarin), GD (soman), GF, and VX,
5. Incapacitating agents such as BZ, and
6. Riot-control agents (similar to MACE).

Biological

Biological agents are organisms or toxins that can kill or incapacitate people, livestock and crops. The three basic groups of biological agents which would likely be used as weapons are bacteria, viruses, and toxins.

1. Bacteria.
Bacteria are small free-living organisms that reproduce by simple division and are easy to grow. The diseases they produce often respond to treatment with antibiotics.

2. Viruses.
Viruses are organisms which require living cells in which to reproduce and are intimately dependent upon the body they infect. Viruses produce diseases which generally do not respond to antibiotics. However, antiviral drugs are sometimes effective.

3. Toxins.
Toxins are poisonous substances found in, and extracted from, living plants, animals, or microorganisms; some toxins can be produced or altered by chemical means. Some toxins can be treated with specific antitoxins and selected drugs.

Most biological agents are difficult to grow and maintain. Many break down quickly when exposed to sunlight and other environmental factors, while others such as anthrax spores are very long lived. They can be dispersed by spraying them in the air, or infecting animals which carry the disease to humans as well through food and water contamination.

- Aerosols—Biological agents are dispersed into the air, forming a fine mist that may driftfor miles. Inhaling the agent may cause disease in people or animals.
- Animals—Some diseases are spread by insects and animals, such as fleas, mice, flies,and mosquitoes. Deliberately spreading diseases through livestock isalso referred to as agroterrorism.

414

- Food and water contamination—Some pathogenic organisms and toxins may persist in food and water supplies. Most microbes can be killed, and toxins deactivated, by cooking food and boiling water.

Anthrax spores formulated as a white powder were mailed to individuals in the government and media in the fall of 2001. Postal sorting machines and the opening of letters dispersed the spores as aerosols. Several deaths resulted.

The effect was to disrupt mail service and to cause a widespread fear of handling delivered mail among the public.

Person-to-person spread of a few infectious agents is also possible. Humans have been the source of infection for smallpox, plague, and the Lassa viruses.

What to do to prepare for a chemical or biological attack

- Assemble a disaster supply kit (see the "Emergency Planning and Disaster Supplies" chapter for more information) and be sure to include:
- Battery-powered commercial radio with extra batteries.
- Non-perishable food and drinking water.
- Roll of duct tape and scissors.
- Plastic for doors, windows and vents for the room in which you will shelter in place—this should be an internal room where you can block out air that may contain hazardous chemical or biological agents. To save critical time during an emergency, sheeting should be pre-measured and cut for each opening.
- First aid kit.
- Sanitation supplies including soap, water and bleach.

What to do during a chemical or biological attack

1. Listen to your radio for instructions from authorities such as whether to remain inside or to evacuate.
2. If you are instructed to remain in your home, the building where you are, or other shelter during a chemical or biological attack:

- Turn off all ventilation, including furnaces, air conditioners, vents and fans.
- Seek shelter in an internal room, preferably one without windows. Seal the room with duct tape and plastic sheeting. Ten square feet of floor space per person will provide sufficient air to prevent carbon dioxide build-up for up to five hours. (See "Shelter" chapter.)
- Remain in protected areas where toxic vapors are reduced or eliminated, and be sure to take your battery-operated radio with you.

3. If you are caught in an unprotected area, you should:
Attempt to get up-wind of the contaminated area.
Attempt to find shelter as quickly as possible.
Listen to your radio for official instructions.

What to do after a chemical attack

Immediate symptoms of exposure to chemical agents may include blurred vision, eye irritation, difficulty breathing and nausea. A person affected by a chemical or biological agent requires immediate attention by professional medical personnel. If medical help is not immediately available, decontaminate yourself and assist in decontaminating others. Decontamination is needed within minutes of exposure to minimize health consequences. (However, you should not leave the safety of a shelter to go outdoors to help others until authorities announce it is safe to do so.)

1. Use extreme caution when helping others who have been exposed to chemical agents:
2. Remove all clothing and other items in contact with the body. Contaminated clothing normally removed over the head should be cut off to avoid contact with the eyes, nose, and mouth. Put into a plastic bag if possible. Decontaminate hands using soap and water. Remove eyeglasses or contact lenses. Put glasses in a pan of household bleach to decontaminate.
3. Remove all items in contact with the body.
4. Flush eyes with lots of water.
5. Gently wash face and hair with soap and water; then thoroughly rinse with water.
6. Decontaminate other body areas likely to have been contaminated. Blot (do not swab or scrape) with a cloth soaked in soapy water and rinse with clear water.
7. Change into uncontaminated clothes. Clothing stored in drawers or closets is likely to be uncontaminated.
8. If possible, proceed to a medical facility for screening.

What to do after a biological attack

In many biological attacks, people will not know they have been exposed to an agent. In such situations, the first evidence of an attack may be when you notice symptoms of the disease caused by an agent exposure, and you should seek immediate medical attention for treatment. In some situations, like the anthrax letters sent in 2001, people may be alerted to a potential exposure.

If this is the case, pay close attention to all official warnings and instructions on how to proceed. The delivery of medical services for a biological event may be handled differently to respond to increased demand. Again, it will be important for you to pay attention to official instructions via radio, television, and emergency alert systems. If your skin or clothing comes in contact with a visible, potentially infectious substance, you should remove and bag your clothes and personal items and wash yourself with warm soapy water immediately. Put on clean clothes and seek medical assistance.

For more information, visit the website for the Centers for Disease Control and Prevention, www.bt.cdc.gov.

Nuclear and Radiological Attack

Nuclear explosions can cause deadly effects—blinding light, intense heat (thermal radiation), initial nuclear radiation, blast, fires started by the heat pulse, and secondary fires caused by the destruction. They also produce radioactive particles called fallout that can be carried by wind for hundreds of miles.

Terrorist use of a radiological dispersion device (RDD)—often called "dirty nuke" or "dirty bomb"—is considered far more likely than use of a nuclear device.

These radiological weapons are a combination of conventional explosives and radioactive material designed to scatter dangerous and sub-lethal amounts of radioactive material over a general area. Such radiological weapons appeal to terrorists because they require very little technical knowledge to build and deploy compared to that of a nuclear device. Also, these radioactive materials, used widely in medicine, agriculture, industry and research, are much more readily available and easy to obtain compared to weapons grade uranium or plutonium.

Terrorist use of a nuclear device would probably be limited to a single smaller "suitcase" weapon. The strength of such a weapon would be in the range of the bombs used during World War II. The nature of the effects would be the same as a weapon delivered by an inter-continental missile, but the area and severity of the effects would be significantly more limited.

There is no way of knowing how much warning time there would be before an attack by a terrorist using a nuclear or radiological weapon. A surprise attack remains a possibility.

The danger of a massive strategic nuclear attack on the United States involving many weapons receded with the end of the Cold War. However, some terrorists have been supported by nations that have nuclear weapons programs.

If there were threat of an attack from a hostile nation, people living near potential targets could be advised to evacuate or they could decide on their own to evacuate to an area not considered a likely target. Protection from radioactive fallout would require taking shelter in an underground area, or in the middle of a large building.

In general, potential targets include:

- Strategic missile sites and military bases.
- Centers of government such as Washington, D.C., and state capitals.
- Important transportation and communication centers.
- Manufacturing, industrial, technology and financial centers.
- Petroleum refineries, electrical power plants and chemical plants.
- Major ports and airfields.

Taking shelter during a nuclear attack is absolutely necessary. There are two kinds of shelters—blast and fallout.

Blast shelters offer some protection against blast pressure, initial radiation, heat and fire, but even a blast shelter could not withstand a direct hit from a nuclear detonation.

Fallout shelters do not need to be specially constructed for that purpose. They can be any protected space, provided that the walls and roof are thick and dense enough to absorb the radiation given off by fallout particles. The three protective factors of a fallout shelter are shielding, distance, and time.

- **Shielding.** The more heavy, dense materials—thick walls, concrete, bricks, booksand earth—between you and the fallout particles, the better.
- **Distance.** The more distance between you and the fallout particles, the better.An underground area, such as a home or office building basement, offersmore protection than the first floor of a building. A floor near the middle of a high-rise may be better, depending on what is nearby at that level on which significant fallout particles would collect. Flat roofs collect fallout particles so the top floor is not a good choice, nor is a floor adjacent to a neighboring flat roof.
- **Time.** Fallout radiation loses its intensity fairly rapidly. In time, you willbe able to leave the fallout shelter. Radioactive fallout poses thegreatest threat to people during the first two weeks, by which time it has declined to about 1% of its initial radiation level.

Remember that any protection, however temporary, is better than none at all, and the more shielding, distance and time you can take advantage of, the better.

Electromagnetic pulse

In addition to other effects, a nuclear weapon detonated in

416

or above the earth's atmosphere can create an electromagnetic pulse (EMP), a high-density electrical field. EMP acts like a stroke of lightning but is stronger, faster and briefer.

EMP can seriously damage electronic devices connected to power sources or antennas. This include communication systems, computers, electrical appliances, and automobile or aircraft ignition systems. The damage could range from a minor interruption to actual burnout of components. Most electronic equipment within 1,000 miles of a high-altitude nuclear detonation could be affected. Battery powered radios with short antennas generally would not be affected.

Although EMP is unlikely to harm most people, it could harm those with pacemakers or other implanted electronic devices.

What to do before a nuclear or radiological attack

1. Learn the warning signals and all sources of warning used in your community.Make sure you know what the signals are, what they mean, how they willbe used, and what you should do if you hear them.
2. Assemble and maintain a disaster supply kit with food, water, medications, fueland personal items adequate for up to 2 weeks—the more the better. (Seethe "Emergency Planning and Disaster Supplies" chapter for more information).
3. Find out what public buildings in your community may have been designated asfallout shelters. It may have been years ago, but start there, and learnwhich buildings are still in use and could be designated as shelters again.

- Call your local emergency management office.
- Look for yellow and black fallout shelter signs on public buildings.Note: With the end of the Cold War, many of the signs have beenremoved from the buildings previously designated.
- If no noticeable or official designations have been made, make yourown list of potential shelters near your home, workplace and school:basements, or the windowless center area of middle floors in high-rise buildings, as well as subways and tunnels.
- Give your household clear instructions about where fallout shelters arelocated and what actions to take in case of attack.
-
4. If you live in an apartment building or high-rise, talk to the manager aboutthe safest place in the building for sheltering, and about providingfor building occupants until it is safe to go out.

5. There are few public shelters in many suburban and rural areas. If you areconsidering building a fallout shelter at home, keep the following inmind.

- A basement, or any underground area, is the best place to shelterfrom fallout. Often, few major changes are needed, especially ifthe structure has two or more stories and its basement—or one corner of it—is below ground.
- Fallout shelters can be used for storage during nonemergency periods, butonly store things there that can be very quickly removed. (Whenthey are removed, dense, heavy items may be used to add to the shielding.)
- See the "Tornadoes" section in the "Thunderstorms" chapter for informationon the "Wind Safe Room," which could be used as shelter in the eventof a nuclear detonation or for fallout protection, especially in a home without a basement.
- All the items you will need for your stay need not be stocked insidethe shelter itself but can be stored elsewhere, as long as you canmove them quickly to the shelter.
6. Learn about your community's evacuation plans. Such plans may include evacuationroutes, relocation sites, how the public will be notified and transportationoptions for people who do not own cars and those who have special needs. See the "Evacuation" chapter for more information.
7. Acquire other emergency preparedness booklets that you may need. See the "ForMore Information" chapter at the end of this guide.

What to do during a nuclear or radiological attack

Do not look at the flash or fireball—it can blind you.

If you hear an attack warning:

1. Take cover as quickly as you can, BELOW GROUND IF POSSIBLE, and staythere unless instructed to do otherwise.
2. If you are caught outside, unable to get inside immediately, take coverbehind anything that might offer protection. Lie flat on the groundand cover your head.
3. If the explosion is some distance away, it could take 30 seconds ormore for the blast wave to hit.
4. Protect yourself from radioactive fallout. If you are close enough to see thebrilliant flash of a nuclear explosion, the fallout will arrive in about20 minutes. Take shelter, even if you are many miles from ground zero— radioactive fallout can be carried by the winds for hundreds of miles. Remember the three protective factors: shielding, distance and time.

5. Keep a battery-powered radio with you, and listen for official information.Follow the instructions given. Local instructions should always takeprecedence: officials on the ground know the local situation best.

What to do after a nuclear or radiological attack

In a public or home shelter:

1. Do not leave the shelter until officials say it is safe. Follow their instructionswhen leaving.
2. If in a fallout shelter, stay in your shelter until local authorities tellyou it is permissible or advisable to leave. The length of your staycan range from a day or two to four weeks.
3. Contamination from a radiological dispersion device could affect a wide area,depending on the amount of conventional explosives used, the quantityof radioactive material and atmospheric conditions.
4. A "suitcase" terrorist nuclear device detonated at or near groundlevel would produce heavy fallout from the dirt and debris suckedup into the mushroom cloud.
5. A missile-delivered nuclear weapon from a hostile nation would probablycause an explosion many times more powerful than a suitcase bomb,and provide a greater cloud of radioactive fallout.
6. The decay rate of the radioactive fallout would be the same, makingit necessary for those in the areas with highest radiation levelsto remain in shelter for up to a month.
7. The heaviest fallout would be limited to the area at or downwind fromthe explosion, and 80% of the fallout would occur during the first24 hours.
8. Because of these facts and the very limited number of weapons terroristscould detonate, most of the country would not be affected by fallout.
9. People in most of the areas that would be affected could be allowed tocome out of shelter and, if necessary, evacuate to unaffected areaswithin a few days.
10. Although it may be difficult, make every effort to maintain sanitary conditionsin your shelter space.
11. Water and food may be scarce. Use them prudently but do not impose severerationing, especially for children, the ill or elderly.
12. Cooperate with shelter managers. Living with many people in confined space canbe difficult and unpleasant.

Returning to your home

1. Keep listening to the radio for news about what to do, where to go, and places to avoid.
2. If your home was within the range of a bomb's shock wave, or you live in a high-riseor other apartment building that experienced a non-nuclear explosion,check first for any sign of collapse or damage, such as:

- toppling chimneys, falling bricks, collapsing walls, plaster falling fromceilings.
- fallen light fixtures, pictures and mirrors.
- broken glass from windows.
- overturned bookcases, wall units or other fixtures.
- fires from broken chimneys.
- ruptured gas and electric lines.

3. Immediately clean up spilled medicines, drugs, flammable liquids, and other potentiallyhazardous materials.
4. Listen to your battery-powered radio for instructions and information aboutcommunity services.
5. Monitor the radio and your television for information on assistance that maybe provided. Local, state and federal governments and other organizationswill help meet emergency needs and help you recover from damage and losses.
6. The danger may be aggravated by broken water mains and fallen power lines.
7. If you turned gas, water and electricity off at the main valves and switchbefore you went to shelter:

- Do not turn the gas back on. The gas company will turn it back on foryou or you will receive other instructions.
- Turn the water back on at the main valve only after you know the watersystem is working and water is not contaminated.
- Turn electricity back on at the main switch only after you know the wiringis undamaged in your home and the community electrical system isfunctioning.
- Check to see that sewage lines are intact before using sanitary facilities.

8. Stay away from damaged areas.
9. Stay away from areas marked "radiation hazard" or "HAZMAT."

http://www.nationalterroralert.com/quickreference/

WHAT TO DO IF A NUCLEAR DISASTER IS IMMINENT!

This guide is for families preparing for imminent terrorist or strategic nuclear attacks with expected blast destruction followed by widespread radioactive fallout downwind.

IF ONLY A 'Dirty Bomb' Attack *(Not the vastly more devastating nuclear weapon blasts with fallout discussed below.) - You can expect localized and downwind contamination from the explosion and dispersed radioactive materials. If you are near enough to see or hear any local bomb blast, assume that it includes radiological or chemical agents. You should move away from the blast area as quickly as possible. If the wind is blowing toward you from the direction of the blast, travel in a direction that is crosswise or perpendicular to the wind as you move away from the blast area. If possible cover your face with a dust mask or cloth to avoid inhaling potentially radioactive dust. Upon reaching a safe location, remove your outer clothing outside and shower as soon as possible. Refer to local news sources for additional instructions about sheltering or evacuation. The government is better prepared to direct and assist the public in 'dirty bomb' emergencies, unlike more serious nuclear weapon attacks below.*

In a national crisis of imminent nuclear weapon attacks, read all the way through this guide first, THEN TAKE EFFECTIVE PROTECTIVE ACTION, BEFORE THEY STRIKE, WITH CONFIDENCE... FAST!

#1 - STAY OR GO?
You must **decide FIRST if you need to prepare where you are, or attempt evacuation**. The nature of the threat, your prior preparations, and your confidence in your sources of information should direct your decision. If you know al-ready you will be preparing to stay at your own home or, at least, the immediate local area, go now to #2 below.

If you are considering evacuation, your decision requires very high confidence that it is worth the risk. You do not want to get stuck between your current location and your hoped for destination, as there will probably be no easy moving forward or getting back. If you fail to get to your destination, you may be exposed without shelter, in a dangerous situation, perhaps among panicked hordes of refugees. Whatever supplies you have may be limited then to what you can carry on foot. IF you are in a big city or near a military target, AND you have relatives or friends in the country that you know are awaiting you, AND the roads between you and them are clear, AND the authorities are not yet restricting traffic, AND you have the means and fuel, evacuation may be a viable option for a limited time. DO NOT attempt evacuation if all of the above is not clearly known, or if the situation is deteriorating too quickly to assure the complete trip. You do not want to get stuck and/ or become a refugee being herded along with panicked masses. **If evacuation is truly a viable option, do not wait - GO NOW!** Do so with as many of the supplies listed in #7 as possible. Better to be two days too early in arriving than two hours too late and getting snagged mid-way, potentially exposing your family to a worse fate than having stayed where you were. Because of the very real danger of getting caught in an evacuation stampede that stalls, almost all families will be better off making the best of it wherever they currently are.

#2 - WHAT YOU NEED TO DO FIRST
Because time is of the essence, you need to **first delegate and assign to different adult family members specific tasks** so they can all be accomplished at the same time. Your first priorities to assure your family survival are Shelter, Water, and Food/Supplies. While some are working on the water storage and shelter at home, others need to be acquiring, as much as possible, the food and supplies.

#3 - FOOD/SUPPLIES
Because much of the food and supplies listed at #7 of this guide may quickly become unavailable, you need to assign someone NOW to immediately go to the stores with that list! Get cash from the bank and ATM's first, if it can be done quickly, but try and use credit cards at the stores, if at all possible, to preserve your cash.

#4 - WATER

With one or more adults now heading to the stores with the list at #7, **those remaining need to begin storing water** *IMMEDIATELY*! Lack of clean water will devastate your family much more quickly and more severely than any lack of food. Without clean water for both drinking and continued good sanitary practices in food preparation and for bathroom excursions (which could become less sanitary than normal), debilitating sickness could rampage through your family with little hope of prompt medical attention. That is a likely but, avoidable, disaster, ONLY IF you have enough water.

Every possible container needs to be filled with water RIGHT NOW! It will be very hard to have stored too much water. When the electricity/pumps go down or everybody in your community is doing the same thing, thus dropping the water pressure, what you've got is all you might be getting for a very long time. Empty pop bottles (1-3 liter) are ideal for water storage, also filling up the bathtub and washing machine. (Remember, later you'll have some in your hot water tank.) If you have any kiddie pools or old water beds, pull them out and fill them up, too. (Water from a water bed should be used only for bathing or cleaning, not for drinking as it may contain traces of algaecide and/or fungicides.) <u>Anything and everything that'll hold water needs to be filled up quickly RIGHT NOW!!</u>

One of the shopping items listed at #7 is new metal garbage cans and liner bags which you'll also use for storing water. If you can't get any more new cans, you could clean out an existing garbage can and scrub it throughout with bleach, then put in a new garbage bag liner and fill it with water. Even sturdy boxes and dresser drawers could be used with bag liners. Choose well where you fill up garbage cans with water because they won't easily be moved once full and many of them together could be too heavy for some upper floor locations. Ideally, they need to be very near where your shelter will be constructed and can actually add to its shielding properties, as you'll see below. B**E ASSURED, <u>YOU CANNOT STORE AND HAVE TOO MUCH WATER!</u>** Do not hesitate, fill up every possible container, **RIGHT NOW!**

#5 - SHELTER

The principles of radiation protection are simple - with many options and resources families can use to prepare or improvise a very effective shelter. You must throw off any self-defeating myths of nuclear un-survivability that may needlessly paralyze and panic, and then seal the fate of, less informed families.

Radioactive fallout is the particulate matter (dust) produced by a nuclear explosion and carried high up into the air by the mushroom cloud. It drifts on the wind and most of it settles back to earth downwind of the explosion. The heaviest, most dangerous, and most noticeable fallout, will 'fall out' first closer to ground zero. It may begin arriving minutes after an explosion. The smaller and lighter dust-like particles will typically be arriving hours later, as they drift much farther downwind, often for hundreds of miles. Once it arrives, whether visible or not, all that will fall will have done so usually in under an hour, coating everything, just like dust does on the ground and roofs. However, rain can concentrate the fallout into localized 'hot spots' of much more intense radiation with no visible indication.

This radioactive fallout 'dust' is dangerous because it is emitting penetrating radiation energy (similar to x-ray's). This radiation (not the fallout dust) can go right through walls, roofs and protective clothing. Even if you manage not to inhale or ingest the dust, and keep it off your skin, hair, and clothes, and even if none gets inside your house, the radiation penetrating your home is still extremely dangerous, and can injure or kill you inside.

Radioactive fallout from a nuclear explosion, though very dangerous initially, loses its intensity quickly because it is giving off so much energy. For example, fallout emitting gamma ray radiation at a rate over 500 R/hr (fatal with one hour of exposure) shortly after an explosion, weakens to only 1/10th as strong 7 hours later. Two days later, it's only 1/100th as strong, or as deadly, as it was initially.

That is really very good news, because our families can readily survive it IF we get them into a proper shelter to safely wait it out as it becomes less dangerous with every passing hour.

What stops radiation, and thus shields your family, is simply putting mass between them and the radiation source. Like police body armor stopping bullets, mass stops (absorbs) radiation. The thicker and heavier the mass, the more radiation it stops, and the more effective it is with every inch more you add to your fallout shelter. The thickness in inches needed to cut the radiation down to only 1/10th of its initial intensity for different common materials is: Steel 3.3", concrete 11", earth 16", water 24", wood 38". The thickness required to stop 99% of the radiation is: 5" of steel, 16" of solid brick or hollow concrete blocks filled with mortar or sand, 2 feet of packed earth or 3 feet if loose, 3 feet of water. (BTW, lead is nothing special, same as anything else pound for pound.) You may not have enough steel available, but anything you do have will have mass and can be used to add to your shielding - it just takes more thickness of lighter wood or books, for example, than heavier earth, to absorb and stop the same amount of radiation. Increasing the distance between your family inside and the radiation outside also reduces the radiation intensity.

The goals of your family fallout shelter are:

- **To maximize the distance away from the fallout 'dusting' outside on the ground, roof and trees.**
- **To place sufficient mass between your family and the fallout to absorb the deadly radiation**
- **To make the shelter tolerable to stay in while the radiation subsides with every passing hour**

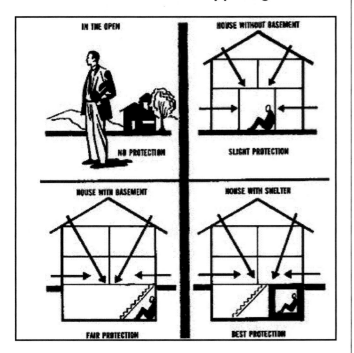

While a fallout shelter can be built anywhere, you should see what your best options are at home or nearby. Many structures already provide significant shielding or partial shielding that can be enhanced for adequate protection. **If you do not have a basement available, you can still use the techniques shown below in any above ground structure, you'll just need more mass to achieve the same level of shielding.** You may consider using other solid structures nearby, especially those with below ground spaces, such as commercial buildings, schools, churches, below ground parking garages, large and long culverts, tunnels, etc.. Some of these may require permissions and/or the acquiring of additional materials to minimize any fallout drifting or blowing into them, if open ended. Buildings with a half-dozen or more floors, where there is not a concern of blast damage, may provide good radiation protection in the center of the middle floors. This is because of both the distance and the shielding the multiple floors provide from the fallout on the ground and roof.

Bottom Line: choose a structure nearby with both the greatest mass and distance already in place between the outside, where the fallout would settle, and the shelter occupants inside. If you have a basement in your home, or at a nearby relatives' or friends' house that you can use, your best option is probably to fortify and use it, unless you have ready access to a better structure nearby.

For an expedient last-minute basement shelter, push a heavy table that you can get under into the corner that has the soil highest on the outside. The ground level outside ideally needs to be above the top of the table shelter inside. If no heavy table is available, you can take internal doors off their hinges and lay them on supports to create your 'table'. Then pile any available mass atop and around the other two open sides such as books, cordwood, bricks, sandbags, heavy appliances, full file cabinets, full water containers, your food stocks, even boxes and pillow cases full of anything heavy, like earth. Everything you can pile up and around it has mass that will help absorb and stop more radiation from penetrating inside - the heavier the better. However, be sure to reinforce your table and supports so you do not overload it and risk collapse.

Leave a small crawl-through entrance and more mass there that can be easily pulled in after you, but with a gap at the top to allow exhaust air out. Have another gap of 4-6" square low at the other end for incoming fresh air. Make bigger if crowded and/or hotter climate. A small piece of cardboard can help fan fresh air in if the natural rising warmer air convection current needs an assist moving the air along. This incoming air won't need to be filtered if the basement has been reasonably sealed up, however any windows or other openings will require some solid mass coverage to assure they stay sealed and to provide additional shielding protection for the basement. More details on this in the next (#6) section.

With more time, materials, and carpentry or masonry skills, you could even construct a more formal fallout shelter, such as the FEMA lean-to on the right, but you will need to assure structural integrity is achieved and adequate mass is utilized.

An effective fallout shelter constructed in a basement may reduce your radiation exposure 100-200+ fold. Thus, if the initial radiation intensity outside was 500 R/hr (fatal in one hour), the basement shelter occupants might only experience 5 R/hr or even less, which is survivable, as the radiation intensity will be decreasing with every passing hour.

Adding mass on the floor above your chosen basement corner, and outside against the walls opposite your shelter, will also increase your shielding protection. Every inch thicker adds up to more effective life-saving radiation shielding.

As cramped as that table space fallout shelter might seem, the vital shielding provided by simply moving some mass into place could be the difference between exposure to a lethal dose of radiation and the survival of your family.

The majority of people requiring any sheltering at all will be many miles downwind, and they will not need to stay sheltered for weeks on end. In fact, most people will only need to stay sheltered full-time for 2-3 days before coming out to safely join the evacuation. Others, still awaiting help arriving, could briefly come out to quickly attend to essential chores, spending ever more time out of the shelter daily, only coming back in to sleep. As miserable as it might seem now, you and your family can easily endure that, especially compared to the alternative.

It's really not so difficult to build an effective family fallout shelter, especially if you get started planning it before needed!

#6 - ESSENTIAL DETAILS

If you've accomplished the above; securing your supplies, stored water, and built your family fallout shelter, <u>CONGRATULATIONS!</u> You have now succeeded in improving the odds of survival for your family 100-fold, or more! Now, you need to expand your knowledge and fine-tune the tactics that will make the most of your family survival strategy.

1. <u>If close to a target,</u> your first indication of a nuclear detonation may be with its characteristic blinding bright flash. The first effects you may have to deal with before radioactive fallout arrives, depending on your proximity to it, are blast and thermal energy. Promptly employing the old "Duck & Cover" strategy, **immediately upon the first indication of the flash,** will save many from avoidable flying debris injuries and minimize thermal burns. Those very close will soon experience tornado strength winds and should quickly dive behind or under any solid object, away from or below windows. Even in the open, laying flat, reduces by eight fold the odds of being hit by any debris. A very large 500 kiloton blast, 2.2 miles away, will arrive about 8 seconds after the detonation flash with a very strong three second wind blast. That delay is even greater further away. That is a lot of time to duck & cover IF alert and you should stay down for 2 minutes. If not near any target 'ground zero' you will only, like the vast majority, have to deal with the fallout later.

2. Government information and guidance is a vital resource in your response to a nuclear crisis, but for many reasons it may be late, incomplete, misleading or simply in error. While evacuation might be prudent for individuals who act quickly in response to a threat, governments will be slow to call for mass evacuations before an event because of their potential for panic and gridlock. As past government calls for duct tape and plastic led to sold-out stores, anxiety, and derision from the press, there will be great reluctance to issue similar alarms. If you want to assure that you have adequate food, water & shelter for your family you must act BEFORE the panic without first waiting for government instructions that may never come or as urgently as warranted. **You alone are ultimately responsible for your family.**

3. <u>Filtering the air in your basement shelter won't be required.</u> Air does not become radioactive, and if your basement is reasonably snug, there won't be any wind blowing through it to carry the radioactive fallout dust inside. Simply sealing any basement windows and other openings prevents significant fallout from getting inside. To improve both the radiation shielding inside the basement, and to protect the windows from being broken and letting fallout blow in later, you should cover them all with wood, and then with earth, sandbags or solid masonry blocks, etc. on the outside and even the inside too, if possible. If the basement air gets stale later on, you could re-open a door into the upper floors of the closed house, or secure a common furnace air filter over an outside air opening leading into your basement.

4. <u>Regarding fallout contamination,</u> any food or water stored in sealed containers, that can later have any fallout dust brushed or rinsed off the outside of the container, will then be safe to use. As long as the fallout dust does not get inside the container, then whatever radiation penetrated the food/water container from the outside does not harm the contents. If you suspect that your clothes have fallout on them, remove your outer clothing before you come inside and leave them outside. A cheap plastic hooded rain poncho that can be easily rinsed off or left outside is very effective. Have water and baby shampoo near the entrance to wash and thoroughly rinse any exposed skin and hair. Exposure to fallout radiation does not make you radioactive, but you need to assure that you don't bring any inside. If any are stricken with radiation sickness, typically nausea, it is when mild, 100% recoverable and cannot be passed on to others. Before fallout arrives, you might also try to cover up items you want to protect outside for easier rinsing off of the fallout dust later when it's

safe to come out and do so. For instance, if you have a vegetable gardening spot or cordwood for heating, you might try covering some of it with plastic or tarp.

5. If without sufficient time to acquire radiological instruments of your own, like survey meters, Geiger counters and dosimeters, you'll need to be extra sure that your portable radios function properly from inside your shelter and that you have plenty of fresh batteries stocked for them. Without radiological instruments, listening for official guidance about the radiation threat levels in your particular area will be the only way you'll know when it's becoming safe to venture out. It might also be the only way you'll know when you first need to take your initial maximum protective action. When not in use, they should not be attached to any outside antenna or even have their own antenna extended. And, they should be wrapped in any non-conducting insulation, like layers of paper or bubble wrap plastic and then stored in a metal container or wrapped in aluminum foil to minimize the potential of EMP ruining the electronics. Having back-up radios would be very prudent. With extra radios, you can have one always tuned to the closest likely target city and, if it suddenly goes off the air, that could be your first indication of an attack.

6. When fallout is first anticipated, but has not yet arrived, anyone not already sheltered should begin using their N95 particulate respirator masks and hooded rain ponchos. Everyone should begin taking Potassium Iodide (KI) or Potassium Iodate (KIO3) tablets for thyroid protection against cancer causing radioactive iodine, a major product of nuclear weapons explosions. If no tablets available, you can topically (on the skin) apply an iodine solution, like tincture of iodine or Betadine, for a similar protective effect. (WARNING: Iodine solutions are NEVER to be ingested or swallowed.) For adults, paint 8 ml of a 2 percent tincture of Iodine on the abdomen or forearm each day, ideally at least 2 hours prior to possible exposure. For children 3 to 18, but under 150 pounds, only half that amount painted on daily, or 4 ml. For children under 3 but older than a month, half again, or 2 ml. For newborns to 1 month old, half it again, or just 1 ml. (One measuring teaspoon is about 5 ml, if you don't have a medicine dropper graduated in ml.) If your iodine is stronger than 2%, reduce the dosage accordingly. Absorption through the skin is not as reliable a dosing method as using the tablets, but tests show that it will still be very effective for most. Do not use if allergic to iodine. If at all possible, inquire of your doctor NOW if there is any reason why anybody in your household should not use KI or KIO3

tablets, or iodine solutions on their skin, in a future nuclear emergency, just to be sure.

7. When you know that the time to take protective action is approaching, turn off all the utilities into the house, check that everything is sealed up and locked down, and head for the shelter. You should also have near your shelter fire extinguishers and additional tools, building supplies, sheet plastic, staple guns, etc. for sealing any holes from damage. Your basement should already be very well sealed against fallout drifting inside. Now, you'll need to seal around the last door you use to enter with duct tape all around the edges, especially if it's a direct to the outside door.

8. You don't need to risk fire, burns, and asphyxiation trying to cook anything in the cramped shelter space, if you have pre-positioned in your shelter enough canned goods, can opener, and other non-perishable foods, that are ready-to-eat without preparation. More food, along with water, can be located right outside your crawl space entrance that you can pull in quickly as needed when safe to do so.

9. For lighting needs within the shelter have some small LED flashlights or LED head-lamps to stretch your battery life. Try not to have to use candles if at all possible. Bring in some books for yourself and games for the children. Throw in a small/thin mattress, some cushions, blankets, pillows, etc.

10. Toilet use will be via a portable camp toilet or a 5 gallon bucket with a seat borrowed from one of the house bathrooms, if you did not purchase a separate one. Garbage bag liners, preferably sized for it, should always be used and a full-size and bag lined garbage can should be positioned very close outside the shelter entrance for depositing these in when it is safe to do so quickly. Hanging a sheet or blanket will help provide a little privacy as shelter occupants 'take their turn'. The toilet needs to have its new 'deposits' sealed up tight with the plastic liner after each use and hand sanitizer towelettes nearby. Use a very secure top on the bucket and position it near the wall entrance with the outgoing upper air vent.

11. Pets, and what to do about them, is a tough call if you fail to make provisions for them. Letting pets run free is not a humane option, both for their potential to die a miserable death from radiation exposure outside and/or to be a danger to others, especially with dogs running in the inevitable packs of multitudes of others abandoned. Preparing for them is ideal, if truly realistic and not a drain on limited resources, while 'put-

ting them down' might eventually become a painful, but necessary reality if the disruption of food supplies becomes very long term.

12. Boiling or bleach water treatments will be used for <u>cleaning questionable water</u> later for drinking. (This is for killing bacteria, not for radiation contamination, which is never a concern for any stored and covered water containers, same for sealed food.) <u>Tap water recently put into clean containers won't likely need to be purified before using.</u> To purify questionable water later, bring it to a roiling boil for 10 minutes at least. If you don't have the fuel to boil it, you can kill the bacteria by mixing in a good quality household bleach at the rate of 10 drops per gallon, and letting it sit for at least 1/2 an hour. The bleach should be at least 5.25% pure, like Clorox, but be sure it has no additives such as soap or fragrance. You can later get rid of the flat taste from boiling, or some of the chlorine taste when using bleach, by pouring it from one container to another several times.

13. <u>There's much more that can be learned t</u>o better understand what you are up against and to acquire to help your family survive and to better endure all of this. While time allows, and if the Internet is still up & running, task someone with getting and printing out this additional information and watch the Civil Defense films.

- The Good News About Nuclear Destruction! http://www.ki4u.com/goodnews.htm

- When An ill Wind Blows From Afar! http://www.ki4u.com/illwind.htm

- Nuclear Effects & Fallout Shelters FAQ http://www.rad-shelters4u.com

- Nuclear War Survival Skills (30mb manual) http://www.ki4u.com/nwss.pdf

- "Know What To Do" 3 minute PSA video http://www.youtube.com/watch?v=QhDi0zoTcSo

- Core shelter video by Cresson Kearny, NWSS author http://video.google.com/videoplay?docid=6404694492992532990

- Civil Defense films made during the Cold War. Old fashioned, but physics and tactics of radiation protection are timeless.

- Survival Under Atomic Attack http://www.archive.org/details/Survival1951

- Duck & Cover Training for Children http://www.archive.org/details/DuckandC1951

- All About Fallout http://www.archive.org/details/AboutFal1963

- Study of a nuclear test at Nevada Test Site http://www.archive.org/details/Operatio1964

If still available and enough time to be overnight shipped your own radiation detection and monitoring instruments, potassium iodide anti-radiation pills, Nuclear Survival handbooks, etc., check at...

http://www.ki4u.com/products1.php

BOTTOM LINE:

When the TV or radio program switches abruptly to an terse announcement saying: "**We Interrupt This Program For This Special Bulletin!**", and your kids look up to you with questioning wide-eyes and eager for assurances, know then that you are confidently ready for them with your own Action Plan ready to go! That's what this is all about... saving our families!

This guide was purposely designed with the sober realization that the overwhelming majority of our fellow Americans would not be compelled to read such a guide until a nuclear crisis was imminent and, unfortunately, their preparation options and time to do so then would be very limited. www.ki4u.com and other survival suppliers will again be quickly sold-out, as all were after 9/11 and Fukushima. This guide then will be the best/only help that we can offer. If you are fortunate enough to be exploring your family preparation needs and options before such a future national crisis, there is much more that you can and should do now to insure that they are even better prepared.

#7 - LIST OF SUPPLIES TO ACQUIRE LOCALLY

If stores are still at all stocked, and safe to go to, try to buy as many of the following items as possible... **IMMEDIATELY**! There are no quantities listed here on the food items below as family size varies and because, as the emergency and panic widens, many items will become quickly sold-out or quantities restricted and you'll need to try to get more of what does remain on the shelves. At a minimum you should be looking at two weeks of provisions, but <u>much better to be aiming for two months or more</u>. The reality is, if/when we are attacked, it will be a very long time before anything is ever 'normal' again, especially at any grocery stores. Hurricane victims can attest to the prolonged misery and disruptions from such a localized disaster, even with the rest of the country still able to help out. Nobody can begin to imagine how bad the suffering will be, and for how long, if nuclear weapons have gone off... and in multiple locations!

The half-dozen top listed and <u>UNDERLINED</u> food items below are primarily for use while in the shelter. They are mostly ready-to-eat that requires no cooking or preparation, just a can opener at the most. (The iodine solution is included here because of its importance for its thyroid-blocking topical use detailed above, IF you do not have KI pills, but it's NEVER to be ingested or swallowed.) The other foods listed below there are better cost/nutrition staples for later use during the extended recovery period. Then follows general non-food supplies, tools and equipment.

Go Acquire It All Now QUICKLY!

Better to risk being a little early when securing your families essential food and supplies, rather than a few hours too late and going home empty-handed...

<u>Ready-to-eat foods (granola/energy/protein bars, snack-paks, raisins, cheese, etc.)</u>

<u>Some perishable foods (breads and fruits like bananas, apples, oranges, grapes, etc.)</u>

<u>Canned goods (soups, chili, vegetables, fruit, tuna, meats, beans, peanut butter, etc.)</u>

<u>Assorted drink mix flavorings (with no cold drinks, just plain water, kids will appreciate it!)</u>

<u>Plenty of potent Multi-Vitamins, Vit C, Pepto Bismol, aspirin, tylenol, other OTC meds, etc.</u>

<u>Iodine solution, like Betadine (16 ounces)- NOT TO BE INGESTED OR SWALLOWED!</u>

Largest bags of rice, beans, flour, potatoes, pasta, quick oats and other grains

Multiple big boxes of dried milk (Could include/use some inside shelter, too.)

Multiple big boxes of pancake and biscuit mix & syrup

Large bag of sugar and jar of honey

Large 2 gallons or more of cooking oil

Baking powder & soda & yeast & spice assortment pack

Bottled water (especially if home supplies not secured yet)

Paper or plastic plates/bowls/cups/utensils and paper towels

Quality manual can opener, 2 if you don't already have one at home

Kitchen matches and disposable lighters

New metal garbage cans and liner bags (water storage & waste storage)

5 gallon bucket and smaller garbage bags sized for it (toilet)

Toilet seat for the bucket (or use one from inside the house)

Toilet paper and, if needed, sanitary napkins, diapers, etc.

Baby wipes (saves water for personal hygiene use)

Flashlights (ideally LED) and more than one portable radio

Plenty more batteries, at least three sets, for each of the above

Bleach (5.25%, without fragrance or soap additives)

Alcohol and Hydrogen Peroxide and hand sanitizers

Prescription drugs filled, and as much extra as possible

First aid kits

Fire extinguishers

Plenty of inexpensive N95 particulate respirator masks

Plenty of cheap plastic hooded rain ponchos for everyone

Water filters and all other camping type supplies, such as portable camp toilet, cook stove and fuel, ammo, etc., if any sporting goods stocks still available.
And, of course, rolls of plastic sheeting, duct tape, staple guns, staples, etc.

Some Final Thoughts...

As mentioned above, this guide was written assuming it would not be read by the majority of its intended audience until a nuclear crisis is already fully upon us--when remaining time and resources to prepare will be extremely limited, maybe with only hours remaining before 'the music stops'.

For that reason, the food, equipment and supplies listed above in #7 has been restricted to only the most typically available from local resources.

If you are fortunate enough to be reading this well before a nuclear threat (or other major disaster) occurs or appears imminent, there's a great deal more that you can and should do beyond the scope of this brief guide.

Surviving the initial threats of a nuclear 'event' and radioactive fallout is relatively easy with the proper knowledge and even the most modest of preparations, as we've detailed above.

The ongoing bigger challenge, though, will be the one brought on by the extensive and much longer-lasting disruptions of services after you survive the nuclear event and emerge safely once the fallout threat has diminished.

You might go many months with little or no new food supplies, along with disruptions of water, sewer, gas, electric, and telephone services, little or no gasoline, and severely limited medical and banking services, law enforcement and fire protection.

With more time to research, make plans, and order supplies, families are well advised to acquire more in-depth training, reference books, longer-term food and water stocks, fuel, medical supplies, personal security, communication equipment, radiation monitoring instruments, camping equipment, supplies and tools. Many informative web sites and suppliers make available all of the above, including military MRE's ready-to-eat meals, dehydrated and freeze-dried foods, as well as buckets of beans, rice, and grains. They also offer solar cookers, water purifiers and barrels, camp and compost toilets, comprehensive medical kits and manuals, shortwave and local two-way radios, perimeter alarms, alternative energy and heating systems, fuel preservatives, long-term packaged seeds, gardening tools, canning equipment, etc. Survivalblog.com has many of the best advertising there. For radiation meters, potassium iodide, etc., see www.ki4u.com.

If all of this preparation seems daunting, here's one strategy to make it a little less overwhelming: Think in two's. First, acquire all the equipment and supplies your family would need to survive for two weeks if totally cut off from stores and utility and municipal services. It might help to consider all you would need during an extended camping trip in any season. Then, once you've accomplished that, expand your preparations and supplies to meet the goal of surviving at home for two months with no utilities or services. After that, continue adding provisions for two more additional months, with the eventual goal of gathering enough supplies so that your family can survive under these distressed conditions for a year or more.

A year might seem like overkill, but you'll no doubt discover that in any disruptive event, numerous friends, neighbors, and relatives will be in need and you will want to help them if you can. Of course, ideally, they should also be preparing their own families for surviving coming disasters, so sharing this information with them might help get them started. Also, for your own family's security, you always want to try to surround yourself with a buffer of like-minded people who are also doing the right things to prepare so they will become helpful allies instead of only a drain on your limited resources. Reality is, they could possibly even become an outright threat for your family retaining enough supplies for the full duration if difficult circumstances were to drag on and became ever more desperate.

Some are e-mailing the link to this guide, or printing up extra copies of the pdf version of this guide and mailing it out, with a quick note; "Hope you never need this information, but just-in-case, keep it handy." Few recipients find that low-key approach offensive or alarmist, and many have reported back to us that they were very grateful. Others have printed up extra copies for church members, school or work and still others with the intent to anonymously distribute them to all their neighbors surrounding them if/ when a nuclear crisis looms. Point is, you want everybody you care about, and those near and around you, to be preparing, it's both better for them and your families security. Also, everyone that does prepare will be one less family then later standing in line for hours (or days) ahead of others who failed to, awaiting a hoped for arrival of a FEMA handout of food or water. Being prepared makes a ton of sense and will one day soon be seen by all, many painfully, perhaps even fatally, as clearly obvious and self-evident.

If you're trying to convince yourself or a spouse to make the investment in prep equipment and supplies, also keep in mind this fact: Many of the supplies save money because buying in bulk and stocking up now is less expensive than buying smaller quantities later, especially as inflation ramps up and/or shortages appear. Further, if nothing bad ever happens, you can eventually eat the food and use most of the supplies, like toilet paper, fuel, etc., so they won't go to waste.

They will also be useful in many disasters besides nuclear events. For example:

Job loss -- Having two to four months of food at home would certainly relieve much of the stress of losing your job and being without an income while looking for another.

Pandemic -- We could someday see a pandemic unleashed that would require families to self-quarantine themselves at home for many weeks to avoid catching the disease. Having these supplies and having made these preparations would make that extremely difficult time more endurable.

Natural disasters, economic dislocations, civil disruptions -- Your family could ride out any number, or cascading combination, of these events in much better shape if you are sufficiently prepared.

Being prepared and stocking up makes sense on numerous levels, especially during this age when costs for many essentials, such as food, fuel, and ammunition, will surely only continue to increase. Stocking up now both saves money today and may well save your family tomorrow.

How People Act in Times of Trouble

When tough times come, you'll likely discover that people today, overall, are not as resilient as they were in times past. For many of us, our grandparents generation included a higher percentage of self-reliant rural folks who both 'made do' on less while growing and raising their own food. Today, most people are far removed from the land and the routine of being responsible for supplying their own food; many even have a dangerous government-dependent mentality of entitlement. Fact is, the morality that both sustained and restrained previous generations during tough times is not as widely embraced in this present population. As a result, many people will more quickly rationalize theft, robbery, looting, and rioting when they fear hunger and deprivation. Crime is already a problem today--even with nobody being hungry, and with law enforcement in place. Crime, then, could explode when hunger threatens and law enforcement is overwhelmed. It is therefore prudent for anyone making serious preparations to also include plans for maintaining their own security if law enforcement is either unavailable or cannot keep pace with the demands of an explosive crime wave. If you do not own or use guns, I would strongly urge you to re-evaluate your personal security. If you find it lacking, acquire some guns and ammunition immediately, and get some safety and practical tactical training in their use. Ask the clerks at your local gun store for advice on defensive arms and to point you to local resources for that essential training.

For those who already have weapons, be sure they are effective models and calibers for self-defense, and that you have stocked plenty of ammunition and high-capacity magazines if needed. Weapons and ammo will quickly disappear, or they will become prohibitively expensive or restricted, once the essential need is more widely recognized.

Financial Concerns

Once you are well on your way to acquiring your family's preparation tools, equipment, and supplies, consider acquiring extra items to help others and to use as future barter goods. You might be able to trade extra water filters, garden seeds, survival books, cooking fuel, batteries, antibiotics, and ammo for other needed products or services. Some people are even converting a modest percentage of their traditional paper investments into some gold and/or silver coins for trading purposes, as well as for prudent wealth diversification. Having wealth in forms other than solely paper dollars, plastic credit cards, or a 401k account might make the critical difference in one day being able to buy gas or get your gravely ill child to the front of a mile-long line to see the only overworked doctor or dentist or pharmacist in town. It'll sure beat only waving around your last mutual fund or bank statement then.

A Final Word

To better avoid unhealthy and overwhelming angst trying to prepare for all future dislocations and disruptions, keep in mind, too, that each step is like acquiring medical insurance. We all hope and pray we won't need that insurance, but if we ever do, our families won't find us then lacking in providing for their basic safety and welfare.

Once you've started making these preparations, strive to stay balanced. Thank God that you have begun, try to awaken others, and begin to confidently relax in your new alert status. You'll then be able to more fully enjoy life with your family knowing that you're firmly on the road to better being able to handle just about any event that might occur in this quickly changing world.

"A prudent man foresees the difficulties ahead and prepares for them; the simpleton goes blindly on and suffers the consequences." - Proverbs 22:3

http://www.ki4u.com/guide.htm

THE CHURCH OF
JESUS CHRIST
OF LATTER-DAY SAINTS

Guidelines for Use of Meetinghouses as Emergency Shelters

Following a disaster, the use of a Church meetinghouse as a community emergency shelter is occasionally needed. Permission to use a meetinghouse is granted by the stake president, after consulting with a member of the Presidency of the Seventy or the Area Presidency. Following approval, the priesthood leader should contact his Church physical facilities representative (PFR).

General Conditions and Guidelines

- While the use of a meetinghouse as a temporary community shelter may occasionally be needed, a Church building generally should not be the first choice. Other community facilities are better suited to accommodate the lodging of large numbers of people.

- If wards or stakes are approached by a local organization desiring to enter into a pre-disaster agreement, the stake president should seek area approval. Following approval, the insurance section of the Risk Management Division should be contacted for needed documents.

- When a meetinghouse is used by a community agency, Word of Wisdom standards should be observed in the building and on surrounding Church property. The chapel and offices are not to be used except for Church purposes. Cooking equipment and heaters that are not part of the meetinghouse furnishings may not be used in the building. Pets, other than service animals, are not allowed in the building.

- The stake president or bishop should assign a priesthood holder to be present any time the building is being used.

References:
1. *Church Handbook of Instructions, Book 1*, pages 10 and 182.
2. *Facilities Management Guidelines for Meetinghouses and Other Church Property* (United States and Canada), page 2.

Disaster Cleanup Guidelines—Church Volunteers Fact Sheet

For more information about this topic, call the Risk Management Division:
- 1-801-240-4049
- 1-800-453-3860, ext. 2-4049 (toll free in the United States and Canada)

This fact sheet addresses the general conditions and the health and safety guidelines that volunteers should understand before they participate in voluntary cleanup efforts. Before cleanup begins, leaders should discuss these items with volunteers and, if possible, give a copy of this document to each volunteer. Volunteers should read this document before filling in the Record of Donated Labor Hours on the third page.

General Conditions

- Volunteers serve at their own risk. Youth under age 18 should only participate when accompanied by a parent or when parental permission has been given.
- The focus for Church volunteers is to assist in cleanup, not reconstruction. Church volunteers should not work on condemned buildings.
- Volunteer work is to be conducted with the consent and oversight of the homeowner.
- Chain saws are to be used only by adults with experience operating them. They are not to be used to cut large trees or tree trunks.
- Training should be given on incident and injury prevention. Injury-related incidents should be reported promptly to ecclesiastical leaders. Primary insurance coverage is the volunteer's own health insurance.

Health and Safety Guidelines

- Wear appropriate clothing. Also, when appropriate, wear hard hats, hard-soled, high-topped shoes, work gloves, and safety glasses, and use hearing protection. Use repellant in mosquito-infested areas. Use sunscreen with an SPF of at least 30. Dust masks are recommended when working in high dust, ashes, or in smoky conditions.
- Avoid becoming overheated or dehydrated. Drink lots of water (but beware of contaminated water), and rest when needed. Seek medical attention immediately if you have symptoms of heat exhaustion.
- Avoid contact with hazardous chemicals, fallen power lines, stray or wild animals, and rodents and reptiles.
- In enclosed areas, avoid using equipment that produces carbon monoxide gas. This may include charcoal grills, camp stoves, or equipment powered by internal combustion engines, such as generators. Carbon monoxide gas is colorless and odorless, making it difficult to detect, and in an enclosed space it can be deadly.

- Beware of unstable structures, uneven surfaces, and broken glass, nails, and other protruding sharp objects. Tetanus and other needed immunizations should be current.
- Beware of working high off the ground. Tie off to a secure object if possible.
- Always lift with your legs, with knees bent to minimize back strain. Work with a partner, and know your limits. Volunteers with pre-existing health conditions, in particular, should perform only those tasks that are within their limitations.
- Use caution when working with mold. Wear a properly fitting N-95 respirator or dust mask (available at building supply stores) and rubber gloves. Do not attempt to clean up areas of mold that exceed ten square feet. After working with mold, wash using soap or hand sanitizer. Wash hands frequently, and change into clean clothes after working with mold or after participating in any disaster cleanup duties.
- Work teams should always have with them a list of emergency contact numbers, the address or GPS location of where they are working, clean drinking water, soap or hand sanitizer, and a basic first aid kit.
- Treat wounds with soap, clean water, and if available, an antibiotic ointment. Puncture wounds and animal and snake bites require rapid, specialized medical attention.
- Be aware of motorized traffic in the area at all times. When walking or working in areas where motor vehicles are passing or where heavy equipment is being used, walk facing oncoming traffic.
- Go to http://www.osha.gov/OshDoc/flood-tornado-recovery.html for further information on health and safety precautions.

Wards and stakes should have a plan in the event of an emergency. Plans are prepared by ward and stake welfare committees under the direction of the bishop or stake president. Plans should be updated periodically. The following should be included:

- Disasters likely to occur and response actions needed.

- Assignment of responsibilities to priesthood and Relief Society.

- Maps, addresses, and contact information of members.

- Procedure to account for missionaries and members following a disaster.

- A list of members with special needs.

- Procedures to assist members who may experience emotional trauma.

- A list of members with available resources such as medical training or the ability to operate heavy equipment.

- How stake leaders will contact the area office (outside the United States and Canada) or Church headquarters (United States and Canada) following a disaster.

- Contact information for the local government, the Red Cross, and other emergency response agencies.

This page intentionally left blank

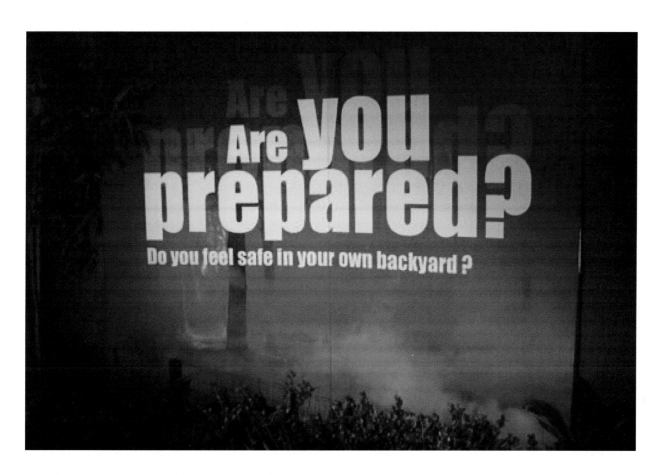

The following collection of articles is presented to help you think outside your comfort zone.

They are intended to make you a little uncomfortable and force you to consider some of the more "_unpleasent_" aspects of preparedness for disasters of a catastrophic nature.

Some of the following material could very well save your life or the lives of your loved ones during a major disaster.

I strongly encourage you to
Read, Ponder and Pray
about each of them accordingly.

SECTION 4:

Preparedness Outside Your Comfort Zone

Organize Yourself, Prepare Every Needful Thing...BOTH

Temporal & Spiritual
FAMILY READY

2+ Year Food Storage Leadership & Knowledge	**PEACE**	Exalted Eternal Family
1+ Year Food Storage Teacher & Example	**RESOURCE**	Endowed Temple Worthy
90 Supply Food & Water Responsible	**PROGRESS**	Active- recieved the Holy Ghost Serving the Lord
Two Weeks Supply & 72 Hour kits	**STARTED**	Baptized Cycle of Faith & Repenting
Nothing to Provide for Self or Others	**NOT READY**	Lost Intentionally or in Ignorance

TEOTWAWKI

THE END OF THE WORLD AS WE KNOW IT

It will be darker.

Without a grid, candles and batteries will provide some transition period until fire once again rules the night. Tough indoors for most of us without a fireplace or woodstove, so it will be darker than we are used to. The day will likely start when the sun comes up and end shortly after the sun goes down, much like the early days of America. With darkness, comes a some weird, but expected medical risks. There will be more bugs and animals getting close to you. Bugs and wild critters don't much like the light bulb, so without it, they will feel emboldened and walk right up to you much more often than now. If they bite or scratch you while nearby, that will be weird and you will react accordingly, but your infection risk goes up in the dark. Your injury risk also goes up as you can't see as well, making it much more likely that you will fall down and go boom, but also that you will bump into things and go ouch. Either way, infections and injuries will increase in a darker world.

It will be colder.

Again, no grid. This one only applies to cold nights and cold climates, but you get the basic idea. From a health standpoint, this really doesn't make for much risk as long as you are inside and avoiding exposure. Blankets and another human to cuddle with (friendly or non-friendly) will keep you warm most of the time. In the winter, hopefully you have an upstairs to go to which is usually quite a bit warmer even in the coldest places. The small, higher rooms will maintain heat much better than larger, open spaces. Basically,

those old movies where everybody piled in the same bed were right. Gone will be the days where little Suzie Loo Hoo gets her own room and privacy, at least at bedtime. Get some cold weather gear that is decent even when you live in southern localities that get rare cold weather, because you won't have the option WTSHTF. Have enough blankets for everyone to layer their beds for the lowest record colds in your area. Take Vitamin C in the wintertime, especially if you are not getting enough fruits and vegetables. Winter colds spread with close contact, but you also need to interact with other humans. Stay away from people that are running fevers and sick, especially those with bad coughs that could be flu or pneumonia. Frostbite can almost always be avoided as long as you are not outside exposed to wind and freezing temperatures without any insulation, but it is possible on noses, toes, ears and fingers left outside covers at night. Fireplaces and woodstoves will be essential to anyone above the Mason Dixon line, so be prepared.

It will be warmer.

What? Didn't we just talk about colder? There are two seasons, not everyone has cold but everyone has hot. Being from MN originally, it is just miserable in July and August sometimes, but can miserable from June to September. Northern MN is about as far north any human could really live, WITH a grid. If you live there now, plan on moving south—seriously. But with the beauty of southern living comes the heat that can really make for some real sticky situations. Heat stroke can kill people, but again exposure avoidance is the key. If you have a two story house now or after the grid goes down you acquire one, live in the lower level or basement in the summertime. Heat stroke is really only a risk if you stay "very heated" for shorter periods of time or "somewhat heated" for longer periods of time. When it is blast-furnace hot, stay in lower levels, caves, or at least shade with a breeze or hand or foot powered fan. Know your local topography and any potential natural cooling sources. Caves, springs, lakes, etc. will really be a necessity for cooling without a grid in very southern climates. If nothing else, dig yourself a hole like those weird Aussie animals and lay in the cool dirt. At night, if it cools down, get as much cool air into your structure or just sleep outside (protected from bugs if possible).

It will be wetter.

Maybe. No guarantees, but as roofs leak and walls crack, water will get in without a repair mechanism (Home Depot). Houses don't last forever, especially when exposed to cold and hot extremes due to no temperature control inside. Walls don't like freezing and thawing, and they don't like getting to 100 plus degrees. In a wet climate, you will likely see more water inside sooner, along with hard frost areas. Being outside more gathering materials and food will make it more likely that you will get caught in rain, and having to slog through the woods hunting and fishing for food will make for some wet feet at the least. Best protection against foot related problems is wear dry, clean socks. My best medical advice is to get some socks and have plenty of them.

It will be dirtier.

Now, this we can guarantee. No grid equals no dishwasher, no laundry room, no water pump. That makes dirt the winner and us the stinky losers. More dirt means more infection risk. Have some soap. Have a source of water for bathing or at least strip down nude during non-lightning downpours and scrub up with what soap you are able to stockpile. Hopefully, all the neighbors will be doing it too so nobody will notice your shame. There is just no substitute for clean skin, so figure out how you can clean clothes, shoes, and bodies. Soap can be made from some common materials that are readily available, but I like the idea of a gross of hard soap bars on my shelf. Granted, we won't likely be washing up for supper every day, but having soap for a regular bath or rain shower will be worth it's weight in gold, maybe more at some point in the future.

It will be more work.

Well, that just sucks for you lazy people, because we are going to eat you first. Just kidding, you taste bad, but you will want to make sure that you can contribute in some meaningful way to your new society of local weirdoes. King Gamer has no meaningful contribution, kids. There will be more gathering, more hunting, more walking. There will be more thinking work too, figuring out how to do things differently with all the stuff you forgot to get or never even thought about living without. With work, especially work you are not used to doing, there is more risk of injury or overuse strains and sprains. Think about what you are good at and use your skills accordingly. If you can't do much else, get really good at shooting and weapons and you will have a place at the table every night, King Gamer. Put your skills to use or whoever has the food is likely to give you less. Even if it's your dad! (Message to son). People teamed together will survive much easier than those on their own, unless Rambo himself is involved in the discussion. But even Rambo can't live without others, so start talking to your friends and family about who can do what best, have some non-powered tools in your shop, and keep in reasonable physical condition for walking and work if it falls to you.

It will be riskier.

Criminals will thrive WTSHTF and that is just the reality of the situation. After banding together in gangs of losers, it is likely they will continue to kill each other off over cigarettes and booze, especially as it gets rare. Tyrants will form larger gangs of minions and will likely form outlaw towns similar to those visualized in many apocalyptic movies we are all familiar with. Good for them! Rely on yourself and your small community and you will only hear legends of the people having to venture there. Stay small and stay safe. Travel only for truly emergency reasons other than wanting to visit Granny or see the big city. Granny is gone if she isn't with you and the big city burned to the ground. You lived, now deal with it. Someone has to have weapons and skill in your group. All the guns and ammo in the world does no good in the hands of a cowardly hippy. Be smart, and think about this reality with your neighbors and friends. Find the skilled contribution. From a health standpoint, getting shot decreases your survival rate. But; injuring yourself in the dark, wet, dirty world that is left also increases your risk of infections. Exposure to more outdoors increases your risk of exposure to insects, snakes, and animals that mean to harm you when you get in their way. This also makes for shorter life expectancy. Again, going out for nature walks is just a bad idea in this world. Know you limits and environment, staying inside while the "real men" go out hunting might be your best plan, don't get defensive anymore or learn how to do it. Whining will likely decrease your survival rate and increase your risk too.

It will leave you hungry.

This increases many of the risks above. Hungry people do stupid, risky things they would not otherwise do to get a meal. You will have to work to get food, instead of driving to the window. Mommy isn't going to plop down your plate after you played your vidya games all day. You may have to go out in the woods. You may have to help with the seeds, if you have them. You may have to cut up the squirrel, if you can catch it. You may have to start the fire to cook over. You cannot prepare enough food to stockpile forever, although you can make a good try. Seeds and animals are a great idea, especially ones that reproduce on their own like rabbits, goats and chickens. From a health standpoint, the same rules apply then as now—cooking your food until it's done, not eating old nasty stuff, etc. But as nutrition decreases infection increases, so plan ahead for your nutrition now. See our other pages about nutrition recommendations, but the basics of being able to eat after TEOTWAWKI is beyond my scope and knowledge.

It will leave you thirsty.

Now this is even worse than being hungry. When you see food, you can usually get to it and eat it, but that sure don't apply to water. Clean, drinkable water is something that you BETTER have at the top of your list. I place it at the end of the list because mine is a medical survival site, not a survival site. If you made it down to here without a water plan, you won't make it. Dying of drinking bad water is really a tough way to go too. It's painful, loud, and involves lots of gross fluids. I don't think I could stress enough your clean water plan. We have one, you should too. You can only survive without water for about 3-4 days, less with exertion. If you are walking all day trying to get somewhere safe without water, you will likely make it about 48 hours. Then it's over. There are some places left in the world where you can drink water you can see, but you better know where they are and the rules before you do. Otherwise, spend some money after doing some research on the right kind of filter for the future without pumps and magic faucets. We are mostly water, so figure out how to keep your levels up to survival standards.

The Precepts of My Preparedness Philosophy

What distinguishes the "Rawlesian" philosophy from other schools of preparedness thought?"

Here is a general summary of my precepts:

Modern Society is Increasingly Complex, Interdependent, and Fragile.

With each passing year, technology progresses and chains of interdependency lengthen. In the past 30 years, chains of retail supply have grown longer and longer. The food on your supermarket shelf does not come from local farmers. It often comes from hundreds or even thousands of miles away. This has created an alarming vulnerability to disruption. Simultaneously, global population is still increasing in a near geometrical progression. At some point that must end, most likely with a sudden and sharp drop in population. The lynchpin is the grid. Without functioning power grids, modern industrial societies will collapse within weeks.

Civilization is Just a Thin Veneer.

In the absence of law an order, men quickly revert to savagery. As was illustrated by the rioting and looting that accompanied disasters in the past three decades, the transition from tranquility to absolute barbarism can occur overnight. People expect tomorrow to be just like today, and they act accordingly. But then comes a unpredictable disaster that catches the vast majority unprepared. The average American family has four days worth of food on hand. When that food is gone, we'll soon see the thin veneer stripped away.

People Run in Herds and Packs, but Both Follow Natural Lines of Drift.

Most people are sheep ("sheeple"). A few are wolves that prey on others. But just a few of us are more like sheep-dogs--we think independently, and instead of predation, we are geared toward protecting and helping others. People naturally follow natural lines of drift--the path of least resistance. When the Schumer hits the fan, 99% of urbanites will try to leave the cities on freeways. The highways and freeways will soon resemble parking lots. This means that you need to be prepared to both get out of town ahead of the rush and to use lightly-traveled back roads. Plan, study and practice.

Lightly Populated Areas are Safer than High Density Areas.

With a few exceptions, less population means fewer problems. WTSHTF, there will be a mass exodus from the cities. Think of it as an army that is spreading out across a battlefield: The wider that they are spread, the less effective that they are. The inverse square law hasn't been repealed.

Show Restraint, But Always Have Recourse to Lethal Force.

My father often told me, "It is better to have a gun and not need it, than need a gun, and not have it." I urge readers to use less than lethal means when safe and practicable, but at times there is not a satisfactory substitute for well-aimed lead going down range at high velocity.

There is Strength in Numbers.

Rugged individualism is all well and good, but it takes ore than one man to defend a retreat. Effective retreat defense necessitates having at least two families to provide 24/7 perimeter security. But of course every individual added means having another mouth to feed. Absent having an unlimited budget and an infinite larder, this necessitates striking a balance when deciding the size of a retreat group.

There are Moral Absolutes.

The foundational morality of the civilized world is best summarized in the Ten Commandments. Moral relativism and secular humanism are slippery slopes. The terminal moraine at the base of these slopes is a rubble pile consisting of either despotism and pillage, or anarchy and the depths of depravity. I believe that it takes both faith and friends to survive perilous times. For more background on that, see my Prayer page.

Racism Ignores Reason.

People should be judged as individuals. Anyone that make blanket statements about other races is ignorant that there are both good and bad individuals in all groups. I have accepted The Great Commission with sincerity."Go forth into all nations" means exactly that: all nations. OBTW, I feel grateful that SurvivalBlog is now read in more than 100 countries. I have been given a bully pulpit, and I intend to use it for good and edifying purposes.

Skills Beat Gadgets and Practicality Beats Style.

The modern world is full of pundits, poseurs, and Mall Ninjas. Preparedness is not just about accumulating a pile of stuff. You need practical skills, and those only come with study, training, and practice. Any armchair survivalist can buy a set of stylish camouflage fatigues and an M4gery Carbine encrusted with umpteen accessories. Style points should not be mistaken for genuine skills and practicality.

Plentiful Water and Good Soil are Crucial.

Modern mechanized farming, electrically pumped irrigation, chemical fertilizers, and pesticides can make deserts bloom. But when the grid goes down, deserts and marginal farmland will revert to their natural states. In my estimation, the most viable places to survive in the midst of a long term societal collapse will be those with reliable summer rains and rich topsoil.

Tangibles Trump Conceptuals.

Modern fiat currencies are generally accepted, but have essentially no backing. Because they are largely a byproduct of interest bearing debt, modern currencies are destined to inflation. In the long run, inflation dooms fiat currencies to collapse. The majority of your assets should be invested in productive farm land and other tangibles such as useful hand tools. Only after you have your key logistics squared away, anything extra should be invested in silver and gold.

Governments Tend to Expand their Power to the Point that They Do Harm.

I often warn of the insidious tyranny of the Nanny State. If the state where you live becomes oppressive, then don't hesitate to relocate. Vote with your feet!

There is Value in Redundancy.

A common saying of my readers is: "**Two is one, and one is none.**" You must be prepared to provide for your family in a protracted period of societal disruption. That means storing up all of the essential "beans, bullets, and Band-Aids" in quantity. If commerce is disrupted by a disaster, at least in the short term you will only have your own logistics to fall back on. The more that you have stored, the more that you will have available for barter and charity.

A Deep Larder is Essential.

Food storage is one of the key preparations that I recommend. Even if you have a fantastic self-sufficient garden and pasture ground, you must always have food storage that you can fall back on in the event that your crops fail due to drought, disease, or infestation.

Tools Without Training Are Almost Useless.

Owning a gun doesn't make someone a "shooter" any more than owning a surfboard makes someone a surfer. With proper training and practice, you will be miles ahead of the average citizen. Get advanced medical training. Get the best firearms training that you can afford. Learn about amateur radio from your local affiliated ARRL club. Practice raising a vegetable garden each summer. Some skills are only perfected over a period of years.

Old Technologies are Appropriate Technologies.
In the event of a societal collapse, 19th Century (or earlier) technologies such as a the blacksmith's forge, the treadle sewing machine, and the horse-drawn plow will be far easier to re-construct than modern technologies.

Charity is a Moral Imperative.
As a Christian, I feel morally obligated to assist others that are less fortunate. Following the Old Testament laws of Tzedakah (charity and tithing), I believe that my responsibility begins with my immediate family and expands in successive rings to supporting my immediate neighborhood and church, to my community, and beyond, as resources allow. In short, my philosophy is to "give until it hurts" in times of disaster.

Buy Life _Assurance_, not Life Insurance.
Self-sufficiency and self-reliance are many-faceted. You need to systematically provide for Water, Food, Shelter, Fuel, First Aid, Commo, and, if need be, the tools to enforce Rule 308.

Live at Your Retreat Year-Round.
If your financial and family circumstances allow it, I strongly recommend that you relocate to a safe area and live there year-round. This has several advantages, most notably that will prevent burglary of your retreat logistics and allow you to regularly tend to gardens, orchards, and livestock. It will also remove the stress of timing a "Get Out of Dodge" trip at the 11th hour. If circumstances dictate that you can't live at your retreat year round, then at least have a caretaker and stock the vast majority of your logistics in advance, since you may only have one trip there before roads are impassable.

Exploit Force Multipliers.
Night vision gear, intrusion detection sensors, and radio communications equipment are key force multipliers. Because these use high technology they cannot be depended upon in a long term collapse, but in the short term, they can provide a big advantage. Some low technologies like barbed wire and defensive road cables also provide advantages and can last for several decades.

Invest Your Sweat Equity.
Even if some of you have a millionaire's budget, you need to learn how to do things for yourself, and be willing to get your hands dirty. In a societal collapse, the division of labor will be reduced tremendously. Odds are that the only "skilled craftsmen" available to build a shed, mend a fence, shuck corn, repair an engine, or pitch manure will be you. and your family. A byproduct of sweat equity is muscle tone and proper body weight. Hiring someone to deliver three cords of firewood is a far cry from felling, cutting, hauling, splitting, and stacking it yourself.

Choose Your Friends Wisely.
Associate yourself with skilled doers, not "talkers." Seek out people that share your outlook and morality. Living in close confines with other families is sure to cause friction but that will be minimized if you share a common religion and norms of behavior. You can't learn every skill yourself. Assemble a team that includes members with medical knowledge, tactical skills, electronics experience, and traditional practical skills.

There is No Substitute for Mass.
Mass stops bullets. Mass stops gamma radiation. Mass stops (or at least slows down) bad guys from entering a home and depriving its residents of life and property. Sandbags are cheap, so buy plenty of them. When planning your retreat house, think: medieval castle. (See the SurvivalBlog Archives for the many articles and letters on Retreat Architecture.)

Always Have a Plan B and a Plan C.
Regardless of your pet scenario and your personal grand plan of survival, you need to be flexible and adaptable. Situations and circumstances change. Always keep a G.O.O.D. kit handy, even if you are fortunate enough to live at your retreat year-round.

Be Frugal.
I grew up in a family that still remembered both our pioneer history and the more recent lessons of the Great Depression. One of our family mottos is: "Use it up, wear it out, make do, or do without."

Some Things are Worth Fighting For.
I encourage my readers to avoid trouble, most importantly via relocation to safe areas where trouble is unlikely to come to visit. But there may come an unavoidable day that you have to make a stand to defend your own family or your neighbors. Further, if you value your liberty, then be prepared to fight for it, both for yourself and for the sake of your progeny.

James Wesley Rawles
http://www.survivalblog.com

Which One Are You?

On Sheep, Wolves, and Sheepdogs

By LTC (RET) Dave Grossman, author of "On Killing."

Honor never grows old, and honor rejoices the heart of age. It does so because honor is, finally, about defending those noble and worthy things that deserve defending, even if it comes at a high cost. In our time, that may mean social disapproval, public scorn, hardship, persecution, or as always,even death itself. The question remains: What is worth defending? What is worth dying for? What is worth living for? - William J. Bennett - in a lecture to the United States Naval Academy November 24, 1997

One Vietnam veteran, an old retired colonel, once said this to me:

"**Most of the people in our society are sheep. They are kind, gentle, productive creatures who can only hurt one another by accident.**" This is true. Remember, the murder rate is six per 100,000 per year, and the aggravated assault rate is four per 1,000 per year. What this means is that the vast majority of Americans are not inclined to hurt one another. Some estimates say that two million Americans are victims of violent crimes every year, a tragic, staggering number, perhaps an all-time record rate of violent crime. But there are almost 300 million Americans, which means

that the odds of being a victim of violent crime is considerably less than one in a hundred on any given year. Furthermore, since many violent crimes are committed by repeat offenders, the actual number of violent citizens is considerably less than two million.

Thus there is a paradox, and we must grasp both ends of the situation: We may well be in the most violent times in history, but violence is still remarkably rare. This is because most citizens are kind, decent people who are not capable of hurting each other, except by accident or under extreme provocation. They are sheep.

I mean nothing negative by calling them sheep. To me it is like the pretty, blue robin's egg. Inside it is soft and gooey but someday it will grow into something wonderful. But the egg cannot survive without its hard blue shell. Police officers, soldiers, and other warriors are like that shell, and someday the civilization they protect will grow into something wonderful.? For now, though, they need warriors to protect them from the predators.

"Then there are the wolves," the old war veteran said, "and the wolves feed on the sheep without mercy." Do you believe there are wolves out there who will feed on the flock without mercy? You better believe it.

There are evil men in this world and they are capable of evil deeds. The moment you forget that or pretend it is not so, you become a sheep. There is no safety in denial.

"**Then there are sheepdogs,**" he went on, "**and I'm a sheepdog. I live to protect the flock and confront the wolf.**"

If you have no capacity for violence then you are a healthy productive citizen, a sheep. If you have a capacity for violence and no empathy for your fellow citizens, then you have defined an aggressive sociopath, a wolf. But what if you have a capacity for violence, and a deep love for your fellow citizens? What do you have then? A sheepdog, a warrior, someone who is walking the hero's path. Someone who can walk into the heart of darkness, into the universal human phobia, and walk out unscathed

Let me expand on this old soldier's excellent model of the sheep, wolves, and sheepdogs. We know that the sheep live in denial, that is what makes them sheep. **They do not want to believe that there is evil in the world.** They can accept the fact that fires can happen, which is why they want fire extinguishers, fire sprinklers, fire alarms and fire exits throughout their kids' schools.

But many of them are outraged at the idea of putting an armed police officer in their kid's school. Our children are thousands of times more likely to be killed or seriously injured by school violence than fire, but the sheep's only response to the possibility of violence is denial. The idea of someone coming to kill or harm their child is just too hard, and so they chose the path of denial.

The sheep generally do not like the sheepdog. He looks a lot like the wolf. He has fangs and the capacity for violence. **The difference, though, is that the sheepdog must not, can not and will not ever harm the sheep.** Any sheep dog who intentionally harms the lowliest little lamb will be punished and removed. The world cannot work any other way, at least not in a representative democracy or a republic such as ours.

Still, the sheepdog disturbs the sheep. **He is a constant reminder that there are wolves in the land.** They would prefer that he didn't tell them where to go, or give them traffic tickets, or stand at the ready in our airports in camouflage fatigues holding an M-16. The sheep would much rather have the sheepdog cash in his fangs, spray paint himself white, and go, "Baa."

Until the wolf shows up. **Then the entire flock tries desperately to hide behind one lonely sheepdog.**

The students, the victims, at Columbine High School were big, tough high school students, and under ordinary circumstances they would not have had the time of day for a police officer. They were not bad kids; they just had nothing to say to a cop. When the school was under attack, however, and SWAT teams were clearing the rooms and hallways, the officers had to physically peel those clinging, sobbing kids off of them. This is how the little lambs feel about their sheepdog when the wolf is at the door.

Look at what happened after September 11, 2001 when the wolf pounded hard on the door. Remember how America, more than ever before, felt differently about their law enforcement officers and military personnel? Remember how many times you heard the word hero?

Understand that there is nothing morally superior about being a sheepdog; it is just what you choose to be. Also understand that a sheepdog is a funny critter: He is always sniffing around out on the perimeter, checking the breeze, barking at things that go bump in the night, and yearning for a righteous battle. That is, the young sheepdogs yearn for a righteous battle. The old sheepdogs are a little older and wiser, but they move to the sound of the guns when needed right along with the young ones.

Here is how the sheep and the sheepdog think differently. The sheep pretend the wolf will never come, but the sheepdog lives for that day. After the attacks on September 11, 2001, most of the sheep, that is, most citizens in America said, "Thank God I wasn't on one of those planes." The sheepdogs, the warriors, said, "**Dear God, I wish I could have been on one of those planes. Maybe I could have made a difference.**" When you are truly transformed into a warrior and have truly invested yourself into warriorhood, you want to be there. You want to be able to make a difference.

There is nothing morally superior about the sheepdog, the warrior, but he does have one real advantage. Only one. **And that is that he is able to survive and thrive in an environment that destroys 98 percent of the population.** There was research conducted a few years ago with individuals convicted of violent crimes. These cons were in prison for serious, predatory crimes of violence: assaults, murders and killing law enforcement officers. The vast majority said that they specifically targeted victims by body language: slumped walk, passive behavior and lack of awareness. They chose their victims like big cats do in Africa, when they select one out of the herd that is least able to protect itself.

Some people may be destined to be sheep and others might be genetically primed to be wolves or sheepdogs. But I believe that most people can choose which one they want to be, and **I'm proud to say that more and more Americans are choosing to become sheepdogs.**

Seven months after the attack on September 11, 2001, Todd Beamer was honored in his hometown of Cranbury, New Jersey. Todd, as you recall, was the man on Flight 93 over Pennsylvania who called on his cell phone to alert an operator from United Airlines about the hijacking. When he learned of the other three passenger planes that had been used as weapons, Todd dropped his phone and uttered the words, "Let's roll," which authorities believe was a signal to the other passengers to confront the terrorist hijackers. In one hour, a transformation occurred among the passengers - athletes, business people and parents. -- from sheep to sheepdogs and together they fought the wolves, ultimately saving an unknown number of lives on the ground.

There is no safety for honest men except by believing all possible evil of evil men. - Edmund Burke

Here is the point I like to emphasize, especially to the thousands of police officers and soldiers I speak to each year. In nature the sheep, real sheep, are born as sheep. Sheepdogs are born that way, and so are wolves. They didn't have a choice. But you are not a critter. As a human being, you can be whatever you want to be. It is a conscious, moral decision.

If you want to be a sheep, then you can be a sheep and that is okay, but you must understand the price you pay. When the wolf comes, <u>you and your loved ones are going to die if there is not a sheepdog there to protect you.</u> If you want to be a wolf, you can be one, but the sheepdogs are going to hunt you down and you will never have rest, safety, trust or love. But if you want to be a sheepdog and walk the warrior's path, then you must make a conscious and moral decision every day to dedicate, equip and prepare yourself to thrive in that toxic, corrosive moment when the wolf comes knocking at the door.

For example, many officers carry their weapons in church.? They are well concealed in ankle holsters, shoulder holsters or inside-the-belt holsters tucked into the small of their backs.? Anytime you go to some form of religious service, there is a very good chance that a police officer in your congregation is carrying. **You will never know if there is such an individual in your place of worship, until the wolf appears to massacre you and your loved ones.**

I was training a group of police officers in Texas, and during the break, one officer asked his friend if he carried his weapon in church. The other cop replied, **"I will never be caught without my gun in church."** I asked why he felt so strongly about this, and he told me about a cop he knew who was at a church massacre in Ft. Worth, Texas in 1999. In that incident, a mentally deranged individual came into the church and opened fire, gunning down fourteen people. He said that officer believed he could have saved every life that day if he had been carrying his gun. His own son was shot, and all he could do was throw himself on the boy's body and wait to die. That cop looked me in the eye and said, **"Do you have any idea how hard it would be to live with yourself after that?"**

Some individuals would be horrified if they knew this police officer was carrying a weapon in church. They might call him paranoid and would probably scorn him. Yet these same individuals would be enraged and would call for "heads to roll" if they found out that the airbags in their cars were defective, or that the fire extinguisher and fire sprinklers in their kids' school did not work. They can accept the fact that fires and traffic accidents can happen and that there must be safeguards against them.

Their only response to the wolf, though, is denial, and all too often their response to the sheepdog is scorn and disdain. But the sheepdog quietly asks himself, **"Do you have and idea how hard it would be to live with yourself if your loved ones attacked and killed, and you had to stand there helplessly because you were unprepared for that day?"**

It is denial that turns people into sheep. **Sheep are psychologically destroyed by combat because their only defense is denial, which is counterproductive and destructive, resulting in fear, helplessness and horror when the wolf shows up.**

Denial kills you twice. **It kills you once, at your moment of truth when you are not physically prepared: you didn't bring your gun, you didn't train. Your only defense was wishful thinking. Hope is not a strategy. Denial kills you a second time because even if you do physically survive, you are psychologically shattered by your fear helplessness and horror at your moment of truth.**

Gavin de Becker puts it like this in Fear Less, his superb post-9/11 book, which should be required reading for anyone trying to come to terms with our current world situation: **"...denial can be seductive, but it has an insidious side effect. For all the peace of mind deniers think they get by saying it isn't so, the fall they take when faced with new violence is all the more unsettling."**

Denial is a save-now-pay-later scheme, a contract written entirely in small print, for in the long run, the denying person knows the truth on some level.

And so the warrior must strive to confront denial in all aspects of his life, and prepare himself for the day when evil comes. If you are warrior who is legally authorized to carry a weapon and you step outside without that weapon, then you become a sheep, pretending that the bad man will not come today. No one can be "on" 24/7, for a lifetime. Everyone needs down time. But if you are authorized to carry a weapon, and you walk outside without it, just take a deep breath, and say this to yourself...

"Baa."

This business of being a sheep or a sheep dog is not a yes-no dichotomy. It is not an all-or-nothing, either-or choice. It is a matter of degrees, a continuum. On one end is an abject, head-in-the-sand-sheep and on the other end is the ultimate warrior. Few people exist completely on one end or the other. Most of us live somewhere in between. Since 9-11 almost everyone in America took a step up that continuum, away from denial. The sheep took a few steps toward accepting and appreciating their warriors, and the warriors started taking their job more seriously. The degree to which you move up that continuum, away from sheephood and denial, is the degree to which you and your loved ones will survive, physically and psychologically at your moment of truth.

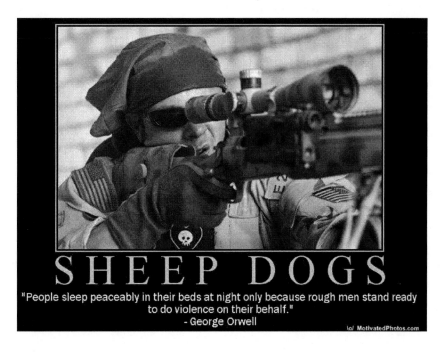

SHEEP DOGS

"People sleep peaceably in their beds at night only because rough men stand ready to do violence on their behalf."
- George Orwell

lo/ MotivatedPhotos.com

100 Emergency Items: *That Will Disappear First*

Tess Pennington, Ready Nutrition
http://readynutrition.com/resources/emergency-items-what-will-disappear-first_11112009/

Do you ever wonder if a major emergency situation occurred what would disappear first? Due to the overwhelming nature of prepping for a emergency situation, many do not know where to even began, let alone think of emergency situations they would need to prepare for. Having a ready supply of food, water and batteries are a good start, but not enough. There are many more items to have on hand besides beans, band aids and bullets.

When planning for an emergency, especially a sudden and long term emergency, think about the worst situation imaginable. For those that need some help - think of mass chaos of people running into grocery stores to get as much food and supplies as possible, gas lines that run out into the street, highways at a virtual stand still, banks not giving out money, looting, fires, the health of the elderly deteriorating due to not being able to get needed medicines, babies crying because that have no formula to drink. It's not a pretty picture when you allow yourself to imagine it. Having supplies on hand can put a person way ahead of the game. While many who are unprepared for such a grim reality will be battling the lines at the grocery stores, those that have prepared accordingly could be packing their items up and headed for hills before many have even attempted to.

This author came across some advice from someone who has experienced a long term emergency first hand. This advice could help a person prepare not only for their well being, but also mentally prepare them for getting through the nightmare of a long term emergency.

Advice From a Sarajevo War Survivor:

Experiencing horrible things that can happen in a war – death of parents and friends, hunger and malnutrition, endless freezing cold, fear, sniper attacks.

1. Stockpiling helps. But you never no how long trouble will last, so locate near renewable food sources.

2. Living near a well with a manual pump is like being in Eden.

3. After awhile, even gold can lose its luster. But there is no luxury in war quite like toilet paper. Its surplus value is greater than gold's.

4. If you had to go without one utility, lose electricity – it's the easiest to do without (unless you're in a very nice climate with no need for heat.)

5. Canned foods are awesome, especially if their contents are tasty without heating. One of the best things to stockpile is canned gravy – it makes a lot of the dry unappetizing things you find to eat in war somewhat edible. Only needs enough heat to "warm", not to cook. It's cheap too, especially if you buy it in bulk.

6. Bring some books – escapist ones like romance or mysteries become more valuable as the war continues. Sure, it's great to have a lot of survival guides, but you'll figure most of that out on your own anyway – trust me, you'll have a lot of time on your hands.

7. The feeling that you're human can fade pretty fast. I can't tell you how many people I knew who would have traded a much needed meal for just a little bit of toothpaste, rouge, soap or cologne. Not much point in fighting if you have to lose your humanity. These things are morale-builders like nothing else.

8. Slow burning candles and matches, matches, matches

Emergency Items That Disappear First

1. Generators (Good ones cost dearly. Gas storage, risky. Noisy...target of thieves; maintenance etc.)

2. Water Filters/Purifiers

3. Portable Toilets

4. Seasoned Firewood. Wood takes about 6 – 12 months to become dried, for home uses.

5. Lamp Oil, Wicks, Lamps (First Choice: Buy CLEAR oil. If scarce, stockpile ANY!)

6. Coleman Fuel. Impossible to stockpile too much.

7. **Guns, Ammunition**, Pepper Spray, Knives, Clubs, Bats & Slingshots.

8. **Hand-can openers**, & hand egg beaters, whisks.

9. **Honey**/Syrups/white, brown sugar

10. **Rice – Beans – Wheat**

11. **Vegetable Oil** (for cooking) Without it food burns/must be boiled etc.,)

12. **Charcoal**, Lighter Fluid (Will become scarce suddenly)

13. **Water Containers** (Urgent Item to obtain.) Any size. Small: HARD CLEAR PLASTIC ONLY – note – food grade if for drinking.

14. **Mini Heater** head (Propane) (Without this item, propane won't heat a room.)

15. **Grain Grinder** (Non-electric)

16. **Propane Cylinders** (Urgent: Definite shortages will occur.

17. **Survival Guide Book.**

18. **Mantles**: Aladdin, Coleman, etc. (Without this item, longer-term lighting is difficult.)

19. **Baby Supplies**: Diapers/formula. ointments/aspirin, etc.

20. **Washboards**, Mop Bucket w/wringer (for Laundry)

21. **Cook stoves** (Propane, Coleman & Kerosene)

22. **Vitamins**

23. **Propane Cylinder** Handle-Holder (Urgent: Small canister use is dangerous without this item)

24. **Feminine Hygiene**/Haircare/Skin products.

25. **Thermal underwear** (Tops & Bottoms)

26. **Bow saws**, axes and hatchets, Wedges (also, honing oil)

27. **Aluminum Foil** Reg. & Heavy Duty (Great Cooking and Barter Item)

28. **Gasoline Containers** (Plastic & Metal)

29. **Garbage Bags** (Impossible To Have Too Many).

30. **Toilet Paper,** Kleenex, Paper Towels

31. **Milk** – Powdered & Condensed (Shake Liquid every 3 to 4 months)

32. **Garden Seeds** (Non-Hybrid) (A MUST)

33. **Clothes pins**/line/hangers (A MUST)

34. **Coleman's Pump** Repair Kit

35. **Tuna Fish** (in oil)

36. **Fire Extinguishers** (or..large box of Baking Soda in every room)

37. **First aid kits**

38. **Batteries** (all sizes...buy furthest-out for Expiration Dates)

39. **Garlic**, spices & vinegar, baking supplies

40. **Big Dogs** (and plenty of dog food)

41. **Flour**, yeast & salt

42. **Matches**. {"Strike Anywhere" preferred.) Boxed, wooden matches will go first

43. **Writing paper**/pads/pencils, solar calculators

44. **Insulated ice chests** (good for keeping items from freezing in Wintertime.)

45. **Work boots,** belts, Levis & durable shirts

46. **Flashlights**/LIGHTSTICKS & torches, "No. 76 Dietz" Lanterns

47. **Journals**, Diaries & Scrapbooks (jot down ideas, feelings, experience; Historic Times)

48. **Garbage cans** Plastic (great for storage, water, transporting – if with wheels)

49. **Men's Hygiene:** Shampoo, Toothbrush/paste, Mouthwash/floss, nail clippers, etc

50. **Cast iron cookware** (sturdy, efficient)

51. **Fishing supplies**/tools

52. **Mosquito coils**/repellent, sprays/creams

53. **Duct Tape**

54. **Tarps**/stakes/twine/nails/rope/spikes

55. **Candles**

56. **Laundry Detergent** (liquid)

57. **Backpacks**, Duffel Bags

58. **Garden tools** & supplies

59. **Scissors**, fabrics & sewing supplies

60. **Canned Fruits**, Veggies, Soups, stews, etc.

61. **Bleach** (plain, NOT scented: 4 to 6% sodium hypochlorite)

62. **Canning supplies,** (Jars/lids/wax)

63. **Knives** & Sharpening tools: files, stones, steel

64. **Bicycles**...Tires/tubes/pumps/chains, etc

65. **Sleeping Bags** & blankets/pillows/mats

66. **Carbon Monoxide Alarm** (battery powered)

67. **Board Games,** Cards, Dice

68. **d-con Rat poison,** MOUSE PRUFE II, Roach Killer

69. **Mousetraps,** Ant traps & cockroach magnets

70. **Paper plates**/cups/utensils (stock up, folks)

71. **Baby wipes,** oils, waterless & Antibacterial soap (saves a lot of water)

72. **Rain gear,** rubberized boots, etc.

73. **Shaving supplies** (razors & creams, talc, after shave)

74. **Hand pumps** & siphons (for water and for fuels)

75. **Soy Sauce,** vinegar, bullions/gravy/soup base

76. **Reading glasses**

77. **Chocolate**/Cocoa/Tang/Punch (water enhancers)

78. **"Survival-in-a-Can"**

79. **Woolen clothing,** scarves/ear-muffs/mittens

80. **Boy Scout Handbook,** / also Leaders Catalog

81. **Roll-on Window Insulation Kit** (MANCO)

82. **Graham crackers,** saltines, pretzels, Trail mix/Jerky

83. **Popcorn,** Peanut Butter, Nuts

84. **Socks,** Underwear, T-shirts, etc. (extras)

85. **Lumber** (all types)

86. **Wagons & carts** (for transport to and from)

87. **Cots** & Inflatable mattress's

88. **Gloves:** Work/warming/gardening, etc.

89. **Lantern Hangers**

90. **Screen Patches,** glue, nails, screws, nuts & bolts

91. **Teas**

92. **Coffee**

93. **Cigarettes**

94. **Wine**/Liquors (for bribes, medicinal, etc,)

95. **Paraffin wax**

96. **Glue,** nails, nuts, bolts, screws, etc.

97. **Chewing gum**/candies

98. **Atomizers** (for cooling/bathing)

99. **Hats** & cotton neckerchiefs

100. **Goats**/chickens

ANOTHER VOICE OF WARNING
...if ye are prepared, ye shall not fear

www.ldsavow.com

Some Ground Truth--
The "Us" & the "Them" in a Societal Collapse

Originally posted at www.SurvivalBlog.com
Copyright 2012

I am a retired Army warrant officer working for the Army teaching Electronic Warfare and Signal Intelligence. I only started reading your blog last week. It's addictive, but slightly disturbing.

Having worked for the Army for 27 years in a number of different failed countries I may have a unique perspective on survival that I would like to share with your readers. I believe most of the "survivalist community" is vastly underestimating the impact that other humans are going to have on their plans. Hunkering down and waiting for everyone to die off is a simplistic plan and I believe has almost no chance of working. You may be able to hide your retreat, but you can't hide the land it sits on. That land itself may become a scarce commodity if the US transitions to an agrarian economy.

Food is the key resource. Most communities are at risk because they simply don't have enough calories stored to get them through any kind of crisis. But, storage is no more than limited capital to allow people time to grow more food. Food production requires land....if your retreat is sitting on farmable land, it will be a scarce resource.

Carrying capacity of the US using non-petroleum farming techniques is far lower than most of your readers probably think. Also, most areas of the US, especially cities, don't have anywhere near enough farm-able land to go back to some kind of agrarian pattern. Without public infrastructure and modern transportation, we are going to experience a huge die-off caused mostly by starvation. In a total collapse scenario without immediate restoration of the economy, basically everyone who lives in a city is doomed unless they can take over some kind of farm land.

If you live in an area without enough farm land, you will be a "have not". Period. I don't care how much food you have stored in your basement.

Here is my key point. These teeming millions will not just starve and go away. I believe that anyone who thinks they can defend a working farm against raiders is deluding themselves.

1. People are dangerous. They are the most dangerous animal on earth. You can never lose sight of that! In almost any society breakdown scenario you can think of, you will be surrounded by starving predators that are much more dangerous than tigers. In the USA, every one of them (or at least the vast majority) will be armed with firearms. The ones currently without firearms will obtain them by any means necessary including looting government armories. These are thinking-breathing and highly motivated enemies.

2. Raiders, defined as "outlaw looting groups" may be a threat for a very short period, but I really don't see groups of more than 4-6 ever forming...they will be quickly replaced by much larger groups of "citizens" doing essentially the same things, but much better armed and organized.

An Example: A few hours after Albania's political crisis in 1998, (which was caused by a national lottery scam), almost every adult male in the country procured an AKM from government stocks. Armories were the first targets looted. I flew into Tirana packing a pistol and a sack of money, naively thinking I would be able to move around the country and defend myself. What a laugh. Everyone had me outgunned, and the vast majority of them had military training of some sort. I never got out of the capital city. Every road seemed to have roadblocks every few miles, blocked by armed local citizens.

3. Without central authority, people don't just starve and go away. They form their own polities (governments). These polities are often organized around town or city government or local churches. They may call it a city counsel or a committee or a senate.

The bottom line is,
"We The People" will do whatever
"We" have to do to survive.
And that specifically includes taking your storage goods.

4. When (not if) a polity forms near you, you had better be part of that process. If not, you will be looked upon as a "resource" instead of a member of the community. The local polity will pass a resolution (or whatever) and "legally" confiscate your goods. If you resist, they will crush you. They will have the resources of a whole community to draw upon including weapons, vehicles, manpower, electronics, tear gas, etc. Every scrap of government owned equipment and weaponry will be used, by someone. Anyone who plans to hold out against that kind of threat is delusional.

5. The local polity that forms is almost certainly going to make mistakes. Some of them are lethal blunders. Odds are, the locals will probably not have given a lot of serious thought to facing long term survival. They will squander resources and delay implementing necessary actions (like planting more food or working together to defend a harvest). They may even decide to take in thousands of refugees from nearby cities, thereby almost insuring their own longer term starvation.

A much better approach is to be an integral part of the community and use the combined resources of the community to defend all of your resources together. This would be much easier if a high percentage of the community were like minded folks who were committed to sharing and co-operating. Because any community with food is likely going to have to somehow survive while facing even larger polities, like nearby cities, counties or even state governments. Don't expect to face a walking hoard of lightly armed, starving individuals. Expect to face a professional, determined army formed by a government of some kind.

A small farming community can probably support a few outsiders, but not very many. The community will need to politically deal with outside polities or they will face a war they can't win. Hiding the fact that you are self sufficient is going to be hard. You can't hide farm land.

Defending your resources against the nearby city will be even harder. You may be able to save the community by buying protection with surplus food...if you have prepared for that. You may indeed have to fight, but stalling that event for even a year could mean the difference between living and being overwhelmed. In any case, your community needs to go into the crisis with a plan. You may be able to shape that plan if you become a community leader instead of a "resource". With Very Kind Regards, - R.J.

Charity in Disaster Situations--Insuring the Cohesion of the "We"

At the risk for sounding preachy, I'd like to re-emphasize the importance of storing extra logistics so that you can be charitable when disaster strikes. Charity is Biblically supported, and makes common sense. (I strongly advise it, regardless of your religious beliefs.) When the Schumer Hits the Fan (SHTF), you will want neighbors that you can count on, not people that you fear or distrust. By dispensing copious charity to your neighbors that did not have the same foresight that you did, you will solidify them as strong allies instead of envious potential enemies. In describing communities, psychologists and sociologists often talk in terms of the "we/they paradigm". Typically, this is used in a negative connotation, such as when they describe racism. (And rightfully so--I loathe racism.) But I can see something positive in building an appropriate "we/they" distinction during a societal collapse--the distinction between your local community and predatory outsiders. Just ask anyone that has ever lived "inside the wire" at a Forward Operating Base (FOB) in Iraq. Those soldiers will tell you that they felt a strong cohesive bond, and were absolutely determined to repel anyone that attempted to attack their FOB. Their steadfast resolve can be summed up with the words: "They are not getting through the wire. Period." Dispensing charity helps build a cohesive "we" and draws into sharp contrast the "they." (In my view of the near future, the "they" will likely be roving bands of criminal looters. Imagine a situation like in the movie The Road Warrior, and you are inside the perimeter at the refinery. Can you see the appropriate "we/they"?)

By logical extension, you can dispense significant charity only if you have it to give. Clearly, you must stock up above and beyond your own family's needs. So, for example, if you calculate that you need 300 pounds of wheat for your family, don't buy just 300 pounds. Instead, buy 600, 900, or even 1,200 pounds. That might sound expensive, but presently you can buy 50 pound sacks of hard red winter wheat for around $7 to $8 each. About 45 pounds of wheat will fit in a plastic 6 gallon food grade bucket that costs just over $2. Or even if you pay more to buy wheat that already packaged for long term storage in buckets (from a vendor like Walton Feed), a 45 pound bucket of wheat still costs just $17.15. Beans and rice are similarly priced. Consider that extra food as a key to building a "sense of community." Even for even those of you that are non-religious, dispensing charity will be part of your "we/they paradigm" insurance. If purchased in bulk quantities, it is also cheap insurance. Don't neglect buying your family that insurance! OBTW, speaking of wheat, the threat of the wheat "superblight" is looming. This makes it urgent for families to stock up.

Where is the Biblical support for charity? It can be seen throughout the Old and New Testaments. Remember the Bible's guidance about leaving unharvested rows of crops, to benefit "gleaners"? For example, see Leviticus 23:22: "And when ye reap the harvest of your land, thou shalt not make clean riddance of the corners of thy field when thou reapest, neither shalt thou gather any gleaning of thy harvest: thou shalt leave them unto the poor, and to the stranger: I am the LORD your God." (KJV)

The Old Testament law regarding charity can be found in Deuteronomy Chapter 15, verses 7-11 (KJV):

15:7 If there be among you a poor man of one of thy brethren within any of thy gates in thy land which the LORD thy God giveth thee, thou shalt not harden thine heart, nor shut thine hand from thy poor brother:

15:8 But thou shalt open thine hand wide unto him, and shalt surely lend him sufficient for his need, in that which he wanteth.

15:9 Beware that there be not a thought in thy wicked heart, saying, The seventh year [of Jubilee], the year of release, is at hand; and thine eye be evil against thy poor brother, and thou givest him nought; and he cry unto the LORD against thee, and it be sin unto thee.

15:10 Thou shalt surely give him, and thine heart shall not be grieved when thou givest unto him: because that for this thing the LORD thy God shall bless thee in all thy works, and in all that thou puttest thine hand unto.

15:11 For the poor shall never cease out of the land: therefore I command thee, saying, Thou shalt open thine hand wide unto thy brother, to thy poor, and to thy needy, in thy land.

From these verses it is it clear that we will always have poor people in our community ("the poor shall never cease out of the land"), and it abundantly clear that it is our duty to help them ("Thou shalt surely give...") End of preachy mode. My apologies if this offended those of you that aren't Christians or Jews. But again, even folks that are strident atheists should see the wisdom of having extra food storage to provide for charity. It is in your own best interest.

Originally posted at
www.SurvivalBlog.com
Copyright 2012

FEARs of A Prepper

I am that dreadful, blighting thing,
Like rat holes to the flood.
Like rust that gnaws the faultless blade,
Like microbes to the blood.
I know no mercy and no truth,
The young I blight, the old I slay.
Regret stalks darkly in my wake, And ignominy dogs my way.
Sometimes, in virtuous garb I rove, With facile talk of easier way;
Seducing where I dare not rape, Young manhood, from its honor's sway.
Again, in awesome guise I rush, Stupendous, through the ranks of war,
Turning to water, with my gaze, Hearts that, before, no foe could awe.
The maiden who has strayed from right, To me must pay the mead of shame.
The patriot who betrays his trust, To me must owe his tarnished name.
I spare no class, nor cult, nor creed, My course is endless through the year.
I bow all heads and break all hearts, All owe me homage — I am FEAR.
(General George S. Patton, Jr – 1944)

It isn't commonly spoken of but to be a prepper is to have fear. That's just the way it is. Some prefer to call it "concerns" or "worries" or "possibilities". But 'fear' is just as correct. There is nothing wrong with fear. It's a natural feeling that evolved as a self-preservation mechanism. Not to confuse fear with "terror" or "scared to death" which, while are common phrases, typically represent an irrational state of mind (synonymous with "panic"). And philosophers say the best way to overcome fear is to face it head on (it is though often a life time of effort).

If you ask most preppers they will say they fear some natural disaster, or plague, or EMP/solar flare, or zombies (if the CDC can warn about then just maybe...), or economic collapse leading to Mad Max land, etc etc. All very realistic possibilities. We can debate the likelihood of each but all are at a minimum worthy of at least being on the radar. (OK, maybe not the zombies.)

However, for me my fears are global. Not that I don't consider at least some of those possibilities but my fears are in a broader viewpoint or "life approach" sense.

While I have always considered myself to be "prepared" (at least more than the next guy usually) for whatever life throws at me, I never took specific steps that at least I consider unusual or exceptional to prepare. The things I did, the way I lead my life, all seemed very reason and logical. And non-specific. That is, what I did could be applied to many scenarios not just one or two specific cases. And if these scenarios never happened, no big deal. My actions didn't cost all that much and certainly could be used (and in fact were used) for other events in life that hadn't entered my thinking at that time. In other words, what I had prepared for – and again, nothing specific – didn't happen but I was able to apply my prepping to other events of life and all worked out just as well.

But now the game has changed.

I have turned a corner. To me it is no longer question of "if" but simply when.

As of writing this the economy is my #1 top concern. I don't like to make economic predictions but in this case I do think at the very least it's going to be much worse before even a glimmer of getting better – if at all. I have written on other sites that I do think the point-of-no-return has been reached and is now being exceeded at warp 10. And all the possibilities that an economic collapse brings are in the forefront of my concerns and prepping thoughts. I have no idea when that collapse will come or what it will look like. No one does. Every national economic collapse has some similarities but all unfold in their own way.

Yes Virginia, I do believe this time is different.

(I do NOT want to get into a discussion of the economy, the national or local debts, economic collapse, etc etc etc. That is not the point of this article.)

I have always said that if it were just me, by myself as a single man, I wouldn't care so much. If all other things in my life unfolded the same (more or less) I would survive whatever comes. And if I didn't, so what really in the bigger picture of the universe.

If it were just me and my wife and all other things being the same we would survive more or less good for the rest of our lives. Not easily. Might take everything we have to do it, dying totally penny less. But I think we would. At least much better than anyone else we know.
But it isn't only me, nor only me and my wife. It's our children now. They can't take care of themselves. Not even in a feral sense in the extreme scenario. And won't be able to for many many years to come at the earliest.

So it is for them that I prepare.

And it is for them that I have preparation fears.

Comes to the crux of this article.

Not simply am I doing enough or am I planning correctly, but even more basically:

Is prepping – food, water, defense, etc. – even the right thing to do at all? Or should I be saving and husbanding every dollar for the future? Or just live life as I always have been?

If I really believe the economy and American society are going over the cliff at full steam why haven't I bought more gold? Is it because in my heart I don't believe it really is so bad? Or am I suffering from the "normalcy bias"?

What if I'm wrong? Sure we can eat the food. And my wife will thoroughly enjoy ribbing me for all my prep work (she already does). But that money could be used for other things right now. But of most fear to me is:

Should I be spending more of my hard earned assets on preps while the American dollar still holds value? Or converting more of it to gold? Or spend it on other aspects of daily life now? Or do nothing?

It is to the last point that I focus most on these days: To see all that I have worked for and saved for all my life become worthless in front of my eyes such that I can't even feed and provide for my family rips at my heart and soul!

To put it another way: I would just want to crawl off and die if one day all that I have managed to save and achieve in my life became worthless (for all intents and purposes), little more than numbers on a piece of paper when I could have spent those numbers on something meaningful for my family while it still held some sort of value.

I'm reminded of a movie from the 70's I had once seen on TV. Don't recall the name. It was low budget. I think it was a Canadian production too. No major actor names in it. The plot was simple: Something has happened to the world's food production capability and food was in very short supply and running out fast. The story focused on two friends, one a farmer and his family living on a family farm trying to produce enough food to survive while fending off bandits; The other a business man in a city trying to make sense of what was happening in the world around him and get enough food for his family to survive the winter. The movie showed food was so valuable that at a wedding guests brought gifts of food – loafs of bread, baskets of produce, etc. – instead of the usual money and household gifts. Near the end the businessman meets with a guy who we today would call a "prepper" who clearly has put away a vast store of food. The guy is now basically a "God Father" of food, with bodyguards paid in food, etc. The businessman offers him a pile of stock and bond certificates, a box of fine jewelry, etc all for just enough food for his family to make it through the winter. The prepper scoffs at the businessman saying quote "People like me stockpiled food while you stockpiled gold. Now who's in charge!" (I remember that quote so vividly after all these years!) In the end, the prepper doesn't give the businessman any food, and the businessman uses his computer to compare the population of North America to the current food supply in storage and determines there's only 60 days worth of food left. Not a happy ending.

Then again, just how much food can you store? At best a year's worth (and I don't have all that much space to store, not without tripping over boxes). Plus water, plus the means to reliably heat water at a minimum. Etc. At some point living off stored food will end and you need to have a substance source of food, either your own production or by trade. Living in a suburban or near-urban location that level of production just isn't possible. (And urban is totally impossible.)

And there is the cost. As I write this I'm looking at a well known food storage company's website. They have several "extreme" food storage packages. One of their packages is a 1-year supply costing $6,600 (rounded) for 3200 calories per day, $5,500 for 2400 calories. Or just a 6 month supply is $3,600 for 3200 calories or $2,900 for 2400 calories. (This is of course a one person supply so for a family of four it would only last a few months at best.) This stuff isn't cheap! But then again what good would it be to need the food, unable to get it, but still have numbers on paper? Can't feed the paper to my family.

On the other hand, just how much gold can you – should you – convert your assets into? It doesn't bother me too much if I bought gold at these lofty levels ($1,674/oz. as of writing this) then see it fall two or three hundred or even four hundred. Wouldn't be the first time I over paid for an investment nor had an investment fall promptly after I purchased it. Goes with the territory. But if I did convert much more of my assets to gold and something did happen to make gold drop back below $1,000/oz that would be an immediate evaporation of a large amount of wealth. And there is the issue of a confiscation or other government enforcement that makes gold effectively worthless in terms of trade for supplies or conversion to currency (don't forget the new 1099 rules start in 2012!).

I suppose the middle ground is the best answer: <u>Do some prepping but keep living life otherwise as best I can.</u> That way if something does happen my family will be better off than many others. But of nothing happens I haven't lost everything on events that didn't unfold. But I just don't know if I will be happy with myself on the middle ground.

Yes, my family will be better off than most of the people we know if an economic disaster happen but I'll always have the nagging though that I could have done more. But if nothing happens, even just trudging along for 10 years in a malaise, I will have spent much needed funds for something that never happened. Maybe even a silly notion. In that scenario cash flow will be king.

Can't dwell on fear.

Fear eats the soul.

We're going to need all our souls to make it through the next couple of years – I fear.

UNPREPARED

Welcome to the Promised Land

by Rod E.
*Originally posted at www.**SurvivalBlog**.com*
Copyright 2012

Over the years, many people have told us that WTSHTF, they are coming to our place in the country. When people say things like this, we hear, "...so that you can take care of me." This document is presented as a source of information for those who might need a realignment of their expectations, a clarification of ours or both. **It should serve as a harsh wake up call for anyone who plans to flee to someone else's survival retreat should the need arise.**

If you have neglected, failed or refused to complete your plans for survival, here are things you need to know, should you decide to depend on someone who has been more diligent.

No One Will Provide You With Shelter
No One Will Feed You
No One Will Provide Drinking Water
No One Will Protect You
No One Will Provide Medical Attention

Did the Children of Israel expect Moses to provide all of these things for them? Nope! He started walking and they had to keep up. Everyone carried what they needed and everyone did everything they needed to do to survive.

Let's take a look at what your life might be like WTSHTF.

For any number of reasons, you lose electricity without notice and your water stops running. (Public water supplies need electricity) When people eventually realize the outage extends beyond their immediate circle of travel, they will panic and stores will be looted. Stores cannot be protected because...the police departments have no electricity. Gas stations will be closed when they cannot deliver fuel because...they have no electricity. It's funny how that works, isn't it? As more people begin to panic they will assemble into angry mobs armed with guns, knives, baseball bats and sticks. No police presence means no protection for you or anyone else. The police have raced home to protect their families.

You are now officially unemployed with no benefits, you cannot withdraw your worthless money from the bank, you cannot make a phone call, listen to the radio or watch television. Your stove, microwave oven, refrigerator and Internet connection are no longer working. You cannot run to Wal-Mart's camping section to pick up a sleeping bag or kerosene lantern. Your car has less than a half tank of gasoline and your terrified wife and children are begging you to do something.

A horde of lawless desperadoes is making its way down your street, hurling rocks and bricks through windows, setting cars on fire and breaking into homes in search of food and supplies. Through sheer numbers and merciless force, they overwhelm every feeble attempt at defense or escape, leaving death and destruction in their path. Like killer bees, they swarm your home and discover that it is vacant because you somehow managed to escape, either through a miracle, proper planning or dumb luck. They ravage what was once your comfortable home sweet home, laying waste years of financial sacrifice and hard work as you are driving or hiking or crawling down the highway or back roads to The Promise Land, your friend's place in the country.

For the sake of this frightening glimpse into your new reality, let's assume that you and your family somehow beat the one in a million odds and successfully escape the chaos and anarchy in the city. Exhausted and emotionally paralyzed with fear and anxiety, you eventually make your way to an overgrown pasture bordered by woods, provided that you were not attacked and killed on your journey or shot as an intruder when you arrive, which is always an unfortunate possibility.

So, in summary:

There is no comfortable shelter waiting for you
There is no water
There is no food
There is no security, no protection at all
The mobs will eventually make their way out into the countryside and find you

The place looks deserted, and there is silence as you cautiously scan the edge of the woods. You can't help but wonder how many guns might be aimed at your head.

Welcome to The Promised Land. It is everything you expected it to be?

More than one person has referred to our place in the country as, The Promised Land. It is important to remember that the people followed Moses. He did not carry them...and I am not Moses...and our place is not The Promised Land. Adhering to the analogy, the city from which you fled was the land of Egypt, our place in the country is the desert. The Promised Land comes later if you survive and behave yourself.

In spite of arriving with nothing more than the inappropriate clothes on your back and the meager amount of food that you were able to carry, and given the obvious absence of expected amenities at your adopted survival haven, you are are still somehow confident that you will survive because you've been responsibly paying the premiums on your Emergency and Disaster Preparedness insurance policy.

You haven't been paying the premiums? You did not sacrifice what you wanted today for what you might need tomorrow? The bad news is, your prognosis for survival is definitely grim. There is no good news.

We do not have a rider on our Emergency and Disaster Preparedness insurance policy for you. You have no insurance coverage at our place. Like most people, we have fallen onto extremely hard times and have been barely able to feed ourselves and keep a roof over our heads. We won't even discuss the monumental tasks of paying medical bills and other past-due responsibilities. Severe illness and extended unemployment completely drained our finances and everything that was left of our emergency supplies. The Schumer has hit the fan for us already. If it gets any worse, we may have to come and live with you. Did you ever think about that?

No One Will Provide You With Shelter.

First off, who knows how long we will be able to keep up the payments on our house or how long it will remain standing? In times of civil unrest, windows get broken, doors get kicked in and houses burn. If our house is somehow miraculously still standing when you arrive, consider what that environment would be like if you chose to stay (provided that we let you). There is only so much room in our house. Imagine being jammed and crammed into an increasingly smelly and dirty house with a maniacal herd of hungry, desperate refugees undergoing various stages of mental deterioration, panic and anger, screaming at each other and crying at the drop of a hat. Sound like fun? Not so much.

To set the record straight, my wife and I will never subject ourselves to that psychological nightmare whether our house is standing or not. Not even a fool would do that during the best of times so why would anyone expect us to do it during a time of great distress? We are both getting old and crotchety, we lack patience and we have no desire to convert our house into a loony bin so take that option off the table right now.

If you show up WTSHTF and if we decide to let you stay, you will have to build your own shelter using your bare hands and your own supplies. Do a web search on the phrase "debris hut" for more information. It is presumptuous and selfish to expect anyone to expend their resources and energy to provide this for you out of the kindness of their heart. Your shelter will need to be built in such a way that it will keep you warm in the winter, cool in the summer and it must be able to withstand 60-70MPH winds, torrential downpours and heavy layers of snow and ice often accompanying the wicked storms that we get periodically. Nature is not your friend. It is a heartless enemy that is constantly trying to kill you. Build your shelter accordingly.

So now that you have built your comfy debris hut with three bedrooms, one and a half baths and a deck, let's discuss the next facet of your reality.

No One Will Feed You

We cannot and will not feed you because we were not blessed with unlimited financial resources, the divine calling to set aside food for you, nor the facility to store that extra food. If God wanted us to do that, He would have told us to do it and made it possible. He doesn't. He hasn't. He didn't. He told you to do it and He made it possible. You listened and obeyed, right? Those are the insurance premiums you should have been paying all along.

If you choose to come to our place WTSHTF, you will need to provide all of your own food. Don't count on living off of the land because first of all, you don't know how, and second, it is much harder than you think. There will be a myriad of other critical responsibilities and events that will demand your attention so having a good food storage is wise. When considering what kind of food you should be putting aside, remember that canned goods expire, bulge and rust. They are also heavy and difficult to transport. Dried goods mold, become infested with bugs and everything attracts mice. We have lots and lots of bugs and mice here in the desert. (Potential food source?) Figure out what you will eat, how much you will eat, double or triple that and figure out a way to get it, store it, rotated to keep it fresh and carry it to our place if you still want to come here. (The lack of a warm, dry house is usually a show stopper for most armchair survivalists)

Consider how much food your family consumes in a week, a month, a year. Now imagine what will happen to you and them if you immediately stopped going to the store to replenish your supplies. Remember, you have no job so you have no money and even if you did, money is no longer worth the paper it is written on. There are no stores to go to and no one is going to sell you food or trade their food for your meager possessions. So get that out of your head. Gold coins, if you have any, might make good sinkers should you decide to go fishing but a pound of gold won't buy a pound of rice because no one does that much fishing.

Do you plan on hunting for food? So do a million other people and those heavily armed, hungry hordes with their guns, snares, spears and home made bows and arrows will be stumbling over each other in the woods. You are better than the competition so one shot, one kill and you miraculously shoot the last squirrel left in the entire county (because the other animals were smart enough to leave when all those crazy people showed up). Everyone hears that gun shot and your mission is now to somehow escape those heavily populated woods with your life and your squirrel, in that order. Good luck with that.

Deciding not to risk your life to kill what's left of God's little animals, you might innocently/ignorantly believe that you can sustain yourself and your family by foraging for wild, edible plants but so does every other unprepared refugee who has fled to the country and they are all scouring the countryside, grazing on everything that is green or was green or might be green someday. Do you know the precise differences between edible plants and their poisonous look-a-like cousins? Even your reference book will tell you that pictures are no substitute for experience. Ingesting the wrong plants may present an unpleasant way to die with the retching and vomiting and sweating and diarrhea that precedes the wheezing, contorting and groan. (See: We Cannot Provide Medical Attention)

Note: You cannot eat grass. Your stomach can process the sugars but not the cellulose which contains most of the calories that you will need. A cow can do it but a cow's stomach is equipped to do that and yours is not. Do your research beforehand or suffer the consequences.

I hope you like bugs, snakes and mice. Yum!

No One Will Provide Drinking Water

Do you really believe that you will somehow be able to locate, carry, purify and store at least one gallon of water per day for each person in your family? Did you remember to bring a big pot to boil water and if so, did you know that it takes about forty pounds of wood to boil five gallons of water, which also weighs about the same? Where will you get all of that wood? Chopping wood with an ax (that you forgot to bring with you) burns calories that you cannot afford to burn because you have been eating grass. How will you carry that much wood and store it and burn it every single day of the year through the rain and snow and freezing rain and under the blistering summer sun, even when you are exhausted or sick with the flu or you have a broken arm? (We are busy fetching and purifying our own water so don't call us.) Remember, while you are gathering water and wood, so is every other rueful wretch struggling to survive and what will you do when they square off with you to fight you for what you have, or worse yet, when they show up with thirty of their thirsty friends to steal your water? (See: We Cannot Protect You)

You will need an efficient, sustainable means to collect, purify and store water...lots and lots of water. You will need the wherewithal to store enough extra water to carry you through the hard freeze of winter (no one wants to fetch water during an ice storm), when you are sick or disabled or overwhelmed with other tasks like vomiting because you ate a flower that looked friendly but wasn't. You will need to know how to efficiently as effectively manage and protect your precious water supply and have a backup plan in case your primary supply is disrupted or destroyed. Ponds dry up or become polluted, containers leak and bad things happen. (Which is obviously our fault) Prepare for it, deal with it or die.

Yes, we know about bio-sand filters. How much sand and gravel did you bring? Perhaps you can find a clean barrel somewhere. Were we supposed to supply that? Wow, you must really be disappointed in us.

No One Will Protect You

Remember those angry hordes that frightened you out of the city and burned your home? They will eventually exhaust the resources of the ravaged neighborhoods and make their way into the countryside. When they find you, and they will find you, they will be even more desperate and dangerous than when you last saw them. Additionally, our neighbors, the heavily armed people who inhabited the countryside long before you got here, will be "foraging" for your resources so be careful out there. Desperate people do desperate things and those people will congregate because there is strength in numbers. Now, it's just you against ten, thirty or fifty desperate people determined to take your food, water and resources and they will have no qualms about hurting or killing you. Are you physically, emotionally and spiritually equipped to survive such an attack...over and over and over again because those attacks will continue to happen with increased intensity as people become more and more desperate.

You will need the ability to effectively defend yourself, your family and your resources against undefeatable forces. You will need more than a gun, a knife or a pointy stick. Those are mere implements and implements are a very small part of the complex security equation. Your opponents will undoubtedly have more and bigger implements and they might arrive in incomprehensible waves of death and destruction. Consequently, you will need to be physically fit and experienced as well as mentally and emotionally prepared. You must possess the reflexes of a gazelle on amphetamines, the strength of a superhero on steroids, the spatial awareness of a rabbit surrounded by hungry wolves and divine wisdom to know what to do in any given crisis. You may be forced to run in order to survive or fight in order to survive but you may run or fight and die anyway. Raise your hand when you think it is our responsibility to step in and save you because you can't protect yourself.

Okay, realistically, security is everyone's business and we would not expect you to defend yourself all by yourself if you were a member of our community, but I hope you understand that making it someone else's responsibility to protect you is presumptuous and dangerous. Make sure you are worth saving by participating in the fray with the same intensity that you would expect from others.

By the way, hungry people will kill you for your food. Very hungry people eat even their dead friends. There are many examples of survival-induced cannibalism throughout history. In fact, most instances of cannibalism are for survival, not ritual. The Donner Party, the wreck of the Mignonette, and the plane crash of the Uruguayan rugby team in the Andes mountains are all stories proving that people who are without food for about ninety days or less will turn to cannibalism. Watch the movie "The Road", and see if that opens your mind to possibilities that await you.

If you wander outside of the perimeter, we cannot protect you. If you are kidnapped, we will not negotiate for your return. We may retaliate with a rabid vengeance but we will not negotiate.

No One Will Provide Medical Attention

So, you somehow got your head bashed in or you were stabbed or shot while defending your debris hut/condo, your dwindling food supply of field mice and a half gallon of dirty pond water stored in a leaky, plastic milk container that you found on the side of the road (Again, obviously our fault). You got stung a zillion times by angry hornets or you rolled in a patch of poison ivy (that you were collecting as food). Perhaps you fell out of a tree or you slipped and broke your arm or you chopped off your finger while trying to split fire wood with a rock and a dull steak knife. Maybe you charred your hand while digging through the hot coals of your smoldering camp fire, retrieving a field mouse that fell off of your roasting stick. We did not budget for a private hospital or a retired veterinarian and you are no longer covered under ObamaCare, so all you might get is a slightly used band-aid. Will that make it all better? If you did not bring any medical supplies, you probably won't like what we will do to your stab gash, bullet hole, hornet sting, broken arm, missing finger or charred hand. And by the way, you deserve that case of poison ivy.
Let's see what else...

We will not build your fires to keep you warm, cook your food or provide comfort. Learn to build a fire now without the use of a lighter or matches and practice until you are good at it. We will teach you while we have the time but don't ask us later because we will be quite busy.

If you come to our place WTSHTF, we will not give you a knife or any other sharp object. If you do not already own a good knife, you obviously won't know how to use one safely anyway. (See: We Cannot Provide Medical Attention) Buy at least two good knives, spend a lot of money for them and learn how to use them and sharpen them! If we have to tell you why, you are probably going to die anyway and "very hungry people" will eat you.

We will not provide you with a bathroom or outhouse or a nice warm shower. You may not like the idea of pooping in a hole behind a tree but you will eventually get over it. If that is simply unacceptable, bring along a port-a-potty with a padded seat and plenty of environment-friendly chemicals, biodegradable toilet paper and be prepared to add an addition to your debris hut.

I will address survival community governance at a later date, but in short, a survival community is not a democracy. You will not get to vote like they do on The Discovery Channel's series, The Colony. Get over it. You chose to leave your democracy when they voted to kill you and take your stuff, remember? Ours will not be a society where members of the House and Senate force those who work to provide for those who won't and it will not reward those who steal with bailouts.

Technically, a survival community does not function as a colony but more like a tribe. Embrace the concept of communal life in a tribe. Consider everything tribe members do together and everything they must do for themselves and you will have an idea of what will be expected of you should you wish to be a part of a survival community. Get used to living with rules. If you think your home owner's association is too strict, you surely won't like living with a tribe of dedicated survivalists with zero tolerance for freeloaders or pansies.

A man recently asked me, "What do I have or what could I do that might be beneficial to your community?" My answer was, "I haven't a clue. Only you can answer that question." He never did. I know what he was thinking and we are not interested in what he has to offer. He has stockpiled lots of guns and ammunition, virtually no food for his extended family and all he has for water purification is one ceramic filter. We don't need him. He needs us. If all you have is guns and ammunition, everyone already considers you a threat and you will have absolutely no idea how they have prepared to deal with that threat. When those people die, someone will take their stuff and the "very hungry people" will eat them. Just something to consider in case you decide to become a looter or a bully. To survive, you need a balance of skills, resources, preparation and experience.

Before you ask someone if you can join their survival community, ask yourself, "Why would they let me come to their place?" This is a fair question that deserves an honest answer. A healthy community is the only way any of us will make it through the coming hard times, but in every community, every person must have more than a single redeeming quality.

Remember the parable of the ten virgins. [In contemporary terms] Five of them paid the premiums on their Emergency and Disaster Preparedness insurance policy. The other five didn't. Make sure you are prepared. Your future depends on it.

If, after reading this, you still want to come to our place and realize that you won't be able to bring much with you when you flee the city, you should probably consider getting your stuff to our place now while you still can. No, we do not have additional storage space so that is another thing for you to consider. We will allow you park your motor home or trailer here and you can even build a shed to store your survival items but that offer is only available to a certain few for a limited amount of time. (My wife wanted me to remove this paragraph.)

If you do not know how to build a shelter or start a fire or purify water, I would advise you to get here as soon as possible so that we can teach you while there is still time to learn. Would you like to practice and see what it would be like to put all of these skills together in a controlled environment? Now is a good time. During a torrential rain storm is another good time.

After thinking about it, there is only one way that we might allow someone to show up on our doorstep without resources. Consider the role of an indentured servant and let us know if that appeals to you because that would be your only option.

Originally posted at
*www.**SurvivalBlog**.com*
Copyright 2012

How about it Grandpa? You got any money?

I Am Your Worst Nightmare

[**Editor's Note**: *This article, while fictional, depicts quite accurately the potential "worst-case" threats that some would face in a significant socio-economic collapse. Indeed, such bands of sophisticated marauders and looters have been seen observed in many societies racked by such collapses, or even local internecine civil war (e.g., Zambia, Bosnia, etc.). Such groups likely would evolve from modern drug cartels, which often rely on prior military personnel, or from drug-based street gangs (M7, Crips, Bloods), which today are known to SEND members into the Armed Services, in order to gain weapons and gear knowledge, and eventually to "bring home" advanced tactical training to share with other gang members, once their enlistment is up*

.

While this threat is at the extreme end of the spectrum for most Church members and/or preppers, especially if they are living in rural areas, it may well be a very real and near-term threat for those living in or near major urban centers such as Los Angeles, New York and Chicago. Thus, we offer this cautionary tale for your consideration."]

Christopher

=====

I am the leader of a band of 8-to-12 looters. I have some basic military training. We move from place to place like locusts devouring everything in our path. My group is armed with light weapons and can develop and follow simple plans of attack. We take what we want by force of arms. We prefer none of our victims survive because that could cause problems for us in the future.

It has been six months since the grid went down. You and the other five members of your party have settled into what may be a long grinding existence. The every day tasks of growing and gathering have now become routine. The news from the outside is extremely limited but you don't really miss it much. Life is simple but physically demanding.

Although things may seem stable you will need to keep your team focused and alert. This is your first and most important layer of defense. You should hold an immediate reaction drill once per week. Keep things simple. Practice a specific response to such threats as injury, fire, attack and evacuation. Despite the challenges you must maintain contact with those around you such as neighbors for vital clues that trouble is brewing. Regular monitoring the radio will be critical in providing an early warning of trouble. You may be able to safely interview refugees with risking your party. Keep in mind the information you get from them may not always be reliable.

While you have been farming I have been learning the best tactics to employ to seize your property and your goods. I have been refining them since we hit the road right after the lights went out. I have conducted eight "hits" so far and have been successful seven times. Here are some of my "lessons learned".

Intelligence gathering and target selection is critical to my success. Targets include those who have large quantities of fuel, food and other valuable supplies. My posse is constantly questioning anyone and everyone we contact searching for this our next victim. Anyone who has ever had knowledge, even second hand, of your preparations is someone of interest to me. I may approach them directly or indirectly. If anyone knows something I will find out about it. Who seems well-fed? Who still has transportation? Who has lights? Who was prepared? Where are they exactly? Somebody talks, either in person or on the radio. They always do.

We search for victims night and day. During the day we are listening for the sounds of machinery, cars, tractors, gunfire or generators. Day or night without a lot of wind those sounds can carry for miles. At night I look for any sort of light. Even a small flash indicates somebody with electricity and that means a rich target. I always have somebody listing to the scanner for any news, leads or insecure chatter.

Operational Security is an important concept for your entire group to understand and maintain. If somebody outside your circle doesn't have a real need to know about your plans, preparations or procedures then they shouldn't know period. Develop a cover story and live it like was a bulletproof vest. It is no less important to your protection and survival. During an event you need to blend in with the surrounding environment. Carefully observe noise (such as generators and other engines) and light discipline especially at night. If you need to test fire weapons do it in one sequence to avoid a prolonged noise signature.

Once I find and target you reconnaissance of your retreat is my next step. Only a fool would try to rush in and try to overwhelm a group of "survivalists". We had a bad experience with that during our second hit. Now we spend at least a day or two trying to size up a large opportunity and the best way to take it down. I will observe retreat activity from a nearby-concealed position. I will get an idea of your numbers, weapons, routines and so much more by careful surreptitious observation. If your group seems alert, I will try and trigger a false alarm with a dog or child to watch your reaction to a threat. That helps me know how you respond, where you are strong and how to attack. I may also obtain a topographical map of the area to identify likely avenues of approach and potential escapes routes you will try to use. I may coerce your neighbors into uncovering a weak spot or access point or other important intelligence. I also have a Bearcat handheld scanner. I will be listening for any insecure chatter from your radios.

Regular patrols at irregular intervals focused on likely observation points and avenues of approach could keep me at bay. You could put down sand or other soft soil in key choke points as a way of "recording" if anyone has recently traveled through the land. Dogs, with their advanced sense of hearing and smell are able to detect and alert you to intruders well in advance of any human. Motion sensing IR video cameras as a part of a security plan could play a part in your layered defense as long as you have power. A 24 hour manned observation point equipped with high quality optical tools is a must. It should be fortified and if possible concealed. It should have a weapon capable of reaching to the edges of your vision. Seismic intrusion devices, night vision and thermal imaging are phenomenal force multiply-

ing tools. They can give you critical intelligence and warning. You should use them if you have them. Understand they are not fool proof and I can often neutralize them if I know you have them.

These tools and techniques provide you reaction time. Time to plan your response and time to execute that plan. Recognize that a "defender" is always at a disadvantage. By definition a defender will be reacting to my attack. Modern warfare has emphasized the ability of the attacker to operate faster than opponents can react. This can be explained by the OODA loop. Below are the four steps of the classic OODA loop. These are the steps a defender goes through when under attack.

1. Observing or noticing the attack.
2. Orient to the direction, method and type of attack.
3. Deciding what the appropriate response will be.
4. Acting on that decision.

As an attacker I will try and operate at a pace faster than you as a defender can adjust to. I will change my direction, pace, timing and method to force you to continue to process through the OODA loop. This creates confusion and wastes your precious reaction time. As a defender you will need to disrupt or reset your attackers timing with a counter-attack. When you are successful you become the attacker. Your defensive plans should utilize and exploit this concept. Here are a few scenarios:

1. Snipe & Siege
I will begin the attack when I can engage at least half of your party's military age personnel in one coordinated effort. I will infiltrate my team into concealed positions around your retreat within 50 to 75 yards. I will target any identified leadership with the first volley. Two thirds of my people will be engaging personnel. The other group will target communications antennas, surveillance cameras and any visible lighting assets. I want your group unable to see, communicate or call for help. The members of my band will each fire two magazines in the initial exchange. Two thirds of my group will change to new concealed positions and wait. One third will fall back into an ambush of the most likely avenue of escape. We will stay concealed and wait until you come out to attend to your wounded and dead. We repeat the attack as necessary until any resistance is crushed.

Ensure you adjust the landscape around your retreat so that I don't have anyplace offering cover or concealment within 100 yards of your residence. You can create decorative masonry walls that can be used to offer cover for personnel close to your residence. Fighting positions can be built now and used as raised planting beds and then excavated for use in the future. These can be extended or reinforced after any significant event. These structures or other measures such as trenching must be sited carefully to avoid allowing them to be used effectively by an attacker if they are overrun.

2. Trojan Horse

For one hit we used an old UPS truck. We forced a refugee to drive it to the retreat gate. We concealed half our group inside the truck. The truck was hardened on the inside with some sandbags around the edges. The other half of our group formed an ambush concealed inside the tree line along the driveway. We killed the driver to make it look good and had one person run away. Those preppers almost waited us out. After nearly three hours they all walked slowly down the driveway. They were bunched up in a group intent on checking out the truck and driver. It was like shooting fish in a barrel.

They could have worked together as group to sweep the area 360 degrees around the truck and they would have surely found us. A dog would have also alerted the residents to our presence. They could have taken measures to eliminate the vegetation offering us concealment on the road near the gate. They could have used CS gas or something similar to "deny" any suspicious areas. Lastly they could have done a "reconnaissance by fire". Shooting into likely hiding spots, including the truck, trying to evoke a response. They should have established an over watch position with the majority of their group. This over watch group would have provided visual security and an immediate response if there were an attack. They were not expecting any additional threats. They didn't consider that there might be additional danger lurking nearby aside from the truck and they died.

3. Kidnap & Surrender

A few weeks ago we surprised and captured a couple of women out tending a garden. It was totally by chance. We were traveling through a very rural area on our way to another town when somebody heard a tractor backfire. We immediately stopped and I sent a small team to recon the noise. They bumped into a small party tending a field at the edge of their retreat. They seized two women and immediately dragged them back to our vehicles. We began negotiations by sending a finger from each one back to the retreat under a white flag. The rest was easy.

This didn't need to happen. Better noise discipline would have kept us from discovering their retreat. Some simple boundary fencing or tangle foot could have delayed us. The women should have been armed and aware of such a threat. If they has established an over watch for the garden they could have engaged us before we took our hostages or at least alerted the others that there was a problem. They

also could have had a quick reaction SOP developed prior to this incident. That Quick Reaction (QR) force could have followed the kidnappers back to our vehicles and set up an ambush of their own. Rural retreat security is a full time job. If you snooze you may lose everything.

4. Fire and Maneuver

I don't like this option but sometimes the prize is just too tempting. We typically infiltrate quietly at night to prearranged start points. We begin our attack just before dawn when your senses are dulled by a long night watch or from sleep. Based on our reconnaissance we divided your retreat into positions or zones that need specific attention. We prepare for battle by using an air rifle to target any lights or cameras. Our first priority is to engage any LP/OP site and destroy or degrade them as much as possible. I split my forces into two supporting groups. One group keeps the target position under constant fire. The other group also fires and maneuvers, closing on the target and destroying it with gunfire or improvised weapons. Many times these positions only have one occupant and the task is relatively easy. Often these positions are easy to spot and are too far from each other to provide any effective mutual support. We will work from one position to the next. In the darkness and confusion most of the defenders are disoriented and ineffective. They fall like dominos. We have also used motorcycles to negotiate obstacles and speed through cuts in the perimeter fence. Then throw Molotov Cocktails into any defensive position as they roar past. If you fall back into your residence we will set up a siege. If we can maneuver close enough, perhaps by using a distraction, we will pump concentrated insecticide into your building or we may introduce LP gas from a portable tank into the house and ignite it with tracer fire.

If there was enough warning time from your OP you could execute a pre-planned response. Your planned response should be simple, easy to understand and execute. Half your group occupies your fighting positions, two to a position. The rest of your party establishes an over watch and concentrate its fire at the enemies trying to fix your positions. If you had more than enough prepared positions the enemy might not know where to attack. It would also provide more flexibility in your defense based on the direction of attack. I would use Night Vision if available or illumination from flares or lights as a last resort. Rats hate light.

Usually people keep main access points blocked from high-speed approach. Likely avenues of approach should also be blocked or choked and kept under observation. Remember though what keeps me out keeps you in. Typically the common techniques of parking vehicles in roadways will only delay my approach not stop it altogether. An ordinary

12-gauge shotgun, shooting slugs, can stop most types of non-military vehicles at close range.

Don't forget the threat of fire or other non-traditional weapons in your defensive plans.
You could create the illusion of a "dead end" for your main access road by positioning a burned out trailer home or a couple of burned out cars at the false "end" of the road. Concealing the fact that the road actually continues to your residence.

Lastly, develop a plan to evacuate and evade capture. When faced with a significantly superior force it may be the only viable option. This should include simple, reliable communications or signals such as three blasts on a dog whistle. Your fighting positions and barriers need to be constructed to allow coordinated withdrawal in an emergency. You should establish a rally point and time limit to assemble. I believe this should be a priority in your practice drills. During a real emergency you may be able to rally, rearm and plan your own version of the "snipe and siege" to retake your retreat.

Key messages:
Your rural retreat defense can be visualized as a set of concentric rings:

Location – Location – Location:
High and remote are best

OPSEC –
Think of it as a form of armor or shield: Practice it and protect it.

Observation Post / Listening Post:
Your first best chance to counter attack

Gates / Fences / other barriers:
May slow me down. Might keep you in.

Fighting positions:
Must provide mutual support and allow for evacuation.

Residence:
Last line. Don't become trapped People, Planning and Practice

Remember:
An aggressive and unexpected counter strike can win the battle.

Stay alert for multiple threats or diversionary tactics. **Criminals excel at feigning weakness to lower your guard.**

Don't underestimate me.

[Thanks to Don, a Survival Spot reader, for this story] http://www.survival-spot.com/surviva...rst-night-mare/

The Thin Blue Line

SOMETIMES THERE'S JUSTICE

SOMETIMES THERE'S JUST US

The Thin Blue Line,

by Deputy W.

Originally posted at www.SurvivalBlog.com
Copyright 2012

The "Thin Blue Line". It describes something much greater than the title of a second rate movie. **It describes the thin blue line of civilian law enforcement officers that is the only thing that separates America from utter chaos.** It is not too difficult to imagine what would happen if that thin blue line were to disappear or become overwhelmed. A scary thought indeed, but one that you are already thinking about since you are reading SurvivalBlog.

Yet, we are alarmingly close to just such a scenario. As most readers of SurvivalBlog know, our modern Western society is extremely complex, interwoven, and most of all, vulnerable. We are facing the most serious economic situation since the Great Depression, but discussion of the current economic crisis and the innumerable other threats to our society is beyond the scope of this essay. Rather, I hope to explain to you, from a rural law enforcement officer's perspective, **what we could be in for in the event of a cataclysmic societal event.**

I have been in a law enforcement career for 10 years. I have worked in a jail, I have worked road patrol, and I have been an investigator. Through my career, I have become a student of human nature. I have seen the evil that man is capable of perpetrating against his fellow man. **There is one general rule to remember about all of humanity: it is at the core of our sinful nature to do that which is best for ourselves, regardless of what effect that may have on other people.** We are a murderous and self seeking race, and it is my hope that you have a personal relationship with Jesus Christ to set you free from this sin.

.

But facts are facts. The Bible tells us that there will be many more souls that will be lost than there will be souls that will be saved in the end times. So we must prepare ourselves spiritually and physically, with the assumption that we will soon be facing unimaginable evil, and it will be in the form of a human face. **As disturbing as it may be to you, you must be prepared to do whatever it takes to defend yourself and your family.** You must be willing and able to deliver a lethal recourse if it becomes absolutely necessary. I will extrapolate on those thoughts.

The average petty criminal has a simple mind set. He operates from much lower moral standard than most other people. He is concerned about only one thing: himself. **He is typically lazy and self serving. He doesn't see a reason to go to work every day.** Working people are chumps to him, but he likes having them around because they earn plenty of things for him to steal. It is no coincidence that burglaries are primarily daytime affairs. He knows that most people will not be home when he chooses to burglarize. He doesn't want to hurt anybody, but he carries a knife or a gun in case somebody tries to interfere with his plans The only thing that keeps him from being more brazen is the threat of enforcement action against him. He doesn't really want to go to jail, because it really is an unpleasant place to be. After all, if jail were so great, why do so many criminals flee capture?

Then consider the more malicious type of criminal. **He has absolutely no morals, with the exception of honor among criminals.** Even that is very questionable if it comes to a point where he can save his own skin. He has been raised on violence, and it is all he knows. **He has no empathy for you, your family, or for anyone else. He doesn't care if he causes you pain, and he probably even enjoys it. He will give no more thought to killing you than you would give to killing a housefly.** He sees people like you as an annoyance to be dealt with. He sees you as an inanimate object, put on this earth only to provide him with gratification. He sees you, your family, and your possessions as a means to an end to self gratification. He will do whatever he wants to do in order to be gratified, unless and until you are willing to do whatever it takes to defend yourself. Otherwise, **it is very likely that you and your family will perish horribly.**

You see both types of these criminals all over America. You see them in the big cities and in the small towns. The only reason they are kept in check is because we have an established system to adjudicate and punish criminals. Even that is not usually enough to keep them from committing dastardly acts. All that we can hope for as a law enforcement officer is to catch the criminal after the act punish him. Then we hope that this acts as a deterrent to future criminal acts. Honestly, I'm not sure that it does. Some men are just plain wicked and that's the way it is.

Criminals are the minority under normal circumstances. Most citizens are decent and hard working people. But it would not take much to destabilize our society. There are a lot of threats to our way of life. Proceed with me through the following scenario.

A major economic collapse occurs in America. Millions are unemployed and have no way to earn honest money. The rest of the citizenry is crippled by inflation. Through various economic events, the entire economy grinds to a halt. Trucks and trains stop moving, which means that coal is not delivered to power plants, and food is not delivered to stores.
.

Things quickly grow desperate. The average family realizes all too late that they have only a few days worth of food in their cupboard, with no available means to acquire more. Hundreds of millions converge on supermarkets within a matter of a week or two, and riots and looting erupts. Martial Law is declared and the National Guard is called up, but is completely inadequate to maintain order. Not only do the aforementioned criminals become free from constraint and begin to run amok, but millions of regular people realize that the only way their kids will be fed is if they go and take supplies from someone else. **Hungry people with weapons will have no reservation about doing unspeakable evil on others if it means their own family will survive a little longer.** Do not doubt that the sinful nature will turn normally docile people into voracious killers. It has been written into our DNA since the Fall of man.

Now to the big point I'm making. Here's where it gets really scary, and the vulnerability of the thin blue line becomes apparent. I am employed in a county with a population of 40,000 people. We have a city of 25,000 as a county seat. At most, the agencies in my area could muster about 50 officers. This means that there would be an 800 to 1 ratio of citizens to police officers in our area. It would be impos-sible to maintain order with this ratio. We would be lucky to be able to hold a few buildings, let alone provide law enforcement service to 1,000 square miles of rural area.

Now imagine this happening in every city in town in America, all at the same time. The number of law enforcement officers, National Guard, and [Reserve Component and active duty] soldiers would be wholly inadequate to even make a small dent in widespread civil disorder. There are many Friday and Saturday nights when our local law enforcement agencies have to stack service calls for two hours due to high call volume, and this is during normal times. If law enforcement agencies can't answer calls in a timely manner during normal times, how could a reasonable person expect law enforcement to be there during a societal collapse?I also urge you to consider this. There is no way that I, even as a police officer, can abandon my God-given responsibility to care for and protect my own family. **There are times when retreat is the better part of valor, and if that terrible time comes, the vast majority of officers will not be able to justify in their own minds fighting a lost cause.**

They will retreat and take care of their family, which is what the brotherhood of the thin blue line is all about. Don't misunderstand. The huge majority of law enforcement officers perform a very dangerous profession honorably and to the very best of their ability. But drastic times will call for drastic measures from everyone, and the preparedness minded person can't assume that the thin blue line will always remain intact.

Thus, it quickly becomes apparent that each citizen will be responsible for his own family's safety and security during these perilous times. To assume that there will always be police there to protect you will most likely be fatal. Please don't make that mistake. Do what you must do. If you own a gun, learn how to use it proficiently. Take firearms training courses, and know the laws in your area. Most importantly, be ready for the unexpected, and don't rely upon the government to take care of you. That's your responsibility. - Deputy W. in Missouri

The Overnighters:

Coming to a Neighborhood Near You,

by Frank C. in California

*Originally posted at www.**SurvivalBlog**.com Copyright 2012*

The collapse has come. It could be economic, geopolitical, a natural disaster, or any combination of the above. Suppose it has now been three weeks since your last trip to the grocery store. It has been two weeks since you lost power to your home. A week ago, two large families broke into, and are squatting in a vacant, foreclosed home down the street. Three days ago, you heard gunshots and loud shouting very close by. You wanted to call the police, but there is no longer any type of phone service, and the last you heard, the police had their hands full battling a large, violent group of Occupiers camped out at your local mall. Yesterday, you noticed five grubby men slowly stalking down the street. Two of them were pushing shopping carts heaped with canned goods, sleeping bags, wine jugs, bottled water and other items. One of them brandishes a large crowbar, another carries a knife, and the third pulls a pistol from inside his belt. The three armed men peel off from the others and knock at the security door of your neighbor across the street. The neighbor and his family had loaded up their large motor home a week ago and gotten out of Dodge. Now, the man with the crowbar is breaking through the front window, easily pulling away the French window panes to create a large hole. The man with the pistol peers inside, sweeping his gun to "clear" the room. He gets a boost from one of his buddies and hops inside.

You are getting edgy, very nervous. You have decided to "bug in" instead of "bugging out," and are wondering if you made the right decision. You have a large stockpile of home-canned fruit, and many five-gallon containers full of beans, rice and grain. Now, what do you do? Do you pull out your own shotgun and confront the group? Or do you lay low and wait to defend your home, in case you turn out to be the next target? What if they knock at your door, and ask for a handout? What if they threaten to toss a "Molotov cocktail" through your window, unless you give them a lot of food?" What do you do? Who are these looters? Where do they come from? How far will they go in their desire to gain the goods they are used to receiving for free, via handouts, welfare and food stamps, which they no longer get?

How will the "homeless" react in a SHTF situation? I have been a volunteer at our local rescue mission for several years, and I am only now beginning to understand some of the motivations, thinking and possible future behavior of "homeless" people. In the past, I have donated food, clothing, and have also preached at the mission's chapel, hoping that somehow my messages will make a difference.

But, how effective are rescue missions, really? A lot of people have the impression that their local rescue mission is helping homeless people to get off the streets, get them cleaned up, sober from drugs and alcohol, gives them training to get a job, find housing, then finally move out and become an independent and productive member of society. Is this true? Well, yes, and no. You need to understand that rescue missions basically help two very different groups of people: People who are in "The Program," and "The Overnighters."

A person in "The Program" is typically referred to the rescue mission by court order. They're forced to be there. Suppose a guy is arrested and convicted of possession of drugs. Whether he does jail time or not, upon his release, he is ordered by the judge to choose between several different drug treatment programs, and your local rescue mission is usually on the list. Once he is accepted into "The Program," he is required to submit to drug testing, stay at the mission, and attend Christian-based classes and chapel service (most rescue missions are Christian-based). At the same time, those "residents" who stick with the program graduate and are moved from on-site dorm housing to "transitional housing," get a job and hopefully, later on move to permanent housing. These are the success stories you hear about at rescue missions. However, there are some graduates, who unfortunately, do go back to their life of crime.

On the other hand, there is, simultaneously, an entirely different group at the average rescue mission: The "Overnighters." The Overnighters are people, usually men, who show up in the late afternoon for a free meal and a bed. Some of these guys do have jobs, both permanent or temporary. They either walk, catch a bus for work, or get a ride from a friend. Many of them have cell phones. Now, you may ask, if they have a job, why on earth are they at the rescue mission? Good question. Some of these men have truly fallen on hard times and lost their apartment or

465

home due to finances, divorce or other circumstances. A few, very few of these, do want to find permanent housing. However, the vast majority of the Overnighters prefer to roam the streets and "game the system."

That's right. In a normal economy, the non-working Overnighters could find work if they really tried. Most rescue missions will really help those who want to work, to find work. But as our economy continues to worsen, it makes it that much harder for the Overnighters to find work, if they wanted to find a job. And that's a big "if". The working could get together with one or two others and split the rent on an inexpensive home or apartment, or even rent their own room, but they choose not to do so. Instead, they tend to drift from the rescue mission to a friend's house, or to Aunt Edna's, or Brother Joe's, where they moan about how "horrible" it is over at the mission, all these "terrible" rules they have to follow, and that "boring" chapel service they're required to attend, to get a meal and bed for the night. They sleep until noon on the sofa, lounge around and enjoy Brother Joe's satellite television and Internet, and raid the refrigerator as long as they can, until they wear out their welcome, when Aunt Edna finally gets up the gumption to kick them out.

Then, Mr. Professional Overnighter goes back to the rescue mission for a few days, or a week or two, until he can find some other gullible sap who will fall for his sad story and let him in. "Someone jacked my wallet! Please, help me!" is just one of many tricks in their book. Some of the Overnighters even drift from a rescue mission in one city to another. They exchange information between themselves about the different rescue missions, the conditions and rules, which missions are "cool," and which ones are "strict." Many of those who are drug addicts only go to the rescue mission just to get free drugs, which are administered at the beginning of their "rehabilitation." Then, as soon as they get a free fix, they leave. Many of the Overnighters have also been kicked out of certain rescue missions due to drunkenness, being high on drugs, fighting, stealing, and throwing psychotic tantrums. In such cases, the police are called and they are arrested. And remember, many of these same Overnighters have long criminal histories, including vagrancy, burglary, home invasion robbery, rape, assault, battery, and murder. A lot of the Overnighters are ex-cons, and many of them, after their release from jail or prison, started out under court order as residents in "The Program." However, they were dropped from The Program after testing positive for drugs, fighting, stealing or some other offense. Once again, many of these are people who are not necessarily the downtrodden, oppressed, down-on-their-luck souls they would like us to think they are.

Now, you may ask, what do the Overnighters have to do with you? In a grid-down situation, they will have everything to do with you and anyone else that has food and other stuff they want. The Overnighters will be the ones pushing those grocery carts down your street, looting whatever they need, by whatever means necessary, including force. And remember, the Overnighters comprise just one of many looting groups, which will most probably include gangsters, hard-core criminals, radical Occupiers, and other assorted oddballs and juvenile punks who are wigged out, because they can no longer stuff their faces from mom's fridge as they play video games or surf the internet. Now, all of these people will have to get off their rear ends and actually find something to eat and drink, and they will all be ravenously hungry, angry and utterly vicious. Not to mention the ones that are going through painful withdrawals from a lack of caffeine, cigarettes, alcohol and drugs. Each of these groups will be competing intensely for any fat target, which is your home, with the potential promise of a tantalizing supply of stored food, water and other supplies.

In the case of the Overnighters, they didn't work for their food before. What makes you think anything will change in a collapse situation? What's interesting to me is that, whenever I preach at a chapel service full of Overnighters, I have noticed that many of them know their Bible. Several of them can quote chapter and verse. They know what is right and what is wrong. But when crunch time comes and food is scarce, all this learning, will for the most part, go out the window. In fact, I would say that their current choice of lifestyle shows they have little or no intention of living by the rules the rest of us live by. The Overnighters are, for the most part, lazy bums who want absolutely no responsibility, and they want to be accountable to no one. Most of them don't want to work, and would not work if a job were offered to them. The rescue missions of the world are giving these leeches every opportunity to escape their squalid lifestyle, but they willingly and stubbornly refuse to change. Personally, I find this highly disturbing.

So, what should you do when faced with the Overnighters of the world? Know, first and foremost, that the Overnighters are quintessential con men. They know every trick of the trade to get you to open your door and give them a handout, including quoting the Bible. Ever notice the beggars on the street corner with the signs, "Need Food...God Bless!" These are people who could very easily get off the street, if they would simply enter The Program at their local rescue mission, instead of choosing the Overnighter lifestyle. These are the same people who, if you give them food, will sometimes throw it back at you and demand money. No matter what you give them, oftentimes it is never enough. Also, if you give to one homeless person who stops at your door, the buzz will quickly travel through the network about where the next big fat target is located, which is your house. And, before you know it, you could very well have a motley mob outside your house, shouting loudly that you are one of the "filthy rich one percent," and that you need to "share the wealth" with them, the poor, oppressed 99 per cent. Am I saying that we should never help others in a time of need? No, I think there are certainly some people we should help. There are many poor families in and out of our church we have quietly helped over the years. And they usually are very meek, almost ashamed to accept help from someone else. They are also profusely thankful. I can't tell you if and how to help others, but whatever you do, maintaining OPSEC is of utmost importance. I believe we need to show love and compassion to some, but we also need to protect our families from potential psychotic killers. Remember, the Overnighters and criminals of the world are right now, as you read this, making their rounds of naive victims, not only emptying Aunt Edna's pantry, but doing home-invasion robberies where innocent people sometimes end up brutally murdered. And, in TEOTWAWKI, you will need a lot of wisdom and prayer, so you and your family won't become the next victims.

[JWR Adds: *It is important to be charitable, but my consistent advice has been to distribute charity through intermediaries, such as your local church or food bank. Do not hand out charity right on your doorstep! And make sure that your name and address never get mentioned by local chariti*es.]

Originally posted at www.SurvivalBlog.com
Copyright 2012

● ● ● ● ● ● ● ● ● ● ● ● ●

Why Prepare, when I can take it from the Mormons?

I have given this subject a great deal of thought; it is of great concern to me, for the reasons which will be evident by the comments I will make..... I have worked in a Survival Store for the past year, helping a friend (the owner) while I looked for work in my primary skill set (engineering).

Please forgive my tone, in advance, if I sound patronizing.... it is not my intent. There may be those who will feel I am being 'alarmist'....this is also not my intent. It is a subject that should, I believe, be understood and recognized as an increasing threat to members, wards, etc. Also, if this has already been covered in-depth elsewhere on this site and I simply missed it, please forgive me but let me know – and I will quietly 'sit down' and be still.

The source of my concern is this:
For the last year I have met many, many people who are not LDS, but are practicing preparations in response to their promptings, as we are. However, I have met and conversed with what appears to be an increasing number of persons who are very much planning...and I say again: planning on plundering 'Mormons' to relieve them of food and provisions... and planning to do so violently....peacefully only incidentally. I have seen a trend to this type and degree of sentiment; I can no longer just shrug it off as the panderings of nuts and kooks... it seems to be growing and becoming pervasive.

In the past I have been fairly successful in discouraging many of these wayward comments by casually asserting that I would see them soon (if they persisted in that track) through the other end of my 'scope, as I would be actively hunting those who would prey on others so perniciously. As I have mentioned, such was my presentation and demeanor during my short discourse that the parties were rapidly convinced of the unwise nature of that line of thought.

Lately, however, with the onset of rising fear bordering on panic brought on by the unwise escalation of what appears to be a 'non-pandemic' (ONE death in the US over 2 weeks CANNOT by any stretch of the imagination be considered even a health risk) has given rise to the repeated sentiment already mentioned...that Mormons are a ready source of food and provisions just waiting to be scooped up by anyone willing to go up against such apparently 'peaceful' and defenseless people.

I would hasten to add that it is NOT just the rank-and-file of Americana with this sentiment and festering plan... I have had information for many years, in at least 20 States, that community 'leaders' (at varying levels) have plans to 'confiscate' such supplies from Church Members who have so faithfully adhered to the admonitions of the General Authorities. These plans, in many instances, include handing out Stake and Ward rosters to various local 'agencies' to 'confiscate' these 'hoarded' supplies, ostensibly to be distributed to the community as they see fit.

Please note: **This is NOT conjecture; this is NOT fear mongering, it is NOT 'conspiracy theory'**. For nearly 15 of my thirty-plus years as an engineer, I functioned as a Security Consultant for Local, State, Federal and certain overseas 'Agencies'. I was privy to plans at many levels...and all seemed to take for granted that civilian confiscation was not only legal and proper, but "the right thing to do", as it would serve the "Greater Good". AND the greatest source of this Greater Good was to take (steal) from those that most seemed to deem as useless, unnecessary, disposable and, to their way of thinking, defenseless.

As an example, a popular author, Claire Wolfe, on page 78 of her book - "The Freedom Outlaw's Handbook" says: "There's a really bad joke that goes like this: **Do you know what's in the most basic Disaster Survival Kit? – A rifle and a directory of the local Mormon Ward**". Now, she uses that tongue-in-cheek to demonstrate her suggestion to cultivate some 'Mormon Friends'...but it should be shockingly illustrative of what many non-LDS folk think.

Here's the real problem...this sentiment is NOT just a few misguided souls...this kind of idea is like an arrow – once shot, it cannot be recalled, deflected or dispelled...the damage will have been done. The thought will lie there, dormant, until called forth into sharp clarity by desperate, starving neighbors who will suddenly recall that YOU are 'Mormons'...and that all of 'those' have a hundred years' food supply(in their minds), and 'they' don't believe in violence...etc, etc, etc.

My point? – This kind of idea, much like the discovery of a single cockroach in the kitchen, is indicative of a thousand-fold others, as yet unseen - having the SAME idea. It may take a while to simmer before taking form, but rest assured...it WILL come bubbling up to the top of the pot.

This brings me to my greatest concern in this line of conjecture... We are, as a people, more prepared to weather the storms of adversity than possibly any people in history – insomuch as having knowledge, food, equipment, and faith in God to live in uncertain times.

HOWEVER, we are, as Families, Wards, Stakes and Communities, woefully inadequate in our planning, equipment, experience and training to prevent either targeted or widespread looting, plunder and murder of our families in time of large-scale disaster and civil unrest. We have become a people completely dependant upon our continuing civilization – and everyone behaving in a civilized manner.

As mentioned above –

How many of you (us) are actually emotionally, physically and mentally prepared to confront, fight, kill, and prevail over a band of marauders determined to take EVERYTHING you have prepared...including your lives, and the lives of your family?

How many of us have experience and expertise in any degree of returning violence, and are fit to undertake it? And are the rest of us, who are NOT thusly trained and experienced, willing and able to rapidly assimilate the skills, mindset and determination necessary BEFORE our tragic ineptitude separates us from those we love?

A plan of action would seem to be in order......and we ALL need to be involved. Or at least ALL who are actually serious about surviving.

Think of this as that annoying clarion sound of the "Emergency Broadcast System" on the radio...that we all have become inured to – we ignore it, at out peril.

I believe the danger is REAL; I believe it to be persistent, and I strongly believe it has become pervasive – flowing into every facet of society as completely as the Sodium Fluoride that has been introduced into most community water supplies across America. A poison we fool ourselves into believing to be harmless at best; and will be ultimately destructive of all of us if not checked, prevented, and eliminated.

Believing that we will be 'pulled out' before we are faced with this eventuality is, in my opinion, as foolhardy as believing that God will simply drop a years' supply of food on your doorstep, if you have 'enough faith'. I don't think too many of us could believe that...else why this forum?

I recall that we have been told that the Book of Mormon is a type and shadow of things to come...should we not take the past history of the Saints as such? The early Saints had much in the way of atrocities committed...Haun's Mill comes to mind, as do several other events; I think it is at least time to plan and prepare for the awful possibility of attacks from our own communities, and work up a plan to either dispel the danger, band together for protection, and/or find other solutions for the short term if and when this happens BEFORE the Call-Out. Peaceful, law-abiding solutions would be preferred; but when you attempt to confront barbarism with civility, the gentle party always loses. It's like confronting a Lion on one's path and dealing with it by saying: "Nice Kitty". It's been said that the art of diplomacy is like saying "Nice Doggy", while reaching for a rock.

I cannot face it alone...no one man or one family can, for long, with impunity. I, for one, am not bulletproof, as much as I would like to believe so. I have hope that things will work out; however, as a Military Science Professor once passed on to me, "Hope is not a strategy".

What say you?   By RamBuff.

Thoughts On Disaster Survival, *Post Katrina...*

The follow information was provided via several emails by a friend heavily involved in the New Orleans disaster of hurricane Katrina, durring the course of the disaster itself. Many of the comments were LIVE to that moment in time....

I've had over 30 people staying with me since Sunday, evacuating from New Orleans and points south in anticipation of Hurricane Katrina. Only two families were my friends they told other friends of theirs that they knew a place where they could hole up, and so a whole bunch arrived here! I didn't mind, because there were six RV's and travel trailers, so we had enough accommodation. However, I've had the opportunity to see what worked - and what didn't - in their evacuation plans and bug-out kits, and I thought a few "lessons learned" might be appropriate to share here.

1. Have a bug-out kit ready at all times.
Many of these folks packed at the last minute, grabbing whatever they thought they'd need. Needless to say, they forgot some important things (prescription medications, important documents, baby formula, diapers, etc.). Some of these things (e.g. prescriptions) obviously can't be stocked up against possible emergency need, but you can at least have a list in your bug-out kit of what to grab at the last minute before you leave!

2. Renew supplies in your bug-out kit on a regular basis.
Batteries lose their charge. Foods have an expiration date. So do common medications. Clothes can get moldy or dirty unless properly stored. All of these problems were found with the folks who kept backup or bug-out supplies on hand, and caused difficulties for them.

3. Plan on needing a LOT more supplies than you think.
I found myself with over 30 people on hand, many of whom were not well supplied and the stores were swamped with literally thousands of refugees, buying up everything in sight. I had enough supplies to keep myself going for 30 days. Guess what? Those supplies ended up keeping 30-odd people going for two days. I now know that I must plan on providing for not just myself, but others in need. I could have been selfish and said "No, these are mine" - but what good would that do in a real disaster? Someone would just try to take them, and then we'd have all the resulting unpleasantness. Far better to have extra supplies to share with others, whilst keeping your own core reserve intact (and, preferably, hidden from prying eyes!).

4. In a real emergency, forget about last-minute purchases.
As I said earlier, the stores were swamped by thousands of refugees, as well as locals buying up last-minute supplies. If I hadn't had my emergency supplies already in store, I would never have been able to buy them at the last minute. If I'd had to hit the road, the situation would have been even worse, as I'd be part of a stream of thousands of refugees, most of whom would be buying (or stealing) what they needed before I got to the store.

5. Make sure your vehicle will carry your essential supplies.

Some of the folks who arrived at my place had tried to load up their cars with a humongous amount of stuff, only to find that they didn't have space for themselves! Pets are a particular problem here, as they have to have air and light, and can't be crammed into odd corners. If you have to carry a lot of supplies *and* a number of people, invest in a small luggage trailer or something similar (or a small travel trailer with space for your goodies) - it'll pay dividends if the S really does HTF.

6. A big bug-out vehicle can be a handicap.

Some of the folks arrived here with big pick-ups or SUV's, towing equally large travel trailers. Guess what? - on some evacuation routes, these huge combinations could not navigate corners very well, and/or were so difficult to turn that they ran into things (including other vehicles, which were NOT about to make way in the stress of an evacuation!). This led to hard feelings, harsh words, and at least one fist-fight. It's not a bad idea to have smaller, more maneuverable vehicles, and a smaller travel trailer, so that one can "squeeze through" in a tight traffic situation. Another point a big SUV or pickup burns a lot of fuel. This is bad news when there's no fuel available! (See point 10 below.)

7. Make sure you have a bug-out place handy.

I was fortunate in having enough ground (about 1.8 acres) to provide parking for all these RV's and trailers, and to accommodate 11 small children in my living-room so that the adults could get some sleep on Sunday night, after many hours on the road in very heavy, slow-moving traffic. However, if I hadn't had space, I would have unhesitatingly told the extra families to find somewhere else - and there *wasn't* anywhere else here, that night. Even shops like Wal-Mart and K-Mart had trailers and RV's backed up in their parking lots (which annoyed the heck out of shoppers trying to make last-minute purchases). Even on my property, I had no trailer sewage connections, so I had to tell the occupants that if they used their onboard toilets and showers, they had to drive their RV's and trailers somewhere else to empty their waste tanks. If they hadn't left this morning, they would have joined long, long lines to do this at local trailer parks (some of which were so overloaded by visiting trailers and RV's that they refused to allow passers-by to use their dumping facilities).

8. Provide entertainment for younger children.

Some of these families had young children (ranging from 3 months to 11 years). They had DVD's, video games, etc. - but no power available in their trailers to show them! They had no coloring books, toys, etc. to keep the kids occupied. This was a bad mistake.

9. Pack essentials first, then luxuries.

Many of these folks had packed mattresses off beds, comforters, cushions, bathrobes, etc. As a result, their vehicles were grossly overloaded, but often lacked real essentials like candles, non-perishable foods, etc. One family (both parents are gourmet cooks) packed eighteen (yes, EIGHTEEN!!!) special pots and pans, which they were going to use on a two-burner camp stove... They were horrified by my suggestion that under the circumstances, a nested stainless-steel camping cookware set would be rather more practical. "What? No omelet pan?" Sheesh...

10. Don't plan on fuel being available *en route*.

A number of my visitors had real problems finding gas to fill up on the road. With thousands of vehicles jammed nose-to-tail on four lanes of interstate, an awful lot of vehicles needed gas. By the time you got to a gas station, you were highly likely to find it sold out - or charging exorbitant prices, because the owners knew you didn't have any choice but to pay what they asked. Much better to leave with a full tank of gas, and enough in spare containers to fill up on the road, if you have to, in order to reach your destination.

11. Have enough money with you for at least two weeks.

Many of those who arrived here had very little in cash, relying on check-books and credit cards to fund their purchases. Guess what? Their small banks down in South Louisiana were all off-line, and their balances, credit authorizations, etc. could not be checked - so many shops refused to accept their checks, and insisted on electronic verification before accepting their credit cards. Local banks also refused (initially) to cash checks for them, since they couldn't check the status of their accounts on-line. Eventually (and very grudgingly) local banks began allowing them to cash checks for not more than $50-$100, depending on the bank. Fortunately, I have a reasonable amount of cash available at all times, so I was able to help some of them. I'm now going to increase my cash on hand, I think... Another thing - don't bring only large bills. Many gas stations, convenience stores, etc. won't accept anything larger than a $20 bill. Some of my guests had plenty of $100 bills, but couldn't buy anything.

12. Don't be sure that a disaster will be short-term.
My friends have left now, heading south to Baton Rouge. They want to be closer to home for whenever they're allowed to return. Unfortunately for them, the Governor has just announced the mandatory, complete evacuation of New Orleans, and there's no word on when they will be allowed back. It will certainly be several weeks, and it might be several months. During that period, what they have with them - essential documents, clothing, etc. - is all they have. They'll have to find new doctors to renew prescriptions; find a place to live (a FEMA trailer if they're lucky - thousands of families will be lining up for these trailers); some way to earn a living (their jobs are gone with New Orleans, and I don't see their employers paying them for not working when the employers aren't making money either); and so on.

13. Don't rely on government-run shelters if at all possible.
Your weapons WILL be confiscated (yes, including pocket-knives, kitchen knives, and Leatherman-type tools); you will be crowded into close proximity with anyone and everyone (including some nice folks, but also including drug addicts, released convicts, gang types, and so on); you will be under the authority of the people running the shelter, who WILL call on law enforcement and military personnel to keep order (including stopping you leaving if you want to); and so on. Much, much better to have a place to go to, a plan to get there, and the supplies you need to do so on your own.

14. Warn your friends not to bring others with them!!!
I had told two friends to bring themselves and their families to my home. They, unknown to me, told half-a-dozen other families to come too - "He's a good guy, I'm sure he won't mind!" Well, I did mind... but since the circumstances weren't personally dangerous, I allowed them all to hang around. However, if things had been worse, I would have been very nasty indeed to their friends (and even nastier to them, for inviting others without clearing it with me first!). If you are a place of refuge for your friends, make sure they know that this applies to them ONLY, not their other friends. Similarly, if you have someone willing to offer you refuge, don't presume on his/her hospitality by arriving with others unforewarned.

15. Have account numbers, contact addresses and telephone numbers for all important persons and institutions.
My friends will now have to get new postal addresses, and will have to notify others of this their doctors, insurance companies (medical, personal, vehicle and property), bank(s), credit card issuer(s), utility supplier(s), telephone supplier(s), etc. Basically, anyone who sends you bills, or to whom you owe money, or who might owe you money. None of my friends brought all this information with them. Now, when they need to change postal addresses for correspondence, insurance claims, etc., how can they do this when they don't know their account numbers, what number to call, who and where to write, etc.?

16. Have portable weapons and ammo ready to hand.
Only two of my friends were armed, and one of them had only a handgun. The other had a handgun for himself, another for his wife, a shotgun, and an evil black rifle - MUCH better! I was asked by some of the other families, who'd seen TV reports of looting back in New Orleans, to lend them firearms. I refused, as they'd never handled guns before, and thus would have been more of a danger to themselves and other innocent persons than to looters. If they'd stayed a couple of days, so that I could teach them the basics, that would have been different but they wouldn't, so I didn't. Another thing - you don't have to take your entire arsenal along. Firearms for personal defense come first, then firearms for life support through hunting (and don't forget the skinning knife!). A fishing outfit might not be a bad idea either (you can shoot bait!). Other than that, leave the rest of your guns in the safe (you *do* have a gun safe, securely bolted to the floor, don't you?), and the bulk ammo supplies too. Bring enough ammo to keep you secure, but no more. If you really need bulk supplies of guns and ammo, they should be waiting for you at your bug-out location, not occupying space (and taking up a heck of a lot of weight!) in your vehicle. (For those bugging out in my direction, ammo supply will NOT be a problem...)

17. Route selection is very, very important.
My friends (and their friends) basically looked at the map, found the shortest route to me (I-10 to Baton Rouge and Lafayette, then up I-49 to Alexandria), and followed it slavishly. This was a VERY bad idea, as something over half-a-million other folks had the same route in mind... Some of them took over twelve hours for what is usually a four-hour journey. If they'd used

their heads, they would have seen (and heard, from radio reports) that going North up I-55 to Mississippi would have been much faster. There was less traffic on this route, and they could have turned left and hit Natchez, MS, and then cut across LA on Route 84. This would have taken them no more than five or six hours, even with the heavier evacuation traffic. Lesson think outside the box, and don't assume that the shortest route on the map in terms of distance will also be the shortest route in terms of time.

18. The social implications of a disaster situation.

Feedback from my contacts in the LSP and other agencies is very worrying. They keep harping on the fact that the "underclass" that's doing all the looting is almost exclusively Black and inner-city in composition. The remarks they're reporting include such statements as "I'm ENTITLED to this stuff!", "This is payback time for all Whitey's done to us", and "This is reparations for slavery!". Also, they're blaming the present confused disaster-relief situation on racism "Fo sho, if Whitey wuz sittin' here in tha Dome waitin' for help, no way would he be waitin' like we is!" No, I'm not making up these comments... they are as reported by my buddies. This worries me very much. If we have such a divide in consciousness among our city residents, then when we hit a SHTF situation, we're likely to be accused of racism, paternalism, oppression, and all sorts of other crimes just because we want to preserve law and order. If we, as individuals and families, provide for our own needs in emergency, and won't share with others (whether they're of another race or not) because we don't have enough to go round, we're likely to be accused of racism rather than pragmatism, and taking things from us can (and probably will) be justified as "Whitey getting his just desserts". I'm absolutely not a racist, but the racial implications of the present situation are of great concern to me. The likes of Jesse Jackson, Al Sharpton, and the "reparations for slavery" brigade appear to have so polarized inner-city opinion that these folks are (IMHO) no longer capable of rational thought concerning such issues as looting, disaster relief, etc.

19. Implications for security.

If one has successfully negotiated the danger zone, one will be in an environment filled, to a greater or lesser extent, with other evacuees. How many of them will have provided for their needs? How many of them will rely on obtaining from others the things they need? In the absence of immediate State or relief-agency assistance, how many of them will feel "entitled" to obtain these necessities any way they have to, up to and including looting, murder and mayhem? Large gathering-places for refugees suddenly look rather less desirable... and being on one's own, or in an isolated spot with one's family, also looks less secure. One has to sleep sometime, and while one sleeps, one is vulnerable. Even one's spouse and children might not be enough... there are always going to be vulnerabilities. One can hardly remain consciously in Condition Yellow while bathing children, or making love! A team approach might be a viable solution here .

20. Too many chiefs, not enough Indians" in New Orleans at the moment.

The mayor has already blown his top about the levee breach: he claims that he had a plan in place to fix it by yesterday evening, but was overruled by Baton Rouge, who sent in others to do something different. This may or may not be true... My LSP buddies tell me that they're getting conflicting assignments and/or requests from different organizations and individuals. One will send out a group to check a particular area for survivors but when they get there, they find no-one, and later learn that another group has already checked and cleared the area. Unfortunately, in the absence of centralized command and control, the information is not being shared amongst all recovery teams. Also, there's alleged to be conflict between City officials and State functionaries, with both sides claiming to be "running things" and some individuals in the Red Cross, FEMA, and other groups appear to be refusing to take instructions from either side, instead (it's claimed) wanting to run their own shows. This is allegedly producing catastrophic confusion and duplication of effort, and may even be making the loss of life worse, in that some areas in need of rescuers aren't getting them. (I don't know if the same problems are occurring in Mississippi and/or Alabama, but I wouldn't be surprised if they were.) All of this is unofficial and off-the-record, but it doesn't surprise me to hear it. Moral of the story if you want to survive, don't rely on the government or any government agency (or private relief organization, for that matter) to save you. Your survival is in your own hands - don't drop it!

21. Long-term vision.

This appears to be sadly lacking at present. Everyone is focused on the immediate, short-term objective of rescuing survivors. However, there are monumental problems looming, that need immediate attention, but don't seem to be getting it right now. For example: the Port of Louisiana is the fifth-largest in the world, and vital to the economy, but the Coast Guard is saying (on TV) that they won't be able to get it up and running for three to six months, because their primary focus is on search and rescue, and thereafter, disaster relief. Why isn't the Coast Guard pulled off that job now, and put to work right away on something this critical? There are enough Navy, Marine and Air Force units available now to take over rescue missions.

Another example there are over a million refugees from the Greater New Orleans area floating around. They need accommodation and food, sure but most of them are now unemployed, and won't have any income at all for the next six to twelve months. There aren't nearly enough jobs available in this area to absorb this workforce. What is being done to find work for them, even in states remote from the problem areas? The Government for sure won't provide enough for them in emergency aid to be able to pay their bills. What about mortgages on properties that are now underwater? The occupants both can't and won't pay; the mortgage holders will demand payment; and we could end up with massive foreclosures on property that is worthless, leaving a lot of folks neck-deep in debt and without homes (even damaged ones). What is being done to plan for this, and alleviate the problem as much as possible? I would have thought that the State government would have had at least the skeleton of an emergency plan for these sorts of things, and that FEMA would have the same, but this doesn't seem to be the case. Why weren't these things considered in the leisurely days pre-disaster, instead of erupting as immediate and unanswered needs post-disaster?

22. Personal emergency planning.
This leads me to consider my own emergency planning. I've planned to cover an evacuation need, and could probably survive with relative ease for between two weeks and one month but what if I had been caught up in this mess? What would I do about earning a living, paying mortgages, etc.? If I can't rely on the State, I for darn sure had better be able to rely on myself! I certainly need to re-examine my insurance policies, to ensure that if disaster strikes, my mortgage, major loans, etc. will be paid off (or that I will receive enough money to do this myself). I also need to provide for my physical security, and must ensure that I have supplies, skills and knowledge that will be "marketable" in exchange for hard currency in a post-disaster situation. The idea of a "team" of friends with (or to) whom to bug out, survive, etc. is looking better and better. Some of the team could take on the task of keeping a home maintained (even a camp-type facility), looking after kids, providing base security, etc. Others could be foraging for supplies, trading, etc. Still others could be earning a living for the whole team with their skills. In this way, we'd all contribute to our mutual survival and security in the medium to long term. Life might be a lot less comfortable than prior to the disaster, but hey - we'd still have a life! This bears thinking about, and I might just have to start building "team relationships" with nearby [people of like mind]!

23. The "bank problem."
This bears consideration. I was at my bank this morning, depositing checks I'd been given by my visitors in exchange for cash. The teller warned me bluntly that it might be weeks before these checks could be credited to my account, as there was no way to clear them with their issuing banks, which were now under water and/or without communications facilities. He also told me that there had been an endless stream of folks trying to cash checks on South Louisiana banks, without success. He warned me that some of these local banks will almost certainly fail, as they don't have a single branch above water, and the customers and businesses they served are also gone - so checks drawn on them will eventually prove worthless. Even some major regional banks had run their Louisiana "hub" out of New Orleans, and now couldn't access their records. I think it might be a good idea to have a "bug-out bank account" with a national bank, so that funds should be available anywhere they have a branch, rather than keeping all one's money in a single bank (particularly a local one) or credit union. This is, of course, over and above one's "bug-out stash" of ready cash.

24. Helping one's friends is likely to prove expensive.
I estimate that I'm out over $1,000 at the moment, partly from having all my supplies consumed, and partly from making cash available to friends who couldn't cash their checks. I may or may not get some of this back in due course. I don't mind it - if I were in a similar fix, I hope I could lean on my friends for help in the same way, after all! - but I hadn't made allowance for it. I shall have to do so in future, as well as planning to contribute to costs incurred by those who offer me hospitality under similar circumstances.

25. People who were prepared were frequently mobbed/threatened by those who weren't.
This was reported in at least seven incidents, five in Mississippi, two in Louisiana (I suspect that the relative lack of Louisiana incidents was because most of those with any sense got out of Dodge before the storm hit). In each case, the person/ family concerned had made preparations for disaster, with supplies, shelter, etc. in good order and ready to go. Several had generators ready and waiting. However, their neighbors who had not prepared all came running after the disaster, wanting

food, water and shelter from them. When the prepared families refused, on the grounds that they had very little, and that only enough for themselves, there were many incidents of aggression, attempted assault, and theft of their supplies. Some had to use weapons to deter attack, and in some cases, shots were fired. I understand that in two incidents, attackers/would-be thieves were shot. It's also reported that in all of these cases, the prepared families now face threats of retribution from their neighbors, who regarded their refusal to share as an act of selfishness and/or aggression, and are now threatening retaliation. It's reportedly so bad that most of the prepared families are considering moving to other neighborhoods so as to start afresh, with different neighbors.

Similar incidents are reported by families who got out in time, prepared to spend several days on their own. When they stopped to eat a picnic meal at a rest stop, or an isolated spot along the highway, they report being approached rather aggressively by others wanting food, or fuel, or other essentials. Sometimes they had to be rather aggressive in their turn to deter these insistent requests. Two families report attempts being made to steal their belongings (in one case, their vehicle) while over-nighting in camp stops on their way out of the area. They both instituted armed patrols, with one or more family members patrolling while the others slept, to prevent this. Seems to me to be a good argument to form a "bug-out team" with like-minded, security-conscious friends in your area, so that all concerned can provide mutual security and back-up.

My take I can understand these families being unwilling to share the little they had, particularly in light of not knowing when supplies would once again be available. However, this reinforces the point I made in my "lessons learned" post last week plan on needing much more in the way of supplies than you initially thought! If these families had had some extra food and water in stock, and hidden their main reserve where it would not be seen, they could have given out some help to their neighbors and preserved good relations. Also, a generator, under such circumstances, is a noisy (and bright, if powering your interior lights) invitation saying "This house has supplies - come and get them". I suspect that kerosene lanterns, candles and flashlights might be a more "community-safe" option if one is surrounded by survivors.

26. When help gets there, you may get it whether you like it or not.

There are numerous reports of aggressive, overbearing behavior by those rescuers who first arrived at disaster scenes. It's perhaps best described as "I'm here to rescue you - I'm in charge - do as I say - if you don't I'll shoot you". It appears that mid-level State functionaries and Red Cross personnel (the latter without the "shoot you" aspect, of course) were complained about most often. In one incident, a family who had prepared and survived quite well were ordered, not invited, to get onto a truck, with only the clothes on their backs. When they objected, they were threatened. They had pets, and wanted to know what would happen to them and they report that a uniformed man (agency unknown) began pointing his rifle at the pets with the words "I'll fix that". The husband then trained his own shotgun on the man and explained to him, in words of approximately one syllable, what was going to happen to him if he fired a shot. The whole "rescuer" group then left, threatening dire consequences for the family (including threats to come back once they'd evacuated and torch their home). The family were able to make contact with a State Police patrol and report the incident, and are now determined that no matter how much pressure is applied, they will not evacuate. They've set up a "shuttle run" so that every few days, two of them go upstate to collect supplies for the rest of the family, who defend the homestead in the meantime.

Another aspect of this is that self-sufficient, responsible families were often regarded almost with suspicion by rescuers. The latter seemed to believe that if you'd come through the disaster better than your neighbors, it could only have been because you stole what you needed, or somehow gained some sort of unfair advantage over the "average victims" in your area. I'm at a loss to explain this, but it's probably worth keeping in mind.

27. There seems to be a cumulative psychological effect upon survivors.

This is clear even - or perhaps particularly - in those who were prepared for a disaster. During and immediately after the disaster, these folks were at their best, dealing with damage, setting up alternative accommodation, light, food sources, etc. However, after a few days in the heat and debris (perhaps worst of all being the smell of dead bodies nearby), many found their ability to remain positive and "upbeat" being strained to the limit. There are numerous reports of individuals becoming depressed, morose and withdrawn. This seemed to happen to even the strongest personalities. The arrival of rescuers provided a temporary boost, but once evacuated, a sort of "after-action shell-shock" seems to be commonly experienced. I don't know enough about this to comment further, but I suspect that staying in place has a lot to do with it - there is no challenge to keep moving, find one's survival needs, and care for the group, and one is surrounded by vivid reminders of the devastation. By staying among the ruins of one's former life, one may be exposing oneself to a greater risk of psychological deterioration.

28. **There is widespread frustration over the lack of communication and empathy by rescuers and local/State government.**

This is partly due to the absence of electricity, so that TV's were not available to follow events as they unfolded but it's also due to an almost deliberate policy of non-communication by rescuers. There are many accounts of evacuees wanting to know where the bus or plane was going that they were about to board, only to be told "We don't know", or "To a better place than this". Some have found themselves many States away from their homes. Other families were arbitrarily separated upon rescue and/or evacuation, and are still scattered across two or three States. Their efforts to locate each other are very difficult, and when they request to be reunited at a common location, all of those with whom I have contact report a blanket refusal by the Red Cross and State officials to even consider the matter at this time. They're being informed that it will be "looked into" at some future date, and that they may have to pay the costs involved if they want to join up again. This, to families who are now destitute! I'm very angry about this, but it's so widespread a problem that I don't know what can be done about it. I hope that in future, some means will be implemented to prevent it happening again. Lesson learned never, EVER allow yourselves to be separated as a family, even if it means waiting for later rescue and/or evacuation. Insist on this at all costs!

29. **Expect rescuers (including law enforcement) to enforce a distinctly un-Constitutional authority in a disaster situation.**

This is very widely reported, and is very troubling. I hear repeated reports from numerous States that as evacuees arrive at refugee centers, they and their belongings are searched without Constitutional authority, and any personal belongings seen as potentially suspicious (including firearms, prescription medication, etc.) are confiscated without recourse to the owner. I can understand the point of view of the receiving authorities, but they are acting illegally, and I suspect there will be lawsuits coming from this practice. Another common practice reported on the ground in the disaster areas is for people to be ordered to evacuate, irrespective of their needs and wishes - even those folks who were well-prepared and have survived in good shape. If they demur, they are often threatened and bullied in an attempt to make them abandon their homes, pets, etc. Lesson learned in a disaster, don't expect legal and Constitutional norms to be followed. If you can make it on your own, do so, without relying on an unsympathetic and occasionally overbearing rescue system to control you and your destiny.

30. **Don't believe that rescuers are all knights in shining armor who will respect your property.**

There have been numerous reports of rescuers casually appropriating small items that took their fancy in houses they were searching. Sometimes this was blatant, right in front of onlookers, and when protests were made, the response was either threatening, or a casual "Who's going to miss it now?". Some of our field agents report that this happened right in front of their eyes. Another aspect of this is damage caused to buildings by rescuers. I've had reports of them kicking in the front door to a house, or a window, instead of trying to obtain access with as little damage as possible; climbing on clean, highly-polished tables with hobnailed boots in order to get at an attic hatch to check for survivors; etc. When they left the house, often the door or window was left open, almost a standing invitation to looters, instead of being closed and/or secured. When the families concerned get home, they won't know who caused this damage, but they will certainly be angered by it. I think that if one evacuates one's home, it might be a good idea to leave a clearly-visible notice that all residents have evacuated, so as to let would-be rescuers know that this house is empty. On the other hand, this might make it easier for looters, so what you gain on the swings, you lose on the round-abouts...

31. **If you choose to help, you may be sucked into a bureaucratic and legal nightmare.**

Example: a local church in the beginning stages of the crisis offered its hall to house evacuees. Local and State officials promptly filled it up with over 100 people. Their "social skills" proved extremely difficult to live with... toilets were blocked, restrooms left filthy, graffiti were scrawled and/or carved on the walls, arguments and disputes were frequent (often escalating to screaming matches, sometimes to physical violence), evacuees roamed the neighborhood (leading to all sorts of reports of petty theft, vandalism, etc.), church workers were subject to aggressive begging and demands, etc. Requests to the authorities to provide better security, administrative assistance, etc. apparently fell on deaf ears - the crisis was so widespread and overwhelming that a small facility such as this seems to have been very low on the priority checklist. After two days of this, with complaints from the neighbors becoming more and more insistent, the church informed local officials that it wanted the evacuees removed at once, if not sooner. They were promptly subject to bureaucratic heavy-handedness (including threats to withhold previously-promised reimbursement for their expenses); threats of lawsuits for daring to insinuate that the evacuees were somehow "lower-class" in their conduct, and for alleged racism, slander, and general political incorrectness; and threats of negative publicity, in that officials threatened to put out a press release denouncing the church for its "elitist" and "un-co-operative" attitude in a time of crisis. The church initially caved in to this pressure, and allowed the evacuees to stay but within a couple more days, the pressure from neighbors and from its own members became impossible to bear, and they insisted on the evacuees being removed to a Red Cross shelter. I'm informed that repairs to their hall will cost over $10,000. This is only one example among many I could cite, but it makes the point clear - if you offer your facilities to authorities, you place yourself (to a certain extent) under their control, and you're potentially liable to a great deal of heavy-handed, insensitive bureaucratic bullying. Those of you in the same position as this church (i.e. with facilities you could make available) might wish to take note.

32. Law enforcement problems will often be "glossed over" and/or ignored by authorities.

In many cities housing evacuees, there have been private reports of a significant increase in crime caused by their presence but you'll find that virtually all law enforcement authorities publicly deny this and/or gloss over it as a "temporary problem". This is all very well for publicity, but it ignores the increased risk to local residents. I've been tracking crime reports in about a dozen cities, through my contacts with local law enforcement and the Louisiana State Police. All the LEO's I speak with, without exception, tell me of greatly increased crime, including rape, assault, robbery, shoplifting, vandalism, gang activity, etc. However, you won't see these reports in the news media, and will often see senior LE figures actively denying it. The officers with whom I speak are angry and bitter about this, but they daren't "go public", as their jobs would be on the line if they did so. They tell me that often they're instructed not to report certain categories of "incident" at all, so as not to "skew" or "inflate" the "official" crime figures. I've also heard reports from Texas, Alabama and Tennessee of brand-new high-end motor vehicles (e.g. Cadillacs, Lincolns, BMW's, etc.) with New Orleans dealer tags being driven through various towns, on their way North and West. The drivers were described as "gang-bangers" (and sundry less complimentary terms). However, there have been no reports of stolen vehicles from New Orleans, because there are no workers to check out dealer lots, or report thefts, and no working computers to enter VIN's, etc. into the NICS database of stolen vehicles - so officers have had no choice but to let these vehicles proceed. Draw your own conclusions.

33. Your personal and/or corporate supplies and facilities may be commandeered without warning, receipt or compensation.

I've had numerous reports from in and near the disaster zone of individuals (e.g. boat-owners, farmers with barns, tractors, etc.) and corporate groups (e.g. companies with heavy equipment, churches with halls, etc.) finding an official on their doorstep demanding the use of their facilities or equipment. If they demurred, they were told that this was an "emergency situation" and that their assistance was being required, not requested. Some of them have lost track of the heavy equipment "borrowed" in this way, and don't know where it is, whether or not it's still in good condition, and when (if ever) it will be returned - and in the meantime, they can't continue their normal operations without this equipment. Others have had their land and facilities effectively confiscated for use by rescue and relief workers, storage of supplies, etc. In some cases, in the absence of their owners, the property of the individuals and groups concerned (e.g. farm gasoline and diesel supplies, the inventory of motor vehicle dealers, suppliers of foodstuffs, tarpaulins, etc.) have been commandeered and used by law enforcement and relief workers, without permission, receipts, reimbursement, etc. Protests have been met with denials, threats of arrest, insinuations of being "uncaring" and "un-co-operative", etc. Lesson learned if you've got what officials need in a time of crisis, forget about Constitutional protections of your property! Sure, you can sue after the fact, but if you need your goods and facilities for your own survival, you're basically SOL. Those of us who stockpile necessities for potential crises like this might want to consider concealing our stockpiles to prevent confiscation and if you need certain equipment for your own day-to-day use (e.g. tractors for farmers, generators, etc.), you might have a hard time retaining possession of these things. This problem applies to relief workers also I've had several reports of private relief workers (e.g. those sent in by churches, etc.) having their vehicles and supplies commandeered by "official" relief workers, without compensation or receipt, and being kicked out of the disaster area with warnings not to return. The fact that the "private" workers were accomplishing rather more than the "official" workers was apparently of no importance.

34. If you look like you know what you're doing, you may be a target of those less prepared.

There have been many, many reports of individuals who were more or less prepared for a disaster being preyed upon by those who were not prepared. Incidents range from theft of supplies, through attempts to bug out with these persons (uninvited), to actual violence. It's genuinely frightening to hear about these incidents, particularly the attitude of those trying to prey on the prepared they seemed to feel that because you'd taken steps to protect yourself and your loved ones, you had somehow done so at their expense, and they were therefore "entitled" to take from you what they needed. There's no logical explanation for this attitude, unless it's bred by the utter dependence of many such people on the State for welfare, Social Security, Medicare/Medicaid, etc. Since they've always been dependent on others, and regarded this as an "entitlement", in a disaster situation, they seem to automatically assume that they're "entitled" to what you've got! In one case, the family's pet dog was held hostage, with a knife at its throat, until the family handed over money and supplies. In two cases, families were threatened with the rape of their women unless they co-operated with the aggressors. In four cases that I know of, children were held hostage to ensure co-operation. There have also been reports of crimes during the bug-out process. Families sleeping in their cars at highway rest areas were a favorite target, including siphoning of gas from their tanks, assaults, etc. The lessons to be learned from this are obvious. One family can't secure itself against these threats without great difficulty. It's best to be "teamed up" with neighbors to secure your neighborhood as a whole, rather than be the one house with facilities in an area filled with those less prepared. If you're in the latter situation, staying put may not be a safe option, and a bug-out plan may be vital. When bugging out, you're still not safe from harm, and must maintain constant vigilance.

35. Those who thought themselves safe from the disaster were often not safe from refugees.
There have been many reports of smaller towns, farms, etc. on the fringe of the disaster area being overrun with those seeking assistance. In many cases, assistance was demanded rather than requested, and theft, looting and vandalism have been reported. So, even if you think you're safe from the disaster, you may not be safe from its aftermath.

36. Self-reliance seems to draw suspicion upon you from the authorities.
I've mentioned this in a previous e-mail, but I've had many more reports of it from those who survived or bugged out, and it bears re-emphasizing. For reasons unknown and unfathomable, rescue authorities seem to regard with suspicion those who've made provision for their safety and have survived (or bugged out) in good shape. It seems to be a combination of "How could you cope when so many others haven't?", "You must have taken advantage of others to be so well off", and "We've come all this way to help, so how dare you not need our assistance?" I have no idea why this should be the case... but there have been enough reports of it that it seems to be a widespread problem. Any ideas from readers?

37. Relief workers from other regions and States often don't know local laws.
This is a particular problem when it comes to firearms. I've had many reports of law enforcement officers sent to assist in Louisiana from States such as New Jersey, California, etc. trying to confiscate firearms on the streets, etc., when in fact the armed citizens were legally armed, under local law. One can't reason with these officers in the heat of the moment, of course, and as a result, a number of people lost their firearms, and have still not recovered them (and in the chaos of the immediate post-disaster situation, they may never do so, because I'm not sure that normal procedures such as logging these guns into a property office, etc. were followed). I understand that in due course, steps were taken to include at least one local law enforcement officer in patrols, so that he could advise officers from other areas as to what was legal, and what wasn't. Also, in Louisiana, law enforcement is conducted differently than in some other States, and officers from other States who came to assist were sometimes found to be domineering and aggressive in enforcing a law enforcement "authority" that doesn't normally apply here. So, if you're in a disaster area and help arrives from elsewhere, you may find that the help doesn't know (or care) about local laws, norms, etc. Use caution!

38. Relief organizations have their own bureaucratic requirements that may conflict with your
needs. A good example is the Red Cross. In many cases, across three States, I've had reports that locals who needed assistance were told that they had to register at a particular Red Cross shelter or facility. The help would not come to them they had to go to it. If they wished to stay on their own property, they were sometimes denied assistance, and told that if they wanted help, they had to move into the shelter to get it. Also, assistance was often provided only to those who came in person. If you left your family at home and went to get food aid, you might be denied aid for your whole family because there was no evidence that they existed - only the number that could be physically counted by relief workers (who would not come to you, but insisted you come to them) would be provided with food. Needless to say, this caused much anger and resentment.

I hope that these "lessons learned" are of use to you. I'm more and more convinced that in the event of a disaster, I must rely on myself, and a few friends, and never count on Government or relief organizations for the help I'll need. Also, I'm determined to bug out for a fairly long distance from a disaster in my home area, so as to be clear of the post-disaster complications that may arise. Once again (as it has countless times throughout history), we see that to rely on others (let alone Government) for your own safety and security is to invite complications at best, disaster at worst.

A Look Back At Katrina...
An Expereinced Prepper Tells All
by raptor

I live in a suburb of N.O. called Metairie. Parts of it were flooded briefly though a small portion was flooded due to the 17th street canal failure for about 2 weeks. My home was not flooded and sustained relatively minor damage.

I evacuated my family (including pets) to Atlanta on Sunday at noon after making sure other people I know including employees had left and did not need transport. I thought I was the last one out as everyone I knew told me they were long gone. I listened to the mayor order a mandatory evacuation of the city as I passed Slidell about 30 miles east of the city. My wife was behind me in another vehicle the whole way pissed off that she had to leave. The whole world was going west to Houston. I decided had at the last minute to head east into the storm's projected route to avoid the traffic since I calculated I had only 18 hours to escape. I did not want to risk being on the road for this storm.

As it turned out, we made a great decision because the traffic was mainly headed west. We momentarily slowed down to 50 mph on parts of the I-10 but for the most part I did not slow down to under 80 mph until we were past the contra flow area about 25 miles north of the coast line on I-59. We picked the right window and the right direction for our quick escape. We spent the night in Birmingham after a 6 hour drive, (we were tired and emotionally spent) and drove with a heavy heart to Atlanta the next morning. I got us settled into a hotel near a relative's home. I then told my wife to go find 2 furnished corporate apartments for us; we knew we were going to be in Atlanta a while. She asked how long (she always assumes I have the answer to everything). I said maybe permanently from the looks of things which really pissed her off.

We waited until the last minute to evacuate due to the reluctance of both my wife and mother to leave. My house is built of reinforced concrete; it is about 8 feet off the ground with parking and storage underneath. It has hurricane shutters, a 30 kW diesel generator with 300 gallons of fuel and is on relatively high ground (about 5 feet above sea level). I have always stock piled food shelf stable and MRE, water, firearms, ammunition, medical supplies and basic disaster supplies and consider my self reasonably prepared. I also keep a small 16 ft Boston Whaler in the garage.

I shut down my business on Friday at noon after we completed our much tested hurricane back up plan. I sent everyone home early and told them to contact me Saturday and Sunday if they decided to evacuate. I told them we would regroup Monday or Tuesday. My usual hurricane rule was in force for my employees. That is "you will not be penalized in any way if you miss work for one or two days due to an evacuation" (little did I know that would be 3 weeks before we would gather as even a partial group again). I gave a 2 week pay advance to everyone before they left telling everyone to be safe but to communicate with me, I normally do not do this but since payday was next Friday and Katrina had me spooked I did it. This 2 weeks pay helped some lower paid employees evacuate to safety. I kept everyone on the payroll and forgave the 2 week pay advance for all. I did this to retain everybody and I was not disappointed by anybody. Most were moved and some to tears when we met again and regrouped. Work provided some normalcy and security during these dark days.

Katrina of course hit and you know the story; carnage, looting, flooding death, etc. Around Wednesday after Katrina, I was going crazy with worry. My employees had not all checked in. Our office had no communications; the whole 504 area code was down. Property was obviously in need of attention and I was concerned about the business. I decided to go back and deal with the issues. I left my family back in Atlanta and went back alone.

I got to my home despite the fact that the city and parish were "sealed off". I know the city well and knew it could not be "sealed off". I got through un-challenged; the flooding in most of Jefferson Parish had been pumped out by then. Upon arriving home I cranked up the generator and had power, HVAC, internet, landline telephone (I could dial out but no one could dial in). I neglected to empty the refrigerator when I left so I did have that mess to clean up. That is a particularly nasty job but a large thick garbage bag, gas mask and chemical gloves make the job easy.

Once home, I assessed the damage and secured what little damage was done. The wind caused little damage to the entire city. The flooding is what caused the bulk of the damage. I fixed what I could then went check out other people's property. I sent digital photos via the internet to my wife in Atlanta who contacted and forwarded the pictures.

I found out some friends from Lafayette, LA were coming down to the city on rescue parties by boat the next day. They were turned away for some obscure reason and stopped by my house to check on me. They agreed to stay a few days to help out our friends. That began the role I played for several friends; being the forward staging area for friends and business associates trying to get back to their businesses.

The generator made life comfortable but it burned copious amounts fuel. My 300 gallons was supposed to last 10 to 12 days but 300 gallons was only a 7 day supply. I had to drive to Baton Rouge with empty drums to buy diesel. Gasoline was in very short supply but diesel was nonexistent for civilians for about a week. I had plenty of natural gas for the grill, seafood boiler, water heater and dryer but it was useless for the generator. I have since added a smaller 15 kW air-cooled gas powered generator to supplement the diesel powered set. The diesel ran like a champ though for 3 weeks straight (500 hours). I stopped it twice a day to check the oil and coolant levels. I changed the oil and filter only once after 200 hours. I had neglected the oil & filter stockpile and had enough for only one filter change. I also had trouble finding the right oil and filter for about 4 weeks so I ran it with dirty oil.

I made many forays into the city with friends and family. Some were clandestine and others were overt and authorized. I passed looters actively looting stores and was shot at on at least one occasion. I will never forget one trip I made. I hired 9 off duty police officers to go with me into a flooded area. This officer was an acquaintance and a true blue cop a real Joe Friday. However, before we left he said "Now if something happens and we shoot someone, we are just going to leave him there ok? Do you understand what I am saying?" It was clear to me that things like that happened and that is what was done. Why do you think there are so many missing people whose bodies were never found? Look at the ages and sex of the missing people, most were under 35, male and lived in areas subject to the unrest.

The 3 things I remember most about the time was the oppressive heat & sun during the day and pitch black nights and the chaos and uncertainty of the whole situation. The following is my list of what worked and did not work:

Communications:

Text messaging worked well all through the worst of the incident. The messages were often delayed but they got through eventually. A Blackberry proved to be a valuable and useful means to communicate. A pager also worked but was only a one way system. The text message interface on a PC also worked great also assuming you have internet service.

A cell phone with different area code was invaluable. I bought a prepaid cell phone in Atlanta. The Cingular system was dysfunctional, but Verison and Sprint did work. I used Cingular and Virgin Mobile which is a Sprint reseller. The cell phone with a different area code allowed you to dial out and to receive calls. Forward your key telephone numbers to this cell and you can remain in communication. The entire 504 area code was unusable for about 30 days. We forwarded our phones before we left but the entire network including forwarding went down. So all of our phones just rang or you received an out of service message which is not good for business.

CB & FMRS radios were useless in the city due to significant range limitations. Around the house a cordless phone with a paging/intercom function worked better than the FMRS radio, since it would ring when you were wanted. I would carry the cordless phone and use the intercom function.

Marine VHF was useful for local area communication though it is strictly illegal to use it for this purpose. A 12 volt VHF unit on a boat in the driveway is good for about a mile to hand held sets. Though hand held sets could get through to the base station at this distance only if you could see the other person. They could also be used in the car on the highway and were useful since the channels are not much in use inland and the squelch function is useful. Be sure to get the VHF units with the ability to use alkaline batteries.

Telephone land lines worked well and in non-flooded areas the telephones land lines never went down. Cable was not robust at and went down early and stayed down a very long time. DSL since it uses land lines did not go down at all. Satellite dishes were blown away and like cable were inoperative. The internet was invaluable.

I set up routine a check in time for all parties with someone outside of the city. I surfaced to communicate and check in at 9am, noon and 6pm to communicate with my wife while she was in Atlanta.

Keep your cell phone batteries charged so have a car adapter, 110 volt adapter, AA adapter, and spare batteries. Anytime you see a place to charge them, charge them up. Keeping these items charged will be a PITA.

A TV made a poor news machine at first. AM & FM radios worked well, the internet was more comprehensive, but had a several hour lag time. A spare satellite dish had Dish TV back up and working in no time. A spare dish also had satellite internet up and operating. I recommend satellite TV and internet as long as you have a spare dish.

Lighting – Darkness, Darkness and more darkness!

Post disaster, street lights will not work and the place will be incredibly dark. When there was no moon the darkness was surreal.

Park your cars so that their head lights shine on likely areas of egress to your house or the place you are visiting. Use the remote fob switch to make the head lights and back up lights go one in the event that you hear someone outside. You can also use the car panic switch to set off the horn for a distraction.

Use a car battery booster with a 12v to 110v inverter to plug in a 110 volt area light to provide area lighting if your generator is not operational.

Use flood lights sparingly they attract too much attention in a dark city. Spotlights with rechargeable batteries were less useful than those which took D cell batteries. The charges could not be relied upon when you needed them and re-charging them once depleted was a PITA. A 12 volt corded spot light are cheaper and more reliable; of course they need a cord & a separate battery. Note that they can also be plugged into the battery booster.

Attempt to create appearance of many more people than you have. A group of 6 to 10 is more likely to thrive than a small group. A person alone is in great danger and should consider leaving.

Flashlights are not useful for area lighting, regardless of size & type. Lanterns are much more useful for area lighting. LED and fluorescent are great inside but Coleman double mantle lanterns dual fuel are great outdoors, but only out doors.

I buy only D cell, AA and/or AAA to simplify inventory needs.

Avoid candles and hurricane lamps, the light is poor for candles and both bring heat and more importantly fire risk into the house. All open flame of any kind should be kept only outside!

Keep a low profile

Be able to establish bonafides with a picture ID with your company name and address work as well as a letter on corporate letterhead, notarized and corporate seal on it.

A white pickup truck with a corporate logo and people inside dressed in PPE will be the key to transportation. Make sure it has a sign on it, magnetic signs with business name work well.

Impersonating a responder is illegal but impersonating a business is not, use the term safety guy or personnel guy. These folks are always in and out and nobody either hates them or really needs them so you will not get drafted by the locals. DoNOT I repeat do not, say you are an insurance adjuster or in the insurance business (even if you are) you will be taking your life into your own hands, seriously. They are considered equal to child molesters.

Personal Morale and Stress

Morale is vital to all on scene.
Cleaning yourself up and putting on clean clothes is a good morale booster. Washing clothes is a pain but it is important to have clean clothes available even if you have to do by hand. As long as the water from the tap is clear and not murky, cloudy or odiferous, you can use it to clean clothes in an electric washing machine, assuming you have a generator.

If you are the leader act like one. Express concern about your people whether you give a rat's *** or not about them. They must think you care about them and will help them, it helps if you are sincere, but even if you are not, pretend to be sincere; your life may depend on it!

Get lots of rest at night. The night is the worst part. It will be very, very dark, which to city dwellers can be scary and disorienting. Sleep is the best way to handle this problem. However if possible always have someone awake 24/7. Preferably set up shifts to ensure all get adequate rest but the group is covered by someone awake. I had a rule that no one went outside alone at night, for any reason. If you heard something unusual, wake up the person who just got off duty or the person about to go on duty and have them go with you. The person on watch also had the car remote control to set off the car lights or the car alarm.

The nights were stressful due to the darkness and unusual quiet. Without power there were no A/C compressors, no cars and no people sounds. The only sounds were frogs croaking (yes in the city frogs) and silence. My generator installation was no noisier than an A/C unit. But with the central A/C units and the generator we were the noisiest thing for many blocks. Add inside and outside lights and we stood out for some distance. Hence the concern about security at night.

Drinking water gets boring so have something like Gatorade mix or tea.

Keep a positive attitude and a smile on your face! Your mood is contagious.

Heat saps strength, stamina & morale. Stay out of the sun, cool and hydrated. Make sure everybody has enough water and is drinking it, not just holding on to it. Read about heat exhaustion and heat stroke, know the symptoms, and act fast if you think the person is being affected by the heat.

Do not underestimate the emotion of seeing a beloved or even familiar place ruined.

Several cops committed suicide as a result of the stress; do not underestimate the level of stress involved.

Fire is a hazard and a real possibility. Have a fire watch and remember you cannot call the fire department or an EMS. There were instances of several houses catching fire and setting a neighboring house on fire. A 24 hour a day fire watch could save your life. Have the garden hoses ready outside, in the event a neighbor's house catches fire.

Smoke alarms in the halls outside bedrooms and Carbon monoxide alarms in every bedroom and other strategic points are a must! The carbon monoxide alarms are mandatory if a generator is used.

Fuel & Power:

Always have enough fuel in a vehicle that can carry your group to a safe point without refueling. Always have a plan to get you and your group out to safe place.

Spare fuel in 5 gallons can is dangerous; store it outside in a shady spot. Hide it because if you do it may get requisitioned. Diesel was almost impossible to find initially but gas was easy to find after the 3rd week.

Consider a tri-fuel generator and hook the generator up to natural gas. Natural gas remained on in most un-flooded sections but failed in flooded areas, so do not rely solely on natural gas have the capability to run on liquid gasoline as well. However a natural gas generator would have solved my fuel problems.

Generators are noisy and will disturb you, people nearby and attract unwanted attention. Find someway to keep the sound down. If you have a portable gas operated generator retrofit a car muffler (search the internet for article) to

it and build a sound box of some kind. You want the noise signature to be as quite as possible. See this link: http://www.alpharubicon.com/altenergy/gensetquiet.htm

Ideally have a large one permanently installed with quality sound deading material around it as I did.

Alternatively:
Dig a hole and put the generator in it and cover it with plywood. Allow for drainage. Build a sandbag berm around it cover the berm with plywood, Enclose it in a building not connected to the house, route the exhaust outside!
Keep its noise to a minimum.

Have an electrician come and put a manual disconnect switch so you can hook the generator to the house. You can do something as simple as putting in the disconnect switch and providing a 50 amp 220 volt plug so you can hook up a portable generator to the house circuits. Avoid having a stand alone generator in the back yard with extension cords. Plan ahead and do it right! Also to keep the peace with your neighbor, plan on running 1 or 2 15 amp circuits to their house(s) if they do not have a generator. That is enough to run a fridge, lights & fans. Or a fridge and a small window A/C.

Weapons:
Type and quantity less important than training and proficiency. All those debates about which is best, is a meaningless discussion. The best one to have is one you have right now in your hand, learn to use it proficiently, including the ability to take it apart and repair it. Make sure you can hit a target at 35 meters one handed with either the left or right hand. Stop debating what is best settle on what works for you and spend the time training with it.

Do not openly brandish weapons the National Guard & cops will take them away despite any laws protecting you. Have spares so that if cops take them away you have others. Do not resist attempts to by LEO to confiscate weapons. It will not end very well for you.

Be prepared to be forcibly removed for your premises and leave your pets or have your pets killed in front of you!

National Guard & LEO are not necessarily helpful, to be trusted or your friends. Trust yourself and your friends. Keep a low profile, avoid confrontations and be respectful and friendly (not subservient) to the NG and police when contact with them is unavoidable. Obey their instructions (at least when they are around) if possible and not counter to your goal. Never confront them or actively or violently resist them, you will lose and become just another unidentified body found in the rubble.

Cash, Documents and Commerce:

A Good way to make a friend is cold soft drinks – trade hot for cold if you can when you are giving them away as gifts. I went through a lot of Cokes.

Image important documents on a scanner and store them on a flash drive or on line by emailing them to yourself at for instance AOL or Google.

Drivers license, passport, social security card, birth certificate, marriage certificate, Insurance policies, vaccination/medical records for family & pets should be imaged.

Use an online bank and have multiple accounts. Keep multiple credit cards with a zero balance so that in an emergency you can at least buy gas, a hotel room and some food.

You need at least $1,000 cash on hand. More is always better but do not carry all split it up in different pockets and use credit cards wherever possible. Keep it in small bills like $5, $10 & $20 along with a credit card. Checks, travelers checks and money orders are useless don't waste your time with them.

Take photos of your insured property and make sure that they are not more than 2 year old. Use a digital camera and store the photos in multiple places.

Any photo albums, documents, or similar such things can be digitalized so that if the original is destroyed you at least have a copy. Look around your house and see what falls into that category. It is amazing how much you lose when you are looking at just a house slab.

Back up your data in multiple places and set out a contingency plan for your business. We use nothing but laptops and have contracted with an off site server to store all of our data files. Everybody can use a virtual private network to set up wherever we may finally stop assuming they can get to high speed internet connections.

Phone forwarding malfunctioned so all our lines did was to ring when they did not get a system busy. Have a contingency plan to notify all customers of a number change or arrange with the telephone company to use a trunk forwarding service.

We set up a toll free number and manned it with a small staff to disseminate contact info. Emails worked fine as did text messages. Web sites also worked well as a means to disseminate telephone numbers.

Looting. Looters and Requisitioning:

Police will loot. It is called requisitioning. They will take your spare gasoline, supplies, ammunition, first aid kits, ice, water, guns and even your vehicle! They are worse than looters in that they have the force of law behind them. They looted cars, booze, TV as well as necessities such as food water and clean clothes.

Avoid looting parties. They tend to be undisciplined and have numerous, armed people. If you join them, watch your back and go only with a group you know and then stick together. Take only what you need and make restitution when you can do so. Even when you need it... looting is wrong. It belongs to someone else.

The LEO & national guard will be hot, tired, scared and grumpy! Avoid them at all costs. They will be well armed, better trained and are more likely to shoot you than the looters. Always approach them slowly with your hands visible and in a non-threatening manner. Politeness (though not submission like you are guilty of something) and a smile on your face and a comment like "Boy am I glad to see you guys, thanks for the help". If you are unsure of the situation extend your hand in a handshake. Their actions will tell volumes as to their intent.

Never curse them, do offer them a cold coke or water. If you do not have a cold drink, say I would offer you guys one but I don't have one.

The USCG were the best guys, they were most useful, professional and least dangerous (as long as you were not hostile to them) the worst were the National Guard units and local PD. They were stressed out lost their homes separated from loved ones etc. They were heavily armed and dangerous. No offense intended to any member of these units but that is my observation.

When you travel, travel in groups. No fewer than two, four in 2 vehicles are better. If you leave your vehicle(s) make sure someone or preferably 2 people stay with it (them).

Have a prearranged sign and counter sign for the group, include a trouble sign and counter sign. Do not shout everybody and anybody's name when you think you see trouble. Use a signal when concerned or needing help. You do not have to be silly about it, but a shout of "Hey Mr. Murphy" is a whole more innocuous than "Hey George and Louis there are five guys coming towards me". In the latter you have conveyed to the party coming at you that there are 2 other people who will be coming shortly. On the other hand if you shout " Hey Mr. Murphy" while looking at the group and waving in a friendly like manner at the people coming at you, they may assume that you are addressing them and waving at them and not calling your buddies to come outside and help. It may just give you the edge in that situation.

Look out for people's pets, save the ones you can. Bring food and water for them since it is likely one else will. Many pets were abandoned and dies a long linger death as a result.

Be very careful avoid any injuries of any kind. If you are injured, cut, get a blister, etc treat it aggressively, even a simple scratch in a disaster zone can be life threatening.

Get vaccination for hepatitis, tetanus and anything else you can talk your MD into giving you.

Do not take supplies from the Red Cross, Salvation Army or others unless you or someone you know truly needs them. Supplies are limited and others in need may do without because you wanted something you did not really need. I saw a single mother with a baby and toddler go without water when an "alpha" male barged in line and took stuff meant for her. The "alpha" males simply put the water in their pockets and walked away. I "found" her some water when the "alpha" males suddenly "dropped" their water and ran for their lives.

Be compassionate, but do not be silly, sometimes sympathy targets (old people, disabled people, kids and women) are used by looters as bait.

Do not be in the disaster area if you can avoid it. Leave the area until the situation stabilizes. If you have to be there stay only as long as necessary. It is not a game and it is sure as hell not fun.

Food, Water & Ice:

Ice is a very valuable commodity when the temperature is 95 degrees and the humidity is 100%. Keep some handy to trade or barter for favors. Use empty water bottles to make it at home in the freezer. It is a good barter commodity.

Safe, potable water is critical. You cannot have too much of it on hand. I had 10 five gallon bottles of water on hand, in addition to 6 cases of 20 oz bottles of water. That was no where near adequate.

Water is either safe or not. If you have the slightest doubt about the water; then it is not safe to drink it!

Unsafe water from the tap can be used for flushing toilets and washing clothes. It can also be used for washing you, but do not drink it and keep it away from your eyes, nose and mouth when showering with it. However, unsafe water

from the tap and a 5% to 10% solution of bleach can be used for cleaning dishes with soap as long as the final rinse is in boiled or clean water (be sure the water has cooled and add 2% to 3% bleach to the rinse water). You can rinse the plate to get the food residue off with the running un-boiled water before washing them, but wash them with boiled water, if possible dip them in a mild bleach solution in the rinse cycle and hand dry.

To make clear water safe, boil the water for 10 to 20 minutes at a rolling boil. You can also add chlorine before boiling it if you are really nervous. Be careful and let the water stand at least an hour to avoid burning yourself. Boil as much as you can at one time because it is a PITA to boil water. I used a seafood boiler and natural gas for this chore. Keep the pot covered when the water is boiling and cooling Store it in a CLEAN preferably sterilized container. Used but clean 2 liter soft drink bottles are perfect for storing boiled water (but wait till it cools to pour it!).

Potable Water should be used as much as possible. For example water used for cooking rice and spaghetti can be re-used for cleaning the pots and dishes.

An outside propane or natural gas burner with a large boiling pot will make quick work of producing many gallons of safe drinking water without the heat and humidity in the house. This boiling pot can also be used to sanitize plates, silverware and pots.

You can attach a large activated charcoal filter to an outside water hose to filter water that you boil for drinking. Boiling may or may not remove toxic chemicals in the water. Use bottled water from a known source if at all possible for all drinking, food preparation washing and bathing.

Water in a pinch can be made safer by filtering it and adding a small amount of Clorox or iodine tablets to the water. Murky or smelly water should not be used for anything, if at all possible!

You may be tempted to use the dishwasher and put it on heated water and the sanitize setting, but do not take the risk. It is just not worth the risk! Plan on hand washing and sanitizing the dishes yourself.

Paper towels, plates and deposable knives and forks work very well and many times are better than real china and silverware. Have lots of paper towels, garbage bags and deposable stuff on hand.

Garbage disposal is a problem; there was not garbage pick up for 2 months. Plan on bringing it to the dump your self. Sanitation is important and garbage stinks after a week in the sun! When you bring it to the dump put it on the trailer; do not put it in the car or trunk you will never get the stink out!

Note you can freeze bottle of unsafe water for ice, just label it as unsafe and do not use or drink the water.

Food is important to morale! Cook it and present it well! Sit down together and eat together, this is great morale builder.

Simple Menus are Important since fresh items are limited
Spaghetti & meatballs
Red beans rice & meat (sausage, hamburger, chicken)
Chicken and rice
Hamburgers and macaroni & cheese
Scrambled eggs, grits and toast
Steak and canned veggies
Jambalaya & meat of any kind
Use MRE only for lunch when out and about or as a last resort. Everybody should sit down and eat together at least once a day for better morale.

Vehicle:
4wd was not important but was useful mainly due to the higher ground clearance it afforded. Bring rope to tie to branches to move them. Make sure the vehicle has auxiliary storage like a roof rack, a roof cargo carrier , a trailer hitch "back porch" or have a trailer. Anything that you can use to carry additional bulky cargo, like roofing shingles, gas, clothes, food water, etc.

I used my boat as means to carry cargo such as garbage and fuel. It was all I had so I used it as a utility trailer. It had 2 -18 gallon gas tanks so filled up those tanks and put 3 -55 gallon drums in the boat. Use what you have.

Make sure your vehicle is in good shape, a broken fan belt, bad tire, leaking water pump or battery with a dead cell is useless and dangerous in a disaster zone.

Be sure to have a can of fix a flat, 12 volt air compressor, battery booster, tire plug kit, flash light with spare batteries and a plug in 12 volt spot light (they are cheaper and more reliable than those needing a charge) as well as basic tools like a screwdriver, pliers and crescent wrench are invaluable. A 12volt to 110 volt inverter (no more than 100 watts to avoid blowing fuses or worse a fusible link), small first aid kit and rope will also be invaluable. A 110 volt trouble light with a 25 foot cord to plug into the inverter will serve multiple purposes of light and power; just do not overload the inverter. Be sure to have a spare oil, brake fluid, ATF fluid and antifreeze, (it does not have to be in the car) you will not be able to find it.

The cargo area if not "hoseable" should be covered in plastic to prevent the spread of contaminants.

A cheaper car or pick up truck will attract a whole lot less negative attention than a blingmobile! Park the Mercedes and Lexus drive the pickup truck!

Tools:
Basic tools like a socket set, wrench, screwdrivers, etc. A cordless electric screwdriver and drill will also save you a lot of energy and sweat.

Other useful tools:
Crow bar large & small for breaking glass and prying open windows and doors. Pry bar for opening doors, Large bolt cutters, Claw hammer, Axe or Hatchet, Small sledge hammer and wedges (s.m.l).
PPE – very important! Hard hat, safety glasses, gloves leather & latex respirators or face mask, steel toed shoes WITH steel soles!

Gas chainsaw (nice but not required unless you live in a wooded area) I used the rope and car to pull large branches out of my way. A tree hand saw is just as useful and less costly in an urban area. In a wooded area buy 2 chainsaws, one is not enough.

Tarps several sizes are good you can always trade them if you do not need them.

An electric sawzall is particularly useful assuming you have a generator.

Chain and padlocks will always come in handy.
Electric extension cords get several and buy the thick contractors grade. Also a power strip with a surge suppressor for each cord will be useful. Tape (electrical & duct), Spray paint (white, orange & black for signs, warnings & messages),Preprinted signs like Looters will be shot are not as useful as handmade signs since the preprinted ones may indicate no one is around. Also date any spray painted signs so people know it is up post disaster.

Boats in Urban Settings and Flood Water:
If you have the misfortune of dealing with a flood, there will be all kind of hazards that you will encounter such that even the oldest of salts will be in a challenging environment.

Operate the boat only at idle or slow speeds. Do not let the boat get on a plane, displacement speed only. They will be signs, wires trees shrubs, debris and many other things that will destroy or damage an out drive. Better to hit something at a slow speed.

Trim the engine up to reduce your draft. Travel in pairs and maintain radio watches be wary of manhole covers if you go in the water. The covers may be gone. There are ditches and various other obstacles that are not apparent. Do not walk in the water if at all possible. Always wear a PFD even an inflatable one is better than nothing.

Navigation will be difficult since road signs may be obscured and your GPS will likely have a nautical chart rather than I-10 on it. Have someone on the boat who knows the area.

Power lines may still be energized, so stay away from them, do not touch them.

For the record, rescued people are not always grateful to be rescued. They may be in shock, terrified, disoriented and/or potentially dangerous. Always have at least one other you can trust in the boat with you. You can concentrate on steering and he/she should concentrate on the people in the boat. Never assume people can swim, provide a PFD for all and make them wear it; if nothing else it will be reassuring for them. If you encounter hostile people, exit the area ASAP. Always know how to get out of an area quickly.

Do not fool around in flood waters! They are nasty, ing and dangerous. Do not handle any floating bodies unless you want a very, very unpleasant experience. Do not ford the water in your vehicle if you can avoid it. Check the depth on foot before you even consider fording water. Most vehicles can get their drive train damaged by as little as a foot of water. The vehicle will also kick up wakes into people's homes. The people in the house may object violently to you flooding their already damaged house. If you do ford water do so at an idle speed and paying close attention to water depth. If in doubt back up to higher ground! Judging the water depth is deceptive since cars have different heights. Often times the center of the road is the highest side. Consider using the sidewalk, lawns or road median to keep at least part of your vehicle high enough not to flood.

Elderly, Infirm, Pets and Kids:
None belong in a disaster zone and should be evacuated ASAP. Pets will be destroyed at the slightest bit of inconvenience to the authorities. Chip your pet and evacuate them. Keep their shots current and board them with friends families or a boarding facility. There were numerous instances of pets summarily destroyed for a variety of reasons including simply spite. Two deputies in St Bernard parish are facing charges for shooting pets for no apparent reason. The incidents were captured on videotape, despite this, they would never have been charged if left to the local officials. One can only imagine what else went on and was not uncovered. An elderly women recounted to me her story about how she refused to leave her home because her pet

could not come with her. The LEO simply shot her beloved pet in front of her said "now the problem is solved" and put the woman in a boat. I heard from others in different areas that they were forced to abandon their pets under threat of physical threat. Some of these pets survived others did not. In a truly bad situation you should assume this attitude will extend to children and non-able bodied people as well. In fact in war time this type of behavior has been documented in various parts of the world.

There was also the case of 32 nursing home patients that were abandoned and subsequently drown in St Bernard Parish. In another case an elderly woman and her middle aged quadriplegic son were told a special van would come get them. No transportation arrived and they both died.

If you are handicapped, elderly have children or pets make your own plans to evacuate. Do not rely on any government plan to assist you. Rely only on yourself.

Evacuation issues:
Leave early or Late – A tough call it depends on your circumstances and how likely your risk is to be vs. that of staying put. Just do not wait too long. allow 12 hours to get to safety!

Which route to use? – be flexible and do not be afraid to use back routes, speed is less important than steady progress away from danger. Keep a close watch on your gas. Look for gas at ½ a tank, search diligently for gas at ¼ of a tank, look for a safe place stop at 1/8 of a tank. Do not run out of gas. If you have to use your reserve tank find shelter nearby and wait until it is safe. Gas gives you options, no gas leaves you vulnerable. If necessary abandon one vehicle and strip all fuel from it. Discard stuff in the following order (if necessary) goods to make things fit: magazines, clothes, ice chests, food, spare tire, tools, adults, children & elderly, pets. Never discard water or fuel. If someone has be left behind (at a safe place obviously) leave two people and give them cash & credit card, water, cell phone and set an alternate rally point.

If possible travel in two cars, evacuation is very dangerous. Your car could break down and leave you and your loved ones stranded with an impending disaster enroute. Two cars capable of carrying all is the safest way to travel. Do not rely on the LEOs to assist, they will be busy and the phrase SOL comes to mind.

What to bring? See the above list but include at least 5 gallons of gasoline, food (simple stuff like bread and peanut butter) and at least 1 gallon of water for every two people. Be sure to carry the gas on top of the vehicle on the roof rack not inside the car. It will make everyone nauseous otherwise. Have maps, a laptop with an internet card to stay in touch with the outside world and a GPS is very useful. FRMS & CB radios do work well here. but are obnoxious to have on all the time. The driver's job is to drive and do nothing else other than keep an eye outside the vehicle. The traffic will range from a creeping 10 to 20 mph to 60 mph bumper to bumper traffic. It is demanding and tiring to drive like this for 6 to 12 hours at a time. If possible appoint one of the passengers navigator. The navigator is responsible for keeping track of the locataion of both vehicles, nearby alternate routes and maintains communication with the other vehicle. Other passengers can be utilized to find accommodations, gas and other necessary information via cell phone (or internet) as well as tend to needs of the other passengers or driver. A 12 volt TV can provide invaluable news.

The traffic will be moving very slowing. 10 to 20 mph is not unusual, so be patient and do not plan on being able to get off the highway for anything for at least 5 to 8 hours.

A poop bucket" is absolutely vital. For males a simple 32 oz cup WITH A LID, a 2 liter bottle and a funnel or a wide mouth 1 to 2 liter juice bottle will work nicely. Women may use the same thing but with a funnel. Be sure to have a towel handy! Do not dump it on the road unless you are traveling very slowly (which is normally the case) keep it sealed in Ziploc bag in between uses to avoid messes. Kids especially preteen girls may pose special problems due to modesty issues. Talk to those involved. It will be a problem and stopping may not be an option, assuming you can even pull over.

Destinations:

It depends on the situation but generally the farther away the better yet the closer the destination the easier it will be to get there. Where you go is up to your budget. I suggest some place with family and friends to help you assimilate in case the stay is a long one. For stays over 2 weeks, a furnished corporate apartment is generally a better deal and more comfortable and normal than a hotel room.

Evacuation by Air:

This is the safest and easiest way to evacuate but you cannot take much with you. This is generally best if you have a house elsewhere or you have small children, elderly or infirm people to remove. When you leave be sure to leave your car parked at an inside garage and at least one level above the ground floor. Do not count on this method unless you own your own plane since flights are generally booked well in advance.

Personal gear:

You should always carry the following:

A butt pack with flashlight, pistol (assuming you have a CCH permit), reloads, cigarette lighter, pepper spray, leatherman tool, latex gloves, small hand sanitizer and digital camera, spare batteries, spare data card. The camera should be kept in a baggy to protect it. Why the camera? So you can show others what you saw and get their input into situations.

Water at least one bottle

Clean towel, spare shoes, spare clothes, and wading boots. I typically wore a jumpsuit and running shoes. I changed my shoes to steel toed boots when I got out of the car and again when I got back in.
A hat and sunscreen were also very handy.

Sanitation:

Wash your hands wash your face with a clean towel before you go into the house if you have been out on "expedition". Hand sanitizer and plain old alcohol work great if potable water is not available..

Thick Plastic/chemical resistant gloves as well as latex gloves to protect yourself from chemicals like chlorine.

Leave your shoes out side and do not track any crud inside. If you wear a jumpsuit with shorts underneath. Shuck the jumpsuit and put it in a garbage bag along with any towels used. Leave your boots outside. Everything dirty goes in the washing machine. Anything recovered from the flood water stays out side. Set up a hose and bucket with dish washing liquid to clean off anything nasty and leave it out side..

Copyright 2007
http://zombiehunters.org

Some additional comments he posted after the main article was done that shed some valuable aditional insight!

The DARKNESS

I mentioned that the dark nights were one of the 3 things that I remember vividly. For those who live in the woods I am sure this is not big deal to you. However, to a "city boy" the only time I experienced darkness like this was at sea over 100 miles offshore on a sailboat. If you are not prepared for this darkness you will find it unsettling. I of course had power and lights at home most of the time but other places all I had was whatever light I brought.

I had to stay places where there was no generator power so lets talk about how to deal with darkness that is akin to being in cave,

The obvious solution is a flash light. I used maglights constantly. I prefer the 3 D cell since it is a good trade off for bulk vs. output. One thing though they go through batteries very quickly and within an hour or so you need new batteries. I always buy Rayovac batteries because the work well but are cheaper than all of the others.

I also use the handheld 6 volt lights made by Dorcy but instead of the 6 volt square battery I bought a couple of D cell converters so I can run them off D cell Batteries.

I also am fond of the AA maglight especially since they now make LED conversion bulbs for these. I wish I had these during Katrina! I went though a lot of batteries. I typically buy the lithium batteries for these lights since the lithium batteries have a long shelf life.

I have some pelican lights with Xeon bulbs but they are not as handy as the maglights. The other truly useful lights I used were Energizer brand folding LED lights and a headlight which has 2 red led a white LED and a krypton bulb. These are relativity inexpensive and very useful when your hands are full but you also need additional light. They use AA or AAA batteries and when you use lithium batteries in them they will last forever running the led lights. I used the red LED at night when out and about to attempt to preserve my night vision. The red LEDs were actually at times too bright.

http://www.energizer.com/products/flash ... cat=4&id=9

There is also the question of illumination for night time encounters. I made a quick field expedient utilizing a Maglight, a SS hose clamp and a Remington 870. I was able to use this simple and expedient to make night illumination of a target possible. You do not need special rails only a hose clamp and flash light. It does not look pretty but the person I point it at will not care about looks for long.

However like I said flash lights are useless for area lighting. That is why lanterns are made. I used several Energizer folding Fluorescent lamps with 2 tubes(http://www.energizer.com/products/flashlights/
flashlight.asp?cat=4&id=8.)
They provide more than adequate illumination of a 12 x12 room. If you run two of them you will think the power is back on. I also used LED lanterns with 12 and 19 LEDs the light was not uniform, but the batteries would last close to 50 hours. I tended to use these as marker lights and area

illumination due to the long life but poor light dispersion. Both of this type is readily available at Wally world for under $12.

I also found Coleman duel fuel lanterns useful since they could burn gasoline. Note the fire hazard though. Candles were completely unsatisfactory in terms of light and heat. A kerosene hurricane lantern actually put out excellent light but not as much as a Coleman lantern and still had a fire risk. Cyalume lights were absolutely useless I had two dozen on hand and was hard pressed to find a use for them. The light is inadequate and they are not reusable.

Now what does work well for area illumination. The 110v light fixture which is shaped like a silver bell and has a clamp to hook to multiple surfaces was invaluable as was a conventional trouble light. Now you are going to say wait a minute you need AC power for that. You are right you do, but not need a lot if you use a 45 watt flood or spotlight bulb and even less if you use an 11 or 15 watt compact fluorescent bulb. You will need a 12 volt power source and an inverter say a 90 watt one to use it. A convenient 12 volt power source is one the car starter devices with the jumper cables and typically an air pump also. It is a very versatile device. You can jump start your car, put air in the tire or plug a 12 volt inverter into the cigarette lighter type plug or use the jumper cable to attach to the inverter. A 15 watt compact florescent bulb running an inverter will typically last all night. You will have to recharge it in the morning but you will have at least 9 hours of enough illumination to read by. Alternatively you can have enough light from the flood light to illuminate a typical yard for about 3 hours.

Finally there is question of illumination outside the house. In a pinch what I did was park the vehicle such that when the lights came on they shined in the direction of an area of concern. I could then trigger the lights with vehicle's remote control. The scene went from pitch black to illuminated with a click of the remote control. I could also trigger the car alarm for added distraction if I wanted to do so. At one point I had 3 vehicles set up like this pointing in different directions.

The other more esoteric device is night vision goggles. I spare no expense on items that I need but $3,000 for a good gen 2 or 3 is just not something I could justify. I did have on hand a Gen 1 unit, which on occasions came in handy. However, I used because I had it, not because it was needed.

However, my over all strategy for night time was simply. Pull back to my house, batten down and keep a small secure perimeter. You do not need to be running around at night and if you are inside a secure perimeter you do not have to worry about the bumps and noises outside of that perimeter.

BRIBERY
I would look at the person and see what they may want at the time. The bribe might be as simple as a cold coke or Gatorade or may have been a few hundred dollars. Let me also stress no one ever said to me I will let you do "it" for $100. My experience is that the only people uttering phases like that outside of the movies are about to either set you up or they are so corrupt that your life is possibly in danger. View it as if you are giving a tip.

I have lived in 3rd world countries and can generally "read" people, especially officials.

When paying cash I would hand them a drink and discretely use a $20 bill or $100 as the "napkin" wrapped around the drink. I would then offer my hand in a handshake and keep the same smile on my face. No winks, nods or anything else like that.

When I traveled, I kept an ice chest with soft drinks, Gatorade or water along with MREs and about $1,000 cash in $10, $20 or $100 in my pocket separate from my wallet and ID.

Never, ever take out your wallet, reach in and take out money, nor should you whip out a huge wad of cash. Do not say "how much will it take", do not be overt or crude. You will be surprised how much you can do with a smile, pleasant banter and something a person wants. The most overt I got was to hand the guy my papers, let him tell me "to get the hell out of his face" and then ask him what I had to do to get where I wanted to go. I would wait for his reaction. If he offered information I would then say "well you seem to be charge could you approve it?" I would wait for the response and either conclude the deal knowing it would be expensive or go elsewhere. If his reaction was belligerent and negative, no amount of persuasion would work, you should leave immediately and either try later or some where else.

I also gave out suntan lotion, mosquito repellant, ice, clean towels, baby wipes. These were always welcomed.

I also would give out MREs and drinks to people (looters or survivors) as well a $10 or even $20 bill on occasion. My logic for this was; I did not like the MREs and if I could avoid a confrontation and danger to me and or my group for an MRE, cold coke and $10, that is a cheap transaction. Beside a magazine or cylinder of bullets can cost more than the $10.

What is interesting is that most "looters" were generally satisfied with a cold coke and few kind words. Having said that, I always kept a compact 9mm or 357 snubbie in my pocket and when I was "being nice" to the looters/survivors I also was ready to end the conversation suddenly and if necessary violently.

Finally try to use the same checkpoints so people there know you. Just like in business it is not what you know or what you have, so much as who you know. I used 2 main check points and I became known as "Ben" (Ben Franklin is on the $100 bill). I knew I had made when one sentry waved and shouted to his commander "it's OK, it is Ben!" When that happened, there were Cokes all around for everyone and everyone needed a "napkin" to reinforce the positive experience of seeing me. They never asked for money but they remembered me and treated me well. I always took care of them (There were 6 guys at that command post/ check point working the day shift and they were there for 6 weeks). I was kinda sorry to see them go.

One final note, the value of bater goods changed rapidly due to supply and demand. Initially real MREs (with a heater of all things!) were in high demand. Then they became the proverbial fruit cake; people them gave to you, but nobody really wanted to eat them. Gas was worth its weight in gold and diesel was even more valuable initially, but once the supplies were up and available they lost thier value beyond retail for barter purposes. Personal toiletries like sun tan lotion, mosquito repellant, BABY WIPES! of all things, hand sanitizers and clean towels all were very useful to trade.

The one item that held its value was a cold soft drink or bottled water! I suspect in cold climes a hot drink will hold the same value.

===

SKILLS
I am going to climb on my soapbox now and I am not addressing to anyone in particular.

Too many people think planning and preparation involves having the best rifle, the best shotgun, the best pistol and enough ammunition to hold off an army. Too many people turn it into some kind of video game. When the SHTF it will not be pretty or fun, it will be dirty, grimy and smelly and not something that you want to do. I would prefer never to have to go thought that situation every again. However, two monster storms have hit in my lifetime (Camille and Katrina) I certainly expect another so I deal with it.

Preparation involves many more skills than firearms and gunsmithing, stock piling food and water. In addition to worrying about the adequacy of an arsenal you should worry about how do I perform basic plumbing jobs, how to disconnect or reconnect an electrical meter from a house, how to fix the generator, flat tire or nail on a tarp or shingles to patch a roof. Basic electrical, plumbing, car repairs and carpentry skills are always skills that you can use and if necessary trade for goods in a prolonged SHTF situation. Knowledge and skills are fundamentally valuable.

In Orleans Parish there was one guy who stayed open and did nothing but fix flat tires on cars. He had a skill very much in demand and no one messed with him because he was "harmless and useful". A perception of harmless and useful is a very good position to be in.

Fundamentally you cannot stock pile enough food, water and ammunition to last the rest of your life. However, knowledge and skills do not go stale nor can anyone take them away. Technology may change but you can adapt your skill set.

The other skill is the mindset of survival/awareness, identifying potential risks and how they evolve, coping with the stress and thinking outside of the box. I like to quote a movie line, the hero when asked what was his favorite weapon said "My brains". I am not saying firearms are not necessary, all I am saying is training and knowledge are every bit as important.

I will get off my soapbox now.

GUNS

Lord Bane wrote:
After reading raptor's posts and first hand experiences I see it going like this:

LEO/NG: Disarm
Proud Gun Guy: I have a constitutional right to this firearm

LEO/NG: Disarm or we will do it for you
Proud Gun Guy: According to Government Code Section 433 (State of Emergency)
Sec. 433.0045. FIREARMS. (a) you may not seize me weapons.

*LEO/NG: *raise fire arms* DISARM or we WILL fire!*
Proud Gun Guy: I am a law abiding citizen who has done nothing wrong, you will not f.....

LEO/NG: **BANG BANG BANG BANG BANG BANG BANG**

*Proud Gun Guy **dies standing up for his rights but no one witnesses his martydom.***

LEO/NG did what they thought they had to in order to protect thier boys down the line.
*Proud Gun Guy **gets left there and is just another nameless victim of a disaster.***

LEO/NG __never do time.__
__Proud Gun Guy's family weeps.__

You left out the double tap "coup de grace" but yes I would say that sums up the most probable scenario.

Probable scenario B is **they take away the weapon, beat the hell out of you and throw you in the temporary jail/holding pen for resisting arrest, threatening an officer and anything else they can think of as a criminal charge.**

Either way, the probable outcomes are not likely to be good, if you are told to surrender your weapon and you chose not to comply.

I offer this scenario to any ZS'er:
Reverse the roles, put yourself in their shoes:

I will set the scene for you. You are hot, thirsty, drenched in sweat from the heat. You have been told about armed looters. You have heard gun shots in the distance many times. Then you see a cammie clad person with mags across the chest and an EBR walking around outside.

What would you assume and how would you approach this person?

There are few things that bear repeating:

11. Have enough money with you for at least two weeks. Many of those who arrived here had very little in cash, relying on check-books and credit cards to fund their purchases. Guess what? Their small banks down in South Louisiana were all off-line, and their balances, credit authorizations, etc. could not be checked SNIP ... Another thing - don't bring *only large bills. Many gas stations, convenience stores, etc. won't accept anything larger than a $20 bill. Some of my guests had plenty of $100 bills, but couldn't buy anything.*

I think it might be a good idea to have a "bug-out bank account" with a national bank, so that funds should be available anywhere they have a branch, rather than keeping all one's money in a single bank (particularly a local one) or credit union. This is, of course, over and above one's "bug-out stash" of ready cash.

Forget PM and debit cards. In the early days of a situation like this, cash and an AMEX card is the answer.

2. When help gets there, you may get it whether you like it or not. There are numerous reports of aggressive, overbearing behavior by those rescuers who first arrived at disaster scenes. It's perhaps best described as "I'm here to rescue you - I'm in charge - do as I say - if you don't I'll shoot you".

In one incident, a family who had prepared and survived quite well were ordered, not invited, to get onto a truck, with only the clothes on their backs. When they objected, they were threatened. They had pets, and wanted to know what would happen to them and they report that a uniformed man (agency unknown) began pointing his rifle at the pets with the words "I'll fix that".

Prepare for your pets, do not turn them over to the authorities and expect them to be returned alive.

3. There seems to be a cumulative psychological effect upon survivors. This is clear even - or perhaps particularly - in those who were prepared for a disaster. During and immediately after the disaster, these folks were at their best, dealing with damage, setting up alternative accommodation, light, food sources, etc. However, after a few days in the heat and debris (perhaps worst of all being the smell of dead bodies nearby), many found their ability to remain positive and "upbeat" being strained to the limit. There are numerous reports of individuals becoming depressed, morose and withdrawn. This seemed to happen to even the strongest personalities. The arrival of rescuers provided a temporary boost, but once evacuated, a sort of "after-action shell-shock" seems to be commonly experienced. I don't know enough about this to comment further, but I suspect that staying in place has a lot to do with it - there is no challenge to keep moving, find one's survival needs, and care for the group, and one is surrounded by vivid reminders of the devastation. By staying among the ruins of one's former life, one may be exposing oneself to a greater risk of psychological deterioration.

Do not under estimate the psychological toll that a disaster will take on you and your loved ones. The impact will be much worse than you think. These post disaster problems were evident in a lot of people. PTSD related problems, domestic violence, suicide and depression were epidemic. The stress also likely accelerated the deaths of many elderly people who could not deal with the stress and related issues.

3. Your personal and/or corporate supplies and facilities may be commandeered without warning, receipt or compensation. I've had numerous reports from in and near the disaster zone of individuals (e.g. boat-owners, farmers with barns, tractors, etc.) and corporate groups (e.g. companies with heavy equipment, churches with halls, etc.) finding an official on their doorstep demanding the use of their facilities or equipment. If they demurred, they were told that this was an "emergency situation" and that their assistance was being required, not requested.

I ran into this myself with fuel. Both gasoline and diesel were "requisitioned" from me. It pissed me off each and every time, but I did give it to them. So I guess I have no one to blame for this but me.

REQUISITIONING

Power Fail wrote:

> *raptor wrote:I ran into this myself with fuel. Both gasoline and diesel were "**requisitioned**" from me. It pissed me off each and every time, but I did give it to them. So I guess I have no one to blame for this but me.*

Who "requisitioned" it from you? How did they go about it (did they ask nicely, did you just go out and find them taking it, or what)? How do you think things would have played out had you politely but firmly declined?

It varied. They were all locals and they did stop after fuel became available after about 2 weeks. Finding fuel especially diesel was difficult in the first 2 weeks. Apparently they had diesel generators. My PU was diesel and I was carrying fuel to a generator for my building to get it back up on line. I made several trips over several days with about a dozen fuel jugs in the truck bed to get fuel for the generator.

I later obtained several drums. I found they did not try to requisition a whole drum probably because it weighs 500+ lbs. 5 gallon jugs on the other hand when carried in the PU truck bed were easy to requisition. They are a nice handy size.

It was not done in a threatening manner but it was clear that no you had no choice in the matter. You could be a street attorney and protest and they would give you problems and take all your fuel or you could be a good citizen and give them two or three of the jugs of fuel and go on your way. They also did not have any receipts to give you for your "donation". I did ask for that once.

They also did not give me back the empty jugs which were even more difficult to find than diesel. I tried to trade empty for full once and was told they did not have jugs with them but I could come back later (with more full jugs to give them).

I likely gave up the fuel too easily but I did not want any trouble from the LEOs. I knew what happened to trouble makers. If I had made a stink about it I probably could have kept the fuel (I can be very persuasive). However I am also sure that would come at a price more than the fuel was worth to me at the time.

My comment was that in retrospect it still pisses me off. However, I would likely do the same thing under the same circumstances.

There was and is a lot of blame to go around starting with the local citizens who ignored the warnings and stayed. However the mismanagement, stupidity and incompetence at the local, state and federal level was simply simply amazing. The chaos was direct result of a total lack of organization at all of those levels.

Things did not improve until General Honore arrived with the army. The situation improved then not because the troops and weapons showed up but because he was able to implement a basic command and control structure.

Lessons from Argentina's economic collapse
By ferfal
http://www.silverbearcafe.com/private/10.08/tshtf1.html

(**Editor's note:** *the article that follows is a very sobering account of the effect that the collapse of the Argentine economy (1999 - 2002) had on its citizens, as seen through the eyes of one of them. The economic collapse wiped out the middle class and raised the level of poverty to 57.5%. Central to the collapse was the implementation of neo-liberal policies which enabled the swindle of billions of dollars by foreign banks and corporations. Many of Argentina's assets and resources were shamefully plundered. Its financial system was even used for money laundering by Citibank, Credit Suisse, and JP Morgan (sound familar?). The net result was massive wealth transfers and the impoverishment of society which culminated in many deaths due to oppression and malnutrition. I am not sure the same thing is about to happen here, but I am sure that there is a distinct possibility that it might. Just food for thought - JSB*)

Wednesday, 13 December 2006

For western countries such as the UK, the first major problems of Peak Oil, assuming there are no oil shocks, will not be the shortage of oil but the economic crises that will occur.

Argentina is a recent example of a country that suffered a serious economic crisis, and although Argentina and the UK are not identical, anyone interested in how economic crises can affect individual lives will be very interested in the following vivid description of life for an Argentinian following the economic collapse.

My brother visited Argentina a few weeks ago. He's been living in Spain for a few years now.

Within the first week, he go sick, some kind of strong flu, even though climate isn't that cold and he took care of himself.

Without a doubt he got sick because there are lots of new viruses in my country that can't be found in 1st world countries.

The misery and famine lead us to a situation where, even though you have food, shelter and health care, most others don't, and therefore they get sick and spread the diseases all over the region.

What got me started on this post is the fact that I actually saw this coming, and posted on the subject here at Frugal's, months before the new viruses spread over the country and the news started talking about this new, health emergency, which proves that talking, thinking and sharing ideas with like minded people (you guys), does help to see things coming and prepare for them with enough time.

So I started thinking about several issues, what I learned (either the hard way or thanks to this forum) after all these years of living in a collapsed country that is trying to get out an economical disaster and everything that comes along with it.

Though my English is limited, I hope I'm able to transmit the main ideas and concepts, giving you a better image of what you may have to deal with some day, if the economy collapses in your country.

URBAN OR COUNTRY?
Someone once asked me how did those that live in the country fare. If they were better off than city dwellers.

As always there are no simple answers. Wish I could say country good, city bad, but I can't. Because if I have to be completely honest, and I intend to be so, there are some issues that have to be analyzed, specially security.

Of course that those that live in the country and have some land and animals were better prepared food-wise. No need to have several acres full of crops. A few fruit trees, some animals, such as chickens, cows and rabbits, and a small orchard was enough to be light years ahead of those in the cities.

Chickens, eggs and rabbits would provide the proteins, a cow or two for milk and cheese, some vegetables and fruit plants covered the vegetable diet, and some eggs or a rabbit could be traded for flower to make bread and pasta or sugar and salt.

Of course that there are exceptions.

For example, some provinces up north have desert climate, and it almost never rains. It is almost impossible to live of the land, and animals require food and water you have to buy. Those guys had it bad, no wonder the northern provinces suffer the most in my country.

Those that live in cities, well they have to manage as they can. Since food prices went up about 200%-300%. People would cut expenses wherever they could so they could buy food. Some ate whatever they could, they hunted birds or ate street dogs and cats; others starved.

When it comes to food, cities suck in a crisis. It is usually the lack of food or the impossibility to acquire it that starts the rioting and looting when TSHTF. When it comes to security things get even more complicated.

Forget about shooting those that mean you harm from 300 yards away with your MBR. Leave that notion to armchair commandos and 12 year old kids that pretend to be grown ups on the internet.

Some facts:

   1) Those that want to harm you/steal from you don't come with a pirate flag waving over their heads.

   2) Neither do they start shooting at you 200 yards away.

   3) They wont come riding loud bikes or dressed with their orange, convict just escaped from prison jump suits, so that you can identify them the better. Nor do they all wear chains around their necks and leather jackets. If I had a dollar for each time a person that got robbed told me, "They looked like NORMAL people, dressed better than we are", honestly, I would have enough money for a nice gun. There are exceptions, but don't expect them to dress like in the movies.

   4) A man with a wife and two or three kids can't set up a watch. I don't care if you are SEAL, SWAT or John Freaking Rambo, no 6th sense is going to tell you that there is a guy pointing a gun at your back when you are trying to fix the water pump that just broke, or carrying a big heavy bag of dried beans you bought that morning.

The best alarm system anyone can have in a farm are dogs. But dogs can get killed and poisoned. A friend of mine had all four dogs poisoned on his farm one night, they all died.

After all these years I learned that even though the person that lives out in the country is safer when it comes to small time robberies, that same person is more exposed to extremely violent home robberies. Criminals know that they are isolated and their feeling of invulnerability is boosted.

When they assault a country home or farm, they will usually stay there for hours or days torturing the owners. I heard it all: women and children getting raped, people tied to the beds and tortured with electricity, beatings, burned with acetylene torches.

Big cities aren't much safer for the survivalist that decides to stay in the city. He will have to face express kidnappings, robberies, and pretty much risking getting shot for what's in his pockets or even his clothes.

So, where to go? The concrete jungle is dangerous and so is living away from it all, on your own.

The solution is to stay away from the cities but in groups, either by living in a small town-community or sub division, or if you have friends or family that think as you do, form your own small community.

Some may think that having neighbors within "shouting" distance means loosing your privacy and freedom, but it's a price that you have to pay if you want to have someone to help you if you ever need it. To those that believe that they will never need help from anyone because they will always have their rifle at hand, checking the horizon with their scope every five minutes and a first aid kit on their back packs at all times.... Grow up

SERVICES
Whatever sort of scenario you are dealing with, services are more than likely to either suffer in quality or disappear all together. Think ahead of time, analyze possible SHTF scenarios and which service should be affected by it in your area.

Think about the most likely scenario but also think outside the box. What's more likely? A tornado? But a terrorist attack isn't as crazy as you though it would be a few years ago, isn't it?
Also analyze the consequences of those services going down. If there is no power then you need to do something about all that meat you have in the fridge, you can dry it or can it. Think about the supplies you would need for these tasks before you actually need them.

You have a complete guide on how to prepare the meat on you computer... how will you get it out of there if there is no power? Print everything that you consider important.

WATER
No one can last too long without water. The urban survivalist may find that the water is of poor quality, in which case he can make good use of a water filter, or that there is no water available at all. When this happens, a large city were millions live will run out of bottled water within minutes.

In my case, tap water isn't very good. I can see black little particles and some other stuff that looks like dead algae. Taste isn't that bad. Not good but I know that there are parts of the country where it is much worse. To be honest, a high percentage of the country has no potable water at all.

If you can build a well, do so, set it as your top of the list priority as a survivalist. Water comes before firearms, medicines and even food.

Save as much water as you can. Use plastic bottles, refill soda bottles and place them in a cool place, preferably inside a black garbage bag to protect it from sun light. The water will pick some plastic taste after a few months, but water that tastes a little like plastic is far way better than no water at all.

What ever the kind of SHTF scenario you are dealing with, water will suffer. In my case the economical crash created problems with the water company, that reduces the maintenance and quality in order to reduce costs and keep their income in spite of the high prices they have to pay for supplies and equipment, most of which comes from abroad, and after the 2001 crash, costs 3 times more.

As always, the little guy gets to pay for it.

Same would go for floods or chemical or biological attacks. Water requires delicate care and it will suffer when TSHTF in one way or another. In this case, when you still have tap water, a quality filter is in order, as well as a pump if you can have one. A manual pump would be ideal as well if possible.

Estimate that you need a approximately a gallon per person per day. Try to have at least two-four weeks worth of water. More would be preferable.

POWER
I spent WAY to much time without power for my own taste. Power has always been a problem in my country, even before the 2001 crisis.

The real problem starts when you spend more than just a few hours without light. Just after the SHTF in 2001 half the country went without power for 3 days.

Buenos Aires was one big dark grave. People got caught on elevators, food rot, hospitals that only had a few hours worth of fuel for their generators ran out of power.

Without power, days get to be a lot shorter. Once the sun sets there is not much you can do.

I read under candle light and flashlight light and your head starts to hurt after a while. You can work around the house a little bit but only as long as you don't need power tools. Crime also increases once the lights go out, so whenever you have to go somewhere in a black out, carry the flashlight on one hand and a handgun on the other.

Summarizing, being in a city without light turn to be depressing after a while. I spent my share of nights, alone, listening to the radio, eating canned food and cleaning my guns under the light of my LED head lamp. Then I got married, had a son, and found out that when you have loved ones around you black outs are not as bad. The point is that family helps morale on these situations.

A note on flashlights. Have two or three head LED lights. They are not expensive and are worth their weight in gold. A powerful flashlight is necessary, something like a big Maglite or better yet a SureFire, specially when you have to check your property for intruders. But for more mundane stuff like preparing food, going to the toilet or doing stuff around the house, the LED headlamp is priceless. Try washing the dishes on the dark while holding a 60 lumen flashlight on one hand and you'll know what I mean. LEDs also have the advantage of lasting for almost an entire week of continuous use and the light bulb lasts forever.

Rechargeable batteries are a must (ed. Get a solar powered battery charger) or else you'll end up broke if lights go out often. Have a healthy amount of spare quality batteries and try to standardize as much as you can.

I have 12 Samsung NM 2500Mh AA and 8 AAA 800mh for the headlamps. I use D cell plastic adaptors in order to use AA batteries on my 3 D cell Maglite. This turned out to work quite well, better than I expected.

I also keep about 2 or 3 packs of regular, Duracell batteries just in case. These are supposed to expire around 2012, so I can forget about them until I need them.

Rechargeable NM batteries have the disadvantage of loosing power after a period of time, so keep regular batteries as well and check the rechargeable ones every once in a while.

After all these years of problems with power, what two items I would love to have?

1) The obvious. A generator. I carried my fridge food to my parents house way to many times on the past. Too bad I can't afford one right now.

2) A battery charger that has both solar panel and a small crank. They are not available here. I saw that they are relatively inexpensive in USA. Do yourself a favor and get one or two of these. Even if they don't charge as well as regular ones, I'm sure it will put out enough power to charge batteries for LED lamps at least.

GAS

Gas has decreased in quality as well, there is little gas. Try to have an electric oven in case you have to do without it.

If both electricity and gas go down, one of those camping stoves can work as well, if you keep a good supply of gas cans.

The ones that work with liquid fuel seem to be better on the long run, since they can use different types of fuel.

You can only store a limited amount of compressed gas and once you ran out of it, you are on your own if stores are closed of they sold them out.

Anyway, a city that goes without gas and light for more than two weeks is a death trap, get out of there before it's too late.

A DIFFERENT MENALITY

I was watching the People & Art channel with my wife the other night. It was a show where they film a couple for a given period of time and some people vote on who is the one with the worst habits, the one they find more annoying.

We were in our bed, and this is when I usually fall asleep but since the guy was a firearms police instructor I was interested and managed to stay awake.

At one point the guy's wife said that she found annoying that her husband spent 500 dollars a month on beauty products for himself. 500 USD on facial cream, special shampoo and conditioner, as well as having his nails polished! If you are that guy and happen to be reading this, or if you know him, I'm sorry, but what an idiot!!

"500 USD, that's a small generator or a gun and a few boxes of ammo" I told my wife.

"That's two months worth of food" she said.

We were each thinking of a practical use for that money, the money this guy was practically throwing away.

Once the SHTF, money is no longer measured in money, but you start seeing it as the necessary goods it can buy. Stuff like food, medicine, gas, or the private medical service bill. To me, spending 500 dollars on beauty products, and to make it worse, on a guy? That's simply not acceptable.

The way I see it, someone with that mentality can't survive a week without a credit card, no use in even considering a SHTF scenario. And this guy is a firearms instructor?... probably the kind of guy that will say that a handgun is only used to fight his way to his rifle... and his facial night cream...

Once you experience the lack of stuff you took for granted, like food , medicines, your set of priorities change all of a sudden. For example, I had two wisdom tooth removed last year. On both occasions I was prescribed with antibiotics and strong Ibuprofen for the pain. I took the antibiotics(though I did buy two boxes with the same recipe just to keep one box just in case) but I didn't use the Ibuprofen, I added it to my pile of medicines.

Why? because medicines are not always available and I'm not sure if they will be available in the future. Sure, it hurt like hell, but pain alone isn't going to kill you, so I sucked it up. Good for building up character if you ask me . Make sacrifices so as to ensure a better future, that's the mentality you should have if you want to be prepared. There's stuff that is "nice to have" that has to be sacrificed to get the indispensable stuff.

There's stuff that is not "basic need stuff" but it's also important in one way or another.

My wife goes to the hairdresser once every month or two. It's not life or death, but it does make her feel better and it boosts her morale. I buy a game for the Xbox or a movie to watch with my wife every once in awhile, just to relax. 7 or 10 dollars a month are not going to burn a hole in my pocket.

Addictions such as alcohol, drugs or even cigarettes should be avoided by the survivalist. They are bad for your health, cost a lot of money that could be much better spent, and create an addiction to something that may not be available in the future.

Who will have to tolerate your grouchy mood when your brand of smokes is no longer imported after TSHTF?

GRAY/BLACK MARKET
Once the SHTF the black/gray market will take no time to appear all around you.

In my country, gray markets were even accepted in the end. At first it was all about trading skills or craft products for food. Districts and towns would form their own barter markets, and created their own tickets, similar to money, that was used to trade.

This didn't last long. Those tickets were easy to make on your home computer, there was no control and eventually people went back to paper money.

These markets were usually placed on warehouses or empty land, and were managed by some wise guy and a few thugs or hired security.

Anyone can go rent a kiosk inside these markets for about 50-100 pesos (about 20-30 dollars) a day and sell his goods and services.

Piece within these markets is usually respected... lets just say that these managers don't call the police if someone tries anything funny, like stealing, fighting or taking advantage of women. That's not good for their business and anyone that tries to mess with their business finds out how much pain the human body can actually experiment or gets a free ticket to meet the Lord.
Sometimes even uniformed cops manage security on these markets, for a small fee of course. As always, you still have to be careful. They may still try to pick your pockets or even attack you once you leave the market. Once you leave the market, you are on your own, as always.

This market evolves, and now a lot of different products are available. Today I visited my local market, a warehouse that is fairly well set up and cleanly managed. They had problems for selling stolen merchandise and fake Brand name clothes a few days ago.

What can be found at a local markets? Mostly food and clothing. Some have more variety than others but cheese, canned food, spices, honey, eggs, fruits, vegetables, beer, wine and cured meat are generally available, same as bakery products and pasta. These are less expensive than those found at supermarkets. Fresh fish is sometimes available but not always, people don't trust much products that need refrigeration, and they get those at supermarkets instead.

Clothes are also popular and you can find copies of brand name clothes, imitations, or even original stolen new clothes, the same goes for shoes and snickers. Children clothes, underwear, socks, sheets and towels are all very popular. Some sell toys, but they are always China made, mostly poor quality though there are some few exceptions.

Others sell tools, also made in China can be found as well, but they are of poor quality.

Some offer their services and repair stuff or offer work as handyman.

You would be amazed of the junk that these guys manage to fix: TVs, CD players, Power tools, etc. They even manage to solder the small integrated circuits boards sometimes. Give one of these guys a screw driver and a bar of chocolate and he will fix a nuclear submarine.

After food and clothes, the 3rd most popular item has to be CDs and DVDs, movies, music, play station 2 and Xbox games, programs, it all ends up there just one or two days after the official release in USA. Seems that they have a guy hidden under Bill Gate's desk or something.

Anyway, almost everything can be found there, and if you want, you can ask around, talk to the right guy and buy illegal stuff like drugs or black market guns and ammo. The quality of the drugs is questionable, of course, and a lot of addicts die from the mixtures these guys sell. Guns are mostly FM High Powers, Surplus 1911s and Colt .45s, Sistemas, and old Colt Detective revolvers in 38 special that found their way from police and military armories into the black market. Condition isn't very good but if you have money you'll be amazed of what you can end up with. Everything that is used by the military and police, including SMGs a, Browning 50 BMG Machine guns, and even frag grenades, is available in the black market, if the customer has the amount of money and a little patience, of course. The big guns may take a while, but the handguns and grenades are readily available.

GOLD & SILVER
Someone hit me in the head please because I messed up about the gold issue.

Everyone wants to buy gold! "I buy gold. Pay cash" signs are everywhere, even on TV! I can't believe I'm that silly!

I just didn't relate it to what I read here because they deal with junk gold, like jewelry, either stolen or sold because they needed the money, not the gold coins that you guys talk about. No one pays for the true value of the stuff, so big WARNING! Sign on people that are buying gold coins.

Since it is impossible to determine the true mineral percentage of gold, small shops and dealers will pay for it as regular jewelry gold.

What I would do if I were you: Besides gold coins, buy a lot of small gold rings and other jewelry. They should be less expensive than gold coins, and if the SHTF bad, you'll not be losing money, selling premium quality gold coins for the price of junk gold. If I could travel back in time, I'd buy a small bag worth of gold rings.

Small time thieves will snatch gold chains right out of your neck and sell them at these small dealers found everywhere. This is VERY common at train stations, subways and other crowded areas.

So, my advice, if you are preparing for a small economical crisis, gold coins make sense. You will keep the value of the stuff and be able to sell it for its actual cost to gold dealers or maybe other survivalists that know the true value of the item.

In my case, gold coins would have been an excellent investment, saving me from loosing money when the local economy crashed. Even though things are bad, I can go to a bank down town and get paid for what a gold coin is truly worth, same goes for pure silver. But where I live, in my local are small time dealers will only pay you the value of junk gold, no matter what kind of gold you have. So, I'd have to say that if TSHTF bad, gold jewelry is a better trade item than gold coins.

GUNS, AMMO AND OTHER GEAR
After TSHTF in 2001, only the most narrow minded, brain washed, butterfly IQ level idiots believed that the police would protect them from the crime wave that followed the collapse of our economy.

A lot of people that could have been considered antigun before, ran to the gun shops, seeking advise on how to defend themselves and their families. They would buy a 38 revolver, a box of ammo, and leave it in the closet, probably believing that it would magically protect them from intruders.

Oh, maybe you don't think that firearms are really necessary or your beliefs do not allow you to buy a tool designed to kill people. So you probably ask yourself, is a gun really necessary when TSHTF? Will it truly make a difference?

Having gone through a shtf scenario myself, total economical collapse in the year 2001, and still dealing with the consequences, 5 years later, I feel I can answer that question.

YES, you need a gun, pepper spray, a machete, a battle axe, club with a rusty nail sticking out of it, or whatever weapon you can get hold of.

A LOT has been written on survival weapons. Everyone that is into armed survival has his or her own idea of the ideal gun battery. Some more oriented to a hunting point of view, others only as self defense means and others consider a little of both, and look for general purpose weapons.

Talking about guns, there is one special subject I want to rectify, and it's the point on what's the primary weapon for the survivalist, specially a urban survivalist that has to function in a society, yes, even after the SHTF.

People, if you are interested in real world SHTF situation, and you want to prepared for the real deal, then understand that this isn't black or white.
You wake up one day and listen on the radio that the economy collapsed and that the stock market closed indefinitely.

CRIME AND INSECURITY

Even though crime has always been an issue in South America, my country was quite the exception. It was dangerous, yes but nothing like after the 2001 economical crisis. One used to be able to let kids play on the sidewalk, or walk back home from a party, a few blocks, and be somewhat safe. This all changed now. There are no kids playing on the sidewalks anymore. I should emphasize this a little more. There are absolutely NO kids playing on the sidewalks at all, at any time of the day. Maybe a kid rides his bike a few meters on the sidewalk, but always under the supervision of an adult. A kid riding a bike on his own will get that bike stolen in no time, probably get hurt in the process, therefore no responsible parent leaves a kid alone on the street. Teenagers present a greater problem. You can't keep a 15 or 16 year old inside a house all day long, and even though they are big enough to go out on their own, when the sun goes down things get much worse.

This is when parents organize themselves; either taking them to someone's house or to a club and picking them up at a certain time. Taxis and remises are used sometimes , but there have been lots of cases of girls getting raped, so no parent worth a buck leaves his son or daughter in hands of a stranger. After years of living like this, almost everyone learned to be careful; sometimes they had to learn the hard way. Practically no one leaves a door or window opened or unlocked. Nor do they hang out in front of the house talking to friends. A bad guy might just see you there, like a sitting duck, pull a gun on you and take you inside your house.

There are no "bandit's law" anymore. One used to hear people talk about "You shouldn't resist a robbery, give them what they want and they'll go away". That holds true no more. These guys are under the influence of drugs, epoxy glue, or just hate your guts so much, because you have a better life than they ever dreamed of, because they were

abused since the day they were born, that they will hurt and humiliate you as much as they can. Letting a criminal inside you house almost guaranties you that he will rape/ beat/ torture and abuse whoever they find inside.

I personally drew a line a few years ago and decided, after one long, serious conversation with my wife; that no one would be allowed inside the house, no matter what. We figured that there are worse things than death. Having decided that, I make sure I always have a weapon on me. They'll have to pay dearly for my life, plus interests.

By far, the most dangerous moment of the day, is when I (or my wife) leave/enter my house. A solid, secure house cannot be broken in easily, so criminals wait until you are standing on front of the door with the keys on your hand to jump on you. This is why we are extra alert when approaching our house, look all around us and if we see anything strange, keep walking around the block or keep on driving. No door is ever opened when there is a strange person around. Whenever someone knocks on our door (and we don't know him/her), they are answered from a second story window. Criminals sometimes disguise as electric company guys or something like that, saying that they have to fix something. NO! If there is something to be fixed they can fix it on the sidewalk. Anything inside your house is your responsibility and the company is not going to fix it for you. Either way, it's always better to play it safe, Better to be rude than dead.

On the car/driving issue, that calls for an entire post dedicated to SHTF driving. For now I'll just say that windows and doors have to be closed at all times, a weapon must be within arms reach, and that stop signs and traffic lights have a hole new meaning once TSHTF. If your country ever falls as mine did, you'll remember me whenever you see a traffic light. You never stop at a red lights or stop sign unless there is traffic, especially at night.

At first, police would write you a ticket for not stopping at a red light if they saw you (another way of saying that they will ask for a bribe if they see you pass a red light), but after a few months they realized that nothing could be done, people would rather risk a ticket than risking their lives, so they decided to turn traffic lights to permanent yellow at night, after 8 or 9 PM. This is, of course, very dangerous. Night car accidents are both frequent and brutal since sometimes both cars hit each other at full speed.

MissinLink asked some good questions that might interest others as well, and since we are on the security issue, here they are:

"Do the invaders of homes in the country just drive up in cars or trucks? Do they hide and sneak up? How do these home invaders attack a home in the country? A similar question could be asked for homes in the city."

Sometimes they just drive up to where you are working, if you are far away from the home, but most of the time they sneak up on you. Criminals are not stupid, and they will spend days checking the place and specially YOUR ROUTINE. For example, if they see that you lock the gate at night, as most do, they will wait for you behind a tree until you are close. This is done a lot. Dogs are the best alarm you can find, and criminals know that. They will poison them with pills when you go to sleep and attack the place in the middle of the night. I know of many that had their dogs killed. If they think that security is tight, they will just hide near the main gate, and wait for you to leave or return. When you stop at the gate and must get out of the truck to open/close the main gate, they attack. I'd say that the most frequent kind of attack is attacking by surprise when you enter/leave your home.

"Most common times of attack? Day night evening morning? I understand occur when coming or going from ones home, etc."

7 am, 9 am, 1pm 7pm, all are common times for attacks. There is no "safe" hour of the day. Night is particularly dangerous. Maybe attacks during the day are faster, they want to get some money or jewelry and leave fast, while at night they might stay inside more time, maybe till the next day. But there are no fixed patterns. If I could give one advice concerning SHTF security, it would be: Eyes and ears wide open when you enter/leave your home. If possible, keep a gun on your hand when doing either one. If something looks, even "feels strange, then go around the block and check again, carefully. If you see them still there, either call the police (if still available) or get help. If you approach the house with a large number of people they will leave. One time, I saw a couple of strange looking guys at my door. I went round the block and saw them still there. I started flashing the car lights and the horn and they left. I had a gun with me, though, so be careful when trying this. Also, remember that a car is one heavy, powerful piece of machinery. I know a guy that had one of those big chrome-tube bumpers installed on his truck, especially for hitting those that were stupid enough to try and make him stop by standing in front of the car.

If I had a truck, I would do so myself. Though I would keep my mouth shut about it, as always. Just say that you think it looks cool or something. Every now and then someone tries to force me to stop my car by standing in front of it (I suppose there are still fools out there that get robbed this way), in the middle of the street. I just aim at them and accelerate at full speed. They always jump out of the way before I hit them. By the way, at first, doing this made me feel nervous, but can you believe that now it's just common driving, as normal as changing gears? I guess it's a little sad.

Studying the SHTF at the University: Dark omens:

I forgot it! Darn, same as the gold stuff but worse, much worse. I've never been good at remembering some things, like numbers and names of people I meet, I forget those (instantly), they just flee my mind, uneventfully, but I do remember some other things that don't seem to be as important. I do remember living in USA as a kid. I remember my school, Pierce School, Don't remember exactly were it was, because we lived some in Boston, Massachusetts and some in New Hampshire. I remember my best friend, Freddy, and a girl (why is there always a girl?) Samantha, Sam. She was red haired and tall, I had a picture of her playing together but I lost it. Some time between the age of 3 and 26 I lost that picture that was so dear to me. I remember the smell of an orange shaped "scratch and smell" sticker my kindergarten teacher stuck in a small book we made once. But I almost forgot this forever. This, this was important, a moment where the life we once knew stopped existing, and a group of students, in a class room that looked like and abandoned building, realized it, all 60 of us at the same time.
It's 1:06 AM over here. I just finished showering and my wife and son are asleep. I was putting shampoo on my hair, thinking about what I wrote today on this post, and remembered the exact moment when I realized along with several other people, not only that TSHTF (that we all knew) but that the world we once new no longer existed, and that this was not a hurricane, this was an ice age period, it wouldn't just go away.

We understood it the same way a kid understands photosynthesis: Because a teacher coldly explained it to us, even used graphics. I slept 5 hours yesterday, 2 hours the day before yesterday. Saturday night I didn't sleep at all. I'm already used to it. Deadlines at the University, staying late at night, drawing in CAD 3D, waiting until Renders are ready. It's a competitive world out there, and no one sympathizes with what you are going through, they just want you to perform as expected, and the standard is always high. It happened 4 years ago, almost a year after the December 2001 crisis. It was a social studies class and this teacher, don't remember if it was a he or a she, was explaining the different kinds of social pyramids. God! Now I remember more!

We even had a text book with those darn, cruel pyramids! The first pyramid explained the basic society. A pyramid with two horizontal lines, dividing those on top (high social class) those in the middle (middle class) and the bottom of the pyramid (the poor, proletarian). The teacher explained that the middle of the pyramid, the middle class, acted as a cushion between the rich and the poor, taking care of the social stress. The second pyramid had a big middle section, this was the pyramid that represents 1st world countries. I which the bottom is very thin and arrows show that there is a possibility to go from low to middle class, and from middle to the top of the social pyramid. Our teacher explained that this was the classic, democratic capitalist society, and that on countries such as Europeans one, socialists, the pyramid was very similar but a little more flat, meaning that here is a big middle section, middle class, and small high and low class. There is little difference between the three of them.

The third pyramid showed the communist society. Where arrows from the low and middle class tried to reach the top but they bounced off the line. A small high society and one big low society, cushioned by a minimal middle class section of pyramid. Then we turned the page and saw the darned fourth pyramid. This one had arrows from the middle class dropping to the low, poor class.

"What is this?" Some of us asked.

The teacher looked at us. "This is us"

"It's the collapsed country, a country that turns into 3rd world country like in pyramid five where there is almost no middle class to speak, one huge low, poor class , and a very small, very rich, top class."

"What are those arrows that go from the middle to the bottom of the pyramid?" Someone asked.

You could hear a pin drop. "That is middle class turning into poor".

I won't lie, no one cried, though people rubbed their faces, held their heads and their breath.

No one cried, but we all knew at that very moment that all we thought, all we took for granted, simply was not going to happen.

"You see, the income from the middle class is not enough to function as middle class any more. Some from the top class fall to middle class, but the vast majority of the middle class turns into poor" Said the teacher.

I don't know how many people in that room suddenly understood that he/she was poor.

The teacher continued "You see, we have a middle class that suddenly turns to poor, creating a society of basically poor people, there is no more middle class to cushion tensions any more. Middle class suddenly discovers that they are overqualified for the jobs they can find and have to settle for anything they can obtain, there for unemployment sky rockets, too much to offer, too little demand. You see they prepare, study for a job they are not going to get. You kids, you are studying Architecture because you simply wish to do so. Only 3 or 4 percent of you will actually find a job related to architecture."

We all sat there, letting it all sink in. After a few months, it all proved to be true. Even the amount of students that dropped out of college increased to at least 50%. They either so no point in studying something that would not make much of a difference in their future salaries, had no money to keep themselves in college, or simply had to drop college to work and support their families.

Someone once said, in this forum, that if this had happened in USA, the social unrest would have been much worse, because people from S. America are stronger. At first, I told him that I didn't think so, I said that all humans adapt when they have no other choice. But now that I consider it more, maybe he was right. Not that S. Americans are stronger, but they are more used to adversities. Most of us are children from grandparents that escaped civil war, either in Spain or dictators in Italy, our parents survived the dirty war, even more dictators, and therefore their children are of strong character too. Can USA citizens survive what we survived? Of course they can, though I think that there are too many that are not like you, many that don't prepare, and take everything for granted. Those are the ones that will be responsible for the increase in the social unrest once the SHTF, those that were too lazy to take care of themselves before the SHTF, or that had gone soft through out the years, believing that the government will "take care of them because they pay their taxes". But in the end, they will pull through. People will adapt, they always do. You'd be surprised. And those that don't want to adapt to the new reality they live in, will die young, thus cleaning the gene pool and ensuring the continuity of the specie. It's been this way for thousands of years.

MISCELLANEOUS Q&A
Don't prepare for an idiot shooting a Raven at you 200 yards away, prepare for the sneaky son of a gun that waits until you are distracted, fed the dogs some nice pills, and gets to you when you less expect him. THAT is much more likely than someone attacking you 200 yards away.

I didn't mean it as an insult to anyone, I'm well aware that there are cases of people shooting enemies 1000 yards away. That is war. Killing someone that wants you dead before he gets close to you is perfectly logical.

Please name me one case of self defense where the person shot the bad guy 100 yards away.

I had a guy try to steal my car a while ago while visiting a friend at his farm.

I saw the guy next to my car about 300 meters away. I had my FAL PARA with me, since we where going to spend some time shooting that morning.

I could have shot that guy from a safe distance, right? But you can't do that in real life. People that shoot others 300 meters away for no reason, claiming self defense, are called psychos. I had to fold my rifle, hide it under my coat, walk to where my car and the guy where, and ask him what he wanted. When he said that he was there to take the car I leveled my FAL at him, and as it usually happens in real life, the guy almost pissed his pants, and left, babbling some BS story I no longer remember.

If someone starts shooting at you 300 yards away, and you shoot back in self defense , that's ok, but that rarely, if ever, happens.

Any bad guy that has survived through puberty will be smart enough to get close, very close, maybe when you are distracted with some chore/fieldwork and point a gun at you, asking you to calm down and walk into the house.

No way can you know what a man's intentions are 200 yards away, unless he starts shooting at you like an idiot. And if he wants you dead that bad, he will get close enough and make sure that that one shot is the last thing you hear on this planet.

As I said, dogs are the best alarm on the field, though those too can be eliminated, as it happened to my friend. A shame by the way, they were nice dogs.

But if your idea of a self defense plan is shooting anyone that happens to be within your 200 yard range, do as you wish. You will not have to worry much about survival, State penitentiary will provide all you need.

It is one thing to go to war, and it is another, completely different, to live your life in a SHTF situation. When you deploy in a war zone, you set yourself mentally to do a job, when the job is done, you return home, you turn the mental combat switch off.

You cannot live your entire life as if you where in combat, it's impossible.

I'm as alert as I can be, all day long, and all night. Thanks to that I kept my family and myself safe, while everyone else I know has at least been involved in one or more violent crimes. I'm so winded up that the slightest sound will make jump out of bed at night and have my pistol ready even before I'm conscious of what I'm doing.

My house is the only one in the block that has not been broken into, my wife and son are safe, safer than all the other stupid sheep that blame God for whatever happens to them, and do nothing to prevent it themselves.

But still, you have to live your life, go to work, go to the supermarket... live a life! do everyday stuff.

The stress of living that way will be the end of you, I'm 26 years old and already have problems related to high stress like high blood pressure, migraines, insomnia, etc.
NSA

"You make it sound like carrying a pistol on your person is a fairly common occurance (at least now)."

My mistake, it is not common, at least for descent working people. There are parts were criminals carry their guns openly, sticking out of their joggings and no one does anything about it. No one dares mess with them, these are neighborhoods were police don't dare to enter.

Carrying a handgun, ready for use (loaded and on your person) is illegal, unless you have a permit that is almost impossible to get. You need to own a large company, and justify carrying the gun because you transport large amounts of money (several thousands of USD on daily basis). Carrying a gun for self defense is not a reason for a carry permit, only the protection of money. It's ridiculous, isn't it?

Still, owning handguns is not that complicated, once you get a gun user card, but a ccw permit card is out of the question.

Some gun users still choose to carry guns, even though they don't have a carry permit. This is not allowed and you might loose your gun user card for this.

Carrying a gun, bought in the black market, and without even having a gun user card, will take you straight to jail.

On the issue of cops and guns, some may understand that you are carrying for self defense, because you are in a very dangerous area, and if you have you gun user card that shows that you bought that gun legally, he MAY be sensitive and let you go, or not.

More than likely, he will ask for a small "tip", for his troubles. It's a matter of luck actually. You have to consider all this, and decide if the risk of getting caught is greater than the risk of getting killed for not being able to defend yourself.

We often call unprepared people, the mass, sheep. Sheep describes them pretty well. They do as the rest of them do, don't fight for their rights, accept almost everything and so on. But what happens when "sheep" get desperate? Well, that 's what happened here.

After years of closing factories and the destruction of the national industry, extremely low wages, people got fed up. This destructive economy by Menem, our previous president, one of the most corrupt president in the history, (he was into the bombing of the jew embassy, managed the drug market in the country, just to mention some) plus the stupidity of the following president, De la RÃºa, was a formula for disaster.

One day the Minister of Economy declared that no one would be able to get more than 100 bucks a day from the ATM(correct?) nor close accounts. You could just get 100 bucks out of the bank a day. That was it.

Then came the devaluation. Before this happened 1 U$S= 1 $ Argentine peso. Suddenly this changed into 1 U$S dollar= 2 peso then 2.5 even 4 pesos. Today 1U$S= 3 Pesos.
The banks kept the people's money, including their deposits in US dollars. If you had 1000 U$S dollars in Bank Boston for example, they turned it into 1000 pesos, that equaled 333 U$S dollars. They stole 666 dollars from you!

Prices went up 200%, 300% and sometimes more. Imagine for one moment what your life would be like if today you go to your local 7-11 and everything has gone up 200%. How would you survive with your pay check?

The sheep got desperate. First, because they had been stolen by banks and wouldn't return the money to the people. (the so called "corralito") then because the classes with the lowest income found out that their salaries weren't high enough to buy the minimum food stuff to survive. The country marched asking for the presidents resignation. He had to leave the presidential palace in a chopper...

Banks were destroyed by people that wanted their hard earned money back. Supermarkets and other shops were looted, as well as regular houses.

This lasted for about a month, the chaos spread all over the country, concentrated in the largest cities.

I remember being at a supermarket and the mob outside, negotiating with the manager. Sometimes, they would not destroy the place if the supermarket surrendered them the goods peacefully.

Food got scarce. I mean, you could buy just a certain amount of milk or water, 4 bottles for example. And most imported goods disappeared. Electro domestics such as TV, videos, and refrigerators kept their prices in dollars, inaccessible for most people. The same happened with real estates, cars and luxury goods.

Today this all seems far away. Not because it got better, but because us humans have this damn capacity to " get used to".

How did our lives change? I cant even being to explain... everything changed!

The streets are more dangerous than ever, thanks to the general poverty.

Education suffered thanks to this as well. Kids working or stealing to survive instead of going to school.
How could I explain this to you?....

For example, tools are really expensive, since most come from abroad... remember, our national industry was sold out or destroyed.

Stuff like MRE, Emergency food bars are impossible to get. No one imports them anymore. (I paid 10 dollars for 1 MRE a guy had)
Guns and ammo are really expensive and are sold in small quantities.

Forget about buying a "case" of ammo! Forget it! I know it's hard for some of you to imagine this, but you just can't buy a " case" of anything. A large store may have 10 or 15 boxes of 308, 20 rounds each box. Small stores have 10. or less.

Only common ammo is available such as 22, 38, 357. 9mm, some 40 s&w, 12 ga 308 and a little 223, that's pretty much it. Ammo for my 357 sig is hard to get. I buy a box of it every time I find one around... and it's extremely expensive.

IF you just HAVE to buy something strange like 300 magnum or 270 (strange for us J) there's one place you can get them from but be prepared to pay +100 dollars for 20 rounds. While we are at it, there are also few models of guns, 70 % of it is used. You can find about 4 or 5 12 ga pumps, mossberg 500, Maverick or Rem 870 in each store. Handguns are relatively plentiful, not the newest models but still there's some Beretta, Glock, Colt, S&W, Walther, Taurus, Rossi and Sig. Same goes for Mausers and bolt action rifles as well as side by side shotguns.

Semi auto rifles are hard to get. Some big gun shops have 1 FAL each. M16 are quite rare and expensive. Saw a Galil and a SKS(600 dollars) the other day, but it's not common and the red tape is HUGE. I found a good FMK3, one of the few left around, and bought it for 250 dollars, but this isn't common.

Shoes and clothes are also, expensive, even in U$S. Labor is cheep; you can have a maid and a gardener for 300 dollars. There's no "safe" job. With 20% unemployment they pay you whatever they want and if you don't like it there are 100 persons waiting to get your job. Owning a shop-business is hard. You have to consider armed robbery (some get hit 10 times a month) and still you have to pay the police for protection (from themselves) Hope it helps, at least so you can have an idea how your world would be if this happened in your country, hope you never have to experience it in the flesh...

Well, one thing I learned with all this is that people adapt, people get "used to".

And finally, people accept.

I have a hard time seeing people eat out of trash cans, that's one thing I'll never get used to.

Every night entire families, wife, husband and 2 or 3 kids, little kids about 3 years old go throw trash cans in search of food.

At almost every light stop there's little bare foot kids begging, all dirty and skinny.

That's the thing that affected me most, the starving children.

One guy in another board told me he didn't care for this "bleeding Heart thing" and that "Life is rough. Get used to it." I told him that I didn't need someone that lives in San Diego, California, explain me how rough life is.

I've seen dead people, man, I once saw a guy "sew" his mouth shut with a piece of rusted wire he got out of a broom, and all that I can handle, but a 3 year old sobbing because he's starving, Im sorry, I can't.

Believe me, it's one thing to see a little kid starving in Africa, you probably saw that terrible image a million times, but now imagine that that kid speaks English, with an American accent, and you see the Hollywood sign in the background.

Both cases are terrible, but the one that looks as if he could be your son and not some kid in Africa or Croatia hits a nerve. Because "those things don't happen here". It happens to others, not in my country, not in my neck of the woods.

Sorry , Im babbling here. Back to your question:

You guys have most stuff covered, but there's some stuff I'd like to share:

1) Don't invest all your money in your country. Don't put all your eggs in the same basket, just in case economy goes to hell. Invest in a country in Europe, in Australia, whatever, I don't know, but not in the same place. I did this, but most people didn't and got screwed.

2) Keep cash. Both dollars and Euros. I know some of you just don't like the European money, but it's the only way you have to cover most bases. Here the national paper money was worth 1/3 from one day to another.

3) If you have land, have some animals. Even a few chickens and rabbits can make a huge difference and will complement your staple food.

4) Buy guns and ammo. Not 20, but a couple of fighting guns, 1 or 2 Mausers and 2 or 3 handguns. You know the kind. Get lots of 22 ammo.

5) Try to get 2 or 3 similar guns, like 2 or 3 AR, Fals, or SKS. This way you can use the same ammo and if 2 guns brake you may be able to fix 1. For example, If I were you, Id buy 3 or 4 SKS and 3000 rounds of ammo. If your SKS brakes, you have a spare gun that you already know how it works and are used to.

6) Spare parts are ok, but make sure you know how to replace them, a gunsmith may not be available. If not, get a similar gun as back up.

7) Don't trust the media. If you watch the news here, reporters say everything is ok, everything is fine. But then you talk to your neighbor and it turns out Mr. X got shot yesterday, the nice girl on the next block got kidnapped and raped, and today the boy next door was also kidnapped. This is the kind of conversations I have in my neighborhood, I'm not kidding.

8) Keep 6 months- a year worth of food stored if you can and have a well or at least a good supply of bottled water stored as well a 2 water purifier and a good supply of filters for them. The water network works but it's not safe. Some time ago an entire town got sick because of the contaminated tap water and lots of people died.

9) B-proof vest. I'd sell my left testicle for one these days. I never believed I would ever need one and now here I am. Get one of those that can go under the regular clothes.

10) Keep your passport and cash ready. If you can afford it, the best thing to do in such a country is getting the hell out of it! Maybe you have family somewhere else, keep in touch just in case. I did with my family in Spain and I going there as soon as I can.

"What about essential services like power and water?"
Power get cut some times but not for long , a couple of flash lights and your ok.

Water is still working but you cant drink. Most of the water supply in Bs As shouldn't be drank, I used to drink it but this year the water was just too dirty. Even if we still pay our water bill and the gov. says it's ok for drinking this water wouldn't be accepted in the US. Here the water companies can bribe their way out of it.
"Were they always delivered reliably or were there blackouts etc...."

There were blackouts, I remember once most of the country was without light for about a day. Buenos Aires was without light for 4 days.

"What about medical care, how do people get treated for injuries or illneses? "

If you have private health you are ok, but if you don't have the money for it you might as well put a bullet in your head. Free hospitalization, forget it, you'll die because of an infection. They don't have supplies, even sterile needles are hard to get in a public hospital. No way, if you don't have private health you have a foot in your grave already.

"Is the crime mostly simple street crime or is it highly organized with gangs and cartels/mafia style?

Both. The police handles most organixed crime. The governors are the head of the organizations on each Province. The worst part is the kidnapping. About 2 or 3 persons get kidnapped each day in my neighborhood.

For example, I keep 10 pesos (about 3 dollars) bills to give to the police if I get stopped when driving. You HAVE to

bride the cop that stops you, the last time I got stopped by a couple of cops I played a little hard to get (pretended I didn't understand he wanted money) the cop got really nervous so I just have him the money and he calmed down, he let me go.
The cops are involved in most illegal activities like drugs, prostitution, robbery and kidnaps.

That's why I keep the high power Hirtemberg 9mm stuff and AP 308, because there a big chance the "perp" might be wearing a "Policia Federal" body armor vest.

They ask for donations. That's right, the government asks the people for donations instead of doing things themselves.

And the best part is that once they get all the donations. (mostly food, milk, blankets and such) The damn Governors SELL the donated goods to the poor. No , you cant imagine the kind of corruption we have here.

The problem is that nothing is being done to get us on the right track, because a small group of people wants this country as poor as possible to take advantage of it.

Imagine having to pay your employees 1 dollar a day and selling the soya, meat and other agricultural products you get at international prices.

The people that own small portions of land have it worse than those professionals that are in the city. This is because they are destroyed by the larger land owners such as Benetton and other large international corporations.

But you are right, they can at least live out of their land. The poor people in cities have to collect cardboard or look in the garbage.

You are also right about people now fixing things instead of buying new ones. Seems as handyman will always find a way to survive.

The only things that can be imported are the cheep ones from China, or Brasil. Other products like large plasma TVs and such are rare and only accessible to the extremely wealthy.

For example, I had to buy a electric shaver because the Gillette blade are too expensive. No way am I going to spend 6 dollars for a pack of Gillette Sensor.

And so you adapt to whats available and what you can afford.

503

People that live in the Patagonia are a little better off than those that live in other Provinces. The rich people do well everywhere (except for the kidnaps and murder) but the poor people that live in the south have better land and can at least grow and raise a few animals. The central part of Argentina, and the North has been severely punished. TucumÃ¡n is a disaster, as well as Chaco, Entre Rios, and others, the amount of children that starve to death is astonishing.

The Chileans returned to Chile long ago, Chile is MUCH better off. Argentineans are going to Chile looking for job.

Buenos Aires is also a disaster area. Even the "nice part" of Buenos Aires, the Capital where the nice Hotels are, the part that tourists see, turns into a complete nightmare after 10 pm.

During the day tourist from around the world shop and sight see, ignoring the beggars. But at night the picture is Mad Max 4:

All the "cartoneros", people that pull carts in search of cardboard and paper to sell, flood the city. And I mean flood: 20 to 30 persons per block.

They pull the carts themselves, followed by the wife and a few children. They pick the paper out of the trashcans and eat whatever they scavenge.

The government considers them "employees" God only knows why, since they have no salaries, just the paper they get. This is just another "trick" the government has to reduce the unemployment %, considering these poor people that eat out of trashcans employed. (Our politicians have no shame)

As I write this I hear shoots being fired outside and people screaming.. jjejee, I never would have think that I would be writing this today, 3 years ago, but now it's almost normal.

Gold & silver kept their true value, as they always do. I didn't have gold, but had dollars and euros. Now that you mention it gold might be a good way to go for the Americans. Dollars, Euros and gold and you'd have most bases covered.

You can't barter gold at a supermarket for example, you would loose too much money. But you can wait until things settle and change for dollars/Euros or other stable paper money and save yourself from devaluation. Or get out of dodge with your gold and deposit it in a safe country.

The point is that gold never looses it's value because, unlike paper money, it holds value itself.

Foreign accounts could not be touched since they are protected by other countries law, not affected by national executive orders.

Imagine a federal agent calling a Suzie Bank.

"Hi, I'd like to seize Mr. Smiths accounts"
"Why?"
"Well, because I want to steal his money"...
Wouldn't work.

A LIST OF THINGS THAT "If you had it to do over again" YOU WOULD GET.

Nomad came up with this one. It's a good idea because it may help some of you from making the same mistakes I did. There are things you don't think about until you need them, and then it's too late.

OK, If I had to do all this from scratch? Say, for example, if I had a 2 year warning, fairy godmother appears one night , all dressed in blue waving a magic wand, saying " Your country will go down the sewer in 2 years, consider yourself warned dear"

There are several things I would have done differently, and things I would have bought:

Food: I'll get to the food issue soon enough, but you can never have too much canned, or other long shelf life food. This was probably one of my greatest mistakes, I overlooked the food problem.

I was talking to my wife today while driving, asked her the same question Nomad asked me "what would you do if you could go back in time, before the 2001 crisis".
My wife, though smart, isn't much into preparedness, but she answered "I'd buy food" in a heartbeat.

"Don't you remember that you could only buy one small bottle of oil at a time, same with sugar, flour and milk. Don't you remember all those empty shelves at the supermarket.?"

Definitely, more food, specially food that lasts for a few years.

CAR

I would have bought a 4x4, even though I live in the city. A 4x4 allows you to dive over the sidewalk or through wasteland, away from roadblocks or riots. I've see those that have 4x4s simply go off road, climb over a boulevard and leave while the rest of us poor car owners have to stay.

A 4x4 truck also has more mass and power in case that someone tries to cut you off or rams you with the car. It's less likely to stop running if you hit someone or several people (in a riot situation) since it's prepared for cross country use and the engine is much more protected.

Fuel containers: Not only jerry cans, but those big metal containers, that hook up like small "u-hauls" ? I'm not sure about their capacity, maybe they can hold one or two barrels of gas. I saw them at construction sites, and they were not that expensive if bought used, before the 2001 crisis. Now , I don't know. Haven't seen them for a while.

A generator: These are imported and very expensive for us. I think that they are now making them here, but I'm not sure about the quality.

A nice TV and DVD player: I know what you are thinking "this guy has gone ... "nuts" "

Please, let me explain.

Going out for dinner or to the movies is not only dangerous but also expensive. You WILL find much better use for that money if SHTF.

There are places in Buenos Aires where you can go out for dinner, movies, or theater shows and have a good time, safely. They either have their own security or arrange with the police for added security. These are the kinds of places you are likely to visit if you ever come to Argentina, places were tourists can move around, relatively safe (there are always exceptions, of course). But these places are either for tourists or for the extremely wealthy. I have a good socio-economical level, better than 96% of the population at least, yet I cant afford to spend that amount of money every weekend or even two weekends a month. Going out for a walk is a possibility, and we do go out for a walk every now and then, but lets just say that the view isn't that good, and you can only walk about 6 blocks in the same direction before you get out of the are which is guarded by private security, after that you are on "you are on your own" land. You CAN go for a walk (just like millions that live in Somalia or Afghanistan go for a walk as well) millions of citizens do, but I'd rather not risk it.

Just the day before yesterday, a young woman was waiting at the bus stop in my neighborhood, holding her 6 month old daughter. A cop that was chasing a bad guy opened fire with his High Power, with no regard to bystanders as they always do. The 9mm FMJ (JHP are not allowed for the average police) went right through the baby's buttocks and through the mother. Miraculously, the bullet didn't hit any of the baby's internal organs and the mother also survived after a few days at the hospital. Was that just luck? Maybe, I prefer to think that God does work in mysterious ways.

We have a lot of cases like this, were innocent people get shot by the police, and the stupid "no JHP" rule makes it worse, since 124 gr. FMJ 9mm will penetrate walls, windows, even bad guys and end up injuring or killing innocent people.

So, back to the TV. Good places are too expensive, and just going out for a walk at night with your wife/girlfriend is out of the question. All of a sudden popcorn , pizza and a movie sounds like a good plan.

I'm not saying that you should spend all day in front of the screen like a zombie. Reading is nice, I love reading myself, but once the SHTF, going out with a date at night wont be that easy, nor will it be that cheap. You will end up paying for that added security the shop/bar/theater owner hired, the higher price of gas and food, while a DVD copy can be found everywhere, and costs only a couple of bucks.

After the SHTF there will be a lot of "why don't we watch a movie" nights. Like it or not TV is cheap, safe entertainment. A play station or xbox is also nice to have.

Even if the country collapses, there will always be a guy with a DVD writer making copies. Just something to think about if you like movies.

BOOKS

Oh, almost forgot. If you like reading a lot, buy books now, even if you wont read them for some time. If your economy crashes, paper will become a source of income for many. We have thousands of scavengers collecting cardboard and paper all day long, specially at night when people take out the trash. As a result, books are not cheap, because they have a value of its own in the form of paper.

Also, consider that books are heavy, making transportation expensive and many are printed abroad.

Just as an example: I returned from visiting my parents in Spain with three suitcases. ONE suit case was entirely full of books. Books cost about 80%-200% more than what they cost in USA or Spain.

Guns & ammo: I always liked guns, so I always had weapons. But I didn't have an adequate survival battery. If you don't have a good survival selection of weapons, buy them now, or as soon as your budget allows. Make it one of your priorities, just after food, water and shelter.

There are several posts on the ideal choice of weapons. Get at least a service size pistol and a military semi auto rifle and a 22 handgun/rifle. (try to get both if you can, they are not that expensive).

A bolt rifle (preferably in the same caliber as the semi) a pump 12 ga shotgun and a sub rifle, like a SMG or pistol caliber semi auto carbine (same caliber as pistol) would complete the package.

I forgot to buy a 22 pistol until after 2001, and ended up paying for a Norinco 22 pistol the same price I would have paid for a Ruger pistol before the crisis.

My advice is: See what you use regularly and what you expect to need after TSHTF. Of those goods, see where they are made. If they are made outside your country, they will either increase in price of stop importation entirely after TSHTF.

In my case, one good example (of many, many others) is Gillette disposable blades. They are made in USA, and right now they cost a fortune. But as I said before, check what is being imported.

No point in buying cases of Cubans for trade after TSHTF if you live in Cuba, right?

I wouldn't think of these items as trade goods, but as "gifts" to buy favors, build up relationships with police, government officials, doctors, people you might need favors from. Stuff, like liquor/wine, a nice pen, perfume, makeup and other "free shop" kind of items can go a long way when you need some strings pulled, or a "friend" within certain circles. And it's not only the item, sweet talking also must be applied.

For example, you need renew your drivers license after the XXXX crisis. The problem is that the office is low on personal (they had to let go 25% and 50% are on strike) so you'll have to wait 4 months until you get an appointment.

You approach the information desk were you find Betty. Now, Betty hasn't had a date since the age of 10, and she weights as much a healthy manatee (though she's not THAT pretty) you kindly ask her to please help you fill the paperwork, and though she's as cold as a Popsicle, you keep calling her by her first name and when you leave she smiles and says good bye.

The next day you drop by and give Betty a Revlon lipstick for "helping" you fill the form, which had difficult questions like "name?"" Age?". It cost you about 4 bucks before the crisis but, since it's made in France, it went up to 20 dollars and then, 2 months ago, they no longer imported it. Revlon saw that they no longer had a market for their 4 Euro lipstick, which now costs Americans 20 dollars and the segment that used to buy it is spending that money in other items like food, so their marketing experts told them that the 4 Euro lipstick is no longer profitable in USA.

Betty used to love that particular lipstick, she thought it made her look like Cindy Crawford (poor Betty) but 20 dollars was more than she could spare in her good looks, and when she finally decided to drop the 40 pounds of M&M's she ate a month in favor for the lipstick, the girl at the drugstore told her that the item is no longer imported into the USA.

Her face lights up when she sees your present, and tells you that you shouldn't have bothered, and she asks how did it go with your license. You tell here that you actually have a problem, it seems that it takes 4 months to renew, and you ask her if , well, maybe she can do something about it... you get the picture.

In other occasions people will let you know that they want a plain and simple "bribe", and there 50 bucks or 100 bucks according to the situation will get the job done. I've used "gifts" (a perfume) to get my passport faster, saved a few months, and I've used bribes every single time the police stopped me for "inspection". I know this does not apply to 1st world countries were most officers are honest self sacrificed people, I mean no insult to the law enforcement community on this forum, but please understand that it does apply to 3rd world countries, and I'm not getting shot by an angry cop over 10 or 20 pesos, let them have their bribe. I tried it once and I will never try it again. A cop stopped me and started BS me. I told him "ok officer, guess you'll have to write me a ticket, I understand". He didn't want to write a ticket , he wanted money and things got ugly. I'm never doing anything that stupid again.

FOOD
A delicate issue. Even though not in the same way, it does affect us all. Keep in mind that if TSHTF, prepared or not, food will always be in your thoughts. If you don't have it you'll do ANYTHING to get it, and if you are prepared you'll worry about being able to get more for the future. Once

you see food prices go up between 200% and 300%, or simply see it missing, you'll realize what a valuable commodity food really is.

To those that think that food will never be a problem in USA:

Come visit my country, even though there are desert areas up north, most of the country is fertile "Pampa".

Just after WWII Argentina practically fed Europe. Argentina was know in Europe as " the world's granary". Cattle and wheat was enough to feed our own country and another continent.
So, what happened? Why are there so many that have little or no food and end up eating out of dumpsters?

I mean, the land is still there, isn't it?

Well, the country is the same country that used to be called the "world's granary" but some things changed. Several big, multinational corporations, such as Benetton, bought hundreds of thousands of acres of natural resources. I don't know the exact number, but I do remember that the media started talking about the integrity of the sovereignty of the country being at risk because of these massive purchases of land, so you can imagine how many acres were bought. Mysteriously, the media suddenly dropped the subject.

Another important factor is that now, with our new economy, it's not good business to sell Argentine food to Argentina. Why sell a kg of meat to the local market for 17 pesos when they can now sell it to Spain for 17 Euros when 1 Euro = 3,5 pesos?

All this combined with high unemployment, salaries that are not enough to buy the minimal amount of calories for a typical family, and the high prices resulted in a country that slowly started to suffer hunger.

Again, I can pin point the exact moment when the entire country realized what was happening. After the 2001 crisis things had been bad, but people in Buenos Aires, the capital city and the richest province, didn't realize how bad things actually where in the other provinces.

This was until teachers noted that kids had problems with education. You see, they noticed that they had problems to concentrate, that they fell asleep, and that they found it difficult to resolve mathematical equations.

They later found out that this was due to mal nutrition, kids where not receiving the minimum amount of nutrients for a healthy working body.

The braking point was when a reporter interviewed a little girl about 8 or 9 years old. The reporter lady asked her what she wanted to be when she grew up, the usual kiddy questions.
The girl, crying, said that she didn't want to be anything, that she didn't care.

The lady asked her why was she crying.

She said that she cried because she was hungry, that she had nothing to eat for days, and it was then that I noticed how skinny the little girl actually was.

Seeing children starve is terrible, I guess we all saw those images f the starving kids in Africa. But when you see them speak your same language, with your same accent, in your own country, it hits a nerve.

People talked about it for weeks, and they interviewed pediatricians that confirmed that the number of children dieing because of hunger had increased drastically in the last few months.
So whatever happens, let it be a hurricane, economical collapse, earthquake or meteor hitting earth, food and water always come first.

Ideally you already have a food plan and have a year worth of food in your basement... You don't? hmm... neither did I when the SHTF and lets just say that I had my manhood up my throat all the time, fearing that supermarkets would definitely close and me and my family would be left without food.

If you don't have your food needs sorted out already, just do what I did, start buying a little extra every time you go to the supermarket. The points you want to look for your storage food are, in order of importance:

1) **No need of fridge.**
2) **High nutritious value/volume**
3) **Long shelf live, between 1-5 years.**
4) **That they don't need water**
5) **That they don't need cooking**

This will usually take you to canned meats, canned tuna, canned vegetables, dried pasta, dehydrated soups, chocolate, milk powder, marmalades, soups, rice and dried beans. Canned food is excellent when it comes to long shelf life. Most of the time they are already hydrated, so they don't need water, and you can eat them out of the can. Just watch out not to dent the can, if this happens air may get inside and ruin it. If you have a dent or bump in a can, consume it fast. Also remember that once the can is opened, you have to remove the food from the can.

507

My favorite canned food is tuna. It lasts forever, it's full of proteins, and no matter how often I eat it, it always tastes good. Besides you can combine it with frizzed vegetables or rice.

Canned fruits and vegetables are also good, but they have much less vitamins than the fresh ones, and you loose most of it unless you drink the liquid they come in.

Dried pasta may need a lot of water to cook, but its one of the best ways to store carbs in convenient to use form. Flower or wheat can also be stored in large quantities and are nutritious, but they require more preparation to consume.

We've become quite independent from the fridge, and only use it to keep frozen our fresh pasta (Ã±oqui) pizza and frizzed vegetables.

We practically freeze everything, because it lasts longer, practically indefinitely, and because if the lights go out a large mass of frizzed food will last for hours, even a day or two. The more mass of food you have frizzed to longer it will hold.

The survivalist, especially the urban one, should try to rely as little as possible on the fridge. That's why canned food and freeze dried food is your best friend.

Yet, anyone who has been for a while with no fresh fruit knows that after some time the skin starts to suffer. Sores will appear after a while, especially on delicate skin like the lips and mouth. Once you start eating fresh fruits and vegetables again they go away.

This happened to me once, spent to much time without fresh vegetables and my mouth was a mess, full of sores. After a week of eating fresh vegetables regularly the symptoms disappeared. That's why you should try to have some fresh food to supplement you storage food. Not much, just 2 or 3 fruit trees on your garden and a small orchard would be fine. You don't have to feed out of this, you just need a little fresh veggies or fruit every once in a while.

On the news right now while I write this: We had elections last Sunday, we voted senators. It seems that in one of the north provinces people where surrendering their ID documents for bags of groceries, some for water, or for 10 pesos (3 USD) they were later taken to warehouses were they spent the night to ensure that they voted. The next day the candidate's men took them to vote, howled inside cattle trucks, like animals. When they arrived they were given their ID documents back with the number of list they had to vote. Thugs guide them and ensure they vote who they want.

HEALTH & FITNESS

Visit you doctor NOW. Get yourself fixed. Visit the dentist and make sure your mouth is in perfect conditions. Nothing is worse than having toothache and no one available to take care of it. Remember that doctors may not be as available as they are now, in the future.

For example I got eye surgery to take care of my sight problem. Now I see perfectly without glasses.

The advantage of laser eye surgery isn't limited to not needing glasses. (which can brake and would be nearly impossible to replace after TSHTF)

Even people react to you in a different way. Humans are after all instinctive animals.

Bad guys will look at you as a weaker person if you wear glasses. Maybe they don't know that at a conscious level, maybe they do, but they do react differently.

This is not me imagining stuff, it's the way things are. Old people and women are specially vulnerable. After old people and women and children, come small framed people, the smaller you are, the weaker you look, the more likely you are to be chosen as a victim by a bad guy. It sounds, cruel, and it sure is, but that's the way it works.

A young man with a well formed body, broad shoulders, muscled arms and a "don't f*** with me" face, is less likely to be a victims of small time thieves. If a professional group choses you as a target that's a completely different story, of course.

Talk to your doctor a lot. Just like "The little Prince", never stop yourself from asking a question. Adopt that as a general philosophy and you'll end up learning a little about everything. Mechanics, doctors, policemen, you can always learn something new from people with skills.

As a survivalist, and as a smart person, you should try to know a little about everything, Always be curious.

That's how I learned that I had to diversify my stock of antibiotics. A doctor told me, that the body will adapt if you always use the same, making that particular antibiotic not that effective, specially in small children, so now I keep two different kinds of antibiotics.

Working out 3 times a week, for a couple of hours will keep you in shape. I work out at home, I have a bench and some weights. Try to compliment some aerobics and weight lifting.

Working the boxing bag is good exercise, works most muscles if done right, and you'll have a much more powerful punch. Keep in mind that a bag is no replacement for a sparring partner and that the bag does not faint nor does it punch back. Still, it good exercise and your punch will be more powerful if you connect.

Running belts and bicycles are also good.

Research on the subject and make your own routine, join a gym and talk to a professional if possible.

Whatever you do, the idea is to have a fit, healthy body. No use in shooting Â½ MOA at 100 yards if you have a gut that hangs half way to the floor and you cant run that same distance without needing an oxygen mask.

I know, shooting is fun, and working out isn't. At least for most, but after some time you'll start to enjoy it, your stamina and morale will definitely increase, and you'll start looking forward to working out.

The survivalist that spends 3 hours a week on his gun skills and no time at all on his own body is not doing things right.

Imagine if you have to run away from a riot/gunfight/attack while carrying your BOB, or fighting bare handed against someone that got you by surprise. This applies for life in general , before or after TSHTF a man has to now how to fight bare handed. You don't have to be Bruce Lee or Mike Tyson, just know how to through a decent punch, cover your face, or some kind or martial art classes.

I once had a fight that got a little ugly. It happened in my mother in law's house, which proves that thing can go bad everywhere at any time. A guy my wife's sister was dating argued with me and things got physical. He had problems with the police for beating up an ex girlfriend (which he was proud of, go figure) and had spend 2 years in jail for stealing cars. My wife's sister was showing up with mysterious bruises on her body, from "falling while working out". So you could say this guy wasn't my favorite person. Anyway, he grabbed my neck by surprise, I grabbed his arm with both hands, one in his hand and the other in his elbow, and twisted it around. The leverage made him let go of my neck and a kept on twisting it forcing him around. He punched me with his other hand but the positing wasn't on his favor so it was just a glancing blow. He pushed with his back against me, so I placed my left arm around hid neck,

my elbow flexed over his Adam's apple. The guy went berserk so I decided that I had to hold on until he passed out, or I would get seriously hurt. I had practiced this choking move with my friend, the one that has the farm I talked about before. He told me that after 30 seconds of choking the person passes out, and after 60 seconds, if you keep choking him, he dies.
So I placed my left arm firmly around his neck while holding my left hand firmly with my right arm, pressing as hard as I could.

The guy went nuts. He slammed me against the walls, trying to get me away from his back.

He started clawing with his fingers on my biceps, desperate. Me? I just hold my lock around his neck, mentally counting. As if by magic, after 20-25 seconds. He lost all strength and fell to his knees like a rag doll, and I let him go.

Meanwhile my wife, her sister and my mother in law were all screaming at me to stop.

Once he caught his breath he said that I was psycho, and that he was just fooling around. Not believing a word he said, I said I was sorry and we both got into the elevator, since we were leaving.

As soon as I close the elevator door, the s*** bag attacks me again. I guess he felt humiliated in front of the woman he beat up. He tried to grab me the same way I did. I knew that this was getting out of hand and I completely lost patience with this clown.

I brought my serrated Cold Steel El hombre from my pocket and placed the dull side against his arm. He got the message instantly a let go of me. Once he did this I shoved him against the elevator, my forearm pressing against his neck and the knife under the neck as well. He calmed down instantly, saying he was sorry, bla ,bla, bla.

When we got out of the elevator I told him that if he ever got close to me or my family again I would put a bullet in his head.

I never saw him again.

This guy was a thief and women beater and I had no use him. Besides these are the kind of rats that would brake into your house when you leave, or worse.
I'm ranting all over the place again. What I mean is that practicing defensive moves is useful, specially if you spar with someone that knows his thing. My friend practices Judo. He won the state championship and was left in 3rd place in the nationals final.

Practice as you would fight in real life. Getting chocked isn't nice, but you get to know what you are working with and know how effective it actually is.

Being in shape will also make you less prone to diseases, such as high pressure, heart problems, and will boost your immune system in general.
Knowing first aid procedures is always helpful. I'll take the red cross course this summer.

Keep a first aid kit and any other special medicine you may need. If you take drugs regularly try to have at least a year's worth of the stuff.

Medicines are hard to get and expensive, many are made in other countries and if SHTF they might not be available. My father in law has Parkinson and needs a special medicine that is no longer imported. He asks friends that travel to get it for him.

I stock pile as much medicines as I can. Apart from the regular 1st aid kit stuff you usually have at home, I concentrate on Ibuprofen and antibiotics, both for children and adults. Antibiotics are precious here, with all the viruses that are floating around. Lung infections are particularly dangerous.

Also remember that keeping a clean, ventilated house goes a long way when it comes to preventing diseases. This is hard when the city is full of filth and there are cockroaches and rats everywhere but it can be done.

My neighborhood isn't that bad, there are places that are much, much worse, where people literally sleep and eat with rats. Cockroaches are a problem, but I keep them somewhat controlled with that poison that comes in syringes and you place around the house.

That reminds me, stock up on rat and cockroach poison. Services are bad in general, and the garbage collectors are no exception.

Once, they went on strike for about a week (though there are worst places where they go months without collecting) and you could see rats running around eh piles of garbage that people threw on the street's boulevard.

This is not healthy, of course. And helps spread diseases all over the city, so keep that in mind as well.

A First-Hand Account of Long-Term "SHTF" Survival in Bosnia

Mac Slavo from SHTFPlan.com recently posted a compilation of a forum thread put together by Chris Kitze from Before Its News. The original thread, found on the Survivalist Boards, features one man's (name Selco) first-hand account of living in a SHTF situation with his family during the Bosnia collapse of 1992. Many of the forum members peppered Selco with questions which he was graciously willing to answer. This is a compilation of those questions and answers.

In this compendium, Selco describes what it was like living in a city for a year without power, fuel, running water, food distribution or any semblance of traditional commerce. Their currency was useless, there were no police forces or government, and the streets were ruled by gangs and violence. The survival strategies that he, his family, and community used to stay alive are eye-opening and may change some of the priorities that you have when it comes to preparing for a SHTF scenario where you live. Although it's long read, I highly recommend it given the wealth of knowledge taken from someone who's lived it.

"Nobody wins, we just survived, with a lot of bad dreams."
– Selco

From Selco:

OK, i wanna share with you my own experience. (be patient with my English, i am from far away)
I am from Bosnia, and as some of you may know it was hell here from 92-95, anyway, for 1 whole year i lived and survived in a city of 50 000- 60 000 residents WITHOUT: electricity, fuel,running water,real food distribution, or distribution of any goods, or any kind of organized law or government.The city was surrounded for 1 year and in that city actually it was SHTF situation.

We did not have organized army or police force, there was groups of defenders, actually anybody who had a gun, fight for his own house and his own family.

Some of us was better prepared, but most of families had food for couple of days, some of us had pistol, few owned AK-47 when all started.

Anyway, after one month or two, gangs started with their nasty job,hospital looked like butchery, police force vanished, 80 percent of hospital staff gone home. I was lucky, my family was big in that time (15 members in one big house, 5-6 pistols, 3 Kalashnikov s) so we lived and survived, most of us.

I remember US Air force dropped MRE every 10 days (god bless USA for that) as help for surrounded city, it just was not enough.Some of houses had little gardens with some vegetables, most did not.

After three months rumors started abouth first deaths from starvation,deaths from low temperatures, we stripped every door , window frame from abandoned houses for heating, i burned all my own furniture for heating, lot of people died from diseases, mostly from bad water (two of my family members), we used rain water for drink, several times i ate pigeons, once i ate rat.

Money did not worth sh.... we traded things, black market worked, few examples: for 1 corned beef can you could have woman for couple of hours(sounds bad, but it was reality) i remember, most of that womans were just desperate mothers, candles, lighters, antibiotics, fuel, batteries, rifle ammo and of course food, we fight like animals for that.

In situation like that lot of things change, **most of people turned to monsters, it was ugly.**

Strength was in the numbers, if you were alone in the house, you ve been probably robbed and killed, no matter how well armed.

Anyway, war ended, again thanks to America (and again god bless USA for that). It is not important witch side had right in that war. It was almost 20 years ago, but believe me, for me it was just like yesterday, i remember everything, and i think i learned a lot.

Me and my family are prepared now, I am well armed, stocked and educated. It is not important what going to happen, earthquake,war, tsunami,aliens terrorists, important thing is that something gonna be.

And from my expirience, you can not survive alone, strength is in the numbers, be close with your family, prepare with them, choose your friends wisely and prepare with them too.

And at the end, this is my first post, and my English is not so good, so don t judge me too hard. "

Q: How did you get around safely?
Actually city was broken in something like lot of street communities, in my street (15 or 20 houses) we organized patrols (5 armed man every night) to watch on gangs or enemies.

We traded things between people in that street, 5 miles from my street there was one street with something like organized traders, but it was to dangerous to go there, it worked only during the nighttime (during the day it was sniper alley) and you had more chance to be robed there than to trade, i used that street only 2 times, and belive me, only when i am really need something bad.

Q: What about wood? It looked like there are many forests around your city, why did you have to burn doors and furniture?
First, thank you for your questions, i did not expect this amount of interest for my post.
I ll be glad to share lot of things with you guys beecause i want to learn lot of things from you.

Anyway:
Bosnia have lot of woods and forests when you check map, but i lived in city closer to the croatian border, more to the south, i don t want to mention name of the city, but if you check map, south part of my country closer to croatia is all in rock.

Yes we had some trees in my city, parks, fruit trees, but most of the city is building and houses" but belive me all trees in the city is going to be burned very fast when you dont have eletricity for cooking and heating. After that all what you have is furniture, doors, wooden floors... (and belive me that stuff is burning too fast).

There was almost no car use in town because: most of the roads jammed with ruins, abandoned cars, destroyed houses stuff like that, and petrol was like gold.

If i needed to go somewhere i almost always used night time, never go alone but also never go in big group (2-3 man maybe), always armed, very fast, always in shadows, trough ruins, rarely openly on the street, actually always hiding.

We did not have suburbs and farmers, in suburbs were enemy army, we were surrounded with enemy army, and inside town you did not know who is your enemy.

And yes, there were organized groops of gangs, 10-15 people, sometimes even 50, but also there were normal people like you and me, fathers, granddads, decent folks, who robed and killed, there was not too much good and bad guys, most of us was gray, ready for everything.

Q: Did you prep and what kind of skills did you need?
We use what we had, we was not prepared for that situation,we did not know for prepping.

So you can imagine in some aspects we go back in stone age, actually in most of.

We just used everything what we had, one example, i had in my propan(or butan i am not sure) stowe big bottle, cylinder (i am not sure is that right word), and i did not use it for cooking or heating, it was to valuable, i manage to built (fix) that bottle with my friend so i can attach a hose on some kind of ventil (sorry my english is going down here) so i can fill those disposable lighters,(they are not disposable if you knowhow to) those lighter worth a small fortune.

To make story short, somebody bring me empty lighter to me and i fill that lighter with gas, usually i took one can for that or one candle or whatewer he can offer me.

I hope you understand my example, my english is poor on some things.

one more example, i am a registered nurse, in time like that, my knowledge was my thing for trade.

And yes, be trained and educated, in times like that it worth a fortune if you know how to fix things, all your goods is going to be exhausted one day, but your specific knowledge can be your food. I mean learn to fix things (shoes or people, whatewer you can).

My neighbor use to know how to make some kind of oil for oil lamps(oil in glass, peace of rope) and he was not hungry, he never show me how he made that oil I belive he use some tree behind his house and small amount of disel, i don t know.

My point is learn things, people always need somebody who know to fix things. It was not survival movie, it was ugly, we did what we have to do to survive.

Nobody wins, we just survived, with a lot of bad dreams.

Q: Wasn't it religious, the war?
Sorry man wrong info, that was not Cristian vs Muslim war, it was civil war, with lot of switching between sides.

And sorry i am not to go in to the politics, i dont care to much for that, i am not going into religious stories, i mean i believe in God as higher power, and I am trying to live by his laws, i am not belong to any dogma, Muslim or Christian.

Q: Who was your support group?
My group was only my family, my blood (relatives like uncles, grandmother...), in my street and in my town trips i had some close friends, but my best friends was my family. I never take stranger in my close group.

Q: If you had three months to prepare today, what would you do?
If i have extra three months to prepare?

Hmmm, probably run overseas :) Joke

OK, Now i am very well aware how things can go very bad in very short time so i have food, hygiene, energy etc. supply for 6 months, i live in apartment with some improved security, i have house with shelter in a village some 5 miles from my apartment, in that house also supply for 6 months, that village small community, most of them are my relatives,most of them are prepared (they learned that from war), i have four kind of fire weapons with 2000 bullets for each (sorry, can not go in details, laws are different here for rifles).

I have big garden with that house and some good knowledge about gardening and farming.

I think i have knowledge now to smell trouble, you know when everybody is saying that everything is going to be fine you somehow know that is everything going to fall apart.

I think i have strength to do everything what it takes to keep me and my family alive, because when everything is going to sh.., be sure, you are going to do some bad things to save your kid. You don t want to be hero, you want to survive with your family.

I am nurse, also i am paramedic (US standards)
And i am willing to learn from all of you.

One man survivor, no chance (OK it is my opinion) no matter how well armed and prepared, at the end you gonna die, i've seen that, many times. Family groups or closest friend with lot of preparing and lots of different knowledge, i believe that is best.

Q: What items should we stockpile?
Thank you

Well depends, i quess if you stock only one thing you are not going to survive, unless you want to survive like robber, then you need only gun and lot od ammo.

I believe besides ammo food hygiene and energy things (batteries etc.) you need to focus on small things for trade, pocket knives, lighters, flints.

Also LOT of alcohol, kind that can stay long, i mean stuff like whiskey and that, does not important what kind, you can have cheapest kind, it is very good thing for trade in desperate time.

Also lack of hygiene things killed a lot of people, i ve seen that.

You gonna need to have some simple things, like for example lot of garbage bags, i mean a lot, many uses for that, and a LOT of duct tape, many many uses for that.

In case of weapon keep it simple, i mean now i always carry Glock 45 with me, because i like that gun, but it is not usual gun and usual caliber here, so i also have two 7,62 mm TT russian pistols hidden, because almost everybody have that gun here and a lot ammunition.

I don t like Kalashnikov, but here there is that rifle on almost every 3rd house so...

Most of the time i collect my water from roof in 4 big barrels during the war, then cooked to desinfect, we also had river in that town , too poluted but if you can't choose...

513

I don t think i am expert, i am here to learn.

I quess it depends how far you going to go to survive with your actions, you need to be prepared to do some ugly things.

Oh yes it changed my perspective on life, i know now that bad things can happens, and on more important thing, actually i believe it is most important: I don't anymore believe government and authority, not at all. When they really doing their best to assure you that everything going to be fine, you can be sure that something bad is happening. Do not just believe, research.

Q: What about the civil war…and the religious fighting? Did gold and silver help much and how did you get the alcohol and other supplies?

I believe in some point this discussion gone wrong way, and no i am not offended, everybody have right for opinion, so here is few of my opinions:

It was a civil war, yes there was a great influence of religion, but somebody mention "what did you do with people of other religion?"

Well in my family there are people with different religious beliefs so what do you mean with that?

I ll try to explain you simple; it was an attackers and defenders, lot of switching sides, civil war. War ended without winners, it ended with truce, thanks mostly to USA. It was the wrong war, wrong reasons. I did not fight for religion or ethnicity, i fought to keep my family and myself alive.

For last 15 years we have peace, we live with people who use to be our enemies, i do not to want to have war and enemy again because ethnicity or religion or any other reason.

Please do not try to generalize anything about that war, there was not good and bad side, we all suffered and we all try to live together again. And yes every side did bad things, and every side had booth good and bad guys.

I am here for one and only reason- survival, i want to learn, and i can share some useful stuff with you. I don t think about your religious beliefs, your ethnicity or your politic opinion.

Few words about my city before war, it was a usual Bosnian town, normal life, decent people, schools, theaters, parks, college, airport, crime rate very low, town like most of the smaller towns in USA (i think). I was a young man, just like any of you maybe.

Now very important think: i am not here to discuss about war reasons, or sides, religion or anything similar. Thanks to the war, in my town was REAL SHTF situation, and we can discuss only about that, only that is important.

You have a lot internet pages, you can learn everything about that war, and you can choose side if you want.

OK that s it. About survival.

I don t know about other people on this forum, but i have lot of alcohol stacked now.

At the beginning of war tank grenade smashed front wall of small distillery (alcohol factory) close to my house, so we took something around 500 liters of rakia (it is something like bosnian whiskey, i guess, it made from grape, very strong)
It was great stuff for trading, people used alcohol a lot, desperate times i think, we also use it for disinfection.

About hygiene, cups and plates, paper or plastic, you gonna need a LOT, i know, we did not have it at all.

My opinion that hygiene things is more important maybe than food, you can easily shoot pigeon, if you have grandmother she may know some eatable plants on nearest small hill (my experience) but you can not shoot hand sanitizer.

Water purifying pills, all kind of cleaning stuff, sanitizers, lot of soap, bleach, gloves, masks, all disposable, take very good care about first aid training, learn how to treat smaller cuts, burns or even gunshot wound, there is not hospital, even if you found doctor somewhere he probably do not have any meds, or you do not have stuff to pay him.

Learn how and when to use antibiotics and have it a lot. Belive me with good knowledge and good amount of meds you are gonna be rich.

About gold and silver, yes, me personally gave all my gold for ammunition in that time, but it did not worth too much.

About pets, i did not have it, i did not notice a lot pets in that time, did somebody ate it? I don t know, probably.

About small family, hmm, not good, usualy few smaller families get together in biggest house and stay together, all relatives (my case)

Small family or single man, not good for survive in town SHTF, maybe in wilderness (i don t have expirience in that) Even if you stay low profile, hidden in your house with lot of food etc, sooner or later mob will come, and you have maybe have one or two guns, very hard. I agree with low profile policy, it is very important not to attract people with anything, but when they come, you need to have numbers, people and guns, best people is your family.

About moving trough the city: always night time as i mentioned, never alone, 2-3 man, very fast, never attract with anything, look like everybody else, if most folks look desperate, poor, dirty you need to look same, there is no need that everybody know you have good amount of food, ammo , clean cloths and everything else back at home. Look and act like everybody else.

When somebody attack you or your family then you need to show that you are very ready.

I never walked in big groups, in that time and that situation big group is gang.

Now, this is all my experience, it was then, i did a lot of mistakes, i am not expert, i am here just like any of you, to learn and share.

For example i don t know too much about wilderness survival, i am here to check it.

Oh yes, few things to the Sedoy: my wife is different ethnicity, and she is also a Catholic, i am not, and to answer you : no i am not going to shoot her.

Q: What happened to those who died? Where did people get firewood?

Well, who ever died or get killed in that period, did not get proper funeral.

Folks used used every peace of free land, close to house for burial, sometimes even in the garden, 2-3 city parks turned to graveyards,after war most of them are exhumed and properly buried. There was not noting like burning bodies or anything similar, as far as i know.

Oh one more interesting thing about fire, some people use to go few miles during the night only to find fire somewhere so they can fire peace of wood and bring it home, and start fire for cooking or heating, lighters and matches was really precious, and most of the folks did not have enough firewood do keep always fire. For most of the people it was constant search for something, fire,wood,food,ammo...

Q: Was salt valuable?

It was valuable yes, but not too much, for example coffee or cigarettes worth-ed much more.

Q What about cigarettes?

Hm, i had a lot of alcohol as i mentioned before, i traded almost everything without any problem, let me say it like this: consumption of alcohol was probably 10 times more than in normal time.Not to mention cleaning and disinfection.

On the other side you made a very good point, if you have money and time and you have a storage it is probably better to store cigarettes or candles and batteries for trade, or food.

I was not prepper at that time, we did not have time to prepare, few days before SHTF politicians on TV stated that everything is fine, when sky fell down we just take what you can.

Q: Tell us more about cooking and the foods you were able to prepare. Were you concerned about the smell getting around and alerting people that there was food over there?

About cooking, before the SHTF i used in my house electricity for booth, cooking and heating, so when everything started i traded some stuff for some kind of old wood stove, i put it in kitchen ad fix exhaust pipe (right word?) trough hole in wall, i use that for cooking and heating. During the summer i cooked in my backyard (walled fence, brick, luckily)

Concerning the smell of the food, hm, i ll try to picture situation: no electricity, no running water, sewage off for months, dead bodies in ruined houses, grime and mess, believe me it was very hard to smell something nice. It was not like in movies, it was ugly,dirty, and smelly.

Yes i had few problems because of cooking, only few, but as i sad before, enough people, properly armed and with will to defend and you can manage most of the problems with that.

Probably situation would be different in wilderness.

I ate mostly some kind of pancakes with local herbs (does not require cooking oil and too much firewood), and of course everything what i could get and trade, rice was good to eat, not too much firewood for that.

I think i had luck, only few times i ate funny things like pigeons.

I always had something to trade, i guess that saved me, and guns of course.

Q: 1. Why would the night be safer than daytime? Outside of the obvious of being easier to hide at night, but were the gangs more out during the days? Also, why only small groups of 2-3? What happened to larger groups?

2. Why would you have to go out at night? For instance, where were you going and why?

3. How did you handle the mob situation when they came for you, or your family?

4. You mentioned trading for bullets, etc. How much shooting were you doing during that time and how much ammo did you have, or would like to have had?

5. How were you able to determine who was an enemy and who wasn't? How did you manage to get out there trade with people and when/where?

6. What fortifications did you do to your home and what kind of guard, or protections did you have in place?

7. Finally, how did you avoid snipers? What precautions did people take against them?

First almost nobody were out during the day because of snipers, line of defence was very close, so whatever you have to do, you do it during the night, trade something, look for firewood (i can express how much this was important in town, and hard), looking for anything, check somebody, go to hear news (very very important, lot of people get killed because they go somewhere just to see what happening, or what s new) remember, no news, no radio ,no tv, nothing, rumors fed lot of people.

Already explained, you can stay home and die of hunger and cold, or even infection of some small wound or go out and risk your life, try to find – trade anything useful.

I did have situations concerning my house only, it is no need for too much details, we had more fire power, and brick wall.
Also we had something like street watch, people from my street were good organized, in case of gangs, now there were a lot shootings.

There was pretty much shooting in town, i did not have enough weapon at the beginning, one rifle and one pistol (ww2), maybe 100 bullets, later i trade some things for more rifles and ammo, remember i gave car battery for 2 rifles.

How much ammo ?
A LOT, as more as you can.

Most of the time you are not able to determine who is enemy or friend, expect my family and few real friend, everybody else is potential enemy. When your friend must choose between his child s death and your death quess who is going to choose.

Rumors, somebody tells you that some old guy few block away have some cans and he is looking for ammo or whatever, you go there, as i say you are always looking for something. Same some people would came in my street as traders, witha some goods.

There was something like trade street during the night, actualy it was a big ruins of sport center, you can go overthere and look for something or offer something, but it was not controlled by anyone so it was too dangerous.

It was primitive pretty much, brick wall around house, bags of sand on windows and doors, over that bags we used whatever you can, big pieces of metal, stones, inside house we put all kind of stuff on windows, only small openning left for rifle, always 5 members of family ready for fight, one always outside on street hidden. Stone age situation

To avoid snipers, we stay home at day, it was not so much night snipers, even during the night we never walked openly on the streets if we can avoid that, always shortcuts, trough ruins, fast and quiet.

Q: What was your bathroom situation? Where did you go? Did you have anything to wipe with? Sorry ask such personal questions, but this is something that I've wondered about in this type of situation.

we used shovel and any piece of land close to house, sounds dirty, and it is dirty, washing with collected rainwater, sometimes go to river (most of the time that was too dangerous) Most of the time we did not have toilet paper, even if i had it, i trade it.

It was a bad situation all the time.

If i can give some advice: first to prep is a weapon and ammo, then everything else, i mean everything, depends how much money and space you have, if you forget something no problem there is always somebody ready for trade, but if you forget guns and ammo then you may not be able to get to trading places.

I do not see big family or group of really(i mean really) good friends as more mouth to feed, i see them as more guns and strength, it is in people nature to adapt.

And keep it simple and use common sense, in the first period weak people vanished, other fight.

Go with small thing, lighters, candles, flints. It is great idea to have fuel generator(electrical generating unit?) but i think is better idea to have 1000 bic lighters. Fuel generator is great, but in shtf scenario in town it is going to attract whole army,1000 bic lighters don t take too much space, cheap, you can always trade it for something.

Real SHTF scenario demands completely change of normal mindset, hard to explain, i ll try through examples.

Q: How easy/hard was it to get weapons AFTER the SHTF and what could you trade for weapon and ammunition
(I remember you saying a car battery for a rifle) and where would I go to find the people who trade in weapons?

Hm, you re right, after the war every house here had a weapon from war, and yes police did some actions to take illegal weapon from population, depends from man to man i quess, lot of people find ways to hide their weapon somewhere, just in case.

I also have legal weapon (license), and authority here have some thing they call it "temporary collecting", it is says

something like : in a case of unusual event (riots, unrest, etc) government have right to temporary collect all legal weapon, so i keep always in mind that, and i acted like some people.

You know some people have legal weapon for everyday carry(i have glock 45 and taurus 38) but some people with legal weapon also have illegal weapon hidden somewhere just in case SHTF and "temporary collecting".

It is not hard to get weapon in SHTF if you have good stuff for trade, but other thing is important, first days of SHTF is worst in terms of chaos and panic, maybe you not gonna have time to get gun. And to be unarmed in chaos panic and riots is bad.

In my case man needed car battery for radio i think, and he had some extra rifles, so we trade.

Q: What about medical care for people who were shot or became injured?
Wounds was mostly gunshot wounds of course, without specialists and everything else, if wounded manage to find doctor somewhere he had like 30% chances to live, again it is not movie, mostly they died, lot of died even from minor cuts infections, i had antibiotics maybe for 3-4 treatment. Of course for my family only.

Simple things killed people, diarrhea can kill you in a few days without meds and rehidratation, (fluid therapy, IV) especially small kids. Lot of fungal skin deseases,and food poisoning, we could not do too much. Basically we treated diseases mostly with local herbs, and if you had wound, put rakia on it and try to find antibiotics somewhere.
So i was good at fixing wounds in term of emergency help, but longer procedure-bad prognosis.

What i learned? Hygiene again, and a lot of meds, especially antibiotics. You need to learn to treat lot of stuff, go online, finish some training, EMT maybe, first aid etc.

In SHTF things are different, learn how to open IV, when to use certain drug, or antibiotics.

Get your self ANA TE (anti tetanus) shot injections , snake poison kit, adrenaline kit (allergic reactions, different kinds) thick removal kit, (thick related illness can kill you, learn how to remove thick)...

Get in your prepper storage some reanimation kit (simple one) like small oxygen cylinder, BVM mask etc. It is not really hard to learn to use all of these.

OK let s clear something, of course you can not use anything of this in real world unless you are certified and trained for that (EMT, nurse, physician).

But in SHTF nobody ask you for license, just learn and have in your storage big part for medical things.

So to answer question how did i help and treat, most of the time very poor,i help some with resources that i have, i took food or something else for exchange, i was badly prepared for that, now i am what do i need to have.

Q: Did your local currency/money still hold value? Were you still able to use money to purchase items from other people?

No, not really, i mean sometimes you can use foreign money if you had it to buy something, (dollars or German marks) but even in that rare occasion rate was unbelievable for examples 1 can of beans for 30-40 dollars (normal value was maybe 0,50) i quess somebody had connections with outside world, black market you know, so he can earn lot of money.But it was very rare. Trade was main thing to get something.

Local currency crashed very fast, in few weeks or month maybe.

Q: How much space should I keep for alcohol storage? What was security like?

About alcohol first, you right but you are right in booth ways, people need alcohohol more in desperte times then usual, so it is kind of gambling i guess , it is very good item for trading, i never had problems with alcohol trading and having than problems with trading other things.

Also i am thinking about something else, maybe it is better to fill my storage with something less space consuming but still interesting for trade, like batteries, antibiotics etc.

Thing is i had all that alcohol for free, i did not buy it. I don t know about this.

In most of the situations people attack me because they think they are stronger, they did not know for sure what i really had.

About ammunition trade, it depends how much ammo you are going to have, sometimes i trade ammo for food, and in few weeks again food for ammo, but i never never do trade at my home, and never bigger amounts, very few people knowed how much of anything i had in my house.

The point is store as much of anything as you can store (space , money) later during the situation you ll see what is most popular, correction ammo and guns always gonna had 1 place for me, but who knows maybe number 2 for trading gonna be for example masks with filters.

About medical issue , i ll write in my next post what do i have now in my medical part of storage.

Defence were very primitive, again we were not prepared, we use what ever we could, windows were broken, roofs mostly damaged from shelling, all windows were blocked with something, sand bags and rocks,every night i blocked my yard gate with junk- rubble from the street and i use old alluminium ladder to get over the wall, when i come back i called somebody from house to get me that ladders so i can move in.

Guy from my street barricaded his house completely, if he go out at night he use a hole that he maded in one room that is connected with neighbor s house, and go trough his (ruined and destroyed) house out, actually he had secret entrance.

It may look weird to say but most secured houses are gone first, of course we had some very nice houses in neighborhood, with walls, dogs, alarms, steel bars on windows, alarms. And you can quess what happened, mob attacked those houses first, some were defended other not, depend how many guns and hands thea have inside.

So i think security is great, but be sure that you keep it low profile, forget about alarm, if you live in town and SHTF you gonna need simple looking non interesting secured house, with lot of guns and ammunitions.

Just keep it low profile and not interesting.

On my apartment door now i have steel door for security reason, but only to keep me trough first short period of chaos, then i am moving out to connect with bigger group of armed people (family and friends) in the country (i hope).

Well in my case migration did not happen because it happen very fast, other army just closed city in ring and that s it, if you ask me where was that army and how we did not seen them coming, the answer is simple, that army was an ally of army of my side and people, and one day we woke up and figured they are enemy now and they are closing all ways out. Politics . It is true, one more side of civil war.

But i heard from others parts of country, and my frends who stayed in villages in the other parts in state, that they have much better situations,countryside had land,corn,wheat, fruit trees, farms etc they had enough food, it was bad, but much better than in city.

I know one thing if we had some way out from the town, we would use it, we did not have it.

Q: What was the situation with banks and stores?

About banks, loans, credit cards. Complete monetary system died for about one year, so nothing works.

It is complex question in many ways, i ll try it to answer it in some future posts, need much more time and much much more space to describe it. Even now almost 20 years later folks are at European court suing banks, because they dont want to admit their savings in banks, lot of different things happened in that period , they changed money, i mean monetary name, they changed it 2-3 times , hyper-inflation occurs, lost of paper trails about savings, loans … i remember some people use that situation to get rich, they still rich.:)

So i ll try to describe that in separate post.

There was a lot problems with proving people s property after everything, for example: my father had nice apartment and because war he must leave it, after war ended he was at court for about 4 years proving that apartment was his, reasons for that were different, because politics in that time, but also he did not have enough paper work to prove that apartment was his (he did not took papers from apartment when he fled, he had more important things to care).

On the other side during the worst period, people just moved in empty house, and that s it.

I mention rural areas in other post. As far as i remember it was better there.

In that period there is not running vehicle, actually i remember tank at the front line, and Lada Niva (check it on web) with cut of doors and roof and installed machine gun (i think it was an old m53) and those two only moved when they fired(they keep it hidden behind ruined houses).

For let me call it "civilian population" there was no moving with vehicles, streets were mostly under rubble and unusable and fuel was too expensive.

Not to draw attention was a big thing, about clothing, there use to be some sort of town defense, it was not like real military,mostly mixed civilian clothes with part of uniforms, different weapon, so no rules.

But as soon as go in to that things and try to talk about two armies, their strength, war crimes, politics i am not gonna like it any more, because people gonna start to choose sides, and i think it is not important for us here.

As i said before there was not organized army, but we all been like soldiers, we had to, most of us carry weapon and try to protect from enemy army and robbers.

Inside the town you did not want to look fancy because somebody shoot you and took your good stuff, you did not want to have fancy rifle, because probably you not gonna find ammo in that caliber and also you are drawing attention.

So let s me try to put it this way: if SHTF tomorrow, i will try to look like most of the people outside, scared, desperate, confused and i ll scream maybe, no fancy looking stuff, i ll not go out in fancy new uniform and yell "I am here, you are finished now looters and robbers" I ll stay low profile, heavily armed and well prepared waiting to see my options, even if i have to go out with all my gear to do things i ll go in night, with best friend or brother. Maybe sounds ridiculous, but from my expirience it works, be wery well prepared, but let nobody outside your house know or see that.

No matter how good is your house security, how good is your weapon, if people see that they have good reason to rob you they probably rob you in town SHTF, it is only matter of time and number of guns.Don t ever give them reason to be interesting for robbing. Stay uninteresting. Now this is my opinion, maybe is not working in different situation.

About robbing grocery store and gas stations, it happened very very fast, as soon as shooting started all valuable things was emptied, there vas some effort of authority to keep it together but everything fall apart in first weeks. Additional Resources

If you're interested (and you should be after reading this), be sure to check out Selco's blog, SHTF School. It's a great urban survival resource.

PREPARDNESS

Strength and wisdom has the man who prepares and invests the necessary assets to protect his family against the dangers of future disasters regardless of how many people may laugh at his efforts

Society's Five Stages of Economic Collapse

Society as we know it will break down and collapse in a five stage process outlined here. While it can be accelerated by certain events like war, a natural disaster, pandemic, terrorist attack, or even an impending asteroid impact, history has shown that economic collapse will essentially happen in this five stage process. To survive the collapse, it is important to read and interpret the signs and understand what assets are important to the current situation so you can be prepared for the worst thereby allowing you to survive intact and with as little damage as possible.

STAGE 1. The Decay Begins

Everything is good and the economy is thriving. A high standard of living has been achieved. This is the way things should be. Goods are cheap and readily available. Everything seems to be in abundance. Stores are filled with retail items ready to be purchased. Life in general is good.

The nation's working infrastructure is solidly intact and working well. However, the idea that everyone is entitled to have what others have earned now permeates society. Redistribution of Wealth Policies are implemented and quietly woven into the fabric of society. Unchecked and under the guise of fairness and equality, these policies slowly decrease productivity and increase dependency on government entitlement and welfare programs.

Primary Assets:

Career
Home Value
Savings
Investments - Stocks and bonds
Health Insurance
Lifestyle Image
Good Credit Rating for Debt Accumulation

STAGE 2. The Slippery Slope

The economy goes into a slow but steadily increasing decline. Unemployment is on the rise. Ever increasing numbers of people receive government assistance in one form or another. People are paid not to work. Government spending has increased dramatically. The price of gold, silver, and other precious metals rise to prices unheard of just a few years earlier. Inflation reaches the double digit levels.

Primary Assets:

> Cash
> Precious Metals, Gold and Silver coins
> Job Stability
> Elimination of debt
> Health Insurance
> Home Equity
> Automobile with good MPG
> Acquiring secluded land more than 40 miles
>   from densely populated areas

STAGE 3. It is Going to Get Worse

The total collapse of the economy begins after a significant and prolonged decline. The government implements price controls. Shortages on essential goods become widespread. Foreclosed houses sit vacant and deteriorating by the tens of thousands. Middle class neighborhoods begin to look like slums. The government begins to print currency to pay its bills and support the tens of millions on public assistance. Inflation increases even more and unemployment exceeds 25%. Banks and businesses fail at ever increasing rates. Nobody seems to have any money. Many are now homeless. Labor unions instigate strikes, civil unrest, and large scale riots. Government services are interrupted and unreliable. Local and national infrastructure is in decay. Violent gangs begin to appear and assert themselves. The government begins confiscation of firearms from law abiding citizens. Violence is everywhere. Cities and urban areas become very dangerous places to live.

At this stage, the country seems pretty much beyond the point of no return. However, things can still be reversed even at this stage if the right person at the top really believes in the basic fundamental concepts of Freedom, Independence, Liberty, and Individual Rights and is not afraid to do what is necessary to reverse the current trend. He will be vilified and hated because of his attitude toward personal responsibility, cutting entitlements, and ending welfare programs. Of course, if the right person were in power and did what needed to be done, none of this would have happened in the first place.

Primary Assets:

> Gold and Silver coins
> Cash
> Job
> Automobile
> Home
> Short term food supplies
> Short term fuel stores
> Firearms and ammo
> Plans to relocate to a secluded rural hideaway
> Small livestock - chicken, rabbit, fish...
> A close network of like minded people
> Survival knowledge and skills

STAGE 4. The Grab for Power

The collapse can transition to this stage at any time after Stage 3. Most of the middle class have lost everything. What used to be well manicured middle class neighborhoods are filled with the carcasses of empty houses damaged and destroyed by vandals. The nation's infrastructure has been seriously neglected and is in need of a major overhaul. The power grid becomes unreliable. Rolling blackouts are a daily occurrence. You can no longer buy or sell gold or own foreign currency. Inflation is out of control. Now the economy collapses. There is a rush for everything and the shelves go empty in a matter of hours. Society falls into chaos. The control of urban areas shifts when violent gangs takeover control of the streets and urban neighborhoods. The government issues restrictive measures in an attempt to control the economy. Everything is in short supply and heavily rationed. Food and gasoline is very expensive and there are very long lines to get them when they are available. Affordable quality health care is non-existent and your job is a distant memory. You will do without what you are unable to provide for yourself. You will discover what it is to live in a third world country.

Primary Assets:

> Relocation to the rural hideaway
> Firearms and ammo
> Long term food supplies (1 year minimum)
> Adequate fuel stores
> Security plan to protect the group and assets
> Trained dog for security
> A working knowledge of survival gardening
> Survival knowledge and skills

Once all of the above has come to pass, the realization of the current circumstances at this moment must be all too obvious. It is too late to prepare at this point. What you did not acquire earlier, you are not going to possess now. Anything of value necessary for your survival has already been claimed. The situation gets worse... much worse.

Stage 5 is next... and it is not pretty.

STAGE 5. Freedom, Liberty, and Independence is Lost

The government implements martial law. Fighting between civilians and government forces break out nationwide. Maintaining more than a 30 day supply of food is considered hoarding food and is illegal. Severe poverty and starvation become a common sight. The government offers marginally acceptable food, water and shelter in exchange for your Freedom, Liberty, and Independence. Democracy ends and a Socialist form of government takes over under the guise of fixing society's problems with the false promise that peace and prosperity will return better than it was just a few years ago. A Totalitarian regime assumes power and the individual freedoms and liberties once enjoyed by the people are completely eliminated.

Primary Assets:

Rural Hideaway
Security plan to protect the group and assets
Living below the radar in a community of like
 minded people
Firearms and the ability to use them
Guard dog for security

Survival knowledge and skills
A working and producing garden capable of
 feeding 150% of the group
A stable supply of clean water
Vegetable seeds for long term food
 production and barter
The will to live and survive in a harsh
 political climate

As you can see, priorities change as the world changes. Your most prized assets of today – your good credit, luxury automobile, and career are no longer important after the economy collapses.

FAILURE TO PREPARE TODAY WILL INCREASE THE MAGNITUDE OF YOUR SUFFERING TOMORROW.

It is better to prepare 10 years too early than 10 minutes too late. Many who lack vision will say that it will never happen and for those who decide to live unprepared should consider the following statement.

LACK OF PLANNING ON YOUR PART DOES NOT CONSTITUTE AN EMERGENCY ON MY PART.
http://www.targetofopportunity.com/5_stages.htm

ELECTROMAGNETIC PULSE

How Long Can You Tread Water?
by Tom S.

Originally posted at www.SurvivalBlog.com
Copyright 2012

Noah may have questioned God about why he should build such a big boat. To quote the comedian Bill Cosby, God might have asked: "How long can you tread water?"

In the event of an Electromagnetic Pulse (EMP) burst 250 miles above Kansas or a super solar flare, the loss of the electrical grid would stop almost all food production and importation in the USA. Some estimate there is, at any given time, more than 1,000 pounds per capita of food in consumable form available in the USA. Unfortunately, it is very poorly distributed and will not be available to the populace in a "Grid Down" scenario. So the question is then, if you personally have not stored at least a three years supply of food per person (and, no, a one year supply just won't due), "How long can you live on a zero calorie diet"?

Iran, as this is written, has a small satellite circling the earth 250 miles high. They are building a satellite launching facility for larger rockets. They have launched missiles from a barge in the Caspian Sea and detonated them at high altitude. They have tested a sophisticated two point detonation method which allows a much smaller nuclear bomb (reduced payload on a rocket). They have enough material right now, if further enriched, to build at least 2 nuclear bombs (although too heavy for missiles). North Korea has enough plutonium for at least 10 bombs, they are making more every day, and they successfully detonated a small nuclear bomb (Hiroshima size) in 2009. As well, they are developing missile and space technology. Chavez just met with Putin to obtain nuclear energy and space technology. Pakistan's nuclear guru A.Q. Khan is known to have shared nuclear bomb technology throughout the Middle East. According to Times Now, "Already Pakistan has 60 nuclear warheads, and now with two new plutonium reactors nearing completion in Khusab, its weapons grade plutonium production will jump seven-fold, according to latest figures released by Swedish institute SIPRI."

North Korea needs money, a lot of money. Plutonium is one of the most precious commodities on the planet. Will Pakistan or Korea sell their plutonium or complete nukes? It does not take a rocket scientist to figure that one out. Syria has transferred Scud [SS-1] missiles to the Lebanese Shiite militant group Hezbollah (Jihadi terrorists). North Korea is suspected of transferring nuclear technology to Syria, Iran and Myanmar (Burma). In short, the nuclear genie is out of the bottle and it is all over the globe. We have simply lost control and now it is only a matter of when, not if.

A super solar storm can do the same thing as an EMP and would have done so in 1859 and 1921 if our electronics had the sensitivity that they do today. As reported by NASA Science in May, 2010, "The sun is waking up from a deep slumber, and in the next few years we expect to see much higher levels of solar activity. At the same time, our technological society has developed an unprecedented sensitivity to solar storms...." Such an event just recently took place. On April 19, 2010, Science Daily Online observed one of the most massive solar eruptions in years. Earth was not in the line of fire ... this time." Again, it is only a matter of time.

A massive cyber attack to the Grid: "The severity of what we're seeing is off the charts," said Tom Kellermann, vice president of security awareness for Core Security Technologies and a member of the Commission on Cyber Security that is advising President Obama. "Most of the critical infrastructure in the U.S. has been penetrated to the root by state actors." Joe Weiss, a security expert and managing partner of Applied Control Solutions, who has testified before Congress about such threats, said "The industry has failed to address these vulnerabilities." He said "The long-term ramifications of such an attack would be severe: If electrical equipment were destroyed, power could be lost for six to nine months, because the replacement gear would take so long to manufacture." Note: As you read the following, consider what that six to nine months without electricity and what the power grid really means to our society.

EMP is optimized by the detonation of a nuclear weapon at 25 to 250 miles above the Earth's surface. An electromagnetic field radiates down to the earth, creating electrical currents. These instantaneous currents accumulate and migrate on long electrical lines and overheat transformers, large and small. Breakers are of no use due to the speed of the pulse which is 1,000 times faster than lightning. EMP will cover the wide geographic region within line of sight to the nuclear burst. A 40 mile high detonation over Virginia would black out the entire East Coast. A 250 mile high detonation over Kansas would take out most, if not all, of the continental USA.

The lead time for obtaining a single replacement of the very large "step-up or step down" type transformer is two to three years from overseas (Total worldwide production of these huge transformers is less than 100 per year); there are about 2,000 in the USA that would need to be replaced plus the millions of small transformers (frequently mounted on utility poles) in the distribution system. There is a huge and perhaps insurmountable problem with almost all electrical power generation plants. They must be shut down gradually according to carefully designed procedures. A sudden shutdown from an EMP or super solar flare would cause the destruction of major components of most power plants and, in a grid down scenario, it would not be possible to repair them. Further, most that survive must have outside power for start up and that outside power won't exist.

The point is Noah only had to contend with a boat ride and live off of stored food with no one coming to his door asking for a handout. We, on the other hand, will be without electricity for many years, able to create very little new food, and will have to defend against a continuous onslaught of attackers.

Even a small nuclear weapon at 250 miles high would permanently take down the electrical grid by shorting out transformers, large and small, because they are all tied into long distribution lines which would pickup, magnify and transmit the surge. Although cars, computers, televisions, generators, etc. may or may not continue to be operational, a regional or national grid failure would cause a cascade of failures throughout the broader infrastructure due to our highly interdependent systems and "just in time" delivery systems. Even if cars and trucks still ran there would be no new fuel supplies. The disruption would include communications (radio, television, phones, GPS), banking (including ATM machines and credit cards), cash registers at stores, medical, police (911 dispatching), fire fighting support, fuel and energy (including gas stations), transportation, food production, processing and delivery systems (including farm equipment, fertilizer and insecticides), water for consumption and irrigation, emergency services, satellites and the Internet. The fundamental force behind any and all modern industrial societies is electricity.

A small nuclear weapon specifically designed to produce a very powerful EMP would take out virtually every electrical device that was not protected. In either case, effectively, the U.S. would be thrown back to the pre-electrical age and 99% of US food production and processing would cease.

Such an event is frequently referred to as "The end of the world as we know it" (TEOTWAWKI) or "When the Schumer hits the fan" (WTSHTF).

There would be immediate loss of access to our money. Under Martial Law, if communications existed to transmit the orders, there would be extreme limits on access to our money, they would allow maybe a maximum of 5% of funds on deposit to be withdrawn per month, but banks would run out of currency almost immediately, if they were open at all, and would not have access to more. Currency itself would only have value as long as people believed the government could restore the electrical grid and get things back to normal. Within a few weeks, when people realize the power will not be coming back on, currency would have no value. Further, the rest of the world, seeing our hopeless condition, would realize we would have no ability to generate revenue and they would deem the US dollar worthless. Investments in US stocks and bonds would be worthless. The value of real estate would be at or near zero. There would be no access to funds held off shore. The loss of wealth as we know it today would be nearly total. Wealth after TEOTWAWKI would have its basis in clean water (and the means to make it), food (and the means to grow and preserve it), fuel, tools and arms and in the knowledge and skills useful in a world without electricity. Gold and silver may have their place, but "you can't eat gold" e.g. If I only have enough food for me and my family to survive, I won't be trading it for gold or silver.

After an EMP or super solar flare, except for those on life support systems or perhaps in airplanes, there would be no immediate loss of life due to the burst(s). There would be no shock wave or radiation. For awhile it would seem to be just an ordinary power outage, but gradually, hour by hour, the seriousness of the problem would be realized. Water from the tap would stop very soon if not immediately. Most emergency generators, if they worked, would run out of fuel within 72 hours. Food in freezers would last a few days then spoil. Grocery stores would be looted within a couple of days. Most food in the USA is stored in regional warehouses, and some of it requires refrigeration. Most people, probably 80%, would choose to stay in their homes for as long as the food in their pantry lasted and they had access to clean or treatable water. They would be hoping, day by day, that the power would come back on and they could resume their everyday lives again. When the water and/or food ran out or they were overrun by looters, they would have no choice but to hit the road in hopes of finding food somewhere. Ninety percent of the US population will run out of food in their homes in less than two months, many in a week or two. They would become refugees. A refugee is a person who is carrying with them all of their means for survival and cannot survive more than a few weeks without help since they cannot produce new food. Many would loot, burn and destroy the cities and suburbs while most would hope to find survival in the country believing that farmers have an abundance of food. Eventually virtually all must leave the cities because there will be nothing left to eat and the means to produce new food there will not exist. (Often referred to as the "Golden Horde" which would follow "Refugee Lines of Drift". See: SurvivalBlog.com)

Vladimir Lenin is often quoted as saying, "Where there is hunger, there is no law." In their struggle to survive refugees would first be beggars, but very quickly, with the increase in hunger, they would become looters and spread out like locusts stripping the land of everything edible. Remember, these people would not be on a simple weekend camping trip. Rather, they and their children would be starving, desperate and probably sick. They would have lost everything. They would face a horrific and uncertain future and they would pretty much do anything to survive. A few may indeed maintain their moral integrity and quietly watch their children starve to death, but the vast majority of refugees will become looters, most of them violent? Many would be in loosely formed bands for the purpose of overwhelming homes or retreats. They will resent and hate those who have stored food in advance and feel it is not fair that preppers should "hoard" food while their families starve. From the preppers point of view they may only have enough food for their own family to survive and to give it away would doom their own family.

Some "Preppers" will have stored food, fuel and arms for themselves and their loved ones, but unfortunately most will have chosen to do so in their suburban or country home, hobby farm or cabin on the lake. First, when WT-SHTF, the neighbors that knew of your prepping will come to your door when they run low on food, first asking then demanding your food; see the Twilight Zone episode "The Shelter" by Rod Serling who understood human nature. Second, looting attacks (violent home invasions) will take place again and again and again on every house, occupied or not, as the locust like hoard spreads across the land looking for that last morsel of food. Remote homes/retreats will be least susceptible but eventually every home/retreat that can be found will be looted. It may take some time for them to reach the mountain lake cabins, but they will reach them, and overwhelm them all. The defenders of homes and retreats will be forced to repeatedly kill and dispose of the bodies of the attackers and deal with the heartbreak of their own dead and wounded until they themselves are eventually overwhelmed by a superior force. No matter how well prepared, the retreat will be overrun. Why? There will be a great many attacks from random groups large and small, day and night, day after day, week after week for months. Also, well organized and well armed groups may note your solid resistance and plan your demise over time since they know you are not going anywhere. Eventually they will use tear gas, explosives, armored vehicles, etc. When they want you, they will take you. The other contingency is that the "attackers" may be the U.S. Military or a local government enforcing Martial Law for the confiscation of food and arms. Frankly, I do not foresee long term survival unless the retreat remains unknown to all.

Typical homes and cabins cannot be defended well. A high velocity .308 projectile will pass through the entire house unless it hits a wall stud or appliance and wall studs are typically spaced 16" apart. Eventually a large enough group or gang will take the house, kill/rape/plunder, transport the goods to their lair and then move on to other targets. They would systematically attack every home/retreat they can find. Any surviving defenders will become refugees. Even with a remote food/equipment cache, the defenders will still be refugees with insufficient food to survive until food could be grown and without the means to preserve it if they could grow it. Almost everyone who becomes a refugee will surely die quickly from exposure, violent mobs, physical attack, starvation, disease, infection or dysentery (which would be epidemic due to fouled water).

You may think this is an exaggeration about the vulnerability of your home and our society, but just take a minute here to step out of your house, walk to the street and study your home for a minute. Imagine you, your brother, and your friend from down the street trying to defend your house at night with two deer rifles and a 12 gauge shotgun against 20 guys with semi-automatic assault rifles, night vision goggles and maybe tear gas and an armored vehicle. You would be surrounded. There would be no help from anywhere and you would not have a "snowball's chance". They will tell you that if you just give up your supplies they will leave you unharmed. When you surrender they will have you haul your goods to their vehicles with smiling gratitude then they will tie you up and torture your wife or children in front of you until you tell them where your "secret supply caches" of food and gold are located, even if you do not have one. (For an example in fiction, see the movie Nevada Smith with Steve McQueen.) The thing is they already know that many retreats have such caches so, until dead from torture, they will not believe that you do not. They will kill the men, children and older women and take any young women with them. Yes, in many cases it will be that horrific. Throughout history it has always been such.

Your home was built completely dependent on services, including sewer, water, electricity, heating fuel and the fuel for your car to get you to and from work and stores. Without electricity you have no heat, no air conditioning, inability to cook (a large propane tank is an exception), no lights, no water, no sewer (requires water for the toilet). Without these services your home is a poorly located weatherproof shell that was built the way it was and where it was only because of the "absolute certainty" that there would always be electrical service. Here is an eye opening weekend experiment: Turn off all the electricity to your house (except the refrigerator and freezer which would be taped shut), turn off the gas and water and prohibit the use of your vehicles. You will find out in a hurry about life without electricity. Now look at your neighbor's house, think about the houses across town, think of your parents or brother's house across the country. All across the nation homes are about the same (about 99%), they all depend upon services that will not be available after the loss of electricity. And almost all will only have a few weeks to a few months of food on their kitchen shelves, pantry and refrigerator. Translation, almost all of their occupants will become refugees when the food runs out or when they are overwhelmed by attackers and will die soon thereafter. All of them. Again, the fundamental force behind any and all industrial society is electricity.

Think about it: When you are forced out of your home or run out of food and there is no new food to be had anywhere, what are you going to do, where are you going to go? This won't be like in the movies or books, there will be no cavalry, no supplies parachuted in, and no relief trucks arriving just in time. There will be no help at all. Over 310 million people in the U.S. will be on their own just like you with almost no new food being produced or imported. Think of the total USA food supply like a giant hour glass being filled with food production and imports just as fast as it is being consumed. After an EMP or super solar flare the consumption will continue at the same rate while food production and importation will essentially stop completely. That means no more new food added to the hour glass! Perhaps one third of total US food supply will rot due to the lack of refrigeration and 80% of the balance is somewhere in the production, storage or distribution system, none of which still function. The balance available to the masses will be consumed as it is looted. The hour glass will be essentially empty for the masses. For anyone to survive they must have enough to eat until new food could be grown, perhaps the second summer after TEOTWAWKI, assuming you have the means and know how.

Hansel and Gretel were dumped in the forest to die or fend for themselves, probably so their parents could try to feed the then smaller family. During severe famine in the middle ages this forced reduction in the size of families was not unheard of. Most of us have no concept of real famine. If we did, each and every one of us would have at least three

years supply of food while obtaining it was so simple, so easy. The representation of the Witch as a cannibal is not a coincidence. Cannibalism was widespread in the past among humans throughout the world; in many cultures it was an everyday thing even without famine. Severe famine and cannibalism, however, go hand and hand, for example the Uruguayan Air Force Flight 57, the Donner Party, Siege of Leningrad, etc. So, when the masses are starving, be careful, they may not look on you as either friend or foe; they may think of you as dinner.

New food cannot be grown until after the violent gangs are gone and those with seeds and know how are no longer afraid of having their gardens discovered. The first new food probably could not be safely grown until the second summer. The first crop by inexperienced gardeners without insecticides, fertilizer, equipment or pumped water will be a disaster. You had better have enough food to get your family through at least until the third year and way more (non-hybrid) seeds than you think you need. My mother was a teenager in the Great Depression. She said they would plant one seed for the birds, one for the bugs and one for themselves, but since they could buy seeds, you should add one more category, production of the seeds for next year's crops. By the way, do you know how to avoid cross pollination and loss of the usefulness of the seeds? Do you know how to collect and store the seeds? If you are not doing it now, you probably won't be able to do it later when your lives depend on it.

After the burst, widespread looting would begin within a day or two in larger cities without containment due to limited communications and totally inadequate law enforcement. Within a week there would be near total anarchy except in some small towns and military bases. Well armed gangs and escaped prisoners, with the most brutal and ruthless taking leadership, would essentially take over and loot, rape, kill and plunder every house and food source within their territory no matter how well defended. In only a couple of weeks these well armed gangs would become very proficient at taking homes and farms and all they could find would be overrun. Over time, every farm animal of every description would be consumed. Wildlife and fisheries would be wiped out. The seed grains needed for next year's crop would be consumed. Unspeakable atrocities, cannibalism, and torture would be rampant. The desperate conditions will unleash the darkest side of human nature. Throughout history, such atrocities consistently take place when there are no consequences in desperate times. Absolute power corrupts absolutely.

As we go about our day to day lives it is very difficult to comprehend that any of the people we know or those that live down the street would do such things, but studies such as the "Stanford Prison Experiment" and others have shown perhaps one third of a random selection of emotionally stable individuals will, within a matter of a few days, show brutal tendencies. Think of that! One third of the "problem free, mentally stable" people! Further, these guys were not trying to survive, they were merely placed in a position of near absolute power over others. In the anarchy after "Grid Down", if the above is any indication, one third of the population (or much more considering the survival circumstances) would become violent predators plus virtually all of the neighborhood nut cases, criminals, perverts and those in prison. It would be the worst nightmare of the zombie horror films. The [Los Angeles] Lakers [basketball team] recently won their umpteenth season and there were riots, even with a huge law enforcement presence. One news report read: "Despite a massive Los Angeles police presence Thursday night, sporadic violence broke out near Staples Center after the Lakers defeated the Boston Celtics in the NBA Finals. Crowds hurled bottles and other objects at police, smashed marquees, jumped on vehicles, broke windows, and set rubbish dumpsters and vehicles on fire..." But, what if there had been no police presence? This was a happy mob.

Eventually, over a year or so, these gangs would be killed off by a variety of means such as losses taking retreats, heavily armed organized communities, occasional army units, rival gangs trying to survive, fighting amongst themselves or, when there were no more places to loot or stored food to eat, they would starve to death.

In six months to a year 90% of the US population would be dead. The higher the current population density of an area the higher percentage death rate since the density of looters and gangs would wipe out almost every prepper, farmer, or retreat no matter how well defended leaving nothing to survive on until food could be grown and leaving very few who have the supplies and know how to grow it. A much higher percentage will survive in rural Kansas while almost no one would survive in densely populated areas.

What about help from overseas? The USA currently exports a great deal of food to feed a hungry world. Without those exports the rest of the world will have food shortages. Some countries may send aid over the short term of a month or two, but over the long term of a year or two, it would be very doubtful since what country is going to starve its own people so that food can be shipped to the USA? Even if ships are sent, what captain will dock his ship amongst a mob of looters. Even if they docked, how do you unload a container ship with no operable cranes? Even if you could unload ships, how could you move goods inland with no fuel for trucks or trains? Even if food could be

moved inland, what coastal community would export food when they need it desperately for their own survival?

It would be far far worse for us now than it was in 1890 because then they had systems in place that worked without electricity such as steam locomotives, horse drawn wagons and plows and lots and lots of work horses and mules. Most important, they had era farming tools and the knowledge of how to live their lives and store food without electricity. Just as vital, they had a functioning society with on-going production capacity and supply lines for basic staples. Even the Amish buy staples, they do not produce everything themselves. After TEOTWAWKI almost no one will have those tools, supplies, sources for staples or that knowledge. Realistically, the USA could not even begin to support the 1890 population of about 64 million people. Unfortunately our existence might be more like the Jamestown colony, circa 1609-10 or so with hostiles at the gate, starvation, disease, and massive die offs so severe they called it the "Starving Time". It could be like that for us without adequate food storage.

What about the military? The nation's military is largely unprotected from an EMP. Since the early 1990s, "Essentially all our new weapon systems have been built with a waiver for EMP hardening," says Bartlett, a scientist and inventor who is the ranking member of the House Armed Services' Subcommittee on Air and Land Forces according to a NewsMax article.

The Military would be pretty much immobilized although they would have more stored fuel and supplies than most. The good news is that if the soldiers who remained with their units could maintain order in the immediate area of their base, food could be grown the first summer. Therefore, if you cannot afford to have a hidden retreat, relocating to be close to a military base in a farming area with good rainfall may save you. The bad news is that while the military won't rape and plunder, they will take your food, fuel and guns "for the common good". Since they could defeat gangs that had taken over regional food storage warehouses they may be able to accumulate a very large supply of food. They would balance out the food supply and your only hope then is that enough food could be produced for everyone or else everyone would starve together. Still, it is better than being a refugee with no future at all.

The consequences of an EMP burst are consistently understated. Writers of reports or articles don't tell the whole story because they either worry about being accused of "Fear mongering" or they are in denial themselves, being unwilling to let their mind take them to the inevitable consequences of a modern society suddenly finding itself permanently without electricity. Frequently there are articles about the possibility of an EMP and they state that the consequences would be "catastrophic" or "disastrous" or "devastating" without going into detail about what that really means. What they don't say is this: Considering our limited ability to create, process and transport new food without electricity and doing so in a state of near total anarchy, the survival rate would be maybe 10%. Even Dr. William R. Graham who is Chairman of the Commission to Assess the Threat to the United States from Electromagnetic Pulse Attack and who is intimately familiar will all aspects of EMP and the vulnerability of our infrastructure and the EMP effect on transformers, etc. has concluded that a 250 mile high burst over Kansas would cause the death of about 80% of the 310,000,000 US population. The actual report to Congress, however, just says "Catastrophic".

Who will survive? Primarily those who use the "The Art of War" tactics of avoiding a direct conflict with superior forces by using deception and concealment "The general who is skilled in defense hides in the most secret recesses of the earth". Without electricity the majority of the population will either kill each other off or die from disease, exposure or starvation. The survivors, for the most part, will be those who do not fight at all. The Golden Hoard or a Government entity cannot fight you or take your supplies if they do not know you exist. The key is to be well hidden during the six months to a year or so after TEOTWAWKI, then keep hidden as much as possible while you grow food but maintain a high level of surveillance and defense. This tactic is completely contrary to the Rambo survivalist types with an arsenal at their disposal and an attitude of "Bring it on" for the Golden Horde and gangs.

"There are a few possible survival scenarios presented here in no particular order since each individual must adapt their skills, knowledge and resources to their situation.

1. Very remote, well hidden, well armed, well trained and well stocked retreats with enough people to guard and defend the retreat and the equipment and other resources to produce food. Food production could begin by the second summer but if it is far away from where you live, you might not be able to get to it. ("Patriots").

2. Very small towns that are cohesive enough to band together, consolidate resources and defend against gangs or refugee throngs (as in the novels One Second After and Lights Out). This is a tactic that would allow food production to begin ASAP. A defendable town on the coast or a large river would be best to allow fish to supplement the diet. However, because it will be ruled by a government, they may also confiscate your supplies for the common good. The Alaska panhandle would be ideal but you "gotta like the rain".

3. Areas in the immediate proximity of military bases where good gardens could be grown. You would still have to survive some home invasions and looting early on but the military presence could provide the security, technical knowledge, tools, equipment and fuel for food production to begin ASAP following TEOTWAWKI. You will be under their "anal" direction and have few freedoms, but you and your family may survive.

4. Those who have stored food and fuel, have access to good water and can stay completely out of sight for up to a year (undetectable fully serviced basement or bomb type shelter). This would allow a family to live in quiet comfort while the rest of the world kills itself off. It is much more doable than one might think, see the references section about "Basements".

5. Those very rare few who could survive in the wilderness well off any trails and undetectable by smoke, smell or sight for a year or more by placing a large cache of food and survival equipment at a wilderness hide. While I could survive year around in the Alaska wilderness if I did not get sick or hurt and if properly prepared (having done so), here in Georgia, the forests would just be too "crowded" to keep hidden; the survivor in the woods here would simply be "The Last Man Standing".

6. Those who had a well stocked sailboat that could be sailed to the tropics (Watch out for Pirates). This is a situation where having gold and silver would pay big dividends.

7. The Amish are wonderfully equipped with tools and knowledge to survive and thrive in the long term without electricity, however, they will be wiped out and their food stocks taken since they do not have guns or knowledge of defensive tactics. They do not have the ability to survive in the short term against armed gangs. This is a classic example of the skill sets necessary to survive early in TEOTWAWKI are much different that those required much later in TEOTWAKI but that for anyone to survive in the long term, they must have both sets. Since the Amish farms function without electricity, when they and the gangs are dead and gone, the tools and systems will still be in place if you know how to utilize them. Of course, all of the animals will have been consumed.

Others who may survive are refugees with skills useful in a post TEOTWAWKI world who may find refuge in one of the above. What skills? Read books about life in 1890 (Lawyers, politicians and stock brokers need not apply but those who could fix a tooth or build a steam engine would be in high demand... a steam engine fired by wood or coal could power a generator to create electricity). Travel tip: have a map showing the nearest military base and be there very soon because even the military will have its limits of how many people they can handle.

WTSHTF, at some point each and every one of us must decide if we actually want to survive to a life that would be harder than any we have ever imagined. But more than that we must decide if we are willing to kill other human beings to defend our food cache and loved ones? Are we willing to kill others to take food so our loved ones could survive? What about witnessing the killings, rapes, torture of our friends, neighbors and loved ones and enduring the smell of rotting bodies that goes on without end. Are we strong enough to mentally go through all of that and keep our sanity and our will to live? Will we survive the guilt of our own survival when the vast majority has died? Further, the mental stress after an EMP burst would be monumental. People would have to instantly transition from the availability of vast amounts of information at their fingertips and information overload to a near total information vacuum. A great many will not be able to handle all or even part of it. Even highly trained military personnel do not handle such events well, how can ordinary citizens hope to live through it and stay sane.

What about Mutual Assured Destruction that kept USA and USSR from war? Maybe but MAD might not work. There are some fanatics in Iran. Ahmadinejad has said that he wants to bring about the coming of the 12th Imam: "Our revolution's main mission is to pave the way for the reappearance of the 12th Imam, the Mahdi" – Ahmadinejad. (So what then are the conditions for the Mahdi's arrival? The destruction of Israel and world conflagration). The threat of our retaliation and the destruction of Iran and the Middle East may not be much of a deterrent in Ahmadinejad's belief system. If Ahmadinejad could simultaneously detonate a bomb in Tel Aviv and 6 to 10 nuclear satellites around the globe at 250 miles high to cause the eventual death of the majority of the world's infidel population and significantly level the playing field, do you think he would? Are you kidding? In a New York minute. He can't do it yet, but, even though it may take years, Iran is working feverishly on the satellite delivery system and in making bombs themselves.

Of course, our own Sun could beat Ahmadinejad to the punch. Severe space weather events that we know about originating from the Sun with the Earth in the "line of fire" have occurred in 1989, 1921 and 1859 (geomagnetic solar super storms). In 1989 only one of the very large difficult to replace step up/step down transformer was destroyed. The 1921 event was 10 times stronger and if it happened today it would probably destroy all of the large transformers. The 1859 event was much stronger than the one in 1921. Such an event could easily destroy the huge trans-

formers that would take years to replace (If the capacity to produce them still existed) which means years without electricity for most of the population. The problem is, we can't survive that long. Scientists consider the recurrence of such a solar super storm as not just a possibility but as inevitable. Indeed, if the Earth had been in the line of fire on April 19, 2010 we quite probably would be living "Grid Down" in TEOTWAWKI right now. How prepared were you and your family on April 19?

Can an EMP burst be prevented? The Heritage Foundation has written extensively on the subject and it is well worth the read. At present defensive missiles are in place in Alaska and California to take out intercontinental missiles in the atmosphere from N. Korea. We must have defensive missiles around the entire USA that are capable of taking out long and short range missiles (such as a Scud or Iran's new 1,200 mile missile launched from a freighter like Iran did in the Caspian Sea). When the "Star Wars" defense was proposed in the 1980's there were those who said such a defense was not possible because "you can't hit a bullet with another bullet", but now the experts say "We can hit a spot on a bullet with another bullet". We have the technology to do this.

We should protect our transformers by requiring all new ones to be EMP and solar flare protected (it adds about 5% to the cost). We could use that stimulus money to retrofit existing transformers, if possible and protect our railroad engines and systems, fuel production, transportation, and electrical generation systems.

If we prepare now, quickly, two things will be accomplished: First, there would be a good chance that the civilized world we know today would survive an EMP burst or super solar storm and, two, there would be far less incentive for an EMP strike. But, as it stands now, if you wanted to destroy the USA whom you perceive to be the devil, you would be salivating at the prospect of launching a few missiles off a freighter in the Gulf of Mexico and causing the death of 90% of the US population. For those who wish to destroy us it has to be positively orgasmic and we should absolutely not underestimate their resourcefulness. Remember, they have access to all of the EMP information you and I do and probably much more. They also have the ability to coordinate a massive cyber attack on the electrical grid which is extremely vulnerable.

That said, the nuclear genie is indeed out of the bottle. Al-Qaeda is said to control 80 freighter ships. It is only a matter of time before organized terrorist groups obtain a bomb that they can sail into one of our port cities. A crude bomb from Iran's uranium would weigh a few thousand pounds. The fact is, we will have to accept the horrific reality that, from time to time, a major coastal city will be nuked from a freighter or small submarine, terrorists have both. Such is the reality of the failure to contain the nuclear genie. They have the desire to kill every man, woman and child in the USA and they have the means to deliver a nuke to our coastal cities; they just need the nuke.

What would be so difficult about having someone like "Jihad Jane" purchase a good sized boat with a dock slip at Gangplank Marina on the Potomac River in Wash. D.C., motor out through Chesapeake Bay to the ocean to pick up a nuke from a freighter at night then arrive at Gangplank Marina on a weekday afternoon and detonate it ?

If one of our cities is nuked, the nation will be under martial law. If your retreat is very far away, the police or military may prevent you from getting there. If you live anywhere on either coast they will probably not let you exit inland. Both politicians and the military have shown their propensity to confiscate guns at such times and most certainly will do so again. Further, the "temporary" martial law may well become permanent. Your stored food may be deemed "Hoarding" and be confiscated in an unconstitutional but nonetheless real house to house search performed by guys who are looking for secret hiding places. You do not want these people to be able to find either your beans or your bullets because, even under permanent martial law, we may still be hit by an EMP burst or solar storm or another coastal nuke.

The world is different today than ever before. The basic problem in our psyche is that we have the "white hat" cowboy mentality; we never throw the first punch, we never draw the gun first; we wait for the bad guy to shoot or draw and only then do we react. This time, if we wait for them to strike first with an EMP without being well prepared, this country, as we know it, will cease to exist. Our military may well destroy their country in retaliation, if they knew where the nuke(s) came from, but the above EMP scenario will still take place here regardless of what happens to the other guy later.

During the cold war we lived with the fear in the back of our minds that one day there may be Global Thermonuclear War that would destroy the world. However, while Global Thermonuclear War is still a possibility, a super solar storm, EMP burst and/or nuked coastal cities are eventual certainties. Nuking a coastal city is easiest and most likely, of course, but our unconscionable lack of preparation makes an EMP burst so appealing they will do everything in their power to make it happen.

Noah knew he could not tread water for long and built the Ark. Since people cannot live on a zero calorie diet for long and the Federal Government, who's primary duty is to protect us, is doing nothing to prevent or prepare for an EMP, super solar flare or cyber attack, we all had better store at least three years of beans, band aids, bullets and benzin. In other words, become a "Prepper", but do so wisely, very well hidden and very very secretly.

"If you think the unthinkable and devise plans to survive, then when the unthinkable occurs, you are prepared and will make the correct choices automatically." (SurvivalBlog. com) A basic rule of thumb in survival situations is that 10% will do the absolute wrong thing, 80% will do nothing and wait to be led, while 10% do the right thing.

An EMP, a massive cyber attack, and a nuked coastal city are all possible but a super solar flare is inevitable. Just a word of caution here, once you let yourself think about such threats and project the inevitable outcomes of life here in the USA without electricity, it is very difficult to get your mind back inside that "denial" box."- Tom S.

About wood stoves: Having lived in an Alaskan cabin with only wood heat for four years I know that the smoke makes it very difficult to keep your presence a secret. Even a year or two after TEOTWAWKI you still will want to keep your existence as secret as possible, therefore do not use just any wood stove; use the 95% efficient and virtually smokeless wood stoves available that, with very dry wood, produce almost no smoke. Further, use wood fuel that does not have a strong odor such as birch and avoid those that do such as cedar or some hardwoods. For wilderness survival there is nothing better than a small fan forced wood stove such as the Sierra stove or similar. I have used these on extended Alaska camp-outs with the Boy Scouts with great success and always unlimited fuel. Because they are fan forced they are very good at burning any wood and producing almost no smoke. This type of fan forced fire is very useful for surviving in the wilderness or, with larger versions and side feed, using outside your retreat to process food.

Basements: Undetectable fully serviced basements/retreats: A family or group in an undetectable basement or bomb shelter can survive in quiet comfort while the rest of the world kills itself off without the tear jerking confrontations from starving beggars, violent confrontations with gangs, looters or the military. And yes, it is very possible.

I once saw an article about a family who bought a house and after living there for two years discovered there was a full basement under the house. The previous owner had sealed up the stairs going down and filled in the small windows that had previously been visible. Why did he do that? He was hiding a flooded basement. So, if a basement can be invisible to someone who actually lives in a house for over two years, what would it take to make a basement invisible to looters and gangs who would be there for less than 30 minutes?   That will be the subject of a separate article.

Selected References:

SurvivalBlog.com, numerous writings

"Electromagnetic Pulse Weapons: Congress Must Understand the Risk" by Baker Spring, Heritage Foundation Web-Memo #2822

"Report of the Commission to Assess the Threat to the United States from Electromagnetic Pulse (EMP) Attack," Volume 1: Executive Report, 2004

"Report of the Commission to Assess the Threat to the United States from Electromagnetic Pulse (EMP) Attack: Critical National Infrastructures," April 2008
Executive Report (See the EMP Commission web site.)

From the Executive Report Summary: "However, now even a single, low-yield nuclear explosion high above the United States... can produce a large-scale EMP effect that could result in a widespread loss of electronics, but no direct fatalities, and may not necessarily evoke a large nuclear retaliatory strike by the U.S. military. This, coupled with published articles discussing the vulnerability of U.S. critical infrastructure control systems, and some U.S. military battlefield systems to the effects of EMP, may create a new incentive for other countries to rapidly develop or acquire a nuclear capability."

"The electrical power system has become virtually fully dependent upon electronic systems working nearly flawlessly. The overall system reliability is testimony to the skill and effectiveness of the control systems. However, the lack of margin (combination of generation and transmission margins) results in making catastrophic cascading outages far more likely, and should the electronics be disrupted, the system is highly likely to fail on a broad scale. Thus, the small margin and reliance on electronics give rise to EMP vulnerability."

"All production for these large transformers used in the United States is currently offshore. Delivery time for these items under benign circumstances is typically one to two years. There are about 2,000 such transformers rated at or above 345 kV in the United States with about 1 percent per year being replaced due to failure or by the addition of new ones. Worldwide production capacity is less than 100 units per year and serves a world market, one that is growing at a rapid rate in such countries as China and India. Delivery of a new large transformer ordered today is nearly 3 years, including both manufacturing and transportation. An event damaging several of these transformers at once means it may extend the delivery times to well beyond current time frames as production is taxed. The resulting impact on timing for restoration can be devastating. Lack of high voltage equipment manufacturing capacity represents a glaring weakness in our survival and recovery to the extent these transformers are vulnerable...."

"Many electric generating plants would be severely damaged by uncontrolled shut down. Almost none, even if not damaged, would be able to restart without external power."

"EMP is one event that may couple ultimately unmanageable currents and voltages into an electrical system routinely operated with little margin and cause the collapse of large portions of the electrical system. In fact, the Commission is deeply concerned that such impacts are certain in an EMP event unless practical steps are taken to provide protection for critical elements of the electric system and to provide for rapid restoration of service, particularly to essential loads."

"The current strategy for recovering from such failures is based on the assumption of sporadic failures of small numbers of components, and for larger failures, drawing on resources from outside the affected area. This strategy leaves us ill-prepared to respond effectively to an EMP attack that would potentially result in damage to vast numbers of components nearly simultaneously over an unprecedented geographic scale."

"The Commission has concluded that the electrical system within the NERC region so disrupted will collapse with near certainty. Thus one or more of the three integrated, frequency-independent NERC regions will be without electrical service. This loss is very large geographically and restoration is very likely to be beyond short-term emergency backup generators and batteries. Any reasonable EMP event would be much larger than the Texas region so basically the concern is the Eastern and Western regions with Texas either included or not depending upon the location of the weapon. The basic threat to U.S. society that moves an EMP event from a local or short-term adverse impact to a more prolonged and injurious event is the time it takes to restore electrical and other infrastructure service.

North American Electric Reliability Corporation three regions, Texas, West and East. All of these collapse mechanisms acting simultaneously provide the unambiguous conclusion that electrical power system collapse for the NERC region largely impacted by the EMP weapon is inevitable in the event of attack using even a relatively low-yield device of particular characteristics.

EMP attack on the electrical power system is an extraordinarily serious problem but one that can be reduced below the level of a catastrophic national consequence through focused effort coordinated between industry and government."

Independent Working Group, "Missile Defense, the Space Relationship, and the Twenty-First Century," 2009 Report, p. 130, at

Rawles, James Wesley, "Patriots: A Novel of Survival in the Coming Collapse", Ulysses Press, 2009

Forstchen, William R., One Second After, Tom Doherty Assoc., 2009

Lights Out, by Half Fast (formerly an Internet e-novel, now being published)

CBS Twilight Zone episode "The Shelter"

Brieitbart.com "Spies compromised US electric grid", Associated Press

Severe Space Weather Events—Understanding Societal and Economic Impacts Workshop Report Committee on the Societal and Economic Impacts of Severe Space Weather Events: A Workshop, National Research Council http://www.nap.edu/catalog/12507.html

"EMP Attack Would Send America into a Dark Age" "EMP Attack Would Wipe Out U.S. Military", NewsMax, Monday, 28 Sep 200

Some key quotes:

"An estimated 80 percent of the population would die within a year of an EMP strike from starvation or disease or would freeze to death, according to William Graham, who was chairman of the congressional Commission to Assess the Threat to the United States from Electromagnetic Pulse Attack."

"The nation's military is largely unprotected in the event an enemy launches a nuclear bomb that would fry microchips and the power grid with an electromagnetic pulse (EMP), Rep. Roscoe Bartlett, R-Md., tells Newsmax."

"Since the early 1990s, "Essentially all our new weapon systems have been built with a waiver for EMP hardening," says Bartlett, a scientist and inventor who is the ranking member of the House Armed Services' Subcommittee on Air and Land Forces.

"If an enemy used an EMP enhanced weapon — and Russian generals told our EMP commission that they had developed weapons which emit 200 kilovolts per meter weapon — I've been assured by experts in the area that everything would be down," says Bartlett, who has been the leading member of Congress fighting to recognize EMP as a threat."

In fact, "One of the first things [an enemy] would do is an EMP laydown to deny you the use of all your equipment which is not EMP hardened, which is essentially all our equipment," Bartlett says. "They don't harden against EMP any more."

The Stanford Prison Experiment:

The Stanford prison experiment was a study of the psychological effects of becoming a prisoner or prison guard. The experiment was conducted in 1971 by a team of researchers led by Psychology Professor Philip Zimbardo at Stanford University. Twenty-four undergraduates were selected out of 70 to play the roles of both guards and prisoners and live in a mock prison in the basement of the Stanford psychology building. Those selected were chosen for their lack of psychological issues, crime history, and medical disabilities, in order to obtain a representative sample. Roles were assigned based on a coin toss.

Prisoners and guards rapidly adapted to their roles, stepping beyond the boundaries of what had been predicted and leading to dangerous and psychologically damaging situations. One-third of the guards were judged to have exhibited "genuine" sadistic tendencies, while many prisoners were emotionally traumatized and two had to be removed from the experiment early. After a graduate student (prisoner #819) broke down from the inhumane conditions in the prison, and realizing that he had been passively allowing unethical acts to be performed under his direct supervision, Zimbardo concluded that both prisoners and guards had become too grossly absorbed in their roles and terminated the experiment after six days.

Milgram, Stanley, 1974 book, Obedience to Authority: An Experimental View. Milgram described experiments conducted at Yale University in 1961after the start of the trial of German Nazi war criminal Adolf Eichmann in Jerusalem. Milgram devised his psychological study to answer the question: "Was it that Eichmann and his accomplices in the Holocaust had mutual intent, in at least with regard to the goals of the Holocaust?" In other words, "Was there a mutual sense of morality among those involved?" Milgram's testing suggested that it could have been that the millions of accomplices were merely following orders, despite violating their deepest moral beliefs. He set up an experiment and showed that most ordinary people can become accomplices in killing totally innocent individuals.

Tom Peters and Robert H. Waterman Jr wrote in 1981 that the Milgram experiment and the Stanford prison experiment were frightening in their implications about the danger which lurks in the darker side of human nature.

33 Minutes   Protecting America in the New Missile Age (2008) by The Heritage Foundation, 214 Massachusetts Avenue, NE, Washington, DC 20002 Ph. (202) 546-4400

Food production and life styles in the USA in 1900 compared to life today:

In 1900, 39 percent of the U.S. population (about 30 million people) lived on farms; today that percentage has plummeted to less than 2 percent (only about 4.5 million people). The transformation of the United States from a nation of farmers to a nation in which less than 2 percent of the population is able to feed the other 98 percent is made possible only by technology.

Human survival without food:

Physical condition, age, amount of fat, and air temperature are major factors but an absolute deprivation of food, on average, will greatly diminish a person's capacity for physical work within a few days. After 4 to 5 days without food, the average person will suffer from impaired judgment and have difficulty performing simple intellectual tasks. After two weeks without food, the average person will be virtually incapacitated. Death typically results between 30 to 60 days with a few being able to last up to 70 days. This is without any physical activity and plenty of good water.

Irish Hunger Strike of 1981

Originally posted at
www.SurvivalBlog.com
Copyright 2012

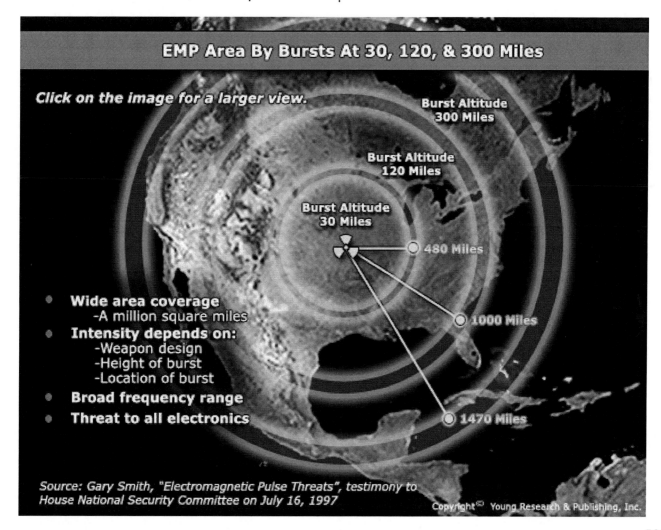

EMP Area By Bursts At 30, 120, & 300 Miles

Click on the image for a larger view.

Burst Altitude 300 Miles
Burst Altitude 120 Miles
Burst Altitude 30 Miles

480 Miles
1000 Miles
1470 Miles

- **Wide area coverage**
  -A million square miles
- **Intensity depends on:**
  -Weapon design
  -Height of burst
  -Location of burst
- **Broad frequency range**
- **Threat to all electronics**

Source: Gary Smith, "Electromagnetic Pulse Threats", testimony to House National Security Committee on July 16, 1997

Copyright© Young Research & Publishing, Inc.

533

MZBs:
Are you prepared?

http://www.doomers.us/forum2/index.p...c,62074.0.html

MZB! Those three letters are enough to put a healthy dose of doom-enriched fear into any well prepped doomer right? It took me a while just to learn what those letters meant; when I did finally look them up in the acronym appendix of the doomer's bible I was silent. **Mutant-Zombie-Bikers?** What kind of fantasy freak group was I associating myself with? I just disliked the term because I couldn't get over the strange thoughts being conjured up in my head of a pack of deranged bikers on dirt bikes, old Harley's, quads, you name it with bleeding flesh and hollowed eyes all coming to attack us after a collapse. We would be all snug and happy in our doomsteads and BOLs but these MZBs would seek us out to destroy us. So yeah, I just couldn't deal with the term and didn't care for it much because it was too abstract and unrealistic.

As time went on and my doomerish view of the world became more and more into focus I kept revisiting the MZB concept. What if the zombie in them didn't refer to some ghoulish character but rather someone who had lost everything and gained the 100 yard stare? Someone who has lost all sense of purpose but still feels the need to move forward? What if the mutant part referred to the transformation some unprepared over-suburbanized schmuck goes through as they realize everything they had worked for, all their competing with the Jones', all their mass consuming waste was all for naught and now had nowhere to go, nothing to live off of, and no knowledge of how to begin to survive? What if the biker part didn't represent the biker gangs of today but rather the same misguided victim of suburbia taking their hobby bike with the last bit of gas and hitting the road in search of food for their overweight, weak, and defenseless family to never return? What if a MZB is simply a former misguided suburbia rat who is now discovering what it means to live and is angry at himself, angry at the world, and especially angry at those who are living a more comfortable post-collapse existence because they were prepared?

As we move closer to the point where a total societal breakdown occurs one way or another it will become very apparent who is prepared and who isn't. My head has been filled with fantasies that when the day comes when anarchy dominates over civilized life that those who weren't prepared would be begging for help, doing anything they could to survive, but for the most part not resorting to violence. I stand corrected.

A casual dinner visit with some close friends was my point of awakening to how ugly everything will be. We were having beers and discussing how we keep getting warning article after warning article but nothing ever happens. Something commonly discussed here. We are tired of the warnings; we are tired of prepping for something that will never come; we are starting to not believe that there will be a collapse. At this point the brother of my friends comes in. He had been a former employee of mine during a construction project five years ago. During that there had been a conflict whereas he thought he was owed more for his efforts than we had paid him (bonus pay). Over the years it had seemed this rift had healed. He joined the conversation and then boldly stated, "if there is a day like you guys describe then I'll just hit the road and take whatever the **** I want. I'll finally get to get back all that the rich **** like you have taken from me! *** you rich bastards! You guys have only gotten ahead because of the sweat from people like me! The day you describe when payback will finally be here!"

We just sat there stunned! I had never considered myself rich. I had started my business with maxing out one credit card, buying used salvage equip and rehabbing it, and sold off all my furniture to buy opening inventory. I worked over 80 hours a week for the first several years while working another full time job. For all of the risk, hard work, and sacrifice for 10 years we make a nice comfortable living; my friends I was visiting had worked equally hard towards becoming a professor. All this time my friends brother was partying, in and out of jail, playing, playing, playing but now as he has nothing and we are comfortable there is an incredible anger and rage within him! Behold the birth of a MZB!

I don't know why but that moment brought together a flood of memories over the past few years of isolated events that I put no thought into. Working in the garden while a pickup truck of loud and obviously drunk guys driving by along the irrigation ditch road, as I looked up they flipped us off yelling obscenities; being threatened by employees that were being fired; being flipped off and cussed at by the low rider crowd (Bienvendos a Nuevo Mexico). All of a sudden what I thought were isolated incidents of angry individuals not to be taken seriously transformed into everything I thought that MZBs could never be.

The day is coming when the collapse does occur and that day will represent freedom by all those who have not prepared and those who have not been fortunate to make it. That day will represent the day that they can begin exchanging their anger for all the pieces we prepared ones have carefully put away safe and sound. There will be no begging for help by those angry hordes; we will be the ones begging for mercy as we give up all we worked so hard for and thoughtfully put away. These people who you see now at the bar at 5, those people you see wasting their few dollars on the bread and circus shows like Nascar races, football games, strip clubs, malls; those people that have invested more money into their vehicles than their vehicles are worth with stereos, chromed rims, oversized exhausts, etc.; it is these people that are the ones who we will be fearing. They have been undergoing a professional training in instant gratification and the day of collapse will be the moment when the supermall of mass instant gratification opens its doors: That supermall will the homes of the prepared.

Are you ready for that day? I know I'm not. I have plenty of supplies, firearms and ammo, water, fuel, you name it but I am not ready to defend it from masses of the angry hordes staking claims on all we have worked for. The day I saw the rage in my friends face I realized I wasn't ready. I had considered needing to defend myself from some abstract threat as foreign and vague as the term MutantZombieBiker; I hadn't considered needing to defend myself from what I bet is 85% of the mass population.

What happens when collapse comes and total anarchy let's go and you are one out of 10 families who is prepared and able to be comfortable. My 6+months of food, water, fuel, ammo will be taken by force and I will only be hoping that my family isn't brutalized. Take a piece of paper; make a grid of 3 dots by 3 dots. The dot in the center is you; the dots surrounding you are your unprepared neighbors who have always waved hello but who now realize you have what they need and are pissed off that you unfairly sacrificed your wages and effort to be prepared while they partied and played. You will not hold these people off at bay whether you are surrounded by 10 acres or are smack in the middle of suburbia. The only way you stand a chance is to begin converting those surrounding dots into equally prepared families who will stand strong with you. The problem is that each one of those families will have friends or families who will ultimately not have any preps and will come to claim their share and consequently part of your stores.

In the past year I have moved from NM to a smaller CO town. I was on the verge of making a decision on buying a property. One is 40 acres right on the edge of town but with a running water source and good farmable land. The other is 5 acres and a nice house with greenhouses shops, a creek, and several outbuildings where a doomer could survive so easily but is right in town. The third is 40 acres on the backside of a mountain overlooking town and has no running water, is completely undeveloped, 4wd access, and surrounded by eight other 40 acre parcels. One realization I had, is that those unprepared masses , are inherently lazy; they are unprepared because they refused to put in the extra effort to become prepared. It is the ant vs. grasshopper fable in the classic sense except the grasshopper will be armed and will outnumber the ant 1:10. By being on either of the first two locations I will be easily accessible by all but the absolute laziest ones. The running water on those two properties will also attract people. I have decided on the remote 40 acres (:30 4wd drive but only a :15 mt bike ride from town).

It will be a lot harder to make an ideal doomstead but there won't be any running water for people to follow, it will take a lot of physical effort, my preps will be hidden and the surrounding 40 acres properties are owned by similar doomer folks. Let the MZBs come because the advantage will be belonged to me. It is impractical to live there full time with kids in school and businesses to run but as part of the plan we will live in a plain, old small, non-fancy, house in town;

I realize that by living in a home equal to what I can afford I make myself and family a target. By living in the smallest home we can fit in and having zero preps visible we can let our friends and family wonder why we live so insanely modest. On weekends and days when we have time we stay at the retreat home which will be 100% off grid and will contain everything needed to be self sufficient for a minimum of 6 months.

There is an unfathomable amount of anger and bitterness in all of our communities. Other terms thrown out that evening in the conversation were that people who were prepped are "elitists", "better than others", "you can only prep if you are a rich ***", "we [bro & his buddies] can't wait to show who will be the new boss in town", "a new sheriff will be in town"; you all get the drift. The Mutant Zombie Bikers are alive and well and I know I have grossly underestimated their threat. Have you?

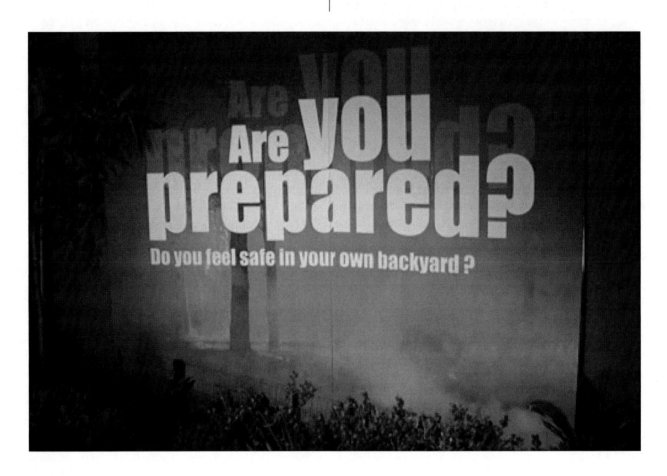

This is my personal testimony of
The Church of Jesus Christ of Latter Day Saints,
and of the miracle that it brought to my life.

This is my personal testimony of the Church of Jesus Christ of Latter Day Saints and the story of my gospel conversion. I wrote down this story at the request of my wife and sister in the summer/fall of 1990. They both felt that my conversion was so unique and offered such a powerful example of how the hand of the Lord could be seen in my life,EPILOGUE that it was my duty and obligation to share it with other people whenever the opportunity arose. All of the details are taken from my personal daily journals that I kept while I was in the service. (it should be noted with some curiosity, that at no other time in my life have I ever kept a journal, save during this brief period of my life where having a written record of what happened would later prove invaluable in transcribing this story). The story you are about to read is true, this is how it really happened. I have done my very best to draw all of the facts and my personal thoughts & impressions directly from my daily journal entries.

This is my story.......

Growing up in Newport Beach California never seemed to lend itself to any particular religious growth. I have only known one Mormon family that I can recall of, and they never brought up the subject of religion when I visited them. They were simply friends of mine, who had several children I played with when I was 12, and a garage that looked like a grocery store. Beyond that I never thought of them any different from anybody else.

My first real encounter with the church occurred during the summer of 1977 at the age of 14, when I took a vacation trip with my grandmother to the Hawaiian Islands. On one of our many drives we happened across the LDS Temple and went inside to take a look. The Temple building was quite beautiful & the grounds were immaculate. Inside the Visitor Center they gave us a special tour and explained some of the history of the Church of Jesus Christ of Latter Day Saints. While taking the tour a young Missionary approached me and asked if I would like to learn more about the Mormon Church when I returned back to the mainland. I gave the missionary my name and address, and told him that I would be glad to find out more about the church when I returned home.

It wasn't long at all after I had returned from the trip that two young men on ten speed bicycles dressed very neatly in dark suits and white shirts showed up at my doorstep. I invited them in and received the first lesson. Over the next month or so they returned several times to my house and I received several of the remaining lessons. Unfortunately, being only 14 years old at the time, and not at all sure about what I was being told, I no longer looked forward to them coming to my house. For that matter neither did my grandmother, as she didn't want her grandson to be converted to some religious sect. So she dis-invited the missionaries from returning to our house, and I never saw them again. Nevertheless, they did manage to leave a small seed in my mind that was to going to stay with me for the next 11 years.

During the following years I had many occasions to think about the Church of Jesus Christ of Latter Day Saints. I became very involved in the Disaster Preparedness movement, and at every corner there were always references to the Church. Over the years I had many opportunities to look into the Church, but I never did. The one time that I wanted to look into it I couldn't find anyone who knew about it at the time. While I was attending the University of Colorado at Boulder something sparked my curriosity in the LDS church again. So I went to the campus interfaith group and asked about the Mormon members. They told me there weren't any and that they didn't have any idea who I should contact. The moment was lost and the thought passed from my head. (Years latter I would find that there was a rather large building directly across from the campus that was a LDS church educational facility. I passed it nearly every day I went to school and never one noticed the large sign in front of it. I suppose it just wasn't time for me yet..) So the years simply passed on by.

Having graduated college in 1987 I joined the United States Army, and eventually arrived at Ft. Bragg N.C. in January of 1988. (When I joined the Army I committed myself to keeping an accurate journal of my daily events and thoughts. Were it not for that Journal, this testimony would have far fewer details). For the first time in my life I began to examine my concepts of religion, and began reading the Bible. They say there are no atheists in foxholes and I for one think thats true, but perhaps it was the jumping out of airplanes in the middle of stormy nights that got me started thinking about life in general. For a guy who was never actve in any church or inclined to any religious activities, one of the most religious experiances I had ever had in my life was standing in the doorway of an airplane in the middle of the night, starring out into the blackness with the wind rushing past my face waiting for a tap on my thigh telling me to take that first step out into the darkness. In moments like that you could hear and feel all the silent prayers of every soldier on that plane. There was never a time I made a jump that I didn't utter a silent prayer to the Lord asking him to watch over me as I once again hurled my fragile body out into his hands. And I also managed to carry a small plastic copy of Psalm 23 (The Lord is my Shepard) in my shirt pocket on all of those jumps.

Right about this time another service member moved out of his room across the hall from mine and failed to close his door when he left. When I went over to check his room I noticed that the only thing left behind in the room was his Bible. For no particular reason I picked it up and took it back to my room. In the coming weeks I slowly read the New Testament from start to finish. While in the middle of this I began regularly attending church services for the first time in nearly 15 years. I visited several different churches and talked with their members in an attempt to find out which one was the right for me. I found that I enjoyed going to Church and associating with other Christians on a regular basis. This only lasted for a couple of months before I became disenchanted though. It slowly became clear to me that there was something missing from these services that I was attending. There was a lack of fellowship or brotherhood. We all came together for an hour a week and that was it.

What I was looking for had to have much more depth than this. I always looked forward to going to Sunday services, but felt somehow let down afterwards. Somehow there had to be a way to bridge the gap between the rest of my life and Sunday mornings. I wanted to have the same feeling of spirit throughout the rest of the week, and to be actively involved and participating in my religion.

In May I participated in a long field exercise that gave me the chance to read the scriptures every day out in the woods by myself. For the first time I began to understand who and what Jesus Christ was, and what it really meant to be a Christian. For years I had always thought of myself as a Christian, but had never really known what it meant to be a Christian. I was the type that had always considered religion to be a matter of personal philosophy. Something best avoided in any organized manner. If religion was such a wonderful thing, then why had so many people been slaughtered by those who had "Divine Knowledge". This was a period of great thought, a time when I began to re-examine many of my personal beliefs. The more that I read and studied, the more that I began to realize how very little I truly knew. The Lord must have seen that I was now ready to receive his true word, and be returned to his flock. For once again two Mormon Missionaries came into my life.

On a Saturday afternoon in mid-July, while I was at a friends house working on some scuba gear, two young missionaries rang the doorbell. My friend invited them into his house and we had a long discussion about the nature of God and about the Christian Religion from the LDS point of view. We talked for the better part of 3 hours, before they had to leave for another appointment. They told me many things about the Mormon church that I had never known before. I can honestly say that I recalled little or nothing at all about the discussions I had had with the other missionaries 11 years before. At the time this was simply another exercise in religious argument, and I loved a good debate. Neither myself, nor my friend had any real intent or interest in pursuing what they were telling us, but it made for a great afternoon's discussion.

Over a month went by and once again I found myself at my friend's house working on the same scuba gear on a Tuesday night, when to our great surprise a different set of missionaries appeared at the doorstep. Again he welcomed them into his house. But this time my friend made it very clear that he had no intention of being converted, but that they might put their energies to better use by concentrating on me instead, and so they did. We talked for several hours this time and in much more depth. My friend challenged them on several of the points they brought up. He was quick to make them look up all of their claims in the Bible, and wouldn't accept anything from the Book of Mormon. Much to his consternation they did quite a good job. His only reply was that they had somehow misinterpreted the true meaning of the scriptures, not that he could be wrong. Before they left for their other appointments they invited me to come to a church welcome-home party for a returning missionary. I wasn't really very interested in going, but my buddy kept egging me on to go and enjoy the free dinner, so I eventually decided to go. They left me with a copy of the Book of Mormon, and asked only that I earnestly read it, ponder over what I had read, and pray to know if it was true. I told them that I would think about it, (not wanting to make any commitments one way or the other) and thanked them for the invitation to the party and the afternoon's discussion. (If it hadn't been for my friend's unending sarcasm and constant teasing about what a great Mormon I would make, I would never have gone, and the course of my life would have been very different indeed. To this day he holds himself responsible for my joining the church).

With more than a little uncertainty I showed up for the welcome-home party. A little bit nervous about just standing around in a room full of people I didn't know, in a Church I knew little about, I began venturing off down the corridors and reading the various announcements and posters on the walls. I quickly began to realize what this church considered to be important. I found a Genealogy room, several different classrooms all set up to teach the different age groups various lessons in Christianity, a Relief Society, the Bishops office, and a Library filled with educational materials. No sooner had I returned to the main area than the two Missionaries appeared and began introducing me to some of the members of their Church.

Never before had I met people that were so genuinely friendly, and who so heart-fully welcomed me (a complete stranger) to be part of their celebration. After the festivities ended I managed to gather 6 different missionaries for an impromptu discussion. This talk lasted several hours, and finally took us to one of their homes, where I received my first semi-formal lesson about the Church of Jesus Christ of Latter Day Saints. Every time they would bring up a different part of the lesson I would begin questioning them on it. I challenged most everything that they told me, and constantly wanted to know why?. My most common statement was "show me where it says that in the Bible". And what amazed me was that every time they were able to do so. Many of questions and challenges were answered with direct quotations of scripture, most of which they had learned by heart. At the end of the discussion they asked me to say a closing prayer, and invited me to attend chapel services with them on Sunday.

Sunday morning I showed up determined to find out what this was all about. I thought that all the discussions and talks in the world didn't amount to anything if the Sunday services didn't tie it all together in a harmonious way. The best way I can describe my feelings about that service are to say that it completely amazed me. Never had I been to anything that even vaguely approached it. First there was no minister to speak of: no old fatherly man dressed in robes, no one holding a Bible and walking back and forth telling the congregation how to achieve eternal salvation. But rather a young lady who was simply a member, who stood before an unadorned chapel, and shared with us her personal testimony of the living Jesus Christ. I found out that it was the responsibility of the membership to keep the word of Christ alive and well. Not that of just one appointed man, but of every man and woman. The Bishop acted more as a daily administrator, and gave the congregation a direction or theme for each meeting.

There were other things that were far different from churches I had been to in the past. Most notably there were many children of all ages. It actually seemed as if the chapel was filled with infants and toddlers and youngsters of all ages. This was a family oriented church, where the children were not hustled away into small rooms for Sunday school, while their parents attended the real services. Rather everyone attended the same service together, and then went off to the individual classes most suited for their age. I also noticed that the taking of the sacrament was a much more important event than in the other churches. Many people around me were truly in prayerful thought during this time, and fully respected the importance of what the sacrament was meant to be. The Sacrament was blessed and passed by the young men of the congregation, not the bishop. They also took the time to open and close each part of the service with a prayer offered by one of the members.

Afterwards I attended an Investigators Class with several other people that were considering joining church. The next event was the Priesthood meeting. This was yet another thing that was totally unlike anything I had experienced before. To think that this Church fully expected every able -bodied man to take up the Priesthood was beyond my imagination. This was something reserved for the specially chosen few, or so I thought. Again a member lead the meeting and I quickly learned that the Mormon Priesthood in not at all the same as the rest of Christianity views it. Throughout the religion the family rings out as the most important unit in life, and that for the most part all of the great things a person can hope to achieve will come to them through their family. And so it is that the Priesthood doesn't so much concern itself with instructing the main body of the church (though it clearly accomplishes this), as it does with raising a truly Christian family, and keeping God alive in our homes.

The next thing that happened that Sunday was destined to change my life. For looking back on it now, I can see that the hand of the Lord had begun to guide me. You see, they took me to the Genealogy room and showed me how to trace my ancestors. For most people this would have been a simple task. Tracing the last three generations or so of your family would simply require that you talk to your parents or your grandparents for a start, and then continue on from there. The problem for me was that my mother and father had been divorced when I was three, and had not remained in touch with one another. For that matter I all but knew nothing whatsoever about my father or his side of my family, and my mother had nothing to offer. Genealogy had always been something that had intrigued me, and this seemed like the golden opportunity to finally pursue it. Though I had no information on my Father whatsoever, I nevertheless dove into it head-first and decided to do as much as I could on my mother's side of the family.

No sooner than had I began gathering information than I began to find out about and meet relatives I had never heard of. During the next two weeks I made several trips to the genealogy room to pick up supplies, as I seemed to be quickly exhausting everything they so willingly gave me. I mailed off question filled letters to dozens of near and distant relatives trying to fill in all of the holes on my Pedigree Chart. I soon found myself consumed with this project and spending a great deal of my free time pursuing it. The many bits and pieces quickly began falling into place, and responses to my letters came back filled with more data than I knew what to do with. The only problem was that the top of my master sheet remained starkly bare, with but my father's name, and no more. I asked everyone in my family for information on my father, any clue that might lead me to where he might be. Then, quite out of the blue, my mother mentioned that she recalled someone having said that my father had joined the Mormon Church and moved to Utah many years ago.

During the next week I attended my second Sunday service, had my room burglarized for some $3500.00 worth of personal property, and was informed that I would be spending Christmas in Central America. I also managed to read the "Principles of the Gospel" and many other booklets that the missionaries provided me at my request. On the 7th of Sept. I received my second lesson, this one lasted nearly 5 hours and didn't end till midnight. The following night I intended on receiving the third lesson, but instead was given the opportunity to help move in a newly arriving missionary. By now Elder Hippard and Elder Bye were fast becoming personal friends of mine, as well as my teachers. It was that night that I decided to join the Church. Had I received some divine revelation that this was in fact the true church of the Lord, that I should forsake all others for it, that it alone possessed the Lord's authority on earth?? No, nothing particularly special took place to convince me to join. I simply felt it was the right church to join, and committed myself to doing so.

On the 10th of Sept. I flew home to Calif. for a week's vacation to visit my family and gather more genealogical information from my relatives. The next 72 hours would see the loss of someone I have held very dear for seven years, and the finding of someone I never knew. Sunday morning I attended service with my girlfriend at her Lutheran Church. I had mentioned a few weeks earlier that I was looking into the Mormon Church. She told me that though she had several friends who were Mormons, and whom she considered to be good people, that the religion was a cult and that I should beware. When her service had ended I talked with her minister for an hour or so about his religion and the differences between it and the LDS Church. As fate would have it he grew up in Salt Lake, and was very well versed in Mormon theology. To my surprise he was not at all anti-Mormon, but rather a well informed man who freely choose to join a different church. After this very informative discussion my girlfriend and I drove up to Los Angeles to visit my Aunt and get some Genealogical Papers she had for me.

My Aunt turned out to be a storehouse of information that had been collected by many different people in our family over the years. I could now solidly trace a part of my family back to the 14th Century. We spent many hours with my Aunt gathering everything that she could give me, and then left for home. On the way home we drove past the Los Angeles Temple, and I decided to stop in and take advantage of being so close to a temple. I invited my girlfriend to come and take the tour with me, and find out more about the church for herself. She declined my offer, and became noticeably uncomfortable just being on the temple grounds. While I was waiting for the tour to begin we talked about the church, and it became all to clear just how prejudiced she was. She could offer no substantial reason for her thoughts about it, but remained vehement in her convictions against it. The tour was very nice. It explained everything the average person might want to know about the church. Its history, foundation and theology. Halfway through the tour I began to feel guilty for leaving her sitting out in the car by herself, so I left early and went out to talk with her.

I don't think she could have gotten off of the Temple Grounds any faster than she did. The very moment I sat down in the car she scolded me for spending so much time on the tour, and immediately drove off the grounds. She actually believed that this was an evil place, and just being there was sacrileges. During the drive home we talked and it became very clear that what ever future we had together would be utterly destroyed if I joined the LDS Church. She would show absolutely no tolerance whatsoever of me joining it. Though we had known one an other for over six years, not once during those years had we ever talked about religion. I would have never guessed that her reaction would be so bitter. And so I lost something very dear me that day.

No sooner had I chosen the Lord over a worldly possession than my mother suddenly remembered another clue to my father's whereabouts. She remembered having seen his stepbrother eight years ago, and that he had been the head of security at a local business. She called and asked if anyone there might remember him. No one there had ever heard of him, but they told us to call back tomorrow and talk to another employee that had worked there much longer. Sure enough the next day's call yielded someone who knew him, and knew where he had moved to. A call to Directory Assistance in Arizona gave me his phone number. After several hours of trying I finally got through to my Step Uncle Danny. Though I had never heard of him, nor met him, he knew me when I was much younger.

When I asked him where my father was, he was sad to say that they didn't keep in touch much anymore, as they had a falling out some time ago. Though he looked through his phone book and address book, he could find no listing for his stepbrother, my father. While we were talking on the phone and just getting to know one an other, his wife stumbled across his mother's funeral notice. On the notice was a phone number that had been my father's number some years ago when their mother had passed away. He gave me the number and wished me the best of luck in tracking him down.

I called directory assistance for the city he had last known my father to be in to see if the number matched up, and it did. Though many years had passed, my father had not left that last address. With the greatest of expectation I dialed the number and waited for my father to pick up the phone. I hadn't any idea what I was going to say to him, after all I had only met the man once in my life that I could recall, and that was when I was much younger. Instead of him answering the phone, a young lady picked up the phone. I told her who I was, and that I wanted to speak to my father. To my great disappointment she told me that my father was in Wyoming fighting the fire at Yellowstone National Park and would not be returning home in the immediate future.

As the two of us talked I found out that she was the wife of my stepbrother. She gave me a mailing address, and I was satisfied that at some time in the future I would be able to get in contact with my father. I felt that I had succeeded in my task, and was fully content with my level of accomplishment. No sooner had I said good-bye and hung up the phone, than it rang. She had wasted no time in calling some of the other members of my father's family to tell them of my call. This time it was my step sister that was calling me. The first thing she did was to ask me when I was going to come up for a visit. I told her that quite by chance I had made previous plans to be in her mountain town that evening to look at a lodge that was for sale. A simple adjustment of plans and I was on my way to meet a part of my family that only minutes before I didn't even know existed.

When I arrived she welcomed me into her house as though I had always been a part of the family. I quickly found out that this whole side of my family had been members of the LDS Church for the past 10 years. We talked for many hours, into the wee hours of the morning. Her husband was with my father in Wyoming, so she was home with her four children, her brother & his wife. I had never met someone who I felt so close to so fast. Before the night was over I had acquired a whole new family, not replacing my old one, but making it complete. She related all of the events that had happened over the years, and I was allowed to participate in my first Family Home Evening with her young children that evening. I can't begin to explain what it is like to grow up as an only child with a single parent. For as many years as I can recall I have wanted to have a brother or a sister. Someone special to share things with. Suddenly I had what I had wished for, and much more. Through all of the years they had known about me, it was only I that did not know of them. My sister shared a great deal of her youth with me that night. We spent hours going through the family photo-albums, and reading old journals. As the night passed by I slowly felt myself becoming a full part of that family. And I began to realize to what a great extent that I had always been there to begin with. I doubt that there is a way to make up for all of the lost years that we could have shared together, but I certainly look forward to all the those that we are going to be together through.

The next morning she was able to contact my father, and we spoke for the first time in over 12 years, only the 2nd time I can remember in my life. He was utterly amazed to hear from me, but very pleased none the less. During our short conversation he promised me that he would fly out to North Carolina for my baptism. He assured me that fire or no fire he would do whatever it took to be present for my Baptism. The day that I was reunited with my father in Heaven, was also the day that I was reunited with my father on earth.

Upon returning to North Carolina I went by the church and stopped in at the genealogy room to get more supplies and share this story with those who were present. It wasn't until that moment, when I had told someone else about this very strange series of coincidences, that I realized it was no coincidence at all. At that moment I realized a miracle had happened right before my eyes and I hadn't even known it. By the time I was able to get together with the Missionaries to tell them this story, they already knew about it. It seems that word of things like this spreads very fast. That night as I received my third lesson I began to see how the hand of the Lord had been guiding me the whole time.

On Sunday Sept. 26th I attended Sacrament services after several weeks of absence. This was my first Fast Sunday, and the testimonies that were presented during the service were especially meaningful. It was a very moving experience to listen to the other members tell their personal experiences of knowing the Lord. I learned that one Sunday a month, Fast Sunday, is set aside that the members might bear their own testimonies to the other members. After Priesthood was over we came back to the barracks to talk with one of my friends that had asked me several questions regarding the church.

We talked with my friend for about an hour, and for the first time I began to realize what I had in fact learned from the missionaries, and what was still not completely clear. This experience only served to reinforce my belief that even though the LDS Church is a missionary church and seeks to spread the word of the Lord as much as possible, that there is clearly a second reason for sending these young men and women out on missions. Namely, that of building up a large body of the church that is well versed in its Doctrine and Scripture, and that are fully able to instruct all of the membership.

Nothing comes for free in this life, or so I have been told. Though I may have been blessed with a miracle only last week, I was now challenged to see just how strong my new faith was. For though only a few weeks ago my mother was completely receptive of my investigation into the church, she has now told me that if I join I will be damned to Hell and never allowed to enter the Kingdom of God in Heaven. Someone has in the course of only a few short days provided her with a wealth of disinformation and lies concerning the Mormon religion. In all of my life I do not ever recall my mother as having displayed any conviction regarding religion, other than a general label of Christianity, and as having attended church when she was much younger. Now completely out of the blue comes this dire warning that my eternal soul is in great and grievous danger should I continue my association with the church. Two days later I received yet another letter that was stuffed full of more Anti-Mormon Literature. At my mother's request I thoroughly read everything that she gave me.

There were several things that aroused my attention, and I brought them to the Missionaries for explanation. On weds the 28 of Sept. I spent 5 hours with the Missionaries responding to every allegation that my mother had made, and referencing every statement in the little booklets that she had sent me. I was very pleased to find out that the majority of it was based on various statements of church members, and not on any scripture. Those that were based on scripture were in fact correct, and agreed with what I had been taught in the preceding months. I found that the two Elders did a tremendous job of looking up supporting scripture to combat the overwhelming majority of accusations against the church. Their knowledge here has proved invaluable in responding to my mother's statements.

When my mother sent the first packet of these Anti-Mormon Booklets I strongly suspected that my ex-girlfriend was responsible. But I had absolutely no way of proving it. With the second batch there was a small note from her to my mother. Why she had taken it upon herself to set my mother against me by providing this garbage to her I don't know. If she is so concerned about me why hasn't she just sent them directly to me?.

The Elders had invited me to come and meet their Mission President the next day, and I agreed that if I could find the time I would be glad to do so. I thought this would be an excellent opportunity to meet someone who should really be able to answer any question put to him. As coincidence would have it, my Sgt. gave me the afternoon off quite unexpectedly. And I drove to the church at the appointed time to meet the Mission President. When I arrived the church was locked up tight, with no sign of anyone being there. So I drove back to the missionaries apartment hoping to find them there, they were gone.

Once again I drove back to the Church. But still no one was there. This time I gave up and headed for home. On the way home I stopped in a Christian book store looking for a book on the Dead Sea Scrolls. We had been talking about these and I wanted a first hand look. While looking through the various books, I came across a shelf of Anti-Mormon Literature. I glanced at a few books and then continued on my way. The book I had wanted wouldn't be in for another week or so.

On my way home I stopped for lunch, and while eating I began to feel this strange compulsion to go back to the book store and purchase one of the books that I had glanced at. For no particular reason I drove back and bought "The God Makers". I spent the rest of the day and all of the night reading this book. Up until now none of the literature that I had read really made much of a case against the church. This book changed that entirely. This book didn't hold anything back, and did everything possible to destroy the church, its foundations, its history, and painted a picture of a secret Satanic Cult cleverly disguised as a Christian Church.

For the first time I began to very seriously doubt that I should be joining this church. If the things that this book alleged were in fact based on reality, I didn't want to have anything whatsoever to do with it. The farther I got into the book the more concerned I became. I started sharing the most startling stories with some of my friends in the barracks, and they were just as amazed as I. How could it be that A church so well known for its upstanding members could be so heavily stepped in Satanism, without anyone ever finding out?. On Friday the 29th I went back to that book store and rented two movies; The God Makers, and The Mormon Dilemma.

But I also decided to give the Missionaries a chance to defend themselves, so I stopped by there house and invited them to come and watch these movies with me and give their comments as it went along. They agreed initially, but upon checking with their President they were denied permission to watch them. Now the fact that they were not allowed to watch these movies really disturbed me. What was it that their President was trying to shield them from?. Did he know that this movie held some truths that his young Missionaries shouldn't be exposed to lest they might lose their faith? This bothered me more than anything that I had read. Before I left they gave me three pro-church videos to balance out the night.

Myself and some other friends spent the night watching the movies. The God Makers turned out to be a joke. It was so far fetched, and so poorly made, I couldn't imagine how anyone could believe it. The Mormon Dilemma was much better, and did bring up some very important points that the Missionaries would have to answer to. All in all it was not nearly so damming as the book, but still left me with many doubts about whether or not the Mormons really were a Christian Church or not.

Saturday the 30th was the 1st day of the General Conference, and I had agreed to come weeks ago. I was really hoping that this would give me an inside look at what really went on inside of the church. This was a program made by the church just for church members. If they were going to deceive me now, they would have to deceive all of their members as well.

What I saw and felt that day as I sat in the chapel was one of the most Christian experiences of my life. Regardless of what the book, the movies, or all of the pamphlets said, this had to be a Christian church. The speakers spoke with true conviction, knowing that what they said was in fact the word of our Lord, and not some Satanic Cult. I watched three sessions that day, and left feeling a 1000% better about the Church. I was also given a book entitled "the Truth about the God Makers". Though I knew I would read every page of it for my mind commanded me to answer ever charge that has been raised, in my heart I knew that it made no difference whatsoever.

That evening I called my mother to try and talk her into watching the nationally televised portion tomorrow. Ready to be assaulted with a barrage of questions and accusations about the Mormon Church, I was instead greeted with a warm hello and "I love you". It seems that since my mother had written me that terrible letter she had come into contact with some practicing Mormons in California, and they had begun to explain to her how the religion actually works. Instead of being angry and mad at me, she was warm and loving. She asked many questions, and requested that I send her things to read on it for herself. Once again the Lord had tested my faith, and when the test was over everything was returned to as it had been.

I arrived early for the second day and sat in the parking lot reading over "The Truth about the God Makers" seeking solid answers to many of the questions I had concerning it. My gut feelings about the Church were quickly reaffirmed, and "The God Makers" debunked. The Conference was a special opportunity for me to take a look inside of the Church from the perspective of a member, rather than that of an investigator. I found it to be very re-assuring, and completely in-line with all of the things that I had been taught, or had come to expect. Mostly it served to reinforce my growing conviction in the Church.

That evening I had my 5th discussion and set a date for my baptism. As always I said the closing prayer for the evening. This has become almost a tradition, one of the Missionaries says the opening prayer and I venture forth the closing prayer. This evening was a little bit different. For the first time in ten years I actually felt something special as I said the closing prayer this evening. It was as though I were spinning around and moving while I was saying the prayer. I had only experienced this once before, 10 years ago during my first set of lessons. After everything was over Elder Bye cautioned me to be on the look-out for Satin. He warned me that he would work his hardest to pull me away from the Church now that I had made a firm commitment. He asked the Lord that I might be protected from Satin's Darts.

As I drove back to the barracks I began to feel a strange sense of happiness descend upon me. I was suddenly reassured that what I had done was in fact the right thing. I felt very good about this evening, and was in especially good spirits all the way back. I think that this evening was probably the first time that I had experienced the power of the Holy-Ghost.

On weds evening my father called me at the barracks. That he had managed to track down the correct number at 11:00pm was no small feat. He was calling to let me know that he had made reservations for himself and most of his family to come to my baptism on the 15th. I was really rather surprised to hear from him, let alone to find out that the whole family would be traveling across the country for my Baptism. We talked for some time that evening. It was really the first time we had ever had a one on one talk. Until that moment I really wasn't sure if he was going to come out, or if he had just said he was going to come out. Once again the power of the Gospel showed itself to me. That someone would travel 3000 miles for a baptism seemed ridiculous to me. But my father had a much better understanding of the significance of that event than I did.

Thursday marked the end of my 6 basic lessons about the Church. This was sort of a review and rap up of all of the others. By now it was clear to me that I looked forward to seeing the Missionaries not only to receive my lessons, but also for the discussions we had afterwards about the Bible and Biblical History. I also found myself just looking forward to their companionship, and the opportunity to get away from the Barracks with all of its less than desirable influences. During the past few weeks they have made a strong attempt to introduce me to many different members, and have allowed me to come along on a few home visits. The people that we visited made me feel much more like a part of their family than like a visitor. Most importantly though, they have all invited me back several times. I have never seen a church where the membership can make a perfect stranger feel like one of the family.

During the past week I had begun sending my mother several different pieces of Church Literature. Each day I would mail her a few pamphlets on different subjects. On Sat I called her and we talked about what I had sent her. She told me that she had really enjoyed all of the things that I had sent her, and was looking forward to the Missionaries stopping by to discuss things in person. She also wished me all of her happiness for my upcoming baptism. She had completely changed her opinion of the Church in the last two weeks.

Sunday brought the reality that in only a week I would become a full member of the Church. I was fitted for my baptismal clothing, and had to chose the various speakers for my ceremony. I visited two different members this afternoon. One for an afternoon meal, and the other for a pumpkin decorating party. Everyone expressed their happiness that I had decided to join the Church, and planed on coming to my Baptism. So many people have had a part in my deciding to join, and all had asked to come to my Baptism, that I expected there to be quite a gathering. And to make things all the better, the Ward was having its Harvest Festival right after my ceremony.

One of the last things that I was taught about was the Law of Tithing. Being on a very fixed income I had expressed my concern at being able to meet this commandment. I was not at all sure how I was going to be able to take out 10% of my monthly income and still manage to pay all of my bills. I had discussed this several times with the Missionaries over the weekend. On Tuesday morning a letter arrived in the mail. It contained a refund check that amounted to exactly 10%

of my take home pay. The set of coincidences that has occurred to me in examining this Church never seems to end. Regardless of my problem or challenge, the answer always manifests itself in the clearest of ways.

Weds evening brought my interview with the Bishop. My father had asked that he might confer the Aronic Priesthood on me after my Baptism. The Bishop and I talked for an hour or so. Mostly he wanted to know if I understood the duties and responsibilities of the Priesthood, and whether or not I had developed a testimony of Christ. I conveyed to him all of the marvelous things that have happened to me in the last few months, and told him that I had a strong conviction in the trueness of the Church. He seemed pleased with my understanding, and told me that there was no reason why my father shouldn't be able to confer the Priesthood to me.

Right after his interview myself and four missionaries went to a young lady's (Susan) hotel room. She had called the Bishop's office and asked if a Priest could come over and give her a blessing of comfort. When we arrived we found out that her husband had just called to tell her that he was divorcing her. It just happened that her job had sent her to my area on a temporary basis, and the next week she was returning to Virginia. The four Missionaries gave her the requested blessing, and she asked me to say a closing prayer as well. The faith of the members never ceases to amaze me. She knew that I was not a member, and yet she wanted me to offer a special prayer for her in her time of need. I did so, and felt it was I who was receiving the blessing, and not her.

We all drove back to the Church, as I still had to have my Baptismal Interview. Unlike the Priesthood interview, this was a more organized interview. The senior missionary had a list of questions from the 6 lessons. He asked me how I felt and what I thought about all of the things that I had been taught. Whether the Book of Mormon was true, if I would support the Prophet, pay my Tithes and attend services regularly. It would seem impossible to fail such an interview.

The other thing we discussed that night was the nature of the Chapel. I have never thought that the Chapel Building was a very religious place. Unlike some other Christian Churches, there is no particular feeling of reverence when you sit alone inside of an LDS Chapel. It is a rather sterile meeting place, with no adornments that belie its true purpose. True, on Sunday when the members are gathered there this all changes. But it does not strike me as a place of solitude to come to contemplate the greater questions in life. The others thought that this was not the case at all, that it was more a matter of conditioning. Possibly I had come to expect that a Chapel had to look a certain way, and I had lost the true feeling or presence of the Holy-Ghost.

Thursday the 13th of October was one of those days that you can never forget during your entire life. Today I met my father. As if the fact that I had found him and been able to talk with him were not a great enough blessing in themselves, the Lord saw fit to bring him and his family all the way across the Country so that he could personally Baptize me. This was a moment that I had thought about for a very long time. Where I had once been an only child to a single parent, I now had 2 brothers, a sister, 2 nephews, 2 nieces, a father, and a very special lady that can go by no other name but "mom".

We spent that evening talking with one another till the wee hours of the morning. I don't think that it will ever be possible to make up the lost years we never shared together, but I am certainly looking forward to the many years we will share together in the future. The next day my Brother arrived from Utah, and the two of us spent that night getting to know each other. How rare an occasion that a man can inherit an entire family, and have a feeling of instant oneness with them all. I was completely accepted into their family as though I had always been a part of it, just not there physically. The love that I had felt among the members of the Church now manifest itself upon me from my own family. Who just like the Church members were complete strangers to me, but took me in as one of their own.

On Saturday my Father Baptized me into the Church of Jesus Christ of Latter Day Saints. And on Sunday my Father conveyed the Aronic Priesthood upon me. Over the course of this weekend I had met and begun new relationships with both of my Fathers. My Father in Heaven, and my Father on Earth. What more could a man ask for.

A few weeks later I once again met Susan. This time it was at Sunday services. I hadn't noticed her at first, but the Missionaries pointed her out to me, and re-introduced me to her. Susan and I sat together throughout the rest of the services that day. As services came to a close I asked her if she would like to go out for lunch. We spent the rest of the day and early evening together talking about a great many things and just enjoying each other's company. Never before had I ever met someone quite like her. It was as if we had known each other for years & years. We quickly found that we had a great deal in common, even though our backgrounds were totally different. If there is a Pre-Mortal existence where we all lived with each other, it seems clear that Susan & I surly must have known one an other.

Knowing that I was to spend Christmas alone on Ft. Bragg, Susan invited me to come and spend it with her family instead. Once again I was struck with the love that the membership shows for others. I was a total stranger to all, and yet they opened their home and their hearts to me. This was an entirely new experience for me. Susan comes from a family of nine brothers & sisters. Where I come from a family of only one. Her family lives in a small farming community in the mountains of North Carolina. I found their Christmas to be much more family and Christ centered than any I had had before. Susan & I traveled back to Virginia for New Years Eve together. Had this been an incredible year ?. I should say so, but there was still more to come.

As time passed Susan and I passed from church friendship to very close personal friends. As the months passed by me in 1989 I found myself spending quite a few weekends with Susan and attending Church services with her on Sundays. Easter Weekend found me once again with her in Virginia. Her family had come out for a visit over the weekend. By now it had become obvious that we were falling in love with one an other. In June we left the United States for a 32 day trip to the Sinai Desert in Egypt, and Jerusalem in Israel. Since I had joined the Army I had used up very little of my vacation time and so was abligated to take some major time off. My commanding officer made a yearly trip to Egypt and had invited me to come along with him to go SCUBA

Diving. On this trip Sue and I had the opportunity to get to know one an other as very few people ever will. We shared many special times together, seeing each other at our worst and our best moments. Our days in Jerusalem were by far and away the most special, and spiritual. To walk were our Lord had walked leaves one with an unforgettable impression upon your soul. There is something very special about that ancient city. Something that seems to call to a man's soul, reminding you of how very real the scriptures are.

We returned in July to the U.S., and on that evening I asked Susan to marry me. We both agreed that it would be a Temple wedding. This meant that we would have to wait many extra months as we both had to prepare to go to the Temple, but this somehow seemed a small price to pay for all of the blessings we would surely receive for doing so. We were married and sealed for all time and eternity in the Washington DC temple in February of 1990, two years, almost to the day from when I had found that old tattered bible laying on the floor in the room across the hall.

I guess I could right off almost all of the things that had happened to me as pure coincidence, but I would be lying to myself, and you as well. In 1992 Sue and I were greatly blessed by the Lord with twins, a boy and a girl. Eight years later, in 2000 we had another son and in 2001 we had another daughter.

Had I not happened across the Temple in Hawaii, had I not joined the Army, had I never found that Bible, had I not been at my friends house on just that night, had I not been there a month later, had I not been interested in Genealogy, had the members not been so open and loving, had my father not been a member, had the Missionaries not been so willing, had I not been in the church for my interview on that night, had there not been anyone else to answer the phone call, had any of these or a dozen other things not happened I would not be where I am today. Are all of these simply coincidences, I leave them to you to decide. As for me I offer you this story to show that miracles do happen in our lives when we allow them to. The Lord is seeking an opportunity to enter into each of our lives, if we will but allow him to do this, surely he will pour out so many blessings that there shall not be room enough to receive them.

And lastly I leave you with this, I seal this story with my current personal testimony in the strongest and most direct manner possible, 14 years after I wrote this.

I know that God, the Eternal Father, lives!

I bear witness to the divinity and reality of his living resurrected son Jesus Christ, who leads his church today, and once again reveals the will of the Father to this, our generation through his living prophet whom he has chosen.

I know that Jesus is the Christ, the only begotten son of the Almighty, even our elder brother.

I bear my testimony to the gift & power of the Holy Ghost.

I have seen with my own eyes the eternal power of the Priesthood and watched it change the lives of those that have accepted the Lord's invitation and welcomed him into their hearts and souls..

Brother, Christopher Michael Parrett

A short exerpt from my Patriarchal Blessing.
"I bless you that you will have opportunities to share the gospel with many under very unusual circumstances. Your Testimony shall burn into the hearts of those that hear it. Study your testimony and be able to pronounce it so that the children of men will be able to understand it without error. Many of these that you testify to will take that testimony with them, even unto their death. It will be to your credit and they will be able to testify that you were a great blessing to them in their time of greatest need."

PS...
As I write this my eldist son is now serving as a full time missionary himself, thus bringing this story full circle. Now he is the one walking down streets looking for someone who is ready to recive a fuller portion of Joy and Happiness into their life. Perhaps he will knock on your door. If he does, please welcome him in and listen to what he has to say. Perhaps it will change your life just as it did mine....